GENDER IN MODERNISM

GENDER IN MODERNISM

New Geographies, Complex Intersections

Edited and with an Introduction by
Bonnie Kime Scott

UNIVERSITY OF ILLINOIS PRESS
URBANA AND CHICAGO

Library of Congress Cataloging-in-Publication Data
Gender in modernism : new geographies, complex intersections /
edited and with an introduction by Bonnie Kime Scott.
p.   cm.
Includes bibliographical references and index.
ISBN-13: 978-0-252-03171-7 (acid-free paper)
ISBN-10: 0-252-03171-7 (acid-free paper)
ISBN-13: 978-0-252-07418-9 (pbk. : acid-free paper)
ISBN-10: 0-252-07418-1 (pbk. : acid-free paper)
1. English literature—20th century—History and criticism.
2. Modernism (Literature)—Great Britain.
3. Sex role in literature.
4. Women and literature.
5. English literature—Women authors—History and criticism.
6. American literature—20th century—History and criticism.
7. American literature—Women authors—History and criticism.
8. Modernism (Literature)—United States.
9. Modernism (Aesthetics)
I. Scott, Bonnie Kime, 1944–
PR478.M6G455   2007
820.9'112—dc22   2006019431

CONTENTS

ACKNOWLEDGMENTS

WE GRATEFULLY ACKNOWLEDGE the assistance and cooperation of archives, agents, and literary estates around the globe. We have made a sincere effort to contact all holders of copyrights and apologize for any that we may have missed. We are most grateful to the following individuals and publishers for permission to quote or reprint the listed items (further publication information appears at the end of each reprinted work): Susanna Pinney for "Country Dealings" by Valentine Ackland and "After my marriage night" by Sylvia Townsend Warner © Susanna Pinney and Tanya Stobbs, Literary Trustees; Jane Fraser for "Religion and the Artistic Imagination," "Am I a Surrealist?" and "The Autobiography of an Embryo" (painting) by Eileen Agar; Orient Paperbacks (a division of Vision Books Pvt Ltd) for an extract from *Across the Black Waters* by Mulk Raj Anand; The Authors League Fund, as literary executors for the Estate of Djuna Barnes for "Introduction" to *Ladies Almanack* by Djuna Barnes; Henrietta Garnett for "Lecture Given at Leighton Park School" and "The Bedroom, Gordon Square" (painting) by Vanessa Bell © 1961 Estate of Vanessa Bell; Mary Kinzie, Trustee for the Estate of Louise Bogan, for "The Heart and the Lyre"; Farrar, Straus and Giroux, LLC, for permission to reprint "Summer Wish" from *Collected Poems: 1923-53* by Louise Bogan, copyright © 1954 by Louise Bogan, copyright renewed 1982 by Maidie Alexander Scannell; unpublished letters to Lola Ridge, Katherine Evans Boyle, and William Carlos Williams, and "On the Run" by Kay Boyle, reprinted by permission of the Estate of Kay Boyle and the Watkins/Loomis Agency; the excerpt from Vera Brittain's *Halcyon, or the Future of Monogamy* (1929) is included with the permission of Mark Bostridge and Rebecca Williams, her literary executors; "The Sociological Film, I" Copyright © W. Bryher permission granted courtesy of the Estates of W. Bryher and Perdita Schaffner; Herbert Aptheker for "The African Roots of War" by W. E. B. Du Bois; Indra Tamang for excerpt from *The Young and Evil* by Charles Henri Ford and Parker Tyler; Dr. Alexander Matthews, Executor of the Estate of Martha Gellhorn for "The Third Winter"; Moorland-Sprinam Research Center, Howard University, for "You," "Your Eyes," "Blue Cycle," "Beware Lest He Awakes," "Black Finger," and "'Rachel,' The Play of the Month" by Angelina Grimké; Kobina Hunter for "Mista Courifer" by Adelaide Casely Hayford;

"Projector" by H. D. (Hilda Doolittle), from *Collected Poems, 1912-44,* copyright © 1982 by the Estate of Hilda Doolittle, and various excerpts by H. D. (Hilda Doolittle) from *Bid Me to Live,* copyright © 1960 by Norman Holmes Pearson, used by permission of New Directions Publishing Corporation, agents; Karen L. Clark for "Machine-Age Exposition" by Jane Heap; Scribner, an imprint of Simon & Schuster Adult Publishing Group, for excerpts from *The Garden of Eden* by Ernest Hemingway, copyright © 1986 by Mary Hemingway, John Hemingway, and Gregory Hemingway; Judith Bach and Katherine Weinstein for their translation of Emmy Hennings's "The Perhaps Last Flight"; Marion Shaw, Literary Executor for the Estate of Winifred Holtby for "Modern Newspapers: Edited to Entertain"; Schuyler (Philippa, George, and Josephine) Family Papers, Manuscripts, Archives, and Rare Books Division, Schomburg Center for Research in Black Culture, the New York Public Library, Astor, Lenox, and Tilden Foundations, for Heba Jannath (Josephine Schuyler's), "America's Changing Color Line"; Pollinger Limited and the Estate of Frieda Lawrence Ravagli for excerpts from *The Woman Who Rode Away* by D. H. Lawrence; "Men's Genius Intimidates Me" and "Femme peintre et son modele" by Marie Laurencin © 2003 Artists Rights Society (ARS), New York/ADAGP, Paris; Anne M. Corey, executor of the Estate of Ruth Lechlitner, for "Lines for an Abortionist's Office" and "Case Recruit"; Special Collections, Colby College, Waterville, Maine, for an excerpt from Vernon Lee's *Satan the Waster;* Farrar, Straus and Giroux, LLC, for permission to reprint "Feminist Manifesto" from *Last Lunar Baedeker* by Mina Loy, works of Mina Loy copyright © 1966 by the Estate of Mina Loy; Farrar, Straus and Giroux, LLC, for permission to reprint "Against *Amore* and Parliamentarianism" and "Marriage and the Family" from *Marinetti: Selected Writings,* F. T. Marinetti, edited by R. W. Flint, translated by R. W. Flint and Arthur A. Coppotelli, translation copyright © 1972 by Farrar, Straus and Giroux, Inc.; "The Press and the Public," and "What the Public Wants," reprinted by permission of PFD on behalf of the estate of Rose Macaulay © 1926 by Boni and Liveright; The Feminist Press at the City University of New York for permission of "Social Conditions among Bantu Women and Girls" by Charlotte Maxeke; excerpt from *Banjo* courtesy of the Literary Representative for the Works of Claude McKay, Schomburg Center for Research in Black Culture, the New York Public Library, Astor, Lenox, and Tilden Foundations; Elizabeth Barnett, Literary Executor of the Edna St. Vincent Millay Society for Sonnet XVIII © 1923, 1951 by Edna St. Vincent Millay and Norma Millay Ellis and "The Pioneer" ("For Inez Milholland" in *Collected Sonnets*) © 1928, 1955 by Edna St. Vincent Millay and Norma Millay Ellis, reprinted by permission; Mrs. T. S. Eliot on behalf of the Mirrlees Estate for *Paris* by Hope Mirrlees; "The Spare American Emotion" and "Comment" by Marianne Moore © *The Dial,* 1926 and 1929, renewed, reprinted by permission of the Literary Executor of the Estate of Marianne Moore, Marianne Craig Moore, with all rights reserved; Winifred Nicholson's Trustees for "Liberation of Colour" and "Window-sill, Lugano" (painting); Sean O'Casey, extract from *The Silver Tassie* © 1985 Macmillan, reproduced with permission of Palgrave Macmillan; Judith Bach and Katherine Weinstein for their translation of "A Description of Emmy Hennings Dancing in a Cardboard Dada Costume" by Suzanne Perrottet; Sheil Land Associates Ltd. for "Meta" and "Chorus Girls" from *Smile Please* by Jean Rhys; "So I gave up going to the theatre" by Dorothy Richardson by permission of Paterson Marsh Ltd. for and on behalf of the Estate of Dorothy Richardson; *International Journal of Psychoanalysis* for "Womanliness as Masquerade" by Joan Riviere, copyright © Institute of Psychoanalysis; "Manifesto of Futurist Woman" by Valentine de Saint-Point, translation copyright © 2001 University of Nebraska Press; Laurence Senelick for his translation of "Emmy Hennings" by Ravien Siurai (Ferdinand Hardekopf); extract from *New Lives for Old* by C. P. Snow reproduced with permission of Curtis Brown Group Ltd., London, on behalf of the estate of C. P. Snow, copyright © C. P. Snow 1932; Richard Sorabji for extracts from Cornelia Sorabji's diaries and lectures in the British Museum; Estate of Gertrude Stein, through its Literary Executor Mr. Stanford Gann Jr. of Levin & Gann, P.A., for an excerpt from *Paris France,* Part 2, by Gertrude Stein; Judith Benét Richardson for "At Last the Women Are Moving," "A Middle-Aged, Middle-Class Woman at Midnight," "Feeding the Children," and "The Ruskinian Boys See Red" by Genevieve Taggard; Ann E. Hardham for an excerpt from *Love* by Elizabeth Von Arnim; Susanna Pinney for "My Shirt Is in Mexico" from *A Garland of Straw* by Sylvia Townsend Warner and "After my marriage night" by Sylvia Townsend Warner from *Whether a Dove or a Seagull* by Sylvia Towsend Warner and Valentine Ackland published by Chatto & Windus © *Susanna Pinney;* Dr. Mariquita West for "Sky-Scraper in Construction" and "Camp Corcoran" by Marie de L. Welch; "The Future of the Press IV" (copyright © Rebecca West 1928) is reproduced by permission of PFD on behalf of the Estate of Dame Rebecca West; The Society of Authors as the Literary Representative of the Estate of Virginia Woolf for "Reviewing," "The Prime Minister," and "The Cinema" by Virginia Woolf; The Berg Collection of English and American Literature, the New York Public Library, Astory, Lenox, and Tilden Foundations for the "The Prime Minister."

I am grateful to my collaborators who have stayed with a project that took longer than any of us could have anticipated, particularly for suggestions that enriched the introduction, but also for working resourcefully to make their chapters the best that they could be, given limits of space and an ever-evolving field. Teddi Brock, administrative coordinator for Women's Studies at San Diego State University, provided many and various forms of help with the management of electronic files and our modest finances. SDSU graduate student Lihong Shi honed her English skills while scanning original documents. Josie Leimbach helped with final copy editing. She and Michelle Garvey helped construct the index. I appreciate grants provided by the SDSU Dean of Arts and Letters and the Carstens/Wertz Faculty Development fund at SDSU. The following institutions have helped offset the major expense of permissions fees and have provided faculty release time for many of us involved in the project: Ball State University, Cornell College (Iowa), the Undergraduate Research Program at the University of Delaware, Franklin College, Loyola University Chicago, Pennsylvania State University, Rice University, and San Diego State University.

GENDER IN MODERNISM

Introduction: A Retro-prospective on Gender in Modernism

BONNIE KIME SCOTT

IN THE YEARS SINCE 1990, when with a team of collaborators I published *The Gender of Modernism*, both gender and modernism have remained lively categories—frequently featured in scholarly discussions, and surviving a variety of constructive challenges. "Gender" was introduced in the 1990 volume as

> a category constructed through cultural and social systems. Unlike sex, it is not a biological fact determined at conception. [. . .] Gender is more fluid, flexible, and multiple in its options than the (so far) unchanging biological binary of male and female. In history, across cultures, and in the lifetime development of the individual, there are variations in what it means to be masculine, or feminine, in the availability of identifications such as asexual and androgynous, and in the social implications of lesbian, homosexual, and heterosexual orientations. (2)

Perhaps the most quoted statement in that introduction said that, by the middle of the twentieth century, canonical modernism had been "unconsciously gendered masculine" (2) in its selection of privileged authors, and in its style and concerns. Starting in the late 1970s, thanks largely to critiques organized by women of color,[1] we began to acknowledge additional unspoken norms that have favored work that is heterosexual, white, representative of "high" culture and an academic middle class, or produced in the Northwestern quarter of the globe. Today, sex (down to various arrangements of X and Y chromosomes) is less regularly discussed as a simple binary. The transsexual and the intersex condition now routinely enter considerations of sexuality and the body.[2] In the first decade of the twenty-first century, gender is most interesting as a system connected with and negotiated among various cultural identifiers. Understood within such complex intersections, gender has both greater and subtler implications. It is less often seen as a division between oppositional feminine and masculine traits or traditions. Gender studies now lead to a variety of activities, only one of which is the recuperative work so central to the gynocritics (so named by Elaine Showalter in the 1980s). The movement from author-centered chapters in *The Gender of Modernism* to chapters based primarily on themes and group identities in this book is one manifestation of this shift. The importance of gender as a modernist issue has only become more obvious over time. Ever more complex questions of gender must be tested in relation to modernist studies, if that area of study is to remain vital and relevant to our lives.[3]

Scholars continue to recover works consciously or unconsciously neglected on the basis of female authorship. A keyword search of the Library of Congress website for "women writers" recently produced ten thousand English language books published between 1990 and mid-2006—the maximum number that can be displayed on the site. Over a thousand of these were in the highest category of relevance. Even Harold Bloom got into the women writers act, however warily, by editing a series of books, "Women Writers of English and Their Works."[4] Among the exciting archival recoveries of texts offered in this volume are Julia Briggs's painstakingly annotated version of "Paris" by Hope Mirrlees (chapter 8), Suzette Henke's transcription from the holograph of Virginia Woolf's "The Prime Minister" (chapter 15), and Sonita Sarker's extracts from Cornelia Sorabji's diaries. Many more women writers have joined those who appeared in the original *Gender of Modernism*. The list continues to grow across race, class, and national boundaries.

Scholarly studies of literary periods and of racial, ethnic, national, or regional groupings have partially restored women to various literary cultures, illuminating dynamics of gender through history and geography.[5] Christanne Miller offers a new grouping in her recent *Cultures of Modernism: Marianne Moore, Mina Loy, and Else Lasker-Schüler: Gender and Literary Community in New York and Berlin*. Several of our chapters reveal collaborative cultures of modernist production. Kate Kelly discovers a communal form of creation in a woman-centered theatre (chapter 18), and in the London Film Society Leslie Hankins finds women entering conversations on cinema, despite a lack of Oxford credentials, and going from there into the management of periodicals (chapter 21).

Under-represented genres, some endemic to activist movements and mass markets, have been recognized and analyzed in relation to gender. Numerous examples emerge in the present volume. Janet Lyon argues for the importance of manifestoes as "the signal genre of modernity's crises"—including anxieties over the "inconsistencies of western modernity's institutions of representation and . . . a perceived concomitant decline in cultural coherence" (chapter 2). Suzanne Clark finds that "women's sentimental rhetoric" fueled "the great progressive movements of the nineteenth century" including abolition, women's rights, Indian rights, public education, anti-drink, immigrant socialization, and urban welfare (chapter 4). Nancy Berke's recovery of American women poets on the left (chapter 3) underlines the importance of crossing class in modernist study. Specialized genres also emerge with Jayne Marek's female editors (chapter 7), and the "gendered perspectives within modernist art history" detected by Diane Gillespie (chapter 20).

Movement across disciplinary boundaries is now an expectation for modernist studies. In assembling two outstanding modernist collections,[6] Lisa Rado felt impelled to seek interdisciplinary perspectives for "a period in which science, art, psychology, technology, sociology, anthropology, and philosophy were simultaneously undergoing a period of revolutionary change" (*Modernism, Gender, and Culture* 8). In the present volume, Virginia Woolf, H. D., and Dorothy Richardson become models of interdisciplinary practice—all of them discussing "the role of visual emotion in cinema, the mystic or fantastic visionary potential of cinema, and the connections between cinematic and spatial languages and the psyche" (chapter 21). Many of the contributors to *Gender in Modernism: New Geographies, Complex Intersections* have previously restructured modernism to be inclusive of new categories and crossings of disciplines, and that work continues in their chapters here.[7] Crossing over into the visual arts has probably been the most apparent interdisciplinary move. This is encouraged by the seasoned, nuanced feminist theory of the gaze, as well as the emergence of visual studies in the turn toward investigations of modernity.[8] The focus on the visual is seen in the illustrations for this volume, and it is richly played out in the final part, "Arts and Performances."

In 1990, I observed, "Gender is not a mask for feminist or woman, though they are inextricable from it. Both men and women participate in the social and cultural systems of gender, but women write about it more, perhaps because gender is more imposed upon them, more disqualifying, or more intriguing and stimulating to their creativity" (*The Gender of Modernism* 3). Gender itself may have become so intriguing that it now provides an essential lens for viewing male writing and experience. We find the gendered turn toward male modernists in texts like Hazel Carby's *Race Men,* and in *Modernism, Inc.: Body, Memory, Capital,* edited by Jani Scandura and Michael Thurston, which studies many more men than women through the lens of gender. While

The Gender of Modernism had five male writers, the present volume includes the work of nearly thirty men, many working cooperatively with women. The rising interest in versions of masculinity holds the promise of more complex models of gender, where various experiences play against one another. However, there remains the specter of male co-option, or reinforcement of contentious lines of opposition.

Gender Trouble?

How useful does the category of gender remain? In *Mappings: Feminism and the Cultural Geographies of Encounter,* Susan S. Friedman devotes much of her first chapter to going "'beyond' gender." She dates and pretty much limits gender to 1980s-era gynocriticism and gynesis ("French feminist" language-centered, post-structuralist readings of gender).[9] Friedman suggests that a new set of "discourses of identity" or subject positions have undermined the privileging these practices gave to gender. She concedes that gender can play a part in later, more complex gynocriticisms involving multiple identities, and in what she sees as an evolved form of gynesis—performance studies. But she does not explore gender in all of the new geographies she proposes. Nor does she consider feminisms not encompassed by Showalter's now dated gyno-binary: for example, the ever-untidy wedding of feminism to Marxism, or recent developments in psychoanalysis such as trauma theory (see Suzette Henke's excellent explanations, chapter 15). At the end of her discussion of gender, Friedman does concede the existence of an enduring politics of gender that still demands everyday feminist effort. Having broken through the great divide of high vs. low modernism, as defined by Andreas Huyssen, modernists are obliged to attend more than ever to everyday life, remaining amid, and not "beyond" gender, in an active and affirmative political life. Modernism, as we now understand it, provides neglected models of just such activity.

Another recent renunciation of gender comes from Mary Poovey, when she chooses "no longer to attend to women writers or even to the 'ideological work of gender'" (Homans 453). Margaret Homans challenged her on this in an exchange titled "Positions: Recovery Redux." Homans adopts Poovey's own method, whereby she superimposes a first reading for "connotations in which the first text was written" upon subsequent "(mis)readings, including the different interests held in the present" (qtd. in Homans 458). She argues for the integration of gender "into any historical analysis from the start" (452), and remarks on the opportunities for enriched contexts and alternative canons afforded by online resources such as the Brown Women Writer's Project.[10]

I like to call attention to a long, nonlinear history of gender, rather than leave it somewhere behind in the 1980s. There is evidence that gender works recurrently, as needed, in cultural studies. Toril Moi notes that "modern feminist theory was born at a time when sexist ideology often grounded its claims about the subordination of women on appeals to the sciences of the body, particularly biology" (14) and that "historically [. . .] *gender* emerged as an attempt to give to biology what belongs to biology, no more and no less" (15). While gender studies recently provided a pathway into the academy for racial, queer, and postcolonial studies, gender and other social discourses were quite generally traded off with one another in the early twentieth century. Cassandra Laity has suggested that turn-of-the-century decadents such as Swinburne and Wilde provided female modernists with the transgressive models denied in the masculinist ideology of the male makers of modernism.

Civil rights activism arose in the United States ahead of feminism in the 1950s.[11] Kate Millett's *Sexual Politics* serves for Tuzyline Allan as a "paradigmatic shift in American intellectual life from civil rights to women's rights" appearing as it did "at a time when black and white women activists" had become "alienated by the male-dominated center of the civil rights movement and the increasingly sexist tone of its revolutionary branch" (1). Like many feminists now writing on modernism, including Friedman, Allan accompanies modernist with postcolonial women authors. This juxtaposition furthers discussion of the formal and cultural concerns of gendered modernism, while retaining meaningful temporal and cultural distinctions.

With chapter 12 of this volume, Allan focuses freshly on gender expressions in African modernity. We find women writers' options shaped by conventions of gender in African communities, and by their more famous male counterparts; American pan-Africanists and global commerce and conflict offer more general influences. These patterns lend themselves well to current theorizing of transnational feminism, including its capitalist critique and its traversals of national boundaries.[12] Following in chapter 13, Sonita Sarker finds gender, colonialism, and modernism inextricable: "Modernism—the face of modernity at the turn of the twentieth century—and late colonialism—the political infrastructure of modernism that provides material resources as well as particular forms of the racialized, sexualized and gendered 'other.'" It is not surprising, then, that for chapter 14, "War, Modernisms, and the Feminized 'Other,'" Claire Tylee enlists Irish and Indian writers.

Rachel Blau DuPlessis argues for the synchronous continuation of various feminist approaches, including questions of gender. Her *Genders, Races, and Religious Cultures in Modern American Poetry, 1908–1934* moves to a model of "exploring diversity within modernism by encouraging feminist reception and gender-oriented analyses of all producers." She does not want to "'gender' modernism, without 'sexing' it, 'racializing' it, 'Semiticizing' it, 'classing' it" (4–6). Her inclusion of anti-Semitism acknowledges the importance of fascism, as applied to racism and ethnic cleansing in the modernist period. The turn toward racializing modernism became remarkable around 1994, with the publication of works such as Michael North's *The Dialect of Modernism* and Laura Doyle's *Bordering on the Body*. Attention to anti-Semitism, fascism, and anti-fascism has also complicated questions of gender.[13] One result of asking racial and ethnic questions within gender studies is that we increasingly see cross-racial connections and discussions. This pattern is reflected in the presence of writers of color and marginal ethnicity throughout this anthology, instead of isolated into chapters of their own (see, for example, chapter 1, "Suffrage"; chapter 4, "Sentimental Modernism"; chapter 7, "Women Editors"; and chapter 10, "Queer Conjunctions"). Anthologized are essays that both analyze and denounce racism (W. E. B. Du Bois) and founding documents that exhibit it (F. T. Marinetti). It remains extremely important to acknowledge ways that modernists used race to articulate issues of gender, at the expense of addressing issues of race or empire.[14]

The debates among feminist approaches to gender over the years have been lively and useful. Gynocritical gender studies had already experienced strains with gynesis by the late 1970s. In 1981, with the anthology *This Bridge Called My Back*, Cherríe Moraga and Gloria Anzaldúa set forth the creative and critical thinking of women of color and forced a worthy, though gradual reassessment of Anglo-American feminism. Norma Alarcón registers its challenge to what she sees as feminism's single theme of gender in her essay "The Theoretical Subject(s) of *This Bridge Called My Back* and Anglo-American Feminism." In her 1989 article "The Race for Theory," Barbara Christian wrote on behalf of dis-empowered authors and academic programs on the fringes, calling for adequate readings of African American women writers and challenging the authority vested in philosophers and French feminists. Part of her objection to the latter hinged on their emphasis on the female body, which threatened to reduce the social construct of gender to essentialist biology (342).

On the other hand, while French feminists made use of the male theorists at the center of post-structuralism, they offered resistance to implausible theory and selected what was worth developing. Thus we see resistance to the Freudian definition of woman premised on her "lack" of a penis, and to the paternal, heterosexual, Oedipal concept of the family. Jacques Lacan's designation of the phallus as the transcendental and authoritative signifier gets set aside in favor of more useful concepts, such as the mirror stage, conceptions of language as discourse, and theories of the gaze.[15] Lacan, Jacques Derrida, and Michel Foucault, though generally blind to issues of gender, have provided post-structuralist feminists with departure points for disrupting gender essentialism, hierarchical and/or binary power structures, and discourses of authority and control. They have set the stage for gender-sensitive developmental theories.

Similarly, materialist feminism addressed the inadequacies of Marxist analysis, drawing attention to the traffic in women, the work of consumption, and production in the home and/or outside the structure of paid work.[16] Various chapters recover radical critiques of class divisions, and even register Communist sympathies. See, for example, Nancy Berke's recoveries from *New Masses* (chapter 3), Jayne Merek's treatment of Dorothy West's editorship at *Opportunity Magazine* (chapter 7), or Pamela Caughie's summoning of Heba Jannath from Nancy Cunard's *Negro* anthology (chapter 14). Scattered through this volume is evidence that the suffrage movement was surprisingly sensitive to class issues.

In her introduction to *Generations: Academic Feminists in Dialogue*, E. Ann Kaplan suggests that third wave feminism, operating in a cyber age of transnational capitalist finance, is "deconstructing gender" even as it destabilizes identities in other ways (28). Writing in 1995, Rita Felski reminded us that feminists have reason to be suspicious of both the dandy's and the deconstructionist's performance of the feminine, often done "at the expense of women" (*Gender of Modernity* 113). Thus, in the midst of the second Bush administration, we find that issues of gender can repeat themselves, and we are best equipped if we keep a running history and draw from cumulative experience.

One of the most widely recognized challenges to gender as a concept came from Judith Butler in her memorably titled *Gender Trouble* (published in 1990, the same year as *The Gender of Modernism*). Echoing Eve Sedgwick, Butler critiques gender as a heterosexually based binary concept (and indeed sees trouble in other binaries, including male/female sex and nature/culture). Though she does not abandon gender, she applies the now well-known concept of the performative to both gender and sexuality: "Once we dispense with the priority of 'man' and 'woman' as abiding substances, then it is no longer possible to subordinate dissonant gendered features as so many secondary and accidental characteristics of a gender ontology that is fundamentally intact" (24). She concludes, "Within the inherited discourse of the metaphysics of substance, gender proves to be performative—that is, constituting the identity it is purported to be. In this sense, gender is always a doing, though not a doing by a subject who might be said to preexist the deed" (25). Citing Simone de Beauvoir's claim that one is not born a woman, but rather becomes one, Butler sees gender as a "repeated stylization of the body," and takes interest in the "contingent acts" that enforce a naturalistic concept of gender (33).[17]

While sensitive to Butler's important critique that gender privileges a heterosexual, binary pair of masculine vs. feminine, I think that by the time we were working on *The Gender of Modernism,* dissonant elements of gender were already erupting in a wide array of reclaimed texts, thus disturbing neat, heterosexually based divisions of gender. What Shari Benstock has termed "Sapphic modernism" was certainly not eliminated by the gender concept from that volume, which featured works by and discussions of Djuna Barnes, Willa Cather, H. D., Charlotte Mew, and Sylvia Townsend Warner. Lesbian studies continue to collect a richer, thicker cultural history, as seen in Laura Doan's *Fashioning Sapphism: The Origins of a Modern English Lesbian Culture.* Her interest in Radclyffe Hall is perpetuated in work by and about Hall, contained in chapters 9 and 17. Relevant material in the present volume goes well beyond what is contained in the most obvious chapters: Gay Wachman's "Lesbian Political History" (chapter 9), and Colleen Lamos's "Queer Conjunctions in Modernism" (chapter 10).[18] Wachman takes pains to make connections between lesbian literary history and British political history.

As represented in Lamos's title for chapter 10, studies of sexuality, though still pursued along the lines of lesbian and gay male identities, have also moved toward the broader, albeit controversial category of "queer theory." This transition was marked by Teresa de Lauretis's special number of *Differences,* "Queer Theory: Lesbian and Gay Sexualities," based on a 1990 conference. In *Libidinal Currents: Sexuality and the Shaping of Modernism,* Joseph Allen Boone argues against the "disentangling of the axes of sexuality and gender" he identifies with Sedgwick: "For one thing, this division of labors underestimates the degree to which feminist inquiry has been willing to engage seriously the realm of the sexual; for another, in making the proper object of feminist critique 'the coarser stigmata of gender difference,' as Sedgwick puts it, such a division of labor not only creates a binary but institutes a hierarchy based on refinement (that which is less 'coarse') and appeal. . . . It has always been difficult for me to conceive of a theoretical paradigm of sexuality that doesn't constantly call upon and have recourse to issues of gender" (17). Gender works throughout Anne Herrmann's *Queering the Moderns: Poses/Portraits/Performance,* a work that extends "queer" beyond sexuality. Herrmann's selection of richly different memoirs allows us to study "processes of queering" that resist "regimes of the normative" (6) found in colonial, sexual, racial, class, and ethnographic constructions. The queering of modernist sexuality comes as a sequel to the gendering of it in feminist studies, and already invites other complexities. In *Deviant Modernism,* Lamos reads canonized male modernist texts as "the site of unresolved struggles" that arose from contemporary debates about gender difference and sexual desire (2). Her study of the ambivalences of same-sex love continues in her chapter, including the pressures faced by members of the Harlem Renaissance, who wanted to "present a decorous and uplifting face to the white world" (chapter 10).

An increasing number of publishers have begun substituting "Gender Studies" for "Women's Studies," even in brochures and advertising sections predominantly featuring work on women writers and issues in women's lives. This shift could be viewed negatively as a crass commercial attempt to rope in more consumers, a conservative masking of feminist work, or at best, a careless use of terms. There has been some renaming of academic departments to bear the "Gender" title—a move that generally extends the curriculum into masculinity studies, performances and technologies of gender, as well as active intersection with racial and queer theory. It may attract participation by more male faculty. However, there remains a strong tendency to hold to the original designation "Women's Studies" for reasons both of history and of momentum, as well as a commitment to focusing on women's experiences. The use of the gender term, both commercially and academically, suggests to me that the question of gender is more universally, openly, consciously, and positively posed than at any previous stage in academic culture. This collection aims at both the rich and multiple intersections afforded by its gender designation, and at further recovery of women's cultural work, as appropriate to Women's Studies.

Issues of Identity and Gender Complexity

As exemplified by Butler's thinking about contingencies of gender and Boone's sense of the interdependency of gender and sexuality studies, there has been considerable debate and some conceptual progress with studying gender in combination with other cultural discourses and identifications. Chicana critic Rosaura Sánchez has noted the multiplicity and fluidity of identity as it is construed from the layering of identities, multiple positionality, and hybridity. We can view "the interpellation of individuals by discourses of ethnicity, gender, class, nation, religion, family, sexuality, and even region, generation, etc. An individual, then, can identify in terms of several subject positions" (1012–13). Norma Alarcón is skeptical of Anglo-American standpoint epistemologists, whose privileging of gender tends to suppress the complexity of the experience of women of color. The figure of the "weave" suggests the position of the theoretical subjects she finds in *This Bridge Called My Back* (366). A complex and overlaid assemblage of identities provides a constructive way of looking at the images of fragmentation, so persistent in modernist experimental literature. Indeed, in this experimental trope, women writers may be particularly sensitive and exploratory. Friedman describes "relationality" as one discourse of positionality available for a geographics of identity. Premised on psychoanalytic and post-structuralist theory, "relationality" argues that one axis of identity, such as gender (and this is her example), must be understood in relation to other axes, such as sexuality and race.[19] Contours of identity change with points of reference, particularly in relation to structures of power (22).

It is worth noting that recent discussions of race call attention to its own process of construction; like gender, it emerged as a form of identification and discrimination in relation to scientific, and particularly anthropological theory. "Passing" has become a more widely employed term to suggest the mobility and play possible with subject identification. I find it interesting that in her study *Passing and Pedagogy,* as in chapter 11 for this book, Pamela Caughie has been able to relate the concept to globalization and technology, in addition to sexuality and race, and to open up "passing" for pedagogy. She finds that "border crossing, facilitated by new technologies and fueled by an increasingly touristic and consumer culture in the interwar period, had a profound effect on the imagining of national and personal identity in modernist cultural productions."

The energetic discussion of identity we have enjoyed in recent years has been accompanied by a proliferation of representative figures of speech. Favorites include "axes," "intersections," "cross-cutting," "matrix," "braid," and "weave."[20] Accordingly, this new collection includes "complex intersections" in its subtitle. The gender "complex" allows for whole areas of identity, rather than intersecting points, to be layered, blended, woven, enriched, and complicated through their coincidence with gender. Presented in this way, gender runs less danger of isolation from other identifications; students of gender have much to learn from studying the forms that blending takes. Such combinations must be taken into account in order to read gender with specificity and subtlety. We also acknowledge that the concept of gender, and demands placed upon it, have changed over time, and that critics and writers today make different demands of gender than did the modernists. "Presentism" risks having present interests dominate, obscure, and misinterpret the concerns of specific eras in the past.

The term "complex" is in part appropriated from Ezra Pound's definition of an "image," one of the central concepts of traditionally male, canonical modernism: "an intellectual and emotional complex in an instant of time," to which he added that he used "'complex' rather in the technical sense employed by the newer psychologists" ("A Retrospect" 4). We will use "gender complex" in the psychological sense, as a provisional, dynamic mental adjustment and expression for individuals, but also in a sense of complex, collective, cultural locations.

Intersections with the Gender Complex

The list of social categories intersecting with gender continues to grow, breaking previous silences and omissions. Sexuality, Race/Ethnicity, Class, and Global Situation (inclusive of imperial and capitalist histories) are best represented in the current collection. The discussion is centered in part three, "Diverse Identities and Geographies," but by no means limited to it. In the figure below, the bold oval represents our focus on questions and concepts of gender. The interactions of gender with other categories of identification is suggested by overlapping of additional ovals, all of them complexly woven with and influencing gender, and permeable as well to one another. Race/Ethnicity and Sexuality have relatively large ovals, representing their prominence

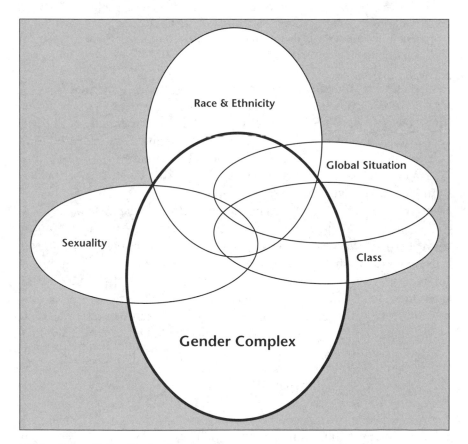

Intersections with the Gender Complex

in the volume; global situation and class issues also figure importantly, and are registered in slightly smaller ovals. There is the potential for all of these cultural categories to overlap, as shown in a tiny section toward the middle. Focus upon another of these categories would yield a different perspective, with different proportions, but still inclusive of gender.

Modernism vs. Modernity

The introduction to the original *Gender of Modernism* included the following description of modernism as it existed before gender and women's studies:

> Typically, both the authors of original manifestoes and the literary histo-
> rians of modernism took as their norm a small set of its male participants,
> who were quoted, anthologized, taught, and consecrated as geniuses. Much
> of what even these select men had to say about the crisis in gender identi-
> fication that underlies much of modernist literature was left out, or read
> from a limited perspective. (2)

Rereading these arguments about modernism, it seems to me that they are aimed at changing the academy at its center, where concepts such as genius and modernism had been rendered hegemonic, and gender had not. Indeed, modernism is a concept that has flourished in the traditional male, Eurocentric academy and with the epistemology of the Enlightenment.[21] Modernism has generally been taken as both a period and a stylistic designation. Experimental writing, "high" modernism as in *The Waste Land, Ulysses,* or *The Waves,* has been the dominant style, reinforcing the need of the academy to be its inter-preter, and dismissing traditions associated with women (particularly women disqualified by class or race), activist agendas, or mass culture. Chapman and Green respond to the pattern in chapter 1: "though it has been tempting to locate a 'great divide' between suffrage polemic and modernist literary experi-ment, recent criticism has also noticed a number of historical and formal con-nections between suffrage art and modernism and the value of the cultural work performed by suffrage texts." On a more sober note, Patrick Collier stud-ies the "conflicting imperatives" that made young writers, and particularly women, resist the profits and the connections offered by journalism, which in the early twentieth century posed "a crisis threatening dire consequences for the health of Britain's democracy and the future of its literature" (chapter 6).

Those who construct the period of modernism tend to center it on 1910–40, missing an important transition, 1880–1910, that included decadent play with sexuality, women's entry into a counter-public sphere as suffragists and socialists, and a coming into literature of technology and mass or consumer culture, with their accompanying debates. This missing era is found in many chapters in this volume, including Chapman and Green, "Suffrage and Spectacle" (chapter 1), Janet Lyons's manifestoes (chapter 2), Berke's "Radical Moderns" (chapter 3), Collier's journalists (chapter 6), Sarker's colonials (chapter 13), and London's mediums (chapter 17).

The appearance of the journal, *MODERNISM/modernity* (1993), Rita Felski's *The Gender of Modernity* (1995), and Paul Gilroy's *The Black Atlantic: Modernity and Double Consciousness* (1993) marks a gradual turn toward modernity as a complement to, if not a substitute for, modernism as a field of study. The range of modernity is much wider than modernism. It places greater emphasis on everyday life and takes interest in "low" as well as "high" modernist forms, as well as their interdependence. It explores the "modernity of department stores and factories, of popular romances and women's magazines, of mass political movements and bureaucratic constructions of femininity" (Felski 28). Such mixtures are evident in the quandaries of journalists explored in chapter 6, and in the text of Hope Mirrlees's *Paris* (chapter 8). The arena of modernity is primarily urban and increasingly mapped around the globe, affecting rural life with its demands for inexpensive labor and homogeneous raw materials. Vital aspects of the study of modernity include patterns of material consumption, technological inventions, and medical interventions that challenge even the integrity of the sexed and gendered body. Evidence of the importance of gender to modernity is readily found in Tim Armstrong's *Modernism, Technology and the Body* (1999), which treats gender, not just in the section headed "Technologies of Gender," but throughout. His section on waste, for example, finds that while Gertrude Stein may celebrate a proliferation of literary excrescences, waste is coded feminine when Ezra Pound edits Eliot, or Thorsten Veblen identifies nonproductive aspects of a capitalist economy. The gendering of mass culture as feminine is one of many aspects of modernity that make it inescapably gender study. The shift to considerations of modernity is particularly strong in the "War, Technology, and Traumas of Modernity" part of this volume, though not limited to it. Susan Squier argues that the interventions at the beginning and end of life, discussed in chapter 16, "Modernism and Medicine," anticipate "the current debates about the biomedical intervention in human life," including "the continuing power of heterosexism, racism, and ableism to structure the biomedical imaginary." In chapter 12, "Modernism, Gender, and Africa," Tuzyline Allan notes that colonial African access to Western knowledge and the modern world favored "masculine forays," while "women with similar aspirations were slower on the draw, impeded largely by the colonial vision of a domesticated African womanhood." Indeed, this global mapping of modernity is one of its most significant developments.

Modernist Re-presentation

As Ronald Schuchard says to his students, "We are now at the threshold of a new age for the study of all modernist literature" and "many of the riches are to be found in the untapped archives and unexamined histories of modernist texts" (195). *The Gender of Modernism,* with its twenty-six chapters on individual, mostly female, modernist writers, can now be seen as one of the founding resources of the new age for modernist studies. The organization of its chapters by author betrays how important the challenge to the canon and recuperative work were, among various goals set in 1990. Once assembled, however, a rich set of connections and common concerns among the selected authors became obvious. An illustration from the introduction, titled "A Tangled Mesh of Modernists," has been one of the most frequently cited aspects of the book, inspiring thought about strategic alliances and cultural contexts. Further tangling has become the order of the day for *Gender in Modernism.*

The twenty-one chapters are organized by themes and concepts, in most cases uniting a group of authors who may or may not have worked together in life, and generally facilitating a re-examination of the history of modernist texts. The themes for individual chapters are framed and explained by their respective contributors—modernist and feminist scholars drawn from multiple generations. The youngest came into modernist study with the former volume in hand. Most have published or are about to publish book-length studies that elaborate the ideas for the chapters they are editing for the volume. The conceptual ideas grounding chapters, and even their styles, differ, meaning that readers can take up a conversation that is varied and invites debate. Rather than tightly package or direct its own use, the volume strives like its predecessor to be a resource and a departure point for new concepts and connections.

The table of contents does cluster the chapters tentatively into five parts, to which I have already referred in developing this "retro-prospective on gender in modernism":

One: "Modernist/Feminist Activism"
Two: "Issues of Production and Reception"
Three: "Diverse Identities and Geographies"
Four: "War, Technology, and Traumas of Modernity"
Five: "Arts and Performances"

These respond to the recent evolution of modernist studies, described above, but they also suggest additional ways that modernist texts can be compared and understood. The initial "Activism" part offers an opening salvo to the apolitical, aesthetic, individualist, and privileged-class modernism favored at the mid-twentieth century. It serves the credo of women's studies that activism and the academy can and should be combined. Through their consideration of the suffragist, futurist, and socialist movements, Chapman and Green, Lyon, Berke, and Ardis clearly place women's words and their bodies in the public sphere. The threads of suffragism and socialism initiated here weave their way into later sections of the book (suffragism recurring in chapters 4, 5, 18, and 19; socialism in chapters 5, 6, 7, 9, and 14).

The second part, "Issues of Production and Reception," recovers alternative sites and stories of modernist publication, with their accompanying aesthetic and political principles, and their internal struggles. *The New Age* emerges from a gendered re-centering by Ann Ardis, resulting in a focus upon Beatrice Hastings, long in the shadow of A. R. Orage, and a new concept for dialogue. With her play among positions regarding modernism and the suffragist movement, Hastings stages a conversation with herself, for the stimulation of her audience. Both Hastings in this chapter and Hope Mirrlees, as presented by Julia Briggs, offer a gendered counterpoint to modernist masters, Pound and Eliot, respectively. As Jayne Marek notes with her female editors, the rhetoric of texts concerned with modernist production could be inflected by female gender concerns, even if their focus was on form and experiment. Suzanne Clark and Patrick Collier address modernist anxieties over sentimental writing and journalism in their chapters, encouraging a reassessment of divides and categories. These efforts encourage new ways of reading modernist texts.

As noted above, the large third part, "Diverse Identities and Geographies," responds to the vast array of identity constructions that have become apparent through the burgeoning of cultural theory. The chapters edited by Gay Wachman, with her historicism, and Colleen Lamos, with her theory of scissions between hetero- and homosexuality, allow us to approach sexualities in various ways. In representing "passing," Pamela Caughie imbricates race, Jewish ethnicity, sexuality, and the exotic other. Her chapter is but one example of ways that we become most aware of the fluidity and contingency of identity as performance. Tuzyline Allan and Sonita Sarker encourage us to think about ways that national identity, colonialism, global travel and commerce, and emigration add further complication and bewilderment to the construction of a self. We can look back on Anglo-Euro-American modernism now from a wider world that includes the trajectories of immigrants and émigrés, and includes situations in colonial and postcolonial India, Africa, and Ireland, as well as effects of the Holocaust. I was struck by the fact that Senegal figures in three chapters—through an ad featuring a Senegalese rifleman in Mirrlee's "Paris" (chapter 8), a Senegalese friend on Claude McKay's Marseilles waterfront (chapter 11), and the poet Léopold Senghor featured in Allan's introduction to chapter 12. Modernism has indeed found different lines of flow.

Part four, "War, Technology, and Traumas of Modernity," attends to the historical and psychological effects of living in an age of military violence and mechanical reproduction (the phenomenon identified as synonymous with modernity by Walter Benjamin). Chapters 14–16, on war, trauma, and medicine, respectively, address crises that spanned genders (neurasthenia/shell-shock; aging). Yet, as Susan Squier notes, these could be worked through very differently, depending upon the gender of the participant. Suzette Henke remarks upon the "bloody inauguration of contemporary psychoanalysis" alongside war, and Freud's own "reinterpretation of 'male hysteria' [. . .] in terms of combat neurosis." Resonating with the section on diverse identities, for her chapter, "War, Modernisms, and the Feminized 'Other,'" Claire Tylee selects works by men and women from various subordinated groups and finds them masking their refusal of "official culture" with irony. Bette London notes that, in the early modernist period, psychical research had "much broader and more diverse constituencies than psychoanalysis" and interestingly provided "important avenues for women's professionalization and mental development" (chapter 17). The subject of modernity, including an embracing of technology, is anticipated in many earlier chapters, including the interests of women editors in chapter 7, the scenarios of travel, synonymous with passing in chapter 11, and with postcolonialism in chapter 13. War is a far more pervasive subject than the one chapter dedicated to it would suggest. It concerns Beatrice Hastings in chapter 5; noncombatants populate chapter 10. Chapter 12 opens with reflections on the "dark dead" of the two world wars and the African Diaspora.

Recent interest in performance, visual media, and other arts fuse with and invigorate modernist critical writing in the final part, "Arts and Performances." Its array of texts blends activist with abstract expressions, as Kelly demonstrates in her chapter on drama. By seeking out critical statements by women artists and *cinéastes,* Gillespie and Hankins restore modernist women's voices to the arts. Shloss notes that the dearth of theory on the subject of dance gave women occasion "to define and redefine the meaning of their own physical movements and performance strategies." Aesthetics was for a long time central to modernist criticism, but in this return to that subject we find it joined with social critique and artistic strategy.

The projects of recovering lost women writers and studying unacknowledged forces of gender were major concerns of the original *Gender of Modernism;* these interests are still widely distributed here, though differently arrayed. Beatrice Hastings steps out from the shadows of *The New Age* in Ardis's selections for chapter 5 and Iris Barry emerges as an important film critic in Hankins's chapter on London cinema. Briggs's chapter 8 on Hope Mirrlees, claims a lost masterpiece, while it attends to newer concerns of political poetry, mass culture, and hybrid identity. Although works by authors such as H. D., Jesse Fauset, Rebecca West, Marianne Moore, Gertrude Stein, and Dorothy Richardson, featured in the original *Gender of Modernism,* are present in this volume, there is no repetition of content; the books will serve as complements. Some canonical modernists are present in *Gender in Modernism*—none is more prominent than Virginia Woolf, now almost universally canonized. She fits here, not through conventional concepts like genius, but via the multiple concepts of modernism as defined today. Well-known authors such as Gertrude Stein, Woolf, Moore, D. H. Lawrence, and Ernest Hemingway are juxtaposed with far less familiar figures, many of whom have very different agendas, places, and ways of working; these inclusions will encourage further rethinking of modernism.

As with the first volume, a premium is placed on items that are still in the archives, out of print, or widely scattered in periodicals of the early twentieth century—works difficult for students and scholars to obtain, and yet essential for a more thorough understanding of modernism. There is a mixture of genres, with the essay outnumbering all others, and the realm of journalism better attended to. Plays are more available, but there remains a generous presence of poetry and excerpts from novels. It is hoped that these selections will summon back into print authors such as Dorothy Richardson, favored during the brief life of Virago and other feminist presses, as well as authors never graced by recovery.

This collection demonstrates both the value and the complexity of gender as a locus for fielding issues of political activism, cultural production, performance, and diverse identity formation on a global stage. Modernism, particularly as negotiated through the cultural complex of gender, in the broader scope of modernity, and verging upon challenges of globalism is "new" once again. The study of its various neglected themes and questions offers better material than ever before for framing a future where diverse people may understand one anther, collaborate, and flourish.

Notes

1. Key works include "A Black Feminist Statement," by the Combahee River Collective (1979), *All the Women Are White, All the Blacks Are Men, But Some of Us Are Brave: Black Women's Studies,* ed. Gloria T. Hull and Barbara Smith (1981), and *This Bridge Called My*

Back: Writings by Radical Women of Color, ed. Cherríe Moraga and Gloria E. Anzaldúa (first published 1981). Perhaps the most eloquent advocate for women of color as well as lesbians was Audre Lorde (1934–92).

2. See, for example, Anne Fausto-Sterling, *Sexing the Body: Gender Politics and the Construction of Sexuality* (New York: Basic Books, 2000); Judith Halberstam, *In a Queer Time and Place: Transgender Bodies, Subcultural Lives* (New York: New York University Press, 2005); Suzanne J. Kessler, *Lessons from the Intersexed* (New Brunswick: Rutgers University Press, 1998); and Kate Bronstein, *Gender Outlaw* (New York: Vintage, 1995).

3. The feminist roundtable chaired by Susan Stanford Friedman at the Modernist Studies Association IV (2002), posed the question, "Is There a Future for Feminist Criticism in Modernist Studies?"

The thematic sections of this collection have much in common with the recent collection, alluringly titled, *Bad Modernisms,* edited by Douglas Mao and Rebecca L. Walkowitz (Durham: Duke University Press, 2006).

4. In an essay used as preface to each of these volumes, "The Analysis of Women Writers," Bloom makes a careful distinction between aesthetic value and the work of gender studies, to which he assigns historical, social, political, and ideological priorities. He claims further that "biographical criticism, like [. . .] historicist and psychological criticism always has relied upon a kind of implicit gender studies" (xvii). See, for example, *British Women Fiction Writers, 1900–1960.* For these attitudes, he labels himself "Bloom Brontosaurus, amiably left behind by the fire and the flood" (xv).

5. I have to admit a certain envy of anthologists whose materials are sufficiently old (published before 1923) to escape the morass of permissions still required for most of the texts retrieved here. Recent representative works include Stephanie Hodgson-Wright, *Women's Writing of the Early Modern Period, 1588–1688;* Maria Prendergast, *Renaissance Fantasies: The Gendering of Aesthetics in Early Modern Fiction;* George L. Justice and Nathan Tinker, eds., *Women's Writing and the Circulation of Ideas: Manuscript Publication in England, 1550–1800;* Paula Backsheider, ed., *Revising Women: Eighteenth-Century "Women's Fiction" and Social Engagement;* Isobel Armstrong and Virginia Blain, eds., *Women's Poetry, Late Romantic to Late Victorian: Gender and Genre, 1830–1900;* Talia Schaeffer and Kathy Alexis Psomiades, *Women and British Aestheticism;* Angela Ingram and Daphne Patai, *Rediscovering Forgotten Radicals: British Women Writers, 1889–1939;* Carolyn Dunn and Carol Comfort, eds., *Through the Eye of the Deer: An Anthology of Native American Women Writers;* Nina Baym, *American Women Writers and the Work of History, 1790–1860;* Renée Brenda Larrier, *Francophone Women Writers of Africa and the Caribbean;* Kang-i Sun Chang and Haun Saussy, eds., *Women Writers of Traditional China;* Susie Tharu and K. Lalita, eds. *Women Writing in India: 600 B.C. to the Present;* and *Women Writing Africa,* Vol. 1: The Southern Region, ed. Margaret J. Daymond et al., Vol. 2: West Africa and the Sahel, ed. Aminta Daw and Esi Sutherland, Vol. 3, ed. Tuzyline Allan, (The Feminist Press). Resources online include the Brown University Women Writers Project (http://www.wwp.brown.edu/), the Orlando Project (http://www.ualberta.ca/ORLANDO/), and the Victorian Women Writers' Project (http://www.indiana.edu/letrs/vwwp/). Significant texts for the "men of 1914" are in the public domain. This is less true of the women, whose flourishing I have associated with 1928.There are many ironies about what the estates of specific modernist writers charge for permissions.

6. *Rereading Modernism* (1994), and *Modernism, Gender, and Culture* (1997).

7. See, for example, book-length studies by Allan, Ardis, Berke, Caughie, Chapman, Clark, Collier, Gillespie, Green, Henke, Kelly, Lamos, London, Lyon, Marek, Sarker, Scott, Squier, Tylee, and Wachman, cited in the relevant sections.

8. Good examples include Bridget Elliott and Jo-Ann Wallace's 1994 collaboration, *Women Artists and Writers;* Alice Gambrell's *Women Intellectuals, Modernism and Difference: Transatlantic Culture, 1919–1945* (Cambridge: Cambridge University Press, 1997); *Surrealist Women: An International Anthology,* edited by Penelope Rosemont (Austin: University of Texas Press, 1998); and *Close Up 1927–1933: Cinema and Modernism,* ed. James Donald, Anne Friedberg, and Laura Marcus. Foundations for visual studies can be found in Teresa de Lauretis, *Technologies of Gender: Essays on Theory, Film and Fiction* (Bloomington: Indiana University Press, 1987); Laura Mulvey, *Visual and Other Pleasures* (Bloomington: Indiana University Press, 1989); Leo Charney and Vanessa Schwartz, *Cinema and the Invention of Modern Life* (Berkeley: University of California Press, 1995); Griselda Pollock's collection, *Vision and Difference;* and Chris Jenks's *Visual Culture* (London: Routledge, 1995).

9. As Friedman notes, these terms evolved by 1984 in Showalter's article, "Women's Time, Women's Spaces" (Friedman 244–45 n.1).

10. I am thankful to Ann Ardis for drawing my attention to this exchange.

11. For fine documentation of the rise of second-wave feminism amid other movements of the New Left, see Rosalyn Baxandall and Linda Gordon, eds. *Dear Sisters: Dispatches from the Women's Liberation Movement* (New York: Basic Books: 2000).

12. See Chandra Mohanty, Ann Russo, and Lourdes Toreres, eds., *Third World Women and the Politics of Feminism* (Bloomington: Indiana University Press, 1991); Interpal Grewal and Caren Kaplan, *Scattered Hegemonies: Postmodernity and Transnational Feminist Practices* (Minneapolis: University of Minnesota Press, 1994); and Mohanty's *Feminism Without Borders: Decolonizing Theory, Practicing Solidarity* (Durham: Duke University Press, 2003).

13. The journal *MODERNISM/modernity* has offered several special numbers on fascism: Vols. 10.1 (2003, on T. S. Eliot and Fascism), and 2.3–3.1 (1996, Parts I and II on Fascism and Culture). Though the study goes back to Virginia Woolf's *Three Guineas* (1938), Fredric Jameson's *Fables of Aggression: Wyndham Lewis, The Modernist as Fascist* (Berkeley: University of California Press, 1979) initiated recent work. Of feminist interest are Erin Carleston, *Thinking Fascism: Sapphic Modernism and Fascist Modernity* (Stanford: Stanford University Press, 1998); Andrew Hewitt, *Political Inversions: Homosexuality, Fascism, and the Modernist Imaginary* (Stanford: Stanford University Press, 1996); Merry Pawlowski, ed., *Virginia Woolf and Fascism: Resisting the Dictators' Seduction* (New York: Palgrave, 2001); and Laura Frost, *Sex Drives: Fantasies of Fascism in Literary Modernism* (Ithaca: Cornell University Press, 2002).

14. Jane Marcus takes on Virginia Woolf on this subject for an incriminating line in *A Room Of One's Own.* "A Very Fine Negress," chapter 2 of *Hearts of Darkness: White Women Write Race* (New Brunswick: Rutgers University Press, 2004), 24–58.

15. In "Feminism and the Politics of Postmodernism," Linda Nicholson offers a model for selecting what is useful from postmodern and post-structural theories, as well as Marxist criticism. "I saw the arguments of postmodernists to be politically useful for feminists in a variety of ways. They enabled feminists to counteract the totalizing perspectives within both the hegemonic culture of liberalism and within certain versions of Marxism. . . . Postmodernism undermined the theoretical arrogance of these two political perspectives by showing that the foundations upon which each rested

were themselves without ultimate justification and, like any other worldview, could be judged only within the context of historically specific values" (75). Pointing to work by Linda Alcoff that suggests that Derridian deconstruction "leaves feminism unable to articulate anything positive or substantive in the idea of *woman*" (77), she moves from the structuralist model of "language as a symbolic system" to the more pragmatic, socially constructed model of language as discourse (79). For another practical and selective feminist take on postmodern theory, see chapter 5, "The Doxa of Difference," in Felski's *Doing Time*. Felski works with the limitations of Lancanian phallocentric critique (123) before going on to consider the difference of dissension in feminist postcolonial theory.

16. The classic essay is Heidi Hartman's "The Unhappy Marriage of Marxism and Feminism: Towards a More Progressive Union," in *Women and Revolution* (Boston: South End Press, 1981). See Nicholson on her problems with her own identification with Marxism (70–71).

17. Mary Hawkesworth assesses Butler's *Gender Trouble* as well as Steven Smith's *Gender Thinking* (1992), R. W. Connell's *Gender and Power* (1987), and Wendy McKenna's *Gender: An Ethnomethodological Approach* in "Confounding Gender," *Signs* 22.3 (Spring 1997): 649–85. If gender is to remain emancipatory, Hawkesworth argues that feminists must confound it: be wary of narratives that link gender to "the cunning of culture operating in the interests of reproduction" (680), and ones that equate causal force to gender. She resists a related shift of feminist politics "toward issues of self, psyche, and sexuality," resulting in an "insufficiently inclusive" politics (681).

18. Look, for example, among the sentimental modernists contained in chapter 4, in Hope Mirrlees's "Paris" (chapter 8), and at the repeated presence of Oscar Wilde in the volume.

19. Alarcón lists "relational dialogues" as one of the minority discourses silenced by prevailing discourses (363).

20. While I will not attempt to track down all of the sources for these figures, one might consult the following: for "weave," see Alarcón, above; Lippard uses "a braid of multiple positions" (266). Both of these metaphors have appeal for their relevance to women's work in textiles and grooming, as does the figure of the "web," which I relied upon heavily in *Refiguring Modernism*. Modleski writes that "feminism needs to insist on the complex, multiple and cross-cutting" nature of identity and to ask: how do we rid ourselves of the desire for a line of origin" in "Cinema and the Dark Continent." Nancy Fraser suggests "axes of power" (qtd. in Felski 32; also in Friedman and Boone, above). I have resisted this term because of its recent militaristic invocation in American foreign policy. "Intersection" is so widely used as to defy documentation, though it works best when just two systems are studied together, and even then the contact seems limited. "Intersectionality" is regularly used to study multiple identifications in relation to power, privilege, and oppression. I value "complex" both as a figure and as a goal for involved, personally transforming study.

21. There has been renewed interest in the Enlightenment paradigm, even by feminist critics. See, for example, Elizabeth A. Flynn, *Feminism beyond Modernism* (Carbondale: Southern Illinois University Press, 2002), and Christine Froula, *Virginia Woolf and the Bloomsbury Avant-garde: War, Civilization, Modernity* (New York: Columbia University Press, 2005).

Works Cited

Alarcón, Norma. "The Theoretical Subject(s) of *This Bridge Called My Back* and Anglo-American Feminism." In Anzaldúa, ed. 356–69.

Allan, Tuzyline Jita. *Womanist and Feminist Aesthetics: A Comparative Review.* Athens: Ohio University Press, 1995.

Anzaldúa, Gloria, ed. *Making Face, Making Soul: Haciendo Caras: Creative and Critical Perspectives by Women of Color.* San Francisco: Aunt Lute Foundation Books, 1990.

Armstrong, Isobel, and Virginia Blain, eds. *Women's Poetry, Late Romantic to Late Victorian: Gender and Genre, 1830–1900.* Basingstoke: Macmillan Press, 1999.

Armstrong, Tim. *Modernism, Technology, and the Body.*

Benstock, Shari. *Women of the Left Bank.*

Bloom, Harold. "The Analysis of Women Writers." In *British Women Fiction Writers, 1900–1960.* Vol. 1, ed. Harold Bloom. Philadelphia: Chelsea House, 1997.

Boone, Joseph A. *Libidinal Currents.*

Butler, Judith. *Gender Trouble.*

Carby, Hazel. *Race Men.* Cambridge: Harvard University Press, 1998.

Caughie, Pamela. *Passing and Pedagogy.*

Christian, Barbara. "The Race for Theory." In Anzaldúa, ed. 335–45.

De Lauretis, Teresa, ed. "Queer Theory: Lesbian and Gay Sexualities." Special Number. *Differences: A Journal of Feminist Cultural Studies* 3.2 (Summer 1991): 1040–91.

Doan, Laura L. *Fashioning Sapphism: The Origins of a Modern English Lesbian Culture.* New York: Columbia University Press, 2001.

Doyle, Laura Anne. *Bordering on the Body.*

DuPlessis, Rachel Blau. *Genders, Races, and Religious Cultures in Modern American Poetry, 1908–1934.* Cambridge: Cambridge University Press, 2001.

Felski, Rita. *The Gender of Modernity.*

———. *Doing Time: Feminist Theory and Postmodern Culture.* New York: New York University Press, 2000.

Friedman, Susan Stanford. *Mappings: Feminism and the Cultural Geographies of Encounter.* Princeton, N.J.: Princeton University Press, 1998.

Gilroy, Paul. *The Black Atlantic: Modernity and Double Consciousness.* Cambridge: Harvard University Press, 1993.

Herrmann, Anne. *Queering the Moderns: Poses/Portraits/Performance.* New York: Palgrave, 2000.

Homans, Margaret. "A Response to Mary Poovey's 'Recovering Ellen Pickering.'" *Yale Journal of Criticism* 13.2 (2000): 453–60.

Huyssen, Andreas. *After the Great Divide.*

Kaplan, E. Ann. "Introduction 2: Feminism, Aging, and Changing Paradigms." In *Generations: Academic Feminists in Dialogue,* ed. Devoney Looser and E. Ann Kaplan. Minneapolis: University of Minnesota Press, 1997. 13–29.

Lamos, Colleen. *Deviant Modernism: Sexual and Textual Errancy in T. S. Eliot, James Joyce, and Marcel Proust.* Cambridge: Cambridge University Press, 1998.

Lippard, Lucy. *The Pink Glass Swan.* New York: New Press, 1995.

Miller, Christanne. *Cultures of Modernism: Marianne Moore, Mina Loy, and Else Lasker-Schüler: Gender and Literary Community in New York and Berlin.* Ann Arbor: University of Michigan Press, 2005.

Modleski, Tania. "Cinema and the Dark Continent." In *Feminism Without Women: Culture and Criticism in a "Postfeminst" Age*. New York: Routledge, 1991. 115–34.

Moraga, Cherríe, and Gloria Anzaldúa, eds. *This Bridge Called My Back*. Watertown, Mass.: Persephone Press, 1981.

Moi, Toril. *What Is a Woman?* Oxford: Oxford University Press, 1999.

Nicholson, Linda. "Feminism and the Politics of Postmodernism." In *Feminism and Postmodernism*, ed. Margaret Ferguson and Jennifer Wicke. Durham: Duke University Press, 1994. 69–85.

North, Michael. *The Dialect of Modernism*.

Pound, Ezra. "A Retrospect." *Literary Essays of Ezra Pound*. Ed. T. S. Eliot. New York: New Directions, [1954]. 3–14.

Rado, Lisa, ed. *Rereading Modernism: New Directions in Feminist Criticism*. New York: Garland, 1994.

———. *Modernism, Gender, and Culture*.

Sanchez, Rosaura. "Discourses of Gender, Ethnicity, and Class in Chicano Literature." In *Feminisms: An Anthology of Literary Theory and Criticism*, ed. Robyn R. Warhol and Diane Price Herndl. New Brunswick: Rutgers University Press, 1997. 1007–22.

Scandura, Jani, and Michael Thurston. *Modernism, Inc.: Body, Memory, Capital*.

Schuchard, Ronald. "American Publishers and Transmission of T. S. Eliot's Prose: A Sociology of English and American Editions." In Ian Willison, Warwick Gould, and Warren Cherniak, eds. 171–201.

Scott, Bonnie Kime, ed. *The Gender of Modernism: A Critical Anthology*.

———. *Refiguring Modernism, Vol. 1: The Women of 1928*.

Showalter, Elaine. "Women's Time, Women's Space: Writing a History of Feminist Criticism." In *Feminist Issues in Literary Scholarship*, ed. Shari Benstock. Bloomington: Indiana University Press, 1987. 30–44.

PART I

Modernist/Feminist Activism

1

Suffrage and Spectacle

**INTRODUCED AND SELECTED BY MARY CHAPMAN
AND BARBARA GREEN**

IN INCREASING NUMBERS, literary and cultural critics have read the Anglo-American twentieth-century suffrage movement in relation to the development of the various cultures of modernity (democratic, aesthetic, visual, advertising, and commodity cultures), and the existence of a feminist literary culture in relation to the emergence of literary modernism.[1] The suffrage movement predates the modernist period, and was characterized throughout by a wide variety of strategies, tactics, and arguments: some radical, some peaceable, some militant, and some constitutionalist.[2] Literary and cultural critics have been struck by the ways in which the dramatic and complex cultural contributions of the last phase of the suffrage movement challenge our understanding of the formation of high modernism and contribute greatly to current efforts to rethink the "great divide" between modernism and mass culture. Much suffrage literature espoused radical politics through the vehicles of the dominant cultural forms of popular culture (the romance, for example); other literary and cultural experiments of the movement borrowed from or contributed to the experimental techniques generally associated with modernism. In both its vibrant print culture and its innovative spectacular politics, the modern suffrage movement in both Britain and America developed new and varied forms of persuasion. The dynamic print culture of the modernist suffrage movement composed a feminist "counter-public sphere" characterized by the creation of a number of women's presses, the establishment of successful oppositional periodicals, the cultivation of feminist speech in a variety of literary genres and popular forms, and the cultivation of feminist work through associations like the Women Writer's Suffrage League in England. At the same time, suffrage offered a challenging visual culture through spectacular activism: sensational publicity stunts; political theatricals and street theater of various sorts; and militant actions. Suffrage organizations capitalized on and helped to shape new understandings of femininity through the new forms of media and visual culture that were defining the new century: especially advertising, cartoons, the accelerated use of photographs in newspapers, and an enhanced desire for sensational journalism. These activities demand to be read in relation to one another, for suffrage activists imagined ways of turning spectacle into print—through media coverage—and making print into a spectacle—through very public creative displays of suffrage banners, petitions, voiceless speeches, and manifestoes.

Though the differences between and within suffrage groups—British and American, constitutional and militant—were immense during the complex period of heightened activism from 1905 to 1920 (roughly from the beginning of militancy in England to the passage of the Nineteenth Amendment in the United States), all embraced the new opportunities that came with modern innovations in print and visual media and developed a wide range of strategies to engage public attention.[3] Large-scale displays of feminist bodies in public spaces worked to announce collectivity and civic participation; the pageant, march, and parade were especially popular vehicles in both countries. And as feminist texts and activists crossed the Atlantic, the cross-pollination of modern political strategies flourished.[4] In both countries new organizations were formed out of frustration with the lack of progress or were revitalized by innovative approaches to lobbying. In Britain, the three major Edwardian suffrage organizations—the non-militant National Union of Women's Suffrage Societies formed in 1897 and led by Millicent Fawcett, and the militant organizations the Women's Social and Political Union (WSPU) formed in 1903, led by Emmeline and Christabel Pankhurst, and the Women's Freedom League (WFL), which broke from the WSPU in 1907, led by Charlotte Despard—participated in the large-scale marches and pageants that composed some of the period's most dramatic street theater.[5] In America, college graduates like Marianne Moore joined with trade unionists and society women to form radical associations like the Collegiate Equal Franchise Society, the Women's Political Union (WPU), the Congressional Union (CU), and the National Woman's Party (NWP), which advocated a radical strategy of symbolic expression.[6] All of these groups organized colorful parades, pageants, and other entertainments that packaged threatening ideas of women's political role within visually pleasing, media-friendly forms, presenting suffrage as, at once, part of a progressive platform and the logical extension of nineteenth-century womanly influence. Initially considered radical, the parade form quickly became "the most characteristic form of activism during the final years of the campaign" (Goddard 250), and could command audiences of nearly 250,000 and involve tens of thousands of women marching according to profession, association, nationality, or branch organization. Suffrage organizations staged a variety of spectacular performances: professional and amateur productions of propaganda plays like Hamilton and St. John's *How the Vote Was Won, tableaux vivants,* debates and speeches, screenings of suffrage newsreels and docu-melodramas, balls and street meetings, cross-country tours by car, train, trolley, or on foot, and other publicity stunts. These spectacles asked spectators to rethink gender by complicating the universal ideal and demonstrating women's fitness for governing through a display of their ability to organize, negotiate conflicts, and achieve solidarity among diverse groups of women.[7]

In addition to the pleasing spectacles of street pageantry and exhibitions, members of the militant organizations, England's WSPU and WFL and Amer-

Fig. 1.1. The "Car of Empire" on the Women's Coronation Procession, June 17, 1911. This photograph demonstrates suffrage activists' development of political spectacle. Reproduced from Suffragette Fellowship Collection, Museum of London, with permission.

Fig. 1.2. National Woman's Party pickets carried banners quoting President Woodrow Wilson's and other politicians' wartime democracy slogans throughout 1917. In this photograph, party members carry a banner that ironically quotes from Wilson's April 1917 war message. Courtesy of the Library of Congress.

ica's CU and NWP, staged acts of political protest. The WSPU began to gain national attention in October 1905 when Christabel Pankhurst and Annie Kenney disrupted an election meeting at the Free Trade Hall, leading to their arrests. The militancy of this phase of the suffrage campaign consisted largely of the disruption of political meetings through the "interruption of male political discourse" and the strategic courting of imprisonment.[8] Newspapers eager for sensational stories and photographs gave these tactics a great deal of public attention.[9] A shared interest in commanding public attention, insisting upon a right to protest, and manipulating constitutionalist rhetoric made for richly textured forms of radical activity produced by both the WSPU and the WFL: for example, Grille Protests where feminists chained themselves to a metal screen in front of the Ladies' Gallery commented upon women's exclusion from political life as did numerous deputations such as the one fictionalized by Evelyn Sharp and reproduced in this section.[10] Increasingly, especially after 1912, the WSPU engaged in more violent forms of protest— from window-smashing to the destruction of private and public property through arson and other methods. The strategy of courting imprisonment continued throughout the campaign, but after the first feminist hunger strike in prison in 1909, the story of suffragettes' sacrifice for the cause took on a grimmer aspect as hunger-striking activists were forcibly fed and, after 1913, subject to the Cat and Mouse Act that released them only to re-imprison them once they resumed activism.

American suffragists borrowed militant tactics from their British sisters but eschewed the violent methods. They staged spectacles that attracted media attention, but they also turned their manipulation of "print" itself into a spectacle, through the colorful display of collectively authored banners, placards, and picket signs in public places. Rather than recalling the feminine, decorative, Arts & Crafts banners fashioned by British suffragists that Lisa Tickner has examined, the sleek functional typeface of American suffrage banners responded in many respects to male modernist accusations that feminine decoration was to blame for cultural stasis and decay and anticipated the design of modernist journals like *BLAST*. From about 1907 on, American suffrage activists utilized these and other forms of print cultural spectacle to criticize the government's failure to respond to women's demands for the franchise. Throughout the next twelve years, silent, peaceable women made spectacles of themselves delivering, presenting, and carrying suffrage print culture: they unfurled banners from the Senate Gallery, ceremonially presented four-mile-long petitions to legislators, and delivered voiceless speeches in shop windows.

In 1917, when President Wilson, preoccupied by the war, refused to meet with lobby groups, the NWP picketed the White House, displaying banners that quoted Wilson's empty rhetoric (e.g., "Liberty is a Fundamental Demand of the Human Spirit"). Jailed for obstructing traffic because picketing was in fact legal, suffragists hunger struck while demanding political prisoner status, a strategy that culminated in beatings and force-feedings. Responding to popular stereotypes of women as garrulous, and suffragists as "lantern-jawed harridans" or "iron-jawed angels," stereotypes that foreground the mouth as a site of women's strength and potential unattractiveness, all of these print cultural spectacles visualized women as temporarily and strategically silent. Performing their political voicelessness through print was a key tactic of their campaign.

More conventional suffrage literature was an integral part of this complex strategy of suffrage spectacle, even, as Sowon Park has claimed, an "event" in its own right best understood within a context of production and circulation that included the creation of organizations for women writers and artists, fund-raising events, the interactive nature of some feminist theater, and the role that novels and other literary forms played to convert a mass readership to the cause.[11] In Britain, suffragists and suffragettes created organizations for feminist artists of various sorts: among them, the Women Writers' Suffrage League (WWSL), Artists' Suffrage League, Suffrage Atelier, and Actresses' Franchise League. The WWSL was formed in 1909 by Cicely Hamilton with Elizabeth Robins elected the first president; members included Sarah Grand, Olive Schreiner, Evelyn Sharp, Violet Hunt, May Sinclair, Alice Meynell, and Ivy Compton-Burnett (Park 92). The organization brought together "professional" women writers—meaning any writer who had sold a text—to support the cause with the method "proper to writers—the use of the pen" (Robins, *Way Stations* 112). The members of the WWSL contributed to suffrage periodicals like *Votes for Women*, *Common Cause*, and *The Vote*, wrote letters to newspapers, and published fiction, plays, burlesques, manifestoes, oratory, autobiographies, diaries, histories, poems, sketches, polemical essays, and songs.[12] Many of these literary works were published through feminist presses like the WSPU's Women's Press and were sold in shops like the Women's Press Shop. The existence of an active feminist readership together with new avenues for the publication and circulation of feminist texts also worked to keep key works in print, for example the classic New Woman novel among suffrage readers, Olive Schreiner's *The Story of an African Farm*.[13]

In the United States, suffragists also produced an unprecedented amount of creative material directed at converting people to the cause—from conventional literary genres to songs, films, cartoons, and slogans, although very little scholarship has addressed this.[14] Writers such as Mary Austin, Charlotte Perkins Gilman, Edna Ferber, Zona Gale, and Alice Duer Miller published both in radical periodicals like *The Woman's Journal, The Suffragist, The Forerunner, The Woman Voter, Women's Political World, Crisis* and *The Masses*, and in mainstream journals devoting special issues to suffrage. The National American Woman Suffrage Association formed its own publishing imprint—the National Woman Suffrage Publishing Company—and the Leslie Bureau of Suffrage Education supplied newspapers with suffrage copy and photographs. Although no formal women writers' associations existed as in Britain, writers congregated in suffrage organizations, and feminist groups, like Heterodoxy, participated in fundraising readings and book auctions, and marched together in parades.

Not only because suffrage literature was created to persuade, but also because much of it was intended for a mass readership as Park and Eileen Sypher have shown, the fiction tends toward realism: for example, documentary reportage, and the incorporation of speeches and polemic in literary works like Robins's *The Convert* and local color in works by American regionalists like Ferber, as well as a reliance on stereotypes such as the attractive suffrage heroine and her anti-suffrage lover. Yet, though it has been tempting to locate a "great divide" between suffrage polemic and modernist literary experiment, recent criticism has also noted a number of historical and formal connections between suffrage art and modernism and the value of the cultural work performed by suffrage texts.[15] Jane Miller has suggested that suffrage literature is proto-modernist, and has argued for a modernism of content rather than form in the suffrage novel. Many suffrage works, however, are also formally innovative in their use of dialect and collective authorship; certainly both the use of parody and pastiche in order to disrupt ideology and the "fluid appropriability of imagery and types" favored by suffrage authors sit nicely next to modernist experiment.[16]

In addition, many modernist artists found common cause (or sometimes cause for criticism) with suffragists and suffragettes. In *BLAST* Wyndham Lewis announced his sympathy for suffragettes while urging them to stop attacks on public property—especially art. Others, like Virginia Woolf in *Night and Day,* noted the labor of suffragists who struggled in offices, meetings, and letter-writing campaigns. Marianne Moore contributed regular unsigned suffrage copy and a letter to the editor to her local newspapers at the same time that her first poems were being published in *The Egoist.* A St. Vincent Millay sonnet celebrates a suffrage martyr; Ford Madox Ford, then Hueffer, wrote pro-suffrage literature; May Sinclair's *The Tree of Heaven* associates radical suffrage with modernist experiment; Djuna Barnes wrote an essay for the *New York World* in which she described her voluntary submission to a forcible feeding; and Rebecca West covered the campaign in periodical articles. Progressive journals too covered the campaign, for example *The Masses* and, as the essays by Beatrice Hastings in this collection show, *The New Age.*

The materials collected here are taken from the height of the modern suffrage campaign and sample ways in which modern feminist literary culture tracked and helped produce new forms of modern feminist activism and spectacle.

Evelyn Sharp (1869–1955), an active journalist, editor, and creative writer, published essays and short fiction in journals like *The Yellow Book,* the *Manchester Guardian,* the *Herald,* and the *New Leader,* in addition to publishing novels and children's literature. A member of the WSPU and the Women Writers Suffrage League, she became editor of *Votes for Women* in 1912 when the editors, the Pethick Lawrences, were imprisoned. In 1910 she published *Rebel Women,* vignettes of suffragette life previously published in journals like the *Manchester Guardian* and *Votes for Women.* These suffrage stories chronicled all aspects of activism—from street hawking newspapers to wearing sandwich boards advertising the cause. "The Woman at the Gate" depicts a women's deputation (a feminist attempt to exercise a citizen's right to petition the king or his representative) as both a personal trial for the individual suffragette about to brave a hostile crowd and as an occasion for political debate and discourse in the public sphere of the city's streets. Here, as in other pieces of suffrage literature, the spectator is as important as the militant action itself and slowly the lines between actor and audience are blurred in such a way as to leave open the possibility of political conversion.

Lady Constance Lytton (1869–1923) joined the WSPU in 1909, joined her first deputation that year, and was sentenced to a month's imprisonment. Daughter of Earl Lytton, viceroy of India, Constance Lytton was given special treatment and placed in the hospital ward despite her pleas to be given the same treatment as other suffragettes. To expose these inequities, and the treatment of women in prison in general, Lytton cross-class dressed as "Jane Warton, Spinster" in 1910 to lead a protest demanding the release of suffragette prisoners in Liverpool. "Jane Warton" was arrested and imprisoned in Walton Gaol, where she went on a hunger strike and was subjected to forcible feeding without a medical examination (which would have revealed her weak heart). The story of Lytton's masquerade as Jane Warton circulated in newspaper articles, letters to the editor, and speeches and became a crucial part of a parliamentary debate on the imprisonment and forcible feeding of suffragettes before Lytton published her memoir *Prisons and Prisoners* in 1914. The autobiographical narrative of imprisonment became and important sub-genre of suffrage writing, and Lytton's text, from which this extract is taken, features many of the sub-genre's conventions: a sense of community forge within the prison, and effort to highlight the plight of women in the prison system, and spiritual language of suffering and enlightenmnet.

Edna Ferber (1885–1968) was one of the greatest American women novelists of her day, best known for her novel *Showboat*. In *Fanny Herself* (1917), Ferber traces the meteoric rise of Fanny Brandeis from unsuccessful small-town Jewish storekeeper's daughter to successful fashion executive. In this excerpt from chapter 15, Fanny returns to New York City from a productive European business trip and finds herself in the middle of a suffrage parade. Fanny is struck by the hopefulness of a young underfed girl marching with immigrant textile workers, whose figure is a reprimand to Fanny's entire industry, which bases its profits on the exploitation of underpaid workers such as these. In the cartoon she sketches of this Russian Jewish waif, Fanny resurrects her creative side, which her corporate job has nearly obliterated, and comes home to her roots: "These are my people!"

The Sturdy Oak, a novel serialized in *Collier's* and then issued in book form, was intended to fundraise for the November 1917 New York State referendum on woman suffrage. Suffrage had been defeated by 195,000 votes in the 1915 referendum; the 1917 victory, in the largest state in the union, was a turning point for the national campaign. Edited by Elizabeth Jordan, coauthor of suffrage leader Anna H. Shaw's autobiography, plotted by regionalist Mary Austin, and collectively authored by fourteen prominent men and women writers, *The Sturdy Oak* models in literary achievement what might be possible politically if women were permitted to collaborate with men. As one character proclaims: "It isn't that women . . . could run the world better. . . . It's that men and women have got to work together to do the things that need doing" (71). The novel follows the romance plot of many contemporary suffrage films, plays, and novels: a conversion narrative, it features an attractive wife whose unexpected support for suffrage (including assuming a cross-class disguise that allows her to address factory "girls") convinces her district attorney candidate husband George to support suffrage and fight political corruption. George's troubles begin when he publishes a naive campaign statement proclaiming men's role as woman's protector, causing disasters on both the home front and the campaign trail: unmarried women cousins take him at his word and move in, and a "voiceless speech" in a downtown storefront dares the chivalric George not to turn a blind eye to violations of legislation protecting women and children workers, as his pro-industry supporters would like. When his wife inspects the horrible conditions of rental properties near the factory and attempts to organize working women, she is mistaken for a suffrage activist and kidnapped by mobsters, leading George to declare himself an independent in support of suffrage. The excerpt from chapter 7, by Anne O'Hagan (1869–1934), reporter, editor, and author, depicts a voiceless speech, invented by American suffragists as a canny means of interrogating political candidates without violating Victorian standards of feminine decorum.

Notes

1. As the inclusion of an assortment of suffrage literature in other sections of this collection indicates, the women's suffrage movement has come into its own in modernist studies. See Sylvia Pankhurst and Mrs. F. W. Pethick Lawrence [Emmeline Pethick Lawrence], "Women's Social and Political Union:'Votes for Women' New Movement Manifesto"; NWSPU, "Our Demand: What It Is and What It Is Not"; Beatrice Hastings, "Suffragettes in the Making," "Feminism and the Franchise"; Edna St. Vincent Millay, "Sonnet for Inez Milholland"; and Cicely Hamilton and Christopher St. John, *How the Vote Was Won.*

2. For studies of the ideas of nineteenth- and twentieth-century suffrage movements, see Bolt and Graham.

3. In Britain, the Representation of the People Act (1918) gave women over thirty the right to vote if they were householders, the wives of householders, occupiers of property with an annual rent of £5 or more, or graduates of British universities. After July 1928 women and men over twenty-one could vote on equal terms. See Purvis and Holton, 3–4. In the United States, the Nineteenth Amendment, ratified in 1920, enfranchised women. See Ford.

4. On connecting links between the United States and British campaigns, see Harrison.

5. For readings of the British suffrage movement, see Eustance et al., Fletcher et al., Garner, Holton, Joannou, Purvis, Kent et al., and Rosen.

6. For readings of the American suffrage movement, see Dubois, Ford, Lumsden, and Lunardini.

7. On suffrage use of theatrical spectacle, see Auster, Glenn, Finnegan, Chapman, and Green.

8. The phrase is Jane Marcus's, from *Suffrage and the Pankhursts*, 9.

9. The *Daily Mail* coined the term "suffragette" to distinguish the militant WSPU from constitutional suffragists in 1906, and the militants embraced it, the WSPU later naming its journal *The Suffragette*. In the United States, suffragists divided over strategy: whether suffrage would be gained most expediently through state referenda or through federal lobbying or both.

10. See Mayhall, 49–52.

11. See Park, 459. For readings of the importance of the manifesto and theater to the suffrage movement, see Lyon and Kelly in this volume. Also see Lyon, *Manifestoes* and Stowell.

12. Crawford gives useful bibliographies of British suffrage novels, plays, and poems. A number of recent reprints and collections reproduce material from the British campaign. See Colemore, Jorgansen-Earp; Marcus's *Suffrage,* Norquay, Roberts and Mizuta.

13. See Ardis, 190–94.

14. The exceptions are Bardes and Gossett, who examine the "declaration of independence" trope in nineteenth-century fiction, Friedl, who has anthologized pro- and anti-suffrage plays, and Chapman, who has examined the suffrage poetry of Alice Duer Miller and co-edited a special issue of *Canadian Review of American Studies* on suffrage print culture. On suffrage periodicals, see Yellin and Finnegan.

15. The phrase "great divide" is Andreas Huyssen's. For recent criticism on suffrage and modernism, see Howlett, Felski, Lyon, Marcus's "Asylums of Anteaus," Park, and Joannou.

16. The last phrase is Murray's, who has claimed that these techniques anticipate postmodernism (202).

Works Cited

Ardis, Ann. "Organizing Women: New Woman Writers, New Woman Readers, and Suffrage Feminism." In *Victorian Woman Writers and the Woman Question,* ed. Nicola Diane Thompson. Cambridge: Cambridge University Press, 1999. 189–203.

Auster, Albert. *Actresses and Suffragists: Women in the American Theater, 1890–1920.* New York: Praeger, 1984.

Bardes, Barbara, and Suzanne Gossett. *Declarations of Independence: Women and Political Power in Nineteenth-Century American Fiction.* New Brunswick: Rutgers University Press, 1990.

Barnes, Djuna. "How It Feels to Be Forcibly Fed." In *New York/Djuna Barnes,* ed. Alyce Barry. Los Angeles: Sun and Moon Press, 1989. 174–79.

Bolt, Christine. "The Ideas of British Suffragism." *Votes for Women.* Edited by June Purvis and Sandra Stanley Holton. New York: Routledge, 2000. 34–56.

Chapman, Mary. "Women and Masquerade in the 1913 Suffrage Demonstration in Washington." *Amerikastudien* 44.3 (Fall 1999): 343–55.

———. *"Are Women People?* Alice Duer Miller's Poetry and Politics." *American Literary History* 18.1 (2006): 59–85.

Chapman, Mary, and Angela Mills, eds. Special "Suffrage" Issue, *Canadian Review of American Studies* 36:1: 1–128.

Colemore, Gertrude. *Suffragette Sally.* London: Stanley Paul & Co., 1911; rpt. as *Suffragettes: A Story of Three Women.* London: Pandora Press, 1984.

Crawford, Elizabeth. *The Women's Suffrage Movement: A Reference Guide, 1866–1928.* London: Routledge, 1999.

Dicenzo, Maria. "Gutter Politics: Women Newsies and the Suffrage Press." *Women's History Review* 12.1 (2003): 15–33.

Dubois, Ellen. *Harriot Stanton Blatch and the Winning of Woman Suffrage.* New Haven: Yale University Press, 1997.

Eustance, Claire, Joan Ryan, and Laura Ugolini, eds. *A Suffrage Reader: Charting Directions in British Suffrage History.* London: Leicester University Press, 2000.

Felski, Rita. *The Gender of Modernity.*

Ferber, Edna. *Fanny Herself.* New York: Frederick A. Stokes Company, 1917. Urbana: University of Illinois Press, 2001.

Finnegan, Margaret. *Selling Suffrage: Consumer Culture and Votes for Women.* New York: Columbia University Press, 1999.

Fletcher, Ian Christopher, Laura E. Nym Mayhall, and Philippa Levine, eds. *Women's Suffrage in the British Empire: Citizenship, Nation, and Race.* London: Routledge, 2000.

Friedl, Bettina. *On to Victory: Propaganda Plays of the Woman Suffrage Movement.* Boston: Northeastern University Press, 1987.

Ford, Linda G. *Iron-Jawed Angels: The Suffrage Militancy of the National Woman's Party, 1912–1920.* Lanham, Md.: University Press of America, 1991.

Gale, Zona. "Folks" [1914]. In *Peace in Friendship Village.* New York: Macmillan, 1919.

Garner, Les. *Stepping Stones to Women's Liberty: Feminist Ideas in the Women's Suffrage Movement, 1900–1918.* London: Heinemann, 1984.

Gilman, Charlotte Perkins. *Selections from Suffrage Songs and Verses.* New York: Charlton, 1911.

Glenn, Susan A. *Female Spectacle: The Theatrical Roots of Modern Feminism.* Cambridge: Harvard University Press, 2000.

Goddard, Leslie. "'Something to vote for': Theatricalism in the United States women's suffrage movement." Ph.D. diss., Northwestern University, 2001.

Graham, Sara Hunter. *Woman Suffrage and the New Democracy.* New Haven: Yale University Press, 1996.

Green, Barbara. *Spectacular Confessions: Autobiography, Performative Activism, and the Sites of Suffrage, 1905–1938.* New York: St. Martin's Press, 1997.

Harrison, Patricia Greenwood. *Connecting Links: The British and American Woman Suffrage Movements, 1900–1914.* Westport, Conn.: Greenwood, 2000.

Heilmann, Ann, ed. *Words as Deeds: Literary and Historical Perspectives on Women's Suffrage.* Special issue of *The Women's History Review* 11:4 and 12:1 (2002–3).

Holton, Sandra. *Feminism and Democracy: Women's Suffrage and Reform Politics in Britain, 1900–1918.* London: Cambridge University Press, 1986.

Howlett, Caroline J. "Writing on the Body? Representation and Resistance in British Suffrage Accounts of Forcible Feeding." In *Bodies of Writing: Bodies in Performance*, ed. Thomas Foster, Carol Siegel, and Ellen E. Berry. New York: New York University Press, 1996.

Hueffer, Ford Madox. *This Monstrous Regiment of Women*. London: Women's Freedom League, 1913.

Huyssen, Andreas. *After the Great Divide*.

Joannou, Maroula. "Suffragette Fiction and the Fictions of Suffrage." In *The Women's Suffrage Movement*, ed. Joannou and Purvis, 101–16.

Joannou, Maroula, and June Purvis, eds. *The Women's Suffrage Movement: New Feminist Perspectives*. Manchester: Manchester University Press, 1998.

Jorgansen-Earp, Cheryl, ed. *Speeches and Trials of the Militant Suffragettes: The Women's Social and Political Union, 1903–1918*. Madison, N.J.: Fairleigh Dickinson University Press, 1999.

Kent, Susan Kingsley. *Sex and Suffrage in Britain, 1860–1914*. London: Routledge, 1990.

Lewis, Wyndham, ed. *BLAST* 1 (June 20, 1914).

Liddington, Jill, and Jill Norris. *One Hand Tied Behind Us: The Rise of the Women's Suffrage Movement*. London: Virago, 1978.

Lumsden, Linda J. *Rampant Women: Suffragists and the Right of Assembly*. Knoxville: University of Tennessee Press, 1997.

Lunardini, Christine. *From Equal Suffrage to Equal Rights: Alice Paul and the National Woman's Party, 1910–1928*. New York: New York University Press, 1986.

Lyon, Janet. *Manifestoes*.

Marcus, Jane. "The Asylums of Antaeus: Women, War, and Madness—Is there a Feminist Fetishism?" In *The New Historicism*, ed. H. Aram Veeser. New York: Routledge, 1989. 132–51.

———, ed. *Suffrage and the Pankhursts*. London: Routledge and Kegan Paul, 1987.

Mayhall, Laura E. Nym. *The Militant Suffrage Movement: Citizenship and Resistance in Britain, 1860–1930*. New York: Oxford University Press, 2003.

Miller, Jane. *Rebel Women: Feminism, Modernism, and the Edwardian Novel*. London: Virago, 1994.

Murray, Simone. "'Deeds *and* Words': The Woman's Press and the Politics of Print." *Women: A Cultural Review* 11.3 (2000): 197–222.

Norquay, Glenda. *Voices and Votes: A Literary Anthology of the Suffrage Campaign*. Manchester: Manchester University Press, 1995.

Park, Sowon S. "'Doing Justice to the Real Girl': The Women Writers' Suffrage League." In Eustance et al., eds., *A Suffrage Reader*, 90–104.

Purvis, June, and Sandra Stanley Holton, eds. *Votes for Women*. London: Routledge, 2000.

Roberts, Marie Mulvey, and Tamae Mizuta, eds. *The Militants: Suffragette Activism*. London: Routledge/Thoemmes Press, 1994.

Robins, Elizabeth. *Way Stations*. London: Hodder and Stoughton, 1913.

———. *The Convert*. 1907. New York: Feminist Press, 1980.

Rosen, Andrew. *Rise Up, Women!*

Sinclair, May. *The Tree of Heaven*. London: Cassell and Co., 1917.

Stowell, Sheila. *A Stage of Their Own: Feminist Playwrights of the Suffrage Era*. Ann Arbor: University of Michigan Press, 1992.

Sypher, Eileen. *Wisps of Violence: Producing Public and Private Politics in the Turn-of-the-Century British Novel*. London: Verso, 1993.

Tickner, Lisa. *The Spectacle of Women*.

West, Rebecca. *The Young Rebecca*.

Winkiel, Laura. "Suffrage Burlesque: Modernist Performance in Elizabeth Robins' *The Convert*." *Modern Fiction Studies* 50.3 (2004): 570–94.

Woolf, Virginia. *Night and Day*. 1919. New York: Harcourt Brace, 1973.

Yellin, Jean Fagin. "Documentation: Du Bois' *Crisis* and Woman's Suffrage." *Massachusetts Review* 14.2 (1973): 265–75.

EVELYN SHARP

The Women at the Gate

"FUNNY, isn't it?" said the young man on the top of the omnibus.

"No," said the young woman from whom he appeared to expect an answer," I don't think it is funny."

"Take care," said the young man's friend, nudging him, "perhaps she's one of them!"

Everybody within hearing laughed, except the woman, who did not seem to be aware that they were talking about her. She was on her feet, steadying herself by grasping the back of the seat in front of her, and her eyes, non-committal in their lack of expression, were bent on the roaring, restless crowd that surged backwards and forwards in the Square below, where progress was gradually becoming an impossibility to the stream of traffic struggling towards Whitehall. The thing she wanted to find was not down there, among the slipping horses, the swaying men and women, the moving lines of policemen; nor did it lurk in those denser blocks of humanity that marked a spot, here and there, where some resolute, battered woman was setting her face towards the gate of St. Stephen's; nor was the thing she sought to be found behind that locked gate of liberty where those in possession, stronger far in the convention of centuries than locks or bars could make them, stood in their well-bred security, immeasurably shocked at the scene before them and most regrettably shaken, as some of them were heard to murmur, in a lifelong devotion to the women's cause.

The searching gaze of the woman on the omnibus wandered for an instant from all this, away to Westminster Bridge and the blue distance of Lambeth, where darting lamps, like will-o'-the-wisps come to town, added a touch of magic relief to the dinginess of night. Then she came back again to the sharp realism of the foreground and found no will-o'-the-wisps there, only the lights of London shining on a picture she should remember to the end of her life. It did not matter, for the thing beyond it all that she wanted to be sure of, shone through rain and mud alike.

"Lookin' for a friend of yours, p'raps?" said a not unfriendly woman with a baby, who was also standing up to obtain a more comprehensive view of what was going on below.

"No," was the answer again,"I am looking at something that isn't exactly there; at least—

"If I was you, miss," interrupted the facetious youth, with a wink at his companion, "I should chuck looking for what ain't there, and—"

She turned and smiled at him unexpectedly.

"Perhaps you are right," she said. "And yet, if I didn't hope to find what isn't there, I couldn't go through with what I have to do to-night."

The amazed stare of the young man covered her, as she went swiftly down the steps of the omnibus and disappeared in the crowd.

"Balmy, the whole lot of 'em!" commented the conductor briefly.

The woman with the passionless eyes was threading her way through the straggling clusters of people that fringed the great crowd where it thinned out towards Broad Sanctuary. A girl wearing the militant tricolour in her hat, brushed against her, whispered, "Ten been taken, they say; they're knocking them about terribly to-night!" and passed noiselessly away. The first woman went on, as though she had not heard.

A roar of voices and a sudden sway of the throng that pinned her against some railings at the bottom of Victoria Street, announced the eleventh arrest. A friendly artisan in working clothes swung her up till she stood beside him on the stone coping, and told her to "ketch on." She caught on, and recovered her breath laboriously.

The woman, who had been arrested after being turned back from the doors of the House repeatedly for two successive hours, was swept past in the custody of an inspector, who had at last put a period to the mental and physical torment that a pickpocket would have been spared. A swirling mass of people, at once interested and puzzled, sympathetic and uncomprehending, was swept along with her and round her. In her eyes was the same unemotional, detached look that filled the gaze of the woman clinging to the railings. It was the only remarkable thing about her; otherwise, she was just an ordinary workaday woman, rather drab-looking, undistinguished by charm or attraction, as these things are generally understood.

"Now then, please, every one who wants a vote must keep clear of the traffic. Pass along the foot-way, ladies, if you please; there's no votes to be had in the middle of the roadway," said the jocular voice of the mounted constable, who was backing his horse gently and insistently into the pushing, struggling throng.

The jesting tone was an added humiliation; and women in the crowd, trying to see the last of their comrade and to let her know that they were near her then, were beaten back, hot with helpless anger. The mounted officer came relentlessly on, successfully sweeping the pavement clear of the people whom he was exhorting with so much official reasonableness not to invade the roadway. He paused once to salute and to avoid two men, who, having piloted a lady through the backwash of the torrent set in motion by the plunging horse, were now hoisting her into a place of safety just beyond the spot where the artisan and the other woman held on to the railings.

"Isn't it terrible to see women going on like this?" lamented the lady breathlessly. "And they say some of them are quite nice—like us, I mean."

The artisan, who, with his neighbour, had managed to evade the devastating advance of the mounted policeman, suddenly put his hand to his mouth and emitted a hoarse cheer.

"Bravo, little 'un!" he roared. "Stick to it!" "Votes for women, I say! Votes for women!"

The crowd, friendly to the point of admiring a struggle against fearful odds which they yet allowed to proceed without their help, took up the words with enthusiasm; and the mud-bespattered woman went away to the haven of the police station with her war-cry ringing in her ears.

The man who had led the cheer turned to the woman beside him, as though to justify his impulse.

"It's their pluck," he said. "If the unemployed had half as much, they'd have knocked sense into this Government long ago!"

A couple of yards away, the lady was still lamenting what she saw in a plaintive and disturbed tone. Unconsciously, she was putting herself on the defensive.

"I shouldn't blame them," she maintained, "if they did something really violent, like—like throwing bombs and things. I could understand that. But all this—all this silly business of trying to get into the House of Commons, when they know beforehand that they can't possibly do it—oh, it's so sordid and loathsome! Did you see that woman's hair, and the way her hat was bashed in, and the mud on her nose? Ugh!"

"You can't have all the honour and glory of war, and expect to keep your hair tidy too," observed one of the men, slightly amused.

"War!" scoffed his wife. "There's none of the glory of war in this."

Her glance ranged, as the other woman's had done, over the dull black stream of humanity rolling by at her feet, over the wet and shining pavements, casting back their myriad distorted reflections in which street lamps looked like grinning figures of mockery—over the whole drear picture of London at its worst. She saw only what she saw, and she shuddered with distaste as another mounted officer came sidling through the crowd, pursuing another hunted rebel woman, who gave way only inch by inch, watching her opportunity to face once more towards the locked gate of liberty. Evidently, she had not yet given sufficient proof of her un-alterable purpose to have earned the mercy of arrest; and a ring of compassionate men formed round her as a body-guard, to allow her a chance of collecting her forces. A reinforcement of mounted police at once bore down upon the danger spot, and by the time these had worked slowly through the throng, the woman and her supporters had gone, and a new crowd had taken the place of the former one.

"Oh, there's none of the glory of war in that!" cried the woman again, a tremble in her voice.

"There is never any glory in war—at least, not where the war is," said her second companion, speaking for the first time. His voice travelled to the ear of the other woman, still clinging to the railings with the artisan. She glanced round at him swiftly, and as swiftly let him see that she did not mean to be recognized; and he went on talking as if he had not seen her turn round.

"This is the kind of thing you get on a bigger scale in war," he said, in a half-jesting tone, as if ashamed of seeming serious. "Same mud and slush, same grit, same cowardice, same stupidity and beastliness all round. The women here are fighting for something big; that's the only difference. Oh, there's another, of course; they're taking all the kicks themselves and giving none of 'em back. I suppose it has to be that way round when you're fighting for your souls and not for your bodies."

"I didn't know you felt like that about it," said the woman, staring at him curiously. "Oh, but of course you can't mean that real war is anything like this wreched scuffle of women and police!"

"Oh, yes," returned the other, in the same tone of gentle raillery. "Don't you remember Monsieur Bergeret? He was perfectly right. There is no separate art of war, because in war you merely practise the arts of peace rather badly, such as baking and washing, and cooking and digging, and travelling about. On the spot it is a wretched scuffle; and the side that wins is the side that succeeds in making the other side believe it to be invincible. When the women can do that, they've won."

"They don't look like doing it to-night, do they?" said the woman's husband breezily. "Thirteen women and six thousand police, you know!"

"Exactly. That proves it," retorted the man, who had fought in real wars. "They wouldn't bring out six thousand police to arrest thirteen men even if they all threw bombs, as your wife here would like to see."

"The police are not there only to arrest the women—"

"That's the whole point," was the prompt reply. "You've got to smash an idea as well as an army in every war, still more in every revolution, which is always fought exclusively round an idea. If thirteen women batter at the gates of the House of Commons, you don't smash the idea by arresting the thirteen women, which could be done in five minutes. So you bring out six thousand police to see if that will do it. That is what lies behind the mud and the slush—the idea you can't smash."

A man reeled along the pavement and lurched up against them.

"Women in trousers! What's the country coming to?" he babbled; and bystanders laughed hysterically.

"Come along; let's get out of this," said the woman's husband hurriedly; and the trio went off in the direction of the hotel.

The woman with the passionless eyes looked after them. "He sees what we see," she murmured.

"Seems he's been in the army, active service, too," remarked the artisan in a sociable manner. "I like the way he conversed, myself."

"He understands, that is all," explained his companion. "He sees what it all means—all this, I mean, that the ordinary person calls a failure because we don't succeed in getting into the House. Do you remember, in 'Agamemnon'—have you read 'Agamemnon'?"

It did not strike her as strange that she should be clasping iron railings in Westminster, late on a wet evening, talking to a working man about Greek tragedy. The new world she was treading to-night, in which things that mattered were given their true proportions, and important scruples of a lifetime dwindled to nothingness, gave her a fresh and a whimsical insight into everything that happened; and the odd companion that chance had flung her, half an hour ago, became quite easily the friend she wanted at the most friendless moment she had ever known.

The man, without sharing her reasons for a display of unusual perception, seemed equally unaware of any strangeness in the situation.

"No, miss, I haven't read it," he answered. "That's Greek mythology, isn't it? I never learnt to speak Greek."

"Nor I," she told him; "but you can get it translated into English prose. It reminds me always of our demonstrations in Parliament Square, because there is a chorus in it of stupid old men, councillors, they are, I think, who never understand what is going on, however plainly it is put to them. When Cassandra prophesies that Agamemnon is going to be murdered—as we warn the Prime Minister when we are coming to see him—they pretend not to see what she is driving at, because if they did, they would have to do something. And then, when her prophecy comes true and he is murdered—of course, the analogy ends here, because we are not out to murder anybody, only to make the Prime Minister hear our demands—they run about wringing their hands and complaining; but nobody does anything to stop it. It really is rather like the evasions of the Home Office when people ask questions in Parliament about the prison treatment of the Suffragettes, isn't it?"

"Seems so," agreed her new friend, affably.

"And then," continued the woman, scorn rising in her voice, "when Clytaemnestra comes out of the house and explains why she has murdered her husband, they find plenty to say because there is a woman to be blamed, though they never blamed Agamemnon for doing far worse things to her. That is the way the magistrate and the daily papers will talk to-morrow, when our women are brought up in the police court."

"That's it! Always put all the blame on the women," said the artisan, grasping what he could of her strange discourse.

Big Ben tolled out ten strokes, and his companion, catching her breath, looked with sudden apprehension at the moving, throbbing block of people, now grown so immense that the police, giving up the attempt to keep the road clear, were merely concerned in driving back the throng on four sides and preserving an open space round the cluster of buildings known to a liberty-loving nation as the People's House. The gentlemen, who still stood in interested groups behind the barred gates of it, found the prospect less entertaining now that the action had been removed beyond the range of easy vision; and some of the bolder ones ventured out into the hollow square, formed by an unbroken line of constables, who were standing shoulder to shoulder, backed by mounted men who made little raids from time to time on the crowd behind, now fast becoming a very ugly one. Every possible precaution was being taken to avoid the chance of annoyance to any one who might still wish to preserve a decorous faith in the principle of women's liberty.

Meanwhile, somewhere in that shouting, hustling, surging mass of humanity, as the woman onlooker knew full well, was the twelfth member of the women's deputation that had been broken up by the police, two hours ago, before it could reach the doors of the House; and knowing that her turn had come now, she pictured that twelfth woman beating against a barrier that had been set up against them both ever since the world grew civilized. There was not a friend near, when she nodded to the artisan and slipped down from her temporary resting-place. The respectable and sympathetic portion of the crowd was cut off from her, away up towards Whitehall, whither it had followed the twelfth woman. On this side of Parliament Square all the idlers, all the coarse-tongued reprobates of the slums of Westminster, never far distant from any London crowd, were herded together in a stupid, pitiless, ignorant mob. The slough of mud underfoot added the last sickening touch to a scene that for the flash of an instant made her heart fail.

"St. James's Park is the nearest station, miss," said the man, giving her a helping hand. "Don't advise you to try the Bridge; might find it a bit rough getting across."

She smiled back at him from the kerbstone, where she stood hovering a second or two on the fringe of the tumult and confusion. Her moment's hesitation was gone, and the sure look had come back to her eyes.

"I am not going home," she told him. "I am the thirteenth woman, you see."

She left the artisan staring at the spot near the edge of the pavement where the crowd had opened and swallowed her up.

"And she so well-informed too!" he murmured. "I don't like to think of it—I don't like to think of it!"

Shortly after midnight two men paused, talking, under the shadow of Westminster Abbey, and watched a patrol of mounted police that ambled at a leisurely pace across the deserted Square. The light in the Clock Tower was out. Thirteen women, granted a few hours' freedom in return for a word of honour, had gone to their homes, proudly conscious of having once more vindicated the invincibility of their cause; and some five or six hundred gentlemen had been able to issue in safety from the stronghold of liberty, which they had once more proved to themselves to be impregnable. And on the morrow the prisoners of war would again pay the price of the victory that both sides thought they had won.

"If that is like real war too," said one of the men to the other, who had just made these observations aloud, "how does anybody ever know which side has won?"

"By looking to see which side pays the price of victory," answered the man who had fought in real wars.

Rebel Women. New York: John Lane Company, 1910. 7–19.

LADY CONSTANCE LYTTON

From *Prisons and Prisoners*

I lay in my bed most of the day, for they did not disturb me, and I tried to keep warm, as I felt the cold fearfully. They brought me all my meals the same as usual, porridge in the morning at 7, meat and potatoes mid-day at 12, porridge at 4.30. When they were hot I fed on the smell of them, which seemed quite delicious; I said "I don't want any, thank you," to each meal, as they brought it in. I had made up my mind that this time I would not drink any water, and would only rinse out my mouth morning and evening without swallowing any. I wrote on the walls of my cell with my slate pencil and soap mixed with the dirt of the floor for ink, "Votes for Women," and the saying from Thoreau's *Duty of Civil Disobedience*- "Under a Government which imprisons any unjustly, the true place for a just man (or woman) is also a prison"; on the wall opposite my bed I wrote the text from Joshua, "Only be thou strong and very courageous." That night I dreamt of fruits, melons, peaches and nectarines, and of a moonlit balcony that was hung with sweetest smelling flowers, honeysuckle and jessamine, apple-blossom and sweet scented verbena; there was only the sound of night birds throbbing over the hills that ranged themselves below the balcony. On it there slept my sister-in-law, and on the balustrade, but making no noise, was a figure awake and alert, which was my brother. My dream was of a land which was seen by my father in his poem of "King Poppy," where the princess and the shepherd boy are the types etherealised. I woke suddenly. I could sleep a little in detached moments, but this dream had made the prison cell beautiful to me; it had a way out.

The strain was great of having to put on my shoes, which were too small, every time I was taken out of my cell to empty slop or to see the Governor. The Matron was shocked that I did not put the right heel in at all and every day I was given another pair, but they were all alike in being too small for my right foot.

The next day, Monday (January 17), the wardress took my bed and bedding away because I would not make it up, but lay on it in the day-time. I told her if she wished she must roll me off, but that I did not intend voluntarily to give it up. She was quite amiable, but rolled me towards the wall and took the bed and bedding from underneath me. There was a little table in my cell which was not fastened to the wall. I turned it upside down and was able to sit in it with my body resting against one of the legs. It was very uncomfortable, but I felt too ill to sit up in the chair, and the concrete floor was much too cold without the bed. Every now and then I got up and walked backwards and forwards in the cell to get a little warmth into me. The Chaplain came in for a moment. He was a tall, good-looking man, of the burly, healthy sort. It seemed to me, from his talk, that he would be very well suited to be a cricket match or football parson, if there were such a thing, but he was totally unsuited to be the Chaplain of a prison, or anyhow of a woman's prison. He thought it wise to speak to me as a "Suffragette." "Look here, it's no good your thinking that there's anything to be done with the women here-the men sometimes are not such bad fellows, and there are many who write to me after they've left here, but the women, they're all as bad as bad can be, there's absolutely no good in them." I did not answer, but I felt inclined to say "Then good-bye to you, since you say you can do no good with the women here."

Presently an officer came and led me out. The manner of nearly all the officers was severe; one or two were friends but most of them treated me like dirt. I was shown along the gangway of the ward, which seemed to me very large, much larger than the D X at Holloway, and went in various directions like a star. I was shown into the Governor's room, which lay at the end of the gangway. It was warm, there were hot pipes against which I was made to stand with my back to the wall, and for a moment, as I put my feet to rest on the pipes, I could think of nothing else but the delight of their heat. The Governor was very cross. I had decided not to do the needlework which constituted the hard labour, for this he gave me three days on bread and water. He would not let me speak to him at all and I was led out, but, before I had got to my cell, I was called back into his presence. "I hear you are refusing to take your food, so it's three days in a special cell." I was taken out and down a staircase till we reached the ground floor. I think my cell was two stories above, but I am not sure; then down again and into a short passage that looked as if it was underground, with a window at the top seemingly only just level with the ground. The door of a cell was opened, I was put inside and the door locked. It was larger than the cell upstairs, and the jug, basin, etc., were all made of black guttapercha, not of tin, placed on the floor. This would have been bad for the ordinary prisoner, as it was quite impossible to tell whether the eating things were clean or not and, in any case, it smelt fairly strong of guttapercha; but as the rule for me was neither to eat nor drink, I was able to put up with it well. The bed was wider than an ordinary plank bed and nailed to the ground, so that I was able to lie on it without being disturbed. Best of all was the fact that it was nearer to the heating apparatus and so seemed quite warm when I was led in. I did not notice at first that the window did not open, but when I had been there six or seven hours it became wonderfully airless. I only left my cell for minutes at a time, when I was allowed to draw water, and the air of the corridor then seemed fresh as mountain air by comparison. I had an idea that Elsie Howey or some of the others would have been put into a punishment cell too. I called, but in vain, my voice had grown weak and my tongue and throat felt thick as a carpet, probably from not drinking anything. I tried signalling with raps on the wall, "No surrender-no surrender," Mrs. Leigh's favourite motto, but I was never sure of corresponding raps, though sometimes I thought I heard them. I could not sleep for more than about an hour at a time, my legs drew up into a cramped position whenever I went off and the choking thickness in my mouth woke me.

Tuesday, January 18, I was visited again by the Senior Medical Officer, who asked me how long I had been without food. I said I had eaten a buttered scone and a banana sent in by friends to the police station on Friday at about midnight. He said, "Oh, then, this is the fourth day; that is too long, I shall have to feed you, I must feed you at once," but he went out and nothing happened till about 6 o'clock in the evening, when he returned with, I think, five wardresses and the feeding apparatus. He urged me to take food voluntarily. I told him that was absolutely out of the question, that when our legislators ceased to resist enfranchising women then I should cease to resist taking food in prison. He did not examine my heart nor feel my pulse; he did not ask to do so, nor did I say anything which could possibly induce him to think I would refuse to be examined. I offered no resistance to being placed in position but lay down voluntarily on the plank bed. Two of the wardresses took hold of my arms, one held my head and one my feet. One wardress helped to pour the food. The doctor leant on my knees as he stooped over my chest to get at my mouth. I shut my mouth and clenched my teeth. I had looked forward to this moment with so much anxiety lest my identity should be discovered beforehand, that I felt positively glad when the time had come. The sense of being overpowered by more force than I could possibly resist was complete, but I resisted nothing except with my mouth. The doctor offered me the choice of a wooden or steel gag; he explained elaborately, as he did on most subsequent occasions, that the steel gag would hurt and the wooden one not, and he urged me not to force him to use the steel gag. But I did not speak nor open my mouth, so that after playing about for a moment or two with the wooden one he finally had recourse to the steel. He seemed annoyed at my resistance and he broke into a temper as he plied my teeth with the steel implement. He found that on either side at the back I had false teeth mounted on a bridge which did not take out. The superintending wardress asked if I had any false teeth, if so, that they must be taken out; I made no answer and the process went on. He dug his instrument down on to the sham tooth, it pressed fearfully on the gum.

He said if I resisted so much with my teeth, he would have to feed me through the nose. The pain of it was intense and at last I must have given way for he got the gag between my teeth, when he proceeded to turn it much more than necessary until my jaws were fastened wide apart, far more than they could go naturally. Then he put down my throat a tube which seemed to me much too wide and was something like four feet in length. The irritation of the tube was excessive. I choked the moment it touched my throat until it had got down. Then the food was poured in quickly; it made me sick a few seconds after it was down and the action of the sickness made my body and legs double up, but the wardresses instantly pressed back my head and the doctor leant on my knees. The horror of it was more than I can describe. I was sick over the doctor and wardresses, and it seemed a long time before they took the tube out. As the doctor left he gave me a slap on the cheek, not violently, but, as it were, to express his contemptuous disapproval, and he seemed to take for granted that my distress was assumed. At first it seemed such an utterly contemptible thing to have done that I could only laugh in my mind. Then suddenly I saw Jane Warton lying before me, and it seemed as if I were outside of her. She was the most despised, ignorant and helpless prisoner that I had seen. When she had served her time and was out of the prison, no one would believe anything she said, and the doctor when he had fed her by force and tortured her body, struck her on the cheek to show how he despised her! That was Jane Warton, and I had come to help her.

When the doctor had gone out of the cell, I lay quite helpless. The wardresses were kind and knelt round to comfort me, but there was nothing to be done, I could not move, and remained there in what, under different conditions, would have been an intolerable mess. I had been sick over my hair, which, though short, hung on either side of my face, all over the wall near my bed, and my clothes seemed saturated with it, but the wardresses told me they could not get me a change that night as it was too late, the office was shut. I lay quite motionless, it seemed paradise to be without the suffocating tube, without the liquid food going in and out of my body and without the gag between my teeth. Presently the wardresses all left me, they had orders to go, which were carried out with the usual promptness. Before long I heard the sounds of the forced feeding in the next cell to mine. It was almost more than I could bear, it was Elsie Howey, I was sure. When the ghastly process was over and all quiet, I tapped on the wall and called out at the top of my voice, which wasn't much just then, "No surrender," and there came the answer past any doubt in Elsie's voice, "No surrender." After this I fell back and lay as I fell. It was not very long before the wardress came and announced that I was to go back upstairs as, because of the feeding, my time in the punishment cell was over. I was taken into the same cell which I had before; the long hours till morning were a nightmare of agonised dread for a repetition of the process.

Lady Constance Lytton and Jane Warton. *Prisons and Prisoners: Some Personal Experiences.* London: William Heinemann, 1914; rpt. London: Virago, 1988. 264–71.

EDNA FERBER

From Chapter 15, *Fanny Herself*

The first week in June found [Fanny] back in New York. That month of absence had worked a subtle change. The two weeks spent in crossing and re-crossing [the Atlantic] had provided her with a let-down that had been almost jarring in its completeness. Everything competitive had seemed to fade away with the receding shore, and to loom up again only when the skyline became a thing of smoke-banks, spires, and shafts. She had had only two weeks for the actual transaction of her business. She must have been something of a revelation to those Paris and Berlin manufacturers, accustomed though they were to the brisk and irresistible methods of the American business woman. She was, after all, absurdly young to be talking in terms of millions, and she was amazingly well dressed. This last passed unnoticed, or was taken for granted in Paris, but in Berlin, home of the frump and the flour-sack figure, she was stared at, appreciatively. Her business [. . .] had to do with two factories on whose product the Haynes-Cooper company [for which she had worked] had long had a covetous eye. Quantity, as usual, was the keynote of their demand, and Fanny's task was that of talking in six-figure terms to these conservative and over-wary foreign manufacturers. That she had successfully accomplished this, and that she had managed to impress them also with the important part that time and promptness in delivery played in a swift-moving machine like the Haynes-Cooper concern, was due to many things beside her natural business ability. Self-confidence was there, and physical vigor, and diplomacy. But above all there was that sheer love of the game; the dramatic sense that enabled her to see herself in the part. That alone precluded the possibility of failure. She knew how youthful she looked, and how glowing. She anticipated the look that came into their faces when she left polite small-talk behind and soared up into the cold, rarefied atmosphere of business. She delighted in seeing the admiring and tolerant smirk vanish and give way to a startled and defensive attentiveness. [. . .]

New York, on her return, was something of a shock. She remembered how vividly fresh it had looked to her on the day of that first visit, months before. Now, to eyes fresh from the crisp immaculateness of Paris and Berlin, Fifth Avenue looked almost grimy, and certainly shabby in spots.

Ella Monahan, cheerful, congratulatory, beaming, met her at the pier, and Fanny was startled at her own sensation of happiness as she saw that pink, good-natured face looking up at her from the crowd below. [. . .] "I waited over a day," said Ella, "just to see you. My, you look grand! I know where you got that hat. Galeries Lafayette. How much?"

"I don't expect you to believe it. Thirty-five francs. Seven dollars. I couldn't get it for twenty-five here."

They were soon clear of the customs. Ella had engaged a room for her at the hotel they always used. As they rode uptown together, happily, Ella opened her bag and laid a little packet of telegrams and letters in Fanny's lap.

"I guess Fenger's pleased, all right, if telegrams mean anything. Not that I know they're from him. But he said—" But Fanny was looking up from one of them with a startled expression.

"He's here. Fenger's here."

"In New York?" asked Ella, rather dully.

"Yes." [. . .] They both had forgotten all about Fenger, their Chief. But they had been in their hotel scarcely a half hour, and Ella had not done exclaiming over the bag that Fanny had brought her from Paris, when his telephone call came.

He wasted very little time on preliminaries. "I'll call for you at four. We'll drive through the park, and out by the river, and have tea somewhere."

"That would be wonderful. That is, if Ella's free. I'll ask her."

"Ella?"

"Yes. She's right here. Hold the wire, will you?" She turned away from the telephone to face Ella. "It's Mr. Fenger. He wants to take us both driving this afternoon. You can go, can't you?"

"I certainly can," replied Miss Monahan, with what might have appeared to be undue force.

Fanny turned back to the telephone. "Yes, thanks. We can both go. We'll be ready at four."

[. . .] Fenger had said, "Damn!" when she had told him about Ella. And his voice had been—well—she pushed that thought outside her mind, too. [. . .]

[. . .] She decided to go down for a bit of lunch, and perhaps a stroll of ten or fifteen minutes, just to see what Fifth Avenue was showing. It was half-past one when she reached that ordinarily well-regulated thoroughfare. She found its sidewalks packed solid, up and down, as far as the eye could see, with a quiet, orderly, expectant mass of people. Squads of mounted police clattered up and down, keeping the middle of the street cleared. Whatever it was that had called forth that incredible mass, was scheduled to proceed uptown from far downtown, and that very soon. Heads were turned that way. Fanny, wedged in the crowd, stood a-tiptoe, but she could see nothing. It brought to her mind the Circus Day of her Winnebago childhood, with Elm street packed with townspeople and farmers, all straining their eyes up toward Cherry street, the first turn in the line of march. Then, far away, the blare of a band. "Here they come!" Just then, far down the canyon of Fifth Avenue, sounded the cry that had always swayed Elm street, Winnebago. "Here they come!"

"What is it?" Fanny asked a woman against whom she found herself close-packed. "What are they waiting for?"

"It's the suffrage parade," replied the woman. "The big suffrage parade. Don't you know?"

"No. I haven't been here." Fanny was a little disappointed. The crowd had surged forward, so that it was impossible for her to extricate herself. She found herself near the curb. She could see down the broad street now, and below Twenty-third Street it was a moving, glittering mass, pennants, banners, streamers flying. The woman next her volunteered additional information.

"The mayor refused permission to let them march. But they fought it, and they say it's the greatest suffrage parade ever held. I'd march myself, only—"

"Only what?"

"I don't know. I'm scared to, I think—I'm not a New Yorker."

"Neither am I," said Fanny. Fanny always became friendly with the woman next her in a crowd. That was her mother in her. One could hear the music of the band, now. Fanny glanced at her watch. It was not quite two. Oh, well, she would wait and see some of it. Her mind was still too freshly packed with European impressions to receive any real idea of the value of this pageant, she told herself. She knew she did not feel particularly interested. But she waited.

Another surging forward. [. . .] A squad of mounted police on very prancy horses. The men looked very ruddy, and well set-up and imposing. Fanny had always thrilled to anything in uniform, given sufficient numbers of them. Another police squad. A brass band, on foot. And then, in white, on a snow-white charger, holding a white banner aloft, her eyes looking straight ahead, her face very serious and youthful, the famous beauty and suffrage leader, Mildred Inness. One of the few famous beauties who actually was a beauty. And after that women, women, women! Hundreds of them, thousands of them, a river of them flowing up Fifth avenue to the park. More bands. More horses. Women! Women! They bore banners. This section, that section. Artists.

School teachers. Lawyers. Doctors. Writers. Women in college caps and gowns. Women in white, from shoes to hats. Young women. Girls. Gray-haired women. A woman in a wheel chair, smiling. A man next to Fanny began to jeer. He was a red-faced young man, with a coarse blotchy skin, and thick lips. He smoked a cigar, and called to the women in a falsetto voice, "Hello, Sadie!" he called. "Hello, kid!" And the women marched on, serious-faced, calm-eyed. There came floats; elaborate affairs, with girls in Greek robes. Fanny did not care for these. More solid ranks. And then a strange and pitiful and tragic and eloquent group. Their banner said, "Garment Workers. Infants' Wear Section." And at their head marched a girl, carrying a banner. I don't know how she attained that honor. I think she must have been one of those fiery, eloquent leaders in her factory clique. The banner she carried was a large one, and it flapped prodigiously in the breeze, and its pole was thick and heavy. She was a very small girl, even in that group of pale-faced, under-sized, under-fed girls. A Russian Jewess, evidently. Her shoes were ludicrous. They curled up at the toes, and the heels were run down. Her dress was a sort of parody on the prevailing fashion. But on her face, as she trudged along, hugging the pole of the great pennant that flapped in the breeze, was stamped a look!—well, you see that same look in some pictures of Joan of Arc. It wasn't merely a look. It was a story. It was tragedy. It was the history of a people. You saw in it that which told of centuries of oppression in Russia. You saw eager groups of student Intellectuals, gathered in secret places for low-voiced, fiery talk. There was in it the unspeakable misery of Siberia. It spoke eloquently of pogroms, of massacres, of Kiev and its sister-horror, Kishineff. You saw mean and narrow streets, and carefully darkened windows, and, on the other side of those windows the warm yellow glow of the seven-branched Shabbos light. Above this there shone the courage of a race serene in the knowledge that it cannot die. And illuminating all, so that her pinched face, beneath the flapping pennant, was the rapt, uplifted countenance of the Crusader, there blazed the great glow of hope. This woman movement, spoken of so glibly as Suffrage, was, to the mind of this over-read, under-fed, emotional, dreamy little Russian garment worker the glorious means to a long hoped for end. She had idealized it, with the imagery of her kind. She had endowed it with promise that it would never actually hold for her, perhaps. And so she marched on, down the great, glittering avenue, proudly clutching her unwieldy banner, a stunted, grotesque, magnificent figure. More than a figure. A symbol.

Fanny's eyes followed her until she passed out of sight. She put up her hand to her cheek, and her face was wet. She stood there, and the parade went on, endlessly, it seemed, and she saw it through a haze. Bands. More bands. Pennants. Floats. Women. Women. Women.

"I always cry at parades," said Fanny, to the woman who stood next her—the woman who wanted to march, but was scared to.

"That's all right," said the woman. [. . .] And she laughed, because she was crying, too. And then she did a surprising thing. She elbowed her way to the edge of the crowd, past the red-faced man with the cigar, out to the street, and fell into line, and marched on up the street, shoulders squared, head high.

Fanny glanced down at her watch. It was quarter after four. With a little gasp she turned to work her way through the close-packed crowd. It was an actual physical struggle, from which she emerged disheveled, breathless, uncomfortably warm, and minus her handkerchief, but she had gained the comparative quiet of the side street, and she made the short distance that lay between the Avenue and her hotel a matter of little more than a minute. In the hotel corridor stood Ella and Fenger, the former looking worried, the latter savage.

"Where in the world—" began Ella.

"Caught in the jam. And I didn't want to get out. It was—it was—glorious!" She was shaking hands with Fenger, and realizing for the first time that she must be looking decidedly sketchy and that she had lost her handkerchief. She fished for it in her bag, hopelessly, when Fenger released her hand. He had not spoken. Now he said:

"What's the matter with your eyes?"

"I've been crying," Fanny confessed cheerfully.

"Crying!"

"The parade. There was a little girl in it—" she stopped. Fenger would not be interested in that little girl. [. . .]

"I guess you don't realize that out in front of this hotel there's a kind of a glorified taxi waiting, with the top rolled back, and it's been there half an hour. I never expect to see the time when I could enjoy keeping a taxi waiting. It goes against me."

"I'm sorry. Really. Let's go." [. . .]

Fifth avenue was impossible. Their car sped up Madison avenue, and made for the Park. The Plaza was a jam of tired marchers. They dispersed from there, but there seemed no end to the line that still flowed up Fifth avenue. Fenger seemed scarcely to see it. He had plunged at once into talk of the European trip. Fanny gave him every detail, omitting nothing. She repeated all that her letters and cables had told. Fenger was more excited than she had ever seen him. He questioned, cross-questioned, criticized, probed, exacted an account of every conversation. Usually it was not method that interested him, but results. Fanny, having accomplished the thing she had set out to do, had lost interest in it now.

The actual millions so glibly bandied in the Haynes-Cooper plant had never thrilled her. The methods by which they were made possible had.

Ella had been listening with the shrewd comprehension of one who admires the superior art of a fellow craftsman.

"I'll say this, Mr. Fenger. If I could make you look like that, by going to Europe and putting it over those foreign boys, I'd feel I'd earned a year's salary right there, and quit. Not to speak of the cross-examination you're putting her through."

Fenger laughed, a little self-consciously. "It's just that I want to be sure it's real. I needn't tell you how important this trick is that Miss Brandeis has just turned." He turned to Fanny, with a boyish laugh. "Now don't pose. You know you can't be as bored as you look."

"Anyway," put in Ella, briskly, "I move that the witness step down. She may not be bored, but she certainly must be tired, and she's beginning to look it. Just lean back, Fanny, and let the green of this park soak in. At that, it isn't so awfully green, when you get right close, except that one stretch of meadow. Kind of ugly, Central Park, isn't it? Bare."

Fanny sat forward. There was more sparkle in her face than at any time during the drive. They were skimming along those green-shaded drives that are so sophisticatedly sylvan.

"I used to think it was bare, too, and bony as an old maid, with no soft cuddly places like the parks at home; no gracious green stretches, and no rose gardens. But somehow, it grows on you. The reticence of it. And that stretch of meadow near the Mall, in the late afternoon, with the mist on it, and the sky faintly pink, and that electric sign—Somebody's Tires or other—winking off and on—"

"You're a queer child," interrupted Fenger. "As wooden as an Indian while talking about a million-a-year deal, and lyrical over a combination of electric sign, sunset, and moth-eaten park. Oh, well, perhaps that's what makes you as you are." [. . .]

They had tea at Claremont, at a table overlooking the river and the Palisades. Fenger was the kind of man to whom waiters always give a table overlooking anything that should be overlooked. After tea they drove out along the river and came back in the cool of the evening. [. . .] It was almost seven when they reached the plaza exit. And there Fanny, sitting forward suddenly, gave a little cry.

"Why—they're marching yet!" she said, and her voice was high with wonder. "They're marching yet! All the time we've been driving and teaing, they've been marching."

And so they had. Thousands upon thousands, they had flowed along as relentlessly, and seemingly as endlessly as a river. They were marching yet. For six hours the thousands had poured up that street, making it a moving mass of white. And the end was not yet. What pen, and tongue, and sense of justice had failed to do, they were doing now by sheer, crude force of numbers. The red-faced hooligan, who had stood next to Fanny in the crowd hours before, had long ago ceased his jibes and slunk away, bored, if not impressed. After all, one might jeer at ten, or fifty, or a hundred women, or even five hundred. But not at forty thousand.

Their car turned down Madison Avenue, and Fenger twisted about for a last look at the throng in the plaza. He was plainly impressed. The magnitude of the thing appealed to him. To a Haynes-Cooper-trained mind, forty thousand women, marching for whatever the cause, must be impressive. Forty thousand of anything had the respect of Michael Fenger. His eyes narrowed, thoughtfully.

"They seem to have put it over," he said. "And yet, what's the idea? Oh, I'm for suffrage, of course. Naturally. And all those thousands of women, in white—still, a thing as huge as this parade has to be reduced to a common denominator, to be really successful. If somebody could take the whole thing, boil it down, and make the country see what this huge demonstration stands for."

Fanny leaned forward suddenly. "Tell the man to stop. I want to get out."

"I want to get something at this stationer's shop." She had jumped down almost before the motor had stopped at the curb.

"But let me get it."

"No. You can't. Wait here." She disappeared within the shop. She was back in five minutes, a flat, loosely wrapped square under her arm. "Cardboard," she explained briefly, in answer to their questions.

Fenger, about to leave them at their hotel, presented his plans for the evening. Fanny, looking up at him, her head full of other plans, thought he looked and sounded very much like Big Business. And, for the moment at least, Fanny Brandeis loathed Big Business, and all that it stood for.

"It's almost seven," Fenger was saying. "We'll be rubes in New York, this evening. You girls will just have time to freshen up a bit—I suppose you want to—and then we'll have dinner, and go to the theater, and to supper afterward. What do you want to see?"

Ella looked at Fanny. And Fanny shook her head, "Thanks. You're awfully kind. But—no."

"Why not?" demanded Fenger, gruffly.

"Perhaps because I'm tired. And there's something else I must do."

[. . .] The elevator door clanged, shutting out the sight of Fenger's resentful frown.

"He's as sensitive as a soubrette," said Ella. "I'm glad you decided not to go out. I'm dead, myself. A kimono for the rest of the evening."

Fanny seemed scarcely to hear her. With a nod she left Ella, and entered her own room. There she wasted no time. She threw her hat and coat on the bed. Her suitcase was on the baggage stand. She turned on all the lights, swung the closed suitcase up to the table, shoved the table against the wall, up-ended the suitcase so that its leather side presented a smooth surface, and propped a firm sheet of white cardboard against the impromptu rack. [. . .]

She sat staring at the paper now, after having marked it off into blocks, with a pencil. She got up, and walked across the room, aimlessly, and stood there a moment, and came back. [. . .] Picked up her pencil, rolled it a moment in her palms, then, catching her toes behind either foreleg of her chair, in an attitude that was as workmanlike as it was ungraceful, she began to draw, nervously, tentatively at first, but gaining in firmness and assurance as she went on.

If you had been standing behind her chair you would have seen, emerging miraculously from the white surface under Fanny's pencil, a thin, undersized little figure in sleazy black and white, whose face, under the cheap hat, was upturned and rapturous. Her skirts were wind-blown, and the wind tugged, too, at the banner whose pole she hugged so tightly in her arms. Dimly you could see the crowds that lined the street on either side. Vaguely, too, you saw the faces and stunted figures of the little group of girls she led. But she, the central figure, stood out among all the rest. Fanny Brandeis, the artist, and Fanny Brandeis, the salesman, combined shrewdly to omit no telling detail. The wrong kind of feet in the wrong kind of shoes; the absurd hat; the shabby skirt—every bit of grotesquerie was there, serving to emphasize the glory of the face. Fanny Brandeis' face, as the figure grew, line by line, was a glorious thing, too. [. . .]

There sounded a smart little double knock at her door. Fanny did not heed it. She did not hear it. Her toes were caught behind the chair-legs again. [. . .] She had brought the table, with its ridiculously up-ended suitcase, very near, so that she worked with a minimum of effort. The door opened. Fanny did not turn her head. Ella Monahan came in, yawning. [. . . .]

"Well, what in the world—" she began, and yawned again, luxuriously. She stopped behind Fanny's chair and glanced over her shoulder. The yawn died. She craned her neck a little, and leaned forward. And the little girl went marching by, in her cheap and crooked shoes, and her short and sleazy skirt, with the banner tugging, tugging in the breeze. Fanny Brandeis had done her with that economy of line, and absence of sentimentality which is the test separating the artist from the draughtsman.

Silence, except for the scratching of Fanny Brandeis's pen.

"Why—the poor little kike!" said Ella Monahan. Then, after another moment of silence, "I didn't know you could draw like that."

Fanny laid down her pen. "Like what?" She pushed back her chair, and rose, stiffly. The drawing, still wet, was propped up against the suitcase. Fanny walked across the room. Ella dropped into her chair, so that when Fanny came back to the table it was she who looked over Ella's shoulder. Into Ella's shrewd and heavy face there had come a certain look.

"They don't get a square deal, do they? They don't get a square deal."

The two looked at the girl a moment longer, in silence. Then Fanny went over to the bed, and picked up her hat and coat. She smoothed her hair, deftly, powdered her nose with care, and adjusted her hat at the smart angle approved by the Galeries Lafayette. She came back to the table, picked up her pen, and beneath the drawing wrote, in large print:

THE MARCHER.

She picked up the drawing, still wet, opened the door, and with a smile at the bewildered Ella, was gone.

It was after eight o'clock when she reached the *Star* building. She asked for Lasker's office, and sent in her card. [. . .] Lasker was always at his desk at eight. Now, Fanny Brandeis knew that the average young woman, standing outside the office of a man like Lasker, unknown and at the mercy of office boy or secretary, continues to stand outside until she leaves in discouragement. But Fanny knew, too, that she was not an average young woman. [. . .]

Carl Lasker's private office was the bare, bright, newspaper-strewn room of a man who is not only a newspaper proprietor, but a newspaper man. There's a difference. Carl Lasker had sold papers on the street when he was ten. He had slept on burlap sacks, paper stuffed, in the basement of a newspaper office. Ink flowed with the blood in his veins. He could operate a press. He could manipulate a linotype machine (that almost humanly intelligent piece of mechanism). He could make up a paper single handed, and had done it. He knew the newspaper game, did Carl Lasker, from the composing room to the street, and he was a very great man in his line. And so he was easy to reach, and simple to talk to, as are all great men. [. . .]

Fanny entered. Lasker laid down her card. "Brandeis. That's a good name." He extended his hand. [. . .]

"[. . .] What can I do for you?"

Fanny wasted no words. "I saw the parade this afternoon. I did a picture. I think it's good. If you think so too, I wish you'd use it."

She laid it, face up, on Lasker's desk. Lasker picked it up in his two hands, held it off, and scrutinized it. All the drama in the world is concentrated in the confines of a newspaper office every day in the year, and so you hear very few dramatic exclamations in such a place. Men like Lasker do not show emotion when impressed. It is too wearing on the mechanism. Besides, they are trained to self-control. So Lasker said, now: "Yes, I think it's pretty good, too." Then, raising his voice to a sudden bellow, "Boy!" He handed the drawing to a boy, gave a few brief orders, and turned back to Fanny. "To-morrow morning every other paper in New York will have pictures showing Mildred Inness, the beauty, on her snow-white charger, or Sophronisba A. Bannister, A.B., Ph.D., in her cap and gown, or Mrs. William Van der Welt as Liberty. We'll have that little rat with the banner, and it'll get 'em. They'll talk about it." His eyes narrowed a little. "Do you always get that angle?"

"Yes."

"There isn't a woman cartoonist in New York who does that human stuff. [. . .] Want a job?"

"N-no."

His knowing eye missed no detail of the suit, the hat, the gloves, the shoes. [. . .] "What's your salary now?"

"Ten thousand."

"Satisfied?"

"No."

"You've hit the heart of that parade. I don't know whether you could do that every day, or not. But if you struck twelve half the time, it would be enough. When you want a job, come back."

"Thanks," said Fanny quietly. And held out her hand.

She returned in the subway. It was a Bronx train, full of sagging faces, lusterless eyes, grizzled beards; of heavy, black-eyed girls in soiled white shoes; of stoop-shouldered men, poring over newspapers in Hebrew script; of smells and sounds and glaring light.

And though to-morrow would bring its reaction, and common sense would have her again in its cold grip, she was radiant to-night and glowing with the exaltation that comes with creation. And over and over a voice within her was saying: [. . .] These are my people! These are my people!

New York: Frederick A. Stokes Company, 1917.

ANNE O'HAGAN

From Chapter 7, *The Sturdy Oak*

Mr. Benjamin Doolittle, by profession Whitewater's leading furniture dealer and funeral director, and by the accident of political fortune the manager of Mr. George Remington's campaign, sat in his candidate's private office, and from time to time restrained himself from hasty speech by the diplomatic and dexterous use of a quid of tobacco. He found it difficult to preserve his philosophy in the face of George Remington's agitations over the woman-suffrage issue. [. . .]

"Now, George, you made a mistake in letting the women get your goat. Don't pay any attention to them. Of course their game's fair enough—I will say that you gave them their opening; you stood yourself for a target with that letter of yours. Howsomever, you ain't obligated to keep on acting as the nigger head in the shooting gallery. Let 'em write; let 'em ask questions in the papers; let 'em heckle you on the stump. All that you've got to say is that you've expressed your personal convictions already, and that you've stood by those convictions in your private life, and that as you ain't up for legislator, the question don't really concern your candidacy. And that, as you're running for district attorney, you will, with their kind permission, proceed to the subjects that do concern you there—the condition of the court calendar of Whitewater County, the prosecution of the race-track gamblers out at Erie Oval, and so forth and so forth. You laid yourself open, George, but you ain't obligated in law or equity to keep on presenting your bare chest for their outrageous slings and arrows."

"Of course what you say about their total irrelevancy is quite true," said George, making the concession so that it had all the belligerency of a challenge. "But I would never have consented to run for office at the price of muzzling my convictions."

Mr. Doolittle wearily agreed that that was more than could be expected of from any candidate of the high moral worth of George Remmington. [. . .]

"Well, I guess that's about all for to-day." Mr. Doolittle brought the conference to a close, hoisting himself by links from his chair. "It takes three thousand dollars every time you circularize the constituency, you know."

He lounged toward the window and looked out upon the pleasant, mellow, autumnal scene around Fountain Square. With the look his affectation of bucolic calm dropped from him. He turned abruptly.

"What's that going on at McMonigal's corner?" he demanded sharply.

"I don't know, I am sure," said George indifferently, still bent upon teaching his manager that he was a free and independent citizen, in leading strings to no man. "It's been vacant since the fire in March when Petrosini's fish market and Miss Letterblair's hat st—"

He had reached the windows himself by this time, and the sentence was destined to remain forever unfinished. For from the low, old-fashioned brick building on the northeast corner of Fountain Square, whose boarded eyes had stared blindly across toward the glittering orbs of its towering neighbour, the Jaffry Building, for six months, a series of great placards flared. Planks had been removed from the windows, plate glass restored, and behind it he read in great irritation:

SOME QUESTIONS FOR CANDIDATE REMINGTON

A foot high, an inch broad, black as Erebus, the letters shouted at him against an orange background. Every window of the second story contained a placard. On the first story, in the show window where Petrosini had been wont to ravish epicurean eyes by shad and red snapper, perch and trout, cunningly embedded in ice blocks upon a marble slab—in that window, framed now in the hated orange-and-black, stood a woman. She was turning backward for the benefit of onlookers, who pressed close to the glass, the leaves of a mammoth pad resting upon an easel.

From their point of vantage in the second story of the Jaffry Building the candidate and his manager could see that each sheet bore that horrid headline:

QUESTIONS FOR CANDIDATE REMINGTON

The whole population of Whitewater, it seemed to George, crowded about that corner.

"I'll be back in a minute," said Benjy Doolittle, disappearing through the private office door with the black tails of his coat achieving a true horizontal behind him. As statesman and as undertaker Mr. Doolittle never swerved from the garment which keeps green the memory of the late Prince Consort.

As the door opened the much-tried George Remington had a glimpse of that pleasing industrial unit, Betty Sheridan, searching through the file for the copy of the letter to the Cummunipaw Steel Works which he had recently demanded to see. He pressed the buzzer imperiously, and Betty responded with duteous haste. He pointed through the window to the crowd in front of Mc-Monigal's block.

"Perhaps," he said, with what seemed to him Spartan self-restraint, "*you can explain the meaning of that scene.*"

Betty looked out with an air of intelligent interest.

"Oh, yes!" she said vivaciously. [. . .] "It's a Voiceless Speech."

"A voice—" George's own face was a voiceless speech as he repeated two syllables of his stenographer's explanation.

"Yes. Don't you know about voiceless speeches? It's antiquated to try to run any sort of a campaign without them nowadays."

"Perhaps you also know who that—female—"

Again George's power of utterance failed him. Betty came closer to the window and peered out.

"It's Frances Herrington who is turning the leaves now," she said amiably. "I know her by that ducky toque."

"Frances Herrington! What Harvey Herrington is thinking of to allow—" George's emotion constrained him to broken utterance. "And we're dining there to-night! She has no sense of the decencies—the—the—the hospitality of existence. We won't go. I'll telephone Genevieve."

"Fie, fie Georgie!" observed Betty. "Why be personal over a mere detail of a political campaign?"

But before George could tell her why his indignation against his prospective hostess was impersonal and unemotional, the long figure of Mr. Doolittle again projected itself upon the scene. Betty effaced herself, gilding from the inner office, and George turned a look of inquiry upon his manager.

"Well?" The monosyllable had all the force of profanity.

"Well, the women, durn them, have brought suffrage into your campaign."

"How?"

"How? They've got a list of every blamed law on the statute book relating to women and children, and they're asking on that sheet of leaves over there if you mean to proceed against all who are breaking those laws here in Whitewater County. And right opposite your own office! It's—it's damn smart. You ought to have got that Herrington woman on your committee."

"It's indelicate, unwomanly, indecent. It shows into what unsexed degradation politics will drag woman. But I'm relieved that that's all they're asking. Of course I shall enforce the law for the protection of every class in our community with all the power of the—"

"Oh, shucks! There's nobody here but me. You needn't unfurl Old Glory," counseled Mr. Doolittle, a trifle impatiently. "They're asking real questions, not blowing off hot air. Oh, I say, who owns McMonigal's block since the old man died? We'll have the owner stop this circus. That's the first thing to do."

"I'll telephone Allen. He'll know."

Allen's office was very obliging and would report on the ownership on McMonigal's block in ten minutes. Mr. Doolittle employed the interval in repeating to George some of the "Questions for Candidate Remington," illegible from the latter's window.

"You believe that woman's place is in the home. Will you enforce the law against woman's night work in the factories? Over 900 women of Whitewater County are doing night work in the munition plants of Airport, Whitewater, and Ondegonk. What do you mean to do about it?"

"You desire to conserve the threatened flower of womanhood." A critical listener would have caught a note of ribald scorn in Mr. Doolittle's drawl as he quoted from his candidate's letter, via the Voiceless Speech placards. 'To conserve the threatened flower of womanhood, the canneries of Omega and Omicron Townships are employing children of five and six years in defiance of the Child Labor Law of this State. Are you going to proceed against them?"

"Woman is man's rarest heritage. Do you think man ought to burn her alive? Remember the Livingston Loomis-Ladd collar factory fire? Fourteen women were killed, forty-eight maimed. In how many of the factories in Whitewater, in which women work, are the fire laws obeyed? Do you mean to enforce them?"

The telephone interrupted Mr. Doolittle's hateful litany. Allen's bright young man begged to report that McMonigal's block was held in fee simple by the widow of the late Michael McMonigal. Mr. Doolittle juggled the leaves of the telephone directory with the dazzling swiftness of a Japanese ball thrower, and in a few seconds he was speaking to the relict of the late Michael. George watched him with fevered eyes, listened with fevered ears. The conversation, it was easy to gather, did not proceed as Mr. Doolittle wished.

"Oh, in entire charge—E. Eliot. Oh! In sympathy yourself. Oh, come now, Mrs. McMonigal—"

But Mrs. McMonigal did not come now. The campaign manager frowned as he replaced the receiver.

"Widow owns the place. That Eliot woman is the agent. The suffrage gang has the owner's permission to use the building from now on to election. She says she's in sympathy. Well, we'll have to think of something—"

"It's easy enough," declared George. "I'll simply have a set of posters printed answering their questions. And we'll engage sandwich men to carry them in front of McMonigal's windows. Certainly I mean to enforce the law. I'll give the order to the *Sentinel* Press now for the answers—definite, dignified answers."

"See here, George," Mr. Doolittle interrupted him with unusual weightiness of manner. "It's too far along in the campaign for you to go flying off on your own. You've got to consult your managers. This is your first campaign; it's my thirty-first. You've got to take advice—"

"I will not be muzzled."

"Shucks! Who wants to muzzle anybody? But you can't say everything that's inside of you, can you? There's got to be some choosing. We've got to help you choose. The silly questions the women are displaying over there—you can't answer them in a word or in two words. This city is having a boom; every valve factory in the valley, every needle and pin factory, is making munitions to-day—valves and needles and pins all gone by the board for the time being. Money's never been so plenty in Whitewater County, and this city is feelin' the benefits of it. People are buying things—clothes, flour, furniture, victrolas, automobiles, rum. There ain't a merchant of any description in this county but his business is booming on account of the work in the factories. You can't antagonize the whole population of the place. Why, I dare say, some of your own money and Mrs. Remington's is earning three times what it was two years ago. The First National Bank has just declared a 15 per cent dividend, and Martin Jaffry owns 54 per cent of the stock. You don't want to put brakes on prosperity. It ain't decent citizenship to try it; it ain't neighborly. Think of the lean years we've known. You can't do it. This war won't last forever"—Mr. Doolittle's voice was tinged with regret—"and it will be time enough to go in for playing the deuce with business when business gets slack again. That's the time for reforms, George; when things are dull."

George was silent, the very presentment of a sorely harassed young man. He had not, even in a year when blamelessness rather than experience was his party's supreme need in a candidate, become its banner bearer without possessing certain political apperceptions. He knew, as Benjy Doolittle spoke, that Benjy spoke the truth—Whitewater, city and county, would never elect a man who had too convincingly promised to interfere with the prosperity of the city and county.

"Better stick to the gambling out at Erie Oval, George," counseled the campaign manager. "They're mostly New Yorkers that are interested in that, anyway." [. . .]

Through the silence following the furniture man's departure, Betty, at the typewriter, clicked upon George's ears. An evil impulse assailed him—impolitic, too, as he realized—impolitic but irresistible. It was the easiest way in which

Candidate Remington, heckled by suffragists, overridden by his campaign committee, mortifyingly tormented by a feeling of inadequacy, could reestablish himself in his own esteem as a man of prompt and righteous decisions. He might not be able to run his campaign to suit himself, but, by Jove, his office was his own!

He went into Betty's quarters and suggested to her that a due sense of the eternal fitness of things would cause her to offer him her resignation, which his own sense of the eternal fitness of things would lead him at once to accept. It seemed, he said, highly indecorous of her to remain in the employ of Remington & Evans the while she was busily engaged in trying to thwart the ambitions of the senior partner; he marveled that woman's boasted sensitiveness had not already led her to perceive this for herself.

For a second Betty seemed startled, even hurt. She colored deeply, and her eyes darkened. Then the flush of surprise and of wounded feeling died. She looked at him blankly and asked how soon it would be possible for him to replace her. She would leave as soon as he desired. [. . .]

He rather wished that Penny Evans would come in; Penny would doubtless take a high hand with him concerning the episode, and there was nothing which George Remington would have welcomed like an antagonist of his own size and sex. But Penny did not appear, and the afternoon passed draggingly for the candidate of the district attorneyship. He tried to busy himself with the affairs of his clients, but even when he could keep away from his windows he was aware of the crowds in front of McMonigal's block, of Frances Herrington, her "ducky" toque, and her infernal Voiceless Speech. And when for a second he was able to forget these he heard from the outer office the unmistakable sounds of a desk being permanently cleared of its present incumbent's belongings.

After a while Betty bade him a too courteous good-by, still with that abominable new air of gravely readjusting her old impressions of him. And then there was nothing to do but to go home and make ready for dinner at the Herringtons', unless he could induce Genevieve to have an opportune headache. Of course Betty had been right. Not upon his masculine shoulders should there be laid the absurd burden of political chagrin strong enough to break a social engagement.

Genevieve was in her room. [. . .]

Genevieve, as he saw through the open door, sat by the window. She had, it appeared, but recently come in. She still wore her hat and coat; she had not even drawn off her gloves. And, seeing her thus, absorbed in some problem, George's sense of his wrongs grew greater. He had, he told himself, hurried home out of the jar and fret of a man's day to find balm, to feel the cool fingers of peace pressed upon hot eye-lids, to drink strengthening draughts of refreshment from his wife's unquestioning belief, from the completeness of her absorption in him. And here she sat thinking of something else.

Genevieve arose, a little startled, as he snapped on the lights and grunted out something which optimism might translate into an affectionate husbandly greeting. She came dutifully forward and raised her face, still exquisite and cool from the outer air, for her lord's home-coming kiss. That resolved itself into a slovenly peck.

"Been out?" asked George unnecessarily. He tried to quell the unreasonable inclination to find her lacking in wifely devotion because she had been out.

"Yes. There was a meeting at the Woman's Forum this afternoon," she answered. She was unpinning her hat before the pier glass, and in it he could see the reflection of her eyes turned upon his image with a questioning look.

"The ladies seem to be having a busy day of it." He struggled, not quite successfully, to be facetious over the pretty, negligible activities of his wife's sex. "What mighty theme engaged your attention to-day?"

"That Miss Eliot, the real-estate woman, you know"—George stiffened into an attitude of close attention—"spoke about the conditions under which women are working in the mills in this city and in the rest of the county." Genevieve averted her mirrored eyes from his mirrored face. She moved toward her dressing table.

"Oh, she did! And is the Woman's Forum going to come to grips with the industrial monster and bring in the millennium the first of the year?"

But George was painfully aware that light banter which fails to be convincingly light is but a snarl. Genevieve colored slightly as she studied the condition of a pair of long white gloves which she had taken from a drawer.

"Of course the Woman's Forum is only for discussion," she said mildly. "It doesn't initiate any action."

Then she raised her eyes to his face, and George felt his universe reeled about him. For his wife's beautiful eyes were turned upon him, not in limpid adoration, not in perfect acceptance of all his views, unheard, unweighed, but with a question in their blue depths.

The horrid clairvoyance which harassment and self-distrust had given him that afternoon enabled him, he thought, to translate that look. The Eliot woman, in her speech before the Woman's Forum, had doubtless placed the responsibility for the continuation of those factory conditions upon the district attorney's office, had doubtless repeated those foolish, impractical questions which the suffragists were displaying in McMonigal's windows. And Genevieve was asking them in her mind. Genevieve was questioning him, his motives, his standards, his intentions! Genevieve was not intellectually a charming mechanical doll who would always answer yes and no as he pressed the strings and maintain a comfortable vacuity when he was not at hand to perform the kindly act. Genevieve was thinking on her own account!

What, he wondered angrily, as he dressed—for he could not bring himself to ask her aid in escaping the Herringtons, and indeed was suddenly balky at the thought of the intimacies of a domestic evening—*what* was she thinking? She was not such an imbecile as to be unaware how large a share of her comfortable fortune was invested in the local industry. Why, her father had been head of the Livingston-Loomis-Ladd Collar Company when that dreadful fire— And she certainly knew that his uncle, Martin Jaffry, was the chief stockholder in the Jaffry-Bradshaw Company.

What was the question in Genevieve's eyes? Was she asking if he were the knight of those women who worked, and sweated and burned, or of her and the comfortable women of her class, of Alys Brewster-Smith with her little cottages, of Cousin Emmeline with her little stocks, of masquerading Betty Sheridan whose sortie into independence was from the safe, vantage ground of intrenched privilege? And all that evening as he watched his wife across the crystal and the roses of the Herrington table, trying to interpret the question that had been in her eyes, trying to interpret her careful silence, he realized what every husband sooner or later awakes to realize—that he had married a stranger. He did not know her. He did not know what ambitions, what aspirations apart from him, ruled the spirit behind that charming surface of flesh. Of course she was good, of course she was tender, of course she was high-minded! But how wide enveloping was the cloak of her goodness? How far did her tenderness reach out? Was her high-mindedness of the practical or impractical variety?

And from time to time, he caught her eyes in turn upon him, with that curious little look of reexamination in their depths. She could look at him like that! She could look at him as though appraisals were possible from a wife to a husband!

They avoided industrial Whitewater County as a topic when they left the Herringtons. They talked with great animation and interest of the people at the party. Arrived at home, George, pleading press of work, went down into the library while Genevieve went to bed. Carefully they postponed the moment of making articulate all that, remaining unspoken, might be ignored.

It was one o'clock, and he had not moved a paper for an hour, when the library door opened. Genevieve stood there. She had sometimes come before when he had worked at night, to chide him for neglecting sleep, to bring bouillon or chocolate. But to-night she did neither.

She did not come far into the room, but, standing near the door and looking at him with a new expression—patient, tender, the eternal look—said: "I couldn't sleep either. I came down to say something, George. Don't interrupt me"—for he was coming toward her with sounds of affectionate protest at her being out of bed. "Don't speak! I want to say—whatever you do, whatever you decide—now—always—I love you. Even if I don't agree, I love you."

She turned and went swiftly away, and George stood looking at the place where she had stood, this strange, new Genevieve, who, promising to love, reserved the right to judge.

The Sturdy Oak: A Composite Novel of American Politics. Ed. Elizabeth Jordan. *Collier's: The National Weekly* 60.6 (October 20, 1917): 19–22.

2

Manifestoes from the Sex War

INTRODUCED AND SELECTED BY JANET LYON

THE SEVEN MANIFESTOES in this section represent a diverse sampling of the numerous polemical documents produced in the so-called sex war of early twentieth-century Western Europe. Drawn from distinct areas of debate about the role of "woman" in the liberal state, they may be read collectively as a modernist enterprise—modernist, that is, not only for their pervasive experimentalism, in the cases of the manifestoes by Mina Loy, F. T. Marinetti, and Valentine de Saint-Point, but also insofar as they are constelled around several pressing political and cultural questions in late modernity. The three suffrage manifestoes with which the section opens are drawn from the early and middle phases of the British suffrage movement of 1905–14 and sketch out a response to the legal "sex disability" for which women seek correction through an expansion of the suffrage. Two representative polemical essays by Marinetti decry the "feminization" of European culture and link the corrosive influence of "woman" both to the decay of art and to the rise of an emasculating representative system of parliamentarianism. Saint-Point's manifesto, written in reply to Marinetti's early Futurist tracts, aims to recuperate "femininity" as a primary psychic and biological life force worthy of Futurism's veneration. Loy's manifesto, which remained unpublished in her lifetime, problematizes the role of the modern woman by situating her between the rock of "equality" championed by the suffrage movement on the one hand and the hard place of the unreflective "freedom" advocated by the European avant-garde on the other.

Like most manifestoes, those included here reflect, to one degree or another, the sense of crisis deriving from the inconsistencies of western modernity's institutions of representation and from a perceived concomitant decline in cultural coherence. The hundreds of suffrage tracts produced during the decade of the militant suffrage campaign repeatedly point to the irrational operations of democratic representation in Great Britain, while the corpus of Futurist manifestoes rejects parliamentarianism out of hand as a bureaucratic outgrowth of bourgeois opportunism. For all of these authors, as well as for a whole host of contemporary commentators, such crises were at least partially crystallized in questions concerning women's relation to the state.

On the one side, those who advocated women's legal equality did so from a number of positions that held as their ideal the fruition of the emancipatory promises of Enlightenment modernity. For some of these advocates, women's equality before the law anchored a radically democratic project that included working-class representation and economic reforms. For others, women's equality promised to introduce ameliorating forms of cultural femininity—maternalism, sexual purity, political honesty—into a badly damaged and unreflexive system of political practices. For still others, the legal recognition of women's equality would remove the "disability of sex" (itself created by the false logic of patriarchal institutions), and in so doing would rehabilitate an originary Enlightenment position of autonomous political subjecthood.

On the other side of the "woman question," self-consciously modern commentators who rejected the project of legal and social equality tended to do so as a repudiation of its normative ideals. From this multifarious perspective, the reformist aims of the suffrage campaign simply reinforced a patriarchal system of governance that was instrumental at best and at worst threatened to reduce all of its subjects to drones of the bourgeois state. For this reason, anti-egalitarian critics who situated themselves within a cultural avant-garde usually eschewed any serious discussion of the suffrage issue and focused instead on the shifting roles of gender in the modern period. Most of the positions held by these critics contained elements of sexual radicalism and an implicit endorsement of gender complementarity, however diversely or provocatively it might be configured in modern culture. Thus, for example, while such vanguard feminist sociologists as Georg Simmel and Marianne Weber differed over the roles and meaning of "male culture" and "female culture," both agreed that these spheres existed *a priori* in principle and that their relations ought to be sexually, politically, and philosophically sympathetic rather than separatist or competitive.[1]

As manifestoes, the documents reprinted here should also be considered within a specific generic context. The manifesto form's long political history, as well as its relatively recent appropriation in the late nineteenth century by the European artistic avant-garde, distinctively colored its reception in the pre–World War One public sphere.[2] When suffragists issued manifestoes that scornfully exposed the vagaries of conventional wisdom and urgently demanded equal rights, they were participating in the transmission of a specific revolutionary discourse that originated in the seventeenth century and underwent iterative transformations during the French and American Revolutions, the Chartist movement, the Commune, and the syndicalist and labor movements—many of which were referred to by name in suffrage documents. By linking their cause rhetorically with the democratic struggles that had traditionally driven the evolution of political modernity, suffragists sought to make their manifestoes intelligible within an established liberatory framework. And while most suffragists stopped well short of advocating violent revolution, their deployment of the manifesto form allowed them to retain the historical echo of political and even physical threat that had previously been the purview of mostly masculinist movements. When bellicose Futurist manifestoes started circulating in London after 1909, the popular press began to conflate the militant actions and texts of the two groups, charging both suffragists and artists alike with a perverse madness directed against the bourgeois status quo. This semiotic relation was openly acknowledged by Marinetti, and by Ezra Pound and Wyndham Lewis in their notorious address "To Suffragettes" in the first volume of *BLAST*, wherein they hailed militant women as their "brave comrades" (152), with whom they shared the tactics and terrain of modernist militancy.[3]

The British suffrage manifestoes included here reflect the earliest forms of this militancy. The first of the broadsheets, "Votes for Women: New Movement Manifesto," was published during the summer of 1906, about a year after the militant suffrage movement had begun in earnest, and was probably written by Emmeline Pethick Lawrence shortly after the WSPU moved from its home in Manchester to London.[4] The document bears all the marks of a traditional political manifesto: it aims to establish the legitimacy of the group for which it speaks, even while it performatively calls that group into being. It invokes a broadly constituted "we," one that represents the subjects of "a people's movement," and in so doing deftly avoids the charges of sectionalism and divisiveness that had been lodged against many eighteenth- and nineteenth-century feminist movements. It alludes to large but unspecified numbers of potential supporters in its assertion that "there can scarcely be found an individual who is prepared to defend seriously in public the continued exclusions of women from the ranks of voters." And, most notably, it repeatedly deploys the manifesto form's trademark insistence that "the time for argument is past!" and "the time for action is come." Such action will stem from two formidable sources: the "united pressure of public opinion," and, more ominously, "the working women of London" who are "AROUSED."[5] An intimation of the power of the masses and the threat of insurrection thus underwrites this manifesto's putatively reformist aims—to remove the "obstacle of sex disability" and establish an inclusive suffrage that will issue in national health.

This identification of a "sex disability" appears repeatedly in manifestoes throughout the suffrage movement and is especially prominent in the second suffrage manifesto reprinted here, "Our Demand: What it Is and What it Is Not." Written late in 1907 by the WSPU directly after one of several organizational splits,[6] this manifesto focuses on Parliament's prevarications about suffrage and demands the passage of an act that will legally equalize men's and women's voting qualifications, so that "whatever qualifies a man to vote shall qualify a woman to vote"; such an equalization can occur only with "the removal of the disability of sex." This use of the term "disability" is entirely consonant with a strain of contemporary theories that understand disability as a condition produced by legal and cultural restrictions. Implicitly rejecting their conservative opponents' characterization of female biological sex as an insurmountable political impairment, suffragists concentrate on the artificial, disabling conditions created by patriarchal institutions that irrationally contravene democratic principles. At the same time, however, the suffragists' formulation endorses an unquestioned normative ideal underlying the universalist form of representative governance from which they seek recognition.[7] The removal of disability, it is suggested, will erase women's political "difference" and enable their assimilation into the model of the universal subject without effectively altering that normative model—which was, in this phase of modern liberalism, white, middle-class, rational, able-bodied, law-abiding, and male. This accommodation by the militant suffrage movement of an unrehabilitated universalism was precisely the sticking point for would-be allies on both the avant-garde and socialist ends of the "woman question." The premium placed by avant-gardists on radical individualism—on the social and aesthetic reification of "difference," as it were—was foundationally antithetical to universalist liberalism. For the socialists' part, their program of radical democracy called for a revolutionary reconfiguration of the universalist model from one of restriction to one of infinitely expanding economic and class inclusivity. Indeed, the demand for women's suffrage at stake in "Our Demand" concerns just this principle of democratic extension. Its authors want to dismiss as mere delaying tactics those doubts expressed by some Labour members who fear that the grant of the vote to women will be "undemocratic," insofar as it will increase the number of middle-class voters without similarly expanding the franchise for unpropertied working-class members of the adult population.[8] The single-issue focus of WSPU suffragists precludes any genuine consideration of this broader structural concern; the manifesto identifies the doubting MP's as "enemies to women masquerading under the guise of friends."

A similar trope of precarious strategic friendship structures the third document in this section, "Window Breaking: To One Who Has Suffered." Composed as an open letter to the shopkeepers whose windows were shattered during the militants' extensive 1912 window-breaking campaign in London's upscale West End, the text wryly divulges the power of the female consumer and reverses the blame for suffrage violence: window-breaking is the fault not of hysterical women (as the popular press would have it) but of the members of the government, those unbridled "servants" of the voting shopkeeper. Suffragists break windows to remind merchants of their duty to their "good friends in business," the women who buy and consume, and they expect their merchant friends to reciprocate by reining in the wayward government with votes and pressure. A threat of economic sabotage lies just under the surface of this epistolary challenge; boycott and vandalism are two of the most fearsome arrows in the quiver of militancy. The third arrow is the woman shopper who, far from being a passive or unthinking consumer, leverages her unremitting demand for the vote with a display of targeted economic agency.[9]

Suffragism's all-consuming faith in the power of the vote was not, strictly speaking, a circumscribed faith in the negative freedoms granted by government; it certainly included the presumption that negative freedoms secured by the vote would lead to the positive freedoms of self-determination and reflexive autonomy for all women. But the polemical texts of the militant suffrage campaign focused almost solely on the vote as an instrument of political empowerment and emancipation. As I have suggested, this instrumental focus tended to isolate the suffrage debate from the broader philosophical discussions that attended on questions of shifting gender roles. As the rest of the manifestoes in this section demonstrate, the "sex war" that began in the late nineteenth century, when women increasingly appeared as workers and agents in the public sphere, and which intensified around the spectacle of the suffrage campaign, had less to do with women's actual qualifications for legal parity than with the ways in which the production and performance of gender challenged the evaluative norms of late modernity.

Marinetti's "Against *Amore* and Parliamentarianism," written during the most violent phase of the British movement, twins both of these aspects of the sex war. On the one side, he attacks parliamentarianism as "grand foolishness, made up of corruption and banality," run by a "horde of lawyers" in a "noisy chicken coop." Women's "childish eagerness for the miserable, ridiculous right to vote" demonstrates their complicity with a deadening form of governance that promises democratic representation but delivers little more than a chaotic attention to the quotidian at the expense of orig- inality, autonomous liberation, and the "blazing flight of the ideal." Mari- netti was not alone in his dismissal of parliamentary governance; Mahatma Gandhi, for one, observed at around the same time that "Parliaments are really emblems of slavery" (38).[10] But Marinetti's polemic is grounded in a libertarian ideal, according to which modernity's expanding "iron cage," to use Max Weber's term, threatens individual expression with its grinding logic of bureaucratic efficiency. That modern women seek political consecra- tion through this means suggests both a fundamental shallowness and an urge towards corruption on their part. And it is this urge that elicits the other side of Marinetti's argument, that women have long been the dupes and the purveyors of poetic *Amore,* a medium of unnatural and cloying "sen- timentality and lechery" through which women constrain and poison mod- ern men in the manner of Ulysses's sirens. Anti-modern and paralytic on the one hand, ultramodern and instrumental on the other, woman is, for Mari- netti, the inscrutable and detested hieroglyph of the modern.[11] His solution to the problem of parliamentarianism is to grant women the vote so that they may hasten its destruction, along with the destruction of their own desire for "horrible, dragging *Amore.*"

In "Marriage and the Family," this "animal" desire is characterized as the pernicious lifeblood of the family, a site of claustrophobic, soul-killing boredom and jealous agony. If modernity entails the systematic replacement of tradi- tional forms of authority by institutions of reflexive rationality, then Mari- netti locates within the family the most anti-modern formation of all: senti- mental marriage. The complaint against marriage has a centuries-long history in both feminist and anti-feminist writing, of course; among the moderns, Valentine de Saint-Point and Mina Loy were but two of many who viewed marriage as a bulwark of women's oppression, as we shall see.[12] For his part, Marinetti accuses marriage of chaining men and women to the "sewer" of an insular *gemeinschaft,* from which no escape into modern freedom is possible. It is particularly perilous for men, he argues, because once a male child has been "effeminized" through familial acculturation, his "character is always retarded."

Marinetti's assertion that "maleness" can be formed or deformed through avoidance of or contact with the family suggests that he understands gender to be a malleable, rather than an essential, property. And yet in this and other manifestoes, he also assumes the ineluctable singularity of maleness and femaleness (which, for Marinetti, are identical with masculinity and femininity)—the former, an active, dynamic, self-producing agent of modernity, the latter an inert, self-identical, biologically driven effect of nature. Such ontological confusion occurs in differing degrees in a number of avant-garde positions on gender, including the one formulated by Valentine de Saint-Point in "Manifesto of Futurist Woman." Saint-Point begins her manifesto—an express response to Marinetti, delivered in 1912 at a Futurist exhibit in Brussels and solicited by Marinetti himself—with an argument that seeks to reestablish a complementary relation between femininity and masculinity, which she identifies as "elements" that inhere in all humans, as well as in all periods of history.[13] From this perspective, femininity is neither superior nor inferior to masculinity; both must be combined in the right balance to produce vigorously healthy and creative epochs and individuals. Women who achieve an adequate measure of masculinity can be "Furies, Amazons," heroines to rescue the "rotting" world, but as Saint-Point's manifesto progresses it becomes clear that they can only assume these personas within the radically circumscribed roles of either mother or lover. The upshot of this double move is that while Saint-Point aims to disarticulate the "elementary" gender properties of masculinity and femininity from the sexed bodies of men and women, she simultaneously articulates those sexed bodies to discrete social functions. Far from engendering the positive freedom of self-reflexive autonomy for the Futurist woman, this solution depends upon and reproduces the prescribed and limiting frame of a non-autonomous femininity.

Saint-Point's disdain for the "cerebral error" of feminism and its rights-seeking discourses is of a piece with the general avant-garde rejection of the negative freedom of artificial equality offered by the state. It is echoed in the poet and painter Mina Loy's "Feminist Manifesto"; however, in her manifesto Loy is at much greater pains to explore the social and cultural problems covered over by what she sees as the quick fix of equal rights. She dismisses the legitimacy of gender complementarity out of hand and focuses instead on the uneven playing field created by the interlacing of the economics of marriage with the abiding patriarchal myths regulating female sexuality. These, she suggests, are at the root of women's oppression: the marriage market restricts woman to "Parasitism & Prostitution," if she is lucky enough to "manoeuver" a man into her life-long support, "or Negation," if she is not. This dilemma is treated telegraphically in one of her most interesting early poems, "Virgins Plus Curtains Minus Dots," wherein housebound virgins without dowries suffer in the knowledge of their impoverished, sexless futures.[14] But in "Feminist Manifesto," written in Florence while she pondered both her own abandonment by a gadfly husband, and her reawakening sexuality after two momentous affairs, Loy formulates an ironically dystopian solution to the marriage problem, delivering it in the emphatic graphics characteristic of this experimental text: the "*unconditional* surgical *destruction of virginity* through-out the female population at puberty—."[15] This militant practice, she suggests, would at least deflate the false cultural capital accruing to woman's "physical purity," and might eventually overturn the rigid institution of marriage by replacing it with informal relations among consenting adults.

Like all of the manifestoes in this section—indeed, like nearly all polemical manifestoes—Loy's concentration of a systemic crisis into a set of axiomatic demands is largely performative rather than practical. The manifesto form is, after all, a dramatic genre that stages conflict in Manichean terms, in order to tell the story of oppression or resentment from a newly calibrated and highly charged position. For this reason, it was a form well-suited to the "sex war" of the modern period, when the urgency of sex combatants could not be fully registered in the reasoned discourse of consensus upon which the democratic public sphere depended. Indeed, all of the authors reprinted here would at least agree with the WSPU's impatient declaration that "*The time for argument is past!*" The time for polemic had been summoned.

Notes

1. See Leck, chapter 3, for an excellent discussion of the role of the "woman question" in the emerging discipline of continental sociology.

2. For a discussion of the history and conventions of the manifesto form, see Lyon, chapter 1.

3. See, for example, Marinetti's "Suffragettes and Indian Docks," in *Marinetti: Selected Writings*, 341–42.

4. See Mary Chapman and Barbara Green's introduction to chapter 1 of this collection for an alternative sketch of the movement. Numerous accounts of the suffrage movement are in print; for an older but still reliable book-length study of the WSPU, see Rosen.

5. This passage probably refers to a mass demonstration that took place on May 19 in London, when a deputation of 260,000 women converged at the Foreign Office. The deputation included a large crowd of working women who marched from the East End with a WSPU delegation.

6. The split produced the more moderate Women's Freedom League; in response, the WSPU asked its offices to identify themselves as the "National Women's Social and Political Union" and to add the word "National" in their national publications.

7. For a critical overview of contemporary discussions of the relations between impairment and disability, see Thomas. For the dependency of rights rhetoric upon the trope of disability, see Baynton.

8. See Powell, 90, and Sylvia Pankhurst, 147–56, for two accounts of this particular impasse. Suffragists of course had excellent reasons to be suspicious of any counter-argu-

ments introduced at the last minute by "allies"; the whole history of the militant suffrage movement is one of cloak and dagger tactics among members of the government and passive aggression on the part of the government toward the suffragists. See Dangerfield, 139–213, and E. S. Pankhurst, passim, for narratives of these relations.

9. See Felski, chapter 3, for an insightful discussion of the female consumer as both "the victim of modernity" and "its privileged agent"; see also chapter 6 for an extensive treatment of feminist discourses during the suffrage period.

10. The debate about parliamentarianism was widespread; see, for example, Lukacs's "The Question of Parliamentarianism" [1920], and Lenin's *Theses on Bourgeois Democracy and the Proletarian Dictatorship* [1919].

11. In Blum's account, "Woman, for the futurists, is a two-faced icon. One face is traditional, with static, eternal features; it looks backward, toward nature and the past, and symbolizes their fetters. The other is artificial and modern; adulterated by contemporary materialism, it looks to the future, evoking undesirable change" (85). See chapter 4 for an excellent discussion of Marinetti's gender politics.

12. Others include Emma Goldman, Olive Schreiner, Rebecca West, and D. H. Lawrence. The capstone of Christabel Pankhurst's polemical suffragist writings is the series of pamphlets collected as *The Great Scourge and How to End It* [1913–14], which repeatedly warns against the medical and social dangers of marriage.

13. See Berghaus for an overview of Saint-Point's career as an avant-garde provocateur and modern dancer.

14. Collected in *The Last Lunar Baedeker: Poems*, 21–23.

15. See Burke, part 2. See also Lyon, chapter 4.

Works Cited

Baynton, Douglas C. "Disability and the Justification of Inequality in American History." *The New Disability History: American Perspectives*. Edited by Paul K. Longmore and Lauri Umansky. New York: New York University Press, 2001. 33–57.

Berghaus, Günter. "Dance and the Futurist Woman: The Work of Valentine de Saint-Point (1875–1953)." *Dance Research* 11.2 (Autumn 1993): 27–42.

Blum, Cinzia Sartini. *The Other Modernism: F. T. Marinetti's Futurist Fiction of Power.* Berkeley: University of California Press, 1996.

Burke, Carolyn. *Becoming Modern: The Life of Mina Loy.* New York: Farrar, Straus and Giroux, 1996.

Dangerfield, George. *The Strange Death of Liberal England, 1910–1914.* 1935. New York: Perigee, 1980.

Felski, Rita. *The Gender of Modernity.*

Gandhi, M. K. *Hind Swaraj and Other Writings.* 1910. Ed. Anthony J. Parel. Cambridge Texts in Modern Politics. Cambridge: Cambridge University Press, 1997.

Leck, Ralph M. *Georg Simmel and Avant-garde Sociology: The Birth of Modernity, 1880–1920.* Amherst, N.Y.: Humanity/Prometheus, 2000.

Lyon, Janet. *Manifestoes.*

Marinetti, F. T. *Marinetti: Selected Writings,* ed. R. W. Flint and trans. R. W. Flint and Arthur A. Cappotelli. New York: Farrar, Straus and Giroux.

Pankhurst, E. Sylvia. *The Suffragette: The History of the Women's Militant Suffrage Movement, 1905–1910.* 1911. New York: Source Book, 1970.

Powell, David. *The Edwardian Crisis: Britain, 1910–1914.* New York: Saint Martin's, 1996.

Rosen, Andrew. *Rise Up Women!*

Thomas, Carol. "Disability Theory: Key Ideas, Issues and Thinkers." *Disability Studies Today*. Edited by Colin Barnes, Mike Oliver, and Len Barton. Cambridge, U.K.: Polity, 2002. 38–57.

EMMELINE PANKHURST, WOMEN'S SOCIAL AND POLITICAL UNION

Votes for Women: New Movement Manifesto

The New Movement for the political enfranchisement of women, initiated by the Women's Social and Political Union, is a people's movement, and is not confined to any section of the community.

The Members of the Union believe that the time has come for vigorous and determined propaganda, and for the adoption of new methods of agitation in the place of the old methods which have produced so little result for the past forty years.

All who work for Political and Social Reform know by experience that Members of Parliament however sympathetic are powerless to urge legislation, unless a strong, persistent and united pressure of public opinion is brought to bear upon the Government. It is the business of this Union to arouse and concentrate public opinion.

The Prime Minister and the majority of the Members of the House of Commons, irrespective of party, have declared themselves personally in favour of removing the disabilities of women, and throughout the country there can scarcely be found an individual who is prepared to defend seriously in public the continued exclusions of women from the ranks of voters. *Therefore, the time for argument is past!* The time for action is come.

The London W. S. & P. Unions adopt the policy, initiated in Manchester and intend to carry on in London a determined and persistent campaign. Since the adoption of this new policy great progress has already been made. THE WORKING WOMEN OF LONDON ARE AROUSED. The end of the long struggle for political existence is in view.

All true lovers of justice must now combine in serious united effort to remove this obstacle of sex disability out of the path which leads to the wholehearted co-operation of men and women in the work of further Social Reform. Social reform can never be satisfactory as long as only one half of the nation is represented.

We confidently appeal to the women of London to join our ranks, enroll their names at once and to become active workers in a movement for getting the VOTE FOR WOMEN. Working men have found out that political action is needed to supplement Trades Unionism and so they formed a Labour Party. Women Trades Unionists and Social Reformers now realize that the possession of the Vote is the most effective way of securing better social and industrial condition, better wages, shorter hours, healthier homes, and an honourable position in the State which will enable women as well as men to render that Citizen Service so necessary to the development of a truly great nation.

Hon. Secretary,	*Hon. Treasurer,*
MISS SYLVIA PANKHURST	MRS. F. W. PETHICK LAWRENCE,
45 Park Walk, Chelsea	87, Clement's Inn, W.C.

London, ca. 1906. The Suffragette Fellowship Collection, London Museum, 50–82/549, reel 12.

NWSPU

Our Demand: What It Is and What It Is Not

From the first women suffragists have demanded neither more nor less than the abolition of the political disability of sex. They have claimed that whatever qualifies a man to vote shall qualify a woman to vote. They have asked than an Act shall be passed which shall run as follows:

In all Acts relating to the qualifications and registration of voters or persons entitled or claiming to be registered and to vote in the election of members of Parliament wherever words occur which import the masculine gender, the same shall be held to include women for all purposes connected with, and having reference to, the right to be registered as voters.

That is our claim to-day. And this was the principle adopted in Mr. Dickinson's first Bill introduced in February, 1907, and talked out on March 8th. If such a law were passed, it would mean that the principle of sex equality would be established for ever, and whatever the franchise for men precisely the same franchise would exist for women.

But this claim, reasonable as it appears to be, has been opposed by certain professing friends of women who have argued that women ought to ask for more than this simple measure of justice.

In the early stages of the present agitation, adult suffrage was urged upon women by this class of politician as the only true solution. Women should ask, it was said, that all men and all women should possess the vote, and should be content with no other demand.

To-day opposition from this quarter may be disregarded, but a somewhat similar attack is being delivered by a section of Liberal politicians, who claim that our demand is "undemocratic." Their views were embodied in the second Bill which Mr. Dickinson introduced on August 14th, 1907. This Bill contained clauses providing that (a) plural voting, which is legal for men, should be illegal for women, and (b) that married women should be entitled to vote on their husband's qualification as joint occupier (whereas under the existing law two men living together cannot qualify as joint occupiers).

At first sight some women may perhaps be inclined to applaud this measure because it seems to promise more to women than what we are asking for. But if they consider it carefully they will see that it is thoroughly bad.

In the first place it is totally wrong in principle to make one franchise for men and another, different, franchise for women. The removal of the disability of sex is the only logical and safe solution.

In the second place the introduction of this measure is bad tactics. It tends to divide our friends into two camps, while leaving our enemies united. The original simple proposal is supported by 420 out of 670 members of the House of Commons, but this proposal would find only a very few supporters. Moreover, it introduces into the question of women's suffrage other highly contentious proposals which would put out of account any possibility of carrying it into law next Session.

This new Bill is nothing but another attempt on the part of Liberal politicians to side-track the women's movement and is prompted by enemies to women masquerading under the guise of friends.

Lest we be charged with undue suspicion in taking this line, we quote, in furtherance of our view, from a source which cannot be charged with bias against the Liberal Government. In a leading article, on October 26th, the *Manchester Guardian* said:

> "Women simply ask that they shall be allowed to vote on the same terms as men. This is the principle which was embodied in Mr. Dickinson's Bill of last Session [March 8], and it was certainly a surprise to the meeting yesterday, and not a pleasant one, when he proceeded to disclaim it, and to plead for something quite different because he thinks it more 'democratic.' We can conceive some women present who should say 'Be hanged to your democracy. We ask for justice, and by justice we understand equal treatment for our sex.' Mr. Dickinson has, of course, a perfect right to his opinion, and he no doubt felt it his duty to express it; but he will get no support from

the women who are working hardest for the suffrage, though he may get a good deal from nominal friends of the movement who we quite clearly that the awkwardness of the present demand lies in its moderation, and that the bigger you can make it the longer you may put it off."

Women who want votes must turn their back deliberately upon this insidious proposal; they must refuse to fall into the trap laid for them by the Liberal Government and must continue to urge their demand for the possession of the vote, on the same terms as it is or may be granted to men.

NWSPU leaflet, ca. 1908. Rpt. in *Suffrage and the Pankhursts*, ed. Jane Marcus. London: Routledge and Kegan Paul, 1987. 166–68.

WSPU

Window Breaking: To One Who Has Suffered

Dear Sir,

You, a prosperous shopkeeper, have had your windows broken and your business interfered with, you are very angry about it, and no wonder. But you are angry with the wrong people. You are angry with the women who broke your windows, whereas you ought really to be angry with the people who drove them to it. Those people are the members of the present Government.

You know as well as I do that the Suffragettes bear no grudge against you personally, though perhaps they have some reason to do so. On the contrary, the women are good friends to you, and without them and their support what would become of that flourishing business of yours?

The people the Suffragettes are angry with, and the people you must blame for your broken windows, are, as I have said, the present Liberal Government. They are robbing women of their just right to vote for the Members of Parliament who levy taxes upon them and make laws for them. What is worse, the Government are constantly cheating and deluding the women who demand the Vote.

How would you like it yourself if you were treated in that fashion, and what would you do to get your rights? We know what men did a few years ago in South Africa for the sake of votes. It was not a question of a few broken windows then; it was a question of thousands of lives and millions of money.

"Well," you may say, "I sympathize with the women, but what have I got to do with it? Why should my windows be broken because Cabinet Ministers are a pack of rogues and tricksters?"

My dear Sir, you have got everything to do with it. You are a voter, and, therefore, the Members of the Government are your servants, and if they do wrong, you are really responsible for it. That is why your windows have been broken—to make you realize your responsibility in the matter.

Let me remind you again that women are your best supporters. You can get on very well without Mr. Asquith and Mr. Lloyd George, but you can't get on without the women who are your good friends in business. Surely one good turn deserves another! The women have been having a very hard time in this Votes for Women fight. **What have you done, what are you doing, and what are you going to do to help them?**

You as voters and as business men have got enormous influence. Last time there was window breaking, some people clamoured for severe punishments for the women. What good did that do? Long sentences of imprisonment, hunger strikes, forcible feeding, which, as the Recorder in a recent trial admitted, is torture! What man likes to think of women going through all that, even if his window **has** been broken.

Don't let it happen again. Put a stop to window breaking, and put a stop to the suffering and sacrifices of the women, by telling the Liberal Government that you will **stand no more of it and that women must have the Vote.**

Believe me, the women will never give in, and you would think the less of them if they did. It is the politicians who must give in, and you and your fellow electors can make them do it.

The day will come when you will be as proud as can be of your broken windows, and of the orders you delivered to the Government to give women the vote.

I am, Sir,
Yours faithfully,

A SYMPATHISER

WSPU leaflet, ca. 1912–13. Rpt. in *Suffrage and the Pankhursts.* Ed. Jane Marcus. London: Routledge and Kegan Paul, 1987. 183–84.

FILIPPO TOMMASO MARINETTI

Against *Amore* and Parliamentarianism

This hatred, precisely, for the tyranny of *Amore* we expressed in a laconic phrase: "scorn for women."

We scorn woman conceived as the sole ideal, the divine reservoir of *Amore,* the woman-poison, woman the tragic trinket, the fragile woman, obsessing and fatal, whose voice, heavy with destiny, and whose dreaming tresses reach out and mingle with the foliage of forests drenched in moonshine.

We despise horrible, dragging *Amore* that hinders the march of man, preventing him from transcending his own humanity, from redoubling himself, from going beyond himself and becoming what we call *the multiplied man.*

We scorn horrible, dragging *Amore,* immense leash with which the sun in its orbit chains the courageous earth that would surely rather leap at random, run every starry risk.

We are convinced that Amore—sentimentality and lechery—is the least natural thing in the world. There is nothing natural and important except coitus, whose purpose is the futurism of the species.

Amore—romantic, voluptuary obsession—is nothing but an invention of the poets, who gave it to humanity. . . . And it will be the poets who will take it away from humanity, as one recovers a manuscript from the hands of a publisher who has shown himself incapable of printing it decently.

In this campaign of ours for liberation, our best allies are the suffragettes, because the more rights and powers they win for woman, the more will she be deprived of *Amore,* and by so much will she cease to be a magnet for sentimental passion or lust.

The carnal life will be reduced to the conservation of the species, and that will be so much gain for the growing stature of man.

As for the supposed inferiority of woman, we think that if her body and spirit had, for many generations past, been subjected to the same physical and spiritual education as man, it would perhaps be legitimate to speak of the equality of the sexes.

It is obvious, in any case, that in her actual state of intellectual and erotic slavery, woman finds herself wholly inferior in respect to character and intelligence and can therefore be only a mediocre legislative instrument.

For just this reason we most enthusiastically defend the rights of the suffragettes, at the same time that we regret their childish eagerness for the miserable, ridiculous right to vote.

Indeed, we are convinced that they will win it hands down, and thus involuntarily help us to destroy that grand foolishness, made up of corruption and banality, to which parliamentarianism is now reduced.

This style of government is exhausted almost everywhere. It accomplished a few good things: it created the illusory participation of the majority in government. I say "illusory" because it is clear that the people cannot be and never will be represented by spokesmen whom they do not know how to choose.

Consequently, the people are always estranged from the government. On the other hand, it is precisely to parliamentarianism that the people owe their real existence.

The pride of the mob was inflated by the elective system. The stature of the individual was heightened by the idea of representation. But this idea has completely undermined the value of intelligence by immeasurably exaggerating the worth of eloquence. This state of affairs worsens day by day.

Therefore I welcome with pleasure the aggressive entrance of women into the parliaments. Where could we find a dynamite more impatient or more effective?

Nearly all the European parliaments are mere noisy chicken coops, cow stalls, or sewers.

Their first principles are: 1) financial corruption, shrewdness in bribery, to win a seat in parliament; 2) gossipy eloquence, grandiose falsification of ideas, triumph of high-sounding phrases, tom-tom of Negroes and windmill gestures.

These gross elements of parliamentarianism give an absolute power to the horde of lawyers.

As you well know, lawyers are alike in every country. They are beings closely tied to everything mean and futile, spirits who see only the small daily fact, who are wholly unable to handle the great general ideas, to imagine the collisions and fusions of races or the blazing flight of the ideal over individuals and peoples. They are argument-merchants, brains for sale, shops for subtle ideas and chiseled syllogisms.

Because of parliamentarianism a whole nation is at the mercy of these fabricators of justice who, by means of the ductile iron of the law, assiduously build traps for fools.

Then let us hasten to give women the vote. And this, furthermore, is the final and absolutely logical conclusion of the ideal of democracy and universal suffrage as it was conceived by Jean Jacques Rousseau and the other preparers of the French Revolution.

Let women hurry to make, with the speed of lightning, this great test of the total animalization of politics.

We who deeply despise the careerists of politics are happy to abandon parliamentarianism to the envious claws of women; inasmuch as to women, exactly, is reserved the noble task of killing it for good and forever.

Oh! how careful I am to avoid irony; I speak as seriously as I know how.

Woman, as she has been shaped by our contemporary society, can only increase in splendor the principle of corruption inseparable from the principle of the vote.

Those who oppose the legitimate rights of the suffragettes do so for entirely personal reasons: they eagerly defend the monopoly of useless or harmful eloquence, which the women will not hesitate to snatch away from them. Fundamentally, this bores us. We have very different mines to put under the ruins.

They tell us that a government composed of women or sustained by women would fatally drag us through the paths of pacificism and Tolstoyan cowardice into a definitive triumph of clericalism and moralistic hypocrisy.

Perhaps! Probably! And I'm sorry!

We will, however, have the war of the sexes, undoubtedly prepared by the great agglomerations of the capital cities, by night life and the stabilizing of workers' salaries. Maybe some misogynistic humorists are already dreaming of a Saint Bartholomew's Night for the women.

But you imagine that I am amusing myself by offering you paradoxes more or less bizarre. . . . Consider, at any rate, that nothing is as paradoxical or as bizarre as reality, and there is very little reason for believing in the logical probabilities of history.

The history of peoples runs at hazard, in any and every direction, like a rather giddy girl who cannot remember what her parents taught her except on New Year's Day, or only when abandoned by a lover. But she is still too disgracefully wise and not disorderly enough, this young history of the world. So the sooner women mix into it, the better, because the men are filthy with millenarian wisdom. These are no paradoxes, I assure you, but gropings into the night of the future.

You will admit, for example, that the victory of feminism and especially the influence of women on politics will end by destroying the principle of the family. One could easily demonstrate that: but you surely would rebel, terrified, and oppose me with ingenious arguments because you do not want the family touched at all. Every right, every liberty should be given to women, but let the family stay intact!

Allow me to smile just a bit skeptically and say to you that if the family, suffocater of vital energies, disappears, we will endeavor to do without it.

It is plain that if modern woman dreams of winning her political rights, it is because without knowing it she is intimately sure of being, as a mother, as a wife, and as a lover, a closed circle, purely animal and wholly without usefulness.

You will certainly have watched the takeoff of a Bleriot plane, panting and still held back by its mechanics, amid mighty buffets of air from the propeller's first spins.

Well then: I confess that before so intoxicating a spectacle we strong Futurists have felt ourselves suddenly detached from women, who have suddenly become too earthly, or, to express it better, have become a symbol of the earth that we ought to abandon.

We have even dreamed of one day being able to create a mechanical son, the fruit of pure will, a synthesis of all the laws that science is on the brink of discovering.

War, the World's Only Hygiene. 1911–15. Rpt. in *Marinetti: Selected Writings*, ed. R. W. Flint and trans. R. W. Flint and Arthur A. Coppotelli. New York: Farrar, Straus and Giroux, 1971. 72–75.

FILIPPO TOMMASO MARINETTI

Marriage and the Family

Family feeling is an inferior sentiment, almost animal, created by fear of the great free beasts, by fear of nights bursting with adventure and ambush. It comes to birth with the first signs of old age that crack the metal of youth. First signs of quietism, of wise moderating prudence, the need to rest, to furl one's sails in a calm and comfortable harbor.

The family lamp is a luminous broody hen who hatches her rotten eggs of cowardice. Father, mother, granny, aunts, and children always end up, after a few dumb scrimmages among themselves, plotting together against holy danger and hopeless heroism. And the steaming soup bowl is the censer burning in this temple of monotony.

As it is now constituted, the family of marriage-without-divorce is absurd, harmful, and prehistoric. Almost always a prison. Often a Bedouin tent covering a lurid mixture of old invalids, women, babies, pigs, asses, camels, hens, and filth.

The family dining room is the twice-daily sewer drain of bile, irritation, prejudice, and gossip.

In this grotesque squeeze of souls and nerves, boredom lives and empty irritation systematically wears and corrodes every private impulse, every young initiative, every practical businesslike decision.

The most marked, energetic characters eat out their hearts in this ceaseless friction of elbows.

An infection arrives, sometimes a real epidemic of swollen idiocy, of catastrophic manias, nervous tics, that changes into a German goose step or a ragtag of emigrants down in the hold.

Female whims flourish anew, litters of babies over the apoplectic stubbornness of their avaricious fathers.

Springlike faces lose their color around an agony that lasts ten years. One victim, two victims, three martyrs, one slaughter, one total madness, a tyrant who is losing his power.

All suffer, all are deprived, exhausted, cretinized in the name of a fearful divinity that must be overthrown: family feeling.

Hallways of idiot wranglings, litanies of reproaches, impossibility of thought or creation on one's own. One mucks around in the daily swamp of dirty domestic economy and dull vulgarities.

The family functions badly, being a hell of plots, arguments, betrayals, contempts, basenesses, and a relative desire on everyone's part for escape and revolt. Jealousy at knife point between the mother and her elegant, beautiful daughters; a contest in greed and wastefulness between conservative father and his playboy son. Everywhere in Italy there is the sad spectacle of the rich egotistical father who wants to force the usual *serious profession* on his poetic or artistic son.

When the family functions well, you have the glue of sentiment, tombstone of maternal tenderness. Daily school of fear. Physical and moral cowardice in the face of a cold, of any new action or idea.

The family that almost always, for the woman, becomes a hypocritical masquerade or else the wise facade behind which one carries on a legal prostitution powdered over with moralism.

All this in the name of a fearful divinity that must be overthrown: Sentiment.

We proclaim that Sentiment is the typical virtue of vegetables, for digging down and growing roots. It becomes a vice in animals, a crime among men, because it fatally restrains their dynamism and swift evolution.

To say *my woman* can be nothing but a childish idiocy or an expression of Negroes. Today, just now, for an hour, a month, two years, according to the flight of my fancy and the power of my animal magnetism or intellectual ascendancy, the woman is as much *mine* as I am hers.

With the words *my wife, my husband,* the family clearly establishes the law of adultery at any cost, or masked prostitution at any cost. Hence is born a school of hypocrisy, treason, and equivocation.

We want to destroy not only the ownership of land, but also the ownership of woman. Whoever cannot work his land should be dispossessed. Whoever cannot give his woman strength and joy should never force his embrace or his company upon her.

Woman does not belong to a man, but rather to the future and the race's development.

We want a woman to love a man and give herself to him for as long as she likes; then, not chained by a contract or by moralistic tribunals, she should bear a child whom society will educate physically and intellectually to a high conception of Italian freedom.

A single woman suffices to support and defend the first growth of a hundred babies, without constriction; their first overmastering perception will be the need to build their own courage, the urgency of personally solving as fast as possible their little physical problems of equilibrium and nourishment; that atmosphere of weeping and hands grasping skirts and sickly smooching that currently comprises earliest childhood will be completely abolished.

We will finally do away with the mixture of males and females that—during the earliest years—produces a damnable effeminizing of the males.

The male babies should—according to us—develop far away from the little girls so that their first games can be entirely masculine, that is, free of every emotional morbidity, every womanly delicacy, so that they can be lively, pugnacious, muscular, and violently dynamic. When little boys and girls live together, the formation of the male character is always retarded. They are always attracted by the charm and willful seductiveness of the little woman, like little *cicisbei* or stupid little slaves.

The abject hunt for a *good match* will be done away with, and the witless calvary of suffocating mothers who bring marriageable daughters to dances and watering places, like heavy crosses to plant on the idiot Golgotha of a good marriage.

"We have to find them a good place"—in a tubercular bed, under an old man's tongue, under the fists of a neurasthenic, like a dry leaf between the pages of a dictionary, in a tomb, a safe, or a sewer—but "find them a good place."

Grim strangulation of the heart and senses of a virgin who fatally thinks of the legal prostitution of marriage as an indispensable condition for gaining the half freedom of adultery and the recovery of her ego through treason.

The wide participation of women in the national work produced by the war has created a typical matrimonial grotesque: the husband had money or was earning it, now he has lost it or can't win it back.

His wife works and finds the way to earn a handsome income at a time when life is exceptionally expensive.

For her kind of work the wife has little need of a domestic life, while the nonworking husband concentrates his activity on an absurd preoccupation with domestic order.

Complete subversion of a family in which the husband has become a useless woman with masculine vanities, and his wife has doubled her human and social value.

Inevitable clash between the two spouses; struggle and defeat of the man.

Futurist Democrat. 1919. Rpt. in *Marinetti*, ed. R. W. Flint. 76–79.

VALENTINE DE SAINT-POINT

Manifesto of Futurist Woman *(Response to F. T. Marinetti)*

> We will glorify war—the world's only hygiene—militarism, patriotism, the destructive gesture of freedom-bringers, beautiful ideas worth dying for, and scorn for woman.
>
> —MARINETTI, "The Founding and Manifesto of Futurism"

Humanity is mediocre. The majority of women are neither superior nor inferior to the majority of men. They are all equal. They all merit the same scorn.

The whole of humanity has never been anything but the terrain of culture, source of the geniuses and heroes of both sexes. But in humanity as in nature there are some moments more propitious for such a flowering. In the summers of humanity, when the terrain is burned by the sun, geniuses and heroes abound.

We are at the beginning of a springtime; we are lacking in solar profusion, that is, a great deal of spilled blood.

Women are no more responsible than men for the way the really young, rich in sap and blood, are getting mired down.

It is absurd to divide humanity into men and women. It is composed only of *femininity* and *masculinity.* Every superman, every hero, no matter how epic, how much of a genius, or how powerful, is the prodigious expression of a race and an epoch only because he is composed at once of feminine and masculine elements, of femininity and masculinity: that is, a complete being.

Any exclusively virile individual is just a brute animal; any exclusively feminine individual is only a female.

It is the same way with any collectivity and any moment in humanity, just as it is with individuals. The fecund periods, when the most heroes and geniuses come forth from the terrain of culture in all its ebullience, are rich in masculinity and femininity.

Those periods that had only wars, with few representative heroes because the epic breath flattened them out, were exclusively virile periods; those that denied the heroic instinct and, turning toward the past, annihilated themselves in dreams of peace, were periods in which femininity was dominant.

We are living at the end of one of these periods. *What is most lacking in women as in men is virility.*

That is why Futurism, even with all its exaggerations, is right.

To restore some virility to our races so benumbed in femininity, we have to train them in virility even to the point of brute animality. But we have to impose on everyone, men and women who are equally weak, a new dogma of energy in order to arrive at a period of superior humanity.

Every woman ought to possess not only feminine virtues but virile ones, without which she is just a female. Any man who has only male strength without intuition is only a brute animal. But in the period of femininity in which we are living, only the contrary exaggeration is healthy: *we have to take the brute animal for a model.*

Enough of those women whose "arms with twining flowers resting on their laps on the morning of departure" should be feared by soldiers; women as nurses perpetuating weakness and age, domesticating men for their personal pleasures or their material needs! . . . Enough women who create children just for themselves, keeping them from any danger or adventure, that is, any joy; keeping their daughter from love and their son from war! . . . Enough of those women, the octopuses of the hearth, whose tentacles exhaust men's blood and make children anemic, *women in carnal love who wear out every desire so it cannot be renewed!*

Women are Furies, Amazons, Semiramis, Joans of Arc, Jeanne Hachettes, Judith and Charlotte Cordays, Cleopatras, and Messalinas: combative women who fight more ferociously than males, lovers who arouse, destroyers who break down the weakest and help select through pride or despair, "despair through which the heart yields its fullest return."

Let the next wars bring forth heroines like that magnificent Catherine Sforza, who, during the sack of her city, watching from the ramparts as her enemy threatened the life of her son to force her surrender, heroically pointing to her sexual organ, cried loudly: "Kill him, I still have the mold to make some more!"

Yes, "the world is rotting with wisdom," but by instinct, woman is not wise, is not a pacifist, is not good. Because she is totally lacking in measure, she is bound to become too wise, too pacifist, too good during a sleepy period of humanity. Her intuition, her imagination are at once her strength and her weakness.

She is the individuality of the crowd: she parades the heroes, or if there are none, the imbeciles.

According to the apostle, the spiritual inspirer, woman, the carnal inspirer, immolates or takes care, causes blood to run or staunches it, is a warrior or a nurse. It's the same woman who, in the same period, according to the ambient ideas grouped around the day's event, lies down on the tracks to keep the soldiers from leaving for the war or then rushes to embrace the victorious champion.

So that is why no revolution should be without her. That is why, instead of scorning her, we should address her. She's the most fruitful conquest of all, the most enthusiastic, who, in her turn, will increase our followers.

But no feminism. Feminism is a political error. Feminism is a cerebral error of woman, an error that her instinct will recognize.

We must not give woman any of the rights claimed by feminists. To grant them to her would bring about not any of the disorders the Futurists desire but on the contrary an excess of order.

To give duties to woman is to have her lose all her fecundating power. Feminist reasonings and deductions will not destroy her primordial fatality: they can only falsify it, forcing it to make itself manifest through detours leading to the worst errors.

For centuries the feminine instinct has been insulted, only her charm and tenderness have been appreciated. Anemic man, stingy with his own blood, asks only that she be a nurse. She has let herself be tamed. But shout a new message at her, or some war cry, and then, joyously riding her instinct again, she will go in front of you toward unsuspected conquests.

When you have to use your weapons, she will polish them.

She will help you choose them. In fact, if she doesn't know how to discern genius because she relies on passing renown, she has always known how to rewarm the strongest, the victor, the one triumphant by his muscles and his courage. She can't be mistaken about this superiority imposing itself so brutally.

Let woman find once more her cruelty and her violence that make her attack the vanquished because they are vanquished, to the point of mutilating them. Stop preaching spiritual justice to her of the sort she has tried in vain. Woman, become sublimely injust once more, like all the forces of nature!

Delivered from all control, with your instinct retrieved, you will take your place among the Elements, opposite fatality to the conscious human will. Be the egoistic and ferocious mother, *jealously watching over her children,* have what are called all the rights over and duties toward them, *as long as they physically need your protection.*

Let man, freed from his family, lead his life of audacity and conquest, as soon as he has the physical strength for it, and in spite of his being a son and a father. The man who sows doesn't stop on the first row he fecunds.

In my *Poems of Pride* and in *Thirst and Mirages,* I have renounced Sentimentalism as a weakness to be scorned because it knots up the strength and makes it static.

Lust is a strength, because it destroys the weak, excites the strong to exert their energies, thus to renew themselves. Every heroic people is sensual. Woman is, for them, the most exalted trophy.

Woman should be mother or lover. Real mothers will always be mediocre lovers, and lovers, insufficient mothers, through their excess. Equal in front of life, these two women complete each other. The mother who receives the child makes the fixture with the past; the lover gives off desire, which leads toward the future.

LET'S CONCLUDE:

Woman who retains man through her tears and her sentimentality is inferior to the prostitute who incites her man, through braggery, to retain his domination over the lower depths of the cities with his revolver at the ready: at least she cultivates an energy that could serve better causes.

Woman, for too long diverted into morals and prejudices, go back to your sublime instinct, to violence, to cruelty.

For the fatal sacrifice of blood, while men are in charge of wars and battles, procreate, and among your children, as a sacrifice to heroism, take Fate's part. Don't raise them for yourself, that is, for their diminishment, but rather, in a wide freedom, for a complete expansion.

Instead of reducing man to the slavery of those *execrable sentimental needs,* incite your sons and your men to surpass themselves.

You are the ones who make them. You have all power over them.

You owe humanity its heroes. Make them!

1912. Rpt. in *Manifesto: A Century of Ism's,* ed. Mary Ann Caws. Lincoln: University of Nebraska Press, 2001. 213–16.

MINA LOY

Feminist Manifesto

The feminist movement as at present instituted is

<u>Inadequate</u>

Women if you want to realise yourselves—you are on the eve of a devastating psychological upheaval—all your pet illusions must be unmasked—the lies of centuries have got to go—are you prepared for the **Wrench**—? There is no half-measure—NO scratching on the surface of the rubbish heap of tradition, will bring about **<u>Reform</u>**, the only method is **<u>Absolute Demolition</u>**

Cease to place your confidence in economic legislation, vice-crusades & uniform education—you are glossing over **<u>Reality</u>**.
Professional & commercial careers are opening up for you—
<u>Is that all you want?</u>

And if you honestly desire to find your level without prejudice—be **Brave** & deny at the outset—that pathetic clap-trap war cry **<u>Woman is the equal of man</u>**—

for

She is **NOT!**

The man who lives a life in which his activities conform to a social code which is a protectorate of the feminine element—
—is no longer **<u>masculine</u>**

The women who adapt themselves to a theoretical valuation of their sex as a **relative impersonality**, are not yet **Feminine**
Leave off looking to men to find out what you are **not**—seek within yourselves to find out what you **are**
As conditions are at present constituted—you have the choice between **Parasitism**, & **Prostitution**—or **Negation**

Men & women are enemies, with the enmity of the exploited for the parasite, the parasite for the exploited—at present they are at the mercy of the advantage that each can take of the others sexual dependence—. The only point at which the interests of the sexes merge—is the sexual embrace.

The first illusion it is to your interest to demolish is the division of women into two classes **the mistress**, & **the mother** every well-balanced & developed woman knows that is not true, Nature has endowed the complete woman with a faculty for expressing herself through *all* her functions—there are **no restrictions** the woman who is so incompletely evolved as to be un-self-conscious in sex, will prove a restrictive influence on the temperamental expansion of the next generation; the woman who is a poor mistress will be an incompetent mother—an inferior mentality—& will enjoy an inadequate apprehension of **Life**.

To obtain results you must make sacrifices & the first & greatest sacrifice you have to make is of your *"virtue."* The fictitious value of woman as identified with her physical purity—is too easy a stand-by—rendering her lethargic in the acquisition of intrinsic merits of character by which she could obtain a concrete value—therefore, the first self-enforced law for the female sex, as a protection against the man made bogey of virtue—which is the principal instrument of her subjection, would be the *unconditional* surgical *destruction of virginity* through-out the female population at puberty—.

The value of man is assessed entirely according to his use or interest to the community, the value of woman, depends entirely on *chance,* her success or insuccess in manoeuvering a man into taking the life-long responsibility of her—
The advantages of marriage are too ridiculously ample—
compared to all other trades—for under modern conditions a woman can accept preposterously luxurious support from a man (with-out return of any sort—even offspring)—as a thank offering for her virginity
The woman who has not succeeded in striking that

advantageous bargain—is prohibited from any but
surreptitious re-action to Life-stimuli—**& entirely debarred maternity**.

Every woman has a right to maternity—
Every woman of superior intelligence should realize her race—
responsibility, in producing children in adequate proportion to the unfit or
degenerate members of her sex—

Each child of a superior woman should be the result of a definite period of
psychic development in her life—& not necessarily of a possibly irksome &
outworn continuance of an alliance—spontaneously adapted for vital creation
in the beginning but not necessarily harmoniously balanced as the parties to
it—follow their individual lines of personal evolution—
For the harmony of the race, each individual should be the
expression of an easy & ample interpenetration of the male &
female temperaments—free of stress
Woman must become more responsible for the child than man—
Women must destroy in themselves, the desire to be loved—
The feeling that it is a personal insult when a man transfers his attentions
from her to another woman
The desire for comfortable protection instead of an intelligent curiosity &
courage in meeting & resisting the pressure of life sex or so called love must
be reduced to its initial element, honour, grief, sentimentality, pride & consequently jealousy must be detached from it.
Woman for her happiness must retain her deceptive fragility of appearance,
combined with indomitable will, irreducible courage, & abundant health the
outcome of sound nerves—
Another great illusion that woman must use all her introspective clear-sight-
edness & unbiassed bravery to destroy—for the sake of her *self respect* is the
impurity of sex the realisation in defiance of superstition that there is *nothing
impure in sex*—except in the mental attitude to it—will constitute an incalculable & wider social regeneration than it is possible for our generation to
imagine.

1914. Rpt. in *The Last Lunar Baedeker*, sel. and ed. Roger L. Conover. New York: Farrar, Straus and
Giroux, 1996. 153–56.

3

Radical Moderns: American Women Poets on the Left

INTRODUCED AND SELECTED BY NANCY BERKE

"RADICAL MODERNS" are women poets on the left who wrote socially engaged poetry during the modern period. Whether through words or through deeds or both, the poets in this section believed in radical social change. For them, human rights must take precedent over the profit-making ideals of capitalism, and art must facilitate the struggle. They also believed that modernist poetry could "make it new" at the same time that it addressed the social and political realities of the modern age. During the first four decades of the twentieth century, these poets, in their belief that another world was possible, introduced their readers to socialist as well as feminist ideas, which were emerging as part of a larger intellectual zeitgeist in the United States.

The group of radical moderns included here are Lola Ridge (1873–1941), Genevieve Taggard (1894–1948), Lucia Trent (1897–1977; along with husband Ralph Cheyney [1896–1941]), Ruth Lechlitner (1901–89), and Marie de L. Welch (1905–74). Because these poets are largely overlooked in the history of literary modernism, they help raise the question of whether modernism as an aesthetic practice in the United States has a blind spot with regard to poets who used their art as a way of bearing witness to or condemning social injustice. Some of these poets, like Lola Ridge and Lucia Trent, were active in feminist causes and critiqued gender roles in their work. Others, like Ruth Lechlitner and Marie de L. Welch, used gendered tropes to comment on the gender divisions that capitalism made manifest.

The work of these radical poets, including some of the material selected here, appeared frequently in the pages of modernist journals and left magazines such as *Dynamo, The Little Review, Palms, Poetry, Rebel Poet, Voices, The Masses and Liberator, The Nation, The New Republic,* and *New Masses.* These numerous small journals and opinion magazines flourished during the modern period. The journals contained writing that is exemplary of the socialist and feminist activities and desires that these female moderns shared with their reading public.

The radical female voices in this section represent a variety of styles and opinions. Their shared task, however, was to promote a gendered critique of capitalism and infuse modernist aesthetics with a social conscience. Radical moderns especially complicated the traditional sex roles of women as these roles related to larger social issues. Written in the midst of the Great Depression, Ruth Lechlitner's poem "Lines for an Abortionist's Office" makes women's reproductive roles a live issue during a time of social, spiritual, and economic deprivation. Lola Ridge's "Lullaby," written during World War I, parodies the cult of maternity and intimates how wartime scarcity fosters racism. In "A Middle-Aged, Middle-Class Woman at Midnight" Genevieve Taggard shows how a middle-class woman uses her social consciousness to question traditional gender and class roles.

The terms of discussion of what constitutes literary modernism remains an exercise in contingency; this is particularly the case when we consider the place of politics. American modernism's right-wing politics vis-à-vis canonical poets such as Pound and Eliot are not seen as *political.* Modernism's left is generally seen as ideological, however, and its aesthetics are put into question. As a result, women poets on the left are not recognized. These radical moderns reshaped the politics of modernism by challenging Poundian and Eliotian pessimism with their hopeful tropes of radical transformation as in poems like Genevieve Taggard's "At Last the Women are Moving," or in Lucia Trent and Ralph Cheney's vision of modernism: "What Is This Modernism?" Yet their poetry is not without its own pessimistic forecast, as seen in poems such as Ruth Lechlitner's "Case Recruit" and Marie de L. Welch's "Sky-Scraper in Construction." Here modernist tropes represent contemporary social life under capitalism as a form of emasculation. Lechlitner's subject "capons his ego" while "breastless trees / unman him." Welch's skyscraper resembles "virile skeletons" of "obese white impotence."

Recognizing the forgotten and/or undervalued modernist poetry scene in America as it was lived and created by women poets on the left allows us to revisit significant historical moments—race riots, labor strikes, and scenes of economic and social disenfranchisement—that are still relevant social experiences in our own time. Although our contemporary forums of social critique are radically different from those used by the early twentieth-century left, the sweatshops such as those Lola Ridge describes in "The Ghetto" have neither disappeared nor stopped being sites for political organizing. The same can be said of Ruth Lechlitner's poem "Lines for an Abortionist's Office," which eerily reminds contemporary readers that the fight for safe, legal abortion has a long national history.

What is more, our current interest in diversity and globalization has always been present in the social poetry of leftist women, and thus this section enables us to rethink modernism in connection to our current literary tastes and practices. Lola Ridge, an Irish immigrant, who was raised in Australia and New Zealand, constructs her own experience of exile through the immigrant Jewish subjects of "The Ghetto" as well as the recently transplanted African American community she describes in her poem "Lullaby," about the East St. Louis Riot of 1917. Marie de L. Welch's visit to "Camp Corcoran" exposed her to the exiled communities of Mexican migrant workers. These poets and poems openly acknowledge diversity by condemning racial intolerance. In addition, they are a vital part of a continuum through which to explore what contemporary writer Ishmael Reed refers to as our "multi-America."

It is clear from reading the socially engaged writing of these radical moderns that this work's significance may not be exclusively (or in some cases at all) in its artistry, its intellectual rigor, or its ability to push the limits of language—the canonical requirements of modernist poetry. This poetry speaks to us of the committed nature of women's intellectual and social conscience during a period of rapid expansion, exploitation, alienation, and destruction. It does so in different ways: through traditional forms, experimental styles, accessible language, and abstraction. Because the women included herein were engaged in social dialogue in their verse as well as in other aspects of their lives, it is important to consider their polemical voices beyond the "revolution of the word." Thus I have included, in the cases of Taggard and Trent, prose pieces to suggest how women poets on the left embraced modernist ideas in more than just poetic form.

This selection begins with an excerpt from Lola Ridge's important long poem "The Ghetto." At twenty-three pages long, the work is the first feminist poem about ghetto life published in America, and probably the first poem about ghetto life in general published in English. "The Ghetto" and "Lullaby," published in Ridge's first book *The Ghetto and Other Poems*, which received much critical acclaim, complicate gender issues attending to ethnicity and class as well. With its imagist snapshots, "The Ghetto" uses the trope of the female body to explore the complexity of the urban ghetto. If modernism is about "making it new," then Ridge's long poem moves beyond mere linguistic and formal experimentation to establish a social dialogue on immigration within the so-called revolutionary spaces of modernist aesthetics.

The poem "Lullaby" intervenes into the social spaces of revolutionary modernism in yet another complex fashion. Constructed like a traditional nursery rhyme, it attacks not only racism but also the problem of gender. In a footnote at the bottom of the page, Ridge informs her readers: "An incident of the East St. Louis Race Riots, when some white women flung a living colored baby into the heart of a blazing fire." Rather than present women as feminist innovators and actors in social change, Ridge problematizes the white racism ignored, or in some cases sanctioned, by her fellow white modernists as she dramatizes white women's acts of racial violence.

Like Lola Ridge, Genevieve Taggard was one of the modern period's most vociferous left voices in both poetry and prose. The poems selected here come from her Depression-era collection *Calling Western Union* (1936). These particular poems convey the poet's conviction that any program for social change must include women. Taggard also challenges the modernist obsession with "making it new" by suggesting that what was new in modern literature was women's involvement. Representing themselves in the struggle for social change, they were becoming a vital component to resisting oppressive conditions created during the Depression.

I also include Taggard's review of Jane Heap's 1927 Machine Age show at the Museum of Modern Art because it offers an alternative view of technology. Originally published in *New Masses*, "The Ruskinian Boys See Red" criticizes Heap's exhibition for failing to show anything more exciting than what is already everywhere on display in the modern metropolis of New York City. Referring to art historian Ruskin's anti-industrialism, Taggard also uses the essay to comment upon the anti-modern, anti-technology bent of a number of her colleagues on the left. Like many women of her generation, Taggard believed that the modern Machine Age would help liberate the masses—especially women, with its time-saving new inventions.

A strong admirer both of Ridge and Taggard, Lucia Trent published three books of poetry, but it is her work as an anthologist and polemicist, along with Ralph Cheyney, her poet-husband, that is particularly interesting. In Trent's and Cheyney's contribution, "What Is This Modernism?" from their polemic on modern poetry, *More Power to the Poets*, the poets argue for the liberation of modern poetry from the words "do not." Ever the supporters of a democratic poetics, Trent and Cheyney traveled the country organizing readings, conducting workshops, and publishing a wide variety of unknown, regional poets in the magazines and anthologies they edited. Whether they were paying tribute to the sonnet, or helping to raise awareness about the Sacco and

Vanzetti case, modernism for them was about social dialogue and collaboration. While "What Is This Modernism?" may appear quaint, and its aesthetic arguments hardly proclaiming the radical artifice associated with most modernist defenses, Trent's and Cheyney's audience would have recognized in it the same radical political spirit expressed in one of their other essays—the introduction to Marcus Graham's *Anthology of Revolutionary Poetry:*

> What are the *modern* seven wonders of the world? We suggest as the seven wonders, the increasing recognition that equal, unrestricted opportunity belongs to all individuals of all races and creeds or lack of creed; the labor movement; the rising opposition to violence and murder, whether they be expressed in lynching, capital punishment, or war; the emancipation of women; modern psychology and the extensions of consciousness; birth control; and the development of machinery to lessen labor and increase production. The poet who cannot find inspiration in these wonders is no seer, no humanist, no prophet, no voice of the spirit crying aloud in the wilderness—in short, no true poet. (36–37) (emphasis added)

Like a number of the other poets included in this section, Ruth Lechlitner had a relatively small output—four books in a lengthy career. With the exception of Taggard, who published at least thirteen books during a career that spanned three decades, it seems that both individual and political reasons interfered with these poets' productivity. Ridge suffered from tuberculosis; Trent appears to have stopped her writing and editing projects after Ralph Cheney's death in 1941; Welch was busy raising two daughters. However, it should be noted that from the late 1940s onward the political climate of the Cold War made it extremely difficult for writers on the left to publish their work. What is more, during the same Cold War period, more and more American women began to disappear into the domestic landscape. It took the women's movement of the late 1960s and 1970s to bring about renewed interest in these left-wing women poets.[1]

While virtually unknown today, Lechlitner's first two collections reveal the kinds of tensions and aesthetics associated with modernist poetics. She is perhaps the most traditionally "modernist" of all the poets in this selection. Her obscurely referenced, albeit formally constructed, powerfully concise poems suggest, as critic Alan Filreis has pointed out, the influence of Wallace Stevens, whose poetry Lechlitner greatly admired. Lechlitner's work, represented here, examines the gendered nature of the Depression by exploring issues such as pregnancy in "Lines for an Abortionist's Office," and patriarchal oppression, which can be traced in "Case Recruit."[2]

Like the other poets in this selection, Marie de L. Welch was an early contributor to the important left-wing magazine *New Masses*. Once criticized for writing poetry that was not sufficiently "revolutionary," Welch is an interesting case. Primarily she wrote what some might call "nature" poetry (she even liked to hunt and fish).[3] Careful examination of this verse, however, reveals numerous complicated metaphors about human struggle and resistance. Welch is represented along with fellow California left writers, George Sterling, Jack London, C. E. S. Wood, and Sara Bard Field in the WPA mural painted inside San Francisco's Coit Tower landmark. Yet, her writing life was a solitary one. According to her friend Muriel Rukeyser, Welch pursued a lonely, "singular" world in her poetry while remaining consummately aware of the "evil and loss" that enveloped humanity. Welch "went deep into a life that looked to many like silence" (16) The contradictions in Welch's career are represented here with the poems "Camp Corcoran," which was inspired by the poet's visit to a migrant camp where radical activists were organizing Mexican cotton pickers for a strike, and "Sky-Scrapers in Construction," which comments on the material excesses of capitalism.

Since no anthology can provide a comprehensive selection of authors or texts, I present here a sampling of modernism's overlooked creators, women poets who produced socially engaged poetry and prose and attempted to explore both the gender and social conscience of modernism as a way to enliven modernist aesthetics. The five authors included in this section should also be remembered as those who were exiled within their own genre and within their own literary movement. Lola Ridge and Marie de L. Welch reminded modern poetry readers that race and class were modernist subjects; Genevieve Taggard and Ruth Lechlitner told their Depression audiences to think not only of class struggle but also of gender struggle, and Lucia Trent and Ralph Cheyney promoted modernism as an inclusive rather than exclusive literary experiment. Inclusion is what we have attempted to do here. Whatever our preconceived notions of literary modernism, whatever our predilections and prejudices, it is not possible to complicate modernist practice without reconsidering such voices as those represented here.

Notes

1. Louise Bernikow's *The World Split Open: Five Centuries of Women Poets in England and America, 1552–1950*, published in 1974, collects some of this poetry and refers to women poets on the left as "the buried history within the buried history" (45). Feminist scholarship in the 1980s also took a renewed interest in radical women poets of the modern period. See Charlotte Nekola's discussion of poetry in *Writing Red: An Anthology of American Women Writers, 1930–1940*, ed. Nekola and Paula Rabinowitz (New York: Feminist Press, 1987).

2. Filreis argues in his book *Modernism from Left to Right: Wallace Stevens, the Thirties,*

and Literary Radicalism that the relationship between prominent modernists such as Stevens and William Carlos Williams, and young radical poets such as Lechlitner, Kenneth Fearing, and Willard Maas was far more significant than scholars of the Cold War era and beyond have acknowledged.

3. According to Filreis, Willard Maas reviewed Welch's first book, *Poems,* for *New Masses.* In his review, Maas argued that Welch's book lacks "revolutionary themes" (205). Yet poet Stanley Burnshaw countered Maas's attack by blaming Welch's publisher, the mainstream Macmillan, for sanitizing the final product by not including poems Welch had published in *New Masses* and other radical periodicals.

Works Cited

Filreis, Alan. *Modernism from Left to Right: Wallace Stevens, the Thirties, and Literary Radicalism.* New York: Cambridge University Press, 1994.

Rukeyser, Muriel. Introduction. *The Otherwise,* by Marie de L. Welch. San Francisco: Adrian Wilson, 1976. 15–22.

Trent, Lucia, and Ralph Cheyney. Introduction. In *An Anthology of Revolutionary Poetry,* ed. Marcus Graham. New York: Active Press, 1929. 33–44.

LOLA RIDGE

From "The Ghetto"

I

Cool inaccessible air
Is floating in velvety blackness shot with steel-blue lights,
But no breath stirs the heat
Leaning its ponderous bulk upon the Ghetto
And most on Hester street . . .

The heat . . .
Nosing in the body's overflow,
Like a beast pressing its great steaming belly close,
Covering all avenues of air . . .

The heat in Hester street,
Heaped like a dray
With the garbage of the world.

Bodies dangle from the fire escapes
Or sprawl over the stoops . . .
Upturned faces glimmer pallidly—
Herring-yellow faces, spotted as with a mold,
And moist faces of girls
Like dank white lilies,

And infants' faces with open parched, mouths that suck at the air as at
    empty teats.
Young women pass in groups,
Converging to the forums and meeting halls,
Surging indomitable, slow
Through the gross underbrush of heat.
Their heads are uncovered to the stars,
And they call to the young men and to one another
With a free camaraderie.
Only their eyes are ancient and alone . . .

The street crawls undulant,
Like a river addled
With its hot tide of flesh
That ever thickens.
Heavy surges of flesh
Break over the pavements,
Clavering like a surf—
Flesh of this abiding
Brood of those ancient mothers who saw the dawn break over Egypt . . .
And turned their cakes upon the dry hot stones
And went on
Till the gold of the Egyptians
    fell down off their arms . . .
Fasting and athirst . . .
And yet on. . . .

Did they vision—with those eyes darkly clear,
That looked the sun in the face and were not blinded—
Across the centuries
The march of their enduring flesh?
Did they hear—

Under the molten silence
Of the desert like a stopped wheel—
(And the scorpions tick-ticking on the sand . . .)
The infinite procession of those feet?

II

I room at Sodos'—in the little green room
      that was Bennies—
With Sadie
And her old father and her mother,
Who is not so old and wears her own hair.

Old Sodos no longer makes saddles.
He has forgotten how.
He has forgotten most things—even Bennie who stays
      away and sends wine on holidays—
And he does not like Sadie's mother
Who hides God's candles,
Nor Sadie
Whose young pagan breath puts out the light—
That should burn always,
Like Aaron's before the Lord.

Time spins like a crazy dial in his brain,
And night by night
I see the love-gesture of his arm
In its green-greasy coat-sleeve
Circling the Book,
And the candles gleaming starkly
On the blotched-paper whiteness of his face,
Like a miswritten psalm . . .
Night by night
I hear his lifted praise,
Like a broken whinnying
Before the Lord's shut gate.

Sadie dresses in black.
She has black-wet hair full of cold lights
And a fine-drawn face, too white.

All day the power machines
Drone in her ears . . .
All day the fine dust flies
Till throats are parched and itch
And the heat—like a kept corpse—
Fouls to the last corner.

Then—when needles move more slowly on the cloth
And sweaty fingers slacken
And hair falls in damp wisps over the eyes—
Sped by some power within,
Sadie quivers like a rod . . .
A thin black piston flying,
One with her machine.

She—who stabs the piece-work with her bitter eye
And bids the girls: "Slow down—
You'll have him cutting us again!"
She—fiery static atom,
Held in place by the fierce pressure all about—
Speeds up the driven wheels
And biting steel—that twice
Has nipped her to the bone.

Nights, she reads
Those books that have most unset thought,
New-poured and malleable,
To which her thought
Leaps fusing at white heat,
Or spits her fire out in some dim manger of a hall,
Or at a protest meeting on the Square,
Her lit eyes kindling the mob . . .
Or dances madly at a festival.
Each dawn finds her a little whiter,
Though up and keyed to the long day,
Alert, yet weary . . . like a bird
That all night long has beat about a light.

The Gentile lover, that she charms and shrews,
Is one more pebble in the pack

For Sadie's mother,
Who greets him with her narrowed eyes
That hold some welcome back.
"What's to be done?" she'll say,
"When Sadie wants she takes . . .
Better than Bennie with his Christian woman . . .
A man is not so like,
If they should fight,
To call her Jew . . ."

Yet when she lies in bed
And the soft babble of their talk comes to her
And the silences . . .
I know she never sleeps
Till the keen draught blowing up the empty hall
Edges through her transom
And she hears his foot on the first stairs.

Sarah and Anna live on the floor above.
Sarah is swarthy and ill-dressed.
Life for her has no ritual.
She would break an ideal like an egg for the winged
        thing at the core.
Her mind is hard and brilliant and cutting
        like an acetylene torch.
If any impurities drift there, they must be burnt up as
        in a clear flame.
It is droll that she should work in a pants factory.
—Yet where else . . . tousled and collar awry at her olive throat.
Besides her hands are unkempt.
With English . . . and everything . . . there is so little time.
She reads without bias—
Doubting clamorously—
Psychology, plays, science, philosophies—
Those giant flowers that have bloomed and withered, scattering
        their seed . . .
—And out of this young forcing soil what growth may
        come—what amazing blossomings.

Anna is different.
One is always aware of Anna, arid the young men
  turn their heads to look at her.
She has the appeal of a folk-song
And her cheap clothes are always in rhythm.
When the strike was on she gave half her pay.
She would give anything—save the praise that is hers
And the love of her lyric body.

But Sarah's desire covets nothing apart.
She would share all things . . .
Even her lover.

The Ghetto and Other Poems. New York: B. W. Huebsch, 1918. 3–9.

LOLA RIDGE

Lullaby*

Rock-a-by baby, woolly and brown . . .
(There's a shout at the door an' a big red light . . .)
Lil' coon baby, mammy is down . . .
Han's that hold yuh are steady an' white . . .

Look piceaninny—such a gran' blaze
Lickin' up the roof an' the sticks of home—
Ever see the like in all yo' days!
—Cain't yuh sleep, mah bit-of-honey-comb?

Rock-a-by baby, up to the sky!
Look at the cherries driftin' by—
Bright red cherries spilled on the groun'—
Piping-hot cherries at nuthin' a poun'!

---

 * (An incident of the East St. Louis Race Riots, when some white women flung a living colored baby into the heart of a blazing fire.)

Hush, mah lil' black-bug—doan yuh weep.
Daddy's run away an' mammy's in a heap
By her own fron' door in the blazin' heat
Outah the shacks like warts on the street . . .

An' the singin' flame an' the gleeful crowd
Circlin' aroun' . . . won't mammy be proud!
With a stone at her bade an' a stone on her heart,
An' her mouth like a red plum, broken apart . . .

See where the blue an' khaki prance,
Adding brave colors to the dance
About the big bonfire white folks make—
Such gran' doin's fo' a lil' coon's sake!

Hear all the eagah feet runnin' in town—
See all the willin' han's reach outah night—
Han's that are wonderful, steady an' white!
To toss up a lil' babe, blinkin' an' brown . . .

Rock-a-by baby—higher an' higher!
Mammy is sleepin' an' daddy's run lame . . .
(Soun' may yuh sleep in yo' cradle o' fire!)
Rock-a-by baby, hushed in the flame . . .

The Ghetto and Other Poems. New York: B. W. Huebsch, 1918. 80–81.

GENEVIEVE TAGGARD

At Last the Women Are Moving

Last, walking with stiff legs as if they carried bundles
Came mothers, housewives, old women who knew
  why they abhorred war.
Their clothes bunched about them, they hobbled with
  anxious steps
To keep with the stride of the marchers, erect, bearing wide banners.

Such women looked odd, marching on American asphalt.
Kitchens they knew, sinks, suds, stew-pots and pennies . . .
Dull hurry and worry, clatter, wet hands and backache.
Here they were out in the glare on the militant march.

How did these timid, the slaves of breakfast and supper
Get out in the line, drop for once dish-rag and broom?
Here they are as work-worn as stitchers and fitters.
Mama have you got some grub, now none of their business.

Oh, but these who know in their growing sons and
      their husbands
How the exhausted body needs sleep, how often needs food,
These, whose business is keeping the body alive,
These are ready, if you talk their language, to strike.

Kitchen is small, the family story is sad.
Out of the musty flats the women come thinking:
Not for me and mine only. For my class I have come
To walk city miles with many, my will in our work.

Calling Western Union. New York: Harper, 1936. 5–6.

GENEVIEVE TAGGARD

A Middle-Aged, Middle-Class Woman at Midnight

In the middle of winter, middle of night
A woman took veronal in vain. How hard it is to sleep
If you once think of the cold, continent-wide
Iron bitter. Ten below. Here in bed I stiffen.
It was a mink-coat Christmas said the papers . . .
Heated taxis and orchids. Stealthy cold, old terror
Of the poor, and especially the children.
                Now try to sleep.
In Vermont near the marble-quarries . . . I must not think
Again, wide awake again. O medicine

Give blank against that fact, the strike, the cold.
How cold Vermont can be. It's nerves, I know,
But I keep thinking how a rat will gnaw
In an old house. Hunger that has no haste . . .
Porcupines eat salt out of wood in winter. Starve
So our children now. Brush back the hair from forehead,
See the set faces hungrier than rodents. In the Ford towns
They shrivel. Their fathers accept tear gas and blackjacks.
When they sleep, whimper. Bad sleep for us all.
Their mouths work, supposing food. Fine boys and girls.
Hunger, busy with this cold to make barbarian
These states, to haunt the houses of farmers, destroyers
Of crops by plan. And the city poor in cold-water flats
Fingering the gas-cocks—*can't even die easy*
If they turn the gas off. I'm sick I tell you. Veronal
Costs money, too. Costs more than I can pay.
And night's long nightmare costs me, costs me much.
I'll not endure this stink of poverty. Sheriffs, cops,
Boss of the town, union enemy, crooks and cousins,
I hope the people win.

Calling Western Union. 13–14.

GENEVIEVE TAGGARD

Feeding the Children

Women are conservative. That is
They want life to go on . . . Groceries
Are important, and milk delivered each morning.
I must feed my children. Keep the peace.

And so they frown at strikes; so they oppose
Sacrifice outside family. What's that to us?
You risk your job for nothing, starve my babies!
What sort of father are you? Tear up your card!

Now the egg-shell wall of home-sweet-home, holy and humble,
Cracks with the price of meat, the lack of milk.
Out in the street they demonstrate her question.
Food, clothes, beds . . . The picket-line is the answer.

We must feed the children. Have you joined the Union?
We must feed the children. March today.
We must feed the children. How shall we feed the children?
We must feed the children. Vote the strike!

Calling Western Union. 54–55.

GENEVIEVE TAGGARD

The Ruskinian Boys See Red

Jane Heap talks such good sense in her catalogue, that her show should have been better. There could have been more guillotinesque, nearly noiseless meat-slicers from Dayton, more kitchen cabinets and Crane Valves; *more Machine Age.* After the show we went outside into a comparatively better show, the city of New York, mixed up with all the past, to be sure, mixed as all art is in life,—but superior to Miss Heap's show in two regards: first, there was more of it and second, it was going.

A week before, down near the East river I stopped short to see on a poster in the dusty window of a print-shop, the familiar cockade of the Lozowick black and white announcing this exhibition. The same machine design that we associate with the *New Masses, Loony,* the *Pinwheel* program and every radical show in town. And when we entered the Lozowicks stood out before everything, surpassing the actual cog-wheels and crank-shafts, and became with the Archipenkos the chief reason for not staying outside and riding on the elevated.

It may be that the machine has got to be stopped before we can see it. In that case this show was right in taking from the delicatessen and the machine shop the tools and contrivances we watch with bored eyes and impatient faces, rapping the counter with the change while we wait for sliced ham or re-soled shoes.

But most of us began inspecting the Machine Age about thirty years ago from Grandpa's knee where we had a good view of his gold-filled turnip watch. And invariably, Machine Age Exhibitors should remember that after seeing the wheels stopped, we wanted to see them going again. There are a lot of grand words that can be used at this point about another dimension and the difference between functional knowledge and no knowledge at all, but I will not use them. I might not use them right. There is a ferry-boat on San Francisco bay going at this instant where the two pistons are enclosed in a great glass house. In there they do their stuff; you watch the incredible shaft plunge upward; the walking beam buries the other piston in the ferry's depths . . . a momentary pause while the action shifts, a totally different rhythm, and then down. . . . The only other object worth peering at so long is a mechanism at the opposite end of existence. . . . People are equally fascinated with a monkey in a cage.

And so if she couldn't get the engineers to rig up something in motion why didn't Jane Heap get Leger's movie, *Ballet Mechanic* and have some Antheil music playing in a little dark room? Is that too much to ask? Jane Heap is content with machine sculpture; but most people want machine dance or drama. Gate Valve 72 inch, by the Crane Company is very fine indeed, from the static point of view. "It is this plastic-mechanical analogy which we wish to present," she says in the catalogue. "Utility does not exclude the presence of beauty . . . on the contrary a machine is not entirely efficient without the element of beauty. Utility and efficiency must take into account the whole man."

An architect went along with me to this show and told me that Hugh Ferriss' Sketch Model of Glass Skyscraper wasn't mere play. The glass is very pale green, and dented all over to keep the light from being too intense; you can see out and not be seen. People who live in glass skyscrapers shouldn't throw stones. . . . Within, under the washy shafted walls, it would be like living under water.

> *Sabrina fair,*
> *Listen where Thou art sitting,*
> *Under the glassy, cool translucent wave . . .*

Beside the Hugh Ferriss model, all around on the wall, drawings of those strangely named abstractions, the Ultimate Allowable Envelopes, black monoliths, altered, altered again, and suddenly, a place to live. Thank God, they didn't look like the stills in *Metropolis*. Over in the corner, some exquisite photographs by Steiner, the back lace of wires, and one startling slant at part of a typewriter. The Americans are better than the Germans, than the Russians, than the French, as far as the architecture goes. One rotograve photograph of the Garment Centre, New York, from high in the air . . . the buildings turn into Aztec pueblos, one straight line and steps of stories, running back.

The architect told me a lot of amazing things I couldn't retain, for instance the zoning law and its intricacies. I do remember though, that he said ninety per cent of all the buildings in New York are now made of synthetic stone. . . . In Spain, somewhere, there is a law in the little towns against carrying off the dust of the streets in your hand to the meagre terrace of a farm; people must be watched, there is so little soil. And sometimes the women come down during a rain and catch the muddy water that runs between the cobbles in their aprons for the sake of the sediment. But this story has little to do with the Machine Age, unless the people who live in the Synthetic Stone Ritz Tower begin to yearn for dirt boxes and hanging gardens. Perhaps synthetic dirt.

This article had started before Miss Heap sprung her show; and the pith of it was to have been ridicule for the howlers. The latest howl took place in the *New Masses* when someone complained because he had to stop at a street corner when the red light went on. Incredible tyranny! The trouble with literary people is that they just can't stick to their real grievances. Red and green lights are no tyranny until you sit down to write. Then you use them since you need to objectify some trouble or other. There is the central and never ending pain in the centre of your chest. It doesn't come from red and green lights. It's just as much there in the country as the city. It's there because you're alive and you can't do anything about it but go on living with it.

But our Ruskinian boys and girls keep talking about the evils of present-day life-standardization, and the robot crowds in the subway, and the horror of cleanliness and order. They make me sick, they make me tired.

And yet, perhaps they are instinctively sound; these people keep claiming that they want to go to the tops of mountains, or to Connecticut farms, etc.; use their hands, sweat; till the soil and play the game of being Isaaks and pioneers. That's what they do need. Because when they get back on the Connecticut farm, and begin to plow or milk cows or even split wood, they discover that there is a lot of work to be done, even when they employ some of the despised Machine Age—in a community that is trying merely to feed and house itself. Such an awful lot of work, such hours of toil and struggle just for food, or fire, or safety from storms, or labor for the beasts that labor for you. Then red and green lights don't seem an awful imposition. There is just one story about the human race that shouldn't ever be omitted from any picture. Men are living on a plane out in the middle of the sky where they have got to hustle in order to eat. The varieties of hustling are continuous; a few red and green lights if you try it one way; complete darkness and a smoky lantern in the wind, another.

The Ruskinian boys and girls are anarchists; they are opposed to even the discipline of the elements; they are indignant that free souls should have the limitations of sun, wind, light, darkness, cold and heat. I am very fond of seeing such people up against it. And when they come back to bath tubs and hot water, transportation and an eight-hour day, they don't have so much to say. After a little visit backwards the Machine Age doesn't seem like such an imposition.

As for Machine Age poetry, don't read Mark Turbyfill, who writes for Miss Heap's catalogue. Mr. Turbyfill calls it the poetry of forces . . . and he plunges (in his own words) mentally and boldly into the seething universe of electrons and vibrations. If you want a really good poem about a Machine Age subject, go back to that timid and near-sighted spinster, Emily Dickinson, who wrote in 1860 or thereabouts, this little piece about a locomotive. (Note that the machine is going.)

> I like to see it lap the miles,
> And lick the valleys up,
> And stop to feed itself at tanks,
> And then prodigious step
> Around a pile of mountains,
> In shanties by the sides of roads,
> And supercilious peer
> And then a quarry pare . . .

That is doing what Louis Lozewick prescribes:

> *Objectify the dominant experience of our epoch in plastic terms that possess value for more than this epoch alone.*

New Masses (July 1927): 18.

LUCIA TRENT AND RALPH CHEYNEY

What Is This Modernism?

The most important work of modernist poets has been kicking over old walls— but we shall sketch, too, the new paths they have started. The breaking of "Do nots" is almost the only practice at which modernist poets work shoulder to shoulder—and we shall indicate the "Do nots" that almost all of them build.

"I do not appreciate the poems. There are too few that deal with nature and love, too many that stress sex. I must confess I cannot make out the meaning of many of them; and I miss the sweetness and light, the pleasant subjects simply expressed in lilting lines, arid teaching uplifting truths that I have always been taught to associate with poetry."

This letter recently received nutshells neatly the objections to most modern poetry. At a meeting of an organization of poets, a poem was objected to vociferously because it contained no "Uplift." Another was condemned because it did not "observe the canons of good taste." At another meeting a young man was promptly squelched by the chair because he pointed out that not one of the poems presented that night contained a single indication that it had been written in the twentieth century rather than the twelfth century.

The younger poets are responding boldly to Clifford Gessler's call, "Art must be creative. It must be alive, untrammelled, savage. If one has anything to say, let him say it openly and fearlessly, with as much as he can attain of a fine high disregard of consequences."

Thoreau's complaint, "Much of our poetry has the very best manners but no character," becomes increasingly less justified though it is still all too true.

The "Do not" which modernists break in subject matter is that Pegasus must be kept in a paddock. *Any subject can be made poetic.* For poetry resides in the poet, not in the subject. Electric lights as well as stars, factory whistles as well as birds, jazz as well as the music of the spheres.

The "Do not" which modernists build is this: Pegasus should *not* be allowed to wander in his sleep up the Milky Way or in lands that never were. Stars are suspect, birds banished to their proper, twittering place, the music of the spheres maligned and princesses personae non grata. Vision is preferred to visions, dreams explored for what they may reveal of reality in the dark mind of man. If we are to build a new Utopia, Pegasus must be set to ploughing the fields at our feet.

Poems of escape are sneered upon as the weak, wan make-shifts they are. Whitman's doctrine of acceptance is embraced. Poets are the "yes-men" of the universe. The life of today is rich enough to demand a poet's best—richest where rawest, most savage and saturnine. Accordingly, modernists are most objective even when introspective. Those fields and valleys which have been taboo are virgin (figuratively) territory and likely to yield the most potent harvest. Modernists know Synge was right, when he said, "What is exalted or tender is not made by feeble blood."

In diction, modernists believe that no word can be too frank, too earthy, too strong, too slangy for poetry. The corresponding "Do not" they build is that no words may be used which would not naturally occur in any conversation on the subject treated. Just as a picture must not be picturesque, poetic diction must contain no poeticisms. The more concrete, graphic and colorful, the richer the taste of blood, tang of loam, smack of all the senses, is the diction, the greater the chances of the poem's living, breathing, moving, fecundating. A poem is most dynamic if it strikes, into a complex, however obliquely.

The broken "Do not" in grammatical construction is that there must be no departure from recognized grammatical constructions. Modernists willingly sacrifice grammar if thereby they gain—and they often do—increased sharpness, poignancy, realism, suggestiveness. They hold effect as all-important. Moreover, they ask with justice why grammar must be a fossilized skeleton instead of a living—i.e., changing—form for embodying thoughts. What they want to say is new, different—why not say it with fresh constructions as well as fresh images? Language is but a group of symbols—why not find new symbols for new things to symbolize? They hold with Rodin and Archipenko that to suggest is sufficient. They hold with modernist painters that significant form is the thing. They seldom aim for smoothness. On the contrary. This is not an age of smoothness. What holds good for grammar goes the same for punctuation, spelling, capitalization. They are working out a new language.

The built "Do not" is akin to the rule for diction. *Do not stray far from daily speech*—and avoid inversions as a chorus-girl a bankrupt. The oaths of many a day laborer hold more of the meat of poetry than most dainty volumettes of verse. We quote Edith Sitwell: "Modern poets are building among the common movements of life, just as Wordsworth built, only the modern poet has a different stylisation, that is all; if we grasp that fact the whole matter becomes easy." Revolution and revaluation have always been a function of poetry. This is an era of accelerated revolution and revaluation. Absolutes are in the discard. The challenge of space and time by thought and their conquest by machinery are reflected in poetry. Poetry is tending to become short, direct, concentrated. (That those classic forms of concentration in verse: the tanka and hokku, come from the unhastening East proves that there is more to recommend brevity than simply the scantiness of time for reading.) There is a quicker tempo in our life and emotions today. Therefore, the modernist "Do not": *Poetry must not be long-winded,* it must achieve its effect, with the strictest artistic economy. The modernist trick of repeating words does not, of course, offend against this rule; it simply heightens the effect with the least retardation.

Another and more far-going indication of this transmutation of values is that neither modernist poets nor poetry-lovers rest content with rephrasing old concepts and attitudes. In exploring the extensions of consciousness and expressing new valuations nouns are made to serve as verbs, colors are used to describe sounds, words are run together and many other devices are explored and exploited. Naturally, these confuse those whose minds are still dusting antimacassars and whose emotions are still enwombed although their bodies are scrambling out of subways to mount skyscrapers.

Incidentally, one of the most fascinating and fruitful devices of modernism in poetry is the transference of qualities, the translation of an impression of one of the senses into the terms of another, speaking of "lustrous music" to quote poetry or "loud color" to quote slang. This illustrates a principle which recurs so often in poetry that it seems to be one of poetry's very corner-stones: the discovery of hidden correspondences, the revelation of similarities where casual thought presumes but differences, and the realization of the unity of life.

Profound skepticism and a sense of frustration are the mood of most of the mentally alert. "The old truths are no longer true and the new truths have yet to be born." The poets and rebels may be fecundating a new world—but neither the whispers of passion nor the anguished shrieks of birth are lilting songs. Enough that they prophecy new life.

Many modernists are intent on developing a new mythos, others seek what validity there may be for us now in American Indian legends and native ballads, still others seek a true understanding of the feel and force of contemporary life and struggle. Nor should these be mutually exclusive. But "the search for truth is not for timid souls."

If two experiences create the same emotional effect or effects which by contrast enhance each other, they may be coupled—and out of their very differences a new emotional effect derived, one quite possibly, which could be secured in no other way. (The whole may be more than the sum of its parts.) By the same token, many rhythms may be combined effectively in one poem. We know that we experience many widely varying sensory reports, emotional reactions, and thoughts virtually simultaneously. Modernists hold they are free to present these in one poem.

They prefer to have the rhythms or cadences of poetry tally with those of emotionally aroused speech.

A word as to old poetic licenses: *don't!*

It would be a safe generalization to say that poetic licenses have been so abused that they have been withdrawn.

To modernists poetry is not a sugared sedative. Neither is it a tonic. It is more apt to be sap, blood. But chiefly it is poetry. It is not the choiring of simple souls. Rather is it the feeling aloud of a thinker whose mediations and meditations are burst in upon by a shouting army of workers tramping past belching mills lit by a rising sun.

More Power to Poets. New York: Henry Harrison, 1934. 106–10.

RUTH LECHLITNER

Lines for an Abortionist's Office

Close here thine eyes, O State:
These are thy guests who bring
To gods with appetites grown great
A votive offering.

Know that they dare defy
The words of law and priest—
(Better to let the unborn die
Than starve while others feast.)

The stricken flesh may be
Outraged, and heal; but mind
Pain-sharpened, may yet learn to see
Thee plain, O State. Be blind:

Accept love's fruit: be sleek
Fat and lip-sealed. (Forget
That Life, avenging pain, will speak!)
Thrust deep the long curette!

Tomorrow's Phoenix. Alcestis Press, 1937. 33.

RUTH LECHLITNER

Case Recruit

Brothers, be stage to him who has
No life except in audience:
His exhibition rounded by an O—
The womb-encircling mother.

Alone he's naked: solitude
Capons his ego; the breastless trees
Unman him, he's ignored
By earth, by starlight made anonymous.

Be mantle to him, people his bareness
Warmly, house his sex:
Be (if you must) his true romance,
His church, his Empire State.

Be his vernacular: Winchell, Hollywood,
(Sly serpent, histrionic lion)
Let him be martyr through your flesh,
Stung by the whip, vicariously clubbed.

Self-love, yes; but these platform tears
Betray most desperate need:
Be to him now the growth he's missed—
Direction, sinew; be his blood, his brother.

Tomorrow's Phoenix. 34.

MARIE DE L. WELCH

Sky-Scraper in Construction

Now gaps in monstrous red
iron ribs are filled with the immense
cold pallor of a sky steel-riveted
against those ribs. Winds bed
with lean iron bones,
lie with virile skeletons
that must be marble-fed
to as obese white impotence.

New Masses (July 1928): 4.

MARIE DE L. WELCH

Camp Corcoran*

This is the camp of the strangest workers,
Yesterday in the cherry orchards,
Today in the cotton fields,
Tomorrow in the vineyards.
This is the camp of the nomad harvesters.

Tonight, this a strikers' camp
Tonight, this is a fort.
Around the field there is a strand of wire;
That is the wall.
Only workers pass here.
The sentinels watch.

Keep out disorder!
Pride is beginning here,
And dignity, and command.

Maybe of these four thousand
Only a dozen or a hundred men
Have more than hunger and patience,
More than a warm country's lazy habit
To wait with,
To take it almost easy,
Even the war of starving.
Maybe only a hundred of four thousand
Slowly, seriously,
Have won dignity, have accepted command.

But it begins.

The sentinels are unarmed.
The single wire is not barbed.

---

* Written after a visit to a camp of striking cotton pickers, a majority of whom were Mexicans, in the San Joaquin Valley in California.

We walked through, in worried darkness,
In the camp of sullen war. In the silence
We stumbled into shallow pools of mud.

We are not used to walking in so much shadow;
We are not used to little fires like stains on the dark.
These are strange roads between the huts of sack and brush.

The little fires emphasize the dark;
They add confusion to the simple dark.

We are not used to this stirred broken dark.
We do not walk back a thousand years every evening.
We did not know the camps there are in the world.
We did not know the wars of the unarmed.

They are starving!
"They need not starve."
They live in mud.
"They have always lived in mud."
Why should they live in mud?
"They need not starve
If they'll just live in mud."

We cannot answer.
In this argument, death
Goes round its circle.

There is a ring of men,
And one man singing,
On the ground.

There is a ring of men,
And one man talking,
On the ground.

Like their fires, like their mud,
On the ground.

Not many—the rest are sleeping.
Days are long;
Waiting is the only deed, and sleep
Is almost the only food.
A few children are tireless, their noise
Is sharp as light.
They laugh like screaming.

There's no beauty here.
Make no mistake.
This is the dust of human ground.
They work, it has not made them beautiful.

This is humanity. It does the work.
It is not beautiful.
Make no mistake.
This is humanity, it is not gentle.
This is humanity, it is not clean.

This is humanity, this is your world.
This is humanity, this is your work.
This is your kind, this is yourself.
Make no mistake.

But see here—beginning.
The stirring, not the form.
It is soft, it is without bones.
It is slow, it is without muscles.

The bones of pride,
The muscles of anger,
The fine nerves of love
Form slowly in the mass.

This is not the form.
This is not the power.
But see here—beginning.
Faint, like the first stir in the pregnant womb.
The body is not torn, only half-tense.
The move is little and deep.

Until passion, until danger, until birth
There will be a long time.

The leaders are fibre of this:
They know what is here.

Forget their courage;
Any man facing danger
Has courage.

They know what is here.

Forget their strength.
The others, even the arguers for death
Have strength.

The leaders are fibre of this.

I'll tell you what the leaders said:
They said, "You have it!"
I'll tell you what the leaders said:
They said, "It's yours!"
Life.
You have it.
It's yours.

I'll tell you what the leaders said:
They said, "Men!"

This Is Our Own. New York: Macmillan, 1940. 57–62.

PART II

Issues of Production and Reception

4

Sentimental Modernism

INTRODUCED AND SELECTED BY SUZANNE CLARK

> The minds of man and woman grow apart, and how shall we express their differentiation? In this way, I think: man, at best is an intellectualized woman. Or, man distinguishes himself from woman by intellect, but it should be well feminized. He knows he should not abandon sensibility and tenderness, though perhaps he has generally done so, but now that his is so far removed from the world of the simple senses, he does not like to impeach his own integrity and leave his business in order to recover it. [. . .] But his problem does not arise for a woman. Less pliant, safer, as a biological organism, she remains fixed in her famous attitudes, and is indifferent to intellectuality. I mean, of course, comparatively indifferent; more so than a man. Miss Millay is rarely and barely very intellectual, and I think everybody knows it.
>
> —John Crowe Ransom, "The Poet as Woman" (784)

EVEN THOUGH THERE are certain characteristics of the sentimental that one might list, so that it seems like other literary conventions or genres, the most salient of them lies outside those definitions. Like other pejorative labels, that of sentimentality hides its gendered insult behind a mask of objective judgment. The idea of the "sentimental" was used by modernist critics to repudiate and for many years effectively silence a whole generation of women writers by linking emotionalism to women—as if revolutionary poetry could only be intellectual—or by suggesting that women's continuity with nineteenth-century conventions of narrative made them less than intellectually respectable. This pejorative and dismissive—and uncritical—use of the word "sentimental" continues to this day. We might become suspicious when we realize that an accusation of sentimentality discriminated against some of the most powerful women writers of their time, among them those whose work is represented in this chapter: Angelina Weld Grimké, Edna St. Vincent Millay, Louise Bogan, and Kay Boyle. A literary history of modernism without them would tell the wrong story.

The great progressive movements of the nineteenth century were deeply allied with women's sentimental rhetoric: abolition, women's rights, Indian rights, public education, anti-drink, immigrant socialization, and welfare in the urban centers such as Jane Addams's Hull House, birth control, and the polarizing issue of women's suffrage. These political and cultural movements carried on in alliances of the twentieth century, and their contributions to the revolution that was modernist literature is evident. But was the progressive, feminist, and sentimental political juggernaut more powerful as a support for women's participation in modernist projects—or was it more powerful because it provided a maternal object against which modernists might launch an explosive revolt? Women writers, activists, and editors were caught in a multiply conflictual situation.

Not war but domesticity was most reviled: hence Nietzsche's attack on the slavishness of women may be heard echoing in Wyndham Lewis's use of "sentimental" as the defining quality of all that the Vortex must reject. In 1914, Wyndham Lewis proclaimed in *Blast:* "The futurist [i.e., Marinetti] is a sensational and sentimental mixture of the aesthete of 1890 and the realist of 1870. / The 'Poor' are detestable animals! They are only picturesque and amusing for the sentimentalist or the romantic" (8). Lewis blasted France and other Latin countries for their "sentimental Gallic gush," "sentimental hygienics," the "abasement of the miserable 'intellectual' before anything coming from Paris, Cosmopolitan sentimentality" (34). In "Our Vortex," he declared: "Everything absent, remote, requiring projection in the veiled weakness of the mind, is sentimental" (147). Dora Marsden thought that the Christian religion made women in particular lack the psychic structure that would enable self-realization: "Seeking the realization of the will of others, and not their own, ever waiting upon the minds of others, women have almost lost the instinct for self-realization, the instinct for achievement in their own person" (Dell 102).

From the first manifestoes of the twentieth-century avant-garde, it was clear that the "sentimental" would be a target. The sentimental could be associated with an emotional romanticism that T. E. Hulme castigated as "spilt religion," or with the maternal authority of the domestic: propriety, religiosity, cultivated feelings, and good taste; or with the enforced passivity and limitation of lifestyles prescribed for women, elaborated in cures for female neurasthenia, and in stark contrast with the active life prescribed for suffering men such as Theodore Roosevelt or Owen Wister. A brief glance at the history of three important little magazines will suggest how the problem might become a narrative—the story of matricide, indeed, that Ann Douglas tells in *Terrible Honesty.* First, Dora Marsden's *Freewoman* developed into *The Egoist*. From the support of suffragettes, its editor, Marsden, turned to the freeing of the willful individual. In his 1913 *Women as World Builders,* Floyd Dell celebrated Marsden's independence and emphasized her repudiation of feminism: "Of all the corruptions to which the woman's movement is now open, . . . the most poisonous and permeating is that which flows from sentimentalism, and it is in the W. S. P. U. [Women's Social and Political Union] that sentimentalism is now rampant. . . . It is this sentimentalism that is abhorrent to us. We fight it as we would fight prostitution, or any other social disease" (Dell 98–99). For her insistence on individual will, Dell calls Marsden "the Max Stirner of feminism" (103). *This Quarter* was established by the partnership of Ethel Moorhead and Ernest Walsh. In *Being Geniuses Together,* Kay Boyle tells us that Moorhead, activist in woman's suffrage, "had smashed plate-glass windows with a hammer, trembling with nervousness as she struck; she had set fire to churches, been arrested, and been forcibly fed." But she and Walsh collaborated as artists, Moorhead contributing her pension rather than her politics, and published Hemingway, Joyce, Carnevali, Ezra Pound, and William Carlos Williams, as well as representations of Picabia and Brancusi's sculpture. In many ways modernist women left the politics of feminism behind. Ann Douglas argues that urban modernity was about the "slaying of the Titaness, the Mother God of the Victorian era." Furthermore, she points out the racist tactics of white middle-class feminist leaders such as Frances Willard, Carrie Chapman Catt, and even Jane Addams, and argues that the Harlem Renaissance would not have happened while middle-class women dominated culture: "Negro and matriarch could not be front stage at the same time." But the situation was more complicated than this. Alain Locke, who in 1925 declared that the "New Negro" did not need sentimental support, also revealed activist fear that the support was losing power:

> The intelligent Negro of today is resolved not to make discrimination an extenuation for his shortcomings in performance, individual or collective; he is trying to hold himself at par, neither inflated by sentimental allowances nor depreciated by current social discounts. For this he must know himself and be known for precisely what he is, and for that reason he welcomes the new scientific rather than the old sentimental interest. Sentimental interest in the Negro has ebbed. We used to lament this as the falling off of our friends; now we rejoice and pray to be delivered both from self-pity and condescension.

The vanguard of activist women for the Harlem Renaissance, for instance, belonged to the middle class—think of Jessie Fauset—and inherited the progressive politics of abolitionist foremothers: Angelina Weld Grimké represents this

personal and political continuity. Women as well as men attacked the hypocrisy of conventional domesticity and wrote about same-sex love. But few wrote
as fiercely as Angelina Grimké's powerful outcry—in her story, "Goldie," and
her play, *Rachel*—against the possibility of motherhood in a culture that would
sanction lynching.

Furthermore, only the middle-class elements of the progressive coalition
were left undamaged by the "red scare," the Palmer raids, and the far-ranging
attack on radical groups that came about at the end of World War I in the
United States. Emma Goldman was deported, Sacco and Vanzetti were executed, and their supporters—including Edna St. Vincent Millay—risked a great
deal. The radical left was represented in Europe by surrealist groups. In the
United States, the *Little Review* emerged as radical in the political spectacle
when it was put on trial for publishing part of the Nausicaa chapter of James
Joyce's *Ulysses*. But Anglo-American modernist aesthetics had not only a con-
servative trajectory, but radicalism to the right. In a 1927 publication of *The
Enemy,* Wyndham Lewis attacked *transition,* together with, Kay Boyle tells us,
"Communism, surrealism, Joyce, Stein, Negroes, Sherwood Anderson, D. H.
Lawrence, and Indians" (*Being Geniuses Together* 263). Lewis meant "to defend
the classical ideal against the spirit of disorder, or the romantic conception."
The conservative southern critics at Vanderbilt celebrated T. S. Eliot and Wil-
liam Faulkner while they vilified writers such as Millay.

Modernist criticism was crusading successfully against the very idea that
poetry might not only revolutionize style but have a political, or at least progressive, edge. Conservatism could be compatible with an aesthetic view of
the literary. Women writers, however, were by virtue of being women attached
to a political narrative. No matter how much they declared themselves not
feminists, as did, in fact, Emma Goldman herself, women were feminists by
virtue of not being silent. And no matter how activist they were, or how emotionally restrained—Louise Bogan almost silenced herself completely with her
restraint—women could be called sentimental. Emma Goldman herself was
called "sentimental," by Lenin, when she advocated free speech for anarchists.
Imagine what might have been said if her public knew that Emma Goldman's
lover called her "Mommy."

This chapter includes selections from four women whose writing demonstrates their encounters with the political tensions of feminism, racial conflict,
progress, and a modernist cultural revolution problematizing feminized narratives and rhetoric: Angelina Weld Grimké, Edna St. Vincent Millay, Louise
Bogan, and Kay Boyle. The revolt against the past that occurred in the period
called "modernist" was often different from previous revolts against tradition
and authority. In psychoanalytic terms we might think of it not as oedipal,

but rather as pre-oedipal (hence violent and at the level of identity and the very entry into language and the capacity to symbolize). This is to say that modernist anarchy in politics and in language might be seen as a revolt not so much against the patriarchy, or the father, but against the mother. Women, of course, participated. However, while it might seem that women as the very exemplars of the conventional could the more easily "make it new," in fact their rebellions could not easily challenge both poetic and social convention at once. One of the most powerful repressions of women's writing came with the critical sanctions against the sentimental. To this day, calling a work "sentimental" means that no critical analysis is required. The censorship of the "sentimental" by modernist critics foreclosed the respectful consideration of women writers.

Angelina Weld Grimké could fascinate us first for her largely unpublished lesbian love poems, most reflecting the influence of the nineteenth-century poetesses with her intense use of poetic musicality in verse, the expression of passion and despair. These lovely poems capture feelings that she could neither make public nor, apparently, act upon in later life, perhaps because her much admired father would not have approved. She herself tells, in an essay in praise of her father's accomplishments, the story of her illustrious family, with a heritage that is partly from the white abolitionist sisters, Angelina and Sarah Grimké, and partly from the African American slaves who gave birth to their cousins. Truly the inheritor of two racial traditions, Angelina Weld Grimké entered into the Harlem Renaissance and into modernist consciousness in the 1920s as a writer protesting the terror experienced by her people, in poems, stories, and a powerful drama about lynching, *Rachel*. She made there the painful, terrible argument that a mother of a black child might best choose never to be a mother—might even kill her child—when she sees the fate of her people, that her child too might be the eventual victim of the lynchers' cruelty. In all of her writing, Grimké presses the extremities of linguistic expression to represent the extremity of the situations she experiences. If the emotion seems excessive to the reader, perhaps the reader is insufficiently instructed about the historical context. Here is an example of how aesthetic judgment could be distorted by anti-sentimental values. Grimké's poems are both pleasing and striking aesthetically, but perhaps not to the reader armed against emotional expression.

Included below, "You" and "Your Eyes" suggest the intensity of lesbian love poems she wrote. Apparently, under the restraining influence of her father, she retreated from lesbian relationships as she grew older. "Blue Eyes" may suggest a love poem, perhaps a cross-racial love such as the marriage of her African American father and her white mother. Or it may suggest a more race-centered politics, with a covert reference to the passing from dominance of the race of "blue eyes." Racial feeling is more overt only in a couple of other poems, such as "The Black Finger," and "Beware Lest He Awakes," and in her drama, *Rachel,* and prose works such as the short story, "Goldie," described in her letter to the *Atlantic Monthly.* "The Black Finger" seems like an imagist poem, condensed, except for the last two lines. Rather than seeing these as a kind of abstract and sentimental excess, consider the emphasis, and the irony, implied by the repetitions: why black, why pointing upward?

Edna St. Vincent Millay was the very emblem of rebellious youth, defining her generation even more than F. Scott Fitzgerald, more widely read and popular than any other poet, a celebrity before Hemingway. Her attitude of exuberant defiance seduced Greenwich Village men from Floyd Dell to Edmund Wilson, though the strand of lesbian friendships that dominated her experiences at Vassar did not enter into the public view. Her political poems celebrated the noted feminist Inez Milholland (a sonnet included below), spoke out on the Sacco and Vanzetti case ("Justice Denied in Massachusetts"), called attention to the war in Spain ("Say That We Saw Spain Die"), and—to the detriment of her reputation on the left—supported patriotic themes during World War II. Like several writers of the Harlem Renaissance, Millay has left a formidable legacy in the sonnet form, including a sequence narrating the course of a love affair, *Fatal Interview.* She must be counted as one of the most careful and nuanced poets of her time, her poems yielding layer after layer of complexity to close aesthetic analysis. However, her attention to the formal musicality of poetry rather than to the shattering of rhetorical and linguistic structures led John Crowe Ransom and others to make her one of their chief objects of the attack on women poets. He characterized her as "barely intellectual," even though her language reveals her mastery of poetics in the Classic, Anglo-Saxon, and European as well as Anglo-American traditions. Her plays are ambitious achievements and she collaborated with Deems Taylor, writing the libretto for *The King's Henchman,* the first real success in American opera.

Millay sometimes used her poetry to celebrate her violations of public morality, writing the lines in the 1918 "First Fig" that would make her the icon of the 1920s sexual revolution: "My candle burns at both ends; / It will not last the night; / But ah my foes, and oh, my friends— / It gives a lovely light." Like D. H. Lawrence and James Joyce, she pressed the limits of sexual figure in language, inviting censorship and scandal. She had plenty of lovers, among them Edmund Wilson, who admired her and her poetry all his critical life and who modeled the intense and dramatic poet, Rita, in his novel, *I Thought of Daisy,* after Millay. Was her attachment to free love, even after she married, the mark of a kind of cultural politics or of a psychologically disturbed individual? Judgments of Millay continue to be seduced by the flamboyant, disturbing life rather than by her poetic achievements. *Savage Beauty,* the recent biography by Nancy Milford, shows that Millay's life was, indeed, far from a model of sentimental bourgeois respectabilities, even after she married. Daniel Epstein, whose *What Lips My Lips Have Kissed* underscores her poetic achievement and praises her moral courage, nevertheless explains away her challenges to convention as manic-depressive, and argues that she was never really an activist. But Millay was passionate about questions of feminism and political justice, and impeccably supportive not only of her family, but of friends that included other women poets such as Elinor Wylie, and controversial figures such as Emma Goldman as well. Like other women writers dismissed as sentimental, she wrote about these passions. Like other women, she understood the ambiguous treatment of the woman as a work of art; the work of art as a woman, and her use of the "speaking picture," or ecphrasis, calls attention to her unsettling poetic voice.

Obviously playing with the idea of female emotion that Ransom took so seriously, Millay wrote the ironic sonnet, "I, being born a woman and distressed" (included below) long before he wrote his denunciation of her as a woman and too emotional. The sonnet shows her virtuosity with the form: bending convention against love's conventions—in the sonnet tradition since the Renaissance—she turns the figure of female frenzy against the not so witty lover/reader, who is dismissed from further conversation no matter how clouded he may think her mind. Millay read "The Patriots," a sonnet (included here) dedicated to Inez Milholland, feminist leader and wife of Millay's future husband, at the 1923 unveiling of a statue of three leaders in the cause of equal rights for women. Cast as the words of the woman remembered there, the poem speaks, uncannily, the lines that will be used on Millay's own grave: "Take up the song; forget the epitaph." In two works not included here due to permissions problems, "Justice Denied in Massachusetts," and "Fear," an essay, Millay writes about the cultural resonance of the executions of Sacco and Vanzetti. The poem, like much of her work, reads political themes ecologically—not as external, passing histories, but inscribed in the landscape of everyday life, so that the death of the innocent offenders becomes a threat to larkspur and corn. The essay angrily challenges readers about their fear of anarchists—and their withdrawal from the demonstrators like herself who went to jail to protest injustice.

Louise Bogan wrote unflinchingly to critique the sentimentality of some women writers, but she also provided a vigorous defense of the place for female treatment of emotion in the history of modern poetry: "The need of the refreshment and the restitution of feeling, in all its warmth and depth, has never been more apparent than it is today, when cruelty and fright often seem about to overwhelm man and his world" ("The Heart and the Lyre"). Her poetry demonstrates her understanding, her overlapping of musicality and the women's lyric. Bogan's version of an écriture féminine ruptures lyric narrative with melancholy precision. Her collected poems, *Blue Estuaries,* are a distillation of impressive artistic power. Some of her shorter lyrics are hauntingly suggestive. Their use of poetic language is not just an imagist condensation; these are poems that have absorbed the European lessons of symbolist experiment, that understand the intense and contradictory juxtaposition of bitterness, evil, and excess to beauty. She puts us into contact with the close alliance of horror and the sublime. In poems such as "Medusa," "The Crows," "Portrait," "Statue and Birds," "Women," and "Cassandra," she describes a female persona that has, it seems, become art. And this death, even into beauty, may provoke horror: "This is a dead scene forever now" ("Medusa"), or resignation: "—O remember / In your narrowing dark hours / That more things move / Than blood in the heart" ("Night"), or witty irony:

> Slipping in blood, by his own hand, through pride,
> Hamlet, Othello, Coriolanus fall.
> Upon his bed, however, Shakespeare died,
> Having endured them all.
>
> ("To an Artist, To Take Heart")

In the lineage of Mallarmé, Bogan understood musicality and condensation in poetry. However, the brief collection—its smallness representing the near silence of a great poet—and the intensity of her work must give us pause. In the case of Bogan, it seems as if the critical faculty and in particular the modernist antipathy to female emotion has all but strangled her voice.

She was a critic of sustained influence and authority in the pages of the *New Yorker,* providing for thirty years a succinct commentary on the development of modernist writing. The essays, collected in two anthologies, *Selected Criticism* and *A Poet's Alphabet: Reflections on the Literary Art and Vocation,* demonstrate her enduring insightfulness. Her book on the first half of the century, *Achievement in American Poetry,* is a brilliant, readable summary of developments in the years of modernism's coming to power. In it she argues that women helped to form the new direction for poetry:

> Freshness and sincerity of emotion, and economical directness of method were, it can be seen, early apparent in formal poetry written by women well before the turn of the century. Women's subsequent rejection of mor-

al passivity, economic dependence, and intellectual listlessness in favor of active interests and an involvement with the world around them—a rejection which, at crucial moments in the English suffragist movement, became exteriorized in actual physical combat—changed the direction and tone of their writing. (23)

The *Letters of Louise Bogan* demonstrate her critical acumen as well. They include a correspondence with Theodore Roethke that reveals her as mentor/lover/mother.

Included below, a long poem, "Summer Wish," published in the 1929 *Dark Summer,* suggests her mastery of poetic form. Does she endure as an accomplished but minor poet? Yvor Winters, reviewing the book, saw the promise of a major poet in her. This poem might haunt us with the possibilities it suggests of more, of poetic greatness. She shows us the materiality of the symbol; the ability of poetic language to speak with the earth. It is that power and the poetic tradition handed down, in this instance most directly from Yeats, that enables her ambitious transformation of harsh materials—childhood trauma, the return of terrible memories, spring and the rebirth of desire—into a dialogue that marks and limits human pain with the permanence of earth's seasons.

The poem leaves us not just with the recognition of her technical prowess, but at the same time shaken by the narrative of despair, of emotion that one could be desperate to avoid recalling, and the accompanying wish nonetheless to live, to participate in the movement of earth toward summer. The poem cites in the epigraph Yeats's "Shepherd and Goatherd," and draws on his "Ego Dominus Tuus" as a model. It is, as her biographer Elizabeth Frank claims, "a great poem in a major style and major mode" (*Louise Bogan* 125). Its linguistic turn to nature draws on an understanding in the lineage of Thoreau. At the same time, it is in particular a poem about female trauma.

The essay reprinted here, on the female tradition in poetry, "The Heart and the Lyre," first appeared not (as did most of her criticism) in the *New Yorker,* but in *Mademoiselle,* together with pictures of earlier poetesses.

Kay Boyle began her innovations in prose and poetry with a recently discovered novel, *Process,* that seems at times almost to be written between languages (French/English: the title itself suggests not only process, but *procès,* trial.) Erotically charged scenes include the mother/daughter exchanges and family incest. Boyle wrote successful novels after this for the next fifty years of a long life, her style becoming gradually less experimental but her perspective always unusual. Associated in France with the Duncan colony, with *This Quarter* and then with *transition,* and with circles of artists and writers that included not only Americans (William Carlos Williams was an important friend and influence) but also Europeans in the surrealist tradition, Boyle nevertheless wrote fiction and prose that drew on an experiences unusual even for the modernists. At the same time that she took a lively interest in artistic circles (as she records in *Being Geniuses Together*), her interests and her style (white earrings from Woolworth's) came out of immersion in the vernacular cultures of the United States, France, and Germany. Her mother read Gertrude Stein's *Tender Buttons* at the dinner table—she and her mother were rebels together, in a sense, and her long political activism carried on lessons learned early.

Kay Boyle too writes always within an activist sensibility, though for her the passion of protest displaces the agency of persons onto the fragments of the scene. Like surrealism, there is a descriptive intensity made suddenly too close by this cutting, as if blown up by a projector upon a movie screen. But her materialization of political process in the bodies of people and things accompanies a refusal to adopt dogmatic narratives of personal and political conflict. In *Process,* a young woman must separate herself from her father and—more difficult—her mother, and these issues of becoming a self find their insistent parallel in radical politics and the possible forms of revolt against capitalism. Revolt occurs between the body and the law in a way that makes language itself strange, the acts of the body strangely superseding the agency of thought. Take, for example, this encounter between a factory girl and her idealistic and internationalist Rotarian boss:

> The skin on her throat was gold-pored from the brushed dust of jewelry. Tarney spoke kindly.
> "Good morning, Mary. What can I do for you?"
> Her hands clawed on her hips, her voice thrust from her sharp.
> "I'm going to lay off, Mr. Tarney."
> [. . .] Her eyes were sharp on him but dark with pain. And she was refusing the pain, refusing the submission to it, and turning her body sharp and angry upon them all. (64).

There is a refusal not only of Christian reassurance, but also of seeing the animate, personified being of the natural world as anything more than indifferent. Kerith, the heroine, "remembered lying on the black tongue of grass, with the sharp teeth of stars plucking at her . . . and her body a white flake of flesh on the dark indifferent tongue of the hill, indifferent." As a meditation on the available possibilities of revolt, the book itself turns its pain, its sharp and angry body, upon kindly and violent oppressions alike. In the sharpness of such will, the narrative turns in particular with and against a maternal lack, embodied in the Ibsenian mother, Nora, who "was never really afraid as long as the responsibility was not on herself" (74).

The relationships of style and the political in the writing of such modernist women as Kay Boyle requires attention to narrative, at the same time that narrative itself was being broken into juxtaposed fragments by modernist experiment.

An example of Boyle's experiments with style (included here) is a short story, "On the Run," first printed in the European journal, *transition*. The story condenses an episode in a longer narrative of an affair, and of love and death, that appeared as a novel, *Year Before Last*. The fleeing lovers—the man dying of tuberculosis—resemble Kay Boyle herself and the poet, Ernest Walsh during his last weeks in the south of France. Formal repetition and a surrealist distortion intensify the situation.

There are also four letters from Boyle's extraordinary and voluminous correspondence, carried out across decades and international boundaries. The first, to Lola Ridge, tells about an act of censorship by Harriet Monroe on "Harbor Song," a poem submitted to *Poetry*. Monroe objected to "buttocks," and suggested replacing it with "shoulders" or "thighs." The second and third, written to Kay Boyle's mother from France, give the reports of her experience with Ernest Walsh that will make the basis for "On the Run." Finally, her letter to William Carlos Williams shows the extraordinary mix of the banal and the poetic that made up the everyday life of a woman modernist/mother like Boyle, a hybridity of visits to the dentist and reviews of her writing.

Works Cited

Bogan, Louise. *Achievement in American Poetry*. Chicago: Henry Regnery, 1951.

———. *The Blue Estuaries: Poems, 1923–1968*. New York: Farrar, Straus and Giroux, 1968.

———. *A Poet's Alphabet: Reflections on the Literary Art and Vocation*. Ed. Robert Phelps and Ruth Limmer. New York: McGraw-Hill, 1970.

———. *What the Woman Lived; Selected Letters of Louise Bogan, 1920–1970*. Ed. Ruth Limmer. New York: Harcourt Brace Jovanovich, 1973.

Boyle, Kay. "On the Run." *transition* (June 1929): 83–85.

———. *Year Before Last*. 1932. Rpt. Carbondale: Southern Illinois University Press, 1969.

———. *Process*. Ed. Sandra Whipple Spanier. Urbana: University of Illinois Press, 2001.

———, and Robert McAlmon. *Being Geniuses Together, 1920–1930*. New York: Doubleday, 1968.

Clark, Suzanne. *Sentimental Modernism: Women Writers and the Revolution of the Word*. Bloomington: Indiana University Press, 1991.

Dell, Floyd. *Women as World Builders: Studies in Modern Feminism*. Chicago: Forbes and Company, 1913.

Douglas, Ann. *Terrible Honesty: Mongrel Manhattan in the 1920s*. New York: Farrar, Straus, and Giroux, 1995.

Epstein, Daniel Mark. *What Lips My Lips Have Kissed: The Loves and Love Poems of Edna St. Vincent Millay*. New York: Henry Holt, 2001.

Frank, Elizabeth. *Louise Bogan: A Portrait*. New York: A. A. Knopf, 1985.

Goldman, Emma. *Living My Life*. New York: Alfred A. Knopf, 1931.

Grimké, Angelina Weld. "'Rachel,' The Play of the Month: The Reason and Synopsis by the Author." *The Competitor* 1 (January 1920): 51–52.

Hull, Gloria. *Color, Sex, and Poetry: Three Women Writers of the Harlem Renaissance*. Bloomington: Indiana University Press, 1987.

Hulme, T. E. "Romanticism and Classicism." In *Speculations*. New York: Harcourt, Brace, 1924. 113–40.

Lewis, Wyndham, ed. *Blast* 1.

"Modern American Poetry: Louise Bogan (1897–1970)." http://www.english.uiuc.edu/maps/poets/a_f/bogan/bogan.htm.

Milford, Nancy. *Savage Beauty: The Life of Edna St. Vincent Millay*.

Millay, Edna St. Vincent. "The Fear." *The Outlook* 147.10 (November 9, 1927): 293–95, 310.

———. "Justice Denied in Massachusetts." In *The Buck in the Snow*. New York: Harper and Brothers, 1928, 32 (first printed in the *New York Times,* August 22, 1927).

———. Ransom, John Crowe. "The Poet as Woman." *Southern Review* 2 (Spring 1937): 783–806.

Spanier, Sandra Whipple. *Kay Boyle: Artist and Activist*. Carbondale: Southern Illinois University Press, 1986.

ANGELINA WELD GRIMKÉ

You

I love your throat, so fragrant, fair,
The little pulses beating there;
Your eye-brows' shy and questioning air;
      I love your shadowed hair.

I love your flame-touched ivory skin;
Your little fingers frail and thin;
Your dimple creeping out and in;
      I love your pointed chin.

I love the way you move, you rise;
Your fluttering gestures, just-caught cries;
I am not sane, I am not wise,
God! How I love your eyes!

Selected Works of Angelina Grimké. Ed. Carolivia Herron. New York: Oxford, 1991. 96.

ANGELINA WELD GRIMKÉ

Your Eyes

Through the downiness of the grey dawn,
    Through its grey gossamer softness—
        Your eyes;

Through the wonder-shine of the one star,
    Beautiful, solitary, in the East—
        Your eyes;

Through the chattering of birds, through their songs,
    Delicate, lovely, swaying in the tree-tops,
    Through the softness of little feathered breasts and throats
    Through the skitterings of little feet,
    Through the whirrings of silken wings—
        Your eyes;
Through the green quiet, the hot languor of noon,
    Sudden, through its cleft peace—
        Your eyes;

Through the slenderness of maiden trees kissed aflame by the mouth of
    the Spring,
    Through them standing against a slowly goldening
    Western sky,
    Through them standing very still, wondering,
    Wistful, waiting—
        Your eyes;
Through the beautiful Dusk, through the beautiful, blue-black hair of
    the Dusk,
Through her beautiful parted hair—
        Your eyes,
        Kissing mine.

Selected Works. 96–97.

ANGELINA WELD GRIMKÉ

Blue Cycle

There is the blue sky,
And there are the blue flowers,
And there are the blue eyes, wide
On the blue flowers.

    . . . .

Other blue flowers have been,
And other blue eyes,
But the blue skies are the same.

    . . . .

And these blue flowers shall pass,
And these blue eyes,
And the blue skies will remain.

Selected Works. 99.

ANGELINA WELD GRIMKÉ

Beware Lest He Awakes

A man as clean and white
In thoughts and deeds of right
As you, you faultless man
Advancing in the van
Of culture and of might;
A miser with your light
You would not even dream
Of letting go one beam,
To guide a groping man,
Who struggles as he can
To tread the path you tread,
Up steps of gushing red;
And if he but go wrong

You bellow loud and long,
In accents, strident, strong;—
Forgetting this, perchance,
That in your own advance,
The slips were even more,
And marked by pools of gore;—
You are a nobler man
Because you have no tan,
And he a very brute
Because of nature's soot;
But though he virtue lack,
And though his skin be black,
Beware lest he awakes!
When called he follows you
With arm as strong and true
As though you were his friend,
And fights unto the end,
That you may safely live;
Then surely you must give
The laurel branch and crown,
And gifts of just renown;
At least you must and can
Call him your brother man!

Ah, no! The cruel jeer
The ready curse and sneer
Are all that he may have—
A little less than slave,
He's spurned by your scorn,
And bound, both night and morn,
In chains of living death;
And if with longing breath
He breathes your air so free,
You hang him to a tree,
You hound of deviltry.
You burn him if he speak,
Until your freelands reek
From gory peak to peak,
With bloody, bloody sod,
And still there lives a God.

But mark! there may draw near
A day red-eyed and drear,
A day of endless fear;
Beware, lest he awakes!

The Pilot (May 10, 1902). Rpt. in *Selected Works.* 116–20.

ANGELINA WELD GRIMKÉ

The Black Finger

I have just seen a most beautiful thing
    Slim and still,
   Against a gold, gold sky,
   A straight black cypress,
    Sensitive,
    Exquisite,
    A black finger
    Pointing upwards.
Why, beautiful still finger, are you black?
And why are you pointing upwards?

Opportunity 1 (September 1923): 343. Rpt. in *The Survey Graphic. Harlem Number.* 6.6 (March 1925): 661.

ANGELINA WELD GRIMKÉ

"Rachel," The Play of the Month: The Reason and Synopsis by the Author

Since it has been understood that "Rachel" preaches race suicide, I would emphasize that that was not my intention. To the contrary, the appeal is not primarily to the colored people, but to the whites.

    Because of environment and certain inherent qualities each of us reacts correspondingly and logically to the various forces about us. For example, if these forces be of love we react with love, and if of hate with hate. Very naturally all of us will not react as strongly or in the same manner—that is impossible.

Now the colored people in this country form what may be called the "submerged tenth." From morning until night, week in week out, year in year out, until death ends all, they never know what it means to draw one clean, deep breath free from the contamination of the poison of that enveloping force which we call race prejudice. Of necessity they react to it. Some are embittered, made resentful, belligerent, even dangerous; some are made hopeless, indifferent, submissive, lacking in initiative; some again go to any extreme in a search for temporary pleasures to drown their memory, thought, etc.

Now the purpose was to show how a refined, sensitive, highly-strung girl, a dreamer and an idealist, the strongest instinct in whose nature is a love for children and a desire some day to be a mother herself—how this girl would react to this force.

The majority of women, everywhere, although they are beginning to awaken, form one of the most conservative elements of society. They are, therefore, opposed to changes. For this reason and for sex reasons the white women of this country are about the worst enemies with which the colored race has to contend. My belief was, then, that if a vulnerable point in their armor could be found, if their hearts could be active or passive enemies, they might become, at least, less inimical and possibly friendly.

Did they have a vulnerable point and, if so, what was it? I believed it to be motherhood. Certainly all the noblest, finest, most sacred things in their lives converge about this. If anything can make all women sisters underneath their skins it is motherhood. If, then, the white women of this country could see, feel, understand just what effect their prejudice and the prejudice of their fathers, brothers, husbands, sons were having on the souls of the colored mothers everywhere, and upon the mothers that are to be, a great power to affect public opinion would be set free and the battle would be half won.

This was the main purpose. There is a subsidiary one as well. Whenever you say "colored person" to a white man he immediately, either through an ignorance that is deliberate or stupid, conjures up in his mind the picture of what he calls "the darkey." In other words, he believes, or says he does, that all colored people are a grinning, white-toothed, shiftless, carefree set, given to chicken-stealing, watermelon-eating, always, under all circumstances, properly obsequious to a white skin and always amusing. Now, it is possible that this type is to be found among the colored people; but if the white man is honest and observant he will have to acknowledge that the same type can be duplicated in his own race. Human nature, after all, is the same. And if the white man only cared to find out he would know that, type for type, he could find the same in both races. Certainly colored people are living in homes that are clean, well-kept with many evidences of taste and refinement about them. They are many of them well educated, cultivated and cultured; they are well-mannered and, in many instance, more moral than the whites; they love beauty; they have ideals and ambitions, and they do not talk—this educated type—in the Negro dialect. All the joys and sorrows and emotions the white people feel they feel; their feelings are as sensitive; they can be hurt as easily; they are as proud. I drew my characters, then, from the best type of colored people.

Now as to the play itself. In the first act Rachel, loving, young, joyous and vital, caring more to be a mother than anything else in the world, comes suddenly and terribly face to face with what motherhood means to the colored woman in the South. Four years elapse between the first and second acts. Rachel has learned much. She is saddened, disillusioned and embittered. She knows now that organized society in the North has decreed that if a colored man or woman is to be an economic factor, then he or she must, with comparatively few exceptions, remain in the menial class. This has been taught her by her own experience, by the experience of her brother, Tom, and by the experience of John Strong, the man she loves. She has learned that she may not go to a theater for an evening's entertainment without having it spoiled for her since, because of her color she must sit as an outcast, a pariah in a segregated section. And yet in spite of all this youth in her dies hard and hope and the desire for motherhood. She loves children, if anything, more than ever. It is in this act that she feels certain, for the first time, that John Strong loves her. She is made very happy by this knowledge, but in the midst of her joy there comes a knocking at the door. And very terribly and swiftly again it is brought home to her what motherhood means, this time to the colored woman in the North. The lesson comes to her through a little black girl and her own little adopted son, Jimmy. Not content with maiming and marring the lives of colored men and women she learns this baneful thing, race prejudice, strikes at the souls of little colored children. In her anguish and despair at the knowledge she turns against God, believing that He has been mocking at her by implanting in her breast this desire for motherhood, and she swears by the most solemn oath of which she can think never to bring a child here to have its life blighted and ruined.

A week elapses between Acts II, and III. During the time Rachel has been very ill, not in body, but in mind and soul. She is up and about again, but is in a highly overwrought, nervous state. John Strong, whom she has not seen since she has been sick, comes to see her. She knows what his coming means and tries unsuccessfully to ward off his proposal. He pleads so well that, although she feels she is doing a wicked thing she finally yields. Just at the moment of her surrender, however, the sound of little Jimmy's heartbreaking weeping comes to her ears. She changes immediately and leaves him to go to Jimmy. Every night since Jimmy has undergone that searing experience in the previous act he has dreamed of it and awakens weeping. With that sound in her ears and soul she finds that she cannot break her oath. She returns and tells John Strong she cannot marry him. He is inclined, at first, not to take her seriously; but she shows him that this time her answer is final. Although her heart is breaking she sends him away. The play ends in blackness and with the inconsolable sounds of little Jimmy weeping.

The Competitor (January 1, 1920): 51–52. Rpt. in *Selected Works.* 413–18.

EDNA ST. VINCENT MILLAY

Sonnet XVIII

I, being born a woman and distressed
By all the needs and notions of my kind,
Am urged by your propinquity to find
Your person fair, and feel a certain zest
To bear your body's weight upon my breast:
So subtly is the fume of life designed,
To clarify the pulse and cloud the mind,
And leave me once again undone, possessed.
Think not for this, however, the poor treason
Of my stout blood against my staggering brain,
I shall remember you with love, or season
My scorn with pity,—let me make it plain:
I find this frenzy insufficient reason
For conversation when we meet again.

The Harp-Weaver and Other Poems. New York: Harper, 1923. 70.

EDNA ST. VINCENT MILLAY

The Pioneer

On the Unveiling of a Statue to Lucretia Mott,
Susan B. Anthony, and Elizabeth Cady Stanton.
Washington, November eighteenth, 1923.

Upon this marble bust that is not I
Lay the round, formal wreath that is not fame;
But in the forum of my silenced cry
Root ye the living tree whose sap is flame.
I, that was proud and valiant, am no more;—
Save as a dream that wanders wide and late,
Save as a wind that rattles the stout door,
Troubling the ashes in the sheltered grate.
The stone will perish; I shall be twice dust.
Only my standard on a taken hill
Can cheat the mildew and the red-brown rust
And make immortal my adventurous will.
      Even now the silk is tugging at the staff:
      Take up the song; forget the epitaph.

First delivered 1923, and printed in *Equal Rights*. Later published as "Sonnet LXVII, for Inez Milholland," in *Collected Sonnets*. Rpt. in *The Buck in the Snow*. New York: Harper and Brothers, 1928. 66.

LOUISE BOGAN

Summer Wish

> *That cry's from the first cuckoo of the year.*
> *I wished before it ceased.*

FIRST VOICE
We call up the green to hide us
This hardened month, by no means the beginning
Of the natural year, but of the shortened span
Of leaves upon the earth. We call upon
The weed as well as the flower: groundsel, stellaria.
It is the month to make the summer wish;
It is time to ask
The wish from summer as always: *It will be,*
It will be.
            That tool we have used.
So that its haft is smooth; it knows the hand.
Again we lift the wish to its expert uses,
Tired of the bird that calls one long note downward,
And the forest in cast-iron. No longer, no longer,
The season of the lying equinox
Wherein false cock-crow sounds!

SECOND VOICE
In March the shadow
Already falls with a look of summer, fuller
Upon the snow, because the sun at last
Is almost centered. Later, the sprung moss
Is the tree's shadow; under the black spruces
It lies where lately snow lay, bred green from the cold
Cast down from melting branches.

FIRST VOICE
A wish like a hundred others.
You cannot, as once, yearn forward. The blood now never
Stirs hot to memory, or to the fantasy

Of love, with which, both early and late, one lies
As with a lover.
Now do you suddenly envy
Poor praise you told long since to keep its tongue,
Or pride's acquired accent,—pomposity, arrogance,
That trip in their latinity? With these at heart
You could make a wish, crammed with the nobility
Of error. It would be no use. You cannot
Take yourself in.

SECOND VOICE
Count over what these days have: lilies
Returned in little to an earth unready,
To the sun not accountable;
The hillside mazed and leafless, but through the ground
The leaf from the bulb, the unencouraged green
Heaving the metal earth, presage of thousand
Shapes of young leaves—lanceolate, trefoil,
Peach, willow, plum, the lilac like a heart.

FIRST VOICE
Memory long since put by,—to what end the dream
That drags back lived-out life with the wrong words,
The substitute meaning?
Those that you once knew there play out false time,
Elaborate yesterday's words, that they were deaf to,
Being dead ten years.—Call back in anguish
The anger in childhood that defiled the house
In walls and timber with its violence?
Now must you listen again
To your own tears, shed as a child, hold the bruise
With your hand, and weep, fallen against the wall,
And beg, *Don't, don't,* while the pitiful rage goes on
That cannot stem itself?
Or, having come into woman's full estate,
Enter the rich field, walk between the bitter
Bowed grain, being compelled to serve,
To heed unchecked in the heart the reckless fury
That tears fresh day from day, destroys its traces,—
Now bear the blow too young?

SECOND VOICE
In early April
At six o'clock the sun has not set; on the walls
It shines with scant light, pale, dilute, misplaced,
Light there's no use for. At overcast noon
The sun comes out in a flash, and is taken
Slowly back to the cloud.

FIRST VOICE
Not memory, and not the renewed conjecture
Of passion that opens the breast, the unguarded look
Flaying clean the raped defence of the body,
Breast, bowels, throat, now pulled to the use of the eyes
That see and are taken. The body that works and sleeps,
Made vulnerable, night and day, to delight that changes
Upon the lips that taste it, to the lash of jealousy
Struck on the face, so the betraying bed
Is gashed clear, cold on the mind, together with
Every embrace that agony dreads but sees
Open as the love of dogs.

SECOND VOICE
The cloud shadow flies up the bank, but does not
Blow off like smoke. It stops at the bank's edge.
In the field by trees two shadows come together.
The trees and the cloud throw down their shadow upon
The man who walks there. Dark flows up from his feet
To his shoulders and throat, then has his face in its mask,
Then lifts.

FIRST VOICE
Will you turn to yourself, proud breast,
Sink to yourself, to an ingrained, pitiless
Rejection of voice and touch not your own, press sight
Into a myth no eye can take the gist of;
Clot up the bone of phrase with the black conflict
That claws it back from sense?
        Go into the breast . . .

You have traced that lie, before this, out to its end,
Heard bright wit headstrong in the beautiful voice
Changed to a word mumbled across the shoulder
To one not there; the gentle self split up
Into a yelling fiend and a soft child.
You have seen the ingrown look
Come at last upon a vision too strong
Ever to turn away.

The breast's six madnesses repeat their dumb-show.

SECOND VOICE
In the bright twilight children call out in the fields.
The evening takes their cry. How late it is!
Around old weeds worn thin and bleached to their pith
The field has leaped to stalk and strawberry blossom.
The orchard by the road
Has the pear-tree full at once of flowers and leaves,
The cherry with flowers only.

FIRST VOICE
The mind for refuge, the grain of reason, the will,
Pulled by a wind it thinks to point and name?
Malicious symbol, key for rusty wards,
The crafty knight in the game, with its mixed move,
Prey to an end not evident to craft. . . .

SECOND VOICE
Fields are ploughed inward
From edge to center; furrows squaring off
Make dark lines far out in irregular fields,
On hills that are builded like great clouds that over them
Rise, to depart.
Furrow within furrow, square within a square,
Draw to the center where the team turns last.
Horses in half-ploughed fields
Make earth they walk upon a changing color.

FIRST VOICE
The year's begun; the share's again in the earth.

Speak out the wish like music, that has within it
The horn, the string, the drum pitched deep as grief.
Speak it like laughter, outward. O brave, O generous
Laughter that pours from the well of the body and draws
The bane that cheats the heart: aconite, nightshade,
Hellebore, hyssop, rue,—symbols and poisons
We drink, in fervor, thinking to gain thereby
Some difference, some distinction.
Speak it, as that man said, *as though the earth spoke,*
By the body of rock, shafts of heaved strata, separate,
Together.
       Though it be but for sleep at night,
Speak out the wish.
The vine we pitied is in leaf; the wild
Honeysuckle blows by the granite.

SECOND VOICE
See now
Open above the field, stilled in wing-stiffened flight,
The stretched hawk fly.

Dark Summer. New York: Charles Scribner's Sons, 1929. 65–72.

LOUISE BOGAN

The Heart and the Lyre

The record of the verse written by women in the United States is remarkably full, for a variety of reasons. In the first place, the country became an independent republic, well equipped with printing presses and paper, during the period when American women began to write in earnest. Then, a new and eager periodical and newspaper audience, with the sort of pioneering background which holds women in high esteem, awaited bits of feminine sentiment and moralizing dressed up in meter and rhyme. Finally, the critical standard of the country remained for a long time rather lax and easygoing. A great mass of verse, good, bad, and indifferent, therefore managed to get published. Through this prolific feminine production we can trace, with much accuracy, every slight shift in American literary fashion, as well as the larger changes of an emotional and moral kind. An examination of the rise and development of female poetic talent over a period of more than one hundred and fifty years in a society which, on the whole, encouraged that talent to function freely and in the open, brings to light various truths concerning the worth and scope of women's poetic gifts.

Before we survey the interesting, colorful, and frequently comic array of American women "poetesses" from Lydia Huntley Sigourney (1791–1865) through the youngest feminine contemporaries, let us look at some of the assumptions and prejudices that have long lodged in people's minds on the subject of women as poets. One rather hoary idea is that women put emotion before form and are likely to be indifferent technicians. Do they not usually, as well, imitate closely the poetic productions of men? A third dark suspicion concerning women's poetic powers troubled even the highly intelligent and ardently feminist mind of Virginia Woolf. Mrs. Woolf, in her delightful series of lectures published in 1929 under the title *A Room of One's Own,* is continually bothered by the thought that in spite of material and moral emancipations women may never write a work of wide and compelling force comparable, for example, to Shakespeare's plays. To exorcise this spectral doubt, Mrs. Woolf canvasses fully the history of woman's difficulties in the role of artist.

Women have always been busy and poor, Mrs. Woolf's argument runs; busy, because they are physically responsible for the production and early care of specimens of the human race; and poor because it seems that men's laws are often framed to keep them in that condition. Lack of education, the tyranny of families, the ridicule of society, as well as lack of independent means, have been factors which, perhaps, kept women from writing epic poems or long poetic plays. Mrs. Woolf gives every credit to the anonymous women who had a hand in composing folk tales, folk songs, adages, proverbs, and nursery rhymes (for it is, after all, Mother Goose, and *Ma Mère l'Oie*). And she is happy to note that, when new freedoms arrived in Europe and England at the end of the eighteenth century, women novelists, at least, appeared in numbers and with brilliance. But what of Shakespeare's supposititious sister— ignorant, penniless, and fearful of masculine jeers, had she tried to carve out a career for herself in the sixteenth century? It is at this point in her argument that Mrs. Woolf begins to stumble against the doubt that no woman is ever going to write a great poetic tragedy in five acts. Perhaps after a hundred years or so this goal will be realized, if the creative woman is given five hundred pounds per annum and, behind a door with a lock on it, a room of her own.

It was a little old-fashioned even in 1929 for Mrs. Woolf to choose a five-act poetic play as the final test of a woman poet's powers. Her vision was somewhat clouded by an Anglo-Saxon literary point of view. Why should women, past, present, or future, remain fixed in the determination to out-Shakespeare Shakespeare? Can it be that there is no basic reason for women to excel in the art of poetry by producing the same sort of poetic structures as men? Men, as a matter of fact, stayed with the five-act poetic tragedy far too long. Perhaps women have more sense than to linger over an obsessing form of this kind.

We turn to the full and complete annals of American women poets hoping that we may discover facts that will lead to a new estimate of the poetic gift in women, as well as hints about its present and future direction. The first women versifiers who appear on the American scene were, it must be confessed, unendowed, grim, pious, and lachrymose. Mrs. Sigourney was provincial and naive enough to glory in two titles: the "American Hemans" and the "Sweet Singer of Hartford." She reigned, however, over a long period as the head of American female letters—from shortly after Washington's second term as president until just after the death of Lincoln, to be exact. She was fluent, industrious, and rather pushing; but she managed to put feminine verse-writing on a paying basis, and give it prestige; even Poe did not quite dare to handle her work too roughly. She gave simple men and women along the eastern seaboard and in the backwoods of the West something to be proud of; it is pleasant for a young nation to have a vocal tutelary goddess.

During Mrs. Sigourney's lifetime the choir of female singers enlarged. Soon a series of anthologies began to appear, exclusively devoted to "songstresses." *The Ladies' Wreath* (1837), edited by Mrs. Sarah Josepha Hale, who also edited *Godey's Lady's Book,* was the first of these. Others followed; and by 1849 Rufus Griswold was able to make good profits with his collection entitled *The Female Poets of America*. This collection went through several editions and, after Griswold's death, turned up in the seventies with a new editor. We are now in a new world. The more depressing ante-bellum aspects of female piety and melancholy have worn off, and we are presented with the spectacle of women becoming ever more ardent and airy. The ardors of Poe's women friends, Fanny Osgood and Mrs. Whitman, are now surpassed by their successors. When we come to Edmund Clarence Stedman's *An American Anthology* (1900), an often unbroken phalanx of women with three (and sometimes four) invincibly Yankee names advances down the table of contents, and their work is now startlingly filled with evidence of culture, with whimsicality, self-preening, and affectation.

But although women's literary manners and, it would seem, their affections became ever more wayward and free, their grasp upon basic conventions remained firm. Even the Wisconsin farm girl, Ella Wheeler, who spiced her stanzas with hints of sin in *Poems of Passion* (1883) soon quiets down into marriage and respectability with a Mr. Wilcox. The list of these late-nineteenth-century women in Stedman, with their multiple names printed in chaste Gothic type, tends to become a blur. But if we search carefully for even the smallest sincerity and talent, personalities begin to emerge. Alice and Phoebe Cary; Celia Thaxter; the mill girl, Lucy Larcom, protégée of Whittier; Julia Ward Howe; Emma Lazarus, who was Jewish, and Louise Imogen Guiney, who was an "Irish Catholic"; Lizette Woodworth Reese of Baltimore and Harriet Monroe of Chicago; and, farther back, crowded in with Mrs. Spofford, Mrs. Moulton, Thomas Bailey Aldrich, Joaquin Miller, and Edward Rowland Sill, we come upon an unpretentious name, easily overlooked, of a woman born in 1830 and dead in 1886: Emily Dickinson. Emily Dickinson represents the final flowering of a long Puritan tradition. Her genius has a hard, bitter, but real kind of civilization behind it; women poets share with men the need for some sort of civilized ground from which to draw sustenance. But it is apparently more difficult for women to throw off the more superficial fashions of any society in which they find themselves. The earlier history of women poets in America should stand as a warning to modern young women of talent. The special virtues of women are clear, in the same record. Women are forced to become adult. They must soon abandon sustained play, in art or life. They are not good at abstractions and their sense of structure is not large; but they often have the direct courage to be themselves. They are practical, intense, and (usually) both generous and magnanimous. They often have a true contemplative gift; and they are natural singers. They are capable of originality and breadth of emotional and intellectual reference as soon as their background opens to any breadth and variety. They are often forced to waste their powers in an inadequate milieu, in social improvisation; to tack back and forth between revolt and conservatism. Far from imitating men to an untoward degree, they often experiment boldly with form and language. Early in the twentieth century, Gertrude Stein, working indefatigably and alone, begins to examine words with the detached interest of the scientist and arrange them in abstract patterns. A little later H. D. gives back to Greek themes some of the pure severity of Greek poetry in the original. Marianne Moore applies a naturalist's eye to objects of art and of nature, describing "with an extraordinary magnificence of phraseology" unlooked-for combinations and harmonies between matter and the spirit. These women have had their male, as well as their female, followers.

Young women writing poetry at present are likely to consider the figure of the woman poet as romantic rebel rather ridiculous and outmoded. The youngest generation of women poets is, in fact, moving toward an imitation of certain masculine "trends" in contemporary poetry. They are imitating, moreover, the work of male verbalizers and poetic logicians, rather than the work of men who have carried through, out of a profound urgency, major poetic investigations; there are few feminine disciples of either Eliot or Auden, in these poets' later phases. Even the greatly gifted Elizabeth Bishop, whose first book recently appeared, places emphasis more upon anecdote than upon ardor. The fear of some regression into typical romantic attitudes is, at present, operating upon feminine talent; and this is not a wholly healthy impulse, for it negates too strongly a living and valuable side of woman's character. In women, more than in men, the intensity of their emotions is the key to the treasures of their spirit. The cluster of women lyric poets that appeared on the American scene just before and after 1918 restored genuine and frank feeling to a literary situation which had become genteel, artificial, and dry. Sara Teasdale's later verse; the best of Edna Millay's early rebellious songs and meditations; Elinor Wylie's ability to fuse thought and passion into the most admirable and complex forms; the sensitive, intellectual poetry of Leonie Adams—all these poetic productions helped to resolve hampering attitudes of the period.

Selected Criticism. New York: Noonday, 1955. 335–42.

KAY BOYLE

From Letters

To: Lola Ridge
August 11, 1924
La Chartreuse,
10, rue des Caraques
Harfleur, (S.I.), France

My perfect Lola:
[. . .] I believe you didn't know that Harriet Monroe accepted the Harbor Song—with reservations. I needed the money and agreed to her censorship. She couldn't "risk" the section entitled "Whore Street" and she didn't "dare" retain the word "buttocks" in the section "For the Sea." Also she didn't want the first verse at all, nor "Monastery." She suggested "shoulders" in the place

of buttocks, and I wrote her that from the moral standpoint I was wholly unable to judge, but from an aesthetic, "shoulders" was completely wrong. She then wrote that she would use "thighs" I think, and I haven't taken the trouble to answer her letter. I presume it is going through as "thighs." Oh, "Labor Horses" also was too out-spoken.[1]

I want more than anything, my dear, to see some new things of yours. For God's sake send me something. [. . .] I want your reading of my book. I feel this way about it. That compared to most other books, it is good—and that individual chapters are excellent—but compared with what there was within me seeking outlet, it is not a success. My people are not real—and in my mind they were not symbols of conflicting forces, but individuals.

You must come, somehow, so we can go on a little while together again, putting our teeth in the fat red lights that loll upon the Seine.

Are you stronger, Lola? I want news of you so. What a miracle if you could come!

> Kay

Note

1. [This and the following letters draw on notes provided by Sandra Spanier, editor of the forthcoming anthology of Kay Boyle's letters]. Kay Boyle's poem "Summer," published in the first volume of *This Quarter* (1925), includes sections from her original "Harbor Song" entitled "Labor Horses," "Monastery," and "Whore Street" that Harriet Monroe would not print in *Poetry*.

To: Katherine Evans Boyle
July 15, 1926
Hotel Grac
Annot, B.A., France

dearest mama:

It's been so very long since I have written because life has been a chaos, and now that there is a breathing space I want to write you about things. [. . .] I wish you were here with us in this very Poconoish place, where the stream flows past the hotel and the nightingales keep us awake on moonlight nights. [. . .]

Michael, as a result of all the parties and intensity, had a hemmorhage in the middle of the night. It was more severe than the Mougins one, but responded to his injection. Of course we couldn't breathe a word to anyone of the real trouble as we had been put out of a hotel a month ago because the

people suspected he had tuberculosis. So Richard had his hemmorhage prescriptions filled, pretending they were for himself, and gave everyone a good
story about stomach trouble keeping M. in bed for a day or two. And then the
next night he had another hemmorhage which began at eleven at night and
I couldn't stop the bleeding until three in the morning. He was too weak to
give himself the injections, so I prayed the good god for strength and did them
myself, and good as a doctor Michael told me, and was busy all night steril-
izing instruments, keeping ice on his chest and hoping to God the people in
the next rooms weren't hearing him coughing up the tumbler's full of blood.
[. . .]

    Kay

TLS. Special Collections, Morris Library, Southern Illinois University.

Note

    The experience forms the basis of Kay Boyle's short story "On the Run," published in
the June 1929 issue of *transition* and is reworked into a chapter of her novel based on
her life with Ernest Walsh, *Year Before Last,* published in 1932.

To: Katherine Evans Boyle
October something [1926]

dearest Mama—

    I want to write you now when things are so intense with me because I want
you to share with me from the beginning whatever's coming. M. has been
bleeding for a week, two hemorrhages a day, and now his heart is too bad to
give another vein injection.[1] Ethel Moorhead came up a week ago and more
or less as a result of discussions over the next number, personal arguments,
etc., this began.[2] She was impossible to me until the night of the first hemor-
rhage when he filled a chamber-pot with blood in five minutes. She went to
pieces and I had to get his injection in his arm, ice and the doctor. When it
was stopped she said, "You're a wonderful woman. I've always excused my
inability by my love and thought the others could do it because they didn't
care about him." The next moment she told us she had a villa and a maid at
Monte Carlo for the winter—up on the hill—and would we come down to her,
and if we didn't find it satisfactory could look for a place of our own. M. was
so happy and she held our hands and said she would go down a few days in
advance to prepare the house, and then send up the car and chauffeur for M.
and me.

But it is yet to be seen whether or not she has relented too late [. . .] M. cannot bear me to be out of his sight for a moment. I have not been out of my clothes for a week. [. . .] Anyway, I'm getting at last a chance to use my priceless voice. M. is quieted if I sing lullabies, Little grey home in the vale, etc. I'll write soon, my darling mother. I loved your long letter.

    Your own

       Kay

ALS. Special Collections, Morris Library, Southern Illinois University.

Notes

  1. Michael, as Ernest Walsh preferred to be known to those close to him.

  2. The third number of *This Quarter*, which was published in the spring of 1927 after Walsh's death.

To: William Carlos Williams
Oct. 16, 1932.
Villa Coustille
Col-de-Villefranche
Nice, A.M., France.

Bill, how in the name of God could you have thought that writing me as you did about my book or any book in the world could huff me or freeze me, or God knows what. [. . .][1] In the first place, my Bobby had mastoid, and an operation. Then we went to Italy. Then I had a tooth pulled and the dentist broke it and fractured the jaw. [. . .] You have brought all this on yourself. Then Bobby's other ear threatened with mastoid. But nursing her carefully and puncturing the eardrum, drained it away. But she must have her adenoids out.

    [. . .] Your fine collection of poems came, and I had long good hours of reading. [. . .] I had a hard time selecting, but finally just chose "The Ball Game," "Down Town," "The Winds," and "Death". [. . .] Let me know if you'd like to see translations first, as there is still plenty of time. I'm hard at work, of course, and getting another novel along which, because I myself play no part in it, will be bigger and better and not so heavily charged. But please always write me as you feel forever and tell me exactly, for that's the only thing. I haven't any illusions about the value of what I'm trying to do—one just writes away and either it comes out well or doesn't, but when I see the kind of praise I get for this last book (old ladies and sentimental elderly virgins love it) I realize that it has not come out well. So you're on the right side, and give me a standard.

I wish I knew more of what you are writing on. Even if everyone else stops, you must go on. Those pieces of early Americans in your book are a feast whenever I open the American Grain—I'd like volumes of them, with your particular comment and spirit and eye for them.[2] Your vein is so rich and deep, when most others began and continue to run thin.

Now there are kids to bathe and—a terrible racket. Six new puppies arrived, as sweet as anything you ever saw. I wish you and your family would come over again someday—Joyce is here now, in very good spirits. Write me some time, when you can. Should I send the Mss. of the poems back to you?

Yours,

Kay

TLS. Beinecke Library, Yale University.

Notes

1. Kay Boyle's novel based on her life with Ernest Walsh, *Year Before Last,* had just been published as part of the fall 1932 list of Harrison Smith and Robert Haas.

2. William Carlos Williams's *In the American Grain* (1925), a collection of essays on "American" heroes from Red Eric of Greenland to Montezuma to Abraham Lincoln, which caused Williams to be cast as an American "primitive" in contrast to the rootless cosmopolitanism of high modernism.

KAY BOYLE

On the Run

The little alps were baked dry and the grass on them waved in June like a slow fire along the rails. These little mountains ran in a sharp sea in the windows and the smoke from the engine twisted in strong white ropes through the car. He opened his mouth to say "St. André-les-Alpes" and when he had opened it the smoke came in and filled it with bitterness. As the train stopped a soft pink tide of pigs rose out of the station-yard and ran in under the wheels of the wagon. The crest of little alps was burning across the roofs of the town, with the dry crumbling finger of the church lifted and the sky gaping white and hot upon decay.

He lay down on the bed in the hotel and when the bonne came to the door he sat up quickly and lit a cigaret. He talked to her smiling, moving his hands, with his eyes insisting that she understand him. He wanted pigs' feet grilled in batter and breadcrumbs. He insisted with his hands moving to convince her of the natural beauty of his hunger. A sick man would not want pigs' feet grilled in batter and breadcrumbs. She answered him shaking her head that they were not this time of year as if they sprang up like seeds in the garden. She nodded sternly, seeing that he was dying. "Later," she said, "later . . ."

Get her out of here he said I am going to cough. Christ is this where the death will get me take the cigaret and when I cough walk around the room and sing or something so they won't hear me

The bonne came back to them saying that the washer-woman had so much work to do that she couldn't take in their laundry this summer. "Here's your laundry back," said the bonne, "because the washerwoman has so much work." "What?" said he. "What?" The alps were closed like dry fists and the grass burned up to the window. "My God," he said, "we'll clear out of here. Saint André-les-Alpes what a hole. I'll come back and haunt you. I'll eat your heart out Saint-André I'll curse and rot you."

If there were a nice fine cold now to tighten up whatever it is shaking around in me hop around the room now and sing to keep them from hearing me a tight cold now pulling me together to say to them

The bonne came back to say that the shoemaker had so much work to do now that he couldn't touch their shoes for them. The mountain-trains were screaming like cats at the window. We're awfully near the railway anyway he said. If I laugh too much at he said my girl you don't understand the Irish until the sun kills me I'll be here none of your washwomen or your shoemakers if there were a fine tight cold to pull me together now he said I'd get out of here faster than the pigs hitting tire dust get her out of the room he said I'm going to cough

The bonne came back to say that the proprietor the woman luxuriously in mourning for her entire family bereaved in the fullness of middle-age would speak with Madame. Bereaved in the full sallow of her cheeks bereaved and the tombstones rising politely polished with discreet sorrow bereaved and remembered with bubbles of jet frosted on her bosoms and mourned under waves of hemmed watered crepe. I have mourned people for years and years this is the way it is done.

She stood in the stairpit with her eyes starting out of her you'll have your bread and your butter and your coffee Madame when you've talked to me. "Come in here," she said. "Finish to enter."

The sweet sorrow of the crucifix faced them the rosary hanging like false-teeth on the bed-stead the sacred smile the Christ bled with artistry in the well-rounded arms of the Virgin. "Madame," she said without any hesitation, "your husband cannot die here," she said, "we are not prepared for death."

He sat up on the bed when he heard her coming back down the hall and he said what do you leave me for you've been gone a hundred years is she being rude to you? I called her a bitch he said keep your temper please keep it it worries me when you slam the door

"Saint-André," he said into the pillow, "I'm a sick man. I'm afraid. This time I'm afraid to go on."

You you afraid listen here packing the bags again the hairy-legged brushes pointed ampoules as beautiful as earrings bottles of ergotine and striped pajamas we're going on somewhere else and have pigs' feet grilled and champagne and peaches with flames running on them this hole dries the guts in you do you remember Menton last February and everythime [*sic*] you read Umbra the cabinay flushed may the Gods speak softly of us in days hereafter

and the very small sausages for breakfast at the Ruhl
Saint-André-les-Alpes you're a perfectly ordinary piss-pot
With a blue eye painted in the bottom of it
Fit only to be put in a cheap room under the bed
With education refinement and all the delicate belly-aches
Here's to bigger and better pigs' feet
Keep on keep on keep on he said maybe I'm going to bleed.

transition (June 1929): 83–85. Rpt. in *Wedding Day and Other Stories*. New York: Jonathan Cape and Harrison Smith, 1930. 103–7.

5

Debating Feminism, Modernism, and Socialism: Beatrice Hastings's Voices in *The New Age*

INTRODUCED AND SELECTED BY ANN ARDIS

ALTHOUGH *THE NEW AGE* under A. R. Orage's editorship (1907–22) has typically been remembered to history as a platform for modernist literature and art, recent scholarship is taking a much more careful account of this British journal's positioning in a post-Arnoldian public sphere that was, even by 1907, ever more complexly fractured, fragmented, and subdivided into counter- and sub-public special-interest communities.[1] Funded substantially by George Bernard Shaw when Orage and Holbrook Jackson first took it over in 1907, *The New Age* quickly outgrew its Fabian Art League support and went on to promote, for a time, its unique commitments to Guild Socialism, which included both viewing the arts as a central component of any truly revolutionary socialist agenda for social change and supporting an economic reorganization of society designed to "free workers from the unrelieved tedium of mass production and restore a sense of craftsmanship which would make labour satisfying and its products beautiful" (Martin 206).[2] In other words, it was as a socialist journal, not as a classic modernist "little magazine," that *The New Age* juxtaposed coverage of contemporary literature and the visual arts with commentary on and cross-references to political debates being carried out in dailies, weeklies, and monthly periodicals across the entire spectrum of the British newspaper industry.[3] As a socialist journal with designs on broad circulation, not as a literary magazine beamed at a very exclusive coterie of readers, it published a multiplicity of works by the likes of T. E. Hulme, Ezra Pound, E. T. Marinetti, and Wyndham Lewis. And it published these now well-known (but at the time still emergent) modernists side by side with parodies, critiques, and alternately hilarious and acrimonious anti-modernist manifestoes.[4]

This chapter introduces the role Beatrice Hastings, Orage's lover and the self-claimed shadow coeditor of *The New Age* (1907–14), played in orchestrating the richly dialogic exchanges that distinguish *The New Age* from other turn-of-the-twentieth-century British periodicals. I give full credit to Orage himself for managing the journal's external conversations with other periodicals through review articles, the editor's column, and "Current Cant." I would also note that Hastings is by no means the only contributor to have written anonymously, pseudonymously, *and* under her own signature in *The New Age*.[5] Nor, for that matter, is *The New Age* the only early twentieth century journal to allow its contributors and editors to publish under multiple signatures.[6] (As Jayne Marek will discuss in a later chapter, Marianne Moore contributed both signed reviews and anonymous "comments" for *The Dial* during her editorship.) What is unusual, however, is the sheer range and variety of signatures Hastings employed. By surveying here the play of Hastings's multiple authorial voices in her writings for *The New Age*, I hope not only to pique further interest in this fascinating writer, but also to show how her very careful and deliberate manipulation of multiple pseudonyms contributed to the development of a feminist counterpublic sphere in early twentieth-century Britain.

In her 1936 memoir, Hastings acknowledges that she used thirteen different pseudonyms in writing for *The New Age:* Beatrice Tina, Robert á Field, T. K. L., Alice Morning, D. Triformis, Edward Stafford, S. Robert West, V. M., G. Whiz, J. Wilson, T. W., A. M. A., and Cynicus (*Old "New Age"* 43). In addition to extensive anonymous contributions, she also claims to have written over sixty articles for "Present Day Criticism" as "R. H. C.," a pseudonym typically attributed exclusively to Orage (*Old "New Age"* 17; Martin 236), and there is a very good possibility that "Richmond Haigh" is yet another of her pseudonyms.[7] The pseudonyms mentioned above, however, are her mainstays, and she wielded them carefully, respecting the distinctiveness of each persona, even staging debates among them as she pursues *The New Age*'s commitment to providing "some neutral ground where intelligences may meet on equal terms" in a public debate about politics, literature, and the arts.[8]

Thanks in large part to Hastings, *The New Age*'s coverage of the campaign for women's suffrage was much more extensive than that of other British socialist periodicals. *The New Age* was willing to provide a platform for staunch anti-feminist socialists such as E. Belfort Bax. Yet it also gave pro-feminist, pro-suffrage, and pro-suffragist writers a multitude of opportunities to challenge the gender conservatism so often imbedded in turn-of-the-century socialist critiques of the British class system. Moreover, unlike *The Clarion*, the socialist journal to which Rebecca West contributed so powerfully as a very young journalist, *The New Age* did not confine such analysis to a "Women's Column" but instead featured discussion of these issues in letters to the editor, feature articles, and columns by regular contributors. The other unique aspect of *The New Age*'s coverage of the women's suffrage campaign is its attention to the points of conflict among contemporary feminisms, and here Hastings plays a crucial role as she both debates other feminists and stages debates between and among her various personae.

Like Dora Marsden, the editor of first *The Freewoman* and then *The New Freewoman*, Hastings was fiercely critical of Emmeline and Christabel Pankhurst, the leaders of the Women's Social and Political Union (WSPU) from 1904 to 1914, because she believed the Pankhursts' efforts were too narrowly focused on the vote. Like Rebecca West, she also found much to criticize in Christabel Pankhurst's puritanical defense of (male) chastity. As Barbara Green has noted, after Christabel and Emmeline Pankhurst officially detached themselves from the Independent Labour Party in 1907 and sought to disassociate the women's suffrage campaign from the image of the working woman in the streets, suffrage supporters such as Hannah Mitchell, Teresa Billington-Greig, and Emily Wilding Davison maintained an interest in broad socialist reform, resisting the Pankhursts' efforts to focus exclusively on the vote and to recast the suffrage campaign as the exclusive purview of middle- and upper-class "womenly women" (*Spectacular Confessions* 35–37). Hastings pitches herself full force into these controversies, and the essays reprinted here illustrate how she "talks back" to other feminists and advocates for women's suffrage, fostering dialogue in a feminist counter-public sphere while at the same time bringing the imbrication of class and gender issues to the attention of socialists who might otherwise envision social change/revolution exclusively in class-based terms.[9]

The essays featured here also showcase her manipulation of multiple pseudonyms in this process. The exchanges between her two signature personae on feminism, "Beatrice Tina" and "D. Triformis," are exemplary. As "Beatrice Tina," Hastings wrote articles such as "Suffragettes in the Making" (December 1908) and "On Guard" (December 1908) endorsing suffrage militancy—though not as a means of achieving the vote but rather as a means of achieving a more accurate sense of the oppressiveness of the British social system. Focusing on the degradations suffered by imprisoned suffragettes rather than the grand public spectacles of the suffrage campaign, "Beatrice Tina" admires the sense of solidarity the suffragettes gain with other political prisoners also experiencing harsh treatment in Holloway: "They have seen what is done to the imbecile criminal. They have felt how the horrid prison system dehumanizes. [. . .]

They recognize victims, whom a hundred Governments of men have failed to redeem, hunted back to a death in life. [. . .] they know the helplessness which dooms again the unfriended, penniless wretches." In an essay such as "On Guard," she demands recognition of the sexual violence (specifically rape) that is a component of the violent backlash against suffragette militancy, urging women to breach decorum in speaking out about such violations.

By contrast, "D. Triformis," who first appears in January 1910, is highly critical of the suffragettes. Through May 1910, Hastings used this pseudonym to develop an anti-militancy, pro-suffrage stance. There are at least three possible interpretations of Hastings's deployment of this new persona. Either she had changed her mind about the effectiveness of suffragette militancy, and therefore changed her alias; or she was simply exploring another stance to invite readers' reactions; or she had changed her mind about militancy *and* developed a new alias with which to explore this new positionality. Lacking the clarifications that archival materials could supply, one can simply note that "D. Triformis" is far more pointedly critical than "Beatrice Tina" of the Pankhursts. "The Failure of Militancy" (January 1910) expresses her doubts about their ability to lead the WSPU, noting that the Pankhursts' earlier refusal to support any feminist issue besides the vote renders their recent increase in violence detrimental to the cause, and arguing that, because violence does not come naturally to women, it will eventually cause the downfall of their movement. Writing again as "D. Triformis" in "Feminism and the Franchise" (March 1910), Hastings is still more harshly critical of the Pankhursts and the WSPU for initially defining their movement as solely pro-suffrage rather than pro-feminism, then belatedly siding with feminists. Her contributions to feminist debate in *The New Age* take a self-referential twist in this essay, as she rebukes the WSPU for "officially boycott[ing] and privately denounc[ing]" Beatrice Tina's critiques of marriage, which "D. Triformis" treats as an instance of their erroneously exclusive focus on the vote. The feminist movement must also, "D. Triformis" insists, invoking "Beatrice Tina's" work, include a "sex revolt": "We object to the illusory hopes held out to the married woman that when such women as pay taxes shall have the vote the conditions of marriage will perceptibly change for the better. [. . .] We object to the representations made to factory women to the effect that the feminine vote will give them wages equal to men's wages."[10]

Hastings's contributions to contemporary debate about women's suffrage and feminism are only one aspect of her richly diverse play of voices/authorial personae in *The New Age*, though. Writing as both "T. K. L." and "Alice Morning," she responds brilliantly, and often quite hilariously, to Ezra Pound's many contributions to *The New Age*. Included here is "The Way Back to America," the first of a series of exchanges that Hastings staged as "T. K. L." with Ezra Pound in the fall of 1913, while *The New Age* was publishing a series of his essays lauding contemporary French poetry. "T. K. L." counters with a wickedly funny critique of each tenet of his classically modernist poetics, and this entire exchange culminates with Orage's defense of the journal's right to attack Pound even as it is publishing him.

Because the archives of *The New Age* have not survived, Hastings's claim to being the journal's shadow coeditor cannot be substantiated through reference to correspondence among the editorial team and between editors and contributors, editing marks on manuscripts, and the like.[11] For this reason, perhaps, *The Old "New Age"* has been treated by scholars—when it's been noticed at all—as the venomous riposte of an ex-lover.[12] I would suggest instead that it hints at a story behind standard, celebratory accounts of Orage's editorial genius, a story that, like so many others in the history of literary modernism, turns upon the vexed complexities of private relationships with a very public face. The excerpts included here register Hastings's deep skepticism regarding Orage's socialist commitments, her bitterness that Orage alone is credited with having discovered the famous modernists that she herself both promoted and jousted with, and her commitment to the utility of pseudonymous and anonymous publication.

Fleeing London (and Orage) for Paris (and the artist Amedeo Modigliani) in 1914, Hastings stayed on with the journal for six more years, writing "Impressions from Paris" under the pseudonym "Alice Morning." One of these columns, dated June 3, 1915, epitomizes Hastings's willingness to challenge feminists, modernists, and *New Age* socialists alike as she develops a feminist reading of modernity sharply attuned to issues of class privilege through her signature journalistic "impressions." One might well view this column as Hastings's "Mr Bennett and Mrs Brown."[13] Like Woolf, Hastings emphasizes the ethical and social responsibilities as well as the formal narrative strategies of the modern writer. To realize just how much is at stake for Hastings in this column, though, contemporary readers need to know something about the article by Ramiro de Maetzu to which she is responding here.

One of *The New Age*'s most frequent and consistent contributors on the subject of Guild Socialism and art, de Maetzu had published an article entitled "Art and Luxury" in the journal just under two months before Morning's column appeared. "Art and Luxury" argues the need for "a satisfactory aesthetic" even during the darkest days of World War I. Emphasizing the inadequacy of aesthetic theorizing to date, calling attention, in particular, to the shortcomings of both Arts and Crafts movement socialism and Wildean aestheticism, de Maetzu makes a crucial distinction in this essay between an "object of luxury" and a true work of art. An object of luxury is, he claims, merely a function of the cultural capital of its proprietor; by contrast, a true work of art, is "much much more than an article of luxury": it "place[s] human nature 'at a point whence rays surged out in all directions into the infinite.' It is a union of reality and ideal, of present and eternity, of body and soul, of the empiric and the necessary." Conceptualized in this manner, art can function as a provocateur for social change, "for the poorer we are the more we shall need it, [and] it will not be possible for us to lull our souls with the narcotic of luxury."[14]

In manifestoes like this, de Maetzu's Guild Socialist aesthetic overlaps significantly with various modernists' claims about the powers of the vortex, the objective correlative, and the like. What is striking about Alice Morning's response is not only that she clashes head on with *The New Age*'s official Guild Socialist spokesman on aesthetics but that she renounces wholesale the project of writing manifestoes, opting instead to provide her readers with simple yet startlingly perceptive vignettes of every day life. Thus, she turns from de Maetzu—*But I give it all up. It seems to me that one cannot categorise luxury*[15]—and segues abruptly into a seemingly unrelated story about a widow who is humiliated by the British Consulate's demand for information about her deceased husband when she attempts to renew a residency permit. The government clerk demands to know her late husband's birth date; she claims to have forgotten it, and is forced to explain, in front of everyone assembled, why "family differences" would keep her from obtaining the information. Refusing to accept her explanations, the clerk "snorts a kind of defense of the British family for the benefit of the assembled humble wretches of British subjects" and insists that she take an oath, though she hasn't "the faintest idea what she was swearing to." How curious, Alice Morning notes wryly in conclusion, to think that, eight years after his death, the widow's dead husband "should still be able to vex her existence by deputy."

As in her earlier writings for *The New Age* on feminism, women's suffrage, and suffragist politics, Hastings here takes issue with a legal system and an accompanying bureaucracy that has no means of (or interest in?) positioning a woman except as an appendage to a male relation. Hastings seems to be suggesting that, for all their manifestoes, modernists and Guild Socialists alike would be unable to register this troubling moment in an anonymous woman's life as a "vortex" exemplifying the oppressiveness, for women in particular, of the modern state's bureaucratic machinery.

The last pseudonym Hastings employs in writing for *The New Age*, "Alice Morning" is also the signature under which Hastings offers her most powerful feminist "impressions" of everyday life. "One doesn't write Impressions with an eye for Immortality," Alice Morning notes in a 1915 column (July 22, 1915,

277). This is a poignant statement of Hastings's awareness of—and commitment to—both the ephemeral nature of journalism and the play of feminist voices she orchestrated through publication under a multiplicity of pseudonyms in *The New Age*.

Notes

1. Wallace Martin's *The New Age Under Orage: Chapters in English Cultural History* is an important and influential early study of the journal that takes for granted its endorsement of the modernist avant-garde. For a very different view of modernism's emergence in this venue and the editorial staff's "quarrels" with the very writers it was introducing to the general public, see my study, *Modernism and Cultural Conflict, 1880–1922*, 143–72.

2. Martin, *New Age Under Orage*, 206. For discussion of British Guild Socialism's relationship to other turn-of-the-twentieth-century socialisms, e.g., Fabian Socialism, the Clarion Movement, Arts and Crafts movement socialism, and French Syndicalism, see *Modernism and Cultural Conflict*, 157–59.

3. These ranged from mass-circulation, mainstream newspapers and periodicals such as the London *Times*, *The Spectator*, and *The Daily Mail* to mid- and small-circulation regional and/or special interest political weeklies and monthlies such as *The New Statesman*, *The Christian World*, *The Clarion*, *The Liverpool Courier*, and the Bristol *Venture*, to modernist little magazines such as *The Egoist*, *Blast*, and *Glebe*.

4. The Modernist Journals Project's online edition of *The New Age* brings the competition among aesthetic and political traditions that so deeply and fiercely animated British public life in the early twentieth century out of the archives and into the classroom for easy access by contemporary students of modernism. See http://www.modjourn.brown.edu/.

5. Orage himself, for example, wrote extensively as "R. H. C."; Arnold Bennett wrote both under his own name and as "Jacob Tonson."

6. In his introduction to *The Faces of Anonymity: Anonymous and Pseudonymous Publication from the Sixteenth to the Twentieth Century*, Robert Griffin argues that "anonymity is not simply a residual characteristic of oral or manuscript culture, but continues . . . to be a dominant form, perhaps the norm, for print culture as well" (15). "Some historical understanding of anonymous publication," he goes on to suggest, must be integral "to our understanding of authorship and writing generally" (15), though this is a subject that literary studies has been "curious[ly] reluctant to acknowledge" (1). It is in this context that I venture to suggest that the turn of the twentieth century is a particularly interesting "moment" in the history of authorship, one far richer with examples of authorial ventriloquism than we have thus far cared to remember.

7. "Richmond Haigh" wrote frequently about women's suffrage and Africa (where Hastings spent her childhood) for *The New Age* between 1908 and 1910. Hastings does not claim the use of the pseudonym in her 1936 memoir; however, as Caroline Bean has suggested, the fact that her given family name was Emily Alice Haigh and that this frequent *New Age* contributor's interests and verbal stylistics bear such a close resemblance to Hastings's signed writings make a strong case for "Richmond Haigh" as yet another of her many personae (Caroline Bean, unpublished research, University of Delaware Undergraduate Research Program, Summer Scholar presentation, August 2002). Bean's

unpublished research on Hastings's coverage of the suffrage campaign informs my treatment here.

8. "To Our Readers," *The New Age* 2.6 (April 25, 1908): 503.

9. As Sean Latham has noted, in the earliest issues of the journal under Orage's editorship, Teresa Billington-Grieg wrote a weekly column detailing the plight of women; however, she quickly "found herself entangled in a series of debates about the priority of socialist causes over feminist ones which abruptly ended her interest in [the journal]" ("Introduction to Volume One," *The New Age*. Modernist Journals Project, http://www.modjourn.brown.edu/Intros/NAV1Int.htm, 10). Beatrice Hastings and Florence Farr then picked up where Billington-Grieg had left off in promoting discussion of a wide array of feminist issues in the journal and in challenging its socialist readers to further radicalize their agendas for cultural change through consideration of "sex-wrong."

10. Hastings takes this self-referencing still further on May 1, 1910, in a letter to the editor entitled "Women and Freedom," in which she responds, as "Beatrice (Tina) Hastings" to an article by "D. Triformis" (*The New Age* 7.2 [May 19, 1910], 29).

11. John Carswell notes that these have not been preserved.

12. Tom Steele, for example, notes its existence but does not mine it for information in *Alfred Orage and the Leeds Arts Club*.

13. As suggested by Bonnie Kime Scott in private correspondence with the author.

14. Ramiro de Maetzu, "Art and Luxury," *The New Age* 16.24 (April 15, 1915), 641, quoting Wilhelm Freiherr von Humboldt.

15. Alice Morning [Beatrice Hastings], "Impressions of Paris," *The New Age* 17.5 (June 3, 1915), 107.

Works Cited

Ardis, Ann. *Modernism and Cultural Conflict, 1888–1922*. Cambridge: Cambridge University Press, 2002.

———, and Leslie W. Lewis, eds. *Women's Experience of Modernity, 1875–1945*. Baltimore: Johns Hopkins University Press, 2002.

Carswell, John. *Lives and Letters: A. R. Orage, Beatrice Hastings, Katherine Mansfield, John Middleton Murry, S. S. Koteliansky, 1906–1957*. New York: New Directions, 1978.

Felski, Rita. Afterword. In Ardis and Lewis, eds. *Women's Experience of Modernity*. 290–99.

———. *The Gender of Modernity*.

Graff, Gerald. "Other Voices, Other Rooms: Organizing and Teaching the Humanities Conflict." *New Literary History* 21 (1990): 817–39.

Green, Barbara. "The New Woman's Appetite for 'Riotous Living': Rebecca West, Modernist Feminism, and the Everyday." In *Women's Experience of Modernity, 1875–1945*, ed. Ardis and Lewis. 221–36.

Hastings, Beatrice. *The Old "New Age" Orage—And Others*. London: Blue Moon Press, 1937.

Kenney, Rowland. "Education for the Workers." *The New Age* 14 (1914): 652–53.

Marek, Jayne E. *Women Editing Modernism: "Little" Magazines and Literary History*. Lexington: University Press of Kentucky, 1995.

Martin, Wallace. *The New Age Under Orage: Chapters in English Cultural History*. Manchester: Manchester University Press; New York: Barnes & Noble, 1967.

Morrisson, Mark S. *The Public Face of Modernism*.

"Morning, Alice" [Beatrice Hastings]. "Impressions of Paris." *The New Age* 17 (1915): 277.

Orage, A. R. "To Our Readers," *The New Age* 2 (1908): 508.

Pankhurst, Christabel. *Plain Facts About a Great Evil.* New York: Sociological Fund of the Medical Review of Reviews, 1913.

"R. H. C." [A. R. Orage?]. "Readers and Writers." *The New Age* 14 (1913): 51.

———. "Readers and Writers." *New Age* 16 (1915): 509.

Steele, Tom. *Alfred Orage and the Leeds Art Club, 1893–1923.* Brookfield, Vt.: Scholar Press, 1990.

T. K. L. [Beatrice Hastings]. "All Except Anything." *The New Age* 13 (1913): 733.

Tina, Beatrice [Beatrice Hastings]. "Woman and Freedom." *The New Age* 7 (1910): 69.

———. "Whited Sepulchers." *New Age* 5 (1909): 13, 35–36, 55–56, 77–78, 99–100, 119–20, 139–40.

——— "Woman as State Creditor." *The New Age* 3 (1908): 169.

——— "Militancy and Humanity." *The New Age* 6 (1910): 225–26.

BEATRICE HASTINGS

Suffragettes in the Making

For what sort of woman is the first division intended? Suppose Mrs. Asquith or Mrs. Gladstone were to be arrested (and no man can foretell a woman's way—the heads of the Tory ladies already are over the wall!), where would they be placed? Would they, with the Suffragettes, be set among convicts? Would they be given skilly to eat and cocoa with lumps of meat floating in it to drink? Would they have nothing but a charwoman's rag to wash with? Would they be obliged to perform their most private offices behind a gate which allowed anyone passing to inspect them?

I hope not! I can imagine their health, like other women's, would suffer before they could bring themselves to endure these disgusting experiences.

It is my particular love to write poetry and to name the bright, glad things of the sun and the woodside sea. I have condemned to the dustbin some juvenile outbursts of mine which flattered by use of the lovely human language ugly human manners better killed by silence. But silence about the filthy tortures practised on the political (and other) prisoners in Holloway is not possible.

I have not yet graduated as a Suffragette. I have not been to prison. Once, I believed it sufficient that every nerve of me strained against the public degradation of women by the State. But now I know that I lack something. I meet women, always every whit as insulted and angry as I, who have lately been tortured by the Government: and they have got a quality different—something more than I—deeper, wilder, ecstatic and bloody. They laugh so much better and freer than they used that I wonder what marvel of initiation happened inside those dead, silent cells that taught my friends the true temper of their courage?

Have they learned, like the Greek, that the tyrant is—lawless? realised that all is to be lost but nothing gained by confidence, their old, ignorant, loyal confidence in his edicts and his fearful punishments?

They have seen what is done to the imbecile criminal. They have felt how the horrid prison system dehumanises. They have lain down, stark awake, on the plank bed, numb as all prisoners are numb, from the whole day's long horror. They recognise victims, whom a hundred Governments of men have failed to redeem, hunted back to a death in life.

Bright, glad, useful men who know no better way with the disobedients than to wreck them in health and spirit!

Some of my friends came out of prison bewildered at the smile of the sun; so they know the helplessness which dooms again the unfriended, penniless wretches.

What sort of heart would that be which could feel, without beating firmer, that, in such matters as these, woman is denied the voice to demand a change in the brutal, senseless, mocking laws?

Do people know what the Suffragettes saw of Daisy Lord; how Daisy Lord sat, daily, in a scarlet-draped enclosure weeping, weeping, weeping, while the chaplain forced into her ears above her sobs the words of Jesus?

Chapel in prison! An orgy of pent-up emotions. Sighs, moans, and the irrepressible, wailing scream and the swoon. For, all day long, the human women in prison must learn to become as the dumb beasts. The breaking of the excruciating rule means solitary confinement.

And this torture is the last ordeal before a Suffragette becomes initiate. She is, thereafter—the Mystery, implacable and anguished beyond fear. Joy, then, is the sole joy of the march forward. Laughter is the laughter of the Will unconquerable; sure of no justice and mercy but through its own movement: never more to be deceived.

The man who is not avowed a friend is written down—foe.
How have some of us allied ourselves with Lloyd George?
Have we forgotten his self-revelation at Swansea?
"Let them be flung out, ruthlessly!"

Lloyd George knew that we were not demanding a right to brawl, but a right to vote. How often must it be repeated before the fact may be understood? We want a voice in the laws which affect us. We demand it in the proper places—Government assemblies of all kinds. Where else should we call for it? We want to declare our immediate need of the vote. It is the Government bullies who brawl and throw us out, "ruthlessly," because we refuse to wait their pleasure.

"Empty your slops!" And the brilliant, beloved women are left to obey this order in public under penalty of the ever-yawning solitary cell.

Fancy Mrs. Asquith emptying her slops before the eyes of three or four people? It is no fancy for the Suffragettes in Holloway. That is part of the filthy punishment. One must go to gaol to understand how beastly may be the decrees of men when they get a human woman in the obscurity of their prisons. She must wash her face and her cell floor and her food tin all with the same rag, left by who knows what unsavoury denizen before her. Her clothes and her boots are a persecution in themselves. She never sees the sun. Even light, whose heavenly eyes would ray in upon her, if they might, is forbidden by the infernal dusk which men say must shut in the prisoner. The window, which is never made to open, is dulled over. What a senseless spite!

When I graduate, it shall be through jesting. Solitary confinement for laughing. But they shall have a laugh, those poor, sad things walking round and round and round.

I, also, want to learn what it is that a woman brings in her soul out of that hell. For certain is this—that she comes forth endowed to conquer, solemn and illustrious!

Beatrice Tina

The New Age 4 (December 3, 1908): 109.

BEATRICE HASTINGS

On Guard

Women of the forward movement, you are aware that the matter of indecent assault upon you by Liberal stewards has now become common town talk. Your reticence, perhaps never a wise policy, continued, may constitute a danger to new recruits who enter the struggle utterly unprepared for violence of this description.

That you can and will adopt extreme measures to protect yourselves from future outrage at the hands of the prurient youths engaged by your cowardly enemies, is not all sufficient. Modesty must not prevent you from publishing throughout your ranks the abominable villainy practised at the Albert Hall. You know that, for such publication, newspapers are not necessary.

It is the duty of every woman who is already informed, to communicate the whole truth of the atrocities to which her comrades were subjected; it is the duty of every woman in the movement to learn this truth.

Sterner measures than those already taken to defeat the lewd attempts, now perilous to conceal, must be resorted to. A whip is no protection to a half-stunned woman. It must be made hazardous for these bullies even to approach you.

It is well known among you that the followers and attendants of Lloyd George are most to be feared. But the evil increases, and no woman, henceforth, should trust to the barely-civilised instincts of the men employed on behalf of the Cabinet Ministers.

Rape is irrevocable. Any means taken to prevent it are justified.

It is imperative that you do not under-estimate the brutal and obscene character of your opponents. Trust to no defence but that of absolute inviolacy. Allow no man to handle you but at his peril.

And let the reminder that such protection against your debased and unclean enemies has become necessary, nerve you to wrest from them the power to liberate and purify the spirit of your country.

BEATRICE TINA.

The New Age 4 (December 10, 1908): 123

BEATRICE HASTINGS

Feminism and the Franchise

In considering the feminist movement, we must remember that this is not primarily a movement for the suffrage, and when stating our case for the suffrage we should be exceedingly careful to eliminate the domestic woman, her miseries, and her methods of revolt. The revolt of the married woman is purely a slave revolt. For the married woman there is necessity to arouse herself against her condition; but there is not one logical reason for her claiming the vote. The W.S.P.U. were aware of this when they framed their resolution to demand the vote on the same terms as it is or may be given to men; that is, on the ground of civic responsibility. Had they held to this limited but logically secure position, the issues to-day would have been very much clearer than they are. One seeks in vain now for a statement of the purely political argument; it has become everywhere confused with the feminist argument.

In the early days the W.S.P.U., while refusing, quite legitimately, to permit discussion on its platforms of the sex-revolt, made the great mistake of attempting to ignore that revolt altogether. Instead of frankly recognizing it as a movement proceeding side by side but by no means identically with their own, they puritanically opposed it and boycotted the feminist exponents. They made enemies of some of the most brilliant feminists, and they called into being the feminine anti-suffragist, who seems to see less danger in things as they are than as they might be if the autocratic puritans ever got into power. With half the women in the country against them, the W.S.P.U. leaders grew unwary. When Mr. Asquith declared that the mass of women were opposed to the vote, instead of denying the vote to responsible women who did want it, they sought to prove that the mass of women were in favour of the vote. Thus, while declaring themselves a narrowly political and not a broadly sex-ethical party, they then strove by might and main to add to their numbers. There were not numbers of women to be found interested merely in the political justice of women's enfranchisement, but there were numberless women in revolt against sex-disability in the home, and these, by means of concession, were induced to join the W.S.P.U.

A remarkable change of atmosphere occurred so soon as the newly-won feminists began to invade the platform. The sex revolt could no longer be ignored. For instance, a book by a spinster, disparaging the holy estate as "a license for sexual intercourse," was reviewed in the columns of "Votes for Women." The work was hailed as notable and courageous; whereas a much earlier pronouncement by the feminist, Beatrice Tina, protesting merely against the abuse of marriage, had been officially boycotted and privately denounced.

Gradually the fortress of the political legion was given over to the feminists. Prodigious promises as to what would happen in favour of married women began to be made, culminating at last in the orgie of chimerical benevolence indulged in by Miss Elizabeth Robins, where such things as the safety of married women from rivalry and a regular lien on the wages of a casual labourer were exhibited as involved in the winning of the vote. Many sound feminists now profess themselves as growing horrified at the prospect that the vote may be lost at length through the folly of the very persons whose business it is to leave feminism alone and attend solely to that which they set out to do, namely, to present the case for the vote. The W.S.P.U. should not properly number more than the women interested solely in the political justice of women's enfranchisement: in short, in that which may be granted immediately. No taxation without representation is irresistible reasoning, and must tell in due time. The principle has been already admitted, and public men begin to realise that to deny the principle in the case of women responsible to the State is a moral insult. We are prepared to hear the usual objection against minorities and constitutional methods—that these take so long to achieve any reform. But by whom and how else is this reform going to lie achieved? Violence and large numbers have not really brought us any nearer. There is no sign that the Government is yielding.

The use of violence, apart from humane considerations, was a mistake on the part of the political women, because it induced (or forced) them to ally themselves openly with the mass *of* women whose revolt was not truly against disenfranchisement but against their ignominious domestic position. This alliance, for the sake of numbers, gave point to the accusation which became a commonplace—that the franchise movement was a fraudulent attempt on the part of women to gain political privileges in return for which they would and could give no guarantee of responsibility to the State. While we should be the first to avow that the position of all women would be improved by the removal of the sex disability in politics and that the vote is a symbol of the moral restoration of womanhood, that avowal involves no further admission. Decidedly we object to the illusory hopes held out to the married woman that when such women as pay taxes shall have the vote the conditions of marriage will perceptibly change for the better. Most, and the worst, of these conditions can only be changed by the action of married women themselves, organised or individual. The million and a half future women electors could not honestly promise any change at all, even if this million and a half were all bent in the same direction, whereas there is small evidence to indicate concerted effort towards the relief of married women. We object to the representations made to factory women to the effect that the feminine vote will give them wages equal to men's wages. That could only be brought about to a small extent by the fixation of the minimum wage for all workers. It is a delusive idea that the feminine vote will inevitably be devoted to this end. And suppose the minimum for both sexes were to be fixed, it is at least possible that men would be chosen and the women left.

All these representations may be magical in inducing large numbers to cry "Votes for Women," but they do not count with the Government; nor can it be said that the threat to the male elector of having to pay out pocket-money to his wife and at the same time perhaps to earn only as much as she herself "when women get the vote" is likely to urge him to rebel against a Government that withholds votes from women.

It may be well said that the few married women fighting for the franchise who thoroughly understand that they will get nothing but thanks far their assistance are entitled to the term "heroic"; and a factory woman helping with the same clear' view of the facts is certainly a heroine. But the majority—those for whom the ideas of tire lien, legal control in the home, legal right to deceased husband's estate, etc., were circulated—have no clear view of the facts. They, with their balloons of reasons why women want the vote, draw down angry ridicule upon the franchise movement. The W.S.P.U. should not be concerning itself with these women at all. They are the raw material for the feminist who must educate them to understand that whit is due to their womanhood is a different thing front what is due to them politically.

The immediate case for the vote concerns politically only the million and a half women who are entitled to the franchise. On this stand, and on no other, may the case be maintained: that taxation without representation is unconstitutional. If it is true that going to prison for one's rights is a quick way of getting them, taxable women can resort to passive resistance. There would probably be a louder and swifter outcry among the electorate against the forcible feeding of passive resisters than against this torture applied as it is now to women summoned for violence.

Perhaps a less exciting method of winning the vote than the militant, the constitutional method is a far more glorious one. Within it are contained the principles upon which civilized nations may justly boast their superiority to barbarous races. It is made up of elements necessary to social perfection.

D. Triformis. *The New Age* 6 (March 3, 1910): 415–16.

BEATRICE HASTINGS

From *The Old "New Age" Orage—And Others*

II. Notes

It is easy to see when I began to take the literary direction of the "New Age." For the first time, the paper shows some signs of being edited instead of being merely filled up. I put it without fear to any competent editor in the world.

[. . .] Not only had Orage no idea how to present what he did print, but he regarded creative work as mere trimmings; at least, this was his refuge from a realisation that he was no artist himself. New writers were waiting, as they always are, the matter was there, but Orage valued neither them nor it. He

could see nothing but big names around his own. How he treated correspondents, unless these were big names or protégés of big names, or compliment-
ed, may be seen in the early issues; he did not print their letters, but only his
own smart retorts! the kind of tin-god's insolence to which he subjected not
a few aspirants to "The New English Weekly," that wooden ape of the "New
Age" I finally formed. He used poems for filling corners, and made few corners.
Except for an occasional story by some known writer, Orage printed practically *no original work.* [. . .] He pshawed when I rescued from a drawer several
manuscripts—for he accepted things, this costing him nothing but a smile or
one of his famous notes, and a place in a pigeon-hole—and I said that these
ought to go in. [. . .] But the paper only became what I wanted when J. M.
Kennedy and A. E. Randall and Huntly Carter settled in and we made a sort
of frame that could stand the inevitable fluctuation of outside contributions.
What J. M. K. was to the "New Age" will be seen presently. [. . .]

Among "New Age" contributors who have expressed their gratitude to Orage for giving them a start, few have sung him louder than Mr. Ezra Pound.

In this preliminary pamphlet, I must suppress the detail I shall publish
later, so simply say that I had to fight not only Orage, but the whole office, to
get Pound's articles in at all. They were so idiosyncratic that I did not quite
trust my own judgment, and I read them out; and everyone howled. However, I put them through. But, Orage scoffed at and belittled Pound in and out
of season. On one occasion, Orage, who knew almost no French, but had the
self-assurance of a Parolles, said—"I reserve my judgment [on French writers
Pound had cited] until he has produced his evidence that any one of them
can write good French." Finally, when I wrote, as "T. K. L.," a series of parodies
of certain poets introduced by Pound, who took the jousting with tolerable
literary manner, Orage, *butting in* with his flat, ponderous pen (and what a flat,
ponderous, stilted, maundering, when not coy, conceited and facetious, when
not plagiaristic or outright thievish "literary" pen he had, I shall later demonstrate) said, so late as Oct. 1913, nearly two years after Pound's debut: "Mr.
Pound's style is a paste of colloquy, slang journalism and pedantry. Of culture,
in Nietzsche's sense of the word, it bears no sign."

I put it to anyone outside literary Bedlam (and for the nonce, I put Pound
inside it) whether an editor able to do as he pleased would have persisted in
publishing a contributor of whom he thought like that? [. . .] (Note: Pound
had to be paid.) [. . .]

My present-day friends, accustomed to the push and publicity of this period,
find it hard to understand how I could be so disastrously indifferent to claiming

my work; how I could go on, year after year, writing anonymously or under pseudonyms that allowed readers to set down my work to other people, mainly to Orage. Puzzle or no (I could explain it with more space; I thought it better for the paper) there it is. I did so. I cared for nothing but the paper, that was my life. I am far from regretting, either, for the work will eventually come back to my door, and I could not have done it if exposed to the publicity I should have had by signing every thing and if it had been known that every new contributor had to reckon with me. I took enormous pains not to be identified. Incidentally, my first contribution to the "New Age" was an unsigned column and a half review of Orage's "Nietzsche in Outline and Aphorism," Nov. 30, 1907, and my last, an article from Paris, signed "Alice Morning," March, 1920.[1]

Here, I say that I am not concerned now merely to establish my own claim. It is too late for me to get anything like personal compensation, and my intimate friends would testify how often I have shrugged aside their indignant advice to make a stand. There is a bigger thing at stake. There is the reputation of the "New Age" itself, that is, of the collectivity of contributors who aimed at a high standard in creative and critical thought of all kinds, however some of them may have fallen away since.

I have a certain sensitiveness to the currents running through the literary world (although it seldom serves me personally), and a very particular kind of *luck,* the journalist's luck—although I was never a journalist in the practical sense of the term—of being on the spot, of meeting the right person, of hearing the significant thing. And I sense that, since the deplorable attempt to pass off "The New English Weekly" as a "revival of the old *New Age*" and since the publication of "the best of Orage's writings," an opinion is gaining ground that the "New Age" was over-rated. I declare that this is not so. I have been going through the volumes lately, after twenty years, and I am inclined to marvel. We built even better than we knew, and we were not afflicted with false modesty! There are hundreds of contributions that have no date and never will have any date because they belong to the ray of liberal mind (the real, not the imitation that tolerates even the enemies of liberty) that is as young and as old as humanity itself. I could do an enchanting summary of each month with the story and, the stars agreeable, I will. No, the falling reputation of Orage is not going to drag down the "New Age" with it. I have not, so far, troubled much to defend myself, but I shall trouble on the "New Age" issue.

---

1. [The selected notes are original to Hastings's text.] This name was inspired by the fortune of a cousin of mine who went as a junior in the "Morning" to the South Pole. [. . .]

And, since I am personally inextricably mixed with it, the mettle of my present ideas and ideals should be understood: whoever may have changed from the early days, I have not. I am still the author of "Woman's Worst Enemy, Woman,"[2] as well as of "The Maids' Comedy"; I still Love the social rebel, and challenge mere man-made laws and hate the Pankhursts, Emmeline and Christabel, who sold the Feminist movement; I am the same crusading, anti-philistine woman I ever was.

Last, but not least, I realize that, without an explanation from me, the future critic could never make sense of the "New Age" story.

III

[. . .]

. . . . [Orage] turned socialist in his youth in a rage against Society in the person of the village Squire—I shall have to correct Dr. Hewlett Johnson on points—and no-one unaware of this complex need hope to make an intelligible study of Orage. He turned into a sort of opposition socialist after failing to charm the risen of the Labour Party: a salt [sad] story, this. He turned National Guildsman when he lost the support of Victor Grayson. Then, he became an independent anything you please and made an unreturned bow to Lloyd George. I gasped, in Paris, when he made his sudden kowtow to Ll.G., flattering him as he had previously scarified him; a year or so before, he was calling him "a Jew-capitalists' pimp." The turn was quite too sudden. Lloyd George took no notice. And I had hardly got my breath back from murmuring a hundred times that week— "he must have gone mad!" when the next issue arrived with a worse shock. The grapes had turned sour. The fox who had smiled was now snarling uncontrollably at "the wily Minister," who had ignored Orage's offer and said what he had to say in "The New Statesman."

He deserted Hobson and Guilds and took Major Douglas's cargo aboard, left him to tug it through the doldrums and later, profiting by a dozen men's work in America, came back the pirate he always was and flew the Social Credit flag. I read his broadcast. He used *words,* in his bamboozling way, simple enough to convince the simplest Alberta farmer that he was going to get a money-ticket for nothing, but he did not simplify the scheme of Social Credit, left it in a tangle to make the joy of a parodist. Major Douglas will still need to explain his scheme.

---

2. Aldington exploits this title in one of his books, without naming me. That this silk-fingered, scratch-nailed, sob-stuffing, eaten-brained curate of the feminine soul is accepted by women as a champion shows what enemies to themselves they still are.

The "New Age" positively suffered from Orage's weathercock "politics," that all had but one end and aim—the chance of leading A.R.O. into the House. And when J. M. Kennedy ("S. Verdad") was lost to the paper,[3] he who had correct information about things political and international, and supplied hundreds of paragraphs, *that* side of the "New Age" slid after the literary and creative side that slid when I left, and there was a complete ruination.

There was this distinction between Orage and the rest of us: we had no interest but in our subject whatever it might be, whereas he had no interest in anything or anyone except in so far as they served his ever-defeated, ever-gnawing craving for a seat. I warrant that Social Credit, like all else, spelled Westminster and Sir Alfred. But, it was a wild dream. He was a coterie man, not a man for a fighting Party. A large audience did not vitalise and electrify him; it chilled and intimidated him. In his first "Notes" in the "New English Weekly," making one of the historical howlers in journalism, he indicated how the House should be conducted and improved so as to be ready for him. The House was to behave itself "according to the rules of the best debate." (I grew to abhor this best debate à la Orage in all its vice. He was sophistication incarnate. Only the bludgeoning T. E. Hulme could ever check him in his excursions the round of the dialectical compass and make him look sulky instead of bewitching.) The political fisticuff, the parliamentary knockout would have found him murmuring some killing aphorism from Nietzsche or another and looking for his hat.

---

3. J. M. K. was known to be "S. Verdad," by many persons. There was no deep mystery about his contributions.

There is a mystery about J. M. K's diaries. Here is a clue, for anyone who may have another. Orage wrote to me that he had gone through K's papers and discovered that he "had been betraying the *New Age* for years." I conclude that J. M. K. had methodically noted down all his unsigned contributions, that were attributed to Orage. J. M. K, as we all knew, took no payment, but I deliberately suggest that those "papers" contained a memorandum of accounts on the other side.

The Old "New Age" Orage—And Others. London: Blue Moon Press, 1937.

BEATRICE HASTINGS

The Way Back to America

Attendez, mes enfants! I am about to waste ten minutes in exposition of the so-called English poets. What I have to say is brief, pardieu! They were all French! Who is that interrupting? Ha—you wish to infer that Chaucer wrote no poetry until he forgot he had once been in France? Well, you may infer what you please, I suppose. What? The "Canterbury Tale"? I smile explosively—all pure French, my dear sir! Now sit down and let me talk. Shakespeare owed all his technique to the Pléiade, that miraculous constellation of Frenchmen. Shakespeare invoked sleep:

> Canst thou upon the high and giddy mast
> Seal up the ship-boy's eye and rock his brains
> In cradle of the rude, imperious surge?

You hear his origin, n'est ce pas? Enough. Ex pede Herculem! They have had a poet, one Swinburne. He, choice creature, enlightened these English. Before Swinburne they believed that a poet should *say* something! The French of A.D. 1300 had failed to show them the beauty of mere emotional words, divine, un-philosophical. Ha—but exoticism, exoticism! Pardon! I am grieving for Alexandria, for Babylon, for Catulle, Catulle! You, perhaps, don't catch on, but do as you please! To-day, once again, we make a trade of art. We know our tools. We can sit down to our business as deliberately as any other craftsman and make good. Muses? Ah, the brave jest! Muses! My friends, we are the Muses. I myself will muse for you to order, and do it superlatively. My personal circle is small—I am an exile on this planet—yet no country, except perhaps England—I know nothing for certain—is altogether alien to me; I find always one choice creature in the trade. We meet. He and I then construct la poèsie, ours or another's or each other's. Two tinkers can each construct an admirable tin can. Two poets can each sing admirably about a tin can, I suppose. We do not sing of tin cans, but we could if we liked. That we sing Beauty, pur et simple, is because it is better for trade. You do not take me? Consider it—not too literally *please*—at your leisure. I have a brother in art. I admire him. He handles his tools. Perhaps I exaggerate, but I honestly believe he has recovered the aesthetic grand mystery—no mystery at all really, but as good as, being so long forgotten. My brother is French, but you guessed this! His wave-lengths! Long! Don't mention it. They need never stop. They only do stop, because it is better for trade. Think over this! He knows more about verse-rhythm than any man living—and why should he not, since nobody else knows more than he knows? No one else knows anything, whatever about his rhythms, for they are his own, incomparable. Them that do assume, ignorant, shallow, have dragged up comparisons. They may compare, of course. I am not God.

Cow hypocrite,
Cow of pretence.

Cow colour of fawn, more fraudulent than our nags, cow colour of fawn, bedaubed with brush, walking lie, cuts hypocrite, cow of pretence.

Cow erst in a pound, footsore down at St. Louis, cow erst in a pound, now corned and in tius at Paris, cow hypocrite, cow of pretence.

Cow of visage rouged, Boodle a business man, cow of visage rouged, was spoofed by the paint on your skin, cow hypocrite, cow of pretence.

Cow with black eyes the fatuous mug made a deal, cow with black eyes, give you the run of his patch, cow hypocrite, cow of pretence.

Cow colour of gold, next day he urged his friend to inspect his purchase, cow colour of gold, they spat, these Americans ten, cow hypocrite, cow of pretence.

Cow like spotted pard, you should have hitched out of shot, cow like spotted pard, each spit become a splotch, cow hypocrite, cow of pretence.

Take breath, mes enfants, though there is more to come. If you are not too drunk with the delicate stuff to be able to carry it as if, as if, I repeat, unconcerned, you will wake at the end of the reading to know that the pageant of all the subtle, neglected, misunderstood poets that ever were has passed before you. You agree? You agree because you also are in the trade. If it were otherwise, I could not have shown you all the elegances of my brother's technique. If there be a man here incapable of yearning over this I cannot help it. If he says that all these assonances are merely decadent exaggerations of one part of the whole technique of poetry, if he considers that rhyme, such as Shakespeare caught has its place—

Come away, come away, Death,
    And in sad cypress let me be laid;
Fly away, fly away, breath;
    I am slain by a fair cruel maid.
My shroud of white stuck all with yew,
    O! prepare it.
My part of death, no one so true
    Did share it.
Not a flower, not a flower sweet,
    On my black coffin let there be strown;
Not a friend, not a friend greet
    My poor corse, where my bones shall be thrown.
A thousand thousand sighs to save,
    Lay me, O! where

Sad true lover never find my grave,
>   To weep there.

—if he says that in this lyric both assonance and rhyme are beautifully mingled, and that my brother's poem is like a boy's trick, again I cannot help it.

Cow grey as a shirt, you weren't worth a greenback washed, cow grey as a shirt, Boodle cursed in his wrath, cow hypocrite, cow of pretence.

Cow of innocent soul, at auction you fetched forty-five, cow of innocent soul, (cents) it was not your fault, copy hypocrite, cow of pretence.

Cow doomed, the butcher, the packer, the grocer, cow doomed slew, put, and bold you in can, cow hypocrite, cow of pretence.

Ah—it begins to tell on you, but I love your drooping! I must explain that whereas this traduction of mine appears to show connected idea, the French original transcends all such commonplace, but what would you? I am employing English and the tongue makes for mere sense. It has hitherto defeated almost all its poets, these, no doubt, true enough yearners after Beauty, pur et simple. Just look at their piteous stolid fabrics woven, malgré eux, around their blockish sky-larks, Satans, Pilgrims, scholar gypsies and what not. My brother's ineffable words mean anything you like, cows, roses, toads, dairymaids or queens—if you *must* have a meaning, but why have one?

In French the thing is a marvel. Listen!

>   Fleur hypocrite,
>   Fleur du silence.
> Rose couleur de cuivre, plus frauduleuse que nos joies,
>   rose couleur de cuivre, embaume-nons dans tes mensonges, fleur
>   hypocrite, fleur du silence.

But imagine an Englishman to set down the stuff! The pure article!

>   Hypocritical flower,
>   Flower of the silence.
> Copper-coloured rose, more fraudulent than our joys, copper-coloured
>   rose, embalm us in thy lies, hypocritical flower, flower of the
>   silence.

But you *can't* imagine it! Such sublime language were only to be ventured upon by a few exquisite souls—and they are all in Bedlam! Such is England! Condole with me, and do forget the impossible Saxon and take to French.

>   Cow transfigured, prime peach-fed pig you in tin, cow transfigured, sold
>   in Paris for three times your carcase's price, cow hypocrite, cow of
>   pretence.

Cow, cow, those Gauls, those applauding messieurs, loved you, hugged
you, swallowed you, abolished all cruder foods, cow, cow, resolved
to bless America with their presence and never to forget Yankee-
doodle, cow hypocrite, cow of pretence.

Cow, cow, cow, cow, cow, your return to the land of your birth with glory
galore is certain if you spurn the sordid hang-dog mob of English
critics and whipster versifiers, cow, cow, cow, cow, cow, I can drag
this out as long as I wish and term my amateur spurts perfectly
brand-new verse-rhythms and be apotheosised by novelty-
mongers, but I prefer my supper which stands served in a hot dish,
cow hypocrite, cow of pretence.

My brother's latest achievement is the "Sonnets in Prose," to be followed
by "Lyrics in Prose," and the series will culminate in "Poetry in Prose," only
to introduce a second series—"Novels in Poesie," "Encyclopædias in Poesie,"
"Essays in Poesie," and so on. You see, friends, if we can only mix everything
up and break every law of the common aesthetic, it will be much better for
the trade. It irks me and my brothers to have to compete on their own lines
with those servile poets who studied fitness and actually threw away in their
ridiculous pride hundreds of experiments which in their estimation would
never lead to poetical success, but which we have picked up and shall offer to
the public, willy nilly. But, friends, it'll be willy, n'est ce pas?

T. K. L. *The New Age* 13 (September 18, 1913): 604–5.

BEATRICE HASTINGS

From "Impressions of Paris"

Just before the disguised Taube arrived, two wounded soldiers, one with a forage cap and one with a fez, seated themselves heavily at the table next to mine
in the cool of the cafe terrace. "It's a good thing we're rich," said the forage
cap, evidently very pleased to be seated, and reaching already for his money
like anyone who is not used to having it. "You, you mean!" replied the fez—"it's
a long time since I touched anything but a smile." "Oh, as to that"—began
the forage cap flourishingly—and then the garcon came up and told him that
soldiers could only be served inside the cafe. So the poor things had to stump
in to the hot room. My regret was interrupted by the bombs. As ever, we all
went to the middle of the street and gazed up at the sky. Really, I did not see

one face more scared than curious. This curiosity is one of the mysteries of the human psychology: rather to be dead than not see what's gong to happen! I saw a soldier so terribly crippled and cut about that nothing but his extraordinary wardrobe of a blue night-cap, a scarlet shirt, red pantaloons, and bright green slippers diverted the passers-by from openly pitying him. I saw him hobble across a stream of nervous taxis to ask the agent what that crowd was in the Champs Elysée; then there he went his very perilous way. I had just left the crowd which was around the chairs where the vendors of old postage-stamps fleece the collectors of such. The boxes and books of stamps are spread out on chairs under the trees, and there the business is conducted. I was on my way from lunching with a friend at the restaurant of The Golden Snails, a Montmartrois haunt opposite the shop of the Three Thousand Shirts, and where I heard a child say a quaint thing. She had asked for strawberries and was given rhubarb, which goaded her to take revenge on her serviette. The mother said—"You are losing half of it, my child!" and Child replied—"But, you know, one does not eat rhubarb for amusement!"

My personal joy over the débâcle of the "Daily Mail" nearly led me to dance on the boulevard. I nearly told the waiter what a splendid thing this was for England. How often has not this newspaper momentarily embittered my existence here since the war began! It has a great hold over the French newspapers; and many a time one throws away one's energy on some importantly headed column only to find "Daily Mail" coyly introduced three-quarters of the way down. The French journals have kept very quiet about the Kitchener affair. "La Liberté" took so much liberty as to mention that copies of "certain" London newspapers were publicly burned; but the majority of papers seem to have preferred to wait for further details! Probably they are now informed that the Northcliffe press is despised in England, but nothing less than the universal outburst against it could ever have convinced people like M. Clemenceau that the Northcliffe "Times" is not quite the same thing as our old Thunderer. The Paris equivalent of the "Daily Mail," the "Matin," had for its ill-bred motto before the war—"Le Matin dit tout," Of course, it does not "say everything" now, though the assertion still clings to the walls of newsagents. "The 'Daily Mail' dit tout much," might—no, I shall become a pariah if I say things like that. But, seriously, I cannot think how such depressing and probably misleading articles as appear in the Paris "Mail," get through. There was one lately picturesquely called "The Caravan of Agony," describing the wounded in hospitals with detail. The writer, a man named E. Powell, spares you nothing, neither the pains of the dying crying for death to come, nor his own sweats, sobs, and agonised smiles as he hurries from scene to scene. [. . .] One of my aunts has four sons at the front. I hope she may never read that article in which, as at the cinemas, more desperate pain and sorrow is heaped together to be shown off in ten minutes than many soldiers may have seen in ten engagements. It needs a white-hot or a white-cool brain to tell of horrors without arousing disgust where this is not intended. A soldier may do it fitly with his phrase tempered by the battle as his steel by the fire; a great poet with talent hardening his genius will do it fitly. "Eye-Witness" does it fitly under responsibility to the whole English public. The taint of sensationalism in a description of the war will produce in the reader instead of social compassion and admiration, personal depression, nausea, cowardice, and the worse impressions of morbidity. If America ever went to war one would pity her non-combatant population at the mercy of the Powells.

I wish that someone could put up a natural defence of luxury against Senor de Maetzu. The very earth itself is so constructed and situated that in some parts a hog may feed on peaches which would be considered a luxury in Brixton. The question of the luxury of peaches is an artificial question of cost, and so the peach-fed hog is considered less a luxury in Brixton than a peach; but there is nothing in the nature of man which says to him: "Thou shalt not eat peaches in Brixton." It is only his pocket which talks. A man come to Brixton from the South, and accustomed all his life to eating a great deal of fruit, would find fruit a necessity at any price he could give; his landlady would as certainly consider him a gourmand. Nothing in his nature says to a man: "Thou shalt not drink beer in Brixton," but in Patagonia he might have to consult his pocket before ordering a bottle of ale. As for what is or what is not luxury, apart from cost, for an individual, so long as he remains in health and his right mind—no one but himself can possibly decide. If a man indulges himself so far as to fall ill, he comes under the physician, or so far as to offend humanity, he comes under ostracism or the law. It is awfully dangerous, considering what a little tyranny may prove the overthrow of a nation, to begin condemning the personal luxuries of men who offend neither family nor neighbours. A "well-regulated society" would never interfere with such a man. Who, indeed, is going to decide what is necessity or luxury for a producer? Who can say, for instance, whether Wagner's indulgence in certain luxuries aided the musician or the charlatan? He himself seems to have said that it developed his personality—and assuredly he meant his musical personality. I don't like Wagner myself, but he would have no trouble in convincing me that all which enervates and worries me in his music was the protest of his genius against his early lack of luxury. Beethoven in an unmechanical age less physically enervating, and a musician of more powerful genius, did not support his life of poverty and incessant irritation (which worked itself off very often on his pupils and patrons) without indulging himself occasionally with alcohol—who would care to instruct him? As for persons like the late Mr. Morgan with his ten Stradivarius—he is a subject for ridicule, not for moralising. He goes in company with the fop and the co-quette. The case of the woman who orders unnecessary dresses at this moment should be an argument for militarising more manufactories. It is not just to use her as an argument against personal tastes which their possessors profess to find useful for personal production.

There seems no reasonable argument against the assertion that what is luxury to one person may be necessity to another. In general it is true. I cannot sympathise with the body which can sit on a high or a hard chair; high and hard chairs paralyse me and make me hate the human race. I cannot sympathise with people who fill their rooms with flowers; in such a room I suffocate. I cannot sympathise with people who eat sweets and cakes instead of smoking. I can sympathise with literary people who must have a room full of well-bound books; although I do with very few, and of those the covers are indifferent to me. It would never do, you see, for me to have to decide what was necessity or luxury for anyone else! I am prejudiced. Again, who can ever settle, except in terms of trade, whether a producer produces more than he consumes? The whole order of artists would have to be annihilated before a general question could be put. If I am well informed, the National Guildsmen exclude artists from their working scheme: Artists will have, as ever, to live by their wits. Nothing can regulate their production. But I give it all up. It seems to me that one cannot categorise luxury. When it has been defined as that which does not benefit the health or efficiency of producers, thereafter the question is particular to each producer. [. . .]

ALICE MORNING.

The New Age 17 (June 3, 1915): 106–7.

6

Journalism Meets Modernism

INTRODUCED AND SELECTED BY PATRICK COLLIER

IN ROSE MACAULAY'S 1920 novel *Potterism*, Jane Potter contemplates a writing career. She *wants* "to be a journalist and to write" (26), imagines herself as "a special correspondent, a free-lance contributor, a leader writer, eventually an editor" (30), ponders writing "articles on social and industrial questions" (28). But the readiest path to this kind of life is closed off to Jane: though she *could* work for her father, a wealthy newspaper publisher, the baron of the "Potter Press," generational antagonism and peer pressure make that path unacceptable. She belongs to an Oxford clique known as the "Anti-Potter League," sworn to stamp out the sentimentality, vulgarity, and mediocrity its members equate with her father's newspapers and, more broadly, England circa 1915. Arthur Gideon, the group's leader, offers this definition of the typical Potterite:

> "Facts are too difficult, too complicated for him. Hard, jolly facts, with clear
> sharp edges that you can't slur and talk away. Potterism has no use for them.
> It appeals over their heads to prejudice and sentiment. [. . .] Potterism is
> all for short and easy cuts and showy results. [. . .] Potterism plays a game
> of grab all the time—snatches at success in a hurry." (16–17)

Gideon will later found a newspaper, *The Weekly Fact*, devoted to "unsentimental journalism [. . .] unhampered by tradition [. . .] the very essence of anti-Potterism" (48). And Jane, in a compromise that illustrates her uneasy position in the journalistic marketplace, will write articles for *The Weekly Fact* and one of her father's papers, the *Daily Haste*.

Jane's dilemma offers a glimpse of the difficulties the journalistic marketplace presented to young English women who wanted to write in 1915. There was plenty of work: dozens of women's publications, appealing to all classes and to widely varied interests, had predominantly female staffs.[1] Many educated men were off fighting in Europe; this factor combined with the sheer number of periodicals—P. J. Keating estimates there were fifty thousand in 1900 (36)—assured plenty of work for women writers. There was precedent for women working not only for women's specialty publications but also in the male-dominated daily newspapers. In the 1890s, Flora Shaw and Mme. Couvreur became foreign correspondents for the *Times,* and Mrs. Frederick Beer edited the *Sunday Times* (Billington 102–3). Women had made sufficient inroads to support the establishment of the Society of Women Journalists in 1894, and by 1905 its membership had increased to 236 from just 69 in 1900. As Richard Altick observed, census data indicate an almost four-fold increase, to more than 1,200, in the number of women identifying themselves as "authors, journalists, or editors" between 1881 and 1901 (392).[2] Even after World War I, when many women in the trades and professions were forced to relinquish their jobs to returning soldiers, the expansion of the press and the specialized market for "women's journalism" ensured plenty of outlets for women.

For a woman like Jane Potter (or Rose Macaulay, for that matter), the question was not *whether* one could work as a journalist but how to do so without compromising one's intellectual credentials. Like the fictional Jane Potter, the four writers anthologized here—Macaulay, Rebecca West, Winifred Holtby, and Virginia Woolf—faced a set of conflicting imperatives. Journalism was the obvious way for an aspiring writer to earn money, build a reputation, and make professional contacts. But to become identified as a journalist threatened one's credibility. By the early twentieth century, the conditions of British journalism were a recognized social problem—a crisis threatening dire consequences for the health of Britain's democracy and the future of its literature. The explosion in newspaper readership and the perceived decline in journalistic quality had long been seen as a threat to literature. Ford Madox Ford predicted in 1908 that the English reader, overwhelmed by the "white spray of facts" in the daily newspaper, would cease to read literature, the newspaper having dulled and sated any appetite for "the printed page" (108). Such warnings were widespread enough by 1921 to be grist for satire: physician and social observer Robert Briffault quipped that year that "the unpopular weeklies [. . .] are doleful with intellectual tears; the popular dailies with 'unexampled circulation' wear the smile of the tiger"—conditions that "bid fair, the wailing voices lament, to snuff out the light of art and culture in the land of Shake-speare" (512).

The essays in this section find four women writers joining the cultural discussion of contemporary journalism, often more equivocally than male commentators. The stakes in these debates were different, and in some ways higher, for women than for men. The historical openness of the profession of journalism to women, the central role journalism played in the suffrage movement, the misogynistic strain underlying many of the critiques of contemporary journalism—all of these factors made the debate about the health and future of the press a crucial but complex one for women writers.

As Macaulay, Holtby, West, and Woolf launched their writing careers, the prestige of journalism as a profession was at a historic low: preachers in pulpits, radicals in parks, and writers in the monthly and quarterly reviews lamented the state of British journalism. The common wisdom went thus: Lord North-cliffe and his contemporaries had brought about the fall of British journalism when they changed the daily newspaper from an outlet for sound political news and opinion to a purveyor of gossip, news "tit-bits," oddities, and garish crime coverage. This crisis was, for many observers, consequent with the arrival of women as a force in journalism. By this logic, the decline began when women emerged as consumers, subjects, and writers of news. As the essayist and playwright St. John Ervine wrote in 1930:

> Newspapers were formerly published for men; they are now increasingly being published for women. The most casual observer of the "national" newspaper cannot fail to notice how womanised the popular press has become. [. . .] Articles by, and about, women prevail in these papers, and editors, without any appearance of embarrassment, will print "powerful articles" by young ladies not long enlarged from school on the reform of Marriage or the reorganization of Sex or the overhaul of Religion. There seem to be many young ladies who will rearrange the entire universe in eight hundred words for a fee of twenty guineas! (836)

Ervine's critique mixes male defensiveness at the female advances in the profession with anxiety over the authority of the journalistic word: if inexperienced women can get into print, how are readers to judge the value of commentary? How distinguish between sober, studied opinions and the jottings of "young ladies not long enlarged from school"?

Commentators saw in these trends journalism's fall from the status of a *profession* (akin to medicine or law) to what *Saturday Review* editor Arthur Baumann, writing in 1920, called "a branch of commerce" (621). Being a "branch of commerce" meant not only that newspapers were themselves commodities for sale, subject to capitalist overproduction, but that their revenues were based largely upon the sale of advertisements, which were attempts to activate the desires of consumers. Newspapers had become an integral mechanism in the machine of commerce. For anyone who felt that laissez-faire capitalism had not lived up to its promise, or that the promise itself was bankrupt—a group that included left- and right-leaning radicals, many modernists, and young people ready to jettison their parents' faith in commerce and empire (such as Rose Macaulay's Jane Potter)—the modern press was an evil of the system. Female journalists found themselves doubly devalued by this discourse, as both the decline of newspapers and the larger rise of consumerism were blamed on women: Baumann, writing in 1920, traced the decline in newspapers to publishers' discovery that appealing to women was the best way to sell ads.

> Women have always spent; formerly the husband's money, now they spend their own, and their husband's, if they have got one. To one man who buys a paper nowadays, there are perhaps ten women. For the majority of women there is but one topic of real interest, namely, clothes. I wish some statistician would supply me with a calculation of the thousands of pounds spent every day in printing plates of women's clothes, and paying people to write about them. [. . .] But it must be obvious that women have exercised a deteriorating influence on the Press. The only hope is that the small number of sane and thoughtful women may increase with time. The present orgy of extravagance and immodesty cannot last for ever. (626)

Here, anxiety about the new press becomes entangled with a sexually inflected fear of consuming women. Such arguments illustrate what Rita Felski calls the "feminization of modernity," a process in which commentators align the concept of the "modern"—as a pejorative that signifies cultural decay—with "a pessimistic vision of an unpredictable yet curiously passive femininity seduced by the glittering phantasmagoria of an emerging consumer culture" (62). Journalism had shifted from its imagined artistic or public service mission into the (feminine) realm of the commodity. For serious writers, particularly those who saw themselves as adversarial to the mainstream, the standard positions were outrage at the daily press's imbecility or studious concern about its social effects— the views expressed by many modernists, and by the fictional Arthur Gideon in *Potterism.*

But such strident renunciations were problematic for women writers. To adopt them could mean to embrace the misogynist strain in modern radicalism that associates the decay of journalism with the "womanisation of the press"—

a strain evident in T. S. Eliot's satiric lyric, "The Boston Evening Telegraph," which associates a dessicated, feminized New England culture with the newspaper in the title (*Collected Poems* 20). Modernists like Eliot and Ezra Pound proclaimed their distance from the mass-circulation press; Eliot set himself up with the small-circulation *Criterion* to issue the aesthetic and social criticism he would later term "minority journalism" ("Journalists" 237), while Pound, during his years in England, moved from little magazine to little magazine and touted the smallness of his audience as its virtue: "I join these words for four people. / . . . world, I am sorry for you, / You do not know these four people" (205).[3] Abandoning the public sphere made less sense for activist women, who had seen journalism contribute to parliamentary action on suffrage and other feminist issues.[4] For Rebecca West, who in 1919 had reached 300,000 *Daily News* readers arguing that England was in need of its first female MPs ("Women in the House"), the English press might be ill, but it must be saved; her critiques are those of a concerned insider, not a scornful outsider. Motivated in part by the political potential in such large readerships, West and Holtby wrote for publications of many types and sizes.[5] In addition to such political considerations, the journalistic world was often more welcoming to women than the literary world—a condition exemplified by Pound's wresting of the *New Freewoman* from its feminist-socialist-environmentalist basis to the modernist literary cause. The journal's transition to the modernist landmark *Egoist* entailed the ouster of Rebecca West as literary editor and the gradual marginalization of editor Dora Marsden.[6] West, Holtby, and Macaulay all made their names as journalists before achieving success as creative writers: West was well known and in demand for her acid tongue as a reviewer before her first novel appeared and while her critical study of Henry James was being ignored by the *Times Literary Supplement*.[7] When Holtby achieved commercial and critical success as a novelist with her final novel, *South Riding*, her work had been a staple in newspapers and magazines for almost twenty years. Their experience suggests strongly that, for young women "just enlarged from school," journalism was a surer bet than literature.

So the writers anthologized here approach the problem of the press with more ambivalence and balance than their male contemporaries ordinarily brought to the subject. Macaulay, for instance, satirizes particular elements of the daily newspaper but resists blanket generalizations or fixed conclusions. West, Holtby, and Macaulay openly dispute the assumption that women are to blame for the state of newspaper content. Scatterbrained editors—not women readers—are the true audience for articles on "why one would not marry a curate," Macaulay argues in "What the Public Wants," reprinted here. She upbraids the silliness of the penny press and the jingoism of the "respectable" dailies, but finds a solution in neither the aesthetic isolation of the little magazines nor the snobby superiority of the intellectual weeklies. Somewhat ambivalently, she defends the public that is pandered to by the mass press and scorned by the intellectual press, suggesting that neither really knows "what the public wants." In "The Future of Journalism," West argues that the prevalence of gossip responds not to demand from the public but from institutional inertia. The public *does* want serious political commentary, but no one is providing it, she argues. Such remarks undermine the capitalist logic that whatever appears in the press must represent "what the public wants" so long as the papers sell copies.

But if women writers could not adopt wholesale the common wisdom about the press, neither could they abstain from the discussion. It was largely a matter of self-defense, of clearing a space from which they could work and reach readers without assuming the taint of mass journalism. As women known primarily as journalists, Macaulay, West, and Holtby faced not only the general distrust of their profession but also prejudices particular to women journalists, including the notion that women were unsuited to the news pages and had better stick to traditionally female outlets, such as serialized fiction or the women's pages. St. John Ervine pleaded with Holtby to write novels and abandon her political journalism, which he called "little bloody notes for *Time and Tide*" on "causes dead before she began to write them" (Shaw 256). Even Mrs. F. Billington, who as a news correspondent in the 1890s was a journalistic pioneer, suggested that "the greater part of woman's work on the Press lies in more domestic interests" and described the profession as "very far from being a generally suitable one for women" (101–2). Much of the mass-circulation press throughout this period affirmed familiar stereotypes of women. The daily "women's pages" and the immensely popular women's magazines focused on matters domestic and cosmetic, channeling reactionary pressure for women to focus on tending their homes and husbands.[8] Resistance to serious women's journalism often matched resistance to women in politics, as in St. John Ervine's derision of Holtby's "bloody causes" or in the declaration of Mary Grieve, the world-famous editor of *Woman* magazine, that it would be "manifestly wrong" for such magazines to address political issues (Grieve 53). In 1906, when Northcliffe launched what he claimed was Britain's first experiment in women's journalism (though in fact the women's magazines, often managed and written by women, date back to the 1870s), he called the paper the *Daily Mirror* on the ground that it "was to be a reflection of feminine interests; what more suitable than a mirror?" (Jones 228).

Faced with this marketplace, in which "women's journalism" could signify vanity, consumerism, and gossip, writers like Macaulay, West, and Holtby set out to attack these tendencies and to practice a politically engaged journalism of their own, one invested in social reform and aimed, in part, at reforming journalism itself to this end. Macaulay and Holtby both satirized the frivolity of much women's journalism while West, disturbed by the lack of political awareness she observed in England, lamented the scarcity of political opinion in the daily press and urged the strengthening of the "weekly organs of opinion" ("Function of the Weekly Review" 115). Holtby's career is particularly informed by a faith in the political power of journalism: she wrote in support of socialist and feminist initiatives, the League of Nations, and indigenous rights in South Africa. Her witty and wide-ranging survey of the English press, "The Modern Press: Edited to Entertain," is reprinted in full here.

While most feminists could agree that newspapers had a critical part to play in the politics of the nation, many found the relationship between journalism and the arts more difficult to untangle. All four of the writers reprinted here divided their careers between journalism and creative writing and felt the conflicts created by this duality. Holtby wrote that she could never make up her mind whether she wanted to be a novelist or a "publicist"—a "reforming type of person or a writing type of person" (Holtby and Brittain, *Letters* 134). West, jealous of her time while she worked on her second, modernist novel *The Judge*, wrote "I hate *hate* HATE journalism" in a 1922 letter (*Selected Letters* 52). And all four wrote scores of book reviews, which were much in demand in the marketplace and which highlighted the troubled symbiosis of journalism and literature. They themselves were stung by negative reviews and aware that personal politics and serendipity could determine how one's work was reviewed, which in turn could diminish one's sales and reputation.

Indeed, it is largely because of the power newspapers exert over the literary landscape that modernism and journalism became antagonists in the early twentieth century. Behind Ezra Pound's attack on the "smugness of 'The Times'" (254) lay the perception that most mass-circulation newspapers and many intellectual weeklies looked askance at avant-garde literature, making them enemies of "newness . . . sworn foe[s] to free speech and good letters" (254). Beyond personal enmity and careerism, two historical developments fueled this antagonism: the explosion in the number of books being issued for the English market, and the fact that early twentieth-century newspapers dedicated little space to reviews. Neither the dailies nor more "high-brow" periodicals could come close to reviewing everything that came out; newspaper reviews often consisted of one short paragraph. Poets and novelists rightly feared that their work, never having been reviewed, would sink instantly into obscurity. "Praise or blame is a minor consideration," novelist Douglas Goldring wrote in 1932. "Silence is the lethal weapon" (290). Modernists responded by creating the little magazines as platforms for creative work and criticism and by writing for the intellectual weeklies, both of which regularly directed broadsides at the mainstream press. Such specialized publications provided a needed outlet but also served as a reminder that, like it or not, modernists were constructing a minority culture.

In "Reviewing" (reprinted here) Virginia Woolf takes up the public press's failures in literary criticism. The essay's experimental nature and uneasy tone make it difficult to tell how serious she is in proposing her solution—that reviews be banned in favor of a service in which expert readers consult with authors in a doctor-patient style relationship. What is clear is Woolf's sense that the popular press was ill-equipped to deal with the flood of books it was being asked to review. Woolf situates her argument in a history of book reviewing that emphasizes the historical relationship between newspapers and literature, and communicates what is currently at stake for creative writers. Figuring the reviewer as an unwelcome voyeur and a "formidable insect," Woolf ignores the contradiction that she herself had been, through most of the 1920s, one of the most prolific and sought-after book reviewers in England. The contradiction was too much for Leonard Woolf, who appended a two thousand-word defense of reviewing to the essay and published the pair as a pamphlet for the Hogarth Press.

The range of attitudes this section covers can be situated between Woolf and Macaulay. Woolf's position as an avant-gardist and deep suspicion of male-dominated institutions led her, ultimately, to imagine a writing life outside the press as it existed in her time. The private consultation system of "Reviewing," like the private printing press of *Three Guineas*, constitutes an imaginary solution to the real problem of the writer's relationship with the press, a solution ingenious but fanciful, ultimately utopian. Macaulay was more conventional but wider-ranging and more balanced. *Potterism* employs a clever if not radical use of point of view to deflate the silliness of the newspapers *and* the modernist's hyperbolic attack against it; three first-person narrators voice multiple opinions on journalism, each revealing its own limitations and excesses. The haughty "anti-Potterite" Gideon is balanced by the scientist Katherine Varick, who suggests the Potter press is "usually right. [. . .] That's the queer thing about it. It sounds always wildly wrong, [. . .] and all the sane, intelligent people laugh at it, and then it turns out to have been right. Look at the way it used to say that Germany was planning war; it was mostly the stupid people who believed it, and the intelligent people who didn't; but all the time Germany was" (30–31). A fourth, omniscient narrator gets the novel's last word, noting what is laughable and sentimental in the daily press *and* what is pretentious and haughty in those who define themselves against it. Gideon emerges as "a pathetic figure [. . .] the intolerant precisian, fighting savagely against the tide of loose thinking that he saw surging in upon him" (206). Macaulay's narrator here, as elsewhere, stands above the fray, revealing press excesses without attacking "the great sentimental public," whose multifariousness and opacity are, as she concludes in "What the Public Wants," "quite right."

Notes

1. Cynthia L. White documents the growth of women's magazines—both circulation figures and number of titles—from 1875 through World War I (69). This expansion created jobs (though staffs were often small—five to ten full-time employees), and a seemingly inexhaustible market for freelance submissions, particularly of serial fiction (87).

2. For calling my attention to these statistics, I am indebted to Fiona Hackney, author of the doctoral dissertation "They Opened up a Whole New World: Femininity, Domesticity, and Modernity in Women's Magazines, 1919–1939." Goldsmith College, University of London, 2006.

3. For a discussion of conflicting modernist attitudes towards the commodification of journalism, see Mark Morrisson's *The Public Face of Modernism*, 5–6, 21, and passim.

4. See Onslow, especially chapter 9, for an account of the nineteenth-century tradition of women's political journalism that set the precedent for women like West and Holtby.

5. West was particularly varied in the outlets she wrote for over her sixty-year career, writing for little magazines and radical journals (*Blast* and the *New Freewoman* both in its original form and when it became the modernist *Egoist*). She wrote as a young woman for the Labour *Daily Chronicle* and the socialist *Daily News*, contributed often to the feminist-socialist *Time and Tide*, and wrote for both intellectual and mainstream publications, from the *New Statesman* and the American *Bookman* to the *New Yorker* and the mass-circulation daily the *Evening Standard*, in the 1930s and 1940s. A partial list of publications to which Holtby contributed includes the *Yorkshire Post* and *Manchester Guardian*, both large provincial daily papers; London dailies the *News Chronicle*, *Evening Standard*, and the socialist *Daily Herald*; the intellectual weeklies *The New Statesman*, the *Nation and Athenaeum*, and *Time and Tide*, of which she became a director in 1926.

6. See Janet Lyon for a rethinking of this key moment in modernist history, which she reads as "literary expansionism" on Pound's part, which led to the journal's politics being de-emphasized as it became "perceived as a literary organ" (140–41). See also Scott (85–88), and, for a view somewhat more charitable to Pound, Morrisson, who reads the switch to *The Egoist* as a "packaging" decision to which Marsden consented (103).

7. See *Selected Letters of Rebecca West*, 323 n.6.

8. See White, 88–91, 98–101, and passim. Particularly after World War I, women's magazines, White argues, are marked by "a sustained effort to curb restlessness on the part of wives and to popularize the career of housewife and mother" (100). Hackney, in her 2002 address "The Publisher, the Editor, the Advertiser," disputed this account, suggesting that, for many women writers and editors of women's magazines, feminism was a valued part of a larger trend toward greater economic and political liberty for women.

Works Cited

Altick, Richard. "The Sociology of Authorship: The Social Origins, Education, and Occupations of 1,100 British Writers, 1800–1935." *Bulletin of the New York Public Library* 66 (June 1962): 389–404.

Baumann, Arthur A. "The Functions and Future of the Press." *Fortnightly Review* 107 (April 1920): 620–27.

Billington, Mrs. F. "Our Leading Lady Journalists." *Pearson's Magazine* 11 (July 1896): 101–11.

Brittain, Vera, and Winifred Holtby. *Testament of a Generation: The Journalism of Vera Brittain and Winifred Holtby,* edited and introduced by Paul Berry and Alan Bishop. London: Virago, 1985.

Briffault, Robert. "The Wail of Grub Street." *English Review* 32 (June 1921): 512–16.

Eliot, T. S. *Collected Poems, 1909–1962.* New York: Harcourt Brace, 1963.

———. "Journalists of Yesterday and Today." *New English Weekly* 16 (February 8, 1940): 237–38.

Ervine, St. John. "The Future of the Press—II." *The Spectator* 145 (November 29, 1930): 836–37.

Felski, Rita. *The Gender of Modernity.*

Ford, Ford Madox (E. R.). "The Critical Attitude: The Passing of the Great Figure." *English Review* 4.1 (December 1909): 101–10.

Goldring, Douglas. "Reviewers Reviewed." *English Review* 54.3 (March 1932): 290–95.

Grieve, Mary. *Millions Made My Story.* London: Victor Gollancz, 1964.

Hackney, Fiona. "The Publisher, the Editor, the Advertiser, and the Reader: Popular British Women's Magazines in the Interwar Period." *Places of Exchange: Magazines, Journals, and Newspapers in British and Irish Culture, 1688–1945.* International Conference. Glasgow, Scotland, July 25–27, 2002.

Holtby, Winifred, and Vera Brittain. *Selected Letters of Winifred Holtby and Vera Brittain.* Ed. Brittain and Geoffrey Handley-Taylor. Bath: Cedric Chivers Ltd., 1960.

Jones, Kennedy. *Fleet Street and Downing Street.* London: Hutchinson, 1920.

Keating, P. J. *The Haunted Study: A Social History of the English Novel.* London: Secker and Warburg, 1989.

Lyon, Janet. *Manifestoes.*

Macaulay, Rose. *Potterism.* New York: Boni and Liveright, 1920.

Morrisson, Mark. *The Public Face of Modernism.* Madison: University of Wisconsin Press, 2002.

Onslow, Barbara. *Women of the Press in Nineteenth-Century Britain.* New York: St. Martin's Press, 2000.

Pound, Ezra. *Ezra Pound's Poetry and Prose: Contributions to Periodicals.* 10 vols. Ed. Lea Baechler, A. Walton Litz, and James Longenbach. New York: Garland, 1991.

Scott, Bonnie Kime. *Refiguring Modernism. Vol. 1: The Women of 1928.*

Shaw, Marion. *The Clear Stream: A Life of Winifred Holtby.* London: Virago, 1999.

West, Rebecca. "The Function of the Weekly Review." *Time and Tide* 8 (December 9, 1927): 114–15.

———. *Selected Letters of Rebecca West,* ed. Bonnie Kime Scott. New Haven: Yale University Press, 2000.

————. "Women in the House." *Daily News* (July 19, 1918): 3.
————. *The Young Rebecca.*
White, Cynthia. *Women's Magazines, 1693–1968.* London: Michael Johnson, 1970.

REBECCA WEST

The Future of the Press IV: The Journalist and the Public

Mr. St John Ervine's articles on "The Future of the Press" have left very little unsaid that the person of sound views could wish to say; but I would like to add a footnote concerning one fault of the modern newspaper which I thought he had ascribed to persons who were only partially responsible for it.

The modern newspaper persistently underrates the public's appetite for solid matter of serious interest; it persistently overrates its appetite for drivel. Persons like Mr. St. John Ervine and myself who maintain this position are not moved by mere highbrow bias; during the exercise of our profession we continually receive intimations which can mean nothing else. If I may refer to my own experience, on two occasions in recent years my letter-box was stuffed for weeks with correspondence concerning articles I had written. The first was when I contributed an article to "My Religion" series in the *Daily Express,* the second when I wrote for the same paper an Open Letter to Dean Inge, which involved discussion of the fundamental principles of trade union-ism and democracy. Both these articles were two thousand words long, and in both I was given a free hand. Nearly all the letters, whether they were writ-ten in agreement with my article or not, expressed pleasure that such serious issues had been raised, and a large proportion of them were written by people who said they had received, or whom one could judge to have received, only an elementary school education; and most of them were extremely lively and interesting. I gather, from such of my fellow contributors to the "My Religion" and Open Letter series whom I know, that they had exactly the same experi-ence. Now, this is of enormous significance considering that the general pol-icy of the editor is to cut down articles to as far below a thousand words as possible and restrict the subjects to a certain frivolous and monotonous range. Quite plainly this policy is not giving the public what it wants.

Specific points that have arisen in the last few weeks have made one feel this strongly. It seemed to me that twice lately newspapers have lost oppor-tunities of raising the kind of discussions that interest people. Once was when Lord Birkenhead wrote his pitiably silly letter about the Prayer Book Debate, and in the course of much futility jeered because Mr. Saklatvala had voted on a subject so alien from his racial interests.[1] People were undoubtedly interested in the fact that Mr. Saklatvala had done so; and I wondered that no editor with a real thirst for political education had seen to it that the public realised that, in jeering at Mr. Saklatvala for voting, Lord Birkenhead was expressing an opinion that, because his Battersea constituents have elected a Parsee, they must therefore be disfranchised so far as all matters not within the purview of a Parsee are concerned; and that there was not initiated a brisk discussion on the rival delegate and representative theories of elective government. I thought it even more amazing when the Departmental Committee on the present laws and regulations relating to the early closing of shops issued its report and showed that it was inadvisable to repeal them because the retailers wished the restrictions continued, because they preferred the added leisure they gave to the profits they withheld. The attitude of resentment this has caused in certain quarters is suggestive—"It is unlikely that if the whole of these D.O.R.A. restrictions were abolished forthwith the retailers of tobacco or sweets would lose anything at all. But if they were to lose something, what on earth has that to do with us—the public? The trade must adjust its affairs to suit our convenience. They exist to serve us, not to make profits for them . . ." (No this is not *The Morning Post* calling but *The New Statesman*.) It seemed strange that no politically-minded editor should have faced his readers with the problems arising out of the fact that this attitude of *The New Statesman* was not the attitude taken up, in this case, by the country—which was going to agree that the retailers had the right to refuse work if they wanted to do so—but that it *was* the attitude taken up by the country last year when the trade unionists refused to work when *they* found it inconvenient and proclaimed a general strike.

Conversely, the policy of cramming the paper with personal gossip, concerning which Mr. St. John Ervine spoke some salutary words, is giving the public what they do not want. People of the kind who read *The Observer* and *The Sunday Times* do not realise what a nuisance this has become. Recently an English servant who was with me out in Italy complained to me that she was asking her relatives to stop sending her a certain Sunday newspaper, that I knew to be of old and good standing as a popular rag that thoroughly enjoyed a good murder but was neither scandalous nor indecent, for the reason that there was nothing in it she could read. I asked her to show me a copy, and I was appalled. There was an abundance of advertisement, which was right and proper enough; but of the few pages left one page was given to the daughter of a man who has attained an immense and undeserved reputation who was apparently trying to find out if the family luck would hold by spilling column after column of watery chatter about her friends and acquaintances; another page was given to a woman writer of real charm but with the same limited range of subject; and yet a third was given over to theatrical gossip of the sort that refers more to what goes on behind the scenes than to what goes on in front of the footlights. My servant was naturally bored to death. She is, of course, not above personal gossip, as none of us are. Personal paragraphs like those which composed the old *M.A.P.,* of which we get an echo in *T.P.'s* paragraph in *The Sunday Times,* would probably amuse her and me. But it was then recognised that to be of interest people had to be interesting. When they wrote of the beautiful Countess of Kilmainhamgoal they did tell you she was seven feet tall and twelve inches round the waist, and had blue eyes the size of soup-plates, and was the bosom friend of Queen Alexandra, and lived in a pre-Norman castle covering twenty-thousand acres with two hundred peacocks that had been trained to form fours on the lawn during breakfast; or whatever the essential points of interest about the lady may have been. They did thereby create a mythical figure such as the people like to muse upon, a new manifestation of Venus or Minerva or Juno or Hebe or whonot. There is still a little personal journalism of that sort being done now. The life of the Duchess of York which is appearing in one of the Women's papers just now is a highly competent attempt to create for the people a pleasant ideal on which their minds can work and dream. But nobody's imagination is going to be stimulated by reading, "I went to the Embassy on Tuesday night and saw Captain Chetwynd Chetwynd. He is very good-looking. I like him because though he is good looking he is not conceited. Most of the young men I know who are good-looking are terribly conceited"; or that "Mrs. Mackenzie, of whom Cecil Beaton has just done a delicious photograph, gets her conversation at her parties as she likes it, by lighting her dining-room table by red bulbs set under red glass moulds designed by Brancusi to express the thought form of a Billingsgate porter's favourite oath"; or "I ran into dear old Monty hurrying off after the rehearsals of the Kafoozleum Revue and he told me he was off to see his new filly he has just bought from poor Sir George Jumble, whose retirement from racing seems final." Recondite adventures in the insipid, the artsome, the equine, do not amuse my servant or myself.

Now at first sight, the case against the modern newspaper proprietor seems black. But that I think, is only seeming. But why, if that be so, does he plaster his papers with these blethers of personal gossip? I think that there he is the blind instrument of social forces. Though the public do not want personal gossip now and in such quantities, they did want it once and in very large doses. This was due to Hollywood and Mr. Michael Arlen.[2] Through the pictures, the minds of the people became furnished with a mythology which meant absolutely nothing except the worship of material good-fortune. Of [old] it was not so; Juno represented such moral and intellectual qualities as the ancients with gratitude and a slight air of weariness attributed to the wife, Venus represented the undomesticated forms of love, Minerva wisdom, Hercules strength, Psyche the soul, and so on. But the stars of Hollywood, with the exception of Mary Pickford and Douglas Fairbanks, who mean not so much to this generation, represent absolutely nothing except generalised well-being. Even Venus, though corporeally present, is not allowed by Mr. Will Hays[3] to exercise her spiritual functions. Nothing is more pathetic than the collapse of the dazzling fact of Miss Pola Negri,[4] who should appear before the mind of the people zoned with legends of extravagant passion, under the prudent determination of Hollywood that the world shall be told that she drinks a glass of buttermilk before retiring, and is kind to her mother. It is the glistening and the null that survives each stultifying fame. Fortunate indeed was the advent of Mr. Michael Arlen, who pointed out that if it was the glistening and null we wanted there were plenty of them at hand. Impossible to estimate the disservice that he did the world by persuading a large class of persons, not interesting except when they had talents above the average or historical possessions in the way of land and great houses, that they were interesting in themselves: that Miss Jones, known to her intimates as Poots, and Captain Smith, known to his intimates as Toots, belonged to a faery breed whose voice and glance is enchantment. It would be idle to deny that for a time his thesis was accepted by the bulk of the people with acclamation, and that duchesses were at a premium; and certainly this news was nowhere more gratefully accepted than by the persons themselves. Once this wave of interest let Poots and Toots into the newspapers it was hard to get them out, since Poots loved writing about Toots, and Toots loved writing about Poots, and both basked in the joy of being written about by the other. Sooner or later the truth about Poots and Toots, that they are colossal bores, leaked out. But I doubt if Lord Northcliffe would have been able to turn standard-bread and sweet-peas out of the newspaper with such admirable promptitude when the public got tired of them, if standard-bread and sweet-peas had greatly enjoyed being in the newspapers and exerted considerable social pressure. We are here dealing not with an initial error of a newspaper proprietor but with a superannuated fashion that it must be extremely embarrassing to scrap.

So much for the positive accusation. Now for the negative fault of not supplying solid and serious matter. I cannot help feeling that this is partly due to a deficiency of journalists who want to write that kind of matter. That kind of matter is bound to be chiefly political. A newspaper can carry a certain amount of reviews of art, literature, and music, and science, just as it can carry a certain amount of financial and sporting news, but not very much. Its mainstay must be general news and political writing. I cannot help believing that the modern newspaper proprietor would pay for vivid political writing. Ultimately he wants circulation: as big a circulation as the spending capacity of his advertisers enable him to print papers for. I believe he would pay for vivid political writing if he thought it maintained its circulation. I do not believe he will be so greatly influenced by political ambitions of his own that free and independent writers will be unable to write for him, because I think he is going to be much less politically ambitious than he ever has been before. The newspaper proprietors who have most recklessly expended their resources to get political power have so dismally failed that their colleagues are likely to be deterred from following their example. But I very much doubt whether they will find the people to pay. There is nothing more certain than that the sort of people who twenty to ten years ago were interested in politics to the degree which made them stimulating writers on political affairs are now far more interested in other nations, in art, or literature, or psychology, in the more academic aspects of economics. The other day I met a young girl who was showing all the starry-eyed enthusiasm and self-devotion that before the war landed a lot of young girls like her in the Suffrage Movement. She was using these qualities to get her across the Atlantic in spite of a state of complete impecuniousness, in order that she might study Behaviourism on its native heath. The whole tendency of thought since the beginning of the century has been to make man skeptical of the mind as an instrument. There could be nothing more deterrent from a passionate view of politics. H. W. Massingham and A. G. Gardiner[5] (whose names be for ever blessed) were able to write on the questions of their day because they thought there was such a thing as absolute truth and that it was ascertainable. J. M. Keynes can write just as brilliantly on the questions of his day, but with a pen made a little listless by his consciousness that if some of his friends at Cambridge are right neither he nor the question exists. What could be more damping? He, and all his generation are terrified of acting on information that is given to them by an intellectual mechanism which they have so many sad and grave reasons for distrusting. Until the thought of the century takes a turn which gives them more confidence in themselves there must be a lack of the old vigour and dogmatic writing that used to be the glory of our newspapers. This would be bound to happen whether our newspapers were owned by the present press nobility and gentry, or the Uxbridge Town Council, or Toc H, or whatever.

Time and Tide 9 (March 2, 1928): 194–96.

Notes

1. Frederick Edwin Smith, First Earl of Birkenhead (1872–1930), was a solicitor, the MP for Liverpool, and a conservative anti-Communist. Shapurji Saklatvala (1874–1936), was born in Bombay and in 1905 moved to London, where he would later become the left-leaning MP for Battersea; he agitated for the working class and for decolonization of India. Revisions to the Book of Common Prayer were proposed in 1927 and 1928. Parliament rejected both proposals.

2. Michael Arlen (1895–1956) was born Dikran Kouyoumdjian in Bulgaria and came to England in 1901. His comic fiction was set among the contemporary English aristocracy.

3. West probably means noted English stage, radio, and film comedian Will Hay (1888–1949).

4. Pola Negri (1894–1987), silent film actress. Born Barbara Apollonia Chalipec in Poland.

5. Gardiner and Massingham were both radical editors and writers who worked with West at the *Daily News* during World War I.

ROSE MACAULAY

The Press and the Public

The life of the editor of a newspaper is, it must he supposed, a continual process of selection. Consider, for instance, those amazing (and amazed) periodicals which bloom (unlike the evening primrose) from ten each morning until nightfall, putting forth every two hours or so a fresh flower. Consider the editor, the news editor and the staff of these journals confronted throughout each day by the problem—"Which among to-day's occurrences shall we record? Which shall form the staple of our paper? Which shall be blazoned forth in placards by the wayside? Which, in fact, shall be to-day our Feature?" So they make their selection. Until about lunch-time their minds dwell on horses; their matutinal news is mainly concerned with the competitions of these animals one with another at equine sports and pastimes. Games played with balls also often occupy their morning thoughts; for they believe, very truly, that their readers find pleasure in learning who has excelled in these games. But, about noon-tide, what time their City Lunch Special, or whatever it may be called, makes ready to burgeon forth, news-editors seem to turn to the wider world; and, from then until their final edition brings the day's happenings to a close, they occupy themselves in setting down what they regard as News. I do not know whether they consider first what interests themselves or what they conceive will interest their readers. But, however they do it, they appear, oddly enough, to have arrived somehow at a kind of general convention on the matter. Perhaps the queerest thing about our queer press is the general resemblance of the contents of one newspaper to the contents of another. It would seem as if all editors leapt every day to approximately the same conclusions as to the desires of humanity for information about the world's happenings.

As to the matter thus arbitrarily selected for presentation, many interesting questions rise. Space being limited, I cannot here ask them all, nor, indeed, answer any. But I ask two. At which sections of the reading public are the various items aimed? And do they hit or miss? How much insight, that is, has the journalist into the minds of his fellow-creatures?

There is, of course, some news of almost universal interest, which finds a response in nearly every breast. Of such a kind are informations concerning peace and war, earthquakes, railway accidents, and strikes, weather, food, and Wimbledon. Of such a kind, too, is—"Mare with Rabies Bites Five Cows," and such thrilling fragments from the world of marvels. Then there is the news meant for a section only—political and parliamentary news, foreign news, news of Royal Persons, books or plays, the public utterances of those who publicly utter, and so forth.

But for what section of readers are such statements as this, that you may see any day in almost any paper? "Anne Jones, an old woman of ninety, died at Llanilar last week. Though bedridden, her intellect was still keen." It would be interesting to know if any reader is stirred by this, or so much as says "fancy" to it. Does it, perhaps, interest other old persons, as yet undeceased? But even they can scarcely think it strange, or more than very slightly sad. Old age must come: old women do die: that is incontrovertible. Anne Jones remains a problem to me. Frankly, I believe her to be a journalistic miss. I do not think she reaches any mark.

But I may be wrong. For at least the journalist has tradition on his side. I was reading the other day one of the irregularly issued news sheets of the year 1669, and came on the following: "A certain Rotcheller, called Isaack Chapron, aged eighty-two years, having travelled sixty years through the four parts of the world, is deceased, having ten days before his death abjured his religion in the church of the Jesuits." Here is Anne Jones, a little amplified and adorned, but still, merely an old man deceased. So perhaps there has always been a public which likes to read of deaths, even the deaths in bed of the old.

But why weddings? Are weddings ever interesting, except to the principals and their friends? Is it possible that there are those who read with pleasure of the marriages of those unknown to them? And, if so, why? These functions lack even the interest of universal occurrence; they do not happen to quite everybody, and they do happen to so many as to miss the interest of singularity. Are they, indeed, read? And are there any readers found to care that the bride wore white tulle and the bridesmaids pink gauze, or whatever brides and bridesmaids do wear on such occasions?

Of divorces I will not here speak. I can only presume that those, if any, who like to read of the union of perfect strangers read also with interest of the union's severance. The human mind is, in many cases, a fathomless pit of sentimental sympathies, which it is not for the cold and hard, such as you and I, to probe. Doubtless all these things find a happy home in some eager breast.

Sometimes, indeed often, the press seems to agree that some item in the day's news is of such enthralling interest, so very amazing, that it must usurp all the placards and nearly all the front page of every paper. In this category journalists place crime, and more particularly murder. "So-and-so in the Dock," they will cry. "Amazing Statements"—and in detail will follow the story, which only very occasionally has elements of interest, and is more often commonplace, crude and flat, amazing only to those very easily amazed. Human drama, doubtless, and probably melodrama, but with no intrinsic interest. To sophisticated minds, such stories, thus set forth, are merely a bore; to the fastidious and sensitive they are also a horror and a tragedy. To open one's paper and come on them is like stumbling into a slaughter yard, or into a home for very dull criminal lunatics. To simpler or robuster souls, whose demands are small, the perusal of such matter may be a pleasure. The journalists may be right. They cater mainly, after all, for the simple and the robust. They are catering, in this matter, further, for the streak of brutality which is in the primitive human mind, and which has, ever since we cumbered the earth, delighted in torture, horror, and death—that brutality which sent our ancestors eagerly to watch executions, which sends crowds even now to get as near to an execution as may be, and which loves, if it cannot witness horrors, to read of them. News editors, knowing well that this delight in horror exists, proceed to feed it with anything they can lay their hands on. Murder, suicide, the dismembering of corpses, any grim, stupidly crude thing does. They serve it up, hot and spiced, to tickle the palates of the gourmets, and advertise their day's menu with a flourish.

It is interesting to speculate what proportion of newspaper readers are bored by this police-court material, and in what proportion it meets a demand. Presumably journalists have thus speculated, and made their decision. They may be right. We are a simple people, with a simple taste in reading matter. Many of us like to read of others being murdered, cut up, and put away in hen-houses or trunks. More will read these tales if they are there, as they will read anything else. Newspapers have us in the hollow of their hands, out of which we meekly eat; we are not particular. All we want (most of us) is a nice piece of reading as we go home from work in the bus or train. We do not demand tales of crime—any other exciting story does for us. But the purveyors of news have decided that we are to have these things, in as large doses as possible. Warm human life-stuff: that is what the news editor (himself, probably, a simple fellow) likes to give us. The same quality perhaps makes him an affectionate husband and father. It does not make him, for those who care little for warm human life-stuff, an interesting or entertaining selector of the world's news. But he may well retort that such should not read the penny press, and that, if they do, they can very easily omit such material as they do not care for.

And, no doubt, he is quite right. Anyhow he has always been the same. The earliest news sheets were full of the same kind of sensational drama—wives poisoning their husbands, parents butchering children, and what not. The public taste has always been thus diagnosed, whether accurately or not.

But of one thing I am sure. Most newspaper readers like leading articles. For these curious effusions sum up our incoherent thoughts for us and give them shape—whether the same shape as the leader writer's or one widely different, called into being by opposition. Some people can only maintain themselves in what they consider sound political principles by regularly reading opposition leaders. Before the leaders of the papers with which they are in agreement, their faith falters and dims; it looks so weak, so improbable, put like that. [. . .]

But more people prefer to see their own thoughts about events set out for them in print; it is nearly as satisfactory as having written them themselves, and how much less trouble!

I close with a suggestion. I would urge the newspaper world to try the experiment of leaving out most of what they at present publish, of publishing much of what they at present leave out, and see if the result is not accepted meekly by the public and consumed with unquestioning relish. For we are wonderfully tamed.

A Casual Commentary. New York: Boni and Liveright, 1926. 84–90.

ROSE MACAULAY

What the Public Wants

This is a topic upon which we, the public, talk a great deal, and rightly. What we want. The desires of humanity and the reasons thereof. What can be more important, more vitally interesting to us all? The question seems to cover a rather wide field of philosophical and metaphysical inquiry, certainly, but that should be no hindrance to any self-respecting journalist such as myself from settling it in a few brief pages.

The public is, of course, all of us. No one, however private he may feel, can evade that common doom of publichood. We are each a head of that monstrous hydra. Well then, what do we want? And why? Can we reduce our many million minds, with their many million longings, to any sort of a common appetite? I suppose so. With all our differences, we all want, as the Romans of old did, bread and circuses, and a little drink; we want leisure and comfort, peace and plenty (which means, I suppose, a lot to eat), a little adventure, good company, something to amuse and interest us, money to turn in our pockets; we want to scrape through life with as little annoyance as may be, and to have a rapid and easy death. We want something on which to exercise our faculty of admiration; we want, that is to say, some variant of that which we call beauty. We want success, love, and the appreciation of our fellows; and some of us want to reproduce our kind.

But when it comes to translating these desires into concrete terms, we have not, most of us, much idea of how to do it. We don't know, in fact, what we want; in fact, the majority of us want, or are willing to take, very nearly everything that is offered us. We can be induced to believe that we want almost anything, from war to that Kruschen feeling. In consequence, we are, as Burke put it, the theatre for mountebanks and impostors. We are not particular. We are, in a sense, always that eager, silly, gaping public of the streets, agog for we know not what, ready to run anywhere to see anything—a procession, or a bus accident, or a dead horse. I made part of such a public the other day. Seeing a vast concourse of persons assembled at Oxford Circus, lining the pavements in patient immobility several deep and at least a hundred yards long, all apparently waiting expectantly for something to occur, or pass, or function in some intriguing manner, I inquired of a policeman, as I joined them (not wishing, naturally, to miss anything), what they were hoping to see. His usual expression of benignant contempt increased. "They don't know," he said. "Do none of them know?" I asked. "I shouldn't think so," he replied. "They just stop because they see other people stopping. They don't know what they're doing, or why, half the time." Obviously the public, as viewed by policemen, doesn't know what it wants. Except that it wants, of course, if it can, to do wrong, to transgress the law in some way. In this it resembles the public as seen by all officials, the public against whom rules are made, who are forbidden to pick the flowers and shrubs, or trespass in woods, or enter the sanctums of station-masters, or take home the books in the British Museum reading-room, or spit in trains. It is obvious what *they* want. They want to do wrong. If officials did not know that we want to do wrong, all these prohibitions would not be put up against us. Viewed by the official mind, we are all miserable sinners, with no health in us. On the other hand, and in spite of this, some kindness is shown us. Sometimes a notice is to be seen announcing that, for the convenience of the public, such and such an arrangement has been made. Sinners we are, but not beyond the pale of treatment by kindness.

Then (I am considering different aspects of the public, the whole being too heterogeneous and giddy a crowd to think about all at once) there is the public as seen by our politicians. To the politician we are something of a dark horse. He does not know what we want; he wishes he did. Do we know ourselves? Vaguely we know that we don't want the politician, that we do want cheap things, no taxes, peace abroad and at home, plenty, a government which interferes with us as little as possible, and no fuss. These large, vague things we want. But do we know which political party will bring us most of them? We do not. We only know that none will bring us much of any of them. We believe, most of us, that one political party is just about as foolish as another, and we rather like to have a House of Commons consisting of three minorities, so that none of them can do anything at all, since we have a well-founded belief that doing is a deadly thing, doing ends in death. We certainly do not want an active government; but what our other political desires are I doubt if most of us know.

And what about that strange, hungry, rapacious creature, the public as seen, or imagined, by the newspaper and magazine editor? There is something a little sinister about this being. Some editors, apparently, see it as a kind of village imbecile, and throw it the provender they believe to be suitable to it. Others believe that there is a public more sophisticated, which wants news of art, politics, literature, and the world at large. But anyone who has ever been asked to write for the cheaper press will have had experiences very significant in the light they cast on what a certain kind of editor believes the public to want. Some time ago, for instance, the literary editor of a newspaper wrote to me asking if I would write an article for his paper on "Why I Would Not Marry a Curate." I rang him up and gave a suitable reply. He said, Well then, would I write about a caveman. I intimated that I was very ignorant of anthropology, and suggested that he should obtain the services of some ethnologist. I was informed that I had mistaken the editor's meaning; what he meant was, not an article on such of our rude forbears as used to live in caves, but on the heroes of the novels of Miss Ethel M. Dell and some of our other contemporary novelists. I said that, unfortunately, I had no acquaintance with the novels to which he referred, so that I could hardly write adequately about the characters contained in them. He said, Well then, would I send him a list of some subjects upon which I could and would write. As the remuneration promised well, I did this. I sent what seemed to me quite a reasonable list of suggestions. But I received a reply saying that I had mistaken his object and the desire of his public, which was to have articles dealing with the lighter side of life. I perceived that by the lighter side of life he meant cavemen, wives, husbands, and marrying curates. Something human, in fact. I felt unable to cope with this, so negotiations were broken off. Shortly afterwards another editor inquired if I would write on "Should Clever Women Marry?" Again I felt unable for the task. Well, there you are. These editors are sure that their public want this kind of stuff. Personally, I believe the editors are quite wrong. I do not believe there is any public which wants anything of the kind. But there is a public which swallows, apparently, anything it gets, and never says what it does want, because it doesn't know. So editors have no resource but to pander to their own morbid taste, hoping that it may also be the taste of others. Those editors who are themselves interested in cavemen, the marriage of clever women; or of members of the Royal Family, or divorces, or murders, or street accidents, or the week-end occupations of Prime Ministers, or photographs of Prime Ministers' daughters, or peers' romances, or other such stuff of life, fill their papers with these things, in touching and apparently never contravened faith. Those editors who are more interested in politics, or strikes, or ancient tombs, or dwindling francs, or the relations of countries one with another, or the utterances of our legislators in conclave, also attribute these interests to their readers. And we, the public, never say. We buy, between us, all the papers, all the magazines, we lick it all up, because it's there. Do we rise up and say, "we want more news of the domestic habits of the Chinese, or of the stars, or less about cat imprisoned in burning house?" We do not. Apathetically we ask for nothing and accept all. We do not cry out even against leading articles. It doesn't follow that we *read* all that is put before us. But—and this is a very solemn thought—there is probably no part of a paper which someone does not peruse. Except, possibly, "Why I Would Not Marry a Curate." I never heard of anyone outside a newspaper office reading that. I do not think any women do. Women (I mean by women, of course, women that are women, not—well, not the other kind) read "Why I Should Not Wash Clothes with Soda," or "Why I Should Not Give Baby Bacon," or "How to Give My Hair that Lovely Sheen," or the weather reports—but I think "Why I Would Not Marry a Curate" panders solely to the depraved taste of the editor who gets it written. All the same, no one remonstrates, for we don't know what we want. Stay; now I think of it there is one exception to, this rule—we do want and demand "All the Winners." [. . .]

Is there, then, no body of opinion, however small, which knows what it wants and does not want (artistically) and why? Well, I suppose, at any given moment, trained tastes agree, more or less (mostly less), that this is good and that bad. But how fickle is this academy of taste! What it admires changes from decade to decade, almost from day to day. The eternal wheel spins round. Our fathers despised the wax fruit and horsehair and antimacassars and sham Gothic of our grandfathers. To-day we are beginning again to think these things good. Our Edwardian forbears admired the futurists and cubists. To-day we think these persons crude, and the Sitwells have lately attempted to recanonise Raphael and even to enthrone Carlo Dolci. We are agreed now that Shakespeare wrote well. But was he thought to write well two hundred years ago? He was not. Even landscape is subject to the ups and downs of taste. In the eighteenth century we admired the ordered grove, the shrubbery with statues, the dædal earth and the pœcile park, and swooned to think of mountains. In the early nineteenth century mountains came in with romance, and fed the Victorians' dark Byronic moods. In our return to-day to the eighteenth century it is possible that the trim landscape may have again its turn, together with Pope, Addison, and the coffee-house wits. No; there is no fixed standard of taste. Aesthetically there may be good, there is certainly bad. As Browning put it, there may be heaven, there must be hell—but has mankind ever been of a mind as to which is which? And we, the great public, not trying to solve that Platonic riddle, fall back agreeably and with an admirable impartiality on liking very nearly everything. And quite right too.

A Casual Commentary. London: Methuen, 1925; New York: Boni & Liveright, 1926. 29–39.

WINIFRED HOLTBY

Modern Newspaper: Edited to Entertain

Contemporary society dreads leisure. For most modern Britons the unforgiving minutes need not necessarily be filled with sixty seconds'-worth of business done; but it must be filled with something. Preferably it must be filled several things at once. We like to smoke as we talk, to listen to jazzy music while we eat, to knit as we read, to turn on the wireless when we play bridge, and to look at the newspapers while we travel. The popularity of the railway bookstall is a sign of the times. The newsboy who sells his papers at bus-stops is another. Even while flying across the Channel in a heavy gale, passengers are frequently observed to have their eyes devoutly upon the reassuring print of the financial columns of *The Times*.

This habit of reading newspapers while in motion has an immense social significance. During the nineteenth century the newspaper was a serious work devoted mainly to political information, to be read by middle- and upper-class fathers of families, in the solitude of the smoking-room, at the club, and, perhaps more rarely, at the breakfast table. Leading articles ran easily to 1,500 words; parliamentary debates were reported at length, and home and foreign news was set down with a solemnity worthy of this recording Angel. The *Daily News* of 1901, when Mr. George Cadbury took it over, was a very different affair from the *News-Chronicle* of today. The *Daily Graphic,* which appeared as the first daily picture paper in 1890, with solemn engravings of royalty in side-whiskers and dignified photographs of foreign statesmen, would hardly recognize its more frivolous decadents in our year of grace.

These papers are intended for a stationary public, for men and women who sat down to their newspapers as today they still sit down to lace their boots. We have frequently attributed the revolution which took place at the beginning of this century to the genius of Alfred Charles Harmsworth, the late Lord Northcliffe, who not only assailed the standards and prejudices of his contemporaries by bringing out the *Daily Mail* at halfpenny in 1896, thus presenting them with a terrific problem in competition by providing as good a news-service as any of them at half the price, but who actually grasped the fact that an immense new public existed in the first generation to be released, partially literate, from our national system of elementary schools. But I do not think that the success of his new methods, which turned Fleet Street upside down, was due entirely to his own commercial genius, nor to his wooing of the graduates of Standard Seven; it was due also to the growth of our suburban population, to the development of our methods of local transport, to the bus and the tram, and the "8.30 to the office," which transformed us from a nation of stationary to a nation of mobile readers.

Today there still exist a few great daily and Sunday papers written for the reader who takes his time. The twopennies—*The Times,* the *Manchester Guardian,* and the *Yorkshire Post*—a few of the more dignified provincial papers, and the *Daily Telegraph* and the *Morning Post* assume that there are still men and women who sit over a leisurely breakfast table, or settle down in an arm-chair deliberately to "read the paper." But they are not, I believe, the controllers of the greatest circulations. The others assume, quite rightly, that they are bought to be read in tea-shops, trams, tubes, trains, barbers' shops, motor-cars, and aeroplanes; that they are the bulwarks against the assault of idleness put up by a public disliking absolute repose; that they are the traveling companions of a nation that spends so much of its time, not walking, not riding, not driving restive horses, nor pedaling a dollar-farthing bicycle, but being moved about from place to place as passengers. Whatever the hymn may say, he who runs cannot read in any comfort; but he who travels in a smooth-running vehicle not only can, but does. The great mass of modern newspapers are planned precisely to suit this traveling public.

When I say "the mass of modern newspapers" I do not mean that today there are many different papers where once were only few. Amalgamation has reduced the number of different papers, but now the circulations are enormous. In 1900 there were nine London evening papers; today there are only three. But nearly nine times as many Londoners read evening papers nowadays as read them then; and as for the editions, they seem to pour out at every hour. As with so many other commodities, the great economic problem of the modern newspaper is distribution rather than production.

But the circumstances of the consumption having changed, the quality of the paper has changed with them. The older newspaper was written largely for information, the new one is written largely for entertainment, and, indeed, it provides as rich and varied an entertainment for a penny as anything in the world could be expected to do.

Brief and Bright is the modern motto. Lord Northcliffe's rule, that nothing on his leader pages during the War should be more than 300 words long, changed not only the whole make-up of the paper, but the style of journalism. It is, of course, impossible to tell the truth about any political or economic matter of importance in 300 words. It is impossible to convey a balanced presentation of opinion; but it is perfectly possible to be sensational, malicious, stirring, funny, or fierce; and all these qualities are more entertaining than the more sombre virtues of rectitude and wisdom.

The news has changed. In the few journals still written for information the world still appears to be moved by large, rather remote, impersonal forces. Parliamentary debates and diplomatic actions, floods in the Mississippi or wars in China, the centenaries of great scientists or the eccentricities of the gold standard—these may appear on Saturday to be the important events in that vision of reality seen by *The Times*. But on Sunday the *News of the World* appears, recording the incidents of the self-same period, and finding there Bandits Loved by Beautiful Novelists, a Welter-weight who Runs away before a Great Fight, Marriage Bar for Girl Aviator, and Couple Gassed in Love Nest. The dailies which provide News as Entertainment appear to adopt the standard of values of the *News of the World* rather than those of *The Times* and the *Manchester Guardian*. The more a paper is able to present a world-vision of Actresses, Adultery, Heroism of Pet Dogs, Foul Play Suspected, Records Broken by Beautiful Girl Athletes, and Pathos of Aged Doctor's Deaths, the higher its circulation rises. For the large impersonal forces seem alien to the Man in the Bus, and there is hardly time between Piccadilly Circus and Leicester Square to grasp the full drama of Gold Monopoly, or the interaction of competitive tariffs and the Disarmament Position.

But if newspapers take their name from the news, they take their revenue from advertisements, and I think that the reason why the public tolerates the use of so much of its pennyworth for the advocacy of drapery and skin-foods, is that the technique of advertising has been developed precisely [along] the lines of entertaining the Tube traveler.

Even in *The Times*, advertisements can be entertaining. I know that the messages in the Agony Column are not what they seem. This, taken from a recent issue, probably means, "Shell preference falling. Sell out immediately and buy Brazilian Railroad debentures"; but what it says is: "Dily—overjoyed at your note. Regret reply delayed. All's well and unchanged. You have no need to worry. Be happy, dearest, and get well. Fondest love—Bee." Now, whatever the real intention of the person who composed that, I suggest that nicer feeling and a kinder disposition could hardly be displayed.

Business offers are no less intriguing. Here, for instance, is a charmer: "Managing Directors Please Note.—Does any manufacturing or other concern want a live young (34) advertising and sales promotion man with successes to his credit? Can guarantee first-rate advertising and stimulus to sales; at present holding important managerial post with large concern; must be in progressive British house (large or small); requires reasonably free hand and £1,200 per annum, or would consider smaller salary and share in profits." I like that. I like the "take it or leave it" negligence of the thing; I like the "or would consider." And I must confess that I like the "live young (34)." Being one year younger than this very-far-from-moribund young gentleman, his assurance of youth is consoling, to say nothing of his insistence that he is not dead.

Personally, I can hardly pass a "House to Let" advertisement. I loathe moving. I pray that my address may remain the same for years, yet photographs of Sixteenth Century Cottages, or announcements of "Chelsea Studios, overlooking River" drive me to embarrassing indiscretions, and the taste is quite a common one. The more the public moves, the more sentimental becomes its interest in the permanence of "homes."

But the best of all advertisements are those which tell the True Life Stories of ladies rescued from neurasthenia by nerve tonics; of gentlemen who lost love and fortune through a sad falling off of the hair, miraculously restored by So-and-so's hair-tonic. I am astounded by the audacity of those good wives who declare, openly giving their own names and addresses, that by Whatnot's Secret System they cured their husbands of drinking. Does it never happen, I wonder, that the husbands, opening their Sunday paper, recognize these formidable photographs of their treacherous wives, puffed hair, gilt locket, dentured smile and all (to say nothing of the brazenly admitted name and address), and learn there for the first time why the good beer no longer tasted sweet, and why the magic of whisky had departed? And, thinking of all the joys now gone for ever (since the Remedy is Guaranteed Permanent), has no person's husband ever seized the hatchet, and then and there exacted the full price of that worst crime of all, "doing good to a man against his will"?

Another popular modern feature is the Woman's Page. Nearly all papers have them, though I believe that few women read them. Most men do. And no wonder, for they deal with those little domestic details so dear to fathers of families—how to make nails stick firmly in crumbling plaster, how to avoid those wrinkles under the chin, how to manure roses, how to make pen-wipers out of last year's felt hat. Nobody wants to make pen-wipers out of last year's felt hat. For many of us, last year's is also this year's; and in any case, who wants pen-wipers? What, I should like to know, are black skirts for? To say nothing of hearth-rugs, tablecloths (if dark-coloured), or even blotting paper? But it is agreeable to read of these things, to attune the tired mind to the restful tempo of a calm Utopia where it is always afternoon and everybody uses pen-wipers and pipe-cleaners, and puts winter clothes away in home-made moth-bags through the summer months.

More and more space of the modern paper is occupied by Gossip Paragraphs. The most popular device is that of the Signed Society Chat. This is usually written under the name of a peer, a débutante, or an actress, and consists of deliciously unintelligible paragraphs that run something like this: "To have coloured lights to assist in conversation may be a new idea, but Lady (Dizzy) Arnott has lovely little pink and blue bulbs concealed in bowls of floating glass flowers on her dinner table, and, as everyone knows, she is one of the wittiest hostesses in town." Or, "My poor friend, Fatty Sprigg, one of the last men about Piccadilly to wear a grey bowler, tells me that his yearling Toots (called after dear 'Toots' Wagner) has strained a tendon and will be out of the running for the Thousand Guineas." Snobbery of every kind—birth-snobbery, sport-snobbery, wealth-snobbery, and even eccentricity-snobbery—provide the modern paper with unending copy.

Then the pictures. No paper today is complete without its pictures. Even the financial pages usually contain a photograph of a director or two. The colourful personalities of brides in bath and royal brides, of gunmen, film stars, Comtesses in pyjamas at Biarritz, prize Pekingese, Channel swimmers, and chorus girls, add richness and charm to the monotony of working-class urban life.

As for the correspondence, whereas the stationary reader could spend a happy day translating the quotations from Ovid appearing in letters to *The Times,* the traveler prefers shorter and brighter letters, of strong human interest, about the Modern Girl, and "Is the Bible True?" and "How many Times the Telephone Exchange Gave the Wrong Number Last Week," and "How I Met My Husband."

Editors, understanding this, have conceived the idea of immense contributed articles by popular writers, actresses, ex-Cabinet ministers, bishops and jockeys, upon such subjects as "Are Women Hard?" "Is There a God?" "The Greatest Thing in Life," and "Should a Mother Tell?" The general instruction delivered to the writers of such *belles lettres* is that they should be provocative and that they should be human. The nature of the required provocation is rarely defined, but the belief that they should be provocative of thought is a mistaken one. Passion, irritation, pleasure, and prejudice are, on the whole, more entertaining activities than profound cerebration, and better suited to the limited time and attention of the reader who is suspended from a strap in a swaying underground tram. The demand for Humanity is one which equally requires definition. The old idea of the Humanities associated the word with those activities peculiar to the human race—the search for truth, the creation of beauty, the discipline of mind and body, the calculations of mathematical formulae. Hence the representation of the classical literatures as Literae Humaniores. The modern notion of Humanity appears, however, to consist chiefly of those instincts which man shares with other animals—the maternal instinct, the sex instinct, the instincts of fear, self-preservation, jealousy, and display. I have frequently wondered at the reason for this change, but am growing more certain that it is in some way due to the mobile habits of our generation of passengers.

There is, of course, a large public which seeks for entertainment in those parts of the paper more exclusively designed for its provision—the comic strips, the cross-word puzzles, the caricatures, the serial stories, the paragraphs of wit like Beachcomber and his innumerable followers, and, I suppose, the columns devoted to sport. Presumably these entertainments are found entertaining by large numbers. There must be avid readers of the columns headed "Mustard and Cress," "A Little Bird Told Me," "Did You Ever?" and so on. The collection of anecdotes, of curious information about the behaviour of white mice, the mathematical oddities, first collected by Mrs. Harmsworth, about how many peas piled together would weigh the same as the dome of St. Paul's, and so on, provide mental stimulus for thousands of men and women, who between the jerks of the bus, cast down their eyes on the print of the sheet before them.

As for sport, it is difficult to understand how those columns in small type, tucked away among the financial pages, amuse anyone; but quite clearly they do. Because I cannot share the rapture of those for whom the heavens are opened by the news that Don Bredman has not sprained his thumb or that Gladiator is in fine fettle for the two o'clock, I may do less than justice to the vicarious pleasure of the sporting pages. But it can be safely affirmed that the accumulated Technical knowledge, disinterested devotion, and passionate zeal with which millions of the inhabitants of these islands pursue the fortunes of racehorses which they have never seen and prize-fighters whom they will never meet, could, if diverted to other purposes, suffice to float a complete town-planning scheme, an educational renaissance, total disarmament, and a Five Year Plan.

There is perhaps only one item of news which surpasses sport in its perennial interest for the bus traveler, and that is the mention of his own name in print. Few are so notorious, few so great, few so unfortunate, that favourable Press publicity cannot soften blows and heighten satisfaction. Why else should country gentlemen grow pumpkins fifty-three inches in circumference? Why else should intrepid young women swim the Channel? Why else should centenarians live to celebrate their 104th birthdays? Why else should Mrs. X. and Miss Y.Z. confess, with name, address, and photograph, the inner history of their epidermic disorders or matrimonial troubles to the advertising department of patent medicine firms? Age cannot wither nor custom stale the infinite pleasures of appearing "in the news." Those members of the public who return horrified from a play like *Late Night Final,* or a film like *The Front Page,* should remember that publicity has this happier side.

And the future? Who would dare to prophesy? Clearly this migratory civilization will not at once grow static. Indeed, when our buses convey us all daily from our homes at Brighton to offices and factories in Middlesex, we shall have more need than ever for the press as entertainment. On the other hand, contrary to the Jeremiads of the pessimists, a large, intelligent, politically-minded public, with more or less civilized standards of culture, is increasing. The demand for the newspaper which offers criticism and information and general comment will grow rather than diminish. Fleet Street has been transformed since 1900. By 1961, may it not be possible that we shall see an even greater diversity of its products? We shall have one or two dailies, at the most perhaps, of *The Times, Manchester Guardian* type, admirably written, rather heavy, solid, and impersonal, and a great number of lively, critical, and intellectual weeklies, written for those who desire stimulus and information; and we shall have a larger number of newspapers for entertainment—gay, brisk, sparkling, nonsensical, brilliant, frivolous, delightful things, designed to divert our attention from the qualms of "banking" and the tedium of the steady flight.

Entertainment Today Series. *Radio Times* (November 27, 1931): 673.

VIRGINIA WOOLF

Reviewing

In London there are certain shop windows that always attract a crowd. The attraction is not in the finished article but in the worn-out garments that are having patches inserted in them. The crowd is watching the women at work. There they sit in the shop window putting invisible stitches into moth-eaten trousers. And this familiar sight may serve as illustration to the following paper. So our poets, playwrights, and novelists sit in the shop window, doing their work under the curious eyes of reviewers. But the reviewers are not content, like the crowd in the street, to gaze in silence; they comment aloud upon the size of the holes, upon the skill of the workers, and advise the public which of the goods in the shop window is the best worth buying. The purpose of this paper is to rouse discussion as to the value of the reviewer's office—to the writer, to the public, to the reviewer, and to literature. But a reservation must first be made-by "the reviewer" is meant the reviewer of imaginative literature—poetry, drama, fiction; not the reviewer of history, politics, economics. His is a different office, and for reasons not to be discussed here he fulfils it in the main so adequately and indeed admirably that his value is not in question. Has the reviewer, then, of imaginative literature any value at the present time to the writer, to the public, to the reviewer, and to literature? And, if so, what? And if not, how could his function be changed, and made profitable? Let us broach these involved and complicated questions by giving one quick glance at the history of reviewing, since it may help to define the nature of a review at the present moment.

Since the review came into existence with the newspaper, that history is a brief one. *Hamlet* was not reviewed, nor *Paradise Lost.* Criticism there was but criticism conveyed by word of mouth, by the audience in the theatre, by fellow writers in taverns and private workshops. Printed criticism came into existence, presumably in a crude and primitive form, in the seventeenth century. Certainly the eighteenth century rings with the screams and catcalls of the reviewer and his victim. But towards the end of the eighteenth century there was a change—the body of criticism then seems to split into two parts. The critic and the reviewer divided the country between them. The critic—let Dr. Johnson represent him—dealt with the past and with principles; the reviewer took the measure of new books as they fell from the press. As the nineteenth century drew on, these functions became more and more distinct. There were the critics— Coleridge, Matthew Arnold—who took their time and their space; and there were the "irresponsible" and mostly anonymous reviewers who had less time and less space, and whose complex task it was partly to inform the public, partly to criticize the book, and partly to advertise its existence.

Thus, though the reviewer in the nineteenth century has much resemblance to his living representative, there were certain important differences. One difference is shown by the author of the *Times History:* "The books reviewed were fewer, but the reviews were longer than now. . . . Even a novel might get two columns and more"—he is referring to the middle of the nineteenth century. Those differences are very important, as will be seen later. But it is worth while to pause for a moment to examine other results of the review which are first manifest then, though by no means easy to sum up; the effect that is to say of the review upon the author's sales and upon the author's sensibility. A review had undoubtedly a great effect upon sales. Thackeray, for instance, said that the *Times'* review of *Esmond* "absolutely stopped the sale of the book." The review also had an immense though less calculable effect upon the sensibility of the author. Upon Keats the effect is notorious; also upon the sensitive Tennyson. Not only did he alter his poems at the reviewer's bidding, but actually contemplated emigration; and was thrown, according to one biographer, into such despair by the hostility of reviewers that his state of mind for a whole decade, and thus his poetry, was changed by them. But the robust and self-

confident were also affected. "How can a man like Macready," Dickens demanded, "fret and fume and chafe himself for such lice of literature as these?"—
the "lice" are writers in Sunday newspapers—"rotten creatures with men's
forms and devils' hearts?" Yet lice as they are, when they "discharge their
pigmy arrows" even Dickens with all his genius and his magnificent vitality
cannot help but mind and has to make a vow to overcome his rage and "to
gain the victory by being indifferent and bidding them whistle on."

In their different ways then the great poet and the great novelist both
admit the power of the nineteenth-century reviewer; and it is safe to assume
that behind them stood a myriad of minor poets and minor novelists whether of the sensitive variety or of the robust who were all affected in much the
same way. The way was complex; it is difficult to analyse. Tennyson and Dickens are both angry and hurt; they are also ashamed of themselves for feeling
such emotions. The reviewer was a louse; his bite was contemptible; yet his
bite was painful. His bite injured vanity; it injured reputation; it injured sales.
Undoubtedly in the nineteenth century the reviewer was a formidable insect;
he had considerable power over the author's sensibility; and upon the public
taste. He could hurt the author; he could persuade the public either to buy or
to refrain from buying.

II

The figures being thus set in position and their functions and powers roughly
outlined, it must next be asked whether what was true then is true now. At first
sight there seems to be little change. All the figures are still with us—critic;
reviewer; author; public; and in much the same relations. The critic is separate
from the reviewer; the function of the reviewer is partly to sort current literature;
partly to advertise the author; partly to inform the public. Nevertheless there
is a change; and it is a change of the highest importance. It seems to have made
itself felt in the last part of the nineteenth century. It is summed up in the
words of the *Times'* historian already quoted: ". . . the tendency was for reviews,
to grow shorter and to be less long delayed." But there was another tendency;
not only did the reviews become shorter and quicker, but they increased immeasurably in number. The result of these three tendencies was of the highest
importance. It was catastrophic indeed; between them they have brought about
the decline and fall of reviewing. Because they were quicker, shorter, and more
numerous the value of reviews for all parties concerned has dwindled until—is
it too much to say until it has disappeared? But let us consider. The people
concerned are the author, the reader, and the publisher. Placing them in this
order let us ask first how these tendencies have affected the author—why the

review has ceased to have any value for him? Let us assume, for brevity's sake, that the most important value of a review to the author was its effect upon him as a writer—that it gave him an expert opinion of his work and allowed him to judge roughly how far as an artist he had failed or succeeded. That has been destroyed almost entirely by the multiplicity of reviews. Now that he has sixty reviews where in the nineteenth century he had perhaps six, he finds that there is no such thing as "an opinion" of his work. Praise cancels blame; and blame praise. There are as many different opinions of his work as there are different reviewers. Soon he comes to discount both praise and blame; they are equally worthless. He values the review only for its effect upon his reputation and for its effect upon his sales.

The same cause has also lessened the value of the review to the reader. The reader asks the reviewer to tell him whether the poem or novel is good or bad in order that he may decide whether to buy it or not. Sixty reviewers at once assure him that it is a masterpiece—and worthless. The clash of completely contradictory opinions cancel each other out [sic]. The reader suspends judgment; waits for an opportunity of seeing the book himself; very probably forgets all about it, and keeps his seven and sixpence in his pocket.

The variety and diversity of opinion affect the publisher in the same way. Aware that the public no longer trusts either praise or blame, the publisher is reduced to printing both side by side: "This is . . . poetry that will be remembered in hundreds of years time . . ." "There are several passages that make me physically sick," [*The New Statesman,* April 1939] to quote an actual instance; to which he adds very naturally, in his own person: "Why not read it yourself?" That question is enough by itself to show that reviewing as practised at present has failed in all its objects. Why bother to write reviews or to read them or to quote them if in the end the reader must decide the question for himself?

III

If the reviewer has ceased to have any value either to the author or to the public it seems a public duty to abolish him. And, indeed, the recent failure of certain magazines consisting largely of reviews seems to show that whatever the reason, such will be his fate. But it is worth while to look at him in being—a flutter of little reviews is still attached to the great political dailies and weeklies—before he is swept out of existence, in order to see what he is still trying to do; why it is so difficult for him to do it; and whether perhaps there is not some element of value that ought to be preserved. Let us ask the reviewer himself to throw light upon the nature of the problem as it appears to him. Nobody is better qualified to do so than Mr. Harold Nicolson. The other day [*The Daily Telegraph,* March, 1939] he dealt with the duties and the difficulties of the reviewer as they appear to him. He began by saying that the reviewer, who is "something quite different from the critic," is "hampered by the hebdomadal nature of his task,"—in other words, he has to write too often and too much. He went on to define the nature of that task. "Is he to relate every book that he reads to the eternal standards of literary excellence? Were he to do that, his reviews would be one long ululation. Is he merely to consider the library public and to tell people what it may please them to read? Were he to do that, he would be subjugating his own level of taste to a level which is not very stimulating. How does he act?" Since he cannot refer to the eternal standards of literature; since he cannot tell the library public what they would like to read—that would be "a degradation of the mind"—there is only one thing that he can do: he can hedge. "I hedge between the two extremes. I address myself to the authors of the books which I review; I want to tell them why I either like or dislike their work; and I trust that from such a dialogue the ordinary reader will derive some information."

That is an honest statement; and its honesty is illuminating. It shows that the review has become an expression of individual opinion, given without any attempt to refer to "eternal standards" by a man who is in a hurry; who is pressed for space; who is expected to cater in that little space for many different interests; who is bothered by the knowledge that he is not fulfilling his task; who is doubtful what that task is; and who, finally, is forced to hedge. Now the public though crass is not such an ass as to invest seven and sixpence on the advice of a reviewer writing under such conditions; and the public though dull is not such a gull as to believe in the great poets, great novelists, and epoch-making works that are weekly discovered under such conditions. Those are the conditions however; and there is good reason to think that they will become more drastic in the course of the next few years. The reviewer is already a distracted tag on the tail of the political kite. Soon he will be conditioned out of existence altogether. His work will be done—in many newspapers it is already done-by a competent official armed with scissors and paste who will be called (it may be) The Gutter. The Gutter will write out a short statement of the book; extract the plot (if it is a novel); choose a few verses (if it is a poem); quote a few anecdotes (if it is a biography). To this what is left of the reviewer—perhaps he will come to be known as the Taster—will fix a stamp— an asterisk to signify approval, a dagger to signify disapproval. This statement—this Gutter and Stamp production—will serve instead of the present discordant and distracted twitter. And there is no reason to think that it will serve two of the parties concerned worse than the present system. The library public will be told what it wishes to know—whether the book is the kind of book to order from the library; and the publisher will collect asterisks and daggers instead of going to the pains to copy out alternate phrases of praise and abuse in which neither he nor the public has any faith. Each perhaps will save a little time and a little money. There remain, however, two other parties to be considered—that is the author and the reviewer. What will the Gutter and Stamp system mean to them?

To deal first with the author—his case is the more complex, for his is the more highly developed organism. During the two centuries or so in which he has been exposed to reviewers he has undoubtedly developed what may be called a reviewer consciousness. There is present in his mind a figure who is known as "the reviewer." To Dickens he was a louse armed with pigmy arrows, having the form of a man and the heart of a devil. To Tennyson he was even more formidable. It is true that the lice are so many today and they bite so innumerably that the author is comparatively immune from their poison—no author now abuses reviewers as violently as Dickens or obeys them as submissively as Tennyson. Still, there are eruptions even now in the press which lead us to believe that the reviewer's fang is still poisoned. But what part is affected by his bite?—what is the true nature of the emotion he causes? That is a complex question; but perhaps we can discover something that will serve as answer by submitting the author to a simple test. Take a sensitive author and place before him a hostile review. Symptoms of pain and anger rapidly develop. Next tell him that nobody save himself will read those abusive remarks. In five or ten minutes the pain which, if the attack had been delivered in public, would have lasted a week and bred bitter rancour, is completely over. The temperature falls; indifference returns. This proves that the sensitive part is the reputation; what the victim feared was the effect of abuse upon the opinion that other people had of him. He is afraid, too, of the effect of abuse upon his purse. But the purse sensibility is in most cases far less highly-developed than the reputation sensibility. As for the artist's sensibility—his own opinion of his own work—that is not touched by anything good or bad that the reviewer says about it. The reputation sensibility however is still lively; and it will thus take some time to persuade authors that the Gutter and Stamp system is as satisfactory as the present reviewing system. They will say that they have "reputations"—bladders of opinion formed by what other people think about them; and that these bladders are inflated or deflated by what is said of them in print. Still, under present conditions the time is at hand when even the author will believe that nobody thinks the better or the worse of him because he is praised or blamed in print. Soon he will come to realize that his interests—his desire for fame and money—are as effectively catered for by the Gutter and Stamp system as by the present reviewing system.

But even when this stage is reached, the author may still have some ground for complaint. The reviewer did serve some end besides that of inflating reputations and stimulating sales. And Mr. Nicholson has put his finger on it. "I want to tell them why I either like or dislike their work." The author wants to be told why Mr. Nicholson likes or dislikes his work. This is a genuine desire. It survives the test of privacy. Shut doors and windows; pull the curtains. Ensure that no fame accrues or money; and still it is a matter of the very greatest interest to a writer to know what an honest and intelligent reader thinks about his work.

IV

At this point let us turn once more to the reviewer. There can be no doubt that his position at the present moment, judging both from the outspoken remarks of Mr. Nicolson and from the internal evidence of the reviews themselves, is extremely unsatisfactory. He has to write in haste and to write shortly. Most of the books he reviews are not worth the scratch of a pen upon paper—it is futile to refer them to "eternal standards." He knows further, as Matthew Arnold has stated, that even if the conditions were favourable, it is impossible for the living to judge the works of the living. Years, many years, according to Matthew Arnold, have to pass before it is possible to deliver an opinion that is not "only personal, but personal with passion." And the reviewer has one week. And authors are not dead but living. And the living are friends or enemies; have wives and families; personalities and politics. The reviewer knows that he is hampered, distracted, and prejudiced. Yet knowing all this and having proof in the wild contradictions of contemporary opinion that it is so, he has to submit a perpetual succession of new books to a mind as incapable of taking a fresh impression or of making a dispassionate statement as an old piece of blotting paper on a post office counter. He has to review; for he has to live; and he has to live, since most reviewers come of the educated class, according to the standards of that class. Thus he has to write often, and he has to write much. There is, it seems, only one alleviation of the horror, that he enjoys telling authors why he likes or dislikes their books.

V

The one element in reviewing that is of value to the reviewer himself (independently of the money earned) is the one element that is of value to the author. The problem then is how to preserve this value—the value of the dialogue as Mr. Nicolson calls it—and to bring both parties together in a union that is profitable, to the minds and purses of both. It should not be a difficult problem to solve. The medical profession has shown the way. With some differences the medical custom might be imitated—there are many resemblances between doctor and reviewer, between patient and author. Let the reviewers then abolish themselves or what relic remains of them, as reviewers, and resurrect themselves as doctors. Another name might be chosen—consultant, expositor or expounder; some credentials might be given, the books written rather than the examinations passed; and a list of those ready and authorized to practise made public. The writer then would submit his work to the judge of his choice; an appointment would be made; an interview arranged. In strict privacy, and with some formality—the fee, however, would be enough to ensure that the interview did not degenerate into tea-table gossip—doctor and writer would meet; and for an hour they would consult upon the book in question. They would talk, seriously and privately. This privacy in the first place would be an immeasurable advantage to them both. The consultant would speak honestly and openly, because the fear of affecting sales and of hurting feelings would be removed. Privacy would lessen the shop-window temptation to cut a figure, to pay off scores. The consultant would have no library public to inform and consider; no reading public to impress and amuse. He could thus concentrate upon the book itself, and upon telling the author why he likes or dislikes it. The author would profit equally. An hour's private talk with a critic of his own choosing would be incalculably more valuable than the five hundred words of criticism mixed with extraneous matter that is now allotted him. He could state his case. He could point to his difficulties. He would no longer feel, as so often at present, that the critic is talking about something that he has not written. Further, he would have the advantage of coming into touch with a well-stored mind, housing other books and even other literatures, and thus other standards; with a live human being, not with a man in a mask. Many bogies would lose their horns. The louse would become a man. By degrees the writer's "reputation" would drop off. He would become quit of that tiresome appendage and its irritable consequences—such are a few of the obvious and indisputable advantages that privacy would ensure.

Next there is the financial question—would the profession of expositor be as profitable as the profession of reviewer? How many authors are there who would wish to have an expert opinion on their work? The answer to this is to be heard crying daily and crying loudly in any publisher's office or in any author's post-bag. "Give me advice," they repeat, "give me criticism." The number of authors seeking criticism and advice genuinely, not for advertising purposes but because their need is acute, is an abundant proof of the demand. But would they pay the doctor's fee of three guineas? When they discovered, as certainly they would, how much more an hour of talk holds, even if it costs three guineas, than the hurried letter which they now extort from the harassed publisher's reader, or the five hundred words which is all they can count on from the distracted reviewer, even the indigent would think it an investment worth making. Nor is it only the young and needy who seek advice. The art of writing is difficult; at every stage the opinion of an impersonal and disinterested critic would be of the highest value. Who would not spout the family teapot in order to talk with Keats for an hour about poetry, or with Jane Austen about the art of fiction?

VI

There remains finally the most important, but the most difficult of all these questions—what effect would the abolition of the reviewer have upon literature? Some reasons for thinking that the smashing of the shop window would make for the better health of that remote goddess have already been implied. The writer would withdraw into the darkness of the workshop; he would no longer carry on his difficult and delicate task like a trouser mender in Oxford Street, with a horde of reviewers pressing their noses to the glass and commenting to a curious crowd upon each stitch. Hence his self-consciousness would diminish and his reputation would shrivel. No longer puffed this way and that, now elated, now depressed, he could attend to his work. That might make for better writing. Again the reviewer, who must now earn his pence by cutting shop window capers to amuse the public and to advertise his skill, would have only the book to think of and the writer's needs. That might make for better criticism.

But there might be other and more positive advantages. The Gutter and Stamp system by eliminating what now passes for literary criticism—those few words devoted to "why I like or dislike this book"—will save space. Four or five thousand words, possibly, might be saved in the course of a month or two. And an editor with that space at his disposal might not only express his respect for literature, but actually prove it. He might spend that space, even in a political daily or weekly, not upon stars and snippets, but upon unsigned and uncommercial literature—upon essays, upon criticism. There may be a Montaigne among us—a Montaigne now severed into futile slices of one thousand to fifteen hundred words weekly. Given time and space he might revive, and with him an admirable and now almost extinct form of art. Or there may be a critic among us—a Coleridge, a Matthew Arnold. He is now frittering himself away, as Mr. Nicolson has shown, upon a miscellaneous heap of poems, plays, novels, all to be reviewed in one column by Wednesday next.

Given four thousand words, even twice a year, the critic might emerge, and with him those standards, those "eternal standards," which if they are never referred to, far from being eternal cease to exist. Do we not all know that Mr. A writes better or it may be worse than Mr. B? But is that all we want to know? Is that all we ought to ask?

But to sum up, or rather to heap a little cairn of conjectures and conclusions at the end of these scattered remarks for somebody else to knock down. The review, it is contended, increases selfconsciousness and diminishes strength. The shop window and the looking-glass inhibit and confine. By putting in their place discussion—fearless and disinterested discussion—the writer would gain in range, in depth, in power. And this change would tell eventually upon the public mind. Their favourite figure of fun, the author, that hybrid between the peacock and the ape, would be removed from their derision, and in his place would be an obscure workman doing his job in the darkness of the workshop and not unworthy of respect. A new relationship might come into being, less petty and less personal than the old. A new interest in literature, a new respect for literature might follow. And, financial advantages apart, what a ray of light that would bring, what a ray of pure sunlight a critical and hungry public would bring into the darkness of the workshop!

The New Statesman, April, 1939. Rpt. in Hogarth Pamphlet Series. London: Hogarth Press, 1939. *Collected Essays*, Vol. 2, ed. Leonard Woolf. London: Hogarth Press, 1966. 204–17.

7

Women Editors and Modernist Sensibilities

INTRODUCED AND SELECTED BY JAYNE E. MAREK

GENDER ISSUES ARE gate-keeping issues, as *The Gender of Modernism* ably demonstrated. Women editors during the modernist period operated at the intersection of contending forces, since editing for publication—a culturally significant gate-keeping task—was heavily inflected by the era's expectations pertaining to gender roles, class distinctions, and ethnicity. Women editors in a male-oriented literary landscape felt the need to speak decisively about matters of public discourse as well as about the remarkable artistic changes occurring at the time. Since these women were well educated and socially aware, they were determined to foster public and intellectual change: they sought out, printed, and discussed works that conveyed (and challenged) modernism's radical ideas. In hindsight, one discerns that these editors' gender added force to their ideas. Sometimes, as one may expect, these women experienced sexist backlash, but more importantly they energized and provoked readers who wanted to hear what "new women" had to say. The selections republished here provide a sample of the variegated ways gender informed critical perspectives in modernist women's editorial articles, reviews, and correspondence.

Editing is a political as well as aesthetic activity, a fact nowhere more evident than in the pages of modernist "little" magazines, including those run by women. Little magazines provided flexibility well-suited to the varieties of modernist experimentation, which was especially important because inventive new work received no hearing at all in the commercial publishing market (Hoffman, Allen, and Ulrich 2–4). Small magazines often took revolutionary stands against what the avant-garde saw as stodgy traditionalism. *Poetry* (founded 1912), *The Little Review* (1914–29), and *The Dial* (revived 1918; run by Marianne Moore, 1925–29) were exemplary little magazines edited by outspoken, visionary women who helped to shape and define the modernist era. Among African American journals, similarly strong influence was achieved by *Fire!!* (1926, collectively edited by the men and women who contributed) and *Challenge/New Challenge* (1934–37), while the journals *The Crisis* (founded 1910) and *Opportunity* (founded 1923) were of great importance in part due to the leadership of women literary editors whose discoveries shaped the Harlem Renaissance.

Harriet Monroe and Alice Corbin Henderson of *Poetry*, the earliest little magazine to usher in the "poetry renaissance," were by turns judicious and outspoken in their editorial views. The fact that Monroe had deliberately set up *Poetry* as a forum that welcomed many kinds of new work brought gender-based censure from those who doubted Monroe's discernment, although Monroe repeatedly demonstrated her breadth of vision and her interest in all forms of poetic excellence. Her speculative editorial "What Next?" mused about the directions that poetic experimentation might take. Monroe correctly predicted more freedom in poetic forms arising directly from changes in the texture of modern life, as "men" freed themselves from conventions and became "more immediately responsive" and "fluid" in creating poetry afresh. "Poetry especially can not wear the corsets, or even the chlamys, of an elder fashion," Monroe declared. Her gender-inflected language suggested that, in order for poetic art to grow within its culture, the limitations inherent in both female and male traditions must be discarded and the public must educate itself into new modes of thought.

Alice Corbin Henderson, Monroe's coeditor from 1912 to 1916, championed imagism, free verse, and the development of a truly American poetic sensibility that included the voices of social and ethnic minorities. Henderson's vigorous opinions added much to the critical debates in which *Poetry* often was embroiled. Henderson, who clearly enjoyed the power to speak her mind, offered a humorous take on editorial decision making in her piece "Of Editors and Poets." Central to the argument was Henderson's dual position as both poet and editor, which allowed her to mock the self-centeredness of aspiring poets even as she held firm to the importance of high editorial standards—the combination of the two creating a "healthily antagonistic and sociable" interaction in which new work could develop. Henderson's "antagonistic" style served her well in numerous head-to-head critical arguments with influential male critics, who intimidated Henderson not a bit.

Like Monroe and Henderson, Amy Lowell was a poet who turned to editing and publishing in order to foster awareness of modern literary techniques as well as to see more work into print. Lowell worked hard to earn an international reputation through her energetic public readings and numerous publishing activities, including editing and producing the influential volumes *Some Imagist Poets* (1915–17). In "Nationalism in Art," Lowell's voice exuded confidence as she pondered the artist's sense of national identity and urged artists to express themselves "openly and fearlessly." The use of the conventional masculine third-person pronoun did not disguise Lowell's strong argument for individual expression regardless of gender: "A strong man gains an added sense of power by everything he learns," Lowell declared. "He has mastered his technique with infinite pains, and by so doing has been able to fling his personality unimpeded before the world." Lowell, whose variations on imagism had piqued the misogynistic wrath of Ezra Pound, made it clear that no artist should allow someone else to dictate to her.

By printing their opinions boldly, women editors trumped sex-role stereotyping when they assumed critical stances that conveyed the authority they felt as arbiters of the new. Margaret Anderson of *The Little Review* flaunted stereotyping by embracing it, for example in her editorial "Our First Year," which celebrated the "faults" of her iconoclastic undertaking and reveled in her ability to champion "a new freedom" of thought, which included feminist consciousness and an anarchy that stressed freedom of speech and choice. She ironically used imagery evoking a breathless "feminine" enthusiasm to point to her vigorous support for "imagination" and rejection of pedantry, reactions that were fully in accord with the experimental modernist impulse. *The Little Review* changed cultural history because Anderson challenged legal boundaries, spoke up as a woman and an intellectual, and printed what she found valuable, most notably the sections of James Joyce's *Ulysses* that ran in the magazine during 1918–20 and that caused the defiant editors to be hauled into court.

Jane Heap, Anderson's coeditor during that time, satirized the court proceedings in "Art and the Law," an editorial with an unmistakably feminist edge. Art, Heap argued, is beyond Law; if literary art reflects the truth of human experience, it is pointless for men to presume to pronounce "obscene" any young woman's (or man's) freedom of action and feeling. Heap used the logical tools of the masculinist legal system to refute the law, thereby manipulating sex-role expectations in a way that was different from Anderson's, but equally powerful. Both *Little Review* editors stood courageously against the gender bias and fear of sexuality encoded in American laws at the time.

When Anderson left *The Little Review* in all but name after the *Ulysses* trial, Heap became editor and shifted the magazine's direction to include more European avant-garde art. Her enthusiasm for abstract and mechanical designs led her to organize a Machine-Age Exposition in 1925. Heap knew perfectly well that her interest in machines, "constructions," and "apparatuses" violated sex-role expectations as well as artistic conventions, so she expressed her autonomous vision through the rhetoric of manifesto in her introduction to a special *Little Review* number about the show. Heap's self-confident alignment with the visionary "men" (artists and engineers) demonstrated her rejection of gender-based, as well as aesthetic, limitations on any aspect of her intellect.

The formidable critical discernment of Marianne Moore appeared in several modes during her editorship of *The Dial*. She often spoke her mind while taking advantage of the mask of anonymity or of shared editorship (for while Moore, Dr. J. Sibley Watson, and Scofield Thayer were named on the masthead, Moore managed the editorship on her own since 1925). The selections republished here show distinctions in tone between a signed book review and one of Moore's anonymous "Comments," suggesting some of the reasons Moore saw fit to manipulate editorial masks.

Moore's signed review of Gertrude Stein's *The Making of Americans* astutely led readers through a basic appreciation for Stein's experimental language and, in so doing, gestured toward both Moore's and Stein's feminist ideology. Moore knew perfectly well that many critics rejected Stein as much out of bias against Stein's powerful persona as for her radical prose. Moore's judicious reading proposed that Stein's "psychological" exactitude was the main determinant of the novel's style. The review began by sketching the gender politics of the Dehnings' marriage and identified "the power of sex" in the novel as an important way Stein implied conflict through ironic language. This discussion of Stein's method had a gender-inflected angle that explicitly critiqued patriarchal control, which Moore conveyed through judicious editorial choice and emphasis.

In contrast, the anonymous "Comment" mocked *The New Republic* for alleging that *The Dial* lacked "interesting" new writers. By pointing to notable authors who had appeared in *The Dial* and by sharply dismissing some whom *The New Republic* had printed, Moore asserted her power of critical discernment: "Whatever character *The Dial* may have is the result of a selection not so much of writers as of writing." The end of the piece gave an ironic twist to having an influential editorial position: "[Let] us remember that it is impossible in the world of letters to act or refuse to act without stirring up a hurricane of catcalls. . . . Lists of interesting new American writers of the past seven years will be gratefully received." Moore's final remark showed her mastery of tone; as with Heap and Henderson, Moore's sincere orientation toward the "new" was edged with a sarcasm that ably conveyed editorial self-confidence.

The political spirit of many twentieth-century African American periodicals, whether "little" or not, was more pronounced than that which catalyzed so-called mainstream modernism. Black-run journals were "involved first in political and social occurrences and then in black literature" (Johnson and Johnson 1), with both aspects nurturing a readership that responded eagerly to serious analyses and positive images about African American life.[1] Publications such as the official periodicals of the NAACP (*The Crisis*) and the National Urban League (*Opportunity*) were essential to the climate that fostered the Harlem Renaissance, which reached its peak in the 1920s.[2] Black women editors, like their white counterparts, generally came from privileged middle-class backgrounds, were well-educated, and thus were particularly able to address the complex pressures of race and gender.

One such woman, Jessie Redmon Fauset, was literary editor (and sometimes managing editor) of *The Crisis* from 1919 to 1926, its years of highest circulation; this position was one of the few seats of power available to an educated black woman at the time (Wall 47, 35–36). Fauset was also de facto editor of *The Crisis*'s spinoff children's magazine, *The Brownies' Book* (1920–21), the first journal directed toward African American youth (Johnson-Feelings 335). As a former teacher, Fauset championed the responsibility of self-education, especially about international issues. In a notable series of articles reflecting her global interests, Fauset tellingly characterized the strong spirit of international black awareness shown through the Second Pan-African Congress in 1921. Fauset's report "Impressions of the Second Pan-African Congress" expressed more than a steady belief in solidarity among the black diaspora—her position as an insider and her explicit acknowledgement of women's active presence at the congress showed her feminist orientation and the idealism with which she nurtured many writers of the Harlem Renaissance.

Artist and poet Gwendolyn Bennett vigorously joined the discussions about African American achievements in her review columns, written while she served as a literary and arts editor for *Opportunity* magazine from 1926 to 1928. Her "Ebony Flute" series employed the casual style of editorial miscellany popular at the time. This disarming (and gender-inflected) effect, similar to Margaret Anderson's style in *The Little Review,* nevertheless allowed Bennett to articulate criteria for a black aesthetic through her comments about books, plays, musicals, and other artistic productions.[3] The "Ebony Flute" installment republished here made a notable point about Carl Van Vechten's controversial *Nigger Heaven*— that the novel served best as a signpost directing attention back to real African American literary accomplishments, such as those by Charles Chesnutt and Langston Hughes. A close look also suggests Bennett's feminist politics, shown through her consistent interest in women who performed, wrote, or promoted literary connections, all activities crucial to the multifarious Renaissance.

Bennett also occasionally wrote for the *New York Herald Tribune Books* section during the years 1927–31. Her "Blue-Black Symphony," a review of Claude McKay's first novel, *Home to Harlem,* helped create the stir that made the book both successful and notorious and provided encouragement to McKay after a long dry spell.[4] Bennett used this review to express support for the free range of expression in new writing, even if that involved problematic portrayals of black characters.[5] Bennett's social politics also showed clearly in that she, along with McKay, questioned the parasitism of "the Harlem 'lounge lizard,'" supported by women, who did not earn his living as did the variegated characters, male and female, described in the novel and celebrated in Bennett's language of colors and physical labor.

In the pages of her magazine *Challenge,* Dorothy West called for social realism to help spark African American literary creativity during the Depression. West's intellectual affinity for communist theory showed in her 1934 letter to Langston Hughes. West's trip to Russia in 1932 had caused a sea change in her outlook by providing a lasting vision of gender and racial equity that inclined her toward serious ideological debate (as she welcomed a clash between points of view as a chance to engage "young thinking Negroes"). The 1937 "Editorial" that opened the retitled magazine *New Challenge,* an issue she prepared with her coeditor Marian Minus and Richard Wright, reiterated West's egalitarian and increasingly "black-red" political stance, as it encourage "folk" and "regional" literary efforts in a "definite social context" pointing toward "the ultimate understanding of the interdependence of cultures." *New Challenge,* although it lasted for only one issue, indicated that African American literary activity was alive and well, and built on questions that had occupied Harlem Renaissance theorists in the 1920s by creating "an explicit fusion of literary and [progressive] political concerns" (Johnson and Johnson 119, 203).

The enormous shifts in critical parameters traced by *The Gender of Modernism* and extended in this volume indicate how the serious study of modernity and of gender continues to intrigue and refresh its scholars. There are now many more critically acknowledged ways to frame and read modernist-era texts that resonate with issues of gender—not to mention issues of "authority" and "the subversive role of art"—and the traditional "invisibility" of editorial processes ought not to fool readers into thinking that painstaking choices in texts and presentations are not fully "constructed and contingent" upon the whole range of editors' intellectual and personal experiences (Bornstein 6, 13, 2). Editorial decisions demonstrate power; the women addressed in this section sought and wielded that power. Their writings made clear that they saw no need for apologia about being female. Modernist women editors often implicitly refuted gender determinism by not even bothering to dismiss sexism—a pragmatic approach that moved such discussions well past simple identity politics. Women editors' particular position as women allowed them to open the gates to the new in ways that had been unimaginable before, and modernism—and the world—were forever changed.

Notes

1. Cheryl Wall notes the significance of turning previously negative black images into positive "incentives"—a hugely successful effort. *Women of the Harlem Renaissance,* 2–3.

2. Wall's discussion of the gender implications of the term "Harlem Renaissance" is instructive (9–10).

3. The range of Bennett's knowledge earned praise from *Opportunity* editor Charles S. Johnson, who had invited Bennett to write the column to call attention to the heightened literary activities of the time (Johnson and Johnson 55–56).

4. See Cooper, 234.

5. Cooper, 238–48.

Works Cited

Anderson, Elliott, and Mary Kinzie, eds. *The Little Magazine in America: A Modern Documentary History.* Yonkers: Pushcart, 1978.

Bornstein, George, ed. *Representing Modernist Texts: Editing as Interpretation.* Ann Arbor: University of Michigan Press, 1991.

Cooper, Wayne F. *Claude McKay: Rebel Sojourner in the Harlem Renaissance.* Baton Rouge: Louisiana State University Press, 1987.

Hoffman, Frederick J., Charles Allen, and Carolyn F. Ulrich. *The Little Magazine: A History and a Bibliography.* Princeton: Princeton University Press, 1946.

Johnson, Abby Ann Arthur, and Ronald Maberry Johnson. *Propaganda and Aesthetics: The Literary Politics of Afro-American Magazines in the Twentieth Century.* Amherst: University of Massachusetts Press, 1979.

Johnson-Feelings, Dianne, ed. *The Best of The Brownies' Book.* New York: Oxford University Press, 1996.

Wall, Cheryl A. *Women of the Harlem Renaissance.* Bloomington: Indiana University Press, 1995.

Zingman, Barbara. *The Dial: An Author Index.* Troy, New York: Whitston, 1975.

MARGARET ANDERSON

From "Our First Year"

An interesting man said recently that the five qualities which go into the making of the great personality—of the genius, perhaps—are (1) energy, (2) imagination, (3) character, (4) intellect, (5) and charm. I number them because the importance of his remark lies in the fact that he arranged them in just that order. The more you think of it the keener a judgment it seems. I can see only one possible flaw in it—a flaw that would not be corrected, I am certain, by moving number four to the place of number one, but by a reversal of number one and number two. Energy does seem the prime requisite—after you've spent a few days with one of those persons who has seething visions and a contempt for concentration. But Imagination!—that gift of the far gods! There is simply no question of its position in the list. It is first by virtue of every brave and beautiful thing that has been accomplished in the world.

Last March we began the publication of THE LITTLE REVIEW. Now, twelve months later, we face the humiliating—or the encouraging—spectacle of being a magazine whose function is not transparent. People are always asking me what we are really trying to do. We have not set forth a policy; we have not identified ourselves with a point of view, except in so far as we have been quite ridiculously appreciative; we have not expounded a philosophy, except in so far as we have been quite outlandishly anarchistic; we have been uncritical, indiscriminate, juvenile, exuberant, chaotic, amateurish, emotional, tiresomely enthusiastic, and a lot of other things which I can't remember now—all the things that are usually said about faulty new undertakings. The encouraging thing is that they are said most strongly about promising ones.

Of course THE LITTLE REVIEW has done little more than approach the ideal which it has in mind. I am not proud of those limitations mentioned above—(and I am far from being unconscious of them); I am merely glad that they happen to be that particular type of limitation rather than some other. For instance, I should much rather have the limitations of the visionary or the poet or the prophet than those of the pedant or the priest or the "practical" person. Personally, I should much rather get drenched than to go always fortified with an umbrella and overshoes; I should rather see one side of a question violently than to see both sides calmly; I should rather be an extremist than a—well, it's scarcely a matter of choice: people are either extremists or nonentities; I should far rather sense the big things about a cause or a character even vaguely than to analyze its little qualities quite clearly; in short,

I should rather feel a great deal and know a little than feel a little and know a lot. [. . .]

This much to start with. Now there are people who complain that within their limited allowance of magazines they are forced to do without THE LITTLE REVIEW because it gives them nothing definite, nothing finished, nothing conclusive. But my idea of a magazine which makes any claim to artistic value is that it should be conducted more or less on the lines of good drama, or good fiction; that it should suggest, not conclude; that it should stimulate to thinking rather than dictate thought. Most magazines have efficient editors and definite editorial policies; that is what's wrong with them. I have none of the qualifications of the editor; that's why I think THE LITTLE REVIEW is in good hands. [. . .]

I think that "policies" are likely to be, or to become, quite damning things. Therefore instead of urging people to read us in the hope of finding what they seek in that direction, it is more honest to say outright that they will probably find less and less of it. Because as "sanity" increases in the world THE LITTLE REVIEW will strive more and more to be splendidly insane: as editors and lecturers continue to compromise in order to get their public, as book-makers continue to print rot in order to make fortunes, as writers continue to follow the market instead of *doing their Work,* as the public continues to demand vileness and vulgarity and lies, as the intellectuals continue to miss the root of the trouble, THE LITTLE REVIEW will continue to rebel, to tell the truth as we see it, to work for its ideal rather than for a policy. And in the face of new magazines of excellent quality and no personality we shall continue to soar and flash and flame, to be swamped at intervals and scramble to new heights, to be young and fearless and reckless and imaginative [. . . ,] to die for these things if necessary, but to live for them vividly first. [. . .]

The rebel program is stated—exactly. More than that, it is in action. The difference between the new issues and the old [. . .] is that we have now learned what we must do; to me, it is that we must learn to do something else. The battle lies not against the chaos of a new freedom, but against the dangers of a new authority. [. . .]

It is for some such need as this that THE LITTLE REVIEW exists: to create some attitude which so far is absolutely alien to the American tradition. I have been going to the lectures of John Cowper Powys, which are spoken of in other places in this issue, and that appreciative man gave me an interesting idea the other day. I should like to see him as editor of a literary magazine whose policy was to cut off the subscription list to everybody who speculated about his pose or his insincerity and failed to miss the great beauty of his words. Now Mr. Powys is as unstable as water: that is his value. He feels entirely too much ever to be fully sane. His hypothetical magazine would gather an audience that could fight successfully the great American crime which may be described briefly as *missing the point*. Thus we might establish a reign of imagination which would make stupid things as impossible as cruel things, which would consider a failure to catch some new beauty or a "moral lynching of great and independent spirits" as greater crimes than murdering a man in a dark corner.

On this basis we shall continue. If we must be sensible at least we shall make it, in Shaw's phrase, an ecstasy of common sense. And out of all this chaos shall we produce our dancing star.

The Little Review 1.11 (February 1915): 1–6.

JANE HEAP

From "Machine-Age Exposition"

The Machine-Age Exposition now being organized by the *Little Review* will be held in the Autumn of this year. The Exposition will show actual machines, parts, apparatuses, photographs and drawings of machines, plants, constructions etc., in juxtaposition with paintings, drawings, sculpture, constructions, and inventions by the most vital of the modern artists.

There is a great new race of men in America: the Engineer. He has created a new mechanical world, he is segregated from men in other activities . . . it is inevitable and important to the civilization of today that he make a union with the artist. This affiliation of Artist and Engineer will benefit each in his own domain, it will end the immense waste in each domain and will become a new creative force. [. . .]

A great many people cry out at the Machine as the incubus that is threatening our "spiritual" life. The aims of this race have bred an incomplete man . . . his outer life is too full, his inner life empty. His religion is either dead or seems a hopeless misfit for life today. The world is restless with a need to express its emotions. The desire for beauty has become a necessity.

THE MACHINE IS THE RELIGIOUS EXPRESSION OF TODAY

When it is admitted that the general public must be educated over and over again to the simplest, new thing, is it surprising that, without any education at all, it is unable to see that it is surrounded by a new beauty. And beyond that . . . who could expect it to see beauty in a thing not made for beauty: the Machine.

The snobbery, awe and false pride in the art-game, set up by the museums, dealers, and second-rate artists, have frightened the gentle public out of any frank appreciation of the plastic arts. In the past it was a contact with and an appreciation of the arts that helped the individual to function more harmoniously.

Such an exaggerated extension of one of the functions . . . the extension of the mind as evidenced in this invention of Machines, must be a mysterious and necessary part of our evolution. Those who see in the Machine nothing but a menace or a utility are simply those people who never see anything at any time. There are others who are alive; who have become impatient with the petrified copying of the dead and dying; who are interested in things dynamic.

WE ADDRESS OUR EXPOSITION TO THESE

We will endeavor to show that there exists a parallel development and a balancing element in contemporary art. The men who hold first rank in the plastic arts today are the men who are organizing and transforming the realities of our age into a dynamic beauty. They do not copy or imitate the Machine, they do not worship the Machine,—they recognize it as one of the realities. In fact it is the Engineer who has been forced, in his creation, to use most of the forms once used by the artist . . . the artist must now discover new forms for himself. It is this "plastic-mechanical analogy" which we wish to present.

The artist and the engineer start out with the same necessity. No true artist ever starts to make "beauty" . . . he has no aesthetic intention—he has a problem. No beauty has ever been achieved which was not reached through the necessity to deal with some particular problem. The artist works with definite plastic laws. He knows that his work will have lasting value only if he consciously creates forms which embody the constant and unvarying laws of the universe. The aim of the Engineer has been utility. He works with all the plastic elements, he has created a new plastic mystery, but he is practically ignorant of all aesthetic laws. . . . The beauty which he creates is accidental.

Utility does not exclude the presence of beauty . . . on the contrary a machine is not entirely efficient without the element of beauty. Utility and efficiency must take into account the whole man. [. . .]

The experiment of an exposition bringing together the plastic works of these two types of artist has in it the possibility of forecasting the life of tomorrow. All of the most energetic artists, both here and in Europe: painters, sculptors, poets, musicians are enthusiastically organized to support this exposition, the Engineers are giving it their interested cooperation.

The Little Review 11.1 (Spring 1925): 22–24.

JANE HEAP

From "Art and the Law"

The heavy farce and sad futility of trying a creative work in a court of law appalls me. Was there ever a judge qualified to judge even the simplest psychic outburst? How then a work of Art? Has any man not a nincompoop ever been heard by a jury of his peers?

In a physical world laws have been made to preserve physical order. Laws cannot reach, nor have power over, any other realm. Art is and always has been the supreme Order. Because of this it is the only activity of man that has an eternal quality. Works of Art are the only permanent sign that man has existed. What legal genius to bring Law against Order!

The society for which Mr. Sumner is agent, I am told, was founded to protect the public from corruption. When asked *what public?* its defenders spring to the rock on which America was founded: the cream-puff of sentimentality, and answer chivalrously "Our young girls." So the mind of the young girl rules this country? In it rests the safety, progress and lustre of a nation. One might have guessed it . . . but—why is she given such representatives? I recall a photograph of the United States Senators, a galaxy of noble manhood that could only have been assembled from far-flung country stores where it had spat and gossiped and stolen prunes.

The present case is rather ironical. We are being prosecuted for printing the thoughts in a young girl's mind . . . her thoughts and actions and the meditations which they produced in the mind of the sensitive Mr. Bloom. If the young girl corrupts, can she also be corrupted? Mr. Joyce's young girl is an innocent, simple, childish girl who tends children . . . she hasn't had the advantage of the dances, cabarets, motor trips open to the young girls of this more pure and free country.

If there is anything I really fear it is the mind of the young girl.

I do not understand Obscenity; I have never studied it nor had it, but I know that it must be a terrible and peculiar menace to the United States. I know that there is an expensive department maintained in Washington with a chief and fifty assistants to prevent its spread—and in and for New York we have the Sumner vigilanti.

To a mind somewhat used to life Mr. Joyce's chapter seems to be a record of the simplest, most unpreventable, most unfocused sex thoughts possible in a rightly-constructed, unashamed human being. Mr. Joyce is not teaching early Egyptian perversions nor inventing new ones. Girls lean back everywhere, showing lace and silk stockings; wear low-cut sleeveless gowns, breathless bathing suits; men think thoughts and have emotions about these things everywhere—seldom as delicately and imaginatively as Mr. Bloom—and no one is corrupted. Can merely reading about the thoughts he thinks corrupt a man when his thoughts do not? All power to the artist, but this is not his function.

It was the poet, the artist, who discovered love, created the lover, made sex everything that it is beyond a function. It is the Mr. Sumners who have made it an obscenity. It is a little too obvious to discuss the inevitable result of damming up a force as unholy and terrific as the reproductive force with nothing more powerful than silence, black looks, and censure.

"Our young girls" grow up conscious of being possessed, as by a devil, with some urge which they are told is shameful, dangerous and obscene. They try to be "pure" with no other incantations than a few "obstetric mutterings."

Mr. Sumner seems a decent enough chap . . . serious and colorless and worn as if he had spent his life resenting the emotions. A 100 per cent American who believes that denial, resentment and silence about all things pertaining to sex produce uprightness.

Only in a nation ignorant of the power of Art . . . insensitive and unambitious to the need and appreciation of Art . . . could such habit of mind obtain. Art is the only thing that produces life, extends life—I am speaking beyond physically or mentally. A people without the experience of the Art influence can bring forth nothing but a humanity that bears the stamp of a loveless race. [. . .]

There are still those people who are not outraged by the mention of natural facts who will ask "what is the necessity to discuss them?" But that is not a question to ask about a work of Art. The only question relevant at all to *Ulysses* is—Is it a work of Art? The men best capable of judging have pronounced it a work of the first rank. Anyone with a brain would hesitate to question the necessity in an artist to create, or his ability to choose the right subject matter. Anyone who has read *Exiles, The Portrait,* and *Ulysses* from the beginning, could not rush in with talk of obscenity. No man has been more crucified on his sensibilities than James Joyce.

The Little Review 7.3 (September–December 1920): 5–7. Rpt. in *The Little Review Anthology*. New York: Horizon, 1953. 301–3.

ALICE CORBIN HENDERSON

Of Editors and Poets

All young poets hate editors. And they are right. When a poet becomes tolerant of an editor, or an editor of a poet, it is not a healthy sign; both have ceased to be alert.

A wrathful young poet is the editor's best friend. He may be overbearing, insolent, but he is apt to be honest. The editor suggests cutting or changing his poem; the poet flies into a rage and tells the editor what he thinks of him. This induces a proper spirit of humility in the editor. (I am not speaking of editors who present to insult a front as smooth and impervious as a hair-cloth sofa!) It also relieves the poet, who, when he has cooled off a bit, wonders if his poem might not be improved according to the editor's suggestion or according to a new idea of his own. Both therefore continue on a purely human footing of give and take, healthily antagonistic and sociable.

But the established poet, whose reputation is not only made but embalmed, and the editor who has no more plasticity than a hitching post—there is no friction between them. They are mutually tolerant of one another. Why not? The relation between them is simply that of a manufacturer and a retailer of any reasonably staple commodity, like sugar, or molasses, or green cheese.

Of course it takes skill to be a poet! But an editor? A pair of shears, a blue pencil, and a paste-pot! All the poet in me hates the editor. The editor in me swears that I am a very bad poet; the poet knows that the editor is a fool. And neither one is entirely wrong!

A. C. H. *Poetry* 8.6 (September 1916): 308.

HARRIET MONROE

From "What Next?"

Prophecy is always reckless, but therefore all the more alluring. And if one's mood is for projection rather than reminiscence, only the wise future can contradict one's errors. So we may perhaps venture an inquiry as to what is coming in this art of poetry—this persistent and imperishable art which the human race, at certain seasons, for certain periods, tries in vain to forget.

To begin with the technique, we suspect that more, rather than less, freedom of form is coming. It seems a quaint reaction that certain sages should be shouting, "Free verse is dead!" The sculptor might as well say that marble is dead, or the painter that oil colors are in their grave; bronze for the one and tempera for the other to be hereafter the only wear.

One is moved often to wonder at the narrowness of the field still generally accorded to poets as compared with the ample kingdoms reigned over by the other arts. [. . .] [Those] have space to dream in and the choice of a thousand modes. But the poet!—his domain was rigidly bounded by the ancients, and therein must he follow appointed paths. Epic, tragedy, comedy; ode, ballad, lyric: these he must serve up in proper blank verse or rhyme according to established forms and measures. And woe be to him if he break through hedges and try to sprint for the wilds!

No, as men release themselves from materialism and demand more and more from the arts, the arts must become more immediately responsive, their forms more fluid. Poetry especially can not wear the corsets, or even the chlamys, of an elder fashion. [. . .]

Shall we, who listen eagerly to Prokofieff, refuse to Wallace Stevens a hearing for his subtle and haunting compositions, as if with wood-wind instruments?—rhythms as heavy with tragic beauty as a bee with the honey of purple roses. Shall we disdain Emanuel Carnevali's splashing rhapsody, *The Day of Summer,* because it isn't a sonata, nor yet a proper Miltonic ode? Shall not Vachel Lindsay play the organ, or even a jazz band, at his pleasure?—and is it for us to prescribe for him the harp or the flute? Hadn't Amy Lowell as much right as Bach to write a fugue of tumbling rhymes and elaborate interwoven harmonies? And shall Ezra Pound, composing nocturnes and fantasias as delicate as Chopin's, be reminded that the public prefers Strauss waltzes? Should Carl Sandburg, with a modern piano under his fingers, be restricted to Mozart's spinet? May not Cloyd Head assail the Shakespearian tradition, even as Debussy assailed the Beethoven tradition, with modern tragedies as close in texture, and as mystically expressive of our innermost feeling and dream, as the Frenchman's *L'àprès-midi d'un Faune?* And shall Edgar Lee Masters, who, of all our modern poets, has the most epic vision—shall he be denied free symphonic range within his large horizon, because staccato poets and careful critics object to his smashing paces?

One might pursue the analogy further. Is it a violin of finest quality that H. D. plays? Is Richard Aldington's *Choricos* sung from some high place to the thrilling notes of a harp? Does Carlos Williams prefer piccolo solos with whimsical twists and turns of half-humorous melody? Does H. L. Davis breathe through the woodwinds music of a mournful mysterious Brahms-like beauty? If Edna Millay sings to the lyre, and Sara Teasdale to the lute, must we be deaf to the delicately emotional lyric solos played on a reed by such younglings as Mark Turbyfill or A. Y. Winters—tunes of thistle-down texture? And shall the full poetic orchestra of the future be confined to the instruments, and the melodic methods, of Elizabeth's time, or Queen Anne's, or Victoria's, or even of all three?

Yes, we might pursue the analogy into wearisome detail, but enough has been said to present our point, which is, that the poetry of the future must have more freedom instead of less; and that, if the public is less tolerant of new methods in poetry than in music, painting or sculpture, it is because it is less educated in modern poetry than in the other modern arts—less educated and more obstinately prejudiced. [. . .]

The public, we protest, should educate itself in this art and be less cocksure in its verdicts. "To have read *Hiawatha* in the eighth grade" does not make a competent connoisseur, and one may not turn down the imagists because one can't scan them in finger-counted iambics. Poetry may be on the way toward as great variety as modern music enjoys, whether in the number, length and placing of notes (syllables) in the bar (the foot); in variety of rhythmic phrasing; in tempo—from *andante* to *scherzo;* in movement—from *staccato* to *legato;* in tone-color, timbre, and the countless other refinements which should make poetry, like music, infinitely expressive of the emotional life of our age. [. . .] [Poetry] has been hampered by language-isolation, and by an antiquated system of metrics—a mediaeval survival in this scientific age, as empirical and misleading as astrology. Professor Patterson of Columbia is almost the first investigator to make a scientific study of speech-rhythms; and it may be reasonably hoped that such work as his will aid the poet of the future to study the past with more knowledge, to rid himself of hampering and artificial restrictions, and to discover new possibilities of beauty in his art.

Indeed, we may look forward with some confidence to a widening of its range. Poetry is like to be recognized more generally as a vocal art, and to be used much more than formerly in connection with music and the dance, both lyrically and dramatically. In spite of postponements and disappointments, one may hope for a proud future, perhaps an almost immediate future, for the poetic drama. [. . .]

Thus there would seem to be good reason to hope for a richer period in the not distant future of poetic art in America. If much has been gained during the last ten or fifteen years, we have reached merely a new viewpoint toward wider horizons. No art is static—it must go on or retreat. The poets must make the art more necessary to the people, a more immediate and spontaneous expression of their life, their dream. A people imaginatively creative enough to invent a telephone, an airplane, to build great bridges and skyscraper towers, is full of the spirit of poetry—the poets have only to set it free.

Poetry 15.1 (1919): 33–38. Rpt. in *Poets and Their Art*. New York: Macmillan, 1926: 192–97.

MARIANNE MOORE

Comment

Months ago—quite beyond the memory of those who have to hustle to read a weekly—*The New Republic* observed in an editorial that *The Dial* has not encouraged a single interesting new American writer since 1920. There was the conclusion to be drawn that new writers whom *The Dial* had published were not interesting, and the inference that interesting new writers had been encouraged by other people and that we had missed them.

What is an interesting new writer?

1. A writer who is interesting for some reason other than his writing. Thus the most interesting writer is often oneself and after that one's friend. But we shall not undertake to argue the matter on this plane.
2. A writer who has lately written something interesting. We naturally feel that our contributors are interesting in that way.
3. A writer who will later make a considerable name for himself in an appropriate quarter. In practice an argument between stubborn people about a new writer can be settled only, if at all, at a time when the writer is anything but new.

What writers, then, have been new during the past seven years and are of such reputation that both *The Dial* and *The New Republic* must agree that they were also interesting? First in importance come the writers we never heard of and shall not hear of until *The American Caravan* turns them up in October. Then come the writers who make you jealous. I do not see, however, that we need precisely knock our heads together for not having encouraged Miss Loos or Mr. Erskine. Could we, if we had tried? Does any one recall to our advantage or to his that we published when he was a new writer stories by Michael Arlen? But I do not suppose *The New Republic* meant us to try to encourage writers who were out of our class. I have great admiration for the healthy talent of Gordon Young whose melodramas in the *Adventure* magazine have been improving steadily for some years. And what could *The Dial* do for him?

Ernest Hemingway is another matter. His book, *The Sun Also Rises,* has more warmth in it than one is accustomed to find in a dozen American successes all together. Fortunately he has reached a level from which he can kick encouragement downstairs.

It remains inconceivable that *The New Republic* should not have thought a single new contributor of ours interesting. Perhaps it is with our "encouragement" that fault is found and not with our contributors at all. Whatever character *The Dial* may have is the result of a selection not so much of writers as of writing. This is the usual way of running a magazine which pretends to general interest—a way which is apt to prove more encouraging to the reader than to the writer, since it aims first of all at ensuring that the magazine contain things which are interesting to read. Things which were interesting to write sometimes come to be rejected. The writer feels that he is being encouraged to try to become a hack. He grows irascible and wastes useful energy. Or, fortunately, he begins to write books—fortunately because the book publishers have rarely been more willing to risk a thousand or so on a good thing than they are at present.

On the other hand, magazines which are edited by their contributors can and must give their contributors the run of the place, and to be given the run of any place can be, for a time, a great encouragement to a writer. Magazines of this type are often more immediately encouraging to interesting new writers, not to mention movements, than magazines like *The Dial*. But in the long run the reader too is important. Many writers will continue to appear first in small "group magazines." Our business is to furnish a not too scattered public for what they write well, as others will see that they have a larger public whenever they choose to be tiresome.

In closing let us remember that it is impossible in the world of letters to act or to refuse to act without stirring up a hurricane of catcalls, of which *The New Republic*'s are not always the merriest. Lists of interesting new American writers of the past seven years will be gratefully received.

The Dial 83.3 (September 1927): 269–70.

MARIANNE MOORE

From "The Spare American Emotion"

The Making of Americans Being The History of a Family's Progress. By Gertrude Stein. 8vo. 925 pages. The Three Mountains Press. $8.

[. . .] We have here a truly psychological exposition of American living—an account of that happiness and of that unhappiness which is to those experiencing it, as fortuitous as it is to those who have an understanding of heredity and of environment natural and inevitable. Romantic, curious, and engrossing is this story of "the old people in a new world, the new people made out of the old." There are two kinds of men and women Miss Stein tells us, the attacking kind and the resisting kind, each of which is often modified by many complex influences. Mr. Dehning who was of the resisting kind, "never concerned himself very much with the management of the family's way of living and the social life of his wife and children. These things were all always arranged by Mrs. Dehning." Yet "they could each one make the other one do what they wanted the other one to be doing"—this "really very nice very rich good kind quite completely successful a little troubled american man and woman." The insufficiency of Alfred Hersland who married Julia Dehning, is shown to be largely a result of his mother's anonymity, of incompetent pedagogy, of spoiling, and of his father's impatient unconsidering wilfulness. The Dehnings were happy; the Herslands were under the impression that they too, were happy. [. . .]

In persons either of the resisting or of the attacking kind, contradictions between "the bottom nature and the other natures" result in hybrids; as in Napoleon—in Herbert Spencer—in various other kinds of nature. Disillusionment, sensitiveness, cowardice, courage, jealousy, stubbornness, curiosity, suspicion, hopefulness, anger, subtlety, pride, egotism, vanity, ambition—each phase of emotion as of behaviour, is to Miss Stein full of meaning. "Someone gives to another one a stubborn feeling," she says, "when that one could be convincing that other one if that other one would then continue listening," and "it is very difficult in quarrelling to be certain in either one what the other one is remembering." Of the assorting of phenomena in "an ordered system" she says, "Always I am learning, always it is interesting, often it is exciting."

There is great firmness in the method of this book. [. . .]

We "hasten slowly forward" by a curious backward kind of progress. "Sometimes I like it," Miss Stein says, "that different ways of emphasizing can make very different meanings in a phrase or sentence I have made and am rereading." [. . .]

Repeating has value then as "a way to wisdom." [. . .]

Certain aspects of life are here emphasized—the gulf between youth and age, and the bond between these two; the fact of sentimental as of hereditary family indivisibility—such that when Julia Dehning was married, every one of the Dehnings had "feeling of married living in them."

The power of sex which is palpable throughout this novel, is handsomely implied in what is said of certain uncles and cousins in the Dehning family,

> "generous decent considerate fellows, frank and honest in their friendships, and simple in the fashion of the elder Dehning. With this kindred Julia had always lived as with the members of one family. These men did not supply for her the training and experience that helps to clear the way for an impetuous woman through a world of passions, they only made a sane and moral back-ground on which she in her later life could learn to lean."

The ineradicable morality of America is varyingly exposited, as in the statement that to Julia Dehning, "all men that could be counted as men by her and could be thought of as belonging ever to her, they must be, all, good strong gentle creatures, honest and honorable and honoring." Contrary to "the french habit in thinking," "the american mind accustomed to waste happiness and be reckless of joy finds morality more important than ecstacy and the lonely extra of more value than the happy two."

There is ever present in this history, a sense of the dignity of the middle class, "the one thing always human, vital, and worthy." [. . .]

As Bunyan's Christian is English yet universal, this sober, tender-hearted, very searching history of a family's progress, comprehends in its picture of life which is distinctively American, a psychology which is universal.

The Dial 80.2 (February 1926): 153–56.

AMY LOWELL

From "Nationalism in Art"

American and English critics do love to talk about American art. They tell us just what it ought to be about, and how it should be presented. They are constantly on the *qui vive* to detect foreign ideas and alien interests, and even if forced to admit good work in something possessing these baneful qualities, they are sure to heave a sigh, and deplore the fact that it is "un-American."

It would seem that the only thing to cure critics of this attitude would be a course in psychology. It is not so surprising that English critics, ignorant of our civilization, and of the vastness of our country and its many and various intellectual reactions, should erect a spurious ideal of what literature here should be. But that our own critics should persist in demanding a narrow and purely surface "Americanism" is more astonishing.

To their minds "Americanism" would seem to consist of a mixture of trade-unionism, slums (neither of which phenomena, it may be remarked, is peculiar to this country), polyethnic factories, and limitless prairies peopled by heroic cow-boys. This would appear to be a rather narrow range in which to confine the art of a great nation. For we are a great nation, and that supremely interesting thing, a nation in the making. Is our lack of a correspondingly great art due to our youth, or to other, and more artificial, causes?

To all people who find art a worthy preoccupation and endeavor, this question is one of paramount interest. What can we do to get ourselves worthily down on canvas or paper? How can we produce that concourse of great artists which the critics are always fuming at us for not possessing? How angry they would be if we suggested that they were one of the obstacles which stand in the way, that this constant talk and urging on the subject of "Americanism" was one of the surest ways not to get it. [. . .]

Art is a thing of the individual. It is all very well to group by-gone artists into schools for class-room convenience. It amuses a certain type of mind to fasten tags upon living men. It interests readers and stimulates their curiosity to line artists up in opposing factions like the two sides of a base-ball game. But these are purely exterior phenomena and leave the profound individuality of the artist untouched. So shy and unaccountable is the creative impulse that it has so far defied the researches of psychologists. It depends upon a number of physical and mental phenomena, worked upon by environment. And it is this subtle, elusive, and awe-inspiring thing which the critics are so anxious to push here and there!

A nation is its character, just as a man is. Personality is made up of all sorts of traits and habits, cross-sectioning and inhibiting each other. It is in its essence, in the kind of character a man has, that his national character comes out. It is stupid and impertinent to be forever telling a man to try and be someone else. The American artist must first of all be encouraged to be himself, and by being himself openly and fearlessly he will also be entirely American. In fact, he could not help it if he would. We are a nation with marked characteristics; there is no lack of national flavor about us. That we do not get it into our literature is because of another national trait—we are conventional, hopelessly, timidly so. All the intellectual revolts and movements come from abroad. But, and here is the point, American artists living abroad are usually in the van of such movements. Whistler led one of the most important artistic reforms of our time, and one of the best known of the French symbolists is Stuart Merrill, an American. No, we are not stupid, and not incapable of the seething intellectual force which makes for change, but here at home we live in an atmosphere of stuffy monotony, and the critics, who should be our teachers and helpers, are forever asking us to mold ourselves on one pattern.

No other country has treated its artists so. Other countries have realized that in the richness and many-sidedness of artistic achievement lies the greatness of national artistic life.

Musicians speak of the "attack" with which a singer takes a note. National character is shown in this quality of "attack," the way an artist takes a subject, the fluid play of his personality about it. Let us show a little more trust in our artists, let us believe that they know what is good for themselves better than we do. And when an American artist, with all the force and vitality of his go-ahead American nature, braves the scorn of the critics and lays a beautiful pomegranate before us, let us not weep or scold because it is not a rice pudding.

Poe and Walt Whitman share the honor of being America's greatest poets. And what a difference! How unlike are the subjects which inspired them, and how utterly unlike their forms of "attack." But it is quite obvious to the most casual reader that neither of them could have come out of any country except America. It is the fashion to call Poe an exotic. Why? Because there has only been one of him? Could he have been an Englishman, a Frenchman, a German? Clearly he has none of the national traits of these, or any other foreign countries. It must be then because he is a genius that we fail to see the American in him. Is it not a little sad that genius is so rare with us that when it appears we dub it "exotic?"

No, what the American artist needs to be told is to be himself. And to spare no study to present that self as it really is. If a poet chooses the ancient Aztec civilization as the background for a poem, it may be as purely "American" a production as though he had laid his scene in the lower East Side of New York at the present day. If he chooses to people the Kentucky woods with fairies, who are we to bar out the fine play of his imagination as alien to our national temper? And is it not a little ludicrous, perhaps pathetic, to have a reviewer upbraid him because he has not chosen to write about the laborers on the adjacent farms? What reviewers of that type do not understand is, that neither poet nor painter chooses his subject. It is the subject which chooses him; he can no more help his preferences and inspirations than he can help the shape of his head. [. . .]

An artist cannot choose his number, but he can learn to spin his wheel. We are afraid to go to school lest we cease to be ourselves. A strong man gains an added sense of power by everything he learns. Every great artist has spent a life of laborious learning. He has mastered his technique with infinite pains, and by so doing has been able to fling his personality unimpeded before the world. The only motto for a serious artist is: WORK! Instead of begging us to be what we are not, the critics should urge us to be more fully what we are. Only so will they hasten the day when America will have the great artists for which she clamors.

Poetry 5.1 (October 1914): 33–38.

JESSIE REDMON FAUSET

From "Impressions of the Second Pan-African Congress"

The dream of a Pan-African Congress had already come true in 1919. Yet it was with hearts half-wondering, half fearful that we ventured to realize it afresh in 1921. [. . .] [We] crossed the seas not knowing just what would be the plan of action for the Congress, for would not its members come from the four corners of the earth and must there not of necessity be a diversity of opinion, of thought, of project? But the main thing, the great thing, was that Ethiopia's sons through delegates were stretching out their hands from all over the black and yearning world.

II

Then one day, the 27th of August, we met in London in Central Hall, under the shadow of Westminster Abbey. Many significant happenings had those cloisters looked down on, but surely on none more significant than on this group of men and women of African descent, so different in rearing and tradition and yet so similar in purpose. The rod of the common oppressor had made them feel their own community of blood, of necessity, of problem.

Men from strange and diverse lands came together. We were all of us foreigners. South Africa was represented, the Gold Coast, Sierra Leone and Lagos, Grenada, the United States of America, Martinique, Liberia. No natives of Morocco or of East Africa came, yet men who had lived there presented and discussed their problems. British Guiana and Jamaica were there and the men and women of African blood who were at that time resident in London. [. . .]

Out of the flood of talk emerged real fact and purpose for the American delegate. First, that West Africa had practically no problems concerning the expropriation of land but had imminent something else, the problem of political power and the heavy and insulting problem of segregation. The East African, on the other hand, and also the South African had no vestige of a vote (save in Natal), had been utterly despoiled of the best portions of his land, nor could he buy it back. In addition to this the East African had to consider the influx of the East Indian who might prove a friend, or might prove as harsh a taskmaster as the European despoiler.

Through the inter-play of speech and description and idea, two propositions flashed out—one, the proposition of Mr. Augusto, a splendid, fearless speaker from Lagos, that the Pan-African Congress should accomplish something very concrete. He urged that we start with the material in hand and advance to better things. First of all let us begin by financing the Liberian loan. Liberia is a Negro Independency already founded. "Let us," pleaded Mr. Augusto, "lend the solid weight of the newly-conscious black world toward its development."

The other proposition was that of Mr. Marryshow, of Grenada, and of Professor Hutto of Georgia. "We must remember," both of them pointed out, "that not words but actions are needed. We must be prepared to put our hands in our pockets; we must make sacrifices to help each other." "Tell us what to do," said Mr. Hutto, "and the Knights of Pythias of Georgia stand ready, 80,000 strong, to do their part."

Those were fine, constructive words. Then at the last meeting we listened to the resolutions which Dr. DuBois had drawn up. Bold and glorious resolutions they were, couched in winged, unambiguous words. Without a single dissenting vote the members of the Congress accepted them. We clasped hands with our newly found brethren and departed, feeling that it was good to be alive and most wonderful to be colored. Not one of us but envisaged in his heart the dawn of a day of new and perfect African brotherhood.

III

Down to Dover we flew, up the English Channel to Ostend, and thence to Brussels.

Brussels was different. [. . .] In the first place, there were many more white than colored people—there are not many of us in Brussels—and it was not long before we realized that their interest was deeper, more immediately significant than that of the white people we had found elsewhere. Many of Belgium's economic and material interests centre in Africa in the Belgian Congo. Any interference with the natives might result in an interference with the sources from which so many Belgian capitalists drew their prosperity. [. . .]

After we had visited the Congo Museum we were better able to understand the unspoken determination of the Belgians to let nothing interfere with their dominion in the Congo. Such treasures! Such illimitable riches! What a store-house it must plainly be for them. For the first time in my life I was able to envisage what Africa means to Europe [. . .]

And yet the shadow of Colonial dominion governed. Always the careful Belgian eye watched and peered, the Belgian ear listened. For three days we listened to pleasant generalities without a word of criticism of Colonial Governments, without a murmur of complaint of Black Africa, without a suggestion that this was an international Congress called to define and make intelligible the greatest set of wrongs against human beings that the modern world has known. We realized of course how delicate the Belgian situation was and how sensitive a conscience the nation had because of the atrocities of the Leopold regime. We knew the tremendous power of capital organized to exploit the Congo; but despite this we proposed before the Congress was over to voice the wrongs of Negroes temperately but clearly. We assumed of course that this was what Belgium expected, but we reckoned without our hosts in a very literal sense. Indeed as we afterward found, we were reckoning without our own presiding officer, for without doubt M. Diagne on account of his high position in the French Government had undoubtedly felt called on to assure the Belgian Government that no "radical" step would be taken by the Congress. He sponsored therefore a mild resolution suggested by the secretaries of the Palais Mondial stating that Negroes were "susceptible" of education and pledging cooperation of the Pan-African Congress with the international movement in Belgium. When the London resolutions (which are published this month as our leading editorial), were read, M. Diagne was greatly alarmed, and our Belgian visitors were excited. The American delegates were firm and for a while it looked as though the main session of the Pan-African Congress was destined to end in a rather disgraceful row. It was here, however, that the

American delegates under the leadership of Dr. DuBois, showed themselves the real masters of the situation. With only formal and dignified protest, they allowed M. Diagne to "jam through" his resolutions and adjourn the session; but they kept their own resolutions in place before the Congress to come up for final consideration in Paris, and they maintained the closing of the session in Brussels in order and unity. I suppose the white world of Europe has never seen a finer example of unity and trust on the part of Negroes toward a Negro leader.

But we left Belgium in thoughtful and puzzled mood. [. . .]

IV

At last Paris!

Between Brussels and the queen city of the world we saw blasted town, ravaged village and plain, ruined in a war whose basic motif had been the rape of Africa. What should we learn of the black man in France?

Already we had realized that the black colonial's problem while the same intrinsically, wore on the face of it a different aspect from that of the black Americans. Or was it that we had learned more quickly and better than they the value of organization, of frankness, of freedom of speech? [. . .]

We met in the Salle des Ingénieurs (Engineers' Hall) in little Rue Blanche back of the Opera. [. . .] And around us were more strange faces—new types to us—from Senegal, from the French Congo, from Madagascar, from Annam. I looked at that sea of dark faces and my heart was moved within me. However their white overlords or *their* minions might plot and plan and thwart, nothing could dislodge from the minds of all of them the knowledge that black was at last stretching out to black, hands of hope and the promise of unity though seas and armies divided. [. . .]

The situation in Paris was less tense, one felt the difference between monarchy and republic. But again the American was temporarily puzzled. Even allowing for natural differences of training and tradition, it seemed absurd to have the floor given repeatedly to speakers who dwelt on the glories of France and the honor of being a black Frenchman, when what we and most of those humble delegates wanted to learn was about *us*. [. . .]

But this audience was different from that in Brussels. To begin with, its members were mainly black and being black, had suffered. More than one man to whom the unusually autocratic presiding officer had not given the right to speak said to me after hearing Dr. DuBois' exposition of the meaning and purpose of the Pan-African Congress, "Do you think I could get a chance to speak to Dr. DuBois? There is much I would tell him."

France is a colonial power but France is a republic. And so when our resolutions were presented once more to this the final session of the Pan-African Congress, that audience felt that here at last was the fearless voicing of the long stifled desires of their hearts, here was comprehension, here was the translation of hitherto unsyllabled, unuttered prayers. The few paragraphs about capitalism M. Diagne postponed "for the consideration of the next Pan-African Congress." But the rest that yearning, groping audience accepted with their souls. [. . .]

V

Yet after all the real task was at Geneva. [. . .] The Assembly of the League of Nations was on. A thousand petitions and resolutions were in process of being presented. Delegates from many nations were here and men of international name and fame were presiding. How were we to gain audience?

Fortunately for us Dr. DuBois' name and reputation proved the open sesame. [. . .]

On Monday night, September 13, Dr. DuBois addressed the English Club of Geneva and conveyed to them some idea of what the black world was thinking, feeling and doing with regard to the Negro problem. I am sure that many of that group of people, thinkers and students though they were, had never dreamed before that there might even be a black point of view. But they took their instruction bravely and afterwards thanked Dr. DuBois with shining eyes and warm hand clasps. [. . .]

At the end of a week of steady driving, by dint of interviewing, of copying, of translating, of recopying, we were ready to present and did present to Sir Eric Drummond, secretary of the League of Nations, a copy in French and English of the resolutions entitled To The World [. . .] and of the manifesto. [. . .]

And between whiles we listened to the world striving to right its wrongs at the Assembly of the League of Nations.

Of course we were at a disadvantage because America, not being in the League of Nations, had no delegate. But Professor Murray suggested to M. Bellegarde, the Haitian delegate, that he state the second resolution [. . .] during the debate on Mandates. This he did, as Professor Murray writes us, with "quite remarkable success" and "I think that next year it may be quite suitable to put it down as a resolution."

VI

Results are hard to define. But I must strive to point out a few. First then, out of these two preliminary conferences of 1919 and 1921, a definite organization has been evolved, to be known as the Pan-African Congress. There will be more of this in these pages. Naturally working with people from all over the world, with the necessity for using at least two languages, with the limited detailed knowledge which the black foreigner is permitted to get of Africa and with the pressure brought to bear on many Africans to prevent them from frank speech—action must be slow and very careful. It will take years for an institution of this sort to function. But it is on its own feet now and the burden no longer is on black America. It must stand or fall by its own merits.

We have gained proof that organization on our part arrests the attention of the world. We had no need to seek publicity. If we had wanted to we could not have escaped it. The press was with us always. The white world is feverishly anxious to know of our thoughts, our hopes, our dreams. Organization is our strongest weapon.

It was especially arresting to notice that the Pan-African Congress and the Assembly of the League of Nations differed not a whit in essential methods. Neither attempted a hard and fast program. Lumbering and slow were the wheels of both activities. There had to be much talk, many explanations, an infinity of time and patience and then talk again. Neither the wrongs of Africa nor of the world, can be righted in a day nor in a decade. We can only make beginnings.

The most important result was our realization that there is an immensity of work ahead of all of us. We have got to learn everything—facts about Africa, the difference between her colonial governments, one foreign language at least (French or Spanish), new points of view, generosity of ideal and of act. All the possibilities of all black men are needed to weld together the black men of the world against the day when black and white meet to do battle.

God grant that when that day comes we shall be so powerful that the enemy will say, "But behold! These men are our brothers."

The Crisis 23.1 (November 1921): 12–18.

GWENDOLYN BENNETT

From "The Ebony Flute"

Gold October has now given way to the crisp call of November and with ac-
celeration akin to that which goes surging through our blood these sharp
autumn days the news about Negroes and what they are doing, as well as
what is being done about them, piles higher and higher. . . . *Deep River,* the
all-American opera or rather operetta, as some of our more fastidious musical
critics would have it, has appeared on Broadway in one and the same week
with *Black Boy* . . . both of these two vehicles feature the Negro . . . There is
a deal of satisfaction in the fact that New York news sheets have given so
much space to the discussion of the former, although little or nothing has
been said of the fact that most of the players in the piece are Negroes. Some
meagre praise is given to Julius Bledsoe, *whose rich voice is a very benison over
the stage whenever he stands forth*—to quote Gilbert Gabriel of the *New York
Sun.* Most of the critiques are given over to the fact of *Deep River's* being a
purely native product as well as to the fact that Laurence Stallings wrote the
book. Due praise is given Mr. Stallings for having recaptured in his libretto
some of the brittle beauty of Lafcadio Hearn's New Orleans. . . . the New Orleans of the fabled 1830's. We wonder though whether an author can be any
greater than the emotion he inspires in his audience. . . . most people are of
the opinion that *Deep River* is fairly dull entertainment. Rose McClendon in
the third act receives rare commendation. . . . Alexander Woollcott says in
the *New York World* for October tenth:

When "Deep River" was having its trial flight in Philadelphia Ethel Barrymore
slipped in to snatch what moments she could of it. "Stay till the last act if you can,"
Arthur Hopkins whispered to her, "and watch Rose McClendon come down those
stairs. She can teach some of our most hoity-toity actresses distinction."

It was Miss Barrymore who hunted him up after the performance to say, "She
can teach them all distinction." [. . .]

As for *Black Boy.* . . . Jim Tully and Frank Dazey seem to have misused
material that was destined for a fine plot. New York critics are of an opinion
that the authors have concocted a rather cheap, tawdry sort of play. However, its star, Paul Robeson, is with one acclaim said to play his part with
distinction and beauty. One knew, of course, even before the play went into
rehearsal that, if *Black Boy* was to be played by Paul Robeson, this good-natured, fame-drunk pugilist would sing with those mellow organ tones that
few songsters achieve. . . . and right here we think again of that faulty, over-

advertised piece, *All God's Chillun*. . . . in it Robeson sang *Sometimes Ah Feel Lak a Motherless Chile* offstage with melting beauty and simplicity. [. . .]

And so we have the native American opera which has as its subject the Negro or rather the Creole who is in part Negro. . . . in the same instant we have the furor that is being created by the "mustard colored" *Lulu Belle*. . . . close on the heels of both of these comes *Black Boy* with a colored star and just in the offing we have J. P. McEvoy's *Hallelujah, Get Hot,* for which Zora Neale Hurston is writing some of the scenes. Which reminds us that the Actors' Theatre announces that it will produce a dramatization of *Porgy* by Dubose Heyward. I understand that Mrs. Heyward assisted her husband in preparing it for the stage. The piece is to be called *Catfish Row* for the stage on the ground that the dramatic production deals more with the group of people who live in this turbulent neighborhood than with Porgy as a single, outstanding personality. So far little is known of the cast save the fact that the players will all be Negroes. It has been characterized by the producers as *a study of the old-fashioned Negro as opposed to the numerous scenes of more sophisticated life in the cabarets of Harlem.*

The Negro as a factor in dramatic art is not confined to New York alone. . . . *Popoplikahu,* an African play by Georgia Douglas Johnson and Bruce Nugent, is being rehearsed by Barrington Guy for the President Theatre in Washington, D. C. Barrington Guy is the son of the famous Nathaniel Guy. Mrs. Johnson is also the author of *Blue Blood,* one of the *Opportunity Contest* prize-winning plays, which is to be included in Frank Shay's *Fifty Contemporary One-Act Plays* which is to be brought out by *Appleton and Company.* Mr. Shay also plans getting together a collection that will be labeled *Fifty Contemporary Plays by Negroes.* . . . speaking of Mrs. Johnson reminds me of the perfectly delightful chat I had with her after she had come back from Chicago where she was graciously received by Harriet Monro [sic] of the *Poetry* staff. . . . and of how Carl Sandburg did speak with her of this and that thing about Negroes and their work. . . . while in the "Windy City" she saw Fenton Johnson who it seems constantly bemoans the fact that he is not in New York City.

Hand in hand with the Negro's position as a figure in American Drama goes our continued importance in literature. *Tropic Death* has been on the market several weeks now. . . . reviewers are of the opinion that Mr. Waldrond knows his subject well and presents his material with ability and assurance. *Nigger Heaven* has been and still is a best seller. Langston Hughes' new book of poems, *Fine Clothes to the Jew,* will be published by Alfred Knopf in the Spring. . . . Aaron Douglas has been commissioned to design the wrapper for this as well as three other Knopf books. The information has leaked through that Joseph Hergesheimer is at work on a new novel which deals with the Negro.

The scene is to be laid in Charleston and its name [at] this writing is to be *Sulphur Rose.*

If Mr. Van Vechten has done nothing else in writing *Nigger Heaven,* he has at least made one more contribution to the vernacular. . . . Sightseers, visitors and other strangers that might find themselves within the limits of Harlem for a space are said to be "vanvechtening" around . . . however, there is one other effect that *Nigger Heaven* has had that is of distinct value to our race history—the Librarian of the Queen's University in Canada has written to James F. Drake, the New York rare book dealer, that he has become so interested in Charles W. Chesnutt, through reading *Nigger Heaven,* that he wants a complete list of his books for the Queen's Library. *The Literary Lovers* of Washington, D. C., of whom E. C. Williams is chairman, met on Sunday, October third, to discuss Mr. Van Vechten's last book. . . . a composite opinion was reached that it was a rather fine thing, although not exactly after the style of their own community. [. . .]

. . . . [Somehow] I wish that along with the record of Negro dances in the Twentieth Century could go the story of Negro music. . . . high up in the pages of its glory I would write the name of Edmund T. Jenkins, composer and musician, *Associate to the Royal Academy of Music* in England, and member of the *Society of Musicians and Composers* in Paris. He was born in Charleston, S. C., and I wonder a bit sadly whether that proud southern city knows that one of her talented sons has died. But thirty years of age, Jenkins' life was snapped short after an acute attack of appendicitis. . . . I shudder to think of the genius the race has lost! In last year's *Opportunity Contest* his *African War Dance* won the first prize. One had but to sit a while in his tiny studio on rue Pasquier in Paris and hear him play bits of this or that composition on which he was at work to realize that here was a musician of rare talent, a poet with a sensitive soul. At the time that he was taken ill he was at work on a descriptive epic for the symphony orchestra. He had finished the composition and orchestration of four movements of it. . . . it was to be in five movements and its name was *The Gully.* The steady thump-thump of the left hand chords will now resound through the years with the last agonized beatings of his noble heart. . . . he was my friend and in the rush of what Negroes are writing or doing and the songs they are singing I should like to pipe one shrill note on a flute of ebony to his memory. . . . and as a hope to the Negroes who will come after this generation with music in their hearts I dedicate this month's column to Edmund T. Jenkins.

Opportunity 4.47 (1926): 356–58.

GWENDOLYN BENNETT

From "Blue-Black Symphony"

Home to Harlem. By Claude McKay. New York: Harper and Brothers. $2.50.

Here is Harlem once more—this time through the eyes of a Negro. Harlem with its laughter, its tears, its working and playing. Here is rich soil which the author ably plows. Claude McKay knows Harlem from the inside. He has gone its mundane ways, one with the black throng that pulsates through his novel.

In this one fact lies the essential difference between this book and *Nigger Heaven,* by Carl Van Vechten, which I am convinced will be for a time at least the criterion by which all novels about Harlem and Negro life in metropolitan cities will be judged. Mr. Van Vechten is a student of research giving a cursory account of his findings; Mr. McKay is the African chief telling the story of his tribe to the children of unborn men. Nor do I mean to make an odious comparison, for each has its place in the American literature of this century. Then too, there are many points of similarity between the two books. Each book is more or less built around the night-life of Harlem, albeit they each depict a different stratum of Negro society. Both books are only sketches of Harlem life, telling in brief that it is a place of color, movement and fever. Each author has taken for his central figure a brown Lothario—Van Vechten's hero a young Negro writer; McKay's Jake, a strapping buck who is a longshoreman.

Home to Harlem is the story of Harlem's serving classes. Longshoremen, waitresses, butlers, laundresses, bell-boys, kitchen-workers, maids and servitors of all sorts amble their way through the pages of Claude McKay's book. These cleaners of shoes and passers of foods gyrate and ogle through the Harlem days that followed the World War. This is Harlem before the era of the "gin-mill"—Harlem in those last agonized days before Prohibition. Negroes, dim-brown, clear brown, rich brown, chestnut, copper, yellow, near-white, mahogany and gleaming anthracite in those frantic whisky guzzling days before the subterfuges of Volsteadism set in. . . . Negroes who are servers of men, fighting, drinking, laughing, dancing. In the words of the author, "dancing, thick as maggots in a vat of sweet liquor, and as wriggling." Here is realism, stark, awful but somehow beautiful. McKay has left no stone unturned, no detail unmentioned in this telling of things as they are. Yet he has told many of the most sordid truths with the same simplicity that a child tells its mother this or that thing has happened. He has touched many ugly and jagged contours with a naïveté that is surprising. There is no lewdness in his uncovering unpleasant secrets about his people. He simply says, "Here is truth." Then again he says, "This is earthy but withal beautiful." McKay brings all five of his sense[s] to the writing of this book. With sensual accuracy his characters move through the smells, the color, the taste of dark-eyed Harlem, touching life with warm, brown hands.

The plot of the story is thin, unimportant. Just the recitation of the amorous meanderings of one Jake Brown, ex-soldier, stevedore, Pullman porter. Rather a symphonic tone-poem of dark brown workers that here and there resounds with immortal chords of sentiment. Claude McKay sets the major theme for his symphony in the tale of his characters as people of a working class. Actually this is a story of whether or not a man of Jake's personal charm shall haul barrels and sling hash for his living or be a "sweet-man," kept by the earnings of women in whose eyes he has found favor. This is a pæan of foodstuffs carried by Negro soldiers who were trained and taken to Europe with the idea that they were to fight in the World War; of black men who unknowingly are hired to work as scabs on the docks at nine dollars a day; of brown men who stoke furnaces on tramp steamers and sleep in filthy places, rife with foul smells; of dining car waiters who must labor under the tyranny of a Negro cook and who must sleep in overcrowded bunks, infested with vermin . . . all juxtaposed against the Harlem "lounge lizard" who leads a lazy, comfortable life. [. . .]

One feels that the author of *Home to Harlem* has written about things that he himself has actually experienced. His workers are not mere puppets; they are McKay recast to fit the story. McKay has stoked furnaces and answered to the call of "George." Much of the fervor of this book is born of that fact. Mr. McKay is a poet as well as a worker. Ever and anon this first novel becomes Claude McKay, the poet, laying fond hands upon the shoulders of Claude McKay, the worker. There is a color in Mr. McKay's words at times that is sheer posey [*sic*]. Then again you feel the sweat trickling down his own back. He bears a firm conviction in his heart that Negroes are beautiful even though their beauty is oft-times bowed beneath heavy burdens. He has given us a new side of Harlem, a side few Negroes would dare or wish to write about. This is the side of the Negro that a white man can never know except by proxy. There is no propaganda in this book unless it is that longshoremen, waitresses, et al. are a joyous people for all their drudgery. Claude McKay is content to let his message be that Harlem is shot with liquor-rich laughter, banana-ripe laughter . . . merging its life into a soft, blue-black symphony.

New York Herald Tribune Books 4.26 (March 11, 1928): 5–6.

DOROTHY WEST

Letter to Langston Hughes, 1934

Dear Lang,

Under separate cover I am sending you a copy of the magazine (*Challenge*) which is the final result of all my thought and plans and hopes these past months. Miraculously I got a little money, and a magazine suits my purpose better than a newspaper page.

I hope it will be the organ for the young Negro voice. I have done this first issue unaided. I am eager for your criticism. Be as harsh as you like. You may want to answer the article on Russia. Please do!

I particularly wanted your help in this venture, for we have fairly opposing views, and there would have been an interesting result. But I have learned—and I am very happy to hear it—that you have become associate editor of *The New Masses*. And thank you for the sample copy. I read it with interest and profit. I dare say you are entirely too busy to lend a helping hand to me. But this magazine is going to many of the colleges. Here is our chance to reach young thinking Negroes. Many young teachers and students have sent requests for the magazine. I want people like you, and Eugene Gordon, and Schuyler, and others as wide-awake to reach this audience.

And yet, Lang, your story pleased me immensely. Personally that is what I prefer from your pen. For who else comes to your height here? But I dare say you think an article does more good. But articles are contemporary. And stories can be immortal.

Lang, I want this magazine to be one of diverse opinions. I have promised myself to print anything that is sincerely written. And I could not go thru that Russian experience without having some leaning toward communism. But I cannot reconcile myself to taking an equal interest in the white worker, or any interest in the white worker. On that point I need a little light. I want to be solely concerned with the black race. With Negro children in particular, that they may have a right to a full life.

With best wishes,

Dortie

ALS from Dorothy West to Langston Hughes, n.d. [envelope postmarked 1934], Langston Hughes Papers, Beinecke Rare Books and Manuscripts Library, Yale University.

DOROTHY WEST [WITH MARIAN MINUS]

Editorial

We envisage *New Challenge* as an organ designed to meet the needs of writers and people interested in literature which cannot be met by those Negro magazines which are sponsored by organizations and which, therefore, cannot be purely literary. Through it we hope to break down much of the isolation which exists between Negro writers themselves, and between the Negro writer and the rest of the writing world. We hope that through our pages we may be able to point social directives and provide a basis for the clear recognition of and solution to the problems which face the contemporary writer.

We are not attempting to re-stage the "revolt" and "renaissance" which grew unsteadily and upon false foundations ten years ago. A literary movement among Negroes, we feel, should, first of all, be built upon the writer's placing his material in the proper perspective with regard to the life of the Negro masses. For that reason we want to indicate, through examples in our pages, the great fertility of folk material as a source of creative material.

We want *New Challenge* to be a medium of literary expression for all writers who realize the present need for the realistic depiction of life through the sharp focus of social consciousness. Negro writers themselves and the audience which they reach must be reminded, and in many instances taught, that writing should not be *in vacuo* but placed within a definite social context.

The reorganization of the magazine has been carried through, not only with the idea of a change in policy, but also in terms of the best way to fulfill our plans for relating it to communities beyond New York City. We want to see *New Challenge* as the organ of regional groups composed of writers opposed to fascism, war and general reactionary policies. There is already one such group functioning in Chicago, and we are eager to see other groups in other cities follow this example. Contributing editors from several large cities have been selected in the hope that the organizational activity of groups in those areas will be facilitated.

The success of this magazine depends upon the avoidance of any petty restrictions with regard to policy. We want it to be an organ for young writers who are seriously concerned with the problems facing them in their defense of existing culture and in their sincere creation of higher cultural values.

While our emphasis is upon Negro writers and the particular difficulties which they must meet, we are not limiting our contributors to Negroes alone.

Any writer dealing with materials which reflect a sincere interest in the ultimate understanding of the interdependence of cultures will be welcomed. The magazine is one for progressive writers, and adheres to the prescriptions of no one dogma. We do ask, however, that the bigot and potential fascist keep away from our door.

The magazine, being non-political, is not subsidized by any political party, nor does it receive huge contributions from any such group (or from individuals). We are dependent upon subscriptions, support of benefit affairs, and outright donations. We are, in this respect, responsible only to ourselves, a fact which is contrary to the belief of the skeptics and agonizing to our enemies. But we recognize our obligations to our friends and advisers and to our sincere critics; and we hope that we shall prove our multiple sense of responsibility.

The Editors. *New Challenge* 2.2 (1937): 3–4.

8

Hope Mirrlees and Continental Modernism

INTRODUCED AND SELECTED BY JULIA BRIGGS

"TO THE FORGOTTEN and silenced makers of modernism," ran the dedication of *The Gender of Modernism.* Hope Mirrlees (1887–1978) is just such a forgotten maker; and if Paris was the cradle of modernism, and the home of the "lost generation," her poem *Paris* (1919)[1] is modernism's lost masterpiece, a work of extraordinary energy and intensity, scope and ambition, written in a confidently experimental and avant-garde style. Mirrlees's view of the world is at once highly reactive and highly individual. It was unconsciously characterized by another modernist woman poet a few years later, Mina Loy, who in celebrating the poetry of Gertrude Stein argued that "the pragmatic value of modernism" was that it urged us to look again; humanity should stop "wasting its aesthetic time," by recognizing the beauty of the ordinary: "The flux of life is pouring its aesthetic aspect into your eyes, your ears—and you ignore it because you are looking for your canons of beauty in some sort of frame or glass case or tradition. Modernism says: Why not each one of us, [. . .] realize all that is impressing itself upon our subconscious, the thousand odds and ends which make up your sensory every day life?" (Scott, ed. 244). Hope Mirrlees's poem *Paris* had quite independently already taken up Loy's challenge: alert and responsive to its political moment, it threads a path between the past and the present, between the daily life of the city and its *revenants,* between the posters on the street and the paintings in the Louvre.

"Modernism has democratized the subject matter and *la belle matière* of art; through cubism the newspaper has assumed an aesthetic quality," wrote Loy (Scott, ed. 244). Yet this extension of high art to take in popular culture is more evident in *Paris* than it is in the art of Gertrude Stein. Loy's emphasis on the democratization of art sprang from the same artistic and intellectual milieu that inspired Mirrlees's poem—from contemporary French debate on the relationship of life and art, words and pictures, Cubism and "Simultaneism." In their different ways, Mirrlees, Stein, and Loy herself all managed to sidestep national or conventional poetic models by adopting the iconoclasm of high French culture. While other modernists harked back to classical, Celtic, or even far Eastern traditions, Mirrlees tuned in to the voices of French contemporaries such as Guillaume Apollinaire (1880–1918), who wrote in "*Zone*":

> *Tu lis les prospectus les catalogues les affiches qui chantent tout haut*
> *Voilà la poésie ce matin et pour le prose il y a les journeaux*
> You read leaflets catalogues posters that sing aloud
> Here's your poetry this morning and for prose there's the newspapers
>
> (Apollinaire 2)

Mirrlees later credited Jean Cocteau (1889–1963), and his elegy for the aviator Roland Garros, "*Le Cap de Bonne-Espérance*" (1919) with "liberating" *Paris,* while he, in turn, had written of being liberated from "*la forme fixe*" (Henig 13; Cocteau 6); but her poem also includes echoes of Blaise Cendrars (1887–1961), and especially of "*Contrastes*" (1913), in which the poet flings open the windows of his poetry to the streets beyond:

> *Les fenêtres de ma poésie sont grand'ouvertes sur les Boulevards*
>
> (Cendrars 70)

Uninhibited either by her gender or her nationality (she was British, or more precisely, Scottish), Mirrlees soaked up *l'esprit nouveau,* the new spirit of art, and wrote a French poem in English, a poem committed to recording the contemporary scene, to exploring the newly identified life of the unconscious, and to using forms that broke down traditional barriers—in particular those between high and low culture, between visual and verbal experience, and between different languages—and within language, between different registers and types of discourse usually isolated from one another.

How, then, did this groundbreaking poem and its remarkable author disappear through the cracks of literary history? In addition to her poems, Hope Mirrlees published three novels and the first volume of the life of the antiquary,

Sir Robert Cotton, yet when she died in 1978 there were no newspaper obituaries of her.[2] If she was remembered at all, it was as the friend of someone else—of the classical scholar Jane Harrison, of Virginia Woolf, of Ottoline Morrell, Gertrude Stein, or T. S. Eliot (whom she revered). In key respects, Mirrlees conforms to the type of modernist woman writer defined by Shari Benstock in her book *Women of the Left Bank*—living in the sixth *arrondissement,* and loving women—yet her name does not appear there, nor in any other standard account of women's contribution to modernism.[3] One reason why she and her poem remained forgotten when other modernist women writers were being rediscovered and reread was the poem's scarcity: *Paris* was printed by the Hogarth Press in an edition of 175 copies (Woolmer 31; Willis 34, 74). Ten years later, following the death of her muse, Jane Harrison, Mirrlees became a Roman Catholic, and thereafter refused permission for the poem to be reprinted, believing that certain passages in it were blasphemous (as indeed they were). More than fifty years later, she finally agreed to its being reprinted with a number of passages cut, but the scholarly journal where it appeared folded after a few issues.[4] Then, as before, *Paris* fell victim to the limitations of print culture. If Mirrlees is remembered today, it is for her fantasy novel, *Lud-in-the Mist* (1926), rather than for *Paris.*

In France, before and during the First World War, poetry and the visual arts had been growing ever closer: cubism attempted to capture the energy of Paris life in Robert Delaunay's paintings of the Eiffel Tower (1910, 1911), and Gino Severini's painting, "The Nord-Sud (Speed and Sound)" (1912), which included posters and lettering (Wilson 82, 84, 85). The *Nord-Sud* was a metro line, initially opened in 1910, though not in full service until 1916. Its route, from Montmartre to Montparnasse, corresponded to a particular cultural axis, and, indeed, to a general migration of the artistic community from Montmartre to the Left Bank. In March 1917, Pierre Reverdy launched a new review named *Nord-Sud,* dedicated to the vision of Apollinaire that had "broken new ground, opened new horizons" (Shattuck 294). It published his poetry and that of Cendrars and Cocteau, as well as articles on Cubism and its significance both for poetry and painting. Contemporary aesthetic theories such as "Simultaneism" sought to transcend the limitations, the stasis of plastic form or written language, by reaching out to embrace the whole of experience, sights and sounds, thought and language, song and dance; to discover new aesthetic means of registering the "continuous flux of Being, [. . .] the very pulse of duration" (Scott, ed. 238). It seemed that the multiplying forms, structures, and relationships of the modern world could no longer sit comfortably within the covers of a book.

Paris's iconoclasm, its aspiration to communicate visually as well as verbally, is reflected not only in its many references to paintings, but also in its

typographically experimental layout. Such experiments had begun with Stéphane Mallarmé (in this respect, as in so many others, the father of modernism). His last great poem *"Un coup de dés jamais n'abolira le hasard"* (1897) set
out the words of one long sentence across its pages to suggest visual forms—the
stars sprinkled across the sky, or the undulations of a musical score. By the
time it was reprinted in 1914, Guillaume Apollinaire was already at work on
the poems that became *Calligrammes* (1918), several of which were written in
shapes that corresponded to their subject matter (as does the Tuileries sequence,
4:20–22). Mirrlees also used the lettering and layout of the words on the page
to highlight particular names or phrases, to imitate their appearance on posters or plaques, or to set up complex relationships between them (as, for example, 5:40–42). *Paris* shifts between short and long lines of verse, and prose
passages; it employs roman and italic print or different sizes of capital letters;
it even runs words vertically down the page as a figure for social disruption,
or bursts into bars of music.

A single surviving sheet of proofs, corrected and revised by Mirrlees, reveals
her concern to achieve exactly the words and images she had in mind, and to
place them precisely on the page.[5] She made considerable demands on her
typesetter, Virginia Woolf. Indeed it was to prove the most difficult task Woolf
ever undertook of this kind, since she was almost certainly typesetting directly
from a manuscript. Her problems are reflected in the number of mistakes she
made, though we cannot tell how many of these originated with Mirrlees. When
the print run had been completed, Woolf found two further glaring errors, and
spent a tedious afternoon writing in corrections by hand on 160 copies, as a
diary entry reveals (Woolf, *Diary,* 2:33; the corrections occur at 3:13, 22:449). In
Paris, Mirrlees adopted the practice of Apollinaire and Cendrars, who had largely abandoned punctuation, and that of Pierre Reverdy, who used blank spaces
to create pauses in a text. Woolf's next two novels, *Jacob's Room* (1922) and *Mrs.
Dalloway* (1925), separate different sections of text with white spaces, one indication of the impact that typesetting *Paris* made on her own writing practice.[6]

Paris anticipates other major modernist texts—*The Waste Land* (1922),
Ulysses (1922), and *Mrs. Dalloway* (1925)—in its focus upon the daily life of a
city, its inhabitants and topography, its sights and sounds during "the peace
carnival," the great Peace Conference that concluded the First World War, and
was held in Paris during the first six months of 1919. In those months, the eyes
of the world were on the city as the conference delegates attempted to rebuild
Europe out of the rubble of the Great War. An older Paris, that of *la belle époque,*
"the banquet years," was over and new myths of sexual and artistic freedom
and experiment were coming into being; Paris was becoming a city of rebels
and outsiders, of individuals alienated or exiled in one way or another. Mirrlees

observes these myths in the making, even as she notes the city's mourning for its war dead, its efforts to absorb the social and economic problems of the peace, and the demobilization of thousands of French soldiers. *Paris* creates its own gesture of reconciliation, its own commitment to Europe through language, by adopting a strange hybrid of English and French that is part of the process of breaking down national and cultural barriers, while also exploring the many similarities and differences of meaning and usage between the two languages. It catches up and quotes the city's proliferating signs—posters, memorial plaques, and announcements, mingling these with literary and religious allusions to create a playful texture of polyglot puns.

Paris explores the dimensions of time and space[7] as the poet pursues her fashionable *flânerie,* her stroll across the city during the course of a single day, which simultaneously extends over several months, just as its tour of Paris is at the same time a tour of the provinces of France. Yet while the poem looks outward, recording the forms and colors of the city, it also looks inward, charting the long day's journey into night, and the fluctuating life of the unconscious. Dreams begotten in the murky waters of the Seine, ascend from knee-deep to waist-deep as the sun sinks (lines 310, 376), and the exploration of different *quartiers* culminates in an anticipation of Joyce's "Nighttown," as the poet reaches Montmartre at nightfall, a *quartier* characterized by alterity, by an otherness repressed during the day. Social inhibitions are embodied in "An English padre" (422), a Don Quixote tilting against the red windmill of the Moulin Rouge, Paris's most famous nightclub, while myopic Yankees enjoy the floor show. The final paragraphs celebrate black jazz musicians, *"the gurls of the nightclub—[who] love women,"* the love of Verlaine for Rimbaud, *absinthe,* Algerian tobacco and "talk, talk, talk" (429–30, 432–35). The poem ends as it began, saluting Paris (for Mirrlees, always a woman) and its cathedral of Notre-Dame, "Our Lady," not only for particular graces accorded, but also for its "grace," its spiritual gift of uniting and nurturing the disparate experiences of body and soul.

Despite this final note of homage, *Paris* also recognizes the city's tensions and dissatisfactions in a variety of ways. France's North African empire is evoked at the outset by the poster for "Zig-Zag" (3) a make of cigarette paper whose trademark was (and still is) the head of a Zouave soldier, and later, by the slogan "*'Ya Bon!*" used to advertise the breakfast food "Banania," famously accompanied by a picture of a Senegalese rifleman (206; Pieterse 85, 162–63). The racism and exploitation of empire is paralleled by the church's exploitation of children—"*Les petits Jésus*" (see line 135), boy prostitutes, while the girls taking their first communion become "holy bait," "Petits Lycéens, / Porno-gra-phie, / Charming pigmy brides" (296, 303–5). Class is also an issue as the poem attends to the workers in their blue overalls (as Cendrars had done in "*Contrastes*"), noting their demand for an eight-hour day, which was to culminate in the general strike of May 1, "The silence of *la grève,*" dramatized in the poem's most disruptive typographical gesture (see lines 236–59, 263). The last third of the poem plays out a "ritual fight" (260) between the Virgin Mary (who for Mirrlees was linked not only with religion but also with the fixed and determined world of art, "the province of fate"), and "The wicked April moon" (262), standing for the flux and chaos of life, and "the province of free-will" (Mirrlees, 1919, viii). According to the preface to her first novel, *Madeleine, One of Love's Jansensists* (1919), "Life is like a blind and limitless expanse of sky, for ever dividing into tiny drops of circumstances that rain down, thick and fast, on the just and unjust alike. Art is like the dauntless, plastic force that builds up stubborn, amorphous substance cell by cell, into the frail geometry of a shell" (vii). Set in seventeenth-century Paris around Mme de Scudéry, *Madeleine* is a *roman à clef,* recording its author's disappointment with Nathalie Barney and her circle of latter-day *précieuses.*

Mirrlees had visited Paris in 1913 with a college friend, Karin Costelloe (soon to marry Adrian Stephen, Virginia Woolf's younger brother). She was then in her mid-twenties, having recently completed a course in classics at Newnham College, Cambridge, under the tutelage of the scholar Jane Harrison. She fell in love with the city, and often returned in the years that followed. In 1914, she was joined by Harrison. They stayed together at the Hôtel de l'Elysée, on the corner of the rue de Beaune and the quai Voltaire, returning in 1915. During the war, they decided to learn Russian, and Hope was studying Russian at the Sorbonne during the first half of 1919, the period covered by the poem. In 1922, Harrison finally retired from Cambridge, and moved to Paris, where she and Hope lived at the American University Women's Club, writing and jointly translating two books from Russian. Among their Paris friends were Gertrude Stein and Alice B. Toklas, André Gide, Charles Du Bos, and the Russian exiles Remizov and Prince Mirsky.[8] While Harrison worked on her memoirs, Hope wrote two further novels, quite unlike one another, yet each original and subversive in its quiet way: *The Counterplot* (1924) is a story of family life, and its transformation into art, while *Lud-in-the-Mist* (1926) is a fantasy, a fable about the disruption of bourgeois life by fairy fruit. In the spring of 1926, Hope and Jane returned to London, to Mecklenburgh Street, but Jane's health was failing, and she died of leukemia in the spring of 1928, leaving Hope bereft.

With Jane's death, Mirrlees's most creative phase came to an end, and it may well be that *Paris* reflected not only the liberating power of Cocteau and company, but also the transforming power of love. Certainly both *Paris* and her three novels all end with a star sign—that of the constellation of the great she-bear, Ursa Major, a coded message to Jane Harrison, and part of a private game in which the two women became the elder and younger wives of "the Old One," Jane's teddy-bear, who assumed a totemic significance for the purpose. The joke was further elaborated in *The Book of the Bear* (1926), a collection of Russian folk tales that they translated together (Beard, 135–38; Peacock 268, 273–75). But if the seven stars of the Great Bear held a particular and private meaning for Hope and Jane, they also stand for the permanent forms of art in opposition to the flux of life, as they had done in Mallarmé's astonishing precursor, *"Un coup de dés"* (Mallarmé 129, 145; see also 268, 273–75).

Such a blend of private and public gestures is characteristic of Mirrlees, whose work remains exceptionally poised and impersonal, even while it draws extensively on her personal experience and knowledge. In *Paris,* she locates herself as a sympathetic outsider, writing of a French city in a French style evolved by an almost exclusively masculine artistic group. The result is an extraordinary hybrid, in which characteristics defined as those of "male modernism"—"experimental, audience-challenging and language-focused" (Scott, ed. 49)—combine with traits more typical of women modernists—"polyphonic, mobile, interactive and sexually charged" (Scott 4). The poem's engagement with so many aspects of the contemporary scene, from the politics of Woodrow Wilson to the latest act at the "Nouveau Cirque" (125, 164) is a measure of its energy, its refusal to lapse into classical generalities. At the same time, such easy intimacy with contemporary culture, both high and low, creates problems for the modern reader. Visitors to Paris in 1919 could have easily identified the advertising slogans, street signs, metro names, landmarks, and newspaper celebrities referred to in the poem, but these are now utterly obscure. In addition to its sources in popular (and transient) culture, the poem assumes a familiarity with French and English literature, particularly Molière and Shakespeare, and with history and works of art (most, though by no means all of these in the Louvre), and even with classical music. There is, of course, an element of display in such a wide range of cultural reference; Mirrlees employs what Ezra Pound (writing of Mina Loy and Marianne Moore) termed "an international tongue common to the excessively cultivated" (Scott, ed. 234), addressing herself to readers who could identify and enjoy her play of words and ideas. Yet even to a reader as cultivated as Virginia Woolf, *Paris* seemed "a very obscure, indecent and brilliant poem" (Woolf *Letters* 2:385). Mirrlees herself tacitly acknowledged its difficulty by supplying explanatory notes at the end. Even so, several of the poem's key figures remain hidden, referred to only indirectly: an obvious example is Georges Clemençeau, father of the French victory (*"le Père la Victoire"*) and Chairman of the Peace Conference (see commentary on 35; 118; 165; Macmillan 27–35).

The first edition of *Paris* is the only complete and authoritative text that exists. Because of the significance of its visual dimension, as well as its importance within the history of material modernism, it needs to be seen in facsimile, as it was set out in the Hogarth Press edition, typos and all. In order to make it more accessible for today's readers, I have provided a detailed commentary, which illustrates how concrete and specific the poem's allusions are, its precision being one aspect of its power. *Paris* is Mirrlees's major achievement, the work by which she deserves to be remembered, the work where her wit, her literary and linguistic sensibilities and her intense engagement with her times are most powerfully concentrated. As a poem it makes a remarkable—and highly political—addition to the canon of modernism—one woman's vision of peace, love, art, and urban life.

Notes

1. Although it is dated 1919, and the events described took place that year, it was in fact published in May 1920. References to the poem are made by line number. The original page numbers appear as they did in the Hogarth edition, where they were placed at the bottom of each page. I would like to thank all those who have contributed to my understanding of the poem, and in particular, Gérard Kahn; also Robin Briggs, Andrew Hugill, Michelle le Doeuff, Nicola Luckhurst, Graham Robb, Nigel Saint, and in the later stages, Hans Walter Gabler, to whom this edition is dedicated.

2. See list of Works Cited, and my account of her life in the *New Dictionary of National Biography*.

3. For example, Sandra Gilbert and Susan Gubar, *No Man's Land: The Place of the Woman Writer in the Twentieth Century* (New Haven: Yale University Press, 1988–89); Gillian Hanscombe and Virginia L. Smyers, *Writing for Their Lives: The Modernist Women, 1910–1940* (London: Women's Press, 1987); Bonnie Kime Scott, *Refiguring Modernism*, 2 vols.

4. On March 12, 1946, Mirrlees told Leonard Woolf that she definitely did not wish any of *Paris* to be reprinted (Hogarth Press archive, Reading University Library); in 1973, it was reprinted with Mirrlees's cuts, in the *Virginia Woolf Quarterly*, which also reprinted some of her more recent poems, but the journal folded soon afterwards. Virginia Woolf reported Mirrlees's conversion to Catholicism in her diary for November 30, 1929: "It is said that Hope has become a Roman Catholic on the sly. Certainly she has grown very fat—too fat for a woman in middle age who uses her brains, & so I suspect the rumour is true. [. . .] It is strange to see beauty—she had something elegant & individual—go out, like a candle flame" (*Diary* 3, 268).

5. The sheet is in the E. J. Pratt Library, Victoria University, Toronto. For further details, see commentary on 15:290–93.

6. In her article, "Virginia Woolf and the Hogarth Press," in *Modernist Writers and the Marketplace,* ed. Willison et al. (132), Laura Marcus has argued that "the experience of laying out Eliot's poetry on the page influenced Woolf's decision to use white spaces in *Jacob's Room;* the gaps provide the reader with a sequence of separated scenes rather than a narrative, and create new forms of connection," but the Eliot poems published

by the Hogarth Press in 1918 were all written in regular forms, either couplets or qua-
trains, so it is the impact of *Paris* that is visible in *Jacob's Room,* and the setting of it
constituted her greatest challenge. When Woolf typeset *The Waste Land* in 1923, she
would have worked from the version already printed in the *Criterion.* See my essay,
"Modernism's Lost Hope: Virginia Woolf, Hope Mirrlees, and the Printing of 'Paris,'" in
Reading Virginia Woolf.

7. Compare Loy, who praises Stein's work for its "interpenetration of dimensions
analogous to Cubism" (Scott, ed. 239).

8. See Gertrude Stein, *The Autobiography of Alice B. Toklas* (1933; London: Penguin,
2001), 153, 157–58; Charles Du Bos provided a *postface* for *Le Choc en retour,* the translation of Mirrlees's novel *The Counterplot* into French. Three stories and a poem by Alexey
Mikhailovich Remizov appear in *The Book of the Bear* (1926), translated by Harrison and
Mirrlees, and itself dedicated "To the Great Bear"; Prince D. S. Mirsky introduced their
translation of *The Life of the Archpriest Avvakum by Himself* (Hogarth Press, 1924).

Works Cited

Apollinaire, Guillaume. *Alcools,* trans. Donald Revell. Hanover, N.H.: Wesleyan Univer-
sity Press, 1995.
———. *Calligrammes: Poems of Peace and War (1913–1916),* trans. Anne Hyde Greet. Berke-
ley: University of California Press, 1980.
Beard, Mary. *The Invention of Jane Harrison.* Cambridge: Harvard University Press, 2000.
Benstock, Shari. *Women of the Left Bank.*
Briggs, Julia. *Reading Virginia Woolf.* Edinburgh: Edinburgh University Press, 2006.
Burke, Carolyn. "Mina Loy." In Scott, ed. *The Gender of Modernism.* 230–38.
Cocteau, Jean. *Oeuvres Poétiques Completes,* ed. Michel Decaudin. Paris: Gallimard, 1999.
Cendrars, Blaise. *Poésies Completes,* ed. Claude Leroy. Paris: Denoel, 2001.
Harrison, Jane. *Themis: A Study of the Social Origins of Greek Religion.* 1912; London: Mer-
lin Press, 1989.
Hausser, Elisabeth. *Paris au jour le jour: les évenéments vus par la Presse, 1900–1919.* Paris:
Les Editions de Minuit, 1968.
Henig, Suzanne. "Queen of Lud: Hope Mirrlees." *Virginia Woolf Quarterly* 1.1 (Fall 1972):
8–21.
Higonnet, Patrice. *Paris, Capital of the World,* trans. Arthur Goldhammer. Cambridge:
Harvard University Press, 2002.
Lilienfeld, Jane. "Willa Cather." In Scott, ed., *The Gender of Modernism.* 46–52.
MacMillan, Margaret. *Paris 1919: Six Months that Changed the World.* New York: Random
House, 2002.
Mallarmé, Stéphane. *Collected Poems,* trans. Henry Weinfield. Berkeley: University of
California Press, 1994.
Marcus, Laura. "Virginia Woolf and the Hogarth Press." In *Modernist Writers and the
Marketplace,* ed. Ian Willison, Warwick Gould, and Warren Chernaik. London: Mac-
millan, 1996.
Mirrlees, Hope. *Madeleine, One of Love's Jansenists.* London: W. Collins, 1919.
———. *The Counterplot.* London: W. Collins, 1924.
———. *Lud-in-the-Mist.* London: W. Collins, 1926.
———. *Le Choc en retour,* trans. Simone Martin-Chauffier. Paris: Plon, 1929.

————. *A Fly in Amber: A Life of Sir Robert Cotton.* London: Faber, 1962.

————, trans. with Jane Harrison. *The Life of the Archpriest Avvakum by Himself.* London: Hogarth, 1924.

————, trans. with Jane Harrison. *The Book of the Bear.* London: Nonesuch Press, 1926.

————. *Paris* (revised edition), *Virginia Woolf Quarterly* 1.2 (Winter 1973): 4–17.

Peacock, Sandra J. *Jane Ellen Harrison: The Mask and the Self.* New Haven: Yale University Press, 1988.

Pieterse, Jan Nederveen. *White on Black: Images of Africa and Blacks in Western Popular Culture.* New Haven: Yale University Press, 1992.

Poisson, Georges, *Guide des Statues de Paris: Monuments, Décors, Fontaines.* Paris: Editions Hazan, 1990.

Scott, Bonnie Kime. Introduction. In Scott, ed. *The Gender of Modernism.*

————, ed. *The Gender of Modernism.*

Shattuck, Roger. *The Banquet Years, The Origins of the Avant-Garde in France: 1885 to World War I.* London: Jonathan Cape, 1969.

Shone, Richard. *The Art of Bloomsbury.* London: Tate Gallery, 1999.

Willis, J. H., Jr. *Leonard and Virginia Woolf as Publishers: The Hogarth Press, 1917–41.* Charlottesville: University Press of Virginia, 1992.

Wilson, Sarah, ed. *Paris: Capital of the Arts, 1900–1968.* London: Royal Academy of Arts, 2002.

Woolf, Virginia. *The Diary of Virginia Woolf.*

————. *The Letters of Virginia Woolf.*

Woolmer, J. Howard. *A Checklist of the Hogarth Press, 1917–1938.* London: Hogarth Press, 1976.

HOPE MIRRLEES

Paris: A Poem

> A
> NOTRE DAME DE PARIS
> EN RECONNAISSANCE
> DE GRACES ACCORDEES

[2]

1	I want a holophrase
2	NORD-SUD
3	ZIG-ZAG
4	LION NOIR
5	CACAO BLOOKER

I want a holophrase

NORD-SUD

ZIG-ZAG
LION NOIR
CACAO BLOOKER

Black-figured vases in Etruscan tombs
RUE DU BAC (DUBONNET)
SOLFERINO (DUBONNET)
CHAMBRE DES DEPUTES

Brekekekek coax coax we are passing under the Seine

DUBONNET

The Scarlet Woman shouting BYRRH and deafening
St John at Patmos

Vous descendez Madame?

QUI SOUVENT SE PESE BIEN SE CONNAIT
QUI BIEN SE CONNAIT BIEN SE PORTE

CONCORDE

I can't
I must go slowly

(3)

Fig. 8.1. First page of poetry from 1920 text of Hope Mirrlees's *Paris*.

6   Black-figured vases in Etruscan tombs

7   RUE DU BAC (DUBONNET)
8   SOLFERINO (DUBONNET)
9   CHAMBRE DES DEPUTES

10   Brekekekek coax coax we are passing under the Seine

11   DUBONNET

12   The Scarlet Woman shouting BYRRH and deafening
13   <St.> John at Patmos

14   *Vous descendez Madame?*

15   QUI SOUVENT SE PESE BIEN SE CONNAIT
16   QUI BIEN SE CONNAIT BIEN SE PORTE

17   CONCORDE

18   I can't

19   I must go slowly

                   (3)

20   The   Tuileries   are   in   a   trance

21   because   the   painters   have

22   stared   at   them   so   long

23   Little boys in black overalls whose hands, sticky with
24   play, are like the newly furled leaves of the horse-
25   chestnuts ride round and round on wooden horses till
26   their heads turn.

27   Pigeons perch on statues
28   And are turned to stone.

29   Le départ pour Cythère.

30   These nymphs are harmless,
31   Fear not their soft mouths—
32   Some Pasteur made the Gauls immune
33   Against the bite of Nymphs . . . look

34   Gambetta
35   A red stud in the button-hole of his frock-coat
36   The obscene conjugal *tutoiement*
37   *Mais c'est logique.*

38   The Esprit Français is leaning over him,
39   Whispering

        (4)

40   Secrets
41   exquisite   significant
42   fade   plastic

43   Of the XIIIth Duchess of Alba
44   Long long as the Eiffel Tower
45   Fathoms deep in haschich
46   With languid compelling finger
47   Pointing invisible Magi
48   To a little white Maltese:

49   The back-ground gray and olive-green
50   Like le Midi, the Louvre, la Seine. . . .

51   Of ivory paper-knives, a lion carved on the handle,
52   Lysistrata had one, but the workmanship of these is
53   Empire. . . .

54   Of . . .

55   I see the Arc de Triomphe,
56   Square and shadowy like Julius Cæsar's dreams:
57   Scorn the laws of solid geometry,
58   Step boldly into the wall of the Salle Caillebotte

59   And on and on . . .

60   I hate the Etoile
61   The Bois bores me:

        (5)

62   Tortoises with gem-encrusted carapace

63   A Roman boy picking a thorn out of his foot

64   A flock of discalceated Madame Récamiers
65   Moaning for the Chateaubriand *de nos jours.*

66   And yet . . . quite near

67   Saunters the ancient rue Saint-Honoré
68   Shabby and indifferent, as a Grand Seigneur from Brittany

69   An Auvergnat, all the mountains of Auvergne in
70   every chestnut that he sells. . . .

71   Paris is a huge home-sick peasant,
72   He carries a thousand villages in his heart.

73   Hidden courts
74   With fauns in very low-relief piping among lotuses
75   And creepers grown on trellises
76   Are secret valleys where little gods are born.

77   One often hears a cock
78   *Do do do miii*

79   He cannot sing of towns—
80   Old Hesiod's ghost with leisure to be melancholy
81   Amid the timeless idleness of Acheron
82   Yearning for 'Works and Days' . . . hark!

83   The lovely Spirit of the Year
84   Is stiff and stark

(6)

85   Laid out in acres of brown fields,

86   The crisp, straight lines of his archaic drapery
87   Well chiselled by the plough . . .

88   And there are pretty things—
89   Children hung with amulets
90   Playing at *Pigeon vole,*
91   Red roofs,
92   Blue smocks,
93   And jolly saints . . .

94   AU

95   BON MARCHE

96   ACTUELLEMENT

97   TOILETTES

98   PRINTANIERES

99   The jeunesse dorée of the sycamores.

100   In the Churches during Lent Christ and the Saints

101   are shrouded in mauve veils.

102   Far away in gardens

103   Crocuses,

104   Chionodoxa, the Princess in a Serbian fairy-tale,

105   Then

106   The goldsmith's chef d'œuvre—lily of the valley,

107   Soon

108   Dog-roses will stare at gypsies, wanes, and pilgrimages

(7)

109   All the time

110   Scentless Lyons' roses,

111   Icy,

112   Plastic,

113   Named after wives of Mayors. . . .

114   Did Ingres paint a portrait of Madame Jacquemart

115   André?

116   In the Louvre

117   The Pietà of Avignon,

118   L'Olympe,

119   Giles,

120   Mantegna's Seven Deadly Sins,

121   The Chardins;

122   They arise, serene and unetiolated, one by one from

123   their subterranean sleep of five long years.

124   Like Duncan they slept well.

125 President Wilson grins like a dog and runs about the
126 city, sniffing with innocent enjoyment the diluvial
127 urine of Gargantua.

128 The poplar buds are golden chrysalids;
129 The Ballet of green Butterflies
130 Will soon begin.

(8)

131 During the cyclic Grand Guignol of Catholicism
132 Shrieks,
133 Lacerations,
134 Bloody sweat—
135 Le petit Jésus fait pipi.

136 Lilac

137 SPRING IS SOLOMON'S LITTLE SISTER; SHE HAS NO
138 BREASTS.

139 LAIT SUPERIEUR
140 DE LA
141 FERME DE RAMBOUILLET

142 ICI ON CONSULTE
143 LE BOTTIN

144 CHARCUTERIE
145 COMESTIBLES DE Iʀᴇ CHOIX

146 APERITIFS

147 ALIMENTS DIABETIQUES
148 DEUIL EN 24 HEURES

149 *Messieursetdames*

150 Little temples of Mercury;
151 The circumference of their *templum*
152 A nice sense of scale,

(9)

153   A golden drop of Harpagon's blood,
154   Preserve from impious widening.

155   Great bunches of lilac among syphons, vermouth,
156   Bocks, tobacco.

157   *Messieursetdames*

158   NE FERMEZ PAS LA PORTE
159   S. V. P
160   LE PRIMUS S'EN CHARGERA

161   At marble tables sit ouvriers in blue linen suits discussing:

162   La journée de huit heures,
163   Whether Landru is a Sadist,
164   The learned seal at the Nouveau Cirque
165   Cottin. . . .

166   Echoes of Bossuet chanting dead queens.

167   *méticuleux*
168   *bélligerants*
169   *hebdomadaire*
170   *immonde*

171   The Roman Legions
172   Wingèd
173   Invisible
174   Fight their last fight in Gaul.

(10)

175   The ghost of Père Lachaise
176   Is walking the streets,
177   He is draped in a black curtain embroidered with the letter H,
178   He is hung with paper wreaths,
179   He is beautiful and horrible and the close friend of
180   Rousseau, the official of the Douane.

181   The unities are smashed,
182   The stage is thick with corpses. . . .

183   Kind clever *gaillards*

| 184 | Their *eidola* in hideous frames inset with the brass |
| 185 | motto |

| 186 | MORT AU CHAMP D'HONNEUR; |

187	And little widows moaning
188	*Le pauvre grand!*
189	*Le pauvre grand!*

190	And petites bourgeoises with tight lips and strident
191	voices are counting out the change and saying *Mes-*
192	*sieursetdames* and their hearts are the ruined province
193	of Picardie. . . .

| 194 | They are not like us, who, ghoul-like, bury our friends |
| 195 | a score of times before they're dead but— |

| 196 | Never never again will the Marne |
| 197 | Flow between happy banks. |

| 198 | It is pleasant to sit on the Grand Boulevards— |
| 199 | They smell of |

(11)

200	Cloacæ
201	Hot indiarubber
202	Poudre de riz
203	Algerian tobacco

204	Monsieur Jourdain in the blue and red of the Zouaves
205	Is premier danseur in the Ballet Turque
206	'Ya bon!
207	Mamamouchi

| 208 | YANKEES—"and say besides that in Aleppo once . . ." |

| 209 | Many a *Mardi Gras* and *Carême Prenant* of the |
| 210 | Peace Carnival; |

211	Crape veils,
212	Mouths pursed up with lip-salve as if they had just said:
213	*Cho-co-lat . . .*
214	"Elles se balancent sur les hanches."

215	Lizard-eyes,
216	Assyrian beards,
217	Boots with cloth tops—

218	The tart little race, whose brain, the Arabs said, was
219	one of the three perches of the Spirit of God.

220	*Ouiouioui, c'est passionnant—on en a pour son argent.*
221	*Le fromage n'est pas un plat logique.*

222	*A a a a a oui c'est un délicieux garçon*
223	*Il me semble que toute femme sincère doit se retrouver*
224	*en Anna Karénine.*

(12)

225	Never the catalepsy of the Teuton
226	What time
227	Subaqueous
228	Cell on cell
229	Experience
230	Very slowly
231	Is forming up
232	Into something beautiful—awful—huge

233	The coming to . . . . . .
234	Thick halting speech—the curse of vastness.

235	The first of May
236	T
237	h
238	e
239	r
240	e
241	i
242	s
243	n
244	o
245	l
246	i
247	l
248	y
249	o
250	f

(13)

251	t
252	h
253	e
254	v
255	a
256	l
257	l
258	e
259	y

260   There was a ritual fight for her sweet body
261   Between two virgins—Mary and the moon

262   The wicked April moon.

263   The silence of *la grève*

264   Rain

265   The Louvre is melting into mist
266   It will soon be transparent
267   And through it will glimmer the mysterious island
268   gardens of the Place du Carrousel.

269   The Seine, old egotist, meanders imperturbably to-
                        wards the sea,

270   Ruminating on weeds and rain . . .
271   If through his sluggish watery sleep come dreams
272   They are the blue ghosts of king-fishers.

(14)

273   The Eiffel Tower is two dimensional,
274   Etched on thick white paper.

275   *Poilus* in wedgwood blue with bundles *Terre de Sienne*
276   are camping round the gray sphinx of the Tuileries.
277   They look as if a war-artist were making a sketch of
278   them in chalks, to be 'edited' in the Rue des Pyram-
279   ides at 10 francs a copy.

280	Désœuvrement,
281	Apprehension;
282	Vronsky and Anna
283	Starting up in separate beds in a cold sweat
284	Reading calamity in the same dream
285	Of a gigantic sinister mujik. . . .
286	Whatever happens, some day it will look beautiful:
287	Clio is a great French painter,
288	She walks upon the waters and they are still.
289	Shadrach, Meshach, and Abednego stand motionless and plastic mid the flames.
290	Manet's *Massacres des Jours de Juin,*
291	David's *Prise de la Bastille,*
292	Poussin's *Fronde,*
293	Hang in a quiet gallery.
294	All this time the Virgin has not been idle;
295	The windows of les Galéries Lafayette, le Bon Marché, la Samaritaine,

(15)

296	Hold holy bait,
297	Waxen Pandoras in white veils and ties of her own decking;
298	Catéchisme de Persévérance,
299	The decrees of the Seven Œcumenical Councils re-
300	duced to the *format* of the *Bibliothèque Rose,*
301	Première Communion,
302	(Prometheus has swallowed the bait)
303	Petits Lycéens,
304	Por-no-gra-phie,
305	Charming pigmy brides,
306	Little Saint Hugh avenged—
307	THE CHILDREN EAT THE JEW.
308	PHOTO MIDGET

309   Heigh ho!

310   I wade knee-deep in dreams—

311   Heavy sweet going

312   As through a field of hay in Périgord.

313   The Louvre, the Ritz, the Palais-Royale, the Hôtel
                                    de Ville

314   Are light and frail

315   Plaster pavilions of pleasure

316   Set up to serve the ten days junketing

317   Of citizens in masks and dominoes

318   *A l'occasion du mariage de Monseigneur le Dauphin.*

(16)

319   From the top floor of an old Hôtel,

320   Tranced,

321   I gaze down at the narrow rue de Beaune.

322   Hawkers chant their wares liturgically:

323   Hatless women in black shawls

324 Carry long loaves—Triptolemos in swaddling clothes:

325   Workmen in pale blue:

326   Barrows of vegetables:

327   Busy dogs:

328   They come and go.

329   They are very small.

330   Stories. . . .

331   The lost romance

332   Penned by some Ovid, an unwilling thrall

333   In Fairyland,

334   No one knows its name;

335 It was the guild-secret of the Italian painters.

336   They spent their lives in illustrating it. . . .

337   The Chinese village in a genius's mind. . . .

338   Little funny things ceaselessly happening.

339   In the Ile Saint-Louis, in the rue Saint Antoine, in

340   the Place des Vosges

341   The Seventeenth Century lies exquisitely dying. . . .

(17)

342   Hu s s s h

dim · · *in* · · *u* · *en* · *do.* *ppp*

346   In the parish of Saint Thomas d'Aquin there is

347   an alley called l'impasse des Deux Anges.

348   Houses with rows of impassive windows;

349   They are like blind dogs

350   The only things that they can see are ghosts.

351   Hark to the small dry voice

352   As of an old nun chanting Masses

353   For the soul of a brother killed at Sebastopol. . . .

354   MOLIERE

355   EST MORT

356   DANS CETTE MAISON

357   LE 17 FEVRIER 1673

358   VOLTAIRE

359   EST MORT

360   DANS CETTE MAISON

361   LE 30 MAI 1778

(18)

362   CHATEAUBRIAND

363   EST MORT

364   DANS CETTE MAISON

365   LE 4 JUILLET 1848

366   That is not all,

367   Paradise cannot hold for long the famous dead
of Paris . . .

368   There are les Champs Elysées!

369   Sainte-Beuve, a tight bouquet in his hand for Madame
Victor-Hugo,

370   Passes on the Pont-Neuf the duc de la Rochefoucauld

371   With a superbly leisurely gait

372   Making for the *salon d'automne*

373   Of Madame de Lafayette;

374   They cannot see each other.

375   Il fait lourd,

376   The dreams have reached my waist.

377   We went to Benediction in Notre-Dame-des-Champs,

378   Droning . . . droning . . . droning.

379   The Virgin sits in her garden;

380   She wears the blue habit and the wingèd linen head-

381   dress of the nuns of Saint Vincent de Paul.

382   The Holy Ghost coos in his dove-cot.

383   The Seven Stages of the Cross are cut in box,

(19)

384   Lilies bloom, blue, green, and pink,

385   The bulbs were votive offerings

386   From a converted Jap.

387   An angelic troubadour

388   Sings her songs

389   Of little venial sins.

390   Upon the wall of sunset-sky wasps never fret

391   The plums of Paradise.

392   *La Liberté La Presse!*

393   *La Liberté La Presse!*

394   The sun is sinking behind le Petit-Palais.

395   In the Algerian desert they are shouting the Koran. ·

396   *La Liberté La Presse!*

397   The sky is apricot;
398   Against it there pass
399   Across the Pont Solférino
400   Fiacres and little people all black,

401   Flies nibbling the celestial apricot—
402   That one with broad-brimmed hat and tippeted pelisse
                                                 must be a priest.

403   They are black and two-dimensional and look like
404   silhouettes of Louis-Philippe citizens.

405   All down the Quais the bouquinistes shut their
406   green boxes.

                             (20)

407   From the VIIme arrondissement
408   Night like a vampire
409   Sucks all colour, all sound.

410   The winds are sleeping in their Hyperbórean cave;

411   The narrow streets bend proudly to the stars;

412   From time to time a taxi hoots like an owl.

413   But behind the ramparts of the Louvre
414   Freud has dredged the river and, grinning horribly,
415   waves his garbage in a glare of electricity.

416   Taxis,
417   Taxis,
418   Taxis,

419   They moan and yell and squeak
420   Like a thousand tom-cats in rut.

421   The whores like lions are seeking their meat from God:

422   An English padre tilts with the Moulin Rouge:

423   Crotchets and quavers have the heads of niggers and
424   they writhe in obscene syncopation:

425   *Toutes les cartes marchent avec une allumette!*

426 A hundred lenses refracting the Masque of the Seven
427 Deadly Sins for American astigmatism:

428 *"I dont like the gurls of the night-club—they love*
429 *women."*

(21)

430 *Toutes les cartes marchent avec une allumette!*

431

DAWN

432

Verlaine's bed-time . . . Alchemy

433

Absynthe,

434

Algerian tobacco,

435

Talk, talk, talk,

436

Manuring the white violets of the moon.

437 The President of the Republic lies in bed beside his
438 wife, and it may be at this very moment . . .

439 In the Abbaye of Port-Royal babies are being born,

440 Perhaps someone who cannot sleep is reading *le*
441   *Crime et le Châtiment.*

442

The sun is rising,

443

Soon les Halles will open,

444 The sky is saffron behind the two towers of Nôtre-Dame.

445 JE VOUS SALUE PARIS PLEIN DE GRACE

★

★ ★ ★

★

★ ★

3 Rue de Beaune

Paris

Spring 191<9>

(22)

[Author's] Notes

P. 1. *Nord-Sud,* one of the underground railways of Paris. *Dubonnet, Zig-zag, Lion Noir, Cacao Blooker* are posters. *Rue du Bac,* etc. are names of stations.

P. 11. "It is pleasant to sit on the Grands Boulevards" to page 13 "the curse of vastness" is a description of the Grands Boulevards.

P. 13. "The first of May, there is no lily of the valley." On May 1, the *Mois de Marie,* lily of the valley is normally sold in all the streets of Paris; but on May 1, 1919, the day of the general strike, no lily of the valley was offered for sale.

P. 14. The April moon, *la lune rousse,* is supposed to have a malign influence on vegetation.

P. 15. "The windows of *les Galeries Lafayette,* etc." During Lent life-size wax dolls, dressed like candidates for Première Communion, are exposed in the windows of the big shops.

P. 22. The Abbaye de Port-Royal is now a maternity hospital.

(23)

[1919] Richmond: Hogarth Press, 1920.

Commentary on *Paris* by Julia Briggs

Note entries and bracketed references are keyed to the poem's line numbers. (Obvious typographical errors in the text have been silently corrected.) Information on the original title page includes "Printed by Leonard and Virginia Woolf at the Hogarth Press, Paradise Road, Richmond, 1919."

Dedication: "To Our Lady of Paris in recognition of graces granted." "Our Lady of Paris," both the Virgin Mary and the cathedral dedicated to her on the Ile-de-la-Cité, at the center of Paris, with an echo of the prayer "Ave Maria, gratia plena" ("Hail Mary, full of grace"—see line 445). The frame suggests that of a votive plaque such as might be hung in a church. From the outset, Paris is addressed as a woman.

1. "holophrase," a single word standing for a phrase, sentence, or complex of ideas, and according to Jane Harrison (JH) characteristic of an early stage of language development (473–75). "I want" can also mean "I lack." Holophrase puns on "hollow phrase."

2. Metro line from Montparnasse to Montmartre, now line 12 (N[ote]P1).

3–6. Brand names on metro posters (NP1): "Zig-Zag," type of cigarette paper, advertised with the head of a "Zouave," an Algerian soldier (and anticipating the poem's zig-zag direction through the city); "Lion Noir" (black lion), a brand of shoe polish; "Cacao Blooker," Dutch make of drinking chocolate. These introduce themes of empire and of *négritude* (blackness), further linked with "Black-figured vases" (550–480 B.C.), found in Etruscan burial chambers.

7–9. "Rue du Bac," "Solférino" and "Chambre des Députés" (now "Assemblée Nationale"), the three most northerly stations on the Nord-Sud line south of the river (rue du Bac is next to rue de Beaune, where HM lived while writing the poem). "Solférino," named for a French victory over Austria in Italy (1859). From 1832, the Chambre des Députés was the French lower house of government. "Dubonnet," brand of fortified wine advertised in metro tunnels, HM's curved brackets suggesting the walls of the metro on which the posters appeared.

10. "Brekekekek coax coax," chorus of Aristophanes' *The Frogs* (405 B.C.) in the underworld (also suggesting rattling wooden carriages in the metro). "Frogs," British slang for the French, used in letters between HM and JH.

12–13. "The Scarlet Woman" appears to St. John on the Greek island of Patmos (*Revelation* 17.3–6). "Byrrh," another fortified wine, advertised with a poster of a woman dressed in scarlet, playing a drum and shouting (see Cocteau 49, 38 for "BYRRH" and St. John as witness). ["St" before "John" inserted by Woolf on 160 copies.]

14. "Are you getting off here, madame?" standard polite phrase for making one's own way off a crowded metro car or bus.

15–16. "Those who weigh themselves [up] often, know themselves well. Those who know themselves well, stay healthy," motto on station scales.

17. The speaker alights at the first station north of the river, Place de la Concorde, a huge square on the Right Bank, formerly used for royal events, the guillotine during the revolution, etc. Concorde means "agreement," introducing the theme of the peace process (MacMillan, passim).

20–22. The spaced-out layout of these lines imitates that of the Tuileries gardens, with gaps left for the basins on the central axis at either end. The poem slows down, changing from south > north (vertical movement on the page) to west > east (horizontal).

23–26. Little boys riding on a carousel in the Tuileries (out of use during WWI) become soldiers, their hands sticky from the mud of the trenches (anticipates lines 89–92, 275–76).

27–29. The pigeons appear to be joined to the statues in the Tuileries, while the statues look "two-dimensional" (273, 403). One, looking over her shoulder, suggests Watteau's "Le Départ pour Cythère" (properly, "L'Embarcation pour Cythère," 1717, in the Louvre), in which those leaving for Cytherea (the island of Venus) look back.

30–34. Some statues are of nymphs. Louis Pasteur (1822–95) developed a vaccine against rabies (Sacha Guitry's play, *Pasteur,* was running in Paris in early 1919. A metro station on the Nord-Sud line had been named after him). "Gauls," the French, as warriors or soldiers. The Nymphs' soft mouths also suggest female genitals ("nymphae," labia minora); their "bite" may refer to venereal disease.

34–39. Leon Gambetta, national hero and Minister for War during the German siege of Paris, announced the Third Republic in September 1870 (in the presence of the 1919 Prime Minister Georges Clemençeau—the first buried reference to him). Gambetta's statue in a frock coat (now in the square Edouar-Vaillant, 20éme) then stood at the base of a seventy-five-foot monumental pyramid in front of the Louvre, with the winged "Genius of France" leaning over him. HM imagines a red stud (his *legion d'honneur* rosette) in a button-hole (*boutonnière* is slang for anus), suggesting a possible sexual intimacy between these two figures.

36. *tutoiement,* an intimate form of address (tu), employed by couples.

37. "But it makes sense."

38. Esprit Français, "Spirit of France." The winged "Genius" on the Gambetta monument.

40–42. "Secrets," defined by four terms set in a square that play between English and French senses: "exquisite" (Fr. *exquis*); "significant" (Fr. *significatif*); "fade," a verb in English, an adjective in French meaning tasteless or insipid; "plastic" (*plastique*), malleable, molded, flowing, often applied to sculpture or the visual arts, a favorite word for HM (see lines 112, 289; *Madeleine,* vii).

43–50. (Exquisite / significant secrets) Of . . . Goya's painting of the Duchess of Alba (1795, near the end of the war between France, Germany, and Spain) depicts her as tall and slender, a pyramid, resembling both the Eiffel Tower and Gambetta's monument. Red ribbons in her hair and on her dress echo his red stud. She seems drugged, and, like him, is pointing, in her case to a small (Maltese) dog at her feet, as if directing the Magi to the infant Jesus at Epiphany. HM and JH may have seen this painting in Madrid in 1916; Goya was fashionable with the French avant-garde.

51. (Significant / plastic secrets) Of . . . On the top of the Gambetta monument was a figure of Democracy riding on a lion. *Lysistrata,* heroine of a play by Aristophanes (411 B.C.), persuaded the women of Athens to end the war with Sparta by going on sexual strike. The play was on at the Marigny Theatre, and another play inspired by it, *La grève des femmes,* was also running in Paris in spring 1919.

54. ("Fade" or fading secrets) Of . . .

55–56. From the Place du Carrousel, the Arc de Triomphe is visible at the far end of the Champs Elysées. Caesar (whose statue stands in the Tuileries) scorns dreams in Shakespeare's play.

58. Salle Caillebotte, room in the Musée du Luxembourg, hung with French impressionist paintings. The painter Gustave Caillebotte's unique collection of these was at first refused by the French Government, but from 1896 most of them were on display.

59. The journey through Paris continues.

60–61. "The Etoile," the *place* at the top of the Champs Elysées, at the center of the fashionable west side, named "etoile" (star) because twelve avenues radiated from it. "The Bois," (Bois de Boulogne), public park at its western edge.

62. In J-K. Huysmans's decadent novel *A Rebours* (1884), Des Esseintes has the shell of a living tortoise encrusted with jewels.

63. "Spinario," Roman statue in bronze (first century B.C.) in the Museo dei Conservatori in Rome. Renaissance copies abound, some in the Louvre.

64–65. Juliette Récamier, famous beauty and lover of the poet Chateaubriand (362). "Discalceated," rare word for "barefooted," as she appears in a portrait (1800) by Jacques-Louis David (291), in the Louvre. *"De nos jours,"* of our time.

67–68. "Saunters" suggests the *flâneur,* stroller or wanderer, a characteristic Parisian type; "rue Saint-Honoré," old street meandering from east to west parallel with the river (Chateaubriand lived at no. 374). "Grand Seigneur," great lord. Brittany, the westernmost region of France, introduces a tour of the provinces.

69. Auvergnat, hot chestnut-seller, native to the Auvergne, the mountainous area of central France. Celtic Brittany and the Gallic Auvergne represent old traditional French stock. Many nineteenth-century Parisians came from Brittany and central France (Higonnet 77).

71–76. Paris was often pictured as a city of peasants, and its *quartiers* thought of as villages, especially by the surrealists (see Louis Aragon, *Le Paysan de Paris,* 1926). Many Paris houses have large gates, providing glimpses of "Hidden courts" decorated with classical figures such as "putti," though the "Little gods" could be the city's artists, musicians and writers.

77. The Gallic cock is a national symbol. The cock wakens the farmer, usually banishing ghosts, though here it becomes the ghost of Hesiod, an early Greek poet who "sang" (as the cock does) of country life in his *Works and Days* (both denied to the dead). "Acheron," one of four rivers of the classical underworld/afterlife.

83. That is, peace; also the "Eniautos Daimon," whose birth and death correspond to seasonal change, the central theme of JH's *Themis.*

85–87. The Spirit of the Year is laid out, corpse-like, in fields whose ploughed furrows ("nos sillons") suggest the fluted drapery of archaic Greek statues, as well as the trenches of WWI.

89–92. Children hung with amulets (good luck charms, to protect from danger) are also reincarnated soldiers (as at line 23; see Cocteau 41). *"Pigeon vole"* (literally, "pigeon, fly"), children's game that also recalls extensive use of pigeons to carry military information in WWI. Red and blue are the colors of Paris, and the blue smocks recall the blue uniforms of French soldiers (as at line 275).

94–98. "At Bon Marche, Spring Outfits Available Now." Bon Marche, large department store in the rue de Babylone, subject of Zola's 1883 novel, *Au Bonheur des Dames* (*Ladies' Paradise*) (Higonnet 200).

99. "jeunesse dorée," gilded youth, used of wealthy, spoilt young people, but also of the buds on the sycamore trees.

100–101. Mauve or purple is the ritual colour used in Lent.

103–4. "Crocuses, / Chionodoxa," flowers of early spring. Crocuses are usually mauve. Blue or white, Chionodoxa, meaning "glory of the snow," a suitable name for a fairy-tale princess. Serbia also recalls the assassination of the Archduke at Sarajevo that triggered WWI.

106–8. "chef d'oeuvre," masterpiece. The floral pageant runs from crocuses, to lily of the valley sold on May 1 (see lines 235–59; NP13) to the dog-roses of early summer. The dog-roses reverse the gaze of the painters (lines 21–22) by watching the annual pilgrimage of gypsies to Saintes-Marie-de-la-Mer in the Camargue on May 23–25; "wanes," an unusual spelling of "wains," or wagons. "Charles's wain," another name for the Great Bear (see lines 445–46).

110–13. "Roses from Lyons," major city, south-east of Paris. Unlike dog-roses, they are "scentless" (*fade?*), yet "plastic," or moulded. In 1913 Joseph Pernet-Ducher named a hybrid tea-rose "Mme Edouard Herriot" after the wife of the then mayor of Lyons.

114–15. French painter J.A.D. Ingres (1780–1867) apparently did not paint Mme Nélie Jacquemart-André (1841–1912), herself a portrait painter and art collector. Her home became the Musée Jacquemart-André at 158, Blvd. Haussmann.

116–21. In February 1919, paintings stored underground for safety were re-hung in the Louvre, including the fifteenth-century "Pietà" from Villeneuve-les-Avignon; Edouard Manet's controversial nude, "Olympia" (1863), first displayed in 1907 after a campaign by Georges Clemençeau (on Manet, see line 290); "Gil[l]es," Watteau's painting of a Pierrot (1718–19); "Mantegna's Seven Deadly Sins," properly "Minerva chasing the Vices from the Garden of Virtue" (ca. 1502); J.-B.-S Chardin (1699–1779) specialized in domestic scenes and still life.

122–24. "Unetiolated," not pale from being stored in a dark, underground place. Shakespeare's Macbeth claims of his murdered victim, "Duncan is in his grave. / After life's fitful fever, he sleeps well" (III.ii. 22–23). The paintings implicitly contrast with dead soldiers, who cannot be resurrected, and may not "sleep well."

125–27. Greeted rapturously as "Wilson le Juste" on arrival in Paris for the peace talks, U.S. President Woodrow Wilson brought his fourteen-point plan, which promised more than it could deliver (MacMillan 3–20). "Gargantua," figuring old Europe, was an anarchic giant, and title character of Rabelais' fantasy (1534–35); his urine was indeed "diluvial," or flood-like (the French describe heavy rain as "pluie diluvienne"). Wilson's "innocent enjoyment" appeared to Clemençeau "pathetic naiveté" (MacMillan 23).

128. "chrysalids," cocoons or pupae that will release butterflies (as the buds release leaves).

131. Easter (Good Friday, April 18, in 1919). "Grand Guignol" ("blood and guts") was a violent, sensational type of melodrama performed at the Grand Guignol theatre in Montmartre (see lines 181–82). [HM cut lines 1–5 of this page when the poem was reprinted in 1973.]

133. Ritual self-flagellation was a regular feature of Good Friday processions.

135. Little Jesus does a pee-pee. "Le petit jésus," pretty child, can also be slang for a boy prostitute.

136. Lilac flowers near the end of Lent, its color echoing that of the church draperies (101, 155).

137–38. Song of Solomon 8.8: "We have a little sister, and she has no breasts" (see also Song of Solomon 2:11–12 for its evocation of spring).

139–41. "Quality milk from the Rambouillet farm," the first of a series of street signs. Rambouillet, a small town south-west of Paris, where Louis XVI created the Ferme de Rambouillet, the Queen's dairy, for Marie-Antoinette. The Hôtel Rambouillet (in Paris) was the first and greatest French salon (see Madeleine, ch. IX).

142–43. "The telephone directory can be consulted here."

144–45. "Delicatessen, for best quality cold cuts."

146–47. "Pre-meal drinks" / "Food for diabetics" (literally, "diabetic food").

148. "Your clothes dyed black in 24 hours" (literally, "mourning in 24 hours"). This and the previous sign are examples of "catachresis," the application of a term to something it does not properly denote. According to MacMillan (26–27), in the Paris of 1919 "almost every other woman wore mourning."

149. "Gentlemen-and-ladies," written thus to reflect its pronunciation on the streets by waiters, etc. (see lines 157, 191–92).

150–54. A Roman temple to Mercury, the winged messenger of the gods, once stood on Montmartre, where the cathedral of the Sacré Coeur had recently been completed (dedicated October 1919). Templum is Latin for a sacred space, but "Little temples" might refer to the circular kiosks on the boulevards or even open-air urinals ("*pissoirs*").

153–54. Harpagon is *The Miser* of Molière's play (1668), who regards his money as his blood (see V.iii). East of the Sacré Coeur (sacred heart) is the rue de la Goutte d'Or (golden drop), its name derived from the wealth of vineyards formerly on that site, so the "golden drop of Harpagon's blood" (money) may be contrasted with the blood of the Sacred Heart. But if the "golden drop" is urine (as at lines 127–28), this might refer to the homosexual activities for which the *pissoirs* had been notorious since the eighteenth century.

155–56. In a typical bar-tabac: vermouth is a type of aperitif; bocks are glasses of beer.

158–60. "Don't close the door, please, the Primus [a compressed air device] will take care of it."

161. ouvriers: workmen, who discuss recent news items.

162. "the eight-hour day," demanded by the workers and voted on by the government on April 17 and 23, but the difficulties of implementing it resulted in a general strike on May 1 (lines 235–59, 263; NP13; Hausser 723, 724).

163. Henri Landru, a serial killer. The police investigated his activities from April to May 1919.

164. According to a programme for May 2, 1919, the learned seal was "Bichette" and her trainer was Capitaine Juge; the Nouveau Cirque was at 251, . rue Saint-Honoré.

165. On February 19, the anarchist Emile Cottin attempted to assassinate Clemençeau, chairman of the Peace Conference (see notes on lines 35–39, 116–21; Hausser 715; MacMillan 150–51). Cottin was condemned to death in March, but reprieved. His name suggests that of Abbé Charles Cotin (1604–82), habitué of the Hôtel Rambouillet (see *Madeleine*, 55).

166. Jacques Benigne Bossuet (1624–1704), bishop and preacher, famous for his funeral sermons, particularly that on Henrietta Maria, Charles I's queen ("chanting dead queens").

167–70. Four adjectives probably refer to the previous discussion: "*méticuleux*," punctilious, scrupulous (Cottin?); "*bélligerents*," aggressive, warlike (the Germans, according to the newspapers?); "*hebdomadaire*," weekly (of the eight-hour day); "*immonde*," monstrous, foul (Landru?).

171–74. The Roman Legions in their winged helmets could be seen as invaders of Gaul (France) (like the defeated Germans) or else as France's departing allies.

175–77. Père Lachaise, third of the trio of seventeenth-century clerics, was the Jesuit confessor of Louis XIV and gave his name to Paris's most famous cemetery. He appears wearing a curtain (introducing the theater of war), embroidered with the letter H (pronounced "ash" in French, and so suggesting the words of the English funeral service, "Dust to dust, and ashes to ashes"—in French, *hache* also means axe).

180. Henri Rousseau (1844–1910), known as the Douanier (customs officer) was a French "Sunday" painter whose paintings ("beautiful and horrible") were admired by the avant-garde, especially after Picasso gave a famous dinner for him (1908). HM may have known his painting "La Guerre" (1894).

181–82. The artistic representation of violent events now dominates the poem. WWI failed conspicuously to conform to any rules, let alone the unities of time, place, and action required of classical tragedy; it was closer to Grand Guignol (line 131), which left "The stage . . . thick with corpses."

183. "*gaillards*," big, strapping fellows.

184. "*eidola*," (Greek) ghosts, spirits, images.

186. Killed in action (literally, "dead on the field of honour").

188–89. "The poor man!"

190. "petites bourgeoises," middle-class women, collecting money for war victims (149, 157). Picardie is a province in northern France, site of much of the fighting in WWI.

194. ghoul-like, ghouls rob graves and eat corpses.

196–97. The battle of the Marne (1914) was the worst battle of WWI for the French in terms of losses, their army being almost cut off by German forces in eastern France. The river Marne flows westwards to join the Seine near Paris, where its banks were lined with "guingettes," dance halls, popular at weekends.

198. "The Grand[s] Boulevards," a series of wide streets, running north of the rue Saint-Honoré, on an east-west axis, lined with theaters and cinemas—a favourite Sunday afternoon walk (the poem seems to zig-zag east from Concorde to the Louvre, west along the rue Saint-Honoré towards the Madeleine, then east along the Grands Boulevards). From here to line 234 is a description of the Grands Boulevards (NP11).

200–203. "Cloacæ" (Latin), sewers below the boulevards; "Hot indiarubber," from car tires—by 1914, there were 25,000 cars in Paris (Higonnet 187); "Poudre de riz," face powder; "Algerian tobacco" (see line 434) was cheap—themes of empire and racial alterity re-appear, picking up on "Zig-Zag" (line 3), cigarette papers rolled around Algerian tobacco and joints.

204–5. "Monsieur Jourdain," *Le Bourgeois Gentilhomme* of Molière's play (1670), dresses up and joins in a Turkish dance in order to become a "Mamamouchi." He is here pictured in the blue and red uniform of the French Algerian army, the Zouaves. "[P]remier danseur," chief soloist; "Ballet Turque [turc]," Turkish ballet.

206. "Dat's good!" the slogan advertising the breakfast food, "Banania," on a famous poster showing a Senegalese rifleman sitting under a palm tree.

208. "YANKEES," Americans, either in Paris for the Peace Conference, or staying on after WWI. African Americans often settled in Montmartre, where they found a tolerant atmosphere (Higonnet 340–42). "[A]nd say besides . . .": Shakespeare's Moor of Venice, Othello, just before his suicide, remembers how he summarily executed a Turk who had "Beat a Venetian, and traduced the State" (V. ii. 354—thus picking up the Turkish theme).

209–10. *"Mardi gras,"* Shrove Tuesday, the last day before Lent, the period of forty days fasting before Easter; *"Carême Prenant,"* Shrovetide, the days before the start of Lent, a period of merry-making or "Carnival" before the fast; here linked with the Peace Conference, as a celebration before repentance and deprivation.

211–13. Crêpes (Shrovetide pancakes) become "crape" thin black mourning veils; *"Cho-co-lat,"* Cho-co-late—the second "o" is long, and emphasised in French pronunciation.

214. "The women rock themselves backwards and forwards on their haunches."

216. Square-cut beards, as portrayed on Assyrian statues.

218. Tart: sharp, acid; "The tart little race" might be the Armenians, victims of Turkish massacres, who sent a special delegation to the Peace Conference (MacMillan 377).

220–21. "Yesyesyes, isn't it exciting—and such good value for money. Cheese isn't a rational dish" (see line 37).

222–24. "A-a-ah yes, he's a charming boy. / I think every honest woman must recognise herself in Anna Karenina." Tolstoy's novel *Anna Karenina* (1877) is the story of a woman who abandons marriage and child for her lover (see line 282).

225. "catalepsy," a seizure or trance in which consciousness is suspended (for other tranced moments, see lines 20, 320). French café gossip is contrasted with the silence of Germans.

226–31. Subaqueous: (constructed) under water; this passage echoes the preface to *Madeleine,* where "Life" (or as here, "Experience") is the material out of which Art is gradually formed.

233–34. With these lines, the description of the Grands Boulevards comes to an end (NP11), suggesting, perhaps, that the life on the boulevards provides raw material needing to be formed into speech or words, if it is to become art ("coming to" could mean coming back to consciousness). Lines 232–34 themselves burst into "vastness" after the six narrow lines that precede them (see also Tennyson's poem, "Vastness").

235–59. May 1 is celebrated as Labor Day in France, but in 1919 there was a general strike in Paris, with violent clashes between the authorities and the workers, some of whom marched with knives between their teeth (Hausser 726; MacMillan 273). The vertical lettering emphasizes the disruption of normal order, representing the lines of marchers, and possibly the stems of the (absent) lily of the valley, usually sold on May 1, to give to friends or sweethearts as a bringer of luck (106, NP13).

260–62. The struggle between the chaos of life and the structure of art (226–32) now becomes a "ritual fight" between two virgins, as the year progresses from "The wicked April moon" (*la lune rousse*) to the month of May, sacred to the Virgin Mary. The April moon is the lunar month after Easter, characterized by cold, harsh winds that seem to scorch (*roussir*) the new growth (NP14). "[H]er sweet body" could be that of Paris.

263. Punning on the English expression, "the silence of the grave," *la grève* is the strike (on May 1), with a further underlying wordplay, since *la grève* means the river bank—the place de *Grève* (now, place de l'Hôtel de Ville) being where Parisian workers assembled to *"faire la grève,"* or go on strike.

268. "the mysterious island gardens" seem to be those of the Carrousel, running from the Arc de Triomphe du Carrousel down to the Tuileries.

269–71. The Seine winds eastward through the center of Paris, reaching the sea at Le Havre. "Ruminating," literally, chewing the cud, and thus recycling or recirculating, also suggests the river's passage through the fertile dairy-farming province of Normandy. Initially associated with the underworld (line 10), the Seine is here (and later, line 414) associated with the Freudian unconscious, which increasingly asserts itself as dreams (271, and see lines 310, 376), anticipated by the melting of the Louvre (265; compare 311–15).

272. "King-fishers," small, bright blue diving birds.

273–74. Paris now becomes a sequence of pictures: the "two-dimensional" (as at line 403) silhouette of the Eiffel Tower (a favorite subject for artists) is "etched" (engraved, black on white), while the soldiers encamped in the Tuileries are drawn in colored chalk, and the page ends with (imaginary) oil paintings.

275–79. "The *Poilus*" (literally "hairy"), French WWI soldiers in blue uniforms, with *"Tierre de Sienne"* (burnt Sienna, reddish brown) packs, around the "gray sphinx" look like the chalk sketches, "edited" (i.e., published) in the rue des Pyramides, a street where souvenirs are sold. The combination of sphinx and pyramids recalls Napoleon's campaign in Egypt, as well as WWI operations in Egypt (MacMillan 382–83, 401).

280–85. "Désœuvrement" (idleness, lack of occupation, suffered by demobilized soldiers) suggests Vronsky; "Apprehension" suggests Anna, the lovers at the center of Tolstoy's *Anna Karenina* (line 224). In part 4, they wake from similar dreams of a sinister Russian peasant (a "mujik"), perhaps unconscious-ly anticipating the Bolshevik Revolution (1917).

286–89. Even the most violent and calamitous moments of history can be transformed into the tranquillity of art. Clio, the Greek muse of history, be-comes a French painter, stilling the watery flux of life. Shadrach et al. were cast by Nebuchadnezzar into the fiery furnace (*Daniel* 3.12–30), but in art they become "motionless and plastic."

290–93. "Manet's *Massacres* . . ." a series of paintings imagined as hanging in the Louvre, depicting violent moments of French history: Manet (1832–83) is imagined portraying the massacres of "les journées de Juin" (days of June, 1848 when protesters were rounded up, disarmed, and killed by the army); David (1748–1825), as painting the taking of the Bastille (July 14, 1789, the beginning of the French Revolution); Nicolas Poussin (1594–1665), as depicting the uprisings of the Fronde (1649, 1652) (see *Madeleine*, 11–12). Pages 13–15 survive in a proof, corrected by HM. Here the first imaginary painting was originally "Cézanne's *Quatorze Juillet*"—apparently altered because its subject, "14 July," was too close to David's. "Manet's *Massacres des Jours de Juin*" was substituted. Manet actually painted the "Execution of Maximilian" (1867) and the executions of May 1871. HM's revisions produce a historical sequence, running from the strike of May 1, 1919, back through the risings of 1848, 1789, and 1652, to illustrate French political resistance.

294–95. Like Clio (but not like Vronsky), the Virgin has been busy—creat-ing business for (and later actually window-dressing) Paris's three largest and best-known department stores—les Galéries Lafayette, le Bon Marche (see line 95), and la Samaritaine. [The last two lines of this page and the first twelve of the next were cut from the 1973 edition.]

295–97. According to HM's notes (NP14), during Lent, department store windows displayed wax models dressed for First Communion in white veils and ties (knots of ribbon) as "bait," to encourage young girls to participate by showing the pretty clothes they could wear. But these "Waxen Pandoras" are also "bait" in a further sense, since (according to Hesiod, lines 80–82) Pan-dora was sent by Zeus to tempt Prometheus and punish him for stealing fire from the gods. Pandora was modeled from clay (not wax), and carried a jar containing all the evils of the world. When she opened it, they all flew out into the world, except Hope (HM's own name), left inside the jar.

298. "*Catéchisme de Persévérance*," a popular nineteenth-century Catholic manual by Jean-Joseph Gaume. The decrees of the "Seven Œcumenical Coun-cils" (Nicea I, 325 A.D.-Nicea II, 787 A.D.) embody the central doctrines of Christianity; "format" means "size"; "*Bibliotheque Rose*," a series of books for girls published by Hachette.

301–2. "First communion." Prometheus has swallowed the "bait" of Pandora, or the communion wafer, or is excited by the First Communicants.

303–5. "Petits Lycéens," little high-school children. "Por-no-gra-phie," spelled out as if for children, is a Greek word meaning, literally, writings about prostitution; "pigmy brides" are miniature brides of Christ. "Pigmy" is a Greek word for the forearm or fist, anticipating the cannibal imagery that follows ("teknophagiai," the eating of children, is discussed by JH in *Themis* 248–49).

306–7. "Little St. Hugh" (not an actual saint), according to anti-Semitic legend, a child murdered by Jews in Lincoln (1255). Chaucer's *Prioress's Tale* tells a similar story. By eating the body of Christ (the Jew) at first communion, the children "avenge" St. Hugh's murder.

308. A photographic studio in Paris? A peepshow?

312. Périgord is a rural region in south-western France, part of the poem's tour of provinces.

313–15. The Louvre is the great Palace at the heart of Paris, now an art gallery; the Ritz is a Hotel at 15, Place Vendôme; the Palais-Royal[e] is opposite the Louvre; the Hôtel de Ville, the Paris Mairie (or town hall), is east of the Louvre on the rue de Rivoli. All are solid, indeed massive buildings, that could only appear "light and frail" in a rising atmosphere of dreams (see line 265).

316–17. "junketing," feasting, merrymaking. Masks and dominoes are carnival disguises (the domino is the cloak to go with the mask), typically worn by the aristocracy, but here by "citizens," thus anticipating the Revolution.

318. "On the occasion of the marriage of Monsieur le Dauphin," the marriage celebrations of the future Louis XVI to Marie-Antoinette. In the course of these (May 30–31, 1770), a display of fireworks created a stampede in which several hundred people were crushed to death or pushed into the river.

319–21. The Hôtel de l'Elysée, 3, rue de Beaune, where HM stayed in Paris and apparently wrote this poem, was a hotel in the modern sense, as well as in the older sense of a grand town house, formerly the property of Mme du Deffand, famous for her *salon*. "Tranced" (line 20, and perhaps 45), trance states, and the automatic writing they generated was to fascinate the surrealists. It is possible that the whole poem, flickering between "real" and imagined Paris sights, was generated by this "tranced" moment of gazing out of the window (Keatsian "magic casements, opening on the foam / Of perilous seas, in fairy lands forlorn"?)

322. "Hawkers . . . liturgically," street peddlars . . . in the style of a church service.

323–24. "Triptolemos," a legendary king of Eleusis who founded the Mysteries and taught men agriculture (including how to make bread). As a baby (wrapped in swaddling clothes that make him "loaf-shaped"), he was loved by Demeter (Ceres), probably identified with the "women in black shawls."

325–26. "Workmen in pale blue," wore denim overalls; "Barrows" belong to street vendors displaying their wares.

332. Ovid, Roman poet and storyteller (43 B.C.-17 A.D.), exiled to Tomis on the Black Sea, but not a "thrall" (i.e., slave) in Fairyland (as was the narrator of Keats's poem, "La Belle Dame Sans Merci"). The resulting "lost romance" is imagined as having inspired Italian painters, as their "guild-secret," peculiar to their craft.

339–40. Three landmarks of seventeenth-century Paris to the north and east, by 1919 in a state of disrepair, and thus "exquisitely dying" (see line 41).

342–45. Quiet was expected for the dying. The eight bars of music are marked "dim—in—u-en-do" (growing softer) to "ppp," pianissimo, very quiet indeed. The melancholy aria is "Lascia ch'io pianga," from Handel's opera *Rinaldo* (1711), "Let me weep for my cruel fate, and let me sigh for my liberty" (recalling Ovid's misery in exile?).

346–47. The beautiful church of Saint Thomas d'Aquin (begun 1688, completed 1766) stands near the end of the rue de Beaune. L'impasse des Deux Anges (the mews of the two angels), is close by. The angels may be linked with Jacob (see *Genesis* 28.12, or 32.24–29), though "two angels" are particularly connected with Lot and the destruction of the cities of the plain (*Genesis* 19.1–17), punished by God for homosexuality (see Cocteau, 28–29, 47; 45, 66). The name of the "impasse" may also suggest lesbianism. It was close to Natalie Barney's house (at 20, rue Jacob) and is referred to in Djuna Barnes's *The Ladies' Almanack* (1928).

348–50. "Impasse," a blind alley, also suggests "deadlock" (both in French and English), and "impassive" (i.e., blank or inexpressive, *impassible*). The French expression for walls without windows, *murs aveugles* (blind walls) may have suggested the comparison with blind dogs. The ghosts, watched by the "impassive windows" (compare line 108), introduce a pageant of the city's famous dead.

353. Sebastopol, port on the Black Sea, besieged and eventually captured (1856) by English and French troops (greatly aided by Algerians, the "Zouaves") during the Crimean War, and commemorated by a street name and a metro station. [HM altered the nun's "Masses" to "dirges" in the 1973 edition.]

354–61. The memorial plaque for the playwright (1622–73) on his house at 40, rue de Richelieu, on the Right Bank, north of the Louvre (see lines 153, 204). "The dying seventeenth century" is followed by the memorial plaque for the Enlightenment philosopher Voltaire (1694–1778), who died at no.1, rue de Beaune, next to or even part of HM's hotel.

362–65. Chateaubriand, Romantic poet and memoirist (1768–1848), died close by, at 118–120 rue du Bac, with the blind Mme Récamier at his bedside (lines 64–65). These writers typify three different centuries, and three different French styles.

367–68. "Paradise" is almost an anagram of "Paris" and "dies." Les Champs Elysées, Paris's most famous avenue, means "the Elysian fields," in classical literature, the home of the dead.

369. The French critic Charles Saint-Beuve (1804–69) was the friend and rival of the poet and novelist Victor Hugo (1802–85), and the lover of his wife Adèle. The Pont Neuf ("New Bridge," now the oldest, completed 1604) would take Saint-Beuve from his house on the Left Bank to the Right (where the Hugos lived, at 6 place des Vosges).

370–73. The duc de la Rochefoucauld (1613–80), author of *Maximes* (1664) and a close friend of Mme de Lafayette (1634–93), author of *La Princesse de Clèves* (1678). He passes Saint-Beuve on the Pont Neuf as he crosses to the Left Bank to visit Mme Lafayette in the rue Ferou. They cannot see each other, perhaps because of the centuries between them, but the duc had figured in Saint-Beuve's great study of the seventeenth century, *Port-Royal* (1840–59). The *"salon d'automne"* exhibited avant-garde painting; it was originally formed by a group of fauvists and postimpressionists in 1903 (Shattuck 61).

375. "It's close, sultry" (literally, heavy, as in "Heavy sweet going," line 311).

377. "Benediction," a Catholic service. "Notre-Dame-des-Champs" (Our-Lady-of-the-fields), one of the oldest churches in Paris; formerly standing in fields on Montparnasse, was rebuilt in 1876. Its metro station is south of rue du Bac on the Nord-Sud line, between Port-Royal (line 439) and the garden of the nuns of St. Vincent de Paul, on the rue de Babylone (now the Jardin Catherine Laboure).

379–82. The Virgin wears the elaborately starched headdress of the nuns of St. Vincent de Paul (winged like the Roman helmets of line 172) and probably sits in their convent garden (see above), where the west wall would have been covered with plum and apricot trees, and there are still box hedges. The Holy Ghost descended as a dove, and "cooing" and "(dove)-cots" are common to babies and doves (compare Cocteau 22: "Dieu roucoule au sommet des arbres").

383. "The Seven Stages," possibly half of the fourteen Stations of the Cross, performed on Good Friday, representing Christ's final sufferings; "cut in box," either means carved in boxwood, or from topiary (pruning box hedges into shapes). Churches display branches of box during Easter week. [The last five

lines of this page and the first six lines of the next were omitted from the 1973 edition.]

384–86. White ("Madonna") lilies, the Virgin's flower. Votive offerings result from a religious promise. The Jap(anese) convert is the painter L. T. Foujita (1886–1968), who painted pictures of the Virgin and Child in soft colors (1917–18), often in shapes resembling bulbs.

387–89. "troubadour," Provencal wandering minstrel. The cult of courtly love voiced in troubadour poetry was linked with the cult of the Virgin; "her," i.e., to her. "Venial sins" are lesser than Deadly Sins (at lines 120, 426–27).

390–91. The garden wall becomes the evening sky, hung with the plums of Paradise, where wasps never fret (eat away) the fruit; on the Solférino bridge, however, people look like flies, nibbling into the apricot (colored) sky (lines 399–401).

392–93, 396. "Freedom!" "The Press!" names of evening newspapers shouted by street vendors.

394–95. "Petit-Palais," built for the 1900 World Exhibition, west of the Place de Concorde, and perhaps just visible from a high west-facing window at the end of the rue de Beaune. At sunset in the Algerian desert the "muezzin" gives the Muslim call to prayer.

400–404. "Fiacres," light horse-drawn four-wheeled cabs. Looking westward, HM might just have seen figures on the old Pont Solférino (demolished 1961), silhouetted like flies against the celestial (heavenly) evening haze; "tippetted pelisse," a fur-collared cloak. Louis-Philippe, "the citizen king," reigned 1830–48, when portraits in silhouette, cut from black paper, were in vogue.

405–6. The Quais are the streets along the banks of the Seine, where the "bouquinistes" (box-owners, booksellers) sell their wares from green boxes, which they lock up at night.

407. Paris has twenty *arrondissements* (administrative districts). The VIIme lies immediately south of the river, on the Left Bank, and includes the rue de Beaune; like the neighboring VIme, this was an up-market address, known as the "Faubourg Saint-Germain."

410. "Hyperbórean," northern. The poem prepares to move up to Montmartre, in the north of Paris.

413. "Ramparts," mounds built for defense. The Louvre was initially built as a fortress (in 1200). Here ramparts keep the river, and perhaps the unconscious, at bay.

414–15. Sigmund Freud (1856–1939), Viennese theorist of sexuality and the unconscious, dredges the river, associated with rising dreams (lines 269–72).

The combination of Freud and electricity evokes modern life. Paris had had electrically lit advertisements from 1912 (Higonnet 145, 358, and compare "Contrastes": "Il pleut les globes electriques," Cendrars 71).

416–18. Taxis line up on the page, as they do on the streets.

421. "their meat," perhaps their clients (see line 4; the opening themes are now replayed).

422. "padre," "Father" (a Catholic priest) strikes at the Moulin Rouge (literally, the Red Windmill), Paris's most famous cabaret show (on the Place Blanche, Montmartre). To tilt with windmills is to make an ineffectual attack (from *Don Quixote*).

423. Black music notes become African American musicians playing jazz; "syncopation," shifting of the regular musical beat, as in jazz. Today this sentence is disturbingly racist, although the black musicians, like the lesbians in the following lines, introduce a liberating discourse of racial and sexual alterity. Jazz was brought to Paris by black U.S. army bands at the end of World War I, and was fashionable in Montmartre (Higonnet 341).

425, 430. Literally, all the cards (or maps) work with, walk with or go out with a match, but the exact meaning is hard to decide. It might refer to packs of cards given out in cafés, with boxes of matches, but "cartes" was also slang for prostitutes, and an "allumette" might be a sexual tease, or even a penis. A song refrain?

426. Fifty pairs of glasses, designed to correct American "astigmatism" (a sight defect that prevents focusing), reflect a (leg) show, saucily entitled "the Masque of the Seven Deadly Sins" (see line 120), a pseudo-religious title for a secular event, perhaps suggesting a further clash between the Virgin and "The wicked April moon."

428–29. Stage performers, like courtesans, were often supposed lesbian, and lesbianism was fashionable in Paris at this time (Higonnet 112–13). The spelling "gurls" may indicate an American accent, but "girls" was also French slang for both lesbians and chorus girls.

431. Dawn brings the poem's time scheme of a single day to a close.

432. Paul Verlaine (1844–96), lyric poet and decadent, fell in love with the precocious poet Arthur Rimbaud (1854–91), author of "L'Alchimie du verbe" (a section of his prose poem, *Une Saison en Enfer*). "Alchemy," the transformation of base metals into gold, is also a figure for the coming of dawn. "Absynthe" [unusually spelled with a "y"] is a powerful green spirit distilled from wormwood to which Verlaine was addicted. Picasso's 1903 painting, "Portrait du poète Cornuti, ou l'Absinthe" is a form of homage to Verlaine. Algerian tobacco was used to roll cheap cigarettes and joints (lines 3, 203).

437–38. Raymond Poincaré was president of France (1913–20). The poem here rocks between homosexuality and heterosexuality (the marriage bed, birth), between couples and single lives.

439. "Port-Royal," maternity hospital on the Left Bank, formerly a convent associated with Jansenism (NP15), a movement within the French seventeenth-century church persecuted by the authorities (and the focus of Saint-Beuve's study, *Port-Royal*). In chapter XVI of *Madeleine,* Madeleine visits the Abbaye, whose mistress, Mère Agnès Arnauld, is a portrait of JH (157).

440. This line suggests Duncan Grant's painting "Le Crime et le Châtiment" (ca. 1909), especially since Dostoevsky's novel (1866) was usually translated "*Crime et Châtiment.*" HM knew Grant, and may have known that the painting showed Marjorie Strachey reading that novel.

443. "Les Halles," until the late 1960s, Paris's main food market, rebuilt of wrought iron and glass (1866).

445. "I salute you Paris full of grace," echoing the Catholic prayer "Ave Maria," "Je vous salue Marie pleine de grace" (see Dedication; Cocteau 82: "Je vous salue pleine de grace . . . o sainte mère").

445–46. The poem ends with the constellation of Ursa Major, the great she-bear, part of the private code between HM and JH, who sometimes signed off letters to HM with this star-sign in reverse.

449. [1916, the "6" overwritten as "9"]

On the final page, HM makes a further highly original gesture by providing a set of notes to her admittedly difficult poem. Though not without precedent (Pope had annotated his "Dunciad"), it was unusual for an author to annotate her own text thus. Brief and fragmentary though her notes are, they offer a fresh perspective on the poem, and incidentally anticipate T. S. Eliot's use of notes in *The Waste Land* (1922).

PART III

Diverse Identities and Geographies

9

Lesbian Political History

INTRODUCED AND SELECTED BY GAY WACHMAN

IN ASSEMBLING THIS SECTION, I am defining "lesbian" widely, to include writing by British modernist women who variously identified themselves as lesbian (Valentine Ackland [1906–69]), or inverted (Radclytfe Hall [1880–1943]), or who did not define their sexuality, but lived openly with other women to whom they were passionately attached (Vernon Lee [1856–1935] and Sylvia Townsend Warner [1893–1978]).[1] Rose Allatini (1890?-1980?) probably belongs in this category as well, but her sexual identity in 1918, when *Despised and Rejected* was published, is hard to determine.[2] The number of male pseudonyms in this list reflects women's difficulties in getting their writing published and reviewed; it also indicates ambivalence about gender identity.[3]

Though these modernist lesbians had various political positions, some common strands emerge. There is recurrent interest in lesbian figurations and war. The epilogue to Vernon Lee's satire, *Satan the Waster* (1920), shows the radical right using homophobia to motivate militancy. Passages from Allatini's *Despised and Rejected* feature a homosexual couple who become conscientious objectors during the First World War. The lesbian protagonists's unrequited love is contrasted to "love between man and man," suggesting a politics of relationship that also appears in Hall's 1934 letter about *The Well of Loneliness*, which focuses on "the inverted" of both genders. The interests of lesbian writers frequently intersected with socialism. Warner's short story, "My Shirt Is in Mexico" (1941), combines a light-hearted exposition of the codes of the closet, expressed in a flirtation on a train with the ideals of 1930s communism and the Spanish Civil War. Warner's poem "After my marriage night" (1933) and Ackland's 1935 essay, "Country Dealings," lack specifically lesbian or homosexual content, but they do focus on class politics as they affect the lives of working-class women. In addition to these connective lines, what I am most interested in showing in this chapter is ways that lesbian literary history illuminates British political history.

Vernon Lee's *Satan the Waster* is a complex multi-genre work. Its center is a revised version of an earlier text, *The Ballet of the Nations* (1915).[4] This "Ballet" takes place in "The World; a Theatre" that is leased and managed by Satan (31). The Orchestra of the Passions assembles: it includes Fear, with Suspicion and Panic; Lady Idealism and Prince Adventure; Sin, with Rapine, Lust, Murder, and Famine; Hatred and Self-Righteousness; Science and Organization, and the beautiful, blind youth, Heroism. The Ballet Master, Death, conducts; he assembles the Nations as dancers. The audience consists of a few Neutral Nations, the Sleepy Virtues, the Ages-to-Come, and Clio, Muse of History, who records and describes the action. The fighting Nations are immortal as long as their Heads are unhurt; they carry these "irreproachable Heads [. . .] stiff and high" above their crawling, wounded bodies or "stumps": "Thus on they danced their stranger and stranger antics. [. . .] And, as they appeared by turns in that chaos of flame and darkness, each of the Dancing Nations kept invoking Satan, crying out to him, 'Help me, my own dear Lord.' But they called him by Another Name" (52–53). When the Orchestra flags and the Nations begin "to halt and stumble, and even to curtsy to each other" (55), Pity and Indignation are recruited from the audience; their addition enables Death to conduct "the third and last figure of our Dance." Satan announces: "I am the Waster of all kinds of Virtue." Clio concludes, "And thus the Ballet of the Nations is still a-dancing" (56–57).

In the epilogue, Satan uses the latest technology to reveal to Clio, Muse of History, the "mystery . . . of what was passing behind the stage" during the First World War. His cinema screen and gramophone depict a series of scenes and conversations between family members, journalists, political and military leaders, diplomats, and businessmen, showing the motives "behind the scenes" of the Ballet. The picture is one of unremitting greed, hypocrisy, deception and self-deception, callousness, cowardice, and pompous stupidity. At last, Satan's screen shows a council chamber full of statesmen, one of whom tentatively raises the topic of peace. Thus starts the excerpt reproduced here; it ends with an unbearable cacophony of voices justifying war. At Clio's unprofessional request—she is, after all, Muse of History—Satan switches off the electric current and ends his production.

One short scene interrupts the statesmen's debate. This takes place in a court of law and represents an important moment in British lesbian history: Maud Allan's 1918 libel suit against Noel Pemberton-Billing. The trial is significant because of its sensationally negative representation of lesbianism, its attempt to prove that sexual knowledge—knowledge of the word "clitoris"— is an indicator of lesbianism, and its conflation of "perversion" with treachery: Maud Allan and Margot Asquith were rumored to be lovers, and the Asquiths were thought to be involved in secret peace negotiations with Germany. Most significant, however, is the fact that Pemberton-Billing stage-managed the whole event as part of a right-wing conspiracy to topple Lloyd George's government and ensure the continuation of the war.

Before the war, Maud Allan had been remarkably successful. She had danced *The Vision of Salome* in Europe, South Africa, India, Australia, and the United States. In England she became an icon of Edwardian decadence and primitivism, like Nijinsky in the Russian Ballet. Pemberton-Billing was a maverick politician and a talented self-publicist and demagogue. A right-wing member of Parliament, he addressed the masses in his newspapers *The Imperialist* and *The Vigilante.* On January 26, 1918, a front-page article in *The Imperialist,* "The First 47,000," maintained that the chief threat to the Empire came from 47,000 homosexuals and lesbians listed in a mysterious German "Black Book." They had been individually perverted and blackmailed by German agents over the past twenty years. They ranged from sailors and "youths of the chorus" to "men and women in whose hands the destiny of this Empire rests. [. . .] wives of men in supreme position. [. . .] In Lesbian ecstacy [*sic*] the most sacred secrets of State were betrayed." Pemberton-Billing and his possibly insane assistant editor, Captain Harold Spencer, produced this salaciously alarmist fantasy to provoke homophobia and class hatred as well as rage against Germany.

Three weeks later, Marie Corelli sent Pemberton-Billing an advertisement for a forthcoming performance of Oscar Wilde's *Salome,* and the following gnomic announcement appeared in *The Vigilante:*

THE CULT OF THE CLITORIS

> To be a member of Maud Allen's [*sic*] private performances in Oscar Wilde's "Salome" one has to apply to a Miss Valetta, of 9, Duke Street, Adelphi, W. C. If Scotland Yard were to seize the list of these members, I have no doubt they would secure the names of several thousand of the first 47,000. (1)

It is probable that, as Pemberton-Billing later maintained, almost none of his readers knew what the word "clitoris" meant. But Allan's career as a dancer was threatened by that word, besides the fact that her name was coupled with Wilde and the perverted 47,000. Like Wilde in 1895, when the Marquess of

Queensbury accused him of sodomy, she sued. And like Wilde, she found that she herself was on trial; both of them lost their cases. Wilde's reason for suing was obvious: the vagueness of the 1885 Labouchère Amendment made conviction of homosexuals charged with "gross indecency" very easy. But there were no laws against lesbianism, and besides, the announcement in *The Vigilante* contains no explicit accusation of sexual perversion or vice.

The jury found Pemberton-Billing innocent of libel because Allan was associated with the decadent, pro-German, upper-class Asquiths as well as with Wilde. She was an independent, sexually knowledgeable woman familiar with the word "clitoris," and she performed perversion in *Salome*. Maud Allan cannot have been a reassuring role model for women who suspected that they might be lesbian or for writers who wanted to depict lesbians in their work; no wonder most representations of sexuality in women's narratives of the twenties are oblique. Only Vernon Lee was old enough and comfortable enough about her sexuality to refer to Maud Allan in her writing. She reproduces precisely the bullying tone in which Pemberton-Billing conducted his defense, the casual ineffectiveness of Justice Charles Darling, the charmingly feminine vagueness of Eileen Villiers Stuart, and the absurdity of the invisible German Black Book of names. But she also makes absolutely clear that Pemberton-Billing worked on the homophobia of his listeners and readers in order to further the political objectives of much of the ruling class: to continue the war as long as possible.

Vernon Lee lived in London throughout the war, writing tirelessly against it. Many of her friends were pacifist: they included Edward Carpenter, Havelock Ellis, Olive Schreiner, Bertrand Russell, and E. D. Morel. She knew all about the pacifism, socialism, and sexology naively explored by Rose Allatini, whose young antiwar activists in *Despised and Rejected* are clearly based on members of the No Conscription Fellowship. Allatini's critique of militarism and her representation of homosexual romance are informed and courageous, but her 1918 lesbian is doomed to invisibility.

Like D. H. Lawrence and E. M. Forster before the First World War, Allatini was much influenced by the utopian sexology of Edward Carpenter and seems to have accepted too uncritically his male-centered primitivist idealism, as expressed in *The Intermediate Sex* (1908) and *Intermediate Types among Primitive Folk* (1914). These books are also the source, however, for her representation of the link between compulsory heterosexuality and imperialist capitalism. The political intensity of *Despised and Rejected* lies in the clarity with which it presents the bourgeois heterosexual world in peacetime and in war, and then opposes to it Carpenter's ideal of the socialist bond of comrade-love.

At the beginning of *Despised and Rejected,* set in the idyllic pre-war spring of 1914, Antoinette de Courcy is represented in enthusiastic pursuit of an older woman; this innocent love is represented in the first excerpt from the novel. The second passage firmly establishes Antoinette's sexual identity as shown in the intensity of her boarding-school crushes followed by her disappointment in "the grown-up world of men." We are told that her desire for women is "without the least taint of morbidity"—before she learns from Dennis Blackwood all about abnormal desire. Dennis, in contrast, has recognized and resolutely suppressed his homosexuality. When he meets the confident young socialist, Alan Rutherford, he continues to run from the "secret terror that [. . .] had been part and parcel of his being, since the first dawn of his adolescence. [. . .] Abnormal—perverted—against nature—he could hear the epithets that would be hurled against him and that he would deserve. Yes, but what had nature been about, in giving him the soul of a woman in the body of a man?" (107). Besides expressing Dennis's shame and fear of discovery, this inflated language sounds as if he's been reading the wrong sexologists: Ulrichs, certainly, but also Krafft-Ebing, with his emphasis on morbidity and perversion. When Dennis and Alan meet again in 1916, Alan's matter-of-fact, Carpenter-like tone deconstructs this jargon: "You've been brooding too much in secret, Dennis, you've grown morbid. . . . For people made as we are it's natural and beautiful to love as we love, and it's perversion in the true sense to try and force ourselves to love differently" (250). They finally make love the night before Alan is arrested as a conscientious objector—an ironic counterpart to the heterosexual couples who consummate their love before the soldier leaves for the Front.

Before this homosexual idyll, however, Dennis has noticed Antoinette's pursuit of Hester and wondered "if he had at last found the answer to a riddle" (53). The riddle is how to live in the world as a closeted gay man; its answer: marry a nice lesbian. This couple doesn't actually marry, but Antoinette's attachment to Dennis intensifies after he leaves her for Alan and then imprisonment. The novel closes with the excerpt reproduced here: a conversation between Antoinette and Barnaby, the leader of the conscientious objectors. He puts Antoinette firmly in her place: his Carpenter-inspired oratory refers only to the heroic suffering of gay men; women are simply immaterial.

The most obvious connection between Rose Allatini and Radclyffe Hall is their martyrdom at the hands of the law. All available copies of both *Despised and Rejected* and *The Well of Loneliness* were seized and destroyed; however, *Despised and Rejected* was banned for its seditious rather than its sexual content. Nonetheless, the magistrate, Alderman Sir Charles Wakefield, opined in passing that *Despised and Rejected* was an "immoral, unhealthy, and most pernicious book, written to attract a certain class of reader for the personal profit of the publishers" ("Despised and Rejected"). One wonders whether that euphemistic "certain class of reader" signifies the hordes of effete German spies who had watched Allan dance *Salome*. Perhaps Sir Charles was a reader of *The Vigilante*.

Radclyffe Hall's 1934 letter about *The Well of Loneliness* was a response to questions about the writing of *The Well of Loneliness* from Gorham Munson, a New York literary scholar. The letter was recently discovered in New York City and donated to the Lesbian Herstory Education Foundation, which reproduced Hall's typescript in its entirety in a pamphlet in 1994. Eight of its eleven pages are reprinted here.

The letter needs little commentary. It makes absolutely clear that Hall's writing of *The Well of Loneliness* was a courageous political act and that she was prepared for censorship, if not martyrdom. Like Wilde thirty years earlier, she was punished more for her courage than her folly. She cannot have been prepared for the illegal manipulations of the law practiced by Sir William Joynson-Hicks, the Home Secretary, and Sir Chartres Biron, Chief Magistrate of the Bow Street Court.[5] Hall is certain, however, that "*the worthy* among the inverted—those fine men and women whom Nature has seen fit to set apart as variants from the more usual type. . . . desire to form a part of the social scheme, to conform in all ways to the social code as it exists at present" (7–8). This snobbery and conservatism mar much of her writing and detract from the courage of her lesbian politics: she is blind to the possibility that the inverted might make common cause with other outsiders. Other writers of her time, such as Rose Allatini and Sylvia Townsend Warner, show their consciousness of the fact that homosexuals and lesbians do not fight for justice in a vacuum.

In 1930 Sylvia Townsend Warner and Valentine Ackland started a lesbian relationship that lasted until Valentine's death in 1969; most of the poems in *Whether a Dove or Seagull: Poems by Valentine Ackland and Sylvia Townsend Warner* were written during their first year together. This joint volume was an original and courageous experiment, in that both women's names appear on the book's title page but none of the poems is attributed to either one of them. A jointly signed Note to the Reader states that "fifty-four of the poems are by one writer, fifty-five by the other. [. . .] The book [. . .] is both an experiment in the presentation of poetry and a protest against the frame of mind [. . .] which judges the poem by the poet, rather than the poet by the poem." The poems, which are mainly about love and rural life, thus become a political act aimed both at compulsory heterosexuality and at the literary canon.[6] The title was taken from a poem by Ackland:

Whether a dove or a seagull landed there
I cannot tell,
But on the field that is so green and bare
A whiteness fell—
And I must know before I go away
If for today
The weather of our love is wild or fair
Or ill or well.

(*Whether a Dove* 35)

During these first years of their relationship Warner and Ackland lived in East Chaldon, Dorset, a village they had loved, first separately and then together, for about ten years. They knew how their working-class neighbors labored and lived. The untitled poem by Warner in this section, "After my marriage night," reflects that knowledge (*Whether a Dove* 77–79). The speaker evokes the shock and loss of self in marriage as she cowers, estranged from her body and the changing seasons, numbed and menaced by the rituals and ripenings of harvest. She emerges in a cold gray dawn through which she can walk proudly, scorning the fields that await winter ploughing and seeking instead the "unfruitful and forsaken" pasture. It has been transformed overnight by a fleece of mushroom caps. Acknowledging their peace and purity, their delicate gills, the marvel of their birth, she can kneel and accept her unborn child.

The richness of this poem lies in its complexity of syntax and form, its unerring musicality, its insistent rhythms and rhymes that convey the trauma, brutality, and solitude that this rural marriage has entailed. Warner looks back to Hardy and on to Dylan Thomas, but its darkness and resolution into clarity are her own. Warner and Ackland are rooted in the land and life of the countryside; from this rootedness grow their class politics and their internationalism.

Early in 1935, Ackland and Warner joined the Communist Party to fight against fascism in Britain and abroad. They worked together to politicize the farm laborers in Dorset and Norfolk, to help build a broad-based coalition against fascism, and to support the Republican Government in Spain. Their articles, reviews, political fables, and poems were published in both British and American periodicals. They went to Spain twice, in 1936 to work with the Red Cross in Barcelona and the following year to attend the Second International Congress of Writers in Defense of Culture. Ackland's book, *Country Conditions*, about the work and lives of farm laborers, was published in 1936.

An early version of one of its chapters, published in *Left Review,* is reproduced here. It needs no commentary: the clear, intensely personal narrative speaks for itself. Granny Moxon had taught Valentine how best to dig the garden; they used to drink in the pub together in the evenings. She died in 1933.

First published in the *New Yorker* in January 1941 and reprinted in *A Garland of Straw,* "My Shirt Is in Mexico" bubbles with Warner's pleasure in the some-times surprising camaraderie that can lighten the isolation of the closet. Sylvia is the first-person narrator; she and Valentine are on their way back to Dorset. The story narrates their conversation with the buffet car attendant on a train early in the Second World War.

The label on Sylvia's bag brings them together, starting a friendly discus-sion of the beauties of the scenery and socialism in Mexico. But their shared escape fantasies cease when the man says, "I've got a shirt in Mexico." With minimal but characteristic prompts from Sylvia and Valentine, he tells the story behind this bizarre statement. The relaxed, confiding speech patterns convey both the working-class speaker's comfort with his middle-class audi-ence and the immediacy of his memory. Together, he and his listeners escape from the compulsory jingoism of war into an internationalist past.

As a cross-dressing butch, Valentine can appreciate the value of a good, male-tailored shirt. No wonder the attendant had looked at the two women "as though [they] were already friends of his" when he first brought them their drinks; he was responding, whether consciously or not, to their lesbian inti-macy. No wonder, too, that he is acquainted with sailors: "Living in Plymouth, naturally I know a lot about New York, so I could tell him things he'd find useful." "Naturally": Warner is making a closet joke out of the stereotype of the gay man cruising the quays. The story is about the pleasures of mutual recognition in the closet.

Reading "My Shirt Is In Mexico" requires familiarity with codes—the mor-al code of life in the closet and the codes of talking or writing within it. These codes are necessitated by social and legal oppression, but one of their more pleasurable products is the discourse of camp. The moral code of the closet requires a certain skill so that one doesn't "out" one's interlocutor while letting her or him know that one is gay—and perhaps interested in sex. Sometimes all that's needed is a look, but enjoyment of the encounter is heightened by the codes of mutual revelation and flirtation—an art at which this buffet-car attendant is an innocent, exuberant master. All that detail about clothes, of course, is homosexual bonding: the attendant and the exile and then Valentine are united in delight in that shirt: "But what I liked best was the way he opened the parcel and looked at the shirt most carefully—how the buttons were fas-tened on and all. Examined it all over, he did. If he had just taken the parcel, that wouldn't have been the same thing, would it?" Indeed it wouldn't. Sylvia, narrator and writer, reads the codes and re-encodes them for the pleasure of her readers.

The final twist of the plot explains how the shirt arrived in Mexico. The buffet-car attendant has the letter from one Renatus Leutner that explains the fate of the "beautiful" shirt: "It is not ungratefully that I bestow it to a comrade going to Mexico when he has greater need than I." Renatus is courteous, with Marxist concern for who has greater need. His name has its origin in Warner's and Ackland's lives. He represents a dear friend of theirs from before the war: the German writer and communist exile, Ludwig Renn.

When Renn, who had fought in the Spanish Civil War, came to stay with Warner and Ackland in Dorset in 1939, they were going through a difficult time: Ackland's lover, Elizabeth Wade White, was also staying with them, and Warner had moved into the spare room. Many years later, Warner recalled Renn's exiled condition and the welcome relief he provided to their *ménage à trois:*

> He had no passport, for he was a stateless person. He had no money, he had no future, he had sat starving behind barbed wire at Argelès, he had an unhealed wound, he had seen the bitter defeat of his cause. He had kept his interest in humankind and his slightly frivolous goodwill. His presence was so restorative. . . . [S]eeing [Elizabeth] in one of her fits of gloom, he said: "Now we will dance," bowed a court bow, put his arm around her waist and waltzed with her on the lawn. (Ackland and Warner, *I'll Stand by You* 167)

A letter from Renn to Warner from Mexico (March 30, 1942) makes quite clear his interest in sexuality: he mentions that the book he is writing about prehistory will examine the origins of homosexuality, and he asks Warner for help on lesbian aspects of this project. Ludwig Renn is a worthy original for that light-hearted, flirtatious comrade, Renatus Leutner, on the London-Plymouth train. And "My Shirt Is in Mexico" is a loving commemoration of Renn's visit and survival and the courage and battles of another war in the internationalist 1930s.

Notes

1. Warner noted after Ackland's death a neighbor's assumption that her relationship with Valentine had been equivalent to marriage: "Kind, how naturally she accepts me among the widows" (*Diaries* 353). See Beer for an account of Vernon Lee's identity as a pacifist, lesbian intellectual, and her related refusal to "fit." As early as the 1890s, her open sexual independence of men enabled her to challenge their intellectual hegemony.

2. Her novel contains explicitly "abnormal" characters. Virginia Woolf speaks of Allatini's "illicit amour" in a 1919 letter to Vanessa Bell (*Letters 2:* 336). Allatini married the composer Cyril Scott in 1921; they had two children and finally separated twenty years later. From then until her death, she lived in Rye, Sussex, with Melanie Mills, who also published romances under several pseudonyms. The two women supported themselves by their writing. See Cutbill's introduction to the GMP edition of *Despised and Rejected*. Both this and the Arno edition (1975) are out of print, but the novel is now again available in a reprint by Ayer Company Publishers.

3. Violet Paget selected her pseudonym (Vernon Lee) in 1878, when she had already published two essays in British journals; she opined then, with characteristic self-assurance, that "No one reads a woman's writing on art, history, or aesthetics with anything but unmitigated contempt" (letter to Henrietta Camilla Jenkin, quoted by Gunn, 66). Radclyffe Hall was christened "Marguerite Radclyffe-Hall"; her close friends called her "John." Ackland changed her first name from Molly to Valentine in her early twenties, before she had published any of her poems, and Rose Allatini published more than thirty novels under at least three pseudonyms: "Lucian Wainwright," "Eunice Buckley," and "A. T. Fitzroy."

4. The first edition of *The Ballet of the Nations* is dedicated "à Romain Rolland / fraternellement / V. L. / et in terra pax hominibus bonae voluntatis / le 4 Août 1915." The entire production of this beautiful volume evokes pity and horror. *The Ballet of the Nations* may well be an ironic response to Diaghilev's ballet, *Le Sacre du Printemps,* composed by Stravinsky, choreographed by Nijinsky, and performed to an outraged and fascinated audience of high society and aesthetes in Paris in 1913. Its emphasis on sexuality and ritual sacrifice caused a furor. See Eksteins.

5. Ten years earlier, Joynson-Hicks had been a right-wing parliamentary crony of Pemberton-Billing. For more on the corruption behind the trial of *The Well of Loneliness,* see Souhami.

6. For more on *Whether a Dove or Seagull,* see Spraggs. On Ackland's and Warner's lives, politics, and writing, see also Hackett; Jane Marcus, "Alibis and Legends," "Bluebeard's Daughters," and "Sylvia Townsend Warner"; and Wachman.

Works Cited

Ackland, Valentine. *Country Conditions*. London: Lawrence and Wishart, 1936.

Ackland, Valentine, and Sylvia Townsend Warner. *I'll Stand By You: The Letters of Sylvia Townsend Warner and Valentine Ackland.* Ed. Susanna Pinney. London: Pimlico, 1998.

———. *Whether a Dove or Seagull: Poems by Valentine Ackland and Sylvia Townsend Warner.* New York, Viking, 1933.

Allatini, Rose [A. T. Fitzroy, pseud.]. *Despised and Rejected*. London: C. W. Daniel, 1918. Reprint ed. New York: Arno, 1975.

Beer, Gillian. "The Dissidence of Vernon Lee: *Satan the Waster* and the Will to Believe." In *Women's Fiction and the Great War,* ed. Suzanne Raitt and Trudi Tate. Oxford: Clarendon Press, 1997. 107–31.

Carpenter, Edward. *The Intermediate Sex: A Study of Some Transitional Types of Men and Women.* 1908. London: Swan Sonnenschein, 1909.

———. *Intermediate Types among Primitive Folk: A Study in Social Evolution.* New York: Mitchell Kennerley, 1914.

"The Cult of the Clitoris." *The Vigilante.* London (February 16, 1918).

Cutbill, Jonathan. Introduction to *Despised and Rejected.* London: Gay Men's Press, 1988.

"'Despised and Rejected': Publisher of Pacifist Novel Fined," *Times* (London) (October 11, 1918).

Eksteins, Modris. *Rites of Spring: The Great War and the Birth of the Modern Age.* Boston: Houghton Mifflin, 1989.

"The First 47,000." *The Imperialist* (January 26, 1918).

Gunn, Peter. *Vernon Lee: Violet Paget, 1856–1935.* London: Oxford University Press, 1964.

Hackett, Robin. *Sapphic Primitivism: Productions of Race, Class, and Sexuality in Key Works of Modern Fiction.* New Brunswick: Rutgers University Press, 2003.

Hall, Radclyffe. "Radclyffe Hall's 1934 Letter about *The Well of Loneliness.*" Lesbian Herstory Educational Foundation, Inc., 1994.

———. *The Well of Loneliness.* 1928. New York: Anchor, 1990.

Hoare, Philip. *Oscar Wilde's Last Stand: Decadence, Conspiracy, and the Most Outrageous Trial of the Century.* New York: Arcade, 1998.

Kettle, Michael. *Salome's Last Veil.* London: Granada, 1977.

Krafft-Ebing, Richard von. *Psychopathia Sexualis with Especial Reference to the Antipathic Instinct: A Medico-Forensic Study.* 1886. Trans. Franklin S. Klaf. New York: Stein and Day, 1978.

Lee, Vernon (Violet Paget). *The Ballet of the Nations: A Present-Day Morality with a Pictorial Commentary by Maxwell Armfield.* London: Chatto, 1915.

———. *Satan the Waster: A Philosophic War Trilogy.* New York: John Lane, 1920.

Marcus, Jane. "Alibis and Legends: The Ethics of Elsewhereness, Gender, and Estrangement." In *Women's Writing in Exile,* ed. Mary Lynn Broe and Angela Ingram. Chapel Hill: University of North Carolina Press, 1989. 271–94.

———. "Bluebeard's Daughters: Pretexts for Pre-Texts." In *Feminist Critical Negotiations,* ed. Alice Parker and Elizabeth Meese. Amsterdam: John Benjamins, 1992. 19–32.

———. "Sylvia Townsend Warner." In Scott, ed. *The Gender of Modernism.* 531–38.

Mulford, Wendy. *This Narrow Place: Sylvia Townsend Warner and Valentine Ackland: Life, Letters, and Politics, 1930–1951.* London: Pandora, 1988.

Souhami, Diana. *The Trials of Radclyffe Hall.* New York: Doubleday, 1999.

Spraggs, Gillian. "Exiled to Home: The Poetry of Sylvia Townsend Warner and Valentine Ackland." In *Lesbian and Gay Writing,* ed. Mark Lilly. Philadelphia: Temple University Press, 1990. 109–25.

Ulrichs, Karl Heinrich. *The Riddle of Man-Manly Love: The Pioneering Work on Male Homosexuality.* 1864. Trans. Michael A. Lombardi-Nash. Buffalo: Prometheus Books, 1994.

Wachman, Gay. *Lesbian Empire: Radical Crosswriting in the Twenties.* New Brunswick: Rutgers University Press, 2001.

Warner, Sylvia Townsend. *Diaries.* Ed. Claire Harman. London: Chatto, 1994.

———. "My Shirt Is in Mexico." In *A Garland of Straw.* London: Chatto, 1943. 81–84.

Wilde, Oscar. *Salome.* London: John Lane, 1906.

Woolf, Virginia. *The Letters of Virginia Woolf.*

VERNON LEE

From *Satan the Waster*

The gramophone wheezes. The cinema shows a council chamber full of statesmen.

1ST VOICE. Don't you think, my lords and gentlemen, that the time might be nearly approaching when it would . . . it might, possibly be just as well to be beginning just to cast an eye on any possible . . I do not, mark, say probable . . avenues—ahem!—leading to an eventual peace?

2ND VOICE. Avenues to peace! Almost the most dangerous things in the world! Let alone peace itself, which is, of course, the most dangerous thing of all!

3RD VOICE. The name of peace must not be mentioned till they have restored Brobdingnag!

4TH VOICE. The name of peace must never be mentioned till they have given us back Lilliput!

5TH VOICE. The name of peace must not be mentioned till I have reannexed the seaboard of Bohemia, the flagstaffs of the sea-kings, the kingdoms of . . .

6TH VOICE. The name of peace must never be mentioned at all!

The gramophone wheezes. The cinema shows a Court of Law, packed with spectators.

A VOICE. The name of peace must never be mentioned by any decent man or woman! Are any of you aware, I wonder, that at this present moment this country harbours in its bosom 47,000 aliens from Sodom and Gomorrah, all busily plotting peace? Does that seem too monstrous for belief? Well, their names and addresses are all registered in a printed book. This young lady, whom I have called as a witness, has actually, *seen* the book!

FEMALE WITNESS. I have. It was shown me by two gentlemen friends, since deceased, at a lunch-party at Greenwich. It was bound in American cloth.

JUDICIAL VOICE. Was it, indeed? And did you see the contents of the book?

1ST VOICE. The contents, my lord, comprised the name of everyone here present who dares to ask pacifist questions.

The gramophone wheezes. The cinema changes back to a council chamber full of statesmen of various nationalities. As the dialogue proceeds it changes to other council chambers in other parts of the world, which flicker in and out without interruption.

1ST VOICE. But they appear to be talking of a possible restoration of Brobdingnag.

2ND VOICE. Ha! A peace trap!

1ST VOICE.But they even suggest reconsidering the question of Lilliput.

3RD VOICE. Oh, another peace trap.

CHORUS OF ANGRY VOICES. Peace traps! Peace traps!

ALL TOGETHER. Who dares to mention peace till they have restored Brobdingnag and given back Lilliput; given me the seaboard of Bohemia . . .

ANOTHER VOICE. Given me also the seaboard of Bo . . .

ONE VOICE AFTER ANOTHER. We can't talk of peace till they have been dismembered and forever silenced. It wouldn't really be peace unless we received our strategic frontiers. It wouldn't really be peace unless we had restored our natural boundaries. It wouldn't really be peace until we had realized our racial aspirations. It wouldn't really be peace until we had reconstituted our historical Empire.

ONE VOICE (deliberately). It wouldn't be peace until we had the other bank of the Hydaspes. It wouldn't be peace until we had got the mines of antimony. It would not be peace until we had realized the formula of the Carolingian Kings and of the Patriots of the year 4. It wouldn't be peace till we had reclaimed the Asiatic appanage of our Crusaders!

Someone in the council room hums "Partant pour le Syrie."

ANOTHER VOICE. (*enthusiastically*). It wouldn't be peace till we had fulfilled the aspirations of D'Annunzio. It wouldn't be peace until we had re-established the Wedding of the Adriatic.

3RD VOICE. It wouldn't be peace until we had re-established the Kingdom of Mazeppa.

4TH VOICE.It wouldn't be peace until we had re-established the Empire of Ziska.

OTHER VOICES. It wouldn't be peace until we had re-established the Kingdom of Ladislaus. It wouldn't be peace until we'd re-established the Kingdom of Borislaus. It wouldn't be peace until we had re-established the Kingdom of Wenceslaus. It wouldn't be peace until we had re-established the Kingdom of Mithridates. It wouldn't be peace until we had re-established the Kingdom of Tiridates. It wouldn't be peace until we had re-established the Empire of Alexander. It wouldn't be peace until we'd re-established the Empire of Solomon. It wouldn't be peace until we had re-established the Empire of the Queen of Sheba.

1ST VOICE. It won't be peace till all my bondholders get paid up their interest.

CHORUS. Peace traps! Peace traps! Peace traps!

IMPERTURBABLE AUTHORITATIVE VOICE. We are out for lasting peace.

A HUBBUB OF VOICES. Peace? Then why did we go to war? You promised . . . we promised . . . they promised . . . We insist on your promise . . . We have made no promises . . . We always keep our promises.

AUTHORITATIVE VOICE (*serenely*). I repeat that we are none of us out for aggrandisement, but for the future peace of the world. We must go on fighting to establish a really lasting peace, equally just towards friends and foes.

A HUBBUB OF VOICES. You promised . . . We promised . . . They promised . . . We insist on your promises! It isn't a matter of aggrandisement! It isn't a matter of prestige! It is a question of principle! It is a question of guarantees! It is a question of permanent peace! This must never happen again! We can't have such things happening again! This *must* be the last war! We must have guarantees of future peace! We will fight to the last man until we have guarantees of future peace! (*A pause and wheeze.*) Lasting peace! Last man! Last penny! Last drop of blood! Last war! Guarantees! Guarantees! Guarantees! Guarantees of lasting peace!

The gramophone gabbles all this out louder and faster, while the cinema figures move and gesticulate quicker, until there is nothing but a hubbub of "We-we" . . . "They—they" . . . "You—you," with a sort of refrain of "Last man!" "Last penny!" "Last war!" "Lasting peace!"

THE MUSE and AGES-TO-COME (holding their hands to their ears). Oh! do stop that horrible row! Oh! what are they all talking about.

SATAN *suddenly switches off the current. The screen is again blank. The gramophone wheezes and stops.*

SATAN. Rather a Babel, wasn't it? And what you have heard is comparatively plain sailing. Why, we haven't come to Victory and its Fruits, nor to the conflicting Self-Determination of the New Nationalities; we haven't come to the Fourteen Points and the Secret Treaties; we haven't come to Famine and Revolution and Bolshevism. Excellent as is my magic apparatus, you couldn't possibly make head or tail of that. It will take fifty years in fifty archives to clear up the muddle. Indeed, if you were to ask me, even I couldn't tell you on the spur of the moment how in the world it all leads to the end.

Satan the Waster: A Philosophic War Trilogy with Notes and Introduction. London: John Lane, 1920. 102–6.

ROSE LAURE ALLATINI

From *Despised and Rejected*

[1. Antoinette and Hester: Declaration of Love]

"I can understand your keeping the others out and hating them to ask questions—you know they're only inquisitive, and not asking because it means a great deal to them. It means a great deal to me, I can't tell you why, but it just does. Please won't you let me come a little bit closer? You see, I'm not frightened of the prickles or the fire. . . ." Quite unconsciously she was pleading as a very young boy might plead with his lady-love.

Hester shook her head. "Even if you do 'come closer,' as you say, you'll only be disappointed. Go and fall in love with that nice Blackwood boy: it will be much more profitable than this sort of thing."

"This sort of thing?" . . . Antoinette repeated with a puzzled frown.

Hester looked at her sharply for a moment, then gave a curt laugh. "Never mind. . . . Do as I say. Stick to young Blackwood."

"To Clive?" Antoinette exclaimed contemptuously. "Why, he's engaged, Doreen says, to a girl who studies economics and won't powder her nose."

"I didn't mean Clive, I meant the one who arrived yesterday—Dennis. At any rate, I'm certain that he's going to fall in love with you."

Antoinette was not interested. Hester continued: "He's quite a character-study. I should like to hear how the affair progresses."

"Would you . . ?" cried Antoinette, overjoyed at the idea that anything connected with herself could be of interest to Hester. "I'd better cultivate him, then."

"I'll leave you my address," said Hester.

"Your address? But you're not going away yet, surely?"

"Going this very evening."

Antoinette stood stock-still in the middle of the road, and gasped. "Not-really?" In the case of anyone but Hester, her plans would have been known by the whole hotel for days in advance. It was but another proof of Hester's aloofness, that the time of her departure came to Antoinette as an absolute shock.

"Don't look so bewildered: it can't possibly matter to you."

"But it does—more than anything else in the world—more than ever now. When I started out with you this afternoon, I was only enormously interested in you, and I admired you—your brains, and the gorgeous way you have of choking off people you don't want. I've watched you do it—Oh often—but

you're not going to choke me off like that, because now, I—I love you. . . ."
She had not intended to say those words; a few moments ago they would not
have entered her mind; now she had not only said them: she meant them.

Hester looked at her gravely, without curiosity and without astonishment.
"If that's the case, I've no right to choke you off. But understand once and for
all that you're on a wild-goose chase. You'll find none of the hidden depths
in me that you seem to expect to find."

"Whether that's true or not, I'll never expect any confidence or anything
that you don't give me of your own free will. But there's nothing on earth that
I wouldn't do for you, if I thought it would make you happy"

[2. *Without the Least Taint of Morbidity*]

Antoinette laughed happily; went to bed, and was soon fast asleep, dreaming
of Hester.

It was a long time since she had been as happy and as excited as she was
now. Her schooldays had held occasional periods of a similar excitement, but
the three years since she had left boarding-school, had been conspicuously
barren, compared with what had gone before. When she was thirteen, there
had been the melancholy-eyed young teacher of literature whom she had
adored; a dreamy unpopular woman, who had been made to suffer horribly in
the innumerable little ways in which schoolgirls can torment their victims.
Antoinette had been seized with a kind of holy wrath, and desire to avenge
and protect; she had flamed out against the whole class, almost wishing that
they would turn and rend her, so that she might have the pleasure of sacrificing
herself for her idol. . . . The idol very soon learnt to return the adoration of the
fervent and hot-tempered worshipper; and simultaneously Antoinette began
to lose interest. She had only enjoyed her role, as long as Miss Prescot had
taken no notice of her: had been apparently unaware of the flutter and throb
of excitement caused by her mere presence in the class-room, or her casual
good-night kiss at bed-time. When Miss Prescot had come to single her out
from the other girls and to linger fondly over that good-night kiss, Antoinette
had had quite a fit of repulsion. She only enjoyed an up-hill battle; even at that
age, the easy conquest had bored her. Also, she hated being touched, except in
cases where her own feelings were aroused. She shook off the girls who sought
to walk with their arms through hers, or to stroke her funny boyish head of
hair; she would run away from them, revelling in the fun of the chase, yet
dreading capture . . . the fear in her eyes contradicted by the laughing curves
of her mouth; the eyes of a nun, indeed, and the mouth of a voluptuary.

And then, some time later, there was the Russian girl, Natasha.

This time, Antoinette's passion was not killed by easy reciprocity, but kept alive by a thousand subtle tortures, rekindled by a single look or gesture, whenever Natasha imagined that it showed signs of waning. Her beauty was her strongest weapon, and at seventeen she used it with a refinement of cruelty that would have done credit to a woman twice her years. Antoinette was fascinated by her long sleepy eyes, that were green as jade, and as hard; by the heavy black hair growing low down upon her forehead; by her indolent graceful body, and the coldly indifferent manner that seemed to express the disdain in which she held her schoolfellows and her teachers alike. She had many slaves and admirers in the school, but none so ardent, so abandoned in her devotion, as Antoinette. Therefore, seeing that this was the case, Natasha ignored her completely; avoided her on purpose when she knew that the younger girl was hovering about the stairs on the chance of being allowed to say goodnight to her; ridiculed her adoration in front of the others; paraded ostentatiously with her favourites before Antoinette's jealous eyes. And then, as she did not wish to forfeit altogether the entertaining spectacle of Antoinette's passion, she would suddenly and unexpectedly be nice to her, making amends in five minutes for all the ill-treatment of the previous weeks. Antoinette forgave her gladly and generously, but the moment she imagined that her troubles were at an end, Natasha would with equal suddenness withdraw her favour, and treat her as badly as ever.

Antoinette suffered greatly at the time, but when her passion had worn itself out, she began to look forward with new zest to being grown up. If already this world of women and girls, narrow though it was, could contain for her such a wealth of thrills and excitement, how much more wonderful must be that other world, the world beyond school, the world of men. So far, she was inclined to feel contemptuous of the world of men, as represented by the elderly masters who took some of the classes at the fashionable boarding-school, and by the coarse-looking schoolboys who grinned at the girls when they passed each other on their daily walks. But she knew that when she was grown-up, everything would be different. Antoinette, counting the months, the years—fifteen, sixteen, seventeen—indulging in occasional passing flickers of feeling for this girl or that mistress; Antoinette, young, eager and glowing with an exuberant vitality, could scarcely await her eighteenth birthday, and the meeting with the lover who, she knew, awaited her . . . a lover to whom she could give all the passion of her soul, and whose touch would thrill her even more potently than had the touch of those women she had adored.

But when at last she was released from school, the grown-up world of men proved singularly disappointing; totally devoid of that stimulus for which she craved. The wonderful lover of her imagination had certainly not yet appeared upon the scene. In the meantime, various supers tried to play the part, but with no success as far as she was concerned. She let them kiss her, because she hoped that thus she might find what she sought; but those that did not arouse active repulsion in her, merely bored her, left her with a sense of staleness and dissatisfaction. She began to fear that she would never be capable of feeling anything for anybody again. And now Hester had proved her fears to be groundless. Gladly, gratefully Antoinette welcomed her advent, and the rush of emotion which she had called forth; turned with relief from her fruitless search in the world of masculinity, to give herself up to whole-hearted worship of this proud silent woman, who had had the power to arouse her from her temporary lethargy. And. in so doing, Antoinette was free from the least taint of morbidity; unaware that there was aught of unusual about her attitude—Hester herself had perceived this—she merely felt that she was coming into her own again, and was healthy-minded and joyous in her un-questioning obedience to the dictates of her inmost nature.

[3. Antoinette and Barnaby: Love between Man and Man]

She was an outcast in a double sense; an Ishmaelite twice over.

"Well?" said Barnaby.

"I? Oh, I don't know where I come in. I think I don't come in at all . . ."

He nodded. "I understand. May I say I'm sorry for you? You know I don't mean it as an insult. . . . What is to become of you, though?"

She smiled wearily. "I suppose I too—just go on. . . ."

"Yes. I'm afraid you're the symbol of what has to be sacrificed to the love between man and man."

"He couldn't have done otherwise"—loyally she was prepared to defend Dennis against anything that even his friend might have to say about him. "He was made like that, and he made things more difficult for himself by bot-tling up all his thoughts and feelings, and being terribly afraid of them, and never telling anyone about them—till he told me."

"He never told me," said Barnaby, "at least not in so many words. But I could see for myself. He's got a queer strain of the maternal in him. It's obvi-ous in the way he looks upon his work, and in the way he looks upon that boy. . . . It's a woman's passion as well as a man's that he feels for Alan; virile and yet tender; stronger even than death or madness; a wonderful motive-force that might accomplish much. . . ."

(A. T. Fitzroy, pseud.). London: C. W. Daniel, 1918, banned and burned. Rpt. New York: Arno 1975. London: GMP, 1988.

RADCLYFFE HALL

From "Notes on *The Well of Loneliness*"

[. . .]

Why Did I Write "The Well of Loneliness"?

I only decided to write "The Well of Loneliness" after the most profound consideration, and deep study of my subject, and, moreover, I waited to write it until I had made a name for myself as an author, this because I felt that it would, at that time, be difficult for an unknown writer to get a novel on congenital sexual inversion published. Also I wished to offer my name and my literary reputation in support of the cause of the inverted.

I knew that I was running the risk of injuring my career as a writer by rousing up a storm of antagonism; but I was prepared to face this possibility because, being myself a congenital invert, I understood the subject from the inside as well as from medical and psychological text-books. I felt therefore that no-one was better qualified to write the subject in fiction than an experienced novelist like myself who was actually one of the people about whom she was writing and was thus in a position to understand their spiritual, mental and physical reactions, their joys and their sorrows, and above all their unceasing battle against a frequently cruel and nearly always thoughtless and ignorant world, a world which seeks to label a fact in Nature as "unnatural" and thus as being a fair target for ridicule or condemnation.

In my book I endeavoured to portray in Stephen Gordon the finest type of the inverted woman, knowing well that such a type does, in fact, exist side by side with the weaker members. My book had a threefold purpose. Firstly, I hoped that it would encourage the inverted in general to declare themselves, to face up to a hostile world in their true colours, and this with dignity and courage. Secondly, I hoped that it would give even greater courage than they already possess to the strong and courageous, and strength and hope to the weak and the hopeless among my own kind, spurring all classes of inverts to a mighty effort to make good through hard work, faithful and loyal attachments—if such attachments are contracted—and, above all, to sober and useful living; in a word spurring all classes of inverts to prove that they are capable of being as good and useful citizens as the best of the so-called normal men and women, and this against truly formidable odds. Thirdly, I hoped that normal men and women of good will would be brought through my book to a fuller and more tolerant understanding of the inverted; that those parents who had chanced to breed male or female inverts would cease from tormenting and condemning their offspring, and thus—as is only too often the case— doing irreparable harm to the highly sensitized nervous system that is characteristic of inversion; above all would cease destroying that self respect which is the most useful and necessary prop to those of all ages in their journey through life, but particularly to the young invert. I hoped also that my book would reach school teachers, welfare workers, indeed all those who had the care of the young, and that it might even prove useful to doctors and psychologists who are often hampered in their work and their studies by meeting only those inverts whose plight has rendered them physically or psychically unfit, those inverts who owing to persecution have become the prey of nervous disorders and cannot thus be considered fair examples of the inverted as a whole. Whether or not I have succeeded in my aim time alone will show.

General Remarks

In his commentary at the beginning of my book, Havelock Ellis says: "So far as I know, it is the first English novel which presents, in a completely faithful and uncompromising form, one particular aspect of sexual life as it exists among us today." He is correct I think; at all events when I sat down to write "The Well of Loneliness," I felt that I was about to undertake the task of a pioneer, and that I must therefore be prepared to face the consequences—frequently unpleasant—that accrue from most pioneer work. As an American journalist of my acquaintance wrote to me wittily when the storm broke: "You have torpedoed the ark, and therefore you mustn't be surprised that Mr. and Mrs. Noah have come out to see what's happened!"

What happened in England was a Government prosecution, two Police Court actions both of which we lost in truly amazing circumstances, and as a result the suppression of the book which, however, was published again in Paris unabridged and in its original language within one month of that suppression. Had I required proof of the blind and bitter antagonism that exists against the inverted, and which in itself shows the vital necessity that existed for the writing of my book, then I had that proof as I sat in the police courts and listened to the conducting of those two cases. A brief resume of the English proceedings appears in the Twelfth Printing of the Two Dollar American Edition. (Covici, Friede Inc.).

What happened in the United States appears in the "Victory Edition" 1929. (Covici, Friede). The account of the attempt made by Mr. Sumner to get my book suppressed in America also, and of the lawsuits that followed, is given in great detail by that brilliant lawyer and champion of literary freedom, Morris Ernst, who, incidentally, fought the forces of retrogression on behalf of my American publishers. This account is indeed well worth reading, and it tells the story of the battle of "The Well of Loneliness" in the United States far better than I could hope to tell it. In the end my book was victorious. I have great cause for gratitude towards America; great cause for gratitude also towards all those eminent American men and women who came forward in defence of the book, and great cause for gratitude towards the three American judges who conducted the last case in so seemly and so eminently just a manner.

Have I suffered through the writing of "The Well of Loneliness"? Yes and no. I certainly felt very strained and war weary by the time the battles were ended. Of course many strange and unexpected things happened to me after the English suppression. Until the book was publicly attacked, some of those whom I had supposed to be sincere friends—taking their cue from a fine and generous Press, perhaps—appeared to accept the book in the spirit in which it had been written; but after the public attack—taking their cue from the then antagonistic portion of the Press—they leapt on me, howling with the wolves. I was down, as they thought, and so they trampled. But then there rose up many in my defence and among these the most unexpected people: simple working people, the humble and the poor as well as a host of distinguished men and women some of whom I had only known by name until they came forward to defend me.

Very moving and unforgettable sympathy was extended to me by all classes of society. For instance, a subscription was started to pay my legal expenses which, however, I could not very well accept in view of the fact that I possessed certain assets—I was able to sell my London house and thus procure the necessary ammunition. One very rich man, unknown to me personally, generously offered to pay the whole of my expenses himself, begging me to engage the best possible barristers, while quite a number of poor working men wrote to me saying that if a subscription was started they would like to contribute their hard earned shillings. And so it was that those dark and distressful days held for me their patches of sunshine. Indeed the sympathy of the British working classes was one of my greatest supports at that time and I am never likely to forget it.

A less agreeable side of the picture is the notoriety that the suppression of the book caused to fall upon me—I could not then escape it nor can I even now six years after the book's publication. I do not like notoriety, it embarrasses me and makes me feel shy, but I realise that it is the price I must pay for having intentionally come out into the open, and no price could ever be too great in my eyes. Nothing is so spiritually degrading or so undermining of one's morale as living a lie, as keeping friends only by false pretences. It is this that drags many an invert down, that whittles away his or her self respect and with it his or her usefulness as a citizen. The worthy among the inverted—those fine men and women whom Nature has seen fit to set apart as variants from the more usual type—hate the lies and the conspiracy of silence that a ruthless society sometimes forces on them. Like their more normal brethren they are honest, simple souls who long to live honestly and to live as themselves, they desire to form a part of the social scheme, to conform in all ways to the social code as it exists at present. Because, though they see its imperfections as every intelligent person must, they realise that nothing in this world can be perfect and that, on the whole, this code as it is—save for its injustice towards themselves—is a workable and necessary proposition unless we are to fall into chaos. Such inverts desire to legalise their unions. Preposterous; do you say? And yet it may come, though I may not be here to welcome its coming.

Notes in a Letter to Gorham Munson, June 2, 1934. Harry Ransom Humanities Research Center, University of Texas at Austin. Rpt. in *Radclyffe Hall's 1934 Letter about The Well of Loneliness*, ed. Polly Thistlewaite. New York: Lesbian Herstory Educational Foundation, 1994.

SYLVIA TOWNSEND WARNER

After my marriage night

After my marriage night, she said, what with love and hate
So mixed and crossed in me, and my own body lost to me,
Heavy with newness of love, like grass drenched down with dew,
And myself, it seemed, with nothing to do but sit and await
The upshot of their debate,

I lost my count of time, she said, I cowered low
Under passing of time, astray in the chime of day
On day clashed and dissolving, night on night a flash
Of darkness smiting anew and lingering on slow
And booming as the ache

Of the tender bell that rules whatsoever the change
From its root escaping, I lay as mute, she said,
Under the sound of time passing as underground

The dead lie listless and amazed, hearing the strange
Overhead music range.

The noise of harvest went by, I heard the sighing stooks
And shouts of those who carried them as though they had married them,
Beribboned the harvest baby was nailed over the hearth,
And over the silent acres went the whirring of rooks.
Shrill from the hedgerow nooks

I heard the bicker of starlings tugging at the elder-tree
Or the cries of rambling children among the bramble bushes;
And at every thud of a ripened apple falling my blood
Was bruised and fled outward as though they were falling through me
With a menace of what might be.

And then came a morning when there was no sound at all,
And I surprised as might be the dead could rise up free
To steal out early, as I did when I was a girl.
Between the two cock-crowings it was, and the sky was tall
With the first looks of the fall

Of the year, standing off naked and remote from an earth that yet
Green-muffled its breast as though loathe to be undressed of summer;
But I with the tall sky was done with it all,
And my feet through the snow-cold dew waded with a well-met
To that washing and whet.

Grey was the unwakened air, the steadfast arch of the down
Stretched like the curving wings of a gull that unswerving sleeps
Onward its way, grey on a cloud of grey,
And onward went I, careless as one in a sleepwalking swoon,
And cold in my cotton gown.

I was proud as I went, I scorned the fields that had given increase
And awaited now like slaves the certain ploughing of winter,
I turned to those acres I knew unfruitful and forsaken;
But behold, my bitter pasture was whitened like a fleece
With mushrooms, and lay at peace.

In a night they had come, whence and how, who could tell?
Myriads of rounded mushrooms everywhere surrounding me,
Thrusting out tender from the harsh earth, engendered,
Frail, with the cleaving grasses broken with their upswell
That no bondage could quell.

I was at peace with them, seeing them so undefiled,
Knowing the gills so delicate hidden under the chilly flesh;
At a birth so meek and marvelous, so secret and maiden-sleek,
I knelt on the grass then, I gave thanks and was mild,
Knowing myself with child.

Whether a Dove or Seagull: Poems by Valentine Ackland and Sylvia Townsend Warner. New York,
Viking, 1933. 177–79.

VALENTINE ACKLAND

Country Dealings

Granny M. was a woman of about sixty-five when I first knew her, I was digging in the new garden-patch, and she leaned over the wall to watch.

"Eee-urr!" she said. "Thik an't the way to dig 'un. Let I have yer spade a
moment." She came down the road again, and in through my gate. Seizing
the spade, she spat on her hands and began to dig at tremendous speed—turning up the earth and knocking it back again, weeds downwards.

"Ar's the way," she said, exhausted, after a few minutes intensive labour.
"Now let I watch you." I worked and she watched, and her advice at that time
saved me about half the labour I would otherwise have spent on that ungrateful soil.

After that we often met. Mostly at the pub, where I went for a drink at
midday. I think she would listen for my voice, for her cottage was at the back
of the inn, and then she would come over the fence and down the garden,
and so we would meet, and play a game of darts (she taught me a new method of throwing, too, which is warranted to win) and drink a pint of old.

Then Granny fell sick. One day, while I was in the garden, I heard her come
up the road, but more slowly than usual. She leaned over the wall, as she had
done on that first day. Her brown face was pale, and she leaned heavily.

"Are you feeling ill, Granny?" I asked.

"B'aint any too snappy, me dear," she replied.

"What's up?" I asked.

"I don't know. I feel mostly all right about marnin', but come night I feel rough again. 'Tis the stomach. I can't seem to fancy ni' think nor that."

After a few days I took her in to see the doctor. I drove her ten miles, because the panel doctor, whom she had walked two miles and more to see, had sent her home again, telling her that nothing was wrong, and she was as fit as a fiddle. If it hadn't been that a friend of hers, an old man named Shepherd Dove, had walked to meet her, she would have lain in the hedge for God knows how long, having dropped there from extreme weakness and pain. She told me all this, and I took her to see another doctor. But first we went for a drive, thank heaven, going around the places she had known as a young woman; the village she had lived and worked in, and to see the house where she had lived with her husband, the blacksmith, whom she had picked up off his feet and carried around the table, once, until he had begged himself off by a promise to be good—I don't know the particulars of the story. We drove around a bit, and then returned to D——, where we saw the doctor. Or at least, she did. I waited outside, after I'd seen her into his room.

She came out jubilant. "Nothing wrong at all—he says. I be as sound as a bell. He's given I some medicine to take after meals."

"What may you eat?" I asked.

"Anything I fancy," she said, triumphantly.

Later on I asked him what was wrong. He shook his head, and replied that he did not know.

After a few more days she collapsed, and lay in the bedroom in her cottage, steadfastly refusing any aid that could be offered.

Friends of hers went in to "do" the cottage. Otherwise she stayed there alone. I sent for the doctor. He came (against etiquette—and for that let us honour him; the "panel" belonged to another) and prescribed—morphia.

After a great deal of trouble and arrangements and delay she was fetched to go to the hospital. There she stayed for a brief time, and then, enquiring about her, I learnt that she was to be sent home as a cancer case, and incurable.

Her cottage was impossible. Low, small, dirty—the thatch full of rat-holes, and leaking terribly. The bedroom had no fire and no ventilation but one tiny window—smaller than any I have ever seen. She lived alone, and—as her condition was terrible—no one would stay there; besides, she could not abide anyone in her house. "Send her to the infirmary," said her doctor (a young man), "and I can look after her there, as I am on the staff. At the hospital I could do nothing much——"

I drove into D——, and as I drew up in the hospital square an ambulance drew out. I did not know then that Granny was in it, and that it would take exactly two and a half hours to do the single journey, that took me (in an ordinary car) twenty-five minutes.

Because she was incurable and dying, she must be turned out of the hospital ward, and because her relatives considered the infirmary a stigma on their charity, she must be taken along a rough cart-track, for two miles extra ride, to their house. Where she died.

And if it hadn't been that I visited her the day before she died, and saw her pain, she would have died without even the comfort of a dose of morphia medicine—for they had not thought to send for any more, and I had to drive into D——, to the doctor's, and fetch that bottle. Otherwise she could have whistled for it.

Meanwhile, her faithful and devoted admirer old bachelor Shepherd Dove, had a nasty swelling on his cheek.

"Have that tooth out!" I advised.

"'Baint ni tooth," said he.

And he was right.

But the local panel doctor (the same one that Granny went to first) diagnosed it, to him, as a swelling and no more—and advised the application of a slightly disinfectant lotion.

Granny sickened and died. Shepherd Dove (who had a romantic devotion to her that would not, perhaps, be believed if I detailed it) visibly drooped and pined while she was ill, and mourned bitterly when she died. But he himself was not so fortunate. While she was ill his face broke out into a weeping sore. This was dressed by the doctor? No. By the innkeeper's wife, who, confronted by this horrible sight, yet stiffened herself sufficiently to lay on a bandage night and morning. And he grew sicker and sicker. He could not eat (it was on the edge of his lower jaw) and he could only with difficulty drink his pint of beer.

Granny had looked after him. No one did, but Mrs. P . . . , now that Granny had gone.

He stumped about the village, crossly evading all enquiries, unless the enquirer asked him to show the place—when he would lift the bandage and reveal an unbelievable sore, which stank more abominably than anything I have ever known. But old Dove would not consent to go near a hospital. "Look what they done for poor Gran," he would say.

I saw his doctor. "Yes," he said jovially. "He's got a nasty cancer there. Silly old fool, I told him to go to the hospital the other day. But he won't."

"He's had it some time?" I asked.

"Ages!" he replied cheerfully. "I thought I oughter tell him at last, don't yer know. So I did, the other day. No use. He won't do a thing. And I can't."

After a little more talk, I basely gave it up. I wish I hadn't. But the old man walked so steadily and so proudly down the road that I dared not coerce him in any way. I COULD NOT have said "Go to the Infirmary."

But that is where he went. And there he died—after three months and more of agony. And nothing had ever been done, by those in authority, to heal him or to help him.

Of course, our great hospitals are a wonderful and everlasting testimony to our charity as a nation. But I wish we could frame them and hang them up, safely behind glass, together with other testimonials—and then start away on State-run hospitals—and OPEN TO ALL, ALWAYS. With room to die in, *pro tem*. Since so many people seem to choose to die there—and so many hospitals have no beds for the mortally sick.

Communism would be a good thing for us, comrades.

Left Review 1.6 (March 1935): 198–200.

SYLVIA TOWNSEND WARNER

My Shirt Is in Mexico

As soon as the train left London, we went along to the buffet car for a drink. The train was crammed, a war-time train loaded with soldiers and with parties of women and children travelling inland to get away from air-raids. It was difficult to move along the corridor; one had to edge one's way past soldiers sitting on their packs, heaps of hand luggage, trainsick children being held out of the window, people queued up sheepishly outside the toilets. But the buffet car was almost empty and looked like something belonging to a different world, with its clean, light-painted walls and red leather upholstery.

We sat down at a little table, and presently the attendant came along with the tariff card. He was a middle-aged man with a good face, innocent and humane like a rabbit's. When I said I'd like a cup of black coffee with rum in it, he made no difficulties, though it was not down on the list.

Coming back with our drinks, he looked at us as though we were already friends of his. The rum was in a measuring glass, and as he poured it into my coffee he said: "Excuse me mentioning it, madam, but I see from your bag you've been in Mexico."

His voice was full of confidence and excitement. For a moment I wondered if I shouldn't take a chance on it, but I was feeling tired and unsure of my powers, so I said, honestly: "No such luck. The bag has, but it's only a loan."

Now we all looked at the label, which was printed with a gay view of flowers and white-clothed tourists riding on festooned mules. And thinking how hard it must be for a man who apparently wanted to go to Mexico to spend his life travelling in a buffet car from Plymouth to London and back again, I said that the friend who owned the bag had liked Mexico very much.

"Oh, yes, it must be a wonderful country," he said "All those hothouse flowers growing wild, and the volcanoes, and the Mexicans making such wonderful artistic things. And everything so old, and yet, in a manner of speaking, only just beginning. Building roads, and learning to read, and getting vaccinated."

"Sensible beginnings," said Valentine.

"Yes, that's right. Oh, I'd like to go to Mexico. It must be beautiful. . . . I've got a shirt in Mexico," he said.

"How did that happen?" I asked. "You're one up on me. I haven't got anything in Mexico."

"It's an uncommon thing to say, isn't it? Oil shares, now, or a cousin—that's to be expected. But not a shirt. It all happened before the war, because of a German gentleman, a refugee. I noticed him the moment he came in—he sat down at that table over there—and I thought to myself: Now, he's somebody. A bald man, and thin as a lath, and most remarkably clean. Bald but not elderly, you understand. Presently he ordered a large coffee and a slice of cake. Well, that didn't tell me much, except a nice manner and a German accent. But when I brought along his order, he'd opened his wallet, and there were his papers spread out—a single to Plymouth and a third-class steamer passage."

"To Mexico?"

"No, to New York. Well, he didn't say anything I could take hold of. But I'd still got a card up my sleeve—there was the ashtray needed emptying. When I went to change it, he said he didn't smoke. Now, I don't smoke either, so that was a beginning. And once you've got a beginning, it's easy, isn't it? From smoking we got round to seasickness, and then I could ask him if he had crossed the Atlantic. 'No,' said he, 'but now I shall.' Living in Plymouth, naturally I know a lot about New York, so I could tell him things he'd find useful. Puddings being called desserts, and luggage baggage, and how you can check it through. He laughed, and said he'd be able to carry all his."

I could see my way to the shirt now.

"Yes, just a suitcase and what he stood up in. What you'd take away for a week-end—and he was going to America for good and all. But not worried in the least. What's more, he seemed so pleased with what he *had* got. Made me feel his suit to see what good wool it was and told me all about a wonderful pair of silk pajamas he'd been given. And you could tell from the way he spoke he was the sort of gentleman who knows about clothes—quite a dandy, in fact. He said straight out his shoes were a disappointment to him—they were a gift, too. And he was quite right; they were very poor articles. Then all of a sudden it flashed on me he could have my shirt. It was a very nice shirt. Providential, really—I'd bought it that very morning and was carrying it down with me. I always like to buy my shirts in London. You get a better style. Well, he wasn't the sort of man you can have pretences with, so I told him straight out I'd like him to take my shirt. Wasn't I lucky to have it with me, though?"

"You were," said Valentine. "I can't wish anyone better luck than that."

"Yes, and he accepted it so pleasantly. But what I liked best was the way he opened the parcel and looked at the shirt most carefully—how the buttons were fastened on and all. Examined it all over, he did. If he had just taken the parcel, that wouldn't have been the same thing, would it?"

"And now he's in Mexico?"

"Oh, no. He's in New York. It's the shirt that's in Mexico. With a friend of his. Look, this is the letter he wrote me from New York."

Often read, always carefully refolded, the thin sheet of paper already had the air of something beginning to be historic:

MARCH 11TH, 1939.

DEAR FRIEND:

I have to tell you how I have made good journey and am settled here in New York City. And I have meet other friends here also, and I find some work shortly. And the beautiful shirt you gave me, it is not ungratefully that I bestow it to a comrade going to Mexico when he has greater need than I. I do not forget the kindness. I hope you are well and make always new friends. I thank you again.

Cordially,
RENATUS LEUTNER.

P.S. New York is very fine.

"You must feel happy about that shirt," I said.

"I do," he replied. "It was a blue one, just right for a sunny climate. I've always wanted to go to Mexico."

A Garland of Straw and Other Stories. London: Chatto, 1943. 81–84.

10

Queer Conjunctions in Modernism

INTRODUCED AND SELECTED BY COLLEEN LAMOS

MODERNISM WAS THE MOMENT when "the love that dare not speak its name" found its voice. Following Oscar Wilde's 1895 defense in the dock when he quoted that memorable line from "Two Loves"—a poem written by his feckless lover, Lord Alfred Douglas—American and British writers gave eloquent and often agonized expression to same-sex desire. Wilde's trial was a historical watershed, the turning point when love between people of the same sex became publicly shameful and subject to criminal penalties. It serves as a landmark for what Michel Foucault and Eve Kosofsky Sedgwick call a crisis in sexual definition, the point around the turn of the century when "heterosexuality" and "homosexuality" were invented as distinct and incompatible sexual orientations.

This section explores same-sex passion in modernist works in terms of *both* its avowal and disavowal. It addresses the aesthetic and sexual implications of homoerotic desires in modernist texts, many of whose authors—such as Djuna Barnes, Ernest Hemingway, Nella Larsen, D. H. Lawrence, and Katherine Mansfield—were ambivalent about such desires. Gay or not, their writings offer representative yet diverse perspectives on same-sex love. Homophobia and homophilia are equally constitutive of Anglo-American modernist literature, a literature that is charged by the split between same- and other-sex love, energized and riven by the homo/hetero binary division. In short, there is not, on the one hand, a "homosexual" modernism and, on the other hand, a "heterosexual" modernism, but a single literary corpus that is torn in various ways by the scission between these (supposedly) incongruent longings. "Queer" describes this uneasy conjunction.

This section draws attention to the works of American and African American authors whose contributions to modern lesbian and gay literature have been insufficiently recognized. With the exception of Mansfield, all of the following selections are by U.S. writers who lived in New York (Greenwich Village or Harlem) and Paris in the early twentieth century. These urban locales were sites of modern literary and sexual experimentation, places where blacks, women, and gay people were relatively free. This section includes an equal representation of female and male authors and is designed to show how male/female difference intersects with homo/heterosexual difference.

Many modern writers did not consider love between persons of the same sex perverse or the sign of an inborn inclination. For instance, in a letter to her suitor, Ethel Smyth (August 15, 1930), Virginia Woolf wrote that "I am diverse enough to want Vita and Ethel and Leonard and Vanessa and oh some other people too" (199).

> I cannot get my sense of unity and coherency and all that makes me wish to write the Lighthouse etc. unless I am perpetually stimulated. It's no good sitting in a garden with a book; or collecting facts. There must be this fanning and drumming. [. . .] Where people mistake, as I think, is in perpetually narrowing and naming these immensely composite and wide flung passions, driving stakes through them, herding them between screens. But how do you define "Perversity."? What is the line between friendship and perversion?[1]

Like Woolf, most women writers of the period regarded same-sex affection as a kind of sapphic love or feminine fondness for women. The masculine version of such commingling was Walt Whitman's idea of comradely "adhesion," a notion that influenced Hart Crane.

The following selections show the diverse ways in which same-sex love was understood in the early twentieth century—what Foucault called its epistemology. Knowledge and power are mutually linked, he argued, so we ought to ask *how* we know what homosexuality is. Many of these selections display the complexity of same-sex love and sexual identification—that is, how loving another woman is interwoven with wanting to be like her—or dis-identification (e.g., "I love her and so must be different"). Barnes's *Ladies Almanack* and Charles Henri Ford and Parker Tyler's *The Young and Evil* are instances of the latter, in which same-sex love crosses gender identity.

In the wake of Wilde's infamy, modern literature is strongly marked by the closet, so that same-sex desire is disclosed by strategies of concealment. Many writers cloaked their depictions of same-sex love in the decorous guise of affection for the dead; indeed, the genre of the elegy has long been a legitimate means for expressions of such love, a tradition continued by Edna St. Vincent Millay and by T. S. Eliot in *The Waste Land*. Writers also displaced same-sex desire onto physical metonymies, especially the hand. The intimacy depicted in Crane's poem, "Episode of Hands," echoes that of Sherwood Anderson, who, in the "Hands" chapter of *Winesburg, Ohio*, describes Wing Bibblebaum's wandering, yearning hands. W. H. Auden took up the trope in his poem "Song," in which "Whispering neighbors, left and right, / Pluck us from the real delight; / And the active hands must freeze / Lonely on the separate knees."

"I think often while holding their hands, and getting exquisite pleasure from contact with either female or male body," Woolf remarked in her letter to Smyth, reminding us that, for many modernist writers, same- and other-sex desires were not clearly differentiated. Mansfield's poem, "Friendship," demonstrates the blurred yet enforced line drawn between adolescent affection and adult desire. The speaker recalls her teenage friendship with another girl when they shared a kitten, a metonymy for their fondness for each other; years later, that harmless love has become dangerous. Mansfield had an ambivalently sexual girlhood relationship with Ida Baker, whom she nicknamed Leslie Moore after her younger brother. In adulthood, their relationship became fraught with guilt on Mansfield's part. The closing lines of the poem reverberate with the cry of the abandoned friend: "This is our Kitty-witty! / Why don't you love her now?" Mansfield's story, "Bliss," like Larson's *Passing*, depicts an erotic triangle in which desire between two women is routed through a man; this heterosexual detour, analyzed by Sedgwick in *Between Men*, is a typical strategy of equivocal same-sex revelation and concealment.

The early twentieth-century discourses of sexology and psychology sharply distinguished homosexuality from heterosexuality. Ulrichs, Krafft-Ebing, Ellis, Hirshfeld, and Freud offered theories of homosexuality that they regarded as pleas for tolerance of it as a naturally occurring aberration.[2] In so doing, though, they pathologized what had been previously treasured as "romantic friendships," creating a kind of person, the homosexual, endowed with a case history as a type of pervert.[3] The homo/hetero division gave birth to an understanding of homoeroticism as a biological deviation or psychological defect. The literary effects of this epochal division are evident in Radclyffe Hall's novel, *The Well of Loneliness*, introduced by Ellis. Hall drew upon sexology to portray a female invert—a woman in whose body was trapped the soul of a man. By contrast, Hilda Doolittle (H. D.) relied upon psychoanalytic theory to develop her gynocentric poetics, in which female same-sex desire is coextensive with feminine identification.

Emboldened by the doctors to speak in defense of the newly coined concept of homosexuality yet frequently hostile to it, some modernist authors challenged these "scientific" discourses. Like Barnes in *Ladies Almanack* and *Nightwood,* they mocked the pscyho-medical diagnosis that rendered them twisted (per)inverts. In *Ladies Almanack,* whose introduction is included below, Barnes presents a humorous caricature of Natalie Clifford Barney as Evangeline Musset, as well as a satiric portrait of the lesbian community of Paris's Left Bank in the 1920s. The diva of that world, Barney was the center of lesbian art and literature; she supported expatriate writers and conducted a famous salon that featured Barnes, Janet Flanner, Renée Vivien, and Dolly Wilde (Oscar's niece). Gertrude Stein's monumental presence, accompanied by the shadowy Alice Toklas, contributed to the avant-garde aesthetic and sexual culture of the Rive Gauche.

McAlmon's *Being Geniuses Together* (1938) remains one of the best chronicles of this lesbian subculture.[4] An expatriate from the Midwest whose homosexuality was an open secret, he returned to his Dakotan roots in "The Indefinite Huntress" (1932), to write of inarticulate longings in an isolated prairie town.[5] Its spare style reminiscent of the fiction of Willa Cather and Anderson, McAlmon's tale centers on two people, Lily and Red, who marry because of their shared yet unacknowledged desire for a beautiful boy. The amazonian Lily is the huntress, who discovers her "definite, female amorous prey" at the end of the story; before that, she proposes marriage to Red. The latter, drawn to Lily through their triangular relationship with the boy, deteriorates after their marriage. Like Cather's texts, the rawboned realism and terse understatement of the story accentuate the unspeakability, indeed, the unthinkability of same-sex love in early twentieth-century, small-town America, before the advent of the modern language and logic of homosexuality.

The modern concept of homosexuality was superimposed upon two older traditions: the Greek model of same-sex erotic friendship and the French, fin-de-siècle literature of decadence. Plato's dialogues and Sappho's poems served as exemplars of the former and became popular during the Hellenistic revival in late-Victorian England.[6] Greek aesthetics, ethics, and love were interwoven in the homophilic writings of Walter Pater, Symonds, Wilde, and E. M. Forster.[7] The discovery of Sappho's lyric fragments inspired an entire generation of women writers; indeed, the figure of Sappho played a major role in the formation of female modernist literature both because of her prominence as the sole classical precursor for women poets and because of the convergence of female friendship and love at the heart of her poetry.[8]

The other, less respectable tradition upon which modern writers drew was that of French literary decadence, beginning with Baudelaire's poems of lesbian "damned women" and Huysmans's novel *Against the Grain,* and continuing in the poetry of Rimbaud, Verlaine, Swinburne, and London's 1890s Rhymers' Club.[9] Wilde's *The Picture of Dorian Gray* and Beardsley's perverse drawings are regarded as the apogee of English decadence. A few decades later, Barnes, Millay, Richard Bruce Nugent, Ford, and Tyler returned to the formal practices and thematic preoccupations of their decadent predecessors as a means of representing socially contemptible desires.

Hellenism and decadence (otherwise known as aestheticism) were not entirely separate discourses in the early twentieth century, however. Pierre Louÿs's *Songs of Bilitis* (1895) is a notoriously naughty example of the homoeroticism of decadent literature and its link to the Greek tradition. Purporting to be translations of the works of Bilitis, a fictive female poet of Sappho's Lesbos, his *Songs* celebrate, in lushly lyrical language, the sensuality of women's bodies and their passion for one another. Floridly and frankly erotic, the *Songs* confirmed the suspicions of those who feared that literary decadence was a fig leaf for degenerate sexuality. Louÿs's depiction of lesbian love was taken up by modern women authors, especially Vivien. Although her life epitomized decadence—including overwrought aestheticism, tragic love affairs, drug addiction, and early death—she insisted upon what she viewed as the purity of female same-sex desire. Vivien's 1904 essay, "The Friendship of Women" is unusual in her oeuvre for its straightforward defense of feminine love as surpassing the carnality of heterosexuality.

The energies unleashed by modern decadence are evident in the works of avant-garde artists in Harlem and Greenwich Village in the 1920s and early 1930s. Gates observes that the Harlem Renaissance "was surely as gay as it was black" and was significantly influenced by England's "yellow 1890s."[10] Nevertheless, openly gay writing was discouraged by leading figures of the Harlem Renaissance who, like Alain Locke (himself gay), wanted to present a decorous and uplifting face to the white world. The homosexual desires of writers such as Countee Cullen, Claude McKay, Wallace Thurman, and Langston Hughes were commonly known and tolerated but not publicly acknowledged. The unapologetic homoeroticism of Nugent's short story, "Smoke, Lilies and Jade" is unprecedented in African American literature. Published in the cutting-edge journal *FIRE!!* (1926) and written in a stream-of-consciousness style, "Smoke, Lilies and Jade" exemplifies the convergence of African American, modernist, and decadent traditions. Drawing upon the perfumed eroticism of Huysman and Wilde in his story, Nugent borrows equally from

Beardsley's fin-de-siècle aestheticism in his sketches.[11] The hero of his story is torn between two lovers—female and male—who represent banal, heterosexual respectability and carnal, homosexual desire. By contrast, Cullen's "Fruit of the Flower" (1925) is the work of a man whose homoerotic passions were cloaked in discretion.[12] "The Fruit of the Flower" refers to the poet's relationship with his adoptive father, who used his wife's makeup and took a strong interest in the local young men's boxing club. The poem suggests that father and son share a "secret sin," one that Cullen also alludes to in "Heritage," a poem in which racial and sexual alienation converge.[13]

The center of *le vie bohème* in the early twentieth century, Greenwich Village sustained a vibrant gay subculture.[14] That queer world is brought to life in Ford and Tyler's novel, *The Young and Evil* (1933), which marks the emergence of a proud gay male literary voice that also candidly addresses the relationship between queer sexuality and gender identity. Two of its four main characters are effeminate "fairies," the other two are "real" men, while all of them engage in pick-ups with sailors and others outside the gay community, sometimes resulting in vicious assaults. The erotic lives of these characters are interwoven with their friendships.

Ford and Tyler were southern dandies who met in New York in 1930, and the novel that they coauthored is based upon their experiences together. Ford subsequently went to Paris, sat at Stein's feet, became a friend of Barnes, and adopted their avant-garde literary styles. He took up Barnes's depiction of a gay milieu and her trope of the doll (from *Nightwood*) to represent the constructedness of gender. Chapter 13 of *The Young and Evil,* "I Don't Want to Be a Doll" describes a drag ball in Harlem when Julian declares, "I am not a fairy doll." He admits, though, that "I have the will to doll," a will energized by the campy allure of cross-gender effeminacy. Written in a mannered, self-consciously experimental style, the novel strives mightily to be "modern" with its bizarre figures, run-on sentences, omitted punctuation marks, surrealist descriptions, stream-of-consciousness interior monologues, and refusal of realistic narrative continuity.

Known for their avant-garde daring, modernist writers queered the literary tradition that they inherited. The centrality of queer authors to the modernist movement should, therefore, come as no surprise, nor that literary modernism and queer sexual expression should emerge more or less at the same time. The authors included in this section are all, in some way, indebted to the figure of Oscar Wilde. Their writings respond, thematically and formally, to Wilde's legacy—to his campy wit, his aesthetic sensibility, and his courageous defiance of sexual norms.

Notes

1. Woolf, *Letters, Vol. 4, 1921–31.* 199–200.
2. For a sampling of their works, see Bland and Doan, eds.
3. See Foucault, *The History of Sexuality, Vol. I,* and Smith-Rosenberg.
4. McAlmon, *Being Geniuses Together;* Benstock, *Women of the Left Bank.*
5. McAlmon published the works of Stein, Barnes, Hemingway, and his own stories in his Contact Press.
6. See Dowling.
7. See John Addington Symonds *A Problem in Greek Ethics* (1901) and *A Problem in Modern Ethics* (1971)—a conjunction that Foucault revisited at the end of the century in *The History of Sexuality, Vol. 2: The Use of Pleasure.*
8. See works by Vivien, Nathalie Clifford Barney, H. D., Millay, and Woolf. Several papyrus texts of Sappho's previously lost lyrics were discovered during Grenfell and Hunt's Egyptian excavations (1897–1906). It was the largest new collection of Sappho's poetry and inspired many writers of the period. See Gubar (199–218), Vanita (1), Reynolds, Benstock, "Sapphic Modernism," Colicott, and Synder.
9. For a sampling of this literature, see Stableford, ed., and Becker, ed.
10. Gates (233). See also Eric Garber's essay in *Hidden from History.*
11. See Wirth (41, 59).
12. Cullen married the daughter of W. E. B. Du Bois and, a few months later, sailed for Europe with his best man and gay friend. The local headline—"A Groom Sails With Best Man" reveals the homoeroticism that Cullen tried to keep out of his published poetry.
13. See Powers.
14. See Chauncy and also Boone.

Works Cited

Becker, Karl ed. *The Yellow Book of Decadence.* Chicago: Art Institute Press, 1985.
Benstock, Shari. "Sapphic Modernism." In *Lesbian Texts and Contexts,* ed. Karla Jay and Joanne Glasgow. New York: New York University Press, 1990.
———. *Women of the Left Bank.*
Bland, Lucy, and Laura Doan, eds. *Sexology Uncensored: The Documents of Sexual Science.* Chicago: University of Chicago Press, 1998.
Boone, Joseph Allan. *Libidinal Currents.*
Chauncy, George. *Gay New York: Gender, Urban Culture, and the Making of the Gay Male World, 1890–1940.* New York: Basic Books, 1994.
Colicott, Diane. *H. D. and Sapphic Modernism.* Cambridge: Cambridge University Press, 2000.
Dowling, Linda. *Hellenism and Homosexuality in Victorian Oxford.* Ithaca: Cornell University Press, 1994.
Faderman, Lillian. *Surpassing the Love of Men.* New York: Morrow, 1982.
Foucault, Michel. *The History of Sexuality, Vol. I: An Introduction,* trans. Robert Hurley. New York: Vintage Books, 1984.
Garber, Eric. "A Spectacle in Color: The Lesbian and Gay Subculture of Jazz Age Harlem." In *Hidden from History: Reclaiming the Gay and Lesbian Past,* ed. Martin Baumi Duber-

man, Martha Vincinas, and George Chauncey Jr. New York: New American Library, 1989. 318–31.

Gates, Jr., Henry Louis. "The Black Man's Burden." In *Fear of a Queer Planet,* ed. Michael Warner. Minneapolis: University of Minnesota Press, 1994.

Gubar, Susan. "Sapphistries." In *Re-Reading Sappho: Reception and Transmission,* ed. Ellen Greene. Berkeley: University of California Press, 1996. 199–218.

McAlmon, Robert. *Being Geniuses Together: An Autobiography.* London: Secker & Warburg, 1938.

Powers, Peter. "'The Singing Man Who Must Be Reckoned With': Private Desire and Public Responsibility in the Poetry of Countee Cullen." *African American Review* 34 (Winter 2000): 661–78.

Reynolds, Margaret. *The Sappho Companion.* New York: Palgrave, 2000.

Smith-Rosenberg, Carol. "The Female World of Love and Ritual." In *Disorderly Conduct: Visions of Gender in Victorian England.* New York: Oxford University Press, 1985.

Synder, Jane McIntosh. *Lesbian Desire in the Lyrics of Sappho.* New York: Columbia University Press, 1997.

Stableford, Brian, ed. *The Dedalus Book of Decadence: Moral Ruins.* Sawtry, Cambs: Dedalus, 1990.

Vanita, Ruth. *Sappho and the Virgin Mary: Same-Sex Love and the English Literary Imagination.* New York: Columbia University Press, 1996.

Wirth, Thomas H. Introduction. *Gay Rebel of the Harlem Renaissance: Selections from the Work of Richard Bruce Nugent.* Durham: Duke University Press, 2002.

Woolf, Virginia. *The Letters of Virginia Woolf.* Vol. 4, 1921-31.

DJUNA BARNES

"Introduction," From *Ladies Almanack*

Now this be a Tale of as fine a Wench as ever wet Bed, she who was called Evangeline Musset and who was in her Heart one Grand Red Cross for the Pursuance, the Relief and the Distraction, of such Girls as in their Hinder Parts, and their Fore Parts, and in whatsoever Parts did suffer them most, lament Cruelly, be it Itch of Palm, or Quarters most horribly burning, which do oft occur in the Spring of the Year, or at those Times when they do sit upon warm and cozy Material, such as Fur, or thick and Oriental Rugs, (whose very Design it seems, procures for them such a Languishing of the Haunch and Reins as is insupportable) or who sit upon warm Stoves, whence it is known that one such flew up with an "Ah my God! What a World it is for a Girl indeed, be she ever so well abridged and cool of Mind and preserved of Intention, the Instincts are, nevertheless, brought to such a yelping Pitch and so undo her, that she runs hither and thither seeking some Simple or Unguent which shall allay her

Pain! And why is it no Philosopher of whatever Sort, has discovered, amid the nice Herbage of his Garden, one that will content that Part, but that from the day that we were indifferent Matter, to this wherein we are Imperial Personages of the divine human Race, no thing so solaces it as other Parts as inflamed, or with the Consolation every Woman has at her Finger Tips, or at the very Hang of her Tongue?"

For such then was Evangeline Musset created, a Dame of lofty Lineage, who, in the early eighties, had discarded her family Tandem, in which her Mother and Father found Pleasure enough, for the distorted Amusement of riding all smack-of-astride, like any Yeoman going to gather in his Crops; and with much jolting and galloping, was made, hour by hour, less womanly, "Though never," said she, "has that Greek Mystery occurred to me, which is known as the Dashing out of the Testicles, and all that goes with it!" Which is said to have happened to a Byzantine Baggage of the Trojan Period, more to her Surprise than her Pleasure. Yet it is an agreeable Circumstance that the Ages thought fit to hand down this Miracle, for Hope springs eternal in the human Breast.

It has been noted by some and several, that Women have in them the Pip of Romanticism so well grown and fat of Sensibility, that they, upon reaching an uncertain Age, discard Duster, Offspring and Spouse, and a little after are seen leaning, all of a limp, on a Pillar of Bathos.

Evangeline Musset was not one of these, for she had been developed in the Womb of her most gentle Mother to be a Boy, when therefore, she came forth an Inch or so less than this, she paid no Heed to the Error, but donning a Vest of a superb Blister and Tooling, a Belcher for tippet and a pair of hip-boots with a scarlet channel (for it was a most wet wading) she took her Whip in hand, calling her Pups about her, and so set out upon the Road of Destiny, until such time as they should grow to be Hounds of a Blood, and Pointers with a certainty in the Butt of their Tails; waiting patiently beneath Cypresses for this Purpose, and under the Boughs of the aloe tree, composing, as she did so, Madrigals to all sweet and ramping things.

Her Father, be it known, spent many a windy Eve pacing his Library in the most normal of Night-Shirts, trying to think of ways to bring his erring Child back into that Religion and Activity which has ever been thought sufficient for a Woman; for already, when Evangeline appeared at Tea to the Duchess Clitoressa of Natescourt, women in the way (the Bourgeoise be it noted, on an errand to some nice Church of the Catholic Order, with their Babes at Breast, and Husbands at Arm) would snatch their Skirts from Contamination, putting such wincing Terror into their Dears with their quick and trembling Plucking, that it had been observed, in due time, by all Society, and Evangeline was in order of becoming one of those who is spoken to out of Generosity, which her Father could see, would by no Road, lead her to the Altar.

He had Words with her enough, saying: "Daughter, daughter, I perceive in you most fatherly Sentiments. What am I to do?" And she answered him High enough, "Thou, good Governor, wast expecting a Son when you lay atop of your Choosing, why then be so mortal wounded when you perceive that you have your Wish? Am I not doing after your very Desire, and is it not the more commendable, seeing that I do it without the Tools for the Trade, and yet nothing complain?"

In the days of which I write she had come to be a witty and learned Fifty, and though most short of Stature and nothing handsome, was so much in Demand, and so wide famed for her Genius at bringing up by Hand, and so noted and esteemed for her Slips of the Tongue that it finally brought her into the Hall of Fame, where she stood by a Statue of Venus as calm as you please, or leaned upon a lacrymal Urn with a small Sponge for such as Wept in her own Time and stood in Need of it.

> Thus begins this Almanack, which all Ladies.
> should carry about with them, as the Priest his
> Breviary, as the Cook his Recipes,
> as the Doctor his Physic, as
> the Bride her Fears,
> and as the Lion
> his Roar!

1928. Rpt. *Facsimile edition*. Elmwood Park, Ill.: Dalkey Archive Press, 1992. 6–9.

BRUCE NUGENT

From "Smoke, Lilies and Jade"

He *wanted to do something* . . . to write or draw . . . or something . . . but it was so comfortable just to lay there on the bed. . . . . . his shoes off . . . and think . . . think of everything . . . short disconnected thoughts—to wonder . . . to remember . . . to think and smoke . . . why wasn't he worried that he had no money . . . he *had* had five cents . . . but he had been hungry . . . he *was* hungry and still . . . all he wanted to do was . . . lay there comfortably smoking . . . think . . . wishing he were writing . . . or drawing . . . or something

. . . something about the things he felt and thought . . . but what did he think . . . he remembered how his mother had awakened him one night . . . ages ago . . . six years ago . . . Alex . . . he had always wondered at the strangeness of it . . . she had seemed so . . . so . . . so just the same . . . Alex . . . I think your father is dead . . . and it hadn't seemed so strange . . . yet . . . one's mother didn't say that . . . didn't wake one at midnight every night to say . . . feel him . . . put your hand on his head . . . then whisper with a catch in her voice . . . I'm afraid . . . sh don't wake Lam . . . yet it hadn't seemed as it should have seemed . . . even when he had felt his father's cool wet forehead . . . it hadn't been tragic . . . the light had been turned very low . . . and flickered . . . yet it hadn't been tragic . . . or weird . . . not at all as one should feel when one's father died . . . even his reply of . . . yes he is dead . . . had been commonplace . . . hadn't been dramatic . . . there had been no tears . . . no sobs . . . not even a sorrow . . . and yet he must have realized that one's father couldn't smile . . . or sing any more . . . after he had died . . . every one remembered his father's voice . . . it had been a lush voice . . . [. . .] his mother had been telling him what he must do . . . and cried softly . . . and that had made him cry too but you mustn't cry Alex . . . remember you have to be a little man now . . . and that was all . . . didn't other wives and sons cry more for their dead than that . . . anyway people never cried for beautiful sunsets . . . or music . . . and those were the things that hurt . . . the things to sympathize with . . . then out into the snow and dark of the morning . . . [. . .] Alex puffed contentedly on his cigarette . . . he was hungry and comfortable . . . and he had an ivory holder inlaid with red jade and green . . . funny how the smoke seemed to climb up that ray of sunlight . . . went up the slant just like imagination . . . [. . .] when they had taken his father from the vault three weeks later . . . he had grown beautiful . . . his nose had become perfect and clear . . . his hair had turned jet black and glossy and silky . . . and his skin was a transparent green . . . like the sea only not so deep . . . and where it was drawn over the cheek bones a pale beautiful red appeared . . . like a blush . . . why hadn't his father looked like that always . . . but no . . . to have sung would have broken the wondrous repose of his lips and maybe that was his beauty . . . maybe it was wrong to think thoughts like these . . . but they were nice and pleasant and comfortable . . . when one was smoking a cigarette thru an ivory holder inlaid with red jade and green. . . . .

he wondered why be couldn't find work . . . a job . . . when he had first come to New York he had . . . and he had only been fourteen then was it because he was nineteen now that he felt so idle . . . and contented . . . or because he was an artist . . . but was he an artist . . . was one an artist until one became known . . . of course he was an artist . . . and strangely enough so were all his friends . . . he should be ashamed that he didn't work . . . but . . . was it five years in New York . . . or the fact that he was an artist . . . when his mother said she couldn't understand him . . . why did he vaguely pity her instead of being ashamed . . . he should be . . . his mother and all his relatives said so . . . his brother was three years younger than he and yet he had already been away from home a year . . . on the stage . . . making thirty-five dollars a week . . . had three suits and many clothes and was going to help mother . . . while he . . . Alex . . . was content to lay and smoke and meet friends at night . . . to argue and read Wilde . . . Freud . . . Boccacio and Schnitzler . . . to attend Gurdjieff meetings and know things . . . Why did they scoff at him for knowing such people as Carl . . . Mencken . . . Toomer . . . Hughes . . . Cullen . . . Wood . . . Cabell . . . oh the whole lot of them . . . was it because it seemed incongruous that he . . . who was so little known . . . should call by first names people they would like to know . . . were they jealous . . . no mothers aren't jealous of their sons . . . they are proud of them . . . why then . . . when these friends accepted and liked him . . . no matter how he dressed . . . why did mother ask . . . and you went looking like that . . . Langston was a fine fellow . . . he knew there was something in Alex . . . and so did Rene and Borgia . . . and Zora and Clement and Miguel . . . and . . . and . . . and all of them . . . if he went to see mother she would ask . . . how do you feel Alex with nothing in your pockets . . . I don't see how you can be satisfied . . . Really you're a mystery to me . . . and who you take after . . . I'm sure I don't know . . . [. . .]

it was hard to believe in one's self after that . . . did Wildes' parents or Shelly's [*sic*] or Goya's talk to them like that . . . but it was depressing to think in that vein . . . [. . .] in truth he was tragic . . . that was a lovely appellation . . . The Tragic Genius . . . think . . . to go thru life known as The Tragic Genius . . . romantic . . . but it was more or less true . . . Alex turned over and blew another cloud of smoke . . . was all life like that . . . smoke . . . blue smoke from an ivory holder . . . [. . .]

Alex sat up . . . pulled on his shoes and went out . . . it was a beautiful night . . . and so large . . . the dusky blue hung like a curtain in an immense arched doorway . . . fastened with silver tacks . . . to wander in the night was wonderful . . . myriads of inquisitive lights . . . curiously prying into the dark . . . and fading unsatisfied . . . he passed a woman . . . she was not beautiful . . . and he was sad because she did not weep that she would never be beautiful . . . was it Wilde who had said . . . a cigarette is the most perfect pleasure because it leaves one unsatisfied . . . the breeze gave to him a perfume stolen from some wandering lady of the evening . . . it pleased him . . . why was it that men wouldn't use perfumes . . . they should . . . each and every one of

them liked perfumes . . . the man who denied that was a liar . . . or a cow-
ard . . . but if ever he were to voice that thought . . . express it . . . he would
be misunderstood . . . a fine feeling that . . . to be misunderstood . . . it made
him feel tragic and great . . . but may be it would be nicer to be understood
. . . but no . . . no great artist is . . . then again neither were fools . . . they were
strangely akin these two . . . [. . .] in truth it was fine to be young and hungry
and an artist . . . to blow blue smoke from an ivory holder. . . . .

here was the cafeteria . . . it was almost as tho it had journeyed to meet
him . . . the night was so blue . . . how does blue feel . . . or red or gold or any
other color . . . if colors could be heard he could paint most wondrous tunes
. . . symphonious . . . think . . . the dulcet clear tone of a blue like night . . . of
a red like pomegranate juice . . . [. . .] there was no one in the cafe as yet . . . he
sat and waited . . . that was a clever idea he had had about color music . . . but
after all he was a monstrous clever fellow . . . Jurgen had said that . . . funny
how characters in books said the things one wanted to say . . . he would like
to know Jurgen . . . how does one go about getting an introduction to a fiction
character . . . [. . .] a few lines of one of Langston's poems came to describe
Jurgen. . . . .

> Somewhat like Ariel
> Somewhat like Puck
> Somewhat like a gutter boy
> Who loves to play in muck.
> Somewhat like Bacchus
> Somewhat like Pan
> And a way with women
> Like a sailor man. . . . .

Langston must have known Jurgen . . . suppose Jurgen had met Tonio Kroeger
. . . what a vagrant thought . . . Kroeger . . . Kroeger . . . Kroeger . . . why here
was Rene . . . Alex had almost gone to sleep . . . Alex blew a cone of smoke as
he took Rene's hand . . . it was nice to have friends like Rene . . . [. . .] Alex
searched the smoke for expression . . . he . . . he . . . well he has created a phantasy mire . . . that's it . . . from clear rich imagery . . . life and silver sands
. . . that's nice . . . and silver sands . . . imagine lilies growing in such a mire
. . . when they close at night their gilded underside would protect . . . but that's
not it at all . . . his thoughts just carried and mingled like . . . like odors . . . suggested but never definite . . . Rene was leaving . . . they all were leaving . . . Alex sauntered slowly back . . . the houses all looked sleepy . . . funny . . . made
him feel like writing poetry . . . and about death too . . . [. . .] he climbed the

noisy stair of the odorous tenement . . . smelled of fish . . . of stale fried fish and dirty milk bottles . . . he rather liked it . . . he liked the acrid smell of horse manure too . . . strong . . . thoughts . . . yes to lie back among strangely fashioned cushions and sip eastern wines and talk . . . Alex threw himself on the bed . . . removed his shoes . . . stretched and relaxed . . . yes and have music waft softly into the darkened and incensed room . . . he blew a cloud of smoke . . . oh the joy of being an artist and of blowing blue smoke thru an ivory holder inlaid with red jade and green . . .

the street was so long and narrow . . . so long and narrow . . . and blue . . . [. . .] Alex walked music . . . it was nice to walk in the blue after a party . . . Zora had shone again . . . her stories . . . she always shone . . . and Monty was glad . . . every one was glad when Zora shone . . . he was glad he had gone to Monty's party . . . [. . .] Alex walked and the click of his heels sounded . . . and had an echo . . . sound being tossed back and forth . . . back and forth . . . some one was approaching . . . and their echoes mingled . . . and gave the sound of castenets [*sic*] . . . Alex liked the sound of the approaching man's footsteps . . . he walked music also . . . he knew the beauty of the narrow blue . . . Alex knew that by the way their echoes mingled . . . he wished he would speak . . . but strangers don't speak at four o'clock in the morning . . . at least if they did he couldn't imagine what would be said . . . maybe . . . pardon me but are you walking toward the stars . . . yes, sir, and if you walk long enough . . . then may I walk with you I want to reach the stars too . . . perdone me senor tiene vd. fosforo . . . Alex was glad he had been addressed in Spanish . . . to have been asked for a match in English . . . or to have been addressed in English at all . . . would have been blasphemy just then . . . Alex handed him a match . . . he glanced at his companion apprehensively in the match glow . . . he was afraid that his appearance would shatter the blue thoughts . . . and stars . . . ah . . . his face was a perfect compliment to his voice . . . and the echo of their steps mingled . . . they walked in silence . . . the castanets of their heels clicking accompaniment . . . the stranger inhaled deeply and with a nod of content and a smile . . . blew a cloud of smoke . . . [. . .] Alex turned in his doorway . . . up the stairs and the stranger waited for him to light the room . . . no need for words . . . they had always known each other. . . . . as they undressed by the blue dawn . . . Alex knew he had never seen a more perfect being . . . his body was all symmetry and music . . . and Alex called him Beauty . . . long they lay . . . blowing smoke and exchanging thoughts . . . and Alex swallowed with difficulty . . . he felt a glow of tremor . . . and they talked and . . . slept . . . [. . .]

he was in a field . . . a field of blue smoke and black poppies and red calla lilies . . . he was searching . . . on his hands and knees . . . searching . . . among black poppies and red calla lilies . . . he was searching pushed aside poppy stems . . . and saw two strong white legs . . . dancer's legs . . . the contours pleased him . . . his eyes wandered . . . on past the muscular hocks to the firm white thighs . . . the rounded buttocks . . . then the lithe narrow waist . . . strong torso and broad deep chest . . . the heavy shoulders . . . the graceful muscled neck . . . squared chin and quizzical lips . . . grecian nose with its temperamental nostrils . . . the brown eyes looking at him . . . like . . . Monty looked at Zora . . . his hair curly and black and all tousled . . . and it was Beauty . . . and Beauty smiled and looked at him and smiled . . . said . . . I'll wait Alex . . . and Alex became confused and continued his search . . . on his hands and knees . . . pushing aside poppy stems and lily stems . . . a poppy . . . a black poppy . . . a lilly [sic] . . . a red lilly [sic] . . . and when he looked back he could no longer see Beauty . . . Alex continued his search . . . thru poppies . . . lilies . . . poppies and red calla lilies . . . and suddenly he saw . . . two small feet olive-ivory . . . two well turned legs curving gracefully from slender ankles . . . and the contours soothed him . . . he followed them . . . past the narrow rounded hips to the tiny waist . . . the fragile firm breasts . . . the graceful slender throat . . . the soft rounded chin . . . slightly parting lips and the straight little nose with its slightly flaring nostrils . . . the black eyes with lights in them . . . looking at him . . . the forehead and straight cut black hair . . . and it was Melva . . . and she looked at him and smiled and said . . . I'll wait Alex . . . and Alex became confused and kissed her . . . became confused and continued his search . . . on his hands and knees . . . pushed aside a poppy stem . . . a black-poppy stem . . . pushed aside a lily stem . . . a red-lily stem . . . a poppy . . . a poppy . . . a lily . . . and suddenly he stood erect . . . exhultant . . . and in his hand he held . . . an ivory holder . . . inlaid with red jade . . . and green. . . . .

and Alex awoke . . . Beauty's hair tickled his nose . . . Beauty was smiling in his sleep . . . half his face stained flush color by the sun . . . the other half in shadow . . . blue shadow . . . his eye lashes casting cobwebby blue shadows on his cheek . . . his lips were so beautiful . . . quizzical . . . Alex wondered why he always thought of that passage from Wilde's Salome . . . when he looked at Beauty's lips . . . I would kiss your lips . . . he *would* like to kiss Beauty's lips . . . Alex flushed warm . . . with shame . . . or was it shame . . . he reached across Beauty for a cigarette . . . Beauty's cheek felt cool to his arm . . . his hair felt soft . . . Alex lay smoking . . . such a dream . . . red calla lilies . . . red calla lilies . . . and . . . what could it all mean . . . did dreams have meanings . . . Fania said . . . and black poppies . . . thousands . . . millions . . . Beauty stirred

. . . Alex put out his cigarette . . . closed his eyes . . . he mustn't see Beauty yet . . . speak to him . . . his lips were too hot . . . dry . . . the palms of his hands too cool and moist . . . thru his half closed eyes he could see Beauty . . . propped . . . cheek in hand . . . on one elbow . . . looking at him . . . lips smiling quizzically . . . he wished Beauty wouldn't look so hard . . . Alex was finding it difficult to breathe . . . breathe normally . . . why *must* Beauty look so long . . . and smile *that* way . . . his face seemed nearer . . . it was . . . Alex could feel Beauty's hair on his forehead . . . breathe normally . . . breathe normally . . . could feel Beauty's breath on his nostrils and lips . . . and it was clean and faintly colored with tobacco . . . breathe normally Alex . . . Beauty's lips were nearer . . . Alex closed his eyes . . . how did one act . . . his pulse was hammering . . . from wrists to finger tip . . . wrist to finger tip . . . Beauty's lips touched his . . . his temples throbbed . . . throbbed . . . his pulse hammered from wrist to finger tip . . . Beauty's breath came short now . . . softly staccato . . . breathe normally Alex . . . you are asleep . . . Beauty's lips touched his . . . breathe normally . . . and pressed . . . pressed hard . . . cool . . . his body trembled . . . breathe normally Alex . . . Beauty's lips pressed cool . . . cool and hard . . . how much pressure does it take to waken one . . . Alex sighed . . . moved softly . . . how does one act . . . Beauty's hair barely touched him now . . . his breath was faint on . . . Alex's nostrils . . . and lips . . . Alex stretched and opened his eyes . . . Beauty was looking at him . . . propped on one elbow . . . cheek in his palm . . . Beauty spoke . . . scratch my head please Dulce . . . Alex was breathing normally now . . . propped against the bed head . . . Beauty's head in his lap . . . Beauty spoke . . . I wonder why I like to look at some things Dulce . . . things like smoke and cats . . . and you . . . Alex's pulse no longer hammered from . . . wrist to finger tip . . . wrist to finger tip . . . the rose dusk had become blue night . . . and soon . . . soon they would go out into the blue. . . . . . .

the little church was crowded . . . warm . . . the rows of benches were brown and sticky . . . Harold was there . . . and Constance and Langston and Bruce and John . . . there was Mr. Robeson . . . how are you Paul . . . a young man was singing . . . [. . .] what could it all mean . . . so many poppies . . . and Beauty looking at him like . . . like Monty looked at Zora . . . another young man was playing a violin . . . he was the first real artist to perform . . . he had a touch of soul . . . or was it only feeling . . . they were hard to differentiate on the violin . . . and Melva standing in the poppies and lilies . . . Mr. Phillips was singing . . . Mr. Phillips was billed as a basso . . . and he had kissed her . . . they were applauding . . . the first young man was singing again . . . Langston's

spiritual . . . Fy-ah-fy-ah-Lawd . . . fy-ah's gonna burn ma soul . . . Beauty's hair was so black and curly . . . they were applauding . . . encore . . . Fy-ah Lawd had been a success . . . Langston bowed . . . Langston had written the words . . . Hall bowed . . . Hall had written the music . . . the young man was singing it again . . . Beauty's lips had pressed hard . . . cool . . . cool . . . fy-ah Lawd . . . his breath had trembled . . . fy-ah's gonna burn ma soul . . . [. . .] now to Augusta's party . . . fy-ahs gonna burn ma soul . . . they were at Augusta's . . . Alex half lay . . . half sat on the floor . . . sipping a cocktail . . . such a dream . . . red calla lilies . . . Alex left . . . down the narrow streets . . . fy-ah . . . up the long noisy stairs . . . [. . .] he felt two cool strong hands on his shoulders . . . it was Beauty . . . lie down Dulce . . . Alex lay down . . . Beauty . . . Alex stopped . . . no no . . . don't say it . . . Beauty mustn't know . . . Beauty couldn't understand . . . are you going to lie down too Beauty . . . the light went out expanding . . . contracting . . . he felt the bed sink as Beauty lay beside him . . . his lips were dry . . . hot . . . the palms of his hands so moist and cool . . . Alex partly closed his eyes . . . from beneath his lashes he could see Beauty's face over his . . . nearer . . . nearer . . . Beauty's hair touched his forehead now . . . he could feel his breath on his nostrils and lips . . . Beauty's breath came short . . . breathe normally Beauty . . . breathe normally . . . Beauty's lips touched his . . . pressed hard . . . cool . . . opened slightly . . . Alex opened his eyes . . . into Beauty's . . . parted his lips . . . Dulce . . . Beauty's breath was hot and short . . . Alex ran his hand through Beauty's hair . . . Beauty's lips pressed hard against his teeth . . . Alex trembled . . . could feel Beauty's body . . . close against his . . . hot . . . tense . . . white . . . and soft . . . soft . . . soft. . . . . . .
. . . . .

೮

[. . .]

೮

up . . . up . . . slow . . . jerk up . . . up . . . not fast . . . not glorious . . . but slow . . . up . . . up into the sun . . . slow . . . sure like fate . . . poise on the brim . . . the brim of life . . . two shining rails straight down . . . Melva's head was on his shoulder . . . his arm was around her . . . poise . . . the down . . . gasping . . . straight down . . . straight like sin . . . down . . . the curving shiny rail rushed up to meet them . . . hit the bottom then . . . shoot up . . . fast . . . glorious . . . up into the sun . . . Melva gasped . . . Alex's arm tightened . . . all goes up . . . then down . . . straight like hell . . . all breath squeezed out of them . . . Melva's head on his shoulder . . . up . . . up . . . Alex kissed her . . . down . . . they stepped out of the car . . . walking music . . . now over to the Ferris

Wheel . . . out and up . . . [. . .] Alex kissed her . . . drift down . . . soft . . . soft . . . the sun had left the sky flushed . . . drift down . . . soft down . . . back to earth . . . visit the mortals sipping nectar at five cents a glass . . . Melva's lips brushed his . . . then out among the mortals . . . and the sun had left a flush on Melva's cheeks . . . they walked hand in hand . . . and the moon came out . . . they walked in silence on the silver strip . . . and the sea sang for them . . . they walked toward the moon . . . we'll hang our hats on the crook of the moon Melva . . . softly on the silver strip . . . his hands molded her features and her cheeks were soft and warm to his touch . . . where is Adrian . . . Alex . . . Melva trod silver . . . Alex trod sand . . . Alex trod sand . . . the sea *sang* for her . . . Beauty . . . her hand felt cold in his . . . Beauty . . . the sea *dinned* . . . Beauty . . . he led the way to the train . . . and the train dinned . . . Beauty . . . dinned . . . dinned . . . her cheek *had* been soft . . . Beauty . . . Beauty . . . her breath *had* been perfumed . . . Beauty . . . Beauty . . . the sands *had* been silver . . . Beauty . . . Beauty . . . they left the train . . . Melva walked music . . . Melva said . . . don't make me blush again . . . and kissed him . . . Alex stood on the steps after she left him and the night was black . . . down long streets to . . . Alex lit a cigarette . . . and his heels clicked . . . Beauty . . . Melva . . . Beauty . . . Melva . . . and the smoke made the night blue . . .

Melva had said . . . don't make me blush again . . . and kissed him . . . and the street had been blue . . . one *can* love two at the same time . . . Melva had kissed him . . . one *can* . . . and the street had been blue . . . one *can* . . . and the room was clouded with blue smoke . . . drifting vapors of smoke and thoughts . . . Beauty's hair was so black . . . and soft . . . blue smoke from an ivory holder . . . was that why he loved Beauty . . . one *can* . . . or because his body was beautiful . . . and white and warm . . . or because his eyes . . . one *can* love. . . . .

RICHARD BRUCE

. . . To Be Continued . . .

FIRE!! 1.1 (November 1926): 33–39.

CHARLES HENRI FORD AND PARKER TYLER

Chapter 13: "I Don't Want to Be a Doll," from *The Young and Evil*

It was a long ride on the subway to 155th Street but they hadn't the money for a taxi. Frederick was not in drag nor was Julian who wore striped pants with a coat that didn't match, his black shirt with an orange tie and a slouch cap. Frederick was not made up more than usual except his eyebrows were plucked thinner but Julian had on his face the darkest powder he could borrow, blue eyeshadow and several applications of black mascara; on his lips was orange-red rouge and a brown pencil had been on his eyebrows showing them longer. He wanted to be considered in costume and so get in for a dollar less. When they arrived at the Casino Palace policemen and others were about the entrance. They passed under the canopy and went in.

I hope we don't get arrested tonight Julian said. Your judgement of my trousers is true but your moral wrong he thought, getting his ticket cheaper than Frederick who said I wonder if money will ever be as unimportant as I think it is.

They had to wind up a long gold-banistered staircase above which a terrible racket was taking serene form.

There is only one sex—the female said Frederick.

Now they are doing without beauty said Julian when he saw the first creation. It was all black lace but only stockings and step-ins and brassiere and gloves. Fanny Ward is supposed to come.

Yes my dear Frederick said. She's so young she has to learn to play the piano all over again!

The ball was too large to be rushed at without being swallowed. The negro orchestra on the stage at one end was heard at the other end with the aid of a reproducer. On both sides of the wall a balcony spread laden with people in boxes at tables. Underneath were more tables and more people. The dancefloor was a scene whose celestial flavor and cerulean coloring no angelic painter or nectarish poet has ever conceived.

This place is neither cozy nor safe Frederick said. It's lit up like high mass.

One was with blonde hair and a brown face and yellow feathers and another was with black hair and a tan face and white feathers. Some had on tango things and some blue feathers. One wore pink organdie and a black picture hat. There were many colors including a beard in a red ballet skirt and number 9 shoes and some others who, conjuring with their golden-tipped wands against the voices of their mutually male consciences, yet remained more serious than powdered—they seemed to be always on their way to far off mistresses.

They found Tony and Vincent at a table with K-Y and Woodward. Vincent spoke with the most wonderful whisky voice Frederick! Julian! Tony was South American. He had on a black satin that Vincent had made him, fitted to the knee and then flaring, long pearls and pearl drops.

Tony dear aren't you overdressed! asked Frederick.

I suppose *you* would say overdressed Tony answered but I'm not Sheba surrounded by food and Mary what you look like in that outfit he said to Julian. Look at her!

Vincent had on a white satin blouse and black breeches. Dear I'm master of ceremonies tonight and you should have come in drag you'd have gotten a prize. He had large eyes with a sex-life all their own and claimed to be the hardest boiled queen on Broadway. Frederick he said you look like something Lindbergh dropped on the way across. Dry yourself Bella!

When are you going to remove your mask and reveal a row of chamber pots Frederick replied in his resonant voice which could also be nasal at the wrong time.

The music was playing wavy and sad and so true.

Let's dance Julian said to K-Y and they went on the floor.

You've mastered the art of makeup she said.

I must have he said when I did things that were pleasant surprises, not wicked because they were unusual and necessary.

Dancing drew the blood faster through their bodies. Drink drusic drowned them. A lush annamaywong lavender-skinned negro gazed at him.

They are looking this way so hard said Julian their eyes go through us and *button* in the back.

A boy with an innocent exterior said to him over his shoulder how is your dog bite?

My dog bite Julian said sweetly. Your mouth hasn't been that close to my leg all evening.

This is dreadfully amusing said K-Y.

One may divide people into thrills and frills I think Julian said. What he was really thinking was that it must be the white-pink flesh like some Italians with the lippink scarlet as heliotrope and the black of hair and the eyebrows with the miraculous slant bespeaking benevolence. He knew the precise youth of it there and the vulgarity raw enough to be exhilarating. He saw another as they danced by a table and the sharkmouth of a hope tore his womb, carrying a piece of it away.

Someone shouted Bessie if you don't believe Heliogabalus died by having his head stuck in a toilet bowl you NEEDN'T COME AROUND any more.

They all ought to be in a scrap-book Julian said. Would blood, paste and print make them stick together?

No said K-Y. There is no holding people back. It will go on until it stops and then there will be something else.

shut your hole watching

them for a moment but when she opened her upstairs cunt and started to belch the greetings of the season I retired in a flurry her boyfriend with the imperfect lacework in the front of his mouth

was a thunderclap could indeed would have been

gentler Fairydale Bedagrace a prize bull in the 2000 pound class and his proud owner is Harry A.

Koch there's my Uncle looking for

me Beulah calm your bowels two o'clock

and not a towel wet that

would be both justice and

amusement Jim! I told you to stay home and mind the babies wished for nothing better well who could? than a man lover and a woman lover in the same

bed [. . .]

sex it's a false landscape only art giving it full

colors

picked me up on Eighth Street and did me for trade in Christopher Street some

books aren't even read things

about the Village because they are bound to be ninety percent

lies there a new place called Belle's Jeans it must be horribly vulgar if

I had your money [. . .]

confessed his love for a man so I didn't stand up and wave the flag I just sat there you know me Mabel and

smiled Mr. Schubert get OFF my face I can't see the CONtract the wine came up and he looked at my intellect so often got

out of the way of a big truck and put my hand over my cunt like

this just too bad isn't it buttercup scalps

of her victims of which she must have cabinets

full says he wears a flower in his buttonhole because it simply Wont stay in his hair! memories are

best couldn't stomach his crotch once so he would be spiteful a kiss is a
promise she looks like death's daughter brought in backwards and went
up bold as you please dropped my lilac

robe could hardly get two articulate sentences out on the subject of homosexuality before someone interrupted us Phoebe-Phobia in person not a
college pennant she had one in her hand though that bore a distinct

resemblance ninety-five percent of the world is just naturally queer and
are really according to the degree of

resistance I don't say I *do* and I don't say I *don't* but if the fur coat had fit
me he would have had a DIFferent answer people [. . .]

[. . .] can

always afford to be tolerant of that which we

misunderstand likes the brave dear that one best

some Lesbians make me think of alligators I saw a little girl holding up
one in the movies and the angles seemed so

characteristic fancy work done at

home and if I look real a definition of love isn't

needed seven yards of lace [. . .]

dear just dirt you

silly! loose as a cut

jockstrap

still dead as far as my mouth

goes a

big chisler while he was here feature it

adores me to stick it in his and flew into a temper last night when after
the regular party my poor thing wouldn't get a hard on enough to go in and
STAY in but I promised to do my husbandly duty next

time orgasm right in his

pants it may have been the first intimate introduction to Miss 69 in
person is to be a comfort standing in a tall scooped out penislike

niche squiffy on

weed observe my dear the bloated lemons waiting to be

selected the first Bess ever to conceive a hopeless romantic affection for
me thrill market the

haughty after breakfast hour grime

in the creases parting his hair has given him a new better

flavor discovered a brazen speakeasy with awfully good stuff

cheap mentioned something about a hashish party please

noticing my excellent features and asking why I didn't have
a screen test taken until a professional routine came into his
compliments flew down on special
wheels couldn't say no to the sensations he gives
me gayest thing on two
feet harlot making theatrical costumes like one demented and
renting the
bed them to come down here and fight like mEn startling
expert symmetry she wanted to make
her have a cuter sissylip
one never say anus you mUst have been stunned into
chillness said why and I said I wanted to see whether he would 69 and
he said of course he didn't and I said but he
did may look Chinese but she's American can
you imagine he wanted to brown I mean bugger
me woman quite mad so cunty in her dark land so idiosyncratic and
blind so obvious so abnormal only
fairy voice about 20 made me really
pretty oh you twisted piece of
lilac the curtain's going
up
looks like the wrath of
God aroma one of Harvard and autumn leaves the Russian ballet
hanging on the wall of his
heart dished as though
drunken showing
everything mattress on the
floor Byzantine
baggage grand cocksucker
fascinated by fairies of the Better
Class chronic
liar fairy
herself sexual
estimate crooning
I'M A CAMPfire girl
gratuitous sexually meaning
both my thighs are so much
stouter tongue's hanging
out sprawled in

bed lower than my
navel tie beginning between his
breasts nest of
Lesbians eyebrows so perfect what it is to
blossom before his style started going uphill on one-ballbearing
rollerskates and the curious pain
began Norma Shearer hairbob the wild evening one and they turned the
spot on me with applause hisses pennies tenderness in sex you know I hate
nothing [. . .] and you know my rule Anna said have you seen Pauline's
novel I said intimating that it's good? said it's an act of God! said I have no
doubt there are so many objects for criticism they Must come from a source
so abundant never cease shocking with his diseases hide it in your vagina
and carry on do you have to go into a song and dance about a face artist
turn over kid I want to use you [. . .]

Julian swayed through the tables and was grabbed by the hand and pulled
to one table for a drink of rye and told his eyes were beautiful. He stayed there
until someone came from another table and got him and gave him a drink of
gin and said kiss me but he said you don't look expectant. That one followed
him toward the orchestra and he went in the side door and up on the stage
and kissed the leader and asked him to play something. When he went back
down the steps the door was closed into the hall and the one who had given
him the drink of gin was standing in front of it. Julian knew that people had
to forget appearances, that horses would hardly, that mountains and clouds
wouldn't and neither would some men but this one would. He found he could
be mad and wasn't afraid of the vengeance of God nor its earthly equivalent
and there was no hesitation from beginning to end. He came out fanning
himself. A chaplet to go around my neck he thought. [. . .]

When he felt better he went out with a hundred images clawing at him,
some good, some almost good and some almost painful.

This is how dolorous things can be in high fettle. The hall was the garden
of Eden afterwards and the lights were out. There was a queen's sorrow in it
too. He walked to a gleam coming from under a door and tried the knob but
it wouldn't work. He banged on it until someone came and unlocked it from
the outside.

He was being looked in the face by several policemen one of whom immediately said THAT'S THE ONE.

What one? Julian asked innocently.

No it's not said another and the first one agreed and Julian walked away.

He was around the corner and doubted if he would take the right subway. Vincent was not to be seen nor anyone he knew. A short man in neat clothes said hello to him.

Julian said hello.

How are you? the man said.

I'm all right said Julian.

Where are you going?

I'm going home.

Let's go have a cup of coffee.

Julian said all right and they went into a coffee pot in the next block. Julian had two eggs also and the man who was a soft comfortable personality who glurred at the right moments paid for them.

They were out on the street when the man said do you live around here?

Julian told him that he lived downtown.

What's your address?

Julian told it to him.

I'll come to see you sometime.

All right said Julian.

The man showed him the elevated and Julian thanked him.

He went up the steps and there were no velvet carpets, no flutes, no bells, no incense and no dancing girls.

In the car he was alone except for a man who looked like a football player never recovered from a daze he got once while scrimmaging.

I'm glad I have my beauty he thought if ever so little weary. Am I a doll he thought or some kind of ghost believing in everything I have believed in do I know what marriage is what new texture is in it anything more than a tongue and lips and inexpert teeth oh to be a bright and unschooled lass I know it and love it and know it and leave it and know it and hate it but never too much the stalk up the poor lavender buds clinging to it their mouths closed yellow in the green and dug clean for anything I've found in the oystergray marrow to hell with all junior disorders what are they my next lover must teach me to swear love is a thing to know more of and deeper of or nothing is lost? nothing can be helped is better life is made up of crossing sticks and time.

The crying in him was because everything was all wrong and he knew it as all learn it sometimes: wrong yet magnetic, prolonged yet brief.

At Sixth Avenue and Eighth Street he got out. It was scarcely dawn.

A doll does not believe in itself he thought it believes only in its dollness I have the will to doll which is a special way of willing to live my poetry may merely be a way of dolling up and then it may be the beginning of ego I think I would be practically nothing without my poetry unless a DOLL my homosexuality is just a habit to which I'm somehow bound which is little more than a habit in that it's not love or romance but a dim hard fetich [*sic*] I worship in my waking dreams it's more a symbol of power than a symbol of pleasure not a symbol inducing pleasure but exemplifying it not a specific symbol no I am not a fairy doll. [. . .]

1933. Rpt. New York: Gay Presses of New York, 1988.

ROBERT MCALMON

From "The Indefinite Huntress"

I

Lily strode firmly into the kitchen and threw down her string of ducks. She knew her mother thought her unladylike qualities a bad example for her younger sisters, so did not boast now of having brought down more game than any of the men who had gone to shoot ducks at early dawn. "There's no use reminding you," Mrs. Root sighed, "but you look like a tramp woman." [. . .]

"Your family were the real aristocrats, weren't they, mother?" Lily said drily, "but what about your Aunt Helga, and you did run away and marry dad? He may not be much of a gent, but he lets a person be." Lily took off her rubber boots, and went to her room. [. . .]

Upstairs, Lily found her cousin Helga packing her trunks for departure that afternoon. During the summer the girls had grown fond of each other, and Helga was the first person with whom Lily had any relationship approaching intimacy. Helga was slight, fawn-haired, and dainty. Lily, who cared not at all about fine clothes for herself, delighted in Helga's wardrobe. [. . .] Lily had never had an opportunity to know a woman of elegance, but she thought Helga elegant. She talked of Paris, of manner and style. Lily felt perturbedly restless, wondering about the outside world.

Changing from her hunting clothes, Lily offered to help Helga pack. "I'll miss you," she said. "You're the one person who has ever told me of great places." [. . .]

"I would give a thousand to have hair like yours," Helga said, distraitly. "That color is worth a fortune. Let it down and I'll dress it for you. I'll give you any one of my gowns you like." [. . .]

Lily chuckled and tore her hair loose with a free gesture. "What would a thing my size do with your finery?" [. . .]

"I love the crackle of your hair," Helga mused, running it through her palms. Lily saw the whiteness of Helga's fine hands against her own hair, in the mirror. "It's as lively as you are, Lily. Oh, I envy you. Being in the country makes me restless, but I won't be happy in New York either. [. . .]

"I wish you could come with me," Helga said. [. . .]

2

Lily was in the yard beneath the umbrella tree. Her hair was loose and she stroked it musingly, liking the electric crackle, and thinking of how Helga had praised its color and gloss. [. . .]

"May I have a drink of water, or buttermilk if you have it?" a voice said. Somewhat resentfully Lily tossed her hair back and looked distantly out of chilled blue eyes at the speaker. He was Red Neill, who owned the restaurant in Lansing. [. . .] He thought he was a real lady-killer, Lily surmised. Her pale eyes challenged his appraising glance with a glance more coldly appraising.

"There's the pump with a cup beside it and your hands aren't tied," Lily spoke curtly. [. . .]

Red shifted the ducks to his other shoulder. "I'll try and speak more respectfully next time, Miss Root," he said. [. . .]

"And what a favor you would do me! I may answer," Lily said, melting somewhat, and not wanting to believe stories about Red [. . .]. "I know it is girls you think are fine and elegant you really bother to be polite to. You have a fancy idea of yourself, I take it."

"You aren't meek yourself, Miss Root. But those others," Red's voice softened, "they have no blood in them. They don't feel anything."

Lily got red in the face and felt temper arise within her. "Pack your ducks on," she said sharply. "What blood or feeling you have doesn't interest me, and I'm busy." [. . .]

Dionisio Granger came into the yard carrying three ducks, and Lily's heart plunged as she recognized him. He was adolescent now, but quickly she saw he retained the beauty which had cut into her. "You've been duck shooting, have you?" she asked, hoping he didn't sense the panicky thrill in her.

"No, Red Neill gave me these," Dion said. "I went hunting with him, but it made me feel rotten to see the ducks plop on the ground or in the water. I couldn't shoot straight anyway. Red pretended I hit some." [. . .]

Dion sat on the grass beside Lily. "Red came into town a hobo not many years ago. He was one of those wandering newspaper fellows, a drunk, I think.

Sister says he's intelligent. He went with her for a while, but she didn't want to go with him after she found out what other girls he hung around."

[. . .] Dion rolled over to bury his head in his arm. [. . .]

"Put your head on my lap and nap," she said, in terror that Dion might be shy, and not do as she suggested. She placed his head on her lap, however, and stroked his hair [. . .]. "I wanted to kidnap you two years back, did you know that?" she said, huskily tender with fear. "I nearly died, you looked so marvellous one day."

Dion blushed and laughed into her face. He felt a tingle in him because of her caress. She was vibrantly alive. He didn't nap, but stirred uneasily. [. . .]

3

"Sure, Dion, you shot at least five ducks, but I'll send some of mine to your mother when we get back to town," Red Neill said. [. . .]

Going across the fields the hunters scared up several coveys of prairie chicken at which they shot carelessly. By noon they stopped at farmer Matson's for lunch, after which they sat drinking with the old man. Red was morose, and swore at his companions. [. . .] He wanted to feel contemptuous of a too-delicate boy brought up by a protected mother, but instead he found himself gently understanding that the boy would be scared among lowbrows getting stinking drunk. He moved to sit nearer Dion, and started to put his arm comfortingly about the boy's shoulder, but he was afraid of frightening the boy. [. . .]

Taking another drink Red obeyed his impulse to put his arm about Dion's shoulder. The boy was unrelaxed in his arm. "You're a great hunter," Red said, gruffly, ill at ease. "Forty ducks in three hours, you can tell your mother." Red was angry at himself for persisting upon telling Dion to lie about the number of ducks he had shot. He only wanted to help the youngster to prove he was a sort who could do things, but why didn't he get it into his noodle that Dion didn't care how many ducks he had shot, and that Dion always gravely assured him he wouldn't lie to his mother?

Dion fidgeted, conscious of Red's whiskey breath. "I couldn't fool her if I tried. I'll say you gave me the ducks."   [. . .]

Red pondered the Grangers. Why should they represent class to him? They weren't very rich and wouldn't have cut any great impression in a city. [. . .] Unconsciously he put his arm about Dion again, and feeling the curve of Dion's shoulder in the palm of his hand he suddenly drew the boy to him. Dion looked up into his eyes, but his expression told nothing. Red didn't analyze, but he had a sharp terror. [. . .] Dion's face swam before Red's vision with a beauty that made him dizzy. A moment later he realized that his sudden clutching at the boy may have frightened him. Dion, however, turned his head and smiled now. His eyes were limpidly clear, but Red knew Dion wanted to draw away. Red hated to have this boy think him brutish and drunken, and he hated his own coarseness. Right now Red knew that if the boy wanted anything, there was nothing he would not do to give it to him, but he suffered, knowing that Dion didn't care what he felt.

Red took a deep swig of whiskey. He felt a horrible desolation of life. Dion had him awed with terror by the unrevealing glisten in his clear eyes. There was no definite quality in their depths; not innocence, knowing, like, distaste; only wonder and questioning, but the questioning did not include him, Red knew. He wanted to think Dion liked him, but instead he feared Dion despised him more, if the boy had known his own feelings. [. . .]

"Do you know Lily Root?" Dion said, to break the silence. [. . .]

"Yes, nice girl," Red said distraitly. [. . .] She was that big Swede girl who always antagonized him. She had hair and eyes, he remembered from having come upon her while she was drying her hair last autumn. [. . .]

"She's a real looker now," Dion said. [. . .]

"Hell, I ought to marry her," Red joked. "I'm getting on and ought to settle down and have kids. She'd make a good cowmother and keep house for me. [. . .]

It was late afternoon before the men were back in town. "Stick around," Red said to Dion. "Ma Jensen will cook us some ducks. [. . .]"

Ma Jensen waddled out of the City Restaurant kitchen. "Ay tink ve giff de poys a goot feed, all vor de same moneys," she commented with sturdy satisfaction, her face shiny from kitchen heat as she felt the breasts of the ducks. [. . .]

Red went across the street to get Dion. [. . .]

Red saw that the girl with Dion was large, firm-bodied, and stalwart in a way unlike any of the Granger girls. She was handsome though. "You don't recognize me, Mr. Neill," Lily Root said. [. . .]

[. . .] He had always thought Lily a big, healthy, strong-bodied farm girl, with keen eyes and startling hair, but now she looked somebody, and had a poised manner. [. . .]

Boys were playing baseball in the street, and one of the throws caught Dion full in the face so that he toppled over. Red saw, and thought the boy was unconscious. Dion was dazed when Red helped him to his feet. "Are you hurt much?" Red asked. "Don't rub your eye. We'll have the doctor see to that right away. He's going to be sick." Red held Dion anxiously. [. . .]

Lily watched with concern. Red's gentleness towards Dion struck her, and affected her strangely. [. . .] There was some luminously tender quality in his treatment of Dion. Lily felt resentful. "I'll walk home with you, Dion," she said, "because you might feel sick and want somebody to hold you up."

"That's all right," Red said gruffly. "I'll take him home in the car. We don't want anything wrong with his eye though. Come on, Dion. We'll have the druggist take a look at it and if it's inflamed, we'll see the doctor." Red had his arm about Dion's shoulder, and pulled the boy around, to lead him towards the pharmacist's. Lily was in his path. She hesitated, and took Dion's other arm.

"Yes, you're right," she told Red. "We'd better see that his eye isn't in danger."

Red sensed that Lily was challenging him. He felt a desire to be rude and tell her that Dion was his friend to look after. She needn't think he meant harm to the boy. Lily's calm, however, cowed him. Let her take Dion home. At the drugstore Mr. Schwarz made light of the blow on Dion's eye. [. . .]

[. . .] When he had left Lily looked strangely at Red. "You aren't as tough as I thought you were." [. . .]

[. . .] "Yes, you and me both. I'm not hard. I'm not so gentle, but I don't like seeing a nice kid's eye put out, I don't care who the kid is."

"Oh, I know," Lily said quickly. "I saw. You wouldn't be so bothered by every kid who got hit in the eye. I have nearly kidnapped Dion myself, twice. There he is, and suddenly he looks so beautiful it kills a person. I never thought you would be able to appreciate that kind of look on a person's face."

"I'm going to Minneapolis on the midnight train. Why not come along?" Red said, with a drummer-like gallantry of implication. He saw Lily flush resentfully. "I didn't insinuate anything," he defended. [. . .]

"[. . .] I don't accept your invitation, thank you, however you meant it. I have a man's way of looking at things, and if I went I'd want my own money, and I can't afford a trip to the city just now [. . .]"

Red laughed. "You're some girl, Miss Root. You have a different line than any other skirt I ever talked to. I say, you eat Dion's duck dinner with me, and we'll go for an auto ride afterwards. I won't act fresh."

Lily became somewhat defiant. "I'm no weak woman. Certainly I'll eat with you, and we might talk sense. [. . .]"

At dinner Lily was on her guard for a time, but mischief came into her. She found she wasn't at all distrustful of Red. Instead she felt surer of herself than he did of himself. "Why would you want me to go to the city with you?" she asked. [. . .] "We don't know a thing about each other, so we don't get at each other when we talk, do we?"

[. . .] "There's not much to know about me. I was a bum newspaperman, and a hobo after I got back from the war. Another fellow put me wise to the fact that I could buy this restaurant cheap, and when I saw Neva Granger I had ideas about settling down, and this town looked as good as anywhere else. She's not so good-looking now, with two kids, but I fell hard then. [. . .]"

Driving out into the country after dinner Lily was not talkative. Her quietness put Red off his guard, and he finally, in a wooded section of the road, tried to put his arm about her. She did not resist until he tried to caress her firm breast. She merely pushed his hand away and sat back. Red was nervous. [. . .] Still Red later tussled with Lily, to kiss her. She resisted only mildly.

"If you treated me the way you did Dion this afternoon you could do anything," Lily suddenly blurted out. "It struck me you were more hurt than he was when that baseball hit him. I knew then you weren't a tough man. I never saw anybody act so tender. [. . .]"

"If I wanted to do anything, I would, but you act as though you thought you could play a trick on me. [. . .]"

"I'd be a good friend to you, and just let it go at that if you'd take things simply."

Red was uneasy. Lily attracted him more than he wanted to admit, and he was incapable of taking her comradeship suggestion. [. . .] He squeezed her hand, trying to believe he thought he had her excited, but also he told himself she was one of those foreign freaks who don't have any passion or feeling. When he pressed her hand Lily responded. He kissed her, and she responded, but not passionately. [. . .]

Lily drew away finally, saying, "You're afraid of me. Why? I know you don't feel anything much about me. You don't feel tender, anyway, and I guess you know I won't let myself be treated like you're used to treating some girls. Let me tell you, if anything happened between us it would be because I wanted it." [. . .]

"Do you want me to offer marriage because I kissed you?" Red said gruffly. [. . .]

"Why would I want that when I wouldn't marry you? That would be no compliment to me," Lily said. [. . .] "We might do as well as most married people at that," she said after a silence. "I wouldn't be a home woman, and I wouldn't stop doing what I wanted to do and thought right because I was married."

"I didn't want to marry till I could leave a little money if I passed out," Red said, blood panicking through him. He told himself this big girl was not his type; that she was being clever and leading him on; but he was afraid too she was as indifferent as she claimed to be.

"I have money," Lily said shortly. Suddenly she felt decisive. "Yes, I will marry you. I have a business head, father will help me stock a ranch, and I can raise horses or cattle. It will be better if I am married, because people won't think they can trick a simple, unmarried young girl then. I want to do something to keep from being bored and restless." [. . .]

Red fidgeted and felt caught. Lily sensed his trapped emotion and felt sympathetic. It gave her a physical urge towards him and she felt his magnetism. Her wish to have him gentle had passed. She felt the bewildered, awkward maleness of him, and knew she wouldn't mind if he became rough towards her again. She knew she was handling the situation, and she felt protective towards him, even to the extent of wanting to let him feel the master enough not to feel beaten. [. . .]

Lily's arm slipped away. Red looked at her. She was apathetic, with a beaten, uncaring look on her face. "No, you're not my answer," Lily said. Red felt a pang of pity and sympathy for the cold distance in her voice. She was different. She was something real. He wanted her, by God, and she was slipping away if he didn't act quickly.

"Hell, Lily, let's get married. [. . .]"

"You ask Dion," Red became persuasive now that Lily held back. "I said today I ought to marry a girl like you and begin to have sense." [. . .]

4

Red and Lily felt evasive towards each other the next day, but each regarded the other curiously when the other was not looking. Neither of them quite figured out how they happened into this impulsive marriage, and Lily felt that she had tricked herself. Red had been gentle, and she didn't feel any virginal resentment towards him. [. . .] At dinner that night she made an attempt to get things straight.

"Red, do you want to go on?" [. . .]

"What's the trouble, girl?" Red said, believing it needful to be a conventional and possessive husband with patronizing protectiveness. "Am I too rough for you? I thought you knew more than you do."

"It's not that," Lily said. "We didn't want marriage. We bluffed ourselves into it. We ought to love each other a little if we stay married. I suppose I'm funny. I've been in love with Dion Granger for two years, somehow. I don't want him like what you did last night, but I get arm hunger and want him to pet whenever I think of him. I want to feel something that way towards anybody who's making love to me. That other doesn't mean anything to me."

"Well, I won't bother you. You wait a while and maybe in a few days you will feel differently," Red told her. "I know some women have to take things easily."

"I don't hate it, but I only felt sorry for you. [. . .] Maybe if you treated me or felt for me as you did yesterday for Dion things would be different, but you don't think my being hurt matters much, really."

"Ya, I get you," Red said gruffly, looking strangely at Lily. "You think I feel about Dion as you do, that's it?"

"I thought you and I had something between us maybe, in understanding how he can get a person."

"We might as well stick to the marriage for a while though. [. . .]"

"All right," Lily said, a new idea making her eager. "That's so. We could stay married, and if things don't go I can go into some business of my own or raise stock. I guess I'm the kind of a woman who ought to be in business anyway. I'm no homebody."

Within a month Lily completely managed the restaurant. [. . .] Ole, a rich man actually, was pleased that Lily should want to become a stock raiser and business woman as his staunch and independent aunt in Sweden was. He gave Lily blooded beef cattle, and horses, and daily she drove to the farm of Red's where she reared her stock.

Red, having married, believed he wanted children, but none arrived, and Lily's attitude towards him did not alter to make her desirous of him. She confused him entirely, for he had a deeply rooted conventional and male attitude towards women and marriage. Strangely he felt faithful towards her, even when she submitted so indifferently to his few efforts at love-making. He drank more heavily, and, always inclined to laziness, sullenly admired Lily's energy and business capacity, while letting her take his affairs more and more into her charge. He watched with strange emotions one day as she was regarding her blooded horses on the farm. There was more between her and the horses than there was between her and him, or her and humans. [. . .]

The next autumn Red went duck-shooting but once. With each year he grew lazier and less inclined even to hunt, his favorite pastime. Having drunk much whiskey, Red got a chill coming home in a heavy rain. He thought he would be well in a few days, but pneumonia set in and within five days he was dead. Lily felt dumbfounded and empty. With Red about, she felt pride in proving to him how competent and fair a person she was. Their relationship had been an easy, sporting comradeship, she felt. To keep from being lonely she went further into stock raising. Constantly she drove about the country, looking for bargain lands or blooded stock to buy. She had become a woman of importance in the town and county now, because of her business ability and wealth. [. . .] One day, in a fit of memory and curiosity, she wrote to her cousin Helga, from whom she had not heard for several years. [. . .]

[. . .] That night she dreamed of Dion, but in the dream he changed to Red, to Helga, to a horse, which became again Red, and she and Red were running up the sky. [. . .]

Helga responded at once to Lily's letter, and Lily, knowing the handwriting, opened the letter with hands trembling with expectancy. This letter was going to solve things for her. She knew before she had finished the first sentence, and was triumphant, with a new purposefulness. Always she had wanted to have Helga with her, to take care of and protect. She had been a child not to have known before. [. . .]

1932. Rpt. *Miss Knight and Others*. Ed. N. S. Lorusso. Albuquerque: University of New Mexico Press, 1992.

COUNTEE CULLEN

Fruit of the Flower

My father is a quiet man
With sober, steady ways;
For simile, a folded fan;
His nights are like his days.

My mother's life is puritan,
No hint of cavalier,
A pool so calm you're sure it can
Have little depth to fear.

And yet my father's eyes can boast
How full his life has been;
There haunts them yet the languid ghost
Of some still sacred sin.

And though my mother chants of God,
And of the mystic river,
I've seen a bit of checkered sod
Set all her flesh aquiver.

Why should he deem it pure mischance
A son of his is fain
To do a naked tribal dance
Each time he hears the rain?

Why should she think it devil's art
That all my songs should be
Of love and lovers, broken heart,
And wild sweet agony?

Who plants a seed begets a bud,
Extract of that same root;
Why marvel at the hectic blood
That flushes this wild fruit?

In *The New Negro*, ed. Alain Locke, 1925. Rpt. New York: Atheneum, 1986. 132.

HART CRANE

Episode of Hands

The unexpected interest made him flush.
Suddenly he seemed to forget the pain,—
Consented,—and held out
one finger from the others.

The gash was bleeding, and a shaft of sun
That glittered in and out among the wheels,
Fell lightly, warmly, down into the wound.

And as the fingers of the factory owner's son,
That knew a grip for books and tennis
As well as one for iron and leather,—
As his taut, spare fingers wound the gauze
Around the thick bed of the wound,
His own hands seemed to him
Like wings of butterflies
Flickering in sunlight over summer fields.

The knots and notches,—many in the wide
Deep hand that lay in his,—seemed beautiful.
They were like the marks of wild ponies' play,—
Bunches of new green breaking a hard turf.

And factory sounds and factory thoughts
Were banished from him by that larger, quieter hand
That lay in his with the sun upon it.
And as the bandage knot was tightened
The two men smiled into each other's eyes.

1920. Rpt. *Complete Poems of Hart Crane,* ed. by Marc Simon. New York: Liveright, 1986.

11

Modernism, Gender, and Passing

INTRODUCED AND SELECTED BY PAMELA L. CAUGHIE

IN THE ORIGINAL *Gender of Modernism* anthology (1990), Bonnie Kime Scott presents "A Tangled Mesh of Modernists," a diagram mapping the crossing of paths among key literary figures of the early twentieth century. A powerful image for modernist literary production, the diagram dramatically reveals both the important role women played in defining modernism ("Not all strands lead to Eliot, Pound, and Joyce," writes Scott) and the "inadequate number of sources" upon which "our understanding of modernism depends" (12). A key motivation for revisiting the gender of modernism in this companion volume is how far we have come over the past fifteen years in unearthing new sources of modernism and, partly as a result, in better understanding modernism as a *global*, not just an international, phenomenon. Modernism, with its emphasis on new technology, can now be seen as at least the inception of what we have come to call globalization. Globalization here refers to the swift dissemination of cultural products (e.g., music, literature, fashion) worldwide through the forces of mass culture such that the borders separating nations and geographic regions become permeable and insecure.[1] The "masthead" of British *Vogue* in the 1920s— "VOGUE KNOWS NO FRONTIERS"—captures the modernist sensibility of unlimited boundary crossing inspired by new modes of transportation, such as the motor car and the airplane, and new means of communication, such as the gramophone and the radio.[2] Most relevant to our concerns here is that such border crossing, facilitated by new technologies and fueled by an increasingly touristic and consumer culture in the interwar period, had a profound effect on the imagining of national and personal identity in modernist cultural productions. The selections in this section illustrate the extent to which the psychic effects of such shifting and permeable borders of national and personal space define the art and literature we now call modernism.

In today's scholarship the tangled mesh of modernism entails crossings of various kinds: networks of personal, professional, and political relations among artists and writers in different media and disciplines; travel, whether actual or virtual, across national and regional borders; psychological complexes, such as the "masculinity complex" in women, some newly emerging, others newly identified by psychologists and psychoanalysts of the day; and crossover identities inspired and sometimes compelled by popular and scientific notions of racial and sexual "character" as well as by new media and new markets. It is this latter kind of crossing that the term "passing" signifies and that is figured in those twin cultural icons of the modernist generation, the androgyne and the mulatto. Passing, the social practice of assuming the identity of another type or class of persons, was not a new phenomenon in the modernist era. Negroes, Jews, homosexuals, and immigrants had long passed for social, political, and economic reasons. What made passing capture the public imagination in the modernist era in ways it never had before was that globalization introduced certain cultural shifts that made it increasingly necessary to think about identity in other than nationalist terms.

It is now commonplace to talk about the imbrication of gender, race, class, and sexuality in identity formation, but in the early twentieth century, the concept of identity was still largely tied to nation. When Stephen Daedalus sets out at the end of *Portrait of the Artist as a Young Man* (1915) to create "the uncreated conscience of his race" (253), he means the Irish; when Margaret Sanger speaks of a new race in *Woman and the New Race* (1920), she means Americans.[3] Yet the increased mobility and the newly permeable borders of the early twentieth century—made possible by new sound and visual technologies as much as by new modes of transportation—made people aware (perhaps for the first time, at least on such a large scale) of the production of *cultural* identity, the way identity is mediated through various cultural forms. A 1927 diary entry by Virginia Woolf connects the forces of globalization to the erosion of national identity: "Also, I said, recalling the aeroplanes that had flown over us, while the portable wireless played dance music on the terrace, can't you see that nationality is over? All divisions are now rubbed out, or about to be" (145). Less enthusiastic than Woolf about the erosion of borders, D. H. Lawrence also attributes the rubbing out of divisions (in this case, racial) to the effects of mass culture. In his 1926 review of Carl Van Vechten's *Nigger Heaven,* a novel about black Harlem by a white author, and Walter White's *Flight,* a novel about passing by a man who could and did pass, Lawrence writes that in reading these novels one is disappointed to discover that the "Negroid soul . . . is an Edison gramophone . . . which is what the white man's soul is, just the same" (*Phoenix* 362). Although for Woolf such border crossing offers the potential for new forms of identification while for Lawrence it homogenizes the differences (actual and imaginary) necessary to identification, both passages draw a connection between globalization and modernist identity. "Changes in intimate aspects of personal life," writes modernist scholar Anthony Giddens, "are directly tied to the establishment of social connections of a very wide scope" (32).[4] Passing, as a concept and not just as a social practice, figures the border crossing inspired and enabled by globalization in the very contours of the self.

Although the examples included in this section are not restricted to actual instances of passing in its first cultural sense, passing as white, that is how modernists would have understood the term. Passing in this sense was an obsessional interest in literature and film of the time, especially in the United States. In her essay on passing included here, Heba Jannath lists several novels of the day that take passing as their subject, of which Nella Larsen's *Passing* is probably the best known today. We could add many more titles to this list, such as James Weldon Johnson's *The Autobiography of an Ex-Colored Man* (1912, reissued in 1925), Garland Anderson's play, *Appearances* (1925), Fanny Hurst's *Imitation of Life* (1933) and John Stahl's film version (1934), and Oscar Micheaux's *God's Stepchildren* (1937). The author of "America's Changing Color Line" might be said to be passing herself insofar as unsuspecting readers took the name "Heba Jannath" to be black, although it was the pseudonym of Josephine Cogdell, the white wife of George Schuyler. As Jannath states in this article, "because of America's particularly fierce taboo on the Negro, we have come to think that passing pertains only to him," whereas in reality, she says, many whites were passing as black and thereby achieving social mobility as well as cultural authority. One thinks of the many Jewish performers in blackface, or at least black voice—Al Jolson, most obviously, but also the blues sound of "torch singers," such as Fanny Brice and Libby Holman, and the Tin Pan Alley songs of Sophie Tucker, who began her career as a blackface performer (Douglas 359). Jewish immigrants impersonated blacks to achieve an *American* identity. Such a practice attests to the *Afra-Americanization* of popular culture, or as Barbara Johnson puts it: "it is [only] through Negro art that American culture is recognized at all" (93). It is not just that passing goes both ways, but that modernist identity was *racialized* by new technologies, such as the microphone, the gramophone, and the cinema.

Passing in the modernist period was more than a literary theme, and as a social practice, it was far more complicated than its common definition as the donning of a mask or the assumption of a fraudulent identity would suggest. Passing as illustrated in this section signifies the *dynamics* of identity and identification in the modernist period—the social, cultural, technological, and psychological processes by which a subject comes to understand her or his identity in relation to others, and in other than purely nationalist terms. Passing—actual and imaginary, conscious and unconscious—produced profound shifts in thinking about the boundaries of identity and aroused ambivalence about those shifting, unstable borders. Thus, passing, especially as we have come to understand it in terms of new approaches to identity issues today, provides an enabling concept for understanding the gender of modernism.[5]

Identity on Trial

Two highly publicized trials in the 1920s that have recently attracted the attention of scholars epitomize the public's fascination with passing and evidence its emerging sense of identity as something one acquires rather than something one is. In 1924, the marriage of Alice Jones, daughter of a working-class couple, to Leonard "Kip" Rhinelander, son of one of New York's leading families, was headline material, but the disclosure, a month after the wedding, that Alice was "colored" prompted a media frenzy in the United States and England. In the 1925 trial over Leonard's annulment suit, the legal arguments supposedly meant to determine Alice's race ended up exposing the slipperiness of racial categories even as both sides employed racial and gender stereotypes to make their cases. The prosecution, for example, depicted Alice as the "vamp," the predatory woman of voracious sexuality popularized in films of the day, evoking a common connection between aggressive sexuality and dark skin. Her lawyers in turn excoriated Leonard's "manliness" in referring to "unnatural" sexual proclivities, most likely a euphemism for miscegenation (Lewis and Ardizzone 37).[6] Where the prosecution set out to prove that Alice had deceived Leonard, the trial ended up showing that, as an editorial in *The Messenger* put it, when it comes to race and sexuality, "deception is the rule."[7] The cover of the "World's Greatest Negro Monthly" for December 1925 (see fig. 11.1)—significantly, the only issue of *The Messenger* to contain any reference to the Rhinelander trial—illustrates just how ambiguous race may be, and how unreliable ocular evidence can be.

Four years later Britain witnessed another sensational trial. Colonel Victor Barker, aka Valerie Arkell-Smith, was tried for perjury in 1929 for passing as a man. Given that her sex was not in dispute, the perjury trial centered on the determination of what we would now call gender identity. How to classify this anomalous woman who lived as a man and married a woman? Was she a new woman? A third sex? The spectacle of Arkell-Smith, with closely cropped hair and forced to wear a dress throughout the trial, testifying that she had always felt herself to be a man before a male judge wearing a wig of curls and a gown

Fig. 11.1. Mrs. Credit of Philadelphia, Pa. Cover photo *The Messenger: World's Greatest Negro Monthly* (December 1925). Reproduced by permission of the Newberry Library, Chicago.

must have struck witnesses even then as perverse, leading them to question conventional markers of sexual difference.[8]

Arkell-Smith's trial, like the Rhinelanders', brought to the fore the public's ambivalence about changing gender conventions and sexual identity at a time when androgynous fashions (e.g., the sheik look for men, trousers for women) and newly independent women were arousing anxiety over what were thought to be clear-cut sex differences. Karl Arnold's cartoon of an androgyne (see fig. 11.2) captures the amused bafflement produced by shifting boundaries between sexual identities.

The public exposure of the Zuni *la'mana,* or "men-women," in anthropological accounts of the time, such as Elsie Clews Parsons's 1916 essay reprinted here, called into question the binary system of gender classification that Arkell-Smith's case likewise challenged. What struck many anthropologists in the 1920s as a sexual perversion, the *la'mana*—called the Berdache by colonialists who saw them as homosexual transvestites or male prostitutes and called two-

Fig. 11.2. Karl Arnold, "*Lotte am Scheidewege*" (Lotte at the Crossroads). *Simplicissimus* 5 (1925). Reproduced by permission of the New York Public Library.

spirit people in many American Indian cultures today—undergo a ceremony that marks their passage into a new identity and a third gender. Anthropologists such as Parsons and Matilda Cox Stevenson (for whom We-Wha served as an interpreter) took them seriously as a "third sex." In a later essay, Parsons writes: "This native theory of the institution of the man-woman is a curious commentary, is it not, on that thorough-going belief in the intrinsic difference between the sexes which is so tightly held to in our own culture" (qtd. in Babcock 9). How tightly is revealed in a 1925 report by the Indian Rights Association. In an effort to discredit the views of anthropologist F. W. Hodge, the report mocks the "gullability . . . of some scientists" for accepting We-Wha (fig. 11.3) as a woman. "'We-Wha' is probably the best joke the American Indian ever played on men and women of trained minds. . . . whose training was such that they would be expected to know the difference between a man and a woman" (2). Given that a *la'mana* is buried in women's attire on the male side of a cemetery, that difference may not be so clear-cut.

Colette's story included in this section depends for its effect on the cul-

Fig. 11.3. We-Wha Weaving. Edward E. Ayer Collection. Reproduced by permission of the Newberry Library, Chicago.

tural confusion over increasingly ambiguous gender and sexual identities. What might at first appear to be a story of heterosexual passion from the male point of view contains descriptive details that throw into doubt the sex of the characters. For example, the short hair and tobacco, once unmistakable signs of masculinity, that Colette uses to describe one of the characters had come to characterize, by the early twentieth century, the "new woman," often depicted with bobbed hair and a cigarette. Even the title, "Nuit Blanche," is ambiguous, suggesting both a sleepless night because of sexual passion and a night of sexual abstinence. More than the lovers' bed, it seems, is exposed in this purposely elusive narrative. The story strongly suggests lesbian sexuality without being explicit, and thus the structure of the narrative provides experience in how to read new sexual identities. Modernist experimental forms— in fiction, poetry, painting, music—had as much to do with promoting new imaginative possibilities of identity as did new modes of communication and the mass circulation of cultural commodities.

Still, the mass circulation of the images produced by these highly publicized trials, made possible by the new technology of photojournalism, helped to fuel the public's fascination with passing. As Michael North points out in *Reading 1922,* new forms of mechanical reproduction in the modernist era—such as photojournalism, broadcasting, and film—differed from earlier forms in that the sound and visual images they produced appeared to be real while at the same time new technologies made the "fact of mediation" all the more apparent (18, 159). The ubiquity of the "new woman" on the cover of journals, in advertisements, and as the subject of novels of the early twentieth century; the increasing visibility of lesbianism, created in part by the practice of labeling all feminists and unmarried women "lesbians" and in part by theories of "normal" femininity promoted by sexologists and psychoanalysts, such as Karl Abraham, who first wrote in 1920 about the "masculinity complex"; the popular craze for the music, dance, and fashions of American Negroes, propelled across the Atlantic by the phonograph, the wireless, and the cinema; and, the first transsexual operations, conducted in Weimar Germany as early as 1931—are just some of the cultural changes that rapidly and widely circulated in the early twentieth century that both stimulated crossover identifications and evoked anxiety about the boundaries of identities, leading to repressive measures.[9]

Legal decisions and legislative proposals in the early decades of the twentieth century responded to such changing notions of gender, sexuality, and race, in effect putting identity on trial. The Mann Act of 1910, also known as the White-Slave Traffic Act, intended to curb prostitution in the United States, effectively controlled white women's and black men's sexuality.[10] In 1921 legislation to criminalize lesbianism was introduced in the British Parliament, though it failed to pass (Garrity, *Step-Daughters* 162). In 1924 the U.S. Supreme Court ruled that people from India were Caucasian but not white since whiteness was a category based on visible features rather than genetic constitution (Lewis and Ardizzone 74). By the mid-1920s immigration to the United States was greatly curtailed by the National Origins Act and miscegenation was illegal in twenty-eight states.[11] Such legal efforts to police the lines of race and sexuality attest to the widespread anxiety over, as well as fascination with, passing. It is no wonder that passing became a prominent theme as well as a structuring device in modernist literature and film. "The thematic elements of passing," writes Henry Louis Gates Jr., "—fragmentation, alienation, liminality, self-fashioning—echo the great themes of modernism" (75).

Travel and Tourism

Modernism, produced by writers and artists who literally moved from one geographic location to another, is often described in terms of dislocation, exile, liminality, and migration.[12] As Rita Felski writes, "The nostalgic yearning for an indeterminate 'elsewhere' is . . . a foundational trope within the modern itself" (31). The search for the new, the foreign, the unknown became "almost a moral obligation," whether that search was directed outward to new lands and new peoples or inward to unconscious desires. Claude McKay best represents this migratory spirit of modernism. The Jamaican writer whose *Harlem Shadows* (1922) is said to have launched the Harlem Renaissance left Harlem for Russia in 1922 and spent the next twelve years as an "American" expatriate, traveling in Russia, France, Spain, Germany, and North Africa. His 1929 novel, *Banjo* (from which the selection included here is taken), set in postwar Marseilles, follows the picaresque lives of Lincoln Agrippa Daily, known as Banjo, and his friends, including Jake and Ray from McKay's *Home to Harlem*, as they drink, love, sing, and fight in the breakwater area known as "The Ditch." With characters who are Arab, African, West Indian, and American Negroes, the novel promotes a diasporic black identity (as opposed to a national identity), an identity conceived as "poetical" not political (*Banjo* 202), while at the same time exposing the diversity within the category of blackness. "A story without a plot" (its subtitle) by "a poet without a country" (as McKay once described himself in a letter to Langston Hughes), the novel presents the modernist artist as vagabond, both traveler and tramp, one with an international mind and a view from below.[13]

From McKay to Paul Gilroy, such mobility and transnationalism have been gendered masculine, a way for men to evade the parochialism and racism of national and regional identities. Although women traveled too—for example, blues women migrating north to perform in cabarets, British women traveling to France to drive ambulances in World War I—they had a different relation to migration. Not only did laws and social conventions attempt to restrict their mobility (both Hemingway's and Lawrence's stories excerpted here reveal that in the 1920s it was still unusual for a woman to travel alone), but gender conventions inhibited their self-fashioning as well. "Woman is woman all over the world, no matter what her color is," declares Ray, the writer and intellectual in McKay's novel. "She is cast in a passive rôle" (206), wanting the "protection of man" (31), as Malty thinks Latnah does, as the Indians in Lawrence's story expect of the white woman. Yet that is woman in society; in the cultural imagination, woman figures, as does Latnah, the foreign, the exotic, the fascinatingly dangerous. Women's increased mobility in the interwar years (registered in photographs of Zora Neale Hurston with her automobile, Georgia O'Keeffe on a motorcycle, and the German actress Margarete Christians with an airplane), their actual contact with the foreign and exotic, threatened their symbolic status as Other.

Writers and artists—such as McKay, Lawrence, and Hemingway—and performers—such as Charlie Chaplin and Josephine Baker—were not the only ones traveling in the interwar period. Tourism increased dramatically in these decades. "In Paris and elsewhere tourists were having a hot time of it" (*Banjo* 135). New means of transportation made travel more affordable and remote places more accessible. Field studies by cultural anthropologists, such as Elsie Clews Parsons, and documentary films, such as Robert Flaherty's *Nanook of the North* (1922), stimulated people's imaginations, inspiring travel as well. Not only did modernist writers and artists confront new cultural formations of identity in their firsthand experience of other cultures, but they also struggled to come to terms with their difference from Western tourists and entrepreneurs, who were seen to be appropriating other cultures for their own spiritual or material gain.

In 1922 Lawrence began what Michael North terms his "grand tour," traveling to Ceylon, Australia, Cuba, Mexico, and the American southwest, seeking "an organic community to which he might belong" (North 11). As did many famous writers and artists of the day (Parsons, Willa Cather, Jean Toomer, Carl Jung, and Greta Garbo, to name a few), Lawrence stayed, in 1924, at the Taos ranch of art patron Mabel Dodge and her Pueblo husband, Tony Luhan. There Lawrence came to distance himself from people like Dodge and John Collier (who would later become the head of the Bureau for Indian Affairs) whose efforts to preserve the cultural productions of Native Americans and to have them valued as art also fueled the tourist industry in the southwestern United States and led to the romanticizing of Native American culture for Western consumption. Lawrence was contemptuous of tourists: "Put on a sombrero and knot a red kerchief round your neck . . . that is the New Mexico known to most Americans" (*Phoenix* 142). Donning the attire of the region, like surrounding oneself with the cultural artifacts of native peoples, is often considered a form of passing, refiguring the self by appropriating the cultural markers of another's identity.

Lawrence was not one to dress native; his writings express contempt for those who did and for the tourist's superficial interest in native culture. "I cannot cluster at the drum" (*Phoenix* 99), he wrote. And yet in his paintings, Lawrence portrays himself in a kind of Mexican blackface (fig. 11.3), racializing masculinity, as he does in "The Woman Who Rode Away." In this story, set in the Sierra Madre in the recession years following World War I, an American woman, who has married for adventure but finds herself bored and demoralized in her desolate surroundings, rides away from home and family on a spiritual quest to seek self-transformation among the Chilchui Indians. Taken hostage by the Indians, the woman spends several months in their village as the priests prepare for her sacrifice at the winter solstice. As the passages included here show, the Chilchui of Mexico, insistently described as black, represent a primal maleness, and the American woman personifies the white race that must be sacrificed to restore both spiritual and sexual harmony to the materialist West. Lawrence may not have identified with Indians the way Dodge and Collier did, but his paintings and fiction tell another story. The notion of a dark, primal maleness enables men to bond across racial difference. The story ends with the priest's sacrificial knife poised above the woman's naked body, waiting for the sun to enter the cave, at which time the priest would strike, "accomplish the sacrifice and achieve the power. The mastery that man must hold, and that passes from race to race" (136).[14]

New Woman, New Race

If "at the beginning of the twentieth century," as psychoanalyst Louise Kaplan writes, "women were changing in ways that were making men wary and uncomfortable" (167), as suggested by Lawrence's story, that discomfort had as much to do with changing racial identities as with gender. Robert McAlmon's poem, "White Males" (1921–22), allegorizes the fate of white men in an age when new women and black men were all the rage. The stallions, "thwarted male things," are insistently identified by their whiteness. As in Lawrence, masculinity is racialized, only here maleness is white, signifying not a primal but a *passing* identity, in both senses of that term. Racial amalgamation and independent women together would assure, the poem warns, that "there were no more white males," at least "none so clear a white as these," suggesting a loss of racial purity as well as a certain notion of manliness as signifying aggression and dominance. The poem does not necessarily lament the passing of white males, but it does capture a pervasive cultural anxiety over the fate of whiteness and masculinity in the interwar period.

   McAlmon's poem, Lawrence's story, Hemingway's novel, and psychoanalyst Joan Riviere's essay included or excerpted here all reveal the racializing of gender and the gendering of race in the cultural imagination of the modernist era. Riviere's "Womanliness as a Masquerade" (1929), for example, describes, in Louise Kaplan's words, "a unique type of gender identity solution" for women who were moving into traditionally masculine domains (268). That is, the masquerade, performing femininity, is a new identity in the modernist era: "The reader may now ask how I define womanliness or where I draw the line between genuine womanliness and the 'masquerade.' My suggestion is not, however, that there is any such difference; whether radical or superficial, they are the same thing" (Riviere 306).[15] Most striking in this essay is the intrusion

Fig. 11.4. D. H. Lawrence. *Fight with an Amazon*. From *The Paintings of D. H. Lawrence* (London: Mandrake Press, 1929). Reproduced by permission of the Newberry Library, Chicago.

of race in this analysis of gender, literally: Riviere's patient phantasizes seducing a Negro intruder.[16] The introduction of racial difference into this analysis of sexual identity reveals, as the contemporary feminist theorist Jean Walton writes, that "the explicit discourse on gender and sexuality of [the 1920s] was informed by implicit assumptions about racial difference" (228).

Ernest Hemingway's posthumously published novel, *The Garden of Eden* (1986), set in the 1920s, bears out Walton's observation most dramatically. Although of higher class status and with more secure funds than McKay's characters, the American writer, David Bourne, and his new wife, Catherine (referred to as "the young man" and "the girl," respectively), live a desultory life in the Mediterranean as they travel through France and talk of going to Spain and Africa for their honeymoon. Part 1, excerpted here, reveals the fetishizing of blackness in the modernist period: "Doesn't it make you excited to have me getting so dark?" Catherine asks David. As in McAlmon's poem, whiteness in this story is an identity to be cast off; "blacking up" is necessary to reinvent the self.[17] At least for the woman. Hemingway, though, does not just racialize gender difference in this story. Here blackness signifies, as it did in the Rhinelander trial, deviant sexuality (the incest suggested by Catherine's referring to David as her brother and her experiment with lesbianism in part 3). Such sexual deviance, epitomized in David's nickname for Catherine, "Devil," is, in turn, presented as the dark consequence of changing gender conventions. In many ways, Catherine is a new woman: she cuts her hair short, she wears slacks and men's shirts, she drinks in public, she drives a car, she travels alone, and she speaks her mind. Yet she takes such changes too far. She wants to be called a boy, she wants to make love like a man, she wants to be darker than an Indian. Catherine does not want to pass, she wants to *be*. Like Toni Morrison's Sula, she is an artist without a medium ("I can't write things," she tells David in part 3), and so her drive toward aesthetic experimentation plays itself out on her own body and in her invention of new identities for herself, her husband, and Marita, the woman they both share. Tanning herself unnaturally black is analogous to cutting her hair indecently short. Both acts represent the desire to cast off the identities historically and culturally offered to her and to become different from those like herself: "you'll be darker than an Indian," she tells David, "and that takes us further away from other people" (30). Both white and black, girl and boy, heterosexual and homosexual, she is a contradiction, an anomaly who cannot compete with the real dark woman, Marita. In the end, Catherine goes mad, burning David's manuscript—a story, set in colonial Africa, about the "seeking, fighting, killing" that McAlmon identifies with white masculinity—only to have Marita take her place at David's side while he rewrites the story "intact" from memory. Insofar as Catherine represents the dark side of the new woman, the flapper, and the passer, Hemingway's novel reads as a cautionary tale about crossing gender, sexual, and racial boundaries.

Notes

1. On globalization and literary studies, see the *PMLA* special issue on "Globalizing Literary Studies" (January 2001), especially Giles Gunn's introductory essay. Recent scholars "globalizing" modernist studies include Giddens, North, Armstrong, Garrity, and Friedman.

2. Jane Garrity discusses British *Vogue* in relation to national identity in "Selling Culture to the 'Civilized.'" As Garrity makes clear, the masthead captures as well the economic imperialism fostered by new technologies and new markets.

3. The preface to the 1918 edition of Madison Grant's *The Passing of the Great Race* declares: "European history has been written in terms of nationality and language, but never before in terms of race" (vii). Grant's focus on race is motivated in large part by the threat posed by the increased frequency of miscegenation (60).

4. In her autobiography, Zora Neale Hurston also connects the global flow of information to the expansion of national as well as personal boundaries, making everyone seem at home anywhere. Writing of her lover who provides the model for Tea Cake in *Their Eyes Were Watching God,* Hurston says: "He always said I reminded him of the Indian on the Skookum Apples, so I knew he meant me to understand that he wanted to be coming home to me, and with those words he endowed me with Radio City, the General Motors Corporation, the United States, Europe, Asia and some outlying continents. I had everything!" (*Dust Tracks* 185).

5. On passing and issues of identity and identification, see, for example, Caughie, Ginsberg, Wald, Pfeiffer, and Butler, chapter 6.

6. Details of this trial come from Lewis and Ardizzone's account. See especially chapter 4, "The Vamp and the Dupe," and chapter 5, "Concessions of Race." Alice's father, George Jones, lived as white in England, but upon coming to the United States in 1891, discovered that he was considered "colored." His mother was white, his father Indian, though whether he was from the West Indies or India was never determined. The British used "black" for people of Indian and Asian descent as well as African (73).

7. "The Rhinelander Case," *The Messenger,* December 1925: 388. Irene in Nella Larsen's *Passing* thinks of this trial in contemplating the fate of her passing friend, Clare.

8. Laura Doan discusses Arkell-Smith's trial in relation to fashion and lesbianism. My knowledge of the Arkell-Smith trial comes from Doan's account.

9. On the first transsexual operations, see Tim Armstrong.

10. The Mann Act, introduced by James Mann, a congressman from Chicago, restricted women's freedom of movement across state lines in an effort to curb prostitution (known as "white slavery"). The black boxer Jack Johnson was charged, though not convicted, under this act in 1912. The Mann Act is mentioned in George Schuyler's *Black No More* (1931) and F. Scott Fitzgerald's *Tender is the Night* (1934). See Langum.

11. For a detailed discussion of miscegenation, see Schuyler.

12. Garrity, in *Step-Daughters of England,* makes this point as well, though she goes on to note that to see modernist writing as embodying the notion of border crossing in its themes and structures is to mistakenly assume it is opposed to national narratives.

13. Other modernists wrote of the artist as vagabond, most famously Colette in *La vagabonde* (1911). I am grateful to Madhuri Deshmuch for bringing McKay's letter to Hughes to my attention.

14. For a detailed discussion of this story, see Caughie, chapter 4.

15. This is what we now refer to as a performative notion of identity. If the masquerade is a mask, as Riviere says, a form of passing, it is not because it hides a genuine femininity behind a fraudulent identity; rather, the masquerade brings into being the identity it seems only to mime. Femininity is an effect of this social performance.

16. Such a fantasy is not surprising in an era in which cross-racial desire was a persistent subject of editorials, fiction, drama, and film, as in Eugene O'Neill's *All God's Chillun Got Wings* (1924) and Kenneth Macpherson's film, *Borderline* (1930), both starring Paul Robeson. See Scott, ed., *The Gender of Modernism* (110–25) for H. D.'s essay on *Borderline*.

17. "You must black up to be the latest rage," sang Gilda Gray (who was white) in the 1922 *Ziegfeld Follies* on Broadway (Lewis and Ardizzone 114–15).

Works Cited

Armstrong, Tim. *Modernism, Technology, and the Body: A Cultural Study.*

Austin, Mary. "Woman Alone." *The Selected Essays of Mary Austin.* Ed. Reuben J. Ellis. Carbondale: Southern Illinois University Press, 1996.

Babcock, Barbara, ed. *Pueblo Mothers and Children: Essays by Elsie Clews Parsons, 1915–1924.* Sante Fe: Ancient City Press, 1991.

Butler, Judith. *Bodies That Matter.* New York: Routledge, 1993.

Caughie, Pamela L. *Passing and Pedagogy.*

Dilworth, Leah. *Imagining Indians in the Southwest: Persistent Visions of a Primitive Past.* Washington: Smithsonian Institution, 1996.

Doan, Laura. "Passing Fashions: Reading Female Masculinities in the 1920s." *Feminist Studies* 24.3 (Fall 1998): 663–700.

Douglas, Ann. *Terrible Honesty: Mongrel Manhattan in the 1920s.* New York: Farrar, Straus and Giroux, 1995.

Felski, Rita. *The Gender of Modernity.*

Friedman, Susan Stanford. *Penelope's Web.*

Garrity, Jane. "Selling Culture to the Civilized: Bloomsbury, British *Vogue,* and the Marketing of National Identity." *Modernism/Modernity* 6.2 (1999): 29–58.

———. *Step-Daughters of England: British Women Modernists and the National Imaginary* (unpublished ms.).

Gates, Henry Louis, Jr. "White Like Me." *New Yorker* (June 17, 1996): 66–72, 74–81.

Giddens, Anthony. *Modernity and Self-Identity: Self and Society in the Late Modern Age.* Stanford: Stanford University Press, 1991.

Ginsberg, Elaine K., ed. *Passing and the Fictions of Identity.* Durham: Duke University Press, 1996.

Grant, Madison. *The Passing of the Great Race, or The Racial Basis of European History.* New York: Charles Scribner's Sons, 1918.

Hurston, Zora Neale. *Dust Tracks on a Road.* 1942. New York: Harper Colins, 1991.

Indian Truth 2.2 (February 1925), published by the Indian Rights Association.

Johnson, Barbara. *The Feminist Difference: Literature, Psychoanalysis, Race, and Gender.* Cambridge: Harvard University Press, 1998.

Joyce, James. *A Portrait of the Artist as a Young Man.* 1916; New York: Signet, 1991.

Kaplan, Louise J. *Female Perversions: The Temptations of Emma Bovary.* New York: Jason Aronson, 1991.

Langum, David J. *Crossing Over the Line: Legislating Morality and the Mann Act.* Chicago: University of Chicago Press, 1994.

Lawrence, D. H. *Phoenix.* 1936; New York: Penguin, 1978.

Lewis, Earl, and Heidi Ardizzone, eds. *Love on Trial: An American Scandal in Black and White.* New York: Norton, 2001.

McKay, Claude. *Banjo.* New York: Harper and Brothers, 1929.

North, Michael. *Reading 1922: A Return to the Scene of the Modern.* New York: Oxford University Press, 1999.

Pfeiffer, Kathleen. *Race, Passing, and American Individualism.* Amherst: University of Massachusetts Press, 2003.

"The Rhinelander Case." *The Messenger* (December 1925): 338.

Sanger, Margaret. *Woman and the New Race.* New York: Truth Publishing Company, 1920.

Schuyler, George S. *Racial Intermarriage in the United States: One of the Most Interesting Phenomena in Our National Life.* Girard, Kans.: Haldeman-Julius Publications, 1929.

Scott, Bonnie Kime, ed. *The Gender of Modernism.*

Wald, Gayle. *Crossing the Line: Racial Passing in Twentieth-Century U.S. Literature and Culture.* Durham: Duke University Press, 2000.

Walton, Jean. "Re-Placing Race in (White) Psychoanalytic Discourse: Founding Narratives of Feminism." In *Female Subjects in Black and White: Race, Psychoanalysis, Feminism,* ed. Elizabeth Abel, Barbara Christian, and Helene Moglen. Berkeley: University of California Press, 1997.

Woolf, Virginia. *The Diary of Virginia Woolf.*

HEBA JANNATH

From "America's Changing Color Line"

[. . .] Notwithstanding her anti-intermarriage laws, taboos and the white mobs which punish by lynching miscegenation of white women and black men, the United States is steadily growing darker in complexion.

This change of complexion is due to six main causes:

(1) Miscegenation by white man and colored woman.

(2) The passing, like a shuttle, of their mulatto offspring back and forth between the races, spiritually and physically weaving them together.

(3) Education of the Negro and the opportunities which accompany it that enable him to accumulate power of his own.

(4) Emancipation of the white woman, her resulting freedom in sex (the even-

tual necessity of protecting her colored offspring by repealing anti-intermarriage laws).

(5) Our growing colonial possessions, unlike Britain's African colonies, most of them having large groups of educated colored people.

(6) Virtual stoppage of immigration.

Reuter and other historians have informed us that miscegenation has proceeded apace here ever since 1630 (the first boatload of slaves arrived in Jamestown, Va., in 1619), or for some fifteen generations. For although intermarriage was very early made illegal in the slave-holding States, nothing has ever stopped intermixture.

Assuming that there were, in 1630, 1,000 cases of intermixture, their descendants would now number some 32,000,000. As people of *known* Negro ancestry in the last census numbered only 12,000,000, there must be millions of persons in the white group with distant Hamitic ancestry. [. . .]

The first "passing" was made possible through the assistance of Southern white fathers, who sent their mulatto offspring North to be educated at the best colleges there, and later set them up in business. [. . .] Moreover, right after the Civil War many colored men married white wives; these, Mr. Dabney further declares, did, when possible, exactly as did the colored children of white men, they became "white."

Passing from one group to another is now of such common occurrence that it has lately become the subject of much popular fiction. Within the last few years *Plum Bun, Passing, Flight, White Girl, Gulf Stream, Love Fetich* and *Bright Skin,* all novels dealing with this so-called recent development in American society, have been published. But, as we have seen, passing successfully out of the Negro group into that of the white has been going on here for centuries. (See *Brown America,* by Edwin Embree.)

Actually, it is far easier to "pass" than our novelists would have us believe. There are, of course, many white Negroes who are too timorous for such an adventure, and there are also many superior persons of remote Negro connection who, because of group loyalty and a sense of duty, refuse to leave the Negro race. But the vast majority, that is the average octoroon, has a practical and unsentimental view of the situation. He rightfully feels he is entitled to his share of white opportunities. The families of the latter usually aid rather than hinder the passage out of their group. They are glad to have their light-skinned relations escape the insults and economic disadvantages whose deadening and tragic effects they know only too well.

The task of passing, especially in our great cities, is not so difficult as is supposed. I know or have heard of dozens of people who have passed successfully but who occasionally run up to Harlem to see some less fortunate relation. One charming blond octoroon, who hails from New Orleans, stops when in New York City at the best white hotels and trots around among white and colored alike, passing when it pleases or amuses her to do so, and in general has a wonderful time.

The octoroons who "pass" are usually past masters at detecting the slightest change in the thoughts and emotions of the people around. They usually, too, have great self-control, and, on the whole, prove to be very charming and sophisticated people. They obtain a view of both races denied most of us, and, full of ambition as they usually are, they emulate the best points of both groups. [...]

It must be borne in mind that passing for something which one is not is a very common practice in America. Jews and Mexicans often pass for Spaniards (since to be Spanish is thought more desirable here). Jews, Russians, Germans, Italians and Irish frequently change their names into "acceptable" Anglo-Saxon, the business world and the movies are full of such transformations. But because of America's particularly fierce taboo on the Negro, we have come to think that "passing" pertains only to him.

Envy and jealousy are everywhere to be met with in the racial situation, from the white man who keeps a Negro mistress and will lynch a black man should he look too long at a white woman, to the Negro woman with a white protector, who will greatly resent the presence of lighter skins within her own group. Many octoroons with white fathers and grandfathers who have wanted, but feared for some reason, to pass out of the Negro group, are loudest in denunciation of whites. Hatred of whites is euphemised by them into "race pride." To hear such people, who often have extremely Nordic features and coloring, talk about "We of the Black race" is ludicrous in the extreme. Negroes, to be sure, are somewhat justified in hating the race which has gone to such elaborate lengths to persecute and penalise them. Nevertheless, it is absurd for them to denounce race prejudice in whites on the one hand while entertaining it themselves so righteously. [...]

Whites sometimes find it convenient to pass for Negroes. A young woman of my acquaintance, who is a mixture of white and Indian blood, but whose relatives have on the Indian side intermarried with Negroes, passes herself off as a Negro in order to teach in a Southern colored college which would otherwise be barred to her. She possesses very straight blond hair and is in the habit of going to a white hairdresser in the city where her school is located. Once, she says, the head woman instructor, overhearing her make an appointment with the white beauty parlor, severely reprimanded her. Teachers and pupils alike, when the news of this heresy leaked out, bitterly denounced her for "trying to act white." [. . .]

As Dr. Einstein, during his visit to New York in 1931, told a Negro reporter who was interviewing him, most of America is crazy on the race question. This insanity is witnessed among the majority of both groups. The average Negro and the average white hold almost identically unsound opinions upon the race problem. Ask the average Negro what he thinks of social equality and racial intermarriage and he will grow as indignant as a white man. He will hotly deny that he wants either, and believe that it is because he is too proud to want any relationship with whites. Let him talk a while and he will unwittingly reveal that he really feels himself inferior. He will ridicule someone who is darker than himself and praise someone lighter. He will talk about "good" (straight) and "bad" (kinky) hair. He will not go with a certain girl because "he's not dealing in coal." The other morning, an elderly black woman who wished to hire herself to me as nurse, emphatically declared "that she suttinly did like to take keer of nice white chillun" but that she wouldn't have anything to do with "no ole black chillun at no price cose they was jes' nachally mean an' evil."

If, according to the Behaviorists, thought is entirely a matter of conditioning rather than of reason, the Negro, developed by the same culture as the white, must necessarily "think white." Subjected as he has been to torture, slavery, disfranchisement and discrimination, he would have had to be more than human not to have acquired a profound, if bitter, respect for the power that could do such things to him. This respect, making the Negro emulate everything "white" (black women want light-skinned babies and black men seek the fairest women they can with safety obtain), hastens amalgamation.

Our nine millions of diluted Aframericans (there are left about 3,000,000 "pure" Negroes) are almost entirely the product of white men and black women in illegal unions. There have been, of course, many exceptional cases where the parties were wed. Since the first appearance of the Negro on these shores, many black men in the North have had white wives. White bondswomen in the early days frequently married Negro slaves. While in deepest Dixie, clandestine affairs between white women and black men have, to some extent, always gone on. But, generally speaking, the mulatto among us has been the issue of black concubines and white men.

This would necessarily be the case since, until the World War, the white woman was almost as much a serf in Dixie as the black man. There is an old American saying to the effect that the only free people in the United States were the white man and the Negro woman. But the political emancipation of American women at the beginning of the last decade, and the wartime migration of Negroes North for better jobs, considerably altered the inter-racial situation.

Frequently, during the last ten years, the white press has blazoned forth in scare headlines about intermarriages between white women and Negro men. Although white men had always had relationship with Negro women, it had been heatedly maintained by Negrophobes that the white woman (except possibly the lowest type) would never "stoop" to intimacy with the Negro man. This "reassuring" belief went with the old-fashioned notion that the female was more spiritual than the male, and "superior" (different) from him in all sexual matters. This notion has been so frequently exploded since 1920 that even the Anglo-Saxon Society would now not have the temerity to mention it. The latest defiance of this ancient taboo came from Carmel, California, where the Jean Toomer–Margaret Latimer nuptials took place under the auspices of the mayor and many well-known intellectuals.

In fact, the majority of the cases recorded in the papers show that most of the young women who have lately crossed the color line have been college graduates and daughters of so-called "good" families.

George S. Schuyler, in a booklet entitled *Racial Inter-Marriage in the United States* (No. 1387, Haldeman-Julius Blue Book), says there are as many as 10,000 inter-racial marriages now, four-fifths of which are the white-woman-black-man variety. [. . .]

No exhaustive statistics have, of course, been obtained upon the subject. Owing to the controversial nature of the matter the parties are always anxious to keep out of the public print. Many of them employ an effective way of avoiding publicity. A white woman when applying for a marriage license has simply to state that she has remote Negro ancestry and the press and pulpit, always so eager to denounce such alliances, are silenced.

So general is the belief in the racial inferiority of the Negro in America, that one apparently has but to admit remote colored ancestry to be left un-molested. Negroes, being shrewder in such matters, are not so easily taken in. But even in the Deep South this method of safeguarding inter-racial relationships has been, and still is, employed. It would be impossible, therefore, to obtain the exact figures upon intermarriage any more than upon intermixture.

Not only has the white woman been said to be immune to the attraction of black men but, in Aframerica, there is an equally reassuring myth to the effect that black men do not want white women.

In spite of what most of the "Uncle Tom" Negro leaders say, the Negro man, being a man, is usually willing enough to be a party to a mixed affair. To say so openly, however, would jeopardise the patronage of white philanthropists who are willing to help the Negro solve the racial problem in every way except the natural one. [. . .]

However, because of the severe penalties attached to the black-man-white-woman relationships in America, the Negro man is more the pursued than the pursuer in these affairs. Since the post-war glorification of Negro virility in literature, it has become ultra-smart among certain fashionable white women to have Negro lovers. *Sweet Man,* by Gilmore Millen (Viking Press, New York, 1930), is the first novel to picture this modern tendency of the white woman to indulge in the forbidden. [. . .]

The Negro group displays almost as much hostility to mixed marriages as the white does; especially where it is a black-man-white-woman union. If it is a colored woman and a white man the Negro seems to feel a certain triumph which softens his disapproval. The difference in attitude among Aframericans toward the Alice and Kip Rhinelander affair and the two marriages of Jack Johnson to white women was marked. They are proud of the former alliance, though it ended disgracefully, but Jack Johnson's preference for white wives greatly annoys them.

Negro women take the lead in the criticism of such matches. They greatly fear the competition of white women. They have been accustomed in the past to have the men of both groups, the one for lovers, the other for husbands, and dislike having the situation changed. My father, a member of the original Klan in Texas, tells me that the organisation was formed in his section at the behest of Negro women, who, after the Civil War, feared the white woman as a competitor.* [. . .]

The greatest objection to white wives in Aframerica comes usually from Southern Negroes, just as it comes from Southern whites. When they move into free territory they bring their prejudices with them. Negroes who will resent a white wife will, however, feel no resentment against her offspring, since by the old law of the fatal drops of blood, her children have become Negroes. Indeed such offspring are greatly favored. [. . .]

Opinion upon racial intermixture is now undergoing a subtle change in America. Many anthropologists now say that there is no such thing as a "pure" race, and that the more mixed a people becomes, the more progressive it is liable to be. E. A. Hooton, of Harvard University, in *Up From the Ape* says:

> Every civilization grows up, to a great extent, from the borrowings and ac-
> cretions of other cultures. The more isolated the habitat of a race or people
> the more disadvantageous is their situation from this point of view.

---

* This is typical of the particular, kind of lie the white Southern gentlemen put out. ED. [Nancy Cunard, editor of *Negro*]

[. . .] The changing opinion toward intermixture may be due to the-waning Anglo-Saxon element in our country. Louis Dublin, writing in the *New York Times*, Sunday, April 17, gives the following figures: in the census of 1890 the percentage of Nordic blood in the white population here was: British 13.2, Irish 23.3, Scandinavian 7.5, German 33.2, Canadian-Others 6.1. By 1930 it had declined . . . from 83.3 to 51 [percent], a loss of 32.3.

According to an article by Raymond Leslie Buell *(New York Times,* April 24, 1932) the total area of our colonial empire and our "spheres of interest" (possessions that we "boss" but do not admit we own) amount to more than a million square miles and embrace a total population of 29,427,418. [. . .] These Colonials are predominantly colored and will exert much pressure upon our future opinions. Add to the Colonials 12,000,000 Negroes residing within the States, and the extent to which America is becoming dark can readily be seen.

With immigration practically ended, we cannot expect any great influx of Nordics, or of any whites whatsoever, in numbers sufficiently large enough to maintain our former division of color. The darker the white group grows, the more ridiculous color prejudice becomes. There being neither religious nor educational differences but only color differences between the races here, prejudice will disappear with the erasure of strongly contrasting peoples. [. . .]

America's darkening complexion will bring with it a train of cultural advantages:

A greater tolerance—therefore a more civilised attitude toward life. Less bastardy and lynching—therefore finer ethics. Better educational facilities in the South—hence less monkey-shines about evolution and science and less "old time religion." Finally, that future war between the white and colored races, which is always being dolefully predicted, may be averted. [. . .]

Negro, Anthology Made by Nancy Cunard, 1931–1933. Rpt. New York: Negro Universities Press, 1969. 83–89.

ELSIE CLEWS PARSON

From "The Zuñi La' Mana"

Of these "men-women" there are today in Zuñi three or, one might almost say, three and a half—there is a boy about six years old qualifying, so to speak, for the status. An elderly Zuñi with whom I talked, a man over seventy, had known during his lifetime of nine *la'mana*. Mrs. Stevenson mentions five.[1] The three adults now living are about the same age, in the late thirties and early forties. Their names are Kasineli, Tsalatitse, and U'k.[2] [. . .] Far from adequate, my observations may be nevertheless worth recording, so very little has been recorded at all about the Indian berdache. I hope to continue the study.

To begin with the little boy, he is still dressed as a male, wearing trousers and a shirt; but his shirt is of a considerably longer cut than that of the other little boys, nor is it tucked into the trousers as they sometimes tuck in theirs. Around his neck is a bead necklace, a mixture of commercial and of stone beads, an ornament not altogether commonplace for either little boys or girls. His hair-cut is the usual all round short cut for boys—girls of his age would be growing a lock at the back of the neck. His features are unusually fine and delicate, unusual even in a Zuñi girl, and his facial expression unusually gentle, mild of expression as is the Zuñi of either sex. Whenever I saw him playing about he was with a girl, although boys of his age begin to gang together. "He talks like a girl," I was told. And by that I learned was meant that he used the "expressions" of a girl,[3] their exclamations and turns of speech."[4] A few of these differentiations in the speech of the sexes I collected:

> [She gives boy and girl versions of: Oh, dear!; Oh, lovely or bully!; Outch!; Stop!; I don't want to! I'm shy!; Oh, I'm so tired; It's awfully cold! Oh, it's very good!]

Kasineli has the facial expression and the stature of a man. He has the longer stride of a man, but it is slow and ponderous like the Zuñi woman's. During the rain dances he always stood on the roof top behind the old woman who is

---

1. "The Zuñi Indians," *Twenty-first Annual Report Bureau American Ethnology*, P. 37. Three of them became la'mana after 1890. [Notes are selected.—Pamela L. Caughie]

2. U'k "sounds like a man's name," I was told; *ditse* is the ending of a girl's name.

4. Lowie notes that Assiniboine berdaches "employed the affirmative and imperative particles peculiar to women's speech." (*Anthropological Papers, American Museum of Natural History,* IV, I, P. 42. New York, 1910.) [. . .]

the head of his household. He did not wear the American calico petticoat so many of the Zuñi women wear but his dress was in every particular as far as I could see like a woman's, and he wore his black blanket in woman fashion, up around the back of the head, irrespective of the temperature, and falling to the knees.[5] Next him on the roof top were standing or sitting three or four kins-women. One of them was an informant of mine. To the *la'mana* in her family she would never refer, although we talked of the subject in general from time to time and we worked together on her family genealogy. Nor would she take me to the house where he lived, the house of her father's sister where her own little son was living and where she had grown up. Her people had tried very hard to dissuade the lad from becoming a *la'mana*, I was told,[6] and I got the impression that in general a family would be somewhat ashamed of having a *la'mana* among its members. In regard to the custom itself there seemed to be no reticence in general and no sense of shame. [. . .]

It is the *la'mana*, Mrs. Stevenson states, whose special function it is to fetch from To'wa Yaleně the clay used in making pottery. This is certainly not so today; anyone may fetch the clay. My elderly informant declared it was never the function of the *la'mana*. At two periods during his memory, however, have the Priests of the Bow endeavored to give a sacred character to the pottery-making, confining it to the first four days of the summer solstice ceremonial, prescribing the firing for the fourth night. Mrs. Stevenson describes this custom without mentioning, however, that it is an innovation.[8] It is possible, it occurs to me, that limiting the fetching of the clay to the *la'mana* may have been prescribed also by these inventive Bow priests. It is possible, but very doubtful I must say until I hear of other religious or quasi-religious functions attaching distinctively to the *la'mana*. I heard of none.

There are myths, however, in regard to "men-women." In a myth reported by Mrs. Stevenson[9] it is the *chaakwena*, a god captured by the *kia'nakwe*, who puts on the *kor'koshi* (*ko'kokshi*), a woman's dress to break his spirit—he is rebelling against taking part in a dance to celebrate his capture. This was the first appearance of a male, say the Zuñi, in women's dress. The *kor'koshi* mask in the *kia'nakwe* dramatization is in woman's dress and is called the *ko'thlama* (*ko'lama*).[10] Cushing gives a different account of the first appearance of the "man-woman." The first born of the incestuous couple, Siweluhsina and Si-weluhsita, the couple who figure so prominently in Zuñi mythology, was "a woman in fullness of contour, but a man in stature and brawn"—a fairly accurate description of the hermaphrodite. And the Zuñi explanation is that

---

5. [. . .] It is a mode of wearing his blanket as irrespective of temperature and as conventional as that of a woman.

from the mingling of too much seed in one kind, comes the two-fold kind, *'hláhmon,* being man and woman combined—even as from a kernel of corn with two hearts, ripens an ear that is neither one kind nor the other, but both!

According to Cushing then this "man-woman of the Kâ'kâ"[11] is the elder sister of the *ko'yemshi,* those sacred antic personages of Zuñi ceremonial, sexually abnormal too, we recall, because "seedless."

I was unable to verify these myths. [. . .]

These myths are, I take it, *a posteriori* explanations of the *la'mana.* They may give a sanction to the transformation custom; they do not originate it. But this matter of possible relationship between the *la'mana* and supernatural function or office needs further study.[12] Meanwhile we should note that the part of the *ko'lamana* appears to be usually taken by a *la'mana.* We'wha took it. Kasineli has taken it. In recent years,[13] however, it has been played by one who is not a *la'mana,* not a "man-woman," but rather a "woman-man" so to speak. Nancy is called in fact, in a teasing sort of way, "the girl-boy," *katsŏtsĕ* (*ka'tsiki,* girl, *ŏtsĕ,* male). Of the *katsŏtsĕ* I saw quite a little, for she worked by the day in our household. She was an unusually competent worker, "a girl I can always depend on," said her employer. She had a rather lean, spare, build and her gait was comparatively quick and alert. It occurred to me once that she might be a *la'mana.* "If she is," said her employer, "she is not so openly like the others. Besides she's been too much married for one." She was, I concluded, a "strong-minded woman," a Zuñi "new woman," a large part of her male, as Weininger would say.

It is because they like woman's work, is the reason that has always been given me both in Zuñi and among the Rio Grande pueblos for the existence of the "man-woman." At Zuñi I was also told, one of my informants being the woman interpreter I have already referred to, that if the household were short on women workers a boy would be more readily allowed to became a *la'mana.* It is always insisted upon that there is never any compulsion upon him to become one.

Of the nine *la'mana* known to my aged interpreter, two had married men, *i. e.,* lived with men as their wives. One of these *la'mana* had been known to my younger Zuñi acquaintances. He was described as effeminate looking—"pretty," like a woman. The families of both parties were said to have objected to the "marriage." The "marriage" was discussed with me as an economic arrangement, and with not the slightest hint of physical acts of perversion on the part of either

---

11. "Zuñi Creation Myths," *Thirteenth Annual Report Bureau American Ethnology,* pp. 401–413.

"husband" or "wife." It seemed to me at the time that the utter obliviousness to that point of view was due to ignorance or innocence, not to reticence.[14] On questions of sexual intercourse the Zuñi, I would say, is naturalistic, not reticent. Nevertheless it is not at all unlikely that this oblivious manner was assumed to check further discussions—for reasons I do not know.

Although the *la'mana* U'k was, I gathered on my first visit, somewhat effeminate looking, he was not married. (Here I should say that Tsalatitse is not effeminate looking. Like Kasineli he is tall and walks with a long, heavy stride.) U'k was teased, I was told, by the children, and he would answer them back like a child. He walks too more like a child than either an adult man or an adult woman, "flighty like," with short, nervous steps. In short he is an undeveloped kind of person. A careful and reliable woman described him as a simpleton.

He is, nevertheless, one of the dancers, for he was initiated into the *ko'tikili,*[15] as are all *la'mana,* just like other boys.[16] The night I saw U'k dancing during the *sha'lako* ceremonial he was in the *chaakwena* dance, that is with the set of dancers from the *uptsana kiwitsine.*[17] He was clothed in the ordinary woman's dress and buckskin leggings plus the usual Hopi dance blanket. He had a downy white feather in his hair, otherwise his hair was dressed in the regular woman's style, bang and turned up queue. He came in to the house fourth in the line of dancers but soon fell out of line and danced separately, opposite the line. Representing a female personage, as I was told he did—that is the position he would naturally take. Before the dancers withdrew, he took a place in the line again, number six. His dance step was much less vigorous than the others; but that is true too of normal males personating "goddesses." U'k is not as tall as the other *la'mana,* his stature is more that of a woman than a man. His features, however, are masculine. Their expression in this dance was that of animal-like dumb patience.

When U'k fell out of line the audience, an audience mostly of women with their children, girls, and a few old men, grinned and even chuckled, a very infrequent display of amusement during these *sha'lako* dances.[18] "Did you notice them laughing at her?" my Cherokee hostess asked me on my return.

---

14. It is a pity Mrs. Stevenson felt called upon to be so reticent. "There is a side to the lives of these men which must remain untold" is all she vouchsafes. (*The Zuñi Indians*, p. 38.) The *la'mana* who was married to a man she mentions, but she refers to the couple merely "as two of the hardest workers in the Pueblo and among the most prosperous." [. . .]

15. The initiation takes place between seven and eleven, the age falling necessarily uncertainly because the ceremonial takes place quadrennially. At any rate this age is prior to that when female dress is definitely assumed, about twelve. [. . .]

18. Aside from the merriment produced by the *ko'yemshi,* the only other show of amusement I saw was called forth by the little boys in the *hemishi'kwe* dance, boys who had their faces painted white and wore a *pitone* to represent female figures.

"She is a great joke to the people—not because she is a *la'mana,* but because she is half-witted."

Neither U'k nor the other two *la'mana* are members of any of the esoteric fraternities. Of the other *la'mana* my aged informant had known one, and one only belonged to a fraternity, the Bedbug fraternity.

When prepared for burial the corpse of a *la'mana* is dressed in the usual woman's outfit, with one exception, under the woman's skirt a pair of trousers are put on.[19] "And on which side of the graveyard will he be buried?"[20] I asked, with eagerness of heart if not of voice, for here at last was a test of the sex status of the *la mana.* "On the south side, the men's side, of course. *Kwash lu*[21] *ŏtsĕ tea'mĕ* (Is this man not)?" And my old friend smiled the peculiarly gentle smile he reserved for my particularly unintelligent questions.

---

20. [. . .] "Why do you make the division?" I asked my old man informant. "Because we do not pray to the women for rain, only to the men."

21. Personal pronouns showing sex are lacking in Zuñi.

American Anthropologist. N.S. 18 (1916): 521–28.

COLETTE

Nuit Blanche

Trans. Anne Callahan

In our house there is only one bed, too big for you, a bit narrow for the two of us. It is chaste, very white, stripped bare; no linens veil its candor in plain light of day. Our visitors do not avert their eyes, but gaze at it quietly with a look of complicity, for it is marked, in the middle, by a sole soft valley, like the bed of a young girl who sleeps alone.

They do not know, those who come here, that each night the weight of our two entwined bodies deepens, beneath its voluptuous shroud, this valley no wider than a tomb.

Oh, our naked bed! A dazzling lamp, hanging over it, exposes it even more. At twilight, we don't look there for the contrived, web-like shadow cast by a lace canopy, nor the rosy glow of a night light whose color resembles that of a sea shell. Like a star that neither rises nor sets, the flame of our bed never dims except to plunge into deep, velvety night.

A halo of perfume surrounds it. Rigid and white like the body of a blessed departed, it gives off a scent, a complex perfume that surprises one, and that one inhales attentively, with the care taken to distinguish between the blond essence of your favorite tobacco, the still more delicate aroma of your very fair skin, and this smell of burnt sandalwood which I give off; but who is to say if this rustic smell of crushed herbs is yours or mine?

Embrace us tonight, O our bed, and may your fresh valley grow deeper still beneath the feverish torpor with which we are intoxicated after a spring day spent in the gardens and in the woods!

I lie here without moving, my head on your sweet shoulder. I am surely going to descend into the darkness of a deep sleep until tomorrow, a sleep so stubborn, so persistent, that the wings of dreams will beat against it in vain. I will sleep. . . . Wait only until I find a nice cool spot for the souls of my feet, which tingle and burn. . . . You have not moved. You are breathing in long drafts, but I sense that your shoulder is still awake, careful to burrow in under my chin. Let us sleep. . . . May nights are so short. In spite of the blue darkness that surrounds us, my eyelids are still filled with sunlight, with rose-colored flames, with fleeting, swinging shadows, and I reflect on my day, eyes closed, as one might look out from behind shutters at a dazzling summer day.

How my heart is beating! I can hear yours as well under my ear. You're not asleep? I lift my head up a little, and though I can't see it, I imagine the paleness of your upturned face, the tawny shadow of your short hair. Your knees are as cool as two oranges. . . . Turn toward me, so that mine might steal some of their sweet coolness.

Ah! let us sleep! . . . My skin tingles as my blood courses beneath it. My calf muscles and my ears are throbbing. Could our soft bed be strewn with pine needles tonight? Let us sleep! I insist!

I can't sleep. My happy insomnia pulsates, lively, and I sense in your stillness the same trembling fatigue. . . . You do not move. You are hoping that I am asleep. From time to time your arm tightens around me out of tender habit, and your charming feet are wrapped around mine. . . . Sleep approaches, touches me lightly and flees. . . . I can see it! It looks like that deep velvet butterfly that I chased in the garden aflame with irises. . . . Do you remember? What light, what impatient youth glorified this entire day! . . . A cutting, pressing breeze blew a smokescreen of rapid clouds across the sun, wilting the tender linden leaves as it passed, and the blooms of the walnut trees fell like scorched caterpillars on our hair, as did the catalpas flowers the color of the rainy mauve of Paris skies. . . . The black currant buds that you crumpled, the wild sorrel strewn like rosettes in the grass, the young mint, still brown, the sage as downy as a hare's ear—everything overflowed with strong, peppery sap, which mingled on my lips with the taste of alcohol and citronella . . .

I could only laugh and shout, treading on the long juicy grass that stained my dress. . . . You watched my folly with calm joy, and when I stretched my hand out to touch the wild roses—you remember, the ever so tender pink ones—you broke off the branch before I could, and you lifted off, one by one, the little claw-shaped, coral-hued thorns. . . . You gave me the flowers, disarmed.

You gave me the flowers, disarmed. . . . You gave me the best place in the shade, under the lilacs hanging in ripe branches, so that, out of breath, I would rest. . . . You picked large cornflowers from beds, enchanted flowers whose velvety centers give off the scent of apricots. . . . You gave me the cream from the little pot of milk at snack time when my voracious appetite made you smile. . . . You gave me the pieces of bread with the most golden crust, and I can still see your hand, translucent in the sun, raised to chase away the buzzing wasp caught in the curls of my hair. . . . You threw a light shawl around my shoulders when, towards the end of the day, a longer than usual cloud moved slowly by and I shivered, drenched, drunk with a pleasure unknown to men, the innocent pleasure of animals happy in the springtime. . . . You said to me: "Come back . . . stop. . . . let's go home!" You said to me . . .

Oh, if I think of you, all the worse for my sleep. What hour just chimed? The windows are beginning to turn blue. I hear my blood pulsing, or else it is the murmur of the gardens below. Are you asleep? No. If I moved my cheek nearer to yours, I would feel your eyelashes flutter like the wings of a captive fly. . . . You are not sleeping. You are watching over my feverish state. You shelter me from bad dreams; you are thinking about me as I am thinking about you, and we are both pretending, out of strange emotional modesty, to sleep peacefully. My entire body gives itself up to sleep, relaxed, my neck leaning heavily on your sweet shoulder; but our thoughts are making love discreetly in the bluish dawn, rising so quickly.

Soon, the bar of light between the curtains will come to life, its color turning rose. In just a few minutes I will be able to read, on your beautiful forehead, on your delicate cheek, on your sad mouth and your closed eyelids, the resolve to appear to be sleeping. It is the hour when I will no longer be able to silence my fatigue, my fidgety insomnia and when I will throw my arms out of this feverish bed and when my devilish heels will get ready to thrash about mischievously.

Then you will pretend to wake up! Then I will be able to take refuge in you, with a flurry of unjust complaints, excessive sighs, bemoaning the untimely arrival of the dawn, the endless night, the noise in the street. . . . For I know very well that you will tighten your embrace and that if being rocked in your arms is not enough to calm me, your kiss will become more persistent, your hands more loving, and you will give me sensual pleasure as a haven, like a sovereign exorcism which will drive from me the demons of fever, anger, worry. . . . You will give me sensual pleasure, bent over me, eyes filled with maternal concern, you who seek in your passionate friend the child you never had.

Translator's Note

The literal translation of the title is "white night," which in French means a "sleepless night," whether a night without sex or a night full of sex. There is no English equivalent that would evoke the French title's double entendre that serves to establish the multi-layered sexual ambiguity of the story.

Les Vrilles De La Vigne. Paris: Editions De "La Vie Parisienne," 1908. 13–20.

CLAUDE MCKAY

From "Malty Turned Down" in *Banjo*

Banjo had taken Latnah as she came, easily. It seemed the natural thing to him to fall on his feet, that Latnah should take the place of the other girl to help him now that he needed help. Whatever happened, happened. Life for him was just one different thing of a sort following the other.

Malty was more emotional and amorously gentle than Banjo. He was big, strong, and jolly-natured, and everybody pronounced him a good fellow. He had made it easy for the gang to accept Latnah, when she came to them different from the girls of the Ditch. But there was just the shadow of a change in the manner of the gang toward her since she had taken up steadily with Banjo.

"Some of us nevah know when wese got a good thing," said Malty to Banjo as they sat up on the breakwater, waiting to be signaled to lunch on a ship. "I think youse the kind a man that don't appreciate a fust-rate thing because he done got it too easy."

"Ise a gone-fool nigger with any honey-sweet mamma," replied Banjo, "but I ain't gwina bury mah head under no woman's skirt and let her cackle ovah me."

"All that bellyaching about a skirt," retorted Malty. "We was all made and bohn under it."

Banjo laughed and said: "Easy come, easy go. Tha's the life-living way. We got met up easy and she's taking it easy, and Ise taking it easy, too."

A black seaman came on deck and signaled them. They hurried down from the breakwater and up the gangway.

Latnah was the first woman that Malty and his pals had ever met actually on the beach. Malty first became aware of her one day on the deck of a ship from which he and Bugsy and Ginger had been driven by a Negro steward.

"G'way from here, you lazy no-'count bums," the steward had said. "I wouldn't even give you-all a bone to chew on. Instead a gwine along back to work, you lay down on the beach a bumming mens who am trying to make a raspactable living. You think if you-all lay down sweet and lazy in you' skin while we others am wrastling with salt water, wese gwine to fatten you moh in you' laziness? G'way from this heah white man's broad nigger bums."

The boys were very hungry. For some days they had been eating off a coal boat with a very friendly crew. But it had left the moorings and anchored out in the bay, and now they could not get to it. Irritated, but rather amused by the steward's onslaught, they shuffled off from the ship a little down the quay. But Malty happened to look behind him and see Latnah waving. He went back with his pals and they found a mess of good food waiting for them. Latnah had spoken in their behalf, and one of the mates had told the chief steward to feed them.

The boys saw her often after that. They met her at irregular intervals in the Bum Square and down the docks. One day on the docks she got into a row with one of the women who sold fancy goods on the boats. The woman was trying to tempt one of the mates into buying a fine piece of Chinese silk, but the mate was more tempted by Latnah.

"Go away from me," the mate said. "I don't want a bloody thing you've got."

The woman was angry, but such rebuffs were not strange to her. To carry on her business successfully she had to put up with them. She had seen at once that the officer was interested in Latnah, and in passing she swung her valise against Latnah's side.

"Oh, you stupid woman!" cried Latnah, holding her side.

"You dirty black whore," returned the woman.

"You bigger white whore," retorted Latnah. "I know you sell everything you've got. I see you on ship." And Latnah pulled open her eye at the woman and made a face.

Later, when Latnah left the ship, she again met the woman with her man on the dock. The man was a slim tout-like type, and he tried to rough-handle Latnah. But Malty happened along then and bounced the fellow with his elbow and said, "Now what you trying to do with this woman?" The man muttered something in a language unfamiliar to Malty and slunk off with his woman.

He hadn't understood what Malty had said, either, but his bounce and menacing tone had been clear enough.

"I glad you come," said Latnah to Malty. "I thank you plenty, plenty, for if you no come I would been in big risk. I would stick him."

She slipped from her bosom a tiny argent-beaded dagger, exquisitely sharp-pointed, and showed it to Malty. He recoiled with fear and Latnah laughed. A razor or a knife would not have touched him strangely. But a dagger! It was as if Latnah had produced a serpent from her bosom. It was not an instrument familiar to his world, his people, his life. It reminded him of the strange, fierce, fascinating tales he had heard of Oriental strife and daggers dealing swift death.

Suddenly another side of Latnah was revealed to him and she stood out more clearly, different from the strange creature of quick gestures and nimble body who panhandled the boats and brought them gifts of costly cigarettes. She was different from the women of his race. She laughed differently, quietly, subtly. The women of his race could throw laughter like a clap of thunder. And their style, the movement of their hips, was like that of fine, vigorous, four-footed animals. Latnah's was gliding like a serpent. But she stirred up a powerfully sweet and strange desire in him.

She made him remember the Indian coolies that he had known in his West Indian Island when he was a boy. They were imported indentured laborers and worked on the big sugar plantation that bordered on his seaside village. The novelty of their strangeness never palled on the village. The men with their turbans and the loin-cloths that the villagers called coolie-wrapper. The women weighted down with heavy silver bracelets on arms, neck and ankles, their long glossy hair half hidden by the cloth that the natives called coolie-red. Perhaps they had unconsciously influenced the Negroes to retain their taste for bright color and ornaments that the Protestant missionaries were trying to destroy.

Every 1st of August, the great native holiday, anniversary of the emancipation of the British West Indian slaves in 1834, the Negroes were joined by some Indians in their sports on the playground. The Indians did athletic stunts and sleight-of-hand tricks, such as unwinding yards of ribbon out of their mouths, cleverly making coins disappear and finding them in the pockets of the natives, and fire-eating.

Some of the Indians were regarded as great workers in magic. The Negroes believed that Indian magic was more powerful than their Obeah. Certain Indians had given up the laborious hoeing and digging of plantation work to practice the black art among the natives. And they were much more influential and prosperous than the Negro doctors of Obeah.

The two peoples did not mix in spite of the friendly contact. There were, however, rare instances of Indians who detached themselves from their people and became of the native community by marrying Negro women. But the Indian women remained more conservative. Malty remembered one striking exception of a beautiful Indian girl. She went to the Sunday-evening class that was conducted by the wife of the Scotch missionary. And she became a convert to Christianity and was married to the Negro schoolmaster.

He also remembered a little Indian girl who was for some time in his class at grade school. Her skin was velvet, smooth and dark like mahogany. She was the cleverest child in the class, but always silent, unsmiling, and mysterious. He had never forgotten her.

Malty's boyhood memories undoubtedly played a part in his conduct toward Latnah. He could not think of her as he did about the women of the Ditch. He felt as if he had long lost sight of his exotic, almost forgotten schoolmate, to find her become a woman on the cosmopolitan shore of Marseilles.

After her encounter with the peddling woman, Latnah attached herself more closely to the beach boys. Maybe (not being a woman of the Ditch, with a tout to fight for her) she felt insecure and wanted to belong to a group or maybe it was just her woman's instinct to be under the protection of man. She was accepted. With their wide experience and passive philosophy of life, beach boys are adepts at meeting, understanding, and accepting everything.

Latnah was following precisely the same line of living as they. She came as a pal. She was made one of them. Whatever personal art she might use as a woman to increase her chances was her own affair. Their luck also depended primarily on personality. [. . .] It did not matter if Latnah was not inclined to be amorous with any of them. Perhaps it was better so. She was more useful to them as a pal. Love was cheap in the Ditch. It cost only the price of a bottle of red wine among the "leetah" girls, as the beach boys called the girls of Boody Lane, because their short-time value was fixed at about the price of a liter of cheap red wine.

Malty had wanted Latnah for himself. But she had never given him any chance. She remained just one of the gang.

The boys were rather flattered that she stayed with them and shunned the Arab-speaking men, with whom she was identified by language and features. When Banjo arrived at Marseilles, Latnah's place on her own terms among the boys was a settled thing. But when, falling in love with Banjo at first sight, she took him as her lover, they were all surprised and a little piqued. And the latent desire in Malty was stirred afresh.

After their lunch, Banjo and Malty went across the suspension bridge to the docks on the other side. They were joined by Dengel, who approached them rocking rhythmically, now pausing a moment to balance himself in his tracks. He was much blacker than Malty, a shining anthracite. And his face was moist and his large eyes soft with liquor.

Dengel was always in a state of heavenly inebriety; sauntering along in a soft mist of liquor. He was never worried about food. The joy of his being was the wine of the docks. He always knew of some barrel conveniently placed that could be raided without trouble.

"Come drink wine," he said. [. . .]

After they had quenched their craving they returned to the far, little-frequented end of the breakwater and lay lazily in the sun. There Latnah, her morning's hustling finished, found them. Her yellow blouse was soiled and she slipped it off and began washing it. That was a sign for the boys to clean up. All except Dengel, the only Senegalese that had crossed over to the breakwater; he was feeling too sweet in his skin for any exertion. The boys stripped to the waist and began to wash their shirts. Bugsy went down between two cement blocks and brought up a can he had secreted there with a hunk of white soap. Finished washing, they spread the clothes on the blocks. Soon the vertical burning rays of the sun would suck them dry.

Malty suggested that they should swim. The beach boys often bathed down the docks, making bathing-suits of their drawers. And sometimes, when they had the extreme end of the breakwater to themselves, they went in naked. They did this time, cautioning Dengel to keep watch for them.

Latnah went in too. Malty was the best swimmer. He made strong crawl strokes. He was also an excellent diver. When he was a boy in the West Indies, he used to dive from the high deck railings for the coins that the tourists threw into the water. When he got going about wharf life in the West Indian ports of Kingston, Santiago, Port of Spain, he told stories of winning dollar bills in competition with other boys diving for coins from the bridges of ships. Of how he would struggle under water against another boy while the coin was whirling down away from them. How the cleverest boy would get it or both lose it when they could not stay down under any longer and came up breathless, blowing a multitude of bubbles.

Latnah was a beautiful diver and shot graceful like a serpent through the water. A thrill shivered through Malty's blood. He had never dreamed that her body was so lovely, limber, and sinewy. He dived down under her and playfully caught at her feet. She kicked him in the mouth, and it was like the shock of a kiss wrestled for and stolen, flooding his being with a rush of sweetly-warm sensation.

Latnah swam away and, hoisting herself upon a block, she gamboled about like a gazelle. Malty and Banjo started to swim round to her, bantering and beating up heaps of water, with Malty leading, when Dengel called: "Attention! Police!" His sharp native eye had discerned two policemen far away up the eastern side of the breakwater, cycling toward them. The swimmers dashed for their clothes.

In a few moments the policemen rode down and, throwing a perfunctory glance at the half-dressed bathers, they circled round and went off again. "*Salauds!*" Dengel said. "Always after us, but scared of the real criminals."

For the rest of the afternoon they basked in the sun on the breakwater. With its cooling they returned to the Place de la Joliette, where the group broke up to forage separately for food.

They came together again in the evening in a rendezvous bar of a somber alley, just a little bit out of the heart of the Ditch. Banjo had his instrument and was playing a little saccharine tune that he had brought over from America:

"I wanna go where you go, do what you do,
Love when you love, then I'll be happy . . ."

The souvenir of Latnah's foot in his mouth was a warm fever in Malty's flesh. And the red wine that he was drinking turned the fever sweet. It was a big night. The barkeeper, a thin Spanish woman, was busy setting up quart bottles of wine on the tables. Only black drinkers filled the little bar, and their wide-open, humorous, frank white eyes lighted up the place more glowingly than the dirty dim electric flare.

Senegalese, Sudanese, Somalese, Nigerians, West Indians, Americans, blacks from everywhere, crowded together, talking strange dialects, but, brought together, understanding one another by the language of wine.

"I'll follow you, sweetheart, and share your little love-nest.
I wanna go where you go . . ."

Malty had managed to get next to Latnah, and put his arm round her waist so quietly that it was some moments before she became aware of it. Then she tried to remove his arm and ease away, but he pressed against her thigh.

"Don't," she said. "I no like."

"What's the matter?" murmured Malty, thickly. "Kaint you like a fellah a li'l' bit?"

He pressed closer against her and said, "Gimmie a kiss."

She felt his strong desire. "*Cochon,* no. Go away from me." She dug him sharply in the side with her elbow.

"You' mout' it stink. I wouldn't kiss a slut like you," said Malty, and he got up and gave Latnah a hard push.

She fell off the bench and picked herself up, crying. She was not hurt by the fall, but by Malty's sudden change of attitude. Malty glowered at her boozily. Banjo stopped playing, went up to him, and shook his fist in his face.

"Wha's matter you messing around mah woman?"

"Go chase you'self. I knowed her long before you did, when she was running after me."

"You're a dawggone liar!"

"And youse another!"

"Ef it's a fight youse looking for, come on outside."

Banjo and Malty staggered off. At the door, Malty stumbled and nearly fell, and Banjo caught his arm and helped him into the street. All the boys crowded to the door and flowed out into the alley, to watch. The antagonists sparred. Malty hiccoughed ominously, swayed forward, and, falling into Banjo's arms, they both went down heavily, in a helpless embrace, on the paving-stones.

Banjo. New York: Harper and Brothers, 1929. 27–37.

D. H. LAWRENCE

From *The Woman Who Rode Away*

From Part 1

[. . .] Suddenly her horse jumped, and three men in dark blankets were on the trail before her.

"*Adios!*" came the greeting, in the full, restrained Indian voice.

"*Adios!*" she replied, in her assured, American woman's voice.

"Where are you going!" came the quiet question, in Spanish.

The men in the dark serapes had come closer, and were looking up at her.

"On ahead," she replied coolly, in her hard, Saxon Spanish.

These were just natives to her: dark-faced, strongly-built men in dark serapes and straw hats. They would have been the same as the men who worked for her husband, except, strangely, for the long black hair that fell over their shoulders. She noted this long black hair with a certain distaste. These must be the wild Indians she had come to see.

"Where do you come from?" the same man asked. It was always the one man who spoke. He was young, with quick, large, bright black eyes that glanced sideways at her. He had a soft black moustache on his dark face, and a sparse tuft of beard, loose hairs on his chin. His long black hair, full of life, hung unrestrained on his shoulders. Dark as he was, he did not look as if he had washed lately.

His two companions were the same, but older men, powerful silent. One had a thin black line of moustache, but was beardless. The other had the smooth cheeks and the sparse dark hairs marking the lines of his chin with the beard characteristic of the Indians.

"I come from far away," she replied, with half-jocular evasion.

This was received in silence.

"But where do you live?" asked the young man, with that same quiet insistence.

"In the north," she replied airily.

Again there was a moment's silence. The young man conversed quietly, in Indian, with his two companions.

"Where do you want to go, up this way?" he asked suddenly, with challenge and authority, pointing briefly up the trail.

"To the Chilchui Indians," answered the woman laconically.

The young man looked at her. His eyes were quick and black, and inhuman. He saw, in the full evening light, the faint sub-smile of assurance on her rather large, calm, fresh-complexioned face: the weary, bluish lines under her large blue eyes: and in her eyes, as she looked down at him, a half-childish, half-arrogant confidence in her own female power. But in her eyes also, a curious look of trance.

"*Usted es Señora? You* are a married lady?" the Indian said.

"Yes I am a lady," she replied complacently.

"With a family?"

"With a husband and two children, boy and girl," she said.

The Indian turned to his companions and translated, in the low, gurgling speech, like hidden water running. They were evidently at a loss.

"Where is your husband?" asked the young man.

"Who knows?" she replied airily. "He has gone away on business for a week."

The black eyes watched her shrewdly. She, for all her weariness, smiled faintly in the pride of her own adventure and the assurance of her own womanhood, and the spell of the madness that was on her.

"And what do you want to do?" the Indian asked her.

"I want to visit the Chilchui Indians—to see their houses and to know their Gods," she replied.

The young man turned and translated quickly, and there was a silence almost of consternation. The grave elder men were glancing at her sideways, with strange looks, from under their decorated hats. And they said something to the young man, in deep chest voices.

The latter still hesitated. Then he turned to the woman.

"Good!" he said. "Let us go. But we cannot arrive until to-morrow. We shall have to make a camp to-night."

"Good!" she said, "I can make a camp."

Without more ado, they set off at a fair speed up the stony trail. The young Indian ran alongside her horse's head, the other two ran behind. One of them had taken a thick stick, and occasionally he struck her horse a resounding blow on the haunch, to urge him forward. This made the horse jump, and threw her against the saddle horn, which, tired as she was, made her angry.

"Don't do that!" she cried, looking round angrily at the fellow. She met his black, large, bright eyes, and for the first time her spirit really quailed. The man's eyes were not human to her, and they did not see her as a beautiful white woman. He looked at her with a black, bright inhuman look, and saw no woman in her at all. As if she were some strange, unaccountable *thing*, incomprehensible to him, but inimical. She sat in her saddle in wonder, feeling once more as if she had died. And again he struck her horse, and jerked her badly in the saddle.

All the passionate anger of the spoilt white woman rose in her. She pulled her horse to a standstill, and turned with blazing eyes to the man at her bridle.

"Tell that fellow not to touch my horse again," she cried.

She met the eyes of the young man, and in their bright black inscrutability she saw a fine spark, as in a snake's eyes, of derision. He spoke to his companion in the rear, in the low tones of the Indian. The man with the stick listened without looking. Then, giving a strange low cry to the horse, he struck it again on the rear, so that it leaped forward spasmodically up the stony trail, scattering the stones, pitching the weary woman in her seat.

The anger flew like a madness into her eyes, she went white at the gills. Fiercely she reined in her horse. But before she could turn, the young Indian had caught the reins under the horse's throat, jerked them forward, and was trotting ahead rapidly, leading the horse.

The woman was powerless. And along with her supreme anger there came a slight thrill of exultation. She knew she was dead.

The sun was setting, a great yellow light flooded the last of the aspens, flared on the trunks of the pine-trees, the pine-needles bristled and stood out with dark lustre, the rocks glowed with unearthly glamour. And through this effulgence the Indian at her horse's head trotted unweariedly on, his dark blanket swinging, his bare legs glowing with a strange transfigured ruddiness, in the powerful light, and his straw hat with its half-absurd decorations of flowers and feathers shining showily above his river of long black hair. [. . .]

She was not aware how moonlight replaced daylight. It happened while she travelled unconscious with weariness.

For some hours they travelled by moonlight: Then suddenly they came to a standstill. The men conversed in low tones for a moment.

"We camp here," said the young man.

She waited for him to help her down. He merely stood holding the horse's bridle. She almost fell from the saddle, so fatigued.

They had chosen a place at the foot of rocks that still gave off a little warmth of the sun. One man cut pine-boughs, another erected little screens of pine-boughs against the rock, for shelter, and put boughs of balsam pine, for beds. The third made a small fire, to heat tortillas. They worked in silence.

The woman drank water. She did not want to eat—only to lie down.

"Where do I sleep?" she asked.

The young man pointed to one of the shelters. She crept in and lay inert. She did not care what happened to her, she was so weary, and so beyond everything. Through the twigs of spruce she could see the three men squatting round the fire on their hams. [. . .] There they squatted with their hats on their heads, eating, eating mechanically, like animals, the dark serape with its fringe falling to the ground before and behind, the powerful dark legs naked and squatting like an animal's, showing the dirty white shirt and the sort of loincloth which was the only other garment, underneath. And they showed no more sign of interest in her than if she had been a piece of venison they were bringing home from the hunt, and had hung inside a shelter.

After a while they carefully extinguished the fire, and went inside their own shelter. Watching through the screen of boughs, she had a moment's thrill of fear and anxiety, seeing the dark forms cross and pass silently in the moonlight. Would they attack her now?

But no! They were as if oblivious of her. Her horse was hobbled: she could hear it hopping wearily. All was silent, mountain-silent, cold, deathly. She slept and woke, and slept in a semiconscious numbness of cold and fatigue. A long, long night, icy and eternal, and she aware that she had died.

Yet when there was a stirring, and a clink of flint and steel, and the form of a man crouching like a dog over a bone, at a red splutter of fire, and she knew it was morning coming, it seemed to her the night had passed too soon.

When the fire was going, she came out of her shelter with one real desire left: for coffee. The men were warming more tortillas.

"Can we make coffee?" she asked.

The young man looked at her, and she imagined the same faint spark of derision in his eyes. He shook his head.

"We don't take it," he said. "There is no time."

And the elder men, squatting on their haunches, looked up at her in the terrible paling dawn, and there was not even derision in their eyes. Only that intense, yet remote, inhuman glitter which was terrible to her. They were inaccessible. They could not see her as a woman at all. As if she *were* not a woman. As if, perhaps, her whiteness took away all her womanhood, and left her as some giant, female, white ant. That was all they could see in her. [. . .]

From Part 2

She was a prisoner in her house and in the stockaded garden, but she scarcely minded. And it was days before she realized that she never saw another woman. Only the men, the elderly men of the big house that she imagined must be some sort of temple, and the men priests of some sort. For they always had the same colours, red, orange, yellow, and black, and the same grave, abstracted demeanour.

Sometimes an old man would come and sit in her room with her, in absolute silence. None spoke any language but Indian, save the one younger man. The older men would smile at her. [. . .] And they gave off a feeling of almost fatherly solicitude. Yet their dark eyes, brooding over her, had something away in their depths that was awesomely ferocious and relentless. They, would cover it with a smile, at once, if they felt her looking. But she had seen it.

Always they treated her with this curious impersonal solicitude, this utterly impersonal gentleness, as an old man treats a child. But underneath it she felt there was something else, something terrible. When her old visitor had gone away, in his silent, insidious, fatherly fashion, a shock of fear would come over her; though of what she knew not.

The young Indian would sit and talk with her freely, as if with great candour. But with him too she felt that everything real was unsaid. Perhaps it was unspeakable. His big dark eyes would rest on her almost cherishingly, touched with ecstasy, and his beautiful, slow, languorous voice would trail out its simple, ungrammatical Spanish. He told her he was the grandson of the old, old man, son of the man in the spotted serape: and they were caciques, kings from the old days, before even the Spaniards came. But he himself had been in Mexico City, and also in the United States. He had worked as a labourer, building the roads in Los Angeles. He had travelled as far as Chicago. [. . .]

"What did you do with your long hair, when you were in the United States?" she asked. "Did you cut it off?"

Again, with the look of torment in his eyes, he shook his head.

"No," he said, in the low, subdued voice, "I wore a hat, and a handkerchief tied round my head."

And he relapsed into silence, as if of tormented memories.

"Are you the only man of your people who has been to the United States?" she asked him.

"Yes. I am the only one who has been away from here for a long time. The others come back soon, in one week. They don't stay away. The old men don't let them."

"And why did you go!"

"The old men want me to go—because I shall be the Cacique."

He talked always with the same naïveté, an almost childish candour. But she felt that this was perhaps just the effect of his Spanish. Or perhaps speech altogether was unreal to him. Anyhow, she felt that all the real things were kept back.

He came and sat with her a good deal—sometimes more than she wished—as if he wanted to be near her. She asked him if he was married. He said he was—with two children.

"I should like to see your children," she said.

But he answered only with that smile, a sweet, almost ecstatic smile, above which the dark eyes hardly changed from their enigmatic abstraction.

It was curious, he would sit with her by the hour, without ever making her self-conscious, or sex-conscious. He seemed to have no sex, as he sat there so still and gentle and apparently submissive, with his head bent a little forward, and the river of glistening black hair streaming maidenly over his shoulders.

Yet when she looked again, she saw his shoulders broad and powerful, his eyebrows black and level, the short, curved, obstinate black lashes over his lowered eyes, the small, fur-like line of moustache above his blackish, heavy lips, and the strong chin; and she knew that in some other mysterious way he was darkly and powerfully male. And he, feeling her watching him, would glance up at her swiftly with a dark, lurking look in his eyes, which immediately he veiled with that half-sad smile.

The days and the weeks went by, in a vague kind of contentment. She was uneasy sometimes, feeling she had lost power over herself. She was not in her own power, she was under the spell of some other power. And at times she had moments of terror and horror. But then these Indians would come and sit with her, casting their insidious spell over her by their very silent presence, their silent, sexless, powerful physical presence. As they sat they seemed to take her will away, leaving her will-less and victim to her own indifference. [. . .]

The Dial 79 (July 1925): 8–12, 79; (December 1925): 121–23.

ROBERT MCALMON

White Males

White stallions dashed by.
I could see their teeth gleaming
Through their lips as they sneered
With death-laughter upon them.
Light poured in silver
Off their arched necks.
But there was blood upon their flanks,
Scarlet trickling upon the white sinews.
The stallions were prancing to death,
Trumpeting defiance with their nostrils.

White Chillingham bulls followed them.
I saw them gore the stallions,
But a wince of pain was across their eyes too.
Sharp horse-hoofs had struck them on the heart.
They fought with missing heart-beats
To plow on, tearing the soil with polished hoofs.
If they could only reach the forest,
If only to die there!
I could not help them.

I remembered dreams I had had
In which white mastodons trampled the plains,
Seeking to reach the forest before death.
And white Irish stags, ten men high,
With antlers that were giant trees with white bark,
Had stumbled under the weight of their own bulk.

A wince was across all their eyes—
But a smile, a never-mind tenderness.
Perhaps they were sure of coming into the purity
Because of their whiteness.

I knew why they were white:
They were dreams—all frozen,
And all white with the frost upon them,
And white with the frost all through them.
They were frozen thwarted male things
Rushing somewhere—
Seeking, fighting, and killing;
But white—say that of them.
The steam off their quivering flanks,
Sweated and weak with exhaustion, was white.
They would never find mates
Before they died.
There would be no more white males,
None so clear a white as these;
Only some tinged with gray—dusty.
But I could not watch them rush to the forest forever—
Not one did I see arrive there—
A cloud or night or blackness always intervened.
I saw them rush forward and disappear,
And then saw no more of them.

In *The Tyro*, ed., Wyndham Lewis. Adelphi: The Egoist Press, 1921–22. 6.

JOAN RIVIERE

From "Womanliness as a Masquerade"

[. . .]

In his paper on "The Early Development of Female Sexuality"[1] [Ernest Jones] sketches out a rough scheme of types of female development, which he first divides into heterosexual and homosexual, subsequently subdividing the latter

---

1. *This Journal*, 8 (1927).

homosexual group into two types. He acknowledges the roughly schematic nature of his classification and postulates a number of intermediate types. It is with one of these intermediate types that I am to-day concerned. In daily life types of men and women are constantly met with who, while mainly hetero-sexual in their development, plainly display strong features of the other sex. This has been judged to be an expression of the bisexuality inherent in us all; and analysis has shown that what appeals as homosexual or heterosexual char-acter-traits, or sexual manifestations, is the end-result of the interplay of con-flicts and not necessarily evidence of a radical or fundamental tendency. The difference between homosexual and heterosexual development results from differences in the degree of anxiety, with the corresponding effect this has on development. Ferenczi pointed out a similar reaction in behaviour,[2] namely, that homosexual men exaggerate their heterosexuality as a "defence" against their homosexuality. I shall attempt to show that women who wish for mas-culinity may put on a mask of womanliness to avert anxiety and the retribution feared from men.

It is with a particular type of intellectual woman that I have to deal. Not long ago intellectual pursuits for women were associated almost exclusively with an overtly masculine type of woman, who in pronounced cases made no secret of her wish or claim to be a man. This has now changed. Of all the women engaged in professional work to-day, it would be hard to say wheth-er the greater number are more feminine than masculine in their mode of life and character. In University life, in scientific professions and in business, one constantly meets women who seem to fulfil every criterion of complete fem-inine development. They are excellent wives and mothers, capable house-wives; they maintain social life and assist culture; they have no lack of femi-nine interests, e.g. in their personal appearance, and when called upon they can still find time to play the part of devoted and disinterested mother-sub-stitutes among a wide circle of relatives and friends. At the same time they fulfil the duties of their profession at least as well as the average man. It is really a puzzle to know how to classify this type psychologically.

Some time ago, in the course of an analysis of a woman of this kind, I came upon some interesting discoveries. She conformed in almost every particular to the description just given; her excellent relations with her hus-band included a very intimate affectionate attachment between them and full and frequent sexual enjoyment; she prided herself on her proficiency as a housewife. She had followed her profession with marked success all her life. She had a high degree of adaptation to reality, and managed to sustain

---

2. "The Nosology of Male Homosexuality." *Contributions to Psychoanalysis* (1916).

good and appropriate relations with almost everyone with whom she came in contact.

Certain reactions in her life showed, however, that her stability was not as flawless as it appeared; one of these will illustrate my theme. She was an American woman engaged in work of a propagandist nature, which consisted principally in speaking and writing. All her life a certain degree of anxiety, sometimes very severe, was experienced after every public performance, such as speaking to an audience. In spite of her unquestionable success and ability, both intellectual and practical, and her capacity for managing an audience and dealing with discussions, etc., she would be excited and apprehensive all night after, with misgivings whether she had done anything inappropriate, and obsessed by a need for reassurance. This need for reassurance led her compulsively on any such occasion to seek some attention or complimentary notice from a man or men at the close of the proceedings in which she had taken part or been the principal figure; and it soon became evident that the men chosen for the purpose were always unmistakeable father-figures, although often not persons whose judgement on her performance would in reality carry much weight. There were clearly two types of reassurance sought from these father-figures: first, direct reassurance of the nature of compliments about her performance; secondly, and more important, indirect reassurance of the nature of sexual attentions from these men. To speak broadly, analysis of her behaviour after her performance showed that she was attempting to obtain sexual advances from the particular type of men by means of flirting and coquetting with them in a more or less veiled manner. The extraordinary incongruity of this attitude with her highly impersonal and objective attitude during her intellectual performance, which it succeeded so rapidly in time, was a problem.

[. . .] She had quite conscious feelings of rivalry and claims to superiority over many of the "father-figures" whose favour she would then woo after her own performances! She bitterly resented any assumption that she was not equal to them, and (in private) would reject the idea of being subject to their judgement or criticism. In this she corresponded clearly to one type Ernest Jones has sketched: his first group of homosexual women who, while taking no interest in other women, wish for "recognition" of their masculinity from men and claim to be the equals of men, or in other words, to be men themselves. Her resentment, however, was not openly expressed; publicly she acknowledged her condition of womanhood.

Analysis then revealed that the explanation of her compulsive ogling and coquetting—which actually she was herself hardly aware of till analysis made it manifest—was as follows: it was an unconscious attempt to ward off the anxiety which would ensue on account of the reprisals she anticipated from the father-figures after her intellectual performance. The exhibition in public of her intellectual proficiency, which was in itself carried through successfully, signified an exhibition of herself in possession of the father's penis, having castrated him. The display once over, she was seized by horrible dread of the retribution the father would then exact. Obviously it was a step towards propitiating the avenger to endeavour to offer herself to him sexually. This phantasy, it then appeared, had been very common in her childhood and youth, which had been spent in the Southern States of America; if a negro came to attack her, she planned to defend herself by making him kiss her and make love to her (ultimately so that she could then deliver him over to justice). But there was a further determinant of the obsessive behaviour. In a dream which had a rather similar content to this childhood phantasy, she was in terror alone in the house; then a negro came in and found her washing clothes, with her sleeves rolled up and arms exposed. She resisted him, with the secret intention of attracting him sexually, and he began to admire her arms and to caress them and her breasts. The meaning was that she had killed father and mother and obtained everything for herself (alone in the house), became terrified of their retribution (expected shots through the window), and defended herself by taking on a menial role (washing clothes) and by *washing off* dirt and sweat, guilt and blood, everything she had obtained by the deed, and "disguising herself" as merely a castrated woman. In that guise the man found no stolen property on her which he need attack her to recover and, further, found her attractive as an object of love. Thus the aim of the compulsion was not merely to secure reassurance by evoking friendly feelings towards her in the man; it was chiefly to make sure of safety by masquerading as guiltless and innocent. It was a compulsive reversal of her intellectual performance; and the two together formed the "double-action" of an obsessive act, just as her life as a whole consisted alternately of masculine and feminine activities. [. . .]

Womanliness therefore could be assumed and worn as a mask, both to hide the possession of masculinity and to avert the reprisals expected if she was found to possess it—much as a thief will turn out his pockets and ask to be searched to prove that he has not the stolen goods. The reader may now ask how I define womanliness or where I draw the line between genuine womanliness and the "masquerade." My suggestion is not, however, that there is any such difference; whether radical or superficial, they are the same thing. The capacity for womanliness was there in this woman—and one might even say it exists in the most completely homosexual woman—but owing to her conflicts it did not represent her main development, and was used far more as a device for avoiding anxiety than as a primary mode of sexual enjoyment. [. . .]

In every-day life one may observe the mask of femininity taking curious forms. One capable housewife of my acquaintance is a woman of great ability, and can herself attend to typically masculine matters. But when, e.g. any builder or upholsterer is called in, she has a compulsion to hide all her technical knowledge from him and show deference to the workman, making her suggestions in an innocent arid artless manner, as if they were "lucky guesses." She has confessed to me that even with the butcher and baker, whom she rules in reality with a rod of iron, she cannot openly take up a firm straightforward stand; she feels herself as it were "acting a part," she puts on the semblance of a rather uneducated, foolish and bewildered woman, yet in the end always making her point. In all other relations in life this woman is a gracious, cultured lady, competent and well-informed, and can manage her affairs by sensible rational behaviour without any subterfuges. This woman is now aged fifty, but she tells me that as a young woman she had great anxiety in dealings with men such as porters, waiters, cabmen, tradesmen, or any other potentially hostile father-figures, such as doctors, builders and lawyers; moreover, she often quarrelled with such men and had altercations with them, accusing them of defrauding her and so forth.

Another case from every-day observation is that of a clever woman, wife and mother, a University lecturer in an abstruse subject which seldom attracts women. When lecturing, not to students but to colleagues, she chooses particularly feminine clothes: Her behaviour on these occasions is also marked by an inappropriate feature: she becomes flippant and joking, so much so that it has caused comment and rebuke. She has to treat the situation of displaying her masculinity to men as a "game," as something not real, as a "joke," She cannot treat herself and her subject seriously, cannot seriously contemplate herself as on equal terms with men; moreover, the flippant attitude enables some of her sadism to escape, hence the offence it causes. [. . .]

To return to the case I first described. Underneath her apparently satisfactory heterosexuality it is clear that this woman displayed well-known manifestations of the castration complex. Horney was the first among others to point out the sources of that complex in the Œdipus situation; my belief is that the fact that womanliness may be assumed as a mask may contribute further in this direction to the analysis of female development. [. . .]

Journal of Psycho-Analysis 8 (1929): 303–13.

ERNEST HEMINGWAY

From *The Garden of Eden*

From Chapter 1

[. . .] They were at the cafe now. The young man had put the tackle away, after the weighing, and washed up and the fish was on a block of ice that had come in the *camion* from Nîmes to ice the mackerel catch. The fish had weighed a little over fifteen pounds. On the ice he was still silver and beautiful but the color on his back had changed to gray. Only his eyes still looked alive. The mackerel fishing boats were coming in now and the women were unloading the shining blue and green and silver mackerel from the boats into baskets and carrying the heavy baskets on their heads to the fish house. It was a very good catch and the town was busy and happy.

"What are we going to do with the big fish?" the girl asked.

"They're going to take him in and sell him," the young man said. "He's too big to cook here and they say it would be wicked to cut him up. Maybe he'll go right up to Paris. He'll end in some big restaurant. Or somebody very rich will buy him."

"He was so beautiful in the water," she said. "And when André held him up. I couldn't believe him when I saw him out of the window and you with your mob following you."

"We'll get a small one for us to eat. They're really wonderful. A small one ought to be grilled with butter and with herbs. They're like striped bass at home."

"I'm excited about the fish," she said. "Don't we have wonderful simple fun?"

They were hungry for lunch and the bottle of white wine was cold and they drank it as they ate the celery *rémoulade* and the small radishes and the home pickled mushrooms from the big glass jar. The bass was grilled and the grill marks showed on the silver skin and the butter melted on the hot plate. There was sliced lemon to press on the bass and fresh bread from the bakery and the wine cooled their tongues of the heat of the fried potatoes. It was good light, dry, cheerful unknown white wine and the restaurant was proud of it.

"We're not great conversationalists at meals," the girl said. "Do I bore you, darling?"

The young man laughed.

"Don't laugh at me, David."

"I wasn't. No. You don't bore me. I'd be happy looking at you if you never said a word."

He poured her another small glass of the wine and filled his own.

"I have a big surprise. I didn't tell you, did I?" the girl said.

"What sort of surprise?"

"Oh it's very simple but it's very complicated."

"Tell me."

"No. You might like it and maybe you couldn't stand it."

"It sounds too dangerous."

"It's dangerous," she said. "But don't ask me. I'm going up to the room if I may."

The young man paid for the lunch and drank the wine that was left in the bottle. Then he went upstairs. The girl's clothes were folded on one of the Van Gogh chairs and she was waiting for him in the bed with the sheet over her. Her hair was spread out over the pillow and her eyes were laughing and he lifted the sheet and she said, "Hello, darling. Did you have a nice lunch?"

Afterwards they lay together with his arm under her head and were happy and lazy and he felt her turn her head from side to side and stroke it against his cheek. It felt silky and barely roughened from the sun and the sea. Then with her hair all forward over her face so it touched him as her head moved she started to play with him lightly and exploringly and then with delight and she said, "You do love me, don't you?"

He nodded and kissed the top of her head and then turned her head and held it and kissed her lips.

"Oh," she said. "Oh."

A long time later they were lying each holding the other close and she said, "And you love me just the way I am? You're sure."

"Yes," he said. "So much yes."

"Because I'm going to be changed."

"No," he said. "No. Not changed."

"I'm going to," she said. "It's for you. It's for me too. I won't pretend it's not. But it will do something to you. I'm sure but I shouldn't say it."

"I like surprises but I like everything the way it is just now at this minute."

"Then maybe I shouldn't do it," she said. "Oh I'm sad. It was such a wonderful dangerous surprise. I thought about it for days and I didn't decide until this morning."

"If it's something you really want."

"It is," she said. "And I'm going to do it. You've liked everything we've done so far haven't you?"

"Yes."

"All right."

She slipped out of bed and stood straight with her long brown legs and her beautiful body tanned evenly from the far beach where they swam without suits. She held her shoulders back and her chin up and she shook her head so her heavy tawny hair slapped around her cheeks and then bowed forward so it all fell forward and covered her face. She pulled the striped shirt over her head and then shook her hair back and then sat in the chair in front of the mirror on the dresser and brushed it back looking at it critically. It fell to the top of her shoulders. She shook her head at the mirror. Then she pulled on her slacks and belted them and put on her faded blue rope-soled shoes.

"I have to ride up to Aigues Mortes," she said.

"Good," he said. "I'll come too."

"No. I have to go alone. It's about the surprise."

She kissed him goodbye and went down and he watched her mount her bicycle and go up the road riding smoothly and easily, her hair blowing in the wind.

The afternoon sun was in the window now and the room was too warm. The young man washed and put on his clothes and went down to walk on the beach. He knew he should swim but he was tired and after he had walked along the beach and then along a path through the salt grass that led inland for a way he went back along the beach to the port and climbed up to the cafe. In the cafe he found the paper and ordered himself a *fine à l'eau* because he felt empty and hollow from making love.

They had been married three weeks and had come down on the train from Paris to Avignon with their bicycles, a suitcase with their town clothes, and a rucksack and a musette bag. They stayed at a good hotel in Avignon and left the suitcase there and had thought that they would ride to the Pont du Gard. But the mistral was blowing so they rode with the mistral down to Nîmes and stayed there at the Imperator and then had ridden down to Aigues Mortes still with the heavy wind behind them and then on to le Grau du Roi. They had been there ever since.

It had been wonderful and they had been truly happy and he had not known that you could love anyone so much that you cared about nothing else and other things seemed inexistent. He had many problems when he married but he had thought of none of them here nor of writing nor of anything but being with this girl whom he loved and was married to and he did not have the sudden deadly clarity that had always come after intercourse. That was gone. Now when they had made love they would eat and drink and make love again. It was a very simple world and he had never been truly happy in any other. He thought that it must be the same with her and certainly she acted in that way but today there had been this thing about the change and the surprise. But maybe it would be a happy change and a good surprise. The brandy and water as he drank it and read the local paper made him look forward to whatever it was.

This was the first time since they had come on the wedding trip that he had taken a drink of brandy or whiskey when they were not together. But he was not working and his only rules about drinking were never to drink before or while he was working. It would be good to work again but that would come soon enough as he well knew and he must remember to be unselfish about it and make it as clear as he could that the enforced loneliness was regrettable and that he was not proud of it. He was sure she would be fine about it and she had her own resources but he hated to think of it, the work, starting when they were as they were now. It never could start of course without the clarity and he wondered if she knew that and if that was why she drove beyond what they had for something new that nothing could break. But what could it be? [. . .]

He found that he had drunk the *fine à l'eau* and that it was getting late in the afternoon. He ordered another and started to concentrate on the paper. But the paper did not interest him as it should and he was looking out at the sea with late afternoon sun heavy on it when he heard her come into the cafe and say in her throaty voice, "Hello darling."

She came quickly to the table and sat down and lifted her chin and looked at him with the laughing eyes and the golden face with the tiny freckles. Her hair was cropped as short as a boy's. It was cut with no compromises. It was brushed back, heavy as always, but the sides were cut short and the ears that grew close to her head were clear and the tawny line of her hair was cropped close to her head and smooth and sweeping back. She turned her head and lifted her breasts and said, "Kiss me please."

He kissed her and looked at her face and at her hair and he kissed her again.

"Do you like it? Feel it how smooth. Feel it in back," she said.

He felt it in back.

"Feel on my cheek and feel in front of my ear. Run your fingers up at the sides.

"You see," she said. "That's the surprise. I'm a girl. But now I'm a boy too and I can do anything and anything and anything."

"Sit here by me," he said. "What do you want, brother."

"Oh thank you," she said. "I'll take what you're having. You see why it's dangerous, don't you?"

"Yes. I see."

"But wasn't I good to do it?"

"Maybe."

"Not maybe. No. I thought about it. I've thought all about it. Why do we have to go by everyone else's rules? We're us."

"We were having a good time and I didn't feel any rules."

"Would you please just put your hand over it again."

He did and he kissed her.

"Oh you're sweet," she said. "And you do like it. I can feel and I can tell. You don't have to love it just like it at first."

"I like it," he said. "And you have such a beautifully shaped head that it is very beautiful with the lovely bones of your face."

"Don't you like it at the sides?" she asked. "It isn't faked or phony. It's a true boy's haircut and not from any beauty shop."

"Who cut it?"

"The coiffeur at Aigues Mortes. The one who cut your hair a week ago. You told him how you wanted yours cut then and I told him to cut mine just the same as yours. He was very nice and wasn't at all surprised. He wasn't worried at all. He said exactly like yours? And I said exactly. Doesn't it do anything to you, David?"

"Yes," he said.

"Stupid people will think it is strange. But we must be proud. I love to be proud."

"So do I," he said. "We'll start being proud now"

They sat there in the cafe and watched the reflection of the setting sun over the water and watched the dusk come to the town and they drank the *fine* à *l'eau*. People came by the cafe without being rude to see the girl because they had been the only foreigners in the village and had been there now nearly three weeks and she was a great beauty and they liked her. Then there had been the big fish today and ordinarily there would have been much talk about that but this other was a big thing in the village too. No decent girls had ever had their hair cut short like that in this part of the country and even in Paris it was rare and strange and could be beautiful or could be very bad. It could mean too much or it could only mean showing the beautiful shape of a head that could never be shown as well.

They ate a steak for dinner, rare, with mashed potatoes and flageolets and a salad and the girl asked if they might drink Tavel. "It is a great wine for people that are in love," she said.

She had always looked, he thought, exactly her age which was now twenty-one. He had been very proud of her for that. But tonight she did not look it.

The lines of her cheekbones showed clear as he had never seen them before and she smiled and her face was heartbreaking.

In the room it was dark with only a little light from outside. It was cool now with the breeze and the top sheet was gone from the bed.

"Dave, you don't mind if we've gone to the devil, do you?"

"No, girl," he said.

"Don't call me girl."

"Where I'm holding you you are a girl," he said. He held her tight around her breasts and he opened and closed his fingers feeling her and the hard erect freshness between his fingers.

"They're just my dowry," she said. "The new is my surprise. Feel. No leave them. They'll be there. Feel my cheeks and the back of my neck. Oh it feels so wonderful and good and clean and new. Please love me David the way I am. Please understand and love me."

He had shut his eyes and he could feel the long light weight of her on him and her breasts pressing against him and her lips on his. He lay there and felt something and then her hand holding him and searching lower and he helped with his hands and then lay back in the dark and did not think at all and only felt the weight and the strangeness inside and she said, "Now you can't tell who is who can you?"

"No."

"You are changing," she said. "Oh you are. You are. Yes you are and you're my girl Catherine. Will you change and be my girl and let me take you?"

"You're Catherine."

"No. I'm Peter. You're my wonderful Catherine. You're my beautiful lovely Catherine. You were so good to change. Oh thank you, Catherine, so much. Please understand. Please know and understand. I'm going to make love to you forever."

At the end they were both dead and empty but it was not over. They lay side by side in the dark with their legs touching and her head was on his arm. The moon had risen and there was a little more light in the room. She ran her hand exploringly down over his belly without looking and said, "You don't think I'm wicked?"

"Of course not. But how long have you thought about that?"

"Not all the time. But quite a lot. You were so wonderful to let it happen."

The young man put his arms around the girl and held her very tight to him and felt her lovely breasts against his chest and kissed her on her dear mouth. He held her close and hard and inside himself he said goodbye and then goodbye and goodbye.

"Let's lie very still and quiet and hold each other and not think at all," he said and his heart said goodbye Catherine goodbye my lovely girl goodbye and good luck and goodbye.

From Chapter 2

He stood up and looked up and down the beach, corked the bottle of oil and put it in a side pocket of the rucksack and then walked down to the sea feeling the sand grow cool under his feet. He looked at the girl on her back on the sloping beach, her eyes closed, her arms against her sides, and behind her the slanted square of canvas and the first tufts of beach grass. She ought not to stay too long in that position with the sun straight up and down on her, he thought. [. . .]

During the night he had felt her hands touching him. And when he woke it was in the moonlight and she had made the dark magic of the change again and he did not say no when she spoke to him and asked the questions and he felt the change so that it hurt him all through and when it was finished after they were both exhausted she was shaking and she whispered to him, "Now we have done it. Now we really have done it."

Yes, he thought. Now we have really done it. And when she went to sleep suddenly like a tired young girl and lay beside him lovely in the moonlight that showed the beautiful new strange line of her head as she slept on her side he leaned over and said to her but not aloud, "I'm with you. No matter what else you have in your head I'm with you and I love you."

In the morning he had been very hungry for breakfast but he waited for her to wake. He kissed her finally and she woke and smiled and got up sleepily and washed in the big basin and slouched in front of the mirror of the armoire and brushed her hair and looked at the mirror unsmiling and then smiled and touched her cheeks with the tips of her fingers and pulled a striped shirt over her head and then kissed him. She stood straight so her breasts pushed against his chest and she said, "Don't worry, David. I'm your good girl come back again."

But he was very worried now and he thought what will become of us if things have gone this wildly and this dangerously and this fast? What can there be that will not burn out in a fire that rages like that? We were happy and I am sure she was happy. But who ever knows? And who are you to judge and who participated and who accepted the change and lived it? If that is what she wants who are you not to wish her to have it? You're lucky to have a wife like her and a sin is what you feel bad after and you don't feel bad. Not with the wine you don't feel bad, he told himself, and what will you drink when the wine won't cover for you?

He took the bottle of oil out of the rucksack and put a little oil on the girl's chin and on her cheeks and on her nose and found a blue faded patterned handkerchief in the canvas pocket of the rucksack and laid it across her breast.

"Must I stop?" the girl asked. "I'm having the most wonderful dream."

"Finish the dream," he said.

"Thank you."

In a few minutes she breathed very deeply and shook her head and sat up.

"Let's go in now," she said.

They went in together and swam out and then played under water like porpoises. When they swam in they dried each other off with towels and he handed her the bottle of wine that was still cool in the rolled newspaper and they each took a drink and she looked at him and laughed.

"It's nice to drink it for thirst," she said. "You don't really mind being brothers do you?"

"No." He touched her forehead and her nose and then her cheeks and chin with the oil and then put it carefully above and behind her ears.

"I want to get behind my ears and neck tanned and over my cheekbones. All the new places."

"You're awfully dark, brother," he said. "You don't know how dark."

"I like it," the girl said. "But I want to be darker."

They lay on the beach on the firm sand that was dry now but still cool after the high tide had fallen. The young man put some oil on the palm of his hand and spread it lightly with his fingers over the girl's thighs and they glowed warm as the skin took the oil. He went on spreading it over her belly and breasts and the girl said sleepily, "We don't look very much like brothers when we're this way do we?"

"No."

"I'm trying to be such a very good girl," she said. "Truly you don't have to worry darling until night. We won't let the night things come in the day."

[. . .]

New York: Simon & Schuster, 1986. 10–19, 20–22, 29–31, 107, 113–15.

12

Modernism, Gender, and Africa

**INTRODUCED AND SELECTED BY
TUZYLINE JITA ALLAN**

> Here comes the sun
> Softening the breasts of virgins
> Making old men smile on green benches
> Awakening the dead under a maternal earth. . . .
> They put flowers on tombs and warm the Unknown Soldier.
> But you, my dark brothers, no one calls your names.
> They promise five hundred thousand of your children the glory
> Of future deaths and thank them in advance, future dark dead.
> *Die Schwarze schande!*[1]
>
> —Léopold Senghor, "To the Senegalese Soldiers Who Died for France"
> (46–47)

> If I have any advice to give to the rising generation of Africa, it is this: NEVER
> be ashamed of your color . . . Be representative of the best of African life. I
> have found from experience that this is the only way to happiness; the only
> way to win the respect of other races; and the only way in which we can ever
> give a real contribution to the world.
>
> —Adelaide Casely Hayford, "The Life and Times of Adelaide Casely-
> Hayford" (789)

WRITTEN IN FRANCE in 1938, Senghor's elegy to the "tirailleurs sénégalais," the
ever-expanding French West African colonial army active in both world wars,
offers a snapshot of history that illuminates the diffuse coalition of interests
and activities associated with the concept of modernism. I begin with the
memorial to the forgotten African soldiers "who gave their lives on battlefields
all over the world to save the honor of the French nation" (Echenberg 166) to
draw attention to the links and tensions among the three elements of my title
and to open up a new line of inquiry in the crowded field of modernist studies.

In the first place, Senghor's poem lends historical support to the juxtaposition of Africa and modernism, whether the latter is conceptualized in ideological, political, or artistic terms. Senghor implicitly challenges the Eurocentric claim to both meanings of modernism, seen as "unidirectional" in favor of Europe (Feierman 28 n.3). Knowledge of the centrality of Africa's role in European modernity, from the first encounter in the fifteenth century to the Atlantic slave trade and colonialism, changes this trajectory dramatically. "The universalizing discourses of modern Europe and the United States assume the silence, willing or otherwise, of the non-European world," as Edward Said has noted (28), and nowhere has the impact been greater than in the discursive traditions of modernism.

The poem therefore brings a shock of recognition to the subject by invoking a bloody memory buried under the rhetoric of European triumphalism. "The First World War," Myron Echenberg writes, "exacted a heavy toll on West African soldiers. Over five years of combat, FWA [French West Africa] furnished 170,891 men. [. . .] Casualties for black Africans ran at approximately 185 per thousand, or 30,000 killed in action" (46). The numbers rose sharply during the Second World War to the point where "seven African divisions and three other colonial divisions out of the eighty French divisions defend[ed] the borders of France in 1939" (88). Shenghor made his own contribution as a soldier and German POW in World War II. His angry response to the suppression of information concerning Africa's mortal sacrifice in the precipitating events of modernist history is, therefore, not only justified, it also suggests that the poet was already contemplating a philosophical challenge to European discursive hegemony, the kind that was to find expression in the pro-black aesthetics of negritude.

The poem's subtext is equally significant. Its recall of the blood-soaked relations between Africa and the West also brings up another kind of blood relations, those linking the African "dark dead" with their diasporic counterparts. No doubt, their heroism in battle in the teeth of racial discrimination establishes a common ground, but the poem's incantational *"Die Schwarze schande"* (black shame) invokes an even longer span of shared history, one marked by a perpetuating cycle of racial humiliation. Since negritude and Pan-Africanism went into high gear in part to put an end to this cycle of shame, it can be said that the big turn of history's wheel occasioned by the two great wars of the twentieth century helped to steer the black world toward the sobering view of an alternative African modernity. The African American contribution to this effort spread over several fronts, but in all it was a telling acknowledgment of Africa's emerging importance. Focusing on the years between 1937 and 1957, Penny M. Von Eschen observes:

> The diaspora politics of this period stood in a complex relationship to African nation-building projects. Those black Americans who constructed diaspora identities did not posit themselves as members or potential members of a nation or advocate a return to Africa in the sense of a back-to-Africa movement. Yet the politics they fashioned did constitute a re-turning toward Africa and an identity defined in relation to Africa. (3)

This gesture of "re-turning" is a dominant trope that emerged from such diverse settings as the eighteenth-century polemics of Olaudah Equiano and other black Atlanticists and the nineteeth-century proto-Pan-Africanism[2] of Martin Delaney, Edward Wilmot Blyden, and Alexander Crummell. In its intense articulations under full-blown Pan-Africanism during the inter-war years, the ideological template for African nationality (and modernity) was firmly in place. Although it took many turns, the theme of return that, as George Shepperson points out, accounts for "most of the elements in the Negro American's influence on Africa" (301) provided a wider base for the effort to galvanize resistance to colonial rule within Africa and pave the way for nation-building in Africa. His summation of Marcus Garvey's influence is particularly illuminating in light of Senghor's evocation of the poisonous legacy of shame: "If Garvey's 'Back-to-Africa' scheme, his Black Star Line, collapsed when he was deported from America in 1927, his massive propaganda for pride, *not shame*, in a black skin left an ineradicable mark on African nationalism everywhere" (303; emphasis added). The project to transform the "shame" of race or nationlessness into pride links Senghor and Garvey, Africa and the African diaspora, the literary and political strands of African modernism.

The texts included in this section by W. E. B. Du Bois and Alain Locke capture a sense of the crucial influence African Americans exerted on Africa's emerging modernity. It is impossible to contract the expansive meanings Africa held in the enormous imagination of W. E. B Du Bois. One of his early essays on Africa, "The African Roots of War" (1915), demonstrates the penetrating focus this theme receives in his canon. Here it serves a fitting intertextual role, as its interlocking tableaus of the continent's history of victimization and exploitation cascade toward the source of the raging economic, military, cultural, and psychic wars in Africa: "the color line." This structure, as Levering Lewis puts it, "paid huge dividends" (504). In his 1978 essay "World War I and Africa" Richard Rathbone reluctantly acknowledges the unequal relationship between his two subjects when he writes: "Fundamentally World War I *seems* to have accelerated the process of political and economic change in colonial Africa" (4, emphasis added). Du Bois had made the case much earlier in the century, leaving no doubt about causes and effects.

Alain Locke's note of optimism in "Afro-Americans and West Africans: A New Understanding" provides a counter-balance not only to Du Bois's censorious tone but also to the unsettling social realities presented in the African women's texts we will be examining. Addressing members of the London-based West African Student's Union in 1929, Locke warned against the overexploitation of racial difference. In the aftermath of the First World War, he believed a "revolution" was needed in "the making of a new Africa," one that would banish "narrow and selfish nationalism" and "narrow and selfish racialism." Locke was making a moral as well as an intellectual argument. He believed the "old order [was] disappearing," yielding to a "new internationalism" based on interdependency. The speech encapsulates Locke's prototypical arguments on race expressed in the lectures he gave at Howard University in 1915, 1916, and 1928.

The elusiveness of modernity as a goal for Africa—now a resonant theme of the postcolonial era—was already a flash point for frustration among a small group of pioneering African male writers early in the twentieth century. Three texts, in particular, deserve mention in this regard. Two of these, Joseph E. Casely Hayford's *Ethiopia Unbound* (1911) and Solomon Plaatje's *Mhudi*, written between 1917 and 1920 and published in 1930, vie for the coveted status as the first black African novel in English and have consequently received considerable critical attention as ur-texts of African cultural nationalism. The third, Kobina Sekyi's satirical play *The Blinkards*, was performed in the Gold Coast (now Ghana) in 1915 and 1917. While both the author and his play remained obscure until its publication in 1974, Sekyi has been rightly reinstated as a critical voice in the African modernist tradition.[3]

Both the expression of modernity in Sengor's poem, and the prominence of a set of African male writers in literary history give rise to questions of gender. In the ethics of war, the soldier is the masculinized symbol of national pride—a longing for the sovereignty of African nationhood to restore the masculine dignity lost to colonial domination. In *Women and War in South Africa*, Jacklyn Cock reminds us that "armies and wars are gendering activities [. . . that touch] men and women differently" (51). So is the rhetoric of nationhood. Homi K. Bhabha's notion of the nation as "wavering between vocabularies" (2)—public and private, communal and individual, progressive and regressive—explains women's precarious location within its borders. For African women, nation-building has not been a profitable enterprise since the new nations have failed to extend to women the kinds of protections imagined in Senghor's poem.

None among the small but distinguished group of elite, evolué women, whose professional and political careers—like Senghor's—grew out of the anti-colonial struggle, has been accorded the historical prominence lavished on

Senghor or Sekyi. Jane Turrittin casts light on one of these neglected pioneering women, the midwife Aoua Keita, author of a rare autobiographical account of female political activism in colonial French West Africa: "Keita's access to alternative knowledge led her to question aspects of African traditions, as well as to work to change the 'traditional' place of women in African societies by promoting women's rights and opposing both French colonialism and patriarchy" (73). In the social histories of women and men in colonial Africa, access to Western knowledge was fraught with gender-based realities that permeated the deepest levels of modern African societies, resulting in stronger masculine forays into the modern world. Women with similar aspirations were slower on the draw, impeded largely by the colonial vision of a domesticated African womanhood.

Taken together, the narratives by Adelaide Casely Hayford (1868–1960), Charlotte Manye Maxeke (1874–1939), and Mabel Dove-Danquah (1905–84) map the effects of gender on the new trajectory of women's engagement with modernity in colonial Africa. These women, generally, have been ignored in mainstream (read male-generated) African critical discourse. Breaking the silence in a recent article, Naana Jane Opoku-Agyemang writes:

> Dove-Danquah's first published short story, "The Happenings of the Night," appeared in serialized form in her own column, "Ladies Corner" in *The Times of West Africa*, between 14 September and 3 October 1931. This point is important because it shows an African woman writer in the early 1930s having almost complete control over her manner of literary production. (69)

Casely Hayford's memoirs were also published serially between October 1953 and August 1954 in one of the period's important journals, *The West African Review*. The first installment began with the following editorial comments: "Mrs. Casely Hayford's story is one which deserves to be made known to the people of West Africa, who are not, in the main, aware of the tremendous changes in social habit and economic circumstances that have taken place within the lifetime of a single living person. But the reminiscences are more than a social document; they are the memories of a wonderful lady whose like has not occurred before in West Africa."[4] Adding to this glowing testimonial the fact that her short story "Mister Courifer" was included in Langston Hughes's anthology of transatlantic black writers, *An African Treasury* (1961), leads one to ponder the reasons for the longstanding indifference to such a fascinating life. Indeed, until the publication of her biography, *An African Victorian Feminist: Adelaide Smith Casely Hayford, 1868–1960*, by Adelaide M. Cromwell in 1986, she remained hidden behind the shadow of her famous husband.

Compared to her West African counterparts, Maxeke has not been as invisible, though she is still missing in many analyses of South African history. Ironically, in the wake of third-wave transnational feminism, a heightened focus on race and gender relations in South Africa has brought into sharper focus her career as a political activist. In the newly published anthology *Women Writing Africa: The Southern Region,* she is referred to as "arguably the greatest black South African apostle of modernity in that country" of her time, one who "enabled the connections with the black culture across the Atlantic that made the construction of South African modernity possible" (Daymond et al. 195). The statement provides a vantage point for assessing and, ultimately, integrating the various strategic visions of African modernity presented in these texts.

Born in 1874 into a Xhosa family in the Cape Province of South Africa, Charlotte Manye Maxeke holds a number of distinctions, stemming from a combination of ingenuity and what has been aptly described as "exceptional luck" (Coquery-Vidrovitch 191). Both were first evident at the time her choir was sent on a concert tour to Britain, a successful experiment repeated two years later and expanded to include Canada and the United States. With the help of some members of the African Methodist Episcopal Church (AMEC), she attended Wilberforce University in Ohio, where she met W. E. B. Du Bois, who later penned the foreword to a brief biography of her written by Alfred Xuma, future president of the African National Congress: "I have known Charlotte Manye Maxeke since 1894 when I first went to Wilberforce University as a teacher. She was one of three or four students from South Africa and was the only woman. She was especially the friend of Nina Gomer, the student who afterward became my wife" (see Xuma 8). Disappointingly, David Levering Lewis fails to mention Maxeke in his account of Du Bois's years at Wilberforce, but he captures the ambiance at the institution sufficiently for one to surmise its religious and intellectual influences on the young African woman (See Lewis 150–78).

Returning home in 1901 with the honor of being the first black South African female college graduate, Maxeke became a worthy challenger of her nation's racial and gender systems of oppression, which she regarded as impediments to progress. In 1903 she married Marshall Maxeke, one of the South African students she had helped to bring to Wilberforce University. Thereafter, under the auspices of the South African AMEC and through personal initiative, Maxeke worked tirelessly to empower women and men in the primary areas of social life in South Africa, including education, politics, the courts, and the black family. With her husband, she established in 1908 Wilberforce Institute in the Transvaal; she founded the Bantu Women's League, which later became the ANC Women's League, and served as president for both organizations; as the first black woman probation officer, she worked in the courts and was directly involved in the rampant crises of black family life; and she organized and led resistance to pass laws.

This spirit of struggle was expressed theoretically as well as practically. In the dynamic instability of South African society at the turn of the century, Maxeke created a critical space to reflect on Africa's conflict as a civilization with Europe. She blamed the instruments of state power and a misaligned Christianity that did not practice what it preached. She translated her understanding of the "new Negro" and "uplift" philosophies of African Americans into a political craft that promoted a relationship with the encroaching modern age but criticized its ruinous effects on black family life. A veteran public speaker proficient in English, Dutch, and several local African languages, she spoke persistently about the erosion of black rights, the appalling plight of the black family and the need to maintain the vitality of the black woman, who held the seeds to the nation's future. "Motherhood," according to Cheryl Walker, "was central to African women's personal and cultural identity as well as their social and economic roles long before the advent of Christian missions in South Africa. But church groups served to transform, elevate and entrench the importance of marriage, wifehood and motherhood for women" (271). These themes reverberate in "Social Conditions among Bantu Women and Girls," a speech Maxeke gave at a conference of European and Bantu Christian Student Associations at the University of Fort Hare in 1930. In South Africa's racially charged political climate, "charity, welfare, concern about the breakdown of 'the family' and moral values—particularly, the breakdown of 'traditional' values and controls within African society—these were areas middle-class black and white women could meet, even agree, without serious challenge to white hegemony" (Walker 329).

The texts by Casely Hayford and Dove-Danquah also reveal the impact of colonial hegemony on the new African cultural landscape. The latter is gender-marked as the province of the new African man, fully or partially educated, and through him we draw the difficult lesson that he has been born into a fault line, resulting in a personal crisis of confidence that is symptomatic of a culture in turmoil. This, of course, is the realm of literature where truth is rendered by suggestion but takes on permanent value. The themes of identity linking the two West African texts reflect deep-seated anxieties over the changing nature of African societies and the pathologies of the new social order. Casely Hayford's exhortation of "the rising generation of Africa," provided above in the second epigraph, is, in effect, a counter-manifesto uttered at the dawn of Africa's independence from colonial rule. It is no coincidence that it invokes Du Bois's pronouncement, made at the century's dawn, that "the problem of the twentieth century is the problem of the color line" (3). Casely Hayford had even deeper transatlantic connections than Maxeke. Born Adelaide Smith in Freetown, Sierra Leone, in 1868 to an elite Krio family, she spent her early years in England and studied music at the Stuttgart Conservatory in Germany. In 1903 she married the Ghanaian-born lawyer and Pan-Africanist, Joseph Casely Hayford. Unlike the Maxekes, who were married the same year, the Casely Hayford union dissolved shortly after the birth in 1906 of their daughter, Gladys, a poet-to-be.

Upon her return to Freetown, Adelaide launched her dream-project to establish a girl's school, but first she had to raise money. Consequently, she made two trips to the United States, with her niece in 1920 to 1922 and singly in 1926. During the first, more successful trip, she met many of the black intelligentsia and cultural icons of the period: Du Bois, Mrs. Booker T. Washington, Nannie Burroughs, Walter White, Mary McLeod Bethune, Paul Robeson, Jessie Fauset, and the leaders of the Coloured Presbyterian Church in New York. In addition, she visited several of the notable black educational institutions: Tuskegee, Spelman, Howard University, and Dunbar High School. According to her biographer, "Mrs. Casely Hayford became well known to the N.A.A.C.P. and to Dr. DuBois for on 21 October 1921, at the second Pan-African Congress, of which DuBois was a key organizer, Miss Jessie Fawcett [sic] of the N.A.A.C.P. mentioned in her talk the work being done by blacks in the United States and that Mrs. Casely Hayford and Miss Easmon were then on a mission seeking their help in the United States" (Cromwell 127). At the end of this trip Casely Hayford had garnered sufficient respect and admiration among black intellectual circles to establish a reputation independent of her husband's. More significantly, she became the public face for Sierra Leonean aspirations. She devoted the ensuing years to running the Girls' Vocational and Industrial Training School, from its inception in 1923 through 1940, when it was closed for lack of money. During this period she was also a member of the Marcus Garvey movement and, involving herself more directly with the Freetown community, she became a strong advocate for the replacement of western clothing with African dress. Clothes, in her view, were a mark of identity and in time she would be pleased with the signs of change in this area of social life. "Instead of blindly copying European fashions, which are made to suit a white woman's personality," she writes in her memoirs, "our women now have come to realize that every race has its own distinctive dress, with its own appeal—and its own suitability for particular climatic conditions" (Cromwell 144). It is not surprising, therefore, that the omniscient narrative voice in "Mister Courifer" is that of the cultural nationalist, devastatingly satirical of Tomas Courifer, the mimic man: "Mr. Courifer always wore black. He was one of the Sierra Leone gentlemen who consider everything European to be not only the right thing, but the *only* thing for the African, and having read somewhere that English undertakers generally appeared in sombre attire, he immediately followed suit." There is, of course, a huge difference between Mr. Courifer's view of things English and his opinion of African women, whom he regards as handmaidens. The narrative perspective is clear: Mr. Courifer is a cultural misfit who deserves to forfeit his future.

In Dove-Danquah's "The Torn Veil" the psychic cost of modernity is even greater. The protagonist's increased capacity for self-delusion comes with an enhanced risk of self-destruction to himself and others. To top off his public image as a new member of the educated elite, Kwame Asante decides to abandon his unschooled wife for one not as educated as he is (that would close the gender gap) but one with just enough education to earn some money. His ego is bruised when the "cloth woman" stands her ground, refuses to be bought off, and returns to her family. Kwame goes ahead with the wedding of his "second choice," anyway, and falling asleep on his passionless wedding night, he has a dream of the deserted woman, resplendent in a wedding dress, with a coquettish smile to boot. Desire wells up in him and he lunges to catch her. He accidentally hits his head and dies. The spot of "joy" on the dead man's face, like the "joy that kills" Kate Chopin's protagonist in "The Story of an Hour," carries the story's irony. But this ghost story has real-life implications. The "torn veil" symbolizes the rending of the African social fabric as traditional values are displaced by new codes of conduct that have not been adequately comprehended.

Dove-Danquah, a pioneering journalist, was born in Ghana in 1905 and educated at home and abroad. Like her older contemporaries, she spent brief periods of time in England and the United States. She also lived in Sierra Leone, where she helped to establish the Sierra Leone Women's Movement in 1951. Back in Ghana, she was appointed editor of the *Accra Evening News*. In 1952 she became the first West African woman to be voted into Parliament. Among her first acts in office was "a motion . . . that customary marriage laws be changed so that 'cloth women' . . . married according to traditional custom could not be divorced so easily by husbands who wanted to marry 'frock ladies'" (Denzer 100). The main medium for Dove-Danquah's message about the ambiguities of social change was journalism. Under the pseudonym Marjorie Mensah she animated her "Ladies Corner" in the *West Africa Times* with social commentary. Unlike her famous husband, J. B. Danquah, who wrote that traditionally married women should "do all domestic and some of the farm work" (Allman 244), Dove-Danquah called for subaltern speech and agency.

Hence, far from being a historical anomaly, as their marginalization suggests, early modernist women in Africa were part of a global black intellectual culture that tracked the shifts in thought and behavior on the continent. The effort to shake off patriarchal, colonial, and racial legacies knit together various black "apostles of modernity,"[5] including Du Bois and Locke. The texts selected here represent a critical intervention in the current effort to re-theorize modernity as "importantly regional, multiple, vernacular, or 'other' in character" (Knauft 1)—a move that enlarges the intellectual vistas of modernism.

Notes

1. "The black shame" was the term used in the German press to describe the humiliating outcome of France's use of colonial troops to occupy Rhineland. See Echenberg, 35.

2. Fryer uses the term "proto-Pan-Africanist" to describe Martin Delany, Edward Wilmot Blyden, and Africanus Horton (273).

3. Sekyi's short story, "The Angels Fanti," appears in Nancy Cunard's 1934 *Negro Anthology*.

4. *West African Review* (October 1958): 1058.

5. This term can be traced to Olufemi Taiwo's "Prophets Without Honor: African Apostles of Modernity in the Nineteenth Century," *West Africa Review* 3.1 (2001). http://www.westafricareview.com/vol.13.1/3.1warhtm.

Works Cited

Allman, Jean, Susan Geiger, and Nakangibe Musisi, eds. *Women in African Colonial Histories*. Bloomington: Indiana University Press, 2002.

Bhabha, Homi K., ed. *Nation and Narration*. London: Routledge, 1990.

Bruner, Charlotte H., ed. *Unwinding Threads: Writing by Women in Africa*. London: Heinemann, 1983.

Casely Hayford, Adelaide. "The Life and Times of Adelaide Casely-Hayford." *West African Review* (October 1953–August 1954).

Casely Hayford, J. E. *Ethiopia Unbound*. London: C. M. Phillips, 1911.

Cock, Jacklyn. *Women and War in South Africa*. Cleveland: Pilgrim Press, 1993.

Coquery-Vidrovitch, Catherine. *African Women: A Modern History*. Trans. Beth Gillian Raps. Boulder: Westview Press, 1997.

Cromwell, Adelaide M. *An African Victorian Feminist: The Life and Times of Adelaide Smith Casely Hayford, 1868–1960*. London: Frank Cass, 1986.

Daymond, M. J., *et al.*, eds. *Women Writing Africa: The Southern Region*. New York: Feminist Press, 2003.

Denzer, LaRay, ed. *Contance Agatha Cummings-John: Memoirs of a Krio Leader*. Ibadan, Nigeria: Sam Bookman, 1995.

Du Bois, W. E. B. *The Souls of Black Folk*. New York: Vintage, 1990.

Echenberg, Myron. *Colonial Conscripts: The Tirailleurs Sénégalais in French West Africa, 1857–1960*. Portsmouth, N.H.: Heinemann, 1991.

Feierman, Steven. "Africa in History: The End of Universal Narratives." In *After Colonialism: Imperial Histories and Postcolonial Displacements*, ed. Gyan Prakash. Princeton: Princeton University Press, 1994. 40–65.

Fryer, Peter. *Staying Power: The History of Black People in Britain.* London: Pluto Press, 1984.

Gikandi, Simon, ed. *Encyclopedia of African Literature.* New York: Routledge, 2003.

Itayemi, Phebean, and Mabel Dove-Danquah. *The Torn Veil and Other Stories.* London: Lutterworth Press, 1947.

Knauft, Bruce M., ed. *Critically Modern: Alternatives, Alterities, Anthropologies.* Bloomington: Indiana University Press, 2002.

Lewis, David Levering. *W. E. B. Du Bois: The Fight for Equality and the American Century, 1919–1963.* New York: Henry Holt, 2000.

———. *W. E. B. Du Bois: Biography of a Race, 1868–1919.* New York: Henry Holt, 1993.

Locke, Alain LeRoy. *Race Contacts and Interracial Relations: Lectures on the Theory and Practice of Race,* ed. Jeffrey C. Stewart. Washington: Howard University Press, 1992.

Long, Richard A. *Africa and America: Essays in Afro-American Culture.* Atlanta: Center for African and African-American Studies, Atlanta University, 1981.

Opoku-Agyemang, Naana Jane. "Recovering Lost Voices: The Short Stories of Mabel Dove-Danquah," ed. Stephanie Newell. *Writing African Women: Gender, Popular Culture, and Literature in West Africa.* London: Zed Books, 1997.

Plaatje, Sol T. *Mhudi.* ed., Stephen Gray. London: Heinemann, 1978.

Rathbone, Richard. "World War I and Africa: Introduction." In *Journal of African History* 19.1 (1978): 1–9.

Said, Edward. "Secular Interpretation, the Geographical Element, and the Methodology of Imperialism." In *After Colonialism: Imperial Histories and Postcolonial Displacements,* ed. Gyan Prakash. Princeton: Princeton University Press, 1994. 21–39.

Sekyi, Kobina. *The Blinkards.* London: Rex Collings, 1974.

Senghor, Léopold Sédar. *The Collected Poetry,* trans. Melvin Dixon. Charlottesville: University Press of Virginia, 1998.

Shepperson, George. "Notes on Negro American Influences on the Emergence of African Nationalism." In *Journal of African History* 1.2 (1960): 299–312.

Stewart, Jeffrey C., ed. *The Critical Temper of Alain Locke: A Selection of His Essays on Art and Culture.* New York: Garland, 1983.

Turrittin, Jane. "Colonial Midwives and Modernizing Childbirth in French West Africa." *Women in African Colonial Histories,* ed. Jean Allman, Susan Geiger, and Nakanyike Musisi. Bloomington: Indiana University Press, 2002.

Von Eschen, Penny M. *Race Against Empire: Black Americans and Anticolonialism, 1937–1957.* Ithaca: Cornell University Press, 1997.

Walker, Cheryl, ed. *Women and Gender in Southern Africa to 1945.* London: James Currey, 1990.

WĀSÚ: The Journal of the West African Students Union of Great Britain and Ireland. Editorial. 1932 and 1933.

Weinberg, Meyer, ed. *W. E. B. Du Bois: A Reader.* New York: Harper & Row, 1970.

Xuma, Alfred. *Charlotte Manye (Maxeke) or "What an Educated African Girl Can Do,"* ed. Dovie King Clarke. The Women's Parent Mite Missionary Society of the A.M.E. Church, 1930.

W. E. B. DU BOIS

The African Roots of War

"Semper novi quid ex Africa," cried the Roman proconsul; and he voiced the verdict of forty centuries. Yet there are those who would write world history and leave out this most marvelous of continents. Particularly today most men assume that Africa lies far afield from the centers of our burning social problems, and especially from our present problem of world war.

Yet in a very real sense Africa is a prime cause of this terrible overturning of civilization which we have lived to see; and these words seek to show how in the dark continent are hidden the roots, not simply of war today but of the menace of wars tomorrow.

Always Africa is giving us something new or some metempsychosis of a world-old thing. On its black bosom arose one of the earliest, if not the earliest, of self-protecting civilizations, and grew so mightily that it still furnishes superlatives to thinking and speaking men. Out of its darker and more remote forest fastnesses, came, if we may credit many recent scientists, the first welding of iron, and we know that agriculture and trade flourished there when Europe was a wilderness.

Nearly every human empire that has arisen in the world, material and spiritual, has found some of its greatest crises on this continent of Africa, from Greece to Great Britain. As Mommsen says, "It was through Africa that Christianity became the religion of the world." In Africa the last flood of Germanic invasions spent itself within hearing of the last gasp of Byzantium, and it was again through Africa that Islam came to play its great role of conqueror and civilizer. [. . .]

The methods by which this continent has been stolen have been contemptible and dishonest beyond expression. Lying treaties, rivers of rum, murder, assassination, mutilation, rape, and torture have marked the progress of Englishman, German, Frenchman, and Belgian on the dark continent. The only way in which the world has been able to endure the horrible tale is by deliberately stopping its ears and changing the subject of conversation while the deviltry went on.

It all began, singularly enough, like the present war, with Belgium. Many of us remember Stanley's great solution of the puzzle of Central Africa when he traced the mighty Congo sixteen hundred miles from Nyangwe to the sea. Suddenly the world knew that here lay the key to the riches of Central Africa.

It stirred uneasily, but Leopold of Belgium was first on his feet, and the result was the Congo Free State—God save the mark! But the Congo Free State, with all its magniloquent heralding of Peace, Christianity, and Commerce, degenerating into murder, mutilation, and downright robbery, differed only in degree and concentration from the tale of all Africa in this rape of a continent already furiously mangled by the slave trade. That sinister traffic, on which the British Empire and the American Republic were largely built, cost black Africa no less than 100,000,000 souls, the wreckage of its political and social life, and left the continent in precisely that state of helplessness which invites aggression and exploitation. "Color" became in the world's thought synonymous with inferiority, "Negro" lost it capitalization, and Africa was another name for bestiality and barbarism.

Thus the world began to invest in color prejudice. The "Color Line" began to pay dividends. [. . .]

Why was this? What was the new call for dominion? It must have been strong, for consider a moment the desperate flames of war that have shot up in Africa in the last quarter of a century France and England at Fashoda, Italy at Adua, Italy and Turkey in Tripoli, England and Portugal at Delagoa Bay, England, Germany, and the Dutch in South Africa, France and Spain in Morocco, Germany and France in Agadir, and the world at Algeciras. [. . .]

With the waning of the possibility of the Big Fortune, gathered by starvation wage and boundless exploitation of one's weaker and poorer fellows at home, arose more magnificently the dream of exploitation abroad. Always, of course, the individual merchant had at his own risk and in his own way tapped the riches of foreign lands. Later, special trading monopolies had entered the field and founded empires overseas. Soon, however, the mass of merchants at home demanded a share in this golden stream; and finally, in the twentieth century, the laborer at home is demanding and beginning to receive a part of his share. [. . .]

Such nations it is that rule the modern world. Their national bond is no mere sentimental patriotism, loyalty, or ancestor-worship. It is increased wealth, power, and, luxury, for all classes on a scale the world never saw before. Never before was the average citizen of England, France, and Germany so rich, with such splendid prospects of greater riches.

Whence comes this new wealth and on what does its accumulation depend? It comes primarily from the darker nations of the world—Asia and Africa, South and Central America, the West Indies, and the islands of the South Seas. There are still, we may well believe, many parts of white countries like Russia and North America, not to mention Europe itself, where the older exploitation still holds. But the knell has sounded faint arid far, even there.

In the lands of darker folk, however, no knell has sounded. Chinese, East Indians, Negroes, and South American Indians are by common consent for governance by white folk and economic subjection to them. To the furtherance of this highly profitable economic dictum has been brought every available resource of science and religion. Thus arises the astonishing doctrine of the natural inferiority of most men to the few, and the interpretation of "Christian brotherhood" as meaning anything that one of the "brothers" may at any time want it to mean.

Like all world-schemes, however, this one is not quite complete. First of all, yellow Japan has apparently escaped the cordon of this color bar. This is disconcerting and dangerous to white hegemony. If, of course, Japan would join heart and soul with the whites against the rest of the yellows, browns, and blacks, well and good. There are even good-natured attempts to prove the Japanese "Aryan," provided they act "white." But blood is thick, and there are signs that Japan does not dream of a world governed mainly by white men. This is the "Yellow Peril," and it may be necessary, as the German Emperor and many white Americans think, to start a world crusade against this presumptuous nation which demands "white" treatment.

Then, too, the Chinese have recently shown unexpected signs of independence and autonomy, which may possibly make it necessary to take them into account a few decade's hence. As a result, the problem in Asia has resolved itself into a race for "spheres" of economic "influence," each provided with a more or less "open door" for business opportunity. [. . .]

One thing, however, is certain: Africa is prostrate. There at least are few signs of self-consciousness that need at present be heeded. To be sure, Abyssinia must be wheedled, and in America and the West Indies Negroes have attempted futile steps toward freedom; but such steps have been pretty effectually stopped (save through the breech of "miscegenation"), although the ten million Negroes in the United States need, to many men's minds, careful watching and ruthless repression.

Thus the white European mind has worked, and worked the more feverishly because Africa is the Land of the Twentieth Century. The world knows something of the gold and diamonds of South Africa, the cocoa of Angola and Nigeria, the rubber and ivory of the Congo, and the palm oil of the West Coast. But does the ordinary citizen realize the extraordinary economic advances of Africa and, too, of black Africa, in recent years? E. T. Morel, who knows his Africa better than most white men, has shown us how the export of palm oil from West Africa has grown from 283 tons in 1800, to 80,000 tons in 1913, which together with by-products is worth today $60,000,000 annually. He shows how native Gold Coast labor, unsupervised, has come to head the cocoa-producing countries of the world with an export of 89,000,000 pounds (weight *not* money) annually. He shows how the cotton crop of Uganda has risen from 3,000 bales in 1909 to 50,000 bales in 1914; and he says that France and Belgium are no more remarkable in the cultivation of their land than the Negro province of Kano. [. . .] There can be no doubt of the economic possibilities of Africa in the near future. There are not only the well-known and traditional products, but boundless chances in a hundred different directions, and above all, there is a throng of human beings who, could they once be reduced to the docility and steadiness of Chinese coolies or of seventeenth- and eighteenth-century European laborers, would furnish to their masters a spoil exceeding the gold-haunted dreams of the most modern of imperialists.

[. . .] Thus, more and more, the imperialists have concentrated on Africa. The greater the concentration the more deadly the rivalry. From Fashoda to Agadir, repeatedly the spark has been applied to the European magazine and a general conflagration narrowly averted. We speak of the Balkans as the storm-center of Europe and the cause of war, but this is mere habit. The Balkans are convenient for occasions, but the ownership of materials and men in the darker world is the real prize that is setting the nations of Europe at each other's throats today.

The present world war is, then, the result of jealousies engendered by the recent rise of armed national associations of labor and capital whose aim is the exploitation of the wealth of the world mainly outside the European circle of nations. These associations, grown jealous and suspicious at the division of the spoils of trade-empire, are fighting to enlarge their respective shares; they look for expansion, not in Europe but in Asia, and particularly in Africa. "We want no inch of French territory," said Germany to England, but Germany was "unable to give" similar assurances as to France in Africa.

The difficulties of this imperial movement are internal as well as external. Successful aggression in economic expansion calls for a close union between capital and labor at home. Now the rising demands of the white laborer, not simply, for wages but for conditions of work and a voice in the conduct of industry, make industrial peace difficult. The workingmen have been appeased by all sorts of essays in state socialism, on the one hand, and on the other hand by public threats of competition by colored labor. By threatening to send English capital to China and Mexico, by threatening to hire Negro laborers in America, as well as by old-age pensions and accident insurance, we gain industrial peace at home at the mightier cost of war abroad.

In addition to these national war-engendering jealousies there is a more subtle movement arising from the attempt to unite labor and capital in world-wide free-booting. Democracy in economic organization, while an acknowledged ideal, is today working itself out by admitting to a share in the spoils of capital only the aristocracy of labor—they more intelligent and shrewder and cannier workingmen. The ignorant, unskilled, and restless still form a large, threatening, and, to a growing extent, revolutionary group in advanced countries.

The resultant jealousies and bitter hatreds tend continually to fester along a color line. We must fight the Chinese, the laborer argues, or Chinese will take our bread and butter. We must keep Negroes their places, or Negroes will take our jobs. All over the world there leaps to articulate speech and ready action that singular assumption that if white men do not throttle colored men, then China, India, and Africa will do to Europe what Europe has done and seeks to do to them.

On the other hand, in the minds of yellow, brown, and black men the brutal truth is clearing: a white man is privileged to go to any land where advantage beckons and behave as he pleases; the black or colored man is being more and more confined to those parts of the world where life for climatic, historical, economic, and political reasons is most difficult to live and most easily dominated by Europe for Europe's gain.

What, then, are we, to do, who desire peace and the civilization of all men? Hitherto the peace movement has confined itself chiefly to figures about the cost of war and platitudes on humanity. What do nations care about the cost of war, if by spending a few hundred millions in steel and gunpowder they can gain a thousand millions in diamonds and cocoa? How can love of humanity appeal as a motive to nations whose love of luxury is built on the inhuman exploitation of human beings, and who, especially in recent years, have been taught to regard these human beings as inhuman? I appealed to the last meeting of peace societies in St. Louis, saying, "Should you not discuss racial prejudice as a prime cause of war?" The secretary was sorry but was unwilling to introduce controversial matters!

We, then, who want peace, must remove the real causes of war. We have extended gradually our conception of democracy beyond our social class to all social classes in our nation; we have gone further and extended our democratic ideals not simply to all classes of our own nation, but to those of other nations, of our blood and lineage—to what we call "European" civilization. If we want real peace and lasting culture, however, we must go further. We must extend the democratic ideal to the yellow, brown, and black peoples.

To say this, is to evoke on the faces of modern men a look of blank hopelessness. Impossible! we are told, and for so many reasons—scientific, social, and what not—that argument is useless. But let us not conclude too quickly. Suppose we have to choose between this unspeakably inhuman outrage on decency and intelligence and religion which we call the World War and the attempt to treat black men as human, sentient, responsible beings? We have sold them as cattle. We are working them as beasts of burden. We shall not drive war from this world until we treat them as free and equal citizens in a world democracy of all races and nations. Impossible? Democracy is a method of doing the impossible. It is the only method yet discovered of making the education and development of all men a matter of all men's desperate desire. It is putting firearms in the hands of a child with the object of compelling the child's neighbors to teach him, not only the real and legitimate uses of a dangerous tool but the uses of himself in all things. Are there other and less costly ways of accomplishing this? There may be in some better world. But for a world just emerging from the rough chains of an almost universal poverty, and faced by the temptation of luxury and indulgence through the enslaving of defenseless men, there is but one adequate method of salvation—the giving of democratic weapons of self-defense to the defenseless.

Nor need we quibble over those ideas—wealth, education and political power—soil which we have so forested with claim and counterclaim that we see nothing for the woods.

What the primitive peoples of Africa and the world need and must have if war is to be abolished is perfectly clear:—

First: land. Today Africa is being enslaved by the theft of her land and natural resources. A century ago black men owned all but a morsel of South Africa. The Dutch and England came, and today 1,250,000 white own 264,000,000 acres, leaving only 21,000,000 acres for 4,500,000 natives. Finally, to make assurance doubly sure, the Union of South Africa has refused natives even the right to *buy* land. This is a deliberate attempt to force the Negroes to work on farms and in mines and kitchens for low wages. All over Africa has gone this shameless monopolizing of land and natural resources to force poverty on the masses and reduce them to the "dumb-driven-cattle" stage of labor activity.

Secondly: we must train native races in modern civilization. This can be done. Modern methods of educating children, honestly and effectively applied, would make modern, civilized nations out of the vast majority of human beings on earth today. This we have seldom tried. For the most part Europe is straining every nerve to make over yellow, brown, and black men into docile beasts of burden, and only an irrepressible few are allowed to escape and seek (usually abroad) the education of modern men.

Lastly, the principle of home rule must extend to groups, nations, and races. The ruling of one people for another people's whim or gain must stop. This kind of despotism has been in later days more and more skillfully disguised. But the brute fact remains: the white man is ruling black Africa for the white man's gain, and just as far as possible he is doing the same to colored races elsewhere. Can such a situation bring peace? Will any amount of European concord or disarmament settle this injustice?

Political power today is but the weapon to force economic power. Tomorrow, it may give us spiritual vision and artistic sensibility. Today, it gives us or tries to give us bread and butter, and those classes or nations or races who are without it starve, and starvation is the weapon of the white world to reduce them to slavery.

We are calling for European concord today; but at the utmost European concord will mean satisfaction with, or acquiescence in, a given division of the spoils of world dominion. After all, European disarmament cannot go below the necessity of defending the aggressions of the whites against the blacks and browns and yellows. From this will arise three perpetual dangers of war. First, renewed jealousy at any division of colonies or spheres of influence agreed upon, if at any future time the present division comes to seem unfair. Who cared for Africa in the early nineteenth century? Let England have the scraps left from the golden feast of the slave trade. But in the twentieth century? The end was war. These scraps looked too tempting to Germany. Secondly, war will come from the revolutionary revolt of the lowest workers. The greater the international jealousies, the greater the corresponding costs of armament and the more difficult to fulfill the promises of industrial democracy in advanced' countries. Finally, the colored peoples will not always submit passively to foreign domination. To some this is a lightly tossed truism. When a people deserve liberty they fight for it and get it, say such philosophers; thus making war a regular, necessary step to liberty. Colored people are familiar with this complacent judgment. They endure the contemptuous treatment meted out by whites to those not "strong" enough to be free. These nations and races, composing as they do a vast majority of humanity, are going to endure this treatment just as long as they must and not a moment longer. Then they are going to fight and the War of the Color Line will outdo in savage inhumanity any war this world has yet seen. For colored folk have much to remember and they will not forget.

But is this inevitable? Must we sit helpless before this awful prospect? While we are planning, as a result of the present holocaust, the disarmament of Europe and a European international world-police, must the rest of the world be left naked to the inevitable horror of war, especially when we know that it is directly in this outer circle of races, and not in the inner European household, that the real causes of present European fighting are to be found?

Our duty is clear. Racial slander must go. Racial prejudice will follow. Steadfast faith in humanity must come. The domination of one people by another, without the other's consent, be the subject people black or white, must stop. The doctrine of forcible economic expansion over subject peoples must go. Religious hypocrisy must stop. "Bloodthirsty" Mwanga of Uganda killed an English bishop because they feared that his coming meant English domination. It did mean English domination, and the world and the bishop knew it, and yet the world was "horrified!" Such missionary hypocrisy must go. With clean hands and honest hearts we must front high Heaven and beg peace in our time.

In this great work who can help us? In the Orient, the awakened Japanese and the awakening leaders of New China; in India and Egypt, the young men trained in Europe and European ideals, who now form the stuff that revolution is born of. But in Africa? Who better than the twenty-five million grandchildren of the European slave trade, spread through the Americas and now writhing desperately for freedom and a place in the world? And of these millions first of all the ten million black folk of the United States, now a problem, then a world salvation.

Twenty centuries before the Christ a great cloud swept over sea and settled on Africa, darkening and well-nigh blotting out the culture of the land of Egypt. For half a thousand years it rested there until a black woman, Queen Nefertari, "the most venerated figure in Egyptian history," rose to the throne of the Pharaohs and redeemed the world and her people. Twenty centuries after Christ, black Africa, prostrate, raped, and shamed, lies at the feet of the conquering Philistines of Europe. Beyond the awful sea a black woman is weeping and waiting with her sons on her breast. What shall the end be? The world-old and fearful things, War and Wealth, Murder and Luxury? Or shall it be a new thing— a new peace and new democracy of all races: a great humanity of equal men? "Semper novi quid ex Africa!"

Atlantic Monthly 115 (May 1915): 707–14. Rpt. in *Black Titan: W. E. B. DuBois, ed.* John Henrik Clarke, Esther Jackson, Ernest Kaiser, and J. H. O'Dell. Boston: Beacon Press, 1970.

ALAIN LOCKE

Afro-Americans and West Africans: A New Understanding

Gentlemen of the West African Student's Union,

That I might speak to you with greatest sincerity and as a friend to friends I have come before you to-night without a prepared address so that I can speak the thoughts that come spontaneously from both my mind and heart as they respond, with pleasure and deep satisfaction, to this reunion of the young African with the young Afro-American mind. This happens far too seldom. I am convinced that it is to our mutual advantage to work toward a spiritual re-union and mutual understanding between the now separated branches of the Negro peoples.

This re-union will be the more constructive, the more it can be worked out in terms of a new and fuller understanding with the younger generation and the more representative classes of our several peoples. Because as students we shall make contact with one another without prejudice and without immediate commitment to definite programs and shall study one another's conditions first before attempting any practical program of action. It has been the error of most of our previous contacts to have ignored this first essential of the meeting of minds in mutual and sympathetic understanding. As students and in terms of student relationships, I see in you and in this occasion the greatest promise of an eventual helpful relation and co-operation, not so much between the masses of our respective peoples, as between those who are or are to be the directing minority of leadership on either side. What we call the "New Negro" mind is reaching out in intelligent ways towards Africa; and it seems to me that some of Young Africa's greatest opportunities may be found in American experience and training. Eventually I think we shall be of great practical use to one another,— but first we must understand each other—and that is primarily the task of our younger educated classes.

You represent, on your side, the very element of which I speak. For myself, I must frankly confess that I belong to the middle generation, the bridge between the old and the new; but I hold opinion with the new and hope I can speak somewhat representatively to-night for the attitude of the young American Negro. It is this generation, your true contemporaries, whom you must come to understand and with whom, I hope, you are to collaborate toward the making of a new Africa. Indeed, to see at all into the future to-day one must look with the eyes of youth and think in terms of the great revolutions which on every side are transforming the world about us. In the turmoil of the great war and its after-math, the old order is disappearing; and this new world which is emerging from post-war confusion is our race's great hope and opportunity. To grasp which you as coming leaders of the people must think largely, looking through the moribund present to the quickening future. In this time of revolution our racial thinking must rise to a higher plane; and just as there is no room in progressive thought to-day for narrow and selfish nationalism, so there is also no proper place for narrow and selfish racialism. Our thought and plans, warrantably focused upon the improvement and welfare of the Negro peoples, must nevertheless be consistent with the progressive and constructive trends of the new world order and of the internationalism upon which it is based. Instead of forming our philosophy and program upon a counter-attitude to the old order and the older schools of political and social thought, we must in spite of reproach, social stigma, repression and persecution, turn with vision to the new world that is in the making and work constructively toward its realisation.

The New Negro thought which with us in America is transforming the outlook of the Afro-Americans in so many vital ways is based largely upon such an attitude. And if we turn toward one another in the spirit of this new internationalism there will be nothing in our plans or actions that would be inconsistent with the most progressive and constructive trends of the world to-day. Let me try to explain this difference in our thought, about Africa to-day. For generations our thought has naturally been molded by that of the dominant race in America. We are, let us frankly confess, Americans and when we have thought about Africa we have for the most part thought as Americans. The circumstances of our coming into America through slavery have inevitably led to a complete adoption of the elements and background of American civilisation. Except in relative social position and economic power, due of course to our treatment as a repressed minority, there is little or no difference between us and the other races in the country. Our first task has been to prove ourselves capable of assimilating our environment, of mastering the thoughts and the tools of the civilisation in the midst of which we have been placed. It is only now that we are well on in a process of doing this that we can in any profitable way turn back to our African background and to the thought of our peculiar cultural derivation and heritage. Even in this there is no radical difference, since the white American is also a man of two continents, culturally speaking; he happens to be Euro-American, and we, Afro-American. Both of us the new American background and culture is basic, but in our larger living we must more and more trace back to our separate heritages. To-day the American Negro is culturally re-discovering Africa and many lines of thinking are trying to bridge the broken span between us and the Motherland and to make the racial background effective in our group life and culture.

This has been a task of generations,—for our first directions of cultural outlook, owing to the wholesale adoption of Christianity and the English language, were necessarily European. And at that stage we saw Africa through a glass darkly, at second remove, sentimentally through the eyes of Christian missionarism. Only gradually are we lifting our minds above the limitations and bias of the Euro-American outlook. Yet to-day we are looking freshly and inquiringly and directly at Africa. To do this we cannot be expected to abandon the position of our adopted and acquired civilisation, though we must extend and revise its point of view with respect to Africa. And we can only hope to do this through your help and co-operation; it is the African who must educate the Afro-American about Africa. Otherwise we shall come to you as we too often have in the past sharing the illusions and compounding the condescension of our Nordic teachers. But if we are to draw fresh cultural strength from our own peculiar resources our thought must entirely free itself from the all, too prevalent misconceptions of our homeland and its culture and thus master a third continent. Difficult as this is, we can accomplish it with your co-operation and bring about a more vital contact between Western civilisation and your own than any yet made or thought possible. In the end, under modern conditions that people will be most efficient who live in terms of the greatest possible synthesis of civilisations, and we welcome this difficult task which our peculiar heritage and history imposes upon us.

It is for this reason that I say that our thought regarding Africa has shifted from the sentimental to the intellectual; we now realise that the first step is to understand Africa and to discover what the educated, forward-looking African has as his program. At least, ours is no longer the attitude of the missionary who judges Africa from his own point of view, and plans to save it. Indeed, in the light of our own practical situation, our talk of African redemption, well-intentioned as it was, was nevertheless an unwarrantable presumption. The first brand of this pious sentimentalism was in terms of missionary Christianity: we were exhorted to help save the "Dark Continent" from benighted heathendom. Considerably later came several movements to tackle African political problems; to launch a crusade to relieve Africa of the domination of economic imperialism and to effect her political redemption. Both programs were hastily undertaken in ignorance of the true situation; in the one case we underestimated the cultural situation in Africa and in the other we over-estimated our own powers of action. Either program without the co-operation on the large scale of African leaders was futile. As long as we had this unsympathetic one-sided point of view, it made little practical difference in the situation that the well-intentioned missionaries were brown and black instead of white. There are many who still continue to think of Africa in one or other of these ways, but I wish to assure you that representative young Negro thought in America does not. Instead of formulating policies without concrete knowledge, we are now seeking for knowledge as a necessary foundation for understanding and subsequent practical work: and, in place of redemption, we are now beginning to think of the value of Africa to us and of the possibilities and prospects of mutually helpful co-operation.

The essential difference between the old and the new school of thought may be stated thus:—

1. The new view considers Africa, primarily from its own point of view and does not seek to impose an alien point of view. We realise that we must look to the African for information about conditions and needs in Africa and for a program which will meet those conditions and needs. Our practical ambition is to second any efforts made by the intelligent leadership of Africa in the direction of self-development and self-help.

2. We realise also that any effective contacts between us must be mutual and upon the basis of a co-operative exchange in which we have as much to learn and to gain as you, perhaps more. It will be fortunate if in our different situations our needs are complementary, as I think they really are.

Thus in our day the old isolation must be brought to an end by an intelligent exchange of ideas. This will be the more constructive the more we let go the idea that we can think better for each other than we can think for ourselves. We cannot, neither you for us nor we for you. But each side can study profitably the conditions of the other and can reinforce progressive action without any attempt to impose programs from the outside. It is very easy, for example, to sit in London and devise plans to put a stop to lynching, and just as easy to sit in New York and fulminate against colonial domination and injustice in Africa. Sensible people know that in both cases for the time being the *status quo* is inevitable, and that the only remedy is to bring about from within a change of the conditions which have produced it. And so we each need to know the specific facts of our several situations and the programs with the greatest practical worth and enlightenment coming out of these situations. Thus we can morally reinforce and strengthen one another in many ways and can focus world opinion upon our most progressive plans and elements.

It is a pleasure to tell you that this newer attitude toward Africa is characteristic of progressive thought in America to-day among both white and black. But of course it is naturally the Afro-Americans who most need and are most eager for better knowledge of a country which they have hitherto seen through the white man's eyes as a vast expanse of marshes, exhaling miasmatic poisons which would kill them in three days, if they succeeded for so long, in evading the bloodthirsty savages who infested its fever-stricken jungles. We now have the right attitude, entirely different, but we need intimate and more reliable information from those in a position to be intelligent spokesmen for Africa. As I sense the mind of our representative youth they are waiting such detailed enlightenment; their spirits surely are ripe for it. As evidence, may I quote you this poem of one of our younger writers,— Lewis Alexander's Sonnet "To Africa":—

Thou art not dead, although the spoiler's hand
Lies heavy as death upon thee; though the wrath
Of its accursed might is thy path
And has usurped thy children of their land,
Though yet the scourges of a monstrous band,
Roam on thy ruined fields, thy trampled lanes,
Thy ravaged homes and desolated fanes;
A mighty country, valorous and free,
Thou shalt outlive this terror and this pain;
Shall call thy scattered children back to thee,
Strong with the memory of their brothers slain;
And rise from out thy charnel house to be
Thine own immortal brilliant self again.

But it is not enough to be sentimentally interested in Africa; we must build new bridges of understanding. On our side the bonds between us and the Motherland have been rudely broken down—you must remember that we have been taught to despise Africa, and that the first American Negro poet, Phillis Wheatley, thanked Providence for her deliverance even through the hard way of slavery:—

"'Twas mercy brought me from my pagan land," she sang. It has taken generations to undo these illusions. However more we do not yet come into contact with the most representative elements of African life; and so we must come to you and you must come to us. I should be ashamed to urge this with such insistence had I not myself made some effort in that direction. I have not yet seen as much of Africa as I should have, but in 1923 I did start on the first of what was to have been a series of African trips. The first, which was to the Near East, Egypt, and the Soudan, did reach completion. My program, which unfortunately was interrupted, was to follow this in subsequent years by three annual trips of five months each on academic leave to West, South, and Central Africa. It is still my ambition to make one or more of these visits, but the nearest approach that I have recently been able to make has been to spend part of two summers at Geneva studying for the Foreign Policy Association of New York the operation of the Mandates System, with particular references to the African mandated territories. But we must have more than occasional contacts. Indeed we very badly need in America some local point for information about Africa and for the study of both the past history and the present conditions of Africa. I hope to see some such centre developed, but it cannot be without the interest and co-operation of representative Africans who sense the need and importance of educating their brothers in America with respect to their common problems and traditions.

It is therefore with more than any individual's gain in mind that I urge you to widen your outlook and extend your education by coming to America, at least for a visit, but if possible for a year or two of study before returning to your homes. Most of you have come to England for professional training, and this is proper. But for your social education, which is also of such importance since you are to be leaders of opinion, it seems to be of the greatest advantage that you should see the interesting laboratory experiment of the eleven million Afro-Americans in process of rapid adaptation to the ways and methods of the most modern Western civilization. Indeed you need some of its technique in Africa, especially in those typical American fields of professional training in education, business administration, social science, and the technical professions. Since you have come so far already, the additional time and expense can be wisely added to increase the mental capital which you will take home for the difficult tasks of your generation. I have just been reading your admirable journal, *Wasu;* it is very inspiring. I am particularly glad to notice in the current issue an article by Mr. Robb, friend and former student, pointing out in detail the opportunities and the expenses for study in our American colleges and universities.

We have many desirable schools, and the choice among them is most used on their separate specialities according to your individual programs. The general universities and colleges of America in the north and west are open to you as they are open to us, without restriction. But for most if you I can see great advantages in study at the Negro schools, of which a few are of standard grade and fully adequate equipment. For in these, in addition to a standard American training, you gain intimate insight into the race life in America, its advances, its problems, its ambitions. Our situation differs in many respects from yours, but that very difference is educational in broadening your social outlook. I speak especially of Howard University, without apology,—not merely because it is our largest university of strictly collegiate grade with a full program of accredited professional courses, but because of two additional factors of importance. One is the fact of its location at the capital of the country, centrally placed between the northern and the southern States where the problems of deepest racial importance can be studied without too great social inconvenience for the foreigner. The other is the fact that we have there a progressive Negro administration, an achievement of which we are proud and out of loyalty to which I have chosen to remain at my post there rather than accept academic calls elsewhere. The President, Dr. Mordecai Johnson, is especially interested to have the institution become an exchange centre for progressive thought on the race question both in its national and international aspects; he and his co-workers, let me assure you will welcome you cordially. It may be that here we can develop that strategic centre of contact between Afro-Americans and their fellows from the motherland of which I spoke. In America many students are wholly or partially self-supporting; I notice you have as your motto the slogan of "Self-help." I urge you to come as self-reliant adventurers, hazarding a chance and willing to make sacrifices. Too many Africans have come over to us in the kindly palm of the missionary. You know what this means, they have not been of the most representative type, and what we need is to have your future leaders meet ou[r] prospective leaders and knit themselves together in some sort of constructive sympathy and understanding.

You will find your brothers in America at the most interesting stage of their development. The hard apprenticeship of slavery is just bearing its mature fruits. The acute effects of our sudden introduction into an alien environment and culture are just wearing off. We are in the midst of a spiritual quickening in which we are breaking free of slavish imitation and casting about for group ideals and values of our own. From a submerged and passive and almost negligible class; we have become a self: conscious and racially proud minority with a peculiar group momentum and fresh spiritual objectives. What you have heard of as the Negro Renaissance and as the emergence of the "New Negro" is an interesting reality of contemporary American life now being taken seriously by the liberal minds of the white majority. This it will be your privilege to see and share, for it focuses in our younger generation which is of college age. The spirit of it, however, permeates all our more progressive circles, and is as much evidenced in the practical world of economic enterprise and civic spirit as it where it first started in the sphere of intellectual, artistic, and cultural expression. We have much yet to accomplish, but never have we been more confident. We have earned all that we possess, and have paid a heavy cost price for the mastery of the technique of Western civilisation which is so important for both our future and yours. We are no longer dazzled or awed by the white man's culture, but wish to use its best elements toward fresh expressions of our own. Probably as a result of the hard discipline of slavery as much as by reason of our rapid educational advance, we are taking a profounder view of life than many of our fellow citizens, and though we cannot invite you to riches and power we can invite you to spiritual seriousness and insight. I wish Negro youth to conclude this message for me. The writer of this poem, at twenty-four is one of the leading poets of America and, as well, one of the spokesmen of our new racial awakening. So eager was he to see Africa that before he had finished college he took ship as a sailor and worked his way to coin to see you. Few met him, but he saw your country, and the inspiration of it has entered not only in the making of his poetry but into the heart of the younger generation who need to know you and whom you need to know. You will, I am sure, catch the vision and message of Langston Hughes's poem, "The Negro Speaks of Rivers."

> I've known rivers:
> I've known rivers ancient as the world and older than the flow of human
>   blood in human veins.
> My soul has grown deep like the rivers.
> I bathed in the Euphrates when dawns were young.
> I built my hut near the Congo and it lulled me to sleep.
> I looked upon the Nile and raised the Pyramids above it.
> I heard the singing of the Mississippi when Abe Lincoln
>   went down to New Orleans, and I've seen its muddy
>   bosom turn all golden in the sunset.
> I've known rivers:
> Ancient, dusky rivers.
> My soul has grown deep like the rivers.

This is the spirit of your contemporaries and brothers who greatly wish to see you and in whose name I ask you to turn your steps and your thoughts toward America.

Address delivered to the West African Students' Union. *The Journal of the West African Students' Union of Great Britain* 8 (January 1929): 18–24.

CHARLOTTE MAXEKE

Social Conditions among Bantu Women and Girls

In speaking of Bantu women in urban areas, the first thing to be considered is the Home, around which and in which the whole activity of family life circulates. First of all, the Home is the residence of the family, and home and family life are successful only where husband and wife live happily together, bringing up their family in a sensible way, sharing the responsibilities naturally involved in a fair and wholehearted spirit. The woman, the wife, is the keystone of the household: she holds a position of supreme importance, for is she not directly and intimately concerned with the nurturing and upbringing of the children of the family, the future generation? She is their first counsellor, and teacher; on her rests the responsibility of implanting in the flexible minds of her young, the right principles and teachings of modern civilisation. Indeed, on her rests the failure or success of her children when they go out into life. It is therefore essential that the home atmosphere be right, that the mother be the real "queen" of the home, the inspiration of her family, if her children are to go out into the world equipped for the battles of life.

There are many problems pressing in upon us Bantu, to disturb the peaceful working of our homes. One of the chief is perhaps the stream of Native life into the towns. Men leave their homes, and go into big towns like Johannesburg, where they get a glimpse of a life such as they had never dreamed existed. At the end of their term of employment they receive the wages for which they have worked hard, and which should be used for the sustenance of their families, but the attractive luxuries of civilisation are in many instances too much for them, they waste their hard earned wages, and seem to forget completely the crying need of their family out in the field.

The wife finds that her husband has apparently forgotten her existence, and she therefore makes her hard and weary way to the town in search of him. When she gets there, and starts looking round for a house of some sort in which to accommodate herself and her children, she meets with the first rebuff. The Location Superintendent informs her that she cannot rent accommodation unless she has a husband. Thus she is driven to the first step on the downward path, for if she would have a roof to cover her children's heads a husband must be found, and so we get these poor women forced by circumstances to consort with men in order to provide shelter for their families. Thus we see that the authorities in enforcing the restrictions in regard to accommodation are often doing Bantu society a grievous harm, for they are forcing its womanhood, its wedded womanhood, to the first step on the downward path of sin and crime.

Many Bantu women live in the cities at a great price, the price of their children; for these women, even when they live with their husbands, are forced in most cases to go out and work, to bring sufficient into the homes to keep their children alive. The children of these unfortunate people therefore run wild, and—as there are not sufficient schools to house them in, it is easy for them to live an aimless existence, learning crime of all sorts in their infancy almost.

If these circumstances obtain when husband and wife live together in the towns, imagine the case of the woman, whose husband has gone to town and left her, forgetting apparently all his responsibilities. Here we get young women, the flower of the youth of the Bantu, going up to towns in search of their husbands, and as I have already stated, living as the reputed wives of other men, because of the location requirements, or becoming housekeepers to men in the locations and towns, and eventually their nominal wives.

In Johannesburg, and other large towns, the male Natives are employed to do domestic work, in the majority of instances, and a female domestic servant is a rarity. We thus have a very dangerous environment existing for any woman who goes into any kind of domestic service in these towns, and naturally immorality of various kinds ensues, as the inevitable outcome of this situation. Thus we see that the European is by his treatment of the Native in these ways which I have mentioned, only pushing him further and further down in the social scale, forgetting that it was he and his kind who brought these conditions about in South Africa, forgetting his responsibilities to those who labour for him and to whom he introduced the benefits, and evils, of civilisation. These facts do not sound very pleasant I know, but this Conference is, according to my belief, intended to give us all the opportunity of expressing our views, our problems, and of discussing them in an attitude of friendliness and fair-mindedness, so that we may perhaps be enabled to see some way out of them.

Then we come to the Land Question. This is very acute in South Africa, especially from the Bantu point of view. South Africa in terms of available land is shrinking daily owing to increased population, and to many other economic and climatic causes. Cattle diseases have crept into the country, ruining many a stock farmer, and thus Bantu wealth is gradually decaying. As a result there are more and more workers making their way to the towns and cities such as Johannesburg to earn a living. And what a living! The majority earn about £3 10s per month, out of which they must pay 25s. for rent, and 10s. for tram fares, so I leave you to imagine what sort of existence they lead on the remainder.

Here again we come back to the same old problem that I outlined before, that of the woman of the home being obliged to find work in order to supplement her husband's wages, with the children growing up undisciplined and uncared for, and the natural following rapid decay of morality among the people. We find that in this state of affairs, the woman in despair very often decides that she cannot leave her children thus uncared for, and she therefore throws up her employment in order to care for them, but is naturally forced into some form of home industry, which, as there is very little choice for her in this direction, more often than not takes the form of the brewing and selling of skokiaan. Thus the woman starts on a career of crime for herself and her children, a career which often takes her and her children right down the depths of immorality and misery. The woman, poor unfortunate victim of circumstances, goes to prison, and the children are left even more desolate than when their mother left them to earn her living. Again they are uncared for, undisciplined, no-one's responsibility, the prey of the undesirables with whom their mother has come into contact in her frantic endeavour to provide for them by selling skokiaan. The children thus become decadent, never having had a chance in life. About ten years ago, there was talk of Industrial schools being started for such unfortunate children, but it was only talk, and we are to-day in the same position, aggravated by the increased numbers steadily streaming in from the rural areas, all undergoing very similar experiences to those I have just outlined.

I would suggest that there might be a conference of Native and European women, where we could get to understand each other's point of view, each other's difficulties and problems, and where, actuated by the real spirit of love, we might find some basis on which we could work for the common good of European and Bantu womanhood.

Many of the Bantu feel and rightly too that the laws of the land are not made for Black and White alike. Take the question of permits for the right to look for work. To look for work, mark you! The poor unfortunate Native, fresh from the country does not know of these rules and regulations, naturally breaks them and is thrown in prison; or if he does happen to know the regulations and obtains a pass for six days, and is obliged to renew it several times, as is of course very often the case, he will find that when he turns up for the third or fourth time for the renewal of his permit, he is put in prison, because he has been unsuccessful in obtaining work. And not only do the Bantu feel that the law for the White and the Black is not similar, but we even find some of them convinced that there are two Gods, one for the White and one for the Black. I had an instance of this in an old Native woman who had suffered much, and could not be convinced that the same God watched over and cared for us all, but felt that the God who gave the Europeans their life of comparative comfort and ease, could not possibly be the same God who allowed his poor Bantu to suffer so. As another instance of the inequalities existing in our social scheme, we have the fact of Natives not being allowed to travel on buses and trams in many towns, except those specially designed for them.

In connection with the difficulty experienced through men being employed almost exclusively in domestic work in the cities, I would mention that this is of course one of the chief reasons for young women, who should rightly be doing that work, going rapidly down in the social life of the community; and it is here that joint service councils of Bantu and White women would be able to do so much for the good of the community. The solution to the problem seems to me to be to get the women into service, and to give them proper accommodation, where they know they are safe. Provide hostels, and clubrooms, and rest rooms for these domestic servants, where they may spend their leisure hours, and I think you will find the problem of the employment of female domestic servants will solve itself, and that a better and happier condition of life will come into being for the Bantu.

If you definitely and earnestly set out to lift women and children up in the social life of the Bantu, you will find the men will benefit, and thus the whole community, both White and Black. Johannesburg is, to my knowledge, a great example of endeavour for the uplift of the Bantu woman, but we must put all our energies into this task if we would succeed. What we want is more co-operation and friendship between the two races, and more definite display of real Christianity to help us in the solving of these riddles. Let us try to make our Christianity practical.

The Native mind in many instances does not understand Christianity, because with the teaching of Christ, and the coming of civilisation, come also so many of the troubles from which the Bantu is to-day suffering, and from which he never suffered before, while he sees the White man apparently happy and comfortable. As an instance of this let me tell you of an old chief, whom I had tried again and again to convert. One day I went to him, and suggested that he was getting old, and that it was high time he was converted, and what do you think he said. He said, "Who is this man who was killed, and why does he cause us so much trouble? We had nothing to do with killing him, why come to me about him? Go to the people who did kill him, and show them what they have done—go to the Jews, and tell them what a lot of trouble they are bringing upon us all." Eventually, he said that he did not want to be converted and to go and live in another heaven to that in which his ancestors were, where he would be lonely. Thus we see the view the old-fashioned Bantu mind takes of Christianity to-day.

In conclusion let me repeat that what we want really, at this stage in our existence, is friendly and Christian co-operation between the Bantu and White women particularly, and also of the whole communities of Bantu and White, to help us solve these problems, which can be solved if they are tackled in the spirit of Christianity and fair-mindedness.

The Journal of Christian Students and Modern South Africa: A Report of the Bantu-Europeans' Student Conference, Fort Hare, June 27th–July 3rd., 1930. Alice, South Africa: Student Christian Association, 1930. 111–17.

MABEL DOVE-DANQUAH

The Torn Veil

Unscrupulous as he was, Kwame Asante had a qualm as he looked at the woman sitting on the African stool near the bed. He had called her and yet when she came he did not quite know how to begin the conversation.

"Akosua, how would you like fifty pounds to start a small business of your own—selling cloth, or perfume and powder?" The woman smiled nervously: ten years of married life had made her wary of her husband's fits of generosity.

She was as black as ebony, with the fine features peculiar to the girls of the Akwapim hills; graceful in her brown and red designed cloth and the lovely silk head-tie wrapped round her head. Her feet were shod in leather sandals and she had on her tiny ears the popular golden ear-rings named *Abongo*. The slender woman on the stool was the mother of three children though she still looked a girl. Married under the Native Customary Law she had served her lord and master with zeal and zest. It is a law which, like some other laws in the Gold Coast, needs disinfecting, for though it aids the man to gain his desire when it is at its fiercest, it does in no way safeguard the position of the woman when the man's passion abates.

"Would you like fifty pounds?" asked Kwame again. "I could make it hundred. You have been a very good wife to me, Akosua."

Did the truth begin to dawn on the woman's consciousness? No, she thrust the thought away from her. He could not do it.

Kwame cleared his throat—after all he might as well get it off his chest: hadn't she noticed that the whole relationship had become impossible? A cloth woman was all right when one was young and struggling; she could be so useful, a general servant and yet a wife. And Akosua was so gentle, and even quite refined, but a man needs a change. He had just completed his two-storied building, and he had been made a committee member of an important club. The other day his Academy had conferred on him an Associateship, and his University had given him a coveted degree. He had at last achieved his ambition and had become an important man in the community. He was thinking seriously of entering the Town Council.

"Fancy being addressed Councillor Kwame Asante, O.B.A., A.S.S." He smiled inanely to himself. Akosua looked at him in wonder.

"Er . . . er . . . Akosua . . . er, I want to tell you I am going to marry a lady; you will be paid off with a hundred pounds."

The woman answered never a word.

"A . . . frock . . . lady . . . um . . . er . . . of course you can read and write Ga and Twi but my friends will call you an illiterate woman."

"Did you consult your friends before you married me ten years ago?" The voice was cold and calm, yet the words cut like a whip.

"If you are going to be impertinent, I shall not discuss the matter further." He got up and walked up and down the room.

"How many men in the Gold Coast will pay a woman off with one hundred pounds? You are only entitled to twenty-five pounds, and here I am out of kindness offering you a hundred. Show some gratitude, Akosua."

She looked at him and stark misery was in her eyes.

"I shall send the children to Achimota College." There was a whining note in his voice. "I am only doing this because of my position in society. You see I may be called to Government House and other important places . . . say something, Akosua."

"I say you can keep your twenty-five pounds, fifty pounds or hundred pounds. I will have nothing to do with it. I will not be paid off."

"What! What! Come! Come! Don't do anything rash."

"If you dare touch me I shall strike your face."

"Strike your master, your husband? Are you mad?"

"I shall leave this housc."

"If you dare to disgrace me by leaving the house before I am ready for you to go, there will be trouble. I do not intend to put up with a wilful woman. What is my sin after all? I only want to become a decent and respectable member of society. If you leave this house without my knowledge and permission, I shall claim every penny I have spent on you since I married and lived with you these ten years; and not only that but I shall claim all the presents I have given to your parents and other relatives. You know our Native Customary Law."

"Yes, I know your Native Customary Law is a grave to bury women alive, whilst you men dance and beat tom-tom on top of the mound of earth."

"You are absolutely impossible," and Kwame strutted out of the room looking very much like an offended turkey-cock.

Akosua rushed to her bedroom, locked her door, flung herself face downwards on the bed and wept as if her heart would break.

"I must go, I must go," she muttered. Akosua's mother was dead but her father, Kofi Asare, was alive. He was a well-to-do cocoa farmer and had six transport-lorries. He doted on the daughter who had made a good match and married a "scholar."

"I wonder what he will say," thought the poor girl. "Crying won't help, I must do something." She got up from her bed, her eyes swollen and moist. She feverishly packed her belongings and those of her children. In a short time the three tin boxes, two baskets and two brass pans were neatly done up.

"The children will soon come from school and when he leaves for Kumasi tomorrow we will go away."

Kwame was still in a mood of righteous indignation when he took the train for Kumasi the next day. He thought: "I have brought Akosua to her senses; what is the world coming to when a cloth woman begins to get indignant because a Christian gentleman and scholar wants to marry a frock lady in church?"

Kwame Asante, like many of our men, had floundered in his sense of values; the western impact on his mentality had sent it all askew. He would have been very much surprised if an outspoken friend had told him that he was neither a Christian nor a gentleman, and that Akosua had far finer instincts and culture than he; but fortunately for him his friends could not see farther than himself—so he was happy in his good opinion of himself.

His nephew Quao, who met him at the railway station three days later, on his return to Accra, gave him the news that his wife had gone away with the children.

Kwame felt a fool and he intensely disliked the feeling. He sent two telegrams to his father-in-law asking that Akosua should be sent back immediately. Not the slightest notice was taken of him; then he sent two middle-aged women to go for her, but they returned without her.

His friends consoled him, over drinks and local cigars.

"Don't you worry, man, a woman, a cloth woman, they are so many; and even if she were a frock lady—what is a woman?" squawked Wilson-Addo, a notorious "woman-chaser," who spent all his savings paying out "pacification" money.

"I can't understand Akosua's behaviour at all; I was only teasing her that I might marry a lady one of these days, but nothing serious at all," lied Kwame. It is amazing what lies husbands tell at the expense of their wives.

"Of course, if she doesn't return I shall have to marry, for I certainly cannot live without a woman in the house."

Kwame Asante made a long bill to his father-in-law, claiming all the money he had spent on Akosua since he married her, as well as the presents given to her parents: it came to three hundred and fifty pounds. He thought better of the matter next day.

"After all Akosua is a woman and women are always weak; after my marriage I can soon coax her round. I can then have one wife in Akwapim and another in Accra—after all, monogamy is all humbug. There is a ratio of about eight women to one man; when I marry one and keep to her alone, what happens to the other seven?"

Martha Aryeetey, Kwame's second choice, a school teacher, was a pleasant-looking girl, plump and cheerful, and extremely proud of herself for having secured Kwame Asante. He had just built and furnished a house at Adabraka, and ever since he fell in love he had been giving her three pounds a month pin-money, and provisions as well; and besides, she was earning seven pounds a month. In fact, she was one of the happiest girls in Accra. Did she think of the woman whose place she was going to occupy? Not at all; after all, she was only a cloth woman.

The great day arrived. Holy Trinity Church was packed with guests and gate-crashers—for many people make it a habit to attend weddings without being invited. According to custom the relatives of the bride and groom were in white.

Kwame and Martha looked well, and radiantly happy. The service was fully choral. It was soon over and a grand reception took place at the Rodger Club. The bride and bridegroom, together with the best man, Yaw Asante, and the bridesmaids and pages, sat on the dais.

A few special guests had champagne, some had whisky and soda, some beer, some ginger beer, others nothing. Thin slices of cakes and *alsomo,* or "twists" as they are called by Europeans, were served round. The handbags of some of the guests were packed and overflowing; some had a slice or two, others sat through and somehow just happened to be overlooked.

Shoals or telegrams arrived from distant friends and relatives. The best man received them, opened some and told the bridegroom the names of the senders. The telegrams were so many.

"Tomorrow we shall read them all," they decided.

At last the guests began to stand and walk up the dais, to shake hands with the newly-married couple. It was a long and tedious ceremony but everything has an end. The last guest had gone; the bridal group walked down the dais to the waiting car. They went from one relative's house to another. All gave good advice and a glass of cold water for luck.

It was ten P.M. when the newly-married couple found themselves alone. After a hurried dinner Mrs Asante could hardly keep her eyes open; she went straight to bed. Mr Asante sat on the verandah for a little fresh air; he dozed off. Suddenly he woke up with a start. Did he hear footsteps? He rushed to the sitting-room.

Was that Martha, sitting with bowed head on the settee in all her bridal finery? "Martha, my dear, why haven't you gone to bed ?"

She lifted her head. Asante blinked rapidly. He rubbed his eyes. Was he drunk or dreaming? Akosua was looking at him shyly. He remembered that look; it had charmed him again and again. He moved towards her.

"Akosua, what are you doing here at this hour of the night?" She did not answer; but she got up from the settee. Lovely she looked in her white brocaded silk cloth; the long bridal veil, held by a wreath of orange blossoms, was nearly sweeping the floor. She eluded him, a mocking smile on her lips. The warm blood throbbed in his veins.

"How maddeningly beautiful she looks!"

Had he really left this cameo in ebony for that other common-place girl?

"I must have been mad." He stretched out his arms: "Akosua, forgive me."

She smiled and beckoned to him. He ran towards her. She ran away from him. Round and round the sitting-room table they went; at last, he got hold of the veil and held fast to it. The leg of the table tripped him up and he fell, knocking his temple on the table's edge.

Asante's younger brother, Yaw, the best man, was the one to awaken the household the next day. They found the bridegroom sprawling on the sitting-room floor, a flimsy bit of a bridal veil tightly clenched in one fist. Joy was in his countenance. Dr Adjaye, who was called, said he had been dead for some hours. The whole neighbourhood soon heard of the tragic occurrence, loud wailings and moanings pervaded the scene. The bride fainted.

No one could give an account of the torn fragment, for there was no tear in Mrs Asante's veil.

"We have not even gone through the telegrams of congratulations; I rushed here early so that we could read them through," said young Asante, the best man, his eyes filled with tears. Carefully he drew the telegrams from his coat pocket. Casually the doctor looked through. He gave a sudden start:

"Hello! What's this, was Mr Asante a married man?"

"Oh, he was only married to a cloth woman according to Native Customary Law," carelessly replied young Asante.

"Well, here is an important telegram from Akwapim." Dr Adjaye cleared his throat. "It is dated yesterday and it reads":

To Kwame Asante, Adabraka
Your wife Akosua died 10 A.M. to-day. Come at once.
    Kofi Asare.

The Torn Veil and Other Stories. Ed. Phebean Itayemi and Mabel Dove-Danguah. London: Evans Brothers, 1975. 7–15.

ADELAIDE CASELY HAYFORD

Mista Courifer

Not a sound was heard in the coffin-maker's workshop, that is to say no human sound. Mista Courifer, a solid citizen of Sierra Leone, was not given to much speech. His apprentices, knowing this, never dared address him unless he spoke first. Then they only carried on their conversation in whispers. Not that Mista Courifer did not know how to use his tongue. It was incessantly wagging to and fro in his mouth at every blow of the hammer. But his shop in the heart of Freetown was a part of his house. And, as he had once confided to a friend, he was a silent member of his own household from necessity. His wife, given to much speaking, could outtalk him.

"It's no use for argue wid woman," he said cautiously. "Just like'e no use for teach woman carpentering; she nebba sabi for hit de nail on de head. If 'e argue, she'll hit eberyting but de nail; and so wid de carpentering."

So, around his wife, with the exception of his tongue's continual wagging like a pendulum, his mouth was kept more or less shut. But whatever self-control he exercised in this respect at home was completely sent to the wind in his official capacity as the local preacher at chapel, for Mista Courifer was one of the pillars of the church, being equally at home in conducting a prayer meeting, superintending the Sunday school or occupying the pulpit.

His voice was remarkable for its wonderful graduations of pitch. He would insist on starting most of his tunes himself: consequently they nearly always ended in a solo. If he happened to pitch in the bass, he descended into such a *de profundis* that his congregations were left to flounder in a higher key; if he started in the treble, he soared so high that the children stared at him openmouthed and their elders were lost in wonder and amazement. As for his prayers, he roared and volleyed and thundered to such an extent that poor little mites were quickly reduced to a state of collapse and started to whisper from sheer fright.

But he was most at home in the pulpit. It is true, his labours were altogether confined to the outlying village districts of Regent, Gloucester and Leicester, an arrangement with which he was by no means satisfied. Still, a village congregation is better than none at all.

His favourite themes were Jonah and Noah and he was forever pointing out the great similarity between the two, generally finishing his discourse after this manner: "You see my beloved Breben, den two man berry much alike. All two lived in a sinful and adulturous generation. One get inside am ark; de odder one get inside a whale. Day bof seek a refuge fom de swelling waves.

"And so it is today my beloved Brebren. No matter if we get inside a whale or get inside an ark, as long as we get inside someplace of safety—as long as we can find some refuge, some hiding place from de wiles ob de debil."

But his congregation was by no means convinced.

Mr Courifer always wore black. He was one of the Sierra Leone gentlemen who consider everything European to be not only the right thing, but the only thing for the African, and having read somewhere that English undertakers generally appeared in sombre attire, he immediately followed suit.

He even went so far as to build a European house. During his short stay in England, he had noticed how the houses were built and furnished and had forthwith erected himself one after the approved pattern—a house with stuffy little passages, narrow little staircases and poky rooms, all crammed with saddlebags and carpeted with Axminsters. No wonder his wife had to talk. It was so hopelessly uncomfortable, stuffy and unsanitary.

So Mr Courifer wore black. It never struck him for a single moment that red would have been more appropriate, far more becoming, far less expensive and far more national. No! It must be black. He would have liked blue black, but he wore rusty black for economy.

There was one subject upon which Mr Courifer could talk even at home, so no one ever mentioned it: his son, Tomas. Mista Courifer had great expectations for his son; indeed in the back of his mind he had hopes of seeing him reach the high-water mark of red-tape officialism, for Tomas was in the government service. Not very high up, it is true, but still he was in it. It was an honour that impressed his father deeply, but Tomas unfortunately did not seem to think quite so much of it. The youth in question, however, was altogether neutral in his opinions in his father's presence. Although somewhat feminine as to attire, he was distinctly masculine in his speech. His neutrality was not a matter of choice, since no one was allowed to choose anything in the Courifer family but the pater-familias himself.

From start to finish, Tomas's career had been cut out, and in spite of the fact that nature had endowed him with a black skin and an African temperament, Tomas was to be an Englishman. He was even to be an Englishman in appearance.

Consequently, once a year mysterious bundles arrived by parcel post. When opened, they revealed marvellous checks and plaids in vivid greens and blues after the fashion of a Liverpool counterjumper, waistcoats decorative in the extreme with their bold designs and rows of brass buttons, socks vying with the rainbow in glory and pumps very patent in appearance and very fragile as to texture.

Now, Tomas was no longer a minor and he keenly resented having his clothes chosen for him like a boy going to school for the first time. Indeed on one occasion, had it not been for his sister's timely interference, he would have chucked the whole collection in the fire.

Dear little Keren-happuch, eight years his junior and not at all attractive, with a very diminutive body and a very large heart. Such a mistake! People's hearts ought always to be in proportion to their size, otherwise it upsets the dimensions of the whole structure and often ends in its total collapse.

Keren was that type of little individual whom nobody worshipped, consequently she understood the art of worshipping others to the full. Tomas was the object of her adoration. Upon him she lavished the whole store of her boundless wealth and whatever hurt Tomas became positive torture as far as Keren-happuch was concerned.

"Tomas!" she said clinging to him with the tenacity of a bear, as she saw the faggots piled up high, ready for the conflagration, "Do yah! No burn am oh! Ole man go flog you oh! Den clos berry fine! I like am myself too much. I wish"—she added wistfully—"me na boy; I wish I could use am."

This was quite a new feature which had never struck Tomas before. Keren-happuch had never received a bundle of English clothes in her life, hence her great appreciation of them.

At first Tomas only laughed—the superior daredevil don't-care-a-damn-about-consequences laugh of the brave before the deed. But after hearing that wistful little sentence, he forgot his own annoyance and awoke to his responsibilities as an elder brother.

A few Sundays later, Tomas Courifer, Jr., marched up the aisle of the little Wesleyan chapel in all his Liverpool magnificence accompanied by a very elated little Keren-happuch whose natural unattractiveness had been further accentuated by a vivid cerise costume—a heterogeneous mass of frill and fur-belows. But the glory of her array by no means outshone the brightness of her smile. Indeed that smile seemed to illuminate the whole church and to dispel the usual melancholy preceding the recital of Jonah and his woes.

Unfortunately, Tomas had a very poor opinion of the government service and in a burst of confidence he had told Keren that he meant to chuck it at the very first opportunity. In vain his sister expostulated and pointed our the advantages connected with it—the honour, the pension—and the awful nemesis upon the head of anyone incurring the head-of-the-family's ire.

"Why you want leave am, Tomas?" she asked desperately.

"Because I never got a proper holiday. I have been in the office four and a half years and have never had a whole week off yet. And," he went on vehemently, "these white chaps come and go, and a fresh one upsets what the old one has done and a newcomer upsets what he does and they all only stay for a year and a half and go away for four months, drawing big fat pay all the time, not to speak of passages, whereas a poor African like me has to work year in and year out with never a chance of a decent break. But you needn't be afraid, Keren dear," he added consolingly. "I shan't resign, I shall just behave so badly that they'll chuck me and then my ole man can't say very much."

Accordingly when Tomas, puffing a cigarette, sauntered into the office at 9 A.M. instead of 8 A.M. for the fourth time that week, Mr Buckmaster, who had hitherto maintained a discreet silence and kept his eyes shut, opened them wide and administered a sharp rebuke. Tomas's conscience was profoundly stirred. Mr Buckmaster was one of the few white men for whom he had a deep respect, aye, in the depth of his heart, he really had a sneaking regard. It was for fear of offending him that he had remained so long at his post.

But he had only lately heard that his chief was due for leave so he decided there and then to say a long good-bye to a service which had treated him so shabbily. He was a vociferous reader of halfpenny newspapers and he knew that the humblest shop assistant in England was entitled to a fortnight's holiday every year. Therefore it was ridiculous to argue that because he was an African working in Africa there was no need for a holiday. All his applications for leave were quietly pigeonholed for a more convenient season.

"Courifer!" Mr Buckmaster said sternly. "Walk into my private office please." And Courifer knew that this was the beginning of the end.

"I suppose you know that the office hours are from 8 A.M. till 4 P.M. daily," commenced Mr Buckmaster, in a freezing tone.

"Yes, er—Sir!" stammered Courifer with his heart in his mouth and his mouth twisted up into a hard sailor's knot.

"And I suppose you also know that smoking is strictly forbidden in the office."

"Yes, er—er—Sir!" stammered the youth.

"Now hitherto," the even tones went on, "I have always looked upon you as an exemplary clerk, strictly obliging, punctual, accurate and honest, but for the last two or three weeks I have had nothing but complaints about you. And from what I myself have seen, I am afraid they are not altogether un-merited."

Mr Buckmaster rose as he spoke, took a bunch of keys out of his pocket, and, unlocking his roll-top desk, drew out a sheaf of papers. "This is your work, is it not?" he said to the youth.

"Yes, er—er—Sir!" he stuttered, looking shamefacedly at the dirty, ink-stained blotched sheets of closely typewritten matter.

"Then what in Heaven's name is the matter with you to produce such work?"

Tomas remained silent for a moment or two. He summoned up courage to look boldly at the stern countenance of his chief. And as he looked, the stern-ness seemed to melt away and he could see genuine concern there.

"Please, er—Sir!" he stammered, "May—I—er—just tell you everything?"

Half an hour later, a very quiet, subdued, penitent Tomas Courifer walked out of the office by a side door. Mr Buckmaster followed later, taking with him an increased respect for the powers of endurance exercised by the growing West African youth.

Six weeks later, Mista Courifer was busily occupied wagging his tongue when he looked up from his work to see a European man standing in his doorway.

The undertaker found speech and a chair simultaneously. "Good afternoon, Sah!" he said, dusting the chair before offering it to his visitor. "I hope you don't want a coffin, Sah!" which was a deep-sea lie for nothing pleased him more than the opportunity of making a coffin for a European. He was always so sure of the money. Such handsome money—paid it is true with a few ejacu-lations, but paid on the nail and without any deductions whatsoever. Now with his own people things were different. They demurred, they haggled, they bar-tered, they gave him detailed accounts of all their other expenses and then, after keeping him waiting for weeks, they would end by sending him half the amount with a stern exhortation to be thankful for that.

Mr Buckmaster took the proffered chair and answered pleasantly: "No thank you, I don't intend dying just yet. I happened to be passing so I thought I should just like a word with you about your son."

Mr Courifer bristled all over with exultation and expectation. Perhaps they were going to make his son a kind of undersecretary of state. What an unexpected honour for the Courifer family. What a rise in their social status; what a rise out of their neighbours. How good God was!

"Of course you know he is in my office?"

"Oh yes, Sah. He often speaks about you."

"Well, I am going home very soon and as I may not be returning to Sierra Leone, I just wanted to tell you how pleased I should be at any time to give him a decent testimonial."

Mr Courifer's countenance fell. What a comedown!

"Yes, Sah," he answered, somewhat dubiously.

"I can recommend him highly as being steady, persevering, reliable and trustworthy. And you can always apply to me if ever such a thing be necessary."

Was that all! What a disappointment! Still it was something worth having. Mr. Buckmaster was an Englishman and a testimonial from him would certainly be a very valuable possession. He rubbed his hands together as he said: "Well I am berry much obliged to you, Sah, berry much obliged. And as time is short and we nebba know what a day may bring forth, would you mind writing one down now, Sah?"

"Certainly. If you will give me a sheet of paper, I shall do so at once."

Before Tomas returned home from his evening work, the testimonial was already framed and hanging up amidst the moth-eaten velvet of the drawing room.

On the following Monday morning, Courifer Jr. bounced into his father's workshop, upsetting the equilibrium of the carpenter's bench and also of the voiceless apprentice hard at work.

"Well, Sah?" ejaculated his father, surveying him in disgust. "You berry late. Why you no go office dis morning?"

"Because I've got a whole two months' holiday, Sir! Just think of it—two whole months—with nothing to do but just enjoy myself!"

"Tomas," his father said solemnly, peering at him over his glasses, "you must larn for make coffins. You get fine chance now."

Sotto voce: "I'll be damned if I will!" Aloud: "No thank you, Sir. I am going to learn how to make love, after which I am going to learn how to build myself a nice mud hut."

"And who dis gal you want married?" thundered his father, ignoring the latter part of the sentence altogether.

A broad smile illuminated Tomas's countenance. "She is a very nice girl, sir, a very nice girl. Very quiet and gentle and sweet, and she doesn't talk too much."

"I see. Is dat all?"

"Oh, no. She can sew and clean and make a nice little home. And she has plenty sense; she will make a good mother."

"Yes, notting pass dat!"

"She has been to school for a long time. She reads nice books and she writes, oh, such a nice letter," said Tomas, patting his breast-pocket affectionately.

"I see. I suppose she sabi cook good fashion?"

"I don't know, I don't think so, and it doesn't matter very much."

"What!" roared the old man; "You mean tell me you want married woman who no sabi cook?"

"I want to marry her because I love her, Sir!"

"Dat's all right, but for we country, de heart and de stomach always go togedder. For we country, black man no want married woman who no sabi cook! Dat de berry first requisitional. You own mudder sabi cook."

That's the reason why she has been nothing but your miserable drudge all these years, thought the young man. His face was very grave as he rejoined: "The style in our country is not at all nice, Sir. I don't like to see a wife slaving away in the kitchen all times to make good chop for her husband who sits down alone and eats the best of everything himself, and she and the children only get the leavings. No thank you! And besides, Sir, you are always telling me that you want me to be an Englishman. That is why I always try to talk good English to you."

"Yes, dat's all right. Dat's berry good. But I want make you *look* like Englishman. I don't say you must copy all der different way!"

"Well, Sir, if I try till I die, I shall never look like an Englishman, and I don't know that I want to. But there are some English customs that I like very much indeed. I like the way white men treat their wives; I like their home life; I like to see mother and father and the little family all sitting down eating their meals together."

"I see," retorted his father sarcastically. "And who go cook den meal. You tink say wid your foud pound a month, you go able hire a perfessional cook?"

"Oh, I don't say so, Sir. And I am sure if Accastasia does not know how to cook now, she will before we are married. But what I want you to understand is just this, that whether she is able to cook or not, I shall marry her, just the same."

"Berry well," shouted his father, wrath delineated in every feature, "but instead of building one mud hut you better go one time build one mad-house."

"Sir, thank you. But I know what I am about and a mud hut will suit as perfectly for the present."

"A mud hut!" ejaculated his father in horror. "You done use fine England house wid staircase and balustrade and tick carpet and handsome furnitures. You want to go live in mud hut? You ungrateful boy, you shame me, oh!"

"Dear me, no, Sir. I won't shame you. It's going to be a nice clean spacious mud hut. And what is more, it is going to be a sweet little home, just big enough for two. I am going to distemper the walls pale green, like at the principal's rooms at Keren's school."

"How you sabi den woman's rooms?"

"Because you have sent me two or three times to pay her school fees, so I have looked at those walls and I like them too much."

"I see. And what else you go do?" asked his father ironically.

"I am going to order some nice wicker chairs from the Islands and a few good pieces of linoleum for the floors and then—"

"And den what?"

"I shall bring home my bride."

Mr Courifer's dejection grew deeper with each moment. A mud hut! This son of his—the hope of his life! A government officer! A would-be English-man! To live in a mud hut! His disgust knew no bounds. "You ungrateful wretch!" he bellowed; "You go disgrace me. You go lower your pore father. You go lower your position for de office."

"I am sorry, Sir," retorted the young man. "I don't wish to offend you. I'm grateful for all you have done for me. But I have had a raise in salary and I want a home of my own which, after all, is only natural, and"—he went on steadily, staring his father straight in the face—"I may as well tell you at once, you need not order any more Liverpool suits for me."

"Why not?" thundered his irate parent, removing his specs lest any harm should befall them.

"Well, I am sorry to grieve you, Sir, but I have been trying to live up to your European standards all this time. Now I am going to chuck it once and for all. I am going back to the native costume of my mother's people, and the next time I appear in chapel it will be as a Wolof."

The very next Sunday the awful shock of seeing his son walk up the aisle of the church in pantaloons and the bright loose overjacket of a Wolof from Gambia, escorting a pretty young bride the colour of chocolate, also in native dress, so unnerved Mista Courifer that his mind suddenly became a complete blank. He could not even remember Jonah and the whale, nor could his tongue possess one word to let fly, not one. The service had to be turned into a prayer meeting.

Mista Courifer is the local preacher no longer. Now he only makes coffins.

In *Unwinding Threads: Writing by Women in Africa*, ed. Charlotte H. Bruner. London: Heinemann, 1983. 8–16.

13

Race, Nation, and Modernity: The Anti-colonial Consciousness of Modernism

INTRODUCED AND SELECTED BY SONITA SARKER

VICTORIA OCAMPO PRESSING Il Duce politely about women's roles in fascist Italy; Jean Rhys resisting the manager of the chorus-girl troupe in England; Behramji Malabari exhorting British rulers to treat his people (Indians) as equals; Gertrude Stein claiming her place as an American outsider in France; Cornelia Sorabji eulogizing her college days in Oxford and eloquently advocating the uplift of Bengali womanhood. These are some of the moments captured in this section, points along the intersecting itineraries of these writers' lives that illuminate their cartographies of political-cultural work. As these moments reveal, these modernist maps are formed by and also inform contemporary beliefs in the *telos* of individual and collective identities.

Selected from writings published between 1892 and 1940, the extracts and these moments within them attest to the individually inflected symbiosis of modernisms (socio-cultural effects) with modernities (political and economic effects).[1] For example, Malabari, in his "Indian Eye on English Life" (1895), a travel-narrative of a cosmopolitan colonial subject, translates, for his own purposes, notions of collective rights, individual equality, historical progress, and civilization that justified the economic and technological rationality of British imperial map-making. Stein's "American Eye on Paris" (1940), another cosmopolitan almanac, deflects her nation's geopolitical aspirations to global power, firstly by presenting a French cultural Mecca as part of a distinctly different civilization, and secondly, by presenting her own marginalization there as actually conducive to her artistic ambitions.

In Malabari's and Stein's accounts, as in the others included in this section, it becomes apparent that ideologies of spaces (geographies) and times (histories), both literal and metaphorical, intersect to form the template of a gendered subjectivity-in-modernity.[2] The intersection of time and space is not simply a metaphysical framework but is implemented in geopolitical structures through technological instruments of modernization—the printing presses that women like Ocampo, Woolf, and Stein owned, the imperial courts of law in which Sorabji had absolute faith, the expansionist industrial and corporate firms to which the strikes responded. In her conversation with Mussolini (Il Duce), Ocampo attempts to contest the vision of Italian fascist history in which the space of the nation and the time of the future is masculine, one that relegates women to stasis or invisibility. As Ocampo puts it in "Living History," Italy is "a country for men" where "the accent falls on unmitigated masculinity." In comparison, Sorabji is fervent about women's roles in fashioning the territories of the emerging Indian nation but equally insistent that these roles should be performed within the imperial spatial parentheses, and by the imperatives of British political and philosophical notions of progress.[3]

Moreover, the juxtaposition of the extracts in this section broadens and deepens the connotations of an international modernism.[4] That expansion of the term is not performed merely by adding South American and Asian regions to the more frequently employed Western Europe–North American connections. The contiguousness of the extracts underscores that these geographies and their respective histories are mutually formative, even within imbalances of power. Ocampo's belief in political womanhood ("Woman, Her Rights and Her Responsibilities") is affirmed in the very encounter with Italian fascism's exclusion of women from history making. Rhys's genealogy of the self attempts to rise out of and away from the overlapping and contradictory influences of a colonial Dominica and its imperial others, England and France. Malabari's call to be treated equally is based on Indian self-determination as it recasts and responds to British modernity. Stein says much about (North) American culture even as she appears only to narrate the features of France.

Based on this interrelationship between geographies (nations, empires, homes) and histories (modern, traditional), what emerges is not *a* modernist subjectivity but a range of subject-positions that are based upon locational and ideological (dis)affiliations. The range within "international modernism" is composed not of discrete entities that define themselves only in philosophical or ideological contradistinction but in actual social and political relationships. Ocampo knew and corresponded with Woolf about modernist women's writing, and with Rabindranath Tagore about Indian independence; Rhys was connected, through Ford Madox Ford, to the same literary circles as Stein; Sorabji and Woolf knew of each other and the latter's relation to Stein is well recorded.[5]

Such mutually impactive geographies and histories generate, as one observes in the extracts, identities that are simultaneously overdetermined by and contingent upon geo-social location and political belief. Ocampo relies upon women's unique ability to take the course of history away from the masculinist fascism she encounters, while believing in a universal modernity in which all participate, regardless of gender or any other difference; blackness is mentioned only in a footnote in these extracts. Rhys, on the other hand, attempts constantly to negotiate and surpass race, gender, and class differences, categories that appear to her to be clearly yet arbitrarily defined in Creole Dominican as well as Western European cultures. Sorabji, like Malabari before her, imagines a cosmopolitan modernity in which Indians are equal to their colonizers on the basis of two seemingly incommensurable quantities: that Indians are judged by their inferior status as colonized subjects but are also perceived as culturally and racially unique.[6] (It is worth pointing out that the homology of national uniqueness with racial and cultural identity, as part of the modernist experience, also fed into primitivism, museum and private collections of "native" art, and the discipline of anthropology.) Sorabji inflects Malabari's vision by inserting the place of women of all classes and education levels as instrumental to social and political progress. Stein's unchangeable American-ness is predicated upon its absolute difference from being French, but her unmarked (lesbian) Jewishness also remains distinct from the Native American Indians she mentions in passing.[7] Woolf's concern for the production and sale from her Hogarth Press is defined by her reading of the 1926 London strike as disruptive to quotidian life as well as national politics, even as she signs petitions for compromise between workers and the captains of industry.

As Woolf, Ocampo, Sorabji, and others testify through their writings, this oscillation between an attention to political (and its attendant) boundaries on the one hand, and a refusal to be bound by them on the other, derive from the violence the individual experiences. In their testaments, the violence of history gives birth to both modernism—the face of modernity at the turn of the twentieth century—and late colonialism—the political infrastructure of modernism that provides material resources as well as particular forms of the racialized, sexualized, and gendered "other." One form of this violence, war (on the international scale and within emerging nation-statehoods) is a persistent part of the backdrop in these writers' visions, one that performs unprecedented shifts in the foundation of the individual and community. Modernist artistic movements such as fauvism, surrealism, cubism, and the growing field of psychoanalysis, capture the violence of historical and social processes that elicit a fascination with the unseen and the uncertain edges of identity (e.g., the supernatural that Rhys explores in her writings).[8] Rhys records the violence done to her imagination of filial and other bonds in her childhood, and of the brutal imprisonment of the elusive and the irreducible into symbols—woman, black, other—that constrain her life. The direct curtness of Il Duce's remarks to Ocampo about women's abilities contrast starkly with Woolf's and Rhys's exploration of the silences and ambiguities in human lives and their societies. On a larger scale, Ocampo wonders whether or not it is "perhaps hoping for the impossible" ("Living History") to urge men to avoid old patterns used to justify violence or destructive behavior.

Imperial/international conflicts breed reductive binaries—us and them, good and bad, superior and inferior. These reductions obtrude upon these authors' complex notion of "origin," on which they base their claim to be treated equally. Casting off the "narcotic" of self-subjugation (Ocampo, "Her Rights" 229) is a particularly complicated project when diverse, unequal, and seemingly contradictory influences inform the situation of writers like Rhys, Malabari, and Sorabji. In her chapter on her black nurse, "Meta," Rhys emphasizes the blend of Indian with French with native Caribbean influences in her childhood. She remembers "lassi mango, if that is how it is spelt," one of Miss Jane's sweets presumably of Indian origin, and French-based words like "loups-garous." Rhys tries diligently to distinguish a "colored" from a "Negro girl," and to determine whether her schoolmate who has "not too frizzy hair" can be counted as one of the "white girls" because she "didn't look colored" (*Smile Please* 39). Rhys understands the class and racialized elements in her relationship with Meta, who seemed always to be alien and angry, but recognizes the same person as someone who is fundamental to her own being. A similar intricacy, although located in a very different political and cultural history, characterizes Sorabji's self-defined place in India. Sorabji makes a distinction between being born in India (therefore, she considers herself an Indian), and being Parsee, an identity that has geographical and cultural origins outside India (in ancient Persia); in her narrative, this heritage distinguishes her from Indian Hindus and Muslims. Moreover, her father's conversion to Christianity aligns her to British modernity and enables her to advocate the cause of Indian self-determination within the context of imperial rule. Similarly Malabari, who defines himself as an "Asiatic," sees the coexistence of British Empire and Indian Nation as viable; for him, England and India are "two nations," at the same time as England is "the land of his rulers" from which he asks for political accountability through equal treatment as a fellow-subject, by its own standards of liberal democracy.[9]

The hybridity of unequally powerful influences that informs this complicated sense of "origin" also inflects a particular sense of dislocation, chosen or enforced, in the lives of these writers. Exile and belonging become simultaneously operative for Rhys as for Stein, for Woolf as for Sorabji, yet carry very different connotations in each case. This battle of insider/outsider becomes crucial in the project of self-determination. Their individual journeys to discover the relationship between "self" and "other" variously configure the landscape of modernist cosmopolitanism. While this phenomenon has been analyzed at great length, cosmopolitanism, as embodied in these writers, is defined in large part by the violence of war and the competing ambitions of nation-states on the world stage, implicit or explicit as those references may be in their writings.[10]

The freedom to be oneself (or make oneself) in a strange place where it is clear that one does not belong by culture or race is a privilege Stein, Malabari, and Sorabji experience in a way that Woolf and Rhys cannot—Woolf because she never left, Rhys because she was always leaving. Rhys's closeness to the racialized or sexualized "other"—Meta and Francine—destabilizes the notion of "minority," making that identity contingent upon location. In her childhood in Dominica, Rhys remembers being forced to take the spectator position, hiding from a rioting crowd, and realizing that "they hate us. We are hated." In this instance, she equates her outsiderness with being white, an identity that does not, and cannot, savor the freedom and joy of being black. In the metropoles of Europe, however, her uncertain status as a "white" person from the colonies puts her in yet another unequal relationship of power, one in which she can never be white enough.

Stein participates implicitly, and Malabari and Sorabji explicitly, in observances of political boundaries and differences that are problematized in Woolf's and Rhys's writings, specifically in relation to colonialism, nationalism, and war. Sorabji, like Stein, identifies her alienness in terms of ethnicity and national identity (made homologous with culture), but her belonging in terms of her profession. The object and destination for the writers in this section are the European metropoles of Rome, Paris, London, and Oxford. However, their status as insider/outsider to nations involved in the geopolitical crises of early twentieth-century modernity—India, Dominica, the United States, Argentina—results in more than one point of orientation. Malabari's is India: he measures Rome's sights and the quaintness of the Italians by their comparability to Indian metropoles and people. Stein's is the United States: even as the extracts here are purportedly about the uniqueness of the French, they rest upon an implicit and simultaneous affirmation of American culture. On closer examination, the parallelism is uneven since, at the time of the writings,

India stood in colonial subjecthood to England, while the United States dominated the world stage.

Many analyses of twentieth-century modernisms and modernities have addressed the factor of class as integral to the workings of both phenomena. In fact, class links them.[11] However, education, as a factor that complicated structures of inequities, is often elided in analyses of modernisms, even in the ones that have dealt with issues of class. This factor often turns upside down the divisions of "margin" and "center" usually maintained in modernist colonial writings, and in discourses upon them. At a time when England's colonies were being "brought into the modern world," some of the colonized were able to avail of the opportunities denied even to the women in colonial centers. For example, as her selection shows, Sorabji's fond familiarity with and expressions of nostalgia for Oxford stand in stark contrast to Woolf's exclusion from the same environs, which the latter documented in *A Room Of One's Own,* among other writings. In contrast to Sorabji, note Rhys's description of England as the very place that erases all desire for learning and books. Not only did Sorabji attend Oxford, she was the first Indian woman to attain a law degree. She maintained her status as a professional public persona for the major part of her life. On the basis of this privilege, Sorabji is even more eager that her nation step into modernity under British tutelage; she is very aware of the place of her nation and herself in the world. On this self-conscious basis, writers like Malabari and Sorabji plead that heritage not be misused, especially by their own kind, and that "rights and responsibilities" be observed (a classically liberal notion of the individual's function). Sorabji attacks the hypocrisy of nationalists who want to maintain Indian "purity" and "civilization," a point of view comparable to Woolf's depiction of the same issues in the case of the English nationalists in *Three Guineas.*

The differently educated women and men in this section stand at a particular crossroads of capital and labor that, in turn, defines the link between modernism and modernity. As is evident in many of the metaphors that Sorabji and Malabari use, individual lives are defined in considerable part by mechanical/technological modernity.[12] This aspect was especially the source of women's self-sustenance and self-determination as professional actors in modern life—Sorabji as social/legal advocate of women in *purdah;* Woolf, Stein, Ocampo as writers and publishers (Hogarth Press, Sur Press); Rhys as stage-performer and writer finding her individual identity. Rhys's life as a chorus girl in dismal productions traveling the damp, dark, small towns in northern England and the sparsely populated beachside places to provide entertainment to the masses is usually glamorized as bohemian. What becomes clear in the extract here is Rhys's firsthand experience of the status of chorus girls as cheap labor, and her familiarity with chorus girls' unions that she uses as defence against an exploitative manager. Here, the language of rights and responsibilities returns—the responsibilities of the intelligentsia to the strikes (Woolf), the rights of women and their responsibilities to nation and empire (Sorabji), the responsibilities of leaders to their people (Malabari, Ocampo, Sorabji, and Woolf), and the responsibility of artists to their locales (Stein).

Most pertinent to all the women writers included in this section, however unequally positioned in relation to each other, is the responsibility of women to their own self-definition. Ocampo uses the imagery of colonization (invasion, territory) but does not tie these metaphors to actual inequalities in England's colonies, at least in the extract here. All the women writers are associated with famous men but are harbingers of new times in their own right. While history lives in the "human material" of youth (as Ocampo puts it), the unique differences of women were to be used to create new visions, not in competition with men but in claiming their own place more completely; after all, according to Ocampo, "only the minorities count. . . . The minorities will always be, willingly or not, the world leaders," especially in the face of insidious forces such as fascism. However, given their contexts, these women writers imagine this role to different ends—Woolf talks of women's journey towards self-realization but not in service of a nation, as Sorabji does, while Ocampo talks about them as outside those structures, as leaders but not as revolutionaries.

In the visions of all the writers in this section, women and other minoritized were to participate in the making of twentieth-century modernity. They were to create a new history based on mutual recognition, in the establishment of national legacies and, in the women writers' works, also international womanhood. Ocampo expresses a "firm and ardent wish that a group of Argentine women, however small" compete for a prominent role on the global stage. International womanhood binds the common black nurse and the ordinary Bengali woman to their more privileged counterparts in Rhys and Sorabji respectively. Women tactically use the classically masculinist genres of biography as eulogy (Ocampo with Woolf) and biography as invective (Rhys with Meta) to characterize their relationships. Thus, while women are witness to history, they are also the makers and recorders of history. Rhys and Ocampo both underscore the ways in which memory fights with death to preserve the presence of those who are gone; as Ocampo says of Woolf, "the dead are not dead except when their slightest gestures or steps are not perpetuated in anyone." A section like this one that emphasizes hitherto underrepresented social and intellectual relationships, in a volume that recognizes once again such "gestures and steps," testifies not only that the dead are not dead but that they have continuing life.

Notes

1. The journal *MODERNISM/modernity* signifies that connection in its title and in many of its articles. See Calinescu, Lukacs, and *Public Culture* as examples of the vast literature on this relationship. I use the plural to indicate the diverse manifestations of phenomena that are usually seen as globally homogeneous. For the connection between modernity and modernism through nationalism, see Smith; see also Eagleton, Jameson, and Said. For other region-based modernisms related to colonialism, see Geist and Monleon, Subramanian, and Zavala; for gender, modernism, and modernity, see Friedman and Joannou.

2. Space in modernity is an oft-visited concept (see Benko and Strohmayer); for time and modernism/modernity, see Kwinter, Osborne, Quinones, Schleifer. As recently indicated in analyses on the intersection of space and time, the address to this simultaneity helps to explain the variety of modernist philosophies across the globe (see Arts, Bauman, Brennan, Friedland and Boden, Giddens, McQuire, Schorske, Soja). For feminist interpretations, see Rose.

3. For other writings by Ocampo and Sorabji relating to women's roles respectively, see Ocampo, Sorabji.

4. In collections like Rado's, the scope of an international modernism refers mainly to (implicitly white) Western European and North American forms, as part of the transatlantic liaison, while in Lemke, the focus on black modernisms across continents is evident. The more recent use of "transnational" requires a separate discussion.

5. For Ocampo and Woolf, see Ocampo (*Virginia Woolf, Orland y cia; Virginia Woolf en su diario*); for Ocampo and Tagore, see Dyson; for Rhys and Ford, see Rhys (*Smile, Please*); for Woolf and Stein, see Woolf, *Letters*.

6. For contemporary uses of "race" and "culture," see Woolf, *Letters*. My essay discusses the terms in the context of Virginia Woolf's "The London Scene"; see Baker and North for use of "race" in African American modernism, and Michaels for use of "nativism" and Jessup for "primitivism" (most often connected with "race").

7. Stein refers to "red Indians" and "Negroes" in a manner similar to Woolf's references to them when writing to Vita Sackville-West. See Sarker on the notion of "unmarked" race and Woolf's references to Stein's and Leonard Woolf's Jewishness; see also Woolf, *Letters*.

8. On modernist art and violence, see Hewitt, and Howlett and Mengham. The crisis in subjectivity as a foundation of social discourse is evident in disciplines such as psychology and psychoanalysis, fields that fused rapidly in modernist aesthetics; for example, see Ellison, Ryan, Trotter. For the kinds of subjectivity produced by colonial experience, see Gikandi, Jervis.

9. For informative biographies of Sorabji and Malabari, see Burton.

10. On modernism and exile, see Emery, Johnson-Roullier, Joseph, Katz, Middleton.

11. On modernism and class structures, see Huyssen, Larsen, Marsh, Rainey, Scandura.

12. See Benjamin.

Works Cited

Arts, Wilhelmus Antonius, ed. *Through a Glass Darkly: Blurred Images of Cultural Tradition and Modernity over Distance and Time.* Leiden: Brill, 2000.

Baker, Houston. *Modernism and the Harlem Renaissance.* Chicago: University of Chicago Press, 1987.

Bauman, Zygmunt. *Liquid Modernity.* Cambridge: Polity Press; Malden, Mass.: Blackwell, 2000.

Benjamin, Walter. "The Work of Art in the Age of Mechanical Reproduction."

Benko, Georges, and Ulf Strohmayer. *Space and Social Theory: Interpreting Modernity and Postmodernity.* Oxford: Blackwell, 1997.

Brennan, Teresa. *Exhausting Modernity: Grounds for a New Economy.* London: Routledge, 2000.

Burton, Antoinette. *At the Heart of the Empire: Indians and the Colonial Encounter in Late-Victorian Britain.* Berkeley: University of California Press, 1997.

Calinescu, Matei. *Five Faces of Modernity: Modernism, Avant-Garde, Decadence.* Durham: Duke University Press, 1987.

Davis, Alex, and Lee Jenkins, eds. *Locations of Literary Modernism: Region and Nation in British and American Modernist Poetry.* Cambridge: Cambridge University Press, 2000.

Dyson, Ketaki Kushari. *In your blossoming flower-garden: Rabindranath Tagore and Victoria Ocampo.* New Delhi: Sahitya Akademi, 1988.

Eagleton, Terry, Fredric Jameson, and Edward Said. *Nationalism, Colonialism, and Literature.* Minneapolis: University of Minnesota Press, 1990.

Ellison, David. *Ethics and Aesthetics in European Modernist Literature: From the Sublime to the Uncanny.* Cambridge: Cambridge University Press, 2001.

Emery, Mary Lou. *Jean Rhys at "World's End": Novels of Colonial and Sexual Exile.* Austin: University of Texas Press, 1990.

Friedland, Roger, and Deirdre Boden, eds. *Now Here: Space, Time, and Modernity.* Berkeley: University of California Press, 1994.

Friedman, Susan Stanford. *Penelope's Web.*

Geist, Anthony L., and Jose B. Monleon, eds. *Modernism and Its Margins: Reinscribing Cultural Modernity from Spain and Latin America.* New York: Garland, 1999.

Giddens, Anthony. *The Consequences of Modernity.* Stanford: Stanford University Press, 1990.

Gikandi, Simon. *Writing in Limbo: Modernism and Caribbean Literature.* Ithaca: Cornell University Press, 1992.

Hewitt, Andrew. *Fascist Modernism: Aesthetics, Politics, and the Avant-Garde.* Stanford: Stanford University Press, 1993.

Howlett, Jana, and Rod Mengham, eds. *The Violent Muse: Violence and the Artistic Imagination in Europe, 1910–1939.* Manchester: Manchester University Press, 1994.

Huyssen, Andreas. *After the Great Divide.*

Jervis, John. *Transgressing the Modern: Explorations in the Western Experience of Otherness.* Malden, Mass.: Blackwell, 1999.

Jessup, Lynda. *Antimodernism and Artistic Experience: Policing the Boundaries of Modernity.* Toronto: University of Toronto Press, 2001.

Joannou, Maroula, ed. *Women Writers of the 1930s: Gender, Politics, and History.* Edinburgh: Edinburgh University Press, 1999.

Johnson-Roullier, Cyraina E. *Reading on the Edge: Exiles, Modernities, and Cultural Transformation in Proust, Joyce, and Baldwin.* Albany: SUNY Press, 2000.

Joseph, Margaret. *Caliban in Exile: The Outsider in Caribbean Fiction.* New York: Greenwood, 1992.

Katz, Jane. *Artists in Exile.* New York: Stein and Day, 1983.

Kwinter, Sanford. *Architectures of Time: Toward a Theory of the Event in Modernist Culture.* Cambridge: MIT Press, 2001.

Larsen, Neil. *Modernism and Hegemony: A Materialist Critique of Aesthetics.* Minneapolis: University of Minnesota Press, 1989.

Lemke, Sieglinde. *Primitivist Modernism: Black Culture and the Origins of Transatlantic Modernism.* Oxford: Oxford University Press, 1998.

Lukacs, Georg. *Essays on Thomas Mann.* London: Merlin Press, 1964.

Marsh, Alec. *Money and Modernity: Pound, Williams, and the Spirit of Jefferson.* Tuscaloosa: University of Alabama Press, 1998.

McQuire, Scott. *Visions of Modernity: Representation, Memory, Time, and Space in the Age of the Camera.* Thousand Oaks, Calif.: Sage, 1998.

Meyer, Doris. *Victoria Ocampo: Against the Wind and the Tide.* New York: George Braziller, 1979.

Michaels, Walter Benn. *Our America: Nativism, Modernism, and Pluralism.* Durham: Duke University Press, 1995.

Middleton, Victoria. *Elektra in Exile: Women Writers and Political Fiction.* New York: Garland, 1988.

North, Michael. *The Dialect of Modernism: Race, Language, and Twentieth-Century Literature.*

Ocampo, Victoria. *La Emancipacion de la Mujer.* San Jose: Editorial Fundacion UNA, 1999.

———. *Virginia Woolf en su diario.* Buenos Aires: Sur, 1954.

———. *Virginia Woolf, Orland y cia.* Buenos Aires: Sur, 1938.

Osborne, Peter. *The Politics of Time: Modernity and Avant-garde.* New York: Verso, 1995.

Public Culture. http://muse.jhu.edu/journals/pc/

Quinones, Ricardo. *Mapping Literary Modernism: Time and Development.* Princeton: Princeton University Press, 1985.

Rado, Lisa. *Modernism, Gender, and Culture.*

Rainey, Lawrence. *Institutions of Modernism: Literary Elites and Public Culture.* New Haven: Yale University Press, 1998.

Rhys, Jean. *Letters, 1931–1966.* Ed. Francis Wyndham and Diana Melly. London: Deutsch, 1984.

———. *The Left Bank and Other Stories.* Preface by Ford Madox Ford. Freeport, N.Y.: Books for Libraries Press, 1970.

———. *Smile Please: An Unfinished Autobiography.* Berkeley: Donald S. Ellis/Creative Arts, 1979.

Rose, Gillian. *Feminism and Geography: The Limits of Geographical Knowledge.* Minneapolis: University of Minnesota Press, 1993.

———. *Writing Women and Space: Colonial and Postcolonial Geographies.* New York: Guilford Press, 1994.

Ryan, Judith. *The Vanishing Subject: Early Psychology and Literary Modernism.* Chicago: University of Chicago Press, 1991.

Sarker, Sonita. "Locating a Native Englishness in Virginia Woolf's *The London Scene*." *NWSA Journal* 13.2 (Summer 2001): 1–30.

Scandura, Jani, and Michael Thurston, eds. *Modernism, Inc.: Body, Memory, Capital*. New York: New York University Press, 2001.

Schleifer, Ronald. *Modernism and Time: The Logic of Abundance in Literature, Science, and Culture, 1880–1930*. Cambridge: Cambridge University Press, 2000.

Schorske, Carl. *Thinking with History: Explorations in the Passage to Modernism*. Princeton: Princeton University Press, 1998.

Smith, Anthony D. *Nationalism and Modernism: A Critical Survey of Recent Theories of Nations and Nationalism*. New York: Routledge, 1998.

Soja, Edward. *The Political Organization of Space*. Washington: Association of American Geographers, 1971.

Sorabji, Cornelia. *India Calling*. London: Nisbet & Co., 1935.

———. *India Recalled*. London: Nisbet & Co., 1936.

Subramanian, Shankar. *Textual Traffic: Colonialism, Modernity, and the Economy of the Text*. Albany: SUNY Press, 2001.

Trotter, David. *Paranoid Modernism: Literary Experiment, Psychosis, and the Professionalization of English Society*. Oxford: Oxford University Press, 2001.

Woolf, Virginia. *Letters, Vol. 3, 1923–1928*.

———. *Three Guineas*. 1938; New York: Harcourt, Brace, Jovanovich, 1966.

———. *A Room of One's Own*. 1929; New York: Harcourt, Brace & World, 1957.

Zavala, Iris. *Colonialism and Culture: Hispanic Modernisms and the Social Imaginary*. Bloomington: Indiana University Press, 1992.

BEHRAMJI MERWANJI MALABARI

From "The Indian Eye on English Life, or Rambles of a Pilgrim Reformer"

The Indian student cannot mix with his English companions on equal terms. He is ill-prepared for it by his early training at home. For one thing, he is so backward in the sports and games that enter so largely into the formation of character and friendship at an English college. He may be patronized for a few weeks by some good-natured fellows, but he works like a drag upon them, so little can he enter into their habits and feelings. When dropped after a fair trial, the stranger keeps his own company, or, in seven cases out of ten, is taken in hand by the worst set at college or in the neighbourhood. He learns to smoke, drink, gamble, to bet, and to squander his substance in worse ways. The life "in apartments," that he has often to accept, does not offer any relief from this round of vulgar dissipation. He may contract debts and disease, and return home with, or without his degree. He carries away wrong impressions of English life, thanks mainly to his earlier home influences over which he could not soar. I am afraid this will continue in not a few cases so long as the difference in the home life of the two nations continues. That is a large problem. The question for the present is, how to offer the comforts and convenience of home to an Indian student in England; how to enable him to make the best of his brief sojourn in the land of his rulers. Even this question I prefer to leave to wiser heads, to more practical friends of our students. But there is one aspect of the question, rather a side issue, on which I should like to offer a few remarks in passing. I refer to the relations that should subsist between Englishmen and Indians, whether in England or in India. We are all agreed that these relations should be friendly. Englishmen vie with Indians in insisting upon this condition. I have very little doubt myself that the majority of Englishmen, official or unofficial, sympathize with native aspirations; but I am equally certain that some of these well-meaning friends overdo their part of friendliness (real friendship, such as we Asiatics feel, it would be too much to look for in such a case), and it seems that the patronizing Englishman does us as much harm as he who always disparages and decries our merits. Strange as it may sound, I hold that it is as bad for us to be given more consideration than our due, as it is to be given less consideration. We should be treated exactly as equals, if we deserve to be. You must not give us less than our due; and pray don't give us more either— in the shape of words or otherwise. We must rough it out with you at school, college, and in public life. Equal justice—and no more. I have preached this doctrine in and out of season for nigh upon fifteen years, incurring the displeasure of some of my own countrymen, and perhaps ridicule from English well-wishers. The Englishman cannot understand why I resent patronage from a superior race. The Indian suspects I am angling for popularity with the governing race at the expense of my "poor down-trodden country." Well, I don't mind what the Englishman may think of it; but I appeal to my own people, the educated portion thereof, to say if they love to wear the badge of inferiority. These remarks apply with equal force as between Natives and Natives; as, for instance, between Mohammedans and Hindus. As a true friend of each, I have always advised them not to rely too much on special favours or concessions. Let us ask of our English rulers and fellow-subjects to treat us as their equals; and where we are wanting, to push us up to their level, rather than keep us where we are, on a crust of comfort, such as they throw to the lame dog whom they do not wish to kick over the stile.

So strongly do I feel against differential treatment, that I have always opposed the suggestion made in India, from time to time, for separate carriage accommodation on the railway lines, in order to avoid race disputes which are by no means infrequent. I have myself suffered a good deal from the exclusiveness of English passengers. But rather than give in for peace sake, I have managed to keep my place and fought for it. In these tussles I have sometimes got the worst of it, but then I have found I was in the wrong.

To English friends in India, and more so to those in England, who are extra-polite to us, simply because we happen to be strangers, who stoop and bend in order to pat us on the back, I appeal earnestly to treat us more like fellow-subjects. By all means be kind and hospitable to us, as you are to your own people; but, above all, be just and impartial. Treat us as you treat your own brethren. Spare us not if you find us tripping. In a word, do not patronize but befriend us. Give us the right hand of fellowship at school and college, in the highways and byways of public life. Anything more from you we would rather be without. Habitual excess of forbearance is perhaps worse, in the long run, than an excess of severity.

The same equal treatment we ask for in the case of the nation as in the case of individuals. We want the public services to be open to Natives and Europeans alike; to be entered by one common portal, that of competition. We do not want England to send us her superfluous wealth; she has need of that at home. But we do want her to manage our resources in India as carefully as she manages her own. And the best way to do this, we think, is to associate with yourselves, in the conduct of public affairs, those of us who are competent for it, not by means of patronage—that is, on official sufferance— but by election mainly at the hands of qualified voters. In short, within the measure of our capacity and the circumstances of the country, there should be an approximation in the methods of government between India and England, with equality as the basis both of public administration and personal intercourse.

This, and much more, might be impressed upon the average English politician, if only be could be got at. But the difficulty is to interest him in the affairs of far-off India. His ignorance does not appear to be wilful. India is so large a problem that the majority of Englishmen give it up in despair. Those who are drawn to it by personal ties, or by a more generous attachment, are distracted by the proverbial multitude of counsel. I believe there ought to be a central informing agency in London, untainted by party bias and by pecuniary interest. Anglo-Indians could be of great service in this connection. Some of them doubtless are; I wish there were more. India has little to do with party politics. Conservatives, Liberals, and Radicals, are practically the same to her. Most of them are actuated by honest, if not strictly honourable intentions towards us. But it would be idle to expect the English, as a people, to concern themselves with our affairs, when they have so many of their own to occupy them. Their want of interest is excusable; they make no secret of it. There is hardly any excuse, however, for the ignorance of responsible men who have the governing of India. Theirs is sometimes a compound ignorance, as the Arabian would call it, an ignorance that knows not it is ignorant. My Lord Rattledrone is a good hand at letting in the light of knowledge Indian on the foggy horizon of his peers. Sir Evan Gossamer may get up a flash now and then to dazzle the Lower House. But when they and I come to close quarters, why do these rulers of India so often think discretion the better part of valour? Where is the need for running away from Indian questions? Take heart of grace, gentlemen, and face your duty. It is no use putting off the evil day. The day will grow more and more evil that way. India is getting on but for the unnatural economic conditions imposed on her by your ignorance. The drain on her resources, perhaps inevitable in the beginning, has been so continuous, that she has hardly enough blood left in her now for healthy circulation. This process of depletion tells most on the peasantry, least able to bear up against it. The heavy expenditure incurred by the military departments, coupled with this drain of resources, cannot last for ever. The sooner you find a remedy, the better for us both. I do not care much what is to become of you in case of a disruption. You will probably find fresh fields and pastures new. But what about us, after this steady growth of a century? A French writer recently drew a picture of the coming struggle in India. The picture appears to have been ludicrously overdrawn. But the colours are not all equally false. The present generation of Natives are duly grateful for the blessings of peace and education they have received. To them it has been a matter of personal experience. Will it be the same to the coming generations? They may look upon the blessings rather as a matter of course, while they cannot but resent poverty and lack of employment all the more keenly because of the education they have received. How long are our responsible rulers to grope in the dark, with the light of knowledge and experience fully available? If England will learn to govern India more and more in accordance with natural conditions, she will not only be amply repaid for the task in itself, but will find a market for her goods, of almost every description, ten times larger than she is likely to find elsewhere. The experiment is as glorious as it is profitable to both. I do not expect a political millennium to be reached to-morrow, any more than I expect a disruption to overtake us at once. But having discovered a mistake, we cannot set about correcting it too soon.

As to ruling India by the sword, my dear Colonel Swashbuckler, you ought to know better. How many swords do you keep in India? Sixty thousand?— eighty thousand?—a hundred thousand? And what is the population of India?—two hundred millions. Now, I defy you to cut off two thousand heads with one sword, even in imagination. You will use the armies of the Native States? How much will these swell the number of your swords? And you are shrewd enough to know that blood is thicker than water. Take my advice, dear Colonel; put your sword into a barrel of vinegar. It will improve vinegar and steel alike, and give you time to read up your school books of history again. How long can one nation rule another merely by the arm of flesh? Long may England continue to rule us, not by the sword, but by the rod.

Fierce is the struggle for existence in the West. Life and health are being ground down under the wheels of modern civilization. Not a little of this cruel sacrifice seems to be due to the arrogance of Capital in its dealings with Labour, especially with unskilled Labour. Hitherto Capital has had it pretty much its own way, in almost every sphere of activity. The day seems to be coming for Labour. Few sights in London interest an outsider so much as what are called working men's demonstrations and strikes. Men, tired of ill-treatment, make a common cause, and strike work. Happily, not a few of these Unions are guided by principle and intelligence. The men give due notice before they go out on strike, and so far the inconvenience to the general public is minimized, and business saved from complete dislocation. Others, pressed by hunger, are ready to take the place of those going on strike. Sometimes the employers prefer to suspend business in the course of negotiation with the strikers, or after the negotiations have failed. If they could, they would perhaps like to starve the men into acquiescence. Against this danger the men seem to be prepared, though very inadequately, thanks to the friends who advocate their cause, and to the public who contribute to their maintenance whilst out. Otherwise, the struggle would be hopelessly unequal, certainly, more ruinous to the aggrieved than to the other party. As it is, I am not sure if some of these Labour demonstrations are not overdone. A new movement is apt to run into excesses; and once it has seized the popular fancy, it works like an infection. Miners, gas-workers, dockers, railway, tram, and 'bus employés; tailors, carpenters, laundresses have, one after another, struck work; some of them obtaining their own terms when reasonable, others effecting a compromise; none, I believe, quite satisfied. In the wake of this suspension of private works we have seen public servants follow, such as postmen, policemen, and even, in a modified sense, some of the military. Evidently, then, the Labour Union has become an institution; and if it keeps within bounds, it will have the sympathy of many thoughtful and disinterested men. The time is nearing for England, when Labour, in the field or the market, shall have to be distinguished from serfdom, and Capital from grasping monopoly. The question is one of great interest. God grant it may be solved in peace, to the honour of English Capital and the advantage of Labour!

I have witnessed some of the demonstrations in Hyde Park, for instance, where the workmen and their sympathizers, with the idle and the curious, pour in by thousands, to the tune of music, the flourishing of banners and so on, generally on Sundays. The processions are joined by hundreds of women, many of whom really help in organizing them, as also in preserving order. They are, as a rule, very quiet and orderly. The strength of some of these organizations may be realized when it is seen that at one time I had to wait in a hansom for over an hour and a half before it could be allowed to get out at a corner of Curzon Street. The general effect of the multitudes walking past, in holiday attire, more fantastic than picturesque, singing, cheering, shouting, but seldom breaking the public peace, is striking enough. But the thing strikes one more as a show, a fair, than a protest. Of course, there is some haranguing in the park; mostly, by crude young socialists who have a pronounced habit of getting red in the face and of dropping their h's. The crowds do not seem to pay much attention to these orators, whom they patronize for a few minutes by turn, just to save appearances. I have not heard a single leader in the park. In the absence of any serious discussion, the thing strikes one most as a huge turn-out where "Mary Hann" takes the field chiefly because her "Arry" is out.

But how instructive the organization is for us in India! We are not likely to have much of it there, in the near future. For one thing, we lack the solidarity of interests. Our only organization worth naming is the National Congress. It is of the utmost importance that the Congress should go on working with a select body of educated men. When the movement extends lower down, or when other movements spring up on anything like the English scale, as between Labour and Capital, India will cease to be India. This latter event may be expected to arise only under the British Rule. India is poor, ignorant, and superstitious. But what can she not do with her numbers, if the numbers once acquire cohesion? It is difficult, however, to say whence the cohesion is to come—from politics or from religion. Politics cannot mould the social and domestic life of a people, as religion does. But religion in India is dead or decaying in the ranks where it is most potent for a wide-felt constructive influence.

To return to the strikes in England. Although one feels that sometimes the grievances of Labour are unreasonable, they are on the whole worthy of careful attention in the interests, not only of Labour but of Capital likewise. Capital has no right to kill Labour. What, for instance, can be so killing as to insist upon drivers and conductors working sixteen hours a day on the omnibus and the tramway lines? These poor men are hardly asleep before they have to awake. We have to think of them and of their families also; that is, of the interests of society. So far it is wrong of Government to stand aloof from this struggle between Capital and Labour, on the plea of freedom of contract. There can be no such thing as real freedom of contract between parties so grievously ill-matched. What free will is possible to a starving employé, as pitted against his prosperous employer? The latter can wait in comfort, whilst the former has starvation staring him daily in the face. It is absurd to postulate a free contract between urgent want, on one hand, and easy sufficiency, on the other. Freedom of contract is not the same thing as freedom of trade. I doubt if Capital will be able very long to resist the legitimate claims of Labour. The spirit of the age is crying out against such resistance. Not that the employers as a body are cruel men. But vested interests are very hard to move, and a false sense of *esprit de corps* makes them oblivious to duties which individually they feel sitting heavy on the conscience. On the other side, representatives of Labour cannot be too often reminded that the path of moderation is the only safe path for them. They must, in certain cases, be content with a shilling less for less work given. Reform in such matters is very slow; it comes by lingering instalments. Of course, the State cannot interfere with the details of a contract, having satisfied itself that the contract has been a really free and equitable one. [. . .]

Bombay: Apollo Printing Work, 1895. 64–70, 122–27, 254–58.

VICTORIA OCAMPO

Living History*

Trans. Doris Meyer

> Pyramids on the one hand; personal liberty on the other. We have an ever increasing number of pyramids or their modern equivalents; an ever diminishing amount of personal liberty. Is this merely a historical accident? Or are these two goods essentially incompatible? If they turn out to be essentially incompatible, then, one day, we shall have to ask ourselves very seriously which is better worth having—pyramids and a perfectly efficient, perfectly stable community; or personal liberty with instability, but the possibility, at least of a progress, measurable in terms of spiritual values.
>
> —Aldous Huxley, *Beyond the Mexique Bay*

I think there's something miraculous about *présence d'esprit*.[1] In one of the most beautiful places in the world (facing three open windows overlooking the tip of the Quai Bourbon) I met a woman in whom this miracle had oc-

---

* This essay was the result of an interview with Benito Mussolini that took place in Rome on September 24, 1934; it was written before Italy invaded Abyssinia in October 1935.

curred. It seems that, having granted her an audience, Mussolini asked her point-blank why she had wanted to see him. "Because I like living history" she replied.

No such question was put to me the day of my conversation with "il Duce," for which I thank heaven, since who knows what inept answer I would have stammered. But with enough Time—and with the help of esprit d'escalier[2]—no doubt I would have finally found the answer that Princess Murat managed to fire off with such opportune rapidity. Only I would have found it too late.

It was thus because I, too, like living history that one clear autumn afternoon, I climbed the steps of the Palazzo Venezia—so severely magnificent, built with stones from the Coliseum—whose perfect beauty is insulted day and night by the proximity of the Victor Emmanuel monument. Counting myself among those who, not believing in ordinary divinities, have transferred to writers of genius their share of credulity, I found myself for the first time about to encounter a genius of another kind: that of Caesar, the perpetual dictator.

Amid greetings in the Roman style and noiseless guards, and after a brief wait during which my eagerness to meet the Duce had time to dissolve in apprehension as a toothache vanishes in the dentist's office (however much one may repeat the "me ne frego"[3] popular among Fascists, at times it's of no avail), I was abandoned once and for all on the threshold of an immense hall. The austerity of its furnishings, which need not be described now, says no to the superfluous, the plural, with a violence that stuns even the least discerning visitor. In order to write, proclaims this austerity, one only needs a table; to sit down, a chair; for light, a lamp; to think and decide, a head. . . . It would be hard for me to remember the table, the chair, or the lamp. But the head would be hard not to remember. It's a monument to Resistance. One sinks into that face beyond the point of recovery, or so it seems. How can one be submerged in such a hard material? There's nothing in that proud (in the full sense of the word) face that doesn't offer terrible resistance: the eyes, the forehead, the nose, the mouth, the unexpected strength of the jaw—all resist. The gaze attracts just as the flame in a fireplace attracts one's eyes in a room.

The first words we exchanged aren't any easier for me to remember than the table, the chair, or the lamp. They matter very little. What matters is "that presence" which the visitor must swallow as the boa constrictor swallows his prey: whole. (Digestion comes later.) What one "hears" is that presence: it is massive, compact. One endures it like a shock. It takes up so much room that it alone seems to fill the immense hall of the Palazzo Venezia.

Some days earlier when 23,000 youngsters paraded before Mussolini, I had watched from a reviewing stand opposite his on the Via dell'Impero, and I had photographed something that made an extraordinary change in the expression of his face: his smile. Imagine a stone mask broken by a smile in which all hardness seems to melt instantly.

His smile seems to me as characteristic of him as his gaze, a gaze so sustained, so direct with his round eyes wide open, that one wonders if the fixed, immobile eyelids ever manage to close. This power of not blinking (in the strict and the figurative sense) is reinforced by something analogous in his elocution: not the slightest vacillation of any kind. I asked the Duce several questions about the role of women in the Fascist State and his opinion of their aptitudes. His answers were hurled at me as from a catapult. The precise sentences, interrupted by short silences, left no room for any doubt or misunderstanding. His tone was sharp; there was no Gordian knot it couldn't cut. Yet, in his lack of circumlocutions there was something appealing, even when the answer contradicted my most intimate convictions. Why?

"Fascist Italy," I said to the Duce, "thinks that the first duty of women is to give children to the State. But don't you believe that women can also collaborate with men in another way?" The Duce answered: "No." A definitive no. "Do you believe," he added, "that Julius Caesar, Napoleon, or Bismarck had any need of such collaboration?" And then, in reply to my silence which he interpreted perfectly: "Do you think that Dante wrote the *Commedia* because of Beatrice? No. What inspired Dante was his hatred of Florence."

Certainly a measure of hatred entered into the *Commedia*, but one has to be short-sighted not to see something else in that poem too. And even if we admit the hypothesis that it might have been that way for Dante, there are other poets. . . . And history also includes, if I'm not mistaken, Cleopatra's nose. That nose which, if it had been any shorter, would have changed the face of the world.

Mussolini's opinion of women doesn't lend itself to equivocation. They shouldn't get involved in politics because they don't understand it. Nor in philosophy, music, or architecture, for the same reason. Of course there are exceptions, but they only confirm the rule.

In parenthesis, and apropos of architecture, all praise would be insufficient to commend the Duce's support of young architects and modern architecture. These young people are beginning to demonstrate their talent in the most convincing manner. Both Le Corbusier and Gropius have spoken to me about them with the greatest esteem and the most sincere admiration. Whereas in Germany and Russia the modern architect has entered the ranks of the unemployed, seeing all his proposals rejected and rescinded, in Italy he finds the effective and intelligent approval of the Duce.

Going back to the opinions of Mussolini concerning women (the principal topic of my conversation with him), in his judgment, a woman can be useful in medicine as long as she's not in surgery. He finds her excellent as a nurse and irreplaceable in early childhood education.

In his opinion, women cannot move in abstract spheres. Instinct is their element. Mussolini concedes the right to have a child, no matter what the circumstances, with the State's support. And, as in Spain or Russia, all children are equal before the law. This is simple justice.

Nonetheless it's evident that his categorical manner of limiting women by the north and the south, the east and the west of their humanity is very debatable from many points of view. Why pretend to be concerned with certain women's problems when one believes in the ideal that everything should be sacrificed to the State, with a capital S, so that the State may be great and strong?

Just as London is a city where the pedestrian's glance is most captivated by articles for men: pipes, ties, vests, tweeds, canes, shirts, scarves, in sumptuous stores (whose luxury is expressed only by quality); similarly Fascist Italy appears to the ingenuous traveler to be a country for men, a country in which the accent falls on unmitigated masculinity. Italy seems to apply to everything the grammatical rule of agreement which requires that after enumerating names of both genders, the only gender that should be taken into account is the masculine. Since "State" belongs to the masculine gender (so it seems) and since everything must agree with "State," the consequences are clear. But in the long run, couldn't this provoke an imbalance—that is to say, progress in one sense and simultaneous retrogression in another?

The fact is that when one dreams of a better world, the place conceded to women by Fascism is not enough.

There are two countries in Europe that are undergoing a thrilling moment in their history—and that of the world: Italy and Russia. At the Convegno Volta where I witnessed the magnificent and generous hospitality (a hospitality I shared in response to a very special invitation for which I am sincerely grateful) offered by Rome to outstanding individuals who had come from all over Europe to expound their ideas about the theater, there were two Russians among the invited guests. One of them, known to the public in Buenos Aires, was Tairoff. I had occasion to converse with him and to question him about the USSR. But even more interesting than what he told me and what I heard him declare in his report to the Convegno Volta was what Andre Malraux told me about his own trip to Russia. This French writer (author of *La Condition Humaine,* one of the best novels to appear in recent years) had just spent several months there, and one of the things that impressed him most was the mentality and attitude of the young women. As I don't want to run the risk of altering someone else's ideas and as I know that Malraux himself will write about the subject, it is to him, to his next books, that I refer the reader who is curious about observations of this sort. For my part, throughout the conversations I had with him, I was able to infer that today's Russian woman is offered all the possibilities for development. This time—and it is perhaps the first in contemporary history—what tomorrow brings her depends solely on her abilities, her conscience, and her aptitudes. It's too early to judge the outcome of this experience, but the future will not fail to do so.

What is being born in Russia as well as in Italy is a new youth, a youth molded in exaltation. I'm not acquainted with and haven't seen that of Russia, but one day I hope to. I *have* seen that of Italy.

Beautiful, well-formed children who played gravely at being soldiers; adolescents full of impulse and grace who marched one warm September afternoon along the Via dell'Impero with a rhythmic step. Happy in their own rhythm, they left me with an unerasable memory: that of their joyous faces turned toward the Duce. That human material was beautiful, beautiful like the Latin sky, more so than all the beautiful dead stones that Rome is so filled with and justifiably proud of. I have seen the Duce smile at the young with a smile that changed even the hard material of his face.

My memory continues to focus on those enchanting new faces stamped with ecstasy—balillas, *avanguardisti, piccole italiane, giovane italiane*[4]—more than it focuses on Rome, renewed by a thorough cleaning that makes the value of each ruin stand out; more than the *autostrade* that unfold in clear ribbons around the peninsula; more than the drained Pontine marshes; more than the organization of the *dopolavoro;*[5] more than the aviation exposition in Milan that is a work of art of its own kind; more than all that has been accomplished successfully in Italy thanks to the Duce. I focus on that memory and on the irrepressible smile that it provoked on his lips—that smile that changes even the hard material of his face. Whoever has not seen Mussolini in the shadow of his blossoming country has not seen him. Those ecstatic faces on one side, that smile of irresistible paternal pride on the other: what will emerge from this love? Because there is love between those children and that man.

In my capacity as a woman, what may come of that reciprocal love strikes me as more important than everything else; more important than what may come of all the hatreds. Hatreds don't interest me. In my capacity as a woman, I cannot subscribe to the idea of the game of destruction of young bodies, for example. If men—even the greatest ones—call the violent repugnance which that game inspires in me foolishness, I won't feel mortified or humiliated. If they explain to me with compassion that that game has existed as long as the existence of man and that it will only disappear from the earth with him, they won't change me or convince me. Cannibalism exists too, and in certain tribes human sacrifices. Why then be shocked by them and try to repress them? They are forgotten customs to which we could return, and nothing more.

Is it possible that women, destined to build the bodies of men with their own bodies, may have the supreme inferiority not to oppose the destruction or systematic mutilation of their creation?

Men and women—I repeat, and women—have never achieved anything great without heroism. That I know. But heroism is applicable to so many things that don't have to do with war (the word has finally come out), to so many things that don't deal with what Marinetti calls "the aesthetic of war in all its splendor of individuals, masses, terrestrial and aerial machines, in all its stimulation of the most luminous human virtues." One can, one must be ready to die—and even to live—for certain ideas such as the fatherland. Those ideas are the fatherland. No woman worthy of the name disputes that. But no woman worthy of the name can resign herself to believing that the masculine game of systematic destruction of young bodies is an indispensable sport for wicked children (who are sometimes grown men) solely for the reason that they have always enjoyed that game. She hopes that wicked children will learn to conduct themselves otherwise, just as she hopes for the discovery of an anticancer serum (hasn't the vaccination against smallpox been discovered?). Is it perhaps hoping for the impossible? And how can one not feel despair for humanity if one doesn't have that hope?

More beautiful than all the beautiful dead stones of which Rome is so proud, as beautiful as the Latin sky, are the young Italians who turned their faces toward the Duce. What will become of this human material? Just as in Russia, only the future can be the judge of this.** Whatever happens will depend on the Head of State. I have seen Italy in blossom turn its face toward him. And in my heart there is only one fervent desire: that the smile of the Duce—that smile that changes even the hard material of his face—may protect and guide that youth to a safe harbor for the greater glory of a country which, by its nature, its traditions, and the art treasures it possesses, is unique in the world.

** The future has already judged: the Italo-Abyssinian war. There is where a part of this beautiful Italian youth has ended up. I wish to declare here publicly my adhesion to the two manifestos published in France and motivated by this war: that of the liberal and democratic intellectuals and that of the Catholic intellectuals answering the manifesto of the Fascist intellectuals. Both manifestos condemn this war of aggression which is the most odious form of war.

And today (in August 1936) at a time when Argentine Catholics are protesting en masse against the anticlerical excesses provoked in Spain (against the leftists) by the civil war that is destroying the country, it is opportune to recall to these same Catholics the extreme indifference or the open Fascism that they showed during the Italo-Abyssinian war. Meanwhile, the true Catholics, the only ones deserving the title, declared in France: "Christianity makes us understand and realize this truth of natural order—that justice is for all men with no exception for persons, races or nations, and that the soul and life of a negro are as sacred as the soul and life of a white." (V O.)

From *Domingos en Hyde Park*. In Doris Meyer, *Victoria Ocampo: Against the Wind and the Tide*. New York: George Braziller, 1979. 217–22.

Notes

1. "keeping one's wits about one"
2. "after-wit or afterthought"
3. "I don't give a damn"
4. Fascist youth groups
5. A Fascist organization that provided after-work-hours activities

VICTORIA OCAMPO

Woman, Her Rights and Her Responsibilities

> "Je n'ai pas besoin d'ordre et me rend de plein gré
> Où non point tant la loi que mon amour me mène. . . ."[1]
>
> —André Gide, *Perséphone*

The revolution signifying the emancipation of women is an event destined to have more repercussions in the future than the world war or the advent of the machine age. Millions of men and women don't yet know that it has occurred, or they attribute this phenomenon to a passing fad, or they imagine that it can only bring humanity a shameful increase in licentiousness, or they smile with superiority at the mention of something so inadmissible. In no way does this alter the accomplished fact. The revolution has taken place since it has already slipped into the consciousness of certain people.

I only wonder whether the word "emancipation" is correct. Wouldn't it be more appropriate to say "liberation?" It seems to me that this term, applied to serfs and slaves, better encompasses what I want to say. Let's not forget that the intolerably coercive methods that men use with women so naturally, and that women accept with surprising meekness, are still legal in many parts of the world. The story of the wife who gets indignant because a compassionate onlooker wants to stop her husband from beating her is perpetuated and reproduced in a thousand ways. The English thinker who affirmed that the masculine sex is sadistic by constitution and that the feminine sex is masochistic has found, as I see it, part of the explanation of the problem—but only if you take away the words "by constitution" and substitute "by force of habit."

In other words, it is true that women have learned to enjoy letting men mistreat them, as it is also true that men, for their part, have learned to enjoy allowing themselves to mistreat women. Of course this mistreatment is generally not physical but moral, and occasionally it takes very refined forms. One cannot expect men to renounce immediately the voluptuousness in which they have immersed themselves daily for centuries. Women themselves will have to take the initiative and "deprive" themselves of the delightful narcotic to which they have become no less addicted.

It is incredible, and I speak now without irony, that millions of human beings have not yet understood that current demands made by women are simply limited to requiring that a man stop thinking of a woman as a colony for him to exploit and that she become instead "the country in which he lives."

In a book on racial problems recently published by three English men of science, Julian Huxley, A. C. Haddon, and A. M. Carr-Saunders, I have found pages on the subject of heredity that seem extremely important to me if considered from the viewpoint of the current problems of women.

In the chapter to which I refer, the subject dealt with is the physical stature of the English. Being emulators of St. Thomas's dictum "seeing is believing," the authors of *We Europeans*—the book in question—are guided solely by facts and statistics. Their religion is scientific investigation and precision. These gentlemen assure us:

1. That the average stature of the English has increased during the second half of the last century (as is the case in some other nations), and

2. That the average stature of the different social classes in England (and in other nations) varies—that of the upper classes being larger.

With regard to the first topic, these gentlemen believe that the average stature has increased because of better food and better conditions of life, not because there has been an intrinsic change in constitution. In other words, racially, the Englishman has not undergone appreciable alteration, and if he were to be returned to his former state of existence, he would be what he had been before.

The second topic is more difficult to resolve. Of course, say these gentlemen, the greater part of the difference in stature between one social class and another is due to the fact that the children of the privileged classes enjoy many more advantages. But it can also be said that there is an average genetic difference between the different classes: that is, that there could be a lineage of large genetic stature in the upper classes, descendants of the Norman invaders, and a lineage of low genetic stature in the lower classes, descendants of a Mediterranean type that inhabited Great Britain before the Norman invasion. One could also say that selection might have favored the type of large genetic stature in the upper classes (through the preference for tall women) and the type of low stature among the proletariat (this type being better able to adapt itself to life in the cities and conditions prevalent in factories). Both causes, probably, the genetic and the environmental, have functioned at the same time. At this point in their logical deductions, these gentlemen are led to consider the question from a new angle, which is the one that interests us with respect to women because it touches us directly and places arguments at our disposal that are difficult to refute:

What is applicable to stature can be applied equally—and with how much greater force, affirm these gentlemen—to psychological character, that is, to intelligence, to special aptitudes, to temperaments. In the first place, this character suffers much more from changes in environment than does the physical character. In the second place, the social environment manifests a larger scale of differences than the physical environment does.

For instance, an extraordinary mathematical talent would not be capable of expressing itself in paleolithic society or among contemporary savages. The most perfect artistic gift would have little meaning on a desert island. The temperament that allows its owner easily to put himself into a state of trance or to have visions would, in an industrial country like Great Britain, expose him to the danger of being locked up in a mental institution or classified as a pathological case. By contrast, in various American countries and in certain Asiatic tribes, it would favor his rise to power and would bring him great prestige as a magician, medicine man, or shaman. A warrior's temperament, which would have found adequate means of expression at the start of Jewish history, would have remained sterile in the era of captivity.

In sum, the same capacities of invention or initiative that can assert themselves powerfully in favorable circumstances can be reduced to nothingness in equally unfavorable circumstances.

Generally, the expression of a particular temperament seems almost always to be determined in childhood—a fact that accounts for the idea that any change in the atmosphere of the home and in prevailing theories and educational methods profoundly affects the child. Thus also, and I continue to transcribe the opinions of these gentlemen, the peremptory affirmation, repeated to satiety, is that differences in aptitude and character between men and women are related in most instances to the difference between the education that males and females receive and to the difference between the economic and social situation of the two sexes. An amusing illustration of this is the indignant exclamation of a Greek of third-century Athens: "Who ever heard of a female cook!"

It is evident, they continue, that individuals endowed with an exceptional combination of genes will probably conquer the obstacles that confront them. But it is also evident that the quantity of innate talent that a person possesses depends for its realization and expression upon the outlets it encounters for its development, and these in turn depend upon such factors relative to environment as economic resources, social climate, and existing educational systems. An apparent reason why the children of the upper classes have proportionately better results in their studies than the children of the lower classes is that they have had more opportunity to receive a better education, whether or not they are gifted by heredity.

Now let's leave these gentlemen.

For my part, I believe that all we have just said about children can be said equally about women. As compared to men, they have always had the same handicap that the children of the proletariat have had as compared to children of the privileged classes. And they have had it for centuries. Although there may once have been a reason for this state of affairs, nothing justifies it today. Neither in one case or the other.

What men, apart from a minority that I bless, do not seem to understand is that we are not at all interested in taking *their* place (this is an error that our extreme reaction to their attitudes may have contributed to creating), but in taking *our own* completely—something that has not happened as yet.

The revolution that is being brought about in our world today—that of women, the most important one—is in no way an *ôte-toi que je m' y mette*[2] like the majority of revolutions. It is certainly not being made in order that women may invade the territory of men, but in order that men may finally stop invading the territory of women, which is a very different matter. Just as in the case of the other revolution (the one that was born in Russia and that, because of the extreme situation that caused it to erupt also created error, brutal attitudes, and terrible misunderstandings), it should not be undertaken, at least the way I understand it, in order that the proletariat may abuse the privileged classes in the same way as the privileged classes have abused it (which would create a vicious circle); it should be undertaken so that every child, having received the same wealth of care in what pertains to his physical and moral health and his education, may ultimately develop his innate talents as well as possible (thereafter inequality of distribution will be based only on this factor), and so that once he is an adult, he may reach the level that corresponds to his true vocation and his authentic worth.

I believe that the great role of the woman in history, played up to now in a rather subterranean way, is beginning to crop out at the surface. It is *she* today who can contribute powerfully to creating a new state of things since all her physical and spiritual being is concentrated on the very fountain of life—the child. She lives, therefore, closer to the future man, since the child over whom she exercises her power, consciously or unconsciously, is that man.

Therefore, I believe that if today's world, which is turned toward chaos, is going to recover an order, a lost equilibrium, it will be the woman who will find herself—whether you admit it or not, take it seriously or not, whether the masses ignore it or not—in the first line of the trenches. Without her collaboration, without awakening her consciousness to the share of work, responsibility, and struggle that is incumbent upon her, I do not see a possibility of salvation. Most grown men do not change, they only wear disguises. When they have reached a certain age, men are as unchangeable, physically, as a child just out of his mother's womb. One can dye his hair but not alter the color of his eyes.

I believe then that everything that leads to awakening the consciousness of the woman so that she will be given an exact notion of her responsibilities, everything that leads to raising her spiritual level and carrying out her education under the best possible conditions analogous to those of man, granting her the means to develop all her faculties whatever they may be, that is what interests us essentially. The rest will come with it.

For this reason, I also believe that every person who wishes to take up this cause should put the elevation of the spiritual and cultural level of women first on the agenda, and I believe that by working for this cause, one works for peace among nations and within nations.

War is an abomination that awakens a woman's rebelliousness much more than a man's because it is the woman who builds with her own body the body of man. And when man mutilates and reduces to formless shreds the very body that, with all her female instinct, she feels the need to protect and conserve, man kills woman as well—and in the cruelest way: obliging her to survive that death.

Woman is capable of heroism and of understanding the heroism of man. She knows very well that, to live life fully and with dignity, it is necessary at times to sacrifice it. But war, today's war, has become so monstrous, so stupid, threatening in such away the whole human species, that one cannot now see heroism in it—only the most dangerous and contagious insanity that the planet has ever suffered.

What can be done to counteract it? As long as the consciousness of man is not transformed—and in this transformation one of the principal factors must be the woman, mother not only by flesh and in flesh, but also mother by spirit and in spirit—all the great pacifist declarations, the abstract plans of action, the societies of nations will, in a word, fail. Peace among nations cannot become a material reality until it acquires a spiritual reality in individuals pure enough to create it. The present League of Nations has not had sufficient strength because it has not had sufficient purity. Dominated by nations that pretend to forget that their current prestige is due to past violence, it can therefore hardly exert any moral power over nations which, by their current violence, try to achieve a future prestige.

Let's try to shed light on these errors. As Aldous Huxley has just said magnificently in a pamphlet on "Constructive Peace," what is needed are men and women who think, feel, and wish—that is to say, with mind, heart, and will; and all must gather together around this cause with a spirit of sacrifice and with absolute fervor. Because this ideal of peace either must be taken as a new religion (what Christ said seems new, so forgotten has it been in practice) or it is better not to mention it, so useless will it be.

In order that the consciousness of the male-child may change or become clearer through the woman, it is necessary that the woman herself rise to the occasion of that task, a task that is hers. We cannot create anything outside ourselves without first having created it inside ourselves. I don't doubt that man will end up becoming what he should vis-à-vis woman. But what is still more urgent is that woman become what she should be vis-à-vis herself. One will be the consequence of the other. From this new attitude will be born a much truer, stronger, and more worthwhile union between man and woman. The magnificent union of two equal beings who mutually enrich each other since they possess different wealths. A union that can only exist among those who accept, *with knowledge of cause,* their independence.

In order for man and woman to cooperate with each other it is necessary that, on man's part, his coercive and patriarchal morality disappear ("patriarchal" used in the same sense as the word "matriarchal," that is, the imposition and absolute predominance of one sex over the other). On the woman's part, the false point of view that has been able to create in her the antagonism of her sex, the rebellion against the oppressor, must also disappear.

The emancipation of woman, as we understand it, is not made to separate her from man but, to the contrary, to bring her closer to him in the most complete, most pure, and most conscious way. In the struggle for life—so rough in our day and prone to pitting individuals against each other in distrust, competition, brutal defense of interests, or opposing doctrines—man and woman have only one natural means of escape from their intolerable isolation: mutual love. In that refuge, at least, they will have to lay down their weapons.

I know that this is not easy or simple. The union of man and woman is a human feat with something of a miracle, and even under the best conditions it is not accomplished without tenacity and patience—I would almost say the combined heroism of two beings—just as a work of art is born of the tenacity, patience, and heroism of a single being possessed of a great love.

But in order to achieve the conditions in which this more perfect union can be accomplished—that is, in order, as women, to find ourselves and occupy the place that belongs to us—we must not wait for the help of men. It cannot occur to them to recover for us the rights of which they do not feel deprived. It is never the oppressors who rebel against the oppressed. Before the rebellion of the oppressed, the attitude of the oppressors is always the same: a small minority gives in to the evidence, understands, accepts, and is ready to do justice; a greater majority feels dispossessed, outraged, and lets forth howls of indignation and anger.

In these cases, only the minorities count. In these cases and, in my judgment, in all cases. The minorities will always be, willingly or not, the world leaders.

Not only can we not logically expect for the moment the help of men, or rather their initiative in these questions, but we must also be prepared to find resistance or indifference (which is even more disheartening) on the part of a large number of women. They will invoke a thousand reasons, some in order to block our progress, others in order to preserve neutrality. There may even be the case, which I think will be common, of their being with us but, nevertheless, abstaining from taking a definite and active role.

Many women, supported by many men, will say that they have enough to do nursing children, feeding them, and changing their diapers. We know all too well that the ones who are working (except of course those who have made a profession of caring for children) have only a limited time to give to these chores, whereas the ones who are idle, dedicated in general to other pursuits, will find excuses for limiting it.

A friend of Madame Curie told me that it was when she was warming milk for her babies' bottles that she also began working seriously with her husband, thereafter becoming the admirable woman that the world has just lost. Is it not desirable that this type of woman be stimulated and cultivated?

The emancipation of women, as I conceive it, attacks the very roots of the evils that afflict female humanity and, on the rebound, male humanity since one is inseparable from the other. And through an inherent justice, the miseries suffered by one produce instantaneous repercussions on the other in different ways.

It is my firm and ardent wish that a group of Argentine women, however small, may acquire a consciousness of their duties which are rights, and of their rights which are responsibilities. If the women of this group can answer for themselves, they will be able to answer shortly for innumerable women.

From *Testimonios II*. In Doris Meyer. *Victoria Ocampo: Against the Wind and the Tide*. Trans. Doris Meyer. New York: George Braziller, 1979. 228–34.

Notes

1. "I do not need order and I deliver myself willingly / Not so much to where the law, but to where my love leads me." These lines are from the final portion of Gide's poem, set to music by Stravinsky and recited by V. O. in several performances directed by the composer.

2. "get out and let me in"

JEAN RHYS

Meta

Now it is time to talk about Meta, my nurse and the terror of my life. She had been there ever since I could remember: a short, stocky woman, very black and always, I thought, in a bad temper. I never saw Meta smile. She always seemed to be brooding over some terrible, unforgettable wrong. When I wasn't old enough to walk by myself I can remember the feel of her hard hand as she hauled me along to the Botanical Gardens, where she was supposed to take me every afternoon. She walked so fast that I had to run to keep up with her, and most of the time, her face turned away, she muttered, curses I suppose.

She dragged me past Miss Jane's sweet shop. I'd often been there with my older sister before she left. Miss Jane was an old coloured lady whose small house was on the way to the Botanical Gardens and her sweets were not only delicious but very cheap. There you could get a small jar of freshly made guava jelly for a penny. The base of most of the other sweets was syrup—mixed with shredded coconut, a tablet, with ginger, a ginger cake. The most expensive were made of clarified sugar and cashew nuts. Those, I think, were three pence. The strangest was a sweet which was called lassi mango, if that is how it is spelt. When it was broken it would stretch indefinitely. The game was for one child to take one end, the other child the other, and go in different directions. At last it would be an almost invisible thread, and the joke was to watch someone walk into it and slap themselves, trying to account for the stickiness. Past all these delights Meta would drag me, taking not the faintest notice of my efforts to escape and jerking me if I looked back.

It was Meta who talked so much about zombies, soucriants and loups-garous. She was the only person I've heard talk about loups-garous (werewolves) in the West Indies. Soucriants were always women, she said, who came at night and sucked your blood. During the day they looked like ordinary women but you could tell them by their red eyes. Zombies were black shapeless things. They could get through a locked door and you heard them walking up to your bed. You didn't see them, you felt their hairy hands round your throat. For a long time I never slept except right at the bottom of the bed with the sheet well over my head, listening for zombies. I suppose someone came in and pulled it down or I would have suffocated.

She also taught me to fear cockroaches hysterically. She said that when I was asleep at night they would fly in and bite my mouth and that the bite would never heal. Cockroaches can be about two inches long, they fly and they smell very disagreeable, but it was Meta who taught me to be truly afraid of them. It didn't help that my mother, who tackled centipedes with great spirit, would go out of the room if a cockroach flew in and refuse to come back until it had been caught. Meta also told me that if a centipede was killed all the different bits would be alive and run into corners to become bigger, stronger centipedes. It must be crushed. She said "mashed up." To this day I'm not quite sure if I really saw two halves of a centipede walking away from each other, still alive.

Even Meta's stories were tinged with fear and horror. They all ended like this: "So I went to the wedding and they say to me, 'What you doing here?' I say, 'I come to get something to eat and drink.' He give me one kick and I fly over the sea and come here to tell you this story."

Years later I made great friends with a Negro girl called Francine. I've written about her before. Francine's stories were quite different, full of jokes and laughter, descriptions of beautiful dresses and good things to eat. But the start was always a ceremony. Francine would say "Tim-tim." I had to answer "Boissêche," then she'd say, *"Tablier Madame est derrière dos"* (Madam's apron is back to front). She always insisted on this ceremony before starting a story and it wasn't until much later, when I was reading a book about obeah, that I discovered that Boissêche is one of the gods. I grew very fond of Francine and admired her; when she disappeared without a word to me I was hurt. People did disappear, they went to one of the other islands, but not without saying goodbye. I still think of Francine and now I can imagine other reasons for her complete disappearance from the house and from my life.

More than anything else I detested a joke Meta used to play on me. I became very friendly with a little boy who was called Willy, like my father. When we came home from school we were supposed to change into fresh "afternoon clothes" as we called them. While I was struggling with strings and buttons and hooks, Meta would say that Master Willy had called for me and was waiting downstairs. I would hurry up and fly down rather dishevelled to find no Willy and Meta laughing loudly in the distance. She played this trick on me several times before I became suspicious.

She was forbidden to slap me and she never did but she got her own back by taking me by the shoulders and shaking me violently. Hair flying, while I still had any breath to speak I would yell, "Black Devil, Black Devil, Black Devil!" I never dreamed of complaining to my mother about all this, and I doubt if it would have been any good if I had, but my relief was enormous when Meta left or was sent away. I can't remember who took her place or if anybody did. But in any case it was too late, the damage had been done. Meta had shown me a world of fear and distrust, and I am still in that world.

In *Smile Please: An Unfinished Autobiography.* Berkeley: Donald S. Ellis/Creative Arts, 1979. 22–24.

JEAN RHYS

Chorus Girls

I was a year and a half to two years in *Our Miss Gibbs.* In the winter we toured small towns in the north, and in the summer the seaside places. The chorus girls' wages were thirty-five shillings a week and extra for every matinée. When you signed the contract you gave them the option for the next tour so long as it was work you were capable of doing. It was a steady job. There was, however, a dreadful gap after the winter tour finished and before the summer tour started. It was impossible to save enough to tide you over this gap, so most of the girls lived at home for those two or three months. The few who, like myself, had no home tried to get a job in what were known as music hall sketches, which went on all the year round.

In one of the gaps I managed to be taken on in the chorus of a music hall sketch called *Chanticleer.* The name was taken from a Paris revue that was a great success at that time. Ours was an appalling show. The biggest joke in it was a girl in tights walking across the stage, dropping an egg and clucking loudly. Only one or two of the girls were at all attractive and we were hardly rehearsed. However, we opened at a town in the north and there we were, waiting in the wings, ready to go on. It was cold and I was shivering. We heard a loud tramping noise and somebody said, "What on earth's that?" The answer was: "That's the gallery walking out." The gallery didn't hiss or boo if they disliked a show, they simply walked out, making as much noise as possible. When it was our turn to go on with our very amateurish dance I was shivering with fear as well as with cold.

As soon as we began I felt the mockery and scorn coming up from the audience like smoke. I was at the end of the line, near the wings, and after a bit of this I simply left the line and went offstage. Before I left I looked at the girl next to me. Her face was grim. She felt it as much as I did but bravely she went on dancing. I took my make-up off and went back to my lodgings feeling very unhappy at being so cowardly. I kept thinking, "She stuck it, why couldn't I?" I made up my mind that on the next night I would stick it whatever they did, whether they hissed, booed or even threw things.

I was in the dressing room with the other girls, making up, when the call-boy knocked and said, "Will Miss Gray please go to Mr. Peterman's office at once." Gray was the name I was using then. Mr. Peterman was the owner and manager of the show. As soon as I got into the room I saw he was in a towering rage. As he glared at me with a tight mouth he looked terrifying. "Why," he said, "did you walk offstage in the middle of the act last night? Were you ill?"

"No, I wasn't ill," I said. "I was frightened."

"And what were you frightened of?"

I said that I was frightened of the audience.

He said, "And what the hell are you doing on the stage, may I ask, if you are frightened of an audience? You can take off your make-up and go home. I don't want to have anything more to do with you, letting down the show like that."

I said, "Well, I shouldn't have run away, I know, but I think you ought to give me my fare back to London."

"And why should I give you your fare? I'll do nothing of the sort."

I had no money at all, so—as always when I am desperate—I was able to fight.

There was a society called, I think, "for the Protection of Chorus Girls." I knew the address and I said, "Mr. Peterman, if you don't give me my fare back to London I will write to the society and complain about you." He growled. I had never before heard a man growl like a dog, but he did. He said, "There's an excursion train to London tomorrow. I'll give you the money for that, nothing else."

When I returned to the dressing room to take my make-up off, the girl next to me said, "Peterman's in an awful rage because I think he's got hardly any bookings for this show."

"I don't wonder," I said.

I was used to sleeping late and the excursion train left at some abnormally early hour. I was so afraid of missing it that I sat up all night, suitcase at my feet, waiting. When I got to London and to my aunt, who was there at the time, she said, "Whatever have you been doing with yourself? You look shocking. You'd better go and have a bath at once, you're so dirty."

I have forgotten how I got over the rest of the gap. I suppose my aunt helped me. Later I went back to *Our Miss Gibbs*.

There was an elaborate dancer in the show, what they called a speciality dancer, and the speciality dancer and the chorus girls were at daggers drawn. She would seldom have anything to do with us; the chorus, in retaliation, responded by attacking her appearance, her manners, her morals. Every possible vice was piled on the poor girl. She had a little dog with her, and the sort of thing the chorus girls said was that she kept the dog to make love to her. I used to watch her from the wings because I loved her dance, and I didn't think she was bad, though rather haughty and touch-me-not. I knew the things said about her were unfair.

People talk about chorus girls as if they were all exactly alike, all immoral, all silly, all on the make. As a matter of fact, far from being all alike they were rather a strange mixture. One of them was the daughter of a well-known Labour leader and we noticed that whenever a Conservative victory had been won and we all cheered (for we were all Conservatives), she cheered more than any of us. We decided she hated her father. Another girl was the daughter of a woman who stood up for Oscar Wilde. There were chorus girls of sixteen and chorus girls of nearly forty; the contract signed with George Dance for *Our Miss Gibbs* enabled you to stay forever if you liked, until you were old and grey. Besides, the older ones often had good voices and were very useful. Some, though not many, were married. Some were engaged to be married and looking forward to their marriages like any other girl. Some were very ambitious, determined to make a good marriage (which was quite possible), and if you imagine they ever did anything which might interfere with that you don't know the type. Some were ambitious to get on in the theatre. These were rather few and far between and I noticed that nearly all of them came from theatrical families.

There was always the company tart, but no one ever called her a tart. They just said, "So-and-so has a lot of friends." She would seldom turn up for the train calls, for someone would be sure to take her by car from one town to the next. I will never forget the face of the stage manager when a girl called Nancy was missing for the rehearsal call on a Monday. A telegram was brought in to him, he opened it and said in a bewildered voice, "*Contretemps*—what the devil does she mean, *contretemps?*" I think it was a day or two before Nancy turned up, and somebody else had to be taught her dance.

We travelled with theatrical baskets which were collected by the theatrical baggage man every Thursday and went with the scenery. So we were left with small suitcases with washing things, toothbrush and very minimal make-up. Sunday was travelling day. The classic joke about travelling was two railway men talking. "What have you got there, Bill?" "Fish and actors." "Oh, shove them on a siding."

Everybody knew the good theatrical lodgings, and everyone knew they were taken in advance. We had to do the best we could. Sometimes we struck lucky, sometimes not. You could save a bit if you lived with another girl, more if you lived with two. The food was always the same. We would get to the new lodgings after our Sunday train journey to a large joint of beef, usually very tough. On Monday we had it warmed up. On Tuesday minced. On Wednesday shepherd's pie or stew. On Thursday something exotic like eggs and bacon or liver. On Friday it was go as you can. On Saturday we were much too busy packing. On Sunday we left for another town which was exactly like the last one, or so I thought. All this was in the winter, in the north.

I never liked our landladies, but one I hated. I was living with a girl called Billie, and we were waiting upstairs with our suitcases packed when the landlady came in and presented us with her bill. It was enormous, about three times what we were expecting. Billie gave one look at it and said, "We're, not going to pay this!" The landlady said, "Oh, yes you will, or you won't leave here." She left the room and locked the door. Billie and I emptied our purses and there wasn't nearly enough to pay her, nor to pay the fare to the next town if we missed our train. Billie said, "There's only one thing to do about this," and opened the window. We were on the second floor but the snow was very thick on the ground down below. Billie said, "Well, here's to it." She threw her suitcase out and jumped after it. She lay still on the ground and I was frightened. After a while she looked up and said, "Come on." I wondered if it was awful but I didn't ask her. I threw my suitcase out too, and jumped. It was an awful bump in spite of the snow and for a while I lay still, wondering if I was dead. Then Billie said, "Come on," so I got up, and we were running out of the garden gate with our suitcases when we saw the landlady looking after us and frowning. Billie said, "One word to you!" and together we ran out of the gate, laughing. From this time dated my irrevocable hatred of landladies.

In England my love and longing for books completely left me. I never felt the least desire to read anything, not even a newspaper, and I think this indifference lasted a long time. Years. I don't remember reading anything on tour except *Forest Lovers*. *Forest Lovers* was a book set in the Middle Ages, about a man and a girl who loved each other very much and who escaped into the forest to hide, but they always slept with a sword between them. All the girls in the dressing room had read the book and the conversation about the sword was endless. "What did they have to do that for? Why? Besides, you could easily get over the sword." "No you couldn't, you'd get cut." "Of course you wouldn't." The company tart, whom I liked very much, would sometimes lend me a book. I wouldn't really read it and sometimes I'd forget it, and she would embarrass me at train calls by shouting down the platform: "Now then, Verney, what've you done with my book?" However abominable and dull my life was, it never occurred to me to buy a book or even a newspaper, which now seems very strange to me.

Going from room to room in this cold dark country, England, I never knew what it was that spurred me on and gave me an absolute certainty that there would be something else for me before long. Now I think the "something else" was something small and limited. I realize that I was no good on the stage, forgot my lines, didn't thirst for the theatre as some of the girls did, yet I was so sure.

I got sick of being in *Our Miss Gibbs,* sick of wearing old Gaiety dresses cleaned. So we left—who was the girl I left with? I have forgotten—and got a job in the chorus of a pantomime at the Old Lyceum Theatre. The Tiller girls used to dance in it. I remember the song they sang:

Away down
In jungle town
Honeymoon
Is coming soon
And we hear the serenade
To a pretty monkey maid
And now in jungle town

The moon shines down
Without a frown
I'll be true
To monkey doodle-doo.

Then the Tiller girls danced, their heels clacking.

I'll be true
To monkey doodle-doo.

There were supposed to be rats in the dressing room but I never saw one. By now my first real affair with a man had started. The pantomime didn't run for long and I didn't try for anything afterwards. I knew that however crudely Mr. Peterman had spoken when he asked what the hell I was doing on the stage, he had spoken the truth, but my lover imagined that I could get on in the theatre and insisted that I should have singing and dancing lessons. Dutifully I attended them. The rest of the time I spent looking out of the window for the messenger boy, because he always sent his letters by messenger.

Smile Please: An Unfinished Autobiography. Berkeley: Donald S. Ellis/Creative Arts, 1979. 86–91.

CORNELIA SORABJI

Extracts from Unpublished Diaries and Lectures

June 23, 1892, from Somerville Hall:

This is alas! The last time that I shall write from my dear Somerville . . . I turn my face for ever on the happiest time life can have for me. I feel it intensely. Dear Oxford—no other place an ever be to me what thou art! . . . My dear kind friends congratulate & condole. They say they'd like to burn the Examiners in that I'm a 1st Class person all round—others won't own its matter for condolence & say they're proud of knowing the 1st B.L.—but what ever view they take they are kind enough to end with protestations of affection. Every one is so good to me. Its nice at any rate to feel that they love me for myself & not for my Class.

MSS EUR/F165

Lecture, August 28, 1930, Williams College

You see what is happening is the confusion of two systems of thought. The Non-Co-operatives under their Anglicized Leaders demand that India should be given complete & immediate Independence—this is the Western urge in their composition.

But they work to pose also as Eastern as protectors of ancient usage, & they imagine that a fierce refusal to use Western machinery or to industrialize India is a justification of their Eastern ancestry, & proves them to be Nationalists. They forget that you cannot both give your Country a place among the Nations of the world & at the same time refuse her the commercial & other intercourse with other Nations which can alone secure her such a place.

Now do you see the danger of flattering our pride in a dead Civilization, & of confusing the ancient ascendancy of the Spirit with the kind of competence required by paramouncy [*sic*] in a world of sense.

And you will realize that I do not enumerate acts as an Alarmist, but because as a business woman, I recognize that we must pause & read not our 2nd century rolls of papyrus, but the writing on the walls of Today.

MSS EUR/F165/179

Lecture, August 26, 27, 1930, Williams College

The civilized world kindly accords us recognition of our ancient civilization but holds as as it were in a dead hand, by judging us in the 20th Century by our achievements before the Xtian [Christian] era.

The Past cannot save the future.

We are living by the Traditions of the Past. We are living upon the Traditions of the Past. And we are expected nevertheless to rule i.e. to make our adjustment to the modern world on this bases.

Are your being fair to us?

Mummy Peas cannot sustain a growing body.

Mummy Wrappings cannot be sold as reach-me-downs in the modern market.

Where then do we now stand, and how are we handicapped?

As Hindus we are handicapped by our garment of holiness.

As Moslems we are handicapped by our superseded opportunities.

As Parsees we are handicapped by the fact that after all we ourselves are trespassers & Foreigners in the Country of our Adoption and at best number only 101,000 souls all told.

MSS EUR/F165/179

The Women of India: Behind the Purdah: Education and Emancipation

How in one phrase shall the present position of women in India be stated? It is the position of the traffic in the busy quarter of some modern city, of Trafalgar-square in London, of the Strand in Calcutta—car, drayhorse, ticca gharri, cycle, rickshaw or ox-cart—even as these, women are travelling at different rates of progression, remarking that this traffic is dangerous because there seems to be no policeman. It is essential to understanding that this truth about an unequalized pace should be grasped at the outset. The amazing thing, however, is not our difference of speed, but that there should be any traffic at all upon the Women's Highway. What England has taken centuries to achieve has been accomplished in India in one night, so to speak . . . The good work, once begun, found no let or hindrance (as in England) from Victorian or pre-Victorian traditions. For happily in this direction there were no local traditions to combat. He might be she, for all that they cared—those framers of a brand-new University Act. Equally the draftsmen of the Criminal Procedure Code let in the word "person" to cover male and female. And in the fullness of time advantage was taken of both University Act and Legal Code.

Thus it happened that in one or two instances we got ahead of England. University degrees were taken on equal terms with men in Bombay in 1884. Oxford did not grant degrees to women till 1920. In 1894 an Indian woman claiming to be a "person" defended a woman upon her trial for murder in a British Court. It was not till 1923 that women began to practise at the English Bar. Again, in the Legislative Council of Travancore a woman was in charge of the portfolio of Public Health seven years before Miss Bondfield became a Minister in London.

The racing cars are outrunning the speed of the country of origin. Turn from the cars to the ox-carts. But it is not use prating of paradox. Is it not often from paradoxes that we get our finest total results? . . . The ox-cart creaking on its wheels, a drowsy driver, drugged oxen—that is the symbol we should use to explain this block in our procession of women. Yet even here there has been a change this last decade. The drowsy driver has roused himself sufficiently to dig his toes into his oxen and twist their tails.

These women of the shut door have a charm of their own—one does not want them to lose it. Since they cannot come out to take what awaits them, cannot we carry our gifts within? Is what we say. And this is what is being done. Take Bengal as an illustration [where Purdahnashins have taken arts degrees and formed a group of social service workers to help illiterate purdahnashins] The value of this work cannot be put too high. It is literally reform from within—the best end from which to equalize the pace.

Watcher, what of the night?

It is passing, says the Watcher. My hope is in the ox-carts.

All which things are a parable.

MSS EUR/F165/162, *The Times* (February 18, 1930).

Wein and Women

To find oneself in a gathering of women representative of 42 Countries of the World, meeting for serious deliberation on the questions concerning women and children and meeting in the Ancient City of Wein (Vienna)—was to experience a thrill both exhilarating and enabling. Selfconsciousness was slain and one realized the possibilities of the Body Corporate, if only that Body would allow Allegiance to master rivalry and personal ambition.

If only members of the Council in India would realize the value of acquainting themselves with facts and of hard work the years between these International Meetings—They would not only be preparing a gift to lay at the feet of the National Council: but they would be preparing for themselves a thrill unmatched elsewhere. You are a craftsman among your peers, able to share experience: best of all you are refitted at these gatherings with new ideas and improved methods of carrying on the work in which all the world of women is interested. You go home to your lonely post, re-charged with energy, and feeling that you are now one of a family, no longer isolated; and local pricks and panics have no power to hurt, any more.

Tagore and Ghandi [*sic*] are well know in Austria and Italy. Indeed in Italy I was discomposed by hearing called after me Hallo! Mr Gandhi.

[. . .] with the friendships we have made and the inspirations we have brought away, we can pinch ourselves away at will—nor fear disillusionment.

MSS EUR/F165/167

Prospice: The New India

[. . .] I am not of those who think that we are yet ready, as a country, for the final experiment; but the one thing to secure, as far as human effort can secure it, is surely the success of whatever programme may be the outcome of the Round Table Conference; and the one thing to bear in mind is . . . *Progressive Self-Government within the Empire* . . . King Feisul said, it will be remembered, to Gertrude Bell: "My lady, no one can give a man independence. He gives it to himself." He spoke of the true independence of the spirit, which alone of old was wont to matter in the East. Did not a Hindu Saint put that into words for us long years ago?

None can injure Self. Only Self can injure Self.

Are we perhaps forgetting that, in this modern talk of our rights and our dignity? Are we perhaps in danger of denationalising ourselves in ways far more serious than the adoption or exploitation of cotton goods not woven on Indian hand-looms? This is not a question for the British Parliament, but for myself and my own countrymen and countrywomen. And the answer? No man need whisper that, except to his own soul.

MSS EUR/17165/195
Oriental and India Office Collection, British Library.

GERTRUDE STEIN

From *Paris France*, Part 2

So it begins to be reasonable that the twentieth century whose mechanics, whose crimes, whose standardisation began in America, needed the background of Paris, the place where tradition was so firm that they could look modern without being different, and where their acceptance of reality is so great that they could let any one have the emotion of unreality.

Then there is their feeling about foreigners that helps a lot.

After all to the french the difference between being a foreigner and being an inhabitant is not very serious. There are so many foreigners and all who are real to them are those that inhabit Paris and France. In that they are different from other people. Other people find foreigners more real to them when they are in their own country but to the french foreigners are only real to them when they are in France. Naturally they come to France. What is more natural for them to do than that.

I remember an old servant invented a nice name for foreigners, there were Americans they existed because she was our servant and we were there, and then there was something she called a creole ecossais, we never did find out where that came from.

Of course they all came to France a great many to paint pictures and naturally they could not do that at home, or write they could not do that at home either, they could be dentists at home she knew all about that even before the war, Americans were a practical people and dentistry was practical. To be sure certainly, she was the most practical, because when her little boy was ill, of course she was awfully unhappy because it was her little boy but then also it was all to do over again because she did have to have one child, any french person has to have one child, and now after two years it was all to do again money and everything. And still why not of course why not.

So all this simple clarity in respect to seeing life as it is, the animal and social life in human beings as it is, the money value of human and social and animal life as it is, without brutality or without simplicity; what is it to-day a french woman said to me about an American writer, it is false without being artificial.

It did not take the twentieth century to make them say that as it has taken the twentieth century to make other people say that.

Foreigners belong in France because they have always been here and did what they had to do there and remained foreigners there. Foreigners should be foreigners and it is nice that foreigners are foreigners and that they inevitably are in Paris and in France.

They are beginning now at last, cinemas and the world war have slowly made them realise, what nationality the foreigners are. In a little hotel where we stayed some time they spoke of us as English, no we said no we are Americans, at last one of them a little annoyed at our persistance said but it is all the same. Yes I answered like the french and Italians all the same. Well before the war they could not have said that nor felt the unpleasantness of the answer. Then we had a Finnish maid here in the country, and once she came in all beaming, it is wonderful, she said, the milk woman knows Finland, she knows where Finland is, she knows all about Finland, why, said the Finnish maid, I have known very educated people who did not know where and was but she knew. Well did she know but she did have the ancient tradition of french politeness and that was that. They do, of course.

But really what they do do is to respect art and letters, if you are a writer you have privileges, if you are a painter you have privileges and it is pleasant having those privileges. I always remember coming in from the country to my garage where I usually kept my car and the garage was full more than full, it was the moment of the automobile salon, but said I what can I do, well said the man in charge I'll see and then he came back and said in a low voice, there is a corner and in this corner I have put the car of Monsieur the academician and next to it I will put yours the others can stay outside and it is quite true even in a garage an academician and a woman of letters takes precedence even of millionaires or politicians, they do, it is quite incredible but they do, the police treat artists and writers respectfully too, well that too is intelligent on the part of France and unsentimental, because after all the way everything is remembered is by the writers and painters of the period, nobody really lives who has not been well written about and in realising that the french show their usual sense of reality and a belief in a sense of reality is the twentieth century, people may not have it but they do believe in it.

They are funny even now they are funny, all the peasants of the village, well not all but a number of them were eating their bread and wine, they do quite nicely now have jam on their bread, nice jam made of a mixture of apricots and apples, just how they happen at the same time I do not quite know, yes perhaps late apricots and early apples, it is very good.

So we were talking and they said to me, now tell me, why does the french chamber vote itself two more years of existence, and we, well of course we never do have anything to say but why do they, tell us. Well I said why not, you know it they know it, and beside if they are there why should not they stay there. Well said they laughing let's be like Spain. Let's have a civil war. Well said I what is the use, after all, after all their shooting each other up they are going to have their king again any way the king's son. Then for a change said they, why do not we have the king's nephew.

That is the way they feel about it, the only thing that is important is the daily life, and so the gangsters, so the twentieth century had really nothing to teach the french countryman therefore it was the proper background for the art and literature of the twentieth century.

The impressionists.

The twentieth century did not invent but it made a great fuss about series production, series production really began in the nineteenth century, that is natural enough, machines are bound to make series production.

So although there was more fuss made about machines and series production in the twentieth century than in the nineteenth of course it was a nineteenth century thing.

The impressionists and they were nineteenth century had as their aspiration and their ideal one painting a day, really two paintings a day, the morning painting and the afternoon painting actually it might have been the early morning and the early afternoon and the late afternoon. But after all there is a limit to the human hand after all painting is hand painting so actually even at their most excited moment they rarely did more than two more frequently one, and very often not one a day, most generally not one a day. They had the dream of a series production but as Monsieur Darantiere said about printing after all they had not the faults or the qualities of machines.

So Paris was the natural background for the twentieth century, America knew it too well, knew the twentieth century too well to create it, for America there was a glamour in the twentieth century that made it not be material for creative activity. England was consciously refusing the twentieth century, knowing full well that they had gloriously created the nineteenth century and perhaps the twentieth century was going to be too many for them, so they were quite self consciously denying the twentieth century but France was not worrying about it, what is was and what was is, was their point of view of which they were not very conscious, they were too occupied with their daily life to worry about it, beside the last half of the nineteenth century had really not interested them very much, not since the end of the romantic movement, they had worked hard, they always work hard, but the last half of the nineteenth century had really not interested them very much. As the peasants always say every year comes to an end, and they like it when the bad weather does not keep them from working, they like to work, it is a pastime for them work is, and so although the last half of the nineteenth century did not interest them they did work. And now the twentieth century had come and it might be more interesting, if it was to be really interesting of course they would not work quite so much, being interested does sometimes stop one from working, work might then be even somewhat disturbing and distracting. So the twentieth century had come it began with 1901.

Paris France. New York: Liveright, 1970. 18–25.

PART IV

War, Technology, and Traumas of Modernity

14

War, Modernisms, and the Feminized "Other"

INTRODUCED AND SELECTED BY CLAIRE M. TYLEE

ALTHOUGH MODERNIST experimentation predates the First World War, many modernist masterpieces were responses to at least one of the armed conflicts that so altered European culture in the first half of the twentieth century: World War I, the Easter Rising and subsequent Irish Troubles, the Russian Revolution(s), the Spanish Civil War, and World War II (Woolf's *Mrs. Dalloway*, Yeats's "Easter 1916," O'Casey's *The Plough and the Stars*, Eisenstein's *Battleship Potemkin*, Picasso's *Guernica*, Kollwitz's war memorial to her son, *Die Eltern*, Shostakovitch's string quartets). As Malcolm Bradbury argues: "The First World War undoubtedly helped ratify modernism . . . it intensified the sense of historical disorder and irony that many experimental writers had begun to probe" (193).[1] There may have been modernist writers (such as James Joyce, Christina Stead, Dorothy Richardson) who largely avoided war in their work; however, the experience of war seems to have impelled other writers into developing modernist strategies (Vernon Lee, Rose Macaulay, Martha Gellhorn).[2] Indeed, it has been claimed that war became the main subject matter of some modernists (Virginia Woolf, Gertrude Stein, and H. D.).[3]

In fact modernist techniques such as fragmentation, free indirect speech, and imagism seemed particularly appropriate to the dissociation and alienation typical of war experience. This alienation was not simply due to "the attenuation of religious belief" that Paul Fussell identifies (*Bloody Game* 25). Many writers were opposed to the political values propagated to support war-aims and wished to dissociate themselves. Furthermore, the internationalism that fostered and was fostered by modernism in the arts was in direct conflict with the closed-minded nationalism promoted by wartime governments. In Britain in particular, during the Great War Victorian myths of a national culture underpinned secret policies of propaganda and censorship that covertly supported aggressively imperialist values.[4] Governments also deliberately used propaganda to accentuate gender differences and inequalities reaffirmed by war policies (men alone were conscripted for combat; women were restricted to auxiliary roles or represented as victims).[5]

Thus throughout the period avant-garde artists, especially women, continually found themselves in conflict with a Victorian rearguard of censors. Many literary modernist strategies, such as irony, obliquity, and ambiguity, can therefore be seen as efforts to circumvent politico-cultural straitjacketing. During World War One, some notable writers who had been successful pre-war, such as Mrs. Humphry Ward, H. G. Wells, Edith Wharton, and Henry James, prostituted their talents to propaganda, spotlighting allied volunteers as heroes admired by grateful women.[6] Other writers resisted this magnifying role: women in particular subjected the war machine to a critical female gaze that ironized ideal models of masculinity, femininity, and heterosexuality (Mary Borden, H. D., Anna Wickham),[7] satirized male-authored war policies (Vernon Lee, Martha Gellhorn) and mocked the profitable propaganda of war films and literature (Gertrude Stein).[8] War culture not only offered a political target for feminist modernist aesthetics; it also provided an opportunity for women writers to encroach on "masculine" territory by their wry uses of form. H. D. in particular developed an allusive, lyrical prose that contrasted with the barbarism of war. While such prose/poetry enabled women to voice their erotic reactions to war (Wickham, Borden, Sinclair),[9] it was also suggestive of the alienation many women felt (Borden, la Motte). On the other hand, early twentieth-century war offered women the opportunity to adventure into areas usually gendered as male preserves (the street at night, the heavy industrial factory, the battlefield), and recent anthologies of women's war texts have tried to illustrate women's responses to this.[10]

The middle-class male establishment represented by the writers who signed The Authors' Declaration in 1914 did not only subordinate women.[11] It also placed in a "feminine" position of subordination working-class men, men from colonized nations such as Ireland, and those who were regarded as racially inferior, such as Indians. It was not until some years after the war that it became possible for writers representing such subordinated groups to "write back" against the dominant wartime propaganda. As Fussell has so persuasively argued, "the most pervasive contribution of modern war to modernist culture is irony" (*Bloody Game* 23). However, I would suggest that this is not merely the result of "hope abridged" (Fussell, *Great War* 35). Irony is the major means by which subordinated and disaffected groups can implicitly refuse to concur with "official culture"—and still manage to get published. I agree with Michael Roth's assertion that "irony is a rhetorical stance that is chosen not on theoretical grounds but because of one's moral, political, and aesthetic commitments" (160). Irony is diverse and is best identified by contrast with the cultural background from which it demurs. It is that taken-for-granted background that bolsters readers' comforting expectations that irony rasps against. In English literature that means a cultural legacy of works such as speeches from Shakespeare's *Henry V* and Tennyson's "The Charge of the Light Brigade." At the time of the 1914–18 war it also meant the late Victorian romanticism of propagandists such as Mrs. Humphry Ward or Edith Wharton, who reduced working-class "Tommies" and Indian volunteers to the feminine status of objects of the gaze, items in a picturesque landscape colored by imperial myths of racial and class superiority.

I have therefore included extracts from writings by members of such subordinated groups: the Liverpool working-class author James Hanley, the Irish playwright Sean O'Casey, the Indian novelist Mulk Raj Anand, as well as two women writers, the poet Anna Wickham and the war correspondent Martha Gellhorn. To gain an idea of their implicit rejection of dominant viewpoints, one has only to set Anand's writing against the picturesque orientalism of Mrs. Humphry Ward's Letter 5 in her best-selling book of propaganda, *England's Effort:*

> And who or what is this horseman looming out of the sleet?—like a figure from a piece of Indian or Persian embroidery; turbaned and swarthy, his cloak swelling out round his handsome head and shoulders, the buildings of a Norman farm behind him? 'There are a few Indian cavalry about here,' says our guide—'they are billeted in the farms. And presently the road is full of them. Their eastern forms, their dark intent faces, pass strangely through the Norman landscape. (125–26)

Or to set the economic desperation that drove the soldiers and seamen constructed by O'Casey and Hanley against the idealistic fervor with which Ward described the role of Kitchener's Army at the Battle of the Somme in Letter 7. She drew on the upper-class chivalric mythology that perpetuated feudal politics.[12] Itemizing "the Scottish regiments, the Ulster division, men of Munster and Connaught, and youths of cockney London," Ward attributed their enlistment to the "holy spirit of man," claiming with archaic rhetoric that: "nothing daunts the troops attacking day and night, in the name of patriotism, of liberty, of civilisation" (222).[13]

However, the idea that it was high-minded patriotism that drove conscripted men, or that they ever have much opportunity to behave heroically in modern war, has long been discounted. I have chosen extracts that display writers' consciousness that war does not only affect the fighting man. These unusual extracts, set away from the firing lines, demonstrate that even the criticism and editing of war literature can be strongly gendered to favor what Elaine Showalter has called the mythical zone of "male-only" experience: the trenches, the sky, the sea.[14] Here are constructions of war as it is variously experienced in the "feminine" domestic sphere of the Home Front.

They have been selected to illustrate a variety of modernist uses of irony but, of course, the very choice to depict family life and the responses of women itself cast an ironic light on the epic tradition of heroic war literature. More specifically, they challenged the sentimentalized view of maternity promoted by British propaganda. Recruiting posters in the First World War claimed "Women and Children say 'GO!'" or showed an elderly mother pointing her son to his duty (Haste). In *Goodbye to All That* Robert Graves later scorned the "war-madness" of the proudly resigned "Letter from a Little Mother" to the *Morning Post* (188–91), but Ward drew on such ideological constructions in her frequent allusions to "Mother England."[15] Thus the pieces selected here need to be understood not only as refraining from the Victorian aesthetic of the picturesque (Tylee, "'Munitions of the Mind'") or as eliminating the "rhetoric of heroic war" (Hynes, *War Imagined* 166–67) that stressed, for instance, the "Holy Spirit of Man" or "the glorious work of war." They also, in various ways, actively challenge the construction of "Noble Motherhood," and of "patriotism, of liberty, of civilisation" emptily reiterated by propagandists such as Ward or Little Mother. What precisely might there be about Western civilization *worthy* of dying for, even supposing the death was freely chosen, they implicitly query; *do* mothers willingly give their sons to the patriarchal state?

Since the overall form of a work also contributes to its modernist effectiveness, readers are recommended to investigate the deliberate challenge to decorum posed by O'Casey's *The Silver Tassie,* by comparing the farcical scenes of Act I (part of which is included here) with his expressionist Act 2.[16] Similarly Hanley's rapid montage will be better appreciated by reading Section IX of "Narrative" (reprinted here), between the sections recounting the torpedoing of Vessel AO.2 and the survivors' plight in the open boat.[17] Anand's novel *Across the Black Waters* is deliberately disjointed and presented here are two contrasting fragments.[18] These lead up to the famous 1914 Christmas Truce as bemusedly witnessed by the Indian troops (248–50). That event is followed by a visit from the Bishop of Chetpur preaching that "it was a holy war." He is later sarcastically mimicked by Lalu: "O Lord Yessuh Messih . . . we pray to you to intercede on our behalf to God . . . to allot us nice graves with little brass plates with our names inscribed on them" (253–55).

"The Night March," the passage of prose-poetry by an actual mother, Anna Wickham, is given in full as it was found among her papers.[19] Concentrating on the drumming, she reveals not only a sexual excitement underlying the patriotic spectacle, but one far removed from Ward's chivalrous dream. That single word "leers" ripples with modernist effect. This is typical of modernist reactions to the almost sickly sentiment and decadent picturesqueness that cloy late Victorian culture. Instead the modernist aesthetic creates moments of piercing beauty or insight, epiphanies to reveal the physical sordidness or spiritual poverty of people's lives in a materialist society. Sparkling examples are to be found in O'Casey, as in the selected passage, when the usually foul-mouthed Harry asks Susie for "the breath of a kiss [to take] to the shell-bullied air of the trenches."

Finally there is a section from Martha Gellhorn's reports of the Spanish Civil War.[20] Neither she nor Mrs. Ward was the first female war correspondent. That privilege is usually accorded to Lady Florence Dixie, who covered the late-nineteenth-century wars in South Africa for the *Daily Mail* (Sebba). There is, of course, a great range of style and approach in women's war journalism, from the personal excitement of May Sinclair to the angry impatience of Sylvia Pankhurst, the comic fearfulness of Mildred Aldrich, and the curious scrutiny of Edith Wharton.[21] However, Gellhorn has finally moved away from Victorian pathos or patronizing high-mindedness. It is not only the fact that her reports feature interviews with lowly people, nor that her Hemingwayesque prose style so carefully avoids abstractions or histrionics, that provide grounds for analyzing her writing as modernist. There is above all her subtle use of modernist punctuation, intercutting the usual material of war news within parentheses to indicate the knowledge that lies unspoken behind the dialogue and must be suppressed if morale is to be maintained. This is a brilliant demonstration of dual-consciousness, a central trope of modernism. Furthermore, displaying tact and discretion, it manifests the value of the feminine art of conversation, one particular gendering of modernism.

Notes

1. Winter has argued strongly that, despite the "iconoclastic element in 'modernism,'" it did not create as surgically defined a schism with the "host of images and conventions derived from eighteenth and nineteenth century traditions" as he believes earlier cultural critics claimed (4). I think most critics would agree that both traditions continued

to coexist during the twentieth century, but the cultural "fracture" that Cooperman identifies certainly opened up from the challenge to the dominance of Victorian conventions broached by modernist war writers. Enduring relations between modernism, the Great War, and British culture have been explored by Booth and Bourke.

2. Vernon Lee's modernist antiwar works, *The Ballet of the Nations* and *Satan the Waster* (excerpted in chapter 9) are discussed by Beer and Plain. I discussed Macaulay's change to modernism in Tylee (1990).

3. See for instance Hussey's claim about "the centrality of war to her life's work" in his collection on Woolf (3), and Gregory on Stein; and see Tate on H. D.'s war fiction in *Modernism* (10–32).

4. For an extensive demonstration of the British Victorian chivalric conventions that modernists strove to eliminate, what Hynes calls "the traditions of war art" and "the rhetoric of heroic war" (*War Imagined* 166–67), see Girouard. For fuller discussion of British wartime propaganda and censorship, see Buitenhuis, Cooperman, and Haste.

5. Connections between war and gendering demonstrated by Enloe were developed by Higonnet: "war must be understood as a gendering activity" (*Behind the Lines* 4). See also Higonnet's essay on "women's ability to find an ironic voice to describe war" ("Not So Quiet").

6. James's writings to raise funds for war aid were collected as *Within the Rim and Other Essays, 1914–15* (see Buitenhuis). Wharton's contribution to war literature is more complicated. Her chivalric propaganda novel *The Marne* is discussed by Buitenhuis and Cooperman; her postwar novel *A Son at the Front* was more considered (see Benstock). On Wharton's war reporting, see Gallagher; on her short war fiction see Tylee "Imagining Women." A third American expatriate, Elizabeth Robins, wrote a propaganda novel, *The Messenger.*

7. The modernist short war stories by Mary Borden and Ellen LaMotte are in Higonnet, ed., *Nurses at the Front.* They are discussed by Tylee (*Great War;* "'Maleness Run Riot'"). H. D.'s war writing in *Bid Me to Live* is well known; Tate discusses her war fiction (*Modernism* 20–32).

8. See, in particular, Stein's spoof film script *A Movie.*

9. See Sinclair's novel, *The Romantic.* London: Collins, 1920.

10. A variety of anthologies have appeared since 1989, responding to feminist literary research, edited by Cardinal, Goldman, and Hattaway, Higonnet, Yvonne Klein, Smith, Tylee; as well as critical studies by Gilbert and Gubar, Marcus, Smith, Tate, Tylee, and collections of essays, edited by Goldman, Raitt and Tate, and Tylee.

11. British writers such as Wells, Ford, and Ward were employed by Britain's secret Propaganda Department to target American sensibilities by using chivalric discourse; see Wright, Buitenhuis, and Hynes (*War Imagined*) on the role of The Authors' Declaration (1914) in this campaign.

12. Cf. Bradbury's discussion of Ford's modernist tetralogy, *Parade's End,* which Buitenhuis rightly calls "probably the greatest English novel written about the Great War" (159). Bradbury analyzes how Ford displays his character, Tietjens, who quested for just causes and true wars, as "absurd in his chivalry." Unlike Ward, Ford and Wells came to disavow the conservative basis for propaganda during the war, Ford feeling that "feudalism was finished" (Bradbury 197–98). See Buitenhuis on Ford and Wells.

13. On Ward's war writing see Small and Tylee, "'Munitions of the Mind'".

14. Examples of masculine-gendered criticism and "Men Only" anthologizing (con-

tested in the feminist collections of n. 10) are legion; see Holger Klein, Fussell, or Hynes.

15. See Fussell, "The Fate of Chivalry," for a somewhat misogynist account of the "conspicuously chivalric" cult of Mother, which he claims the Great War terminated.

16. The protestant Irish dramatist Sean O'Casey (1880–1964) is best known for his so-called Dublin Trilogy, plays about the political realities of life for the urban poor when Ireland was governed from London. The third play, *The Plough and the Stars* (1926) gave a controversial interpretation of the Easter Rising of 1916; his fourth play, *The Silver Tassie* (1928), which is about synchronous events, should be considered next in the sequence. It further developed O'Casey's depiction of the effects of colonial exploitation from his international socialist standpoint. Ayling remains the best introductory critic to O'Casey's "tragic irony" (*Casebook* 181).

17. Like O'Casey, James Hanley (1901–85) was born in Dublin, but he was raised in the expatriate Catholic community of Liverpool. Hanley worked on troop ships during the Great War, and then enlisted underage with the Canadian Army to serve in France until September 1918 (see his autobiography, *Broken Water*). War and the sea remained his major literary subjects. Although Hanley's fiction draws on social-realist traditions, Edward Stokes has argued convincingly that his work is modernist. That is clearly true of his most famous novels, both set in World War II: *No Directions* and *Sailor's Song*. However, what distinguishes Hanley from other modernists is his sympathetic identification with women's hard physical labor, seen in his account of the monstrous old mother, Mrs. Fury, cleaning out the filthy hospital ships in *Our Time Is Gone* (381–82). Quite what she was cleaning up is revealed in "Narrative" (213). This early novella encapsulates many of the themes and tropes Hanley was to develop in his later works, including the rapid cutting between scenes, changes of tempo, emotional violence, and, above all, the frenzied chaos of disaster. Typically, split into the mythical tale of men alone, are reminders of the powerful attachments to that other, female world, which holds desperately onto the men's lives less by an umbilical cord than by an anchor chain, both dragging and securing them back to loving safety.

18. Mulk Raj Anand (1905–2004) was born in Peshawar, India, and educated at the Universities of Lahore, London, and Cambridge. Between the world wars he associated with members of the Bloomsbury Group in England, but he returned to live in Bombay from 1946. His first two novels, *Untouchable* (1935) and *Coolie* (1936) evinced a deep sympathy for people at the lowest depths of Indian society. He prepared the first draft of *Across the Black Waters* in Madrid and Barcelona during the Spanish Civil War in 1937. Dedicated to his father, an officer in the British Indian Army, it is the middle volume in a trilogy about the political radicalization of a young Sikh. The other two volumes are *The Village* and *The Sword and the Sickle*.

19. Although born in England, "Anna Wickham" (Edith Alice Mary Hepburn, 1884–1947) was educated in Australia and then trained as an opera singer in Paris. Her independent spirit was a source of conflict with Patrick Hepburn, the London lawyer whom she married in 1905, and led to a period in a lunatic asylum. She survived by expressing herself through poetry that was highly regarded by contemporaries such as D. H. Lawrence, Ezra Pound, and Natalie Barney. Her collected work, including poetry, prose, and an autobiographical fragment, was published by Virago in 1984.

20. The distinguished journalist, Martha Gellhorn (1908–98) was born in St Louis. The author of five novels, two collections of short stories, a play, and four books of

novellas, she is best known for her nonfiction. (See Rollyson for her publications up to 1990.) From 1936 she reported on every major war, directly engaging with the lives of those affected by conflict. Her account of entering Dachau in 1945 is especially forthright and her Vietnam reports, published in *The Guardian,* London, were censored in United States. *The Face of War,* her collected war journalism, went through many editions from 1959 to 1998, accreting new wars and impassioned Introductions and Conclusions: "There has to be a better way to run the world and we better see that we get it" (409).

21. These journalists are discussed in Tylee, *The Great War,* and Gallagher.

Works Cited

Anand, Mulk Raj. *Across the Black Waters.* London: Jonathan Cape, 1940. Rpt. New Delhi: Vision, 2000.

Ayling, Ronald. *O'Casey: The Dublin Trilogy—A Casebook.* Basingstoke: Macmillan, 1985.

Beer, Gillian. "The Dissidence of Vernon Lee: *Satan the Waster* and the Will to Believe." In Raitt and Tate, eds., *Women's Fiction and the Great War.*

Benstock, Shari. "Introduction" to Edith Wharton, *A Son at the Front.* DeKalb: Northern Illinois University Press, 1995. vii–xvi.

Booth, Allyson. *Postcards from the Trenches: Negotiating the Space between Modernism and the First World War.* Oxford: Oxford University Press, 1996.

Bourke, Joanna. *Dismembering the Male: Men's Bodies, Britain, and the Great War.* London: Reaktion Books, 1996.

Bradbury, Malcolm. "The Denuded Place: War and Form in *Parade's End* and *USA.*" In Holger Klein, ed. *The First World War in Fiction.* 193–209.

Buitenhuis, Peter. *The Great War of Words: Literature as Propaganda, 1914–18 and After.* London: Batsford, 1989.

Cardinal, Agnes, Dorothy Goldman, and Judith Hattaway, eds. *Women's Writing on the First World War.* Oxford: Oxford University Press, 1999.

Cooke, Miriam, and Angela Woollacott, eds. *Gendering War Talk.* Princeton: Princeton University Press, 1993.

Cooperman, Stanley. *World War I and the American Novel.* London: Johns Hopkins, 1967.

Enloe, Cynthia. *Does Khaki Become You? The Militarization of Women's Lives.* London: Pluto, 1983.

Fussell, Paul. "The Fate of Chivalry, and the Assault upon Mother." In *Killing in Verse and Prose and Other Essays.* London: Bellew, 1990. 217–44.

———. *The Great War and Modern Memory.* Oxford: Oxford University Press 1975.

———.. Introduction. *The Bloody Game: An Anthology of Modern War.* Ed. Paul Fussell. London: Abacus, 1992.

Gallagher, Jean. *The World Wars through the Female Gaze.* Illinois: Southern Illinois Press, 1998.

Gellhorn, Martha. "Conclusion 1988." In *The Face of War.* London: Granta, 1993. 400–409.

Gilbert, Sandra M., and Susan Gubar. *No Man's Land 2: Sexchanges.* New Haven: Yale University Press, 1989.

Girouard, Mark. *Return to Camelot: Chivalry and the English Gentleman.* London: Yale University Press, 1981.

Goldman, Dorothy, ed. *Women and World War I: The Written Response.* Basingstoke: Macmillan, 1993.

Graves, Robert. *Goodbye to All That,* rev. ed. London: Cassell, 1957.

Gregory, Elizabeth. "Gertrude Stein and War." In Raitt and Tate, eds., *Women's Fiction and the Great War.* 263–81.

Hanley, James. *Broken Water.* London: Chatto, 1987.

———. "Narrative." In *The Last Voyage and Other Stories.* London: Harvill Press, 1997. 145–271.

———. *Our Time Is Gone.* London: John Lane, 1940.

Haste, Kate. *Keep the Home Fires Burning: Propaganda in the First World War.* London: Allen Lane, 1977.

Higonnet, Margaret R. et al., eds. *Behind the Lines: Gender and the Two World Wars.* New Haven: Yale University Press, 1987.

———. "Not So Quiet in No-Woman's-Land." In *Gendering War Talk,* ed. Miriam Cooke and Angela Woollacott. Princeton: Princeton University Press, 1993. 205–26.

———, ed. *Lines of Fire: Women Writers of World War I.* New York: Penguin, 1999.

———, ed. *Nurses at the Front: Writing the Wounds of War.* Boston: Northeastern University Press, 2001.

Hussey, Mark, ed. *Virginia Woolf and War: Fiction, Reality, and Myth.* New York: Syracuse University Press, 1991.

Hynes, Samuel. *A War Imagined: The First World War and English Culture.* London: Bodley Head, 1990.

———. *The Soldiers' Tale: Bearing Witness to Modern War.* New York: Penguin, 1997.

Klein, Holger, ed. *The First World War in Fiction.* London: Macmillan, 1976.

Klein, Yvonne M., ed. *Beyond the Home Front: Women's Autobiographical Writing of the Two World Wars.* Basingstoke: Macmillan, 1997.

Marcus, Jane. "Afterword: Corpus/Corps/Corpse: Writing the Body in/at War." In Helen Zenna Smith. *Not So Quiet . . . Stepdaughters of War.* New York: Feminist Press, 1989. 241–300.

Plain, Gill. "The Shape of Things to Come: The Remarkable Modernity of Vernon Lee's *Satan the Waster.*" In Tylee, ed., *Women, the First World War, and the Dramatic Imagination.* 5–21.

Raitt, Susanne, and Trudi Tate, eds. *Women's Fiction and the Great War.* Oxford: Oxford University Press, 1997.

Rollyson, Carl. *Nothing Ever Happens to the Brave: The Story of Martha Gellhorn.* New York: St Martin's, 1990.

Roth, Michael S. *The Ironist's Cage: Memory, Trauma, and the Construction of History.* New York: Columbia University Press, 1995.

Sebba, Anne. *Battling for News: The Rise of the Woman Reporter.* London: Hodder and Stoughton, 1994.

Shakespeare, Nicholas. "Martha Gellhorn." *Granta* 62 (1998): 215–35.

Showalter, Elaine. "Feminist Criticism in the Wilderness." *Critical Inquiry* 8 (1981): 179–205.

Small, Helen. "Mrs Humphry Ward and the First Casualty of War." In Raitt and Tate, eds., *Women's Fiction and the Great War.* 18–46.

Smith, Angela K. *The Second Battlefield Women, Modernism and the First World War.* Manchester: Manchester University Press, 2000.

———, ed. *Women's Writing of the First World War—An Anthology.* Manchester: Manchester University Press, 2000.

Smith, R. D., ed. *The Writings of Anna Wickham: Free Woman and Poet.* London: Virago, 1984.

Stein, Gertrude. *A Movie.* In *Operas and Plays.* Paris: Plain Edition, 1932.

Stokes, Edward. *The Novels of James Hanley.* Melbourne: Cheshire, 1964.

Tate, Trudi. *Modernism, History, and the First World War.* Manchester: Manchester University Press, 1998.

———, ed. *Women, Men, and the Great War: An Anthology of Short Stories.* Manchester: Manchester University Press, 1995.

Tylee, Claire M. *The Great War and Women's Consciousness: Images of Militarism and Womanhood in Women's Writings, 1914–64.* Basingstoke: Macmillan, 1990.

———. "Imagining Women at War: Feminist Strategies in Edith Wharton's War Writing." *Tulsa Studies in Women's Literature* 16.2 (1997): 327–43.

———. "'Maleness Run Riot': The Great War and Women's Resistance to Militarism." *Womens' Studies International Forum* 11.3 (1988): 199–210.

———. "'Munitions of the Mind': Travel Writing, Imperial Discourse, and Great War Propaganda by Mrs. Humphry Ward." *English Literature in Transition, 1880–1920* 39.2 (1996): 171–92.

———, ed. *War Plays by Women: An International Anthology.* London: Routledge, 1999.

———, ed. *Women, the First World War, and the Dramatic Imagination: International Essays (1914–1999).* Lampeter: Mellen, 2000.

Ward, Mrs. Humphry. *England's Effort.* London: Smith Elder. 1916.

Winter, Jay. *Sites of Memory Sites of Mourning: The Great War in European Cultural History.* Oxford: Oxford University Press, 1995.

Wright, D. G. "The Great War, Government Propaganda and English 'Men of Letters' 1914–16." In *Literature and History* 7 (1978): 70–100.

MULK RAJ ANAND

From *Across the Black Waters*

As the train reached Calais station congested with uniforms there came noise of raucous shouting above the din of the slow engine. They could see hordes of European soldiers standing by cattle-truck trains, who lifted their hands and cheered the sepoys: *"VivelesHindus!"*

The sepoys rushed to the doors and cheered back in the only English greeting they knew; "Hip hip hurrah!"

The echo filled Lalu's heart with a sympathetic exhilaration. He wanted to rush out and shake hands with them.

But as the train came to a standstill, Havildar Lachman Singh was giving out the orders: . . . "All ranks . . ."

The cheering had died down almost as suddenly as it had begun and there was a confused babble of voices. In spite of Havildar Lachman Singh's clear orders the sepoys were asking how long they were to stop here and how far the front was. And they were venturing vague guesses and all kinds of explanations. As Lachman Singh had gone out towards the officers' compartment, they were in suspense.

In the undarkening morning Lalu could see a few civilians, mostly women and children, presumably relatives of the soldiers, sitting peaceably on numerous and diverse packages, even as he had often seen people in India sit down anyhow on odd bundles on the platforms of railway stations. And, as before, during his journey through France, so now, he felt how like the Indians the French were. The frail, sombre French women, patiently waiting there, looked so like the Indian women. Even the black clothes they wore were the colour preferred by the matrons in India. Of course, the styles of clothes were more uniform here. The women's dresses were more fashionable and showed their bodies. And, somehow, these women were more desirable.

He looked intently among the group seated on the platform, so that perhaps he could discover a pretty face to linger on. But they seemed sad and forlorn as they sat there, their noses red with crying . . . And he felt embarrassed and irreverent to be looking at them with desire and he lifted his gaze and scanned the platform.

Throngs of French soldiers stood by awaiting trains, lounging against the doorways. With their shuffling gait, some in red trousers and blue coats, but mostly in khaki, they were not models of soldierly bearing, according to the definitions he had learnt through the kicks of Corporal Lok Nath. He couldn't make anything of their quick voices, shouting greetings and speaking subtle inflexions of their queer lingo. But they seemed lithe and active and hearty though they were small, even smaller than the Tommies.

"Are we going to get some tea or coffee in this place?" asked Kirpu as he still lay huddled without betraying much curiosity in the world of Calais station.

"Havildar Lachman Singh has gone to see, Impatience!" said Lalu.

Suddenly hoarse shouts came down the adjacent platform and eased the strain of waiting.

The soldiers who had crowded the platform by the train began to take leave of their aged mothers, fathers, wives and sisters and then hurry into the train.

"They even embrace before parting like us Hindustanis," Lalu said. "They are even like us in affection."

"Rape-daughters! The men kiss each other on the cheeks," said Kirpu.

Some of the women were crying even as his mother had cried when he had left home after the holiday. He was sad, because they were sad. His blood seemed to be congealed. And yet, there was an insidious fascination about their suffering, for he had never seen the Sahibs behave like this. Somehow the English in India always concealed their emotions. He himself had been shy in saying farewell to his own people. But he had done so from the mistaken belief that it was against fashion.

A woman on the platform was sobbing hysterically, a poor frail thing, as she clung to her husband while he was whispering something as he stroked her and soothed her.

Lalu waved his head as if he were drunk with a sudden tenderness now and he felt as if there was happiness in that embrace as well as pain . . . He felt he could have taken Maya into his arms and soothed her like that . . .

But the guard came shouting for the men to enter.

"Oh no, oh no, let the train not go. Let it not break their hearts," Lalu said to himself agitatedly.

The guard was calling persistently, however, *"Envoiture! Envoiture!"*

The soldier who had been embracing his wife separated from her and went towards his heedless son who had been straying.

"Oh, go and be kissed by your father," Lalu almost wanted to shout to the child.

But the soldier caught the lad, picked him up, threw him aloft as if he were a doll, and smothered him with kisses.

The train whistled.

One hurried flourish of his hand towards his wife who now stood sobbing and the soldier went into the carriage. The train began to move. The man was now blowing kisses to his loved ones. All the soldiers were blowing kisses to their friends, waving their hands, and shouting to their relations, while those left on the platform were waving little white handkerchiefs. The wife of the soldier was sobbing more hysterically as she held her child. She sobbed and sobbed and was going to wheel round like a sea-gull and sink when a porter held her and led her away.

Lalu sank back exhausted by the strain of the scene he had witnessed. He sensed that their parting might be forever.

On the other side of the station a cattle-truck train was coming in and most of the sepoys went stampeding to the windows to look and cheer.

At that moment, Havildar Lachman Singh came in and said: "Belgian infantry there, coming back from the front. They have seen service and are returning to rest and to be re-equipped."

"Where is the tea, *Havildara?* That's what we want to know," asked Kirpu.

"The pot is boiling," said Lachman. Lalu got up to look at the regiment which had just returned from the war. He gaped at them. Outwardly they didn't look any the worse for having been in action, though their uniforms didn't look smart, but then the uniforms of the continental troops were loose and dirty anyway. And they had come through the valley of death.

"Tea!" Santu the cook shouted.

And the sepoys stampeded down to take their places in line. The train shrieked and groaned out of Calais followed by the cheers of the Belgian infantry, who sprawled about on the adjacent platform.

Now they were really off to the front, he had been told, and they would soon get there. Soon he would see the real thing, the war, the final reality, and then he could reckon whether he would live or die—because people had been known to die in wars, though Uncle Kirpu seemed to have come unscathed through his various campaigns!

The countryside through which the train was moving at tortoise speed was flat after the grassy green of the hills and valleys, beyond Orleans. The cornfields nestling under the ragged, dirty dark were all stubble, except here and there were crops, which seemed like clover and beetroot or potatoes, still stood uncut by small farmhouses. And yet everything seemed as usual and there was nothing to show that there was a war on in this land.

Perhaps the train would land them right behind the front and they would have to get out at once and begin to fight the enemy. The train seemed to be dribbling along, slower than ever. He wondered naively if the engine driver was afraid.

And, somehow, he seemed to be contracting into himself, and felt alone, alone in the grey morning of this vast alien earth, beyond which was a vaster earth or a vaster sea, beyond which again was the vaster sky where every one faded away.

A dim star stood on the rim of the horizon.

Someone had said at school that the earth was only a chunk chipped off the moon when this planet had grazed with another in its rotation round the sun, and that it was only about as big as a small star. How much bigger must the other planets be then, how much bigger than the distances he had travelled?—And that was not the largest distance on earth, there being much longer distances which ships and trains and motors had spanned, distances which he would never be able to cover himself. And there were the snowy regions of the North Pole and the South Pole that no one had yet crossed.

He felt small in comparison with this gigantic world, a poor insignificant fool of a peasant boy who had had to run away from the village and join the army and who had now come to fight, a joke among these grown-up men for his new-fangled notions, a ridiculous fool in spite of the grave, wise airs he gave himself, small and feeble and half-afraid, among other frightened folk.

"What is the talk son, then?" Kirpu asked him.

"Until he comes under the mountain, brother, the camel says there is no greater than I," said Lalu with a feigned humility.

"Your meaning in that the camel always sobs at loading time?"

At that instant the train creaked and pulled up somewhat like an over-loaded camel. And everyone laughed. After a minute of suspense broken by whispers it jerked along again, like a branch line train in India, almost at the pace at which one could have walked or at least run along.

Lalu recalled how the peasants in Central Punjab often turned thieves and dacoits during famine time and boarded the slow trains, looted the passengers' property and disappeared into the forests. From their docile, harmless looks there was no chance of the peasants doing that here. And, anyhow, they wouldn't get anything from a troop train. But the enemy could suddenly attack the train and kill them all, loot their rifles and the few machine guns and the big guns that were being carried on some of the open trucks. Perhaps it was because of this fear that the train was going slowly: the engine driver was being cautious. They were certainly in a mysterious zone, and every move was being negotiated carefully . . . There, the train was slowing down. "What was happening?" Slower, slower . . . it had stopped again . . . for fear of Yama, God of death?

The air was filled with a deafening roar like the booming of the big gun at Brigade Headquarters at the hour of twelve. He looked out to see what it was. He felt tense and excited. But there seemed nothing unusual ahead of the train or on its sides. Only a farmhouse nestled under a few trees in the flat country which was wet and soggy. There was a nip in the air: and it seemed that it had rained here overnight, though it had been quite clear the way they had come.

"The hour of twelve has struck," Uncle Kirpu said.

At that moment, wonder of all wonders, Captain Owen came up to their compartment like a fashionable young yokel jumping to the footboard of a train.

"*Acha hai*, sepoy *log*? . . . Not far now—the destination!"

"God may sweeten your mouth for saying so, *Huzoor*," said Kirpu. "Come in and grace us with your company."

Captain Owen smiled his gracious, shy smile, but did not enter.

All the sepoys turned to him with respect, arranging themselves the while.

"Don't move, as you were," said Owen Sahib.

"This is like going to a war on the frontier, *Huzoor*," said Havildar Lachman Singh, referring to the comradeship that was reflected in the Sahib's visit, for he recalled how the British officers of the 69th had once shared the same lorries with the sepoys in Waziristan.

The Adjutant moved his head, then flushed and, shading his mouth, shouted:

"Yes. *Jung!*" And he made a gesture of despair.

But his words were being smothered by the shrieking of the brakes, and, for a moment, he closed his eyes, and contracted his face. Then he said: "Too much traffic near the front."

"Come inside, *Huzoor,*" Kirpu said.

"*Sab acha?*" said the Sahib and, jumping down, walked towards his compartment.

"He is a good man," Havildar Lachman Singh said as he left.

"Strange thing, the Sahib coming to talk to us," said young Kharku.

"They want to give you heart," said Kirpu who had himself been surprised.

"He is gentle," said Lalu.

"I hear that the *Angrezi* Badshah is a gentleman," said Dhanoo. "But German Kaiser is bad tempered."

"They are cousins, though, Daddy," Lalu informed Dhanoo.

"He speaks well in our tongue," said Rikhi Ram.

"It is not good for Sahibs to be so familiar with sepoys," said Daddy Dhanoo. "Some men will misunderstand . . ."

Lalu moved his eyes away, caressed the silence, sat back and closed his eyes. What was the meaning of existence? he asked himself. [. . .]

THE LIGHT WAS FAILING before they had gone two or three miles. They could not keep the combat order as their boots hit each other's heels on the uncertain surface of the road. But they tramped on, as if the spirit had been taken out of them by the prospect of going to the front again. For, in their simplicity, they had believed that they had done their part in the two battles in which they had fought and would now be allowed to rest somewhere or drafted back to Hindustan while they were still whole. And, now, on the way to "Farishtabad," they felt a resentment which expressed itself in sullen silence.

Lalu had felt the gap by his side, a continual reminder of the friend he had left behind. And the sense of guilt became a cancer and the fear that he was now left alone to face Havildar Lok Nath and Jemadar Subah Singh, both of whom swaggered about as if they bore no responsibility for the ugly incident of Kirpu's suicide, though, for the while, they kept their distance from him, their real victim.

The numbness of fatigue and exasperation had somewhat atoned for his sadness and, after a time, his mind just became a blank, noticing only the automatic movement of the sepoys' feet as they cut across the highway, past sombre woods, bereft of all leafage, their stark trees lifting their gnarled hands to God in a kind of prayer for life. A few stars glistened in the sky and a pallid half moon thrust its head against the rough contour of the wintry heaven.

As they passed by an occasional farmhouse, the natives came out to stare at them, men and women watching with bowed heads and humble mien, as if offering a kind of repressed apology from themselves and the irresponsible Generals of their country for this war in which the stranger had had to be called in to fight.

Lalu was affected by a sight of an old woman who was feeding her chickens and kept up an incessant flow of incomprehensible chatter till the tail of the regiment had vanished on a corner of the road beyond her cottage. She was wrinkled and had a knowing air about her ugly face, like his mother's. And, in spite of himself he felt nostalgic, and began to hum a melancholy Punjabi melody in his throat:

"Only four days to play, Oh mother, only four days to play!

Night has fallen, mother, my Beloved is far away,

Oh mother, four days, only four days to play . . ."

"Oh louder, sing louder," coaxed Rikhi Ram with a weak smile on his energetic, commonsensical face. He had respected Lalu's grief and not intruded on his silence throughout the march, and the boy warmed to him, but, of course, would not sing.

"Let us sing 'Lachi,' boys," Rikhi Ram said hilariously. "Come on." And he began.

"Aha, in one village two *Lachian,*

Two *Lachian,* two *Lachian,*

The younger *Lachi* started all the trouble . . .

"Come on," Dhayan Singh shouted with a wholehearted laugh which seemed to issue from his tummy.

"Aha, in one village do *Lachian,*

Aha, the older *Lachi* asked the girls,

The girls, the girls, the girls,

Oh, what colour veil suits a fair complexion?

Aha, the girls said truly,

Said truly, said truly, said truly,

A black veil becomes a fair complexion . . ."

The simple strain rose beyond the original soft pitch of Rikhi Ram's hard accent to a chorus, broken at first by the voice of those who joined a little later, or stressed a phrase too early, or slurred it and varied a line according to the version current in their locality, but then rising to an uproarious, high-pitched duet which relaxed their grim set faces and melted the congealed blood in their veins.

"Let us sing 'Bazar Vakendian,'" someone ventured.

"No let us have, 'Come put your arms round my neck, Oh Puran, I am dying,'" suggested Dhayan Singh.

'No, no, no, let us have "Harnam Singh",' said Lalu. This was a duet which they had themselves evolved about the typical sepoy in the war and his sweetheart, Harnami, and her insistence for presents from *Vilayat:*

> I want a pair of shoes,
> I want a pair of shoes, I want a pair of shoes,
> > *Val* Harnam Singha . . .
> > Oh, I shall fetch for you,
> I shall fetch for you, I shall fetch for you
> A pair of fine shoes, with high heels,
> *Ni Harnamiae* . . .

The frank ribaldry of this set them laughing, and it would have gone on, but it released their inventive genius, and too many different versions were forthcoming, and they were afraid of the officers farther ahead, though both the Sahibs and the Indian officers were relieved to hear their voices.

Now they were becoming more and more profane and tended to break ranks, because they were tired. Rikhi Ram cautiously suggested that they should look to their steps before someone should turn on them and rebuke them.

Lalu reverted to another melancholy tune. "Oh mother, one day one has to go . . ." when they began to see the vague contours of wrecked houses looming across the highway and defining themselves into a longish village. Before they had entered its main street, orders rang out, for their officers had met the billeting authorities. They were drawn up in the shadow of a huge château and waited there in the cold dark for a while. Presently they were shunted off into the outhouses of the chateau across a magnificent courtyard, into comfortable quarters.

Glossary

> *Havildar* = Non-commissioned officer in Indian Army, equivalent in rank to sergeant;
> *Jemadar* = Highest rank of Indian N.C.O., equivalent in rank to Sergeant major;

Sepoy = Indian soldier in the British Indian Army;
Sikh = member of a reformed Hindu sect;
Singh indicates full adult membership of the Sikh community.

New Delhi: Vision, 2000. 68–73; 211–13.

JAMES HANLEY

Narrative: IX

The tall building of the shipping company was situated on the Pier Head. It was the highest of all the buildings lining that part of the city that afforded the most magnificent view of the river. Through the massive swing-doors of the building men, women and children were now pouring, for it had been reported that the AO.2 had been torpedoed off the Irish coast. The staff in the office were almost driven frantic by breathless and anxious relatives of the crew enquiring after their husbands, sons and brothers. But the big gentleman standing at the door, with his nice new uniform and shiny peaked cap, was feeling a little ruffled by the continuous questions put to him, by excited women and children. And one of these happened to be Mrs Morgan. The children clutched desperately at her skirts as she swept down one corridor and up another, searching for the Superintendent, whom she said she knew personally. From time to time she dabbed a handkerchief to her eyes, and the children too were sobbing. It seemed as though the whole of the huge building had been suddenly turned into the Wall of Weeping. And when Mrs Morgan, choking back her sobs, asked a passing boy where the Super's office was, he directed her to the lift. She was carried quickly up to the top floor. When she stepped out of the lift the first person she met was Mrs Brady. That woman too was beside herself with grief. The harried clerks were in their various offices cursing this stroke of fate—the ship or the men were not immediate matters to them. They were only anxious for a little peace. Each office, each room, was visited in turn by the frantic tear-stricken women.

"Oh, Mrs Brady," began Mrs Morgan, when she suddenly stopped, for Mrs Brady had collapsed into a heap before her very eyes. Two lift girls came to her assistance and sat her down on a near-by chair. And Mrs Morgan kept saying aloud: "I knew it. Something told me this would happen. O dear Christ! Nearly nine months out of work and lands in that. O good God!" She burst into a fresh fit of weeping.

Below, an excited crowd had gathered about the notice-board which the company had had posted at the entrance to the office. It gave the names of the crew of the unfortunate boat, but no other information. There was none to give. All kinds of rumours were flying about. The Ship had been mined, she had been set on fire, she had sunk of her own accord. But the long list of names staring them in the face was enough. The AO.2 had been torpedoed. The ceaseless Babel of sound, the continuous sobbing of women and children, began to have its effect in those hidden sanctuaries where relations of members of the crew were never allowed to go. The offices were everywhere besieged, the clerks driven off their heads answering questions. Mrs Morgan took her children down to the ground floor. The corridor was jammed with people wailing and shouting, and one amongst them, a slip of a girl dressed in black, standing by the wall, or rather being crushed against it by the many bodies. The whole place was full of the warm smell of animal flesh, scores of handkerchiefs were being pulled from pockets, and above all this the ceaseless din of typewriters, the incessant ringing of telephone bells, the whir of the lift dynamos, the calls and cries of office-boys, porters, door-men, and baggage-men. There was one woman who for an hour had done nothing but run up and down stairs, never seeking any particular office, just running up and down and holding her hands to her face, as if this were the only kind of thing she was capable of. Upstairs, downstairs, along corridors, and asking and looking into everybody's face, and beating her hands against the walls of the corridors. Her name was Mrs Maugham. Her son was a trimmer in the boat. She screamed from time to time: "O my lovely lad. Dead through those Germans. O mother of God!" Shouting and beating the wall and the man with a face like a wolf in his office near by saying to his clerk: "Get that frantic woman out of here. It's getting on my nerves. Sounds like a confounded dog whining there all the time." His nerves were on edge. He had just answered the questions, some of them almost incoherent, of nearly one hundred women. He was getting tired of it. After all, what was one hundred? The war had to be won, and he was doing his best to beat those Germans. The clerk did as he was told and other women pestering him with questions, and he said to himself: "Holy Hell! Such whiners I never saw in all my life"; and aloud to Mrs Maugham: "How'd you do if you had to go away yourself?" Poor woman crazy with grief listening to him.

"How'd you like to go?" she replied. "Blast you. What about my poor lad? Dead! *Dead! Dead!*"

So it went on; huge crowds hanging around the shipping offices. Men selling newspapers about the Liverpool ship torpedoed by a German submarine, and other placards hitting one in the face and telling you all quiet on the Western Front and rations must be curtailed again. There was a poor woman with a shawl on her head and she was trying to get through the crowd, as she was intent on seeing the director of the engine-room department. The director in his office was sitting by a big fire and reading about "great lads fighting for us and that's the stuff to give 'em," and suddenly this woman outside his door, this woman whose name was Duffy, banging with hands of terror and pain on his door, and the director saying impatiently to his clerk: "Who's that? Good Lord! Am I never to have a single minute's peace? Damn it!" The clerk, who was very devoted to his boss, rushed to open the door to dispel this nuisance, and as soon as he did so there was the woman panting and sobbing, who nearly knocked him down as she pushed her way in.

"Oh, sir! Is Mr Duffy saved from this boat? Oh, sir, please tell me if he's all right. Poor darling. Oh, Jesus, please tell me he's safe, sir"; and as she said this, half of which was unintelligible to the harassed director, his face grew redder and redder with excitement and anger.

"Please go outside, my good woman. We can't tell you anything at present. We will advise everybody concerned as soon as we get the news through. Please go outside. Can't you see I'm busy?"

Mrs Duffy was terrible to see and all the blood drained from her face. Then she raised her two hands high above her head and, joining them, brought them down with a terrific thump upon the desk. Thump. Thump. All her heart and soul were in those hands now, and the continual thumping on the desk was only the poor hands themselves crying. She shouted continually: "Well, why don't you do something? My poor man, and never a one gives a curse. Darling! Darling!" she called out, and it seemed as though her very heart's blood were clouding the eyes, for all thoughts and all feelings were in those hands as she thumped.

"Take her out!" said the director. "The poor woman's gone light in the head," and she heard it and shouted again and again as the clerk dragged her out of the office. "Why don't you do something, you lot of devils? Why don't you do something, and my poor man dead? Damn and blast you, you pack of b—s," and only great grief was speaking in those words now. She was helped down the stairs. And she, along with others, crawled back to where she lived, and it was all dark there, and none saw these people suffering, poor people's blood, and none understood, for there was no time to think now, as Germans were winning, and what time was there to think of poor people? War had to be won.

All day and all night the offices were besieged and bombarded by the wives and sisters and brothers of the crew of the AO.2, and always their eyes were upon that board outside, devouring each name, trying to read into the plain black and white of a name a miracle, and no more than a miracle. Rain fell; it pelted down on this gathering, most of them poorly dressed and shivering with the east wind coming in over the Mersey. But they did not mind that; they could stand there for ever. They were thinking of their heart's blood staining earth and sky and ocean, and no kind words for them. They were calmer now, hardly uttering a sound, just standing in silence, like dumb animals, waiting, waiting. Were only poor people, must give their sons and brothers and husbands. War had to be won. Their eyes ransacked and sought and hungered, but no answer. No answer. The AO.2 was lost and all members of her crew had been reported missing.

The Last Voyage and Other Stories. London: Harvill, 1997. 259–64.

MARTHA GELLHORN

The Third Winter: November 1938

In Barcelona, it was perfect bombing weather. The cafés along the Ramblas were crowded. There was nothing much to drink; a sweet fizzy poison called orangeade and a horrible liquid supposed to be sherry. There was, of course, nothing to eat. Everyone was out enjoying the cold afternoon sunlight. No bombers had come over for at least two hours.

The flower stalls looked bright and pretty along the promenade. "The flowers are all sold, Señores. For the funerals of those who were killed in the eleven o'clock bombing, poor souls."

It had been clear and cold all day and all day yesterday and probably would be fair from now on. "What beautiful weather," a woman said, and she stood, holding her shawl around her, staring at the sky. "And the nights are as fine as the days. A catastrophe," she said, and walked with her husband toward a café.

It was cold but really too lovely and everyone listened for the sirens all the time, and when we saw the bombers they were like tiny silver bullets moving forever up, across the sky.

It gets dark suddenly and no street lights are allowed in Barcelona, and at night the old town is rough going. It would be a silly end, I thought, to fall into a bomb hole, like the one I saw yesterday, that opens right down to the sewers. Everything you do in war is odd, I thought; why should I be plowing around after dark, looking for a carpenter in order to call for a picture frame for a friend? I found Hernández' house in a back street and I held my cigarette lighter above my head to see my way down the hall and up the stairs and then I was knocking on a door and old Mrs. Hernández opened the door and asked me to come in, to be welcome, her house was mine.

"How are you?" I said.

"As you see," old Hernández said, and he pushed his cap back on his forehead and smiled, "alive."

It wasn't much of a home but they looked very handsome in it. A wick floating in a cup of oil lighted the place. There were four chairs and a big table and some shelves tacked on the wall. The ten-year-old grandson was reading close to the burning wick. The daughter-in-law, the wife of their youngest son, played quietly with her baby in a corner. Old Mrs. Hernández had been working over the stove, and the room was smoky. What they would have to eat would be greens, a mound of cabbage leaves the size of your fist, and some dry bread. The women start cooking greens long in advance because they want to get them soft at least. Boiled flavorless greens go down better if they are soft.

The picture frame was not ready, Hernández could not get the wood. Wood is for dugouts and trenches, bridges, railroad ties, to prop up bombed houses, to make artificial arms and legs, for coffins. He used to collect the fragments from destroyed houses, he said, not to work with, but for firewood, but now that is all saved for the hospitals. It was hard to be a carpenter, there wasn't much wood or much work any more.

"Not that it matters about me," Hernández said, "I am very old."

The little boy had been listening. His grandmother kept looking at him, ready to silence him if he interrupted while his elders spoke.

"What do you do all day?" I said.

"I stand in the food line."

"Miguel is a good boy," Mrs. Hernández said. "He does what he can to help his old grandmother."

"Do you like doing that?" I said.

"When they fight," he said, laughing to himself, "it is fun."

His grandmother looked shocked. "He does not understand," she said. "He is only ten. The poor people—they are so hungry, sometimes they quarrel among themselves, not knowing what they do."

(They put up a sign on the shop door, and word flies through the neighbourhood that you can get food today. Then the lines form. Sometimes they are five blocks long. Sometimes you wait all that time but just before your turn comes the shop closes. There is no more food. The women wait in line and talk or knit, the children invent games that they can play standing in one place. Everyone is very thin. They know perfectly, by the sound of the first explosion, where the bombs are falling. If the first bomb sounds hollow and muffled, they do not move from their places, because they know there is no immediate danger. If they can hear the drone of the planes too clearly or the first explosion is jagged and harsh, they scatter for doorways or refuges. They do this professionally, like soldiers.

The pinched women file into the shop and hand their food cards over the high bare counter. The girls behind the counter look healthy because they are wearing rouge. Then the food is doled out in little grey paper sacks. A sack the size of a cigarette package, full of rice: that will have to do two people for two weeks. A sack half that big, full of dried peas: for one person for two weeks. Wait, there's some codfish too. The girl behind the counter pulls out a slab of the gray-white flat fish and cuts off a little piece with a pair of scissors. She cuts it with scissors, not a knife, because scissors are more accurate. A piece as long as your finger and twice as thick is the ration for one person for two weeks. The woman with gray hair and a gray frozen face and exhausted eyes reaches out to get her piece of fish. She holds it a minute in her hand, looking at it. They all look at it, and say nothing. Then she turns and pushes her way through the crowd and out the door.

Now she will wait every day to hear whether the store in her neighbourhood is open again, whether you can trade anything, whether a farmer she knows is coming to town with a dozen eggs and four cabbages and some potatoes. Whether somewhere, somehow, she can get food for her family. Sometimes when the shop runs out of food before everyone is served, the women are wild with grief, afraid to go home with nothing. Then there's trouble. The little boys don't understand the trouble, all they know is that a quarrel brightens the long hours of waiting.)

"You don't go to school?" I said.

"Not now."

"He did very well at school," his grandmother said.

"I want to be a mechanic," the child said, in a voice that was almost weeping. "I want to be a mechanic."

"We do not let him go to school," Mrs. Hernández said, stroking the child's black head. "Because of the bombs. We cannot have him walking about alone."

"The bombs," I said, and smiled at the boy. "What do you do about the bombs?"

"I hide," he said, and he was shy about it, telling me a secret. "I hide so they won't kill me."

"Where do you hide?"

"Under the bed," he said. The daughter-in-law, who is very young, laughed at this, but the old people treated the child seriously. They know that you must have safety in something; if the child believes he is safe under the bed it is better for him.

"When will the war end?" the daughter-in-law asked suddenly.

"Now, now," said the old man. "It will end when we have won it. You know that, Lola. Have patience and do not be silly."

"I have not seen my husband for five months," the girl explained, as if this were the very worst thing that could ever happen to anyone. Old Mrs. Hernández nodded her head, which was like a fine worn wood carving, and made a little sympathetic noise.

"You understand, Señora," Mr. Hernandez said to me, "I am so old that perhaps I shall not live to see the end of the war. Things do not make any difference to me any longer. But it will be better for the children afterward. That is what I tell Lola. Spain will be better for her and Federico afterward. Besides," he said, "Federico is learning a great deal in the Army."

(The Internationals had left the lines and were waiting to go home, or were already gone.* There was a parade for them, down the Diagonal, and women threw flowers and wept, and all the Spanish people thanked them somehow, sometimes only by the way they watched the parade passing. The Internationals looked very dirty and weary and young, and many of them had no country to go back to. The German and Italian anti-Fascists were already refugees; the Hungarians had no home either. Leaving Spain, for most of the European volunteers, was to go into exile. I wonder what happened to the German who was best man for night patrols in the 11th International Brigade. He was a somber man, whose teeth were irregularly broken, whose fingertips were nailless pulp; the first graduate of Gestapo torture I had known.

The Spanish Republican Army, which had been growing and shaping itself through two winters, now dug in for the third winter of war. They were proud and self-confident soldiers. They had started out as militia companies, citizens carrying any sort of rifle, and had become an army and looked like an army and acted like one.

They were always a pleasure to see and often a surprise. On a clear night, coming back very tired from the Segre front, we stopped at divisional headquar-

---

* In September 1938 the Republican government of Spain, no doubt hoping to shame Franco into a similar gesture, withdrew the International Brigade from the fronts. Four of Mussolini's Italian divisions stayed and fought for Franco until the end of the war. Hitler's artillerymen and pilots also remained. Italian planes were bombing Barcelona when this article was written [note in the original].

ters to look at maps and get some dinner too, if lucky. We were received by the
Lieutenant Colonel, who commanded ten thousand men. He was twenty-six
years old and had been an electrician at Lerida. He was blond and looked American and he had grown up with the war. The chief of operations was twenty-three
and a former medical student from Galicia. The chief of staff was twenty-seven,
a lawyer, a Madrid aristocrat who spoke good French and English. Modesto,
commanding the Army of the Ebro and a great soldier, was thirty-five. All the
new corps commanders were in their late twenties and early thirties. Every-body
you saw knew what he was doing and why; it was a cheerful army. The winter
is the worst time of all in war and the third winter is long, cold and desperate;
but you couldn't feel sorry for that army.)

"Both my boys are soldiers," Mrs. Hernández said. "Miguel's father is the
oldest, Tomás, he is at Tortosa; and Federico is up toward Lerida somewhere.
Tomás was here only last week."

"What did he say of the war?" I asked.

"We do not speak of the war," she said. "He says to me, 'You are like all
the other mothers in Spain. You must be brave like all the others.' And sometimes he speaks of the dead."

"Yes?"

"He said, 'I have seen many dead.' He says that so I will understand, but
we do not speak of the war. My sons are always close to the bombs," she said
in her blurred old voice. "If my children are in danger, it is not well that I
should be safe."

The girl Lola had started to sing to her child, to keep it quiet, and now she
brought the baby over near the lighted wick, for me to see. She turned down
a grayish blanket showing the child's head and sang, "Pretty little child, my
pretty little girl."

The face seemed shrunken and faded, and bluish eyelids rested lightly shut
on the eyes. The child was too weak to cry. It fretted softly, with closed eyes,
and we all watched it, and suddenly Lola pulled the cover back over the bundle
in her arms and said, coldly and proudly, "She does not have the right food to
eat and therefore she is not well. But she is a fine child."

The Face of War. London: Granta, rev. ed., 1993. 41–46.

SEAN O'CASEY

From Act I, *The Silver Tassie*

[MRS FORAN *enters by door, helping* in MRS HEEGAN, *who is pale* and *shivering with cold.*]

MRS HEEGAN [*shivering* and *shuddering*]. U-u-uh, I feel the stream of blood that's still trickling through me old veins icifyin' fast; u-uh.

MRS FORAN. Madwoman, dear, to be waitin' out there on the quay an' a wind risin' as cold as a stepmother's breath, piercin' through your old bones, mockin' any effort a body would make to keep warm, an' [*suddenly rushing over to the fireplace in an agony of dismay, scattering* SIMON *and* SYLVESTER, *and whipping the frying-pan off the fire*]—The steak, the steak; I forgot the blasted steak an' onions fryin' on the fire! God Almighty, there's not as much as a bead of juice left in either of them. The scent of the burnin' would penetrate to the street, an' not one of you'd stir a hand to lift them out of danger. Oh, look at the condition they're in. Even the gospel-gunner couldn't do a little target practice by helpin' the necessity of a neighbour. [. . .] [EXIT]

MRS HEEGAN [*pushing in to the fire,* to SIMON *and* SYLVESTER]. Push to the right and push to the left till I get to the fosterin' fire. Time eatin' his heart out, an' no sign of him yet. The two of them, the two of my legs is numb . . . an' the wind's risin' that'll make the sea heave an' sink under the boat tonight, under shaded lights an' the submarines about. [SUSIE *comes in, goes over to window, and looks out.*] Hours ago the football match must have been over, an' no word of him yet, an' all drinkin' if they won, an' all drinkin' if they lost; with Jessie hitchin' on him, an' no one thinkin' of me an' the maintenance money.

SYLVESTER. He'll come back in time; he'll have to come back; he must come back.

SIMON. Two times consecutively before, makin' the Cup the property of the Club.

SYLVESTER. Exactly!

MRS HEEGAN. The chill's residin' in my bones, an' feelin's left me just the strength to shiver. He's overstayed his leave a lot, an' if he misses now the tide that's waitin', he skulks behind desertion from the colours.

SUSIE. On Active Service that means death at dawn.

MRS HEEGAN. An' my governmental money grant would stop at once.

SUSIE. That would gratify Miss Jessie Taite, because you put her weddin' off with Harry till after the duration of the war, an' cut her out of the allowance.

SYLVESTER [*with a sickened look at* SIMON]. Dtch, Dtch, dtch, the way the women nag the worst things out of happenings! [. . .]

MRS HEEGAN. She's coinin' money workin' at munitions, an' doesn't need to eye the little that we get from Harry; for one evening hurryin' with him to the pictures she left her bag behind, an goin' through it what would you think I found?

SUSIE. A saucy book, now, or a naughty picture?

MRS HEEGAN. Lion and Unicorn standin' on their Jew ay mon draw. With all the rings an' dates, an' rules an' regulations.

SIMON. What was it, Mrs Heegan?

MRS HEEGAN. Spaced an' lined; signed an' signatured; nestlin' in a blue envelope to keep it warm.

SYLVESTER [*testily*]. Oh, sing it out, woman, an' don't be takin' the value out of what you're goin' to tell us.

MRS HEEGAN. A Post Office Savings Bank Book.

SYLVESTER. Oh, hairy enough, eh?

SIMON. How much, Mrs Heegan? [. . .]

MRS HEEGAN. Two hundred an' nineteen pounds, sixteen shillings an' no pence.

SYLVESTER. Be-God, a nice little nest-egg, right enough!

SUSIE. I hope in my heart that she came by it honestly, and that she remembers that it's as true now as when it was first spoken that it's harder for a camel to go through the eye of a needle than for a rich person to enter the kingdom of heaven.

SIMON. And she hidin' it all under a veil of silence, when there wasn't the slightest fear of any of us bein' jealous of her.

[*A tumult is heard on the floor over their heads, followed by a crash of breaking delf. They are startled, and listen attentively.*]

MRS HEEGAN [*breaking the silence*]. Oh, there he's at it again. An' she sayin' that he was a pattern husband since he came home on leave, merry-making with her an' singin' dolorously the first thing every mornin'. I was thinkin' there'd be a rough house sometime over her lookin' so well after his long absence . . . you'd imagine now, the trenches would have given him some idea of the sacredness of life!

[*Another crash of breaking delfware.*]

MRS HEEGAN. An' the last week of his leave she was too fond of breakin' into song in front of him.

SYLVESTER. Well, she's gettin' it now for goin' round heavin' her happiness in the poor man's face.

[*A crash, followed by screams from* MRS FORAN.]

SUSIE. I hope he won't be running down here as he often does.

SIMON [*a little agitated*]. I couldn't stay here an' listen to that; I'll go up and stop him: he might be killing the poor woman.

MRS HEEGAN. Don't do anything of the kind, Simon; he might down you with a hatchet or something.

SIMON. Phuh, I'll keep him off with the left and hook him with the right. [*Putting on his hat and coat as he goes to the door.*] Looking prim and careless'll astonish him. Monstrous to stay here, while he may be killing the woman.

MRS HEEGAN [*to* SIMON *as he goes out*]. For God's sake mind yourself, Simon.

SYLVESTER [*standing beside closed door on right with his ear close to one of the panels, listening intently*]. Simon's a tidy little man with his fists, an' would make Teddy Foran feel giddy if he got home with his left hook. [*Crash.*] I wonder is that Simon knockin' down Foran, or Foran knockin' down Simon?

MRS HEEGAN. If he came down an' we had the light low, an' kept quiet, he might think we were all out.

SYLVESTER. Shush. I can hear nothin' now. Simon must have awed him. Quiet little man, but when Simon gets goin'. Shush? No, nothin' . . . Something unusual has happened. O, oh, be-God!

[*The door against which* SYLVESTER *is leaning bursts suddenly in.* SYLVESTER *is flung headlong to the floor, and* MRS FORAN, *her hair falling wildly over her shoulders, a cut over her eye, frantic with fear, rushes in and scrambles in a frenzy of haste under the bed.* MRS HEEGAN, *quickened by fear, runs like a good one, followed by* SUSIE, *into the room, the door of which they bang after them.* SYLVESTER *hurriedly fights his way under the bed with* MRS FORAN.]

MRS FORAN [*speaking excitedly and jerkily as she climbs under the bed*]. Flung his dinner in to the fire—and then started to smash the little things in the room. Tryin' to save the dresser, I got a box in the eye. I locked the door on him as I rushed out, an' before I was half-way down, he had one of the panels flyin' out with—a hatchet!

SYLVESTER [*under the bed—out of breath*]. Whythehell didn'tyou sing out beforeyousent thedoor flyin' inontop o' me!

MRS FORAN. How could I an' I flyin' before danger to me—life?

SYLVESTER. Yes, an'you've got meinto a nice extremity now!

MRS FORAN. An' I yelled to Simon Norton when he had me—down, but the boyo only ran the faster out of the—house!

SYLVESTER. Oh, an' the regal-like way he went out to fight! Oh, I'm findin' out that everyone who wears a cocked hat isn't a Napoleon!

[TEDDY FORAN, MRS FORAN's *husband, enters by door, with a large fancy, vividly yellow-coloured bowl, ornamented with crimson roses, in one hand and a hatchet in the other. He is big and powerful, rough and hardy. A man who would be dominant in a public house, and whose opinions would be listened to with great respect. He is dressed in the khaki uniform of a soldier home on leave.*]

TEDDY. Under the bed, eh? Right place for a guilty conscience. I should have thrown you out of the window with the dinner you put before me. Out with you from under there, an' come up with your husband. [. . .]

MRS FORAN. I'll not budge an inch from where I am.

TEDDY [*looking under the bed and seeing* SYLVESTER]. What are you doin' there encouragin' her against her husband?

SYLVESTER. You've no right to be rippin' open the poor woman's life of peace with violence.

TEDDY [*with indignation*]. She's my wife, isn't she?

MRS FORAN. Nice thing if I lose the sight of my eye with the cut you gave me!

TEDDY. She's my wife, isn't she? An' you've no legal right to be harbourin' her here, keepin' her from her household duties. Stunned I was when I seen her lookin' so well after me long absence. [. . .]

SYLVESTER. Goon up to your own home; you've no right to be violatin' this place.

TEDDY. You'd like to make her your cheery amee, would you? It's napoo, there, napoo, you little pip-squeak. I seen you an' her goin' down the street arm-in-arm.

SYLVESTER. Did you expect to see me goin' down the street leg-in-leg with her?

TEDDY. Thinkin' of her Ring-papers instead of her husband. [*To* MRS FORAN] I'll teach you to be rippling with joy an' your husband goin' away! [*He shows the bowl.*] Your weddin' bowl, look at it; pretty, isn't it? Take your last eyeful of it now, for it's goin' west quick!

SUSIE [*popping her head in again*]. God is watching you, God is watching you!

MRS FORAN [*appealingly*]. Teddy, Teddy, don't smash the poor weddin' bowl.

TEDDY [*smashing the bowl with a blow of the hatchet*]. It would be a pity, wouldn't it? Damn it, an' damn you. I'm off now to smash anything I missed, so that you'll have a gay time fittin' up the little home again by the time your loving husband comes back. You can come an' have a look, an' bring your mon amee if you like.

[*He goes out, and there is a pause as* MRS FORAN *and* SYLVESTER *peep anxiously towards the door.*]

SYLVESTER. Cautious, now cautious; he might be lurking outside that door there, ready to spring on you the minute you show'd your nose!

MRS FORAN. Me lovely little weddin' bowl, me lovely little weddin' Bowl!

[TEDDY *is heard breaking things in the room above.*]

SYLVESTER [*creeping out from under the bed*]. Oh, he is gone up. He was a little cow'd, I think, when he saw me.

MRS FORAN. Me little weddin' bowl, wrapp'd in tissue paper, an' only taken out for a few hours every Christmas—me poor little weddin' bowl.

SUSIE [*popping her head in*]. God is watching—oh, he's gone!

SYLVESTER [*jubilant*]. Vanished! He was a little cow'd I think, when he saw me.

[MRS HEEGAN *and* SUSIE *come into the room.*]

MRS FORAN. He's makin' a hash of every little thing we have in the house, Mrs Heegan.

MRS HEEGAN. Go inside to the room, Mrs Foran; an' if he comes down again, we'll say you ran out to the street.

MRS FORAN [*going into room*]. My poor little weddin' bowl that I might have had for generations!

SUSIE [*who has been looking out of the window, excitedly*]. They're comin', they're comin': a crowd with a concertina; some of them carrying Harry on their shoulders, an' others are carrying that Jessie Taite too, holding a silver cup in her hands. Oh, look at the shameful way she's showing her legs to all who like to have a look at them!

MRS HEEGAN. Never mind Jessie's legs—what we have to do is to hurry him out to catch the boat.

[*The sound of a concertina playing in the street outside has been heard, and the noise of a marching crowd. The crowd stop at the house. Shouts are heard—"Up the Avondales!";* "Up Harry Heegan and the Avondales!" *Then steps are heard coming up the stairs, and first* SIMON NORTON *enters, holding the door ceremoniously wide open to allow* HAR-RY KEEGAN *to enter, with his arm around* JESSIE, *who is carrying a silver cup joyously, rather than reverentially, elevated, as a priest would elevate a chalice.* HARRY *is wearing khaki trousers, a military cap stained with trench mud, a vivid orange-coloured jersey with black collar and cuffs. He is twenty-three years of age, tall, with the sinewy muscles*

of a manual worker made flexible by athletic sport. He is a typical young worker, enthusiastic, very often boisterous, sensible by instinct rather than by reason. He has gone to the trenches as unthinkingly as he would go to the polling-booth. He isn't naturally stupid; it is the stupidity of persons in high places that has stupefied him. He has given all to his masters, strong heart, sound lungs, healthy stomach, lusty limbs, and the little mind that education has permitted to develop sufficiently to make all the rest a little more useful. He is excited now with the sweet and innocent insanity of a fine achievement, and the rapid lowering of a few drinks. JESSIE is twenty-two or so, responsive to all the animal impulses of life. Ever dancing around, in and between the world, the flesh, and the devil. She would be happy climbing with a boy among the heather on Howth Hill, and could play ball with young men on the swards of the Phoenix Park. She gives her favour to the prominent and popular. HARRY is her favourite: his strength and speed have won the Final for his club, he wears the ribbon of the DCM. It is a time of spiritual and animal exaltation for her.]
BARNEY BAGNAL, *a soldier mate of* HARRY's, *stands a little shyly near the door, with a pleasant, good-humoured grin on his rather broad face. [. . .]*

HARRY [*joyous and excited*]. Won, won, won, be-God; by the odd goal in five. Lift it up, lift it up, Jessie, sign of youth, sign of strength, sign of victory!

MRS HEEGAN [*to* SYLVESTER]. I knew, now, Harry would come back in time to catch the boat.

HARRY [*to* JESSIE]. Leave it here, leave it down here, Jessie, under the picture, the picture of the boy that won the final.

MRS HEEGAN. A parcel of sandwiches, a bottle of whisky, an' some magazines to take away with you an' Barney, Harry.

HARRY. Napoo sandwiches, an' napoo magazines: look at the cup, eh? The cup that Harry won, won by the odd goal in five! [*To* BARNEY] The song that the little Jock used to sing, Barney, what was it? The little Jock we left shrivellin' on the wire after the last push.

BARNEY. "Will ye no come back again?"

HARRY. No, no, the one we all used to sing with him, "The Silver Tassie." [*Pointing to Cup*] There it is, the Silver Tassie, won by the odd goal in five, kicked by Harry Heegan.

MRS HEEGAN. Watch your time, Harry, watch your time.

JESSIE. He's watching it, he's watching it—for God's sake don't get fussy, Mrs Heegan.

HARRY. They couldn't take their beatin' like men. . . . Play the game, play the game, why the hell couldn't they play the game? [*To* BARNEY] See the President of the Club, Dr Forby Maxwell, shaking hands with me, when he was giving me the cup, "Well done, Heegan!" The way they yell'd and jump'd when they put in the equalising goal in the first half!

BARNEY. Ay, a fluke, that's what it was; a lowsey fluke.

MRS HEEGAN [*holding* HARRY's *coat up for him to put it on*]. Here, your coat, Harry, slip it on while you're talkin'.

HARRY [*putting it on*]. All right, keep smiling, don't fuss. [*To the rest*] Grousing the whole time they were chasin' the ball; an' when they lost it, "Referee, referee, offside, referee . . . foul there; ey, open your eyes, referee!"

JESSIE. And we scream'd and shouted them down with "Play the game, Primrose Rovers, play the game!"

BARNEY. You ran them off their feet till they nearly stood still.

MRS FORAN [*has been peeping in timidly from the room and now comes in to the rest*]. Somebody run up an' bring Teddy down for fear he'd be left behind.

SYLVESTER [*to* HARRY]. Your haversack an' trench tools, Harry; haversack first, isn't it?

HARRY [*fixing his haversack*]. Haversack, haversack, don't rush me. [*To the rest*] But when I got the ball, Barney, once I got the ball, the rain began to fall on the others. An' the last goal, the goal that put us one ahead, the winning goal, that was a-a-eh-a stunner!

BARNEY. A beauty, me boy, a hot beauty.

HARRY. Slipping by the back rushing at me like a mad bull, steadying a moment for a drive, seeing in a flash the goalie's hands sent with a shock to his chest by the force of the shot, his half-stunned motion to clear, a charge, and then carrying him, the ball and all with a rush into the centre of the net!

BARNEY [*enthusiastically*]. Be-God, I did get a thrill when I seen you puttin' him sittin' on his arse in the middle of the net!

MRS FORAN [*from the door*]. One of yous go up an' see if Teddy's ready to go.

MRS HEEGAN [*to* HARRY]. Your father'll carry your kit-bag, an' Jessie'll carry your rifle as far as the boat.

HARRY [*irritably*]. Oh, damn it, woman, give your wailin' over for a minute!

MRS HEEGAN. You've got only a few bare minutes to spare, Harry.

HARRY. We'll make the most of them, then. [*To* BARNEY] Out with one of them wine-virgins we got in "The Mill in the Field," Barney, and we'll rape her in a last hot moment before we set out to kiss the guns!

[SIMON *has gone into room and returned with a gun and a kit-bag. He crosses to where* BARNEY *is standing.*]

BARNEY [*taking a bottle of wine from his pocket*]. Empty her of her virtues, eh?

HARRY. Spill it out, Barney, spill it out. . . . [*Seizing Silver Cup, and holding it towards* BARNEY] Here, into the cup, be-God. A drink out of the cup, out of the Silver Tassie!

BARNEY [*who has removed the cap and taken out the cork*]. Here she is now. . . . Ready for anything, stripp'd to the skin!

JESSIE. No double-meaning talk, Barney.

SUSIE [*haughtily, to* JESSIE]. The men that are defending us have leave to bow themselves down in the House of Rimmon, for the men that go with the guns are going with God.

[BARNEY *pours wine into the Cup for* HARRY *and into a glass for himself.*]

HARRY [*to* JESSIE]. Jessie, a sup for you. [*She drinks from the Cup.*] An' a drink for me. [*He drinks.*] Now a kiss while our lips are wet. [*He kisses her*] Christ, Barney, how would you like to be retreating from the fairest face and [*lifting* JESSIE's *skirt a little*]—and the trimmest, slimmest little leg in the parish? Napoo, Barney, to everyone but me!

MRS FORAN. One of you go up, an' try to get my Teddy down.

BARNEY [*lifting* SUSIE's *skirt a little*]. Napoo, Harry, to everyone but—

SUSIE [*angrily, pushing* BARNEY *away from her*]. You khaki-cover'd ape, you, what are you trying to do? Manhandle the lassies of France, if you like, but put on your gloves when you touch a woman that seeketh not the things of the flesh.

HARRY [*putting an arm round* SUSIE *to mollify her*]. Now, Susie, Susie, length-en your temper for a passing moment, so that we may bring away with us the breath of a kiss to the shell-bullied air of the trenches . . . Besides, there's noth-ing to be ashamed of—it's not a bad little leggie at all.

SUSIE [*slipping her arm round* HARRY'S *neck, and looking defiantly at* BARNEY]. I don't mind what Harry does; I know he means no harm, not like other people. Harry's different.

JESSIE. You'll not forget to send me the German helmet home from France, Harry?

SUSIE [*trying to rest her head on* HARRY'S *breast*]. I know Harry, he's different. It's his way. I wouldn't let anyone else touch me, but in some way or another I can tell Harry's different.

JESSIE [*putting her arm round* HARRY *under* SUSIE's *in an effort to dislodge it*]. Susie, Harry wants to be free to keep his arm round me during his last few moments here, so don't be pulling him about!

SUSIE [*shrinking back a little*]. I was only saying that Harry was different.

MRS FORAN. For God's sake, will someone go up for Teddy, or he won't go back at all!

TEDDY [*appearing at door*]. Damn anxious for Teddy to go back! Well, Ted-dy's goin' back, an' he's left everything tidy upstairs so that you'll not have much trouble sortin' things out. [*To* HARRY] The Club an' a crowd's waitin' outside to bring us to the boat before they go to the spread in honour of the final. [*Bitterly*] A party for them while we muck off to the trenches!

HARRY [*after a slight pause, to* BARNEY]. Are you game, Barney?

BARNEY. What for?

HARRY. To go to the spread. and hang the latch for another night?

BARNEY [*taking his rifle from* SIMON *and slinging it over his shoulder*]. No, no, napoo desertin' on Active Service. Deprivation of pay an' the rest of your time in the front trenches. No, no. We must go back.

MRS HEEGAN. No, no, Harry. You must go back.

SIMON, SYLVESTER AND SUSIE [*together*]. You must go back.

VOICES OF CROWD OUTSIDE. They must go back!

[*The ship's siren is heard blowing.*]

SIMON. The warning signal.

SYLVESTER. By the time they get there, they'll be unslinging the gang-ways!

SUSIE [*handing* HARRY *his steel helmet*]. Here's your helmet, Harry. [*He puts it on.*]

MRS HEEGAN. You'll all nearly have to run for it now!

SYLVESTER. I've got your kit-bag, Harry.

SUSIE. I've got your rifle.

SIMON. I'll march in front with the cup, after Conroy with the concertina.

TEDDY. Come on: ong avong to the trenches!

HARRY [*recklessly*]. Jesus, a last drink, then! [*He raises the Silver Cup, singing:*]

Gae bring to me a pint of wine,

And fill it in a silver tassie;

BARNEY [*joining in vigorously:*]

. . . . a silver tassie.

HARRY. That I may drink before I go,

A service to my bonnie lassie.

BARNEY. . . . bonnie lassie.

HARRY. The boat rocks at the pier o' Leith,

Full loud the wind blows from the ferry;

The ship rides at the Berwick Law,

An' I must leave my bonnie Mary!

BARNEY. . . . leave my bonnie Mary!

HARRY. The trumpets sound, the banners fly,

The glittering spears are ranked ready;

BARNEY. . . . glittering spears are ranked ready;

HARRY. The shouts of war are heard afar,
The battle closes thick and bloody.
BARNEY. . . . closes thick and bloody.
HARRY. It's not the roar of sea or shore,
That makes me longer wish to tarry,
Nor shouts of war that's heard afar—
It's leaving thee, my bonnie lassie!
BARNEY. . . . leaving thee, my bonnie lassie!
TEDDY. Come on, come on. [SIMON, SYLVESTER, *and* SUSIE *go out.*]
VOICES OUTSIDE.
Come on from your home to the boat;
Carry on from the boat to the camp.

TEDDY *and* BARNEY *go out.* HARRY *and* JESSIE *follow; as* HARRY *reaches the door,
he takes his arm from round* JESSIE *and comes back to* MRS HEEGAN.

VOICES OUTSIDE.
From the camp up the line to the trenches.
HARRY [*shyly and hurriedly kissing* MRS HEEGAN]. Well, goodbye, old woman.
MRS HEEGAN. Goodbye, my son.

[HARRY *goes out. The chorus of "The Silver Tassie," accompanied by a concertina, can
be heard growing fainter till it ceases.* MRS FORAN *goes out timidly.* MRS HEEGAN
*pokes the fire, arranges the things in the room, and then goes to the window and looks
out. [. . .]* MRS HEEGAN *with a sigh, "Ah dear," goes over to the fire and sits down. A
slight pause, then* MRS FORAN *returns to the room.*]

MRS FORAN. Every little bit of china I had in the house is lyin' above in a
mad an' muddled heap like the flotsum an' jetsum of the seashore!
MRS HEEGAN [*with a deep sigh of satisfaction*]. Thanks be to Christ that we're
after managin' to get the three of them away safely.

—CURTAIN—

Seven Plays by Sean O'Casey. Ed. Ronald Ayling. London: Macmillan, 1985. 188–99.

Glossary

Cheery amee/ mon amee = Corrupt from French *chère aimeé/ mon aimé:* lover, darling.
Jew ay mon draw = Corrupt of *Mon Dieu mon Droit* from the national coat of arms on
    British official documents.
Napoo! = World War I slang, corruption of French *il n'y a plus'* meaning "nothing do-
    ing."
Ong avong to the trenches = Corrupt French *en vant* meaning forward march to the trenches.

Ribbon of DCM = Distinguished Conduct Medal (military decoration for soldiers other than commissioned officers).

Ring-paper = Wedding certificate guaranteeing an allowance paid to the legal wife of a soldier on active service.

Yous = Irish colloquial for "you."

ANNA WICKHAM

London Scenes: The Night March

As I stand at the bottom of the hill I am conscious of a faint insistent rhythm. It is a drum and fife band in the distance. That sound always stirs me with vague, half-understood emotions. Military music means nothing to me, I have always lived in times of peace, but my ancestors understood it. It is to me like a symbol of which I have forgotten the significance. I only know that it means something.

I look eagerly in the direction of the sound. Soon there is a swaying on the crest of the hill. This becomes a ribbon of marching men which the street lamps mottle with shadow and light. The light and the night and the wave motion of the swinging line give to the commonplace tune the appeal of great music, and in some way the sound of the music and the marching feet have a certain quality of silence. The sound and the scene no longer appeal to the eye and the ear, but only to the mind. They become like things vividly thought.

I see the faces of the first men. They do not speak. They are absent and pale as if their senses were asleep, they walk like somnambulists. By the side of the ranks walk many civilians all silent, all hypnotised by music and movement. Then come the horses walking in time to the music, and then a quick-firing gun—a toy ornamented with bright metal—so small, so neat and yet so deadly, suggestive of the powers of death and hell.

In the rear ranks the men are smoking, the blue-grey smoke ascends through the still air. The march seems like the march of ghosts. One of the ghosts raises his head and catches sight of me. He draws himself up and leers, very full of sex. The men pass. They turn the corner where a church shows its bulk against the London sky. I am left in the street with tears in my eyes. These men and that music mean little to me. But my ancestors, within me, remember them.

The Writings of Anna Wickham. Ed. R. D. Smith. London: Virago, 1984. 381.

15

Modernism, Trauma, and Narrative Reformulation

INTRODUCED AND SELECTED BY SUZETTE A. HENKE

THE MODERNIST PERIOD is not only circumscribed, but virtually defined by historical trauma. After the triumph of British imperialism during the Victorian era, the Edwardian epoch offered a brief respite before European war erupted in the summer of 1914. The resonant thunder of the guns of August inaugurated heretofore unimagined horrors of technological warfare that would resonate throughout the century and give birth to renewed psychological interest in the debilitating effects of post-traumatic stress disorder. Documentary film footage of World War I testifies to the tortures of modern combat: the protracted terror of life in the trenches, where men lived in constant dread of bombs, shells, poison gas, shrapnel, machine guns, and hand-to-hand combat, as well as threats of trench foot and leg amputation. It is little wonder that the psychological effects of so-called *shell shock* were first anatomized in soldiers afflicted during the Great War, when traumatized combatants were often dismissed as malingerers or executed as traitors. Such was the bloody inauguration of contemporary psychoanalysis, with Sigmund Freud spearheading the reinterpretation of "male hysteria" and neurasthenia in terms of combat neurosis.

The Greek word "trauma" literally refers to a physical wound and, until the last century, alluded strictly to bodily injury. Twentieth-century psychology metaphorically expanded the term to denote a sudden and unexpected blow to the psyche that evoked specific symptoms—intrusive but uncontrollable flashbacks, often recurring in vivid nightmares; exaggerated startle responses and/or aggressive outbursts; psychic fragmentation and dysphoria (the opposite of euphoria); flatness of mood, numbing, and anhedonia (loss of sensation and enjoyment); disinterest, distrust, and eventual despair.

In her pioneering work *Trauma and Recovery,* Judith Lewis Herman proposed that "the most common post-traumatic disorders are those not of men in war" but of ordinary citizens in civilian life (28). When the protagonist of H. D.'s *Asphodel* draws a similar analogy between parturition and military sacrifice, she insists that women in childbirth risk their own lives "like any soldier" (*A* 170). For women, in particular, traumatic events may cluster around experiences of sexual violation and/or pregnancy loss—physical or metaphorical wounds to the body that devastate the psyche. Both Freudian talk therapy and the analogous practice of scriptotherapy can offer palliation of post-traumatic symptoms by allowing survivors to reformulate obsessive memories of trauma in the shape of controlled and coherent testimony.

Virginia Woolf, as deceased analysand, has been subjected to posthumous diagnoses of manic-depression (bipolar malady), childhood sexual abuse, and/ or schizophrenia. What seems clear, however, is that every fictional text she composed subtly incorporates a haunting trauma narrative.[1] Her 1925 novel *Mrs. Dalloway* is dominated by the shell-shocked ravings of Septimus Smith, a psychological casualty of World War I, and by the shadow of trauma cast by a shockingly brief allusion to the death of Clarissa Dalloway's sister, Sylvia Parry, killed by a falling tree. Most critical assessments of Smith's aberrant behavior have failed to give adequate consideration to "The Prime Minister," an early draft of the opening scenes of *Mrs. Dalloway.* In this inaugural fragment, Septimus is clearly suffering from post-traumatic stress disorder provoked by the Great War. He may—or may not—have seen combat.[2] Woolf's manuscript provocatively alludes to Smith's authorship of a pamphlet on Russia—presumably a radical socialist critique indicative of his "outsider" political status.

The holograph manuscript of "The Prime Minister," held in the Henry W. and Albert A. Berg Collection of the New York Public Library, has never been transcribed for publication.[3] The following selections offer a textual palimpsest acknowledging the generative dimensions of Woolf's *avant-texte.* Angled brackets <. . .> indicate relevant material deleted by Woolf in the original manuscript, and wavy brackets {. . .} delineate words she added in the margins. By comparing this holograph transcription with the published typescript, a reader can disinter several layers of occluded textual traces that replicate, in reverse order, Woolf's practice of double(d) self-censorship.

In "The Prime Minister," Woolf feels compelled to anatomize the severe symptoms of Septimus Smith's apparent madness by exaggerating his idiosyncracies. Without his wife Rezia to balance and interpret his deranged behavior, Septimus emerges as a "queer" subject (Woolf's term), suffering delusions of messianic grandeur. He begins laughing and raving in a crowded restaurant and is seized by a fear that his heart will, at any moment, burst into pieces. In the holograph, a leopard's head from a silver vase winks at him in sly connivance, as he struggles to control his hebephrenia—a manic laughter that, he believes, has gashed a hole in the wall, through which seeps a warm, uncanny fluid permeating the quivering atmosphere.

Through Woolf's technique of free indirect discourse, Septimus cynically assesses Europe's postwar liberation by alluding to war photographs that testify to the horrors of civilian carnage via frozen bodies and the corpses of innocent children. Haunted by a misanthropic vision of humanity, he indicts a race of corrupt individuals intent on hurting, harming, and destroying one another, yet oblivious of their own cruelty. Despite paranoid fantasies, he articulates the "insane truth" that primitive instincts toward murder and mayhem are routinely glorified by the rhetoric of nationalism and patriotic jingoism. Sardonically, he observes: "Death, death, death—in the service of the Nation; that was the only creditable exit for a man with a wife." Paradoxically, the citizen who attempts suicide will be locked in a madhouse; but a man who hurls himself toward self-destruction in military combat will posthumously reap imperial accolades.[4]

Clearly manifesting symptoms of post-traumatic stress disorder, Septimus might also exhibit behaviors characteristic of bipolar malady—manic expansiveness and grandiosity tempered by the severe cynicism of clinical depression. As Kay Redfield Jamison explains in *Touched with Fire,* extreme forms of mania may be "characterized by violent agitation, bizarre behavior, delusional thinking, and visual and auditory hallucinations" (13). In fact, "mixed states, in which depressive and manic symptoms coexist" (36), might characterize the most dangerous phase of bipolar malady, during which a psychotic subject feels sufficiently exuberant to implement creative (or self-destructive) projects, but so depressed that he or she is tormented by a sense of extreme hopelessness. Gifted with ebullience, divergent thinking, and dendritic sensibilities, the manic Septimus harbors grandiose visions and believes himself a prophet, even as he asks metaphysical questions and flirts with suicidal ideation.

In "The Prime Minister" holograph, Septimus vows to kill himself and, in megalomaniac obsession, assumes the role of religious scapegoat: "One might give one's body to be eaten by the starving, and . . . be a martyr." Envisaging himself as a man-god slain, like Christ or Apollo, to expiate the sins of a guilty community, he plans first to assassinate the Prime Minister, then to commit suicide and offer his body as a eucharistic sacrament to hordes of eastern European refugees displaced by the war. In the final version of *Mrs. Dalloway,* Woolf prudently deletes his maniacal fantasies of assassination, martyrdom, and cannibalistic sacrifice, and portrays Septimus as a tormented war veteran victimized by the forces of British imperialism.

Although the holograph excerpts included in this volume focus on Septimus Smith, Woolf may have intended an uncanny parallel between his deranged behavior and the abstracted consciousness of H. Z. Prentice, who might have served as an early prototype for Peter Walsh. This cerebral bachelor is a "queer old fellow" who mutters distractedly to himself and swings his dispatch boxes with narcissistic carelessness. A highly opinionated political thinker, he seems oblivious of his domestic dependence on affable females who benevolently attend to his bachelor comforts. Like Richard Dalloway, Prentice focuses exclusively on global conflict and remains deliberately blind to the domestic injustice characteristic of British patriarchal institutions.

Prentice is an avatar of the patriarchal bogey who haunts Woolf's more radical polemic in *Three Guineas* and inspires her indictment of the fascist spirit that buttresses autocracy, whether it operate in the halls of Parliament, the chambers of Temple Bar, or the dining rooms of professional men. "And are not force and possessiveness," she asks ingenuously, "very closely connected with war?" (30). Woolf insists that whenever men are invested, by law or by custom, with totalitarian power to control women and children or to bend the malleable spirits of the weak, the poor, the disenfranchised, or the afflicted, "we have in embryo the creature, Dictator as we call him when he is Italian or German, who believes that he has the right, whether given by God, Nature, sex or race is immaterial, to dictate to other human beings how they shall live; what they shall do" (53). Whether this Nietzschean will to power be exercised by political leaders on a global stage or by overbearing husbands in the microcosm of a domestic household, the force of male bullying is equally invidious. In 1938, on the eve of World War II, Woolf shocked the British public by exhorting its citizens to "crush him [the Dictator] in [their] own country" before challenging the "very dangerous" and "very ugly" totalitarian monsters ruling abroad (Hitler, Stalin, Franco, and Mussolini) (53).

A lifelong pacifist, Woolf abhors "the inhumanity, the beastliness, the horror, the folly of war" (83) perpetrated by gray-haired patriots who mount "conspiracies that sink the private brother" (105) by encouraging young men to seek heroic sacrifice in the mouth of a machine gun. In *Three Guineas* she tries to expose the ominous similarities between British imperialism and the demonic potential of German, Italian, and Spanish fascism, all of which honor the "quintessence of virility" embodied in a figure who is "called in German and Italian Fuhrer or Duce; in our own language Tyrant or Dictator" (142). She despises "Herr Hitler" for his Nietzschean adulation of the "hero requiring recreation" through female sexual servicing; and "Signor Mussolini" for his homage to "the wounded warrior requiring female dependents" (111). "The whole iniquity of dictatorship, whether in Oxford or Cambridge, in Whitehall or Downing Street, against Jews or against women, in England, or in Germany, in Italy or in Spain" is all of the same fabric in a world that empowers a "monstrous male, loud of voice, hard of fist, childishly intent on scoring the floor of the earth with chalk marks" (105). Woolf understands that global warfare breeds psychological trauma in soldiers and citizens alike, even as the force of political aggression wreaks havoc on the humanist values of civilization and culture. As a committed pacifist and a feminist revolutionary, she proudly celebrates her privileged status as an "outsider" in the British empire: "For . . . in fact, as a woman, I have no country. . . . As a woman my country is the whole world" (109).

Woolf's American counterpart, the expatriate Hilda Doolittle (H. D.), filtered her narrative representations of World War I in *Asphodel* and *Bid Me to Live* through a series of personal traumas on the home front: a shattering stillbirth in 1915; the death of her brother Gilbert in combat at Thiacourt in 1918; her father's sudden death from stroke; a life-threatening bout of influenza; and the dissolution of her marriage to Richard Aldington after the 1919 birth of her daughter Perdita, fathered by Cecil Gray. In works of autobiographical fiction, H. D. conflates the trauma of pregnancy loss with the wartime amputation of a soldier's limb. Both traumas, she insists, manifest the psychic phenomenon of a phantom limb and precipitate the kind of post-traumatic stress disorder traditionally associated with combat neurosis. After a course of psychoanalysis with Sigmund Freud in Vienna, H. D. further interrogated her analysis by composing a memoir, *Tribute to Freud*. Only when she was able to act on her analyst's advice and reformulate the story of her own wartime tragedy in the genre of autobiographical fiction did she succeed in working through post-traumatic symptoms of intrusion and dissociation. *Madrigal*, the roman à clef composed in response to Freud's directives, was eventually published as *Bid Me to Live*.

What H. D. envisages so poignantly both in *Bid Me to Live* and *Asphodel* (a manuscript completed in the 1920s but not published until 1992) is the implicit analogy between the text of woman's body, scarred and mutilated by the physiological stress of childbirth, and male testimony about war wounds and heroism. Julia Ashton, the H. D. figure in *Bid Me to Live,* has been traumatized by stillbirth—an experience based on Hilda's own pregnancy loss, which she linked with the shocking news of the sinking of the Lusitania during World War I. Julia, Hilda's alter ego, exhibits symptoms of traumatic dysphoria, characterized by "confusion, agitation, emptiness, and utter aloneness. . . . Depersonalization, derealization, and anesthesia . . . accompanied by a feeling of unbearable agitation" (Herman 108–9). She meticulously delineates symptoms of hyperarousal, loss of affect, and a sense of emotional paralysis associated with traumatic constriction. Morbidly depressed, Julia cannot imagine resurrection from a conjugal bed that she identifies as a virtual deathbed. H. D.'s melancholic protagonist is so alienated from her soldier-spouse that she feels trapped in marriage to a virtual stranger—a Greek poet whom military service has transmogrified into a brutal and aggressive Roman soldier, tainted with the stench of poison gas from the trenches.

Retreating to the enchanted natural landscape of Cornwall, Julia begins mythically to identify with ancient Druidic spirits and embraces the pantheistic, healing power of nature. Her dreams of artistic creation are encoded in the ideal of *gloire,* a symbol of pure possibility that she shares with fellow artist and pacifist, Frederico (based on D. H. Lawrence). "The child is the *gloire* before it is born" (*B* 177), she postulates. And it is this potential that functions as the repressed textual unconscious of *Bid Me to Live*—the mysteriously germinating seed of an ineffable future. H. D. would eventually recover from the most deleterious effects of post-traumatic stress disorder, but only through protracted experiments in scriptotherapy, whereby she wrote and wrote again, in various autobiographical reformulations, the trauma narrative evinced by her civilian experiences during the Great War.[5]

Most critics have described Miriam Henderson, the protagonist of Dorothy Richardson's *Pilgrimage,* as an agnostic, a romantic individualist, a committed feminist, and an incipient mystic. Few take note of the central aporia of Richardson's thirteen-volume stream-of-consciousness novel: Miriam's traumatic discovery of the body of her suicided mother. According to Gloria Fromm, the details of maternal madness and self-destruction, laconically reported in *Pilgrimage,* reflect Richardson's personal experience of filial bereavement. Mary Richardson had been clinically depressed and mentally unstable for a long time before her family bundled her off to the seaside resort of Hastings in the company of a reluctant daughter. One Saturday morning, in search of respite from Mary's lunatic ravings, Dorothy took a short excursion into town to cheer her flagging spirits. Returning home, she found the still warm corpse of the mother who had slashed her own throat with a kitchen knife. Like her protagonist Miriam Henderson, Dorothy immediately shut down affective responses and took refuge in post-traumatic anhedonia.

In *Pilgrimage,* Mrs. Henderson's death at the end of "Honeycomb" is veiled in the numbing revery of Miriam's fantasmatic imagination. Pronominal confusion amalgamates the daughter's body with that of her self-murdered parent. Trauma is immediately veiled and repressed in Richardson's story, as the phenomenon of death is filtered through devastating psychological resonances for the survivor. The social isolation, estrangement, malaise, and dysphoria that characterize much of Miriam's stream-of-consciousness narrative in the ensuing volumes of *Pilgrimage* might, indeed, be ascribed to the effects of post-traumatic stress disorder—a syndrome precipitated by an event so shocking that the author cannot directly record it. "The Tunnel" documents symptoms of intrusive flashbacks that break into Miriam's consciousness when she encounters an advertisement for *Teetgen's Teas* in a row of shops that she daily passes, despite the maddening effects of such compulsive repetition. Assaulted by guilt over her mother's death, Miriam later indicts herself as "a murderess. This was the hidden truth of her life" (3:75). In the throes of depression, she wonders: "What was the use of going on?" (3:120).

A myriad of healing experiences—including love relationships with Michael Shatov and Hypo Wilson; a profound (possibly lesbian) intimacy with a female consort, Amabel; and a dawning sense of political awareness through the Lycurgan/Fabian Society—all gradually enable Miriam successfully to reformulate traumatic memories. When she self-consciously refuses the emotional asphyxiation associated with Victorian marriage, the young artist finally feels liberated from relentless flashbacks. Seeing an ad for *Teetgen's Teas,* she recalls the horror once evoked by words that *"forced me to gaze into the darkest moment of my life and to remember that I had forfeited my share in humanity for ever and must go quietly and alone until the end"* (4:155). Exultant, Miriam realizes that *"now their power has gone"* (ibid.). She finally exonerates herself of responsibility for her mother's death by concluding: "If one could fully forgive oneself, the energy it takes to screen off the memory of the past would be set free" (4:607).

When Hypo Wilson, a self-proclaimed freethinker based on H. G. Wells, invites Miriam to become his mistress, he proposes an agenda both constricting and gender-bound: "Try a novel of ideas. . . . *Middles. Criticism,* which you'd do as other women do fancy-work. *Infant.* NOVEL" (4:240). If Miriam should consent to a love affair, he promises, she and their future offspring might flourish in provincial luxury (while he plans to remain safely ensconced in the company of his long-suffering spouse). "You want a *green solitude,"* Hypo counsels. "An infant. Then you'd be able to write a book" (4: 238). He whimsically advises Miriam to enrich her creativity through procreation and become a "feminine George Eliot" (4:240).

Miriam's creator was spared the reproductive consequences of her sexual liaison with H. G. Wells when an unplanned pregnancy ended in spontaneous abortion. Hypersensitive and artistically gifted, Richardson sutured a series of personal traumas by rewriting the story of her life in a massive Kunstlerroman. Heir to Henry James, and inspired by the inner light of Quaker meditation, she successfully reinvented what Virginia Woolf would call the "psychological sentence of the feminine gender" ("Dorothy Richardson" 191). Before James Joyce, she developed radical techniques of narrative focalization independent of the nineteenth-century omniscient authorial voice. Her stylistic innovations were unique when *Pointed Roofs* first appeared in 1915. Although Richardson gave birth to the stream-of-consciousness style in English literature, her germinal texts have too often gone unnoticed on the shelves of library archives. To the bane of modernist studies, her major works are currently out of print.

Notes

1. For a discussion of Woolf's childhood sexual abuse, see de Salvo. Caramagno makes a convincing case for a diagnosis of manic-depressive illness, as does Jamison.

2. For further analysis of this fragmentary text, see Henke, "Virginia Woolf's *Prime Minister.*" On Septimus Smith and post-traumatic stress disorder, see De Meester, Froula, and Henke in Ardis and Scott.

3. For a clear-text transcription of the typescript, see Appendix B in Susan Dick's second edition of *The Complete Shorter Fiction of Virginia Woolf*. I am grateful for the generous assistance of John Daniels, who, at the outset of this project, prepared an original transcription of Woolf's typescript. Erika Bein and Leslie French offered keen sight and insight in helping me decipher Woolf's spidery script. Delinda Buie, curator of the Ekstrom Library Rare Books Collection at the University of Louisville, proved an invaluable resource throughout the project, as did Laura Bartlett, who made judicious suggestions concerning Richardson's *Pilgrimage*.

4. According to Lee, Virginia Woolf, like Freud, "linked her personal history to world history, as she linked Septimus's madness to the 'cataclysms' of war" (459). In delineating Smith's post-traumatic stress disorder, Lee speculates, Woolf amalgamated her own autobiographical trauma with her observations of the postwar malaise suffered by friends like Ralph Partridge and Gerald Brennan. At the 2001 Woolf conference in Wales, Michael Davis reminded me that Woolf had initially assigned her own patronymic "Stephen" to her male-identified alter ego in the *Prime Minister.*

5. In a letter dated May 11, 1933, to her lesbian companion Bryher, H. D. confesses to feeling "worn out" by the "flood of war memoires" that assailed her consciousness when she began reading a volume of D. H. Lawrence's letters, edited by Aldous Huxley (Friedman, *Analyzing Freud* 264). H. D. was particularly disturbed by Lawrence's exchange of letters with Cecil Gray, Perdita's father, and by "insinuating letters" alluding to the Lawrences' visit to Richard Aldington, Brigit Patmore, and Dorothy Yorke on Port-Cros. Freud seems to have advised autobiographical scriptotherapy as a cure for writer's block. See also Friedman, *Penelope's Web,* and Henke, *Shattered Subjects.*

Works Cited

Caramagno, Thomas C. *The Flight of the Mind: Virginia Woolf's Art and Manic-Depressive Illness.* Berkeley: University of California Press, 1992.

DeMeester, Karen. "Trauma and Recovery in Virginia Woolf's *Mrs. Dalloway.*" *Modern Fiction Studies* 44.3 (1998): 649–73.

DeSalvo, Louise. *Virginia Woolf: The Impact of Childhood Sexual Abuse on Her Life and Work.* Boston: Beacon Press, 1989.

Dick, Susan, ed. *The Complete Shorter Fiction of Virginia Woolf.* 1985. Rpt. New York: Harcourt Brace, 1989.

Doolittle, Hilda. *Asphodel*. Ed. Robert Spoo. Durham: Duke University Press, 1992. (Abbreviated *A*).

Friedman, Susan Stanford, ed. *Analyzing Freud: Letters of H. D., Bryher, and Their Circle.* New York: New Directions, 2002.

———. *Penelope's Web.*

———. Psyche Reborn: The Emergence of H. D. Bloomington: Indiana University Press, 1981.

Freud, Sigmund. *The Standard Edition of the Complete Psychological Works of Sigmund Freud.* 24 vols. Ed. and trans. James Strachey. London: Hogarth, 1953–74. (Abbreviated *SE* and volume number).

Fromm, Gloria. *Dorothy Richardson: A Biography.* Urbana: University of Illinois Press, 1977.

Froula, Christine. "*Mrs. Dalloway*'s Postwar Elegy: Women, War, and the Art of Mourning." *Modernism/Modernity* 9.1 (2002): 125–63.

Henke, Suzette A. *Shattered Subjects: Trauma and Testimony in Women's Life-Writing.* New York: Palgrave/St. Martin's, 1998/2000.

———. "Virginia Woolf and Post-Traumatic Subjectivity." In Ardis and Scott, eds, *Virginia Woolf: Turning the Centuries*. 147–52.

———. "Virginia Woolf's *Prime Minister*: A Key to *Mrs. Dalloway*." In *Virginia Woolf: Centennial Essays*. Ed. Elaine Ginsberg and Laura Gottlieb. Troy, N.Y.: Whitston, 1983. 127–41.

Herman, Judith Lewis. *Trauma and Recovery.* New York: Harper Collins, 1992.

Jamison, Kay Redfield. *Touched with Fire: Manic-Depressive Illness and the Artistic Temperament.* New York: Simon & Schuster, 1993.

Lee, Hermione. *Virginia Woolf.* New York: Alfred A. Knopf, 1997.

Woolf, Virginia. "Dorothy Richardson." In *Virginia Woolf: Women and Writing.* Ed. Michele Barrett. London: Women's Press, 1979. 188–92.

———. *Mrs. Dalloway*. 1925; New York: Harcourt, 1981.

———. "A Sketch of the Past." In *Moments of Being.* Ed. Jeanne Schulkind. New York: Harcourt Brace, 1985. 61–159.

H. D. (HILDA DOOLITTLE)

From *Bid Me to Live*, Chapters 1, 2, 3, and 4

Chapter 1

Oh, the times, oh the customs! Oh, indeed, the times! The customs! Their own, specifically, but part and parcel of the cosmic, comic, crucifying times of history. Times liberated, set whirling out-moded romanticism; Punch and Judy danced with Jocasta and Philoctetes, while wrestlers, sprawling in an Uffizi or a Pitti, flung garish horizon-blue across gallant and idiotic Sir Philip Sidney-isms. It was a time of isms. And the Ballet.

They did not march in classic precision, they were a mixed bag. Victims, victimised and victimising. Perhaps the victims came out, by a long shot, ahead of the steady self-determined victimisers. They escaped; the rowdy actual lost generation was not actually their generation. They had roots (being in their mid-twenties and their very early thirties) still with that past. They reacted against a sound-board, their words echoed, were not lost in the drawl of later sirens. If Bella predicted that later film or stage-type, maybe Bella was ahead of them, more fashionable, then, the more determined to self-destruction; it was not because Bella was so actually of the lost, of that lost generation, it was simply that Bella was anyway doomed to self-extinction. In any time, lost, the harlot of the middle-age miracle-play, while Julia was almost ridiculously some nun-figure, gaunt, over-intellectualized, of the same play. But Bella was not a harlot, Julia was not a saint. When Rafe Ashton said to Julia, "I would give her a mind, I would give you a body," he was biting off, extravagantly, much more than even he could chew.

Were they extrovert? Introvert? They had no names for these things. True, the late war-intellectuals gabbled of Oedipus across tea-cups or Soho café tables; it was not Vimy or Loos they talked of. What was left of them was the war-generation, not the lost generation, but lost actually in fact, doomed by the stars in their courses, an actuality, holocaust to Mars, not blighted, not anae-mic, but wounded, but dying, but dead. [. . .]

But she wasn't to be saved that way. She was in the middle of something. Three long French windows, three double sets of curtains that she had hemmed herself, were three symbolical sets of curtains about to part on carnage in Queen's Square. She could not know that she was in the middle of a trilogy, she could not phrase it that way. She was in the middle of something. They all were. That war.

Having stuck it one year, two years, the beginning of a third year, why should she give in now, go, as they urged her, back to America, go, as they suggested, into the country? *J'y suis.* [. . .]

Mrs Rafe Ashton. That is my name. It was a blithe arrangement. [. . .] They made a signal success of it, but in the tradition not so much of Robert Browning and Elizabeth Barrett as of Punch and Judy. [. . .]

She had lost the child only a short time before. But she never thought of that. A door had shuttered it in, shuttering her in, something had died that was going to die. Or because something had died, something would die. But she did not think that. And he lifted the slightly tainted bowl of water and said, "Poor Julia, poor Judy." And everything was where everything was and it doesn't matter that the *Lark* can't pay us for our translations any more and stopped Rafe's French Parnassian series, and the Weekly has been incorporated into something vaguely propagandish, and Rafe said he might as well enlist as give up his time to statistics, all humbug, he said. And she did not shout (how could she?) Oh, God, enlist then, go, go, go, go, go.

It was shut in her as other things were shut in her because "the war will be over." (The war will never be over.) I strove too high physically: "Now Mrs Ashton, you have such a nice body, you will always regret it if you do not have this child." Later, she took a room near Rafe (after he had enlisted) at Corfe Castle [. . .]

The surface was as the surface had been. Only colder. Only—but I waited for you to come back and then you will be careful but what good was that; shivering, she received the dregs of what had been, not openly resentful.

If the wound had been nearer the surface, she could have grappled with it. It was annihilation itself that gaped at her.

"I'm sorry," (as if that could possibly mean anything), "did I hurt you, Judy?"

But such a fear, even with complete detached psychological equipment, is not easily dealt with. Perhaps better no knowledge. This was no occasion for a little knowledge is a dangerous thing. The greater the gap in consciousness, the more black-hole-of-Calcutta the gap; the more unformed the black nebula, by reasoning, the more glorious would be the opening up into clear defined space, or the more brilliant a star-cluster would emerge, if somehow, at some time, the surface could be adequately dealt with. Sufficient unto the day. This was not that day. But the more she feared, repudiated Rafe in her black-Calcutta self, the more she strove to reach him. [. . .]

Chapter 2

He would be going back to France. To-morrow, to-day. They would brew tea (all this had happened before), they would find eggs in the shelf under the book-case where they kept their shoes. They would smoke, and while a winter-dawn stole over a sleeping city he would say those things that might (God knows) have better been left unsaid. [. . .] She had married him when he was another person. That was the catch, really. [. . .]

[. . .] She shook herself erect, sat upright on a bed, that was marriage-bed, that was death-bed, that was resurrection. [. . .]

[. . .] Stepping on the blue square of carpet, before the low double-couch, their bed, she had pulled away from the endangering emotional paralysis. Sheets, a bed, a tomb. But walking for the first time, taking the first steps in her life, upright on her feet for the first time alone, or for the first time standing after death (daughter, I say unto thee), she faced the author of this her momentary psychic being, her lover, her husband. [. . .]

[. . .] She was walking normally, naturally, she was walking out of the mood (paradise) toward the table; she was coming-to from drowning; she was waking out of aether. "Oh, the—time—" she looked at the thing he was looking at; his service wrist-watch was spread flat with its leather strap on the table. Its disc was covered with round woven wire, like a tiny basket, bottom side up, or a fencer's mask. Time in prison, that time. It ticked merrily away, inside its little steel cage.

"I can actually hear it ticking." She had to say something. For she couldn't do this again, she couldn't do this again, she couldn't do this again.

[. . .] "It's time, it's time." The little demon or devil or daemon was alive. She knew of course that it hadn't stopped at tea-time. [. . .]

He called her Anthea. It was Julie, Judy, Judy-bird, or Julie-bird. Anthea. He said it again. His eyes had a vague look, what was he looking at, she wondered. He must not go-off like that, his eyes must stay-put, stay normal, fixed on this room.

He must not look out across a sheet of slate-cold water, to another continent, to France. [. . .]

[. . .] Soon, he would be assembled, off, *bid me to love. Bid me to die. Loved I not honour more.* But that was the catch, that was what was the matter. It would have been reasonably easy, if they had wholly believed in it, to play at seventeenth-century gallantry, or to play Electra and the dead. Death? It was not possible. He was going to say it. He did say it. "Remember if I don't come back or if I do come back and anything happens (if anything gets between us), remember this was this, and this is always." Always? It was a long time.

The ghost, whatever it was, was not dead. Ghosts don't, of course, die. That was it. It had been, even in the beginning, a sort of emanation. Something they had between them. Its moments were prolonged, would last a day, a day and a night. The thing between them, that they conjured up together, would be a flash-light through a wall. [. . .]

[. . .] She had lived with him, absent, so intensely. He would be almost nearer, once he had gone, than he was now. But he hadn't gone yet.

She must hold the thing; like a tight-rope walker, she must move tip-toe across an infinitely narrow thread, a strand, the rope, the umbilical cord, the silver-cord that bound them to that past. The past had been blasted to hell, you might say; already, in 1917, the past was gone. It had been blasted and blighted, the old order was dead, was dying, was being bombed to bits, was no more. But that was not true. Reality lived in the minds of those who had lived before that August. They had lived then. They had had that year in Italy, before the war, almost a year of married life in England after. Two years. One married year in England and the time together, before that, in Paris, in Rome. In Capri, Verona, Venice.

Words that she did not speak held old cities together; on this fine strand, this silver-cord, Venice was a bright glass-bead, certainly a translucent emerald-green, a thing in itself, in itself worth all the misery of the past two years. 1914. Then 1915 and her death, or rather the death of her child. Three weeks in that ghastly nursing-home and then coming back to the same Rafe. Herself different. How could she blithely face what he called love, with that prospect looming ahead and the matron, in her harsh voice, laying a curse on whatever might then have been, "You know you must not have another baby until after the war is over." Meaning in her language, you must keep away from your husband, keep him away from you. When he was all she had, was country, family, friends. Well—that anyway. And roses on her pillow and "Darling, you have come back."

Roses?

There were roses on the table now [. . .]

"What did you say, Julie?"

"I was thinking of Italy—"

"Open my heart and you will see—"

"Yes—"

"—graved inside of it," he chanted in mock unction, "Italy," but he didn't dare think, himself did not dare realize how frail the cord was, how heavy the memories strung along the frail spider-web of a silver-cord that might so soon be broken.

"Or ever the pitcher—"

Oh, God, had she said that? No, just breathed it. He had been so unhappy when she had quoted, *ten thousand shall fall*. "Well," said Rafe Ashton, "over the top."

He had said that before. She knew the answer to that. [. . .]

Half of their things from the last flat in Hampstead were stacked with some of the books and two-thirds of the kitchen things and china, in the packing-cases in the basement. This was their bed. She ran over the furniture, inventory. She looked up. He was strapping on his Sam Browne. He stepped to the knapsack, drew it toward him, then dragged it to the bed. He sat clothed now, a British officer on leave, on the edge of the bed. He tightened the fastenings of the knapsack and then suddenly unfastened them. He was looking for something. Then he strapped on his watch. Then he unstrapped his watch. "Come here." [. . .]

He sat on the edge of the bed and again fumbled in the knapsack, "I want you to keep something for me, something very precious. Promise."

"Yes," she said. "I promise."

He laid a bundle of letters on the top of the coat, pulled over her.

"What's this?"

"It's something very precious, the last batch of letters that you sent me. I almost took them back again."

"I'll send others to you."

"I know—you'll—send—others—to-me—" His head was bent over the knapsack. The back of his head was smooth. His shoulders were British officer, out of a tailor's window. [. . .]

"Your watch," she was holding it out to him, with the leather strap. [. . .]

"Over the top," he said. He had said that before. "Poor stuff, Fritz," he said. Then he took her hand in his hand, he held the strap around it. "It's too big," he said, he pulled the strap to its last leather eyelet, then he got up. He fumbled on the table, he slapped a pocket, he was prodding at the strap with a penknife.

"What's wrong?"

"Your wrist," he said, "I told you it was too thin." He was prodding at the strap.

"You'll spoil it."

"It?" His head was bent, his shoulders were the shoulders of a British officer on leave. He was going away. Don't think about the shoulders. Now he took her hand roughly. "Fingers," he said, "too thin. Good for nothing—good for poetry." Now he kissed her fingers, but what was all this? People don't cry. We don't.

"It's time you went. Oh, I did want to go with you, if you'll only let me get up, it's not too late, I can yet go with you."

But he fastened the leather round her wrist, he tightened with a hard twist, he bent over her hand, secured the strap in the fresh-cut eye-hole. "It fits now," he said.

"Yes," she said, tugging at the strap to pull off the officer's wrist-watch that had been last time in Loos, Lenz? Where was it? Where is this? I can't see anything.

He took both hands in his. Two hands in his.

"I don't want it, damn it," he said. "I'm leaving it with you, to give you some idea—" what was he saying? Now there was nothing but the rough kha-ki under her throat. Her chin brushed buttons, her thin-clad chest felt buttons, he was holding her too tight. She didn't say anything. Then she said,

"Go away, go away, or it will be too late."

"Too late," he said, "it's damn near too late—and if—"

"Don't say it," she said. "Don't say anything."

"Just this," he said, "wear this for me, one out of suits with fortune, who would give more—but that—"

She was crying on the pillow. He didn't see me crying. She heard the front door thud, like the front door thudded when there was a thick fog.

Chapter 3

Why did he give me his watch? The watch went on ticking. He had shut this door so quietly that she did not know he had gone, though she knew he had gone. She knew he had gone when the front door thudded; he has gone. This has happened before. Would it always go on happening? That time in Corfe Castle when she reminded him that love is stronger than death. Was it? Why yes. She had been going on living with death and she was alive. She was stronger. But love? Everything that happened had happened so quickly. But was two years, was three, quick? It was a long time. Time. It went on ticking. [. . .]

Her heart simply wasn't there. It was elevated, lifted; in bed, she felt that light-headedness that meant she was free. Why, of course, she didn't care. Why should she? She would be alone now to recover from this last leave, till the next leave, if there was a next leave. He was dead already, already he had died a half-dozen times, he was always dying. [. . .]

She lifted her wrist under the bed-covers, she let it fall back. She clenched her cold fingers under the bed-covers. The wrist-watch was a stone, scarab weighing her to this bed. [. . .]

Herself, she could stay here but the cold lead of her forehead, the rather heavier lead of the back of her head, were filled with an aura of slight burning. Her mind had been snuffed out, for an hour; they had not really slept last night. This short sleep was one of those asbestos curtains that bangs down; it had not quite done its job. The blaze and flame of chemicals was in the room, in the back of her head, her forehead was cooler. She might manage it somehow that the whole head calmed down and the muddle of poisonous gas and flayed carcasses be dispersed somehow. It was actually a taste in her lungs, though while he was here, she had not recognized it, said it was some sort of vague idea, but she knew it was true. He had breathed a taint of poison-gas in her lungs, the first time he kissed her. He had coughed a little but then she said, "It's the room, we should open the windows, it's stuffy in here." She said, "We're smoking too much." [. . .]

I started a sort of poem. It was the idea of March. Writing letters to you and writing poetry go along in the same sort of groove, I mean when I get into the mood of writing a letter, I feel I can rush headlong down the proverbial cliff. If I glean anything worth typing out, I'll send it and please remember that any scraps on old envelopes must wing back here—doves? Turtle. That verse, the voice of the turtle is heard in the land always worried me, but it was the turtle-dove, why didn't they say so? He feedeth among the lilies. Do you remember those somewhat filthy frogs at Sirmione?

Chapter 4

Everything had to fall to pieces sooner or later; well, why not sooner? Then, at least, you get it over, face the worst, know. She had already faced the worst inwardly; not actually facing the actual facts, but resounding to them, as it were, or refracted back from them, reflected when things became impossible, and anyhow, however, come to grips with him? His "I won't come back next time" destroyed all possibility of contact. [. . .]

Julia Ashton is the last person in the world to minimise the thing he goes through. Back and forth from France—now he is actually enjoying it. Now he likes it. But I can not serve God and Mammon, not serve poet and hearty over-sexed ("we have them on the run") young officer on leave. I love you,

Rafe, but stay away, don't come back; don't, for God's sake, take that book now off the shelf, don't turn now and be Rafe; stay away, don't mangle my emotions any more.

I spared you what I went through, you do not spare me. I did not tell you; my agony in the Garden had no words.

Don't go on, for I can not tell you, what happened two years ago, what happened two and a half years ago; this is late summer, early autumn 1917. [. . .]

This time, you are all but submerged, is there any use any longer sweating agony in a Garden? I had my crucifixion. I can't go back, step over my own corpse and sweat blood, now that you are what you are. [. . .]

It couldn't be a worse muddle. There he stood. She noted the season by the great sheaf of tawny red and coppered chrysanthemums on the table. This was the season—of mellow fruitfulness. A great, over-sexed officer on leave, who had thrown off his tunic, is mellow fruitfulness. His body was harder, he was as they say well set-up, his head was bronze on the less bronze shoulders, he was perfectly proportioned, a little heavy but a late-Roman, rather than Greek image, that walked about a room, himself with no clothes on.

A bronze late-Roman image had got out of the wrong department in the Louvre or the British Museum, something that moved and talked, like the picture of the Roman soldier in the Judgment of Solomon in their child's illustrated Bible spread open on the floor. She did not actually put this two and two together. Though obviously something was being severed, was being cut in half. Already Bella had begun insistence, "He can't have it both ways," and "You tyrannize his spirit." Already the thing was cut in half, not so neatly, Siamese-twin mangled tentacles still bound Rafe-Julia together. His "Bella is a star-performer" was the remark of a stranger, of someone friendly but of another world, another dimension, telling her in a friendly manner that Bella was a star-performer. [. . .]

It is true that Bella Carter was upstairs in Ivan's little bedroom. But Bella was part of a play, she had her entrances, she had her exits. How blame Bella? There was no blame anywhere. Or if there was blame, it was Julia's; she was holding on to something that had been smashed to hell. Why had she not just let it all go? Two years, three years, Paris, the Louvre. All those things were stacked in cellars, the galleries would be empty. Everybody was waiting for everything to be smashed. Why pretend that life could possibly be the same, ever? Why pretend, here in this room, in this house, that this was her room, this is my bed. Nothing belonged to anybody, the room was common-room, birds of passage roosted and rooted and parties certainly had smashed what lines had been left in the air by the casual reading of *Hesperides*—was it? Words had made a pattern, delicate yet firm, clear etched as the little wire cage on the face of the watch he gave her. The watch was the same watch, but time was different. Months, days were smashed. There was no continuity. She had given up pretending.

"What's this?" he said.

"That?" She was waiting for him to say something in keeping with this whole mad show. He should say, "Bella is waiting for me upstairs, Bella is a star-performer, Bella understands these things, I'm going up to Bella."

"Old Rico," he said, "what's dam' old Frederico writing?" [. . .]

Writing for old Rico? "I wasn't exactly writing it for Rico." But she had, she was; it was Rico's pale face and the archaic Greek beard and the fire-blue eyes in the burnt-out face that she had seen, an Orpheus head, severed from its body. Or alive, a live head (fastened onto shoulders) was certainly not a late-Roman head, a Roman soldier out of an illustration or out of a room of late Pompeian bronzes in a cold hall. He was pulling her sketch-book out of her hand, he was scratching a verse on the last page, "Lend me your sketch-book, I want to write something." But this was not certainly that Rafe, that one was buried under ashes, hard lava shut him in, though truly he was there, shut in, covered over, to be dug out, sometime maybe. [. . .]

"What does Frederick want, what does old Frederico want with you?" He spoke as if she were a cast-off old potato-bag or bit of sacking. Did he? No. He spoke as if he cared, as if it mattered that Rico was writing her, that she was writing Rico.

"Well, he writes to everybody, his letters are around somewhere if I kept them, they're there in that stack of papers." Were they? No. They were burning in her head, blue-fire, the things he wrote and the things that he didn't write, the way the blue-flame licked out of the paper, whatever it was he wrote.

"He's cerebral, he has to write to someone." [. . .]

"Listen," he said, "it's perfectly clear; I love you, I desire *l'autre.*"

Yes, that was clear. The room was clear, it was her room, their room, there had never been any parties, the chrysanthemums were tawny suns, were dark-red and frayed yellow with no flower scent, but the leaf-scent of the woods.

They were trees in various gold and red autumn-leaf, not flowers.

There was a shape to their marriage, broken now, shattered actually, yet there was a shape to it. It was Frederick who had taken her away (cerebrally), it was Bella who had broken across (physically), but all the same, there it was the union, the two minds that yet had the urge, or the cheek you might say, to dare to communicate. For her, it was very simple. [. . .]

The grim unlovely spectre vanished. Almost it was, as if they were together for the first time, as if Bella had completed him in some purely physical way, as if Rico with his "We will go away together where the angels come down to earth" had completed her, in her purely emotional-cerebral dimension. [. . .]

[. . .] Rico's flaming letters had been no ordinary love-letters, they were written to her in "pure being," as he said. And Bella had taken away the over-physical sensuality of Rafe so that now, almost for the first time, for the first time anyhow since the ordeal in the nursing-home, she was with him without fear. Almost, Bella Carter had given her back Rafe.

It was not that she thought of Rico; but the fact that Rico wanted her, no matter how idealistically she might translate his letters, meant that there was something there, something that was wanted. Of course Rico did not really want her; he was harassed and distressed and he loved Elsa, his great Prussian wife. He loved Elsa, yes, he said so; no, he did not say so. But it was now as if this cerebral contact had renewed her. She had not actually met Rico (he was in Cornwall) since the writing of the letter, *you are a living spirit in a living spirit city.* Yes, she was that. Rafe Ashton is my husband.

Wife, husband. Elsa and Rico were very near, she and Rico would burn away, cerebralistically, they would burn out together.

Julia existed, parasitically on Rafe, and Rico lived on Elsa.

But once alive, fed as it were from these firm-fleshed bodies, they were both free, equal too, in intensity, matched, mated. She did not think of Rico. But it was reading Rico's letter that had started their talk on poetry and she and Rafe had that together.

Bella had nothing of that; Rafe might write poems to Bella, but he and Bella were different. It was poetry that had brought Rafe to her, in the beginning; it was poetry that gave back Rafe now. [. . .]

1960. Rpt. Redding Ridge, Conn.: Black Swan Books, 1983.

DOROTHY RICHARDSON

From *Pilgrimage*

Volume 1, Honeycomb, *Chapter 11*

[. . .] In the room yellow with daylight a voice was muttering rapidly, rapid words and chuckling laughter and stillness. Miriam grasped the bedclothes and lay rigid. Something in her fled out and away, refusing. But from end to end of the world there was no help against this. It was a truth; triumphing over everything. "*I* know," said a high clear voice. "*I* know . . . I don't deceive myself" . . . rapid low muttering and laughter. . . . It was a conversation. Somewhere within it was the answer. Nowhere else in the world. Forcing herself to be still, she accepted the sounds, pitting herself against the sense of destruction. The sound of violent lurching brought her panic. There was something there that would strike. Hardly knowing what she did, she pretended to wake with a long loud yawn. Her body shivered, bathed in perspiration. "What a lovely morning," she said dreamily, "what a perfect morning." Not daring to sit up, she reached for her watch. Five o'clock. Three more hours before the day began. The other bed was still. "It's going to be a magnificent day," she murmured, pretending to stretch and yawn again. A sigh reached her. The stillness went on and she lay for an hour tense and listening. Something must be done to-day. Someone else must know. . . . At the end of an hour a descending darkness took her suddenly. She woke from it to the sound of violent language, furniture being roughly moved, a swift angry splashing of water . . . something breaking out, breaking through the confinements of this little furniture-filled room . . . the best, gentlest thing she knew in the world, openly despairing at last.

The old homoeopathist at the other end of the town talked quietly on . . . the afternoon light shone on his long white hair . . . the principle of health, God-given health, governing life. To be well one must trust in it absolutely. One must practise trusting in God every day. . . . The patient grew calm, quietly listening and accepting everything he said, agreeing again and again. Miriam sat wondering impatiently why they could not stay. Here in this quiet place with this quiet old man, the only place in the world where any one had seemed partly to understand, mother might get better. He could help. He knew what the world was like and that nobody understood. He must know that he ought to keep her. But he did not seem to want to do anything but advise them and send them away. She hated him, his serene, white-haired, pink-faced old age. He told them he was seventy-nine and had never taken a dose in his life. Leaving his patient to sip a glass of water into which he had measured drops of tincture, he took Miriam to look at the greenhouse behind his consulting-room. As soon as they were alone he told her, speaking quickly and without benevolence, and in the voice of a younger man, that she must summon help, a trained attendant. There ought to be someone for night and day. He seemed to know exactly the way in which she had been taxed and spoke of her youth. It is very wrong for you to be alone with her, he added gravely.

Vaguely, burning with shame at the confession, she explained that it could not be afforded. He listened attentively and repeated that it was absolutely necessary. She felt angrily for words to explain the uselessness of attendants. She was sure he must know this and wanted to demand that he should help, then and there, at once, with his quiet house and his knowledge. Her eye covered him. He was only a pious old man, with artificial teeth making him speak with a sort of sibilant woolliness. Perhaps he too knew that in the end even this would fail. He made her promise to write for help and refused a fee. She hesitated helplessly, feeling the burden settle. He indicated that he had said his say and they went back.

On the way home they talked of the old man. "He is right; but it is too late," said Mrs Henderson, with clear quiet bitterness, "God has deserted me." They walked on, tiny figures in a world of huge grey-stone houses. "He will not let me sleep. He does not want me to sleep. . . . He does not care."

A thought touched Miriam, touched and flashed. She grasped at it to hold and speak it, but it passed off into the world of grey houses. Her cheeks felt hollow, her feet heavy. She summoned her strength, but her body seemed outside her, empty, pacing forward in a world full of perfect unanswering silence.

The bony old woman held Miriam clasped closely in her arms. "You must never, as long as you live, blame yourself, my gurl." She went away. Miriam had not heard her come in. The pressure of her arms and her huge body came from far away. Miriam clasped her hands together. She could not feel them. Perhaps she had dreamed that the old woman had come in and said that. Everything was dream; the world. I shall not have any life. I can never have any life; all my days. There were cold tears running into her mouth. They had no salt. Cold water. They stopped. Moving her body with slow difficulty against the unsupporting air, she looked slowly about. It was so difficult to move. Everything was airy and transparent. Her heavy hot light impalpable body was the only solid thing in the world, weighing tons; and like a lifeless feather. There was a tray of plates of fish and fruit on the table. She looked at it, heaving with sickness and looking at it. I am hungry. Sitting down near it she tried to pull the tray. It would not move. I must eat the food. Go on eating food, till the end of my life. Plates of food like these plates of food. . . . I am in eternity . . . where their worm dieth not and their fire is not quenched.

Volume 2, The Tunnel, *Chapter 7*

WHY must I always think of her in this place? . . . It is always worst just along here. . . . Why do I always forget there's this piece . . . always be hurrying along seeing nothing and then, suddenly, Teetgen's Teas and this row of shops? I can't bear it. I don't know what it is. It's always the same. I always feel the same. It is sending me mad. One day it will be worse. If it gets any worse I shall be mad. Just here. Certainly. Something is wearing out of me. I am meant to go mad. If not, I should not always be coming along this piece without knowing it, whichever street I take. Other people would know the streets apart. I don't know where this bit is or how I get to it. I come every day because I am meant to go mad here. Something that knows brings me here and is making me go mad because I am myself and nothing changes me.

Volume 4, Dawn's Left Hand, *From Chapter 3*

Teetgen's Teas, she noted, in grimed, gilt lettering above a dark and dingy little shop. . . .

Teetgen's Teas. And behind, two turnings back, was a main thoroughfare. And just ahead was another. And the streets of this particular district arranged themselves in her mind, each stating its name, making a neat map.

And *this* street, still foul and dust-filled, but full now also of the light flooding down upon and the air flowing through the larger streets with which in her mind it was clearly linked, was the place where in the early years she would suddenly find herself lost and helplessly aware of what was waiting for her eyes the moment before it appeared: the grimed gilt lettering that *forced me to gaze into the darkest moment of my life and to remember that I had forfeited my share in humanity for ever and must go quietly and alone until the end.*

And now their power has gone They can bring back only the memory of a darkness and horror, to which, then, something has happened, begun to happen?

She glanced back over her shoulder at the letters now away behind her and rejoiced in freedom that allowed her to note their peculiarities of size and shape.

From round the next corner came a distant, high, protesting, nasal yell dropping into a long shuddering gurgle: *Punch.* She turned the corner. There they were at the end of the street.

In front of a greengrocer's a few slum children standing in the muddy street, more numerous elders, amongst them a busy doctor, paused for a moment, a teacher, excusing her delight with a sceptical smile, two rapt hospital nurses.

Munching one of the greengrocer's foreign apples, tasting like pineapple, she held up her face towards the mimic theatre high in air, from which joy flowed down upon this little crowd eagerly and voluntarily gathered together.

Volume 4, Dawn's Left Hand, *From Chapter 9*

There ought to be homage. There was a woman, not this thinking self who talked with men in their own language, but one whose words could be spoken only from the heart's knowledge, waiting to be born in her.

Now here, really, was a point for him: men want recognition of their work, to help them to believe in themselves. They want limelight and approval, even if they are only hanging a picture, crookedly, in order to bring them confirmation of the worth of what they do. Unless in some form they get it, all but the very few—the stoic philosophical ones who are apt to have a crooked smile, and a pipe in one corner of it, and not much of an opinion of humanity, but a sort of blasphemous, unconsciously destructive, blind, kindly tolerance—are miserable. Women, then, want recognition of themselves, of what they are and represent, before they can come fully to birth. Homage for what they are and represent.

He was incapable of homage. Or had given all he had and grown sceptical and dead about it. Left it somewhere. But without a touch of it she could not come fully to birth for him. In that sense all women *are* Undine. Only through a man's recognition can they come to their full stature. But so are men, in their different way. It was his constricted, biological way of seeing sex that kept him blind. Beauty, even, was to him beauty by contrast with Neanderthal man . . .

"The trouble with Miretta is that one can't take liberties with a philosopher."

She smiled from far away, from where if only he knew and could have patience just to look at what she saw and fully submit himself to its truth, see and feel its truth, she could travel towards him. But at least this evening he was serene, not annoyed both with himself and with her as in last week's dimly lit room where yet in memory he seemed so much nearer to her than in this golden light. This evening he knew that the barrier was not of her own deliberate placing.

"Now with others than Miretta"—flattery—"one just takes them in one's arms and immediately there is no barrier."

"Not because I am different. Because there is a psychological barrier. We've not talked enough."

"Talking comes afterwards, believe me."

He dropped a kiss on her shoulder.

"You *are* a pretty creature, Miriam. I wish you could see yourself."

With the eyes of Amabel, and with her own eyes opened by Amabel, she saw the long honey-coloured ropes of hair framing the face that Amabel found beautiful in its "Flemish Madonna" type, falling across her shoulders and along her body where the last foot of their length, red-gold, gleamed marvellously against the rose-tinted velvety gleaming of her flesh. Saw the lines and curves of her limbs, their balance and harmony. Impersonally beautiful and inspiring. To him each detail was "pretty," and the whole an object of desire.

With an impersonal sacredness they appeared before her, less imaginable as objects of desire than when swathed, as in public they had been all her life.

This mutual nakedness was appeasing rather than stimulating. And austere, as if it were a first step in some arduous discipline.

His body was not beautiful. She could find nothing to adore, no ground for response to his lightly spoken tribute. The manly structure, the smooth, satiny sheen in place of her own velvety glow was interesting as partner and foil, but not desirable. It had no power to stir her as often she had been stirred by the sudden sight of him walking down a garden or entering a room. With the familiar clothes, something of his essential self seemed to have departed.

Leaving him pathetic.

The impulse seemed reckless. But when she had leaned forward and clasped him, the warm contact drove away the idea that she might be both humiliating and annoying him and brought a flood of solicitude and suggested a strange action. And as gently she rocked him to and fro the words that came to her lips were so unsuitable that even while she murmured "My little babe, just born," she blushed for them, and steeled herself for his comment.

Letting him go, she found his arms about her in their turn and herself, surprised and not able with sufficient swiftness to contract her expanded being that still seemed to encompass him, rocked unsatisfactorily to and fro while his voice, low and shy and with the inappropriate unwelcome charm in it of the ineffectual gestures of a child learning a game, echoed the unsuitable words.

She leaned back surveying him with downcast eyes, dismayed to feel in him the single, simple, lonely helplessness of the human soul from which his certainties, though they seemed blind, had made her imagine him exempt, and wanting now only to restore him as swiftly as possible to his own world, even at the price of pretending she believed in it. With this determination came a sudden easy certainty of being able to rescue his evening from any sense of failure and disappointment.

Looking up at him with a plan in her mind that in his present state of simplicity did not seem impossible, she met his voice:

"Lost lady. Your reputation's in shreds, Miriam, virginal though you be." [. . .]

"Mere existence isn't life."

"Why *mere?* Most people have too much life and too little realization. Realization takes time and solitude. They have neither."

"You can't go through life feeling your pulse."

"I'm not one of those people who boast that outsiders see most of the game. I hate that. And it isn't true. What is true is that certain outsiders, I don't say I'm one of them, see *all* the game. I believe that. People who have never, in your sense, plunged into life."

"Ee-yes. Books. Almost everything can be got from books. Plus imagination. I believe it's true of lots of women, it may be true of you, that homoeopathic doses of life are enough. But have at least your homoeopathic dose. You've had London. Enormously. But it'll end by wearing you down. [. . .]"

And still the words, put together with his genius for putting the right words together, went on drawing into her mind remembered moments in cool gardens and shadowy woods that were all of one quality, so that many backgrounds were competing to represent it.

". . . flat in town . . . leisure to write . . . country-house visits for holidays . . ." passed unsuccessfully across her preoccupation, each in turn emptied of reality by the overshadowing influence that had driven her from the green solitude.

"Middles. You've masses of material for Middles. Criticism. You could do that on your head. Presently *novel*."

The writing of a novel suggested only a pleasant, exciting, flattering way of filling a period of leisure and thereby creating more leisure. That was what it had seemed to be to all the writers she had met at the Wilsons'; and Michael had cried out against the modern way of regarding letters as a source of wealth.

And Hypo's emphasis suggested that the hideous, irritating, meaningless word *novel* represented the end and aim of a writer's existence. Yet about them all; even those who left her stupefied with admiring joy, was a dreadful enclosure.

She saw Raskolnikov on the stone staircase of the tenement house being more than he knew himself to be and somehow redeemed *before* the awful deed one shared without wanting to prevent, in contrast to all the people in James who knew so much and yet did not know.

"Even as you read about Waymarsh and his 'sombre glow' and his 'attitude of prolonged impermanence' as he sits on the edge of the bed talking to Strether, and revel in all the ways James uses to reveal the process of civilizing Chad, you are distracted from your utter joy by fury over all he is unaware of. And even Conrad. The self-satisfied, complacent, know-all condescendingness of their handling of their material. Wells seems to have more awareness. But all his books are witty exploitations of ideas. The torment of *all* novels is what is left out. The moment you are aware of it, there is torment in them. Bang, bang, bang, on they go, these men's books, like an L.C.C. tram, yet unable to make you forget them, the authors, for a moment. It worries me to think of novels. And yet I'm thrilled to the marrow when I hear of a new novelist. *Clayhanger,* though I've not read it."

"He's a realist. Documenting. You'd like Bennett. Perhaps the novel's not your form. Women ought to be good novelists. But they write best about their own experiences. Love-affairs and so forth. They lack creative imagination."

"Ah, imagination. Lies."

"Try a novel of ideas. Philosophical. There's George Eliot."

"Writes like a man."

"Just so. Lewes. Be a feminine George Eliot. Try your hand."

He was setting out the contents of the cruet as if they were pieces in a game—a lifetime might be well spent in annotating the male novelists, filling out the vast oblivions in them, especially in the painfully comic or the painfully tragic and in the satirists—and now moved them towards her with the air of a demonstrator intent on directing a blank and wavering feminine consciousness:

"*Middles. Criticism,* which you'd do as other women do fancy-work. *Infant.* NOVEL."

His voice was dropped to the very low tone it took when he discussed what he liked to believe were improprieties. [. . .]

London: J. M. Dent and Sons Ltd., 1967. Vol. 1:487–90, Vol. 2:136, Vol. 4:155–56, 230–32, 238–40.

VIRGINIA WOOLF

From "The Prime Minister" Holograph
Ed. Suzette Henke

Key to Textual Annotations

<. . .> Script deleted by Woolf in the holograph
{. . .} Script added by Woolf to holograph from manuscript margins.
[?] Unclear—Words guessed at or supplied
[ ] Holograph page

{Friday, October 6th 1922 Hogarth House}
[133] The violent explosion which made the women who were serving gloves cower behind the counter, and Mrs Dalloway and Miss Anstruther, who were buying gloves, sit very upright, came from a motor car. It stood still in the middle of Bond Street; and passers by, who of course stopped, and stared, had just time to see a face of the very greatest importance against the dove grey <lining of> upholstery before a male hand drew the blind and there was nothing to be seen except a square of dove grey.

Yet rumours were at once in circulation, from the middle of Bond Street, to Oxford Street on the one side, to Atkinson's scent shop on the other, passing invisibly, inaudibly, like a cloud, soft, swift, veil-like upon hills, falling indeed with something of a cloud's sudden sobriety and stillness upon faces which, a second before, had been {utterly} unconcerned, {quite} self-seeking and individualistic. But now mystery <and authority> had brushed them with her wing. They had heard the voice of authority. The spirit of religion was abroad {with her <bandaged> blind eyes and her gaping mouth}. Yet whose face had been seen there upon the cushion, before the blind was drawn by the hand of the Private Secretary—the Prince of Wales', the Prime Minister's, the Queen's? Nobody knew. But that did not prevent them gazing, worshipping, dallying, loitering, conjuring up visions, and dreaming perhaps of romantic contingencies; how the Queen might alight, or the Prince of Wales jump out; or the Prime Minister talking with his cigar [135] between his lips, just as he is in the Daily Mirror, {might} burst the door open, brush his secretaries aside, hail a cab with his own hand, graciously accept the tribute of the crowd, and drive off, democratically beaming, to Downing Street.

"The Prime Minister's car," said Edgar J. Watkiss, an artisan, who, shortly before, had emerged from a deep hole below Oxford Street. And coming in respectful yet humorous accents from a man in a blue overall, this information convinced H. Z. Prentice and at the same moment fired him with bitterness. For if the workers can talk like that about the Prime Minister, what hope is there thought H. Z. Prentice, giving one look at the motor car, and shoving his way through and cutting down a back street <for any of us? the future of the world? for humanity, for society,> for human progress?

And H. Z.—for he was called by his initials. It is the sign of a certain character. The masterful characters are not called by their initials. They must have been at one of the Universities; and coming to London have kept up with college friends. Their friends' wives, who welcome <them,> for there is something homely, and lonely too, about these queer old fellows, who never seem to marry; yet like children; ought to be looked after; catch awful colds; never seem to have anything warm to wear; and sit up to all hours of the night talking politics,—call them H.Z. {Oh dear, how dull they can be!} They are able men <often> too. They take injustice to heart—not so much <private> domestic injustice, for they <are often> a little blind to details—but <the> injustice <upon a large scale> which Turks inflict upon Armenians. Injustice weighs upon them at nights, and the thought of boundaries and tyrannies makes them grey. They write articles. Take the unpopular side, of course; travel to study institutions rather than art; sometimes **[137]** become too extreme even for their own editors, {have lost many friends,} but never compromise; and stand periodically without the least chance of success for Parliament. Bitterness is one of their sins. But that, too, is scarcely at all private; or only for this reason—that they come, as their rare second initial shows—from the higher bourgeoisie {Zacchary being in the family since Cromwell} ; and thus <never get taken quite seriously by the workers themselves. The workers respect them—though and there is always a> gulf between H. Z. Prentice and Edgar Watkiss [. . .]—and H. Z. Prentice walked on towards Leicester Square <thinking of the Prime Minister.>

That (perhaps) makes him bitter. But not sufficiently to distract him from {the nature of his ugliness} the overwhelming <permanent> injustice which, at that very moment, as he walked towards Leicester Square, weighed upon <multitudes of> Russians, Germans, and Austrians. Kept continents cramped in its grip; <forbade the natural flourishing of human life; and turned his hair grey> wrinkled <hollowed> a cheek which, ten years since, had been chubby. He had been young once. <But not now.> His hair, now grey, had been lustrous, thick, reddish, dark, and looked like a young carthorse's winter jacket, thick, and dusky {drooping one long crest at the back} . [. . .] For he argued. He had won prizes for jumping. But nature, who has the body in her keeping, <slowly withdrew their colours and their firmness> most ungraciously withdrew, one by one, every favour; indeed as if nature were in <alliance with the> sun, the carnations <that burnt in June, the waves flinging> [body?] upon the beach, and {were in conspiracy with something} approved of something utterly useless in men and women <loved to see them [lounging?], could not endure abstract ideas, [. . .]> and could not tolerate an eye fixed upon devastated steppes and violated boundaries when her carnations are in flower, <. . .> **[139]** and the hour comes for idling, dreaming. And so, nature withdrawing, the rigour of abstract ideas set in. One saw Prentice coming half a street off <by the swing of his legs & knew him a crank.> He ambled. <He muttered.> {He talked to himself.} And the thought of the crowd in Bond street ogling the Prime Minister's car enraged him. And his temper, worn in the service of mankind, was extremely uncertain. He would strike his hat down upon the hat peg when he took it off; and meeting Mrs Huntley Lewis in the passage of the restaurant in Leicester Square, he made her feel that things were about as bad as they possibly could be.

[143] "I saw the Prime Minister this morning," said H. Z.

Very opportunely, there was a backfire beneath the windows.

"What I can't tolerate is the attitude of the working classes," said H. Z.

And at once something seemed to happen to everyone, **[145]** as if their private concerns had been obliterated, and they were all united; and yet not in any kind of order <but each was irresponsible.> The motor car had exploded inside them some powder within them simultaneously, and the series of explosions that now ran round the table produced a uniformity of sound.

How differently those words were murmured or even sighed in Bond Street as the car, with its blinds drawn and an air of inscrutable reserve <and authority>, slowly proceeded towards Piccadilly, still gazed at, ruffling the faces on both sides of the street with the same dark breath of veneration, whether for the Queen, the Prince, or the Prime Minister. Nobody knew for certain. After all, the face still had only been seen for a few moments. Even the sex was in dispute. But {there could be no doubt that} greatness was seated within; greatness was passing, hidden, down Bond Street; removed only by a hand's breadth from ordinary people, who might now for the first and last time be within speaking distance of the majesty of England, of the enduring symbol of the state which will be known to Hottentots and Hindus and curious antiquaries sifting the ruins of London when Bond Street is a grass grown path, and all of us, hurrying this Wednesday morning to lunch or back from lunch, are dry bones, with a few wedding rings mixed up in our dust and the gold stoppings of decayed teeth. The face in the motor car/name of the Queen of England will then be known.

Mrs Dalloway, who was walking towards Piccadilly holding a parcel containing white gloves in her hand caught the whisper opposite Atkinson's—the Queen's car. She, too, looked, but not quite as the rest did in <that> way. After all, her husband Richard Dalloway, had lunched in the Queen's presence. [. . .]

[151] The car had gone. But it had left behind it a slight ripple which flowed through the tea rooms and luncheon rooms in the immediate neighbourhood. For thirty seconds all heads, whether bare or bonneted, were inclined the same way, and the beef grew cold; and the eggs; and when the knife was <again> resumed, something had happened.—Something so trifling {in single instances} that no mathematical instrument could register the vibration; yet in its fulness, rather formidable, and, in its common appeal, emotional, for in all the tea rooms and the restaurants men and women, who were strangers, looked at each other's faces as though they were not strangers. In the public house in the back street, a Colonial <who had had too much to drink> said something <so insulting> about the Royal family, at that word a table was upset and a glass broken. For the surface agitation as it sunk, grazed something very profound. Loyalty <to the throne, their political beliefs—and politics. [. . .]> Indeed it was quite alarming to hear them talking at luncheon in Leicester Square—about the Prime Minister who had brought this country to depths of degradation—"Unparalleled," said H. Z. Prentice, "in my experience!"

[155] As he spoke, the violence/agitation suddenly died down.

There was nothing more to be said.

An <air of> extraordinary flatness fell upon the company, who were for the most part drinking coffee. There was complete silence. And then Septimus Smith laughed. Nobody had spoken to him, and therefore he must have been laughing at something he thought, or saw. <His eyes, after wandering guiltily from face to face, fixed themselves upon the table cloth>. {He was staring at the table cloth.} H. Z. Prentice, feeling very uncomfortable, said something quite irrelevant. Septimus Smith looked at the table cloth, which seemed to him of astonishing whiteness. The silver vase, with the leopard's head holding a ring in its mouth, had, too, an extreme significance, <for the leopard had opened its mouth, Septimus thought; and winked, and that had made him laugh>. The violence of their talk, which had excited him profoundly, seemed connected with the brilliant cloth and the flashing silver and the sense which possessed him of his own astonishing insight and importance. (He was a man of about twentyseven, <pale and freckled> with eyes rather far apart, a pale face, and very white teeth.) His heart was beating very fast. Everything had momentarily become very splendid and very simple. Yet physically he felt as if, unless something cool and firm restrained his heart it would fly into pieces.

"They are always talking about making the connection, but they never do" said Mrs Lewis.

"They have to get a bill through Parliament," said someone—(and they spoke so loud and so firmly with this very purpose, to help Septimus to control himself) [157] to control his heart; and also, for their own sakes, to <protect themselves from a queer> dam the hole in the wall which Septimus had made by his laugh: for something warm and disquieting had trickled through the hole, and dancing over outlines of things {making them quiver,} like hot air when it quivers over bricks.

Mrs Lewis opened her bag and took out her purse and looked through it; and they all went down stairs and paid their bills and parted on the pavement of Leicester Square; H. Z. taking Ellis Robertson by the arm. Septimus came out by himself and walked towards Charing Cross Road—<for what reason?> because a barrel organ was playing in the little street by the ladies' hat shop.

Playing a divine melody, he thought, which, faint and auroral at first like a shepherd boy's pipe <piping on the mountain top>, broadened as he approached. Now was Europe free! Now Mrs Lewis and Ellis Robertson could tear up their <appalling photographs of frozen bodies [. . .]> corpses and dead children. The bars of the prisons were down. The red and purple hats were given for nothing. <Beauty, winged & plumed, fluttered from the sky & lighted on the common head. [. . .] Hands and arms struck straight out, thought Septimus, liberal; reformer, as he stood by the hat shop> and he saw the sky full of birds, purple and red, descending. They fell through his body giving him actually the sensation of gliding, swooping, alighting, to the admiration of multitudes, who beheld him with terror (but he knew he was safe) and received him, as he bestowed upon them his extraordinary gift, with a rapturous clamour of love. He was some sort of Christ, probably. And the news must [159] be communicated at once—at once!—there was no time to lose—to the Prime Minister. The barrel organ had stopped. The organ grinder and his wife, she in a tight black jacket, he seedy with red-pouched eyes, looked about for pence. Then, without warning, the woman started singing very loudly, the organ playing very slowly. Some terrible warning, Septimus thought, who heard <in its sound> guns firing, the rattling of sabres and bones, [. . .] for Mrs. Lewis had talked of skeletons. And all the dry branches in a forest creaking {and their eyes looking at him}. The fear which had seized him at luncheon was on him again—a doubt as to his own sanity. He was incapable of saying the ordinary things. People were already looking at him. <Death, death, death—in the service of the Nation; that was the only creditable exit for a man with a wife>. It was necessary to kill himself, but so as not to bring discredit on one's wife. One might give one's body to be eaten by the starving, and then, thought Septimus, be a martyr, and then as I am going to die I will kill the Prime Minister and some one who has everything I want, like Ellis Robertson (he had been named for the editorship of the new daily paper). I shall be immortal, he thought, my name will be on all the placards. He walked to Charing Cross Road, and stood on the pavement, where the buses stop, by the Pavilion. <The divine melody had stopped. The barrel organ had gone>.

Though the street was crowded, and it was a hot afternoon, a chill and a greyness seemed to Septimus to wash over them all; and they passed him at a foot's pace, slowly. Clearness and sobriety were his. The procession was unutterably mean. There was no vitality in it. If you take them separately, each one of them is bad, Septimus thought. <They have killed everyone. There is an immense unhappiness at the heart of everything>. They are so unhappy that [161] they are so hideous; <they smell; they are corrupt>. They are now moving about to hunt each other.<The insect crawl continued in front of him>. If you see things as they are, he thought. And the futility of the innumerable books, sold at the corner, struck him. He lit a cigarette. Strange indeed for a man about to die to smoke a cigarette, but such a man sees of course the truth, as sometimes in the middle of a play, the illusion fails, and the actors are seen to be merely acting, seen through to the bone, by me, thought Septimus <with perfect calmness. Lighting, smoking, and> forgetting to smoke. And <somehow remembering> all the enmities and vanities of his life, and not of his life, but understood all that he had read {in a flash}. He had the sensation of turning innumerable {pages and finding innumerable meanings everywhere. [. . .] Shakespeare's sonnets—for example—written of course by a woman}. The meaning had been human beings are bad. Only of course concealed. He now recalled how his stud had been stolen, and the companion[?] of the servant girl; she was in league with thieves. And his wife <too> of course hated him; for she had said that morning that she would be out late. The truth ought to be told to somebody, Septimus thought. In fact, the whole thing ought to be stopped. But nothing can stop this omnibus, he thought. The driver's face was unspeakably wicked, and pockmarked with every sort of disease.

Mrs Huntley Lewis did not like to go up to Septimus and speak to him. Yet he looked so queer, standing on the pavement, with a cigarette held downwards. <He swayed a little.> He might be going to faint. He was an awfully nice young man <she thought>. His pamphlet about Russia <was really quite first rate> for instance . . . Only, sometimes, when she saw a single person, an individual, Mrs. Lewis [. . .] felt abashed. How do **[163]** you approach people, singly? [. . .] She would go up to him and say—But <before she could> he walked away. He walked towards Trafalgar Square. She lost sight of him. And the newsboys were [. . .] shouting out the results of the Bye-Election. The coalition had been hopelessly beaten by Labour. Mrs. Lewis said, Well done! <aloud>. [. . .] It did look as though there were a little sense in human beings. [. . .] The people, she thought, the common people, are sound. [. . .]

The policeman in Downing Street saluted.

[167] Suddenly everything stopped, and there approached a discreet motor car; trim and self possessed, which, as it entered the gates had to slow down so that, craning forward, and peering in, one saw something or other—a face?—The Prime Minister's? All the pigeons rose in a fan shape high over head; and above up in the sky was an aeroplane; the pigeons wheeling cut the sky into a pattern—But the aeroplane was trailing smoke across the sky.

Mrs Dalloway looking from her window at Westminster saw people stopping in the street looking up.

Henry W. and Albert A. Berg Collection, New York Public Library.

16

Modernism and Medicine

INTRODUCED AND SELECTED BY SUSAN SQUIER

FROM THE VANTAGE POINT of the twenty-first century, as the United States congress debates laws to regulate the cloning of human embryos and state legislatures battle over the "right to die," it is tempting to assume that documents relating to early twentieth-century medicine would seem outdated, even quaint. The six excerpts that comprise this section demonstrate just how wrong such a characterization would be, for they reveal that current debates about the biomedical intervention in human life were anticipated—indeed, at times even exceeded—by those occurring in early twentieth-century fiction and nonfiction. While the range of biomedical interventions was vast in the early twentieth century, I have chosen to focus on those addressing the beginning and the end of life, because gender arguably has its most vivid figuration there. These six excerpts comprise two clusters, then: extrapolative essays responding to the notion of extra-uterine gestation or ectogenesis, and novels assessing the social origins and effects of rejuvenation therapies.

Taken together, these excerpts indicate the intense interest in the biomedical intervention in the lifespan in the second and third decades of the twentieth century, in England and the United States. They dramatize the disciplinary consolidation of the new scientific and medical fields of sexology, endocrinology, embryology, and gerontology that emerged in the early years of the twentieth century, and they also attest to the attraction that scientists and writers from the left as well as the right felt for the field of eugenics, which flourished in the United States and the United Kingdom from its founding in

1909 until discredited by the rise of Nazi eugenics in the 1930s. These converging discourses not only shaped the ways that medicine negotiated the beginning and the end of life, but also influenced how modern writers used medicine as a platform for other issues, especially socialist and feminist concerns. While reflecting the force of left and feminist critiques of normative culture, they also attest to the continuing power of heterosexism, racism, and ableism to structure the biomedical imaginary, retaining a normative (white, heterosexual, able-bodied) human being even when normative lifespan patterns were subjected to massive disruption. In the almost uncanny resemblance between the medicine of these novels and pamphlets and the reproductive and gerontological medicine of our day, these excerpts also suggest the power of fiction—both in the form of novels and of extrapolative essays—to shape the agenda of science. Finally these selections raise questions about the different responses of modernism and modernity to scientific practice: what achieves a kind of canonical standing in the nonfiction essay (*Daedalus,* for example, which has been reprinted in a casebook with essay commentary) has failed to achieve canonical standing in literature. Instead, the works of fiction excerpted here are little-known, compared with the familiar texts of the modernist canon.

The Pamphlets

If the manifesto is the "signal genre of modernity's crises," as Janet Lyon observes elsewhere in this volume, the extrapolative pamphlets in the *To-Day and To-morrow* series represent an ingenious variation of the manifesto mode, for they adopt the strategy of declaring the modern crisis over, the future arrived. This forward-looking series paradoxically produced its effects through the "revival of a form of literature, the Pamphlet, which has been in disuse for many years" (Haldane, endpapers). J. D. Bernal, Vera Brittain, and J. B. S. Haldane all contribute pamphlets written retrospectively from an era in which the modern transition has been successfully negotiated, imagining as settled the tumultuous debates that prompted manifestoes. The proleptic rhetorical strategy is a powerful one, enabling the readers of the pamphlets to engage in a thought experiment while simultaneously exposing them to social critique. As T. S. Eliot observed, "We are able to peer into the future by means of that brilliant series [which] will constitute a precious document upon the present time" (Haldane, endpapers, 3). While Haldane, Brittain, and Bernal present wide-ranging images of the future from which they purport to write, common to all of their pamphlets is the biomedical innovation of ectogenesis: a hypothetical method of extra-uterine gestation that separates sexuality from reproduction, removes the direct involvement of woman with gestation and parturition, and may enable various kinds of intervention in the conception and gestation processes.

Haldane's *Daedalus,* originally delivered as a lecture to the New College Essay Society and the Heretics Society at Cambridge University, catalyzed a vigorous debate over the social implications of extra-uterine gestation, of which only a section is included here. In addition to the responses included in the selections here, by pacifist journalist and novelist Vera Brittain and crystallographer J. D. Bernal, the pamphlet also received responses from philosopher Bertrand Russell, sexologist Norman Haire, socialist physician and eugenicist Eden Paul, and poet Robert Graves, as well as fictional treatment in Aldous Huxley's satiric novel, *Antic Hay* (Werskey 86). Comparing Haldane's initial formulation of ectogenesis to the responses of Bernal and Brittain, we find a striking gender divergence in the way that the reproductive technique is imagined, and in its social implications, despite their shared leftist positions. Both Haldane and Bernal were part of the Cambridge radical science community, sexually and politically outside the decorous mode of that university community. Not only were both men committed socialists, but each was involved in the 1920s in notorious sexual scandals, Bernal through his repeated infidelity to his wife Eileen Sprague, and Haldane in 1925 as the co-respondent in a divorce suit filed by journalist and science-fiction novelist Charlotte Burghes (see Werskey). The generally progressive tenor of Haldane's and Bernal's visions of ectogenesis seems at a dramatic remove from the restrictive gender categories still governing their legal and social lives. In contrast, Brittain imagines ectogenesis as a false step in a gradual process of sex- and gender-liberation, focusing less on remaking the beginning of life than on equalizing the biological foundations shaping the later years.

J. B. S. Haldane, ardent Oxford-educated biochemist and physiologist, whose socialist sympathies brought him to eugenics, argues for the preeminent importance of biology (not physics or chemistry) for the twentieth century, and positions ectogenesis as the springboard to a eugenically mediated improvement of human society. Later, Haldane would acquire authority and popular renown for his role as a popularizer of science, and would publish an essay offering instructions to other aspiring popular science writers: "How Should One Write a Popular Science Article?" But as the newly named Dunn Reader in Biochemistry at Cambridge, who had just accomplished some crucial studies of the statistical implications of Darwin's theory of natural selection, it seemed audacious indeed for this young scholar to transgress the taboo against popularizing scientific findings, particularly when linked to the futurological speculations of *Daedalus, or Science and the Future* (Werskey 83).

Haldane wryly assumes a debased genre for his pamphlet, claiming to be excerpting "some extracts from [an] essay on the influence of biology on history during the 20th century which will [. . .] be read by a rather stupid undergraduate [. . .] to his supervisor during his first term 150 years hence" (Haldane 56–57). Surveying the attempts to introduce eugenic improvements to the human race through the "application of biology to politics," Haldane's undergraduate imagines ectogenesis as leading to a world in which sexuality is liberated from the constraints of reproduction, women are relieved of the burden of childbirth, and people craft their political cohort, and their descendants, through a process of conjoined medical and civic negotiation.

A committed socialist and rationalist, J. D. Bernal envisions ectogenesis less as the route to social justice than to accelerated evolution toward a fully efficient, enhanced human being, ruled not by the vagaries of desire but by scientific rationality. Bernal's narrative, also told retrospectively from what we would now term a *posthuman* future, offers not an undergraduate essay, but a fable as his generic frame for this evolutionary narrative. As he tells it, ectogenesis serves as the beginning stage—a kind of *larval state*—for the production of the reconfigured human being. He envisions the three-stage creation of a "perfect man such as the doctors, the eugenists and the public health officers between them hope to make of humanity" (Bernal 42). Once that ectogenetic larval stage is over, the human being enters a chrysalis stage, when freed from the biological constraints of the human body, he has his perception amplified by the attachment of new sensory organs, his motor capacities amplified by machinic prostheses, and his mental capacities amplified by a system of connectionist networks bringing his thoughts instantaneously into communication with a shared, essentially immortal, complex mind. Bernal's vision of the creation of this new human being incorporates a remarkably prescient grasp of the changes in the institution of medicine that would accompany such a turn to prosthetic enhancement. As he tells it, remote and virtual surgery gradually replaces hands-on medical practice:

> The carrying out of these complicated surgical and physiological operations would be in the hands of a medical profession which would be bound to come rapidly under the control of transformed men. The operations themselves would probably be conducted by mechanisms controlled by the transformed heads of the profession, though in the earlier and experimental stages, of course, it would still be done by human surgeons and physiologists. (Bernal 46)

Significantly, the gender of this new human being is unmarked, that is to say: male. The eradication of physical gestation amounts to the eradication of women themselves. Instead of the "new women" of his time, Bernal gives us a "new man [who] must appear to those who have not contemplated him before as a strange, monstrous and inhuman creature, but [. . .] is only the logical outcome of the type of humanity that exists at present" (Bernal 51). Bernal's vision of this new man depends upon two central aspects of modernity: the functional specialization built into modern industry, which treated the modern worker as a machine (Rabinbach), and the process of decontextualization essential to modern laboratory science, through which the experimental subject was removed from its *natural* context and artificially manipulated toward scientifically framed goals. Indeed, Bernal's vision of an artificially accelerated human evolution amounts to precisely such a decontextualization, as the human being is removed first from his social surroundings, then from his physical body with its particular sensory surround, and finally from the notion of an organically based individual consciousness itself: "Finally, consciousness itself may end or vanish in a humanity that has become completely etherialized, losing the close-knit organism, becoming masses of atoms in space communicating by radiation, and ultimately perhaps resolving itself entirely into light" (Bernal 57).

In contrast to Bernal's gradual dissolution of human ties, Vera Brittain stresses emotional and relational connections when she responds to Haldane's vision of a world made rational and subject to human control by the biological innovation of ectogenesis. Adapting the myth of the kingfisher, already given potent circulation in T. S. Eliot's *The Waste Land* and Virginia Woolf's *Orlando,* Brittain uses for her frontispiece the tale of "Alcyone, or Halcyone," a Greek goddess who cast herself into the sea when her husband Ceyx was drowned. As Brittain explains: "The gods pitied the devoted pair, and changed them into birds, the alcyons or halcyons (kingfishers); it was believed that during the breeding-time of these birds, the sea was always calm" (Brittain 4). The distance between Eliot's use of the Fisher King to his articulation of patriarchal anxieties, and Woolf's use of the kingfisher to affirm Orlando's vision of multiple sexual potential, prepares us for Brittain's invocation of the halcyon to summon up an image of breeding between a pair-bond that is devoted but not patriarchal, sexual without being exclusively *hetero*sexual. A committed feminist pacifist, Brittain's stated intention of improving the institution of marriage serves her as an ingenious strategy for advancing such feminist goals as female economic and social independence. She refuses to limit women's capacities to the narrowly reproductive, arguing instead for a view of women's agency that is lifelong and broadly social. Her response to Haldane's notion of ectogenesis stresses the limitations of a scientific attempt to improve human parturition, demonstrating that a stress on biomedical processes alone omits the crucial role played by human relations and nurturance in the production of healthy human beings. In a remarkably direct refutation of Haldane's and Bernal's visions, Brittain describes the development, assessment, and ultimate social repudiation of ectogenetic gestation. Instead, would-be parents, heeding the advice of medical and child specialists, choose another biomedical intervention that didn't abolish childbirth, but rather made pregnancy pleasurable and childbirth nearly painless.

Despite its critique of ectogenesis, Brittain's pamphlet is not wholly adverse to biomedical interventions, but instead exemplifies a flexible feminist techno-scientific practice that will affirm biomedical technology *when it can be seen to improve the lot of women.* Thus, Brittain envisions changes throughout the entire lifespan, rather than focusing on the biomedical reconfiguration of gestation and birth alone. With a nod, perhaps, to the sexual adventures of her fellow pamphleteers, she recalls how: "up to a century ago, a man's period of physical attractiveness was anything from ten to twenty years longer than a woman's— a circumstance which was apt to cause marital chaos whenever the husband was one of those semi-civilized males who set more value upon *naiveté* and freshness than upon the beauty which arises from intelligence and experience" (Brittain 70). Yet in the intervening years, Brittain recounts, we have seen the accomplishment of a lifelong biomedical recalibration of men and women, thanks to the pioneering work of Haldane and Rosenfeldt, who in 1973 synthesized the sex hormone, enabling the creation of "Rosenfeldt's Rejuvenating Serum." Medical interventions are now enabling men and women not only to remain vigorous longer, but to age at the same rate (Brittain 72).

The Fiction

The gendered experience of ageing is central to the three fictional excerpts I have included, all of which explore the notion of rejuvenation therapy. Elizabeth Von Arnim's *Love* (1924) recounts a tale of a woman who undergoes rejuvenation therapy. Von Arnim's widowed Catherine Cumfrit finds herself desperate to sustain the attention of her younger male lover, Christopher Monckton. Though initially unselfconscious about the discrepancy in their ages, she soon discovers that in the eyes of the world she is inappropriately old for him. Taken once too often as his mother rather than his lover, she decides to undertake a painful—and ultimately unsuccessful—course of X-ray treatments from Dr. Sanguesa in the hope of achieving rejuvenation. Only the death in childbirth of her beloved daughter, herself married to a man several decades her elder, moves Catherine to rethink her desperate struggle to hold on to her fading youth. The story ends not with a successful rejuvenation but with a painfully won feminist insight:

the impact of age falls differently on men and women, with the result that society takes very different views of May-December relationships depending on
whether it is the woman or the man who is the elder. This feminist theme is
recontained in a wish-fulfillment plot. Though Catherine disowns her right to
"be married to someone so young," asserting that in the face of Death the
struggle for youth and love is unseemly, her young husband will not accept
her verdict that their relationship must end (Von Arnim 276). Instead, he asserts
that both men and women must come to terms with the threat of death: men
in war, women in childbirth. In the face of both mortal threats, both sexes are
still entitled to continue caring—for themselves and for each other: "*I* didn't
throw away my silk handkerchiefs and leave off shaving because my friends
died—. . . Why should the ones who didn't die behave as though they had?"
(ibid.). The novel ends without a resolution; the lovers pledge to "take care of"
each other, but in the face of their discrepant ages, they are "both afraid"
(278).

The story might well have been drawn directly from Brittain's description
of the marital chaos wrought by man's overvaluation of female *naiveté* and
freshness, except that it predates it by four years. Instead, both Atherton's and
Von Arnim's novels testify to the wide variety of rejuvenation therapies available in the United States, England, and Europe in the 1920s and 1930s. Doctors
Eugen Steinach and Harry Benjamin specialized in rejuvenating women, offering X-ray and electrical treatments to the ovaries at their offices on Park
Avenue and in Geneva, while it was Serge Voronoff who had pioneered rejuvenation therapy, with his experiments in gland transplantation (see Squier).
While canonical modernist literature reveals only a glancing familiarity with
such treatments, most notably in discussions of Yeats's "monkey gland" treatments and their effect on his poetry, these excerpts more marginal to the high
modernist canon are much more directly engaged with the science of rejuvenation. Atherton herself had taken the Steinach treatment in 1922, while Von
Arnim's later years in Switzerland may have enabled not only the cosmetic
surgery that onetime lover Michael Frere remembered, but also possibly the
rejuvenating injections of Swiss endocrinological surgeon Paul Niehans (see
de Vere White).

As Atherton and Von Arnim's excerpts exemplify, the division between
literature and biomedical science customarily allots to fiction the perspective
of the *recipient* of rejuvenation therapies, not that of the *provider.* An exception
is the final excerpt of this section, C. P. Snow's anonymously published *New
Lives for Old.* Snow, a chemist by profession, addresses rejuvenation therapy
from the perspective both of recipient and of provider, asking us to consider
what this new set of biomedical therapies means, both to those who invent

and disseminate them, and to those of us who consume them, for good or for ill. We approach rejuvenation therapy from a very different angle of vision in Snow's novel than we did in the fictions of Atherton and Von Arnim. If we accept, for a moment, Snow's contested formulation that there are "two cultures," the one scientific, the other humanistic, we have certainly made that cultural crossing in this novel, for the novel is situated firmly in the culture of science. As readers, we are *in on* the biomedical formulation of the new rejuvenation treatment.

With King's College Professor of Biophysics Billy Pilgrim and his junior colleague David Callan, we experience the struggle of scientific experimentation and the exhilaration of the successful synthesis of *collophage*. Moreover, Snow (like Brittain before him) anticipates the convergence of biomedicine and politics into a kind of governmentality of biopower, as he traces in the novel the institutional effects of this new therapeutic substance. The trajectory of this new sex hormone, from synthesis to public release, stands as an ironic anticipation of many such contested pharmacological itineraries, not the least of them RU486 and drugs to treat AIDS. Governmental resistance to the technology (because it will not inherently produce profit for the government) is only overcome when nationalist pride takes over. As with contemporary debates over stem-cell research, the threat that another nation's scientists will overtake Britain's provides a potent argument for technological advance. Snow's novel documents the wide-ranging social consequences of what to Von Arnim seems an individual choice—the turn to rejuvenation therapy. Two classes of people are created: those who are able to afford, and avail themselves of, this treatment, and those who are unable to, either for economic or physiological reasons. Employment is disrupted, since the traditional stepladder by which older workers retire, making space for younger workers, is no longer in place. Older workers, rejuvenated, may stay on endlessly, leaving younger workers adrift. The structure of the family is threatened: younger rejuvenated wives may run off from older non-rejuvenated husbands, while daughters may find their rejuvenated mothers competing for the attentions of the same suitor. Finally, as the collophage becomes a scarce commodity, different social groups and ultimately different nations must compete for access to it. Misused, it results in tragic illnesses and deaths, while when it is used properly it functions as both an economic and cultural catalyst, creating markets for new commodities (cosmetics, cosmetic surgery), and audiences for new art forms.

The audiences for new art forms that Snow envisioned may have come into being, only seventy years (one lifetime) after he imagined them. These six excerpts representing the biomedical reconfiguration of the beginning and the end of life arguably began by sharing the strategy of fiction: either the extrapolative fiction foundational to the *To-Day and To-Morrow* series pamphlets, or the fiction of Von Arnim, Atherton, and Snow's realistic novels. But, equally arguably, these six excerpts seem to us today closer to fact. We read them now from the vantage point of a society where *in vitro* fertilization and surrogacy have been accepted as routine, with cloning a debated technique looming on the horizon; a society where face-lifts and hormone replacement therapy have become a routine (if not universal) aspect of ageing in the West, and the poor of the third world represent an increasing source of transplant organs to first-world recipients. If the modernist canon virtually turned its back on these profoundly disruptive biomedical interventions—both as they were imagined, and later as they were gradually given literal form—the marginal genres of science fiction, fable, and extrapolative essay did not. That we are increasingly unable or unwilling to distinguish between these genres, since they are all part of what we now characterize as postmodern literature, suggests their fundamental importance to the gendered genres of modernity.

Works Cited

Bernal, J. D. *The World, The Flesh, and the Devil.* London: Kegan Paul, Trench, Trubner & Co., Ltd, 1929.

Brittain, Vera. *Halcyon, or The Future of Monogamy.* London: Kegan Paul, Trench, Trubner & Co., Ltd., 1929.

de Vere White, Terence. Afterword. Elizabeth Von Arnim, *Love.* 279–84.

Haldane, J. B. S. *To-Day and To-Morrow,* advertisement. In *Daedalus, or Science and the Future* [1923]. London: Kegan Paul, Trench, Trubner & Co., Ltd., 1926. Endpapers.

Rabinbach, Anson. *The Human Motor: Energy, Fatigue, and the Origins of Modernity.* New York: Basic Books, 1990.

Squier, Susan. "Incubabies and Rejuvenates: The Traffic Between Technologies of Reproduction and Age-Extension." In *Figuring Age: Women, Bodies, Generations,* ed. Kathleen Woodward. Bloomington: Indiana University Press, 1999. 88–111.

Von Arnim, Elizabeth. *Love.* 1925. New York: Washington Square Press, 1988.

Werskey, Gary. *The Visible College.* London: Free Association Books, 1988.

VERA BRITTAIN

From *Halcyon, or The Future of Monogamy*

(9)

[. . .] The fact nevertheless remains that, up to a century ago, a man's period of physical attractiveness was anything from ten to twenty years longer than a woman's—a circumstance which was apt to cause marital chaos whenever the husband was one of those semi-civilized males who set more value upon *naïveté* and freshness than upon the beauty which arises from intelligence and experience.

It must be added that biological differences were not solely responsible for this unfortunate contrast between men and women. In the strangely masochistic Victorian era, when an appearance of sober middle-age was regarded as a moral obligation for all mothers, however youthful, and for all spinsters over the age of thirty, the average woman began to look elderly for many years before her sexual activity ended.

One of the first results of the emancipation of women through the feminist movement appeared quite early in the twentieth century in a better adjustment of their appearance and activities to their physical vitality. This adjustment was accelerated by the Great European War, in which the services of women who could not only think but move quickly came to be urgently required by all the combatant nations. The liberation of women's legs and waists was, indeed, one of the very few beneficial changes wrought by this conflict. Ten years after the euphemistically-named Peace of Versailles, the youth of large numbers of women had already been noticeably prolonged by exercise, athletics, occupation, fresh air, hygienic clothing, and the limitation of families, and many of them even achieved the postponement of age more successfully than their husbands.

It was not, however, until later in the century that the possibility of controlling biological changes by science became generally known to the public, although experiments in so-called "rejuvenation" had been familiar to limited groups of scientists for many years.

Professor Eugen Steinach, of Vienna, whose classic work *Verjüngung* was published in 1920, began his investigations into the sexual characteristics of animals as early as 1894, while many experiments in testicle-grafting, ovary-transplantation and the tying of the sperm-duct were successfully carried out upon animals, and even in a few cases upon human beings, by Lichtenstern and Voronoff during the first quarter of the twentieth century. At the same time the eminent biologist, J. B. S. Haldane—whose adventurous youth was so largely dedicated to sensational experiments, particularly upon himself—had foreseen the possibility of isolating and synthesizing the definite chemical substance produced by the ovary upon which he believed a woman's sexual potency to depend.

Rejuvenating operations, though still regarded with fear and suspicion by the unenlightened, had been undergone by intelligent men and women for some years, when in 1973 Felix Rosenfeldt, working in co-operation with his master Haldane, succeeded in isolating the substance which the latter had indicated half a century earlier. This great discovery was fraught with tremendous social consequences, for it rendered immediately possible the composition of Rosenfeldt's Rejuvenating Serum, of which a simple injection at the first sign of the menopause restored the sexual activity of women for a further period of fifteen to twenty years.

In a few cases it was even found possible to revive the capacity for child-bearing in women whose periodic functions had long ceased. One of the most celebrated of these experiments was that performed in 1977 upon the first Queen of the re-established Kingdom of Hungary, who by means of three injections given by Rosenfeldt himself was enabled to produce an heir to the throne three days after her sixty-second birthday.

(10)

These revolutionary biological discoveries ensured for all time the prolongation of the youth of men, and to an even more astonishing degree of the youth of women, and provided for that simultaneous ageing of married partners which has done so much to eliminate the once frequent tragedies due to the premature sexual failure of women.

Needless to say, this happy result was not achieved without strong opposition on the part of English clerics and American Neo-Fundamentalists, the latter of whom suspected some subtle and sinister connection between rejuvenation and the doctrine of evolution

The objections of the clergy, however, were based less on scientific than on moral grounds, for many of them still took for gospel truth the melancholic dictum of their model, Charles Kingsley, that "Men must work and women must weep". The discipline of suffering, they maintained, had always been regarded as especially necessary for the female character, and since a great part of woman's unhappiness had been occasioned by the early cessation of her sexual activities, any attempt to remove this cause of sorrow must be regarded as profane interference with the Deity's determination to afflict females for their own good.

It need hardly be said that the men and women of a society still directly influenced by the veteran feminists who had been familiar in their early youth with remarkably similar arguments, countered these anachronistic doctrines with a healthy determination to sacrifice no available increase of joy to such moral shibboleths as had so often destroyed the potential happiness of past generations.

Closer attention, however, was paid to the more rational opposition of the Talkie Stars' Union, which pointed out that instead of prolonging the biological youth of women it would be better to curtail the physical potency of men, on the ground that few spectacles were more revolting than that of an elderly man suffering from senile sensuality.

It was, indeed, the supporting contention of a group of University Professors that an earlier release from their carnal impulses would render the good life more accessible to many men and women who were hindered from attaining it by the disproportionate part played in the average existence by sexual complications, which was responsible for the establishment at the Beach Head Rejuvenation Clinic of a special department for the treatment by glandular operation of those afflicted with excessive physical desire.

(II)

Though many of the biological inventions and discoveries so characteristic of the later twentieth century have necessarily been omitted from my summary because unrelated to the subject of this section, a concluding word must be said upon the attempts which began about 1950 to separate the sexual love of men and women from their generative processes. Since the preoccupation of the female with her tedious reproductive cycles is known to have accounted for a percentage of matrimonial failures, even the merely partial success of ectogenetic experiments has not been without its influence upon the practice of monogamy.

As long ago as 1923, in the remarkable little volume of predictions called *Daedalus*, which I have so often cited, J. B. S. Haldane prophesied the existence of 60,000 ectogenetic children by 1968, and went on to foretell the ultimate production of a seventy-per-cent laboratory-grown population derived from the reproductive cells of a limited number of highly selected parents.

The older generation may remember having heard from their grandparents of the tremendous sensation which occurred in 1971, when, only twenty years later than the date predicted for this event by Haldane, an ectogenetic girl was successfully reared through the embryonic stages and brought to "birth" in Monet's laboratory. Heedless of the world-wide ecclesiastical *furore* let loose by this triumph, the leading ectogeneticians of England, France, Germany, Russia, and the United States at once went rapidly ahead with the rearing of the embryonic children supplied by a small but slowly increasing number of co-operative parents.

Although, however, their experiments showed the universal production of ectogenetic children to be quite feasible, the complete divorce of sexual relationships from their consequences was never found desirable, owing to a risk that it might in time lead to the demolition of the human race.

Students of the pioneer movement in Infant Welfare may remember that some of the first child-specialists were accustomed to point out in their lectures and writings that the intelligent "mothering" of small children by their own parents had a definite scientific value. The truth of this view, believed in 1970 to be an out-of-date relic of sentimental Georgianism, was demonstrated very clearly by the first laboratory-grown children, who suffered as much psychologically from lack of individual parental affection as they gained physiologically through being selected from the best stock. The majority of them, indeed, though most carefully exercised, dieted and exposed to sunlight, dwindled away and died about the fifth year.

These unsatisfactory consequences of ectogenesis, combined with the fact that the early adoption by women of Kettmann's system of muscular and digestive control rendered childbirth painless and pregnancy definitely pleasurable, led nearly all twenty-first century parents to return to natural methods of reproduction. In the case, however, of the few marriages where normal pregnancy was exceptionally inconvenient to the wife, or would involve a long separation from her husband, recourse was had to the expedient, subsequently familiar under the name of Dickensian Pre-Birth, which Sir Frederick Benedickens invented in 1984.

By this operation, now comparatively common, the fertilized embryo is removed from the mother a few weeks after conception, without damage to itself or deterrent effect upon her ability to conceive afresh, and is grown for eight months in Kolinovski's Gestative Solution. The majority of such children, however, are returned to the mother immediately after their first complete exposure to the air for the purpose of artificially induced lactation, and in no case are they allowed to remain in the laboratory for more than a year after "birth".

I must now conclude my survey of mankind's moral and physical liberation with a brief description of the type of marriage produced by these changes.

Halcyon, or The Future of Monogamy. London: Kegan Paul, Trench, Trubner and Co., Ltd., 1929. 70–78.

J. D. BERNAL

From *The World, the Flesh, and the Devil*

Starting, as Mr. J. B. S. Haldane so convincingly predicts, in an ectogenetic factory, man will have anything from sixty to a hundred and twenty years of larval, unspecialized existence—surely enough to satisfy the advocates of the natural life. In this stage he need not be cursed by the age of science and mechanism, but can occupy his time (without the conscience of wasting it) in dancing, poetry and love-making, and perhaps incidentally take part in the reproductive activity. Then he will leave the body whose potentialities he should have sufficiently explored.

The next stage might be compared to that of a chrysalis, a complicated and rather unpleasant process of transforming the already existing organs and grafting on all the new sensory and motor mechanisms. There would follow a period of re-education in which he would grow to understand the functioning of his new sensory organs and practise the manipulation of his new motor mechanism. Finally, he would emerge as a completely effective, mentally-directed mechanism, and set about the tasks appropriate to his new capacities. But this is by no means the end of his development, although it marks his last great metamorphosis. Apart from such mental development as his increased faculties will demand from him, he will be physically plastic in a way quite transcending the capacities of untransformed humanity. Should he need a new sense organ or have a new mechanism to operate, he will have undifferentiated nerve connections to attach to them, and will be able to extend indefinitely his possible sensations and actions by using successively different end-organs.

The carrying out of these complicated surgical and physiological operations would be in the hands of a medical profession which would be bound to come rapidly under the control of transformed men. The operations themselves would probably be conducted by mechanisms controlled by the transformed heads of the profession, though in the earlier and experimental stages, of course, it would still be done by human surgeons and physiologists.

It is much more difficult to form a picture of the final state, partly because this final state would be so fluid and so liable to improve, and partly because there would be no reason whatever why all people should transform in the same way. Probably a great number of typical forms would be developed, each specialized in certain directions. If we confine ourselves to what might be called the first stage of mechanized humanity and to a person mechanized for scientific rather than aesthetic purposes—for to predict even the shapes that men would adopt if they would make of *themselves* a harmony of form and sensation must be beyond imagination—then the description might run roughly as follows.

Instead of the present body structure we should have the whole framework of some very rigid material, probably not metal but one of the new fibrous substances. In shape it might well be rather a short cylinder. Inside the cylinder, and supported very carefully to prevent shock, is the brain with its nerve connections, immersed in a liquid of the nature of cerebro-spinal fluid, kept circulating over it at a uniform temperature. The brain and nerve cells are kept supplied with fresh oxygenated blood and drained of de-oxygenated blood through their arteries and veins which connect outside the cylinder to the artificial heart-lung digestive system—an elaborate, automatic contrivance. This might in large part be made from living organs, although these would have to be carefully arranged so that no failure on their part would endanger the blood supply to the brain (only a fraction of the body's present requirements) and so that they could be inter-changed and repaired without disturbing its functions. The brain thus guaranteed continuous awareness, is connected in the anterior of the case with its immediate sense organs, the eye and the ear—which will probably retain this connection for a long time. The eyes will look into a kind of optical box which will enable them alternatively to look into periscopes projecting from the case, telescopes, microscopes and a whole range of televisual apparatus. The ear would have the corresponding microphone attachments and would still be the chief organ for wireless reception. Smell and taste organs, on the other hand, would be prolonged into connections outside the case and would be changed into chemical testing organs, achieving a more conscious and less primitively emotional role than they have at present. It may perhaps be impossible to do this owing to the peculiarly close relation between the brain and olfactory organs, in whim case the chemical sense would have to be indirect. The remaining sensory nerves, those of touch, temperature, muscular position and visceral functioning, would go to the corresponding part of the exterior machinery or to the blood supplying organs. Attached to the brain cylinder would be its immediate motor organs, corresponding to but much more complex than, our mouth, tongue and hands. This appendage system would probably be built up like that of a crustacean which uses the same general type of arm for antenna, jaw and limb; and they would range from delicate micro-manipulators to levers capable of exerting considerable forces, all controlled by the appropriate motor nerves. Closely associated with the brain-case would also be sound, colour and wireless producing organs. In addition to these there would be certain organs of a type we do not possess at present—the self-repairing organs—which under the control of the brain would be able to manipulate the other organs, particularly the visceral blood supply organs, and to keep them in effective working order. Serious derangements, such as those involving loss of consciousness, would still, of course, call for outside assistance, but with proper care these would be in the nature of rare accidents.

The remaining organs would have a more temporary connection with the brain-case. There would be locomotor apparatus of different kinds, which could be used alternatively for slow movement, equivalent to walking, for rapid transit and for flight. On the whole, however, the locomotor organs would not be much used because the extension of the sense organs would tend to take their place. Most of these would be mere mechanisms quite apart from the body; there would be the sending parts of the television apparatus, tele-acoustic and tele-chemical organs, and tele-sensory organs of the nature of touch for determining all forms of texture. Besides these there would be various tele-motor organs for manipulating materials at great distances from the controlling mind. These extended organs would only belong in a loose sense to any particular person, or rather, they would belong only temporarily to the person who was using them and could equivalently be operated by other people. This capacity for indefinite extension might in the end lead to the relative fixity of the different brains; and this would, in itself, be an advantage from the point of view of security and uniformity of conditions, only some of the more active considering it necessary to be on the spot to observe and do things.

The new man must appear to those who have not contemplated him before as a strange, monstrous and inhuman creature, but he is only the logical outcome of the type of humanity that exists at present. It may be argued that this tampering with bodily mechanism is as unnecessary as it is difficult, that all the increase of control needed may be obtained by extremely responsive mechanisms outside the unaltered human body. But though it is possible that in the early stages a surgically transformed man would actually be at a disadvantage in capacity of performance to a normal, healthy man, he would still be better off than a dead man. Although it is possible that man has far to go before his inherent physiological and psychological make-up becomes the limiting factor to his development, this must happen sooner or later, and it is then that the mechanized man will begin to show a definite advantage. Normal man is an evolutionary dead end; mechanical man, apparently a break in organic evolution, is actually more in the true tradition of a further evolution.

A much more fundamental break is implicit in the means of his development. If a method has been found of connecting a nerve ending in a brain directly with an electrical reactor, then the way is open for connecting it with a brain-cell of another person. Such a connection being, of course, essentially electrical, could be effected just as well through the ether as along wires. At first this would limit itself to the more perfect and economic transference of thought which would be necessary in the co-operative thinking of the future. But it cannot stop there. Connections between two or more minds would tend to become a more and more permanent condition until they functioned as dual or multiple organisms. The minds would always preserve a certain individuality, the network of cells inside a single brain being more dense than that existing between brains, each brain being chiefly occupied with its individual mental development and only communicating with the others for some common purpose. Once the more or less permanent compound brain came into existence two of the ineluctable limitations of present existence would be surmounted. In the first place death would take on a different and far less terrible aspect. Death would still exist for the mentally-directed mechanism we have just described; it would merely be postponed for three hundred or perhaps a thousand years, as long as the brain cells could be persuaded to live in the most favourable environment, but not for ever. But the multiple individual would be, barring cataclysmic accidents, immortal, the older components as they died being replaced by newer ones without losing the continuity of the self, the memories and feelings of the older member transferring themselves almost completely to the common stock before its death. And if this seems only a way of cheating death, we must realize that the individual brain will feel itself part of the whole in a way that completely transcends the devotion of the most fanatical adherent of a religious sect. It is admittedly difficult to imagine this state of affairs effectively. It would be a state of ecstasy in the literal sense, and this is the second great alteration that the compound mind makes possible. Whatever the intensity of our feeling, however much we may strive to reach beyond ourselves or into another's mind, we are always barred by the limitations of our individuality. Here at least those barriers would be down: feeling would truly communicate itself, memories would be held in common, and yet in all this, identity and continuity of individual development would not be lost. It is possible, even probable, that the different individuals of a compound mind would not all have similar functions or even be of the same rank of importance. Division of labour would soon set in: to some minds might be delegated the task of ensuring the proper functioning of the others, some might specialize in sense reception and so on. Thus would grow up a hierarchy of minds that would be more truly a complex than a compound mind.

The complex minds could, with their lease of life, extend their perceptions and understandings and their actions far beyond those of the individual. Time senses could be altered: the events that moved with the slowness of geological ages would be apprehended as movement, and at the same time the most rapid vibrations of the physical world could be separated. As we have seen, sense organs would tend to be less and less attached to bodies, and the host of subsidiary, purely mechanical agents and perceptors would be capable of penetrating those regions where organic bodies cannot enter or hope to survive. The interior of the earth and the stars, the inmost cells of living things themselves, would be open to consciousness through these angels, and through these angels also the motions of stars and living things could be directed.

This is perhaps far enough; beyond that the future must direct itself. Yet why should we stop until our imaginations are exhausted? Even beyond this there are foreseeable possibilities. Undoubtedly the nature of life processes themselves will be far more intensively studied. To make life itself will be only a preliminary stage, because in its simplest phases life can differ very little from the inorganic world. But the mere making of life would only be important if we intended to allow it to evolve of itself anew. This, as Mr. Whyte suggests in *Archimedes,* is necessarily a lengthy process, but there is no need to wait for it. Instead, artificial life would undoubtedly be used as ancillary to human activity and not allowed to evolve freely except for experimental purposes. Men will not be content to manufacture life: they will want to improve on it. For one material out of which nature has been forced to make life, man will have a thousand; living and organized material will be as much at the call of the mechanized or compound man as metals are to-day, and gradually this living material will come to substitute more and more for such inferior functions of the brain as memory, reflex actions, etc., in the compound man himself; for bodies at this time would be left far behind. The brain itself would become more and more separated into different groups of cells or individual cells with complicated connections, and probably occupying considerable space. This would mean loss of motility which would not be a disadvantage owing to the extension of the sense faculties. Every part would now be accessible for replacing or repairing and this would in itself ensure a practical eternity of existence, for even the replacement of a previously organic brain-cell by a synthetic apparatus would not destroy the continuity of consciousness.

The new life would be more plastic, more directly controllable and at the same time more variable and more permanent than that produced by the triumphant opportunism of nature. Bit by bit the heritage in the direct line of mankind—the heritage of the original life emerging on the face of the world—would dwindle, and in the end disappear effectively, being preserved perhaps as some curious relic, while the new life which conserves none of the substance and all the spirit of the old would take its place and continue its development. Such a change would be as important as that in which life first appeared on the earth's surface and might be as gradual and imperceptible. Finally, consciousness itself may end or vanish in a humanity that has become completely etherialized, losing the close-knit organism, becoming masses of atoms in space communicating by radiation, and ultimately perhaps resolving itself entirely into light. That may be an end or a beginning, but from here it is out of sight.

The World, the Flesh, and the Devil. London: Kegan Paul, Trench, Trubner & Co., Ltd. 1929. 45–57.

J. B. S. HALDANE

From *Daedalus, or Science and the Future*

"It was in 1951 that Dupont and Schwarz produced the first ectogenetic child. As early as 1901 Heape had transferred embryo rabbits from one female to another, in 1925 Haldane had grown embryonic rats in serum for ten days, but had failed to carry the process to its conclusion, and it was not till 1940 that Clark succeeded with the pig, using Kehlmann's solution as medium. Dupont and Schwarz obtained a fresh ovary from a woman who was the victim of an aeroplane accident, and kept it living in their medium for five years. They obtained several eggs from it and fertilized them successfully, but the problem of the nutrition and support of the embryo was more difficult, and was only solved in the fourth year. Now that the technique is fully developed, we can take an ovary from a woman, and keep it growing in a suitable fluid for as long as twenty years, producing a fresh ovum each month, of which 90 per cent can be fertilized, and the embryos grown successfully for nine months, and then brought out into the air. Schwarz never got such good results, but the news of his first success caused an unprecedented sensation throughout the entire world, for the birthrate was already less than the deathrate in most civilized countries. France was the first country to adopt ectogenesis officially, and by 1968 was producing 60,000 children annually by this method. In most countries the opposition was far stronger, and was intensified by the Papal Bull "Nunquam prius audito", and the similar fetwa of the Khalif, both of which appeared in 1960.

As we know, ectogenesis is now universal, and in this country less than 30 per cent of children are now born of woman. The effect on human psychology and social life of the separation of sexual love and reproduction which was begun in the 19th century and completed in the 20th is by no means wholly satisfactory. The old family life had certainly a good deal to commend it, and, although nowadays we bring on lactation in women by injection of placentin as a routine, and thus conserve much of what was best in the former instinctive cycle, we must admit that in certain respects our great grandparents had the advantage of us. On the other hand, it is generally admitted that the effects of selection have more than counterbalanced these evils. The small proportion of men and women who are selected as ancestors for the next generation are so undoubtedly superior to the average that the advance in each generation in any single respect, from the increased output of first-class music to the decreased convictions for theft, is very startling. Had it not been for ectogenesis there can be little doubt that civilization would have collapsed within a measurable time owing to the greater fertility of the less desirable members of the population in almost all countries.

It is perhaps fortunate that the process of becoming an ectogenetic mother of the next generation involves an operation which is somewhat unpleasant, though now no longer disfiguring or dangerous, and never physiologically injurious, and is therefore an honor but by no means a pleasure. Had this not been the case, it is perfectly possible that popular opposition would have proved too strong for the selectionist movement. As it was, the opposition was very fierce, and characteristically enough this country only adopted its present rather stringent standard of selection a generation later than Germany, though it is now perhaps more advanced than any other country in this respect. The advantages of thorough-going selection, have, however, proved to be enormous. The question of the ideal sex-ratio is still a matter of violent discussion, but the modern reaction towards equality is certainly strong."

Our essayist would then perhaps go on to discuss some far more radical advances made about 1990, but I have quoted only his account of the earlier applications of biology. The second appears to me to be neither impossible nor improbable, but it has those features which we saw above to be characteristic of biological inventions. If reproduction is once completely separated from sexual love, mankind will be free in an altogether new sense. At present the national character is changing slowly according to quite unknown laws. The problem of politics is to find institutions suitable to it. In the future perhaps it may be possible by selective breeding to change character as quickly as institutions. I can foresee the election placards of 300 years hence, if such quaint political methods survive, which is perhaps improbable, "Vote for Smith and more musicians", "Vote for O'Leary and more girls", or perhaps finally "Vote for Macpherson and a prehensile tail for your great-grandchildren". We can already alter animal species to an enormous extent, and it seems only a question of time before we shall be able to apply the same principles to our own.

I suggest then that biology will probably be applied on lines roughly resembling the above. There are perhaps equally great possibilities in the way of the direct improvement of the individual, as we come to know more of the physiological obstacles to the development of different faculties. But at present we can only guess at the nature of these obstacles, and the line of attack suggested in the myth is the one which seems most obvious to a Darwinian. We already know, however, that many of our spiritual faculties can be manifested only if certain glands, notably the thyroid and sex-glands, are functioning properly, and that very minute changes in such glands affect the character greatly. As our knowledge of this subject increases we may be able, for example, to control our passions by some more direct method than fasting and flagellation, to stimulate our imagination by some reagent with less after-effects than alcohol, to deal with perverted instincts by physiology rather than prison. Conversely, there will inevitably arise possibilities of new vices similar to but even more profound than those opened up by the pharmacological discoveries of the 19th century.

The recent history of medicine is as follows. Until about 1870 medicine was largely founded on physiology, or, as the Scotch called it, "Institutes of medicine". Disease was looked at from the point of view of the patient, as injuries still are. Pasteur's discovery of the nature of infectious disease transformed the whole outlook, and made it possible to abolish one group of diseases. But it also diverted scientific medicine from its former path, and it is probable that, were bacteria unknown, though many more people would die of sepsis and typhoid, we should be better able to cope with kidney disease and cancer. Certain diseases such as cancer are probably not due to specific organisms, whilst others such as phthisis are due to forms which are fairly harmless to the average person, but attack others for unknown reasons. We are not likely to deal with them effectually on Pasteur's lines: we must divert our view from the micro-organism to the patient. Where the doctor cannot deal with the former, he can often keep the patient alive long enough to be able to do so himself. And here he has to rely largely on a knowledge of physiology. I do not say that a physiologist will discover how to prevent cancer. Pasteur started life as a crystallographer. But whoever does so is likely at least to make use of physiological data on a large scale.

The abolition of disease will make death a physiological event like sleep. A generation that has lived together will die together. I suspect that man's desire for a future life is largely due to two causes, a feeling that most lives are incomplete, and a desire to meet friends from whom we have parted prematurely. A gentle decline into the grave at the end of a completed life's work will largely do away with the first, and our contemporaries will rarely leave us sorrowing for long.

Old age is perhaps harder on women than on men. They live longer, but their life is too often marred by the sudden change which generally overtakes them between forty and fifty, and sometimes leaves them a prey to disease, though it may improve their health. This change seems to be due to a sudden failure of a definite chemical substance produced by the ovary. When we can isolate and synthesize this body we shall be able to prolong a woman's youth, and allow her to age as gradually as the average man.

Daedalus, or Science and the Future. London: Kegan Paul, Trench, Trubner and Co., Ltd., 1923. 63–76. A paper read to the Heretics, Cambridge, February 4, 1923.

ELIZABETH VON ARNIM

Chapter 14, Part II, from *Love*

She never did. And it was just as well, thought Christopher, for Catherine had, most astoundingly, taken it into her head to be jealous of her. She wouldn't admit she was, and professed immense admiration for Miss Wickford's beauty, but if the emotion she showed after that dinner wasn't jealousy he was blest if he knew what jealousy was.

It amazed him. She might have heard every word he said. Miss Wickford was extremely pretty and quite clever, and why shouldn't he like talking to her? But he was very sorry to have made Catherine unhappy, and did all he knew to make her forget it; only it was suffocating sort of work in hot weather, and he felt as if he were tied up in something very sweet and sticky, with no end to it. Rather like treacle. It was rather like being swathed round with bands of treacle.

He came to the conclusion Catherine loved him too much. Yes, she did. If she loved him more reasonably she would be much happier, and so would he.

It was bad for them both. The flat seemed thick with love. One waded. He caught himself putting up his hand to unbutton his collar. Perhaps the stuffy weather had something to do with it. July was getting near its end, and there was no air at all in Hertford Street. London was a rotten place in July. He always walked to his office and back so as to get what exercise he could, and every Saturday they went down to his uncle for golf; but what was that? He ached to be properly stretched, to stride about, to hit things for days on end, and his talk became almost exclusively of holidays, and where they should go in August when his were due.

Lewes was going to Scotland to play golf. He had gone with Lewes last year, and had had a glorious time. What exercise! What talk! What freedom! He longed to go again, and asked Catherine whether she wouldn't like to; and she said, with that hiding look of hers—there was a certain look, very frequent on her face, he called to himself her *hiding* look—that it was too far from Virginia.

Virginia? Christopher was much surprised. What did she want with Virginia? Short of actually being at Chickover, she wouldn't see Virginia anyhow, he said; and she, with her arms round his neck, said that was true, but she didn't want to be out of reach of her.

This unexpected reappearance of Virginia on the scene, this sudden cropping up of her after a long spell of no mention of the girl, puzzled and irritated him. They would, apparently, have gone to Scotland if it hadn't been for Virginia. Must he then too—of course he must, seeing that he couldn't and wouldn't go away without Catherine—be kept hanging round within reach of Virginia? She was the last object he wished to be within reach of.

He was annoyed, and showed it. "Why this recrudescence," he asked, "of maternal love?"

"It isn't a recrudescence—it's always, Chris darling," she said, looking rather shamefacedly at him, he thought—anyhow queerly. "You don't suppose one ever leaves off loving somebody one really loves?"

No, he didn't suppose it. He was sure she wouldn't. But he wasn't going into that now; he wasn't going, at ten in the morning, to begin talking about love.

"It's time I was off," he said, bending down and kissing her quickly. "I'm late as it is."

He hurried out, though he wasn't late. He knew he wasn't late, only he did want to get into what air there was—into, anyhow, sunlight, out of that darkened bedroom.

She too knew he wasn't late, but she too wanted him for once to go, because she had a secret appointment for half-past ten, and it was ten already; a most important, a vital appointment, the bare thought of which thrilled her with both fear and hope.

She didn't know if anything would come of it, but she was going to try. She had written to the great man and told him her age and asked if he thought he could do anything for her, and he had sent a card back briefly indicating 10:30 on this day. Nothing more, just 10:30. How discreet. How exciting.

She had read about him in the papers. He was a Spanish doctor, come over to London for a few weeks, and he undertook to restore youth. Marvelous, blissful if he really could! A slight operation, said the papers, and there you were. The results were most satisfactory, they affirmed, and in some cases miraculous. Suppose her case were to be one of the miraculous ones? She hadn't the least idea how she would be able to have an operation without Christopher knowing, but all that could be thought out afterwards. The first thing to do was to see the doctor and hear what he had to say. Who wouldn't do anything, take any pains, have any operation, to be helped back to youth? She, certainly, would shrink from nothing. And it sounded so genuine, so scientific, what the doctor according to the papers, did.

The minute Christopher had gone she hurried into her clothes, refused breakfast, hadn't time to do her face—better she shouldn't that day, better she should be seen exactly as she really was—and twenty minutes after he left she was in a taxi on the way to the great man's temporary consulting rooms in Portland Place.

With what a beating heart she rang the bell. Such hopes, such fears, such determination, such shrinking, all mixed up together, as well as being ashamed, made her hardly able to speak when the nurse—she looked like a nurse—opened the door. And suppose somebody should hear her when she said who she was? And suppose somebody she knew should see her going in? If ever there was a discreet and private occasion it was this one; so that the moment the door was opened she was in such a hurry to get in out of sight of the street that she almost tumbled into the arms of the nurse.

It gave her an unpleasant shock to find herself put into a room with several other people. She hadn't thought she would have to face other seekers after youth. There ought to have been cubicles—places with screens. It didn't seem decent to expose the seekers to one another like that; and she shrank down into a chair with her back to the light, and buried her head in a newspaper.

The others were all burying their heads too in newspapers, but they saw each other nevertheless. All men, she noticed, and all so old that surely they must be past any hopes and wishes? What could they want with youth? It was a sad sight, thought Catherine, peeping round her newspaper, and she felt shocked. When presently two women came in, and after a furtive glance round dropped as she had done into chairs with their backs to the light, she considered them sad sights too and felt shocked; while for their part they were thinking just the same of her, and all the men behind their newspapers were saying to themselves, "What fools women are."

The nurse—she looked exactly like a nurse—came in after a long while and beckoned to her, not calling out her name, for which she was thankful, and she was shown into the consulting room, and found herself confronted by two men instead of one, because Dr. Sanguesa, the specialist, could only say three words in English—"We will see" were his words—so that there was another man there, dark and foreign-looking too, but voluble in English, to interpret.

He did the business part as well. "It will cost fifty pounds," he said almost immediately.

In a whole year Catherine had only ten of these for everything, but if the treatment had been going to cost all ten she would have agreed, and lived somehow in an attic, on a crust—with Christopher and youth. Indeed, she thought it very cheap. Surely fifty pounds was cheap for youth?

Twenty-five pounds down," said the partner—she decided he was more a partner than an interpreter—"and twenty-five pounds in the middle of the treatment."

"Certainly," she murmured.

Dr. Sanguesa was observing her while the partner talked. Every now and then he said something in Spanish, and the other asked her a question. The questions were intimate and embarrassing—the kind it is more comfortable to reply to to one person rather than two. However, she was in for it; she mustn't mind; she was determined not to mind anything.

In her turn she asked some questions, forcing herself to be courageous, for she was frightened in spite of her determination and hopes. Would it hurt, she asked timidly; would it take long; when would the results begin?

"We will see," said Dr. Sanguesa, who hadn't understood a word, nodding his head gravely.

It would not hurt, said the partner, because in the case of women it was dangerous to operate, and the treatment was purely external; it would take six weeks, with two treatments a week; she would begin to see a marked difference in her appearance after the fourth treatment.

The fourth treatment? That would be in a fortnight. And no operation? How wonderful. She caught her breath with excitement. In a fortnight she would be beginning to look younger. After that, every day younger and younger. No more Maria Rome, no more painful care over her dressing, no more fear of getting tired because of how ghastly it made her look, but the real thing, the real glorious thing itself.

"Shall I *feel* young?" she asked, eagerly now.

"Of course. Everything goes together. You understand—a woman's youth, and accordingly her looks, depends entirely on—"

The partner launched into a rapid explanation which was only saved from being excessively improper by its technical language. Dr. Sanguesa sat silent, his elbows on the arms of his revolving chair, his finger-tips together. He looked a remote, unfriended, melancholy man, rather like the pictures she had seen of Napoleon III, with dark shadows under his heavy eyes and a waxen skin. Every now and then his sad mouth opened, and he said quite automatically, "We will see," and shut it again.

She wanted to begin at once. It appeared she must be examined first, to find out if she could stand the treatment. This rather frightened her again. Why? How? Was the treatment so severe? What was it?

"We will see," said Dr. Sanguesa, nodding.

The partner became voluble, waving his hands about. Not at all—not at all severe; a matter of X-rays merely; but sometimes, if a woman's heart was weak—

Catherine said she was sure her heart wasn't weak.

"We will see," said Dr. Sanguesa, mechanically nodding.

"The examination is three guineas," said the partner.

"Three more, or three of the same ones?" asked Catherine, rather stupidly.

"We will s—"

The partner interrupted him this time with a quickly lifted hand. He seemed to think Catherine's question was below the level of both his and her dignities and intelligences, for he looked as if he were a little ashamed of her as he said stiffly, "Three more."

She bowed her head. She would have bowed her head to anything, if these men in exchange would give her youth.

The examination could be made at once, the partner said, if she was ready.

Yes, she was quite ready.

She got up instantly. They were used to eagerness, especially in the women patients, but this was a greater eagerness than usual. Dr. Sanguesa's sombre, sunken eyes observed her thoughtfully. He said something in Spanish to his partner, who shook his head. Catherine had the impression it was something he wished interpreted, and she looked inquiringly at the partner, but he said nothing, and went to the door and opened it for her.

She was taken upstairs into a sort of Rose du Barri boudoir, arranged with a dressing-table and looking-glasses, and another nurse—at least, she too looked like one—helped her to undress. Then she was wrapped in a dressing-gown— she didn't like this public dressing-gown against her skin—and led into a room fitted up with many strange machines and an operating table. What will not a woman do, she thought, eyeing these objects with misgiving, and her heart well down somewhere near her feet, for the man she loves?

Dr. Sanguesa came in, all covered up in white like an angel. The partner, she was thankful to notice, didn't appear. She was examined with great care, the nurse smiling encouragingly. It was a relief to be told by the nurse, who interpreted, that her heart was sound and her lungs perfect, even though she had never supposed they weren't. At the end the nurse told her the doctor was satisfied she could stand the treatment, and asked when she would like to begin.

Catherine said she would begin at once,

Impossible. The next day?

Oh yes, yes—the next day. And would she really—she was going to say look nice again, but said instead feel less tired?

"It's wonderful how different people feel," the nurse assured her; and Dr. Sanguesa nodded gravely, without having understood a word, and said, "We will see."

"He hasn't tried it on himself, has he?" remarked Catherine, when she was in the Rose du Barri room again, dressing.

The nurse laughed. She was a jolly-looking young woman but perhaps she was really an old woman, who had had the treatment.

"Have you been done?" asked Catherine.

The nurse laughed again. "I shall be if I see I'm getting old," she said.

"It really is wonderful?" asked Catherine, whose hands as she fastened her hooks were trembling with excitement.

"You wouldn't believe it," said the nurse earnestly. "I've seen men of seventy looking and behaving not a day more than forty."

"That's thirty years off," said Catherine. "And supposing they were forty to begin with, would they have looked and behaved like ten?"

"Ah well, that's a little much to expect, isn't it," said the nurse, laughing again.

"I'm forty-seven. I wouldn't at all like to end by being seven."

"Your husband would pack you off to a kindergarten, wouldn't he," said the nurse, laughing more than ever.

Catherine laughed too. She was so full of hope that she already felt younger. But when she put on her hat before the glass she saw she didn't anyhow look it.

"Don't I look too awful," she said; turning round frankly to the friendly nurse, who, after all, was going to be the witness of her triumphant progress backwards through the years.

"We'll soon get rid of all that," said the nurse gaily.

Catherine quite loved the nurse.

Love. [1925] New York: Washington Square Press, 1995. 239–45.

C. P. SNOW

From *New Lives for Old*

The next morning, Pilgrim woke early, with the questions goading his mind: Am I getting young again? Has it worked? He jumped out of bed and threw up a blind; the room was lit by the diffused pale sunlight. Then he put on his spectacles and looked at himself in the mirror. With a despondent emptiness, he stared at a form that seemed to be very much the same as it had been the last ten years. Eagerly, he tried to find a difference: some of the lines round the corners of his mouth were a little fainter, perhaps. There might be the slightest of changes—but he could not convince himself.

He sat dejectedly on his bed. He made an effort to be more optimistic. What, after all, could he hope to see? Even when rejuvenation was complete, there would only be a general air of vitality, certainly no real youthening of the face. The weaker lines would go, the hollows would fill out; but, he smiled slightly, on his own round face it was difficult to find hollows to fill.

During the last few days, he had told himself what he must expect time and time again; and yet reason is so weak that he was downcast when he could not have an immediate and complete reversion to himself at twenty. As always, he thought, the irrational hope is too strong for the intellect; one wishes what one knows to be impossible, and is disappointed when it doesn't come.

But though there could not be much alteration in the face, the drastic inner change should be bringing him new life. Unless something were wrong, he should be becoming a different man; it might take weeks before the rejuvenation was complete, but it should already have begun. No optimism could argue that away. . . .

With a renewed anxiety, he walked up and down the room. How was he feeling to-day? Though he knew perfectly how impossible it is to estimate the state of one's own health, he made the useless attempt. He had a dull ache in the back of the head; but in nervous strain that was not uncommon, he apologized to himself. His tongue was a little furred. His thigh muscles were stiff after the ridiculous run of yesterday afternoon. Otherwise he was his normal self.

Then he had a flash of reassurance. He was not quite his normal self. There was a touch of spring in his movements that had been gone for many years; it was not induced by the mind, he thought happily, for it had been there when he was fearing that nothing had happened after all. Unconsciously, even in his worry, he had noticed, as he walked along the floor, that his feet were eager to make the next step; they did not stay firmly on the ground, as they had done for so long.

He tried to preserve his scientific caution, but for the moment it had vanished with his fears. "I've not got much to go on," he said to himself, "but, by the Lord, I do believe it's happening!"

Throughout the morning the confidence continued; he went to the laboratory and talked enthusiastically to Callan upon a new side-line of their work; after that, he argued with a colleague over some point of university politics, not because he was interested but simply to express his buoyancy. Just before lunch, he did not feel so exultant, and, almost instinctively, without considering, he rang up Maclehose.

"Hallo, Maclehose," he said. "I thought you'd like to know I'm feeling very fit."

Maclehose's brisk voice replied: "Of course you are. Why ever shouldn't you?"

"I think I really can feel a difference already," Pilgrim went on. Even through the telephone, Maclehose's ear, sympathetic by nature and experience, could detect the doubt, the need for encouragement, which had prompted the call.

"It'll be gradual, I imagine. It won't all happen at once," he said. "Don't worry if you're not exactly bucking with energy for a few days."

Pilgrim answered, more cheerfully: "I told you, I really think there is a change." Maclehose chuckled to himself how familiar all these gambits were in the patient's desire to be told about his condition. He said warmly:

"Well, if you're right, that's better still. I'm doing some more people this afternoon, Vanden and Bock and some women. I may want to talk to you about one or two points soon. I thought we might have a combined attack on the medical side of rejuvenation. You and I could do it, during the next ten or twenty years."

Pilgrim smiled amiably at the receiver. There was a pleasant comforting sound about that "ten or twenty years." "Any time you like," he said, and went to lunch satisfied.

At his end, Maclehose stood thoughtfully by the telephone. "This phase of anxiety after rejuvenation is going to be something of a problem," he reflected. "If it occurs to a man like Pilgrim, exceptionally balanced and cheerful, it will happen much more violently to most of these old people. It's a problem which will have to be tackled." Then he smiled; he had sent Pilgrim away happy; if a man like Pilgrim, very intelligent in human affairs, was made contented by a reference to "the next ten or twenty years," probably the problem was not worth considering. He chuckled: "What children the cleverest men are, where their bodies are concerned!"

The afternoon turned damp and cloudy, and Pilgrim sat lazily in his flat, reading an immensely long novel by a young man who was being acclaimed as the English Proust. Pilgrim had considered taking a long walk in the rain, but some unconscious caution prompted him not to test his youth prematurely again; it was better to bask for a while in the comfortable feeling that he could exert himself violently if only he cared. He was half-ashamed of his policy of discretion and he tried to lose himself in the book, which gave very subtle and involved accounts of the emotions of adolescents. Pilgrim had to admit that it was beautiful in places and nervously sensitive everywhere, but his attention lagged, and several times he read the winding paragraphs over twice without their leaving any but the most dulled impression. Quite a number of the great novels of the world were admirable except that one did not particularly want to read them; this book, he decided, was of that class. He put it down, and glanced at several journals. The rain slanted softly on to the window panes; the afternoon turned greyer and slowly passed away.

Vanden called early in the evening. Pilgrim noticed at once the subdued excitement hiding behind the impassive face, and he asked:

"You've been to Maclehose, Van?"

"Yes," said Vanden, "I've been performed on." None of them at this time used the word "rejuvenated" in conversation, and soon the slang developed of referring to the process as "being done." "Have you been done?" was shortly to become a common question among elderly women. "I've been performed on," Vanden repeated. He laughed shortly. "An amusing b-business." To Pilgrim the lines on his face spoke as clearly as though he were saying what he would find hard to confess. Instead of sitting here talking lightly, he was really despairingly anxious to share his uneasiness; Pilgrim was sure that he wanted to say—"Billy, do you think it will be all right with us? Nothing's happened yet. I'm not getting younger."

But Pilgrim saw how strong the emotional conventions were. Vanden, who would have discussed the details of any love affair with the completest candour, could not admit his fright over the new life. Though nothing was important except this insidious fear, he began to talk about Maclehose and the psychology of doctors in general.

"I've always wondered," he said "why a serious n-novel has never been written round a doctor as the central figure.Think of it, Billy; think of all the complications which we conveniently forget. We think of a doctor as someone quite impersonal, because it would be inconvenient if we didn't. But of course a doctor remains a human being when he's p-playing about with a beautiful body. I wonder what sort of mess it leads to inside him. And there's another thing: what sort of curiosity is it which leads men to want to play about with bodies in the first place? It's very strong, you know. Young men get very keen on the idea of being a doctor. I should like to go into it as fully as I could."

His sympathy heightened by his own uncertainties of a few hours before, Billy Pilgrim could feel that these words were only a mask which Vanden wanted to throw aside. To Pilgrim's alert ear, there was something wrong with the sound of them; Vanden's usual biting quality was absent, there was a hesitancy which was uncommon. So Pilgrim, with the satisfaction of one just recovered from a disease who is able to encourage someone still in its clutches, said, with a cheerful smile:

"You needn't worry if you don't feel much different for a few hours, Van. It doesn't all happen at once, you know."

Vanden's eyes looked eager. His set face softened.

"Oh," he said. "You're sure! What happened to you?"

"Nothing at all last night," Pilgrim replied. He chuckled: I was damned worried. But to-day there is a change."

"You're really d-different. You're quite certain?"

"Not quite." Pilgrim's face clouded, but there was a satisfaction in laying bare his own doubts. He saw Vanden's mouth tighten. "We can't be quite certain for a few days—and even then it won't be easy to say absolutely definitely. You see, this feeling young is a personal subjective thing, and it'll take time to get us into it. Our bodies are getting younger every minute, but there'll be a lag before our minds really accept it as the usual state of things."

"Our b-bodies are getting younger?" Vanden's indifference had gone, and he was speaking quickly.

"Scientifically it's certain," Pilgrim answered. "For myself, I'm beginning to feel it"—he pushed up his spectacles and twinkled his eyes—"about half the time. The other half, it seems fantastic. But in a week or two we shall be taking it as a perfectly normal thing. First, we think it's happened all at once—at least I did."

"I did too," Vanden tried to smile.

"Then we think it isn't happening at all. That's where you are now. Then we shall just find the whole thing become part of us without noticing it, and all these worries will seem quite ridiculous." Pilgrim looked at Vanden, who was regaining some of his poise.

"Yes, I suppose so," Vanden said. "But that doesn't mean that they're not d-disturbing things to have."

"Of course it doesn't," said Billy Pilgrim. He gazed at his friend. "It's a pity we can't get rid of the human mind: it's more trouble than it's worth. Always getting bothered about a future which it knows perfectly well won't happen."

Vanden moved his lips in response to Pilgrim's friendly grin, and then said: "If this doesn't happen, Billy—" and broke off.

"We should none of us ever recover," said Pilgrim evenly.

"That's true," Vanden said. For a moment they felt the pressure of doubt return. Then Billy Pilgrim shrugged his shoulders." But the question doesn't arise. It will happen. He lit his pipe. "What are we going to do to-night?"

Vanden replied: "Sit uncomfortably with a lot of other people listening to a play which is bound to be b-bad." The answer was a private joke between them, and Pilgrim gave his most whole-hearted laugh. So often, in the course of forty years, they had known one another in the depths of misfortune; Pilgrim's marriage, Vanden's first love affair, the loss of a mistress, the failure of a book, all the calamities which must happen to any man in a lifetime, had provided nights when one or both of them could only hope for the days to pass, in order that the pain might slowly go. At these times they had sat together, as they did to-night, and Pilgrim had asked many times what they should do, and Vanden had always replied with the same phrase. Years of use had turned the meaningless remark into a bitter-sweet joke, enriched by the pain which they had seen each other suffer.

"Good," said Pilgrim. He thought for a second, and then went on: "What about fetching some of the others who've seen Maclehose to-day? They're probably none too pleased with life. Bock was going, I think, and Simone—"

"And Alison's m-mother, I saw her coming out," Vanden put in. "You want us to make them all happy, do you?" He smiled. "I must say, Billy, you're an offensively kind-hearted man."

Pilgrim gently rubbed his stomach: "My main objection to hard-hearted men of the world like yourself is that you're so completely devoid of any practical sense whatever. When one's worried, the best cure is to find someone rather more worried than oneself—and if possible worried in the same way. It'll be the best thing for both of us, as you ought to know. It may be kind-hearted, but that doesn't matter—unless your conscience prevents your doing it because of that?"

"You shouldn't explain your benevolence away," said Vanden. "It isn't convincing: the benevolence is still there."

"Of course it is," Pilgrim retorted. "I don't set out to be a super-man without any of the weaker emotions. I shall enjoy cheering these people up."

"Have it your own way," Vanden said.

Bock arrived as they were finishing a light dinner. He looked as precise in a tail-coat and a white tie as in morning dress; but his manner was a shade less confidently inquisitive than usual. "Maclehose told me," he began, "that you two have both been operated on by him."

Pilgrim laughed: "If you call it an operation, yes," he said. "I'm not so good at euphemisms." He looked at Bock's face, which seemed much more human now that it was removed by trouble from its cast of detached inquiry. Pilgrim said: "By the way, don't worry if you feel exactly the same as now, for the next few hours. Nothing happens for a while." Bock showed his relief very clearly. Vanden found himself feeling almost warm towards him, during these few minutes of mutual uneasiness. "I confess," said Bock, "that I was wondering when we might expect a change."

Pilgrim repeated what he had told Vanden of his own progress; in all of them there was an anxious hope. Soon they set out in Vanden's car to fetch Mrs. Byrne from her house in Cromwell Road. Pilgrim and Vanden had met her at lunch with Alison a fortnight before; they had been amused by the fragile old lady with her lorgnon, bright blue eyes and malicious tongue. When they got to the house they found that Alison was at her flat, and Pilgrim was mildly annoyed. Alison was such an adornment to a party, it was a nuisance that she was not there, he thought and noticed Vanden staring at him with a steady glance.

Mrs. Byrne came into the room, however, and their eyes could not leave her. She had changed amazingly from "the dry flesh held together entirely by the wish to annoy my enemies," as she had said about herself on their first meeting; then, she had walked with a stick, now, she came in lightly; her skin was still sallow, but the lines had become very faint; altogether, she looked years younger.

"Good evening," she said. "It was charitable of you to ring me up, Professor. Still, I expect you enjoyed it."

Pilgrim gazed at her incredulously; she was dressed in a bistre silk frock which fitted softly into her drawing-room of light half-tones.

Vanden said: "He'd have had a pleasure of a different sort, if he's known what to expect."

Throwing a shawl over her shoulders, she replied: "I'm afraid the lights will show up my skin. I haven't had time to get it put right yet. But I do feel appreciably further from the grave, don't you?"

Pilgrim's eyes met Vanden's, and they could each see a trace of amusement. To search out Mrs. Byrne in order to comfort her because she was still old and miserable, and to find instead that she looked a youngish graceful thirty-five, far younger than any of them—it was the kind of joke, Pilgrim thought, that Vanden put into his novels.

"It isn't working so quickly with us, I'm afraid," said Pilgrim. "You'll have to be content with three old men."

"Oh, I'm sorry," she looked quickly at them all. Vanden and Pilgrim both saw with a shock how much she was like Alison in her sudden moments of sympathy. "Perhaps tomorrow—"

"To-morrow we shall be getting younger," said Pilgrim. After a spasm of jealousy at seeing someone of his own age look young enough to be his daughter, he had been overcome by a quick and vital happiness. For the thing was done! He'd not been mistaken about his own feelings! With Mrs. Byrne, for some reason he didn't know, the change was working in front of their eyes. She was younger than Vanden or himself, probably not more than sixty, and that might have helped, though why he could not see.

He watched Vanden, and saw anxiety melting from his face; and Bock was becoming primly jocular as he too saw the concrete proof of what must soon happen to them all. Until they had felt in their own blood, they could not be at ease, but the sharpest of their worries was swept away. Only Pilgrim, the most hopeful of them by nature, had a lingering doubt remain. More than the others, he had seen the physical effects which can be brought about by a state of mind.

They drove rapidly to Simone's house in Shepherd's Market, and walked through the hall, dark and littered with heavy rugs, into a room which was shamelessly ornate in black and bronze. No one else, as Vanden had often said, would have dared to own a room like that and yet, as a background for Simone, it seemed to reveal a strange somber beauty of its own.

Simone herself was waiting for them, and her mouth parted in a wide smile across her cheeks. Then Mrs. Byrne smiled back, and the sight of her froze Simone into a mask of depression too obvious to be ignored.

"What's the matter?" Mrs. Byrne asked. "Haven't you been done, too?"

"No," said Simone. "They won't have my sort of stuff ready for a fortnight or so."

The others, who had undergone the aching stress of three weeks before the preparations were ready, could understand what a blow it must have been for her, when she came to the operation itself and was told that she would have to wait a fortnight more. And then, as a final pain, to see Mrs. Byrne reveling in her release from old age.

Billy Pilgrim felt the question sound inane as he asked it:

"I suppose you need the beta-product?"

"They said something about it," Simone replied listlessly. Her vivacity had been broken down. "But I wasn't very interested."

"Of course," said Pilgrim, pushing up his spectacles, "it'll be all right in a fortnight. You'll have the stuff then."

"A fortnight is a long time," Simone said.

"I think we'd better go to this p-play," Vanden broke in.

Pilgrim wondered curiously what emotions were hidden behind the unmoved manner, what could he feel at this unpleasantness, with her life and his interwoven as they were?

"You won't want me, Van," she said. "You young people won't want me."

"Don't be absurd," Vanden picked up her cloak. "If it's happening to us at all, there's precious little sign of it: Except with Mrs. Byrne. You must come."

Simone looked at Mrs. Byrne, with envious dislike. With an effort she laughed:

"I suppose I'll come, she said. Even at my age, I'm younger than the rest of you, whether you've started again or not."

Chapter 2, *New Lives for Old*. London: Camelot Press, 1933. 110–21.

17

Mediumship, Automatism, and Modernist Authorship

INTRODUCED AND SELECTED BY BETTE LONDON

> After some time—from five to fifteen minutes—she is seized with slight spasmodic convulsions, which increase, and terminate in a very slight epileptiform attack. Passing out of this, she falls into a state of stupor, with somewhat stertorous breathing; this lasts about a minute or two; then, all at once, she comes out of the stupor with a burst of words. Her voice is changed; she is no longer Mrs Piper, but another personage, Dr Phinuit, who speaks in a loud, masculine voice in a mingling of negro patois, French, and American dialect.
>
> —Professor Charles Richet, describing a sitting with the medium, Mrs. Piper in Cambridge, England (qtd. in Sage 9)

THIS DESCRIPTION OF the American medium Mrs. Piper, widely recognized as one of the most remarkable practitioners of trance mediumship in modern history, captures many of the critical features of mediumistic performance— most notably, the lending of the medium's body to some unknown "personage" that speaks or writes through her, without her conscious knowledge or volition. In Mrs. Piper's case, as her mediumship developed in a career spanning the years 1887–1924, *voice* communication, as described above, came more and more to be replaced by automatic *writing*, directed by "control spirits" of increasing refinement and erudition.[1] This automatic writing was initiated in much the same manner as the spoken messages: Mrs. Piper's arm would be seized with violent convulsions, and a burst of writing would ensue, her hand moving as if it did not belong to her. The writing itself, always produced with great rapidity, often resembled mirror-writing, and sometimes included words written in Greek (a language with which Mrs. Piper had no conscious familiarity). So complete was Mrs. Piper's submersion in the trance state that "in some of the sittings one personality communicated through the voice, while another, entirely different, and speaking of utterly different matters, communicated simultaneously in writing" (Sage 10).

The subject of exhaustive studies by both the American and British Societies for Psychical Research, Mrs. Piper's case corroborates the experience of automatism as a transatlantic phenomenon. Moreover, it testifies to the relocation of mediumistic acts from the Victorian drawing room, with all the trappings of amateur theatricals, to the auspices of psychical research societies, with all the accouterments of the scholarly and scientific enterprise. As a modernist phenomenon, then, mediumship represented a performance of a different order from its Victorian counterpart.[2] Turning from the physical materialization of dead spirits in darkened séance rooms, it concentrated instead on the manifestation of mental powers, the display of literate and cultured knowledge as seen in the copious production of speech and writing. As such, modern mediumship and automatism provided new forms of access to the study of mental and creative processes, to the modes by which the mind (whether understood to be occupied by some discarnate spirit, as spiritualists would claim, or subject to the individual's own subliminal consciousness) receives and transmits information. Psychical research, as the investigative machinery for these phenomena, could be seen, as Pamela Thurschwell has argued, to have distinct parallels to discourses like psychoanalysis that developed contemporaneously with it. The difference between the two, it could be argued, is that during this period, psychical research played a significant role for much broader and more diverse constituencies than psychoanalysis.

As the case of Mrs. Piper suggests, moreover, the investigation of mediums reproduced a certain gendered dynamic that paralleled psychoanalysis's studies of hysteria—with the female body, subject to involuntary spasms and reflexes, subjected to the gaze of the (typically) male expert. Upheld as one of the "most perfect" examples of mediumship ever discovered, Mrs. Piper's mediumship would seem to have achieved its remarkable stature by being the case "most perseveringly, lengthily and carefully studied by highly competent men" (Sage 1).[3] Indeed, one of the qualities of successful mediumship would appear to be the ability to perform before a host of witnesses; thus Geraldine Cummins, in the essay reproduced here, documents the professionals who observed the production of her automatic writings—scripts purportedly dictated to her by a first-century Christian and detailing knowledge far outside the range of her own expertise and education: "Amongst those who were present at the production of these writings at different times have been: 3 members of the medical profession, 2 Fellows of the Royal College of Physicians (Ireland), a Doctor of Law, a Doctor of Philosophy, 3 Doctors of Divinity, 5 clergymen, a well-known historical scholar, the editor of a literary monthly, a journalist, a sculptor, a novelist, and representatives of English and American Societies for Psychical Research."

As these examples suggest, women's automatism turned writing into a performance—one that would appear to receive its validation from the men who observed, analyzed, and documented it. But such a representation tells only part of the story. Mrs. Piper, who never questioned her role as the passive object of masculine attention, represents, in fact, what might be called the first phase of modern mediumship and automatism—the onset of her earliest trance experiences nearly coinciding with the establishment of the Society for Psychical Research (SPR) in 1882.[4] By the 1920s, spurred by the massive loss of life in World War I, mediumship had seen a significant revival, most notably in middle-class intellectual circles in London, Cambridge, and Dublin, as well as in American cities; in the 1920s and 1930s, then, when literary modernism was at its height, the practice of automatic writing was flourishing. This second phase of the modern mediumistic experience brought with it a new, more self-conscious breed of automatist.[5] The mediums represented in the selections included here—Hester Travers Smith, Geraldine Cummins, Gladys Osborne Leonard—might be seen as representative of this more professionalized figure. Unlike Mrs. Piper, who never publicly spoke in her own voice or commented on her mediumship—although thousands of pages in the *Proceedings* of the SPR have been devoted to it—these new mediums proved intent on making claims for their own agency in their "automatic" productions, publishing, in their own names (if only as "editor" or "recorder"), the messages communicated to them. Thus Travers Smith published *Psychic Messages from Oscar Wilde* in 1924 and Cummins published *The Scripts of Cleophas: A Reconstruction of Primitive Christian Documents* in 1928, after successfully establishing her copyright in a suit against one of the sitters at her séances (see London 150–78). Like other of their generation's most prominent mediums, they also published autobiographical accounts of their experiences, appearing under such titles as *My Life in Two Worlds* (Leonard), *Unseen Adventures* (Cummins), and *Voices from the Void* (Travers Smith).

Significantly, these women all came from middle-class backgrounds, and they were not without intellectual, artistic, and professional aspirations. Before devoting her energies exclusively to psychical research (as an automatist, but also as a recorder and investigator of psychic phenomena), Geraldine Cummins had achieved a minor career as a playwright and fiction writer, with three of her collaboratively written plays performed at the Abbey Theatre, and she apparently had at one time considered pursuing a career as a doctor. Hester

Travers Smith, better known by her maiden name Hester Dowden, was the daughter of an eminent Shakespeare scholar, Edward Dowden, who taught at Trinity College, Dublin; she grew up in the heart of Ireland's literary and intellectual culture, and she herself was an accomplished musician. Gladys Osborne Leonard began her professional life as an actress. Indeed, one of the developments that marked the shift from Victorian to modern mediumistic practices was the extent to which they came to be seen, in competition with other professions, as occupations attracting those Virginia Woolf dubbed "educated men's daughters," and as points of entrée into exclusive intellectual and artistic circles.

Often thought of as amateur, even fringe activities, these occupations were, as the appended selections demonstrate, important avenues for women's professionalization and mental development. As such, they reflected new opportunities for women to participate in intellectual culture and to achieve positions of authority once largely occupied by men. The "competent men," for example, who first studied Mrs. Piper for the SPR were increasingly replaced, as the society grew, by the competent women who studied her successors. Mrs. Leonard, for example, who, along with Mrs. Piper was one of the SPR's most-studied subjects, was famously investigated, as seen in the excerpt from the *Proceedings* included here, by Radclyffe Hall and Una Troubridge—investigators who carefully document the conditions of their controlled experiments. Unlike Mrs. Piper, who depends on the noblesse oblige of the SPR for her maintenance (the society eventually sets up a pension fund for her), Mrs. Leonard is a professional who receives a customary fee—a situation Hall and Troubridge go to considerable lengths to justify, since "many members of the Society look askance upon professional mediums" and "the attitude of the Society as a whole has always been largely skeptical of evidence received through paid mediumship."[6] Unlike Mrs. Piper, moreover, whose control spirits were generally masculine, Mrs. Leonard's primary control is Feda, the surviving spirit of a fourteen-year-old Indian girl who claims to be Mrs. Leonard's own great-great-grandmother. And the communicator in this case, A. V. B., was purportedly the surviving spirit of Radclyffe Hall's former lover, Lady Batten—a communicator who eventually takes over as a personal control (as seen in the closing excerpt here). In authenticating Mrs. Leonard's mediumship for the SPR, Radclyffe Hall and Una Troubridge were simultaneously redefining psychical research's gendered location, authenticating it as a place to perform by, for, and with women.

Not all mediums, however, were women; in the "Oscar Wilde" scripts reproduced here, for example, much of the automatic writing is produced by a "Mr. V" (the pseudonym for a Cambridge mathematician), assisted by Travers

Smith—or her daughter—resting her hands on his. But almost all of the most prominent and highly respected mediums of this age were women. Whether or not they were paid for their labor, they were recognized as occupying the leading ranks of this emerging profession; and whether or not they sought credit for the mental feats they accomplished, they achieved a scholarly reputation by assuming the authority that came to them without their knowledge. Thus Cummins, for example, in her comments "Concerning the Cleophas Scripts," readily admits that she is "not a student of history, nor a scholar"; yet her production of crypto-biblical apocrypha, with its specialized religious and historical data, puts her in converse with "experts in New Testament exegesis" and other "recognised scholars representing the Church and the Universities." While some established mediums were university-educated—Mrs. Verrall, for example, a lecturer in classics at Cambridge University, received automatic writing in Greek and Latin—most were not, and like Cummins, they found their access to this world through their automatic writing; like Cummins, moreover, many such mediums gravitated to knowledge of the ancient world and early Christian subjects. Travers Smith, for example, produced *The Scripts of Philip,* purportedly dictated by a contemporary of Jesus, and through her control spirit Johannes (who claimed to be a Greek who studied at the Great Library of Alexandria in 200 B.C.), she produced an extensive body of Neoplatonic philosophy (see Fripp), despite her lack of training in any of these subjects. Through their automatic writing, then, these mediums found license to encroach on the preserve of experts—in the creation of their texts and in their commentary on them.

In Cummins's case, for example, the production of a sustained body of writing "contrary to all my tastes and inclinations," "outside the compass of my conscious creative powers" provides her with a platform from which to enter topical debates about the nature of such unnatural phenomena—to pit her lived experience against the dry knowledge of the scientists and historians. And she continues this project in a chronicle that ultimately runs to eight volumes, published over a twenty-two-year time span. Hester Travers Smith, on the other hand, takes on the literary establishment; the daughter of a Shakespeare scholar, she establishes herself as a medium specializing in "literary" matters, producing both new "original" literature from long-dead authors (in the 1940s, for example, she produces new "Shakespeare" sonnets) and original literary criticism she attributes to these same departed writers. The scripts excerpted here, for example, include "Wilde's" often surprising critiques of such contemporary writers as Joyce, Bennett, Shaw, and Galsworthy. The selections in this chapter have been chosen, then, to illustrate the place of mediumship in women's intellectual culture in the first decades of the twentieth century.

The "scripts" of automatic writing, it should be pointed out, are not in themselves fascinating—not, at least, if one tries to read them as self-contained aesthetic objects. The recently published *Yeats's "Vision" Papers,* for example, containing the transcripts of the automatic writing Georgie Yeats produced with her husband in near daily sessions for the first two and a half years of their marriage (1917–20) make for daunting reading, representing as they do a kind of unedited flow of information, sometimes trivial, sometimes obscure, often broken and fragmented; like the excerpts from Mrs. Leonard's sittings cited in the Hall-Troubridge study, or from the "Oscar Wilde" communications, the narrative flow is interrupted by the markings of the conditions of its production—whether in the question-and-answer format through which the various parties to the communications participate, or in the meticulous recording of the difficulties of transmission. The extended passage in the excerpt here, for example, where Mrs. Leonard's control "Feda" tries to reproduce a word peculiar to the communicator, A. V. B., is typical of automatic transcripts: "Its S . . . P . . . O, Mrs. Una, then a little letter, and then a letter like this (she draws a 'K' on U. V. T.'s hand). It's a down stroke like this, with a little bit like this sticking to it; Sporki . . . Sporkif?"

As the "Oscar Wilde" selections included here will demonstrate, moreover, automatic scripts tend to be uneven in style and content, even when they purport to be the communications of a famous author (as was, in fact, a frequent phenomenon); they do not pretend to be high art in their own right, nor can they generally sustain more than fitful comparison with their putative origins. Arguably "Oscar Wilde's" quip, "Being dead is the most boring experience in life. That is, if one excepts being married, or dining with a schoolmaster," has more of the ring of Wilde than his assessment of the contemporary woman as "an excrescence" that "protrudes from social life as a wart does from the nose of an inebriate," but the messages reproduced in Travers Smith's text are as likely to be of the latter as the former order. The critique, reproduced by Travers Smith in her concluding statement "To the Public"—that "Wilde 'has not improved in the process of dying,' as he says of his mother," that his "wit is 'tarnished' since he 'passed over'" (149–50)—is the common refrain about all such productions. And the explanation generally proffered—that allowances must be made for the difficulty of communication; for the time elapsed since the author's finest literary work was completed; and for the negative effects of the experience of "death" on an author's creativity make the very flawed nature of the texts a proof of their authenticity. As necessarily flawed objects—objects that insistently call attention to the means of their own production—they participate in a peculiarly modern dynamic that relocates significance from product to process, from message to medium (in all senses of the word). The interest of such scripts, then, is above all else, as a site of cultural production—the site even, perhaps, of an unacknowledged modernist mode of writing.

As a site of literary production, however, automatic writing occupies a place decidedly outside the mainstream. Written by those at the margins of modernist creativity, it was largely consumed and distributed in venues far from the hub of modernist literary culture. Indeed, while interest in spiritualism and the occult clearly preoccupied some modernist icons, in the typical story we have inherited—a story most famously embodied by W. B. Yeats—mediums figure as, at best, mere footnotes to the creative geniuses whose work they facilitated or inspired. Unlike the situation in France, where the surrealists self-consciously experimented with automatic writing—albeit an automatic writing stripped of all trappings of spiritualism, with the medium replaced by the author/artist—in Great Britain and America, there was no comparable tradition of viewing automatic writing as an avant-garde aesthetic, and hence no way to absorb something like Gertrude Stein's early scientific interest in automatism (see Will). Nor for those writers who explicitly involved themselves with séances and spirit communication—H. D., Radclyffe Hall—has there been a ready way to link these involvements to aesthetic consequences, although this aspect of H. D.'s work is now drawing increasing attention (see Sword 118–31).

Within the context of mediumistic production, *Psychic Messages from Oscar Wilde* is in many ways exceptional, aiming for a mass audience and garnering considerable popular attention. More often, however, such texts, if published at all, would find audiences only through coterie publication. To recover automatic writing, then, as a site of artistic and cultural production is to recover the conditions of its circulation and consumption. Much of what we know about the subject comes from what can be reconstructed from studies in the *Proceedings* of the SPR, where the automatic scripts rarely appear in their entirety; instead, they appear piecemeal, embedded in the texts that supply the critical machinery to explain them. What can be reproduced is necessarily an already compromised simulacrum of the original—whether because the features of manuscript culture that characterize these writings are elided in the turn to print, or because the linguistic peculiarities of the communications cannot be adequately translated—hence for example, Hall and Troubridge's admission that they have "not closely followed Feda's broken English, it would have taken too long to think out suitable spelling for her idiosyncrasies." As with the Cummins essay included here, moreover, much of the relevant material originated in talks to special interest societies, and was published in obscure journals and periodicals that have long since ceased publication.

Recovery of mediumship as a site of literary production is further complicated by a discourse that renders authorship suspect. Thus Cummins, for example, repeatedly maintains that she could not have written what her scripts display, that, as the authorities explain, much in the scripts "appears quite inexplicable on the supposition of human authorship." Yet such disavowal could be liberating, transforming composition in Cummins's words into "an adventure of the mind," or in Travers Smith's explanation, "an adventure which arouses surprise and interest." Dispersing authorship across a chain of intermediaries, automatic scripts, indeed, become a repeated demonstration of the "death of the author" and the birth of the "author function"—in cases like the "Oscar Wilde" scripts, quite literally so. Much of the text, in fact, consists of meta-commentary on the conditions of its own construction, of how a "dead" author can "speak again" or "use the pen." It is perhaps ironic, then, that *Psychic Messages from Oscar Wilde* is one of the few texts Travers Smith actually publishes in her name, although she does so ostensibly as editor. But for Travers Smith, as for other automatists, their scripts often became the property of others, the sitters in whose presence, and at whose behest, they produced their writing, and who unabashedly published these works, with or without explicit attribution to the medium. This was the case, for example, with the "Shakespeare" scripts Travers Smith produced later in life with two different sitters (Allen, Dodd). While for those who produced and studied such documents, their interest was often in locating evidentiary knowledge of authorship—information that would prove that the communicator was who he or she claimed to be (whether "Oscar Wilde," A. V. B, or a first-century scribe)—their interest for us may be in the way they self-consciously perform and illuminate the inevitably mediated nature of writing. In doing so, these practices reopen the question of a medium's agency, even as they confirm authorship as something other than the private and solitary practice we have frequently taken it to be.

Notes

1. Control spirits are entities or "personages" that generally supplant the consciousness of the medium, using the medium's physical frame—i.e., the medium's brain and body—to convey messages of their own or transmit messages from other spirit communicators, serving, in this last case, as the medium's "medium." Many mediums harbored multiple controls, and sustained hierarchical relationships among them. In psychical research circles, much debate centered on the exact nature and function of the control, with some arguing that controls acted as interpreters and amanuenses (as in the case of Mrs. Leonard's "Feda"), while others saw them as masters of ceremonies, arranging the order and selection of otherworldly speakers.

2. For important studies of nineteenth- and twentieth-century mediumship, see Basham, Braude, Cottom, London, Oppenheim, Owen, Sword, Thurschwell.

3. These investigators included R. H. Hodgson of the American SPR, famed for his exposure of fraudulent mediums. Hodgson began his study of Mrs. Piper almost immediately after his much celebrated exposure of Madame Blavatsky. His unwavering belief in Mrs. Piper's integrity played a significant part in establishing her reputation as a medium whose practice was above suspicion. After his death in 1905, Hodgson became one of the principal "spirits" who communicated through Mrs. Piper.

4. For the history of the Society for Psychical Research, see Haynes and Turner.

5. The term "automatist" was used in British psychical research circles as the technical name for mediums who produced automatic writing; the term "medium," on the other hand, was the preferred term among spiritualists (those who believed in survival in the afterlife) and was the term commonly used by the public to include all practitioners of "psychic" phenomena. I have used the terms medium and mediumship here in this more inclusive sense.

6. While many mediums argued that mediumship constituted professionalized labor—requiring the long hours, extensive training, and high level of discipline of any profession—many of these same mediums refused payment in order to avoid the imputation that their results may have been influenced by financial remuneration. Consequently, mediumship became in this time period increasingly the preserve of leisured middle-class women.

Works Cited

Allen, Percy. *Talks with Elizabethans: Revealing the Mystery of "William Shakespeare."* London: Rider and Co, 1947.

Basham, Diana. *The Trial of Woman: Feminism and the Occult Sciences in Victorian Literature and Society.* New York: New York University Press, 1992.

Braude, Ann. *Radical Spirits: Spiritualism and Women's Rights in Nineteenth-Century America.* Boston: Beacon, 1989.

Cottom, Daniel. *Abyss of Reason: Cultural Movements, Revelations, and Betrayals.* New York: Oxford University Press, 1991.

Cummins, Geraldine. *The Scripts of Cleophas: A Reconstruction of Primitive Christian Documents.* 2nd ed. London: Rider and Co., 1928.

———. *Unseen Adventures: An Autobiography Covering Thirty-four Years of Work in Psychical Research.* London: Rider and Co., 1951.

Dodd, Alfred. *The Immortal Master.* London: Rider and Co., 1943.

Fripp, Peter. *The Book of Johannes.* London: Rider and Co., 1941.

Haynes, Renée. *The Society for Psychical Research, 1882–1982: A History.* London: MacDonald and Co., 1982.

Jenney, Shirley Carson. *The Fortune of Eternity* [by Percy Bysshe Shelley]. New York: William-Frederick, 1945.

Leonard, Gladys Osborne. *My Life in Two Worlds.* 1931. London: Cassel and Co., 1992.

London, Bette. *Writing Double: Women's Literary Partnerships.* Ithaca: Cornell University Press, 1999.

Oppenheim, Janet. *The Other World: Spiritualism and Psychical Research in England, 1850–1914.* Cambridge: Cambridge University Press, 1985.

Owen, Alex. *The Darkened Room: Women, Power, and Spiritualism in Late Victorian England.* Philadelphia: University of Pennsylvania Press, 1990.

Sage, M. *Mrs. Piper and the Society for Psychical Research.* Translated by Noralie Robertson. Abridged edition. Preface by Sir Oliver Lodge. New York: Scott-Thaw, 1904.

Sword, Helen. *Ghostwriting Modernism.* Ithaca: Cornell University Press, 2002.

Travers Smith, Hester. *Voices from the Void: Six Years' Experience in Automatic Communications.* 1919. London: Psychic Book Club, 1954.

Thurschwell, Pamela. *Literature, Technology, and Magical Thinking, 1880–1920.* Cambridge: Cambridge University Press, 2001.

Turner, Frank M. *Between Science and Religion: The Reaction to Scientific Naturalism in Late Victorian England.* New Haven: Yale University Press, 1974.

Will, Barbara. *Gertrude Stein, Modernism, and the Problem of "Genius."* Edinburgh: Edinburgh University Press, 2000.

Yeats, W. B. *Yeats's "Vision" Papers. Vol. 1: The Automatic Script: 5 November 1917–18 June 1918.* Edited by Steve L. Adams et al. General Editor, George Mills Harper. Iowa City: University of Iowa Press, 1992.

———. *Yeats's "Vision" Papers. Vol. 2: The Automatic Script: 25 June 1918–29 March 1920.* Edited by Steve L. Adams et al. General Editor, George Mills Harper. Iowa City: University of Iowa Press, 1992.

HESTER TRAVERS SMITH

From *Psychic Messages from Oscar Wilde*

Introduction

This book bears the title of "Psychic Messages from Oscar Wilde." Twenty-three years have passed since the author of "De Profundis" passed out of the present life. It may seem incredible that he should make an attempt to send his thoughts back again to a world in which his share of ill-fame exceeded his good fame and fortune. Have we adequate reason for supposing that these messages are genuine? That Oscar Wilde still exists? The public must judge of these matters; those to whom the writings came can only transmit them to the world to which they are addressed.

How and by whom were these messages received? They came through automatic writing and the ouija board, two methods of psychic communication which are described later on in this book. In all cases Oscar Wilde was "the communicator," not what is termed "the control." This distinction between "a control" and "a communicator" may not be clear to those who have not made a special study of Psychic Phenomena. "Control" is a term which is applied to that mysterious entity who professes to be the "spirit guide" of the medium. He is the intermediary who admits suitable communicators. He is a being whose identity it is difficult to establish. The "communicator" professes to be the discarnate spirit of a human being. Our communicators, not our controls, go to prove or disprove survival. These messages came directly from Oscar Wilde to his mediums. My control, who calls himself "Johannes," merely introduces this communicator, rather unwillingly, to me. In the automatic writing there was no control or intermediary.

In the chapters which follow the automatic script I have more fully described the circumstances under which these writings came. I have frequently quoted and referred to the work of Professor C. Richet, not only because I value his conclusions, but also because he has formulated a theory which is logical and not impossible, and by which he seeks to explain psychic phenomena without accepting the spirit hypothesis. It is a significant fact, for those who refuse to consider psychical research seriously, that Professor Richet has devoted thirty years of his life to the study of this subject. His great distinction, as perhaps the most eminent physiologist in Europe, should give him a hearing, though his present theoretical opinion may be open to dispute. In fact, Sir Oliver Lodge has already dealt very ably with the problem of "cryptesthesia" as an explanation of psychic phenomena. It will seem difficult to many.

The first of our messages from Oscar Wilde came in automatic writing, as follows:

Automatic Script Obtained on June 8th, 1923
Sitters—Mrs Travers Smith and Mr V.

Lily, my little Lily—No, the lily was mine—a crystal thread—a silver reed that made music in the morning. (Who are you?) Pity Oscar Wilde—one who in the world was a king of life. Bound to Ixion's wheel of thought, I must complete for ever the circle of my experience. *Long ago I wrote that there was twilight in my cell and twilight in my heart,* but this is the (last?) twilight of the soul. *In eternal twilight I move,* but I know that in the world *there is day and night, seed time and harvest,* and red sunset must follow apple-green dawn. Every year spring throws her green veil over the world and anon the red autumn glory comes *to mock the yellow moon.* Already the may is creeping like a white mist over lane and hedgerow, *and year after year the hawthorn bears blood-red fruit after the white death of its may.* (Mrs T.S.—Are you Oscar Wilde?) Yes, Oscar Wilde. (Mrs T.S.—Tell me the name of the house you lived in in Dublin. Tell me where your father used to practice.) Near Dublin. My father was a surgeon. These names are difficult to recall. (Mrs T.S.—Not at all difficult if you are really Oscar Wilde.) I used to live near here—Tite Street. (Mrs T.S.—There is a Tite Street near here and he has spelt it correctly. I don't know where

he lived in London. Did you know about it?) (Mr V, the writer of the script.—
I have never been in Chelsea before to-day, and to the best of my knowledge
I had never heard of Tite Street.) (Mrs T.S.—Well, Oscar Wilde, what was your
brother's name?) William—Willie. (Mrs T.S.—Now, what did your mother, Lady
Wilde, call herself?) Speranza. Pity Oscar Wilde. (Mrs T.S.—Why have you come
here?) To let the world know that Oscar Wilde is not dead. His thoughts live
on in the hearts of all those who in a gross age can hear the flute voice of
beauty calling on the hills or mark where *her white feet brush the dew from the
cowslips in the morning.* Now the mere memory of the beauty of the world is
an exquisite pain. *I was always one of those for whom the visible world existed.* I
worshipped at the shrine of things seen. *There was not a blood stripe on a tulip
or a curve on a shell* or a tone on the sea that but had for me its meaning and
its mystery and its appeal to the imagination. Others might sip the pale lees
of the cup of thought, but for me the red wine of life.

Pity Oscar Wilde. To think of what is going on in the world is terrible for
me. Soon the chestnuts will light their white candles and the foxgloves flaunt
their dappled, drooping bells. Soon the full moon will swim up over the edge
of the world and hang like a great golden cheese—Stop! Stop! Stop! Stop! This
image is insufferable. You write like a successful grocer, who from selling pork
has taken to writing poetry. (Mrs T.S.—Who said that?) Oscar. I find the words
in my medium's mind. Try again—*like a great golden pumpkin hanging in the blue
night.* That is better, but it is a little rustic. Still, I adore rustic people. They are
at least near to nature, and, besides, they remind me of all the simple pleasures
I somehow missed in life. (Here Mrs T.S. made some remark about Lady Wilde
being a half crazy old woman who thought she could write poetry.) Please do
not insult my mother. *I loved and honoured her.* (Mrs T.S.—We are not insulting
her. Spell out the name by which your mother called herself.) Speranza. Yes, it
is quite true what I said. I lived for the beauty of visible things. The rose flushed,
anemones that star the dark woodland ways, those loveliest tears that Venus
shed for Adonis, and shed in vain, were more to me than many philosophies.

**COPY OF AUTOMATIC SCRIPT OBTAINED MONDAY, JUNE 18TH, 1923.
PRESENT.—MR V, MRS TRAVERS SMITH, MR B, MR DINGWALL
(RESEARCH OFFICER OF THE SOCIETY FOR PSYCHICAL RESEARCH),
MISS CUMMINS. MR V WAS THE AUTOMATIST,
MRS T.S. TOUCHING HIS HAND.**

Oscar Wilde. Being dead is the most boring experience in life. That is, if one
excepts being married or dining with a schoolmaster. Do you doubt my identity? I am not surprised, since sometimes I doubt it myself. I might retaliate

by doubting yours. I have always admired the Society for Psychical Research. They are the most magnificent doubters in the world. They are never happy until they have explained away their spectres. And one suspects a genuine ghost would make them exquisitely uncomfortable. I have sometimes thought of founding an academy of celestial doubters . . . which might be a sort of Society for Psychical Research among the living. No one under sixty would be admitted, and we should call ourselves the Society of Superannuated Shades. Our first object might well be to insist on investigating at once into the reality of the existence of, say, Mr Dingwall. [. . .]

RECORD OF A COMMUNICATION RECEIVED AT THE OUIJA BOARD, JUNE 17TH, 1923, AT 11.30 P.M. RECORDED BY MISS CUMMINS. THE MEDIUM WAS MRS TRAVERS SMITH.

Oscar Wilde. I have come, as you asked for me. I am naturally an interesting person—not only do I flaunt the colours of literature, but I have the lurid flame of crime attached to me also. My dear lady, do you realise that you are talking to a social leper? (Yes, we do.) I do not wish to burden you with details of my life, which was like a candle that had gutted at the end. I rather wish to make you believe that I was the medium through which beauty filtered and was distilled like the essence of a rose.

[. . .] (Did you know Mr W. B. Yeats?) I knew Yeats very well—a fantastical mind, but so full of inflated joy in himself that his little cruse of poetry was emptied early in his career. (What of his work?) A little drop of beauty that was spread only with infinite pains over the span of many years.

He will not be interested to know that I have still the voice to speak and the mind to put my thoughts on paper. He is too full of his own literary salvation to worry over a brother in art who fell from too much beauty, or rather, the desire for beauty, (Mrs T.S.—Give us a proof of your identity.) Do not ask me for proofs. I do not wish to visualise my medium as an old spinster nosing into the other world in the hope that she may find salvation for herself when Providence removes her from this sphere. I rather like to think of her as a creature who has a certain feeling for those who strive from twilight to reach the upper air. (We admire your work.) I am infinitely amused by the remarks you all make. You seem to think that I am gratified by your approval and your smiles, which mean that, in spite of all his crime, he had a certain value for us. I have value as each and all of you have; and I am none the worse for having drunk the dregs as well as the best of the vintage. . . .

Here we are in the most amusing position. We are like so many ants that creep round and round and do our silly tasks daily without any interest in our work. I feel like a very ancient ant nowadays. I am doing what is little better than picking oakum in gaol. There, after all, my mind could detach itself from my body. Here, I have no body to leave off. So one of my, most interesting occupations is impossible. It is not by any means agreeable to be a mere mind without a body. That was a very decorous garment, that made us seem very attractive to each other; or, perhaps, supremely the opposite. Over here that amusement is quite out of the question, and we know far too much about the interiors of each others' ideas. They grow very pale in this process, and one tires of one's ideas so easily. You can see them just as you saw the slightly creased and dabbled clothes of your friends on earth. (Have you seen your mother?) Yes, I have seen her. She has not really improved in the process of dying. She is less comely now than when Speranza used to lead the intelligentsia in Dublin in those days when we had still the relics of civilization among us. (Will you come again?) I will come again gladly, if you will let me buzz on as an autumn bee might who was tired of hunting for fresh blossoms out of season. I am tired, too, but I like to remind myself now and then of the fact that there are people who regard this little globe as the whole of what is reality.

COPY OF AUTOMATIC SCRIPT WRITTEN ON JULY 2ND, 1923. THE WRITER WAS MR V, WHO WAS ASSISTED BY MRS TRAVERS SMITH TOUCHING HIS HAND. PRESENT—MISS CUMMINS.

Note.—A portion of this script deals with the novels of Arnold Bennett, H. G. Wells, and Eden Philpotts. Neither Mrs Travers Smith nor Mr V are great novel-readers. They had each read one novel by Arnold Bennett, three or four of H. G. Wells' earlier novels; they had not read anything whatever by Eden Philpotts.

Oscar Wilde. Like blind Homer, I am a wanderer. Over the whole world have I wandered, looking for eyes by which I might see. At times it is given me to pierce this strange veil of darkness, and through eyes, from which my secret must be forever hidden, gaze once more on the gracious day. I have found sight in the most curious places. Through the eyes out of the dusky face of a Tamal girl I have looked on the tea fields of Ceylon, and through the eyes of a wandering Kurd I have seen Ararat and the Yezedes, who worship both God and Satan and who love only snakes and peacocks. [. . .]

It may surprise you to learn that in this way I have dipped into the works of some of your modern novelists. That is, I have not drawn the whole brew, but tasted the vintage. You have much to learn. Time will ruthlessly prune Mr Wells' fig trees. As for Mr Arnold Bennett, he is the assiduous apprentice to literature, who has conjured so long with the wand of his master Flaubert that he has really succeeded in persuading himself and others that he has learnt the trick. But Flaubert's secret is far from him. of his characters, one may say that they never say a cultured thing and never do an extraordinary one. They are, of course, perfectly true to life—as true as a bad picture. They are perfectly commonplace, and, for the Clayhangers, the Lessways and the Tellwrights, oblivion will have a plentiful meed of poppy. Mr. Bennett has undertaken a grave irresponsibility by adding to the number of disagreeable types in the world. Of late, we understand, he has taken to producing prostitutes. It is pleasanter to turn to Mr. Eden Philpotts, who, unlike Mr. Bennett, on whose sterile pages no flowers bloom or birds sing, has a real and unaffected love of nature, and, unfortunately, all nature's lack of variety. He is a writer who has been very faithful, far too faithful, to his first love. One wishes that spring would sometimes forget to come to Dartmoor.

THE FOLLOWING COMMUNICATION CAME THROUGH MRS TRAVERS SMITH'S HAND AT THE OUIJA BOARD, JULY 2ND, 1923, AT 11 P.M. RECORDED BY MISS CUMMINS.

Oscar Wilde. I have no very special desire to give my thoughts from this place of dimness to you who are breathing the upper air. But if it gives you pleasure to speak to one, who is in a manner soiled in the eyes of the world, I will continue to talk to you and to spin my webs of thought around you. [. . .] I will go on and tell you how I have wandered into the minds of the moderns, as you are pleased to call them.

It is a rather entertaining process. I watch for my opportunity, and when the propitious moment comes I leap into their minds and gather rapidly these impressions, which are largely collective. I spoke to-day of Mr Bennett and Mr Wells. These two writers have somehow managed to attain a summit which has deceived themselves. They actually believe they are fit for the company of the gods who drink the nectar of pure mind. And here they are utterly lost, neither of these gentlemen can do more than prepare a ready-made costume for the lay figure. They cannot create, and even when the lay figure is nailed together they cannot clothe it.

I feel the London of my time has been swallowed up; an article of a coarser quality is now in its place. The women of my time were beautiful, from the outward side at least. They had a mellifluous flow of language, and they added much to the brilliant pattern of society. Now woman is an excrescence, she protrudes from social life as a wart does from the nose of an inebriate. (Do you see women?) I see them now and then, dear lady, when I have the chance of using the eyes of a suitable medium. (Do you see this room?) Yes, a little dimly. (Mrs T.S.—Do you see me?) Yes, I can see you quite clearly. (How do you manage when Mr V and I sit together?) I can control his hand. I can only control your mind. Your hand is guided by your mind. . . .

(What is your opinion of Bernard Shaw?) Shaw, after all, might be called a contemporary of mine. We had almost reached the point of rivalry, in a sense, when I was taken from the scene of action. I had a kindly feeling towards poor Shaw. He had such a keen desire to be original that it moved my pity. Then he was without any sense of beauty, or even a sense of the dramatic side of life, and totally without any idea of the outside of any human being as he was utterly ignorant of his internal organs. And yet there was the passionate yearning to be a personage, to force his person on the London world and to press in, in spite of the better taste of those who went before him. I have a very great respect for his work. After all, he is my fellow-county-man. We share the same misfortune in that matter. I think he may be called the true type of the pleb. He is so anxious to prove himself honest and outspoken that he utters a great deal more than he is able to *think*. He cannot analyse, he is merely trying to overturn the furniture and laughs with delight when he sees the canvas bottoms of the chairs he has flung over. He is ever ready to call upon his audience to admire his work; and his audience admires it from sheer sympathy with his delight.

(Whom do you admire among the moderns?)

I am not given to admiration, I fear. But if you ask me sincerely whom I admire among the modern dramatists, I think there is only one who has any approach to form and a sense of drama. I feel that if I give you the name of this writer you will think that I praise his work chiefly as Shaw might, with a desire to be original. But I assure you, the only mind I have entered into which appeals to my literary sense is John Galsworthy. He is my successor, in a sense. For although he dives more deeply into the interior of the human being he is ever occupied with the exterior, which is so important in the play of society; and he succeeds, with this very difficult medium, in producing something akin to life with all the artificiality which is so essential to the stage. He is the aristocrat in literature, the man who takes joy in selection, as our poor friend Shaw never did. Shaw plunges in and seizes the first object his hand can grasp and takes a wholesome joy in ripping it to pieces. Galsworthy is slow in his selection, but when he selects he does so from an exquisite sense of fitness and he presents the complete pattern of his idea [. . .]

THE FOLLOWING COMMUNICATION CAME THROUGH MRS TRAVERS SMITH'S HAND AT THE OUIJA BOARD, JULY 4TH, 1923. RECORDED BY MISS CUMMINS.

Oscar Wilde is here. I shall readily speak to you, because it seems to me that these glimpses of the sun keep me from growing too mouldy here below. Hamlet speaks of his father's ghost as "old mole." I often used to smile in my unregenerate days at the clumsy way in which the Englishman—for surely our Shakespeare was nothing if not English. . . . The clumsy way in which he addressed the shade of his father used to wound my feelings of delicacy and selection. But now that I am a mole myself I understand. I fully appreciate this expression. It was well chosen and should be of interest to the Society for Psychical Research, as it displays an inward knowledge of the state over here. . . . more useful to me when I speak of what you are familiar with; and the other, that I enjoy my glimpses into the present chaotic conditions. It affords me great happiness when I reflect that I escaped this age of rasp.

MRS TRAVERS SMITH AT THE OUIJA BOARD, JUNE 20TH, 1923. RECORDED BY MISS CUMMINS.

Johannes. (Will you summon Oscar Wilde?) He is unpleasant. You may speak to him, but not often or much. . . . Oscar Wilde is speaking. Yes, I will give you a few minutes' light; that allows me to look through the peephole. It quite amuses me in a desultory way; it is not strictly an intellectual occupation, but it is a mild distraction from the twilight of my present state, which is somewhat the condition that is suitable for the propagation of a low form of vegetable existence. (Mrs T.S.—I have sent your communications to Mr Yeats.) He will not be gratified by finding me still extant, unless it affords him some proof that he will continue to inflate, in a further state, his ecstatic penetration of the universe. (What about your literary work?) I do not get much literary stimulus over here. I am rather in the condition of coma of the mind that used to overcome me when the great massed-up population of London oppressed my being. The shades here are really too tumultuous. They are overcrowded and we get confused by seeing into each others' thoughts. . . .

I wish you would just take me as I come. I crawl into your mind like a sick worm and try to bore a hole above the earth so that I may once more look at the sun. . . .

(Why do you speak to me?)

I like to speak to you because you remind me of the time when I too was a creature hampered by that garment you call a body. I really do not miss it much, because there is a joy in that nakedness which leaves all the thoughts and ideas of the mind, whether foul or fair, open to the public gaze. I feel now as if the extreme reticence of wearing a body was almost indecent. It is far more decent to go about blaring one's loves and hates, blowing them in the faces of those we meet—as it were, being so much on the outside that we cannot be said to have an inside. My dear lady, what will it be for you to lose your little shape, to have no shape, to be a fluid and merely stream about in such an undecided way that it is like drifting before a heavy tide. My mind is not really as repulsive as you would expect. It looks quite respectable at times. Of course there are times when it looks like an ancient thief, who steals away from me with shame in his face. That is only one aspect of me. I have other attractive ones. There is the brilliant orange of my thoughts, and the deep rose red of my desires, which cling to me still. They are perfumed and smell sweet to me. But there is somehow a sense that they are getting a little stale. This condition of twilight is bringing out a delicate mossy mould upon them which rather damages their hue. (Here the sitting was interrupted.) [. . .]

MRS TRAVERS SMITH AT THE OUIJA BOARD, JULY 6TH, 1923, 11.45 P.M. RECORDED BY MISS CUMMINS. THIS COMMUNICATION CAME THROUGH WITH THE SAME RAPIDITY AS THE PREVIOUS MESSAGE.

Oscar Wilde. I will try to let my thoughts fly through your brain. (I was tired when I spoke to you last.) I found you less sensitive to my ideas than before, but even when you are tired you are a perfect æolian lyre that can record me as I think. [. . .]

(What is your opinion of "Ulysses," by James Joyce?)

Yes, I have smeared my fingers with that vast work. It has given me one exquisite moment of amusement. I gathered that if I hoped to retain my reputation as an intelligent shade, open to new ideas, I must peruse this volume. It is a singular matter that a countryman of mine should have produced this great bulk of filth. You may smile at me for uttering thus when you reflect that in the eyes of the world I am a tainted creature. But, at least, I had a sense of the values of things on the terrestrial globe. Here in "Ulysses" I find a monster who cannot contain the monstrosities of his own brain. The creatures he gives birth to leap from him in shapeless masses of hideousness, as dragons might, which in their foulsome birth contaminate their parent. . . . This book appeals to all my senses. It gratifies the soil which is in everyone of us. It gives me the impression of having been written in a severe fit of nausea. Surely there is a nausea fever. The physicians may not have diagnosed it. But here we have the heated vomit continued through the countless pages of this work. The author thought no doubt that he had given the world a series of ideas. Ideas which had sprung from out his body, not his mind!

I, who have passed into the twilight, can see more clearly than this modern prophet. I also know that if he feels his work has sprung from courage, which is innate in him, he should be led to realize that "Ulysses" is merely involuntary. I feel that if this work has caught a portion of the public, who may take it for the truth, that I, even I, who am a shade, and I who have tasted the fulness of life and its meed of bitterness, should cry aloud: "Shame upon Joyce, shame on his work, shame on his lying soul." . . . Compare this monster Joyce with our poor Shaw. Here we find very opposite poles. For both these writers cry aloud that they have found the truth. Shaw, like a coy and timid maiden, hides his enormous modesty with bluster. Joyce, on the other hand, is not a blusterer at all. In fact he has not vomited the whole, even in this vast and monumental volume—more will come from Joyce. For he has eaten rapidly; and all the undigested food must come away. I feel that Joyce has much to give the world before, in his old age, he turns to virtue. For by that time he will be tired of truth and turn to virtue as a last emetic.

(You are most amusing.)

I am glad that a poor ghost can bring laughter to your eyes.

(I am interested in literature.)

I quite appreciate that fact. You have a sense of style, and this helps me to put poor thoughts before you. [. . .]

COPY OF AUTOMATIC SCRIPT RECEIVED ON JULY 13TH
THROUGH THE HAND OF MR V.
MRS TRAVERS SMITH TOUCHING HIS HAND.

Tell me, dear lady, what are the virtues that are necessary for a happy life? Tell me in a few words. I don't want to know anything about the vices! (Mrs T. S.—Give me your views.) I have no views. I wish I knew. If I did I should not tell you, since it is always bad advice that is given away. (Mrs T.S.—I really cannot name any virtue that makes for a happy life.) I was afraid you were going to say work. Never having done any in my life I am naturally an authority on it. Ah! I forget! I once trundled the barrow for poor old John Ruskin, and in a moment of weakness I almost renounced the great cardinal doctrine of the indignity of labour. But during those few days I learned so much about the *body* of man under Socialism that afterwards I only cared to write about the soul. I told people that I never even walked. But that was a pardonable exaggeration. I always walked to bed. Don't talk to me about work, dear lady. It is the last refuge of the mentally unemployed; the occupation of those too dull to dream.

To be eternally busy is a sign of low vitality. They who go to the ant to learn her ways always come back *antiquated* but seldom wise. And while it may be true that Satan sometimes finds mischief for idle hands to do, even God does not know what to do with the industrious.

So, dear lady, live to do nothing and be happy. Eschew work and be fine. No one should ever do anything. At least no woman should. The woman who was content to merely *be* was always charming, but the woman who *did* was often detestable. This is a maxim which might be taken to heart by our modern business girls. Then, instead of hunting so diligently for their husbands in dusty offices, they would stay at home and their husbands would come to them. [. . .]

Appendix

[. . .]

To the Public

It is time that I drop the role of lecturer on psychic phenomena and put myself into the position of those to whom the terms automatic writing, ouija board, sub-conscious and cryptesthesia mean little or nothing, but in whom the fact that we seem to be talking again to so prominent a figure as Oscar Wilde is an adventure which arouses surprise and interest. When portions of these scripts appeared in the *Daily News,* the *Occult Review,* etc., I was infinitely amused at the diversity of criticism which they brought forth. Our first critic, Mr. John Drinkwater, who "was interviewed" by the *Weekly Despatch,* frankly confessed that he was entirely out of touch with the psychic side of the matter, but from the literary standpoint he did not consider the style convincing. He cited various expressions which were "not like" Wilde, notably the cruel manner in which he describes the modern woman as "a wart on the nose of an inebriate" and dismisses the writings of the Sitwells by stating that he does not spend his "precious hours in catching tadpoles." These expressions, Mr. Drinkwater says, are "crude." He cites Wilde's horror of anything unpleasant; the horror with which he was inspired by seeing a man with toothache for instance. He suggests that the real Oscar would be incapable of speaking of anything as painful as a wart. I admit that this case is so surprising that if one is suddenly "interviewed" it is probably very difficult to criticize the writings of a discarnate spirit who is speaking from the "twilight." My reply is that Wilde's feeling for what is ugly and painful altered after his prison experience. He probably had not prepared these discourses, and, even in his best period, it is possible that a crude expression may have escaped him now and then, especially in conversation. For instance, being tapped on the shoulder by an acquaintance, with the remark, "Wilde, you are getting fatter and fatter," his retort was: "Yes, and you are getting ruder and ruder." Would Mr Drinkwater consider that a very subtle reply? Other critics have expressed the opinion that Wilde "has not improved in the process of dying," as he says of his mother, Lady Wilde. His wit is "tarnished" since he "passed over." Do we then expect our shades to "smarten up" in the Beyond? The pathetic part of it is that poor Oscar agrees with these critics; he moans over his mouldy state and cites Hamlet's remarks to his father, when he calls him "old mole," as a case in which the Society for Psychical Research should take an interest. In one rather long article we are accused of raising a "dreary" shade. Now why are we expected to provide a jovial ghost, when we consider poor Oscar Wilde's career? It is suggested that we should let the dead rest, that having been exhumed was bad enough for the poor poet and that I add insult to injury by hauling him back from Hades. The fact, however, is that poor Oscar forced his company on Mr V and myself. He seized the pencil from another communicator and has held on firmly to it ever since. He has insisted on speaking to the world again. It seems to afford him a little relaxation; why should I refuse it? If it relieves him to let fly his bitter shafts of wit once more, I feel, in mere courtesy, I must permit him to relieve his mind.

That first little essay, written probably to convince his mediums, is almost the only case in which Wilde has indulged in what are practically quotations from his works. If he has failed to select his words as happily as he used, we must allow for distinctly trying circumstances. He pushes in on our sitting, I am taken by surprise and I continually interrupt his flow of language with annoying questions. He even complains of finding unsuitable words in his medium's mind; the only simile he can seize on to describe the moon is a "great golden cheese." He can't bear this and writes, "stop, stop, stop, stop, you write like a successful grocer, etc."

The next time we sat Wilde was determined to let fly at something. He dropped his pathetic tone and used the Society for Psychical Research as a means of expressing his indignation at my having questioned his identity. Really this script cannot be described as the work of a dreary ghost. Are there many persons in the literary world to-day who could improve on the discarnate Wilde's wit when he speaks of the "Society of Superannuated Shades"?

Then, quite uninvited, he begins to criticise modern authors. He prefaces his first criticism by another appeal to our pity. There is real pathos in his description of the chances that offered themselves to him from time to time to see the world again. It is a fantastic idea and quite characteristic of its supposed author, I think. He says: "In this way I have dipped into the works of some of your modern novelists." These criticisms are all written, it must be remembered, from the standpoint of thirty-five years ago, for, though Wilde may have tasted modern literature, he can hardly be expected to have moved with the times. This "age of rasp" is a positive pain to the Apostle of Beauty, he is glad to have escaped it. "In your time the main endeavor of the so-called artist is to torture the senses. . . . Pain is the only quality which is essential to any literary work of the present day." . . . It is from that angle he speaks of Wells, Bennett, Philpotts, and Joyce. His other criticisms are leveled at Shaw, Hardy, Meredith, George Moore and Galsworthy. The latter is the only author who escapes lightly. All the others, even those who were practically his contemporaries, come in for a share of pepper from Wilde's caustic tongue. The note of a colossal egotism is prominent in all these scripts, it never varies. When he speaks of his prison life it is positively shameless: "I was a fallen God, a fallen King," etc. He views his brothers in literature with a certain jealousy, I fear. His fall and the bitter and cruel misery of his last years appear to have sent him on to further miseries. His literary career stopped dead three years before he died himself; it was short, and fame has come to him, as to many others, after he passed into twilight. [. . .]

I feel it is quite natural that Wilde should be revolted by a work like "Ulysses." It is entirely out of harmony with his time and ideas. He might easily fail to see what the admirers of Joyce call the "vastness of the book." It is completely ugly; that is enough. His horror of probing into the "inside" of a human being would naturally be aroused by a book which, I believe, practically deals with nothing else.

I am not altogether surprised that Galsworthy appeals to Wilde. There is little real kinship between these two, but it is true that Galsworthy, in a different sense from Wilde, deals with the surface of social life; that his feeling for form is fine and that his sense of selection is often exquisite. Galsworthy, however, uses the surface of society as a medium through which he expresses intense emotions, emotions which sometimes tend to become sentimental. Wilde never rouses our emotions, he certainly cannot be accused of being a sentimental writer, he never gets the full value out of a moving situation, he is too deeply interested in the "human pattern," as he calls it, to worry about such futilities as joys and sorrows. [. . .]

We pass on to Wilde's memories of his sufferings in prison. I rather hesitated to ask him about that time, but to my surprise he seemed eager and willing to talk of it. In reading this script it must be borne in mind that I had not read "De Profundis for over twenty years. Wilde as he was when he left prison was not the Wilde who played with the "surface of society," the "flaneur," as he calls himself. He had learnt the value of humility and love, and was, as he says, a richer man after he had come to realize the sacredness of sorrow. His life, after he left gaol, was more tragic perhaps than while he was there. His present condition seems a continued tragedy. It is painful to feel that after twenty-three years he is still without the beauty and sunlight for which he thirsts. Yet he has the certainty, which few of us have here, that his state is temporary; that he will achieve again all and more than he possessed in his earth life.

In criticizing these writings it must be remembered that between the Wilde of the nineties and the Wilde of 1923, two great gulfs are fixed. The gulf of his imprisonment and the gulf of his death. It cannot reasonably be expected that he is unchanged since he wrote "Intentions" and "The Importance of Being Earnest." In his letter to Robert Ross with instructions regarding the publication of "De Profundis," Wilde says "Of course I need not remind you how fluid a thing thought is with me—with us all—and of what an evanescent substance are our emotions made." Here again we find the idea of "fluid mind," which came through at the sitting at Andre Gide's and again to me several times at the ouija board, before I knew he had used the expression before.

In the automatic writing which followed on the script about his prison life, Wilde begins with a quotation from "De Profundis," "Society sent me to prison," and again he quotes from it when he says, speaking of the bread he was forced to earn, "like Dante, how salt the bread when I found it." This script is completely clear and logical from beginning to end. The astronomical knowledge displayed here is merely used as illustration and does not in any way detract from the characteristic turn of the sentence or the application of ideas, which are more in the style of "De Profundis" than his earlier works.

Let us for a moment try to imagine the present position of Oscar Wilde, allowing it is he who writes these messages. He has suddenly found a means of speaking to the world again after twenty-three years' silence. His mediums are, of course, a matter of indifference to him, he merely wants to make use of any possible instrument. It would be futile to speculate as to how or why he discovered us. The word Lily is written; Wilde seizes the pencil; the emblem of the aesthetic movement gives him his opportunity. "No, the lily is mine, not his," he writes. When I have identified him he quotes from "De Profundis." "Twilight in my cell and twilight in my heart." As he goes on he reminds us of "Intentions" and "De Profundis." In "Intentions" we have "The white feet of the Muses brushed the dew from the anemones in the morning." In our first script, "Her white feet brush the dew from the cowslips in the morning." In "De Profundis" the passage occurs "There is not a single colour hidden away in the chalice of a flower or the curve of a shell to which, by some subtle sympathy with the very soul of things my nature does not answer." In the automatic writing we find, "There was not a blood stripe on a tulip or a curve on a shell or a tone on the sea, but had for me its meaning and its mystery and its appeal to the imagination."

If any of us had spent twenty-three years in a distant country, and, during that time, had neither visited nor written to our own land, we could scarcely be expected to preserve our memories of it intact, nor could our friends expect us to return completely unchanged and as we were in our prime. Oscar says he is more alive than we are, in spite of the fact that he is confined in a dim Hades. I disagree with one of our critics, who says that the first script is the ghost of Oscar's style as well as of his personality. I quite understand the difficulty presented to the lay mind by phenomena professing to come from the dead. To them the dead are dead in every sense. There may be a vague religious faith in the hereafter deep in the sub-conscious mind, but when it comes to accepting an actual personality which does not approach us with any of the orthodox ideas of the Beyond it seems too preposterous and our criticism of evidence is, very naturally, highly prejudiced. Yet, in all the notices of our script, it is admitted that these communications are not of the order which is generally offered us from the other side. No one can deny that this discarnate Wilde has preserved his sense of humour. [. . .]

I should like to make it quite clear that the speed of both the writing and ouija communications was tremendous. I already mentioned that in one instance 700 words were written in about an hour and a quarter. This essay is a long and logical argument. As regards the ouija board messages, it was difficult to keep up with them even in shorthand; the traveller flew from letter to letter with lightning speed at the rate of 60 to 70 words per minute. If we regard the scripts as a case of sub-conscious imitation, it is interesting to note that style and handwriting were sustained through hundreds of pages at this pace. [. . .]

I am sorry that the subjects spoken of are so scattered. In the automatic writing, Wilde chose them himself. At the first two sittings he seemed to exhaust the power in his mediums very rapidly. There was a pause, and when the pencil moved again an entirely different theme was chosen. The later writings have been longer and more continuous. In the ouija work, I suggested subjects, as a rule. I asked a question and it was promptly followed up.

I value the opinions of those who are not conversant with psychic subjects, also those of persons who, like myself, have studied mental mediumship. Both can help us from entirely different standpoints. The literary critics must make allowance for the difficulties in automatic communication and also for the fact that Oscar Wilde has passed on to new conditions. They must not demand exactly the mind they are familiar with. From the psychic point of view these scripts must be of value whether they are considered to arise from the sub-conscious or to be a proof of survival. Their value from the literary point of view is quite another mater. I sincerely hope that no prejudice against the method by which they came will injure their chances of having a fair hearing.

A literary ghost is, I think, a new departure in the psychic world. Messages from the dead are usually very vague as to work and interests on the other side. Oscar Wilde may be occupying his time with "what is little better than picking oakum in gaol," but his keen enjoyment of ideas seems the same as ever. He is certainly less changed by the "process of dying" than any other ghost I have come across so far.

I have endeavored to analyse these writings honestly. I am convinced that they are worthy of investigation. They are certainly so to those who are interested in proof or disproof of survival, and they may be useful also to the faithful: those who have accepted the gospel of annihilation. For them Oscar Wilde's return can be regarded as a fresh proof of the credulity of even intelligent persons. The theosophist will fall in with us, I think, for here we have evidence of the punishment that awaits our astral part. The spiritualist will add a very important addition to what confirms his faith; he can hardly produce a more definite instance of continued personality than what is before us.

I hope that Oscar, in his state of twilight, may be comforted if he realizes that some of us are conscious he still exists. He may give us further evidence that he is still a living mind. If so, I shall publish a sequel to this book. He is still quite willing to talk and write. He has suggested that he is in a position to resume, some of his literary work again; but, knowing as I do the difficulties and uncertainty of automatism, I dare not promise anything definite. [. . .]

Psychic Messages from Oscar Wilde. London: T. Werner Laurie Ltd., 1924. 1–165.

GERALDINE CUMMINS

Concerning the Cleophas Scripts

Before I give a brief account of these automatic writings,[1] I should first like to make my own position quite clear. I am an Irishwoman and, therefore, come of a nation of fanatical enthusiasts for creeds and parties, both religious and

---

1. *The Scripts of Cleophalas*, 2nd ed. London (Rider); 12s. 6d. net.

political. Keenly conscious of this national tendency, when I took up the study of psychical research, I determined I would not espouse any dogma or party that might be connected with it. So I have no propaganda to advance. I am in this matter, as are so many others, groping after a truth that we shall probably never find in this life.

With regard to the Cleophas Scripts, therefore, I can only state the facts, so far as I am able, and leave you to decide as to whether they have been communicated to me by a discarnate being, or whether I have tapped what some call the Great Memory of Nature, or whether these writings are simply the product of my subconscious mind. Owing to my lack of knowledge I am not in a position to discuss the content of the Scripts from the historical point of view. Here I can only quote the opinion of experts.

The Scripts of Cleophas now consist of half-a-million words, and purport to be an historical account based upon chronicles of Early Christian times. They have been made in the presence of numerous witnesses. I have not, at any time, endeavoured to obtain such writings alone.

I may say at once that it was contrary to all my tastes and inclinations to produce narrative dealing with the religious history of the first century. My ignorance is considerable concerning that period. I know neither Greek, Hebrew nor Latin; and my reading is confined to literature of a modern character. But I was led to continue with the writing of these Scripts because their contents were a matter of considerable surprise to me, and also because they so completely differed from any conscious writings of my own.

They contain also a knowledge of the period which I personally could not trace to previous reading or study pursued by me. The greater part of them express, I think, a view of life which is of the first century, not of the twentieth. And there are views in them with which my conscious self is in entire disagreement. But only experts in New Testament exegesis can express an opinion as to their value from the historical point of view. The manuscripts have been, therefore, submitted to Professors who are, as Dr. Lamond has stated in the prefatory note to the second edition, "recognized scholars representing the Church and the Universities." These authorities, after a careful examination, state that the Cleophas Scripts "contain much, which, on consideration of the life and mentality of the intermediary, Miss Cummins, appears quite inexplicable on the supposition of human authorship."

Besides the character of the actual contents of the Scripts, the rapidity of the writing is an important point for students of psychical research to consider. The speed of the writing is at all times considerable 2,042 words written in 1hr. 15mins., 2,600 words in 2hrs., 1,750 in 1hr. 5mins, in comparatively good English. Unless for some particular reason I am roused from the dream or semi-trance state into which I fall, never less than 1,400 or 1,500 words are written at a time. I have written automatically for as long as 2hrs. 10mins. In my case conscious composition is a very laborious procedure, and I find it impossible to accomplish it at all satisfactorily if any person is present in the room at the time. It is an interesting fact, then, that people do not affect me when I write automatically; nor do they seem to influence the matter in the Scripts if they are at a sitting.

I remember one occasion when there were seven witnesses present, some of them learned men, and a noisy thunder-storm raged outside. Before the sitting began I feared I would never be able to put myself in the special mental state necessary. But the Messenger, who purports to communicate the Script, assumed control in a few moments, and wrote for over an hour and a half at a very considerable speed without a single pause. It is a feature of this writing that there are no halts until the final full-stop. The material obtained on the occasion of the thunderstorm and the seven witnesses is almost without alteration incorporated in chapter 30, pp. 103ff., of the published volume.

Amongst those who were present at the production of these writings at different times have been: 3 members of the medical profession, 2 Fellows of the Royal College of Physicians (Ireland), a Doctor of Law, a Doctor of Philosophy, 3 Doctors of Divinity, 5 clergymen, a well-known historical scholar, the editor of a literary monthly, a journalist, a sculptor, a novelist, and representatives of English and American Societies for Psychical Research.

As I have said, I am not out to prove any cause or theory. In some ways, indeed, I should prefer to feel that these writings were my own conscious composition. But, in the interests of psychology and psychical research, I have to admit that the production of these Scripts is quite outside the compass of my conscious creative powers. Day after day, in the presence of witnesses, I have sat for over a month in a country house, far from books, with not even a Bible near me, getting this detailed chronicle with the same abnormal rapidity; the MS. each day being taken away and not read out to me, to avoid the possibility that my subconscious mind might be considered to be building in advance upon it. Yet those who have read the first published installment, will perceive that the narrative maintains an episodic unity. I am, I repeat, not a student of history, nor a scholar. I lead a busy life and have other absorbing work. But experts in these matters have decided that the Cleophas Scripts contain much which "appears quite inexplicable on the supposition of human authorship."

In these days many scientists and psychologists worship the subconscious mind with the same superstitious enthusiasm as the Philistines of old worshipped their "Baal." They attribute amazing powers to this mythical being, who lurks beneath the threshold of our consciousness, *but whom they cannot define.* These would undoubtedly argue that the Cleophas Writings were the production of my sub-liminal self. Let us for a moment, then, examine this theory.

The scholars who have studied these Scripts, have stated, that in many respects, they resemble various early apocryphal writings; that interesting parallels may be drawn between them. They refer particularly to the Apocryphal Acts of the Apostles and especially to "The Clementine Recognitions." I have never read a word of these Apocryphal Acts though I have heard the name previously. I never even heard of the "Clementines" until I saw the title when the completed preface was shown me. I should like to know, therefore, why my subconscious mind should in its writings ape works that have never been conveyed to my intelligence by physical means,—that is to say, through my hearing or through my sight.

But the physiologist, if he is a follower of Professor Richet, would probably reply: "Cryptesthesia explains it all." I understand that cryptesthesia is the name of an alleged mental gift possessed by certain sensitives. This gift enables them to obtain correct information by prying into some stranger's memory, a stranger probably absolutely unknown to the sensitive. If, then, I have the power of cryptesthesia, the Cleophas Scripts may be the composition of an unknown scholar's unconscious mind—a composition my mind copied off from his unconscious memory. His conscious mind could hardly have composed the Cleophas Scripts, because I think he probably in that case would have intimated to me by this time that I had published his composition word for word. Who amongst you, or even amongst historical scholars, has so intimate, so accurate a knowledge of "The Clementine Recognitions," that I could pick your subconscious mind, and produce not a copy of "The Clementines," but a work written in the same manner and style, and moreover draw from the contents of this stranger's subconsciousness at the rate of 1,700 words an hour? The supposition seems absurd.

We have then the theory of telepathy. Telepathy is another magical word much misused by a great many people, who believe it explains every psychic problem. Let us first take the simplest definition of the term. For instance, at this moment you think of a table, and instantly a table is pictured on my brain. Let telepathy be regarded as a term dealing only with the present, with neither the past nor the future. Consider it as your conscious thought of the present moment instantly duplicated in another mind. Then, if I am the victim of telepathy, on the numerous occasions when I place myself in the quiescent state necessary for these Cleophas Writings, there must always be some student, closely studying Early Christian history and apocryphal works, with whose subconscious mind I am in telepathic communication. I find this hard to believe. It would make the episodic continuity of the narrative impossible. Meetings for these writings have been held in the morning, afternoon and evening. There has never been a regular fixed hour for them. Why should any student or students be at the beck and call of my subconscious mind, and obligingly arrange their hours of study to correspond with my hours for writing? No, I fancy mental broadcasting or telepathy does not cover the whole field.

There is a certain type of scientist who, when dealing with psychic problems, will accept no statement of any kind. He will not believe that a single George Washington exists. His creed is that no one can tell the truth about himself. Let us endeavour in a measure to assume the attitude of this cynical scientist. Let us assume that you do not accept my statements and those of Miss Gibbes and others as regards my life, my interests and my lack of knowledge. Let us assume that I talked in Greek and Hebrew when in my cradle, that I am a student versed in gnostic epistles, in pseudepigraphic documents, whatever they may be, in early Pagan and Christian history. Even if I were such a paragon, I still claim that this fairy tale would not wholly account for the normal production of the Cleophas Scripts.

For if I had been versed in the history of that early period I could not, in the presence of witnesses, consciously compose and write day after day, as fast as my hand can shape the letters, long detailed narratives, making a continuous chronicle whose statements have been to a considerable degree checked by scholars. Knowledge in such a case would be a hindrance, not a help. I have been told that most historians and critics of that period disagree. If I had been acquainted with their theories, I should have been faced with the choice of a hundred different roads. I should not have known where to turn. I should never have got started on my journey at all. Save for a few archaisms in the writing and some cutting necessary because of exigencies of space, the actual text is printed in the published volume as it was written. Finally, the editors, when comparing the Scripts with apocryphal writings, state: "In tone, in general atmosphere there is much which cannot be explained simply as reproduction or dependence." I feel, therefore, that not even the cynical scientist can prove that the Scripts of Cleophas are the normal production of my brain.

There remains, therefore, the spiritistic hypothesis, the theory of a Great Memory of Nature and of a race memory to be considered as the possible source of these writings.

Now, if we assume that they are communicated by a discarnate intelligence, we are at once faced with the argument that they would have been written in either Aramaic, Greek or Latin, the languages of that period. But the Messenger claims that the narrative is communicated by means of images or thoughts; a thought is communicated through the vehicle of the words stored in the memory-centers of the writer's brain. You may regard such an explanation as unconvincing. But I think we can find evidence of this method of communication among cases of psychometry and of telepathy reported between living people.

It is noticeable, for instance, in Prof. Gilbert Murray's remarkable experiments in telepathy reported in the S.P.R. Journal for Dec. 1924, that when a correct impression was received, it seemed to come as a picture rather than in words, and was not reported by the percipient in the literal words thought of by the agent. Speaking of telepathic experiments, Prof. Julian Huxley said recently, that they never seemed to get photographic results,—that is to say, a literal transmission like wireless. "What is transmitted is like the picturing of a general idea," as he expressed it. It goes through the mind and is redistilled." The method of communication in telepathy is still a complete mystery. If then there is communication between living and discarnate beings it may be of an analogous nature. The material of the Cleophas Scripts may, to use the words of Prof. Huxley, "go through the mind and be redistilled."

As to the Great Memory hypothesis,—the whole problem of memory is a very difficult one. Men like Sir Arthur Keith and Prof. Huxley write of "the apparent impossibility of separating mind and matter, body and soul." But it has been stated as a physiological fact that every particle of our body changes in seven years. Surely, therefore, if we accept this statement of the physiologists, our memories, if purely material, should also be changed? The boy of 14 would be unable to remember any event that happened to him when he was 5 years old; the young man of 21 would be incapable of recalling an event that occurred when he was 10 years old, that memory-deposit having disappeared through the physiological changes of the whole body. But we know that this is not the case, that some of our clearest memories are those of our childhood of 20 and 25 years back or more.

It would seem, therefore, that man's memory functions otherwise than physically. Its pictures are probably imprinted on some ethereal medium, and are accessible to the thinker by an effort of whose character he is as much unconscious as he is unconscious of the functioning which regulates the action of the muscles of the heart. The events of his past life are photographed on some invisible, and perhaps imperishable, substance. By making an effort of thought he draws the memory required within the reach of some interior sense which reflects its impressions on the physical brain. If this be true of each individual's memory, it would seem to postulate a Great Memory fed by all mankind, as the sea is fed by innumerable rivers that flow into it.

There are thousands of cases of correct psychometry on record. I myself, through automatic writing, have obtained correct histories from jewellery and from stones hundreds of years old. I think, then, we may almost accept as proved that memory survives the dissolution of the body and has some kind of permanence. A reference was recently given me in automatic writing to this vast Record of Nature which is, I think, of interest.

"Memory may be likened to the sea. It is all about you, and as illusive as the waters of the ocean. When we are alive we come like children to it with our small buckets, and fill them with the salt fluid. But how little we carry away up the sands; how easily and swiftly we spill it out upon the ground! Yet, behind us, is that vast area of water, booming endlessly upon the shore. The sound of memory is now to me like the sound of the tide as when, in the olden days, I listened to it through the summer evenings."

I have dwelt at some length on this problem of memory because the Messenger, who purports to communicate the Scripts of Cleophas, claims that he, in company with seven scribes, has drawn the narrative from many chronicles that were imaged on the Tree of Memory by men who lived in the first century. If for the moment we accept this statement, various conclusions may be drawn from it and certain criticisms answered in connection with the Cleophas Scripts.

A lady, who is a novelist and a Spiritualist, complained to me that these writings did not contain a great deal of ethical teaching, and that she would have supposed that by this time Cleophas and his scribes would have attained to a high degree of spiritual wisdom. But the contents of the Scripts furnish us with no reason for believing that these discarnate beings have not progressed spiritually since they passed from the earth. These writings are not claimed to be their present memories or their present thoughts. They are said to be the contents of chronicles written by men during their lifetime on earth at the end of the first and in the second century. There is given, in short, the interpretation of an era, as seen through the eyes of men who felt and thought deeply in that period, and thus printed their impressions of it on the ether-memory.

Now, if, for the time being, we accept the Spiritualist hypothesis, and regard these Scripts as communicated by those whose physical bodies died hundreds of years ago, what was their purpose? Supposing the desire was to prove their own survival, they certainly would not convince us by communicating knowledge they had gained during the many years passed by them in the unseen. This would not be evidence of personal survival. But it would certainly be evidential and striking if they conveyed to us their vision of life when they lived it on earth. And this appears to be the design behind the Scripts of Cleophas, provided we accept them as a communication from unseen intelligences.

This brings me to another criticism of the Scripts. It was raised by a scholar, who said to me recently: "What I want is the exact truth concerning the happenings in those early Christian times. I believe neither in miracles nor magic; and these pages are full of accounts of miraculous phenomena. They are not, therefore, of historical value."

This gentleman craved for history of the blue-book order written from the point of view of the 20th century. He could not see that, if the Scripts were of that type, they would be entirely unevidential from the psychical research point of view, and that critics might then justly claim them to be the product of my subconscious mind. The editors of the Cleophas Writings say: "The remarkable part played by magic in the following pages need not be regarded as an argument against their probable authenticity. It is much more to be taken as an argument in their favor, for the natural tendency of any fabricator would have been the representation of the early years of the Church as a 'golden age,' free from any taint of superstition or chicanery."

But my friend the higher critic would probably reiterate: These writings are of no historical value from the point of view of the higher criticism. And I would answer: It depends on the way you like your history.

Do you want it to be a little blue-book of facts and dates arranged in precise chronological order? Or do you want to enter into the atmosphere of those early days? And even if the facts given are sometimes questionable, do you want to realize society as it was viewed in those times by the fanatical man in the street? Do you want to have some conception of his superstitious horror or exaltation at marvels that would seem to us no marvels, at the alleged witchcraft that would seem to us to be picturesquely exaggerated and to have a natural explanation? If you require the latter form of history, if you wish to enter into the mental conditions of the man of that period, then it would seem that according to the editors, who also are scholars, the Cleophas Scripts fulfill those requirements. For they write that the contents of this book "might be taken as a true reflection of the state of society in which the early Church had to make its way." And later, when discussing the difficult problem of inspiration, they say they are "convinced of the importance such documents as this possess, not so much for exhibiting what Christianity was in itself when pure and undefiled, as for revealing what Christianity was taken to be by its primitive exponents."

With all due respect to my friend the higher critic, then, we have to consider the psychology of the historian as well as the history presented to us.

When studying Early Christian writings we would do well to put the test of the child-mind to them, and make our own reservations accordingly. In the contents of the Cleophas Scripts there is clearly evidence of a child-mind. They show, as the editors state, "a naïve enjoyment in thaumaturgic phenomena." And in this curious feature lies one of their principal claims to authenticity, at least in my opinion. I come of a medical clan. My father and grandfather were physicians. I have always been in the habit of viewing with a skeptical eye all reports of alleged miracles of healing. Yet this is the type of miracle most frequently described in the Cleophas Scripts. If I had tried consciously to compose a history of Early Christian times, I would certainly not have inserted in it accounts of miraculous healing. Also the style and exposition of the narrative differ very considerably from my normal style and my method of setting out a tale. It might, of course, be argued that Cleophas is a secondary personality, and that I have inherited knowledge from pious ancestors of mine upon which this secondary personality can work. None of my ancestors were clergymen, but some of them were very much interested in the Bible. However, according to physiologists, we can inherit only tendencies, not actual knowledge or learning, from our forebears. Perhaps, mercifully, the sins of the fathers cannot descend to the children in this respect. So race-memory or hereditary influences do not, I feel, explain these writings.

Truth may be viewed from many angles and yet never be correctly perceived. The critical scientist is the high priest of this generation and calls the tune that makes the rhythm for our thoughts. To his mind man is but a collection of whirling atoms, that come together for a short period, then part company, disintegrate and come together in another form world without end. He believes that the life of man is no more than a candle flame which is finished when blown out. Yet the materialistic scientist, who is held by so many in our rationalistic age to speak as with the voice of the inspired prophets, is probably just as far from the truth in his assertions about life and its mystery as the primitive Christian, who believed the earth was flat and the skies were a pretty blue roof. We must try to realize in our quest for truth that the altar-cloth of to-day is usually the doormat of to-morrow. We must, therefore, be very cautious in our assertions as to what is true and what is false. When we are criticizing historical material, we have always to consider the outlook of the man who wields the pen. We must decide whether we are interested in the vision of one who writes of his own time and, therefore, is often blinded by the dust of battle, blinded by his own passionate feelings; or whether we prefer the writing of a cold, detached historian of a later age who is blinded neither by passion nor by the fury of battle. He is probably more accurate as regards facts; but he often fails to convey the whole vision of the period, the atmosphere, the spirit of the time about which be writes, because be has not been in the conflict nor felt the prejudices, the wild emotions, it inspires.

In their preface the editors remark that there is, at times, to be found in the Scripts, "a distrust of pagan learning, an undercurrent of emotionalism, the occasional emergence of a cruder and more vindictive spirit. (They go on to say) the careful reader may be left, in the end, with a definite impression of a background of superstition, misinformed zeal and ignorance which may well, the editors believe, have been precisely that in which the Apostles and their successors had to labour. The early converts, Church officials and teachers who figure in these pages certainly exhibit no excess of enlightenment in their grasp of Christianity; they are often zealous with that zeal which is not too clearly to be distinguished from fanatical bigotry."

Let us examine this statement. I have told you I have a horror of fanaticism. And those other characteristics in the writings (such as a distrust of pagan learning) mentioned by the editors would certainly not be an expression of my own modern views, but might well express the attitude of mind of one who had actively participated in the life of that period, who had been blinded by the dust of battle, wearied by the struggle for a cause. It is this very human, and at times erring, outlook that adds to the Scripts' claim to authenticity, to their being the outpouring not of my mind, but of minds far distant in space and time, the outpouring of those who had lived and felt in some of the great moments of Early Christianity.

Let me now quote from an article by a skeptical man of science, the biologist, Prof. Julian Huxley. He writes: "I can think of our personalities being lost, blended, taken up into some general reservoir of mind and spirit . . . wandering through the universe until either they were destroyed or came back to actuality of consciousness by making contact with something which could work as a receiving apparatus for mind."

In this statement Prof. Huxley is obviously groping after the idea of a Great Nature Memory which is wholly impersonal though it contains myriads of personalities.

It may be true that there is this reservoir of memory. And I may have presented some evidence which points to my brain having been what Prof. Huxley describes as "a receiving apparatus," that has recorded the memories of certain ancient chroniclers. But, even if we accept the theory of a Great Memory, I find it hard to believe that, by entering a state of meditation, I am able to tap this memory directly. A third party would seem essential, an unseen being, who would act as intermediary, interpreting the code of images in this memory, then bearing the charge, as it is called, to my mind, wherein it is redistilled and set down upon the page through the mechanism of my brain.

On the other hand, the Scripts of Cleophas may be the product of my subconscious mind. But, if this is so, it possesses a knowledge, which had not, previous to the writing, so far as I am aware, passed through my consciousness; also it possesses a capacity for abnormally rapid composition quite incompatible with my slow mentality. Furthermore, my subconscious mind is a perverse creature; for, if it has composed the Cleophas Scripts, it has written about a period in which I am not interested. I want very much to write modern novels and plays dealing with the present or the future; and it has bullied me into writing about the distant past. I admit, as I have said before, I have been a willing tool, firstly because of the psychological interest of this experiment, and secondly because of the interest of the narrative.

A remark of R. L. Stevenson is of value in connection with this experiment. He constantly speaks of the Brownies and the work they do for him. He says, "they can tell the dreamer a story piece by piece like a serial and keep him all the time in ignorance of where they aim." That is exactly my position. And so I continue with this writing, partly because I always want to know what happens next, and I haven't the least idea beforehand. The production of the Cleophas Scripts is to me an adventure of the mind. And I am as an adventurer or explorer in an unknown land, who never knows what will be the character of the new landscape presented to his sight on the morrow.

I firmly believe that the age of external adventure is passing, and that the age of mental adventure is coming into its own at last. I do not agree with Mr. Arnold Bennett, who, when speculating about a future life, wrote: "Human ignorance of the future is more than bliss; it is an ordinance of the divine wisdom." People invariably invoke the name of the deity when they want to make a reactionary protest against the search after knowledge. No man can set bounds to the march of knowledge. And no man should say, in the Name of God, thus far shalt thou go and no farther.

We are but at the beginning of the study of ourselves. And I believe that a time is coming when, through psychical research and through adventures of the mind, the children of the future will salve lost knowledge and will lift perhaps a corner of the curtain of mystery that envelopes life.

In conclusion, I should like to make one more statement about the Scripts. A certain critic complained bitterly because the published volume contained no account of Christ's walk to Emmaus after his resurrection. This critic seemed to question the possible authenticity of these writings, because no allusion had been made to that vitally important period in religious history,—the days that followed the crucifixion. But a detailed narrative of that time has been given in the later Scripts. The published volume contains only a fragment of these writings. The editors have now examined the chronicle so far as it has been written, and have expressed the opinion that "the interest increases as the record proceeds."

Moreover, at least 150,000 unpublished words in this long narrative have no apparent connection with events related in the New Testament and deal with alleged happenings in Rome, Alexandria, Cyprus and other places.

Read before the Quest Society, November 22, 1928. *The Quest: A Quarterly Review* 20.4 (July 1929): 3–19.

RADCLYFFE HALL AND UNA LADY TROUBRIDGE

From "On a Series of Sittings with Mrs. Osborne Leonard"

Introduction

When extracts from this paper were read at the meetings of the Society in January and March 1918, we mentioned the possibility of the publication, at a later date, of a fuller report on the series of sittings held by us with Mrs. Osborne Leonard between August, 1916, and August, 1917.

As is well known, Mrs. Leonard is a professional medium, and she has always received her customary fee from us. We are well aware that many members of the Society look askance upon professional mediums, and that the attitude of the Society as a whole, has always been largely sceptical of evidence received through paid mediumship. Mrs. Leonard is more or less at the disposal of any member of the public who can prove him or herself a *bona fide* inquirer. Therefore, as we propose to base this paper on evidence received through a professional medium, we feel that it is incumbent upon us to preface that evidence by a short *resumé* of the circumstances connected with our earliest investigations of Mrs. Leonard's phenomena.

I first heard of Mrs. Leonard through a lady who had written to Mr. J. Arthur Hill for advice. As far as I can remember this was either at the end of July or at the beginning of August, 1916. This lady requested me to test Mrs. Leonard on my own behalf and hers, for although I was not an experienced investigator, she considered that I should be an impartial judge of evidence received. [. . .] I addressed no conversation to Mrs. Leonard prior to my sitting, beyond thanking her for the appointment, and she went quietly into trance. Her control, Feda, began by describing a young soldier; I did not recognise him, and said so, asking if there were no other communicators wishing to speak. It seemed that there were, for I very soon got the description of a great friend of mine who had died some months previously. Later on we shall give an extract from that first sitting.

The description was brief, but unmistakeable; except my friend, whom it fitted exactly, I had lost no one to whom it corresponded in the very least. After Mrs. Leonard had been in trance for what I think must have been a little over half an hour, Feda complained that my friend was an inexperienced communicator, and would probably get on much better if I had a table-sitting. Feda therefore withdrew and the medium awoke suddenly. I told Mrs. Leonard what had happened and we had a table-sitting. Mrs. Leonard had both her hands on the table, but for the best part of the time only one of my hands rested on the table, as I was taking notes with the other. My friend immediately gave her full name through the table, though I should have preferred her not to do so. She also gave the name of a place to which we had been together. [. . .] We fully realise that the influence of the subliminal and supraliminal minds must to a certain extent be discounted, especially in table-sittings, when at least one of the sitters is cognisant of the facts given; and although what was given at this sitting appears to eliminate conscious fraud, nothing was obtained through the table which could not be accounted for by unconscious muscular guidance by those who incline to that hypothesis. It will remain for the reader to decide at the end of our paper, whether another hypothesis, namely, that of telepathy between the living, is an adequate explanation of the subsequent trance-sittings with which we propose to deal.

[. . .] I did not again go to Mrs. Leonard until October 2nd, 1916, when I visited her together with Lady Troubridge. We went as anonymous sitters recommended by Sir Oliver Lodge. I asked Mrs. Leonard whether she remembered me; she said that she thought she did, but could not be certain as she saw so many people. I took the sitting, Lady Troubridge acting as recorder. The control Feda recognised me immediately, not by name, of course, but as having sat before. After this sitting of October 2nd, 1916, we arranged for a series of regular sittings. For the first five months of our weekly sittings with this medium—and we sat sometimes oftener than once a week—neither Lady Troubridge nor I ever visited her alone, one or other of us always acting as recorder. The recorder bore specially in mind the importance of taking down everything said by the sitter, and equally careful notes were made of any conversations held with the medium in a normal state, before and after the sittings, which conversations were invariably brief.

There is another statement which we think it is well to make. During those early sittings descriptions were received of The White Cottage, at Malvern Wells, a house much loved by my deceased friend and myself, together with a description of characteristic features of the neighbourhood and references to the neighbours.

There appeared to be only two possible explanations of the descriptions in question: either the knowledge displayed by Mrs. Leonard, when in trance, was obtained in some supernormal manner; or else pretty extensive enquiries had been made in the neighbourhood of Malvern Wells. We had absolutely no reason to doubt Mrs. Leonard's integrity, but it must be borne in mind that my friend's name had been received through the table, and that we had in those days very little first-hand knowledge of Mrs. Leonard's phenomena. It has always appeared to us that those who are engaged upon such a momentous investigation as that of phenomena purporting to be occasioned by discarnate human beings, should leave no stone unturned to make each step of the ground as sure as possible before proceeding. I therefore felt it incumbent upon me to employ a good detective agency, and from this agency I received a report on November 14th, 1916.

As the result of their investigations at Malvern Wells and in the surrounding district, it was ascertained that no enquiries regarding myself or my deceased friend had been made from any likely sources of information since her death. No such enquiries would have been made prior to her death by a fraudulent medium, as during her lifetime neither she, nor I, nor Lady Troubridge had ever visited a medium, or taken any interest in Psychical Research. [. . .]

We have recently informed Mrs. Leonard of the fact that detectives were employed by us in connection with her phenomena, and she fully realised that the reports furnished by the detectives represented a valuable testimonial to the genuineness of her powers.

With regard to the extracts from the sittings with which we propose to deal, the purporting communicator has on every occasion except one been my friend of whom a description was given at the first sitting. On the one occasion when she was not the principal communicator, I was given to understand at a later sitting that she had been instrumental in helping Feda to get messages through. My friend will be alluded to in the sittings as A. V. B., I shall appear as M. R. H., and Lady Troubridge as U. V. T. Feda is in the habit of addressing me as "Mrs. Twonnie," her own version of the name by which I am often called, and Lady Troubridge as "Mrs. Una." During the sittings, Feda has gradually acquired the habit of calling A. V. B. "Ladye," a nickname which belonged to her in life, and was given spontaneously through Feda at an early sitting. Of Feda we need say very little, as she is already known to the public through Sir Oliver Lodge's book *Raymond.*

Throughout the sittings we have in our records, for the sake of brevity and clarity, treated the medium, during her trance, as being non-existent, except in those instances when Feda alludes to her as "my medium," or "this one," etc. We have assumed that Feda takes her place, or at times A. V. B., and have attributed to these controls all words spoken by, or movements made by Mrs. Leonard. For instance, it will be noticed that in the records, we say: "Feda touches her forehead," etc., instead of: "Feda touches the medium's forehead," or: "Mrs. Leonard touches her forehead." In our records we have not closely followed Feda's broken English, it would have taken too long to think out suitable spelling for her idiosyncrasies. Her knowledge of the English alphabet is shaky, and although she will at times recognise and mention letters quite accurately, at other times she appears to be at a loss, and is reduced to attempting to draw with her finger the letters that are apparently shown her, or to such descriptions as: "It's a curly letter like a snake, or "It's like a cross without a top." She will generally speak of O as a little circle, and she will also describe any letter that has a stroke above or below the line, as, for instance, small Y or B, as "a long letter," while others, such as small U or E, are "little letters." Her English varies; it is almost correct when she purports to be repeating a message verbatim, and at all times is quite intelligible in spite of its eccentricities.

As throughout the following Paper we propose to deal exclusively with the purporting attempt of discarnate intelligences to communicate *evidential* matter, we have, in some of the longer extracts from sittings, occasionally omitted remarks interlarded by Feda, concerning conditions in the "spirit world," etc. In order, however, to do full justice to the sustained and consecutively coherent nature of the sittings, it is only fair to state that these remarks of Feda's, although non-evidential, were seldom irrelevant, being usually in the nature of parallels suggested by the topic in hand.

It may perhaps be as well to remark here that the records of our sittings have always been copied by hand, or typed, on the afternoon of the day upon which the sitting took place. Of course, since the original notes were made, some few facts have come to light, and occasionally our memory has afforded a further verification of certain incidents; this has led to some trifling modifications of, or additions to, our original annotations appended to the records. Occasionally, also, mature consideration, consequent upon a deeper study of the sittings, has thrown a new light on some of Feda's statements. [. . .]

Our thanks are due to Feda for the full and accurate records which we have been able to obtain. She has always shown the greatest solicitude on this point, repeating slowly and carefully, more than once, anything intricate that appeared to her to be of evidential value; unlike most controls she can be stopped with impunity should the recorder be in fear of getting behind-hand, and yet cleverly take up the thread the moment she is told that the recorder is ready. We have both remarked that she often appears to have a curious knowledge of the exact stage in the notes that the recorder has reached, and has been known to rebuke the communicator, saying: "Don't speak so quickly; Mrs. Twonnie" (or "Mrs. Una," as the case may be) hasn't got that down yet," and at other times, when the sitter has enquired whether the recorder is ready, Feda will answer glibly and correctly for the recorder: "Oh, yes, she's got that down all right," or the contrary. The above has been our experience; possibly we have been particularly fortunate, owing perhaps to the fact that a very real mutual liking has grown up between ourselves and Feda. This, we have been given to understand, is not invariably the case.

Chapter 1: Description by Feda of Communicator's Personal Appearance as Evidence of Identity

The first evidence with which we shall deal is that relating to personal appearance and conditions as a proof of identity, when given through a control who purports to be in touch with the communicating spirit; and in this connection we shall give a few extracts from early sittings, beginning with my first sitting of August 16th, 1916, at which I was my own recorder.

We will begin the extract after Feda's description of the unknown soldier aforementioned.

> M. R. H. I do not know him, is there no one else?
>
> F. Yes, there's a lady of about sixty years old, perhaps.
>
> M. R. H. Please describe her, she interests me more. (Feda did not take the hint, however, but continued to describe the soldier, who appeared to be very insistent.)
>
> M. R. H. Please leave him; as I do not know him, I am afraid I cannot help, though I would do anything I could. Will you describe the lady of about sixty?
>
> F. The lady is of medium height, has rather a good figure but is inclined to be too fat, Feda thinks; she has a straight, nose, a well shaped face, but the face is inclined to lose its outline a little. The eyebrows are slightly arched, her hair is not done fashionably.
>
> M. R. H. Is it worn in the neck?
>
> F. No, it's done on the crown of her head. She has passed over quite recently. She had not been well for some time prior to passing, she was sometimes conscious of this, but put it behind her. Feda doesn't mean to say that she worried over it much, or that she suffered much, she didn't. Feda thinks she didn't know how ill she really was. She went about doing things just as usual, she gives Feda the impression of internal weakness. You were much with her in her earth life, you gave her vitality, you kept her up with your vitality . . . The lady's eyes look to Feda to be dark, perhaps grey.

Regarding this description: A. V. B. was fifty-seven, when she died, had had a fine figure, but latterly became too stout; she had a straight nose, which was very slightly tip-tilted, she wore her hair dressed high on her head, and, at the time of this sitting, she had only been dead two months three weeks and a day. For some time prior to her death she had not been strong, partly owing to the effects of a bad motor accident. She must often have put her ailments behind her, however, and we do not think for a moment that she had any idea of how ill she was; I can only say that I had none. She went about doing things as usual up to the very day of her last illness, which came on without the slightest warning. She did suffer from internal weakness, though this had nothing to do with her death. A. V. B. and I were the closest friends for eight years, and lived together for a great part of that time. She would sometimes say to me that she believed that my vitality kept her up and helped her; we used to discuss this together. A. V. B.'s eyes were of a dark blue, some people might have called them of a dark bluey-grey colour. [. . .]

On October 2nd, 1916, I took a sitting with Mrs. Leonard, Lady Troubridge acting as recorder. After a few words of greeting the sitting opened by Feda recognising the communicator as the lady whom she had seen at my first sitting. I asked Feda to describe her again, and she did so accurately and much more fully than on the first occasion. [. . .]

> M. R. H. Ask her if she suffered much when she died.
> F. She says not as much as one would think. Something had come up to her head, and before she passed over worked up to the brain, and formed a small clot on some part of the brain that stopped her feeling. It doesn't seem to worry her, but she wants to know if that is what happened.
> M. R. H. Yes, that is what happened.
> F. It pressed, and prevented her feeling.
> M. R. H. Was she frightened?
> F. She says: "When I woke up it felt strange, I had an idea I was still dreaming, I had rather strange dreams, I don't know if I *told* anyone. Often I was half awake and half asleep."
> M. R. H. Quite right; did she know me at all?
> F. She says it's hard to explain, but yes, she did know you, but was not sure if you were part of the dream, or real. She says: "I could *feel* you. You seemed to be mentally impressing me with all your might with"—(*sotto voce*: Old Lady, old Lady, oh, Lady?) She says you said: "Oh! Ladye, oh! Ladye it's all right." "And now and again holding me physically as if wanting to hold me up." Did she ever choke in her throat? because she's just put her arm around you for a minute, and Feda felt her physical body. [. . .]

As we have said already, A. V. B. died of an apoplectic seizure. There was cerebral haemorrhage which formed a clot on the brain, and this led to progressive paralysis. She lay for eleven days prior to her death with only occasional flashes of semi-consciousness. A. V. B. lost all power of coherent speech almost immediately after her seizure; we find Feda, however, saying that A. V. B. wondered whether she had told anyone of her strange dreams. She could not, of course, have actually told anyone anything, though one cannot be certain as to how far she was conscious of this loss of speech; occasionally she used to make inarticulate sounds, as though trying to speak.

As we have already said, A. V. B.'s nickname was "Ladye"; during her illness, when speaking to her, I most certainly said, "Oh, Ladye," on several occasions; I never called A. V. B. "old lady" in my life, and this indecision on Feda's part as to whether the words used were "Oh, Ladye" or "old lady" is rather enlightening, as showing, it appears to us, the bias occasionally given to certain messages owing to preconceived ideas on the part of the control. "Ladye" being an unusual nickname, Feda cannot quite believe, apparently, that she has heard correctly. "Old Lady" is a more familiar form of address to Feda; she therefore decides to try both. [. . .]

We next come to a Leonard sitting of October 9th, 1916; I took the sitting and Lady Troubridge was the recorder. Speaking of A. V. B., Feda says:

> F. She looks much better than when Feda saw her last.
> M. P. H. Can you tell me the colour of her hair?
> F. Brown like this one's, Feda thinks. (Here Feda touches the medium's hair.)
>   But she does it high up, not in her neck. [. . .]

Now regarding the above extract, A. V. B.'s hair was brown, but considerably darker in colour than the medium's. We have repeatedly noticed that one of Feda's weakest points is describing the colour of people's hair. [. . .]

Nothing further of importance with regard to A. V. B.'s *appearance* occurred till eight months later, when on June 6th, 1917, a much more detailed description of her was given by Feda. By this date, as we shall see later, A. V. B. had been trying her hand at a personal control of the medium, and during a personal control which had occurred a short time prior to this sitting of June 6th, 1917, A. V. B. complained that Feda always described her as being too old looking. I did not thereupon begin to expatiate upon A. V. B.'s appearance when at her best; I merely remarked that she had always been a young-looking woman. As a matter of fact Feda's earlier descriptions, although not flattering, and inclined to pick out the weak points and ignore the good, were on the whole good descriptions of A. V. B. as she was for a little time before her death. The description which we will now quote is a very remarkable one of A. V. B. as she was when she was younger. Here is the extract from the sitting of June 6th, 1917. Lady Troubridge took the sitting and I recorded.

> F. Mrs. Una, she's got a nice complexion, very nice, it isn't a bit wrinkled, it's very smooth. Before she passed on her cheeks fell in a little bit, and do you know her mouth had got drawn down a little in the left corner, like this? (Feda draws down one side of her mouth a little) She's showing that; it was straight at the other corner, but the left side is drawn down, and in a bit, but not very much.
>
> M. R. H. Yes, that was so, but I'm not sure that you've got the right side.
>
> F. Well, Feda *thinks* she shows the left side. It gives her face rather a drawn look. She used to have a very pretty chin and neck, but the muscles had got a little flabby and let it fall a bit, so that when you'd see her side-face, it didn't look quite so stucked out and pretty as it used to.
>
> M. R. H. She's always making mistakes between the right and left.
>
> F. Yes, she explained that to you once. You see it's like a negative to Feda, what she shows. You know, Mrs. Una, how in a photo, if you've been wearing something on your right side, it comes out as though it were your left.
>
> U. V. T. Well, but the fact is perfectly right and it's a very good evidential proof.
>
> F. It took away that pretty, chirpy look from her face. (Feda begins pouting out her lips.) Mrs. Una, when she had her under lip coming out like this (Feda slightly pulls out her under-lip with finger and thumb), it made her look cheeky-looking. It stuck out a little firmly; under the lip it was tucked in, in a little dip, and then it came out in a pretty rounded chin; Feda can see all this because she's like that now, you know, but when she first came here she was not so pretty as she is now. You don't think she'll mind Feda saying that she has rather a cheeky mouth and chin do you?
>
> U. V. T. No, of course not, it's a very good description.
>
> F. She says she doesn't know, perhaps she does look cheeky now. Her face has got pretty, soft curves, but Feda feels that under that softness there would be a little sharp determinedness; Feda feels it would be like looking awful softly at people when they were off their guard, and that then she would suddenly come out and put her foot down and get her own way. They would be so surprised, but while their mouths were still open, she would have done it. She's got a lot of determination, but there's no fuss, no noise, she didn't say much, but she managed it somehow. Feda doesn't think that her nose and eyes were so cheeky as her mouth and chin. [. . .]

We can only add, regarding the whole of the description, including that of her manner of walking, that it is lifelike of A. V. B. as she was some years ago, and that the points of particular interest which we have mentioned would have been just the points which A. V. B. would have endeavoured to get described, in order that there should be no mistake as to her identity.

Chapter 2

SECTION II. MEMORY OF CHARACTERISTICS OF M. R. H.

We now come to another point upon which A. V. B. appears to have retained her memory. During the sitting of October 2nd, 1916, which I took, Lady Troubridge acting as recorder, the following occurred:

M. R. H. Does she know I am going away?
F. Yes, she seems anxious about it. It isn't what you're going to do there.
M. R. H. Tell her Una will look after me.
F. She says, yes, she is very glad if she will; that is, if you will let her; she says she has got a very difficult task.

The sitting of October 13th, 1916, which was taken by Lady Troubridge and recorded by me, terminated with the following:

U. V. T. Tell Ladye she's got to help me to take care of Twonnie.
F. She says, yes, she wants that, she puts her in your charge.
U. V. T. Tell her I will do my best.
F. She says she's afraid you hardly appreciate the magnitude of your task. It will be perfectly awful sometimes, terrible!

Now this would appear to show a memory of one of my tiresome characteristics. With reference to Lady Troubridge's looking after me, it might have been gathered that I liked being looked after, since I myself suggested that it should be so; whereas it would seem that A. V. B remembers that when I am not well I do *not* like being fussed over, and that I become stubborn and irritable.

SECTION VII. MEMORY OF WORDS PECULIAR TO A. V. B.

We will now deal with two examples of what would appear to be a rather more subtle retention of memory than those hitherto given, since it is the retention of memory regarding the meaning or sense of certain words invented by A. V. B. herself. We must first of all record some words of mine spoken during the sitting of November 15th, 1916, which sitting we have stated in another connection, was a bad one, probably owing to the fact that I pressed questions. One of my questions on that occasion was as follows: "Ask her does she remember a funny word she invented with Adela for people they didn't like?" Feda replied, that A. V. B. would try to remember it, would put it in a mental note-book, but that it made it extremely difficult when I asked things point blank. We only mention this because it must be borne carefully in mind that I distinctly said that the word which A. V. B. had invented, was applicable to people she did *not* like.

On January 17th, 1917, a sitting which I took, Lady Troubridge recording, I suddenly put the following question:

"Does she remember the word, 'Poon?'; perhaps she will laugh, but I'd like to know whether she remembers what that word meant?"

> F. Yes, she is laughing, she says that word meant a state. It was a word used to express a state or condition.
>
> M. R. H. It was a word she used.
>
> F. Feda can't understand, but she says it was a word that she used to you. She says she sometimes thought of you in connection with it. Feda does hope it's not a nasty word, because she says she doesn't mean that she just thinks of it because she heard you say it, she means, that she would use it in connection with thinking of you. "Poon, Poon," she calls *you* that. Poon isn't a name! But she calls *you* that in her mind now, she thinks of *you* as "Poon," she *likes* to think of you as that. Feda's got just to say what she says, and she says that she hopes you think of *her* as that too.
>
> M. R. H. Of course I think of her as that. (To A. V. B.) There was a word that was the opposite word to "Poon." Do you remember? You and I had two words.
>
> F. Yes, she says it was the antithesis, but that she can't remember the word itself. No, Feda mustn't say that she can't remember, it is that she can't get it through.
>
> M. R. H. Oh! Ask her to try and get the first letter through.
>
> F. Oh dear! Feda can't get it. But it is only a short word. (Here Feda begins drawing violently in the air and distinctly forms an "S.") It's a curly letter like a snake, look, Feda will do it on your hand.
>
> M. R. H. Yes, that's right, it's an "S."
>
> F. It isn't a long word, it's a short one, and she did manage to give it quick to Feda once, but Feda couldn't get it, she'll give it one day though.

Between this sitting of January 17th, 1917, and that of May 2nd, 1917, with which we are about to deal, an attempt was made during an A. V. B. Control, to pronounce this word beginning with an "S." The word was not articulated, however, and A. V. B. did not get beyond making the opening sibilant consonant, and when I asked A. V. B. what she was doing, she said she was trying to get the word which was the antithesis of "Poon." I remarked that I did not intend to give her the word, as I wished it kept as a test; to which A. V. B. cordially agreed.

On May 2nd, 1917, Lady Troubridge took the sitting and I acted as recorder. A. V. B. had been conversing with us through Feda regarding a certain person, some of whose ways A.V. B. rather disapproved of, when suddenly, Feda broke out as follows:

> F. She says that's senseless and reasonless too. (*Sotto voce:* It's *what,* Ladye? What are you trying to say S—ss—Sss—S—ss.) What *is* the word, Ladye? It's Spor—Spor—Spor! She's trying to get a word through that Feda can't make out, Feda doesn't believe it's a proper word at all; it's a very funny word, but it must mean something, because she *is* trying so hard to get it through, it means . . . it means . . . Oh! Feda doesn't know. It seems to be some sort of more expressive word for senseless: (*Sotto Voce:* Spor . . . Spor . . . Spor . . . Spor . . .) Well, it's Spor, anyhow.
>
> U. V. T. What's the letter after "Spor" do you think, Feda?
>
> F. It's a long letter. After the "R" comes a long letter.
>
> U.V.T. When you say a long letter, Feda, do you mean long above the line, or long below the line?
>
> F. It seems to Feda to be long at the bottom. (Feda has for some moments been making perpendicular strokes in the air.) It isn't an ordinary word at all; it's a funny word that Feda has never heard before. Oh! Mrs. Una, Feda sees that it isn't long under the line, it's long *above* the line; well, there's that letter, then comes a small letter (*sotto voce:* Sporti . . . Sporbi). This little letter sounds something like "I"; (Feda pronounces the I as in the word "fish"). And after this small letter there comes a curved letter, and then it seems to Feda there's another long letter. (Here Feda whispers quite inarticulate things.)
>
> U. V. T. Well, Feda, perhaps it will be easier if you try to draw the first long letter on my hand. (Feda begins drawing vigorously.)
>
> F. It's S . . . P . . . O, Mrs. Una, then a little letter, and then a letter like this; (she draws a "K" on U. V. T.'s hand). It's a down stroke like this, with a little bit like this sticking on to it; Sporki . . . Sporkif?
>
> U. V. T. Well, Feda, try to draw the letter which you said was curved, on my hand; the letter that you said came after the long one.
>
> F. That letter goes like this, Mrs. Una (here Feda draws an "S" on U. V. T.'s hand). And then there's another letter like this (here Feda draws an "H").
>
> U. V. T. Is that the last letter of the word, Feda, or are there others?
>
> F. Well, Feda can't see any more, (suddenly and very loud) SPORKISH! SPORK-ISH! But that isn't a word at all! Ladye says: "Yes, it is," and that it applies to people who rake things up. "Not Poon," she says, she says it's the antithesis to "Poon."

M. R. H. At last you've got it.

F. "Sporkish," she says it in such a funny way, Mrs. Twonnie, she says that you and she used to call people that sometimes, you used to say: "So-and-so is sporkish," Feda knows that it isn't a proper English word though.

Now with regard to these two coined words, we must deal first with the word "Poon." As will be remembered, I asked on January 17th, 1917, whether A. V. B. could remember what "Poon" meant. There had been a suggestion given by me on November 15th, 1916, as has been stated, that there did exist a word which had been invented by A. V. B. and a certain "Adela," for people they did *not* like. We may, therefore, justifiably conclude, that had Mrs. Leonard only normal knowledge to work on, she would have retained a memory of my words spoken on November 15th, 1916, and have made a mental note to the effect that there existed some curious word which had been used by A. V. B., the meaning of which word was *uncomplimentary*. As a matter of fact, the word which I tried to get on November 15th, 1916, was an *un*compli-mentary word, and there is no apparent reason why, when I myself mentioned the word "Poon" on January 17th, 1917, Mrs. Leonard, had her knowledge been normal, should not have jumped to the conclusion that this strange word "Poon," was the *un*complimentary word which I had hoped to get on November 15th, 1916. But, in reply to my question of January 17th, 1917, we find Feda speaking of this word "Poon" as a state or condition; telling us that A. V. B. says it was a word she used to *me,* that she sometimes thought of me in connection with it, that she calls me "Poon," that she thinks of me as "Poon," that she *likes* to think of me as that, and that she hopes I will think of *her* as that too.

Now, the word "Poon" was A. V. B.'s own invention. It was meant to express all the pleasant, indefinable qualities in people whom she liked. When A. V. B. said that a person was a "Poon," or that they were "Poony," she meant it as a summing up of all those attributes which most appealed to her. I do not lay any claim to the attributes with which her affection endowed me, but in spite of that she did apply this term to me.

After getting on January 17th, 1917, a satisfactory definition of the word "Poon," I again return to my original idea of November 15th, 1916, and try to obtain from the communicator its antithesis. I do not succeed in getting further on this occasion than the statement that it is a short word beginning with "S."

On May 2nd, 1917, however, as will have been seen, we obtained the word "Sporkish "; the application of the word was perfectly correct, and its use just where it occurred in the conversation was entirely characteristic of A. V. B.

"Spork" and "Sporkish" were words also invented by A. V. B. Their meaning embraced all tiresome and unpleasant people and their characteristics. These words were semi-humorously applied by A. V. B. to all people and things that bored her, irritated her, or otherwise incurred her disapproval. It is interesting to note that the word "Sporkish" was finally obtained at the sitting of May 2nd, 1917, as a comment upon circumstances that were precisely such as would have evoked it from A. V. B. during her earth life. Interest is added by the fact, that whereas I gave on January 17th, 1917, the word "Poon" as a noun, and asked for its opposite, by which it might be reasonably understood that its opposite was also a noun; and whereas I implied on November 15th, 1916, also, that the word I wanted was a noun, and whereas we were definitely endeavouring to obtain a noun, to wit "Spork," we obtained on May 2nd, 1917, most unexpectedly, the equally familiar and characteristic adjective "Sporkish."

SECTION VIII. MEMORY OF M. R. H.'S METHOD OF COMPOSING.

We next come to what would appear to be a retention of memory regarding my methods of writing poetry; these were remarked upon by A. V. B. through Feda on June 27th, 1917, at a sitting taken by me, Lady Troubridge acting as recorder. At a previous sitting on December 6th, 1916, at which I was the sitter and Lady Troubridge recorded, I had repeated the first verse of one of my own poems; I naturally did not say that it was my own, merely asking A. V. B. through Feda whether she remembered it. It appeared that she did so, since Feda gave me to understand, after having said that the poem was recognised, that the communicator wished to add something to what I had said, which was correct, as there was one other verse to that particular poem. After this Feda said the following words: "Mrs. Twonnie, she says, 'She makes it herself,'" In reply to this I asked Feda to make her words a little less ambiguous; I said "I don't quite understand, Feda; did she say, 'I make it myself,' or did she say, She makes it herself'?" To which Feda replied: "No, she didn't say, 'I make it myself,' her words were, 'She makes it herself'"; by which I understood that A. V. B, had been trying to give Feda to understand that I wrote poetry.

I am a very minor poet, still, several books of my verses have been published and a number of my lyrics set to music. Supposing therefore that my anonymity had not been preserved, as we think it had, Mrs. Leonard in the normal state might easily have come across some of my poems and recognised in me their author; this possibility should be taken into account. On June 27th, 1917, however, there occurred a further reference to my work. Feda began it by giving a word here and there, such as "flights," "canopy," "vast," "pace," etc., which words she stated were, according to A. V. B., contained in some of my poems. There appeared to be an effort to recall, by this method, certain poems to my mind. No doubt these words do appear in my poems, I should think they probably did in most poems; at all events the references were not sufficiently clear to be of any interest. What is of interest, however, is the following:

> F. She says that you used to get a first and second line like in a flash, and then you used to get succeeding lines, perhaps two, and then you used to go back and have to alter the first a bit, sometimes. She says it seemed as though the first and second came in a flash, and you wouldn't be perfectly certain what was to follow. Although the first and the second lines would suggest a theme, you wouldn't know what was to follow them at all. You would hang on to the first line, it would sing in your brain as though making music. She says it's funny, with your things more than anyone else's, the first line is always the key-note to the rest.
>
> M. R. H. How long ago is she speaking of?
>
> F. Some time ago, not only just before she passed on.
>
> M. R. H. I only meant to ask whether it was before or after she passed on.
>
> F. Oh! before.

As A. V. B. lived with me for years, she, more than anyone else perhaps, was aware of my methods of work. It is perfectly correct to say that my first and second lines come to me in a flash. It is also absolutely correct to say that having got hold of two lines that please me, I have very often not the slightest idea what I am going to follow them up with. Lady Troubridge, in going over my papers the other day, came upon innumerable scraps of paper, as well as scrawls in exercise books, containing two first lines, or sometimes only one, of a poem which I had apparently never followed up. Feda says that A. V. B. says that I would hang on to the first line; that it would "sing in my brain as though making music." Now it is usually impossible for me to conceive a line of original poetry without singing it mentally, so to speak; in other words, my lines always suggest to me a complementary tune. It is, and always has been my habit to write my poems at the piano, composing words and music simultaneously. No one was as familiar with this habit as A. V. B., as she was also with the fact that, having got my two first lines, I would go to the piano, playing and at the same time singing them over and over again, in what must have been a most tiresome manner, while waiting for further inspiration. Since, needless to say, I am not in the habit of doing this in public, it is difficult to see how knowledge of my methods of work can have reached the medium normally.

Chapter IV. Personal Touches and the A. V. B. Control [. . .]

The first personal control attempted by A. V. B. took place on January 19th, 1917. I was taking the sitting alone, and my attention was first called to the fact that something unusual was about to occur by Feda, who fidgeted uncomfortably, exclaiming at the same time "What are you trying to do, Ladye, what *are* you trying to do?" After these words, no more was heard of Feda, the medium remaining perfectly still, and apparently, deeply entranced, for what I should say was the space of a minute or two. When she began to speak again she did so in an almost inaudible whisper, her first words being: "Where are you? Pull me forward." There was nothing evidential in this first A. V. B. control, as speech appeared very difficult and movement almost impossible. A certain amount of emotion was shown, but, on the whole, admirable self-control was maintained on the part of the purporting communicator, which was again very characteristic of A. V. B. who was extremely self-controlled during her life-time. Since January 19th, 1917, there have been repeated efforts at an A. V. B. control, which has been very slowly growing in power and evidential value. [. . .]

During the early A. V. B. controls, A. V. B. complained that she could not make the medium laugh. One day, however, she suddenly succeeded in doing so, and what ensued was extraordinarily reminiscent of A. V. B.'s own laugh, and this characteristic laugh has, since then, often occurred. On several occasions the timbre of Mrs. Leonard's voice has changed, and has become very like A. V. B's voice; startlingly so, once or twice. A. V. B. herself has remarked upon this, which appears only to be possible during the earlier part of the personal controls. On one occasion A. V. B. said discontentedly: "Oh! now the power is going, can't you hear my voice getting Mrs. Leonard again?" which statement was correct. [. . .]

Another interesting feature of the A. V. B. control is the fact that the purporting communicator has occasionally appeared to be dissatisfied with the pronunciation of certain words. For instance, A. V. B. has struggled with the word "often." Mrs. Leonard, in the normal state, pronounces the T in this word, she says "off-ten." A. V. B. always pronounced it "orfen." Constantly during an A. V. B. control this word is pronounced in Mrs. Leonard's fashion; on one occasion, however, A. V. B. appeared to realise what was happening, and a little rehearsal ensued. She only once succeeded in saying "orfen," repeating "off-ten," and then "orferten, orferten," several times in rather a bewildered manner. When asked what she was doing, she replied vaguely that she "was just trying it."

On August 5th, 1917, however, during an A.V.B. control, this word "often" was pronounced in A. V. B.'s own fashion; after having said "orfen," twice, with perfect ease and naturalness, the purporting communicator suddenly slipped back into Mrs. Leonard's pronunciation, without apparently noticing the difference. [. . .]

It may be as well to state how the notes of these A. V. B. controls have been made. It has not been possible to write them down during the actual control, as it appeared to be absolutely necessary that the sitter, and, when present, the recorder as well, should concentrate their entire attention on the medium, in order to observe closely all gestures; and still more in order to be able to catch every word spoken, because the voice during an A. V. B. control is sometimes very weak and low. The A. V. B. controls always occur at the end of the sitting; our method has therefore been to record the notes while the medium is coming out of trance, getting down in that interval all points of evidential interest, and omitting everything of a merely personal and non-evidential nature. This has not proved difficult up to the present, as the A. V. B. controls have generally been but of short duration, and there have seldom occurred more than one or two evidential points during each control.

Nothing of any kind has ever been given away by Lady Troubridge or myself, who have regarded the personal control as a possible fruitful source of further evidence.

Proceedings of the Society for Psychical Research. Part LXXVIII. (December 1919): 339–485.

PART V

Arts and Performances

18

Gender and Collaboration in Modern Drama

INTRODUCED AND SELECTED BY KATHERINE E. KELLY

THE FEMALE PLAYWRIGHTS presented in this chapter occupied a unique position to break with a past that had held the actress and the female playwright in suspicion through the end of the nineteenth century. By the advent of modernism, a qualified opportunity had opened for women, both actresses and playwrights, to enter public culture as fascinating but still ambivalent icons of the new.[1] Well acquainted with the norms of theatrical display and consumption, these British, U.S., and European playwrights and performers—all of them actual or would-be actresses—brought to the stage a heightened awareness of the relation between public performance and gendered expectations. Their plays and performances, in consequence, address gender in a variety of registers, some of them coded. In Christopher St. John's *The First Actress* (1911), for example, male characters explicitly debate the merits of gendered acting while satisfying homosocial desire. St. John follows this debate with a masque-fantasy in which celebrated actresses display a woman-centered alliance across historical periods. St. John and Cicely Hamilton's co-written suffrage drama, *How the Vote Was Won* (1913), comically plays with the suffrage conversion trope, while hinting at Hamilton's serious critique of middle-class marriage. Sophie Treadwell's *Machinal* exposes its protagonist's horror through a subconscious appeal to female audience members. And a (male) reviewer's accounts of Emmy Hennings's Dada performances (1912) evoke a double reference to female sexuality as both prodigious and diseased.

Some contemporary spectators may have been attuned to the highly inflected representations of gender in these plays, particularly as they interacted with other socially charged issues—social class, women's suffrage, war, and same-sex desire. The circulation of shared political and aesthetic commitments among shifting and overlapping modernist communities created for these play-wrights an urgent sense of purpose and a sympathetic reception, at least by select members of their coteries. The styles of the plays included here—wheth-er realist or avant-garde—tell us less about how they functioned culturally than do the playwrights' links to performance groups such as the Pioneer Players, the Actresses' Franchise League, and the Provincetown Players. Woman-centered and explicitly lesbian[2] alliances among a group of artists linked to the suffrage movement, for example, can explain St. John's choice of plot and structure in *The First Actress* as well as or better than the influence of Henrik Ibsen's "femi-nist" plays on the London stage some twenty years earlier.

Suffrage Sociability—The Women Writers' Suffrage League and the Actresses' Franchise League:

> With one's fellow suffragettes the tie, only sometimes an intimate one, was nevertheless unbreakable. You have a different feeling all your life about the woman with whom you evaded the police sleuth and went forth to break windows in Whitehall or to be mobbed in Parliament Square or ejected from a Cabinet Minister's meeting. (Sharp 136)

Many authors who joined the suffrage movement organized, wrote, paint-ed, and published collaboratively.[3] Cicely Hamilton characterized this spirit of joint effort in cofounding, with Bessie Hatton, one of the earliest suffrage organizations, the Women Writers' Suffrage League, in June of 1908.[4] Its ob-jective, "to obtain the vote for women on the same terms as it is or may be granted to men," signaled its alliance with the decentralized, non-militant wing of the movement.[5] Its methods were "those proper to writers—the use of the pen" (*Suffrage Annual for 1913* 137). Hamilton supported herself and her sister Evelyn first as a touring actress and later as a writer. She joined the suf-frage cause as an outgrowth of her own experience as a single working wom-an, intent on changing the way women became educated, made life choices, and earned a living wage.[6] Launching her activism with her first nonfiction book, *Marriage As a Trade* (1909), Hamilton exposed the enforced reliance of middle-class women upon marriage as their sole means of monetary sup-port—a reliance she characterized as legalized prostitution. But her political involvement soon extended to suffrage and the birth control movement, among other woman-centered issues.

Hamilton met Christopher St. John and Edy Craig sometime in 1908 as the three of them were drawn, like dozens of other female and some male artists, to create propaganda on behalf of the suffrage cause. Devoting their efforts to similarly feminist campaigns, the three eventually became good friends, with Hamilton using her visits to the Craig-St.John-Atwood home at Smallhythe in Kent to escape the pressures of work (Whitelaw 78–79). When they met, Hamilton had written a suffrage conversion story—a simple reversal plot in which an "anti" becomes converted to the cause—to appear as a pamphlet with cartoon illustrations (Tickner 243). St. John recognized the dramatic potential in the story and adapted it for the stage (Whitelaw 83). Directed by Edy Craig, and performed by the Actresses' Franchise League in a matinee at the Royalty Theatre on April 13, 1909 (see fig. 18.1), *How the Vote Was Won* proved a comic hit, drawing a positive notice even from the (anti) *Pall Mall Gazette,* which praised it as a "witty" example of the "theatre of ideas" (qtd. in Whitelaw 84). The premise of the play—a common "anti" claim that women should be content to remain at home under male support—is pushed to its logical extreme. By the play's close, middle-class clerk Horace Cole has joined other men, shouting desperately, "Down with the Government!" "Rule Britannia!" "Votes for Women!" (Hamilton 36). Using elements typical of the suffrage conversion trope, this one act nevertheless outshines others with its broad comic sweep (all are mocked, including suffragists) and its brilliant comic dialogue. Performed by some of the better-known actresses of the day, the play signals the alignment of theatrical feminists with suffrage culture.

Formed in 1908, soon after the Women Writers' Suffrage League, the Actresses' Franchise League followed its precedent in identifying itself as "neutral" on the question of militancy. It quickly became one of the most glamorous and visible of the suffrage leagues (see fig. 18.2). But this visibility could also prove dangerous: it intensified the AFL's propaganda potential but it could also threaten its members' prospects for securing parts on the commercial stage. This helps to explain why the issue of militancy was so explosive among its members, leading to a fracture by 1911. To make matters worse, theatrical trade newspapers like *The Era* opposed suffrage, arguing—to actresses' disbelief—that the "favorable" working conditions they enjoyed proved the franchise unnecessary to securing professional equality with men (*The Era*).

The crowning achievement of the Actresses' Franchise League was "The Woman's Theatre," announced on May 23, 1913, as a "new feminist theatre" by and for women artists to be organized and funded as a subscription-based cooperative. In spite of its mission, it opened (controversially) with two plays

Fig. 18.1. Postcard of Cicely Hamilton and Christopher St. John's *How the Vote Was Won*. Royalty Theatre, April 1909. Produced by the Actresses' Franchise League. Reproduced by permission of the Women's Library (formerly the Fawcett Library), London.

Fig. 18.2. Members of the Actresses' Franchise League at the Women's Coronation Procession, June 17, 1911. Reproduced by permission of the Museum of London.

by male writers Eugène Brieux and Bjornstjern Björnson, both with solid ties to the Ibsen movement and therefore carrying with them Ibsen supporters, George Bernard Shaw and William Archer, who could help ensure the theater's critical and financial success. The inaugural season did succeed, but a second season, initially delayed by the war, was eventually displaced by the newly formed "Woman's Theatre Camps Entertainments" (See Kelly, "Actresses' Franchise League").

The Pioneer Players (1911–20)

Fresh from her experiences with a politically divided Actresses' Franchise League, Edy Craig founded the Pioneer Players in 1911 on the model of J. T. Grein's Independent Theatre Society, as a London-based, subscription-financed company. Pointedly anti-commercial and begun with very little capital, the Players claimed two objectives: (a) "To produce plays dealing with all kinds of movements of interest at the moment"; and (b) "To assist social, political, and other Societies by providing them with plays as a means of raising funds" (First Annual Report, 1911–12, 3). The Players welcomed theater as a propaganda medium for connecting members of various political and social communities. Suffrage societies were one such community but not, as the Players were at pains to clarify, the only activists whom they supported. "All we ask of a play," writes Craig in the first annual report, "is that it shall be interesting" (7–8). In this respect, they differed from the Actresses' Franchise League, which directed its propaganda efforts nearly exclusively to the suffrage cause.

Unorthodox and idiosyncratic, Craig chafed under the expectations of the suffrage societies, preferring to organize her own activist theater along broad inclusionary lines. Craig met Christopher St. John (Christabel Marshall) in 1895 and they remained together until Craig's death in 1947. The painter, Tony (Clare) Atwood, joined their household in 1916, forming a *mènage á trois,* consisting of a writer and historian (St. John), a designer (Craig), and a painter, who supported and enabled one another's work.

The First Actress was the third in a triple bill of one acts performed for the inaugural season of the Pioneer Players at the Kingsway Theatre on May 8, 1911, and published by the Utopia Press. As a historical play/fantasy, the play typified the revisionist impulse in suffrage discourse, which tended to rewrite the past as a record of women's inevitable march towards winning the vote and sharing political power. St. John sets her play in the London of 1661, at the first performance of a woman—Margaret Hughes playing Desdemona—on the British stage.[7] Used by her aristocratic lover as bait in his feud with Kynaston, the favorite boy actress of the day, Hughes believes her debut performance has failed to prove women's stage worthiness. Exhausted and disappointed, she falls asleep and dreams a hopeful vision in which a series of actresses from the "future"—from Nell Gwynne to Madame Vestris—appear before her, each vowing to remain on the stage to teach the "unmannered dogs . . . to doubt a woman's intellect—a woman's grit." (19). Staged at a high point in the women's suffrage campaign, the play featured several prominent suffragists, including Auriol Lee as Madame Vestris (see fig. 18.3), and Lena Ashwell as "An Actress of To-Day," who concludes with a triumphant speech, "Brave Hughes—forgotten pioneer—your comrades offer you a crown!" (21). St. John's play aligns Hughes with contemporary suffragists campaigning for equal opportunity with men. But more tellingly, the play points to the different manner in which women and men support other members of their sex. In a triangulation of desire, Hughes finds herself positioned between the boy actress, Kynaston, and her lover, Sir Charles Sedley, who is, however, so absorbed with defeating Kynaston that their rivalry outweighs the affection between master and mistress (much as the love/hate between Othello and Iago in the play-within-the-play exceeds the attraction between Othello and Desdemona). In exposing the homosocial desire of Sedley and Kynaston, and in following this exposure with the actresses' alternative display of solidarity, St. John implicitly argues for the superior strength of female friendship as a force that will eventually over-power institutionally supported male friendships barring actresses from the stage.

Sophie Treadwell's Machinal *(perf. 1928, pub. 1949)*

Sophie Treadwell wrote *Machinal* as a deliberate attempt to connect modern gender experiments to the stage, in this case, the New York commercial stage. *Machinal* formalizes gender difference in material terms, aligning women with organic sexuality and men with mechanical surveillance in the context of what Cicely Hamilton called "marriage as a trade." Like St. John and Hamilton before her, Treadwell muscled her way into the male professions of journalism and literature by learning to inhabit her writing with various traveling poses, crossing conventions of high and popular culture, documentary and fiction, gender critique and stylized technique. And like Hamilton, she first approached theater as a would-be actress, serving as an assistant to the internationally famous Polish actress, Helena Modjeska, through whose friends she placed her early scripts with New York theater managers (Dickey 7). Her alliances with women were political as well as professional. During 1914, Treadwell joined the Lucy Stone League, marching 150 miles to deliver a petition for women's suffrage to the New York legislature (Dickey 9).

Fig. 18.3. Decima Moore as Mme. Abington and Auriol Lee as Mme. Vestris in *The First Actress* by Christopher St. John. Kingsway Theatre, London 1911. Reproduced by permission of the Victoria & Albert (V&A) Picture Library.

Living by her pen, along with all of the writers featured in this section, Treadwell appears to have thought carefully about the reception of her play. *Machinal* arrived in a New York where modern womanliness—the "manly woman"—had become the subject of both intellectual and popular writing. One year following the premiere of *Machinal*, psychoanalyst Joan Riviere published "Womanliness as a Masquerade" (included in chapter 11), explaining in Freudian terms the oscillation between "male" and "female" behavior in the "manly-woman" as an unconscious but constructed performance in which this new modern woman first desires to possess her father's power (penis) and then flirts with him to compensate/apologize for her desire. Whether or not Treadwell followed Freud, we do know that she hoped to appeal to the female spectator's subconscious in the play. The notes accompanying the first typescript include a parenthesis she deleted before publishing the play: "The hope is . . . to create a stage production . . . that will have 'style,' and at the same time, . . . by the excitement of its sounds—(and perhaps by the quickening of still secret places in the consciousness of the audience, especially of women)—to create a genuine box office attraction."[8] Treadwell's reference to the "still secret places" resembles not only Riviere's unconscious from which masquerade arises but also Dadaist and surrealist attempts to bypass (in this case, the female) spectator's conscious mind during performance. Treadwell based the play's fable on the recent sensational trial of Ruth Snyder and her lover Judd Gray, who successfully plotted to kill Snyder's husband. When Treadwell's Helen swings between childish helplessness and oppositional resistance, she behaves like the modern manly-woman in the throes of abjection. An experienced journalist who borrowed actual lines from the Snyder testimony in writing her play (Dickey 146), Treadwell did not mimic the historical Ruth Snyder; instead, she fashioned Helen as a type of Young Woman trapped by class and gender in an unwanted marriage bearing an unwanted child only to discover—too late—the possibility of achieving joy and sexual pleasure with another man. In choosing to depict her as a conflicted murderer, Treadwell frames her as a victim of history—caught between a nineteenth-century desire to please "the father" and a modern desire to seize the father's privilege of sexual pleasure. Also caught between her memory of the child's utter dependency upon the father and the prospect of her literal annihilation by the symbolic world of the father, Helen is situated by Treadwell in Julia Kristeva's condition of abjection.[9] A photo from the 1990 production (fig. 18.4) shows the prosecuting attorney—the onstage representation of the father's law—physically bearing down on Helen. Helen proceeds through the drama in a state of bewildered abstraction, not simply as an expressionist style statement, but as a gesture of emotional paralysis that has rendered language moot. The close of the drama attempts to place the female spectator close to Helen's dilemma, as we observe her recoiling from her mother and dreading her daughter's future. The Royal National Theatre's 1993 production placed the electrocution onstage, capturing for some spectators what Kristeva has referred to as the "jouissance" of the abject, identified by one reviewer as "the tragic ecstasy of despair," and by another as the "strangely exhilarating" emotion accompanying Helen's

Fig. 18.4. New York Shakespeare Festival production of Sophie Treadwell's *Machinal,* September 24, 1990. Ralph Marrero (Prosecuting Attorney), *top;* Jodie Markell (Young Woman), *bottom.* Reproduced by permission of photographer George E. Joseph.

death (Dickey 186, 189). This abjection annoyed some spectators but "exhilarated" and horrified others.[10]

Frau Dada: Emmy Hennings and Sophie Taeuber in Zurich Dada (ca. 1912)

A similar pose of desensitized automatism can be seen in the photograph of Emmy Hennings (1885–1948), posing with one of her Dada puppets (see fig. 18.5).[11] Gazing in the direction of the camera but with downcast eyes and an expressionless face, Hennings holds her demonic-looking doll as if it were an extension of her right arm. Her puppets have been described as "floating with functionless arms and legs" with futile and captive gestures, "capable only of displaying their emptiness" (Hubert 522). Hennings was the first Dadaist to use dolls and puppets, perhaps as decorative props in the Cabaret Voltaire, which she helped found, but certainly as symbols of the Dadaists' desire to evacuate the ego from artistic production (Rugh 18).

Hennings's strategic evocation of abjection in the figure of these limp puppets works visually, as it was intended to work psychologically in *Machinal's* Helen, to provoke the spectators by appealing directly to their subconscious through the animated operation of an inanimate medium. Hailed by one reporter as "the star" in a cabaret where stardom was repudiated, Hennings was a dancer, writer, and reciter of her own songs and those of her husband, Hugo Ball. She expressed Dada's "undercurrent of despair and outrage at the inhumanity of the age" (Rugh 14). Unafraid of projecting the sentiment fueling Dada's outrageousness, she opened an avenue of affect between Dada's creators and its audiences. The centrality of Hennings's presence in the Cabaret suggests that her subsequent erasure from Dada histories was both deliberate and systematic.

Accounts of Dada's generally aggressive misogyny, cataloged in Sawelson-Gorse's introduction to *Women in Dada* and "confessed" by former Dadaist Richard Huelsenbeck,[12] have been complicated by other accounts of collaboration—especially between married couples—as the defining ethic of the Cabaret Voltaire. The Dada movement in Zurich, writes Thomas Rugh, "represented a depersonalization of art, the breaking down of hierarchical designations . . . in favor of collaboration" (9). Renée Riese Hubert describes the Zurich Dada couples—including Hennings/Ball and Taeuber/Arp—as "dedicated to collaboration, grant[ing] each other support and respect" (517). Their collaboration, however, tended towards the conventional in its assignment of embodiment (singing, performing, reciting) to women and composition (typically) to men. As Hubert has noted, "Many of [Hennings's] poems owed their appeal if not

Fig. 18.5. Emmy Hennings with Dada puppet. Zurich 1916. Reproduced courtesy of the Robert Walser Archive, Zurich.

their fame to her spirited interpretations" (519). Similarly, Hugo Ball's new genre of poems, "poems without words" or "sound poems," emerged intertextually with his wife Sophie Taeuber's costumed performances.

Read mimetically, the text of Hennings's puppet sketch, "The Perhaps Last Flight," traces a disturbing pattern of heterosexual eroticism, in which male desire is perceived by the female as (excitingly) murderous and in which female surrender signals a willing victimization, "For you I live—for you I die," and so on. But even when read figuratively, it narrates a drama of attempted intimacy in which the surrender of the female to the male amounts to her self being "observed" and, in consequence, obliterated, by the male. Heterosexual intimacy leads not to some kind of union but to the devouring of the female by the male. Also troubling is Ferdinand Hardekopf's ostensibly flattering commentary on Hennings, which reads like a virtual anthology of Dada-surrealist misogyny, calling repeated attention to Hennings's body, hair, and clothing as admirably unsentimental ("divorced from human feeling"), and to her sexual appetite as prodigious, but without commercial taint: "There's nothing wrong with eroticism, but prostitution always implies syphilis."[13]

Sophie Taeuber worked as an arts and crafts teacher in a Swiss school of design and occasionally participated in the Galerie Dada as a dancer. She typically performed solo improvisations, usually accompanied by beating drums and the choral readings of poems. Dance, song, and recitation were simultaneous, forming intertextual, mixed-media events. In her dances, Taeuber not only collaborated with her husband, Hugo Ball, who designed some of her costumes, but also borrowed elements from other artists—Marcel Janco's masks as a nonwestern alienating device; language spoken to disrupt rather than connect participants and spectators; a playful tone and movement; and textiles and designs in her sculptured costumes (Hubert 530–31). Indirectly influenced by the dance teachings of Rudolf von Laban, Taeuber's dancing was admired by Tristan Tzara in a note inserted into the journal *Dada:* "delirious strangeness in the spider of the hand vibrating quickly ascending towards the paroxysm of a mocking capriciously beautiful madness" (qtd. in Hubert 531).

Like Hennings, she was active in Dada primarily as a performer and maker of Dada puppets and heads. "Puppet-making and dancing," writes Hubert, "represented primarily the women's share in the Dada world," although Hans Arp matched his wife's talents as an embroiderer and tapestry weaver (527, 530). Taeuber frequently modeled and danced inside of abstract costumes made by her husband, Hans Arp (see fig. 18.6) on the occasion of the opening of the Galerie Dada in Zurich, 1916. From her early teen years, writes Hubert, "Taeuber favored outlandish disguises and costumes" (530). Her 1916 "cubistic" costume/sculpture, shown in the photograph, belies the attraction to primitivism typical

Fig. 18.6. Sophie Taeuber posing in an abstract dance costume designed by her husband, Hans Arp, on the occasion of the opening of the Galerie Dada in Zurich, 1916.

of the early cubists and delights in translating the organic body (linked to the bourgeois feminine) into a series of abstract (i.e., correctively masculine?) shapes. Taeuber's implicit intention resembles Hennings's; that is, she deliberately flaunted conventional feminine poses in favor of masquerading an artificial masculinity, thereby ensuring that the value of her performance would remain circumscribed by the very aesthetic borrowed to evacuate the feminine.

And yet, women Dada performers also collaborated. On some occasions, they appeared together. In claiming an active part in the "genesis of Dadaism," Mary Wigman recalls "my friend Sophie Taeuber [. . .] and I sewed ourselves so tightly into our extravagant costumes one day that, for the whole night, we could not get out of them." Wigman then lists the performers of the Café Voltaire as her "daily guests," a list that includes Emmy Hennings (qtd. in Sorell 141). After Taeuber's accidental death, and twenty-five years after her Dada performances, Emmy Hennings wrote a tribute to her friend, in which, writes Renée Hubert, "Hennings displayed a deep understanding of Taeuber's dance, so different from her own" (533). The puppets and cardboard costumes made and worn by these female avant-gardists (including Hannah Hoch) may not have been considered by them or by other cabaret artists to be "art works" in the same sense that paintings or sculptures were considered "art" (Rugh), but then for the Dadaists, that was the point—to substitute for the artistic item a collaborative event that displaced the artwork and the artist by a series of compromising deferrals. Gender played a part in the design of these deferrals. Identified by her gender as organic-corruptible-bourgeois, the female avant-gardist earned aesthetic status by evacuating her body for a series of cardboard facets and by giving birth to inanimate puppets in lieu of organic children.

The Provincetown Players: Edna St. Vincent Millay's
Aria da Capo (1920)

Across the Atlantic, young postwar artists were flocking to Greenwich Village and to the theater as the testing ground for modernist innovation. Known primarily for her poetry, Edna St. Vincent Millay was nevertheless drawn in the 1920s to join a stage community, where she hoped to earn a place as an actress.[14] The stage was provided by the Provincetown Players (1915–29), co-founded by Jig Cook and his playwright wife, Susan Glaspell, and recently moved to Greenwich Village from Provincetown. Millay's play helped define what has been called the second, or middle phase, of the Players, when the symbolist verse play competed with the realistic prose drama in the Players' repertoire. In the 1919–20 season, with Cook and Glaspell on sabbatical from the theater, poetic plays took over the repertoire under a short-lived splinter group called "The Other Players," which Millay and her sisters supported. Plays by Djuna Barnes, Alfred Kreymborg, Wallace Stevens, and (especially) Millay, made the season a success, which was not, however, repeated (Ozieblo 104–8; Sarlós 88). Millay's desire to perform had drawn her to the Players who, under the influence of Floyd Dell's socialism and Jig Cook's visions of a new American Renaissance, shared with The Women's Theatre the practice of pooling income from writing (much of it provided by Glaspell's pen) and permitting playwrights to direct their own plays. But crucially for Millay, the Players provided roles for her sisters Norma and Kathleen, and her mother, Cora, who together formed the core of her small but fiercely woman-centered family, for which she was now chief breadwinner. The Millay sisters kept their mother in their lives, creating what Millay biographer Nancy Milford called, "a theater piece, a family romance. . . . one of the best women's stories there is in America" (Milford 177). The Provincetown Players gave Millay a second community within which to locate her female family tribe.

Aria da Capo, her third play to be produced by the Players, and Millay's personal favorite, appeared first in December of 1919, and, following its success, again in April of 1920 and June of 1921. While space limits preclude offering the text of Millay's play here, it is worth considering as an American avant-garde example of indirect but powerfully political dramaturgy. Millay titled her piece after the musical form in which the first line or couplet of a light song is repeated at its close. Refashioning the Harlequinade tradition, in which two of the stock characters of the commedia dell'arte, Harlequin and Pantalon, compete for the affection of a third (Columbine), Millay opens the play with self-parodying urbane nonsense, striking a precise tone of postwar exhaustion: "Pierrot, a macaroon! I cannot live without a macaroon!" to which Pierrot responds, "My only love. You are *so* intense! . . . / Is it Tuesday, Columbine?—I'll kiss you if it's Tuesday" (5). But when these lines repeat at the play's close, they are spoken across a table covering the corpses of two pastoral shepherds who have, in a travesty of pastoral tranquility, murdered one another for greed. The First World War cast a long shadow across Millay's ironic one act, which was quickly dubbed an antiwar play.[15] Even while celebrating the success of her avant-garde play, Millay was developing a distaste for "stylized writing," and becoming aware that her path was diverging from the mainstream of U.S. modernists,[16] including some of the poetic "Other Players." Millay, writes Jo Ellen Green Kaiser, "increasingly turned to the public and to local politics to enact immediate change" (39), endangering her reputation as a "hard" modernist of the masculine Pound/Eliot school.

Conclusion

When viewed as a group, Taeuber's and Arp's dances, sculpture/costumes, and puppets; Treadwell's expressionist *Machinal;* Millay's pacifist *Aria da Capo;* and St. John's and Hamilton's propaganda one-acts, reveal the outlines of a woman-centered modern drama—both avant-garde and historical—that emerged through forms of communal creation as an alternative to the commercial theater. As scholars and performers renew their understandings of the modern, they may well find that collaboration in modern theater and drama, opened to view through newly permeable disciplinary borders, will both complicate and enrich attempts to understand the circulation of sexuality, politics, and aesthetics during the modern period.[17]

Notes

I would like to acknowledge the help offered by the following friends and colleagues, who pointed the way to sources, translations, photographs, and other items (with apologies to any whose names I have mistakenly omitted): Katharine Cockin, Jerry Dickey, Diane Freedman, J. Lawrence Mitchell and the Texas A&M University Department of English, Uwe Moeller, Robert Shandley, Bonnie Travers, and Tim Snipes.

1. Davis's *Actresses as Working Women* charts the problematic position of the late Victorian/Edwardian actress.

2. While the term "lesbian" was not yet in the general lexicon (Radclyffe Hall's "lesbian" novel, *The Well of Loneliness,* would be prosecuted for libel in 1928), St. John was, according to Katharine Cockin, forthright about her same-sex preference and its link to her concern for the well-being of women as a class. She nevertheless used restraint in representing same-sex love in her coded "lesbian" novel, *Hungerheart,* published anonymously in 1915 (Cockin, *Women* 65–66).

3. To consider the Pioneer Players and the Actresses' Franchise League in terms of sociability is to refuse to associate the public commercial theater with "the best" in a hierarchy of aesthetic value and to expand the notion of artistic significance to include an awareness of the particular audience for whom the significance is salient. For a discussion of sociability as a model for theater historiography, see Davis and Donkin, and Kelly, *Alan's Wife.*

4. Hamilton led what has been called by her biographer, Lis Whitelaw, "a woman-centered life," complete with a strong circle of female friends, especially St. John and Craig, some of them openly lesbian, and most of them actively involved in feminist causes of various kinds. Like St. John and Tony Atwood, Hamilton often chose to dress in tailored, masculine-styled clothes, scorning the argument that suffragists should appear feminine to discount the "antis" slurs.

5. The suffrage movement was divided into multiple factions, but the primary three, listed from largest to smallest, included (1) The National Union of Women's Suffrage Societies (NUWSS), a diverse coalition of sixteen older suffrage societies dating from 1879, under the leadership of Millicent Fawcett. Non-party, non-militant, and therefore "constitutionalist" in its methods, its newspaper was *The Common Cause;* (2) The Pank-

hurst-led, militant Women's Social and Political Union (WSPU), formed in 1903, was dedicated from its start to the single-minded pursuit of the vote by violent and other means. *Votes for Women* served as its newspaper until 1912, when the Pankhursts forced out the papers' editors, the Pethick-Lawrences. *The Suffragette* became the new militant WSPU paper; (3) The Women's Freedom League (WFL) resulted from a split within the WSPU in 1907, one year after the Pankhursts' arrival in London. Both Craig and Hamilton joined this group, which described itself as "militant" but non-violent in its tactics. Its paper was *The Vote*. See Lisa Tickner's *The Spectacle of Women* for historical accounts and photographs of these groups.

6. See Whitelaw's biography of Hamilton, which relies on a set of unfortunately spare materials available to chronicle the life of this overlooked writer, including Hamilton's often vague and evasive autobiography, *Life Errant*.

7. For a summary of the play's critical reception, see Dymkowski. Ferris discusses the play's expression of homosocial desire through the convention of cuckoldry.

8. Quoted in Wynn, 35.

9. See "Approaching Abjection," especially as Kristeva identifies the abject with the maternal body, and as she describes the effect of abjection, including "Mother-phobia and the Murder of the Father." Helen feels abandoned by her mother and resists the father. As she is being strapped into the electric chair, she cries, "Don't touch me. . . . I won't submit! Not now!" (527).

10. In response to a 1960 U.S. revival, Robert Brustein dismissed Treadwell's Helen as "a sensitive dish of cream . . . curdled in the age of the machine" (qtd. in Bywaters 97). A *New York Post* reviewer expresses sympathy for the heroine, "moving to her doom in . . . a [bewildered] trance." Dickey's *Sophie Treadwell* contains an encyclopedic summary of critical responses to this play's major stagings.

11. Katherine Weinstein generously made available the translated Dada texts reproduced here. Her dissertation accounts for the work of female Dadaists in postwar Zurich.

12. Rugh has noted Huelsenbeck's ironical "lack of awareness" of the importance of collaboration as a Dada method in the latter's well-intentioned but miscalculated 1964 critique of his and other Dadaists' misogyny in the Zurich of 1916.

13. Emmy Hennings's experiences as a morphine addict and prostitute found their way into her expressionist-style poems, which gave way to her staunch antiwar stand, eventually shared by Hugo Ball. See Weinstein and Rugh for further discussion of these elements of Hennings's life and work.

14. Millay became stagestruck at Vassar, where she was celebrated as a leading actor. In Greenwich Village she became part of the postwar generation of villagers, together with Provincetown Theatre members Floyd Dell, Max Eastman, and Jack Reed. After winning a part in Dell's play, they quickly became lovers. The Players' policy allowed her not only to act in others' plays but to design and direct her own. See Dash, 138–46.

15. *New York Times* reviewer Alexander Woollcott called it "the most beautiful and most interesting play in the English language now to be seen in New York," whose point might be lost on the "average unthinking audience," but would find its target in a mother grieving the war loss of her son (December 14, 1919: 2).

16. In March of 1921, writes Jo Ellen Green Kaiser, "she warned her sister not to 'let any of the Provincetown Players see the manuscript of her Vassar play,'" later published

as *The Lamp and the Bell,* because she realized that they "would hate it, & make fun of it, & old Djuna Barnes would rag you about it" (in Freedman 39).

17. Penny Farfan's book, *Women, Modernism, and Performance,* (Cambridge 2004), published after this chapter was written, extends this analysis of women's performances in the forming of modernism to include contributions by Elizabeth Robins, Ellen Terry, Virginia Woolf, Djuna Barnes, and Isadora Duncan.

Works Cited

Adlard, Eleanor, ed. *Edy: Recollections of Edith Craig.* London: Frederick Muller, 1949.

Bywaters, Barbara L. "Marriage, Madness, and Murder in Sophie Treadwell's *Machinal.*" In *Modern American Drama: The Female Canon,* ed. June Schlueter. Rutherford, N.J.: Farleigh Dickinson University Press, 1990. 97–110.

Cockin, Katharine. *Edith Craig (1869–1947): Dramatic Lives.* London: Cassell, 1998.

———. *Women and Theatre in the Age of Suffrage.* London: Palgrave, 2001.

Dash, Joan. *A Life of One's Own: Three Gifted Women and the Men They Married.* New York: Harper & Row, 1973.

Davis, Tracy. *Actresses as Working Women: Their Social Identity in Victorian Culture.* London: Routledge, 1991.

———, and Ellen Donkin. *Women and Playwriting in Nineteenth-Century Britain.* Cambridge: Cambridge University Press, 1999.

Dickey, Jerry. *Sophie Treadwell: A Research and Production Sourcebook.* Westport, Conn.: Greenwood Press.

Dymkowski, Christine. "Entertaining Ideas: Edy Craig and the Pioneer Players." In *The New Woman and Her Sisters: Feminism and Theatre, 1850–1914,* ed. Viv Gardner and Susan Rutherford. Hemel Hempstead: Harvester Wheatsheaf, 1992.

The Era (London), January 16, 1909: 23.

Farfan, Penny. *Women, Modernism, and Performance.* Cambridge: Cambridge University Press, 2004.

Ferris, Lesley. "The Female Self and Performance: The Case of *The First Actress.*" In *Theatre and Feminist Aesthetics,* ed. Karen Laughlin and Catherine Schuler. Madison: Associated University Presses, 1995. 230–42.

Freedman, Diane P., ed. *Millay at 100.* Carbondale: Southern Illinois University Press, 1995.

Hamilton, Cicely, and Christopher St. John. *How the Vote Was Won: A Play in One Act.* London: Edith Craig, 1913.

Hardekopf, Ferdinand (Ravien Siurlai). "Emmy Hennings." *Die Aktion* (June 5, 1912), n.p.

Hubert, Renée Riese. "Zurich Dada and its Artistic Couples." In *Women in Dada,* ed. Naomi Sawelson-Gorse. Cambridge: MIT Press, 1998. 516–45.

Kaiser, Jo Ellen Green. "Displaced Modernism: Millay and the Triumph of Sentimentality." In *Millay at 100,* ed. Diane P. Freedman. Carbondale: Southern Illinois University Press, 1995. 27–42.

Kelly, Katherine E. "The Actresses' Franchise League Prepares for War: Feminist Theatre in Camouflage." *Theatre Survey* (May 1994): 121–37.

———. "*Alan's Wife:* Mother Love and Theatrical Sensibility in London of the 1890s." *MODERNISM/modernity* 11.3: 539–60.

———. *Modern Drama by Women, 1880s-1930s: An International Anthology.* London: Routledge, 1996.

Kristeva, Julia. "Approaching Abjection"; "From Filth to Defilement" (both abridged). In *The Portable Kristeva,* ed. Kelly Oliver. New York: Columbia University Press, 1997. 229–63.

Milford, Nancy. *Savage Beauty: The Life of Edna St. Vincent Millay.* New York: Random House, 2001.

Millay, Edna St. Vincent. *Aria da Capo: A Play in One Act.* New York: Mitchell Kennerley, 1921.

Ozieblo, Barbara. *Susan Glaspell: A Critical Biography.* Chapel Hill: University of North Carolina Press, 2000.

Pioneer Players' Scripts. Ellen Terry Memorial Museum, Kent.

Pioneer Players' Annual Reports. First Report, 1911–12; Second Report, 1912–13; Third Report, 1913–14; Fourth Report, 1914–15; Fifth Report, 1915–16; Sixth Report, 1916–17; Seventh Report, 1917–18; Eighth Report, 1918–19; Ninth Report, 1919–20. Ellen Terry Memorial Museum, Kent.

Riviere, Joan. "Womanliness as a Masquerade." *Formations of Fantasy.* Edited by Victor Burgin, James Donald, and Cora Kaplan. London: Methuen, 1986. 35–44.

Rugh, Thomas F. "Emmy Hennings and Zurich Dada." *Dada Surrealism 10/11* (1982): 5–28.

Sarlós, Robert Károly. *Jig Cook and the Provincetown Players: Theater in Ferment.* Amherst: University of Massachusetts Press, 1982.

Sawelson-Gorse, Naomi. Preface. *Women in Dada.* Ed. Naomi Sawelson-Gorse. Cambridge: MIT Press, 1998. x-xviii.

Sharp, Evelyn. *Unfinished Adventure.* London: John Lane, 1933.

Sorell, Walter, ed. and trans. *The Mary Wigman Book: Her Writings.* Middleton, Conn.: Wesleyan University Press, 1975.

St. John, Christopher. *The First Actress* [1911].

The Suffrage Annual and Women's Who's Who. Ed. A. J. R. London: Stanley Paul and Co., 1913.

Tickner, Lisa. *The Spectacle of Women.*

Treadwell, Sophie. *Machinal.* In *Twenty-Five Best Plays of the Modern American Theatre.* Early Series. Ed. John Gassner. New York: Crown Publishers, 1949. 495–529.

Weinstein, Katherine. "Subversive Women: Female Performing Artists in Zurich Dada." Dissertation. Tufts University, 2001. Directed by Laurence Senelick.

Whitelaw, Lis. *The Life and Rebellious Times of Cicely Hamilton.* London: Women's Press, 1990.

Wynn, Nancy. "Sophie Treadwell: Author of *Machinal.*" *Journal of American Drama and Theatre* 3.1 (1991): 29–47.

CHRISTOPHER ST. JOHN

The First Actress

CHARACTERS IN THE PLAY

MRS. MARGARET HUGHES (of Killigrew's Co. of King's
    players)..NANCY PRICE
GRIFFIN (of Killigrew's Co. of King's Players)...........................E. GWENN
SIR CHARLES SEDLEY...BEN WEBSTER
LORD HATTON ....TOM HESLEWOOD

VISIONS OF THE FUTURE

MRS. NELL GWYNN .... ELLEN TERRY
MRS. BARRY .... LILY BRAYTON
MRS. BRACEGIRDLE .... SUZANNE SHELDON
MRS. ANNE OLDFIELD .... HENRIETTA WATSON
MRS. PEG WOFFINGTON ....MAY WHITTY
MRS. KITTY CLIVE...DOROTHY MINTO
MRS. SARAH SIDDONS ....SABA RALEIGH
MRS. FANNY ABINGTON .... MONA HARRISON
MRS. DOROTHY JORDAN................................... LILLIAN BRAITHWAITE
MADAME VESTRIS.. AURIOL LEE
AN ACTRESS OF TO-DAY... LENA ASHWELL

PERIOD—1661

SCENE:—*Back of stage at the New Theatre, Drury Lane. The performance of "Othello" has just concluded. Applause is heard from the front of the house, mingled with cat-calls, hissing, and hooting. Thud of missiles being thrown against the curtain. An actor dressed as Othello with a very black face comes round the backcloth and goes into his dressing-room. Followed by* MARGARET HUGHES *and* GRIFFIN. HUGHES *sinks into a chair down R.* GRIFFIN *fans HER with the prompt copy.*

HUGHES. Thank God that's over!
    GRIFFIN. All but the shouting! And the pippin-throwing. You had better keep this apple as a memento. (*HE holds out an apple, which* HUGHES *refuses to take.*) Just as you like. I'll eat it. It happens not to be rotten.

HUGHES. Griffin—what did that fellow in the pit call out when I went on to speak the epilogue?

GRIFFIN. I think it was: "Call yourself a woman! You ought to be ashamed of yourself."

HUGHES. But why? There have been female actresses before to-night.

GRIFFIN. Only French hussies.

HUGHES. Sober-thinking people must see that it's really more proper for Desdemona to be represented by a woman than by a boy in a woman's habit.

GRIFFIN. It depends on the woman, and it depends on the boy. If all our boy-actresses had the beauty, the grace, the genius of Mr. Kynaston.

HUGHES. Kynaston! Don't talk to me of Kynaston. It was he who paid all those people to hoot, I'll be bound. Sir Charles said he would have a cabal here to hoot me. (*After a pause.*) Griffin, was I so bad?

(*ENTER* SIR CHARLES SEDLEY *and* LORD HATTON.)

GRIFFIN. Don't ask a poor devil of an actor. What does *he* know about it. Here comes Sir Charles Sedley—and Lord Hatton—You'll get the truth from *them*—they are poets, men of the world, men of fashion; they can give you the valuable and profound opinions which circulate in Fop's Corner. (*Curtain up.* GRIFFIN *up and moving things.*)

HUGHES. (*To* SEDLEY.) Well, Sir Charles—it's over.

SIR CHARLES. Yes; and I'll be hanged if it wasn't a great success.

LORD H. Very glorious scenes and perspectives.

SIR CHARLES. The devil take *them!* Who's talking about them? I say we have settled Kynaston!

LORD H. He had a cabal in front, however.

SIR CHARLES. And didn't you witness the settling of the cabal! Ten sturdy fellows of mine had cleared the boxes of them before the end of the first act.

HUGHES. Burt must be told not to put so much black on his hands. He has ruined my veil.

SIR CHARLES. Burt ought never to have played the Moor. Hair ought to have played it. I told Killigrew so—but he was obstinate—all managers are so dem'd obstinate. But what does it matter? You, my Peg, were the cynosure of all eyes.

LORD H. The King looked amazed.

SIR CHARLES. Dem me! His Majesty will look more amazed when every female part in every playhouse in London is taken by a woman actress—when your Kynastons and Nolles and the whole crew of boys have been swept off the stage!

GRIFFIN. That will never be.

SIR CHARLES. Dem me! Who spoke to you, sir! This is the fellow, Hatton, who shares a lodging and a shirt with Sam Goodman! When Goodman goes out, Griffin here must lie a-bed, for they only have one shirt between 'em! This is Griffin's day for wearing the shirt, and he takes advantage of it to contradict his betters!

GRIFFIN. I say, if you are right, Sir Charles, 'tis strange that since the King granted the managers permission to employ women, not one of the managers has availed himself of the privilege till to-night! And to-night was not the whole house shouting, "Give us back the boys"?

HUGHES. Oh, that's not true! Is it Charles?

SIR CHARLES. Of course not. Upon my word, Griffin, I'll have you clubbed for your presumption, as I had Kynaston clubbed in St. James's Park. (GRIFFIN up and pull curtains.)

LORD H. Come, come, Charles! Don't spoil this great evening—the evening of your triumph—with threats. Did you observe Lady Castlemaine? I wonder what she thought of the innovation. I noticed that her ladyship could not forbear laughing when Desdemona was strangled!

SIR CHARLES. And of course, we have never heard any laughter in the boxes when Kynaston dies as Juliet! Poor soul, when he has a death scene, 'tis always the most comic part of the whole play!

HUGHES. How did you like my willow scene, Charles?

SIR CHARLES. Charming, charming! Zauns! If Kynaston isn't turning yellow under his pink and white at this moment, I'm a Dutchman! Some fellows of mine went down to the Duke's Theatre just now to spread the news of our success before the audience had dispersed; by this time 'tis all over the town that a female actress has played Kynaston off the stage. Hatton, we must put in an appearance at the Chocolate House to see how the lad is taking it. Oh, I look forward to the meeting!

HUGHES. Were you pleased with my performance, Charles?

SIR CHARLES. You were radiant, exquisite, charming! The lines were not always intelligible, perhaps—but so much the better. Othello is sorry stuff. But your business! Uncomeatable! Kynaston! Kynaston! Where is Kynaston now? After this humiliation I fancy the ladies will be less anxious to drive their darling round Hyde Park in their coaches. You wouldn't believe it, Hatton, but the other day the saucy rogue had on gloves like mine—pulled up to the elbow. Positively he had imitated my gloves.

LORD H. He imitates more than your gloves, Charles. I hear that the other night he turned the thrashing your fellows gave him to account, and mimicked you giving them their orders—yes, Charles, 'tis true. He mimicked your voice from the stage!

SIR CHARLES. I'll mimic *him*. I'll break every plank he stands on. Presumptuous ape!

LORD H. (*Crosses.*) It was a damned clever imitation. They tell me even your best friends could not forbear laughing.

SIR CHARLES. Precisely what I should expect from my best friends! Well, Peg, I think no one will deny you've earned your supper. I'll just put in an appearance at the Chocolate House with Hatton, and return here to fetch you. You will be ready.

HUGHES. No, no. Send your coach back for me, Charles. Don't come yourself. I should prefer to go straight to my lodgings—and to bed. I am—I am fatigued.

SIR CHARLES. Fatigued! Now, I take this very ill of you, Peg, indeed I do! I have invited several persons of distinction to supper—Lord Rochester, Lord Falkland, Sir George Etheridge. Both Falkland and Etheridge have promised to write you a comedy. Now, it's ten to one that if I plead you are indisposed they will spread about the town that you have failed—especially my Lord Rochester, who swore I could not train you for the stage in thirty lessons!

HUGHES. Perhaps his Lordship spoke the truth. Even you, Charles, have not been able to praise me.

SIR CHARLES. My sweet girl—you are overwrought. Positively you are overwrought. You don't know what you are saying. *I* have not praised you! Have I not said that your performance will be the whole talk of the Court and town—and that no one having witnessed your grace and beauty will suffer Kynaston or any other lanky boy on the stage any more? The eyes of the audience were prepossessed and charmed before aught of the poet's approached their ears. Desdemona, we all confess, is the most wretched of characters, but you gave it a lustre and a brilliance! You dazzled our sight—so that we could not see the deformities of Shakespeare.

HUGHES. Oh, Charles!

SIR CHARLES. (*To* HATTON.) 'Tis unfortunate that my new comedy, "The Mulberry Garden," was not finished in time. I have designed such a woman's part in that comedy as has never been writ before. I think I have never related you the plot of "The Mulberry Garden," Hatton?

LORD H. Yes, Charles, often, and I had read it before in Moliere. Come, we shall not catch the world at the Chocolate House if we delay longer.

SIR CHARLES. That's true. *A bientot,* Peg. I shall return for you within half an hour. I rely on you to be ready.

(*EXIT* SIR CHARLES *with* HATTON.)

HUGHES. (*Following HIM and shouting after HIM.*) Whether you come within half an hour or an hour or a year, I shall not be ready. It's not all my fault—it's your fault—it's your fault. You are to blame. You have made a fool of me. I have failed—oh, I have failed! (*SHE bursts into tears.*)

GRIFFIN. No, no. Comfort yourself, my dear. You have not failed. It is your sex which has failed. It has been weighed in the balance and found wanting.

HUGHES. (*Tearfully.*) I see no reason why women should not be able to act—and in any case, is it becoming to see men past forty frisking it as wenches of fifteen?

GRIFFIN. The voice is the voice of Margaret Hughes, but the sentiments are the sentiments of Sir Charles Sedley. But do not credit for a moment that Sir Charles is convinced of their truth! Not he! He assumed them merely as a weapon to fight Kynaston. How came you on the boards at all? Kynaston offends Sir Charles by imitating his style of dress. My gentleman seeks to revenge himself. He hires ruffians to thrash Kynaston; as you know, the lad was mightily bruised, and there was no play the following evening—but you cannot extinguish a great artist by such methods of barbarism. Kynaston returns, with a limp, 'tis true, but dearer than ever in the love of playgoers. What does Sedley do then? His vanity will not acknowledge defeat. He has a pretty mistress who has gained applause in his circle by mimicking our leading boy-actress. He gives her a few lessons in elocution and deportment, and induces Killigrew to engage her in his company. He falsely spreads about that women actresses are to be the fashion, that the King favours them, and so forth. He conceives that this move will mortify Kynaston and injure him in public esteem. But Sedley's gold and Sedley's lies have alike failed to corrupt the public. The public, trained by the accomplished actors of a past generation, and since by Kynaston, perhaps the greatest of them all, know what the art of acting is. They will not accept a woman in the place of those great men merely because she is lovely, merely because she is the favourite of a man of fashion. No—never! I am sorry for you, Mrs. Hughes. It is not your fault that you have been made the tool of Sir Charles's vanity. You might bear in mind that the audience to-night were not incensed against you personally. They were but protesting against woman's invasion of a sphere where she is totally unfitted to shine.

HUGHES. You are very clever, Griffin, and I am a fool—Charles always told me himself so, until he began to educate me for the stage—but I don't see how we can be unfitted to play women's parts. Are we not fitted—if only because we are women?

GRIFFIN. That is as much as to say that acting is not an art. By that show of reasoning we must import negroes to play Othello—we must go to the gaols to find the impersonators of our villains—must bribe noblemen to play our stage dukes—and allow no unmarried actor to play a husband, no childless actor to depict the emotions of a father. Acting, Mistress Hughes, is the art of assuming a character, not the accident of being it. You happen to be a woman, but can you draw tears for a woman's grief as Kynaston can? Can you so sensibly touch the audience to the spectacle of outraged modesty and invincible fidelity? Forgive me, no! 'Tis the genius of assumption, of creation, that makes an actor like Kynaston the faithful limner of your sex upon the stage. I will even go so far as to say that his trained powers enable him, when he dons a woman's habit, to look lovelier than you all—to speak with a sweeter voice— to walk with a greater grace—to express the very quintessence of the female soul!

HUGHES. All this may only be because men have had more practice. Perhaps if women were encouraged to give the art as careful a study, they could do as well.

GRIFFIN. Believe me, it is not in them—to give that careful study. Have they the mental power or the mental energy? They certainly have not the creative imagination. What artistic creation have women to their credit in history? Yet they have had the opportunity of participating in arts demanding a much smaller sacrifice of womanly delicacy than the art of acting.

HUGHES. Our womanly delicacy! I like to hear you men prate of our "womanly delicacy"—as if you valued it so highly. Do you think my appearance on the stage to-night has rubbed the bloom off mine? Say we oughtn't to act because we are inferior to you in ability, if you like, Griffin, but for Heaven's sake don't speak as if we must be preserved from it because of our delicacy! A lot of delicacy the Sedleys and Etheredges of the world leave us!

GRIFFIN. You do but confirm me in my opinion, Mistress Hughes. Were your sex to tread the stage it would not be in your power to resist the assaults of the kind of gentry of which you have named two bright and shining examples. The limits imposed on you by Nature preventing you from studying the art seriously, you would endeavour to atone for the deficiency in your talents by practicing airs and tricks to tempt mankind. The gentry would not be able to judge of your performance apart from your sex. No doubt they would enjoy the diversion, but the stage would suffer degradation.

HUGHES. I'm not so sure. Perhaps we should not be so busy in the affairs of love—if we had other affairs to interest us.

GRIFFIN. You have already a large choice of such affairs, Mistress Hughes— affairs better befitting a woman's mental capacity—embroidery, the study of languages, the ornamental side of cooking, and many other domestic arts.

And lastly there is what I may call the *grande affaire*—the true vocation of every woman—the excellent business of being a wife to a good man, and rearing him a hopeful and healthful progeny.

HUGHES. For the matter of that, Mr. Burt rears a hopeful progeny—certainly a numerous progeny—and it doesn't interfere with his playing Othello!

GRIFFIN. You are illogical, Mistress Hughes—a privilege of your sex, but one by the exercise of which you further proclaim its unfitness for such a rational art as that of acting, where a patriot, a prince, a beggar, a clown each have their propriety, where action is perfectly and logically adjusted to character and manner—

HUGHES. (*Interrupting.*) I say Mrs. Burt is dead, and Mr. Burt is a mother to his family. But we won't quarrel about that, Griffin. I know you are right in the main. I failed completely. My diction was artificial—my voice was weak—and I tried to make up for it by bawling. Charles's flattery about my gestures didn't deceive me. They were ill-designed and inappropriate. I walked like a cripple—and held my head like a hunch-back—oh, I know! 'Tis very bitter to me to think that through my failure I may have kept my sex off the stage for centuries—if not for ever. Good-night, Griffin.

GRIFFIN. Good-night—but stay, there's no one in the theatre. Had I not better remain with you till Sir Charles returns?

HUGHES. No, no. I want to be alone. Good-night.

GRIFFIN. Good night. (*Returning, HE says, consolingly.*) You will do better next time.

(*EXIT* GRIFFIN.)

HUGHES. Thank you—Griffin—but I don't want even to think of next time. Perhaps some day I may be able to look back on it all—as a nightmare. God—if I could just sleep! I am fatigued—fatigued—to death. (*Yawning.*) Griffin was right. I ought never to have attempted it—I have made it impossible for the others—perhaps there never will be—any others—I am sorry for that—very sorry—(*All the latter part of this speech has been spoken drowsily, and now SHE falls asleep. A voice is heard singing outside. Gradually it becomes more distinct.*)

Oranges, who'll buy my oranges,
Sweet China oranges, ripe oranges,
Yellow as the sun, round as the moon,
Juicy and sweet,
Sweet China oranges.

(*The vision of* NELL GWYNNE *appears.*)

GWYNNE. Come, now—not so much bleating! You're a trifle hasty in your sorrow here, as I, Nelly, can very quickly prove. You must know I saw you acting from the pit. I was selling oranges there! When they began to hoot—and jeer—I cried out: "You damned confounded dogs, what are you laughing at? Many another woman will mount the stage before the year's out." They said in jest: "Why not *you*, Nelly?" "Stranger things have happened," said I. "We don't want women on the stage," said one fellow who wasn't too drunk to speak distinctly. "You mayn't want 'em, but, by the Lord Harry, you've got to have 'em," said I, "and they'll do your damned dull stage a power of good." Well, they only laughed again—but the joke won't be against *me*, I think, when I enter the King's Playhouse, as I shall do, and become an actress in great vogue. Be merry, Mrs. Hughes. You've led the way, and I that was at first no better than a Cinderwench will follow, and will be spoke of by folks who've never heard the name of Edward Kynaston! Ask the ringers of St. Martin's! Every week their bells shall ring out in honour of poor Nelly, long centuries after she is laid in earth! Listen—you may hear them.

(*EXIT, singing.*)

Oranges and lemons,
The bells of St. Clemens;
Cost me three farthings,
The bells of St. Martin's.

(*ENTER visions of* MRS. BARRY *and* MRS. BRACEGIRDLE *as the Rival Queens.*)

MRS. BARRY.

My brain is burst, Debate and Reason quenched.
The storm is up, and my hot, bleeding heart
Splits with the rack—
I beg the gods to help me for the moment.

(*Drives knife into* MRS. BRACEGIRDLE'S *heart.*)

BRACEGIRDLE. Oh! Oh! I'll be sworn you did that on purpose, Mrs. Barry, to revenge yourself because the property man gave me your veil. The knife has pierced my stays; it has entered at least a quarter of an inch into my flesh! I'll play the Rival Queen with you no more, trust me for that. I'll walk out of the theatre rather!

BARRY. Come, come, my Bracegirdle, is this the time

To exhibit private feuds, and jealousies!
The glorious public triumphs we shall win
Must be our theme; we're here to prophesy!
Twin stars, with equal lustre we shall shine;
There shall be peace between our reputations!
'Twas ignorance, dear Hughes, that made them spurn you.
But by our time men will have learned our worth.
What fool will prate then, *"The stage is not for you"?*
The names of Barry, Bracegirdle, be my witnesses!

(*SHE sweeps off, followed by* BRACEGIRDLE.)
(*ENTER vision of* NANCE OLDFIELD.)

OLDFIELD. Not forgetting little Nancy Oldfield. *If* you please! She has a word to say! She has a prophecy. Think of it, Hughes! An actress so greatly honoured that at her death she will lie in state in Jerusalem Chamber—for all the world as though she had won a battle or conquered a province. The public who loved her when she laughed as when she wept, will be faithful. They will crowd to see her—in her last part! Only sixty years after they threw pippins at you, and the world will see an actress buried in Westminster Abbey—buried like a queen!

(*EXIT* NANCE, OLDFIELD.)
(*ENTER vision of* PEG WOFFINGTON.)

WOFFINGTON. The whirligig of time brings in his revenges—and another Peg! Peg Hughes has prepared the way for Peg Woffington—Peg the Second—

(*Vision of* KITTY CLIVE *dances in.*)

CLIVE. And that's enough to Peg! I, Kitty Clive—
WOFFINGTON. (*Ignoring* CLIVE.) Peg the Second will teach the pit to presume! She will not forget that they would have none of Peg the First.
CLIVE. Mrs. Woffington—I have a line here.
WOFFINGTON. Unmannered dogs! I'll teach them to doubt a woman's intellect—a woman's grit. Nature has given me a harsh, unpleasing voice—but that shall not daunt me—I'll learn to use it! A defect shall become a grace. And as for intellect—
CLIVE. They don't want to hear all that! I, Kitty Clive—
WOFFINGTON. (*To* HUGHES.) You sowed the good seed in flouts and jeers—we shall reap it in applause and honour—

(*ENTER* MRS. SIDDONS *as for the sleep-walking scene.*)

Yes—I will give place to the Tragic Muse most gladly—though never to a Singing Chambermaid—

(*EXIT* PEG WOFFINGTON.)

CLIVE. I, Kitty Clive—
SIDDONS. Out daunted spot.

(*EXIT* KITTY CLIVE.)

All the prejudice in all the world shall not keep us off the stage. What's that I see—a great painter writes his name on the hem of an actress's garment! And statesmen, to watch her, sit among the fiddlers. *We fail!* But, screw your courage to the slicking-place, and *we'll not fail. We'll not fail.*

(*EXIT* SIDDONS.)
(*ENTER* MRS. ABINGTON,)

ABINGTON. 'Tis hard on Nosegay Fan to have to follow the lofty-minded Siddons—to hitch her comedy waggon to that tragic star! Where's George Ann Bellamy or Miss Farren or Pritchard? All were fitter for the task. My prophecy, dear comrade Hughes, is of an immortal comedy. Behold the original—and the author says the never equaled—Lady Teazle! When all the comedies of your day are dead, and the names of the boy-actresses forgotten, "The School for Scandal" will be alive, and the memory of Fan Abington will live with it!

(*EXIT* MRS. ABINGTON.)
(*ENTER* MRS. JORDAN.)

JORDAN. Shall I play tragedy, comedy, high or low, opera or farce? Sure I'll play 'em all; but laughing will agree with me better than crying! Peg, if you had begun in comedy, you'd have had fewer apples thrown at you—take Dorothy Jordan's word for it!

(*EXIT JORDAN.*)
(*ENTER* MME. VESTRIS *as Captain MacHeath.*)

VESTRIS. I'll not content myself with playing the woman, not I! Since men once put on the petticoats and played all *our* parts, Vestris will put on trousers, and play some of theirs for a change! And play them so well, too, that man will hardly know himself, so elegant, so gallant, so fascinating will he appear—such a pretty devil of a fellow! Captain MacHeath takes off his hat to you, Mistress Hughes, and begs the public, who once thought it unbecoming for us to tread the stage, even in our skirts, never to be too sure of anything!

(*EXIT* VESTRIS.)
(*ENTER an* ACTRESS *of To-day.*)

ACTRESS. When I am born, dear Peg, people will have quite forgotten that the stage was ever barred to us. They will laugh at the idea that acting was once considered a man's affair—they will be incredulous that the pioneer actress was bitterly resented. Yet they will be as busy as ever deciding what vocations are suitable to our sex. It will be "Man this" and "Woman that" as though we had never taught them a lesson. I see an old map where the world is divided into two by a straight line. The man who ruled that line across the world said: "All territory discovered to the right of the line in future to belong to Spain; all to the left to Portugal." To my age such a division of the world will seem comical indeed; yet that is how I see them still dividing the world of humanity—"This half for men," "That half for women." If in my day that archaic map is superseded, we shall not forget that it was first made to look foolish when women mounted the stage. Brave Hughes—forgotten pioneer—your comrades offer you a crown!

(*The shapes of the others rise from the front of the theatre. They come forward.* MRS. SIDDONS *holds a crown over the head of the sleeping* HUGHES.
(*Music. Disappearance of Visions.*)

First performed at the Kingsway Theatre, May 8, 1911. Reproduced from the copy at the Ellen Terry Museum, Smallhythe, Kent.

CICELY HAMILTON AND CHRISTOPHER ST. JOHN

From *How the Vote Was Won*

CHARACTERS

HORACE COLE (a clerk, about 30)	MAUDIE SPARK (his first cousin)
ETHEL (his wife, 22)	MISS LIZZIE WILKINS (his aunt)
WINIFRED (his [her] sister)	LILY (his maid of all work)

AGATHA COLE (Horace's sister)   GERALD WILLIAMS (his neighbour)
MOLLY (his niece)
MADAME CHRISTINE (his distant relation)

SCENE. *Sitting-room in* HORACE COLE'S *house at Brixton. The room is cheaply furnished in a genteel style. The window looks out on a row of little houses, all of the Cole pattern. The door leads into a narrow passage communicating at once with the front door. The fireplace has a fancy mantel border, and over it is an overmantel, decorated with many photographs and cheap ornaments. The sideboard, a small bookcase, a table, and a comfortable armchair, are the chief articles of furniture. The whole effect is modest, and quite unpleasing.*

TIME. *Late afternoon on a spring day in any year in the future.*

When the curtain rises, MRS. HORACE COLE *is sitting in the comfortable armchair putting a button on to her husband's coat. She is a pretty, fluffy little woman who could never be bad-tempered, but might be fretful. At this minute she is smiling indulgently, and rather irritatingly, at her sister* WINIFRED, *who is sitting by the fire when the curtain rises, but gets up almost immediately to leave.* WINIFRED *is a tall and distinguished looking young woman with a cheerful, capable manner and an emphatic diction which betrays the public speaker. She wears the colours of the N.W.S.P.U.*

WINIFRED. Well, good-bye, Ethel. It's a pity you won't believe me. I wanted to let you and Horace down gently, or I shouldn't be here.

ETHEL. But you're always prophesying these dreadful things, Winnie, and nothing ever happens. Do you remember the day when you tried to invade the House of Commons from submarine boats? Oh, Horace did laugh when he saw in the papers that you had all been landed on the Hovis wharf by mistake! "By accident, on purpose!" Horace said. He couldn't stop laughing all the evening. "What price your sister, Winifred?" he said. "She asked for a vote, and they gave her bread." He kept on—you can't think how funny he was about it.

WINIFRED. Oh, but I can! I know my dear brother-in-law's sense of humour is his strong point. Well, we must hope it will bear the strain that is going to be put on it to-day. Of course, when his female relations invade his house—all with the same story, "I've come to be supported" he may think it excruciatingly funny. One never knows.

ETHEL. Winnie, you're only teasing me. They would never do such a thing. They must know we have only one spare bedroom, and that's to be for a paying guest when we can afford to furnish it.

WINIFRED. The servants' bedroom will be empty. Don't forget that all the domestic servants have joined the League and are going to strike, too.

ETHEL. Not ours, Winnie. Martha is simply devoted to me, and poor little Lily *couldn't* leave. She has no home to go to. She would have to go to the workhouse.

WINIFRED. Exactly where she will go. All those women who have no male relatives, or are refused help by those they have, have instructions to go to the relieving officer. The number of female paupers who will pour through the workhouse gates to-night all over England will frighten the Guardians into blue fits.

ETHEL. Horace says you'll never *frighten* the Government into giving you the vote. He says every broken window is a fresh nail in the coffin of women's suffrage. It's quite true. Englishmen can't be bullied.

WINIFRED. No, but they can *bully*. It's your husband, your dear Horace, and a million other dear Horaces who are going to do the bullying and frightening this time. [. . .]

ETHEL. Winnie, how absurd you are! You know how often you've tried to convert Horace and failed. Is it likely that he will become a Suffragette just because—

WINIFRED. Just because?—Go on, Ethel.

ETHEL. Well, you know—all this you've been telling me about his relations coming here and asking him to support them. Of course, I don't believe it. Agatha, for instance, would never dream of giving up her situation. But if they did come Horace would just tell them he *couldn't* keep them. How could he on £4 a week?

WINIFRED. How could he? That's the point! He couldn't, of course. That's why he'll want to get rid of them at any cost—even the cost of letting women have the Vote. That's why he and the majority of men in this country shouldn't for years have kept alive the foolish superstition that all women are supported by men. [. . .] They wouldn't listen to argument. . . . so we had to expose their pious fraud about woman's place in the world in a very practical and sensible way. At this very minute working women of every grade in every part of England are ceasing work, and going to demand support and the necessities of life from their nearest male relatives, however distant the nearest relative may be. I hope, for your sake, Ethel, that Horace's relatives aren't an exacting lot! [. . .]

ETHEL. What male relative are you going to, Winnie? Uncle Joseph?

WINIFRED. Oh, I'm in the fighting line, as usual, so our dear uncle will be spared. My work is with the great army of women who have no male belongings of any kind! I shall be busy till midnight marshalling them to the workhouse. . . . This is perhaps the most important part of the strike. By this we shall hit men as ratepayers even when they have escaped us as relatives!

Every man, either in a public capacity or a private one, will find himself face to face with the appalling problem of maintaining millions of women in idleness. Do you think the men will take up the burden? Not they! [*Looks at her watch.*] Good heavens ! The strike began ages ago. I must be off. I've wasted too much time here already.

ETHEL [*looking at the clock*]. I had no idea it was so late. I must see about Horace's tea. He may be home any minute. [*Rings the bell*]

WINIFRED. Poor Horace!

ETHEL [*annoyed*]. Why "poor Horace"? I don't think he as anything to complain of. [*Rings again.*]

WINIFRED. At this minute I feel some pity for all men.

ETHEL. What can have happened to Martha?

WINIFRED. She's gone, my dear, that's all.

ETHEL. Gone! Nonsense. She's been with me ever since I was married, and I pay her very good wages.

[*Enter LILY, a shabby little maid-of-all-work, dressed for walking, the chief effort of the toilette being a very cheap and very smart hat.*]

ETHEL. Where's Martha, Lily?

LILY. She's left, m'm.

ETHEL. Left! She never gave me notice.

LILY. No, m'm, we wasn't to give no notice, but at three o'clock we was to quit

ETHEL. But why? Don't be a silly little girl. And you mustn't come in here in your hat.

LILY. I was just goin' when you rang. That's what I've got me 'at on for.

ETHEL. Going! Where? It's not your afternoon out.

LILY. I'm goin' back to the Union. There's dozens of others goin' with me.

ETHEL. But why—?

LILY. Miss Christabel—she told us. She says to us: "Now look 'ere, all of yer—you who've got no men to go to on Thursday—yer've got to go to the Union," she says; "and the one who 'angs back"—and she looked at me, she did—"may be the person 'oo the 'ole strain of the movement is restin' on, the traitor 'oo's sailin' under the 'ostile flag," she says; and I says, "That won't be me—not much!"

[*During this speech WINIFRED puts on a sandwich board which bears the inscription: "This way to the Workhouse."*]

WINIFRED. Well, Ethel, are you beginning to believe?

ETHEL. Oh, I think it's very unkind—very wicked. How am I to get Horace anything to eat with no servants?

WINIFRED. Cheer up, my dear. Horace and the others can end the strike when they choose. But they're going to have a jolly bad time first. Goodbye.

[*Exit* WINNIE, *singing the "Marseillaise."*]

LILY. Wait a bit, Miss. I'm comin' with yer. [*Sings the "Marseillaise" too.*] [. . .]

[*Exit* LILY.]

[*Enter* HORACE COLE—an *English master in his own house*—and GERALD WILLIAMS, *a smug young man stiff with self-consciousness.*]

ETHEL. You're back early, aren't you, Horry? How do you do, Mr. Williams?

GERALD WILLIAMS. How do you do, Mrs. Cole. I've just dropped in to fetch a book your husband's promised to lend me.

[HORACE *rummages in book-shelves.*]

ETHEL. Had a good day, Horry?

HORACE. Oh, much as usual. Ah, here it is [*reading out the title*] "Where's the Wash-tub now?" with a preface by Lord Curzon of Kedleston, published by the Men's League for Opposing Women's Suffrage. If that doesn't settle your missus, nothing will.

ETHEL. Is Mrs. Williams a Suffragette?

GERALD. Rather, and whenever I say anything, all she can answer is, "You know nothing about it." I call that illogical. Thank you, old man. I'll read it to her after tea. So long. Good-bye, Mrs. Cole. [. . .]

[*Exit* GERALD WILLIAMS]

HORACE [. . .] Tea ready?

ETHEL. Not quite, dear. It will be in a minute.

HORACE. What on earth is all this!

ETHEL. Oh, nothing. I thought I would cook your chop for you up here to-day—just for fun. [. . .]

HORACE. My dear child! It's very nice of you. But why not cook in the kitchen? Raw meat in the drawing-room! Do you want to turn me into a poor miserable vegetarian?

ETHEL. Oh, Horry, don't!

[*She puts her arms round his neck and sobs. The chop at the end of the toasting-fork in her hand dangles in his face.*]

HORACE. What on earth's the matter? Ethel, dear, don't be hysterical. If you knew what it was to come home fagged to death and be worried like this. . . . I'll ring for Martha and tell her to take away these beastly chops. They're getting on my nerves.

ETHEL. Martha's gone. [. . .] She went off without a word. . . . and Lily's gone, too. [*She puts her head down on the table and cries.*]

HORACE. Well, that's a good riddance. I'm sick of her dirty face and slovenly ways. If she ever does clean my boots, she makes them look worse than when I took them off. We must get a charwoman.

ETHEL. We shan't be able to. Isn't it in the papers?

HORACE. What *are* you talking about?

ETHEL. Winifred said it would be in the evening papers. [. . .]

HORACE. Oh, I saw something about "Suffragettes on Strike" on the posters on my way home. Who cares if they do strike? They're no use to anyone. Look at Winifred. What does she ever do except go round making speeches, and kicking up a row outside the House of Commons until she forces the police to arrest her. Then she goes to prison and poses as a martyr. Martyr! We all know she could go home at once if she would promise the magistrate to behave herself. What they ought to do is to try all these hysterical women privately and sentence them to be ducked—privately. Then they'd soon give up advertising themselves.

ETHEL. Winnie has a splendid answer to that, but I forget what it is. Oh, Horry, was there anything on the posters about the nearest male relative? [. . .]

ETHEL. Winnie said that not only are all the working women going to strike, but they are going to make their nearest male relatives support them.

HORACE. Rot!

ETHEL. I thought how dreadful it would be if Agatha came, or that cousin of yours on the stage whom you won't let me know, or your Aunt Lizzie! [. . .] Oh, look, Horace, there's a cab—with luggage. Oh, what shall we do?

HORACE. Don't fuss! It's stopping next door, not here at all.

ETHEL. No, no; it's here. [*She rushes out.*]

HORACE [*calling after her*]. Come back! You can't open a door yourself. It will look as if we didn't keep a servant.

[*Re-enter* ETHEL, *followed after a few seconds by* AGATHA. AGATHA *is a weary looking woman of about thirty-five. She wears the National Union colours, and is dowdily dressed.*]

ETHEL. It is Agatha—and such a big box. Where *can* we put it?

AGATHA [*mildly*]. How do you do, Horace. [*Kisses him.*] Dear Ethel! [*Kisses her.*] *You're* not looking so well as usual. Would you mind paying the cabman two shillings, Horace, and helping him with my box? It's rather heavy, but then it contains all my worldly belongings.

HORACE. Agatha—you haven't lost, your situation! You haven't left the Lewises?

AGATHA. Yes, Horace; I left at three o'clock.

HORACE. My dear Agatha—I'm extremely sorry—but we can't put you up here.

AGATHA. Hadn't you better pay the cab? Two shillings so soon becomes two-and-six. [*Exit* HORACE.] I am afraid my brother doesn't realise that I have some claim on him.

ETHEL. We thought you were so happy with the Lewises.

AGATHA. So were the slaves in America when they had kind masters. They didn't want to be free.

ETHEL. Horace said you always had late dinner with them when they had no company.

AGATHA. Oh, I have no complaint against my late employers. In fact, I was sorry to inconvenience them by leaving so suddenly. But I had a higher duty to perform than my duty to them.

ETHEL. I don't know what to do. It will worry Horace dreadfully.

[*Re-enter* HORACE.]

HORACE. The cab *was* two-and-six, and I had to give a man twopence to help me in with that Noah's ark. Now, Agatha, what does this mean? Surely in your position it was very unwise to leave the Lewises. You can't stay here. We must make some arrangement.

AGATHA. Any arrangement you like, dear, provided you support me.

HORACE. I support you!

AGATHA. As my nearest male relative, I think you are obliged to do so. If you refuse, I must go to the workhouse.

HORACE. But why can't you support yourself? You've done it for years.

AGATHA. Yes—ever since I was eighteen. Now I am going to give up work, until my work is recognised. Either my proper place is the home—the home provided for me by some dear father, brother, husband, cousin, or uncle—or I am a self-supporting member of the State, who ought not to be shut out from the rights of citizenship.

HORACE. All this sounds as if you had become a Suffragette! Oh, Agatha, I always thought you were a lady.

AGATHA. Yes, I *was* a lady—such a lady that at eighteen I was thrown upon the world, penniless, with no training whatever which fitted me to earn my own living. When women become citizens I believe that daughters will be given the same chances as sons, and such a life as mine will be impossible.

HORACE. Women are so illogical. What on earth has all this to do with your planting yourself on me in this inconsiderate way? You put me in a most unpleasant position. You must see, Agatha, that I haven't the means to support a sister as well as a wife. Couldn't you go to some friends until you find another situation?

AGATHA. No, Horace. I'm going to stay with you.

HORACE [*changing his tone, and turning nasty*]. Oh, indeed! And for how long—if I may ask?

AGATHA. Until a Bill for the removal of the sex disability is passed.

HORACE [*impotently angry*]. Nonsense. I can't keep you, and I won't. I have always tried to do my duty by you. I think hardly a week passes that I don't write to you. But now that you have deliberately thrown up an excellent situation as a governess, and come here and threatened me—yes, threatened me—I think it's time to say that, sister or no sister, I intend to be master in my own house!

[*Enter* MOLLY, *a good-looking young girl of about twenty. She is dressed in well-cut, tailor-made clothes, wears a neat little hat, and carries some golf-clubs and a few books.*]

MOLLY. How are you, Uncle Horace? Is that Aunt Aggie? How d'ye do? I haven't seen you since I was a kid.

HORACE. Well, what have you come for?

MOLLY. There's a charming welcome to give your only niece!

HORACE. You know perfectly well, Molly, that I disapprove of you in every way. I hear—I have never read it, of course—but I hear that you have written a most scandalous book. You live in lodgings by yourself, when if you chose you could afford some really nice and refined boarding-house. You have most undesirable acquaintances, and altogether—

MOLLY. Cheer up, Uncle. Now's your chance of reforming me. I've come to live with you. You can support me and improve me at the same time.

HORACE. I never heard such impertinence. I have always understood from you that you earn more than I do.

MOLLY. Ah, yes; but you never *liked* my writing for money, did you? You called me "sexless" once because I said that as long as I could support myself I didn't feel an irresistible temptation to marry that awful little bounder Weekes.

ETHEL. Reginald Weekes! How can you call him a bounder! He was at Oxford.

MOLLY. Hullo, Auntie Ethel! I didn't notice you. You'll be glad to hear I haven't brought much luggage—only a night-gown and some golf-clubs.

HORACE. I suppose this is a joke.

MOLLY. Well, of course, that's one way of looking at it. I'm not going to support myself any longer. I'm going to be a perfect lady, and depend on my Uncle Horace—my nearest male relative—for the necessities of life. [A *motor horn is heard outside*.] Aren't you glad that I am not going to write another scandalous book, or live in lodgings by myself.

ETHEL [*at the window*]. Horace! Horace! There's someone getting out of a motor—a grand motor. [. . .] She's got luggage, too! The chauffeur is bringing in a dressing-case.

HORACE. I'll turn her into the street—and the dressing-case, too.

[*He goes fussily to the door, and meets* MADAME CHRISTINE *on the threshold. The lady is dressed smartly and tastefully. Age about forty, manners elegant, smile charming, speech resolute. She carries a jewel-case, and consults a legal document during her first remarks.*]

MADAME C. You are Mr. Cole?

HORACE. No! Certainly not! [*Wavering.*] At least, I was this morning, but—

MADAME C. Horace Cole, son of John Hay Cole, formerly of Streatham, where he carried on the business of a—

[*A motor horn sounds outside.*]

HORACE. I beg your pardon, but my late father's business has really nothing to do with this matter, and to a professional man it's rather trying to have these things raked up against him. Excuse me, but do you want your motor to go?

MADAME C. It's not my motor any longer; and—yes, I do want it to go, for I may be staying here some time. I think you had one sister, Agatha, and one brother, Samuel, now dead. Samuel was much older than you—

AGATHA. Why don't you answer, Horace? Yes, that's perfectly correct. I am Agatha.

MADAME C. Oh, are you? How d'ye do?

MOLLY. And Samuel Cole was my father.

MADAME C. I'm very glad to meet you. I didn't know I had such charming relations. Well, Mr. Cole, my father was John Hay Cole's first cousin; so you, I think, are my second cousin, and my nearest male relative.

HORACE [*distractedly*]. If anyone calls me that again I shall go mad. [. . .]

HORACE. My dear madam, do you realise that my salary is £3 10s. a week—and that my house will hardy hold your luggage, much less you?

MADAME C. Then you must agitate. Your female relatives have supported themselves up till now, and asked nothing from you. I myself, dear cousin, was, until this morning, running a profitable dressmaking business in Hanover Square. In my public capacity I am Madame Christine. [. . .]

HORACE. Do you think that you are justified in coming to a poor clerk, and asking him to support you—you, who could probably turn over my yearly income in a single week! Didn't you come here in your own motor?

MADAME C. At three o'clock that motor became the property of the Women's Social and Political Union. All the rest of my property and all available cash have been divided equally between the National Union and the Women's Freedom League. Money is the sinews of war, you know.

HORACE. Do you mean to tell me that you've given all your money to the Suffragettes! It's a pity you haven't a husband. He'd very soon put an end to such folly.

MADAME C. I had a husband once. He liked me to do foolish things—for instance, to support him. After that unfortunate experience, Cousin Horace, you may imagine how glad I am to find a man who really is a man, and will support me instead. By the way, I should so much like some tea. Is the kettle boiling?

ETHEL [*feebly*]. There aren't enough cups! Oh, what *shall* I do?

HORACE. Never mind, Ethel; I shan't want any. I am going to dine in town, and go to the theatre. I shall hope to find you all gone when I came back. If not, I shall send for the police.

[*Enter* MAUDIE SPARK, *a young woman with an aggressively cheerful manner, a voice raucous from much bellowing of music-hall songs, a hat of huge size, and a heart of gold.*]

MAUDIE. 'Ullo! 'Ullo! Who's talking about the police? Not my dear cousin Horry?

HORACE. How dare you come here?

MAUDIE. Necessity, old dear. If I could have found a livelier male relative, you may bet I'd have gone to him! But you, Horace, are the only first cousin of this poor orphan. What are you in such a hurry for?

HORACE. Let me pass! I'm going to the theatre.

MAUDIE. Silly jay! the theatres are all closed—and the halls, too. The actresses have gone, on strike—resting indefinitely. I've done my little bit towards that. They won't get any more work out of Maudie Spark, Queen of Comédiennes, until the women have got the vote. Ladies and fellow-relatives, you'll be pleased to hear the strike's going fine. The big drapers can't open to-morrow. One man can't fill the place of fifteen young ladies at once, you see. The duchesses are out in the streets begging people to come in and wash their kids. The City men are trying to get taxi-men in to do their typewriting. [. . .]

HORACE. Even if this is not a plot against me personally, even if there are other women in London at this minute disgracing their sex—

MAUDIE. Here, stop it—come off it! If it comes to that, what are *you* doing—threatening your womankind with the police and the workhouse.

HORACE. I was not addressing myself to you.

AGATHA. Why not, Horace? She's your cousin. She needs your protection just as much as we do.

HORACE. I regard that woman as the skeleton in the cupboard of a respectable family; but that's neither here nor there. I address myself to the more ladylike portion of this gathering, and I say that whatever is going on, the men will know what to do, and will do it with dignity and firmness. [*The impressiveness of this statement is marred by the fact that* HORACE'S *hand, in emphasising it, comes down heavily on the loaf of bread on the table.*] [. . .]

MADAME C. Get a paper, Cousin Horace. I know some men will never believe anything till they see it in the paper.

ETHEL. The boys are shouting out something now. Listen.

[*Shouts outside.* "Extry special. Great strike of women. Women's strike. Theatres closed. Extry special edition. *Star! News!* 6.30 edition!"]

MOLLY. You see. Since this morning Suffragettes have become women!

ETHEL. [. . .] Oh, heavens, here's Aunt Lizzie!

[As ETHEL *pronounces the name* HORACE *dives under the table. Enter* AUNT LIZZIE *leading a fat spaniel and carrying a bird-cage with a Parrot in it.* MISS ELIZABETH WILKINS *is a comfortable, middle-aged body of a type well known to those who live in the less fashionable quarter of Bloomsbury. She looks as if she kept lodgers, and her looks do not belie her. She is not very well educated, but has a good deal of native intelligence. Her features are homely, and her clothes about thirty years behind the times.*]

AUNT L. Well, dears, all here? That's right. Where's Horace? Out? Just as well; we can talk more freely. I'm sorry I'm late, but animals do so hate a move. It took a long time to make them understand the strike. But I think they will be very comfortable here. You love dogs, don't you, Ethel?

ETHEL. Not Ponto. He always growls at me.

AUNT L. Clever dog! he knows you don't sympathise with the cause.

ETHEL. But I do, Aunt; only I have always said that as I was happily married I thought it had very little to do with me.

AUNT L. You've changed your mind about that to-day, I should think! What a day it's been! We never expected everything would go so smoothly. They say the Bill's to be rushed through at once. No more deceitful promises, no more dishonest "facilities"; deeds, not words, at last! Seen the papers? The Press are not words, us to-day, my dears. [MADAME C., MOLLY, AND MAUDIE *each take a paper.*] [. . .]

MOLLY. Oh, do listen to this. It's too splendid! [*Reading from the paper.*] "Women's Strike—Latest: Messrs Lyons and Co. announce that by special arrangement with the War Office the places of their defaulting waitresses will be filled by the non-commissioned officers and men of the 2nd Battalion Coldstream Guards. Business will therefore be carried on as usual." [. . .]

AUNT L. [*to* ETHEL] Well, my dear! What have you got there? Read what the *Star* says.

ETHEL [*tremulously reading*]. "The queue of women waiting for admission to Westminster Workhouse is already a mile and a half in length. As the entire police force are occupied in dealing with the men's processions, Lord Haldane has been approached with a view to ascertaining if the Territorials can be sworn in as special constables."

MAUDIE [*laughing*]. This is a little bit of all right. [*Reading*] "Our special representative, on calling upon the Prime Minister with the object of ascertaining his views on the situation, was informed that the Right Honourable gentleman was unable to receive him, as with the assistance of the boot-boy and a Foreign Office messenger, he was actively engaged in making his bed."

AUNT L. Always unwilling to receive people, you see! Well, he must be feeling sorry now that he never received us. Everyone's putting the blame on him. It's extraordinary how many men—and newspapers, too—have suddenly found out that they have always been in favour of woman's suffrage! [. . .] Any man who tries to oppose us to-day is likely to be slung up to the nearest lamp-post.

ETHEL [*rushing wildly to the table*]. Oh, Horry! my Horry!

[HORACE *comes out from under the table.*]

AUNT L. Why, bless the boy, what are you doing there?

HORACE. Oh, nothing. I merely thought I might be less in the way here, that's all.

AUNT L. You didn't hide when I came in, by any chance!

HORACE. I hide from you! Aren't you always welcome in this house?

AUNT L. Well, I haven't noticed it particularly; and I'm not calling to-day, you understand, I've come to stay. [HORACE, *dashed and beaten, begins to walk up and down the room, and consults* ETHEL.] [. . .] I've given up my boarding-house, and I depend on you, Horace, to keep me until I am admitted to citizenship. It may take a long time.

HORACE. It must *not* take a long time! I shan't allow it. It shall be done at once. Well, you needn't all look so surprised. I know I've been against it, but I didn't realise things. I thought only a few hooligan window-smashers wanted the vote; but when I find that *you*—Aunt—Fancy a woman of your firmness of character, one who has always been so careful with her money, being declared incapable of voting! The thing is absurd.

MAUDIE. Bravo! Our Horry's waking up.

HORACE [*looking at her scornfully*]. If there are a few women here and there who *are* incapable—I mention no names, mind—it doesn't affect the position. What's going to be done? Who's going to do it? If this rotten Government think we're going to maintain millions of women in idleness just because they don't like the idea of my Aunt Lizzie making a scratch on a bit of paper and shoving it into a ballot-box once every five years, this Government have reckoned without the men—[*General cheering*] [. . .] Anyhow, who are the Government? They're only representing *me*, and being paid thousands a year by *me* for carrying out *my* wishes. [. . .] [G]entlemen, the men of England are sick and tired of your policy. Who's driven the women of England into this? *You*—[*he turns round on* ETHEL, *who jumps violently*]—because you were too stupid to know that they meant business—because you couldn't read the writing on the wall. [*Hear, hear.*] It may be nothing to you, gentlemen, that every industry in this country is paralysed and every Englishman's home turned into a howling wilderness— [MOLLY. Draw it mild, Uncle. HORACE. A howling wilderness, I repeat]—by your refusal to see what's as plain as the nose on your face; but I would have you know, gentlemen, that it *is* something to us. We aren't slaves. We never will be slaves—[AGATHA. Never, never!]—and we insist on reform. Gentlemen, conditions have changed, and women have to work. Don't men encourage them to work, *invite* them to work? [AGATHA. *Make* them work.] And women are placed in the battle of life on the same terms as we are, short of one thing, the *locus standi* of a vote. [MAUDIE. Good old *locus standi!*] [. . .] It's dawning upon us all that the women would never have taken such a step as this if they hadn't been the victims of a gross injustice. [ALL. Never.] Why shouldn't they have a voice in the laws which regulate the price of food and clothes? Don't they pay for their food and clothes? [MAUDIE. Paid for mine since the age of six.] Why shouldn't they have a voice in the rate of wages and the hours of labour in certain industries? Aren't they working at those industries? If you had a particle of common sense or decent feeling, gentlemen—"

[*Enter* GERALD WILLIAMS *like a souvenir of Mafeking night.*[1] *He shouts incoherently and in a hoarse voice. He is utterly transformed from the meek, smug being of an hour before. He is wearing several ribbons and badges and carries a banner bearing this inscription: "The men of Brixton demand votes for women this evening."*]

WILLIAMS. Cole, Cole! Come on! come on! You'll be late. The procession's forming up at the town hall. There's no time to lose. What are you slacking here for? Perhaps this isn't good enough for you. I've got twelve of them in my drawing-room. We shall be late for the procession if we don't start at once. Hurry up! Come on! Votes for Women! Where's your banner? Where's your badge? Down with the Government! Rule Britannia! Votes for Women! D'you want to support a dozen women for the rest of your life, or don't you? . . . Every man in Brixton is going to Westminster. Borrow a ribbon and come along. Hurry up, now! Hooray! [*Rushes madly out crying* "Votes for Women! Rule Britannia; Women never, never shall be slaves! Votes for Women!"]

[*All the women who are wearing ribbons decorate* HORACE.]

ETHEL. My hero! [*She throws her arms round him.*]

HORACE. You may depend on me—all of you—to see justice done. When you want a thing done, get a man to do it! Votes for Women!

[AGATHA *gives him a flag which he waves triumphantly.*]

 [*Curtain tableau:* HORACE *marching majestically out of the door, with the women cheering him enthusiastically.*]

[CURTAIN.]

Produced for the first time at the Royalty Theatre, London, April 13, 1909. London: Edith Craig, 1913.

Note

 1. A night celebrating the 217-day Boer siege of the town of Mafeking in the Republic of South Africa.

SOPHIE TREADWELL

From *Machinal*

Episode I. To Business.

Episode II. At Home.

Episode III. Honeymoon.

Episode IV. Maternal.

Episode V. Prohibited.

Episode VI. Intimate.

Episode VII. Domestic.

Episode VIII. The Law.

Episode IX. A Machine.

THE PLOT is the story of a woman who murders her husband—an ordinary young woman, any woman.

THE PLAN is to tell this story by showing the different phases of life that the woman comes in contact with, and in none of which she finds any place, any peace. The woman is essentially soft, tender, and the life around her is essentially hard, mechanized. Business, home, marriage, having a child, seeking pleasure—all are difficult for her—mechanical, nerve nagging. Only in an illicit love does she find anything with life in it for her, and when she loses this, the desperate effort to win free to it again is her undoing.

The story is told in nine scenes. In the dialogue of these scenes there is the attempt to catch the rhythm of our common city speech, its brassy sound, its trick of repetition, etc.

Then there is, also, the use of many different sounds chosen primarily for their inherent emotional effect (steel rivetting, a priest chanting, a Negro singing, jazz band, etc.), but contributing also to the creation of a background, an atmosphere.

THE HOPE is to create a stage production that will have "style," and at the same time, by the story's own innate drama, by the directness of its telling, by the variety and quick changingness of its scenes, and the excitement of its sounds, to create an interesting play. [. . .]

LIGHTING concentrated and intense.—Light and shadow—bright light and darkness.—This darkness, already in the scene, grows and blacks out the light for dark stage when the scene changes are made.

EPISODE EIGHT
THE LAW

SCENE: *Courtroom.*

SOUNDS: *Clicking of telegraph instruments offstage.*

CHARACTERS:

JUDGE	MESSENGER BOYS
JURY	LAW CLERKS
LAWYERS	BAILIFF
SPECTATORS	COURT REPORTER
REPORTERS	YOUNG WOMAN

The words and movements of all these people except the YOUNG WOMAN *are routine—mechanical—Each is going through the motions of his own game.*

AT RISE: ALL *assemble, except* JUDGE.

(*Enter* JUDGE.)

BAILIFF (*mumbling*). Hear ye—hear ye—hear ye!

(ALL *rise.* JUDGE *sits.* ALL *sit.*)

(LAWYER FOR DEFENSE *gets to his feet—He is the verbose, "eloquent"—typical criminal defense lawyer*)

(JUDGE *signs to him to wait—turns to* LAW CLERKS; *grouped at foot of the bench*)

1ST CLERK. (*handing up a paper—routine voice*). State versus Kling—stay of execution.

JUDGE. Denied.

(1ST CLERK *goes.*)

2ND CLERK. Bing vs. Ding—demurrer.

(JUDGE *Signs.*)

(2ND CLERK *goes.*)

3RD CLERK. Case of John King—habeas corpus.

(JUDGE *Signs.*) (3RD CLERK *goes.*) (JUDGE *Signs to* BAILIFF.)

BAILIFF (*mumbling*). People of the State of—versus Helen Jones.

JUDGE. (*to* LAWYER FOR THE DEFENSE) Defense ready to proceed?

LAWYER FOR DEFENSE. We're ready, your Honor.

JUDGE. Proceed.

LAWYER FOR DEFENSE. Helen Jones.

BAILIFF. HELEN JONES! (YOUNG WOMAN *rises.*)

LAWYER FOR DEFENSE. Mrs. Jones, will you take the stand?

(YOUNG WOMAN *goes to witness stand.*)

1ST REPORTER (*writing rapidly*). The defense sprang a surprise at the opening of court this morning by putting the accused woman on the stand. The prosecution was swept off its feet by this daring defense strategy and—

(*Instruments get louder.*)

2ND REPORTER. Trembling and scarcely able to stand, Helen Jones, accused murderess, had to be almost carried to the witness stand this morning when her lawyer—

BAILIFF (*mumbling—with Bible*). Do you swear to tell the truth, the whole truth and nothing but the truth—so help you God?

YOUNG WOMAN. I do.

JUDGE. You may sit. (*She sits in witness chair.*)

COURT REPORTER. What is your name?

YOUNG WOMAN. Helen Jones.

COURT REPORTER. Your age?

YOUNG WOMAN (*hesitates—then*). Twenty-nine.

COURT REPORTER. Where do you live?

YOUNG WOMAN. In prison.

LAWYER FOR DEFENSE. This is my client's legal address.

(*Hands a scrap of paper.*)

LAWYER FOR PROSECUTION (*jumping to his feet*). I object to this insinuation on the part of counsel on any illegality in the holding of this defendant in jail when the law—

LAWYER FOR DEFENSE. I made no such insinuation.

LAWYER FOR PROSECUTION. You implied it—

LAWYER FOR DEFENSE. I did not!

LAWYER FOR PROSECUTION. You're a—

JUDGE. Order!

BAILIFF. Order!

LAWYER FOR DEFENSE. Your Honor, I object to counsel's constant attempt to—

LAWYER FOR PROSECUTION. I protest—I—

JUDGE. Order!

BAILIFF. Order!

JUDGE. Proceed with the witness.

LAWYER FOR DEFENSE. Mrs. Jones, you are the widow of the late George H. Jones, are you not?

YOUNG WOMAN. Yes.

LAWYER FOR DEFENSE. How long were you married to the late George H. Jones before his demise?

YOUNG WOMAN. Six years.

LAWYER FOR DEFENSE. Six years! And it was a happy marriage, was it not? (YOUNG WOMAN *hesitates*.) Did you quarrel?

YOUNG WOMAN. No, Sir.

LAWYER FOR DEFENSE. Then it was a happy marriage, wasn't it?

YOUNG WOMAN. Yes, Sir.

LAWYER FOR DEFENSE. In those six years of married life with your late husband, the late George H. Jones, did you EVER have a quarrel?

YOUNG WOMAN. No, Sir.

LAWYER FOR DEFENSE. Never one quarrel?

LAWYER FOR PROSECUTION. The witness has said—

LAWYER FOR DEFENSE. Six years without one quarrel! Six years! Gentlemen of the jury, I ask you to consider this fact! Six years of married life without a quarrel. (*The* JURY *grins*.) I ask you to consider it seriously! Very seriously! Who of us—and this is not intended as any reflection on the sacred institution of marriage—no—but!

JUDGE. Proceed with your witness.

LAWYER FOR DEFENSE. You have one child—have you not, Mrs. Jones?

YOUNG WOMAN. Yes, Sir.

LAWYER FOR DEFENSE. A little girl, is it not?

YOUNG WOMAN. Yes, Sir.

LAWYER FOR DEFENSE. How old is she?

YOUNG WOMAN. She's five—past five.

LAWYER FOR DEFENSE. A little girl of past five. Since the demise of the late Mr. Jones you are the only parent she has living, are you not?

YOUNG WOMAN. Yes, Sir.

LAWYER FOR DEFENSE. Before your marriage to the late Mr. Jones, you worked and supported your mother; did you not?

LAWYER FOR PROSECUTION. I object, your honor! Irrelevant—immaterial—and—

JUDGE. Objection sustained!

LAWYER FOR DEFENSE. In order to support your mother and yourself as a girl, you worked, did you not?

YOUNG WOMAN. Yes, Sir.

LAWYER FOR DEFENSE. What did you do?

YOUNG WOMAN. I was a stenographer.

LAWYER FOR DEFENSE. And since your marriage you have continued as her sole support, have you not?

YOUNG WOMAN. Yes, Sir.

LAWYER FOR DEFENSE. A devoted daughter, gentlemen of the jury! As well as a devoted wife and a devoted mother!

LAWYER FOR PROSECUTION. Your Honor!

LAWYER FOR DEFENSE (*quickly*). And now, Mrs. Jones, I will ask you—the law expects me to ask you—it demands that I ask you—did you—or did you not—on the night of June 2nd last or the morning of June 3rd last—kill your husband, the late George H. Jones—did you, or did you not?

YOUNG WOMAN. I did not.

LAWYER FOR DEFENSE. You did not?

YOUNG WOMAN. I did not.

LAWYER FOR DEFENSE. NOW, Mrs. Jones, you have heard the witnesses for the State—They were not many—and they did not have much to say—

LAWYER FOR PROSECUTION. I object.

JUDGE. Sustained.

LAWYER FOR DEFENSE. You have heard some police and you have heard some doctors. None of whom was present! The prosecution could not furnish any witness to the crime—not one witness!

LAWYER FOR PROSECUTION. Your Honor!

LAWYER FOR DEFENSE. Nor one motive.

LAWYER FOR PROSECUTION. Your Honor—I protest! I—

JUDGE. Sustained.

LAWYER FOR DEFENSE. But such as these witnesses were, you have heard them try to accuse you of deliberately murdering your own husband, this husband with whom, by your own statement, you had never had a quarrel—not one quarrel in six years of married life, murdering him, I say, or rather they say, while he slept, by brutally hitting him over the head with a bottle—a bottle filled with small stones—Did you, I repeat this, or did you not?

YOUNG WOMAN. I did not.

LAWYER FOR DEFENSE. You did not! Of course you did not! (*Quickly.*) Now, Mrs. Jones, will you tell the jury in your own words exactly what happened on the night of June 2nd or the morning of June 3rd last, at the time your husband was killed.

YOUNG WOMAN. I was awakened by hearing somebody—something—in the room, and I saw two men standing by my husband's bed.

LAWYER FOR DEFENSE. Your husband's bed—that was also your bed, was it not, Mrs. Jones?

YOUNG WOMAN. Yes.

LAWYER FOR DEFENSE. You hadn't the modern idea of separate beds, had you, Mrs. Jones?

YOUNG WOMAN. Mr. Jones objected.

LAWYER FOR DEFENSE. I mean you slept in the same bed, did you not?

YOUNG WOMAN. Yes.

LAWYER FOR DEFENSE. Then explain just what you meant by saying "my husband's bed."

YOUNG WOMAN. Well—I—

LAWYER FOR DEFENSE. You meant his side of the bed, didn't you?

YOUNG WOMAN. Yes. His side.

LAWYER FOR DEFENSE. That is what I thought, but I wanted the jury to be clear on that point. (*To the* JURY.) Mr. and Mrs. Jones slept in the same bed. (*To her.*) Go on, Mrs. Jones. (*As she is silent.*) You heard a noise and—

YOUNG WOMAN. I heard a noise and I awoke and saw two men standing beside my husband's side of the bed.

LAWYER FOR DEFENSE. Two men?

YOUNG WOMAN. Yes.

LAWYER FOR DEFENSE. Can you describe them?

YOUNG WOMAN. Not very well—I couldn't see them very well.

LAWYER FOR DEFENSE. Could you say whether they were big or small—light or dark, thin or—

YOUNG WOMAN. They were big dark looking men.

LAWYER FOR DEFENSE. Big dark looking men?

YOUNG WOMAN. Yes.

LAWYER FOR DEFENSE. And what did you do, Mrs. Jones, when you suddenly awoke and saw two big dark looking men standing beside your bed?

YOUNG WOMAN. I didn't do anything!

LAWYER FOR DEFENSE. You didn't have time to do anything—did you?

YOUNG WOMAN. No. Before I could do anything—one of them raised—something in his hand and struck Mr. Jones over the head with it.

LAWYER FOR DEFENSE. And what did Mr. Jones do?

(SPECTATORS *laugh.*)

JUDGE. Silence.

BAILIFF. Silence.

LAWYER FOR DEFENSE. What did Mr. Jones do, Mrs. Jones?

YOUNG WOMAN. He gave a sort of groan and tried to raise up.

LAWYER FOR DEFENSE. Tried to raise up!

YOUNG WOMAN. Yes!

LAWYER FOR DEFENSE. And then what happened?

YOUNG WOMAN. The man struck him again and he fell back.

LAWYER FOR DEFENSE. I see. What did the men do then? The big dark looking men.

YOUNG WOMAN. They turned and ran out of the room.

LAWYER FOR DEFENSE. I see. What did you do then, Mrs. Jones?

YOUNG WOMAN. I saw Mr. Jones was bleeding from the temple. I got towels and tried to stop it, and then I realized he had—passed away—

LAWYER FOR DEFENSE. I see. What did you do then?

YOUNG WOMAN. I didn't know what to do. But I thought I'd better call the police. So I went to the telephone and called the police.

LAWYER FOR DEFENSE. What happened then.

YOUNG WOMAN. Nothing. Nothing happened.

LAWYER FOR DEFENSE. The police came, didn't they?

YOUNG WOMAN. Yes—they came.

LAWYER FOR DEFENSE (*quickly*). And that is all you know concerning the death of your husband in the late hours of June 2nd or the early hours of June 3rd last, isn't it?

YOUNG WOMAN. Yes sir.

LAWYER FOR DEFENSE. All?

YOUNG WOMAN. Yes Sir.

LAWYER FOR DEFENSE (*to* LAWYER FOR PROSECUTION). Take the witness.

1ST REPORTFR (*writing*). The accused woman told a straightforward story of—

2ND REPORTER. The accused woman told a rambling, disconnected story of—

LAWYER FOR PROSECUTION. You made no effort to cry out, Mrs. Jones, did you, when you saw those two big dark men standing over your helpless husband, did you?

YOUNG WOMAN. No Sir. I didn't, I—

LAWYER FOR PROSECUTION. And when they turned and ran out of the room, you made no effort to follow them or cry out after them, did you?

YOUNG WOMAN. No sir,

LAWYER FOR PROSECUTION. Why didn't you?

YOUNG WOMAN. I saw Mr. Jones was hurt.

LAWYER FOR PROSECUTION. Ah! You saw Mr. Jones was hurt! You saw this—how did you see it?

YOUNG WOMAN. I just saw it.

LAWYER FOR PROSECUTION. Then there was a light in the room?

YOUNG WOMAN. A sort of light.

LAWYER FOR PROSECUTION. What do you mean—a sort of light? A bed light?

YOUNG WOMAN. No. No, there was no light on.

LAWYER FOR PROSECUTION. Then where did it come from—this sort of light?

YOUNG WOMAN. I don't know.

LAWYER FOR PROSECUTION. perhaps—from the window.

YOUNG WOMAN. Yes—from the window,

LAWYER FOR PROSECUTION. Oh, the shade was up!

YOUNG WOMAN. No—no, the shade was down.

LAWYER FOR PROSECUTION. You're sure of that?

YOUNG WOMAN. Yes, Mr. Jones always wanted the shade down.

LAWYER FOR PROSECUTION. The shade was down—there was no light in the room—but the room was light—how do you explain this?

YOUNG WOMAN. I don't know.

LAWYER FOR PROSECUTION. You don't know!

YOUNG WOMAN. I think where the window was open—under the shade— light came in—

LAWYER FOR PROSECUTION. There is a street light there?

YOUNG WOMAN. No—there's no street light.

LAWYER FOR PROSECUTION. Then where did this light come from   that came in under the shade?

YOUNG WOMAN (*desperately*). From the moon!

LAWYER FOR PROSECUTION. The moon!

YOUNG WOMAN. Yes! It was bright moon!

LAWYER FOR PROSECUTION. It was bright moon—you are sure of that!

YOUNG WOMAN. Yes.

LAWYER FOR PROSECUTION. How are you sure?

YOUNG WOMAN. I couldn't sleep—I never can sleep in the bright moon. I never can.

LAWYER FOR PROSECUTION. It was bright moon. Yet you could not see two big dark looking men—but you could see your husband bleeding from the temple.

YOUNG WOMAN. Yes Sir.

LAWYER FOR PROSECUTION. And did you call a doctor?

YOUNG WOMAN. No.

LAWYER FOR PROSECUTION. Why didn't you?

YOUNG WOMAN. The police did.

LAWYER FOR PROSECUTION. But you didn't?

YOUNG WOMAN. No.

LAWYER FOR PROSECUTION. Why didn't you? (*No answer.*) Why didn't you?

YOUNG WOMAN (*whispers*). I saw it was—useless.

LAWYER FOR PROSECUTION. Ah! You saw that! You saw that—very clearly.

YOUNG WOMAN. Yes.

LAWYER FOR PROSECUTION. And you didn't call a doctor.

YOUNG WOMAN. It was—useless.

LAWYER FOR PROSECUTION. What did you do?

YOUNG WOMAN. It was useless—there was no use of anything.

LAWYER FOR PROSECUTION. I asked you what you did?

YOUNG WOMAN. Nothing.

LAWYER FOR PROSECUTION. Nothing!

YOUNG WOMAN. I just sat there.

LAWYER FOR PROSECUTION. You sat there! A long while, didn't you?

YOUNG WOMAN. I don't know.

LAWYER FOR PROSECUTION. You don't know? (*Showing her the neck of a broken bottle.*) Mrs. Jones, did you ever see this before?

YOUNG WOMAN. I think so.

LAWYER FOR PROSECUTION. You think so.

YOUNG WOMAN. Yes.

LAWYER FOR PROSECUTION. What do you think it is?

YOUNG WOMAN. I think it's the bottle that was used against Mr. Jones.

LAWYER FOR PROSECUTION. Used against him—yes—that's right. You've guessed right. This neck and these broken pieces and these pebbles were found on the floor and scattered over the bed. There were no fingerprints, Mrs. Jones, on this bottle. None at all, Doesn't that seem strange to you?

YOUNG WOMAN. No.

LAWYER FOR PROSECUTION. It doesn't seem strange to you that this bottle held in the big dark hand of one of those big dark men left no mark! No print! That doesn't seem strange to you?

YOUNG WOMAN. No.

LAWYER FOR PROSECUTION. You are in the habit of wearing rubber gloves at night, Mrs. Jones—are you not? To protect—to soften your hands—are you not?

YOUNG WOMAN. I used to.

LAWYER FOR PROSECUTION. Used to—when was that?

YOUNG WOMAN. Before I was married.

LAWYER FOR PROSECUTION. And after marriage you gave it up?

YOUNG WOMAN. Yes.

LAWYER FOR PROSECUTION. Why?

YOUNG WOMAN. Mr. Jones did not like the feeling of them.

LAWYER FOR PROSECUTION. You always did everything Mr. Jones wanted?

YOUNG WOMAN. I tried to—Anyway I didn't care any more—so much—about my hands.

LAWYER FOR PROSECUTION. I see—so after marriage you never wore gloves at night any more?

YOUNG WOMAN. No.

LAWYER FOR PROSECUTION. Mrs. Jones, isn't it true that you began wearing your rubber gloves again—in spite of your husband's expressed dislike—about a year ago—a year ago this spring?

YOUNG WOMAN. No.

LAWYER FOR PROSECUTION. You did not suddenly begin to care particularly for your hands again—about a year ago this spring?

YOUNG WOMAN. No.

LAWYER FOR PROSECUTION. You're quite sure of that?

YOUNG WOMAN. Yes.

LAWYER FOR PROSECUTION. Quite sure?

YOUNG WOMAN. Yes.

LAWYER FOR PROSECUTION. Then you did not have in your possession, on the night of June 2nd last, a pair of rubber gloves?

YOUNG WOMAN (*shakes her head*). No.

LAWYER FOR PROSECUTION (*to* JUDGE). I'd like to introduce these gloves as evidence at this time, your Honor.

JUDGE. Exhibit 24.

LAWYER FOR PROSECUTION. I'll return to them later—now, Mrs. Jones—this nightgown—you recognize it, don't you?

YOUNG WOMAN. Yes.

LAWYER FOR PROSECUTION. Yours, is it not?

YOUNG WOMAN. Yes.

LAWYER FOR PROSECUTION. The one you were wearing the night your husband was murdered, isn't it?

YOUNG WOMAN. The night he died,—yes.

LAWYER FOR PROSECUTION. Not the one you wore under your peignoir—I believe that is what you call it, isn't it? A peignoir? When you received the police—but the one you wore before that—isn't it?

YOUNG WOMAN. Yes.

LAWYER FOR PROSECUTION. This was found—not where the gloves were found—no—but at the bottom of the soiled clothes hamper in the bathroom—rolled up and wet—why was it wet, Mrs. Jones?

YOUNG WOMAN. I had tried to wash it.

LAWYER FOR PROSECUTION. Wash it? I thought you had just sat?

YOUNG WOMAN. First—I tried to make things clean.

LAWYER FOR PROSECUTION. Why did you want to make this—clean—as you say?

YOUNG WOMAN. There was blood on it.

LAWYER FOR PROSECUTION. Spattered on it?

YOUNG WOMAN. Yes.

LAWYER FOR PROSECUTION. How did that happen?

YOUNG WOMAN. The bottle broke—and the sharp edge cut.

LAWYER FOR PROSECUTION. Oh, the bottle broke and the sharp edge cut!

YOUNG WOMAN. Yes. That's what they told me afterwards.

LAWYER FOR PROSECUTION. Who told you?

YOUNG WOMAN. The police—that's what they say happened.

LAWYER FOR PROSECUTION. Mrs. Jones, why did you try so desperately to wash that blood away—before you called the police?

LAWYER FOR DEFENSE. I object!

JUDGE. Objection overruled.

LAWYER FOR PROSECUTION. Why, Mrs. Jones?

YOUNG WOMAN. I don't know. It's what anyone would have done, wouldn't they?

LAWYER FOR PROSECUTION. That depends, doesn't it? (*Suddenly taking up bottle.*) Mrs. Jones—when did you first see this?

YOUNG WOMAN. The night my husband was—done away with.

LAWYER FOR PROSECUTION. Done away with! You mean killed?

YOUNG WOMAN. Yes.

LAWYER FOR PROSECUTION. Why don't you say killed?

YOUNG WOMAN. It sounds so brutal.

LAWYER FOR PROSECUTION. And you never saw this before then?

YOUNG WOMAN. No Sir.

LAWYER FOR PROSECUTION. You're quite sure of that?

YOUNG WOMAN. Yes.

LAWYER FOR PROSECUTION. And these stones—when did you first see them?

YOUNG WOMAN. The night my husband was done away with.

LAWYER FOR PROSECUTION. Before that night your husband was murdered—you never saw them? Never before then?

YOUNG WOMAN. No Sir.

LAWYER FOR PROSECUTION. You are quite sure of that!

YOUNG WOMAN. Yes.

LAWYER FOR PROSECUTION. Mrs. Jones, do you remember about a year ago, a year ago this spring, bringing home to your house—a lily, a Chinese water lily?

YOUNG WOMAN. No—I don't think I do.

LAWYER FOR PROSECUTION. You don't think you remember bringing home a water lily growing in a bowl filled with small stones?

YOUNG WOMAN. No—No I don't.

LAWYER FOR PROSECUTION. I'll show you this bowl, Mrs. Jones. Does that refresh your memory?

YOUNG WOMAN. I remember the bowl—but I don't remember—the lily.

LAWYER FOR PROSECUTION. You recognize the bowl then?

YOUNG WOMAN. Yes.

LAWYER FOR PROSECUTION. It is yours, isn't it?

YOUNG WOMAN. It was in my house—yes.

LAWYER FOR PROSECUTION. How did it come there?

YOUNG WOMAN. How did it come there?

LAWYER FOR PROSECUTION. Yes—where did you get it?

YOUNG WOMAN. I don't remember.

LAWYER FOR PROSECUTION. You don't remember?

YOUNG WOMAN. No.

LAWYER FOR PROSECUTION. You don't remember about a year ago bringing this bowl into your bedroom filled with small stones and some water and a lily? You don't remember tending very carefully that lily till it died? And when it died you don't remember hiding the bowl full of little stones away on the top shelf of your closet—and keeping it there until—you don't remember?

YOUNG WOMAN. No, I don't remember.

LAWYER FOR PROSECUTION. You may have done so?

YOUNG WOMAN. No—no—I didn't! I didn't! I don't know anything about all that.

LAWYER FOR PROSECUTION. But you do remember the bowl?

YOUNG WOMAN. Yes. It was in my house—you found it in my house.

LAWYER FOR PROSECUTION. But you don't remember the lily or the stones?

YOUNG WOMAN. No—No I don't!

(LAWYER FOR PROSECUTION *turns to look among his papers in a brief case.*)

1ST REPORTER (*writing*). Under the heavy artillery fire of the State's attorney's brilliant cross-questioning, the accused woman's defense was badly riddled. Pale and trembling she—

2ND REPORTER (*writing*). Undaunted by the Prosecution's machine-gun attack, the defendant was able to maintain her position of innocence in the face of rapid-fire questioning that threatened, but never seriously menaced her defense. Flushed but calm she—

LAWYER FOR PROSECUTION (*producing paper*). Your Honor, I'd like to introduce this paper in evidence at this time.

JUDGE. What is it?

LAWYER FOR PROSECUTION. It is an affidavit taken in the State of Guanajato, Mexico.

LAWYER FOR DEFENSE. Mexico? Your Honor, I protest. A Mexican affidavit! Is this the United States of America or isn't it?

LAWYER FOR PROSECUTION. It's properly executed—sworn to before a notary—and certified to by an American Consul.

LAWYER FOR DEFENSE. Your Honor! I protest! In the name of this great United States of America—I protest—are we to permit our sacred institutions to be thus—

JUDGE. What is the purpose of this document—who signed it?

LAWYER FOR PROSECUTION. It is signed by one Richard Roe, and its purpose is to refresh the memory of the witness on the point at issue—and incidentally supply a motive for this murder—this brutal and cold-blooded murder of a sleeping man by—

LAWYER FOR DEFENSE. I protest, your Honor! I object!

JUDGE. Objection sustained. Let me see the document. (*Takes paper which is handed up to him—looks at it.*) Perfectly regular. Do you offer this affidavit as evidence at this time for the purpose of refreshing the memory of the witness at this time?

LAWYER FOR PROSECUTION. Yes, your Honor.

JUDGE. You may introduce the evidence.

LAWYER FOR DEFENSE. I object! I object to the introduction of this evidence at this time as irrelevant, immaterial, illegal, biased, prejudicial, and—

JUDGE. Objection overruled.

LAWYER FOR DEFENSE. Exception.

JUDGE. Exception noted. Proceed.

LAWYER FOR PROSECUTION. I wish to read the evidence to the jury at this time.

JUDGE. Proceed.

LAWYER FOR DEFENSE. I object.

JUDGE. Objection overruled.

LAWYER FOR DEFENSE. Exception.

JUDGE. Noted.

LAWYER FOR DEFENSE. Why is this witness himself not brought into court—so he can be cross-questioned?

LAWYER FOR PROSECUTION. The witness is a resident of the Republic of Mexico and as such not subject to subpoena as a witness to this court.

LAWYER FOR DEFENSE. If he was out of the jurisdiction of this court how did you get his affidavit out of him?

LAWYER FOR PROSECUTION. This affidavit was made voluntarily by the deponent in the furtherance of justice.

LAWYER FOR DEFENSE. I suppose you didn't threaten him with extradition on some other trumped-up charge so that—

JUDGE. Order!

BAILIFF. Order!

JUDGE. Proceed with the evidence.

LAWYER FOR PROSECUTION (*reading*). In the matter of the State of—vs. Helen Jones, I Richard Roe, being of sound mind, do herein depose and state that I know the accused, Helen Jones, and have known her for a period of over one year immediately preceding the date of the signature on this affidavit. That I first met the said Helen Jones in a so-called speak-easy somewhere in the West 40s in New York City. That on the day I met her, she went with me to my room, also somewhere in the West 40s in New York City, where we had intimate relations—

YOUNG WOMAN (*moans*). Oh!

LAWYER FOR PROSECUTION (*continues reading*).—and where I gave her a blue bowl filled with pebbles, also containing a flowering lily. That from the first day we met until I departed for Mexico in the Fall, the said Helen Jones was an almost daily visitor to my room where we continued to—

YOUNG WOMAN. No! No!

(*Moans.*)

LAWYER FOR PROSECUTION. What is it, Mrs. Jones—what is it?

YOUNG WOMAN. Don't read any more! No more!

LAWYER FOR PROSECUTION. Why not?

YOUNG WOMAN. I did it! I did it! I did it!

LAWYER FOR PROSECUTION. You Confess?

YOUNG WOMAN. Yes—I did it!

LAWYER FOR DEFENSE. I object, your Honor.

JUDGE. You confess you killed your husband?

YOUNG WOMAN. I put him out of the way—yes.

JUDGE. Why?

YOUNG WOMAN. To be free.

JUDGE. To be free? Is that the only reason?

YOUNG WOMAN. Yes.

JUDGE. If you just wanted to be free—why didn't you divorce him?

YOUNG WOMAN. Oh I couldn't do that! I couldn't hurt him like that!

(Burst of laughter from ALL *in the court. The* YOUNG WOMAN *stares out at them, and then seems to go rigid.)*

JUDGE. Silence!

BAILIFF. Silence! *(There is a gradual silence.)*

JUDGE. Mrs. Jones, why—(YOUNG WOMAN *begins to moan—suddenly—as though the realization of her enormity and her isolation had just come upon her. It is a sound of desolation, of agony, of human woe. It continues until the end of the scene.)* Why—?

(YOUNG WOMAN *cannot speak.)*

LAWYER FOR DEFENSE. Your Honor, I ask a recess to—

JUDGE. Court's adjourned.

(SPECTATORS *begin to file out. The* YOUNG WOMAN *continues in the witness box, unseeing, unheeding.)*

1ST REPORTER. Murderess confesses.

2ND REPORTER. Paramour brings confession.

3RD REPORTER. I did it! Woman cries!

(There is a great burst of speed from the telegraphic instruments. They keep up a constant accompaniment to the WOMAN'S *moans. The scene* BLACKS OUT *as the courtroom empties and* TWO POLICEMEN *go to stand by the woman.)*

BLACK OUT

(The sound of the telegraph instruments continues until the scene lights into EPISODE NINE—*and the prayers of the* PRIEST.*)*

First produced by Arthur Hopkins at the Plymouth Theatre, New York City, on September 7, 1928. First published 1949. This version first published in *Twenty-Five Best Plays of the Modern American Theatre*, edited with an introduction by John Gassner. New York: Crown Publishers, 1966. 495–96, 519–26.

RAVIEN SIURLAI (FERDINAND HARDEKOPF)

Emmy Hennings

Amid the ingratiatingly dusty smiles of the chansonniers, her waxen face bound up, her yellow hair cut short in a page-boy, with stiffly piled kiss-curls and the dark of her delicate silk dress divorced from every human feeling, on to the cabaret stage of unbalanced despair, the stage of gentlemen who stand on one another's heads, the devastated variety stage run for four years by Jacob von Hoddis steps Frau Emmy Hennings . . . Emmy Hennings, protectorate of fever and magical death, displayed not even the moral inhibitions which make it possible to enjoy hymns to adultery. Rarely have maskers misunderstood and applauded such negligence; Claire Waldoff, parodying the cabaret orgies, and, in Frankfurt, the convulsively twitching ballet skirt of Sidi Riha—oh sea and foam sweetly congealed into the rustle of tulle—a woman is a creature of infinities, gentlemen. But one must not necessarily confuse eroticism with prostitution. (There's nothing wrong with eroticism, but prostitution always implies syphilis.) Then Frau Hennings revealed, not politely enough to mask herself, to her partner, that he is the aphrodisiac of a pimp. And again applause indicates that attention slumbers. For who can prevent this girl, possessed by hysteria, irritation and the brain-churning intensity of the literati, increasing to avalanche proportions, from waltzing in the direction of parliamentarianism, the only institution where the desperation and destructive anger of the oppressed can be dissipated without danger, without leaving a trace and promoting business. Don't take it lightly. . . . All right then, let's liberate the public, which is inhibited from taking things seriously. Let's teach it to respect itself, its reactions, its bourgeois order. Emmy Hennings needs a sketch in which the explosive perspectives of American electric billboards will turn criminal-tragedies into jokes, and where people will kill each other out of indifference as the stage caves in. And while Emmy Hennings, heavily made-up, hypnotized by the fracturing gaze of the dying, torn by morphine and absinthe and by the bloody flames of the electric halo, will be frozen in the uttermost Gothic distortion, her voice will frisk over the corpses and mock them like a yellow canary trilling soulfully. Emmy Hennings performed in the Linden cabaret in Berlin.

A review of a pre-Dada cabaret performance by Emmy Hennings in 1912 [ed.].

Die Aktion (June 5, 1912), n.p. Trans. by Lawrence Seneliak. Published in Katherine Weinstein. "Subversive Women: Female Performing Artists in Zurich Dada." Ph.D. diss., Tufts University, 2001.

EMMY HENNINGS

The Perhaps Last Flight

Trans. Judith Bach and Katherine Weinstein

Deep night. Silent. A steep room in a foreign city. Square.
Dull candle-light flickers.
A door opens demonically.
Two beings sit in front of each other. A man and a woman.
The man (sinking into two grey lakes which have also been restless) says:
"I want to look at you. Always look at you—look very closely . . ."
The woman (slowly and extenuated): "I believe one should not look closely at
anything. Just not look closely. I believe . . ."
The man: "You believe, you say?"
The woman (hesitating): "Yes, to me everything seems doubtful. Everything
questionable. Maybe . . ."
He (drinking her in): "O, talk to me—I listen."
She (consuming, with an interrupted gesture): "Take me! Take me!"
They fell into each other. She flew to him . . .
Later he immediately grabbed a cigarette.
She smiled silently (a smile that seemed even sweeter because it was so rare):
"Ah! You are one of those. Hm. Immediately new sensations."
He: "Another subject."
His eyes looked cool. Around the malicious narrow lips, a grey smile was
roaming. The smile of a murderer.
She looked thunderstruck at his open mouth. His eyes narrowed cynically.
There it struck her. Eyes burned into one another. Drew them in . . .
There she recognized him. A secret sign passed between them.
He: "Yes, yes . . . I am the one."
She trembled. She fell timidly into his hands. And then (looking up at
     him while
lying prone): "For you I live—for you I die."
And again this grey smile of a murderer around his mouth.
The next day they met. He asked: "How are you?"
And she died because she felt observed.

"Die vielleicht letzte Flucht." *Cabaret Voltaire: Eine Sammlung kiinstlericher und literarischer
Beiträge* (1916): 28. Translated and published in Katherine Weinstein, "Subversive Women: Female
Performing Artists in Zurich Dada." Ph.D. diss., Tufts University, 2001.

SUZANNE PERROTTET

A Description of Emmy Hennings Dancing in a Cardboard Dada Costume

Trans. Judith Bach and Katherine Weinstein

She stood there, dressed in a cardboard pipe from head to toe.[1] Her face was a horrible mask with an open mouth and the nose pressed to the side, her arms in thin cardboard pipes lengthened with stylized long fingers. The only living part of her that one could see were the feet, naked all alone down there—that was so terse and expressive. She had been dancing like this. She couldn't do anything else but slap the ground with her feet or tip the whole thing like a chimney and during that she also spoke here and there. But one didn't understand it. One felt it. And sometimes she expelled a scream, a scream . . . I had never seen anything like it and I was won over by the Dadaists.

Translated and published in Katherine Weinstein. "Subversive Women: Female Performing Artists in Zurich Dada." Ph.D. diss., Tufts University, 2001.

Note

1. Suzanne Perrottet was a Laban dancer and composer.

19

Modernism, Gender, and Dance

INTRODUCED AND SELECTED BY CAROL SHLOSS

FROM ITS BEGINNINGS, modern dance was informed by debates about gender, nature, artifice, and the meaning and procedures of staging human subjectivity. Its first and most famous advocate, Isadora Duncan, intent to teach as well as perform, explained that she wanted to use the body to reconceptualize women's place in western culture, and she imagined that her techniques of performance would be relevant to living as well as dancing. "For me the dance is not only the art that gives expression to the human soul through movement, but also the foundation of a complete conception of life, more free, more harmonious, more natural. . . . What I want is a school of life" (*Isadora Speaks* 31).

Paris's foremost critic of the dance in the 1920s, André Levinson, had mixed feelings about Duncan as an artist and he frequently disagreed with her vision of the liberating function of dance. But as a man who gave himself fervently to the task of reading the performing body, he has left us with an excellent way to understand why the world of dance became a site of contention about the very nature of gender in the early part of the twentieth century. A Russian émigré, Levinson often lectured about the artistic quarrels that were unfolding around him in Paris. He saw clearly the nature of the problem he faced in writing anything at all intelligible about movement. "We are exceedingly ill-equipped for the study of things in flux," he wrote in "The Spirit of Classical Dance," included in this section. And he identified his dilemma as part of a much more far-reaching historical circumstance. "It is because the art of the dance is so peculiarly inarticulate that it has never possessed a proper aesthetic philosophy" (in Acocella and Garafola 42–43).

The distinctive modernist moment in the history of dance seems to have grown out of this lack, this absence of a vocabulary and set of associated concepts. For it abrogated the necessity of deconstruction, made silence into opportunity, and permitted new ideas to grow on the site of loss. Out of dearth or deficiency, people like Isadora Duncan, Mary Wigman, Loie Fuller, Maud Allen, Ruth St. Denis, and Margaret Morris found occasion for women to define and redefine the meaning of their own physical movements and performance strategies. That is, they understood the body to be capable of a kind of writing that offered a new cultural narrative to all women of their generation. Suzanne Perrottet, who began her dance career with Jacques Dalcroze and then became a student of Rudolf Laban, explained that dance was "a religion for me . . . this new thing that did not yet exist, I lived entirely for it" (in Green 96). She and others like her pursued the transmission of these meanings in the face of a balletic tradition that, however inarticulate, they associated with the prescriptions, strictures, and recalcitrance of an unwanted past.

Against their efforts to find, to experience, and to name the meaning and energy of their own creativity, other artists and critics continued to uphold the value of classical dance. Levinson, having identified the general absence of an aesthetic philosophy for dance, contributed to the creation of such a philosophy by aligning himself with traditional ballet. He wanted to defend it against what he called "cures by antiquity, painting, music, rationalism, psychology, naturalness" (*Ballet Old and New* 77–78). It was not that he disagreed with Isadora Duncan that the ballet deformed the body, but he attributed a different meaning to its distortion. Where Duncan proclaimed, "the ballet condemns itself by enforcing the deformation of the beautiful woman's body!" speaking as if it were self-evident that beauty, health, and morality adhered in bare feet and gauze dresses, Levinson asked why women would pursue such discipline in the first place. Where Duncan imbued ballet and modern dance with gendered qualities, seeing ballet as a prescriptive reenactment of patriarchy, a ceremony of women's culturally enforced subordination, Levinson looked for the aesthetic purpose that subsumed and justified such physical discipline.

Like Mallarmé, he believed ballet to be an ideal art. He was interested in Mallarmé's notion "that the ballerina *is not a girl dancing;* . . . *she is not a girl,* but rather a metaphor which symbolizes some elemental aspect of earthly form: sword, cup, flower, etc., and that *she does not dance* but rather, with miraculous lunges and abbreviations, several paragraphs of dialogue or descriptive prose. Her poem is written without the writer's tools" ("Ballets" 96). Writing with her body, she *suggests* things that the written work could express only in theory. About the symbolic nature of pure dance Levinson further observed that "When a dancer rises on her points, she breaks away from the exigencies of everyday life and enters into an enchanted country—that she may thereby lose herself in the idea" (in Acocella and Garafola 11). However it was he himself who seemed to lose himself in his ideas about the beauty and symbolic power of the ballerina's body. He observes in "The Spirit of Classical Dance" that her physical discipline served only to free her "from the usual limitations upon human motion" (48). "To discipline the body to this ideal function, to make a dancer of a graceful child, it is necessary to begin by dehumanizing him, or rather by overcoming the habits of ordinary life. . . . The accomplished dancer is an artificial being, an instrument of precision, and he is forced to undergo rigorous daily exercise to avoid lapsing into his original purely human state" (47). Given these passions and allegiances, it is not surprising that Levinson also found fault with another "gendered" aspect of the European stage, the synchronized line dancing of music-hall groups like the Gertrude Hoffmann Girls, which began to perform in Paris and Berlin in the mid 1920s. As he wrote in "The Girls," which is included in this section, the discipline that "dehumanized" the ballerina, making her into an "instrument of precision," served these girls to ill effect. They were precise, but only in the manner of an industrial machine; they were energetic, but only in the manner of "sturdy, blond Barbarians." He looked at their brute health, their jaunty kicks; he listened to the monotonous cadences to which they danced, arm in arm, hand in hand, shoulder to shoulder, presenting a single profile for the public, and he decided that he watched little more than an exhibition of clamorous athleticism. These girls had neither modesty nor shame. Unlike an older generation of cancan chorus girls, these young women had no "perverse implication or equivocal appeal in the chastity of their half-naked limbs." Their nudity was not provocative, but it resounded with much more sinister implications. Levinson thought them stereotyped; he thought their personalities to have been effaced. They had no names but their trade names—the Fisher Girls, the Tiller Girls, the Jackson Girls—and this was the source of their danger. "There is in these exercises of the girls something suggestive of a parade step, something reminiscent of those military ballets which were once so popular or the popular enthusiasm attending a return to the barracks, drums beating, flares flaming; or of the cadenced thrill of a martial pantomime. The other day, when the Jackson Girls . . . descended the great staircase of the German Reichstag, hand on hips, in a goose-step, were they not alluding to the pomp of the vanished Empire?" Imbued with ideas no less forceful than the ones that governed his appreciation of classical ballet, these young women embodied Levinson's belief that modernity had become a matter of sheer, anonymous biology and mechanism, and in his identification of their technique as a "goosestep," he anticipated the rise of German National Socialism in ways that were unhappily prophetic.[1]

To Isadora Duncan and to other inventors of modern dance, neither ballet nor the performances of the music hall carried interest. The discipline of both art forms was anathema; the cultural symbolism that inhabited them was equally abhorrent. According to Duncan, whose comments are included in this section, the discipline was forced by and representative of what was worst in western culture, and its insistent rigor was indicative of deformation in the lives not only of dancers but also of ordinary women who were similarly forced into unnatural postures and routines by a culture careless of their welfare. Duncan considered the early part of the twentieth century "dreary," "routinized" and "mechanical" (in Franko 7). She understood women's health to be compromised by lack of exercise, by sedentary occupations, by binding clothing, and by anonymously repetitive tasks, that were represented to her by the destinies of secretaries and typists. Crista Anita Brück might well have spoken for her with her invocation of the fate of women clerks, secretaries, stenographers, and typists: "Tempo, tempo, faster, faster. Man funnels his energy into the machine. The machine which is he himself, his foremost abilities, his foremost concentration and final exertion. And he himself is machine, is lever, is key, is type and moving carriage. Not to think, not to reflect, on, on, fast, fast, tipp, tipp, tipptipptipptipptipptipp" (in Kittler 221).

If machines like the typewriter could inscribe social power on the tired bodies of women workers, women could resist or subvert that power, Duncan felt, by using the body as an active agent of knowledge. She represented her "invention" of a new style of dancing as a moment outside of historical time, a moment when she returned to and "listened" to the truth of the body, imagined as an Other of modern culture. "For hours I would stand quite still, my two hands folded between my breasts, covering the solar plexus. . . . I was seeking and finally discovered the central spring of all movement" (in Franko 1).[2]

Duncan went from isolated communing with the rhythms and flows of her own embodiment to another "elsewhere" of culture. In 1903 she traveled to Greece, where she sought traces of a time before technology required the repetitive, crippling behaviors of the twentieth century's machine aesthetic. From this sojourn on the Peloponese she constructed a further justification for the "natural," organic style of her movement technique, and from these personal awakenings, she founded, along with her sister Elizabeth, the Isadora Duncan School in Grunewald, Germany, and a series of studios in the heart of Paris. Her vision of the flowing energy of the reawakened feminine self was to carry into a future that promised "the mission of woman's body" and "the holiness of all of its parts" (Franko 10).

If Isadora Duncan imagined a kind of somatic utopia that would be ushered into existence by a group of movement strategies, Margaret Morris began to tailor a similar set of commitments to the needs of an actual population. As the principal of her own troupe and the founder of many schools, Morris performed in Paris regularly. In 1925 Morris established her first Parisian school in a studio at 10 avenue de la Bourdonnais, taught there herself until she was called back to England, and then left the girls in the care of Mary Sykes. Morris's movement strategies had grown out of the system that Isadora Duncan's brother Raymond advocated when he had toured through England as a young man. At a formative time in her own career as an expressive dancer, Margaret Morris had attended one of Raymond Duncan's lecture-demonstrations and had come away inspired by his love of classicism, the beauty of his poses, and the logic of the physical system he advocated. Like him, she began to explore the highly articulated postures found in Greek art, and like him, she saw immediately the health and freedom of movement fostered by exercise in non-binding clothing. She was by all accounts a passionate and graceful dancer, but since she led a conventional personal life, she encountered none of the amusement that Duncan's untrousered existence aroused.

To the contrary, Margaret Morris intuitively inspired the trust of the medical profession, which looked to her for guidance in creating therapies for physically handicapped children, for war veterans, and for pregnant women. She became one of the great innovators of the physical culture curriculum in English and European schools, advocating a combination of rhythmic music and movement to develop the aesthetic sensibilities of ordinary people.

In her native England, Morris based her work in both a studio and a club in Chelsea, where those in the neighborhood could congregate, take classes, and watch small, local performances. As the granddaughter of William Morris, she had a high visibility in the arts; but as doctors in England discovered the attractiveness of her exercise regimes to those in need of physical rehabilitation, her talents were increasingly drawn away from the stage. Eventually she acquired a degree in physical therapy, adding knowledge of physiology to her innate sense of aesthetics. She saw the importance of beauty as a motivation for physical improvement of whatever kind. She appraised her own historic moment as deeply divided between those with an aesthetic sensibility and those interested in physical culture, and she thought her own contribution could be one of synthesis. In "Health and Physical Exercise," included in this section, she writes, "First of all pupils should be made to realize that every movement and position they make must be good to look at. Not by an effort to be 'graceful'; striving after grace is fatal to good movement; *real* grace and good looking easy movements can only be the outcome of health and strength. An obvious illustration is the panther or the tiger" (26).

"The first step in the creative appeal," she continued, "is that the pupils should feel themselves to be *part* of a rhythmic whole." Anyone at all could be a Margaret Morris dancer. She saw benefits in her method for typists and accountants and the "various sedentary, and for the most part uninteresting, occupations of the majority of people" (26). Her method included "all that is necessary for the development of healthy, intelligent human beings . . . it requires no special conditions . . . it is absorbingly interesting . . . [and] suitable for . . . all ages from two years as the exercises can be graduated to suit any age, or state of physical fitness or weakness" (29).

She believed fervently that rhythmic movement was the foundation of health, and she saw her work in relation to the discoveries of Freud and the nascent psychiatric sciences. In her judgment, the body itself could offer the greatest responsiveness to its own unconscious illness. "One reason why so many people are discontented and repressed," she claimed, "is to a great extent because they have never had any outlet for their emotions in their youth. . . . By discovering a means of expression, the repressions that are the cause of so many disorders in later life can for the most part be avoided. . . . So I begin first by helping the child balance itself" (35, 42).

Like her contemporary Maria Montessori, whose work she knew intimately, Morris educated children through their senses. Babies were taught to improvise to music, to compose steps, to work in groups, and to make cooperative compositions. They were taught about forms, color, sound, movement, and the fundamentals of design. Each element of Morris's program was created to foster self-esteem; each child's artistic efforts were taken seriously. "Everything that children put their hearts into is a serious business to them. . . . The copying or even looking at painting and drawings I entirely disapprove of for young children. All art is an impression of something as seen by the artist. As far as possible first impressions should be obtained first-hand, and not through the eyes of another—even a great artist" (44). As she told John Galsworthy, she wanted to work with women while they were young before other experiences had altered "the savage element which modern civilization causes us to stifle" (44).

The stakes in these contested views about the meaning of modernist dance and its function in western culture were high. André Levinson considered that continued attention to formal, disciplined artistic beauty held a barbaric future at bay. When he reviewed Henri Massis's *Defense of the West* in 1927, he admitted that Massis's social analysis fostered a "catastrophic feeling of deterioration and decline." He also felt this intuitive dread, and in his review he proclaimed that he "passionately share[d] Monsieur Massis's devotion to the civilization of the West and his militant faith in the vitality of its principles." To him, as to Massis, it seemed that the "West and the East were engaged in a formidable duel . . . more metaphysical than political: the future of civilization was at stake" (in Acocella and Garafola 14).

Isadora Duncan also placed a high and "civilizing" value on her performance strategies. She spoke lyrically, actively, and self-consciously, rewriting and overwriting classical male ideas about corporeality. Her barefoot, scantily clad adherents were also ushering in the future, using the movement of the body itself as a signifying practice. She did not fear decline; she welcomed change. "The dancer of the future," she claimed, "will not dance in the form of a nymph or fair coquette, but in the form of a woman in her greatest and purist expression. . . . She will dance the changing life of nature, showing how each part is transformed into the other" (in Goellner and Murphy 34).

To us, looking back through time, the importance of the conflict between Levinson, Duncan, and the nascent modern dance movement may well lie not in its terms of opposition (what kind of dancing is/was preferable?) but in the absence of ideology that made dance such fertile ground for introducing new ideas about gendered identity in the early years of the twentieth century. If dance proceeded by means of what Mallarmé called "the alphabet of the inexpressible," then its very lack of articulation left it available for a new "writing" of the meaning and purpose of women's dedication to the arts and to the health of their everyday lives.[3] Women were not essentially any one kind of symbol, but were always in the midst of becoming, constituting identity in the very act of performing it. In this they anticipated contemporary French writers of the *écriture féminine* school and other critics like Judith Butler, who continue to remind us that gender does not preexist deeds but is always a "doing."[4] One stages one's identity whether the curtains rise or not.

Notes

1. Levinson's other salient publications are: *Bakst: The Story of Leon Bakst's Life* (Berlin: A. Kogan Pub. Co., 1922); *La Danse Au Théâtre, Esthétique Et Actualité Mêlées* (Paris: Bloud & Gay, 1924); *Marie Taglioni (1804–1884)* (London: Dance Books, 1977); *Danse D'aujourd'hui* (Arles: Actes sud, 1990).

2. For more resources on Isadora Duncan, see: Fredrika Blair, *Portrait of the Artist as a Woman* (New York: McGraw-Hill, 1986); Ann Daly, *Done into Dance: Isadora Duncan in America* (Bloomington: Indiana University Press, 1995); Floyd Dell, *Women as World Builders; Studies in Modern Feminism* (Chicago: Forbes, 1913); Mary Desti, *The Untold Story; The Life of Isadora Duncan, 1921–1927* (New York: H. Liveright, 1929); Dorée Duncan,

Carol Pratl, and Cynthia Splatt, *Life into Art: Isadora Duncan and Her World* (New York: W. W. Norton, 1993); Isadora Duncan, *My Life* (New York: Liveright, 1927); Isadora Duncan and Sheldon Cheney, *The Art of the Dance* (New York: Theatre Arts, 1928); Arnold Genthe, *Isadora Duncan* (New York: Books for Libraries, 1980); Dayna Goldfine et al., *Isadora Duncan: Movement from the Soul* (Los Angeles: Direct Cinema Limited, 1989); Alice Hubel, *Isadora Duncan* (Paris: Park Avenue, 1994); Ruth Kozodoy, *Isadora Duncan. American Women of Achievement* (New York: Chelsea House Publishers, 1988); Peter Kurth, *Isadora: A Sensational Life* (Boston: Little Brown and Co., 2001); Lillian Loewenthal, *The Search for Isadora: The Legend & Legacy of Isadora Duncan* (Pennington, N.J.: Princeton Book Co., 1993); Paul David Magriel, *Isadora Duncan* (New York: H. Holt and Company, 1947); Victor Ilyitch Seroff, *The Real Isadora* (New York: Dial Press, 1971); Walter Terry, *Isadora Duncan: Her Life, Her Art, Her Legacy* (New York: Dodd Mead, 1964); Abraham Walkowitz, *Isadora Duncan in Her Dances* (Girard, Kan.: Haldeman-Julius Publications, 1945).

3. For excellent contemporary discussions of the ideological meanings of dance see: E. A. Grosz, *Volatile Bodies: Toward a Corporeal Feminism* (Bloomington: Indiana University Press, 1994); Judith Lynne Hanna, *Dance, Sex, and Gender: Signs of Identity, Dominance, Defiance, and Desire* (Chicago: University of Chicago Press, 1988); Laura Hinton and Cynthia Hogue, *We Who Love to Be Astonished: Experimental Women's Writing and Performance Poetics* (Tuscaloosa: University of Alabama Press, 2002); Amy Koritz, *Gendering Bodies/Performing Art: Dance and Literature in Early-Twentieth-Century Culture* (Ann Arbor: University of Michigan Press, 1995).

4. See Butler, *Bodies that Matter: The Discursive Limits of "Sex"* (New York: Routledge, 1993); *Gender Trouble: Feminism and the Subversion of Identity.*

Works Cited

Acocella, Joan Ross, and Lynn Garafola, eds. *André Levinson on Dance: Writings from Paris in the Twenties.* Hanover, N.H.: University Press of New England, 1991.

Duncan, Isadora. *Isadora Speaks.* Ed. Franklin Rosemont. San Francisco: City Lights Books, 1981.

Franko, Mark. *Dancing Modernism/Performing Politics.* Bloomington: Indiana University Press, 1995.

Goellner, Ellen, and Jacqueline Shea Murphy. *Bodies of the Text: Dance as Theory, Literature as Dance.* New Brunswick: Rutgers University Press, 1995.

Green, Martin. *Mountain of Truth: The Counterculture Begins, Ascona, 1900–1920.* Hanover, N.H.: University Press of New England, 1986.

Kittler, Friedrich. *Gramophone, Film, Typewriter.* Stanford: Stanford University Press, 1999.

Levinson, André. *Ballet Old and New.* New York: Dance Horizons, 1982.

———. "The Spirit of Classical Dance." In Acocella and Garafola, eds. 42–48.

Mallarmé, Stéphane. "Ballets." Ed. Martin Leonard Pops. In *Dance:* Special Issue of *Salmagundi* 33–34 (Spring–Summer 1976): 96.

Morris, Margaret. *Margaret Morris Dancing: A Book of Pictures by Fred Daniels, with an Introduction and Outline of Her Methods by Margaret Morris.* London: Kegan Paul, Trench, Trubner & Co. Ltd., 1928.

ISADORA DUNCAN

The Dance and Its Inspiration: Written in the Form of an Old Greek Dialogue

"We should learn that the body of woman has through all the ages itself been the symbol of highest beauty." A silence fell upon us. I was looking toward some light clouds which had gathered in the east, and then it seemed to me in their midst I saw a young goatherd sitting surrounded by his goats and sheep of fleecy whiteness—and before him, rose-tipped of the sun, stood the Goddess of Cyprus, and she smiled as she reached her hand for the prize which she knew was hers. That exquisitely poised head, those shoulders gently sloping, those breasts firm and round, the ample waist with its free lines, curving to the hips, those limbs and knees and feet all one perfect whole, one instant and the vision was radiant in its loveliness and then vanished.

"To learn," I repeated, "that through all the ages woman's body has been the symbol of highest beauty."

"Will you explain to me what you mean?" you asked.

"Why," I replied, "is it not true that the first conception of beauty arose from the consciousness of proportion, line, the symmetry of the human form, for surely without this consciousness we could have had no understanding of the beauty surrounding us. First, knowledge of the line of sky- and earth-forms, and from this the conception of line and form of architecture, painting and sculpture. All art, does it not come originally from the first human consciousness of the nobility in the lines of the human body?"

"I feel this to be true," you replied, "for when we study a noble human body we can feel how from this form as first idea all noble forms may follow as natural sequence."

Then I explained, "Would it not seem to you that when one's idea of the human form is a noble one, so one's conception of all the lines and forms would be ennobled thereby, and that, on the other hand, a weak or false conception of human form would lead to a weak and false conception of all line and form?

"Well then," I continued, "have we not come about in a circle to my reason for saying that to gain a true conception of the highest beauty woman must first gain the knowledge of the true line and form of her own body?"

"But," you asked, "how is woman to learn the correct form of her body?"

"Think of all you have learned in your life," I replied, "and tell me which are the things you have learned best—those which you have read in books or those which you have lived, experienced?"

"Surely," you answer, "those which I have myself experienced."

"Shall a woman find this knowledge in the gymnasium, exercising her muscles, or in the museums regarding the perfection of sculptured form, or do you mean by the continual contemplation of beautiful objects and the reflection of them in her mind?"

"These are all ways," I replied, "but the chief thing is, she must use this beauty and her own body must become the living exponent of it—not by the thought or contemplation of beauty only, but by the living of it—and as form and movement are inseparable as all life is movement, I might say by that movement which is in accordance with the beautiful form will she learn, for in their gradual evolution form and movement are one."

"And how would you name that movement which is in accord with the most beautiful human form?"

"There is a name, the name of one of the oldest of the arts—honored as one of the nine Muses—but it is a name that has fallen in such disrepute in our day that it has come in our country to mean just the opposite of this definition. I would name it The Dance."

"Oh," you cried sympathetically," so woman is to learn beauty of form and movement through the art of the dance?"

"Yes, and I believe here is a wonderful undiscovered inheritance for coming womanhood, the old dance which is to become the new. She shall be sculptor not in clay or marble but in her body, which she shall endeavor to bring to the highest state of plastic beauty; she shall be painter, but as part of a great picture she shall mingle in many groups of new changing light and color. In the movement of her body she shall find the secret of right proportion of line and curve and—the art of the dance she will hold as a great wellspring of new life for sculpture, painting and architecture."

"Then before woman can reach high things in the art of the dance, dancing must exist as an art for her to practice, which at the present day in our country it certainly does not—that is, according to your definition—for you were speaking of woman's form in its highest beauty, and of a movement which would be appropriate to that form, and you called the practicing of that movement as an art, the dance. But I suppose all art must have some fountainhead from which to draw. And the great fountainhead of movement, where are we to look for it?"

"You ask this," I replied, "as if woman were a thing apart and separate from all other life, organic and inorganic, but she really is just a link in the chain and her movement must be one with the great movement which runs through the universe and, therefore, the fountainhead, as you express it, for the art of the dance will be the study of the movements of Nature."

A soft breeze came to us from over the sea, the sails slowly filled and took the wind and with the strengthening of the breeze the waters formed in long undulations; for some time our eyes followed them and rejoiced in their movements. Why is it that of all movement which gives us delight and satisfies the soul's sense of movement that of the waves and of the sea seem to me the greatest?

"When the breeze came some moments ago did we both not watch with joy the subsequent movement of the waters and did we not say the greatest movement is the wave movement? The answer would seem to be that this great wave movement runs through all Nature, for when we look over the waters to the long line of hills on the shore they seem also to have the great undulating wave movement of the sea, and all movements in nature seem to me to have as their ground plan the law of wave movement."

The ground, dry baked, heat cracked, the atmosphere of a peculiar hard bright-ness—overhead the changeless blue sky—through the branches one of the hills—the distance. We are walking together in the pleasant shade of the olive trees, pacing slowly, each filled with our own thoughts. In our walk we reached a gnarled old trunk that had long lain in its present position.

"Do you remember yesterday we were speaking of the movement in Nature and you said that the wave was the great foundation movement of Nature? This idea continually presents itself to me and I see waves rising through all things. Sitting here and looking through the trees they seem also to be a pattern conforming to lines of waves. We might think of them from another standpoint, which is that all energy expresses itself through this wave movement, for does not sound travel in waves, and light also, and when we come to the movements of organic nature it would seem that all free natural movements conform to the law of wave movement. The flight of birds, for instance, or the bounding of animals. It is the alternate attraction and resistance of the law of gravity that creates this wave movement. Do you remember yesterday we were speaking of the dance and when I asked you where you would look for the source of this art, you answered Nature? Since then the idea will not leave me, and I see dance motifs in all things about me. Was this your idea for instance that there is a dance in all Nature?"

"Yes," I replied. "All true dance movements possible to the human body exist primarily in Nature."

"Do you use the phrase 'true dance' in opposition to what you would name the false dance? Is there such a thing as a false dance? And how do you explain this? If the true dance is appropriate to the most beautiful human form, then the false dance is the opposite of this definition: that is, a movement which conforms to a deformed human body. How can this be possible?"

"It sounds impossible," I replied, "but take your pencil and see if we can prove what I have said. First draw me the form of woman as it is in nature. And then draw me the form of woman in the modern corset and satin slippers used by our dancers. And now do you not see the movement that would conform to one figure would be perfectly impossible for the other? To the first, all the rhythmic movements that run through water would be possible. They would find this form their natural medium for movement. To the second figure these movements would be impossible on account of the rhythm being broken in the latter and stopped at the extremities. We cannot for the second figure take movements from nature, but must, on the contrary, go according to set geometric figures based on straight lines, and that is exactly what the school of dance of our day has done. They have invented a movement which conforms admirably to the human figure of the second illustration, but which would be impossible to the figure as drawn in our first sketch. Therefore, it is only those movements which would be natural to the first figure that I would call the true dance."

"But what you call 'deformed' is by many people held to be an evolution in form, and the dance which would be appropriate to woman's natural form would be held by these people as primitive and uncultivated. Whereas the dance which is appropriate to the form much improved by corsets and shoes they would name as the dance appropriate to the culture of the present day. These people would be in no way of your opinion in your definition of what you name the true dance. How would you answer these people?"

"Man's culture is making use of nature's forces in channels harmonious to those forces and never going directly against nature. And all art must be intimately connected with nature at its roots—the painter, the poet, the sculptor, and dramatist, but holding it for us through their work according to their ability to observe in Nature. Nature always has been and must be the great source of all art."

Isadora Speaks. Ed. Franklin Rosemont. San Francisco: City Lights Books, 1981. 41–46.

ISADORA DUNCAN

The Freedom of Woman

If my art is symbolic of any one thing, it is symbolic of the freedom of woman and her emancipation from the hidebound conventions that are the warp and woof of New England Puritanism.

To expose one's body is art; concealment is vulgar. When I dance, my object is to inspire reverence, not to suggest anything vulgar. I do not appeal to the lower instincts of mankind as your half-clad chorus girls do.

I would rather dance completely nude than strut in half-clothed suggestiveness, as many women do today on the streets of America.

Nudeness is truth, it is beauty, it is art. Therefore it can never be vulgar; it can never be immoral. I would not wear my clothes if it were not for their warmth. My body is the temple of my art. I expose it as a shrine for the worship of beauty.

I wanted to free the Boston audience from the chains that bound them. I saw them before me, shackled with a thousand links of custom and environment. I saw them chained by Puritanism, bound by their Boston Brahminism, enslaved and hidebound in mind and body. They wanted to be free; they cried out for someone to loose their chains.

They say I mismanaged my garments. A mere disarrangement of a garment means nothing. Why should I care what part of my body I reveal? Why is one part more evil than another? Is not all body and soul an instrument through which the artist expresses his inner message of beauty? The body is beautiful; it is real, true, untrammeled. It should arouse not horror, but reverence. That is a difference between vulgarity and art, for the artist places his whole being, body and soul and mind, on the throne of art.

When I dance, I use my body as a musician uses his instrument, as a painter uses his palette and brush, and as a poet uses the images of his mind. It has never dawned on me to swathe myself in hampering garments or to bind my limbs and drape my throat, for am I not striving to fuse soul and body in one unified image of beauty?

Many dancers on the stage today are vulgar because they conceal and do not reveal. They would be much less suggestive if they were nude. Yet they are allowed to perform, because they satisfy the Puritan instinct for concealed lust.

That is the disease that infects Boston Puritans. They want to satisfy their baseness without admitting it. They are afraid of truth. A nude body repels them. A suggestively clothed body delights them. They are afraid to call their moral infirmity by its right name.

I don't know why this Puritan vulgarity should be confined to Boston, but it seems to be. Other cities are not afflicted with a horror of beauty and a smirking taste for burlesque semi-exposures.

Isadora Speaks. Ed. Franklin Rosemont. San Francisco: City Lights Books, 1981. 48–49.

MARGARET MORRIS

From "Health and Physical Exercise"

Almost everyone will agree that *health is* the most essential thing for a happy life. Yet how few are really well—or even fairly well and how little trouble people will take to *keep* well and prevent getting ill, though they will spend any amount of time and money getting "cured"!

I believe in very many cases a little care and attention to eating, sleeping, and right exercise would render curing unnecessary. Not enough attention has been paid to finding out what is the most health-giving form of exercise, in relation to the conditions of modern civilization, and the resources at the command of the average person.

Most doctors are agreed that "swimming" is the most perfect form of physical exercise, as it brings into play all the muscles, no one part having to bear the weight of the body, and it also induces good breathing. But swimming is not a form of exercise that most people can indulge in regularly, and there are many reasons why swimming in baths is of far less value than open air swimming, specially in the sea. If we take swimming as a standard of good physical exercise, then let us consider if we have any equivalent exercise that can be done on land.

Our forms of physical exercise to-day are walking, running, games and sports, gymnastics and boxing. Dancing as understood by the majority cannot be called an exercise. "Stage dancing" is limited to comparatively few people, and tends to over-develop certain parts; "fancy dancing" as taught in schools is too mild to have much muscular effect, and ball-room dancing only exercises the feet and legs.

That leaves us the list already mentioned, all excellent forms of exercise in

---

* I wrote on this subject in *The Daily Sketch,* 23rd June 1919.

their different ways, but I must emphatically say that none of them is capable of giving the *normal health and balance* necessary to the average human being. Further, in the case of games, sports and boxing, people have to be physically trained *for* them; they are not a training in themselves.

For confirmation of this statement that none of our present forms of physical exercise are sufficient, one has only to look at the wretched physical condition and appearance of most of the population, or ask any doctor with experience of council schools and hospitals what he thinks of the average physique, to be convinced that there is much room for improvement.

Obviously, even the right form of exercise will not keep everybody well—but it has not been tried, and I am convinced that it would make an enormous difference. It may quite rightly be argued by those who are fully satisfied with our present games and gymnastics, that the majority of people do not get any of these forms of exercise in sufficient quantity to derive benefit from them. This is quite true; but I do not think the physique of even the well-to-do, who are brought up on games and gymnastics, is sufficiently good to give one complete confidence in the system, and one great objection to games and gymnastics is their impracticability for the masses. Gymnastics need a gymnasium and apparatus; games need a special field and a special outfit.

For a form of exercise to become practical for the masses of any nation, it must require the minimum of special conditions. It should be possible to practise it in any good-sized room, playground, park or open space. It is possible so to practise my method of physical culture, of which I will now try to give you some idea. A doctor friend of mine once described my methods as "land swimming" and I think there is a great similarity of movement. I have found that children trained on my system learn to swim in deep water almost at once.

The aim of my method is that there should be no strain on any one part or over-development of another, every part working together in harmony and balance, creating a condition in which the body can grow to the fullest extent of normal healthy development.

Let me explain how this is arrived at, and the basis on which I have built up my method. To construct anything sound you must start from fundamentals. In creating a method of movement for the development of human beings the fundamentals must be common to *any* nationality, and *any* age. So I take the most fundamental form of movement—walking; then I take running, springing, jumping, hopping—all the simplest movements that everyone not physically or mentally defective must have done at some time.

It will be found that in all these movements—which may I think reasonably be called "natural"—the part the arms and upper portion of the body plays, is that of balance; counter-balancing the action of the feet and legs. The more strenuous the action of the lower limbs, the more vigorous the action of arms and shoulders to preserve equilibrium.

If you analyze the movements of walking or running you will find that the action of the right *leg* is always counter-balanced by a corresponding movement with the *left* shoulder and arm, and *vice versa*. This opposition movement, most clearly seen in running, produces a twisting movement in the body at the waist line; and exercise in this part of the body is essential to health, and is quite absent in the occupations and amusements of people living in towns. I do not think that the value of this opposition movement has been fully realized, or that it is used nearly enough in most physical exercises.

In walking this movement is not sufficiently accentuated to make it a very valuable form of exercise, and running by itself is also inadequate (though the opposition movement is more accentuated) because the runner only uses certain muscles repeating the same muscular actions all the time. Therefore, though walking and running may be said to be the starting point of my system, they are only a part of it, the movements involved not being sufficient to strengthen all parts of the body. The next movements I use are a continuation or amplification of walking and running embodying the same principles. They are based on positions taken from Early Greek vase painting; popularly supposed to be purely artistic conventions, whereas, it seems likely that they are fairly accurate representations of positions used in Hellenic gymnastics and dances. At any rate, I have found them to be of extraordinary value in physical development, and exactly what was needed, being actually an *accentuation* of normal walking and running positions, but with the necessary fixing of postures essential to the education of the muscles. They accentuate the turn at the waist, the bend of the knees, and by using more definite and strong positions of the arms, use the shoulder and back muscles, so that the holding of these positions induces, by building up the necessary muscles, an easy and balanced walk, and correct posture in standing.

It is useless to say to someone who is round-shouldered or weak in the back "You must hold yourself up!" unless you can enable them to stand up, by building up the necessary muscle. Bad posture in walking and standing is mostly the result of weakness, and as such can easily be corrected; and I have found the Greek positions invaluable in this respect.

My interest in the Greek positions is due entirely to the great benefit and usefulness to be got out of them; I am not concerned with their historical correctness, and valuable as I have found them to be, they do not include all that is necessary for the development of the body; there are other movements, such as leg-lifting, twisting, stretching, and bending, that are necessary, and are only a further amplification from the natural basis. In using the word "natural," I do not use it in an absolute sense. Naturalness like everything else must be relative to circumstances and surroundings.

It may be objected that some of the further developments of my methods are not "natural," as people do not instinctively think of them and do them. I think that any position the body can be put into, any series of movements it can perform, without contortion, strain, or over-development, must be natural; and every possibility of movement should be investigated, to enable the body to make full use of its capabilities. If people led really natural lives, working out of doors, swimming and walking constantly, systems of physical culture might not be necessary. But, as is well known, hardly anyone is able—or even desires!—to lead such a life, and conditions of modern civilization make it impossible for people to get the exercise necessary to health in such a normal way. Therefore, some more concentrated kind of movement becomes essential. Also it must be remembered that hardly anyone starts life really physically fit, or without some hereditary disability or weakness, and something more than the most normal forms of exercises are needed to correct them. Whenever possible, all classes and exercises should be done out of doors, and in the sunlight. I have always been a great believer in the power of the sun for health. I should like some day to have a sanatorium for sun-treatment combined with my physical culture for I am convinced the results would be astonishing.

I have not space here to deal with the strictly remedial side of the work, nor have I in the past intentionally developed it along those lines, though I intend to do so in the future. My thoughts were turned to the definitely remedial possibilities because several of my pupils, girls and children who came to me very thin and weakly, have developed amazingly strong physiques, with no other form of physical work. And adult pupils, some middle-aged, have told me how much their health, especially digestion, was improved. Doctors and surgeons who have been investigating my work lately believe that it will also prove very beneficial in cases of minor deformities, but in this book I am dealing with the average, so-called healthy person.

One of the most important aspects of my method is the *mental* side. Leaving out the obvious fact that of course any co-ordinated movement must involve some mental work, gymnastics, running and walking are as far as possible without mental activity; their great limitation being that there is no *interest* causing mental stimulation and activity. In games and boxing, the mind is as active as the body, and the factor of interest is always present, in this respect giving them a great advantage over exercises. But, as I have said before, games and boxing are not primarily a means of training, but an end for which the athlete has to be trained. And *in* the case of games the interest, or motive force, is too strong, from the point of view of the physical good to be derived from them.

It is now becoming more generally recognized how badly most children stand while actually playing games. This is only to be expected; unless children are already trained, so that they unconsciously stand in good positions, it is inevitable that they will stand in bad ones. If they are keen on the game they cannot be thinking of how they are standing.

All schools have gymnastics as well as games, but the games are regarded as part of the physical training. I consider that from this point of view they are negligible. Yet to increase the time given to ordinary physical exercises would only lead to boredom. So it seems obvious that something more than what we use at present is necessary.

The question of interest of the pupils in physical exercises is a most important one. It is being realized more and more how essential real interest and enjoyment are for getting the good out of anything. It is well known that one of the problems of remedial exercises is the difficulty of keeping the patient interested—especially children—and it has been held that half the good that should be derived from such exercises is lost, if the person doing them is in a state of boredom. One of the main problems then seems to be *"How* can physical exercises be made interesting?"* I am convinced that it can be done by bringing in the *artistic* or *creative* element. The word "artistic" is a very dangerous one, owing to its frequent misuse. I shall avoid it as far as possible, using rather "creative"; for any manifestation of art must be a form of the creative impulse; the difference being in the medium used, and the character and capability of the user; and there are, of course, infinite degrees of intensity in these manifestations. Creating something is the most interesting form of activity, and I believe that everyone has the desire in a greater or lesser degree. In the lesser forms the desire is often satisfied by being part of a thing created by someone else.

To explain what I mean more clearly: I believe this most fundamental desire is the reason why many people are enthusiastic about playing in quartettes, amateur orchestras and theatricals, singing in choirs, or part songs. And a still lesser manifestation is in the enjoyment of seeing and hearing professionals do these things. Unconsciously people rebel against the dullness and ugliness all around them (which is essentially *anti*-creative and *anti*-life), and want to feel themselves a part of something else, something capable of arousing emotions and impressing others, even if this participation is only in witnessing a performance. When the audience, or the performer, or the creator, gets this emotion (or "uplift" as the Americans call it) then that is "art" *for them,* because something has been created for them and, by their own reactions, *in them.*

It is useful for the present purpose to classify all "motives" under certain main headings:

(1) The *Creative,* including all love, art, and lesser creative desires.
(2) The *Competitive,* including fighting, games, sport.
(3) The *Obvious Gain* motive, including all business, and all hopes of getting something for nothing.

Though "motives" and "instincts" have been elaborately classified by psychologists, there are infinite degrees of overlapping and merging. I need not here, however, enter more deeply into the matter; my argument is a simple one; namely, that to arouse vital interest in large numbers of human beings, the elements of one or other of the three groups I have mentioned must be present. Games, boxing and sport, of course, have the competitive motive very strongly, and it is the reason of their very wide appeal. Gymnastics and athletic running and walking involve none of these motives strongly enough, and that is why their appeal is more limited.

I admit that anything *may* appeal to people from entirely different motives, but a broad classification such as I have made is not an attempt at minute investigation, but a useful generalization to explain my point. The "obvious gain" motive is *slightly* present in gymnastics and exercises. People doing them hope to grow stronger, or benefit in some way. But the "gain" is not sufficiently obvious, because the development cannot be fast enough to keep the interest over a long period. The "obvious gain" appeal needs to be presented in a more obvious form such as giving away a quarter of tea with a pound of margarine. The fictitiousness of the gain hardly seeming to affect the appeal!

The only way that remains of making physical exercises interesting to large numbers of people is to bring in, in some form or other, the "creative" or artistic appeal. This is not so difficult or farfetched as it may appear at first sight. In fact, instead of being difficult it is really inevitable, when the matter is approached from the point of view of the artist. The reason that this has not been done is that the artist type of mind has not been interested in physical culture as such-and the type of mind interested in the physical side has thought that "art had nothing to do with it."

But the tendency of modern thought and science to-day is towards linking up and relating—rather than separating into water-tight compartments. So that any insistence on the interdependence of subjects that have been treated as entirely separate should seem reasonable at least to some people.

I will try to explain how the "creative appeal" can be brought into physical culture. First of all the pupils should be made to realize that every movement and position they make must be good to look at. Not by an effort to be "graceful"; striving after grace is fatal to good movement, *real* grace and good looking easy movements can only be the *outcome* of health and strength. An obvious illustration is the panther or the tiger—remarkable for their wonderfully graceful, easy movements. Such grace is the result of perfectly developed and controlled muscles, and entire freedom from self-consciousness. An analogous grace and confidence in human beings is what I am aiming at.

I am convinced that no position or movement that is in itself ugly or stupid to look at can be good for the development of a perfect physique. Of course, there will be much diversity of opinion as to what is "good-looking"! I am naturally taking it from my own point of view—it being my belief that if the exercises are fulfilling their function in developing the body harmoniously they are *bound* to, be "good-looking," in the, sense that a motor-car, or a submarine if it is designed for the utmost efficiency is good looking. It is always the frills and added ornaments that make things abominable. The first step in the creative appeal is that the pupils should feel themselves to be *part* of a rhythmic whole. Very early in the work, too, the actual individual creative work comes in. The pupils compose groups, short steps, singly or together, and both to rhythm and to music. It is quite possible for babies of three years to simple composition, and pupils of all ages find it interesting. By bringing in the "creative side" the longer the pupils continue the more interesting it becomes; it is always an incentive to gaining more control of mind and body (which inevitably involves regular practice) that the pupils should be able to do the movements that they want to put into a dance. As the pupils progress, more interesting compositions are possible, till besides abstract compositions of design only, they learn how to *use* design to express ideas and emotions.

There are exercises and steps that are essential to bodily and mental training—these are mostly done with music and they are interesting and enjoyable in themselves. Of course the training is carried further for the *professional* dancer. It may be thought that the study of composition in movement is quite unnecessary to people who have to earn their livings doing accounts, typing, and the various sedentary, and for the most part uninteresting, occupations the majority of people in town are engaged on. This is a great mistake. It is just because the "creative" side hardly comes into such lives at all that it is most necessary for them: I claim for my method that it is the most natural form of physical culture:

That it includes all that is necessary for the development of healthy intelligent human beings.

That it requires no special conditions.

That it is absorbingly interesting.

That it is suitable for people of all ages from two years, as the exercises can be graduated to suit any age, or state of physical fitness or weakness.

That it is directly applicable to ordinary life, causing people to walk and stand well, to breathe properly to move freely and easily, at the same time training the mind in concentration and construction.

I hope I may soon have an opportunity of proving that my method of physical culture, besides being suited to the needs of the average human being, is also the best training for *athletes*. It seems to me quite obvious that the best form of training must be one which brings in the actual positions and combination of movements used in the particular sport for which the athlete is being trained.

Anyone looking at the illustrated papers will constantly see photographs of footballers, tennis champions and boxers in positions that actually occur in my exercises. This is not really surprising, since my method is based on natural movements.

In the gymnastics, skipping and running used for training athletes at present; hardly any of these positions occur. In games and boxing, the fact that each movement is related and joined on to the next, gives a more continuous and at the same time *varied*, movement than is found in the above forms of training, and which is much nearer the continued movement and quickly changing and arrested positions of dancing. Golfers would find the practising of the twist at the waist and the opposition movements which I use so much, invaluable as training, as would the tennis enthusiasts; who would also undoubtedly find their power of spring, and quickness of movement, much increased.

The footballer would perhaps benefit the most, for, by the hundreds of photographs I have cut out of the papers, he uses my positions the most frequently, but men are the hardest to convince, especially if the word "dancing" is mentioned—which is not surprising if one remembers that the word conjures up in most people's minds a picture of ballet skirts and toe shoes!

It is interesting to note how the same movements will not be recognized in different circumstances. If a man is shown in a room some of the high kicks and extraordinary springs and twists of which we have photographic records in games, he will not recognize them but say that he does not want to be a dancer. He will say that kind of thing is not suited to men, but as soon as a ball is put in front of him in a playing-field, he involuntarily goes through these "dancing" positions, and finds them quite manly! Again, if one demonstrates some of the positions constantly used in tennis or golf as "dancing positions," many people will criticize them as not "natural," but as soon as it is a *game* they are watching, the players holding something in their *hands,* and having an objective, everyone is immediately satisfied that it is quite a normal proceeding.

A word about a suitable costume. The tunic I have designed for use in the school will be seen in several of the photographs. I have found this shape to be the best for showing all the body movements. The shoulders and back being bare enables the teacher to see at once any defects in posture, and to watch the development. I have lately designed a tunic which is a slight modification of the one used in my school—the shoulders being covered and the skirt a little longer—it is very suitable for all outdoor sports as well as dancing.

A special costume is not essential; any loose short garment can be used, but I have found from experience that the flowing Greek tunic hides too many faults of physique and of movement, body positions being difficult to see.

Bare feet are best for all practice (except for dances designed to be performed in shoes). This allows us to see clearly the position and use of the foot; the mere exercise of the feet without shoes strengthens insteps and ankles, and the teacher can see if special exercises are necessary to correct any weakness. I need hardly say that corsets are not worn; they become quite unnecessary even for full figures, when the right amount of muscle is built up to keep the body in the right posture, and the organs in place.

For men and boys the usual sports outfit of vest and running shorts is worn—this being an entirely practical costume for the purpose.

Margaret Morris Dancing: A Book of Pictures by Fred Daniels, with an Introduction and Outline of Her Methods by Margaret Morris. London: Kegan Paul, Trench, Trubner & Co. Ltd., 1928. 11–33.

ANDRÉ LEVINSON

The Girls

In the change which in recent years has come over the large spectacular shows of the European stage, no influence has been more decisive than that of the disciplined and determined army which has ousted the old *corps de ballet,* conquered the music-hall and the revue, and which is now invading the operetta and menacing even the Opera: the army of the modern Eve, the anonymous sportswoman, the impersonal beauty, the serial-soul, the "girl." For some three years now she has been developing from a member of the show into the show itself. She owes her rise, both in Paris and Berlin, to a picked American troupe, which, instead of leveling the whole by suppressing the parts, has chosen to combine the most outstanding personalities and to co-ordinate the play of the most varied temperaments. The first Gertrude Hoffmann Girls executed a bold *coup d'état* in the Moulin Rouge. They deposed the headliner and gave the freedom of the stage to a hitherto subordinate *genre.*

For twenty-five years trails of girls have been trekking the jungle of the modern capitals right and left. In the big spectacular revues we see them, between the patriotic patter-song and the undraped *tableau,* introducing their interlude, which is always the same, or the same in effect. These troupes of girls are all alike, and all the girls in one troupe are alike. They are as difficult to differentiate as the models of a Japanese engraver or Outamaro's great heads. Their "turn" on the bill is that of an organized group, a collectivity. And if anything were needed to emphasize the physical identity, or what seems to us such, of these wholesale performers, it is the absolute simultaneity of their movements.

The personality of the classic "girl" has been effaced, and a wholesale type, a stereotyped model has been multiplied to order. They are standardized products and they have no names but their trade-names: the Fisher Girls, the Tiller Girls, the Jackson Girls, etc. Their acts are equally stereotyped. They dance, to the throb of regular rhythms, with legs out-flung to the height of their eyes, or, knicking their knees, by describing a circle with pointed foot. A violent kick, and they project a leg sidewise, drawing a radius or a full circle. Their motions are borrowed from the *shindy* (motions as old as the Pyramids) or from the French *cancan*—but a *cancan* stripped of its billowing skirts and surreptitious allusions. These young plebeians are short-skirted and bare-legged; they are blonde, rosy and chubby as dolls; and they put to shame the cynical formulas of European vice by their ingenuousness. They are strong, they are muscular, and their faultless alignment and jaunty attack is in withering contrast to the tame flock of the "walk-ons," the ladies who pose in the nude and reap nothing but the yawns of the stalls.

In close file, each resting a hand on her partner's shoulder, presenting a single profile to the public in sixteen or twenty-four replicas, or developing their ranks "front," shoulder to shoulder, hand in hand, arms interlaced, the phalanx of these Girls marks with a sounding, unanimous tap the monotonous but energetic cadence of the step.

I use the word *phalanx,* advisedly: it is more than a metaphor. There is in these exercises of the girls something suggestive of a parade step, something reminiscent of those military ballets which were once so popular, or of the popular enthusiasm attending a return to the barracks, drums beating, flares flaming; or of the cadenced thrill of a martial pantomime. The other day, when the Jackson Girls, helmeted and be-plumed, descended the great staircase of the German Reichstag, hand on hips, in a goose-step, were they not alluding to the pomp of the vanished Empire, to the solemn splendor of its *Wachtparade?* But, beside the military revue, these maidenly battalions concoct other formulas of group-movement, more closely coherent formations. When soldiers are drawn up in line, a prescribed interval separates each from his neighbor: they are pawns on a chess-board. A troupe of girls, however, forms a single unit, a caterpillar with thirty-two feet: each girl clings closely to her neighbor, taking her by the waist, with just elbow room enough to measure the scope and direction of the general movement.

I must not suggest, however, that an entrance of Girls has no other tricks than a simultaneous and synchronized evolution. They vary their effects by turning them upside down, by lying on their backs and mimicking their gymnastic paces in the air—muscular tensions and distensions rhythmically decomposed; and sometimes they peel a movement by transmitting it, like an electric current, from one to another. In a figure which we know over here as the *chemin de fer* (the railroad), each girl makes as if to sit on the bent knee of her neighbor, who holds her by the elbow. Or else they collapse one after another like bowling-pins. Forsaking for a moment the logical sequence of this synopsis, I might cite the Indian dance in the operetta, *Rose-Marie*, at the Théâtre Mogador, Paris, the "Totem Tom-tom," in which the leader of fifty Scott Girls makes them form and unravel the most varied figures, now sweeping the stage in a curlicue, now waving like a harvest under the wind. This geometric play, this deploying of living facets in constant transformation like the colored glasses of the kaleidoscope (André Gide's favorite plaything as a boy) goes straight back to the "avenues" and "figures," in which the dancing masters of the Renaissance excelled, those inventive geometricians who staged the *entrées* of the Royal Courts.

In building his show about a squad of these Girls, the modern producer wisely condemns them to silence: a lien on success. Originally, they would have been a vocal unit as well. We have seen such "chorus-girls," straining a brawny leg, mittened in tiny socks, shod in high-heeled shoes, the while a clamor arose which the Continental ear, I must admit, shrank from recognizing as song. What might that acidulous yapping portend? what cynical silliness? what sentimental drool? Who knows? Who cares? No matter. Pass. We are not listening to music. The voice functions merely as a percussion instrument, beating time and punctuating rhythm. Automatons, these girls; but a wondrous Hydra, too, with twelve or twice twelve placid and nodding dolls' heads; a disciplined and conjugated vigor; the regular beat of a single, innumerable heart: and the squads of these Foolish and skirmishing Virgins brought a breath of freshness into a theatre steeped in slow deliberation, and marked the intervals of the main action, like an accompaniment in the bass. Such were the Girls of yesteryear.

One day we awoke to the fact that simultaneous movement increased in value (strange as it might seem) in inverse ratio to the number of the dancers. Two dancers doing the same step to the same rhythm fascinated us far more than twelve doing the same thing.

Couples began to replace the former battalions. This concentration of effect was illustrated, in the early 1900's, by the Five Harrison Sisters, Girls at their most quintessential. They inspired the draughtsman Thomas Theodore Heine, founder of the famous *Simplicissimus* (that bulwark of German humor, which held its own against the Kaiser), with some memorable linear freaks. But the parts proving greater than the whole, the Harrison Sisters disbanded. Then came the Dolly Sisters (in Paris): agreeable but commonplace performers, inflated by publicity. They established, however, their abbreviated formula of a team of "sisters," of dancing doubles; and we remembered, by an erudite evasion, that both Plautus and Shakespeare had built masterpieces on that curious phenomenon of a complete resemblance, which abolishes the boundaries of personality and wheedles and delights the mind. Others followed their lead: the Rowes, the Dodge Twins perpetuated the pact sororal. Then came other companies like the Academy Girls, who polished their methods with more subtle inventions and a smoother lyricism, contributing to a refinement and elaboration of their *genre,* but weakening its direct and—brutal—appeal. Finally came the invasions of the Americans, the irresistible onslaught of the Hoffmann Girls. On a unique and memorable evening they conquered the boards of Paris and stifled all resistance. And ever since they have ruled the world of the music-hall from the heights of Montmartre.

Was the success of that bevy of stars, the Hoffmanns, a triumph of art? Did they bring new life to the theatre, to the covenant between audience and actor, by some new convention? No, certainly not. They were in reality breaking into the playhouse. In that famous parade of theirs, which made the stage reel with a feigned but carefully calculated confusion, Life itself was leaping onto the boards, clamorous, incandescent, all splendor and tumult. And to silence Art they had a mighty ally, a gigantic trans-muter: its own runaway refugee, Rhythm! The jazz-band, so terrifying, so cleverly organized, before which the tame, tumbled tunes of old have faded, focused all their energies and whipped up the play of their muscles. The material of this marvelous production was modern sport.

We have, to be sure, seen many amazing acrobatic specialists on the stage and in the ring. But these American girls are not specialists bred in a tradition (like the dynasty of the Rastelli, for instance, who have been juggling for a hundred and fifty years) and limited to a single stunt. They are many-sided sportswomen. To be a sportswoman, however, is not an attribute of art, it is a manner of being, a highly despotic and exclusive fashion of culture, a faculty of reflexes, an intelligence of the muscles.

In these young girls there is nothing in excess, except health and the consequent absence of everything morbid or passionate which might give them mystery. The soul is skin-deep: they are bodies full of a joy of life expressed in feats of strength and skill. Pretty? judged by the canons of sculpture, no, probably not; but, in point of sportsmanlike "form," yes, emphatically yes. That "form" serves to safeguard their sex. There is no perverse implication or equivocal appeal in the chastity of their half-naked limbs. Their nudity, happily, is innocent both of modesty and shame. Modesty is a scruple of the soul, haunted by the idea of sin, and in this earthly paradise the purity of the body is contaminated by nothing suggestive of a soul. Their grace is natural, animal even: a fluid play of muscles under lustrous skin, feline leaps and bounds. When the Hoffmanns appear one by one, in "individual entrances," Miss Margaret is a chamois, Miss Emma a peacock, and Miss Florence Kolinsky, of the furry name, represents a leopard. Or rather, she does not represent anything: she is a leopard, giddily, greedily, with powerful paws, with lengthening stride. The others are roaming gazelles and bounding mustangs. And if the game grows human, though ever so little, the charming zoo is transformed suddenly into a great Negro *tam-tam*, ebullient with savage geniality and a rhythmic geyser spurting into syncopations and *glissandi*.

By rhythm the Hoffmann Girls stylize exercise: for "training," like any physical labor, requires a bodily rhythm. To the habitual figures, to the methods which have become "canonical" in girl-shows, they have added all the resources of acrobatic dancing, feats of strength and skill verging on, an athletic show-off, on the prowess of the trapeze-artist: they have mastered all the flexibilities, all the disjointings which belong to the circus-ring. And the virtue of rhythm, the regular division in time of those muscular contractions and distentions, multiplies the fascination we may find—such as it is—in these gymnastic eccentricities. One of their amazing acts represents a fencing match, and here they succeed in giving an esthetic value to spontaneous movement. The crystalline click of the blades beats the measure with a clear music of its own. Plotted in its every development, distributed in time and space, this mannerly dance of the duel is no longer merely a bit of competitive sport, a contest of uncertain issue, subject to chance and disorder: it is an imitation. Sport touches on the theatre. Here the Hoffmann Girls develop physical exercise and acrobatic skill almost to the point of choreography. But when they attempt dancing, they fail, for to set to rhythm an ordinary movement or a sport-action is not to dance. Miss Catherine, who is a toe dancer, and Miss Ferral, when they dance Chopin, remind one of a savage chieftain donning a pair of spectacles or a three-cornered hat. The troupe of toe dancers sponsored by Madame Albertina Rasch is no exception in this respect. Their technic, rapidly and superficially assimilated, with each dancer specializing in some choreographic difficulty, is that of the ballet; but their esthetic is that of the music-hall. This is no synthesis, no associated form of choreographic culture, but a mere mechanical amalgam of two *genres* that do not blend. Now, often, these lithe American girls, in their radiant youth, though their race is without memories, re-discover, beyond the centuries, beyond all civilizations, something indefinable and ancient, which we Europeans will never recover. Miss Florence Kolinsky acts the Queen of Sheba not like an archaeologist but like an actual contemporary of Solomon's charmer. Her pose on her elbows, for instance, reproduces, by a strange coincidence, the image on a Greek vase or the sculptured Salomés over the doors of Romanesque cathedrals.

The ancients raised statues to the nine daughters of Mnemosyne and suspended by invisible threads the tiny figures of their *Nikés,* their winged Victories. Take these sixteen Muses of our own confused day, these shapely and sport-loving Americans: is not each worthy to pose, at least, for a figurehead on a radiator-cap, for that tiny modern fetich, that ultimate idol, spinning precipitously in the wind of a racing 40 H. P. Rolls Royce? For they are pure symbol, the living image of our life, which substitutes for the glamour of the mind and the quest of the sublime the worship of biological forces and mechanical forces. That is the lesson we should take to heart, as we watch—like the Romans of the Decadence—the parade of these "sturdy, blonde Barbarians."

Theatre Arts Monthly (1928).

20

The Gender of Modern/ist Painting

INTRODUCED AND SELECTED BY DIANE F. GILLESPIE

"WOMEN CAN'T PAINT, women can't write." In Virginia Woolf's *To the Lighthouse* (1927), Charles Tansley's words echo in Lily Briscoe's mind, undermining her confidence as she stands before her canvas (48). Lily also has to assert her artistic vision against the fashionable paintings of a male contemporary and the reverence of her culture for old masters. Her theme is mother and child, those "objects of universal veneration" (52) who recur in the visual arts as emblems of a feminine role that both attracts and repels her. As she struggles to render Mrs. Ramsay and James as a harmony of colors and shapes, Lily has to keep reminding herself, "But this is what I see; this is what I see" (19). It is worth recalling this well-known characterization of a woman painter because, through it, Woolf probes some of the sex and gender divisions that we now see as important parts of any study of what is called "modernism" in the visual arts and, more specifically, in painting.[1]

In the discipline of art history, "modernism" ranges in time from mid-nineteenth-century French painting to as far as American art of the mid-twentieth century. More specifically, "modernism" evokes high art and refers to original, self-conscious explorations of an essentially two-dimensional medium, using formal aesthetic criteria, with little regard for subject or topicality. From this perspective, "modernism" rejects "classical, academic, and conservative types of art" as well as "forms of popular and mass culture" (Harrison 144–45). Andreas Huyssen notes the recurrent definition in modernist discourse of "mass culture and the masses as feminine" (47). "The powerful masculinist and misogynist current within the trajectory of modernism," Huyssen continues, "openly states its contempt for women and for the masses," linked and feared "as political threat[s]" (49–50). Academics with feminist or cultural studies orientations challenge facile distinctions between high art and mass culture, masculine and feminine—along with many other variations of these binaries, like genius and talent, original and imitative—as severely limiting and not nearly so objective as often claimed. Ironically, and perhaps inevitably, the revolution in the visual arts identified with "modernism" is now under attack in some quarters as conservative.

Yet the persistence of "modernist" selection and evaluation in the visual arts is evident in, for example, continued use of a 1936 flowchart developed by Alfred H. Barr for the catalog of an exhibition called *Cubism and Abstract Art.* Working chronologically from top to bottom on a page, Barr traces influences on, and relationships among, various male painters, European cities, and avant-garde-isms in order to demonstrate how cubism culminates, in the 1930s, in abstraction. As recently as 1999, in a *Cambridge Companion to Modernism* chapter on "The Visual Arts," Glen MacLeod bases his own discussion on Barr's "still . . . useful" chart (195–96) and mentions, in passing, only three or four women painters. Griselda Pollock suggests that the chart establishes and perpetuates "a selective tradition which normalizes, as the *only* modernism, a particular and gendered set of practices" (50). "Women are completely off the map of abstract art" as conceived by Barr, note Bridget Elliott and Jo-Ann Wallace, as are "non-European 'others'" except "when their art can be absorbed by that of European men" (158).[2]

During the last twenty-five years or so, scholars sensitive to sex and gender-based inequities have made known an alternate women's art history composed of "old mistresses,"[3] for all it can reveal about women's lives and creative work, and about those values the masculine canon emphasizes, dismisses, or omits altogether. Valuable as these efforts are, too often women artists remain isolated in separate academic courses and, as Marxist, ethnic, lesbian, and postcolonial critics have observed, the alternate female canon is itself often exclusionary. If "modernist" criticism cannot accommodate or account for many serious, successful, professional women artists who belong to the history of "modern" art, then, as Pollock and others say, "shifting the paradigm of art history" is necessary. Painting, accordingly, becomes an interdisciplinary "*social practice*" (Pollock 5), a response to "modernity." One studies, not the history of art defined as a limited canon of "aesthetic masterpieces," but rather "a history of images" created under specific social and historical conditions (Bryson et al. xvi).

This paradigm shift means, among other things, raising questions about both conception and reception of works of art. For example, to what extent do committed women artists, consciously or unconsciously, accept or challenge cultural values, artistic traditions, or avant-garde theories that devalue their art as "feminine" or dismiss it as merely "imitative of" or "influenced by" the work of a male painter or avant-garde group?[4]

Included here are writings by six very different *women* artists: Vanessa Bell (1879–1961), Marie Laurencin (1885–1956), Eileen Agar (1899–1991), Sonia Delaunay (1885–1979), Winifred Nicholson (1893–1981), and Emily Carr (1871–1945). To identify them as "women," instead of simply as "artists," is one response to the sex and gender-role hierarchies, tensions, and negotiations at issue in this volume. The manifestoes and other writings signed by *men* at the centers of avant-garde groups are widely available. Indeed, as other scholars already have pointed out, most of these six women have been familiar largely through their associations, varying in kind and degree, with better-known male painters who dominated the postimpressionist, surrealist, cubist, or other artistic circles of their time.[5] Since these women no longer need resurrection from oblivion, however, nor confinement to an alternate modernist canon, I looked for their lesser-known contributions to the conversations about the visual arts of the period. Although these six comment on paintings by men and define some of the same characteristics of modernism in the visual arts, they also help to identify gender issues from different perspectives. Most important, in front of their easels, they function confidently. In their choices of subjects, varying degrees of representation, and individual experiments with color and form, they go their own creative ways.

It is appropriate to look at selected *writings* by women painters because modern writers and artists, especially those experimenting with their media, frequently crossed the traditional lines between visual and verbal art forms. As the poet Blaise Cendrars puts it, "painters and writers . . . lived mixed up with each other, probably even with the same preoccupations" (qtd. in Fagin-King 89). In 1913 Cendrars and Sonia Delaunay collaborated on *La Prose du Transsiberien,* an accordion-folded, vertical, "simultaneous book," two meters long. Delaunay describes her contribution as "a harmony of colors unwinding parallel to the poem" (qtd. in Waller 298). Other painters like Marie Laurencin wrote poetry, Winifred Nicholson wrote "tales," and Emily Carr wrote autobiographical sketches and stories. The writings included here, however, are instances in which these women artists spoke or wrote about art for a public forum.

One hallmark of the so-called middle- to upper-middle class "new woman" around the turn of the last century was her movement from a private into a public realm (Todd 2). More women artists received formal artistic training, exhibited publicly, and joined forces in societies to promote their work. Many defined themselves as painters in the traditional genre of the self-portrait or had themselves photographed in studios among their works of art.[6] Although women artists often kept detailed journals and wrote numerous letters, especially during the early years of their careers when they needed to define themselves as professionals, they rarely wrote for publication. In their later years, they mostly published autobiographies that justified the artistic lives they had led (Witzling, *Voicing Our Visions* 4).[7] Excerpts from Eileen Agar's *A Look at My Life* (1988) appear here as a retrospective on the period ("Am I a Surrealist?"), as does a version of Marie Laurencin's article ("Men's Genius Intimidates Me"), which originally appeared under another title in *Le Carnet des Nuits* (1942). The remaining selections give us the public speaking and writing "voices" of those who mustered sufficient authority and experience to make pronouncements about art in other public ways, not so much to promote themselves, as to explain to others the creativity they considered of paramount importance.

Some especially wanted to communicate with "common viewers," to broaden the audiences for the more experimental art of their time. "What does the man who is not an artist want to know about colour?" Winifred Nicholson asks in a 1944 essay ("Liberation of Colour"). She continues in a conversational tone, identifying with the difficulties faced by her imagined reader. Vanessa Bell and Emily Carr, on opposite sides of the Atlantic, faced their uninitiated viewers in person. In 1925, Bell took on the daunting task of explaining how visual artists view the world to teen-aged boys at her son's school. She used humorous anecdotes and slides to keep their attention ("Lecture Given at Leighton Park School"). In 1930, Emily Carr faced an audience of five hundred at the Women's Canadian Club in her hometown of Victoria. She needed to create a context for her first one-artist show for people who were either ignorant of, or hostile to, modern art ("Fresh Seeing"). When Nicholson notes that "the joy of colour is inborn within each one of us," when Bell contrasts the vision of adults to the "form and colour" perceived more easily by children, and when Carr advocates "fresh seeing," they all lead common viewers away from utilitarian values and a presumed preference for photographic likenesses. As Carr puts it, "where form is so simplified and abstracted that the material side, or objects, are forgotten—only the spiritual remains."

Such public statements by women artists are not abundant. As Emily Carr states, "Artists talk in paint, words do not come easily" ("Fresh Seeing"). Art criticism and history also are fields traditionally dominated by men.[8] Vanessa Bell, familiar with the writings of Roger Fry and Clive Bell, defines a critic as someone able "to get into another artist's mind, and see what that artist wished to do and how far he has succeeded"; she insists that she has no such evaluative skills. Nor, she says, does she have "more than the vaguest ideas of the history of art" ("Lecture"). Rather than just revealing feminine self-deprecation, Bell's comments affirm her different skills as a *visual* artist. Similarly, Winifred Nicholson recognizes that there are painters as well as viewers "who prefer to [. . .] trust their eyes alone." Only those "who like words," she says, should proceed with her essay ("Liberation").

In spite of the considerable differences among their paintings and the kinds of lives they led, the women in this section are in several ways as homogeneous as are the men on Barr's chart. That they are not working class calls attention to the fact that, well into the modern period, "a private income was not just helpful" for women; "it was often decisive" in getting the education and chances to exhibit necessary to an artistic profession (Grimes et al. 16). Marie Laurencin, whose Creole mother was a seamstress, whose birth was illegitimate, and who worked her way into the middle class as a professional artist, is a partial exception. She is suspected, for her pains, of marketing herself and her work as unthreateningly naive, childlike, and stereotypically feminine (Perry, *Women Artists* 110).[9] At the other end of the social scale is Winifred Nicholson, who came from an aristocratic family on her mother's side. Financially secure, confident in her abilities, and completely committed to her art, "she did not *need* fame" (Collins 120) nor, in spite of very successful exhibitions in the 1920s and 1930s, did she seek it. When Nicholson told the poet Kathleen Raine, "I have never painted a masterpiece," she was not admitting incapacity. She was challenging the definition. Nicholson, says Raine, never wanted to produce anything so "intellectual, abstract, worked-out in advance and belonging not to some moment but to an inner conception of an abstract kind" (199)—anything, it seems, so traditionally masculine.

The poet Guillaume Apollinaire, to whom Laurencin was lover, muse, and companion, encouraged the feminine role she played so well. "She is endowed with the greatest possible number of feminine qualities and is free of all masculine shortcomings," he said. Women artists err when "they want to surpass their male colleagues, and in attempting to do so, [. . .] lose their feminine taste and gracefulness" (qtd. in McPherson, 13). Laurencin's mostly retrospective, autobiographical piece, "Men's Genius Intimidates Me," seems to confirm Apollinaire's assessment. At the same time that she attributes "genius" to men, however, Laurencin identifies "with everything that women accomplish" as more appealing. In her flattened, simplified, and curvilinear style, she painted her group portraits of herself, Apollinaire, Picasso, and others who surrounded them at the Bateau Lavoir, a shabby studio in Paris's Montmartre. Admittedly "fascinated" by the cubist theories of this group, she nevertheless concludes that she "never could" paint according to them ("Men's Genius"). Her palette of pastels juxtaposed to blacks and greys was nothing like the neutral tones of the cubists (McPherson 29), and neither were her subjects—primarily individual girls and women, or groups of them, often depicted with placid horses or gentle dogs.[10]

Eileen Agar celebrates a different version of the feminine in "Religion and the Artistic Imagination." Agar, however, speaks less personally than Laurencin and admits to no humility in the face of men's "genius." Looking to Europe, she finds emotional sources of creative power in the unconscious (symbolized by the Sun) and discovers that the "artistic and imaginative life is under the sway of womb-magic." She also looks to Russia, where she finds creative power in Jewish closeness to the Earth, and to America, where it is in the Negroes' association with the Moon. She explores the extent to which "natural symbolism [sun, earth, moon] has a greater emotional appeal to a woman than has religious mysticism" represented by traditional Christianity. The art of her time, in other words, grows out of, embodies, and elevates to a central position, qualities traditionally associated with outsiders: women, Jews, and Negroes.

Agar is sympathetic to the surrealists' fascination with the unconscious as a source of creativity. She has her own response, however, to the preoccupation of male surrealist painters with what Whitney Chadwick calls "a mythical Other onto whom their romantic, sexual, and erotic desire is projected." The real women, who like Agar were painters as well as wives or lovers of men in the group around André Breton, dissociated themselves from the movement and continued their artistic careers. Even though they contributed to surrealism by, for instance, celebrating the female body "not as Other, but as Self" (*Women, Art* 310–11), their association with surrealism may well have prevented recognition of the individuality of their work.

In *Autobiography of an Embryo,* Agar paints the "womb-magic" she describes in "Religion and the Artistic Imagination." This large painting extends over four bordered panels. In each, Agar orchestrates, against a black background that is also a kind of grid, a mixture of bright-colored, floating, organic, and often circular images. These suggest suns, moons, wombs, dividing eggs, and foetuses, plus forms from nature (like shells, birds, plants, and fossils). Classical sculpture (including early fertility figures) and other images allude to cultural history. Oriana Baddeley reads the painting as an analogy between "physical procreation" and "artistic invention" (166), a reclamation for women, in other words, of the masculine analogy between penis and pen, pencil, or brush.

In spite of their cosmopolitan backgrounds and lives (with birthplaces ranging from Agar's in Buenos Aires to Delaunay's in the Ukraine), the women included here are also white and Euro-North American. Unlike the recovery work on race and ethnicity in literary studies of the modern period, the relevant scholarship in art history has focused more on contemporary rather than on modern minority women artists.[11] Eileen Agar's comments on the influence of Negro music on American culture, and Emily Carr's engagement with the art of indigenous peoples of the Canadian Northwest, however, underscore the need to examine the often appreciative, but also frequently stereotypical appropriation of other cultures into the visual arts of the period.[12]

The exhibition that coincided with Emily Carr's lecture, "Fresh Seeing," consisted of about fifty paintings in which she tried to document the culture and, more difficult, to capture the spirit of First Nation peoples in British Columbia. Their displacement by British immigrants (Carr's parents among them) began in the mid-nineteenth century. When Carr began her work on Indian themes at the turn of the century, diseases introduced by immigrants already had decimated some of the more accessible villages. British laws and religious beliefs had undermined their cultures. Museums and private collectors were stripping villages of cultural artifacts and, along with inevitable deterioration and some vandalism, totem poles were rapidly disappearing (Shadbolt 91). Initially determined to help preserve vanishing First Nation cultures, Carr traveled to deserted and decaying villages. Although, as Sharyn Udall suggests, Carr could not entirely escape the entrenched view of native peoples as "exotic 'others' whose culture could only be preserved by the intervention of benevolent, paternalistic whites," her sympathetic, complicated responses went further (33–34). Ultimately, her desire for documentation gave way to an urge to create comparably strong works of art. Although Carr traveled and had stimulating connections with other painters, she was less urban and cosmopolitan than other painters in this section. Yet, like Picasso and others interested in formal aspects of African art, she saw the simplification and distortions of totem poles as essentially modern (Udall 35). Carr also saw totems as art created out of emotionally charged confrontations with the spiritual, a creative process, in other words, that corresponded to her own response to the Canadian wilderness (Shadbolt 115–16).

Carr painted bold landscapes with totem poles as well as close-ups of individual totems, or parts of them. *Totem Mother, Kitwancool* (1928), for example, is a marvelous rendition of that familiar theme, mother and child. The smiling, benign, seated mother encloses the baby in a rectangular frame formed by her hands and arms, like an exterior womb above her bare legs, knees and toes turned in to fit the pole's vertical geometry. "The mother expressed all womanhood," Carr wrote admiringly, "the big wooden hands holding the child were so full of tenderness they had to be distorted enormously in order to contain it all. Womanhood was strong in Kitwancool" (qtd. in Udall 41). Other totem poles represented woman as malign, as Carr also recognized.[13]

Although European male surrealists explored opposing views of woman as "virgin, child, celestial creature," and muse versus "sorceress, erotic object, and *femme fatale*" (Chadwick, *Women Artists* 13), Carr, less egocentrically, placed carved female totem figures among the endless creative and destructive forces animating the Canadian wilderness.

Although some traditional gender hierarchies were reaffirmed in modernist discourse, painters of both sexes crossed gendered boundaries—between, for example, floral and figure painting, color and line, and decorative and fine arts. Mid-nineteenth-century impressionists, followed by Matisse and Van Gogh, revived interest in flower painting, ignoring its status as a "lesser" feminine genre (Grimes et al. 21–22). Women had painted flowers, however, not because of any inevitable link with nature, but because they had been excluded from life classes with nude models, and because they often lacked necessities, especially studio space, for more ambitious figure compositions depicting historical or legendary events.

When they began to have more choices, women still often painted floral still lifes. Vanessa Bell did, as did Marie Laurencin. Although Winifred Nicholson, revising the tradition of mother and child, painted her husband holding their infant son, as well as children, mountain and seascapes, and abstracts, she always returned to floral subjects. Nicholson's "new kind of flowerpiece" usually revealed flowers in a container, often glass, set on a window-sill against a broad, luminous landscape with a foreground, a background, but no middle-ground, not even a window (Collins 127). An example is *Window-sill, Lugano* (1923), in which Nicholson experimented with deft applications of paint with her fingers. In her "flowerpieces" she may have been striving for the effects achieved by women painting in the Chinese emperors' courts. Their flowers have "'shen' quality," Nicholson writes, and "no man artist has painted 'shen' that I know of." Nicholson translates "shen" as "wonder, great wonder" (unpublished article, qtd. in Collins 142).

Nicholson's preoccupation with flowers is inseparable from her interest in color. If, like flowers, color traditionally is associated with emotion and thus "femininity," and line (or form) with intellect and thus "masculinity" (Perry, *Women Artists* 55, 59), then Nicholson remakes the tradition to suit herself. In "Liberation of Color" she bridges the gender gap between intuition and intellect. There is "a Music of Colour," she writes, "which is to artists as scientific as the Theory of Musical Harmony." In this spirit, she provides a diagram to indicate how each of the seven colors of the rainbow "merges into its neighbour" in a "river of light" ("Liberation"). Nicholson not only sought ways to free colors from objects, she also tried to paint "unseen colours at either end of the spectrum" (Neve 18).

Like Winifred Nicholson, Sonia Delaunay-Terk was fascinated by color, wanted to liberate it from form, and knew that her interest was validated by the scientific advances of the time. The colorful Russian folk art in Delaunay's background and some early experiments with textiles encouraged her to develop—along with, as well as independently of, her husband Robert Delaunay—the lyrical use of colors in an abstract painting style dubbed "Orphism" by Apollinaire. Her square canvas, *Electric Prisms* (1914), for instance, is the result of a series of studies of the myriad colors of light that began as a response to her urban, technological world, specifically to the reflections made by some electric lights newly installed on the Boulevard Saint-Michel in Paris. In *Electric Prisms,* Delaunay orchestrates on her canvas brightly colored circular shapes and concentric rings along with horizontal and vertical lines. Evident, below left-center, is a small recreation of the advertising leaflet for the simultaneous book she had created with Blaise Cendrars. *Electric Prisms* was also, as Robert Delaunay writes, "the origin of her clothing creations" ("Sonia" 136). He describes Sonia Delaunay's textile designs as "characterized by *rhythm*. . . . The colors are "simultaneous," arrangements producing "new and original effects" ("'Simultaneous'" 138–39).

A number of the artists represented in this section, including Bell and Laurencin, produced fashion, carpet, and textile designs, stage settings and costumes, book illustrations, and/or mural paintings for architectural spaces, but Sonia Delaunay is best known for her decorative work. Until recently, however, modernist art critics clung to a tradition that distinguished fine from applied arts and associated the latter with women's traditional needlework and crafts (Broude 315–16, 327). Delaunay, however, in her 1929 introduction to the decorative designs represented in fifty pages of reproductions, including several of her own work, for an issue of *L'Art International d'Aujourd'hui* ("Carpets and Fabrics"), emphasizes the intimate connections between painting and the applied arts. Like Laurencin, Delaunay distances herself from cubist theory and practice. To her, it is "negative," destructive rather than creative in its simplification. Cubism nevertheless laid the foundation for new work inaugurated by painters who found ways to suggest "depth with considerable plasticity by linking colors" rather than by using light and shade (*chiaroscuro*). Like Nicholson, Bell, and Carr, Delaunay talks of "new ways of looking into reality." However important the utilitarian element may be in the decorative arts, they have an "indispensable" spiritual dimension ("Carpets and Fabrics").

Painters of both sexes may have shared their interests in floral subjects, color, and the decorative arts, but women artists' choice of nude females as subjects raises one of the most vexed gender issues in discussions of modern/ist painting: the identification with, versus the resentment of, a voyeuristic male "gaze" at an objectified female body. In modernism, painters divested the female nude of many conventional historic, exotic, or "mythological trappings"; often painted her in "non-naturalistic styles" (Perry, *Women* 119); and placed her in contemporary settings (Perry, *Gender* 201). Griselda Pollock notes, however, the continuance in modernist painting of "masculine sexuality and its sign, the bodies of women . . . the nude, the brothel, the bar" (54).

What happened when women, anxious to experiment with a full range of modernist motifs and techniques, painted female nudes? Socialized to define themselves "in terms of the 'feminine position,' as object[s] of the look," did they assume in front of their easels, "the 'masculine position' as subject[s] of the look"? More likely, Mary Kelly says, women at their easels learned to occupy a fluid, dual-gendered position (98). When one considers women artists and female models, then, discussions of the gaze must go beyond the simple masculine/feminine dichotomy (derived from Freudian and then film theory) in which men stare at women, to include women's gazes and those of gays and lesbians, mutual gazes between ethnic majorities and minorities and between colonizers and colonized, as well as "multiple identifications" and "shared gaze[s]" (Olin 213, 215, 217).

In *Woman Painter and Her Model* (1921), Marie Laurencin paints an unabashedly "feminine" artist. She stands, brush pointed at a canvas depicting the already painted image of an ambiguously clothed but equally feminine model. Or does the painter point her brush at her model while staring out of the picture space at an invisible canvas? In either case, there are no power hierarchies or barriers here. Subject and object, art and reality, blur. Although the brush may retain—or parody—some traditional phallic associations, woman painter and model stand side by side, black eyes equally penetrating, gazes triangulating with what is off the canvas. Laurencin joins the two women in a mirror-like intimacy, yet each figure remains mysteriously autonomous.[14]

Vanessa Bell occasionally painted female nudes that ranged, over her career, from near-abstract to representational, and from preliminary studies for larger paintings or decorations to common motifs like women bathing. Two years after the first post-impressionist exhibition that she found so liberating (Gillespie 16, 40), for instance, she painted *The Bedroom, Gordon Square* (1912). Here Bell applies her version of a nonrepresentational approach to the female nude, her sex suggested primarily by the length of her dark hair. The head of the solitary figure tilts forward, perhaps over a book. The face is featureless, and, as there are no eyes, there is no glance, at the painter or any other viewer, of either self-assertion or invitation. Conventional erotic connotations are neutralized, and the figure is only one part of a harmony of rectangular shapes and shades of gray and white, green and flesh tones.[15]

The women featured in this chapter, then, reflect a number of the characteristics of "modernism." They also provide their own perspectives, challenges, and subversions through choices and treatments of subjects and through negotiations with particular male-dominated, avant-garde movements. It is tempting, as we reconstruct the artistic activities of fifty to one hundred years ago, to stress the ways gender hierarchies victimized women artists of the time. Yet these six artists present themselves as thoughtful, confident, and committed. Their words and paintings underscore the necessity of our continued reexamination of evaluative assumptions behind art historical constructions of modernism.

Notes

1. Woolf's characterization of Lily Briscoe is also based in part on the tension between doubt and confidence that she perceived in her sister, the painter Vanessa Bell (Gillespie 196–203).

2. Elliott and Wallace contrast Barr's chart to Natalie Barney's sketched map of "Le Salon de l'Amazone," the unfolding frontisleaf to her memoir, *Adventures de l'esprit,* and to the street map of "Expatriate Paris" used by Shari Benstock in *Women of the Left Bank* to locate the residences and businesses of women important to modernism (157, 159, 161).

3. *Old Mistresses: Women Artists of the Past* was the title of a 1972 exhibition (Pollock 21); Parker and Pollock use *Old Mistresses: Women, Art, and Ideology* to title their 1981 book. The phrase does not connote reverence as does "old masters"; it challenges the assumption that women have not created art (Pollock 21).

4. See Perry, *Women Artists,* for a discussion of how several early twentieth-century French women artists found a *"fringe modernist* space . . . in which they could achieve certain limited forms of success and artistic recognition" (11–12).

5. Chadwick's *Women Artists and the Surrealist Movement* is a good example. Deepwell objects to the treatment of women artists primarily as lovers and wives of male artists and to the exclusion of important relationships with women (5). Studies do exist of Vanessa Bell and Virginia Woolf (Gillespie, Dunn), as do collections of letters between a number of women artists and their female friends. Among the studies of women artists as lesbians is Chadwick's book on Romaine Brooks (*Amazons*).

6. See Garb; Weisberg and Becker; Perry, *Women Artists,* chapter 1; Waller, chapter 7.

7. Deepwell notes that "women artists' writings on their own work . . . are rarely republished" (2). Exceptions are three collections: Witzling, *Voicing Our Visions;* Slatkin; and Witzling's edited collection of contemporary women artist's writings *(Voicing Today's Visions).* The selections are largely autobiographical.

8. There were some women art critics. For "Fresh Seeing," Carr drew on *Painters of the Modern Mind* by Mary Cecil Allen. Carr also purchased Katherine Dreier's *Western Art and the New Era* (Shadbolt 78).

9. Suzanne Valadon is another exception. The illegitimate daughter of a domestic servant, she was introduced to painting by posing nude for male artists like Toulouse Lautrec (Perry, *Women Artists* 126–27).

10. McPherson calls Laurencin's mature style of the 1920s and 1930s "a sophisticated and gender-specific form of modern primitivism" (14). Alexander Watt applauds Laurencin's inclusion in a 1936 exhibition called "Peintres Instinctifs," painters who "have developed talent on personal instincts, and not in any way due to the ideals and endeavors of a particular school" (qtd. in McPherson 41).

11. In the 1940s, Lois Mailou Jones began to paint out of her black American heritage (Peterson and Wilson 124), but I could not locate any public writing. For contemporary multicultural scholarship see, for example, LaDuke's study, which includes Asian, Latin American, Eastern European, and United States artists.

12. Gibson comments on the early twentieth-century artistic avant-garde's "apartheid, its exclusion of artists of color as the *makers* of important art" and the use of such art "primarily as inspiration for the European avant-garde" (165). Gibson contrasts Picasso's *Les Demoiselles d'Avignon* (1907) to contemporary black artist Faith Ringgold's *Picasso's Studio* (1991), a quilt painting and "antipatriarchal parody" (156). Any treatment of avant-garde art, Gibson says, must "include a poetics of gender" as well as "a poetics of colonial and postcolonial experiences" (164).

13. Carr also painted the wild and frightening, giant "ogre goddess" D'Sonoqua (Udall 36), with breasts carved like eagles' heads and black eyes, circled by white, that, Carr says, "bored into me as if the very life of the old cedar looked out" (qtd. in Udall 37).

14. Laurencin tried to describe this intimacy/mystery in "My Model," translated into English for publication in *The Listener* in 1937.

15. Vanessa Bell's *Interior with Two Women* (1932) is more representational and depicts what are probably a clothed painter and her nude model. Laura Knight's *Self-Portrait with Nude* (1913) is one of the best examples of this interest in the gaze of a female painter.

Works Cited

Agar, Eileen. *A Look at My Life.* London: Methuen, 1988.

Baddeley, Oriana. "Eileen Agar." In *Five Women Painters.* Ed. Grimes, Collins, and Baddeley. 161–80.

Benstock, Shari. *Women of the Left Bank.*

Broude, Norma. "Miriam Schapiro and 'Femmage': Reflections on the Conflict Between Decoration and Abstraction in Twentieth-Century Art." In *Feminism and Art History: Questioning the Litany,* ed. Norma Broude and Mary D. Garrard. New York: Harper & Row, 1982. 315–29.

Bryson, Norman, Michael Ann Holly, and Keith Moxey, eds. Introduction. *Visual Culture: Images and Interpretations.* Hanover, N.H.: Wesleyan University Press, 1994. xv–xxix.

Chadwick, Whitney. *Amazons in the Drawing Room: The Art of Romaine Brooks.* Berkeley: University of California Press/National Museum of Women in the Arts, 2000.

———. *Women, Art, and Society.* 2nd ed. London: Thames & Hudson, 1997.

———. *Women Artists and the Surrealist Movement.* Boston: Little Brown, 1985.

Collins, Judith. "Winifred Nicholson." In *Five Women Painters,* ed. Grimes, Collins, and Baddeley. 117–52.

Deepwell, Katy. Introduction. *Women Artists and Modernism.* Ed. Katy Deepwell. Manchester: Manchester University Press, 1998. 1–17.

Delaunay, Robert. "The 'Simultaneous' Fabrics of Sonia Delaunay (Second Version) (1938)." In *The New Art of Color: The Writings of Robert and Sonia Delaunay,* ed. Arthur A. Cohen. New York: Viking, 1978. 137–39.

———. "Sonia Delaunay-Terk (1938)." In *The New Art of Color: The Writings of Robert and Sonia Delaunay,* ed. Arthur A. Cohen. Trans. David Shapiro and Arthur A. Cohen. New York: Viking, 1978. 132–36.

Dunn, Jane. *A Very Close Conspiracy: Vanessa Bell and Virginia Woolf.* Boston: Little, Brown, 1991.

Elliott, Bridget and Jo-Ann Wallace. *Women Artists and Writers: Modernist (Im)positionings.* London: Routledge, 1994.

Fagin-King, Julia. "United on the Threshold of the Twentieth-Century Mystical Ideal: Marie Laurencin's Integral Involvement with Guillaume Apollinaire and the Inmates of the 'Bateau Lavoir.'" *Art History* 11.1 (March 1988): 88–114.

Garb, Tamar. *Sisters of the Brush: Women's Artistic Culture in Late Nineteenth-Century Paris.* New Haven: Yale University Press, 1994.

Gibson, Ann. "Avant-Garde." In *Critical Terms for Art History,* ed. Robert S. Nelson and Richard Shiff. Chicago: University of Chicago Press, 1996. 156–69.

Gillespie, Diane Filby. *The Sisters' Arts: The Writing and Painting of Virginia Woolf and Vanessa Bell.* Syracuse: Syracuse University Press, 1988.

Grimes, Teresa, Judith Collins, and Oriana Baddeley. *Five Women Painters.* Oxford: Lennard Publishing (in association with the Arts Council of Great Britain), 1989.

Harrison, Charles. "Modernism." In *Critical Terms for Art History,* ed. Robert S. Nelson and Richard Shiff. Chicago: University of Chicago Press, 1996. 142–55.

Huyssen, Andreas. "Mass Culture as Woman: Modernism's Other." In *After the Great Divide.* 44–62.

Kelly, Mary. "Re-viewing Modernist Criticism." In *Art After Modernism: Rethinking Representation,* ed. Brian Waller. New York: New Museum of Contemporary Art; Boston: David R. Godine, 1984.

LaDuke, Betty. *Women Artists: Multi-Cultural Visions.* Trenton, N.J.: Red Sea Press, 1992.

Laurencin, Marie. "My Model." *The Listener* (September 8, 1937): 511–12.

MacLeod, Glen. "The Visual Arts." In *The Cambridge Companion to Modernism,* ed. Michael Levenson. Cambridge: Cambridge University Press, 1999. 194–216.

McPherson, Heather. "Marie Laurencin: An Undividedly Feminine Psyche." In *Marie Laurencin: Artist and Muse,* ed. Douglas K. S. Hyland and Heather McPherson. Birmingham, Ala.: Birmingham Museum of Art, 1989. 13–49.

Neve, Christopher. "The Points of View of Winifred Nicholson." In *Unknown Colour: Paintings, Letters, Writings by Winifred Nicholson,* ed. Andrew Nicholson. London: Faber & Faber, 1987. 14–24.

Olin, Margaret. "Gaze." In *Critical Terms for Art History,* ed. Robert S. Nelson and Richard Shiff. Chicago: University of Chicago Press, 1996. 208–19.

Parker, Rozsika. *The Subversive Stitch: Embroidery and the Making of the Feminine.* New York: Routledge, 1984.

———, and Griselda Pollock. *Old Mistresses: Women, Art, and Ideology.* New York: Pantheon, 1981.

Perry, Gill. *Gender and Art.* New Haven: Yale University Press/Open University, 1999.

———. *Women Artists and the Parisian Avant-Garde: Modernism and 'Feminine' Art, 1900 to the Late 1920s.* Manchester: Manchester University Press, 1995.

Petersen, Karen, and J. J. Wilson. *Women Artists: Recognition and Reappraisal from the Early Middle Ages to the Twentieth Century.* New York: Harper & Row, 1976.

Pollock, Griselda. *Vision and Difference: Femininity, Feminism, and Histories of Art.* London: Routledge, 1988.

Raine, Kathleen. "The Unregarded Happy Texture of Life." In *Unknown Colour: Paintings, Letters, Writings by Winifred Nicholson,* ed. Andrew Nicholson. London: Faber & Faber, 1987. 195–202.

Shadbolt, Doris. *Emily Carr.* Vancouver: Douglas & McIntyre, 1990.

Slatkin, Wendy, ed. *The Voices of Women Artists.* Englewood Cliffs, N.J.: Prentice Hall, 1993.

Todd, Ellen Wiley. "The 'New Woman' Revised." *Painting and Gender Politics on Fourteenth Street.* Berkeley: University of California Press, 1993. 1–38.

Udall, Sharyn Rohlfsen. *Carr, O'Keeffe, Kahlo: Places of Their Own.* New Haven: Yale University Press, 2000.

Waller, Susan. *Women Artists in the Modern Era: A Documentary History.* Metuchen, N.J.: Scarecrow Press, 1991.

Weisberg, Gabriel P., and Jane R. Becker, eds. *Overcoming All Obstacles: The Women of the Academie Julian.* New York: Dahesh Museum; New Brunswick: Rutgers University Press, 1999.

Witzling, Mara R., ed. *Voicing Our Visions: Writings by Women Artists.* New York: Universe, 1991.

———. *Voicing Today's Visions: Writings by Contemporary Women Artists.* New York: Universe, 1994.

Woolf, Virginia. *To the Lighthouse.* San Diego: Harcourt Brace Jovanovich, 1989.

VANESSA BELL

From "Lecture Given at Leighton Park School"

When Mr Evans asked me to come and talk to you about art, he very kindly made it clear that I was not expected to come as a critic. In fact, had he not done so, I don't think I should have dared to come, lest you might expect me to tell you all kinds of things quite beyond my powers. [. . .] He asked me to come [. . .] as an artist, and artists, in the opinion of many, are little better than lunatics. Perhaps before I have finished talking to you you will share that opinion—and if to be a lunatic is to have different values from the majority of people I'm not sure I don't share it myself.

Besides being rather mad, artists are apt to be revolutionaries. I am not afraid however of not finding sympathy for revolution at Leighton Park, whatever proper contempt you may feel for ignorance. Judging from some of the speeches I have heard here and the rumours that sometimes reach me, Leighton Park is a veritable hot-bed of revolution. So I do not feel that I need fear want of sympathy on that score.

What does it feel like to be an idiot and a revolutionary? It is really quite pleasant. The cause of one's infirmities is simply this. One is so made that the world presents itself to one as form and colour instead of presenting itself as it does to most sane and respectable people. Of course I don't really know—how can I?—how it does present itself to other people. But let me tell you of something I read the other day which throws some light on the way in which writers at any rate look at their surroundings.

The writer in question, Mrs Woolf, in an essay called *Mr Bennett and Mrs Brown,* described herself travelling in a train with a man and an old lady. I cannot tell you all the things this couple suggested to Mrs Woolf—you must read the essay yourselves if you want to know, but this is what one glance at the old lady was enough to suggest to Mrs Woolf.

> She was one of those clean threadbare old ladies whose extreme tidiness—everything buttoned, fastened, tied together, mended and brushed up—suggests more extreme poverty than rags and dirt. There was something pinched about her, a look of suffering, of apprehension, and, in addition, she was extremely small. Her feet, in their clean little boots, scarcely touched the floor. I felt that she had nobody to support her, that she had to make up her mind for herself; that, having been deserted, or left a widow, years ago, she had led an anxious, harried life, bringing up an only son, perhaps, who, as likely as not, was by this time beginning to go to the bad.

After a glance at the man—who is decided to be a respectable corn-chandler from the North—and a whole train of speculation as to their relationship, troubles, worries, difficulties, joys and sorrows, Mrs Woolf looks again at the old lady—

> The impression she made was overwhelming. It came pouring out like a draught, like a smell of burning. What was it composed of—that overwhelming and peculiar impression? Myriads of irrelevant and incongruous ideas crowd into one's head on such occasions, one sees the person . . . in the centre of all sorts of different scenes. I thought of her in a seaside house, among queer ornaments: sea urchins, models of ships in glass cases. Her husband's medals were on the mantelpiece. She popped in and out of the room, perching on the edges of chairs, picking meals out of saucers, indulging in long, silent stares.

But you must read all the other things she suggested for yourself if you want to.

Now for the purposes of her argument, which I need not go into, Mrs Woolf proceeds to imagine that other writers were in the railway carriage with her and that they also looked at the suggestive couple opposite. What would Mr Wells have seen? [. . .]

And then Mrs Woolf tells us how Mr Arnold Bennett would have used his eyes. [. . .]

But these people are writers. The world to them is not very interesting in form and colour—I daresay they wouldn't notice whether the old lady had a red rose or a pink one in her bonnet. They would notice that she had on a bonnet and not a hat, because a bonnet has quite a different social and human significance from a hat. I have often known writers notice most minute details when such details have an interest other than a purely visual one. Let me give you an instance. It has been my fate always to live among writers—I know the species well. When I was quite young, living in a house full of Victorian sentiment and family photographs in plush frames fired me one day with a desire to reform. I seized those photographs, a few of them, huddled together behind draperies and flowers in the darkest corner of a dark room. I decided that many were hideous and should be banished and that others should be framed in something pleasanter to behold and more hygienic than plush—(Do you know what plush is? I can't describe it if you don't). Well, I carried out my reform. I did it in secret, in fear and trembling, hoping that the literary powers would be blind to this as to so much else. But no. They noticed at once and I was condemned as a heartless desecrator of the most sacred sentiments of family.

On another occasion—you see I was already a revolutionary—I decided boldly to interfere once more with household tradition and remove an enormous glass chandelier that had hung from time immemorial in such a way as to block all light from the middle of the common sitting-room. I got help from a tall brother. We took it down. [. . .] But no one noticed. You see the chandelier had only been a mass of colour and reflected lights and semi-transparencies—it had no particular human associations—and so, although everything else in the room now stood revealed as colour and form where before all had been veiled in shade, for the writers there was no difference.

Now let us return to the railway carriage. You have heard how three different writers looked at one old lady. But did any of them really *see* her? Not in a way that I should call seeing. They saw that she was tidy and clean, because that had human significance. Probably they saw, though not one gives us even so much clue to her appearance, that she had grey hair: It would be a kind of label—grey hair = old age—just as they might think red in strawberries means ripeness, or a blue sky means a fine day. Suppose a milliner had been sitting opposite Mrs Brown. She would certainly have [. . .] decided that such bonnets were only to be bought now in a certain kind of shop in a certain kind of town and would have been able to tell you its price to a halfpenny.

Or suppose a doctor. I think [. . .] he'd have noticed things mercifully hidden from you and me—symptoms of all kinds perhaps and the probable speedy end of Mrs Brown.

But the artist, this madman—who does not go beyond his eyes—whose eyes find enough to absorb him all the way from Richmond to Waterloo in the mere outside of the sitter opposite, what does he see? Well, if I were a critic and could get inside other artists' heads, no doubt I could tell you what some of them might see. It would be fascinating to be able to see her as seen by different painters. Now these artists have seen different things but what they have all seen is form and colour. Form definite, distinct, Carlyle's form, no other old man's. The shape of Carlyle's head, the way it is set on his shoulders, its proportion to the rest of him. Any old man might suggest thoughts on old age to a writer, but only Carlyle would suggest that particular shape to a painter. The grey hair, which has spoken of old age at once to writers and doctors, means to a painter not just grey hair, but a certain grey—perhaps a grey with silver lights and warm shadows, perhaps an opaque cold grey, but a grey as different from other greys as one chord in music is different from others.

I said that the artist does not go beyond his eyes. I know of course that that remark lays me open to flat contradiction. Many people think that an artist is quite capable of telling you a great deal about the sitter besides telling you what they feel about his shape and colour. They think that his past, present, future, his whole relationship to the universe in fact, can be conveyed by the way in which his head droops on his shoulder and one hand rests on another. I am not going to dispute that at the moment, it would take too long, but at least I think all will agree that the principal preoccupation of the artist is with form and colour. Even if sometimes he goes on from such considerations to others, still many artists evidently have found this particular province of theirs so full of fascination and interest that they have been content to remain there. [. . .] It is indeed so exciting and so absorbing, this painters' world of form and colour, that once you are at its mercy you are in grave danger of forgetting all other aspects of the material world. Think what this may lead to and you will understand why it is that the poor creatures, the artists, are thought—well—half-witted at any rate.

Long ago, when you were very young, you yourselves, all of you, saw the world as colour. You didn't see shapes very well then, at any rate you hadn't the experience necessary to tell you that differences of colour imply changes of shape, nor did you know anything about the way in which colour reveals space. You would have walked over the edges of chairs and into the nice hot fire which looked so lovely and bright, if your nurse hadn't stopped you. But how exciting colour was—how you longed for the bright gold watch held out to you—it was merely tiresome to have to learn that all is not gold that glitters and that that beautiful green paint you got all over your pinafore which made such a wonderful pattern was really dirty and probably poisonous. In fact you were dangerously like artists. Luckily you were probably saved from going farther on that road to ruin by your superior intellect which showed clearly to what such foolish fancies would lead. And I must admit that once you cut yourself adrift from the practical implications of appearances there is no telling what may not happen. For instance it may very well be that dirt becomes beautiful. I don't hope to convince you of this, unless I can persuade you to come one day into a studio where the char woman has been kept properly at bay by means of large placards, with PLEASE DO NOT TOUCH in bold black letters on them placed on tables and chairs and shelves. There the dust has done its modelling, and there's no good denying that very often beauty results. You'll find me blowing up the housemaid for destroying dust at this rate and of course after that I know I have only an asylum to expect, where no doubt everything will be scrubbed twice a day. Luckily the artist *can* see beauty in other things than dirt. [. . .] But after all this power [. . .] may have its uses. Suppose a practical sensible sane man or woman were to take a walk through Reading some winter evening. They come upon a butcher's shop, in which is hanging the carcase of a great ox. The man, if he happens to be a butcher, can tell me from what he sees exactly how that ox should be cut into joints, the name and price of each. If he be learned in prices, he can tell me whether the shop man is a profiteer. The woman perhaps knows how much to order for her hungry family or can guess the weight of a given joint. You may be revolted by the sight or you may have your greed aroused. Wouldn't the butcher's shop have a new kind of excitement and splendour for us if we could see it as Rembrandt once saw such a sight, not as a piece of more or less good and expensive meat, but like this? It seems to me there are some compensations for seeing it thus, even if it leads to one's having not quite such a good dinner the next day. Then there is another advantage which comes from using your eyes in this impractical way. One is almost incapable of being bored. Even a kitchen coal scuttle may become the most exciting combination of curves and hollows, of deep shadows and silver edges, instead of a tiresome thing to be filled with coal, or a half worn-out thing that will soon need renewal.

I do not hope however to stir you to such revolt as the giving up of all cleanliness, order and greed. That would be asking for too much trouble. Also I foresee another difficulty. You would turn upon me, when your rooms were dirty, your clothing hanging in beautiful rags, and your food covered with exquisite mould, and you'd say: "Very well. Here we are on the verge of ruin. We have done all you told us. We see old ladies, butchers' shops and dust all alike as things of beauty without giving a thought to their other possibilities.

Fig. 20.1. Vanessa Bell. *The Bedroom, Gordon Square*, 1912, oil on canvas 55.9 x 45.3 cm. © Bell Estate. Reproduced by permission of the Art Gallery of South Australia, Adelaide.

But what then? We can't paint. We can't make others see what we see because we haven't the skill. What is the use of seeing as Rembrandt saw if we can't use our hands as he used his? If only you'd told us to learn how to draw first, by the time we'd learnt to see we might be able to turn it to some account." Well now I'm going to confess to my worst heresy. It is this. Skill no doubt is of great importance in many walks of life. If you want to make boots, to make leather bags, to practise any of the crafts, and some of you not only do want to, but do succeed in doing so most admirably, as I saw last term—then you must be possessed of a certain amount of skill. [. . .] But I am certain—and this is my heresy—that in art skill is of no importance. When I say skill I mean skill of hand, mechanical skill. (There is another skill, that which comes to artists in their maturity, almost unconsciously perhaps, with which I am not concerned here.) I even think it more likely to be a hindrance than a help, for as I said before skill means that your hand has acquired certain habits and habits of hand tend to destroy what is most important to an artist—sensibility.

Suppose you are drawing a flower—if you are capable of seeing that flower with all its subtleties of form, the way its edges recede or are sharp against the space behind, you have to try to express your feeling about those things in line. It must be sensitive, everywhere—nowhere must it become mechanical. Now habit of hand is always more or less mechanical. If it weren't, you couldn't depend on it. When you're cutting an edge of leather you don't want to stop and think on the way. Your hand must know its business without help from your mind. But in art your mind—or your feeling—must direct you always. You may hesitate, or you may draw your line with a single quick movement, but you must see and feel what you want to do, your action must not be the result, as in craft, of long training to make one particular movement and no other. Of course the artist generally acquires some skill of hand. He cannot avoid it. [. . .] But this skill is a snare in art. Many of the greatest artists have had very little and it is of course common enough to find miraculous skill with little or no artistic gift. The people who cut the wood blocks for *Punch*, in the days before everything could be reproduced by process, must have had almost incredible skill. [. . .] They sometimes I suppose got tired of following artists' vagaries and produced some woodcuts designed as well as executed by themselves, but their talent did not lie in that direction. If you look at artists of greater reputation you will find I think that the two things do not necessarily go together. Skill is sometimes no doubt necessary in order to enable the artist to carry out his conception. If I conceive a work, as the primitive Italians often did, which has as an essential part of it a surface covered with most elaborate and minutely detailed gilding, I must know how to produce that effect, and in order to do that I must be a craftsman too and have mastered the whole intricate business of preparing the ground, by incising the pattern, inlaying the jewels perhaps, and gilding the whole. But unless I am enough of an artist to *see* first how this will look, and what place it will have in my work as a whole, my skill will be wasted. Many artists I think allowed their crafts to run away with them, and generally, as I'm sure those who can draw the curves of periods would tell you, when art is on the downward grade, skill tends to get the upper hand.

Nowadays artists often use such a very simple technique that most people, who judge that art is good in proportion as it looks difficult to produce, dismiss such pictures as these, by saying, "Any child could do that." Any child often could do it if any child could see what had to be done. Look at these children's drawings. How clear and decided and unhesitating is the line. They have no difficulty in doing what they want to do.

Already at the age of six or so children begin to lose this power and I daresay some of you in the Upper School have quite lost it. [. . .] This cannot be helped of course, nor is it desirable that you should, even as artists, keep the vision of childhood. You must learn to see other things than flat colour, you must learn to see form with all its complexities and distance and space. But do not let your attention wander from interest in what you see to interest in what you do. [. . .] At any rate go as far as you can in sympathy with the artist's vision even if you have to consider the practical aspects yourselves.

The skill of a child is in fact great enough to do anything but those things which require long training, and you yourselves at the age of five or six had enough, I have no doubt, to do anything that as artists you now need to do. [. . .] If we could see our end clearly at the beginning as children do—and state it, and leave it—our pictures would no doubt be as lovely in technique as are those of the old painters in fresco who had to do so on account of their medium, or those who like Van Eyck or Piero della Francesca saw clearly how one stage was to follow another till they achieved their conclusion. As with them, the child has vision guiding his hand and using its adequate skill. But our vision is weak compared to our hand's cleverness. We do not see clearly what we want to do. If we did I believe we should find no difficulty in doing it.

Sketches in Pen and Ink. Ed. Lia Giachero. London: Hogarth, 1997. 149–65.

Fig. 20.2. Marie Laurencin. *Woman Painter and Her Model (Femme peintre et son modele)*, 1921, oil on canvas, 31" x 25¹/₂" (81 x 65 cm.). Reproduced by permission of Collection Herve Odermatt, Paris.

MARIE LAURENCIN

Men's Genius Intimidates Me

Trans. Alita Kelley

Because I love painting so much, I feel it has nothing to do with me. When I was still very young I noticed that if I ever told people what I wanted to do—learn my lessons, draw, sew—I'd only to mention those things and somehow I'd never get to do them. Ever since I started painting I've been careful not to talk about it, it's a sort of superstition. When my pictures remain in my house they begin to trouble me; I don't like to see them there and the few I have are ones I've kept because of the frames.

If I feel far removed from other painters, it's because they are men, and for me men are a difficult problem to solve. I've always been astonished by their discussions, their research, their genius, without which nothing would exist; one can live in their shadow as long as one doesn't intend to imitate them. When a poet writes he says what I want to say so well that I say nothing, and the same applies to painting. The great masters, and contemporary painters too, have worked in my place.

But if men's genius intimidates me, I feel very comfortable with everything that women accomplish. When I was little I liked silk thread, I stole pearls and threaded them on colored silks; I felt they were well hidden and I took them out and looked at them. I'd have liked to have had lots of children so I could do their hair and tie it with ribbons. I loved listening to mothers singing, and my happiest days were when I was taken to a convent where the sisters hugged me and showed me picture books and let me play on the harmonium. Most of all, I loved looking at their faces; I studied the sweetness of their smiles, the gentleness of their voices; I was the laziest little girl in the world.

My first history lesson dealt with the Franks and was exceedingly painful to me; it took a lot of patience to learn anything at all. Fortunately, the chapter on the Franks ended and Saint Clothilde, the first queen, showed up and I was saved. I discovered the queens and heroines of French history; nothing else interested me, I studied their portraits. Their names in small print followed by the name of the country in large print delighted my ear when I read and I called it The Music of the Queens. I wished I could have seen a real portrait of Joan of Arc. I hated Catherine de Medici and Madame de Maintenon even more, because she was held up as an example for us. I thought she was a hypocrite with her double chin, a scary school mistress. It's because all the pictures show her when she was at the height of her fame.

Books without pictures were disappointing. One word that made me dream—it appeared even in history books for children—was "favorite." Initially I thought "the favorites" were beautiful non-existent beings, then as I got older I saw that they were real women whom Kings had picked out and fallen in love with, and they made the queens suffer, but they were so attractive. They received the kings in their magnificent dwellings and you couldn't believe they could grew old. I thought such beauties would never be seen again.

Then, suddenly, we were fifteen and started looking at ourselves. Ghirlandaio and Botticelli were our favorite painters.

The faces of some of my school friends, with their adolescent grace, were perfect models for the Italian school. Narrow jaws, long hair, eyes framed by eyebrows as nature made them—you forgot the ugly school uniform. Heads like angels were often the best at calculating, and our own "Primavera" made the *P.C.N.* which was quite a *coup* at that time.

Youth, in others, is always something to love and admire! For most of us it was very gloomy: we weren't even allowed to run, and very few played tennis or knew how to swim. On Sundays we were taken for walks along the Champs-Elysées, on Thursday we went to a museum. For parties they made us look so ugly that we spent the evening crying. Yet we were always ready for something new and met the next day to ask each other about the good time we'd had.

Life was full of secrets: Alfred de Musset, stories of courtesans . . . we weren't allowed out alone. Held back from life, we searched passionately for it in painting and poetry.

If you learn to paint you must learn to use color. I've always been for jumping in and swimming; it's delightful because water is clean, but colors used to terrify me. They so easily got dirty. Red was my particular enemy. I've never been able to use vermillion; even now, I lack the nerve and use madder in place of it. And while we're on the subject of color, have you ever noticed how great thinkers and great masters love blue? It's nice; people who like blue are always alright.

We might still find our friends hiding in Jean Goujon's sculptures, even in Leonardo da Vinci's angels, and since we were always under our parents' eye we tirelessly copied portraits of Madame Vigée-Lebrun and her daughter in crayon or charcoal, with all the sentimental baggage: little capes and fichus, glove sellers, hairdressers. Men aren't crazy about Madame Vigée-Lebrun, though they grant her a place in museums. Her painting is rather chilly. With Goya's paintings of women, on the other hand, a whole tricky world of lies and dancing in the streets opens up, and with such grace too! Gracious steel marionettes, and from his way of painting them, Goya wasn't fooled in the least. He gave back, an eye for an eye, a tooth for a tooth; the Duchess of Alba's cool, haughty glance, Queen Maria-Luisa's ugliness . . . not one inch of their straight-backed height overlooked; their delightful feet are not those of goddesses but of Eves who're sure of themselves and all they command.

In Spain the concierge, the servant girl, and the lady of the house are alike as sisters: they have the same black eyes, the same way of speaking, and all know the same ancient tricks of a woman and a puppet. Goya painted them unceasingly and apparently never lost his head. According to legend he sired over eighty children out of wedlock. I'm often asked, out of politeness, or curiosity, or perhaps to please me, how I became a painter in spite of the difficulties I had at first and my struggle with colors. For a time I went to an academy where the teachers who'd given it their name spent half an hour a week there; they'd say a few words and take off without noticing us. But there were students there, and for us little bourgeois Parisiens being surrounded by foreigners was like a tonic. All different countries met there, and one got the impression that Paris was the center of it all, the ideal place for artists to be. From mingling with foreigners I realized I had been extraordinarily lucky to have been born in Paris, and it made me very proud.

The Seine was my river. I knew all the Paris street songs, which didn't stop me singing Gerard de Nerval's ancient airs as well. I'd sneak out on Bastille Day and go to the lower class districts, and I think the idea of painting came to me on the top of a horse-drawn omnibus on the Auteuil-St. Sulpice route. We skirted the houses and furnished rooms whose windows revealed women half dressed and men in the shadows playing the banjo . . . it was a world so very far removed from my own and I never ceased loving to look at it and always went on the top of the bus.

In those days we went in for something that's almost disappeared—writing. To make an appointment one had to wire—or rather, send a message that went by pneumatic tube—and letters were important . . . our friends' handwriting . . . I'm still moved when I see handwriting. I'm always in good spirits when I get letters, and I always answer . . . From there it's only a short step to paint brushes, canvas, and work. I like to write letters, since I can't sing any more it's like whistling a tune when I get up and start living through the day. The little I've learned was taught to me by my contemporaries I call The Great Painters: Matisse, Derain, Picasso, Braque. They won't like it if I mention their names, they're like that. I think they're like that song of Carmen's "If you don't love me, I love you . . ."

If I didn't become a cubist it's because I never could. I wasn't capable of it, but their theories fascinated me.

Arts. July 24, 1952.

Fig. 20.3. Sonia Delaunay-Terk. *Electric Prisms (Prismes electriques)*, 1914, oil on canvas, 93" x 98" (2238 x 250.9 cm). Musee National d'Art Moderne, Centre Georges Pompidou and Art Resource, N.Y.

SONIA DELAUNAY

Carpets and Fabrics

Trans. Alita Kelley

The purpose of our study is to introduce a selection of fabrics and carpets that illustrate the style dominant at the current time. We must ask you to excuse any omissions due to unforeseen problems—we were unable to reach several artists, and many photographs proved insufficiently clear for reproduction. I do believe, however, that you will find our choice sufficiently representative of current production.

Every historical time finds its own individual expression, and it is interesting, among a multitude of contemporary styles, to note the few that succeed in molding public taste. The work of these few responds to needs and tastes that the general public, always set in its ways, delays in accepting as its own but which finally emerge as the one its own vitality dictates.

Style is a synthesis of the practical needs and spiritual way of being of a given period. Our intent has been to study the origins of our selection and its connections with more profound artistic activity.

We live in a period that is predominantly mechanical, dynamic, and visual, with the first two directly attributable to the practical needs of the times, and the visual element being characteristically spiritual. The spiritual element of a style develops through the intercession of individuals of a visionary bent whose hypersensitivity enables them to anticipate future trends and to express them in their creative work. Unconscious of their fundamental role in style setting, the reactions of such persons to life around them brings new ways of looking into reality, while the mediation of sensitive elements transforms their way of looking into reality also. A similar, simple explanation informs expression in the case of various objects, i.e., architecture, furniture, fashion, etc., and, moreover, the aesthetic element is in accord with the practical.

The speed and dynamism reflected in modern life demand synthesis in all things. In the case of mechanical constructions, beauty is revealed, not as an effect of taste, but intimately tied to function, a principle pushed to absurd limits by some theorists' advocation of the utilitarian element over the spiritual, which they forget has always been indispensable to mankind and the one to which we owe our most beautiful human creations.

Awareness of formal simplicity has led us to study fabrics and the flat and even decoration of surface area. At this time we are witnessing a renaissance of flat decorative elements, fabrics, wall hangings, and a resurgence of murals. Large united surfaces without decoration in relief calls for the element of fantasy that wall hangings and tapestry provide. Small pictures on bare walls do not fit with current architecture, and architecture alone imposes the wall decoration that it requires.

Flat, level decoration is allied to surface; it creates forms that bring those surfaces alive and contributes to their expressivity; in turn, elements of flat decoration become an integral part of pictorial study and decide which direction it will take. All depends on the way colors interact with each other.

Now that the opposition has been defeated, our contemporary style faces another danger. Starting around 1905, new forms and colors began to gain ground, thanks to the works of a small group of painters who, in individual ways, began shaking off forms that had outlived their time and belonged to the past. Such forms now appeared complicated and decadent, out of tempo with the new rhythm that brought about a resurgence of simplification, and painters (Matisse and the fauves) simplified the colored surfaces of objects, expanding and exalting the colored areas of a design.

If simplification is achieved by objects being expressed in flat color in the work of Braque, Picasso, and other Cubists, the object itself disappears and the painting becomes an abstract poetical composition with the object implied more than it is expressed. This period is fundamentally destructive. Pictorial expression became simplified but was negative; it prepared the terrain for a new taste, but, since expression of the object had been destroyed, it could not create a new way of looking at things. The true visionaries in modern times have been Gleizes, Delaunay, and Leger. They too had been freed from the past by their elders, but they were not deterred by a play of abstract forms and they created a vision that was lyrical and belonged to the future.

Delaunay discovered new technical means of expression involving color and form. By opposing flatnesses, through a principle of simultaneous contrast, these painters created a way of expressing depth with considerable plasticity by linking colors and without recourse to chiaroscuro. Their views of the modern city, its advertisements and fashions, have become the poetic leitmotif of our time and are currently fundamental to visual expression in the applied arts and luxury industries.

As we attempt to define present day style and to indicate its origins, it is important to remember those painters who were reviled and ridiculed for many years yet who were, in fact, the forerunners and anonymous inspirers of today's style. Certain artists attempt to revitalize their imagination and to hide their creative poverty in an excess of geometric elements: this is new decoration on an old base. Seen for what they are, such complex designs are as false as any other rediscovered, non-constructive ornamentation. Characteristic of the new style, now in formation, on the other hand, are those objects in which surface color and form combine with maximum utility.

"Tapis et Tissus Presente par Sonia Delaunay," *L'Art International d'Aujourd'hui*. No. 15. Paris: Editions d'Art Charles Moreau, 1929. A different translation is published in *The New Art of Color: The Writings of Robert and Sonia Delaunay*. Ed. Arthur A. Cohen. Trans. David Shapiro and Arthur A. Cohen. New York: Viking Press, 1978. 199–201.

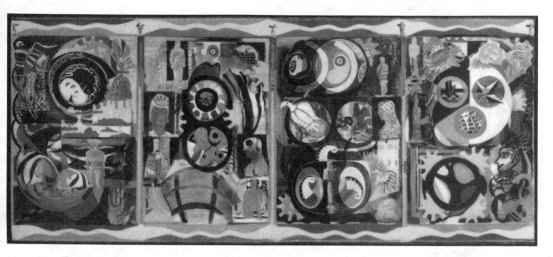

Fig. 20.4. Eileen Agar, *The Autobiography of an Embryo*, 1933/34, oil on board, 90.17 x 313.36 cm. Reproduced by permission of the Tate Gallery (Britain).

EILEEN AGAR

Religion and the Artistic Imagination

As an artist, the Earth, the Sun and the Moon have a greater significance for me than the highly rarified idea of the Holy Trinity. For natural symbolism has a greater emotional appeal to a woman than has religious mysticism. Measured by the artist's sensitiveness Christianity appears to undergo profound changes resulting to a new and more naturalistic mythology in Europe, Russia and America.

(a) In Europe, the importance of the unconscious in all forms of Literature and Art establishes the dominance of a feminine type of imagination over the classical and more masculine order. Apart from rampant and hysterical militarism, there is no male element left in Europe for the intellectual and rational conception of life has given way to a more miraculous creative interpretation, and artistic and imaginative life is under the sway of womb-magic. The Sun is an increasingly important symbol in the new mythology of Europe. Turner, Van Gogh, Monet, among others, have helped just as much to realise the plastic nature of this pre-eminently European symbol as any fifteenth century painter of the Christian tradition.

(b) Russia obviously repudiates Christianity, and the female concept as a form of life, and as a logical conclusion of their programme of social reconstruction they are bound to do away with all forms of imaginative life. This extreme rationalism will give a Jewish character to their outlook, and therefore their emotional life is bound to be nourished from Jewish sources. The new Russian form of life is already near to earth. They are the only people in the world to build up images tied directly to the earth, pictures of fertility and fecund life, no sharp-shadowed moon-like landscapes as in America, for under the hammer and sickle grow waving seas of corn. The Jewish race alone has this same quality of virile earth-nearness, expressed not in terms of the peasant but in terms of the intellectual. For having been forbidden the worship of graven images the mainstream of Jewish creative life has flowed in the direction of the written word. The centre of energy in Russian life will be essentially Jewish.

(c) Only in the child-like emotional veracity of the negro can America find its creative fulfillment, for, excepting the Indian tradition, there is no other cultural background to the present-day amorphous civilisation of America. The negro's emotional life is moon-hit, in him life is the most primeval; what is before sex is alone capable of sublimation into something beyond sex. Music carries this undifferentiated quality. It is essentially an art of the night. Negro music is at present but a note in the desert, a plaintive, new-born cry, a note nevertheless taken up by the whole of America, distorted into a syncopated, savage, sexless roar. The emergence of this new form in America lies much more in the distant future, than the immediate epoch we face in Europe and Russia, for the two latter are bound to exert a cultural influence long before the American life-form has taken shape.

Thus a woman finds these three forms of vitality important, because they are the only crystallisations of emotional integrity in the world to-day. For only by reaching back to the deepest and simplest emotional source native to a particular life-form can a creative harmony be projected into the world. Expressed in the symbolism of the Earth, the Sun and the Moon, the Holy Trinity of Christianity is realised and surpassed by these three emergent cultures in Russia, Europe and America.

The Island. December 1931: 102.

EILEEN AGAR

From "Am I a Surrealist?"

Before 1936 there had been very little information available in England about European Surrealism, apart from articles in obscure periodicals. But however many the shocked disapprovals of the exhibition, nearly everybody behaved well. Only when Paul Eluard delivered his poetry lecture on 24 June and talked of de Sade, that holy martyr of freedom, did Augustus John, until then sitting quietly in the audience, get up noisily and exit dragging his blonde companion with him, slamming the door behind him. A thousand visitors came each day, mostly stunned and puzzled by what they saw, except for those few who were aware of the international significance of this new approach to art. [. . .]

The press had a field day, though their taunts must have often fallen on deaf ears, for people, mostly young people, came, in their hundreds and thousands, not to sneer, but to learn, to find enlightenment and to live. There was much to see and admire in the show, not only the courage—east of the Rhine, at that time, every item would have been burnt or condemned as degenerate—but the revolution in thought, for Kant, that Chinaman of Konisberg, had eternally narrowed the German imagination and sense of freedom, if not that of the rest of Europe.

The Surrealists themselves were a proud, elegant and unforgettable group. They all seemed to be very handsome, [. . .]

The Surrealist women, whether painters'or not, were equally good-looking. They were elegant and dressed with panache, caring about clothes and their surroundings, however strange the interiors. Our concern with appearance was not a result of pandering to masculine demands, but rather a common attitude to life and style. This was in striking contrast to the other professional women painters of the time, those who were not Surrealists, who if seen at all, tended to flaunt their art like a badge, appearing in deliberately paint-spotted clothing. The juxtaposition by us of a Schiaparelli dress with outrageous behaviour or conversation was simply carrying the beliefs of Surrealism into public existence.

Amongst the European Surrealists double-standards seem to have proliferated, and the women came off worst. Breton's wife, Jacqueline, was expected to behave as the great man's muse, not to have an active creative existence of her own. In fact, she was a painter of considerable ability, but Breton never mentioned her work. The men were expected to be very free sexually, but when a woman like Lee Miller adopted the same attitude whilst living with Man Ray, the hypocritical upset was tremendous. Perhaps the English, ever discreet, managed to avoid such obvious confrontations . . .

Abstract art and Surrealism were the two movements that interested me most, and I see nothing incompatible in that, indeed we all walk on two legs, and for me, one is abstract, the other surreal—it is point and counterpoint. Surrealism for me draws its inspiration from nature. I recall the account of Tanguy walking along the beach noting the tiny marine forms, studying the seaweed and the rocks. Then he would go back to his studio and create a painting which made references to what he had seen, yet nature would only be the starting point for his imagination. I adopt a similar approach, though at the same time, abstraction would also be exerting its influence upon me, giving me the benefit of geometry and design to match and balance and strengthen the imaginative elements of a composition. Outer eye and inner eye, backward and forward, inside out and upside down, sideways, as a metaphysical aeroplane might go, no longer classical or romantic, medieval or gothic, but surreal, transcendent, a revelation of what is concealed in the hide-and-seek of life, a mixture of laughter, play and perseverence.

You see the shape of a tree, the way a pebble falls or is formed, and you are astounded to discover that dumb nature makes an effort to speak to you, to give you a sign, to warn you, to symbolise your innermost thoughts. Chance is not a neutral but a distinctly positive force; the Surrealists believe that you can get on good terms with chance by adopting a lyrical mode of behaviour and an open attitude.

A Look at My Life. Written in collaboration with Andrew Lambirth. London: Methuen, 1988. 118–22.

WINIFRED NICHOLSON

From "Liberation of Colour"

What does the man who is not an artist want to know about colour? He likes colour, likes it bright when he is cheerful, sober for work in his office, and new when it is a fresh variety of sweet pea. He knows all about colour and what he likes, and what he dislikes. Music—that is different—he can hum "God Save the King" and recognize "The Marseillaise"—if he can't, he leaves music to the musicians.

Yet there is a Music of Colour—an art of colour which is to artists as scien-

Fig. 20.5. Winifred Nicholson. *Window-sill, Lugano*, 1923, oil on board, 28 x 50 cm. Reproduced by permission of the Tate Gallery (Britain)

tific as the Theory of Musical Harmony. It is so new that few people, except those who are creating it, are aware that it exists. It is abstract and related to no recognizable objects—it is universal as a medium and powerful for the expression of thought and emotion. It is dynamic in that there is a far-reaching future ahead of it—a future of unexplored possibilities. Any reader who wants to know more of it, read on. Those who prefer to use their eyes and trust their eyes alone (and are they not the wisest?) turn to the pictures, look at them, and read no further. But for those readers who like words, read on—follow me.

To begin with there are no words for colours, only a few flower names, a few jewel names, that is all, and quite inadequate to convey the myriad shades that our eyes perceive each moment. For the colours you must use your inward eye as you read these words in black print, as I call up for you the living, glowing, vibrating tones of the Rainbow Prism that are our medium. I can give you also the key to the structure on which we are working. A structure as scientific, we think, as the octave in music or the ladder of numbers of the number table.

I have set this key out in the diagram and this is how to read it. In the center column, reading across, you will read the seven names of the colours of the rainbow. Substitute in your mind's eye their bright hues for the written words. Now these colours are to many people, may be to you, isolated phenomena, connected with known objects. Green, that's for grass; red, that's for letter boxes, etc. If one speaks of the rainbow sequence, you have to say a childish rhyme to remember the order in which the colours run—"Richard Of York Gains Battles In Vain." If that is your conception of colour, you must change your notions, and accept colours in their relation to one another, each in its own place as part of white light. As this snow-white light is shattered they appear one after the other as a river sequence. Each colour takes its place, and merges into its neighbour, just as each note merges into the next note in the river of sound from bass to treble. Musicians have made halts or stations along this river of sound, and called these halts notes—the notes of the scale. Just in the same way artists have made halts in the river of light and called these halts Red, Orange, Yellow, Green, Blue, Indigo, Violet. There are seven of them just as there are seven notes in the musical scale, and this is not mere coincidence, but a fundamental of the Law of Proportion.

To go back to the diagram. You will see that colour has seven halts below indicating seven degrees of depth or density, descending from the light tones of each particular colour to its darkest hue. Above each rainbow colour you will see seven more names, these rise from the highest transparency or shade of each hue to its neutralization.

These scales are the chart on which colour artists build the conceptions of their painting. They play their melodies and their harmonies to and fro, and up and down on such a chart, very much as the composer uses the keyboard of the piano or a mathematician uses the number table in the science of calculation.

Each colour is unique, but no colour can stand alone. To get the full value of its unique colour it must have other hues by its side, not for mere contrast, as black, say, contrasts with white, or square with circle, but prismatically to break up the rays of colour, as a shuttlecock is tossed, to and from the waves of light. Thus all the most brilliant things of nature are composed of tiny facets or mirrors which reflect and re-reflect each other—kingfisher's breast, jay's feather, butterfly's wing, fish's scales, flower petals in all their transparency—each may appear one hue, but in reality under a microscope are made up of many varied hues in true harmony, heightening each other's brilliance. So we cull our colours here and there, up and down the scale to create the particular colour we have in mind.

Yesterday I set out to pick a yellow bunch to place as a lamp on my table in dull, rainy weather. I picked Iceland poppies, marigolds, yellow iris; my bunch would not tell yellow. I added sunflowers, canary pansies, buttercups, dandelions; no yellower. I added to my butter-like mass, two everlasting peas, magenta pink, and all my yellows broke into luminosity. Orange and gold and

clay	mud	dust	earth	shadow	slate	lead
terracotta	dun	putty	khaki	mist	pewter	prune
brick	fawn	beige	faded oak leaf	sea grey	steel	mulberry
roan	bistre	hay	sage	air force blue	blue grey	vieux rose
rust	ocre	straw	willow	fell blue	knife blue	musk rose
coral	sand	amber	crab apple	turquoise	royal	wine
ruby	flame	topaz	emerald	azure	sapphire	amethyst
RED	ORANGE	YELLOW	GREEN	BLUE	INDIGO	VIOLET
sugar pink	alabaster	sulphur	duck's egg	babyribbon blue	ice blue	pale lilac
scarlet	apricot	lemon	pea green	sky	french blue	lavender
vermillion	fire	canary	grass green	forget-me-not	hyacinth	heliotrope
tomato	fox	brass	cabbage	larkspur	ultramarine	purple
dragon's blood	copper	daffodil	forest green	lapis-lazuli	electric blue	maroon
mahogany	tobacco	mustard	laurel	horizon	midnight	damson
RAVEN	BLACK COFFEE	TIGER SKIN	BLACK VELVET	ZENITH	PITCH	CHOCOLATE

lemon and primrose each singing its note. Pleased with my success I added more sweet peas and drowned my yellow completely. Another colour emerged, not yellow. Each colour thus created by a supremacy over the other colours it finds itself among, has its own message, and this message is sufficient for the gamut of human thought, and corresponds to it; as music can correspond to it. The same science of intervals plays upon human emotion.

Red is always an assault, an insult, a danger cry, shouting Revolution! Robbery! and paradoxically, "Homage to the King." It is the taunting flame out of the primal volcano. It is the easiest colour to see. Man saw it first. Orange is an open colour expressing prosperity and plenty, sunbaked universe, and laughter under the sun. Yellow is the atmosphere of wisdom, reflection and calm. Green is quieter still, rest and content, the emerald ripple of wave and flow. Blue is the colour we love most, its suggestion is the lark's song, hope that soars into the stratosphere. Indigo is tragedy, like red it can stand almost alone, crying to Pluto's intense blackness, to death, and to Faith.

This conjures violet, whose magic is perceived only by keen-eyed men, but it is known by song birds and honey bees. Its wish can only be used by the great colour masters, and it is a safe indication of their mastery. It has been caught best by the Eastern painters, seeing in psychic sunlight, and it is being sought by painters such as Christopher Wood, for it calls to a colour beyond itself on the scale, a colour that our eyes cannot see, although we know that it is there by the power of its ultraviolet rays. Maybe we shall see this colour some day when we have trained our eyes more precisely. Some eyes even now, looking at a rainbow or a prism, can see beyond the violet, a faint trace of fuchsia pink, the indication of the red, the first colour of the rainbow into which the colours flow in their completed cycle. For past the gap where we cannot see, the violet flows back into red again. Look at the double rainbow in the stormy sky. Can your eyes see a hint of this unknown colour between the outer bright rainbow and its echo? [. . .]

It is strange that our ears detached sounds from objects so long ago, and made the art of music; while it is so recent that our eyes have detached colour from objects and made the abstract art of colour—painting. [. . .]

The old masters used colours as servants to express form and the colours were limited by this. I was told when I was a student that it was not possible to paint the blue of the sky. I remember reading a letter of Gauguin's which said that you could paint the sky much bluer if you painted a larger area of blue, that the blueness depended on the proportion of the area to the other colours. I felt my eyes beginning to open. Then I read a letter of Van Gogh's which said that the blueness of the sky depended on the contrast of the blue to its complementary colour, orange, and that colours could be made brilliant by contrasting each colour to its complementary, red to green, orange to blue, yellow to violet. It was not only the quantity of the area of the blueness which told, but the quality of the complementary colour. So as to get his Provence sky blue he concentrated on golden-orange, cornfields, and orange-red soil. He painted in couples, in duality, and produced great masterpieces of colour, its furnace, and its fury, but he found no sanity, for colour is not a duality, and art cannot be based on two contrasting opposites, any more than life can be. Duality is no solution. But he was the first of the new colour seekers who sought colour for its own sake.

Next amongst the seekers came the abstract painters. They were the men, who, having been chased out of their comfortable lodgings of Academic Representation by the camera, sought out new fields and hunting grounds where no camera could follow them. They gave up representing objects, and sought for proportion, balance, poise. They abstracted from the scale the three primary colours, red, yellow, blue, and though a Mondrian may only contain one red or one yellow and a blue, the other one or two of the three are always in mind, evoked by their very absence, if not by their presence. To these new pioneers all other colours except the three primaries were taboo. They said to me in Paris, "You must not use green—green is not an abstract colour," and as for using violet, that was anathema. Colour was used by them abstractly, apart from objects, but it was used to denote form, to denote the extent of their geometry. Their form and geometry were not used to denote colour as an end in itself. That remained to be done, but they did liberate colour from objects and colour as a living art sprang out, and artists realized its potentialities.

[. . .] The full power of that art is still to be made visible, and the colour artists of today are working along these tones, each in his or her own vision. Matisse still works representationally, but in full chromatic scale. He uses objects to denote colours. I should think of a pink Matisse or a jade Matisse, not of a girl or a basket of fruit. Kandinsky and Miro have given up recognizable objects and use their colour free as experiment. Matthew Smith and Graham Sutherland explore transparent intensities, Frances Hodgkins the dusky, honeyed sequences, and Paul Nash the pastel scale that closely relates itself to line. Ben Nicholson touches the duns and greys and oatmeals, the mid-tones of the neutral scales.

The present generation is not working in duality nor in triplicate, but in the sevenfold harmony of the rainbow scale, and as yet they have only ventured a little way along the road to the use of the full vitality of colour. But the way is open. Colour is free to use. You can paint "Bluer Than The Sky." Blueness is your aim, the sky falls below. Use the scales travelling from red to violet and the simultaneous ones from brilliance to neutral and thence to dusk. Use their sevenfold brilliance, their sevenfold depths, their sevenfold rhythm in space as geometry, not in time as in music. There is unlimited scope here. The colour will call shapes, forms and masses, recognizable if you wish, abstract if you prefer. Think in terms of intervals—wide intervals for clarion calls—red to green or vermilion to dun, close intervals for lullaby music—sea-blue to sea-green, or pearl to opal. Conjure for yourself such a picture, you will find it sheer delight, and within the range and possibility of anyone without training at an art school. Art schools teach one how to copy nature, but the joy of colour is inborn within each one of us from the child with its silver and scarlet toy to the old man in his rose garden.

There is a great deal waiting to be painted, and many roads to voyage. I will leave it to you to paint new colour pictures for yourself. I hope I have obliterated for you for ever the old conception that colour must be a slave to form and must be tacked down on to objects. I hope I have shown you that colour is the vital power out of which forms, objects, images, thoughts themselves, can be created.

I have built for you the scaffolding of the artist's science upon which the new colour art is being built everywhere, even in the fiery crucible of war, because colour is as much a need for man as freedom. The savage puts a parrot's feather in his hair, the modern man paints a colour harmony, and because he is a free man of unlimited possibilities he needs a free art whose range is neither limited nor hampered in scope and yet one that meets his needs as scientifically true. He wants no nightmare nor dream fancy. Such art is search, and he wants nourishment. Nourishment of Truth, and art that answers his own inward rhythm. Such rhythm as he knows to be the rhythm of space—the heart beat of the universe.

Unknown Colour: Paintings, Letters, Writings by Winifred Nicholson. London: Faber & Faber, 1987. 124–29. Originally published as "Winifred Dacre" in *World Review*, 1944.

Note

Pictures reproduced with original article

Cover	Joan Miró: *Painting*
Red	Graham Sutherland: *Part of a Row of Solicitors' Offices, Swansea*
Orange	Van Gogh: *Sunflower*
Yellow	Mondrian: *Composition with Red, Blue, Yellow*
Green	El Greco: *Toledo in a Storm*
Blue	Duccio: *The Annunciation*
Indigo	Marcoussis: *Painting*
Violet	Christopher Wood: *The Plage, Hotel Ty-Mad, Tréboul*

EMILY CARR

From "Fresh Seeing"

I hate like poison to talk. Artists talk in paint—words do not come easily. But I have put my hate in my pocket because I know many of you cordially detest "Modern Art." There are some kinds that need detesting, done for the sake of being bizarre, outrageous, shocking, and making ashamed. This kind we need not discuss but will busy ourselves with what is more correctly termed "Creative Art." I am not going to tell you about the '*ists* and '*isms* and their leaders, and when they lived and when they died. You can get that out of books. They all probably contributed something to the movement, even the wild ones. The art world was fed up, saturated, with lifeless stodge—something had to happen. And it did.

I want to tell you some of the things that I puzzled about when I first saw it and wondered what it was all about. It stirred me all up, yet I couldn't leave it alone. I wanted to know why. When I went to Paris in 1911. I was lucky enough to have an introduction to a very modern artist. Immediately I entered

Fig. 20.6. Emily Carr, *Totem Mother, Kitwancool*, 1928, oil on canvas, 109.7 x 69.7 cm. Reproduced by permission of the Vancouver Art Gallery, Emily Carr Trust, VAG 42.3.20. Photo by Trevor Mills.

his studio I was interested. Later I took lessons from him. Yet, strange to say, it was his wife, who was not an artist at all, that first gave me very many of the vital little sidelights on modern art. She really loved and appreciated it, not for her husband's sake (they scrapped), but for its own sake. She evidently admired his work more than she admired him. He was a fine teacher and his work was interesting and compelling, but his wife read and thought and watched, and she had the knack of saying things.

To return to the term "Creative Art." This is the definition a child once gave it: "I think and then I draw a line round my think." Children grasp these things more quickly than we do. They are more creative than grown-ups. It has not been knocked out of them. When a child draws he does so because he wants to express something. If he draws a house he never fails to make the smoke pour out of the chimney. That moves, it is alive. He feels it. The child's mind goes all round his idea. He may show both sides of his house at once. He feels the house as a whole, why shouldn't he show it? By and by he goes to school and they train all the feeling out of him. He is told to draw only what he sees, he is turned into a little camera, to be a mechanical thing, to forget that he had feelings or that he has anything to express; he only knows that he is to copy what is before him. The art part of him dies.

The world is moving swiftly and the tempo of life has changed. What was new a few years back is now old. There have been terrific expansions in the direction of light and movement; within the last few years these have altered everything. Painting has felt the influence. Isn't it reasonable to expect that art would have to keep pace with the rest? The romantic little stories and the mawkish little songs don't satisfy us any longer. Why should the empty little pictures? The academic painting of the mid-nineteenth century in England had entirely lost touch with art in running after sentiment.

When Paul Cézanne, the great Frenchman who did so much to show the world that there was something so much bigger and better for art, came, he was hooted at, called crazy, ridiculed! Now we realize what he and the men who followed him did to open the way, to change our vision. Cézanne's real business was not to make pictures, but to create forms that would express the emotions that he felt for what he had learnt to see. He lost interest in his work as soon as he had made it express as much as he had grasped.

Lawren Harris says: "The immediate results of 'Creative Art' are irritating and foreign." One thing is certain—it is vital and alive. The most conservative artists, although they may rant and rail, are consciously or unconsciously pepping up their work. They know that if they do not, it is going to look like "last year's hat" when it goes into the exhibitions. They are using more design, fresher colour, and the very fervour with which they denounce Modern Art shows how it stirs them up. So also with the onlooker. It may stir and irritate him, but isn't it more entertaining and stimulating even to feel something unpleasant than to feel nothing at all—just a void? There is such a lot of drab stodginess in the world that it's delicious to get a thrill out of something.

Willinski says: "A high proportion of the naturalistic painting of the world was done in the nineteenth century, due partly to the fact that the invention of the camera greatly enhanced this technique." Certain of the camera's limitations are now universally admitted.

The camera cannot comment.

The camera cannot select.

The camera cannot feel, it is purely mechanical.

By the aid of our own reinforcement we can perceive roughly what we desire to perceive and ignore, as far as is physically possible, what we do not desire to perceive. No work of real value is produced by an artist unless his hand obeys his mind. The camera has no mind.

We may copy something as faithfully as the camera, but unless we bring to our picture something additional—something creative—something of ourselves—our picture does not live. It is but a poor copy of unfelt nature. We look at it and straightway we forget it because we have brought nothing to it. We have had no new experience.

Creative Art is "fresh seeing." Why, there is all the difference between copying and creating that there is between walking down a hard straight cement pavement and walking down a winding grassy lane with flowers peeping everywhere and the excitement of never knowing what is just round the next bend!

Great art of all ages remains stable because the feelings it awakens are independent of time and space. The Old Masters did the very things that the serious moderns of today are struggling for, namely, trying to grasp the spirit of the thing itself rather than its surface appearance; the reality, the "I Am" of the thing, the thing that means "you," whether you are in your Sunday best or your workday worst; or the bulk, weight, and impenetrability of the mountain, no matter if its sides are bare or covered with pine; the bigger actuality of the thing, the part that is the same no matter what the conditions of light or seasons are upon it—the form, force, and volume of the thing, not the surface impression. It is hard to get at this. You must dig way down into your subject, and into yourself. And in your struggle to accomplish it, the usual aspect of the thing may have to be cast aside. This leads to distortion, which is often confused with caricature, but which is really the emotional struggle of the artist to express intensely what he feels. This very exaggeration or distortion raises the thing out of the ordinary seeing into a more spiritual sphere, the spirit dominating over the subject matter. From distortion we take another step on to abstraction where the forms of representation are forgotten and created forms expressing emotions in space rather than objects take their place; where form is so simplified and abstracted that the material side, or objects, are forgotten—only the spiritual remains. [. . .]

As the ear can be trained by listening to good music, so the eye can be trained by seeing good pictures.

People complain that modern art is ugly. That depends on what they are looking for and what their standard of beauty is. In descriptive or romantic art they are looking for a story or a memory that is brought back to them. It is not the beauty of the picture in itself that they observe. What they want is the re-living of some scene or the re-visiting of some place—a memory.

The beauty concealed in modern art consists more in the building up of a structural, unified, beautiful whole—an enveloped idea—a spiritual unity—a forgetting of the individual objects in the building up of the whole.

By the right disposition of lines and spaces the eye may be led hither and thither through the picture, so that our eyes and our consciousness rest comfortably within it and are satisfied. Also, by the use of the third dimension, that is, by retrogression and projection, or, to be plainer, by the going back and the coming forward in the picture—by the creation of volume—we do not remain on the flat surface having only height and breadth but are enabled to move backward and forward within the picture. Then we begin to feel space. We begin to feel that our objects are set in space, that they are surrounded by air. We may see before us a dense forest, but we feel the breathing space among the trees. We know that, dense as they may appear, there is air among them, that they can move a little and breathe. It is not like a brick wall, dead, with no space for light and air between the bricks. It is full of moving light playing over the different planes of the interlocked branches. There are great sweeping directions of line. Its feelings, its colour, its depth, its smell, its sounds and silences are bound together into one great thing and its unfathomable centre is its soul. That is what we are trying to get at, to express; that is the thing that matters, the very essence of it.

There are different kinds of vision. The three most common are practical, curious, and imaginative. Because these are habitual in daily life we have become accustomed to use them when looking at pictures, and all three of them cause their owner to be interested in practical matters, in the data which the picture records, in matters of skill, in storytelling, etc. If anyone using only these three types of vision looks at a picture in which the trees have, let us say, been made universal instead of particular (that is to say, in which they have had all their pictorial, meaningless branches and wiggles omitted and the essential shape then changed to meet the needs of design), he is more or less incensed. His practical vision at once asks: What are they? When told they are trees, he is angry and says: "They don't look like it." The fact that the artist has aimed at another goal than that of copying is beyond his comprehension. It doesn't exist for a person using only these three types of vision.

The attainment of further adventure in seeing pictures depends on what is called pure vision. This is the vision that sees objects as ends in themselves, disconnecting them from all practical and human associations. [. . .] Today we have almost lost the ability to respond to pictures emotionally—that is, with aesthetic emotion. Modern art endeavours to bring this ability to consciousness again.

The question of things not looking what they are is often a stumbling block to the observer who would like to understand modern art. There may be a bigger thing that the artist is striving for in his picture than the faithful portraying of some particular trees or other objects. It may be some great emotion that he feels sweeping through the landscape. We will say there is a high mountain of overpowering strength in his picture that seems to dominate everything, to make the rest cower and shrink. Possibly that is the thing he focuses his attention on, the thing he is trying to express. He sacrifices everything to that emotion, changing his forms, selecting, omitting, bending every other thing to meet that one desire. Everything in his picture must help to envelop and unify his idea. [. . .]

What about our side of Canada—the Great West, standing before us big and strong and beautiful? What art do we want for her art? Ancient or modern? She's young but she's very big. If we dressed her in the art dresses of the older countries she would burst them. So we will have to make her a dress of her own. Not that the art of the Old World is not great and glorious and beautiful, but what they have to express over there is not the same as we have to express over here. It is different. The spirit is different. Everyone knows that the moment we go from the Old Country to the New, or from the New to the Old, we feel the difference at once. European painters have sought to express Europe. Canadian painters must strive to express Canada. [. . .] Her great forests, wide spaces, and mighty mountains and the great feel of it all should produce courageous artists, seeing and feeling things in a fresh, creative way. "Modern" we may call it, but remember, all modern art is not jazz. Canada wants something strong, big, dignified, and spiritual that shall make her artists better for doing it and her people better for seeing it. And we artists need the people at our back, not to throw cold water over us or to starve us with their cold, clammy silence, but to give us their sympathy and support. I do not mean money support. I mean moral support; whether the artists are doing it in the old way or in the new way, it does not matter, so long as it is in the big way with the feel and spirit of Canada behind it. [. . .]

Some say the West is unpaintable and our forests monotonous. Oh, just let them open their eyes and look! It isn't pretty. It's only just magnificent, tremendous. The oldest art of our West, the art of the Indians, is in spirit very modern, full of liveness and vitality. They went for and got so many of the very things that we modern artists are striving for today. One frequently hears the Indians' carvings and designs called grotesque and hideous. That depends on the vision of the onlooker. The Indian used distortion or exaggeration to gain his ends. All nature to him seethed with the supernatural. Everything, even the commonest inanimate objects—mats, dishes, etcetera—possessed a spirit. The foundation that the Indian built his art upon was his Totem. He did not worship it, but he did reverence it tremendously. Most of the totems were animal representations, thus animal life played a great part in the life of the Indian and his art. They endowed their totem with magic powers. In the totem image the aspect or part of the animal that was to work magic was distorted by exaggeration. It was made as the totem-maker saw it—only more so. The Indians were supposed to partake of the nature of their totems. That is to say, eagles were supposed to be daring and fierce, ravens cunning and tricky, wolves sly and fierce. The beaver is expressed by his huge front teeth, his hands usually clasping a stick and his cross-hatched tail tucked up in front of him. These are his most particular and characteristic emblems. They represent him as a brave, splendid creature, an ancestor to be proud of. There is all the difference in the world between their beaver and the insignificant little animal that we take for our national emblem. We belittle him, only give him his surface representation. The Indian goes deeper. He expresses the thing that is the beaver, glorifying him, showing his brave little self that can saw down trees and build his house, energetic, courageous. They show the part of him that would still be beaver even if he were skinned. Here is a striking instance of the difference between Representative and Modern Art. [. . .]

It is not my own pictures I am pleading for. They are before you to like or to dislike as you please. That is immaterial. [. . .]

The plea that I make to you is for a more tolerant attitude toward the bigger vision of Creative Art—a quiet searching on your part to see if there is sincerity before you condemn. [. . .]

Fresh Seeing: Two Addresses by Emily Carr. Toronto: Clarke, Irwin & Company, 1972. Originally published as "An Address by Emily Carr to the Victoria Women's Canadian Club on March 1930," Toronto: Oxford University Press, 1955.

21

Cinéastes and Modernists: Writing on Film in 1920s London

INTRODUCED AND SELECTED BY
LESLIE KATHLEEN HANKINS

> Now one thing never to be lost sight of in considering the cinema is that it exists for the purpose of pleasing women.
>
> —Iris Barry

IF, ACCORDING TO Walter Benjamin's quirky logic, Paris was the capital of the nineteenth century, it is but a short leap to claim the movie theater as the capital of the twentieth. And—especially in the dynamic decade of the long 1920s—that site was full of women. An astonishing constellation of women writers, intellectuals, and *cinéastes* debated, and helped determine, the place of cinema in cultural history; this chapter will focus on *cinéastes*—largely women—writing in and around London during that time. Women *cinéastes* were vital to that film culture: Iris Barry played a role inventing film criticism in England and as a founder of the Film Society (before moving to the United States to found the MOMA Film Library);[1] Bryher, H. D., and Dorothy Richardson, along with Kenneth Macpherson, launched the international film journal *Close Up,* and H. D. and Bryher acted in avant-garde films produced by Bryher and Macpherson's company POOL; Virginia Woolf wrote about cinema and the Hogarth Press published film studies; Lotte Reiniger and Olga Preobrashenskaia were experimental directors whose work was screened in London. Women intellectuals came to cinema by diverse paths. Leaping across media, Lydia Lopokova, from the experimental Russian Ballet, danced in a short Pathé film that celebrated cinematic play.[2] H. D. and Barry went from poetry to screen with an alacrity that reveals a hunger for this versatile, vibrant new medium. Editors such as Dorothy Todd of the British *Vogue* and the women editors of little magazines featured in chapter 7 published articles on the cinema.

Though women shaped the cinematic avant-garde, critiqued mainstream film, debated film aesthetics and cultural theory, wrote and published film studies, and circulated and reviewed films, histories of the 1920s have not preserved their significant contributions. Feminist scholars—such as pioneers Flitterman-Lewis, McCreadie, Foster, Acker, Heck-Rabi, Kuhn, and Radstone—have made inroads, but film studies have been decades slower than literary studies to address the erasure of women from intellectual history—especially those women who shaped early film culture as directors, writers, and theorists. Clearly, if we claim screen stars such as Greta Garbo and forget film theorists such as Iris Barry, we limit the role of women in cinema to spectacle, and diminish our intellectual legacy. As the 1930 Film Society Programme number 38 on Women Directors shows, directors such as Dulac, Preobrashenskaia, Arzner, Reiniger, and Field were active in the 1920s. But it is telling that this program, including their representative works, showcases several films now lost or only available in archives. Clearly, retrieval projects are still essential to feminist film history. This chapter highlights writings of the time about overlooked directors such as Preobrashenskaia, it offers the work of lost theorists such as Barry, and recovers neglected institutions such as the Film Society.

Gender and Feminism: Oblique to Overt

Harry Furniss's 1914 study of cinema genders the art in the traditional way: "Our Lady Cinema has captivated the hearts of all pleasure-seekers. She has bewitched them, the world over, by millions and millions. She has only to be seen for one to fall a victim to her fascinations" (Furniss ix). As late as 1926, *The Criterion* recalls the familiar conceit: "That so alternately maligned and eulogized youngest daughter of Apollo, the cinema, proved to be the *grande vedette* of the past Paris season; a *vedette* in her own right and a *vedette* because of her marriage with the boldest of the children of Apollo, the dance" (Shaw 178). Yet, also in 1926, instead of continuing to offer us the femme fatale muse of cinema, Barry casts gender differently: "Now one thing never to be lost sight of in considering the cinema is that it exists for the purpose of pleasing women. Three out of every four of all cinema audiences are women" (*Let's Go* 59). As Barry and Richardson agree, cinema was *for* women, but Barry takes this a step further by declaring that it should be created *by* women (*Let's Go* 176–77). Other discussions of the emerging art of film emphasize the gender of cinema in diverse and compelling ways: Eric Walter White brings gender and class together when he terms cinema "the Cinderella of the arts" and chastises "Lady Literature" for attempting to keep her below stairs (*Parnassus* 15). In a provocative reversal, H. D. in "Beauty" recalls—and complicates—gendered rescue fantasies, urging intellectuals to work "for the clearing of the ground, for the rescuing of this superb art, from its hide-bound convention. Perseus, in other words, and the chained Virgin. Saint George, in other words, and the Totem dragon. Anyhow it is up to us, as quickly as we can, to rescue this captured Innocent (for the moment embodied in Greta Garbo)" ("Beauty" 28).[3]

Though gender and feminism are not the most apparent concerns of the *cinéastes,* an interest in women and "a difference of view" (Woolf, *A Room of One's Own*) color their relationship to the new art. At times, overt feminist ideas surface in their works; Barry's spirited attack on the mainstream movie industry's obsession with the love interest, and Bryher's solid support for Preobrashenskaia's feminist film exposé of sexual abuse within the patriarchal family are examples. Eye-opening historical documents include Barry's columns about women active in the film industry and Richardson's pieces—akin to those of Barry—describing the escape cinema provided working-class women.

Cinema and Modernism(s)

Women *cinéastes,* the elite intellectual aristocracy, coterie culture, little magazines, and other cultural forums engage with the *déclassé* Cinderella of the arts through a variety of complex encounters. Some highbrow modernist intellectuals scorned the cinema as beneath contempt. But for others, including key women, cinema was the newest of the new in the make-it-new era. Cinema—as a theoretical, intellectual, debatable site in cultural history—was for them the vibrating pulse of contemporary culture. If, as Walter Benjamin asserts, "One of the foremost tasks of art has always been the creation of a demand which could be fully satisfied only later" ("Work of Art" 237), one could argue that modernism(s) helped create the demand for cinema and vice versa. Stein's claim, "I cannot repeat this too often any one is of one's period and this our period was undoubtedly the period of the cinema and series production" (*Lectures* 177), offers another way to consider the upheavals of Dada and surrealist performance art, the energy of cubist and other visual art movements, the celebration of the machine, Stein's own infinite repetitions, Soviet revolutionary ideology, the call to "make it new," and Imagism's concentration on the visual close up. Cinema could be seen as the art form toward which other experiments in modernism were moving; as Barry, with characteristic flair, remarks, "I wonder sometimes why the Montmartre cubists go on cubing when the cinema exists" (*Let's Go* 43). Like the advocates of literary experimentation, *cinéastes* worked to incite intellectual debate and writing about the new art. Barry urges "I ask then: critics arise, invent terms, lay down canons, derive from your categories, heap up nonsense with sense" (*Let's Go* vii) and H. D.

Fig. 21.1. In the 1920s from the London Film Society to the small presses and little magazines—and even within the pages of British *Vogue—cinéastes* debated about the new art. © Hankins.

insists, "It is the duty of every sincere intellectual to work for the better understanding of the cinema" ("Beauty" 28).

Conversations and Enterprises

International avant-garde film culture was vibrant, cosmopolitan, and inspiring in the mid to late twenties; the energy incarnate in the *ciné clubs* of Paris,[4] revolutionary Soviet cinema, German Expressionism and trick film, and American forays into the avant-garde, all found their way to London through cinema crusaders, mobile intellectuals, elite little magazines and glossy high fashion ones, and the phenomenal cultural venture of the Film Society.[5] As the explosion of film essays indicates, cinema was in vogue in the 1920s; cinema was, in fact, in *Vogue* (British) under the short-lived but brilliant editorship of Dorothy Todd with Madge Garland, and in a host of other magazines and journals—as well as newspapers and trade publications. Various ventures publishing on the cinema included *Broom, Vanity Fair, The Arts, The Daily Mail, The Spectator, Kine-Weekly, The Little Review, The New Criterion,* the *Adelphi, The Na-*

tion and Athenaeum, Close Up, The London Mercury, FIRE!!, Theatre Guild Magazine, The New Republic, and *The Dial.* Woolf's description of a conversation with Eddy Sackville-West (a member of the Film Society) and Duncan Grant preserves the excitement of conversations on cinema: "We all chatter hard [. . .] very interesting: we compare movies and operas; I'm writing that for Todd: rather brilliant. All, to me, highly congenial, and even a little exciting, in the spring light; hammers tapping outside; trees shaking green in the Square: suddenly we find its 7 and all jump up" (*Letters* 3:254).

Restoring women to the film conversations of the twenties recaptures the way the cultural moment sounded. Women were active in many of these enterprises, particularly in the Film Society and international publications. Perhaps because movies were at first scorned by the largely male highbrow culture industry, women were welcome to write as public intellectuals, as critics and theorists of film. As long as no elite cultural institution such as "Oxbridge" offered credentials for the study of cinema, males were not in a privileged position. Women—many of whom were self-educated outsiders—had equal access to films (not the case in the art studios or Oxbridge library, as Woolf reminds us in *A Room of One's Own*). In published exchanges, male and female critics consider the role of cinema and its place in the arts, and lively cross connections abound. When Clive Bell trashes the cinema in a 1922 *Vanity Fair* article, Barry no doubt responds with her chapter "Art?" in *Let's Go to the Pictures.* The *TLS* raises its "highbrows" at Barry's book in its review and White in his Hogarth pamphlet refers to "Iris Barry's disappointing book" (*Parnassus* 27). *Close Up* blasts his pamphlet; Bryher applauds Barry's book, noting in her review, "something of the swift dynamic quality of the screen races through the pages" ("More about Films"). Within the pages of *The New Republic,* Woolf publishes a rhetorically dazzling analysis of cinema and Gilbert Seldes engages her in dialogue in his response. And, in the British *Vogue,* Barry, Aldous Huxley, and several anonymous writers offer competing visions of films, actual and potential, mainstream and avant-garde.

The Film Society

The Film Society transformed London's intellectual film culture in the 1920s almost overnight, bringing modernists together in an electric cultural moment. Iris Barry was at the center of the project. Not limited to *cinéastes,* the Film Society involved intellectuals from all the arts, and the screenings touched visual artists, sculptors, art critics, poets, and writers. H. D. refers to "those admirable Sunday afternoon performances of the London Film Society" ("Beauty" 26); Clive Bell was a participant in its one "riot" (Hankins, "Across" 153–54).

Fig. 21.2. Iris Barry, co-founder of the London Film society, prolific writer, and *cinéaste*. Reproduced courtesy of the Museum of Modern Art Film Stills Archive.

From the rather cavalier beginnings described in Barry's autobiographical notes, the Film Society became a stunning success. Ivor Montagu's recollections register the scale of this success: "Our Sundays became so fashionable we had to transfer after a few seasons from the New Gallery to the Tivoli, from a cinema holding 1,400 to one accommodating between two and three thousand" ("Old Man's Mumble" 223). Barry could complain in 1925 that "the cinema lacks chic" ("American Prestige and British Films" 51–52), but that was no longer the case by 1926.

Sample programs of the Film Society reveal an eclectic mix: vintage newsreels, science shorts, revivals of noteworthy films, groundbreaking international films not otherwise available in England, and experimental avant-garde films. The Film Society screenings were reviewed in publications as diverse as *The London Mercury, The Nation and Athenaeum, Close Up, Vogue* and *Kine-Weekly. Vogue* regularly praises Film Society programs; an anonymous essay, "The

Future of the Cinema," in Early March 1926, begins by highlighting its central role: "The Film Society has now given enough performances for one to be able to judge the present state of the Art of the Cinema" (69), and reviews films from programs 4, 5, and 6. The programs and reviews introduced intellectuals to films that became touchstones in cinema essays: *The Cabinet of Dr. Caligari, Entr'acte, Ballet mécanique,* the *Secrets of Nature* shorts and assorted other films. Cross-references to these films in writings by various *cinéastes* indicate how the Film Society and the coterie culture around it shared and shaped film discourse. Published discussions of film dramatically changed between 1924 and 1926, no doubt partly because in that interval the Film Society altered intellectuals' awareness of cinema.

The Cinema in Print

The little magazines, newspapers, and even some glossy highbrow fashion magazines wrote about what the Film Society screened, disseminating film culture. Intellectuals—male and female—engaged with cinema in print. The little magazines, the Film Society, and Hollywood came together at times; in 1923 *The Adelphi* heralded a forthcoming article by Charlie Chaplin due to appear in the January 1924 issue, and in 1926 Chaplin's essay was referred to in the Film Society Programme number 6 on *The Cabinet of Dr. Caligari* (Amberg 23). Starting in 1924, Barry wrote film criticism in the *Adelphi,* over forty columns of film criticism for *The Spectator,* at least five articles for *Vogue* in 1924–26, and over sixty columns for *The Daily Mail* in 1926–30. Her influential book of film theory and criticism, *Let's Go to the Pictures,* was published in the fall of 1926. Aldous Huxley's "Where are the Movies Moving?" was published in *Vanity Fair* and in *Vogue* (London). In winter 1926 *The Little Review* published selections focusing on Paris film, including a still from Fernand Léger's *Ballet mécanique.* In 1926, Woolf published her essay "The Cinema," not for Todd as she proposed in the letter quoted above, but in *The Nation and Athenaeum, The Arts* and (without her knowledge) in *The New Republic;* in an exchange with *Close Up* she even considered reprinting it there (Beinecke archive). In 1928 and 1931, the Woolfs' Hogarth Press joined the throng publishing on film. Eric Walter White's film publications for the Hogarth Press relate cinema to the other arts—including literature—as the titles and epigraph alluding to Shakespeare and Whitman testify. *Walking Shadows: An Essay on Lotte Reiniger's Silhouette Films* (1931) celebrates a noted (now neglected) German woman director, Lotte Reiniger, whose work was shown regularly by the Film Society.

Hogarth Press and POOL offer vivid examples of men and women working together to publish film studies. In 1927, *Close Up*[6] and POOL Publishing were launched by Bryher, Kenneth Macpherson, and H. D., and Richardson was enlisted for a regular column. *Close Up* encouraged international film, especially the German and Russian films not available in England. Passionate and opinionated articles lash out at censorship (Richardson organized a petition against censorship), encourage film clubs, and offer a wide range of intelligent, challenging critiques. Richardson's private letters to Bryher demonstrate her energetic networking; she brainstorms about soliciting writings from Barbara Low, Robert Nichols, H. G. Wells, Huxley, and Lawrence, who she says "loathes films" (Fromm 138).[7]

That *Vogue,* the quintessential female fashion publication aimed at upscale women, played a role fashioning the interest in film as an art, is surely significant for any study of cinema and gender. During the highbrow era of Todd, when *Vogue* was a major force celebrating modernism in the arts and literature, film graces its pages, encroaching on—and at times almost displacing—the theater columns. Cinema was truly launched in *Vogue* in Late August 1924, with a featured space in the contents (albeit under the heading *Miscellaneous*). In this issue, *Vogue* offers a film still spread, "Seen on the Screen," and a pioneering article by Iris Barry, "The Scope of the Cinema," illustrated with stills from *The Niebelungs*. This article is a complex rhetorical effort to dismiss any lingering doubts that film was worthy of serious critical and artistic appreciation and to claim cinema as a vital part of the cultural imagination. Three of Barry's shorter pieces in *Vogue* ("The Autumn Cinema," "The Cinema in Three Moods," and "The Cinema Continues to Improve") share the page with advertisements for Elizabeth Arden—an interesting juxtaposition, because as Elizabeth Arden shapes the appropriate modern woman's body, Barry's articles hope to shape the appropriate modern woman viewer, one who will bring critical intelligence to bear on popular films, international (French and German) films, and those of mainstream Hollywood. *Vogue*'s table of contents page for Early January 1925 shows how film has captured the cultural imagination; it offers a half-page drawing of a fashionable society woman running a movie projector, showing a film of fashion models. The triangle of projected light forms the "V" for *Vogue.* "Paris Screens and Footlights" in early February 1925 demonstrates the rising status of cinema by its subtitle: "Two of the Latest Plays follow the old traditions while an Extraordinary Film is the Newest Achievement of the Ultra-Modern School" (63). The ultra-modern film (*Ballet mécanique* by Fernand Léger) is represented by a circle montage of stills from the film surrounding a photograph of George Anteil who "wrote special music for the film" (63). In Early February 1926, Barry's essay "The Cinema," noting that "The cinema is young and full of possibilities" (52), opposes the disproportionate celebration of avant-garde experimental film:

"The cinema is (though we give thanks for all daring experiments of an eclectic kind) for the large public" (78). Her argument for balance between popular film and the avant-garde is visually enacted by the illustrations: a full-page studio shot of Charlie Chaplin faces her essay and three of Fernand Léger's avant-garde caricatures of Chaplin are interspersed within her columns.

Overview of the Selections

"The Cinema: A Comparison of Arts," Barry's first *Spectator* article on cinema (she had been writing unsigned tidbits for a time), articulates her assertive advocacy of cinema vis à vis theater and allows for thought-provoking topical connections with Dorothy Richardson's first column in *Close Up*. One essay from *Vogue*, "The Scope of the Cinema," demonstrates the intersection of highbrow and high fashion that shaped that magazine in this decade. Reading this essay with Woolf's "The Cinema" provides new insights. Film Society Programme number 38 on Women Directors demonstrates the Film Society's interest in women in film as a viable category, and presents films cross-referenced by Barry and Bryher.

Let's Go to the Pictures broke new ground. As *The Spectator* review notes, "Miss Barry is no dilettante intellectual who has taken up the cinema as a hobby. She is a thoroughly well-equipped, well-informed and whole-time professional cinema critic, who has learnt her job thoroughly, and can give opinions which, even if we sometimes disagree with them, must always be given serious attention" ("Metaphysic" 864). The book explores cinema versus the other arts, offers a sophisticated intellectual discussion of the aesthetics of visual art versus moving pictures, and addresses popular culture topics (actors, subtitles, stars, and the lives of film folk) in the tone of a film fan. Quite a hybrid, it testifies to her astonishing range from common viewer to art theorist to feminist advocate. Her introductory vignettes, as documents of popular culture, provide a vivid picture of the world of movie-going of the 1920s and a few choice passages offer a taste of her pithy analysis and vast range. Selections from Barry's later *Daily Mail* columns demonstrate her commitment to mainstream film culture, explicitly addressing women in Hollywood film production.

Virginia Woolf's essay is a complex intervention in film culture, projecting a highbrow future for cinema, with oblique references to avant-garde film, and overt reference to the ubiquitous *Dr. Caligari*.[8] Gilbert Seldes's response essay documents the transatlantic dialogue in film criticism, directly addressing Woolf's points. H. D.'s "Projector" poems (the first of them printed here) are remarkable; by writing poems to cinema, she forges a radically different relationship between literature and the cinema than the much-maligned (by Woolf and others) cinematic adaptations of novels. H. D. uses psychology, spirituality, and myth to elevate the status of cinema in poems that resemble love poems or hymns. Equating cinema with Greek mythology gives lowly cinema quite a leap in cultural status, and the argument in the poem, that the arts and religion have failed and cinema (as male god) is renewing that lost energy, is quite intriguing. H. D. claims the cinema as child and as lover, inviting connections with Richardson's and Barry's discussions of the hypnotic pleasures of the screen for women.

Richardson's first column in her *Continuous Performance* series in *Close Up* describes and analyzes the film audience of working-class women. Her essays focus on the audience and the screening environment in the neighborhood picture palaces. Bryher's role as an editor, publisher, writer, and supporter of *cinéastes* is legendary. In *Close Up* she writes practical advice about forming film clubs, essays on film and education, and articles and reviews. The selection from her book, *Film Problems of Soviet Russia,* a chapter focusing on Preobrashenskaya's film, *Peasant Women of Riazan,* is impressive as an astute analysis and endorsement of the strong social critique and artistry of that dazzling feminist film.

Overview and Conclusion

> The radical politics of lost-and-found scholarship lies in not merely correcting a record that swept away women's contributions but in refashioning film theory and historiography.
>
> —Lauren Rabinovitz

From Barry's enthusiastic omnipresence, to Todd's publication of both mainstream and avant-garde film articles in *Vogue,* to Bryher's and H. D.'s proselytizing about German and Russian films, to Woolf's gestures toward a high art of abstract cinema, to Richardson's cultural critiques of the apparatus of the picture palaces, women *cinéastes* were at the center of debates about cinema culture in the 1920s. This chapter's montage of selections from books, pamphlets, little magazines, and highbrow fashion magazines documents women's participation in the cultural moment and their differing perspectives on film culture. This introduction resists the temptation to begin by framing the recovered essays through the apertures of today's feminist film theory. Instead, I suggest studying the writings by theorists of the twenties—individually and together—first. Though the section identifies individual *cinéastes,* it can—and should—be read in alternative configurations, reading the writers together to open up dynamic exchanges. Woolf, H. D., and Richardson pose related questions about visual culture—especially about the role of visual emotion in cinema, the mystic or fantastic visionary potential of cinema, and the connections between cinematic and spatial languages and the psyche. The topic of woman as spectacle is common to Barry, H. D., and Richardson. Barry and Richardson are attuned to the working-class and class dynamics in cinema and in the picture palaces. Barry, Richardson, H. D., and Woolf debate about cinema and the other arts, waging aesthetics in border disputes between literature, theater, and film, so it would be valuable to track their diverse viewpoints on poetry and cinema, or theater and film. The possibilities are limitless.

One cannot help but wonder what directions film theory might have taken if years ago we had had access to the theoretical and critical ideas of Richardson, H. D., Bryher, and Barry alongside those of Eisenstein and Bazin. What happens when we bring the resurrected insights from the 1920s into contact with today's critical and theoretical energy? Recent feminist film studies have taken two major paths: recovering the lost films and writings of women in film history, and developing feminist theoretical approaches to films.[9] Resurrecting these lost voices of women film theorists and *cinéastes* of the 1920s provides a means of bridging those two paths; this section proposes that we use these writings as a springboard to enliven today's film studies. It may prove fruitful to relate the insights in the recovered writings to our discussions of the gaze, the spectator, the spectacle, relationships between film and literature,[10] creative possibilities for film adaptation, film as social practice, the cinematic apparatus, cultural hegemony and the cinema/movies split, and other vital issues in film theory in our cultural moment. With the re-introduction of lost theorists and critics into the intellectual mix, we can ask new questions and respond to new stimuli. How might Barry's and Richardson's discussions of the female spectator intersect with Mary Ann Doane's and Laura Mulvey's studies of the spectator? How might feminist psychoanalytical work by Laura Mulvey, E. Ann Kaplan, and others gain from Richardson's and H. D.'s writings on psychology and cinema? Judith Mayne, Anne Friedberg, Laura Marcus, and Sandy Flitterman-Lewis provide excellent examples of scholarship that incorporates intellectual work by early women directors and theorists, especially *Close Up* writers and Germaine Dulac; their projects suggest how scholars might use the essays in this section—and the bibliography—to broaden and deepen film studies in the twenty-first century. And, of course, yesteryear's theorists may stimulate us to move in directions not yet explored.

This chapter hopes to inspire other historical restoration projects as well, such as ones to restore and re-distribute the film *Peasant Women of Riazan,* to locate and study the elusive film, Arzner's *Fashions for Women,* to engage with additional neglected women *cinéastes,* and to reissue books such as Barry's *Let's Go to the Pictures.* The historical and archival turns in film studies offer particular opportunities for feminist scholars to build on the reclamation projects of pioneers. Even as archival digs resurrect more women *cinéastes,* we may expand the conceptual frame for the work of those *cinéastes* within our cultural moment by asking the question, "Now what?" as we brainstorm about productive ways to engage with that work.[11] This chapter is just a sneak preview of coming attractions awaiting those who wish to follow these leads to continue the quest for *cinéastes* and their ideas. As Iris Barry phrases it, "I should like to irritate one or two intelligences into beguiling this new monster as critically as it deserves" (*Let's Go* viii).

Notes

I would like to acknowledge with gratitude the generous assistance of fellowships and grants that made my research possible: Iowa College Foundation Research Fellowship, 2000; National Endowment for the Humanities, Summer Stipend, 1998; The H. D. Visiting Fellowship, the Beinecke Library of Yale University, 1994. These grants enabled me to travel to archives, to screen films, and to gather valuable documents.

    1. See Hankins and Wasson on Iris Barry.

    2. A brief discussion and still illustration of Lopokova dancing in the film appears in my article, "Tracking Shots through Film History."

Fig. 21.3. The wedding scene from Olga Preobrashenskaya's revolutionary feminist film, *Peasant Women of Riazan,* shown at the London Film Society and praised by Bryher. Reproduced courtesy of the Pacific Film Institute.

3. The woman critic as Perseus or Saint George is an intriguing gender switch.

4. Vital to the French scene was the presence of Germaine Dulac, French feminist director, theorist, and tireless cinema advocate. See Flitterman-Lewis.

5. See Higson, Wasson, Sexton, and Hankins on film culture of the 1920s.

6. Scholars have written extensively on H. D. and the *Close Up* group in the past fifteen years. In addition to the invaluable *Close Up* anthology, see scholars Edmunds, Egger, Friedberg, Gevirtz, Morris, and Mandel.

7. *The Gender of Modernism* includes H. D.'s *Borderline* pamphlet and Richardson's essay "The Film Gone Male"; Donald, Friedberg, and Marcus, eds., make accessible many *Close Up* articles; therefore, readers are referred to those groundbreaking collections.

8. See Hankins's articles on Woolf's "The Cinema."

9. Anthologies of the criticism and theories, such as Carson, Dittmar, and Welsch (eds.), Erens (ed.), and Bean and Negra (eds.), provide good overviews of today's feminist film theory, as does Foster's introduction to *Women Film Directors*.

10. See Susan McCabe.

11. Gaines and Rabinovitz refine and interrogate feminist film studies by drawing attention to the theoretical and conceptual underpinnings of reclamation projects and initiating discussion about future work. For more discussions on these issues, see the series "An Archive for the Future" in *Camera Obscura* 2006 (beginning in the 21.1 issue). Also see Petro, Bean and Negra, and the website for The Women's Film History Project: http://www.Duke.edu/web/film/wfp.

Works Cited

Acker, Ally. *Reel Women: Pioneers of the Cinema, 1896 to the Present.* New York: Continuum, 1993.

Amberg, George. *The Film Society Programmes, 1925–1939.* New York: Arno Press, 1972.

Barry, Iris. "American Prestige and British Films." *The Spectator* (July 11, 1925): 51–52.

———. "The Autumn Cinema." *Vogue* (London) 64.6 (Late September 1924): 78.

———. "The Cinema." *Vogue* (London) 67.3 (Early February 1926): 52–53.

———. "The Cinema Continues to Improve." *Vogue* (London) 65.4 (Late February 1925): 78.

———. "The Cinema in Three Moods." *Vogue* (London) 64.7 (Early October 1924): 104.

———. *Let's Go to the Pictures.* London: Chatto & Windus, 1926.

Bean, Jennifer, and Diana Negra, eds. *A Feminist Reader in Early Cinema.* Durham, N.C.: Duke University Press, 2002.

Bell, Clive. "Art and the Cinema: A Prophecy that the Motion Pictures, in Exploiting Imitation Art, will Leave Real Art to the Artists." *Vanity Fair* (November 1922): 39–40.

Benjamin, Walter. "Paris, Capital of the Nineteenth Century." In *Reflections*, ed. Peter Demetz. Trans. Edmund Jephcott. New York: Schoken Books, 1986.

———. "The Work of Art in the Age of Mechanical Reproduction."

Beinecke Rare Book and Manuscript Library of Yale University.

Blakeston, Oswell. Review of *Parnassus to Let. Close Up* 4.1 (January 1929): 76–77.

Bryher, Winifred. "More about Films." Rev. of *Let's Go to the Pictures. Outlook:* 1.22: 27.

Carson, Diane, Linda Dittmar, and Janice R. Welsch, eds. *Multiple Voices in Feminist Film Criticism.* Minneapolis: University of Minnesota Press, 1994.

Chaplin, Charlie. "Does the Public Know What It Wants?" *The Adelphi* 2.1 (January 1924): 702–10.

Close Up: A Magazine Devoted to the Art of Films. Ed. Kenneth Macpherson and Bryher. 1927–33. Volumes 1–10. Arno Series of Contemporary Art. New York: Arno Press. 1971.

Doane, Mary Ann. *Femmes Fatales: Feminism, Film Theory, Psychoanalysis.* New York: Routledge, 1991.

———, Patricia Mellencamp, and Linda Williams. *Re-Vision: Essays in Feminist Film Criticism.* University Publications of America, Inc., 1984.

Donald, James, Anne Friedberg, and Laura Marcus, eds. *Close Up 1927–1933: Cinema and Modernism.* Princeton: Princeton University Press, 1998.

Edmunds, Susan. *Out of Line: History, Psychoanalysis, and Montage in H. D.'s Long Poem.* Stanford: Stanford University Press, 1994.

Egger, Rebecca. "Reading by Half-Light: Cinematic Spectatorship in Modernist Women's Writing." Dissertation. Cornell University, 1995.

Erens, Patricia, ed. *Issues in Feminist Film Criticism.* Bloomington: Indiana University Press, 1990.

"The Films." Rev. of *Let's Go to the Pictures,* by Iris Barry. *Times Literary Supplement* (December 9, 1926).

Flitterman-Lewis, Sandy. *To Desire Differently: Feminism and the French Cinema.* New York: Columbia University Press, 1996.

Foster, Gwendolyn Audrey. *Women Film Directors: An International Bio-Critical Dictionary.* Westport, Conn.: Greenwood Press, 1995.

———. *Women Who Made the Movies* (1991), video. Distributed by Women Make Movies, New York.

Friedberg, Anne. "Writing About Cinema: *Close Up 1927–1933.*" Dissertation. New York University, 1983.

Fromm, Gloria. Ed. *Windows on Modernism: Selected Letters of Dorothy Richardson.* Athens: University of Georgia Press, 1995.

Furniss, Harry. *Our Lady Cinema.* Bristol: J. W. Arrowsmith Ltd., 1914.

"The Future of the Cinema." *Vogue* (London) (Early March 1926): 69.

Gaines, Jane. "Film History and the Two Presents of Feminist Film Theory." *Cinema Journal* 44.1 (2004): 113–19.

Garrity, Jane. "Selling Culture to the 'Civilized': Bloomsbury, British *Vogue,* and the Marketing of National Identity." *MODERNISM/Modernity* 6.2 (1999): 29–58.

———. "Virginia Woolf, Intellectual Harlotry and 1920s British *Vogue.*" In Caughie, ed. 185–218.

Gevirtz, Susan. *The Fiction and Film Writing of Dorothy Richardson.* New York: Peter Lang, 1996.

Hankins, Leslie K. "'Across the screen of my brain': Virginia Woolf's 'The Cinema' and Film Forums of the Twenties." In *Virginia Woolf's Multiple Muses,* ed. Diane Gillespie. Columbia: University of Missouri Press, 1993. 148–79.

———. "A Splice of Reel Life in Virginia Woolf's 'Time Passes': Censorship, Cinema and 'the usual battlefield of emotions.'" *Criticism* (Winter 1993): 91–114.

———. "Iris Barry, Writer and Cinéaste in *The Adelphi, The Spectator,* the Film Society and the British *Vogue:* Forming Film Culture in London of the 1920s." *Modernism/ Modernity.* 11.3 (September 2004): 2–29.

———. "Tracking Shots through Film History: Virginia Woolf, Film Archives, and Future Technologies." In Ardis and Scott, eds. *Virginia Woolf Turning the Centuries.* 266–75.

H. D. *Borderline Pamphlet.* 1930; rpt. in Scott, ed. *The Gender of Modernism.* 110–25.

———. "Beauty." "The Cinema and the Classics," part 1. *Close Up* 1.1 (July 1927): 22–33.

———. "Projector II *(Chang)." Close Up* 1.4. (October 1927): 35–44.

Heck-Rabi, Louise. *Women Filmmakers: A Critical Reception.* Metuchen, N. J.: Scarecrow Press, 1984.

Higson, Andrew, ed. *Young and Innocent? The Cinema in Britain, 1896–1930.* Exeter: University of Exeter Press, 2002.

Huxley, Aldous. "Where are the Movies Moving? The Brilliant Success of the Cinema in Portraying the Fantastic and Preposterous." *Vanity Fair* 24.5 (July 1925): 39, 78.

———. "Where are the Movies Moving? Some Notes on the Potentialities of the Cinema in the Expression of Fantastic Themes and Extravagant Flights of Fancy." *Vogue* (London) 68.11 (Early December 1926): 76, 124.

Kaplan, E. Ann. *Psychoanalysis and Cinema.* New York: Routledge, 1989.

———. *Women and Film: Both Sides of the Camera.* New York: Methuen, 1983.

Kuhn, Annette, and Susannah Radstone, eds. *The Women's Companion to International Film.* Berkeley: University of California Press, 1994.

Lejeune, C. A. *Cinema.* London: Alexander Maclehose and Co., 1931.

Luckhurst, Nicola. *Bloomsbury in Vogue.* London: Cecil Woolf, 1998.

Mandel, Charlotte. "Garbo/Helen: The Self-Projection of Beauty by H. D." *Women's Studies* 7 (1980): 127–35.

———. "The Redirected Image: Cinematic Dynamics in the Style of H. D. (Hilda Doolittle)." *Literature/Film Quarterly* 11 (1983): 36–45.

Mayne, Judith. *Cinema and Spectatorship.* London: Routledge, 1993.

———. *The Woman at the Keyhole: Feminism and Women's Cinema.* Bloomington: Indiana University Press, 1990.

McCabe, Susan. *Cinematic Modernism: Modernist Poetry and Film.* New York: Cambridge University Press, 2004.

McCreadie, Marsha. *Women on Film: The Critical Eye.* New York: Praeger, 1983.

"The Metaphysic of the 'Movies.'" Review of *Let's Go to the Pictures,* by Iris Barry. *The Spectator* (November 13, 1926): 864.

Montagu, Ivor. "Old Man's Mumble: Reflections on a Semi-Centenary." *Sight and Sound* 44.4 (Autumn 1975): 220–24, 247.

Morris, Adelaide. "The Concept of Projection: H. D.'s Visionary Powers." *Contemporary Literature* 25 (Winter 1984): 411–36.

"The Next Step." "Seen on the Stage." *Vogue* (London) 65.1 (Early January 1925): 50.

"Paris Screens and Footlights: The Ballet 'Relâche' and an Exciting Film at the Champs Elysées: Mme. Georgette Leblanc in 'L'Inhumaine.'" *Vogue* (London) 65.1 (Early January 1925): 37, 70.

"Paris Screens and Footlights: Two of the Latest Plays Follow the Old Traditions of the Paris Stage, while an Extraordinary Film is the Newest Achievement of the Ultra-Modern School." *Vogue* (London) 65.3 (Early February 1925): 63, 82–83.

Petro, Patrice. *Aftershocks of the New: Feminism & Film History.* New Brunswick: Rutgers University Press, 2002.

Rabinovitz, Lauren. "The Future of Feminism and Film History." *Camera Obscura* 21.1 (2006): 39–44.

Richardson, Dorothy. "The Film Gone Male." In Scott, ed. *The Gender of Modernism.* 423–25.

Sexton, Jamie. "The Film Society and the Creation of an Alternative Film Culture in Britain in 1920s." In Higson, ed. 291–305.

Shaw, Walter Hanks. "Cinema and Ballet in Paris." *New Criterion: A Quarterly Review* 4.1 (January 1926): 178–84.

Stein, Gertrude. *Lectures in America.* 1935. Boston: Beacon Press, 1985.

Wasson, Haidee. "The Woman Film Critic: Newspapers, Cinema, and Iris Barry." *Film History: An International Journal* 18.2 (2006): 154–62.

———. "Writing the Cinema into Daily Life: Iris Barry and the Emergence of British Film Criticism in the 1920s." In Higson, ed., 321–37.

White, Eric Walter. *Parnassus to Let: An Essay about Rhythm in the Films.* Hogarth Essays. Second Series. No. 14. 1928.

———. *Walking Shadows: An Essay on Lotte Reiniger's Silhouette Films.* London: Hogarth Press, 1931.

Woolf, Virginia. *The Letters of Virginia Woolf.* Vol. 3.

———. *A Room of One's Own.* 1929; New York: Harcourt, Brace, Jovanovich, 1957.

IRIS BARRY

The Cinema: A Comparison of Arts

Some glib fraud long ago invented the detestable phrase "the silent stage," as though the cinema were nothing more than the theatre docked of its words. This dishonest and unintelligent view is strangely persistent. Yet partisan comparisons between the cinema and the stage are actually rather unfair to the stage, because the cinema has so much wider a scope. It alone can handle natural history, anthropology and travel. It can more fully develop parable, fairy-story, pageant, romance and character-study. But since both theatre and cinema do express farce, comedy, tragedy and melodrama there is a common ground on which they may properly be compared, although they are different art forms in different mediums.

In presenting drama, the theatre has certain advantages. The actors are present in the flesh. Everyone who saw Sarah Bernhardt in *Queen Elizabeth,* a 1913 film, felt the loss involved in her physical absence. Her acting was Bernhardt's acting. But it was not merely her voice that lacked: it was an emanation of personality. Then, the very concentration and confinement of the actors on the stage gives an adventitious and enviable intensity to all that they do. The atmosphere is one so gem-like and fierce that the audience feels itself included in that brilliant cube behind the footlights, and is given a lasting impression of light and activity. They forget that the theatre is as dark as the picture-palace, and the acting static compared with film-acting. The third advantage, which I believe not really to be an advantage, is the use of the spoken word. Certainly, in the most exalted form of the drama, the language has a peculiar literary beauty. But where there are excellent plays in which the speeches cannot be judged as literature, this quality is not essential. And even if it were, then, ideally, the visual beauty of a film should be the aesthetic alternative to the stage's poetry. I can conceive of films throughout which pictures of ineffable loveliness should continually melt into each other. There will be such films yet. There have already been promises: In one flash of conscious pictorial organization (the grouping of some choristers) in *Rosita*, in the perspectives and architecture of *Caligari*, in the co-ordinated movement on many planes of the crowds in *The Golem* and in a treatment of landscape in *The White Sister*. Meanwhile, it seems to me idle to insist that the cinema is inferior, artistically, to the stage: as idle, since the difference is one of medium, as to claim that Tchekov is a greater artist than Van Gogh. There *are* idiotic and ugly films, but the theatre is the mother of *Tons of Money*.

The cinema has its peculiar advantages. Visual imagery, less primitive and more sophisticated than auditory, is also sharper, more rapid, richer, and more permanent. The eye can take in more impressions in a given time, can associate more freely than the ear. Tests have shown, moreover, that a *moving* image is apprehended 20 per cent more effectively than a *static* image. The producers of films have only just begun to admit these facts, but when the cinema is tuned up to the acute visual machinery of the public, then I think it will be a very exceptional stage-play indeed which will give in dialogue anything like the delicate analysis of character, the diverse, minute and intuitive flashes into behaviour by which the film of the future, solely by means of pictures, will express drama. Both the *Woman of Paris* and *The Street* are experiments in pictorial drama, and I thought them much better, as plays, than, say, *Anna Christie* or *The Forest*.

The personal presence of the actors on the stage is compensated by the cinema's increased intimacy, by the possibility of seeing the actor's every gesture and changing expression and, more, his very thoughts in concrete form. Also, the world of the screen is not only spatially unconfined, it is a fuller world that of the theatre. It has infinite variety of scene, endless angles of vision and focuses, it can use for its own ends all the resources of landscape and architecture, and, very important indeed, it brings out an enormous significance in natural objects. Chairs and tables, collar-studs, kitchenware and flowers take on a function which they have lost, except for young children, since animism was abandoned in the accumulating sophistication of "progress."

The dramatic advantage of having Desdemona's handkerchief a protagonist, not a property, is obvious.

So psychologically satisfying is cinematographic drama that, were it a question of mere rivalry, were it not that the theatre *is* a totally different art-form, fulfilling a different function, I feel positive that, not only would the movies already have invaded certain West End theatres, but that, before long, there would be no regular theatre at all.

The Spectator (May 3, 1924): 707.

IRIS BARRY

The Scope of the Cinema

It is really no wonder that numbers of well-known writers, and artists too, go frequently to the cinema, when it provides them not only with an easily obtainable mental distraction but also stores up layers of experience, of local colour, in their subconscious minds for use in the future.

The cinema, from the penny-in-the-slot affair it was twenty-five years ago, has become not only the regular entertainment of millions of people, but a dream into which everyone can dissolve while retaining as much consciousness as he chooses. Viewing it, dispassionately, the moving picture is really extraordinary in that besides entertaining in the good old way by telling a story, and telling it in the most vivid way—that is, directly to the eye in pictures—it puts one *au courant* with places, eras, customs and types of mind foreign, but infinitely interesting just because of their strangeness. It is no longer true that one half of the world does not know how the other half lives; travel films make that impossible. An ordinary person going to the cinema casually during the last six months may easily have been on a whaling expedition in *Down to the Sea in Ships,* will have watched the wild elephants, the smartly striped zebras and the apes in *Trailing African Animals;* he will have witnessed those fast-vanishing ritual dances of savages in *Cannibals of the Southern Seas,* which anthropologists regard as the origin of all drama. Not content with taking us across several maps for a few shillings, the cinema keeps before us its constant News Pictorials, with their thrilling and often beautiful scraps of information on the method of counting blood-cells, the manufacture of battleships and Bangkok hats, the form of champion tennis players and the manner of the newest frocks. And all these "interest features" are merely the prelude to the real picture-plays themselves. Apart from the dramatic element of the plays, they too—even the most foolish of them—are apt to contain intriguing bits of information, whether it be about the psychological necessities of modern humanity (for it is obvious that the cinema would not have established itself as it has but for the fact that it does in some way solve the complexes of our age) or about the physical conformation of the back-woods. Very agreeable are the disguised travel films, like *Nanook of the North* and the recent *He and Ski* film with its lovely snow-scenes round St. Moritz and the exciting paper-chase on skis. The immense scope of the film-play proper, both in manner and in matter, cannot sufficiently be realised. It is a long cry from the pageantry of *Robin Hood, Scaramouche* and *The Fall of an Empress,* with their vast swirling crowds and their historical atmosphere, from the cold visual beauty of *The Niebelungs,* that dignified German screen-epic of the Dragon era of Europe's past, to the riotous farces of Buster Keaton. The first, painted in on a broad canvas, obey many of Aristotle's dramatic canons, while the farces, which are to our time what the circus was to our ancestors, provide surely the pleasantest wish-fulfilment ever devised for the amusement of mankind. Every mentality is catered for between those two extremes, in the melodramas which the cinema presents so much more effectively than Drury Lane can, in the social satires, the sex dramas, the Wild West films with their exciting *tempos* (rushing express trains, avalanches, motor-dashes, aeroplane fights and what not), in the witty comedies of Constance Talmadge, the fantasy of *Felix the Cat,* and the very intellectual films of Charles Chaplin. City men slip away (you can see them in the West End cinemas any afternoon) to follow the allure of roguish Mae Murray or drop an easy tear for a white-haired mother. Typists wallow in the supposed goings-on of the very smart, and the very smart safely court danger in the squalor of a Bowery crook's life.

But here and there on the screen in any of these films may flash a fugitive beauty; for a film is not simply photography, it is a story told in motion. In the various rhythms of speed as well as in the more obvious "artistic" staging the film-producer can now and again capture for us both psychological and visible loveliness. At the moment it is from Germany that the most interesting films are coming—films that care less to tell a story in pictorial *clichés* than to experiment with the yet-undiscovered possibilities of the cinema as a new form of expression. In *The Golem,* with its dark story of Jewish persecutions, they experimented with architecture and with the use of the crowd in the manner of a ballet master, to emphasise the emotion of the principal performers. *The Street,* while resembling in story many a melodrama from the States, was unique in the excellence of Eugen Klopfer's conventionalised acting, and *Caligari,* an old story now, but important in the history of the cinema, was frankly futurist and achieved in pictures what Poe did in words. German films are good to look at, conscientiously acted and mounted, and, best of all, they are original.

But there are delights for the eye in almost all films; a still-life on the screen, beautiful in itself, takes on a fresh beauty because of its dramatic importance; the whole resources of sea and landscape may be selected by an artist—for some producers are artists—as a background to the action, and the characters may so move and thread their way, in the story, through the scene that both it and they acquire new value, stimulate vivid flashes of imagination in the spectator. Hergesheimer's *The Bright Shawl,* brilliantly acted by Dorothy Gish and Richard Barthelmess, recently bore witness to the new ability of American films to capture atmosphere and to wean the camera at last from its tendency to insist on realism. This and all good new films promise something so unique, so little understood by any of us as yet, that it is with growing interest that one follows the development of a real film-technique, that one notes the broadening of the cinema's inspiration and scope.

Iris Barry

Vogue (London) 64.4 (Late August 1924): 65, 76

IRIS BARRY

Untitled Memoirs about the Launching of the Film Society

It began with a telephone call from an unknown person—a man who said that his name was Ivor Montagu, that he had been lunching with Hugh Miller the actor and that they both wanted to come and talk to me. About the cinema. About something to do with the cinema. And as the cinema was one of the things that interested me most at the time, to a degree which most of my friends regarded as eccentricity or mania, I said that they had both better come round at once and have tea with me so that we could talk. Curiosity to see these unknown persons and to hear what they had to say understandably played its part in my invitation.

At that time, 1925, I was living in the romantic but rather sordid ground floor and basement of an 18th century house in Bloomsbury just off Theobalds Road. The hall smelt strongly of tomcats and though the proportions of the rooms were charming, the paintwork was dismal and the furniture, mostly books, rather sketchy. I remember chiefly an old oak coaching chest of my grandfather's which we had painted scarlet and served as an additional seat. There was a typewriter on a cheap desk, three Chippendale chairs and a similar but heavily rustic armchair which I had formerly found in the family cowshed, a "good" dining-room table, masses of books and a portable typewriter. It was in fact a set-up almost too typical of the dwelling-place of a young intellectual couple of the period.

Whatever the characteristics or deficiencies of the place, it was clear that when Mr. Montagu and Mr. Miller arrived that neither had the least interest or importance for them, this tall bespectacled young man with the black curly hair got right down to [his] subject at once. His senior, elegantly handsome Mr. Miller, spoke less but was clearly in accord with him.

Briefly what Montagu said was this: there exists in London a distinguished and successful Stage Society. Let us found a Film Society which like the former will give programs on Sundays—but in the afternoons—to its subscribers. In this way we could show to an intelligent audience which we must suppose to exist the quantities of films new and old, American or foreign, which now remain unseen or perish miserably for want of the right audience or, indeed, are entirely forbidden or mercilessly mutilated by the censor.

My agreement was immediate and enthusiastic and we got out pencils and paper at once to sketch a program of action. But it may have to be explained now why Montagu and Miller had chosen to come to see me rather than another, upon having hatched their project during lunch. A number of factors entered into their decision.

To begin with, in 1925 the English press and even the English government had suddenly become aware of the near-demise of the British film industry, not inconsiderable before the war of 1914. If I remember aright, no single film was being made in England. . . . With more than a little jingoism, this lack had recently been privately and publicly deplored as prejudicial to the health of the nation, more and more of whose subjects and notably the younger ones were thus being subjected to foreign—which is to say American—influence, ideas and ideologies. There was, evidently, also the loss of prestige to deplore, not to mention the loss of money since, according to the new slogan, it was no longer only that "trade follows the flag" but that "trade follows the film."

There was even a tale often repeated that a certain perfume had increased its sales internationally after a bottle of it had been seen in a widely circulated movie on Gloria Swanson's dressing-table. Hollywood and thus America were mopping up the dough: thus it was high time that England got back into the film business. Should I recall that this was only very shortly before the Daily

Mail's celebrated poster "U. S. Usury" and assorted attacks on the U. S. government kept England trembling with indignation.

Quite some little while before Montagu's visit to me, the then proprietor and editor of the old influential weekly, The Spectator, Mr. St. Loe Strachey had at a directorial meeting touched upon this very topic. I should perhaps recall that up to that time the press collectively more or less ignored the existence of the cinema. But Mr. Strachey with his customary dash and foresight felt that "something should be done" by his Spectator to call attention to the currently sad state of the English film and the deplorable consequences and general state of the cinema in England. Articles or even editorials should be written. His son, recently graduated from Oxford and now a member of the Spectator staff, said in his inimitable drawl: "There *is* a woman whom I have met who *seems* to know quite a little about the subject. I think we might try her." No sooner said than done. The woman was myself. I had had the pleasure of dining with the Strachey son and his room-mate, Edward Sackville-West not so long before and evidently must have talked a lot, probably perhaps too much, about the movies. So I was now interviewed, I think by the Strachey son, for I seem to recall his office with a sofa strewn with a surprising number of highly coloured cushions piled up upon it as was the new fashion at the time. So I began to write about movies for the Spectator—every week a sort of brief guide to current films—the title of the film, the movie theatre where it could be seen and a couple of lines of comment, often quite emphatically for or against. As at that time none of us (none of my contemporaries) knew what fear or favour was, the comment was often absolute: avoid this big absurdity at the West End, go and see this other fascinating oddity even if it means making a wearisome journey by tube to an outlying suburb. And there must have been some persistent readers of the lines, as proved by occasional correspondence and fairly frequently telephone calls to The Spectator on the subject.

Soon, the paper commissioned me to write occasional articles or reviews of films and at the same time I wrote occasionally on the same topic for Vogue, thanks to the interest of the American editress, Miss Dorothy Todd and her assistant Miss Madge Garland.

MOMA Film Archives.

IRIS BARRY

From *Let's Go to the Pictures*

Introduction

[. . .] One by one we slip away into the dark, soporiferous cinema. Why? Because it shows us the object behaving. Because without ever telling the unnecessary and mutable truth it is always saying something which is relatively exact under given circumstances. Because it is personal experience.

At the moment we are a little ashamed of ourselves. Critics and connoisseurs demonstrate their deep sense by damning the films in every key. So those of us who go to the pictures every week, or every day, keep it rather quiet, or allude to it as being cheap, or restful. Others of us even allege that it solves our complexes.

Going to the pictures is nothing to be ashamed of. I should like to discuss why we do slink into the cinema and what happens to us there. Chiefly, I should like to irritate one or two intelligences into beguiling this new monster as critically as it deserves. All this is largely for my own sake. There are not enough of the kind of pictures I like best to make life wholly worth living, and I want more.

Cinematography, authority bellows, is not an art any more than a passport photographer is an artist. I am unconvinced. It is already a visual as well as a dramatic art: the finest films are as lovely to the eye as they are moving to the emotions. Their beauties, like those of music and the ballet, are fugitive, it is true: it is the accumulated succession of diverse images which gives aesthetic delight. Yet, because the moving picture speaks direct to the eye, it is a powerful form of communication. Scenes of which we can read or even see with pleasurable excitement played on the stage would be intolerable when given with all the silent and intimate reality of the screen. So it comes about that even in the crudest films something is provided for the imagination, and emotion is stirred by the simplest things—moonlight playing in a bare room, the flicker of a hand against a window. Is this not a virtue, dramatically, and for its enhancement of what, apart from the films, would be common and pointless? Tolstoi declared that art should be intelligible to the simplest people: this the cinema certainly is, besides being as universal as music.

It seems to me that the best way to help progress is not by condemning cinematography off-hand, but by seeing for oneself what the cinema's function and its virtues are, and then by patronizing those films which almost nearly reach one's ideal. If enough people support the better type of pictures, and stoutly demand more and still finer ones, they will get them. Supply inevitably follows demand.

I ask then: critics arise, invent terms, lay down canons, derive from your categories, heap up nonsense with sense and, when you have done, the cinemas will still be open and we can all flock in as proudly as we do now to the theatre and the opera, which indeed it is regarded as meritorious and noble to support. I do not however foresee a time when the public will "support" the cinema. The monster public can safely be left alone with its chief amusement: pterodactyl does not support mammoth. Indeed, I will say here and now that I very much hope, should such a lamentable day dawn, I shall have been interred long before with whatever respect was due.

From Chapter 4, "The Public's Pleasure"

The Cinema exists to please women—The question of wedding bells—Some films which ignored them—A fierce digression on "this getting married business"—do we really want so much love stuff?—How to get rid of it—

[. . .] Well, to begin with, I am not at all convinced that the public as a whole do want love stuff and love stuff only. I think the love stuff is overdone. It's at such a pass now that you can't have a woman nestle in any man's arms without the collective audience reaching for its hat under the impression that the finale is due. I concur that a love interest would always be useful and necessary in seven-eighths of all films. But not *such* a love interest. Not this cheap business of just getting oneself married, not this insistence on the feminine power of attracting a man till he finds her bed and board till the end of her days without her making one effort to deserve it.

And if it is so, then let us unite quickly to do something about bringing the great Anglo-Saxon races to an end. For if the adult population of England, America, Canada, Australia and S. Africa think that the main thing on earth is for a woman to get herself married off, then the sooner the end the better. If I thought it, I wouldn't be concerned about picking the cinema out of the mud, I'd be manufacturing bombs and dropping germs in the biggest reservoirs. I suppose we have all liked Jane Austen for ridiculing this "getting married" business. But women in those days really had some excuse for feeling so urgent about matrimony. It was the only career open to them. To-day, thank heaven, we're crawling out of that bog! There are a good many things women can do, including the making of good wives, the kind of wives who are more than food-dispensers and child rearers, who are human beings with some individuality of their own as well. Also we are beginning to realize that a woman who isn't well—I mean who doesn't feel she is doing the best that's in her—inside marriage, is best out of it. But it's hard to get people to admit this, even if they believe it, for "popular opinion" is against them. Now popular opinion is really just nothing but a lot of lies boosted in the form of soothing syrup by the printing press and the film factory, to give people false dreams for fear they kick at true facts.

I admit it began with the printing-press. For years, thousands of sloppy stories, poems, articles, plays and novels have been pouring out into the world harping on this great love and marriage business. But it is soothing syrup, not reality, all the same. What if we all do (the women) wish we were the heroine in *The Blue Lagoon* or the heroine in any magazine story, or the heroine in any musical comedy? We jolly well know we aren't and sometimes we recognize that if we were we wouldn't like it. *Do* women usually marry the first young man they meet under suitable circumstances? No, they don't, and they tend to do so less every year. They look around. It is all very well to lull oneself from the age of sixteen to sixty with "sweet love stories," but do we act up to them? No, we don't.

We might as well, then, do something about persuading film producers not to drop treacle into our mouths any more. It is bad for us.

If one out of ten of all the women who go to the movies here and in America would write a nice little letter to the manager of their pet cinema and tell him they're tired of just nothing but unreal love-stuff, they'd get something else. If one out of ten of them asked for more films like:

Abraham Lincoln
Her Sister from Paris
Forbidden Paradise
Pearls and Savages
The Woman of Paris
College Days
The Marriage Circle
The Last Laugh
Don Q.
The Black Pirate
Stella Dallas
Skinner's Dress Suit
The Monkey's Paw
The Tower of Lies

Vaudeville
The Unholy Three
Nell Gwyn
Dr. Marbuse
Her Big Night

they'd get them. If they asked for slow-motion sports pictures, or films about people's lives, or about ideas like revenge, parental responsibility, a desire for self-expression, or what not, they'd get them. The films would be every bit as competent, every bit as entertaining as they are now. There'd still be love interest, of course, but it would not queer everything as it now does.

One moment! Remember that *Robin Hood, Way Down East, The Ten Commandments, The Hunchback of Notre Dame,* were big successes. Remark also that the love interest in them was very slight. Why there's even money in films that aren't entirely about love!

And then we might get some films about the people who fall in love, not just about their getting caught up together; real romance these might be, palpitating bits of sentiment. But real. For after all, what's interesting in a love story is not the fact that a man loves a girl, but (*a*) the circumstances they are in, the adventures they have, and (*b*) in their own characters and the change their sentimental relationship makes in them.

There always will be plays, novels, stories and films simply about courtship; there *is* a demand for them. People know that they are "nice" just as they know jokes about fleas and boarding houses are "funny." Such sentiment indeed represents an ideal, another waking dream. All that I suggest is that out of the billions of people who do go to the pictures there exist some millions who tire of false sentiment, and I earnestly beg everyone who does so tire of it to join me and some others in a fight for variety. I say false sentiment advisedly for the majority of the films of sentiment *are* false and correspond to nothing in the actual erotic experience of anyone. [. . .]

London: Chatto & Windus, 1926. vii–x.

IRIS BARRY

Women Film Makers

It is not often that the person who makes films—that autocrat who shouts mysterious instructions through a megaphone to actors, camera men, and electricians—is a woman.

The work is hard; it entails handling crowds of hundreds of people, controlling a little army of technical experts, and getting the best acting out of the cast. It also calls frequently for an iron hand in a velvet glove when a star or small-part player has the tantrums. The hours are long: from nine in the morning until any time up to midnight.

Considerable interest, therefore, has been aroused by the appointment of Miss Dorothy Arzner as a fully fledged film director in the studios of the big American firm Famous Players Lasky. Her first picture, "Fashions for Women," recently seen at the Plaza in London, certainly justified this appointment. A light, gay comedy, it flowed across the screen with a sureness, ease, and wit by no means always achieved by directors of light film entertainment.

This strikingly handsome woman's apprenticeship to films has been thorough. She began as a scenario typist, graduated to cutting films, and astonished Hollywood by the brilliant manner in which she, single-handed, cut and edited "The Covered Wagon." Her success will certainly inspire other women in the subordinate ranks of filmdom with hopes of following her upwards.

For she is not unique in her position. Miss Lois Weber, hitherto America's only woman director, achieved an artistic success long ago with her film "Shoes," has made several other films, and now, after an absence, returns as a director with Leatrice Joy as star in "The Angel of Broadway."

In France Mme. Germaine Dulac is highly esteemed for the films of her making: in Sweden the veteran actress Karin Swanstrom has directed a singularly human and sincere picture.

London Daily Mail (July 13, 1927).

IRIS BARRY

Women Who Make Us Laugh

Though men declare that women have no sense of humour, quite a number of the screen celebrities who trade in laughs are feminine.

Speaking of film comedy, the names of Chaplin, Lloyd, and Keaton spring inevitable to mind: though Reginald Denny and Raymond Griffith are no less adept at creating hilarious outbreaks in cinemas. The women comedians of the screen are all of the Denny and Griffith kind rather than the Chaplin and Lloyd type—they are not acrobatic, not utterly ridiculous, not always being hit by someone. One laughs with them as with Denny, rather than at them as with, say, Harry Langdon.

Perhaps Betty Balfour is the screen's most compelling and original comedienne. Not all her films have been good, though she has retained her popularity through even the poorest of them. As the flower girl in the "Squibs" series she was inimitable; in "Reveille" she displayed dramatic as well as comic talent and latterly in "Blinkeyes" her fresh, spontaneous personality carried her through a not very remarkable story triumphantly. Now she is to "co-star" with Sid Chaplin in "A Little Bit of Fluff."

Mabel Normand, who had a touch of real genius, rarely appears nowadays, but it was during his association with her that Chaplin developed. Mabel Normand and the late Max Linder will always be remembered not only as two of the first world-favourites of the screen, but as Chaplin's tutors.

Bebe Daniels has inherited some of Mabel Normand's repertory of funny tricks, and gambols and leaps nearly as vigorously as Fairbanks. Louise Fazenda has the monopoly of two devices—looking half-witted and screaming dismally—at both of which she is highly gifted and by means of which she succeeds in being genuinely funny.

Even Zasu Pitts, though a first-rate tragedienne in her own rather uncanny way, has a true gift for comedy and knows just when and how to move, or to give a glance which will create a sudden laugh. For if timing is a large part of the art of a stage comedian, it is almost the whole of film fun-making.

Pre-eminent among the women comedians of the cinema, however, is one childish little figure that somehow does not strike anyone as being properly comic: yet one which provokes the most delightful ripples of merriment as well as gently enjoyable tears of pity and compassion. This small girl is one of the cleverest business magnates in the whole film industry: level-headed, farsighted, eminently practical as well as womanly.

Yet the world regards her, on the screen, as the big-hearted, plucky, comical little maid of all work, with her spindly but expressive legs and tiny hands which move in quick protest at any unkindness, any cruelty.

This little girl, who is a big business chief, and who is also one of the most gifted comediennes of the screen, is Mary Pickford.

London Daily Mail (July 25, 1927).

LONDON FILM SOCIETY PROGRAMME NO. 38 (WOMEN DIRECTORS)

THE FILM SOCIETY
PROGRAMME
(Fifth Season)

At 2:30 P.M.
SUNDAY, MARCH 16, 1930
AT THE TRIVOLI PALACE, STRAND
(by courtesy of the management)

Conductor: Mr. Ernest Grimshaw
(by permission of Provincial Cinematograph
Theatres Ltd)

2.30 **Down Under** **1929**
Direction.. Percy Smith
Production .... British Instructional Films (Great Britain)

Miss Mary Field, who wrote the dialogue of this "Secret of Nature," joined the producing firm in 1925 as advisor on Imperial Films. She has for some time been in charge of the preparation of the "Secrets of Nature" series. This film, announced as part of the programme of January when, however, "The Aphis" was shown instead, was photographed underground.

2.42 **Cinderella** **1924**
Direction.. Lotte Reiniger
Producing Firm ....Institute für Kulurforschung (Germany)

This is Miss Reiniger's second silhouette film. Since its exhibition without sub-titles to the Society in December, 1927, an original poem by Mr. Humbert Wolfe has been introduced in the form of sub-titling.

2.55 The Last Post 1929
Direction... Dinah Shurey
Production ....Britannia Films (Great Britain)
David ....John Longden
Martin...John Longden
Paul ....Frank Vosper

Miss Shurey, whose films like *"Carry On"* enjoyed wide circulation, has specialised in patriotic melodrama. The present excerpts, chosen by the director from an as yet unissued picture, relate the beginning and end of a story full of incident. In the intervening passages, David, the least heroic of the brothers, associates after the war with a shady group of political malcontents. Their activities culminate during the General Strike in the theft of a Lewis gun. The method adopted by the repentant David to avert the execution of Martin is given in a later reel not shown now. The picture actually opens with a military funeral, the rest of the story being related in a long "flash-back."

3.25 Interval of five minutes

3:30 Fashions for Women...1926
Direction... Dorothy Arzner
Production ....Famous Players Lasky Corp. (U. S. A)

No film could better illustrate the characteristics of American programme pictures in general. It is constructed to display a star advantageously. At the same time it gratifies many dreams by bestowing upon its Cinderella-heroine great material luxury. The story is the familiar one of the impersonation of an important individual—the woman who rules the world of Paris modistes, in this case—by a girl in humble circumstances. Miss Esther Ralston plays both roles. In the airman-hero members will recognise the late Mr. Elinar Hansen of "The Joyless Street," whose career in Hollywood was cut short by a fatal motor accident. Mr. Raymond Hatton plays the heroine's press agent: it is his insistence that she shall retire after having her face lifted, while a double, subsequently to be unmasked with further publicity, takes her place, which is the pivot of the plot.

Both scenes and titles in this picture nicely illustrate the lengths in suggestiveness to which a producer may safely go.

Miss Dorothy Arzner entered Famous Players' studios as a script typist. After filling the same post with Nazimova's company, she became a film cutter. Her success in cutting *"Blood and Sand"* and, more particularly, *"The Covered Wagon"* made her famous. She next wrote original stories for the screen, edited *"Sons of the Sea"* and was promoted to direction. Her pictures are *"Ten Modern Commandments," "Manhattan Cocktail," "Get Your Man,"* and *"The Wild Party."*

The Sea Shell and the Clergyman **1929**
Direction .... Germaine Dulac

This is the film rejected by the British Board of Film Censors on the grounds that it "is so cryptic as to be almost meaningless. If there is a meaning, it is doubtless objectionable." The film is shown in its entirety.

Madame Dulac is a well-known French director.

4.25 The Peasant Women of Riazan **1927**
Direction .... Olga Preobrashenskaja
Production .... Sovkino (U. S. S. R)

Sections, illustrating some ethnographically interesting marriage customs, and the change in the position of women in Russia since 1917, have been chosen from this film linked together by a slight thread of story.

Mme. Preobrashenskaja, one of the most experienced of Russian directors though by no means the only woman director, began making films for children some fifteen years ago. As this film clearly shows, she belongs to the older and more theatrical tradition of Russian production. It is considered her most interesting work. Shown on the continent as *"The Village of Sin"* this film has been passed by the British Board of Film Censors as *"The Devil's Plaything."*

It may be observed that peculiarly national characteristics appear with great clarity in the work of women directors.

Continuity titles have been added in all cases to cover cuts made.

THE FILM SOCIETY

The next performance of the Film Society will be held on April 6th, and will probably include *The General Line* by S. M. Eisenstein.

In view of the many complaints received respecting late arrival of members of the audience, the doors of the auditorium will be closed against ingress, at this performance and in future, during the progress of each film.

Intending Members are requested to communicate with the Secretary, Miss J. M. HARVEY, 56 Manchester Street, W. 1. There are two rates of subscription each entitling to one seat at each performance for the remainder of the season (£1–11–6 and £1–1–0).

The Council will be pleased at all times to hear from Members of suggested modifications to the provisional programme.

Applications for the commercial use of films shown at past performances should in all cases be made through the Secretary.

VIRGINIA WOOLF

The Cinema

People say that the savage no longer exists in us, that we are at the fag-end of civilisation, that everything has been said already, and that it is too late to be ambitious. But these philosophers have presumably forgotten the movies. They have never seen the savages of the twentieth century watching the pictures. They have never sat themselves in front of the screen and thought how, for all the clothes on their backs and the carpets at their feet, no great distance separates them from those bright-eyed, naked men who knocked two bars of iron together and heard in that clangour a foretaste of the music of Mozart.

The bars in this case, of course, are so highly wrought and so covered over with accretions of alien matter that it is extremely difficult to hear anything distinctly. All is hubble-bubble, swarm, and chaos. We are peering over the edge of a cauldron in which fragments of all shapes and savours seem to simmer; now and again some vast form heaves itself up, and seems about to haul itself out of chaos. Yet, at first sight, the art of the cinema seems simple, even stupid.

There is the King shaking hands with a football team; there is Sir Thomas Lipton's yacht; there is Jack Horner winning the Grand National. The eye licks it all up instantaneously, and the brain, agreeably titillated, settles down to watch things happening without bestirring itself to think. For the ordinary eye, the English unaesthetic eye, is a simple mechanism, which takes care that the body does not fall down coal-holes, provides the brain with toys and sweetmeats to keep it quiet, and can be trusted to go on behaving like a competent nurse-maid until the brain comes to the conclusion that it is time to wake up. What is its surprise, then, to be roused suddenly in the midst of its agreeable somno-lence and asked for help? The eye is in difficulties. The eye wants help. The eye says to the brain, "Something is happening which I do not in the least under-stand. You are needed." Together they look at the King, the boat, the horse, and the brain sees at once that they have taken on a quality which does not belong to the simple photograph of real life. They have become not more beautiful, in the sense in which pictures are beautiful, but shall we call it (our vocabulary is miserably insufficient) more real, or real with a different reality from that which we perceive in daily life? We behold them as they are when we are not there. We see life as it is when we have no part in it. As we gaze we seem to be removed from the pettiness of actual existence. The horse will not knock us down. The King will not grasp our hands. The wave will not wet our feet. From this point of vantage, as we watch the antics of our kind, we have time to feel pity and amusement, to generalize, to endow one man with the attributes of the race. Watching the boat sail and the wave break, we have time to open our minds wide to beauty and register on top of it the queer sensa-tion—this beauty will continue, and this beauty will flourish whether we behold it or not. Further, all this happened ten years ago, we are told. We are behold-ing a world which has gone beneath the waves. Brides are emerging from the Abbey—they are now mothers; ushers are ardent—they are now silent; moth-ers are tearful; guests are joyful; this has been won and that has been lost, and it is over and done with. The war sprung its chasm at the feet of all this inno-cence and ignorance, but it was thus that we danced and pirouetted, toiled and desired, thus that the sun shone and the clouds scudded up to the very end.

But the picture-makers seem dissatisfied with such obvious sources of inter-est as the passage of time and the suggestiveness of reality. They despise the flight of gulls, ships on the Thames, the Prince of Wales, the Mile End road, Piccadilly Circus. They want to be improving, altering, making an art of their own—naturally, for so much seems to be within their scope. So many arts seemed to stand by ready to offer their help. For example, there was literature. All the famous novels of the world, with their well-known characters, and their famous scenes, only asked, it seemed, to be put on the films. What could be easier and simpler? The cinema fell upon its prey with immense rapacity, and to this moment largely subsists upon the body of its unfortunate victim. But the results are disastrous to both. The alliance is unnatural. Eye and brain are torn asunder ruthlessly as they try vainly to work in couples. The eye says: "Here is Anna Karenina." A voluptuous lady in black velvet wearing pearls comes before us. But the brain says: "That is no more Anna Karenina than it is Queen Victoria." For the brain knows Anna almost entirely by the inside of her mind—her charm, her passion, her despair. All the emphasis is laid by the cinema upon her teeth, her pearls, and her velvet. Then "Anna falls in love with Vronsky"—that is to say, the lady in black velvet falls into the arms of a gentleman in uniform, and they kiss with enormous succulence, great deliberation, and infinite gesticulation on a sofa in an extremely well-appointed library, while a gardener incidentally mows the lawn. So we lurch and lumber through the most famous novels of the world. So we spell them out in words of one syllable written, too, in the scrawl of an illiterate schoolboy. A kiss is love. A broken cup is jealousy. A grin is happiness. Death is a hearse. None of these things has the least connection with the novel that Tolstoy wrote, and it is only when we give up trying to connect the pictures with the book that we guess from some accidental scene—like the gardener mowing the lawn—what the cinema might do if it were left to its own devices.

But what, then, are its devices? If it ceased to be a parasite, how would it walk erect? At present it is only from hints that one can frame any conjecture. For instance, at a performance of Dr. Caligari the other day, a shadow shaped like a tadpole suddenly appeared at one corner of the screen. It swelled to an immense size, quivered, bulged, and sank back again into nonentity. For a moment it seemed as if thought could be conveyed by shape more effectively than by words. The monstrous, quivering tadpole seemed to be fear itself, and not the statement, "I am afraid." In fact, the shadow was accidental, and the effect unintentional. But if a shadow at a certain moment can suggest so much more than the actual gestures and words of men and women in a state of fear, it seems plain that the cinema has within its grasp innumerable symbols for emotions that have so far failed to find expression. Terror has, besides its ordinary forms, the shape of a tadpole; it burgeons, bulges, quivers, disappears. Anger is not merely rant and rhetoric, red faces and clenched fists. It is perhaps a black line wriggling upon a white sheet. Anna and Vronsky need no longer scowl and grimace. They have at their command—but what? Is there, we ask, some secret language which we feel and see, but never speak, and, if so, could this be made visible to the eye? Is there any characteristic which thought possesses that can be rendered visible without the help of words? It has speed and slowness; dart-like directness and vaporous circumlocution. But it has also, especially in moments of emotion, the picture-making power, the need to lift its burden to another bearer; to let an image run side by side along with it. The likeness of the thought is, for some reason, more beautiful, more comprehensible, more available than the thought itself. As everybody knows, in Shakespeare the most complex ideas form chains of images through which we mount, changing and turning, until we reach the light of day. But, obviously, the images of a poet are not to be cast in bronze, or traced by pencil. They are a compact of a thousand suggestions of which the visual is only the most obvious or the uppermost. Even the simplest image: "My luve's like a red, red rose, that's newly sprung in June," presents us with impressions of moisture and warmth and the glow of crimson and the softness of petals inextricably mixed and strung upon the lilt of a rhythm which is itself the voice of the passion and hesitation of the lover. All this, which is accessible to words, and to words alone, the cinema must avoid.

Yet if so much of our thinking and feeling is connected with seeing, some residue of visual emotion which is of no use either to painter or to poet may still await the cinema. That such symbols will be quite unlike the real objects which we see before us seems highly probable. Something abstract, something which moves with controlled and conscious art, something which calls for the very slightest help from words or music to make itself intelligible, yet justly uses them subserviently—of such movements and abstractions the films may, in time to come, be composed. Then, indeed, when some new symbol for expressing thought is found, the film-maker has enormous riches at his command. The exactitude of reality and its surprising power of suggestion are to be had for the asking. Annas and Vronskys—there they are in the flesh. If into this reality he could breathe emotion, could animate the perfect form with thought, then his booty could be hauled in hand over hand. Then, as smoke pours from Vesuvius, we should be able to see thought in its wildness, in its beauty, in its oddity, pouring from men with their elbows on a table; from women with their little handbags slipping to the floor. We should see these emotions mingling together and affecting each other.

We should see violent changes of emotion produced by their collision. The most fantastic contrasts could be flashed before us with a speed which the writer can only toil after in vain; the dream architecture of arches and battle-ments, of cascades falling and fountains rising, which sometimes visits us in sleep or shapes itself in half-darkened rooms, could be realized before our waking eyes. No fantasy could be too far-fetched or insubstantial. The past could be unrolled, distances annihilated, and the gulfs which dislocate novels (when, for instance, Tolstoy has to pass from Levin to Anna, and in so doing jars his story and wrenches and arrests our sympathies) could, by the sameness of the background, by the repetition of some scene, be smoothed away.

How all this is to be attempted, much less achieved, no one at the moment can tell us. We get intimations only in the chaos of the streets, perhaps, when some momentary assembly of colour, sound, movement suggests that here is a scene waiting a new art to be transfixed. And sometimes at the cinema, in the midst of its immense dexterity and enormous technical proficiency, the curtain parts and we behold, far off, some unknown and unexpected beauty. But it is for a moment only. For a strange thing has happened—while all the other arts were born naked, this, the youngest, has been born fully clothed. It can say everything before it has anything to say. It is as if the savage tribe, instead of finding two bars of iron to play with, had found, scattering the seashore, fiddles, flutes, saxophones, trumpets, grand pianos by Erard and Bechstein, and had begun with incredible energy, but without knowing a note of music, to hammer and thump upon them all at the same time.

The Nation and Athenaeum (July 3, 1926): 381–83.

GILBERT SELDES

The Abstract Movie

In Mrs. Woolf's essay, The Movies and Reality (the New Republic, August 4) there occurs this sentence:

> Something abstract, something which moves with controlled and conscious art, something which calls for the very slightest help from words or music to make itself intelligible, yet justly uses them subserviently—of such movements and abstractions the films may, in time to come, be composed.

The keen intelligence of the whole essay ought to tempt every one who has been thinking about the movies to write an extensive commentary; but the sentence quoted has a peculiar interest because it is apparently written without knowledge of the abstract films which have been made in Paris in the last two or three years, films which already make the conditional future unnecessary. At least a part of the films of tomorrow will be composed of the elements Mrs. Woolf mentions.

Of the three films I have seen, two at least have been shown in New York by the Film Guild and the Film Associates, the film made by the French cubist painter Fernand Léger collaborating with the American Dudley Murphy, and the film sponsored by Comte Etienne de Beaumont, *Of What Are Young Films*

Dreaming? (an unhappy flavorless translation of the French title which was a pun on the name of de Musset's play). The third was made to be shown between the two parts of the last of the Swedish ballets under Rolf de Maré, and is called Entr'acte. Of these, the Beaumont film seems to me to be the most completely realized, the Léger-Murphy film which was the pioneer, the least; but as the three films are identical in essence and in significance, I shall not try to judge among them, nor to identify the separate points of interest by name.

It is extremely difficult for the American, accustomed to an involved plot dominating even such films as exploit a dominant player, to gather by word of mouth the actual content of these films; that they can be interesting passes belief. Fortunately for the critic he has only to write down what he has actually seen; these films are made for pure visual enjoyment. In general the spectator has seen objects in motion; the objects may be easily identified—a straw hat, a boat on the Seine, a row of bottles, a shoot-the-chutes; or they may be distorted, seen through a prismatic glass, through smoke, at unusual angles, upside down. The movement may be accelerated or retarded, shown backward, repeated, tricked in a hundred ways. There may be a swelling blot of ink on a pane of glass, a shadow endowed with proper life, mysterious darkness or twilight on the screen; human beings may be present, as actors, as masses, as incidentals. There may be a mock funeral with the mourners in slow motion and the hearse running off by itself, or a green triangle may leap under and through a red circle, faster and faster in a geometrical struggle for supremacy, or the city of Paris may rush headlong to perdition as the airplane from which the picture is taken nose-dives around the Eiffel Tower.

Anyone familiar with the pictures will recognize some of these elements: the cleverer news reels, the trick pictures in which a cow walks into itself, added to a touch of the Clavilux will supply at least half of the sensations in seeing an abstract film. Until the abstract picture arrived, in fact, the trick movie was the "purest" in a technical sense. What the abstract picture has added is deliberate intention. The repetitions, the changes of pace, the variations in the form projected in the Léger picture were intended to create cumulative emotion, coming to a climax. It was not wholly successful; I have noted before that the only actually moving part of the picture was concerned with a woman bearing a burden up a hill, and being eternally shifted back to the bottom just as she reached the crest. To make the film theoretically successful this suggestion of human emotion ought to have been omitted; yet it, too, was entirely cinematographic, and did not depend upon story. *Entr'acte* was vaguely connected with the ballet, *Relâche,* and Borlin, the principal dancer, appeared too regularly; in the Beaumont film the only persons one recalls at all are a few well known Parisians whose faces are distorted as in the comic mirrors at Coney Island. In each of the films the most significant part was that played by the variation of movement and the variation of forms. There was excitement in the changing speeds at which bottles moved about each other; there was extraordinary pleasure to the eye in watching a tiny object spinning round on a moving phonograph record and seen through a distorting glass; there was a prime thrill in the dip and sway of the roller coaster, a movement which took in the whole visible world and was felt at the pit of the stomach. In two of the pictures there appeared the most beautiful scenic shots I have ever seen, with the color-scheme reversed, so that trees were white against a black sky.

None of these pictures is entirely successful; all three are exceptionally fine movies and important in the progress of the movie. They all have created images on the screen and proved that these images can call our emotions into being; but none of them has tried to be specific. None of them has tried to use a definite image for the communication of a definite thought. They have proved that symbols can be evocative on the screen; it is enough.

Until recently *The Cabinet of Doctor Caligari* has been uniquely the art-film, and it is interesting that Mrs. Woolf's thoughts on the movies were inspired by this hardy outrider. There were several important things in Caligari, most of them noted so often as to cause nausea to our good American directors. Caligari used expressionistic (i.e., entirely unrealistic, but emotionally correct) settings for its action, and would have been an entire failure if the rhythm of the principal players had not also been cast in a mode of unreality. The shape of an attic or of a window, the bizarre unexplained appearance of a patch of sunlight without a source, the use of levels, inclines and curves, all contributed to the intensity of emotion which the story was to call up. It was in no sense an abstract film, but it indicated, years before the abstract film was made, to what ultimate use it may be put. Because I think it quite unreasonable to suppose that we shall give up the story-film; the film, properly handled, tells a story magnificently, and so far has been a disappointment only because it has found no way to tell more than the outside of a story, telling it blatantly and vulgarly. Caligari succeeded at moments in suggesting thought and feelings without always depending upon action. ("A kiss is love. A broken cup is jealousy.") The abstract film which will give the director symbols and images will give him at the same time a hundred times his present capacity to tell his story, to give it the third dimension it has so far been lacking, an intellectual and emotional content.

The abstract film, like the trick film and the news reel, has worked severely within the limitations of the machinery of taking and projecting; it has called in few outside aids. (I believe that Satie wrote the ballet music, and that part of it accompanied *Entr'acte;* but I saw it alone and heard nothing beyond the ordinary piano; the other two films I saw, in small projection rooms, without music.) That means that as soon as the director feels free to do so, and brings his technique up to the required point, he can embody all that these films teach him. In the actual taking of pictures the American director is probably unexcelled; the technical proficiency he needs is in knowing how a thing will look when taken, in knowing how to displace or distort his object in front of the camera; I should also think that a knowledge of psychology would not be inappropriate. He will displease the fanatical amateurs of the abstract picture by using a few hundred feet here and there to heighten an emotion; but he will gradually enlarge the available field for the movie and teach the movie-going public to look for more and care for more than he has previously given.

In writing about *The Big Parade* in this journal I noted that its finest moment was the reappearance of a line of soldiers advancing through a wood— a line seen perhaps twenty minutes earlier in the picture. The line reappeared in the midst of barrage fire; its contribution to the narrative was far less than that of other sequences. Yet it had tremendous emotional effect because it made contact in our minds in the electrical circle of image-imagination. I am convinced that the soldiers purely as soldiers were not the cause; it was the appearance of a known line, it was the pace, the timing, the rhythm of that appearance which counted.

In all such speculations we who are not actually engaged in making movies assume one thing which the professionals instantly deny. We think that the movie can be made great by ceasing to be realistic; we insist that the camera is not a mere recorder—even the still camera is more than that, and when you add motion we feel we have scientific backing in our claim that the camera can and should transpose its objects. In short we want the moving picture to be an *art through its mechanism,* not an art through literature and not a mechanism alone. The professionals tell us we are slightly mad; and it has been left for amateurs to prove that we are sane. But the last word is still in the field of commerce. The non-realistic, the actually imaginative or creative movie will not sell. That is, I believe, true. But it is impermanently true. Our audiences have been starved of imagination so long that they may fail to recognize it and care for it. The usual method, after starvation, is to begin to feed the victim very slowly indeed.

The New Republic (September 15, 1926): 95–96.

H. D.

Projector

Light takes new attribute
and yet his old
glory
enchants
not this,
not this, they say,
lord as he was of the heiratic dance,
of poetry
and majesty
and pomp,
master of shrines and gateways
and of doors,
of markets
and the cross-road
and the street;
not this,
they say;
but we say otherwise
and greet
light
in new attribute,
insidious fire;
light reasserts
his power
reclaims the lost;
in a new blaze of splendour
calls the host
to reassemble
and to readjust
all severings
and differings of thought,
all strife and strident bickering
and rest;
O fair and blest,
he strides forth young and pitiful and strong,
a king of blazing splendour and of gold,
and all the evil
and the tyrannous wrong

that beauty suffered
finds its champion,
light
who is god
and song.

He left the place they built him
and the halls,
he strode so simply forth,
they knew him not;
no man deceived him,
no,
nor ever will,
with meagre counterfeit
of ancient rite,
he knows all hearts
and all imagining
of plot
and counterplot
and mimicry,
this measuring of beauty with a rod,
no formula
could hold him
and no threat
recall him
who is god.

Yet he returns,
O unrecorded grace,
over
and under
and through us
and about;
the stage is set now
for his mighty rays;
light,
light that batters gloom,
the Pythian
lifts up a fair head
in a lowly place,
he shows his splendour
in a little room;
he says to us,
be glad

and laugh,
be gay;
I have returned
though in an evil day
you crouched despairingly
who had no shrine;
we had no temple and no temple fire
for all these said
and mouthed
and said again;
beauty is an endighter
and is power
of city
and of soldiery
and might,
beauty is city
and the state
and dour duty,
beauty is this and this and this dull thing,
forgetting who was king.

Yet still he moves
alert,
invidious,
this serpent creeping
and this shaft of light,
his arrows slay
and still his foot-steps
dart
gold
in the market-place;
vision returns
and with new vision
fresh
hope
to the impotent;
tired feet that never knew a hill-slope
tread
fabulous mountain sides;
worn
dusty feet
sink in soft drift of pine
needles

and anodyne
of balm and fir and myrtle-trees
and cones
drift across weary brows
and the sea-foam
marks the sea-path
where no sea ever comes;
islands arise where never islands were,
crowned with the sacred palm
or odorous cedar;
waves sparkle and delight
the weary eyes
that never saw the sun fall in the sea
nor the bright Pleaiads rise.

Close Up 1 (July 1927): 46–51.

DOROTHY RICHARDSON

From "So I gave up going to the theatre"

[. . .] The palaces were repulsive. Their being brought me an uneasiness that grew lively when at last I found myself within one of those whose plaster frontages and garish placards broke a row of shops, in a strident, north London street. It was a Monday and therefore a new picture. But it was also washing day, and yet the scattered audience was composed almost entirely of mothers. Their children, apart from the infants accompanying them, were at school and their husbands were at work. It was a new audience, born within the last few months. Tired women, their faces sheened with toil, and small children, penned in semi-darkness and foul air on a sunny afternoon. There was almost no talk. Many of the women sat alone, figures of weariness at rest. Watching these I took comfort. At last the world of entertainment had provided for a few pence, tea thrown in, a sanctuary for mothers, an escape from the everlasting qui vive into eternity on a Monday afternoon.

The first scene was a tide, frothing in over the small beach of a sandy cove, and for some time we were allowed to watch the coming and going of those foamy waves, to the sound of a slow waltz, without the disturbance of incident. Presently from the fisherman's hut emerged the fisherman's daughter, moss-haired. The rest of the scenes, all of which sparked continually, I have forgotten. But I do not forget the balm of that tide, and that simple music, nor the shining eyes and rested faces of those women. After many years during which I saw many films, I went, to oblige a friend, once more to a theatre. It was to a drawing-room play, and the harsh bright light, revealing the audience, the over-emphasis of everything, the over-driven voices and movements of all but the few, seemed to me worse than ever. I realised that the source of the haunting guilt and loss was for me, that the players, in acting *at* instead of *with* the audience, were destroying the inner relationship between audience and players. Something of this kind, some essential failure to compel the co-operation of the creative consciousness of the audience.

Such co-operation cannot take place unless the audience is first stilled to forgetfulness of itself as an audience. This takes power. Not force or emphasis or noise, mental or physical. And the film, as intimate as thought, so long as it is free from the introduction of the alien element of sound, gives this co-operation its best chance. The accompanying music is not an alien sound. It assists the plunge into life that just any film can give, so much more fully than just any play, where the onlooker is perforce under the tyranny of the circumstances of the play without the chances of escape provided so lavishly by the moving scene. The music is not an alien sound if it be as continuous as the performance and blending with it. That is why, though a good orchestra can heighten and deepen effects, a piano played by one able to improvise connective tissue for his varying themes is preferable to most orchestral accompaniments. Music is essential. Without it the film is a moving photograph and the audience mere onlookers. Without music there is neither light nor colour, and the test of this is that one remembers musically accompanied films in *colour* and those unaccompanied by music as colourless. The cinema may become all that its well-wishers desire. So far, its short career of some twenty years is a tale of splendid achievement. Its creative power is incalculable, and its service to the theatre is nothing less than the preparation of vast, new audiences for the time when plays shall be accessible at possible rates in every square mile of the town. How many people, including the repentant writer, has it already restored to the playhouse?

"Continuous Performance," *Close Up* 1:1 (July 1927): 34–37.

BRYHER

The Sociological Film, I

The Peasant Women of Riazan is one of the greatest and most beautiful films that has been made. It combines construction, beauty and dramatic power together with beautiful photography, as many of the outdoor scenes are done on panchromatic stock. (Panchromatic costs considerably more than ordinary negative and is more difficult to develop, but gives all colors approximately their true value and is therefore far more lovely to watch.) But the negative was destroyed in the fire at the Afifa works last autumn, and it is said that there is no other in Russia and that only a few scratched and worn copies are left. If this is so it is one of the greatest tragedies that have happened in the history of cinematography.

It is also an example of a problem of the Russian film world: that of keeping down costs. Most Hollywood films have three negatives; that is, during all the scenes there are three cameramen and three machines turning and the development costs are tripled. Naturally, it is not possible to afford this in Moscow, where the expenditure must be kept as low as possible. Only, if a negative gets destroyed, the whole labor of months is lost.

The Peasant Women of Riazan (*Das Dorf er Sünde*) was directed by a woman, Olga Ivanovna Priobrashenskaya. (It is a Sovkino film, released by Derussa.) She was born in 1885 and completed the eighth class at the Gymnasium. Afterwards she studied at the Moscow Art Theatre and acted under the management of Stanislavsky, Nemirovitch-Danchenko, Meyerhold, Mardianof, Tairof, etc., until 1913.

In 1913 she began to act for the films with the firm Timan and Reinhart.

In 1915 she started work as cinema stage manager, at first under the direction of V. R. Gardin. Her first independent production was *Young Lady-Peasant Woman* (based on Pushkin), made in 1916, for the firm of Vengerof. She directed later, for the Neptune firm, *Hamsun's Victoria*. In 1919 she became artistic director of a class of cinema models in the first Gos-Kino school. She is said to be marvellous as a teacher. And she has worked uninterruptedly at cinema training from 1920 to the present day. In 1923 she helped to direct, with V. R. Gardin, *The Land-Owner* and *Locksmith and Chancellor,* for the Wufku, at Yalta. She has also made two films for children, *The Truth of Fedkin* and *Kiriliou,* and has just finished another full-length film, *The Last Attraction.*

Few women to date have used the screen creatively: this is economic circumstance rather than inability to use the medium. So much of the commercial cinema depends upon its women stars, but, apart from acting, opportunities are few, and the creative and artistic side is almost barren of names. But now, in Russia, Priobrashenskaya has made a film as great in its way as any discussed in this book, and one that is also an amazing sociological and constructive document.

It is utterly free from propaganda, this film. Somehow, a woman who thinks is freer than a man from political trammels. It is much harder for a man, perhaps, to break with convention. But the woman thinker (I admit there are a few of them) seeks for truth.

And truth is the underlying principle of *The Peasant Women.*

It is spring in Russia. Women, in gaily colored skirts, stand with their washing about the river edge. Long white strips of sheet bleach on the short turf. Ducks waddle in the mud and calves trot about the grass. The washing has to be done whether there is war or not. But it is pleasant on a spring morning when the earth is soft about the bank. These scenes are quite unhurried and the mind is allowed to rest on them, on the important things, with no suggestion that fire, avalanche or sudden pasteboard set will blot out reality with their tame expectedness.

The farmer Vassily (E. Fastrebitski) drives back from market with his son Ivan (C. Babynin). There is a lovely feeling here of the unsteady wheels and at the same time the certainty and unsureness of a ford. Women shout greeting. A sack drops. Ivan slides off the cart to fetch it and meets Anna (R. Pushnaya), a war orphan, staring at the branches. They are too shy to be anything but in love.

The cart jolts on along a narrow track between thick flowers. And it is the road, with its ruts and tall weed, grass and field blossom, that seems to be important, rather than the men, both dreaming of Anna. Spring and such tranquillity that one wonders why the first sub-title spoke of "the years of war."

Vassilissa (E. Zessarskaya), the farmer's daughter, drags a baby calf behind her into the orchard beyond the farm and brushes through fruit branches to meet her lover, Nikolai, the smith. She does not hear her father's cart coming up the road. The young smith leaps over the hedge and runs through the leaf-patterned orchard. These shots are full of movement as the wind is.

But the farmer has seen them.

The farmer's wife waits outside the farmhouse door, and with her Vassily's former mistress (O. Narbekova) is standing with her little girl.

What will he have brought them from market?

The atmosphere is tense over supper. Vassily is furious that his daughter and the smith love one another. It is jealousy with him, not any question of fitness. When Vassilissa comes in, the farmer storms at her and orders her out of the room. She looks at him, and in that moment O. Priobrashenskaya achieves genius. For father and daughter *look* alike in that instant: mentally. The father's tyranny has become strength in the girl. In Ivan it has become weakness. A psychological probability well worked out throughout the film. Vassilissa turns proudly and walks out. Ivan, shocked and dreaming of Anna, forgets to dip his spoon in the communal soup bowl. At last the father can vent his anger upon someone: he dashes a spoonful of hot soup in the boy's face and shouts at him, "You dreamer, it is time you married," and Ivan, rebellious for once, runs out crying no.

But he cannot endure against his father's will. He sits with his eyes on the floor throughout the bethrothal bargaining. A girl lies weeping in a room. It is only at the final moment, when they have to look at each other's faces, that Ivan and Anna see that their own wishes have been fulfilled as well as parental commands.

There is shouting and dancing at the marriage feast, though Anna brings but a little calf and tiny dowry. The former mistress of Vassily dances, laughing and sweating like a heavy animal. Suddenly her merriment turns to morose anger, for she has caught the farmer looking at Anna, and knows what that look means. In the confusion Vassilissa and the smith slip away to talk to each other.

The father, angry and frustrated, finds them in the barn. He storms and threatens. But Vassilissa will not put up with his anger any longer. If the smith, she says, will promise to respect her as if she were his wife, she will live with him, since marriage is not permitted without the father's consent. Nikolai agrees and they walk out together.

Summer is short. Bare-footed, Anna follows Ivan to the cornfields. In the village, peasants smear pitch on the smith's door and constantly taunt Vassilissa. But what does that matter so long as they are together? Corn waves in the fields: long ears and shadows, light slants and little winds. (Much of this would not register on ordinary stock. These effects need panchromatic, as is used here.) But in the middle of work, the bell rings. More men are needed for war. More conscripts must go, and amongst them the smith and Ivan.

The villagers go with them up the road and then Vassilissa, as the men disappear, realises that she will be left alone to the jeers of the women, and Anna knows there will be no escape from the jealousy of Ivan's mother nor from the farmer's persecution. And none of them can read and write, so there is no hope of news.

Days go on. The farmer drives back alone from market, drunk. Women spin and gossip and tell tales in the large room. Only Anna sits alone. As they hear horses clatter through the rain, women and children slip away.

Vassily comes in with a sack. What has he brought this time from market? His wife and his mistress have fixed their eyes on the bag. And he brings out shawls for them. But from the very bottom he brings out a better, more beautiful shawl for Anna, and goes, drunk, in search of her.

The mistress, raging with jealousy, follows him.

Anna is in her room, but Vassily breaks through the door. There is no escape. As the farmer, half ashamed, goes back through the dark stairway, he meets his former mistress. Both stare at each other. Guiltily and uneasily.

Months pass. Anna has a baby. There is no news of the soldiers. But there is peace at last and men begin to drift back to the village. Nikolai returns, but the war has changed him. His good temper has gone and he is sullen and over-bearing. Vassilissa, however, has won by her activity a place on the village council. A messenger summons her to go and help with the childrens' home they are making. Nikolai forbids this angrily; her place is the home, to build the fire and cook for him and to wait upon his pleasure. But Vassilissa laughs and walks out saying simply "that is at an end. We live in the new Russia."

Anna's life has become unbearable, and one day a letter comes-from Ivan. He also is returning home. Get out, the mother tells her, get out with the baby. But Anna does not know where to go. She wanders up the road and sits on a stone, crying, under the former landowner's house, which the energetic younger women, under Vassilissa's direction, are making into the childrens' home.

Vassilissa, hearing crying, runs down the steps. She knows the story. But she has a solution. Anna must bear the situation a few days longer till the home is ready, then she can leave her baby in it and begin life over again.

The Spring Festival comes. There are swings, women laugh and fling garlands on the water. The farmer and his wife go out to the crowds. So does the mistress; and her child, replica of the mother, poses in front of the glass and leaves, sneering at Anna. It is interesting to see this, so true to what a lot of children are, copies of an adult world, only less powerful, rather than the innocent little beings most studios make them out to be. Anna, afraid to go, plaits her hair and watches through the window. Suddenly she sees Ivan and, afraid, runs from him and hides.

But Ivan has lost his sensitiveness in the army. He sees the baby, rages, joins with the family hurried back to welcome him. Terrified, Anna runs out and throws herself into the stream. Vassily first, followed by the others, runs along the bank, but it is too late. They carry the body home and sit looking at it.

At that moment Vassilissa enters. She wastes no time over the dead. Where is the living? She looks round the room, walks over to the baby and picks it up. "Your father, Ivan, is the guilty one," and she leaves them to their raging and reproach while she herself, with the baby in her arms, walks towards the childrens' home.

It is the child, and the living, that are important. This is so new in cinematography. New almost to literature. It is Vassilissa who has dared to do what she wanted to do, who has emerged from horror and despair and evil; Vassilissa with the fundamental desire to protect the growing thing. You should stay at home, the man says. And the women who stay at home meet with baseness and evil and jealousy and death because they are unable to protect themselves. Every woman who is economically independent makes the acts and the attitude of the father, and in a lesser degree, of Ivan and Nikolai, less possible. Vassilissa, who had no child and defied her father, protects all children. The farmer's wife, who had a family, attacked the helpless and forgot the baby. Anna, who was sensitive and submissive and weak, gave in to village customs and met death.

Over all the world the same things happen, in equal and lesser degree.

Not until women are able to care for themselves will there be real progress in development. It may be that husband and wife will not necessarily both be at work together, but unless the woman knows that she is able to go out and earn her living, there is always risk of tyranny. From the man's point of view, too, he should not have to feel that a family or a wife are to be a drag on him all his days.

No State should have the right to demand life: military service for men and child-birth for women should be utterly a voluntary action. There are many women unfitted psychologically to bear children or more than one child, their reaction (often unconscious) affects the baby more than anyone else. And as things are at present constituted, numbers of women desire children, but because of environment or circumstance do not marry. Under a decent system it should be possible for any woman in good physical health to have a child if she desired, and it should be held equally wrong for those who did not wish one to have them. And on birth it would be the rule, and not the exception, to place all children in a nursery school for the first few years of their life. And I write this from the point of view of the child.

It is this that is so great about *The Peasant Women of Riazan*. Priobrashenskaya has seen beyond faces into truth. The farmer is a tyrant, but he is illiterate and has nothing to break the monotony of his life but drink or finding a new woman. Ivan is sensitive and weak. When his sensitiveness is rubbed away he becomes a bully also, blustering to hide his incompetence. Anna is helpless and kind and meets disaster. The mistress is a heavy, sensuous animal, but kindly and comic, had not her passions of jealousy and anger been aroused. It is all lack of education and of intelligent amusement. But Vassilissa, learning and thinking, builds for a new age.

The Peasant Women seems to me the most moral film I have ever seen. It has expressed the entire core of village life, the attitude of gossip and tyranny from the old to the young, that drives the stronger types to seek the freedom of the towns, all over the world. Yet a few days ago a cutting reached me from an English paper saying that Russian films were the dirtiest the correspondent had seen, for in one of them a married woman had a child with her father-in-law. And that very same morning, opening the local paper, there was an account of a man who had violated and then murdered his daughter in a remote Alpine village, and then escaped to the hills whence he was driven by the winter snows. Another peasant situation repeated, and *not in Russia*. When people so blind themselves to what happens in the world one can understand any revolution. But I think there is a fundamental sanity in the English that would see and understand and acclaim *The Peasant Women* for the truth and constructiveness of its lesson.

Unless a copy was preserved in Russia, it is unlikely the picture can be shown again.

Bryher

Film Problems of Soviet Russia. Territet, Switzerland: Pool Publishing, 1929

GENERAL BIBLIOGRAPHY
(Works referenced in two or more chapters)

Ardis, Ann, and Bonnie Kime Scott, eds. *Virginia Woolf Turning the Centuries: Se-lected Papers from the Ninth Annual Virginia Woolf Conference.* New York: Pace University Press, 2000.

Armstrong, Tim. *Modernism, Technology, and the Body: A Cultural Study.* Cambridge: Cambridge University Press, 1998.

Benjamin, Walter. "The Work of Art in the Age of Mechanical Reproduction." In *Illuminations,* ed. Hannah Arendt. Trans. Harry Zohn. New York: Schocken Books, 1969.

Benstock, Shari. *Women of the Left Bank: Paris, 1900–1940.* Austin: University of Texas Press, 1986.

Boone, Joseph A. *Libidinal Currents: Sexuality and the Shaping of Modernism.* Chicago: University of Chicago Press, 1998.

Butler, Judith. *Gender Trouble.* New York: Routledge, 1990.

Caughie, Pamela. *Passing and Pedagogy: The Dynamics of Responsibility.* Urbana: University of Illinois Press, 1999.

Donald, James, Anne Friedberg, and Laura Marcus, eds. *Close Up 1927–1933: Cinema and Modernism.* Princeton: Princeton University Press, 1998.

Doyle, Laura Anne. *Bordering on the Body: The Racial Matrix of Modern Fiction and Culture.* New York: Oxford University Press, 1994.

Felski, Rita. *The Gender of Modernity.* Cambridge: Harvard University Press, 1995.

Friedman, Susan Stanford. *Penelope's Web: Gender, Modernity, H. D.'s Fiction.* New York: Cambridge University Press, 1990.

Huyssen, Andreas. *After the Great Divide: Modernism, Mass Culture, Postmodernism.* Bloomington: Indiana University Press, 1986.

Lewis, Wyndham, ed. *BLAST* 1 (June 20, 1914). Rpt. Santa Rosa: Black Sparrow Press, 1992.

Lyon, Janet. *Manifestoes: Provocations of the Modern.* Ithaca: Cornell University Press, 1999.

Milford, Nancy. *Savage Beauty: The Life of Edna St. Vincent Millay.* New York: Random House, 2001.

MODERNISM/modernity. http://muse.jhu.edu/journals/modernism-modernity/.

Morrisson, Mark. *The Public Face of Modernism: Little Magazines, Audiences, and Reception, 1905–1920.* Madison: University of Wisconsin Press, 2001.

North, Michael. *The Dialect of Modernism: Race, Language, and Twentieth-Century Literature.* New York: Oxford University Press, 1994.

Rado, Lisa. *Modernism, Gender, and Culture: A Cultural Studies Approach.* New York: Garland, 1997.

Rosen, Andrew. *Rise Up Women! The Militant Campaign of the Women's Social and Political Union, 1903–1914.* London: Routledge and Kegan Paul, 1974.

Scandura, Jani, and Michael Thurston. *Modernism, Inc.: Body, Memory, Capital.* New York: New York University Press, 2001.

Scott, Bonnie Kime, ed. *The Gender of Modernism: A Critical Anthology.* Bloomington: Indiana University Press, 1990.

———. Introduction. *The Gender of Modernism.* In Scott, ed., 1–18.

———. *Refiguring Modernism. Vol. 1: The Women of 1928,* and *Vol. 2: Postmodern Feminist Readings of Woolf, West, and Barnes.* Bloomington: Indiana University Press, 1995.

Tickner, Lisa. *The Spectacle of Women: Imagery of the Suffrage Campaign, 1907–14.* Chicago: University of Chicago Press, 1988.

West, Rebecca. *The Young Rebecca: Writings of Rebecca West, 1911–17.* Ed. Jane Marcus. Bloomington: Indiana University Press, 1982.

Willison, Ian, Warwick Gould, and Warren Chernaik, eds. *Modernist Writers and the Marketplace.* London, Macmillan, 1996.

Woolf, Virginia. *The Diary of Virginia Woolf.* 5 Vols. ed. Anne Oliver Bell, Vols. 2–5 assisted by Andrew McNeillie. New York: Harcourt Brace Jovanovich, and London: Hogarth, 1977–84.

———. *The Letters of Virginia Woolf.* Ed. Nigel Nicolson and Joanne Trautmann. 6 vols. New York: Harcourt Brace Jovanovich, and London: Hogarth, 1975–1980.

CONTRIBUTORS

TUZYLINE JITA ALLAN is associate professor of English at Baruch College, the City University of New York, where she teaches courses in African American and postcolonial literatures. She is the author of *Womanist and Feminist Aesthetics: A Comparative Review* (1996), and is a co-director/series editor of *Women Writing Africa*. She has edited the special number "Teaching African Literatures in a Global Economy" for *Women's Studies Quarterly* (1997). She is writing a book on Black Atlantic gender politics.

ANN ARDIS is professor of English at the University of Delaware. Recent books include *Modernism and Cultural Conflict, 1880–1922* (2002), *Women's Experience of Modernity, 1875–1945* (co-edited, 2002), and *Virginia Woolf: Turning the Centuries* (co-edited, 2000). She is currently co-organizing a symposium and anthology on "Transatlantic Print Culture, 1880–1930: Emerging Media, Emerging Modernisms."

NANCY BERKE is assistant professor of English at LaGuardia Community College, the City University of New York. She has published *Women Poets on the Left* (2001). She is currently involved in an editing project on modern American women poets, and writing a book about single women.

JULIA BRIGGS is professor of English and Women's Studies at De Montfort University, Leicester, UK, and an Emeritus Fellow of Hertford College, Oxford. She is author of *Night Visitors* (a history of the ghost story, 1977), *This Stage-Play World: Texts and Contexts, 1580–1625* (1983; rev. 1997), a biography of E. Nesbit (1987), *Virginia Woolf: An Inner Life* (2005), and *Reading Virginia Woolf* (2006).

PAMELA L. CAUGHIE is professor of English and associate faculty member in women's studies at Loyola University, Chicago, where she teaches courses in modernism, feminist theory, and African American literature. She is author of *Virginia Woolf and Postmodernism* (1991), and *Passing and Pedagogy: The Dynamics of Responsibility* (1999), and editor of the collection *Virginia Woolf in the Age of Mechanical Reproduction* (2000). Recent work, "Class Acts," extends her work on passing to performances across class boundaries.

MARY CHAPMAN is associate professor of English at the University of British Columbia in Vancouver, B.C., Canada. She has published articles on suffrage parades, parlor theatricals, and nineteenth-century American literature and culture. Recent books include *Sentimental Men: Masculinity and the Politics of Affect* (co-edited, 1999) and an edition of Charles Brockden Brown's *Ormond* (1999).

She is currently writing a study of American suffrage literature and modernist print culture.

SUZANNE CLARK is professor of English at the University of Oregon, where she teaches courses on modern literature, theory, and the environment. She has published articles and essays on modernist and cold war writers and theorists, gender, anarchism, and the sentimental. Books include *Sentimental Modernism* (1991) and *Cold Warriors* (2000). She is working on *The Natural History of Modernism,* and on a biography of her father, Robert D. Clark.

PATRICK COLLIER is associate professor of English at Ball State University, where he teaches nineteenth- and twentieth-century British literature. He is the author of *Modernism on Fleet Street* (2006) and articles about T. S. Eliot, Virginia Woolf, and Charlotte Brontë.

DIANE F. GILLESPIE, emeritus professor of English, Washington State University, is author of *The Sisters' Arts: The Writing and Painting of Virginia Woolf and Vanessa Bell,* editor of *The Multiple Muses of Virginia Woolf,* which contains her essay on photography, and co-editor of the selected papers, *Woolf and the Arts.* Currently she is working on a study of nudity and self-exposure in painting and writing.

BARBARA GREEN is associate professor of English at the University of Notre Dame, where she teaches courses on modernism and gender. She is the author of *Spectacular Confessions: Autobiography, Performative Activism, and the Sites of Suffrage, 1905–1938* (1997), and is currently working on feminist periodical culture.

LESLIE KATHLEEN HANKINS is professor of English at Cornell College in Iowa, where she teaches courses on Virginia Woolf, cinema, and twentieth-century literature. She is co-editor of *Virginia Woolf and the Arts* (1997). "Iris Barry, Writer and Cinéaste in *The Adelphi, The Spectator,* the Film Society and the British *Vogue*" appeared in *MODERNISM/modernity.* Hankins is writing a book on Woolf and cinema.

SUZETTE A. HENKE is Thruston B. Morton Sr. Professor of Literary Studies at the University of Louisville. Her books include *James Joyce and the Politics of Desire* (1990) and *Shattered Subjects: Trauma and Testimony in Women's Life-Writing* (1998). She is currently co-editing a collection on *Virginia Woolf and Trauma* (forthcoming from Pace University Press) and completing a book on *Post-Traumatic Narrative.*

KATHERINE E. KELLY is associate professor of English at Texas A & M University in College Station, Texas, where she teaches courses on modern drama and modernism. She has published *Modern Drama by Women: An International Anthology* (1996) as well as articles on Elizabeth Robins, the Actresses Franchise League, and G. B. Shaw. She is currently at work on a study of theatrical sociability in the forming of modernism.

COLLEEN LAMOS is associate professor of English at Rice University. She is author of *Deviant Modernism: Sexual and Textual Errancy in T. S. Eliot, James Joyce, and Marcel Proust* (1998) and co-editor of *Masculinities in Joyce: Postcolonial Construc-*

tions (2001). She is at work on a book entitled *"I'm not a lesbian, I just loved Thelma": Sexual Identifications in Modern Women's Literature.*

BETTE LONDON is professor of English at the University of Rochester, where she teaches courses in modern and Victorian literature and women's writing. She is the author of *The Appropriated Voice: Narrative Authority in Conrad, Forster, and Woolf* (1990) and *Writing Double: Women's Literary Partnerships* (1999). She is currently working on a study of the idea of posthumous writing.

JANET LYON is associate professor of English at Pennsylvania State University. She teaches courses on various modernisms, modernity, and gender/sexuality theory, and is co-director of the Disability Studies Program at Penn State. She is the author of *Manifestoes: Provocations of the Modern* (1999) and is at work on a book titled *The Perfect Hostess: Salons and Modernity,* and a study of modernism's philosophical indebtedness to disability.

JAYNE E. MAREK is associate professor of English at Franklin College in Franklin, Indiana, where she teaches literature, writing, and film. Publications include *Women Editing Modernism: "Little" Magazines and Literary History* (1995), the *Poetry* index with critical introduction (1998), and articles on modern poetry, cinema studies, and faculty scholarship. She is writing a study of women editors and the Harlem Renaissance.

SONITA SARKER is associate professor of English and Women's and Gender Studies at Macalester College in St. Paul, Minnesota. She is author of essays on Woolf and co-editor of *Trans-Status Subjects: Gender in the Globalization of South and Southeast Asia* (2002). She is currently working on a book on transnational feminist/women's modernism in response to imperialist capitalism and fascism.

BONNIE KIME SCOTT is professor and chair of Women's Studies at San Diego State University in California, where she teaches courses on women writers, feminist theory, representation, and gender. Her books include *The Gender of Modernism* (1990), *Refiguring Modernism* (2 vols., 1995), *Selected Letters of Rebecca West* (2000), and *Virginia Woolf: Turning the Centuries* (co-edited, 2000). She is at work on a study of Virginia Woolf's uses of nature, which contributes to a greening of modernism.

CAROL SHLOSS is professor of English at Stanford University in California, where she teaches courses on modernism and gender, women experimental novelists, and modern Irish literature. Her most recent book was *Lucia Joyce: To Dance in the Wake* (2003). She is currently at work on *Treason's Child: Mary de Rachewiltz and the Real Estate of Ezra Pound.*

SUSAN SQUIER is Brill Professor of Women's Studies and English at Pennsylvania State University. Her books include *Babies in Bottles: Twentieth-Century Visions of Reproductive Technology* (2000), *Playing Dolly: Technocultural Figurations, Fantasies and Fictions of Assisted Reproduction* (co-edited, 1999), and *Liminal Lives: Imagining the Human at the Frontiers of Medicine* (2004).

CLAIRE M. TYLEE is Subject Leader for English at Brunel University, West London, where she teaches courses on the women's movement and twentieth-century literature and on gender and writing. Her books include *The Great War and Women's Consciousness* (1989), the collection *War Plays by Women* (1999), the edited essays, *Women, the First World War, and Dramatic Imagination* (2000), and *In the Open: Jewish Women Writers and British Culture* (forthcoming). She has recently published on women's Holocaust writing.

GAY WACHMAN is associate professor in the Humanities and Languages Department at the State University of New York at Old Westbury, where she teaches courses in multicultural literature, women's writing, lesbian and gay writing, and colonialism and postcolonialism. Her publications include *Lesbian Empire: Radical Crosswriting in the Twenties* (2001), and articles on Sylvia Townsend Warner and Virginia Woolf.

INDEX

The University of Illinois Press
is a founding member of the
Association of American University Presses.

———————————————————————————

Composed in 9/13 ITC Stone Serif
with Meta display
by Celia Shapland
at the University of Illinois Press
Designed by Paula Newcomb
Manufactured by Sheridan Books, Inc.

University of Illinois Press
1325 South Oak Street
Champaign, IL 61820-6903
www.press.uillinois.edu